Lecture Notes in Computer Science   13156

More information about this subseries at https://link.springer.com/bookseries/7407

Yongxuan Lai · Tian Wang · Min Jiang ·
Guangquan Xu · Wei Liang ·
Aniello Castiglione (Eds.)

Algorithms and Architectures for Parallel Processing

21st International Conference, ICA3PP 2021
Virtual Event, December 3–5, 2021
Proceedings, Part II

 Springer

Editors
Yongxuan Lai (ID)
Xiamen University
Xiamen, China

Min Jiang (ID)
Xiamen University
Xiamen, China

Wei Liang (ID)
Hunan University
Changsha, China

Tian Wang (ID)
Beijing Normal University
Zhuhai, China

Guangquan Xu (ID)
Tianjin University
Tianjin, China

Aniello Castiglione (ID)
University of Naples Parthenope
Naples, Italy

ISSN 0302-9743   ISSN 1611-3349 (electronic)
Lecture Notes in Computer Science
ISBN 978-3-030-95387-4   ISBN 978-3-030-95388-1 (eBook)
https://doi.org/10.1007/978-3-030-95388-1

LNCS Sublibrary: SL1 – Theoretical Computer Science and General Issues

This Springer imprint is published by the registered company Springer Nature Switzerland AG
The registered company address is: Gewerbestrasse 11, 6330 Cham, Switzerland

Preface

On behalf of the Conference Committee we welcome you to the proceedings of the 2021 International Conference on Algorithms and Architectures for Parallel Processing (ICA3PP 2021), which was held virtually during December 3–5, 2021. ICA3PP 2021 was the 21st in this series of conferences (started in 1995) that are devoted to algorithms and architectures for parallel processing. ICA3PP is now recognized as the main regular international event that covers the many dimensions of parallel algorithms and architectures, encompassing fundamental theoretical approaches, practical experimental projects, and commercial components and systems. This conference provides a forum for academics and practitioners from countries around the world to exchange ideas for improving the efficiency, performance, reliability, security, and interoperability of computing systems and applications.

A successful conference would not be possible without the high-quality contributions made by the authors. This year, ICA3PP received a total of 403 submissions from authors in 28 countries and regions. Based on rigorous peer reviews by the Program Committee members and reviewers, 145 high-quality papers were accepted to be included in the conference proceedings and submitted for EI indexing. In addition to the contributed papers, eight distinguished scholars, Yi Pan, Daqing Zhang, Yan Zhang, Shuai Ma, Weijia Jia, Keqiu Liu, Yang Yang, and Peng Cheng, were invited to give keynote lectures, providing us with the recent developments in diversified areas in algorithms and architectures for parallel processing and applications.

We would like to take this opportunity to express our sincere gratitude to the Program Committee members and 160 reviewers for their dedicated and professional service. We highly appreciate the six track chairs, Ding Wang, Songwen Pei, Zhiming Luo, Shigeng Zhang, Longbiao Chen, and Feng Wang, for their hard work in promoting this conference and organizing the reviews for the papers submitted to their tracks. We are so grateful to the publication chairs, Yang Wang, Carmen De Maio, Donglong Chen, and Yinglong Zhang, and the publication assistants for their tedious work in editing the conference proceedings. We must also say "thank you" to all the volunteers who helped us in various stages of this conference. Moreover, we are so honored to have many renowned scholars be part of this conference. Finally, we would like to thank all speakers, authors, and participants for their great contribution and support to make ICA3PP 2021 a success!

December 2021

Min Jiang
Aniello Castiglione
Guangquan Xu
Wei Liang
Jean-Luc Gaudiot
Yongxuan Lai
Tian Wang

Organization

General Co-chairs

Jean-Luc Gaudiot   University of California, Irvine, USA
Yongxuan Lai   Xiamen University, China
Tian Wang   Beijing Normal University and UIC, China

Program Co-chairs

Min Jiang   Xiamen University, China
Aniello Castiglione   University of Naples Parthenope, Italy
Guangquan Xu   Tianjin University, China
Wei Liang   Hunan University, China

Track Chairs

Ding Wang   Nankai University, China
Songwen Pei   University of Shanghai for Science and
                            Technology, China
Zhiming Luo   Xiamen University, China
Shigeng Zhang   Central South University, China
Longbiao Chen   Xiamen University, China
Feng Wang   Wuhan University, China

Local Co-chairs

Cheng Wang   Huaqiao University, China
Liang Song   Xiamen University, China

Publication Chairs

Yan Wang   Xiamen University of Technology, China
Carmen De Maio   University of Salerno, Italy
Donglong Chen   Beijing Normal University-Hong Kong Baptist
                            University United International College (UIC),
                            China
Yinglong Zhang   Minnan Normal University, China

Publicity Co-chairs

Fan Lin	Xiamen University, China
Longbiao Chen	Xiamen University, China
Saiqin Long	Xiangtan University, China
Zhetao Li	Xiangtan University, China

Steering Committee

Yang Xiang	Swinburne University of Technology, Australia
Kuan-Ching Li	Providence University, Taiwan, China

Program Committee

A. M. A. Elman Bashar	Plymouth State University, USA
Jiahong Cai	Hunan University of Science and Technology, China
Yuanzheng Cai	Xiamen University, China
Jingjing Cao	Wuhan University of Technology, China
Zhihan Cao	Huaqiao University, China
Arcangelo Castiglione	University of Salerno, Italy
Lei Chai	Beihang University, China
Chao Chen	Chongqiing University, China
Donglong Chen	Beijing Normal University-Hong Kong Baptist University United International College (UIC), China
Haiming Chen	Ningbo University, China
Juan Chen	Hunan University, China
Kai Chen	Institute of Information Engineering, Chinese Academy of Sciences, China
Lifei Chen	Fujian Normal University, China
Rongmao Chen	National University of Defense Technology, China
Shuhong Chen	Guangzhou University, China
Xiaoyan Chen	Xiamen University of Technology, China
Xu Chen	Sun Yat-sen University, China
Yu Chen	Wuhan University of Technology, China
Yuanyi Chen	Zhejiang University, China
Yuxiang Chen	Huaqiao University, China
Lin Cui	Jinan University, China
Haipeng Dai	Nanjing University, China
Hong-Ning Dai	Lingnan University, China
Xia Daoxun	Guizhou Normal University, China

Himansu Das	KIIT Deemed to be University, India
William A. R. De Souza	Royal Holloway, University of London, UK
He Debiao	Wuhan University, China
Xiaoheng Deng	Central South University, China
Chunyan Diao	Hunan University, China
Qiying Dong	Nankai University, China
Fang Du	Ningxia University, China
Guodong Du	Xiamen University, China
Xin Du	Fujian Normal University, China
Shenyu Duan	Shanghai University, China
Xiaoliang Fan	Xiamen University, China
Xiaopeng Fan	Shenzhen Institute of Advanced Technology, Chinese Academy of Sciences, China
Yongkai Fan	China University of Petroleum, Beijing, China
Zipei Fan	University of Tokyo, Japan
Fei Fang	Hunan Normal University, China
Tao Feng	Sichuan University, China
Virginia Franqueira	University of Kent, UK
Anmin Fu	National University of Defense Technology, China
Bin Fu	Hunan University, China
Zhipeng Gao	Beijing University of Posts and Telecommunications, China
Debasis Giri	Maulana Abul Kalam Azad University of Technology, India
Xiaoli Gong	Nankai University, China
Ke Gu	Changsha University of Science and Technology, China
Zonghua Gu	University of Missouri, USA
Gui Guan	Nanjing University of Posts and Telecommunications, China
Yong Guan	Iowa State University, USA
Zhitao Guan	North China Electric Power University, China
Guangquan Xu	Tianjin University, China
Ye Guixin	Northwest University, China
Chun Guo	Institute of Information Engineering, Chinese Academy of Sciences, China
Guijuan Guo	Huaqiao University, China
Jun Guo	Quanzhou University of Information Engineering, China
Shihui Guo	Xiamen University, China
Zehua Guo	Beijing Institute of Technology, China
Yu Haitao	Guilin University of Technology, China

Dezhi Han	Shanghai Maritime University, China
Jinsong Han	Zhejiang University, China
Song Han	Zhejiang Gongshang University, China
Yulin He	Shenzhen University, China
Alan Hong	Xiamen University of Technology, China
Haokai Hong	Xiamen University, China
Zhenzhuo Hou	Peking University, China
Donghui Hu	Hefei University of Technology, China
Yupeng Hu	Hunan University, China
Yuping Hu	Guangdong University of Finance and Economics, China
Qiang-Sheng Hua	Huazhong University of Science and Technology, China
Weh Hua	University of Queensland, China
Yu Hua	Huazhong University of Science and Technology, China
Chenxi Huang	Xiamen University, China
Haiyang Huang	Huaqiao University, China
Jiawei Huang	Central South University, China
Jing Huang	Hunan University, China
Weihong Huang	Hunan University of Science and Technology, China
Xinyi Huang	Fujian Normal University, China
Zhou Jian	Nanjing University of Posts and Telecommunications, China
Fengliang Jiang	Longyan University, China
Wanchun Jiang	Central South University, China
Wenjun Jiang	Hunan University, China
He Jiezhou	Xiamen University, China
Zhengjun Jing	Jiangsu University of Technology, China
Xiaoyan Kui	Central South University, China
Xia Lei	China University of Petroleum, China
Chao Li	Shanghai Jiao Tong University, China
Dingding Li	South China Normal University, China
Fagen Li	University of Electronic Science and Technology of China, China
Fuliang Li	Northeastern University, China
Hui Li	Guizhou University, China
Jiliang Li	University of Goettingen, Germany
Lei Li	Xiamen University, China
Tao Li	Nankai University, China
Tong Li	Nankai University, China

Wei Li	Jiangxi University of Science and Technology, China
Wei Li	Nanchang University, China
Xiaoming Li	Tianjin University, China
Yang Li	East China Normal University, China
Yidong Li	Beijing Jiaotong University, China
Sheng Lian	Xiamen University, China
Junbin Liang	Guangxi University, China
Kaitai Liang	Delft University of Technology, The Netherlands
Wei Liang	Hunan University, China
Zhuofan Liao	Changsha University of Science and Technology, China
Deyu Lin	Nanchang University, China
Fan Lin	Xiamen University, China
Jingqiang Lin	University of Science and Technology of China, China
Yongguo Ling	Xiamen University, China
Guanfeng Liu	Macquarie University, Australia
Jia Liu	Nanjing University, China
Kai Liu	Chongqing University, China
Kunhong Liu	Xiamen University, China
Peng Liu	Hangzhou Dianzi University, China
Tong Liu	Shanghai University, China
Wei Liu	East China Jiaotong University, China
Ximeng Liu	Singapore Management University, Singapore
Xuan Liu	Hunan University, China
Xuxun Liu	South China University of Technology, China
Yan Liu	Huaqiao University, China
Yaqin Liu	Hunan University, China
Yong Liu	Beijing University of Chemical Technology, China
Zhaobin Liu	Dalian Maritime University, China
Zheli Liu	Nankai University, China
Jing Long	Hunan Normal University, China
Wei Lu	Renmin University of China, China
Ye Lu	Nankai University, China
Hao Luo	Beijing Normal University-Hong Kong Baptist University United International College (UIC), China
Zhiming Luo	Xiamen University, China
Chao Ma	Hong Kong Polytechnic University, China
Haoyu Ma	Xidian University, China

Chengying Mao	Jiangxi University of Finance and Economics, China
Mario Donato Marino	Leeds Beckett University, UK
Yaxin Mei	Huaqiao University, China
Hao Peng	Zhejiang Normal University, China
Hua Peng	Shaoxing University, China
Kai Peng	Huaqiao University, China
Li Peng	Hunan University of Science and Technology, China
Yao Peng	Northwest University, China
Zhaohui Peng	Shandong University, China
Aneta Poniszewska-Maranda	Lodz University of Technology, Poland
Honggang Qi	University of Chinese Academy of Sciences, China
Tie Qiu	Tianjin University, China
Dapeng Qu	Liaoning University, China
Zhihao Qu	Hohai University and Hong Kong Polytechnic University, China
Yang Quan	Huaqiao University, China
Abdul Razaque	International IT University, Kazakhstan
Chunyan Sang	Chongqing University of Posts and Telecommunications, China
Arun Kumar Sangaiah	VIT University, India
Shanchen Pang	China University of Petroleum, China
Yin Shaoyi	Paul Sabatier University, France
Hua Shen	Hubei University of Technology, China
Meng Shen	Beijing Institute of Technology, China
Huibin Shi	Nanjing University of Aeronautics and Astronautics, China
Liang Shi	East China Normal University, China
Peichang Shi	National University of Defense Technology, China
Liang Song	Xiamen University, China
Tao Song	China University of Petroleum, China
Song Han	Zhejiang Gongshang University, China
Riccardo Spolaor	University of Oxford, UK
Chunhua Su	Osaka University, Japan
Bingcai Sui	National University of Defense Technology, China
Nitin Sukhija	Slippery Rock University of Pennsylvania, USA
Bing Sun	Huaqiao University, China
Yu Sun	Guangxi University, China

Zeyu Sun	Luoyang Institute of Science and Technology, China
Zhixing Tan	Tsinghua University, China
Bing Tang	Hunan University of Science and Technology, China
Mingdong Tang	Guangdong University of Foreign Studies, China
Wenjuan Tang	Hunan University, China
Ming Tao	Dongguan University of Technology, China
Weitian Tong	Georgia Southern University, USA
Asis Kumar Tripathy	Vellore Institute of Technology, India
Xiaohan Tu	Railway Police College, China
Baocang Wang	Xidian University, China
Chaowei Wang	Beijing University of Posts and Telecommunications, China
Cheng Wang	Huaqiao University, China
Chenyu Wang	Beijing University of Posts and Telecommunications, China
Feng Wang	China University of Geosciences, China
Hui Wang	South China Agricultural University, China
Jianfeng Wang	Xidian University, China
Jin Wang	Soochow University, China
Jing Wang	Chang'an University, China
Lei Wang	National University of Defense Technology, China
Meihong Wang	Xiamen University, China
Pengfei Wang	Dalian University of Technology, China
Senzhang Wang	Central South University, China
Tao Wang	Minjiang University, China
Tian Wang	Huaqiao University, China
Wei Wang	Beijing Jiaotong University, China
Weizhe Wang	Tianjin University, China
Xiaoliang Wang	Hunan University of Science and Technology, China
Xiaoyu Wang	Soochow University, China
Yan Wang	Xiamen University of Technology, China
Zhen Wang	Shanghai University of Electric Power, China
Zhenzhong Wang	Hong Kong Polytechnic University, China
Jizeng Wei	Tianjin University, China
Wenting Wei	Xidian University, China
Yu Wei	Purdue University, USA
Cao Weipeng	Shenzhen University, China
Weizhi Meng	Technical University of Denmark, Denmark

Sheng Wen	Swinburne University of Technology, Australia
Stephan Wiefling	Bonn-Rhein-Sieg University of Applied Sciences, Germany
Di Wu	Deakin University, Australia
Hejun Wu	Sun Yat-sen University, China
Qianhong Wu	Beihang University, China
Shangrui Wu	Beijing Normal University, China
Xiaohe Wu	Hunan University of Science and Technology, China
Zhongbo Wu	Hubei University of Arts and Science, China
Bin Xia	Nanjing University of Posts and Telecommunications, China
Guobao Xiao	Minjiang University, China
Lijun Xiao	Guangzhou College of Technology and Business, China
Wenhui Xiao	Central South University, China
Yalong Xiao	Central South University, China
Han Xiaodong	Minjiang University, China
Fenfang Xie	Sun Yat-sen University, China
Guoqi Xie	Hunan University, China
Mande Xie	Zhejiang Gongshang University, China
Songyou Xie	Hunan University, China
Xiaofei Xie	Nanyang Technological University, Singapore
Yi Xie	Sun Yat-sen University, China
Zhijun Xie	Ningbo University, China
Peiyin Xiong	Hunan University of Science and Technology, China
Dejun Xu	Xiamen University, China
Jianbo Xu	Hunan University of Science and Technology, China
Ming Xu	Hangzhou Dianzi University, China
Wenzheng Xu	Sichuan University, China
Zhiyu Xu	NSCLab, Australia
Zichen Xu	Nanchang University, China
Zisang Xu	Changsha University of Science and Technology, China
Xiaoming Xue	City University of Hong Kong, China
Xingsi Xue	Fujian University of Technology, China
Changcai Yang	Fujian Agriculture and Forestry University, China
Chao-Tung Yang	Tunghai University, Taiwan, China
Dingqi Yang	University of Macau, China
Fan Yang	Xiamen University, China
Fengxiang Yang	Xiamen University, China

Guisong Yang	University of Shanghai for Science and Technology, China
Hao Yang	Yancheng Teachers University, China
Hui Yang	National University of Defense Technology, China
Lan Yang	Quanzhou University of Information Engineering, China
Lvqing Yang	Xiamen University, China
Mujun Yin	Huaqiao University, China
Haitao Yu	Guilin University of Technology, China
Sheng Yu	Shaoguan University, China
Shuai Yu	Sun Yat-sen University, China
Zhiyong Yu	Fuzhou University, China
Liang Yuzhu	Huaqiao University, China
Tao Zan	Longyan University, China
Yingpei Zeng	Hangzhou Dianzi University, China
Bingxue Zhang	University of Shanghai for Science and Technology, China
Bo Zhang	Shanghai Normal University, China
Chongsheng Zhang	Henan University, China, China
Haibo Zhang	University of Otago, New Zealand
Hong-Bo Zhang	Huaqiao University, China
Jia Zhang	Jinan University, China
Jingwei Zhang	Guilin University of Electronic Technology, China
Jun Zhang	Dalian Maritime University, China
Mingwu Zhang	Hubei University of Technology, China
Qiang Zhang	Central South University, China
Shaobo Zhang	Hunan University of Science and Technology, China
Shengchuan Zhang	Xiamen University, China
Shiwen Zhang	Hunan University, China
Tianzhu Zhang	Nokia Bell Labs, USA
Yi Zhang	Xiamen University, China
Yilin Zhang	Huaqiao University, China
Baokang Zhao	National University of Defense Technology, China
Bowen Zhao	Singapore Management University, Singapore
Jinyuan Zhao	Changsha Normal University, China
Liang Zhao	Shenyang Aerospace University, China
Sha Zhao	Zhejiang University, China
Wan-Lei Zhao	Xiamen University, China
Yongxin Zhao	East China Normal University, China

Qun-Xiong Zheng	Institute of Information Engineering, Chinese Academy of Sciences, China
Ping Zhong	Central South University, China
Binbin Zhou	Zhejiang University City College, China
Qifeng Zhou	Xiamen University, China
Teng Zhou	Shantou University, China
Wei Zhou	Guilin University of Electronic Technology, China
Xinyu Zhou	Jiangxi Normal University, China
Haibin Zhu	Nipissing University, Canada
Shunzhi Zhu	Xiamen University of Technology, China
Weiping Zhu	Wuhan University, China
Xiaoyu Zhu	Central South University, China
Zhiliang Zhu	East China Jiaotong University, China
Haodong Zou	Beijing Normal University-Hong Kong Baptist University United International College (UIC), China
Yunkai Zou	Nankai University, China

Reviewers

Yingzhe He	Peifu Han	Shihang Yu
Zhiyu Wang	Xuefei Wang	Lei Huang
Wang Yin	Wen Dong	Shuqi Liu
Jingyi Cui	Zhengbo Han	Yawu Zhao
Xingda Liu	Jincai Zhu	Feiyu Jin
Guohua Xin	Chen Qi	Yunfeng Huang
Zhangyan Yang	Na Zhao	Fei Zhu
Yuexin Zhang	Bingxuan Li	Shengmin Xu
Chenkai Tan	Zhixiu Guo	Yao Hu
Hongpeng Bai	Xu Wu	Weijing You
Lixiao Gong	Yu Pen	Rui Liu
Xue Li	Jian Yin	Fan Meng
Wenqing Lei	Xinjun Pei	Haiyuan Gui
Xue Hu	Xiaoquan Zhang	Guangjing Huang
Meiqi Feng	Yihao Lin	Qingze Fang
Victor Chiang	Shiqiang Zheng	Hualing Ren
Xin Ji	Huifang Zeng	Ziya Chen
Pengqu Yan	Yixiang Hu	Ruixiang Luo
Xinru Ding	Xincao Xu	Wenxuan Wei
Yumei Li	Jiahao Zhao	Zhiming Lin
Haodong Zhang	Lulu Cao	Xin He
Zhe Chen	Jiahui Yu	Guoyong Dai
Gang Shen	Faquan Chen	Zhiyuan Wang
Hongfei Shao	Xue Zhai	Yajing Xie

Hanbin Hong
Min Wu
Siyao Chen
Kaiyue Zhang
Xiaohai Cai
Zhiwen Zhang
Tieqi Shou
Liqiang Xu
Chenhui Lu
Hang Zhu
Jiannan Gao
Hang Zhou
Haoyang An
Yang Liu
Peiwei Hu
Xiaotong Zhou
Qiang Tang
Chang Yue
Miaoqian Lin
Yudong Li
Zijing Ma
Zhankai Li
Chengyao Hua
Qingxuan Wang

Yi Wang
Mingyue Li
Songsong Zhang
Jingwei Jiang
Meijia Xu
Shuhong Hong
Anqi Yin
Shaoqiang Wu
Shuangjiao Zhai
Fei Ma
Shiya Peng
Kedong Xiu
Shengnan Zhao
Chuan Zhao
Bo Zhang
Baozhu Li
Ning Liu
Wang Yang
Xiaohui Yang
Zihao Dong
Sijie Niu
Kun Ma
Dianjie Lu
Ziqiang Yu

Lizhi Peng
Yilei Wang
Zhang Jing
Tian Jie
Jian Zhao
Hui Li
Yan Jiang
Minghao Zhao
Lei Lyu
Yanbin Han
Yanlin Wu
Lingang Huang
Mingwei Lin
Wenxiang Wang
Xinqiang Ye
Songyi Yang
Cancan Wang
Xingbao Zhang
Yafeng Sun
Li Lin
Jinxian Lei
Wentao Liu

Contents – Part II

Software Systems and Efficient Algorithms

The Design and Realization of a Novel Intelligent Drying Rack System
Based on STM32 3
    Shiwen Zhang, Wang Hu, Wei Liang, and Lei Liao

Efficient Estimation of Time-Dependent Shortest Paths Based on Shortcuts 18
    Linbo Liao, Shipeng Yang, Yongxuan Lai, Wenhua Zeng, Fan Yang,
    and Min Jiang

Multi-level PWB and PWC for Reducing TLB Miss Overheads on GPUs 33
    Yang Lin, Dunbo Zhang, Chaoyang Jia, Qiong Wang, and Li Shen

Hybrid GA-SVR: An Effective Way to Predict Short-Term Traffic Flow 53
    Guanru Tan, Shiqiang Zheng, Boyu Huang, Zhihan Cui, Haowen Dou,
    Xi Yang, and Teng Zhou

Parallel and Distributed Algorithms and Applications

MobiTrack: Mobile Crowdsensing-Based Object Tracking
with Min-Region and Max-Utility 65
    Wenqiang Li, Jun Tao, Zuyan Wang, YiFan Xu, Xiaolei Tang,
    and YiChao Dong

Faulty Processor Identification for a Multiprocessor System Under
the PMC Model Using a Binary Grey Wolf Optimizer 81
    Fulai Pan and Weixia Gui

Fast On-Road Object Detector on ROS-Based Mobile Robot 96
    Gang Wang, Qiudi Song, Tao Li, and Min Li

A Lightweight Asynchronous I/O System for Non-volatile Memory 108
    Jiebin Luo, Weijie Zhang, Dingding Li, Haoyu Luo, and Deze Zeng

The Case for Disjoint Job Mapping on High-Radix Networked Parallel
Computers 123
    Yao Hu and Michihiro Koibuchi

FastCache: A Client-Side Cache with Variable-Position Merging Schema
in Network Storage System   144
    Lin Qian, BaoLiu Ye, XiaoLiang Wang, Zhihao Qu, Weiguo Duan,
    and Ming Zhao

An Efficient Parallelization Model for Sparse Non-negative Matrix
Factorization Using cuSPARSE Library on Multi-GPU Platform   161
    Hatem Moumni and Olfa Hamdi-Larbi

HaDPA: A Data-Partition Algorithm for Data Parallel Applications
on Heterogeneous HPC Platforms   178
    Jingbo Li, Li Han, Yuqi Qu, and Xingjun Zhang

A NUMA-Aware Parallel Truss Decomposition Algorithm for Large Scale
Graphs   193
    Zhebin Mou, Nong Xiao, and Zhiguang Chen

Large-Scale Parallel Alignment Algorithm for SMRT Reads   213
    Zeyu Xia, Yingbo Cui, Ang Zhang, Peng Zhang, Sifan Long, Tao Tang,
    Lin Peng, Chun Huang, Canqun Yang, and Xiangke Liao

Square Fractional Repetition Codes for Distributed Storage Systems   230
    Bing Zhu, Shigeng Zhang, and Weiping Wang

An Anti-forensic Method Based on RS Coding and Distributed Storage   240
    Xuhang Jiang, Yujue Wang, Yong Ding, Hai Liang, Huiyong Wang,
    and Zhenyu Li

Data Science

Predicting Consumers' Coupon-usage in E-commerce with Capsule
Network   257
    Wenjun Jiang, Zhenqiong Tan, Jiawei He, Jifeng Zhang, Tian Wang,
    and Shuhong Chen

A High-Availability K-modes Clustering Method Based on Differential
Privacy   274
    Shaobo Zhang, Liujie Yuan, Yuxing Li, Wenli Chen, and Yifei Ding

A Strategy-based Optimization Algorithm to Design Codes for DNA Data
Storage System   284
    Abdur Rasool, Qiang Qu, Qingshan Jiang, and Yang Wang

Multi-Relational Hierarchical Attention for Top-k Recommendation   300
    Shiwen Yang, Jinghua Zhu, and Heran XI

Edge Computing and Edge Intelligence

EdgeSP: Scalable Multi-device Parallel DNN Inference on Heterogeneous
Edge Clusters 317
    Zhipeng Gao, Shan Sun, Yinghan Zhang, Zijia Mo, and Chen Zhao

An Efficient Computation Offloading Strategy in Wireless Powered
Mobile-Edge Computing Networks 334
    Xiaobao Zhou, Jianqiang Hu, Mingfeng Liang, and Yang Liu

WiRD: Real-Time and Cross Domain Detection System on Edge Device 345
    Qing Yang, Tianzhang Xing, Zhiping Jiang, Junfeng Wang, and Jingyi He

Deep Learning with Enhanced Convergence and Its Application in MEC
Task Offloading 361
    Zheng Wan, Xiaogang Dong, and Changshou Deng

Dynamic Offloading and Frequency Allocation for Internet of Vehicles
with Energy Harvesting 376
    Teng Ma, Xin Chen, Yan Liang, and Ying Chen

SPACE: Sparsity Propagation Based DCNN Training Accelerator on Edge 391
    *Miao Wang, Zhen Chen, Chuxi Li, Zhao Yang, Lei Li, Meng Zhang,
    and Shengbing Zhang*

Worker Recruitment Based on Edge-Cloud Collaboration in Mobile
Crowdsensing System 406
    Jinghua Zhu, Yuanjing Li, Anqi Lu, and Heran Xi

Energy Efficient Deployment and Task Offloading for UAV-Assisted
Mobile Edge Computing 421
    Yangguang Lu, Xin Chen, Fengjun Zhao, and Ying Chen

Blockchain Systems

Research on Authentication and Key Agreement Protocol of Smart
Medical Systems Based on Blockchain Technology 439
    Xiaohe Wu, Jianbo Xu, W. Liang, and W. Jian

CRchain: An Efficient Certificate Revocation Scheme Based on Blockchain ... 453
    Xiaoxue Ge, Liming Wang, Wei An, Xiaojun Zhou, and Benyu Li

Anonymous Authentication Scheme Based on Trust and Blockchain
in VANETs 473
    Li Zhang and Jianbo Xu

BIPP: Blockchain-Based Identity Privacy Protection Scheme in Internet
of Vehicles for Remote Anonymous Communication 489
  Hongyu Wu, Xiaoning Feng, Guobin Kan, and Xiaoshu Jiang

Deep Learning Models and Applications

Self-adapted Frame Selection Module: Refine the Input Strategy for Video
Saliency Detection 509
  Shangrui Wu, Yang Wang, Tian Wang, Weijia Jia, and Ruitao Xie

Evolving Deep Parallel Neural Networks for Multi-Task Learning 517
  Jie Wu and Yanan Sun

An Embedding Carrier-Free Steganography Method Based on Wasserstein
GAN 532
  Xi Yu, Jianming Cui, and Ming Liu

Design of Face Detection Algorithm Accelerator Based on Vitis 546
  Jie Wang, Ao Gao, and Jingxin Li

FSAFA-stacking2: An Effective Ensemble Learning Model for Intrusion
Detection with Firefly Algorithm Based Feature Selection 555
  Guo Chen, Junyao Zheng, Shijun Yang, Jieying Zhou, and Weigang Wu

Attention-Based Cross-Domain Gesture Recognition Using WiFi Channel
State Information 571
  Hao Hong, Baoqi Huang, Yu Gu, and Bing Jia

Font Transfer Based on Parallel Auto-encoder for Glyph Perturbation
via Strokes Moving 586
  *Chen Wang, Yani Zhu, Zhangyi Shen, Dong Wang, Guohua Wu,
  and Ye Yao*

A Novel GNN Model for Fraud Detection in Online Trading Activities 603
  Jing Long, Fei Fang, and Haibo Luo

IoT

Non-interactive Zero Knowledge Proof Based Access Control
in Information-Centric Internet of Things 617
  Han Liu and Dezhi Han

Simultaneous Charger Placement and Power Scheduling for On-Demand
Provisioning of RF Wireless Charging Service 632
  Huatong Jiang, Yanjun Li, and Meihui Gao

A Cross-domain Authentication Scheme Based on Zero-Knowledge Proof 647
  Ruizhong Du, Xiaoya Li, and Yan Liu

NBUFlow: A Dataflow Based Universal Task Orchestration
and Offloading Platform for Low-Cost Development of IoT Systems
with Cloud-Edge-Device Collaborative Computing 665
  Lei Wang, Haiming Chen, and Wei Qin

IoT-GAN: Anomaly Detection for Time Series in IoT Based on Generative
Adversarial Networks 682
  *Xiaofei Chen, Shuo Zhang, Qiao Jiang, Jiayuan Chen, Hejiao Huang,
  and Chonglin Gu*

Freshness and Power Balancing Scheduling for Cooperative
Vehicle-Infrastructure System 695
  Qian Qiu, Liang Dai, and Guiping Wang

A Low Energy Consumption and Low Delay MAC Protocol Based
on Receiver Initiation and Capture Effect in 5G IoT 709
  Hua-Mei Qi, Jia-Qi Chen, Zheng-Yi Yuan, and Lin-Lin Fan

Building Portable ECG Classification Model with Cross-Dimension
Knowledge Distillation 724
  Renjie Tang, Junbo Qian, Jiahui Jin, and Junzhou Luo

Author Index 739

Software Systems and Efficient Algorithms

The Design and Realization of a Novel Intelligent Drying Rack System Based on STM32

Shiwen Zhang[1,2]([✉]), Wang Hu[1], Wei Liang[1], and Lei Liao[3]

[1] School of Computer Science and Engineering, Hunan University of Science
and Technology, XiangTan, Hunan, China
`shiwenzhang@hnust.edu.cn`
[2] Hunan Key Laboratory for Service Computing and Novel Software Technology,
Hunan, China
[3] Hunan Vocational College of Art, Changsha, Hunan, China

Abstract. With the development and progress of society, people have
higher and higher requirements for the intelligence of the drying rack
system. Therefore, it is essential practical significance to improve the
level of intelligence of the drying rack system in people's daily life. Traditional drying rack systems are mainly divided into four types: outdoor,
floor-standing, hand-operated, and electric. However, they all have the
disadvantages of consuming human resources, time, and space. In this
paper, we design a novel intelligent drying rack system based on STM32,
consisting of many sensors, a horizontal rotation mechanism, and a lifting mechanism. This intelligent drying rack system first uses raindrop
sensors, photoresistors, and wind speed sensors to collect external environmental information. Then, the system monitors the surrounding environment changes in real-time. When the environment changes, the system will drive the motor to realize collecting and drying clothes. Finally,
we can realize all intelligent control functions through voice module, button module, and infrared remote control. In addition, we also develop an
APP that displays the system's control interface and can realize all intelligent control functions. Through debug-running and system testing, the
simulation results demonstrate the accuracy and efficacy of the designed
drying rack system.

Keywords: Intelligent control · STM32 · Sensors · Drying rack system

1 Introduction

With the development of the Internet of Things (IoT) and wireless communication technology [1–4], the drying rack system has become a necessity for
many families. Traditional drying racks are mainly divided into four types: outdoor, floor-standing, hand-operated, and electric. Traditional outdoor and floor-
standing drying rack systems mainly consist of mechanical structures [5]. These
drying rack systems have the advantage of saving indoor space. However, these

© Springer Nature Switzerland AG 2022
Y. Lai et al. (Eds.): ICA3PP 2021, LNCS 13156, pp. 3–17, 2022.
https://doi.org/10.1007/978-3-030-95388-1_1

drying rack systems, which consist of mechanical structures, are usually heavy. People usually need to cost a lot to use these drying rack systems. It is extremely inconvenient for most people's daily lives. Traditional manual drying rack system is often installed in a fixed location [6–9]. When using the manual drying rack system, users need to start it by hand. Although it saves a certain amount of work, it is still inconvenient for users. Therefore, the efficacy of the manual drying rack systems is not very high. Subsequently, Zhu et al. [10] improved the traditional technology and designed an electric drying rack system. When electricity is supplied to these electric drying rack systems [11–14], they can run automatically. However, the electric drying rack systems cannot change their working state in response to the changes in the environment. Meanwhile, these drying rack systems tend to be fixed and difficult to move once installed. On the whole, these traditional drying rack systems do not have enough intelligence to meet the increasing requirements of people. Therefore, it is meaningful to develop an intelligent drying rack system to enhance the user's experience.

In this paper, we design a novel intelligent drying rack system that uses multiple sensors to obtain environmental information. The designed intelligent drying rack system can analyze the acquired environmental information to determine whether to drive the internal motor to realize the functions of collecting and drying clothes. We use the voice module, button module, and infrared remote control to achieve real-time intelligent indoor control. Regarding the mechanical structure of the drying rack system [19–21], we design a horizontal rotation mechanism device. This device rotates the clothes outwards so that the clothes are dried more evenly. Thus, this intelligent drying rack system can dry clothes as quickly as possible. At the same time, based on the WiFi and android intelligent home detection system [22–24], we also develop an APP that realizes the intelligent control of the system. Finally, we prove the accuracy and efficacy of the designed drying rack system by conducting some experiments. The main contributions of this paper are listed as follows:

- We utilize multiple sensors to obtain environmental data. Multiple sensor modules in the intelligent drying rack system can provide multiple environmental data. Therefore, the system can make precise control based on these large amounts of environmental data.
- We design a voice control, button control, and infrared remote control mechanism to collect clothes or dry clothes intelligently. We can speak a specific voice or press a specific button to achieve the corresponding control function. We also develop an APP to realize the intelligent control, which can show the overall functions of the drying rack system. When we are not at home, we can directly choose to use the APP to collect clothes or dry clothes.
- We debug the system and conduct extensive experiments on real-world sample data. The experimental results indicate the accuracy and efficacy of the designed intelligent drying rack system.

The rest of our paper is organized as follows: Sect. 2 reviews related works and introduces relevant preliminaries. In Sect. 3, we present the design of the system. Then, we show the system hardware design in Sect. 4. Section 5 and Sect. 6 respectively introduce the software design and the performance evaluation. Finally, Sect. 7 concludes this paper.

2 Related Work

In 2010, Zhu [10] first designed an intelligent electric drying rack system to realize the function of automatically collecting clothes. This intelligent drying rack system adopts a pulley structure and is driven by a motor. The designed drying rack system detects weather changes through rain and snow sensors and automatically collects or dries clothes. However, this drying rack system only considers rain and snow conditions, and the scope of use has great limitations. Later, Deng et al. [15] designed a multifunctional intelligent drying rack system. The designed intelligent drying rack system uses AT89C52 as the main control chip. This drying rack system's button, photoresistor, and raindrop detection module transmit the light intensity and weather information to the central control chip in real-time. The main control chip in the system controls the rotation of the stepper motor, which allows the mechanical device to stretch and contract smoothly. Although this drying rack system adds button control functions, it is still not intelligent enough. In 2020, Zhang et al. [18] designed an intelligent drying rack system based on STC89C51. This intelligent drying rack system consists of a sensor module, a wireless transceiver module, a motor control module, and a status display module. However, the designed intelligent drying rack system has few sensors, and the wireless transmission function is not perfect.

To improve the technology of the intelligent drying rack system, wireless control is widely used. In 2019, Li et al. [17] designed an intelligent quick-drying system with the microcontroller HT66F70A as the core. According to the environmental information collected by the sensors in the system, this drying rack system determines whether to drive the stepping motor to realize the function of collecting clothes or drying clothes. The designed drying rack system can also send information through remote control and GSM module to realize the function of collecting or drying clothes. In 2021, Wu et al. [16] designed a similar intelligent drying rack system. The intelligent drying rack system is connected to the smart home system through the Internet of Things to realize the wireless control function. In addition, this drying rack system adds more sensors than the previous intelligent drying rack system. However, the mechanical structure of these intelligent drying rack systems is not perfect and lacks indoor voice and button control functions.

Different from existing work, we design a novel intelligent drying rack system based on STM32. The designed intelligent drying rack system has more sensors to monitor environmental factors. This intelligent drying rack system can realize all control functions through voice module, button module, infrared remote control, and APP. We conduct some simulation experiments to verify the accuracy and efficacy of the designed drying rack system.

3   System Design

3.1   System Framework

In this paper, the system framework of the intelligent drying rack system is shown in Fig. 1. The intelligent drying rack system is designed based on STM32 single-chip microcomputer. This intelligent drying rack system collects environmental information through various sensors. The remote controller sends a pulse signal to the infrared module. The STM32 microcontroller processor in the drying rack system can receive various signals from the infrared module, button module, and voice module in real-time. The cloud server receives the control information from the APP and sends the information to the WIFI module [25]. The WIFI module will send the information from the cloud server to the micro-control processor of the drying rack system. This drying rack system will drive the motor to achieve intelligent control.

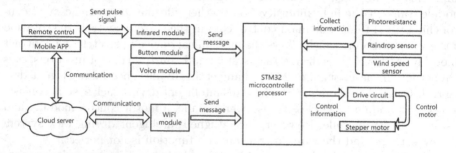

Fig. 1. System framework of the intelligent drying rack system.

3.2   System Function Module

The main functional modules of the drying rack system are the sensor module, wireless module, voice control module, stepper motor module, and infrared remote control module. The sensor module mainly consists of a raindrop sensor, wind speed sensor, and photoresistor. The raindrop sensor detects whether it is raining or not. The wind speed sensor detects the wind speed and transmits the wind data to the system. The photoresistor collects light intensity data through an analog-to-digital converter and transmits the information to the system. We use the Attention (AT) command to configure the wireless module to operate in Station (STA) and Access Point (AP) modes. The wireless module is equal to serial WIFI in STA mode. The wireless module can receive data from the STM32 serial port and upload data to the cloud server. We use the voice module to achieve intelligent control. When we speak a keyword of the voice, the system will execute the corresponding function. The stepper motor module is connected to the port of STM32. We control the rotation of the stepper motor through the port output of STM32. We have set different functions for the buttons on the infrared remote control.

3.3 Principle of Control

We first introduce the requirements of the system. We suppose that the wind speed threshold is 5 (m/s). When the wind speed of the surrounding environment exceeds the threshold, the system will realize the function of collecting clothes (the output function value is 1). The output function is a nonlinear binary function. The wind power binary function is shown in Eq. 1.

$$f(x) = \begin{cases} 1 & x \geq 5 \\ 0 & x < 5 \end{cases} \tag{1}$$

The characteristic of the photoresistor is that the stronger the light, the lower the resistance value. As the light increases, the resistance value continues to decrease. We suppose that the threshold of light intensity is 80 (lx). When the light intensity of the environment exceeds the threshold, the system will dry the clothes(the output value is 1). On the contrary, the system will collect clothes. The output function is a non-linear binary function. The illumination binary function is shown in Eq. 2.

$$h(x) = \begin{cases} 1 & x \geq 80 \\ 0 & x < 80 \end{cases} \tag{2}$$

3.4 System Flow

First, we initialize the drying rack system. Various sensors in the system are in working condition and continuously monitor the surrounding environment. Second, when the surrounding environment changes, this drying rack system automatically analyzes whether to drive the motor to achieve intelligent control. Third, the cloud server receives the control information from APP and sends the information to the WIFI module. When the drying rack system receives control information from the WIFI module, remote control, button module, and voice module, this drying rack system will drive the corresponding motor to collect or dry clothes.

4 System Hardware Design

4.1 Main Control Chip

The principle diagram of the main control chip is shown in Fig. 2. The STM32F103 is selected as the main control chip for the intelligent clothes drying rack system. This master chip has 48 pins and 37 input (I)/output (O) pins. All I/O interfaces in the chip can be mapped to 16 external interrupts. Most of the ports in the chip are compatible with 5V signals. Each I/O port can receive or output 8(mA) current, which can fill up to 20(mA) current. This master chip has powerful functions and has been widely used in the embedded field. The combination of crystal circuits in this master chip and STM32 internal circuit ensures the standard clock frequency of STM32. This intelligent drying rack system uses two ceramic capacitors to ensure that the crystal oscillator can usually start the vibration in the drying rack system. At the output of the crystal oscillator circuit, the resistor and load capacitor form a current limiting network. The primary function of the current limiting network is to limit the current and prevent damage to the crystal oscillator circuit inside the inverter. The stability of this main control chip ensures that the drying rack system can realize various intelligent controls.

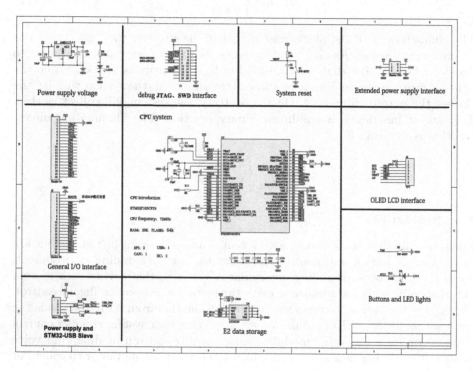

Fig. 2. Schematic diagram of main control chip.

4.2 Raindrop Sensor Module

The circuit diagram of the raindrop module is shown in Fig. 3(a). When the raindrop sensor is connected to the system, the sensor in the drying rack system keeps in the ready state. When the sensor detects a droplet on the board, the output value of the system decreases, and the switch indicator light comes on. If rain drops on the monitoring board, the motor will be driven to achieve intelligent control. The raindrops on the detection board disappear, the sensor outputs a high value, and the switch indicator light goes out. According to the analog output principle, the raindrop sensor connected to the STM32 port detects the number of raindrops in real-time. When there are water droplets on the detection plate of the raindrop sensor, the raindrop sensor can determine the digital output of the system. When the drying rack system detects the corresponding level, the system will automatically collect clothes.

4.3 Photoresistor Module

The circuit diagram of the photoresistor is shown in Fig. 3(b). The working principle of the photoresistor is based on the internal photoelectric effect. As the light intensity increases, the resistance value of the photoresistor drops rapidly. The photoresistor is the output of the comparator, which has the advantages of clear signal, suitable waveform, and strong driving ability. We can use the adjustable potentiometer to adjust the brightness of the detection lamp. The output form of the photoresistor is 0 or 1. According to the output value, this intelligent drying rack system will automatically collect or dry clothes.

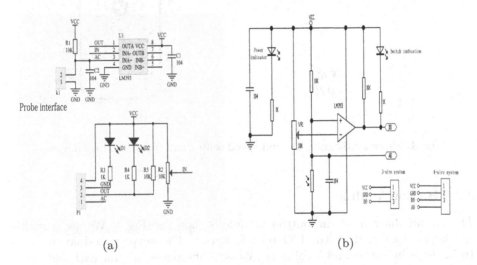

Fig. 3. Schematic diagram of raindrop module and photoresistor.

4.4 Wind Speed Sensor Module

The wind structure diagram is shown in Fig. 4(a). The wind speed sensor consists of a housing, a wind cup, and a circuit module. The wind speed sensor has a photoelectric conversion mechanism, microcomputer processor, standard current generator, and current driver. The wind speed sensor is three wind cups structure. The wind cup is made of polycarbonate fiber material with high strength and good stability. The signal processing unit inside the cup outputs the wind speed signal. When the wind sensor detects high wind speed, the drying rack system will collect clothes.

4.5   Infrared Module

The infrared controller and infrared receiver are shown in Fig. 4(b). The STM32 microcontroller has an infrared receiver. The signal of the drying rack system goes low when the system receives an infrared signal. The level change in the system is essentially a pulse. After decoding the pulse, the drying rack system will collect or dry clothes.

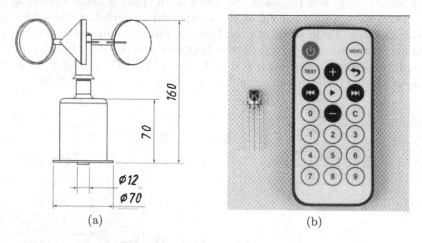

(a)   (b)

Fig. 4. Shematic diagram of wind speed sensor and remote control device.

4.6   Button Module

The circuit diagram of the button module is shown in Fig. 5. We use a multi-key keyboard to reduce the I/O port footprint. The keypad module connects 16 buttons in 5 rows and 5 columns. We set different values for each button in the system, and different buttons represent different functions. The drying rack system is mainly used by scanning the keys and storing the scanned values in variables. When different keys are pressed, this drying rack system can realize different intelligent controls.

4.7   Speech Recognition Module

The schematic diagram of the speech recognition module is shown in Fig. 6. Speech recognition is a technology based on keyword list recognition. The speech module uses tone to compare human pronunciation and find the word that best matches the pronunciation of the keyword. We reduce the false recognition rate by adding some other arbitrary words to the recognition list. The microcontroller (MCU) in the system in the drying rack receives the speech data. After parsing the voice data, the drying rack system collects or dries the clothes.

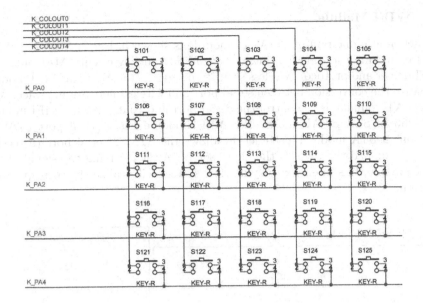

Fig. 5. Schematic diagram of buttons.

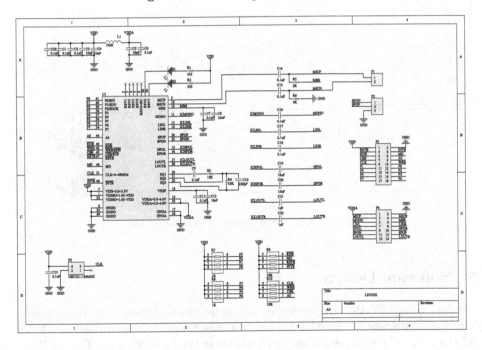

Fig. 6. Schematic diagram of speech recognition module.

4.8   WIFI Module

The schematic diagram of the WiFi module is shown in Fig. 7. ESP8266 WIFI serial communication module integrates radio frequency circuit, MAC address, WIFI driver and protocol, wireless security protocol, etc. We use a WIFI module to realize the conversion between serial port and wireless network interface. And we use AT commands to control the serial port and configure the WIFI module ESP8266 in STA or AP mode. The WIFI module has a serial port to WiFi function in STA mode. This function allows the STM32 serial port to receive data and upload the data to the cloud server. After receiving the signal of the WIFI module, this intelligent drying rack system will realize the corresponding function.

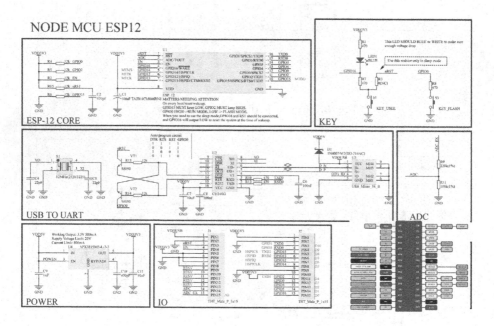

Fig. 7. Schematic diagram of WIFI module.

5   Software Design

We design an APP that displays the control interface of the drying rack system. The main interface of the APP is shown in Fig. 8(a). The main interface of this APP adopts a layered design and is displayed in the form of cards. The APP can display the current wind speed, temperature, and air humidity in real-time. We can use the functions of lifting, panning, spinning, and harvesting in the APP to realize the intelligent control of the drying rack system.

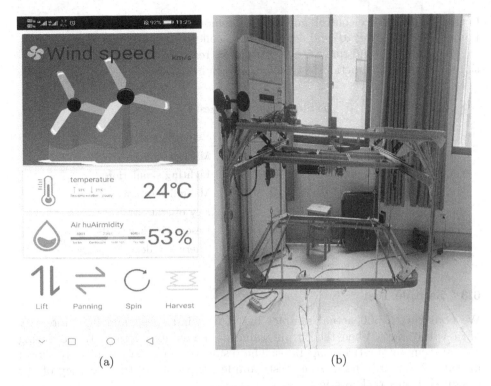

(a)   (b)

Fig. 8. Schematic diagram of WIFI module and APP main interface.

6   Performance Evaluation

6.1   Environment Settings

In this paper, we develop the hardware system of an intelligent drying rack with the C language on the MDK5 platform. We develop and configure the WiFi module ESP8266 on the Arduino platform by using the C++ language. We use the Java language to develop a software application controller on the Android studio platform. All the tests in this paper are implemented on a computer with a 2.3 GHz Intel Core i5 eight-core processor and 8 GB RAM.

6.2   Physical Test

We install the debugged hardware devices on the mechanical device and assemble them into actual products. The physical diagram of the intelligent drying rack system is shown in Fig. 8(b). After installing the intelligent drying rack system, we conduct the following functional tests. First, we turn on the power and let the system run without clothes hanging. Second, we test the function of raindrop, photosensitive, and wind speed sensors, respectively. Third, we test button control, voice control, and infrared remote control functions, respectively. Fourth, We use APP to send commands to collect clothes or dry clothes.

By debugging and running the system, we realize all intelligent control functions. The system function test table is shown in Table 1.

Table 1. Functional test table

Realize the function	Completion	Remarks
Dripping	✓	Manual drip test
Dim light	✓	Lighting simulation
Wind force	✓	Manual rotation
Button control	✓	Key operation
Voice control	✓	Descriptive keywords
APP control	✓	There is a delay

6.3 Sample Test

We constructed 300 actual samples based on wind speed and light intensity on a windy day. When the output value of the sample data is 1, the drying rack system automatically operates. The results of some test samples are shown in Table 2. The results of some test samples demonstrate the accuracy of the designed drying rack system.

Table 2. Partial test samples

Sample number	Wind speed	Light intensity	Output
1	0.8 (m/s)	27.0 (lx)	0.00
2	6.0 (m/s)	58.0 (lx)	1.00
3	2.4 (m/s)	66.0 (lx)	0.00
4	4.3 (m/s)	85.0 (lx)	1.00
5	7.0 (m/s)	100.0 (lx)	1.00
6	8.4 (m/s)	154.0 (lx)	1.00
7	3.4 (m/s)	66.0 (lx)	0.00
8	4.9 (m/s)	79.0 (lx)	1.00
9	3.8 (m/s)	99.0 (lx)	1.00
10	9.5 (m/s)	85.0 (lx)	1.00
11	4.5 (m/s)	85.0 (lx)	1.00
12	4.9 (m/s)	78.0 (lx)	1.00

A comparative summary of the novel intelligent drying rack system based on STM32 and existing intelligent drying rack systems is shown in Table 3. This intelligent drying rack system has more comprehensive control functions than existing drying rack systems [5–9].

Table 3. A comparative summary

Systems	F_1	F_2	F_3	F_4	F_5	F_6
[5]	2					✓
[6]	2				✓	✓
[7]	4			✓		✓
[8]	3		✓	✓		✓
[9]	2		✓			✓
Ours	6	✓	✓	✓	✓	✓

Note. "F_1": Number of sensor types; "F_2": Voice control function; "F_3": Infrared remote control control function; "F_4": APP control function; "F_5": Button control function; "F_6": Sensor threshold control.

6.4 Performance Evaluation

We evaluate the execution time and delay time of the intelligent drying rack system. We test on 300 samples. The system time cost is shown in Fig. 9. The transmission of APP control commands needs to pass through the cloud server so

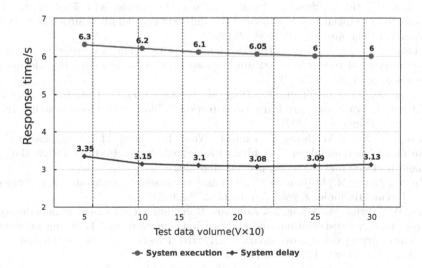

Fig. 9. System time cost.

that the intelligent drying rack system has a delay of 3 s. The execution time of the intelligent drying rack system is about 6 s. With the increase of test samples, the execution time and delay time of the system remain basically stable. The system time cost indicates the efficacy of the designed drying rack system.

7   Conclusion

In this paper, we design a novel intelligent drying rack system based on STM32. Unlike the previous intelligent drying rack system, we use multiple sensors to monitor environmental data in real-time. Meanwhile, we use the voice module, button module, and infrared remote control to achieve real-time intelligent indoor control. Finally, we also develop an APP to show the system's function and realize the control function. In addition, we give the performance analysis of the system and conduct extensive experiments on real actual samples to evaluate the performance of our system. The experiment indicates that the designed intelligent drying rack system has good accuracy and efficacy. In future work, we will continue to expand the system functions and improve the system's performance in all aspects.

Acknowledgment. This work is supported in part by the National Natural Science Foundation of China (No. 61702180), and the Hunan Province Science and Technology Project Funds (No. 2018TP1036).

References

1. Danzi, P., et al.: Communication aspects of the integration of wireless IoT devices with distributed ledger technology. IEEE Network **34**, 47–53 (2020)
2. Wang, W., He, S., Sun, L., Jiang, T., Zhang, Q.: Cross-technology communications for heterogeneous IoT devices through artificial doppler shifts. IEEE Trans. Wireless Commun. **18**, 796–806 (2019)
3. Liang, W., Ning, Z., Xie, S., Hu, Yu., Lu, S., Zhang, D.: Secure fusion approach for the internet of things in smart autonomous multi-robot systems. In: Information Science, pp. 1–20 (2021)
4. Liang, W., Xiao, L., Zhang, K., Tang, M., He, D., Li, K. C.: Data fusion approach for collaborative anomaly intrusion detection in blockchain-based systems. IEEE Internet Things J., 1 (2021)
5. Yang, X., Xiong, W., Song, S., Yang, J., Wang, K., Cheng, M.: Design and analysis for multi-functional drying machine with umbrella frame. In: Information Management and Computer Science, pp. 482–486 (2020)
6. Su, Y., Zhang, M., Mujumdar, A.: Recent developments in smart drying technology. In: Drying Technology, vol. 33, pp. 260–276 (2015)
7. Lv, W., Zhang, M., Wang, Y., Adhikari, B.: Online measurement of moisture content, moisture distribution, and state of water in corn kernels during microwave vacuum drying using novel smart NMR/MRI detection system. In: Drying Technology, vol. 36, pp. 1592–1602 (2019)
8. Menshutina, N., Goncharova-Alves, S., Matasov, A.: Intelligent systems for the design of drying processes. In: Drying Technology, vol. 38, pp. 147–157 (2020)

9. Liang, Y., Lin, S., Huang, J., Li, A.: Design and development of outdoor intelligent waterproof clothes-drying device. In: Technological Development of Enterprise (2013)
10. Zhu, B.: An intelligent electric clothes drying device. In: Forum of Association for Science and Technology, no. 10, pp. 71–72 (2010)
11. Tang, J., Feng, H., Ding, J., Zhou, H., Xuan, H.: Research and implementation of indoor environment monitorable control system based on internet of things technology. In: Technological Innovation and Application, no. 33, pp. 14–16 (2019)
12. Lin, Y., Lee, Y., Chang, C.: Establishing an intelligent laundry drying rack using system innovation theory. In: IOP Conference Series: Earth and Environmental Science, vol. 603, no. 1, pp. 12–47 (2020)
13. Xing, X., Zhang, C., Gu, J., Zhang, Y., Lv, X., Zhuo, Z.: Intelligent drying rack system based on internet of things. J. Phys. Conf. Ser. **1887**(1) (2021)
14. Zhang, Y., Miao, F., Xing, S., Wang, Z., Xiong, X.: Home intelligent integrated wardrobe. J. Phys. Conf. Ser. **1748**(6) (2021)
15. Deng, T., Wang, Z.: Multifunctional intelligent clothes drying rack system. In: Electronic Technology and Software Engineering, no. 16, pp. 105–106 (2018)
16. Wu, K., Xu, Q., Liu, H., Yuan, J., Tong, X.: Research and design of a new intelligent drying device. In: China's Collective Economy, no. 12, pp. 165–166 (2021)
17. Li, J., Li, B., Chen, J.: Intelligent quick clothes drying device. In: Technology and Innovation, no. 9, pp. 82–86 (2019)
18. Zhang, B., Ma, Y., Qiu, X., Hao, S.: Design and implementation of intelligent clothes hanger control system. Microprocessor **41**(3), 48–50 (2020)
19. Wu, Z., Lin, Q., Xie, X., Yu, K., Wang, Q., Lin, J.: Movable smart outdoor drying rack design. In: Technological Innovation and Application, no. 6, pp. 34–37 (2021)
20. Chen, Y., Hong, L., Hu, B.: Design of intelligent rainproof telescopic drying rack based on STC89C52 single-chip microcomputer. In: Electromechanical Engineering Technology, vol. 49, no. 11, pp. 43–45 (2020)
21. Li, Y., Zhang, J., Mo, J.: Design of smart clothes rack based on Arduino single chip microcomputer. In: Science and Technology Innovation, no. 33, pp. 183–184 (2020)
22. Wang, L., Peng, D., Zhang, T.: Design of smart home system based on WiFi smart plug. In: Int. J. Smart Home **9**, 173–182 (2015)
23. Liang, W., Zhang, D., Lei, X., Tang, M., Li, K., Zomaya, A.: Circuit copyright blockchain: blockchain-based homomorphic encryption for IP circuit protection. IEEE Trans. Emerging Topics Comput. **9**(3), 1410–1420 (2021)
24. Liang, W., Long, J., Li, K., Xu, J., Ma, N., Lei, X.: A fast defogging image recognition algorithm based on bilateral hybrid filtering. ACM Trans. Multimedia Comput. Commun. Appl. **17**(2), 1–16 (2021)
25. Bleikher, O., Kvesko, S.: Using of information systems for socio-economic management applications in mechanical engineering enterprises. In: Applied Mechanics and Materials, vol. 770, pp. 651–655 (2015)

Efficient Estimation of Time-Dependent Shortest Paths Based on Shortcuts

Linbo Liao[1], Shipeng Yang[1], Yongxuan Lai[1]([✉]), Wenhua Zeng[1], Fan Yang[2], and Min Jiang[1]

[1] School of Informatics/Shenzhen Research Institute, Xiamen University, Xiamen 361005, China
{laiyx,whzeng,minjiang}@xmu.edu.cn
[2] School of Aerospace Engineering, Xiamen University, Xiamen 361005, China
yang@xmu.edu.cn

Abstract. The shortest path search in the road network in the road network is of great importance in various Intelligent Transportation Systems. However, the commonly used shortest path search algorithms, such as Dijkstra and A * algorithm, are time-consuming due to their complexity, which leads to their poor performance in large-scale road networks. Thus, a new optimization technology is required to solve the path search problem on large-scale road networks. In this paper, the temporal feature of the road network is considered for the shortest path search problem, which is closer to the road network of the real world. And, an algorithm called *Time-Dependent A* With Shortcuts (TDAWS)* is proposed to estimate the time-dependent shortest paths. Concretely, the road network is pre-processed offline and partitioned into several regions based on clustering, which captures the spatial pattern of the road network. Then we construct shortcuts contain the shortest paths information to reduce search time and propose two mechanisms called Hop On Directionally (HOD) and Hop-Off Early (HOE) to avoid unnecessary detours. We constructed an extensive experimental study on a road network with real-world taxi trajectory data and compared our approach with existing techniques. The results demonstrated that the time cost of our method is more stable and achieves up to 17 times faster than the precise shortest path searching algorithm with an acceptable extra ratio (about 20%) on the path length.

Keywords: Approximate shortest path · Graph partition · Path estimation · Time-dependent road network

This work was supported in part by the Natural Science Foundation of China under Grant 6187215 and Natural Science Foundation of Guandong under Grant 2021A1515011578, and Shenzhen Basic Research Program under Grant JCYJ20190809161603551.

Y. Lai et al. (Eds.): ICA3PP 2021, LNCS 13156, pp. 18–32, 2022.
https://doi.org/10.1007/978-3-030-95388-1_2

1   Introduction

With the development of intelligent transportation, many car-hailing systems and navigation systems have emerged in recent years [13]. Those systems process millions of path-planning or time-estimations tasks every day, within which the shortest path search is a fundamental block. The shortest path computation must be efficient to respond in a real-time way [16]. However, the shortest path searching algorithms are time-consuming due to the complexity of the task [22]. Besides, time-dependent shortest path search, which considers time-dependent factors like traffic jams, becomes a general search method and increases the computing time.

The well-known Dijkstra algorithm [5] performs well on static graphs and can be extended to the time-dependent case straightforwardly [6]. However, there are lots of repeated computations when processing shortest path search on the same road network. Moreover, the A^* algorithm [12] is a goal-directed search and is guaranteed to explore no more nodes than Dijkstra's algorithm. In the A^* algorithm, all the computed information is cached to accelerate the search, which requires a huge memory space and makes it impractical.

Road networks have some unique features that distinguish them from other common graph structures. First, the road network is usually a hierarchical network, in which the high-grade highway has greater capacity and higher driving speed than the low-grade highway. Second, high-grade highways can span and link different regions, while low-grade highways are scattered in each region. Therefore, when planning a trip from one area to another, people often choose the main road first and then the minor road leading to the main road. In this way, we can reduce the complexity of the path search process. Besides, some scenarios like the travel time estimation, in which only an estimated cost of the travel time needed, can avoid the detailed exact shortest path calculation [2]. Therefore, we need to optimize the classical shortest path algorithms such as the Dijkstra algorithm [5] to solve the time-dependent shortest path problem.

In this paper, we study the problem of travel time estimation for large-scale time-varying road networks. The challenges lie in several aspects: 1) the search time is positively correlated with the distance between origin and destination, which results in a big difference in the time costs between long-distance and short-distance path searching; 2) the speeds of the road segments change with time, which increases the uncertainty of path searching. In this paper, the idea *shortcut* [7] is applied to quickly guide the search process from the start region to the end region. And we propose an efficient algorithm that estimates the shortest path on time-dependent road networks based on the shortcut mechanism. The major contributions of this paper are as follows:

- We proposed a bidirectional partition method that combines with the K-Means clustering [17] to partition a road network into regions, where shortcuts are inserted at their best positions.
- We proposed a path searching algorithm to estimate the shortest paths efficiently. Different from existing research, we consider the shortest path search

problem within the scenario of large-scale time-dependent road networks. And our approach adopts bidirectional partitions and shortcuts to make the searching time-efficient and stable.
- We conducted extensive experiments on a real road network with real request datasets. The results demonstrated that our approach achieves up to 17 times faster than the precise shortest path searching algorithm with an acceptable deviation on the path length. Besides, the searching time is stable regardless of the distance from the origin to the destination.

The rest of this paper is organized as follows. Section 2 presents the related work of this paper. Section 3 gives some preliminaries and problem definitions. Section 4 presents the details of the graph partition algorithm that combines K-Means and the construction of shortcuts. Section 5 presents the detailed description of the approximating shortest path algorithm based on shortcut mechanism. Section 6 presents the implementation details of hop on directionally and hop off early. Section 7 presents the experimental studies and analysis. Finally, Sect. 8 concludes the paper and presents some future directions.

2   Related Work

There are lots of speed-up techniques proposed for path-finding algorithms during the past several decades [4, 21]. This section mainly introduces two important algorithms related to road networks: 1) algorithm based on hierarchy in road network; 2) graph-based search space trimming algorithm.

A lot of works use the hierarchical structure of the road network to accelerate the search. Shapiro et al. [19] proposed a heuristic algorithm that uses the "level" of nodes and edges to generate approximate shortest paths rapidly. This algorithm can obtain the near-optimal path by searching a few nodes. Chou et al. [2] partitioned a large-scale network into a high-level subnetwork and a set of lower-level subnetworks. The partitioning permits a trade-off between pre-computation and query time processing. Then, they proposed a hierarchical algorithm to approximate the shortest paths in large-scale networks. A traffic mining approach had been proposed by Gonzalez et al. [10]. They used the road hierarchy and pre-computed areas to limit the search space. Delling and Nannicini [3] noted the timing of the road network and proposed a hierarchical approach called *core routing* that combined with bidirectional goal-directed search in time-dependent road networks. This algorithm is flexible and suitable for a dynamic scenario where the piecewise linear time-dependent cost functions on unfixed arcs. But the algorithm did not reduce the search time compared with the shortest path estimation algorithm while it has a complex preprocessing.

The road network contains a lot of road information, and a lot of work uses the pre-computed information of the road network to prune the search space. Wagner and Willhalm [20] pruned the Dijkstra's search by using geometric containers with precomputed information. Experiments show that the search space for online computation reduced significantly.Lauther, U. I. [14,15] proposed a variant of Dijkstra's algorithm by using edge flags to prune the search space in static networks. They partitioned the road network into geometrically connected regions and introduced the concept of edge flags: the flag is set if there is a shortest path over it into the target region. Möhring et al. [18] also introduced an algorithm that uses edge flags and particularly examined different partitioning algorithms and compared their impact on the speed-up of the shortest-path algorithm. They found that the bidirectional search is the best partition-based speed-up method among the methods they tested. Gutman [11] defined the vertex reach and pruned a path search by using vertex reaches. It easily handles multiple origins and destinations. Goldberg et al. [8, 9] improved the reach-based approach of Gutman [11] and introduced a practical algorithm that combines A^* search, landmark-based lower bounds, and reach-based pruning. Through the reach-aware landmarks and improved algorithm, the preprocessing and queries are faster while the overall space consumption is reduced.

Most existing works use a hierarchical structure or preprocess the road network to speed up the search or reduce the search scope. However, these algorithms consume a lot of time as the request distance increases. We consider the directed large-scale time-dependent road network and propose an efficient shortest path estimation algorithm based on road network partitions and shortcuts which has a stable search efficiency regardless of the distances of requests.

3   Problem Definition

3.1   Time-Dependent Road Network

Let a strongly connected directed graph $G = (V, E)$ be the road network with a set of nodes V and a set of edges $E \subseteq V \times V$. The edges of a graph are weighted by a function $w : (E, t_0) \rightarrow \mathbb{R}$ where t_0 is time.

The weight of an edge $e(u, v) \in E$ at time t_0 is the traveling time from u to v instead of distances; we denote the weight of edge $e(u, v)$ at time t_0 as $w(e(u, v), t_0)$. Given a path from o to d can be denote as $p(o, d, t_0) = (v_0 = o, ..., v_i, ...v_j, ..., v_k = o)$, where t_0 is the departure time. Then the weight of path p is defined as $w(p) = w_0(e(v_0, v_1), t_0) + w_1(e(v_1, v_2), t_1) + ... + w_{k-1}(e(v_{k-1}, v_k), t_{k-1})$, where $t_{i+1} = t_i + w_i(e(v_i, v_{i+1}), t_i)$. The path that has the minimum weight from o to d with a departure time t_0 is called the shortest path which is denoted by $p_s(o, d, t_0)$. We construct an edge $e(o, d)$ with weight $w(e(o, d), t_0) = w(p_s(o, d, t_0))$, which is called the *shortcut* from o to d. As shown in Fig. 1, the dotted line represents the shortcut from A to E, its weight is the minimum path weight from A to E. In the following, we represent the path as $p(o, d)$ when the departure time t_0 is known as context.

3.2   Partitions of Road Network

Given a strongly connected directed graph $G = (V, E)$, we denote the partition of G as $P_m(1 \leq m \leq k)$, where k is the total number of the partitions. The

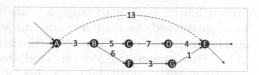

Fig. 1. A shortcut bypassing several nodes: the dotted line is the shortcut from node A to E, which represents the shortest path $p(A, E) = (A, B, F, G, E)$.

$V_{P_m}(1 \leq m \leq k)$ is the set of vertices in P_m and $V_{P_m} \cap V_{P_n} = \emptyset (m \neq n$ and $1 \leq m, n \leq k)$. Each partition has a representative node $C_m(1 \leq m \leq k)$, which is called *core node*.

For any node x in the graph G, the index of its partition can be expressed as i(x). So the partition that x belongs to can be denoted by $P_{i(x)}$ and the corresponding core node is $C_{i(x)}$. For simplicity, we replace them with P_x and C_x in the following.

4   Graph Partitioning and Shortcuts Construction

The preprocessing that creates additional information can reduce the search space. More precisely, our approach uses regions to constrain the search space and uses shortcuts to accelerate the path search algorithm. The weights of paths greatly depend on how the road network is partitioned and how core nodes are selected, as they severely affect the quality of shortcuts. In this section, we introduce the preprocessing of the time-dependent road network: graph partitioning and shortcut construction.

The main idea of our algorithm is to use shortcuts between regions to reduce the search space and accelerate the search. Considering the consumption of storage space, we only establish the shortcut between core nodes of each region. Partition and core node acquisition can be divided into two steps: 1) select the core nodes by the K-Means clustering-based algorithm; 2) generate the regions according to the core nodes. Then, a modified $A*$ algorithm is applied to accelerate the estimate of the time-dependent shortest path. The algorithm accelerates the searching by shortcuts when the origin and destination are not in the same region. Besides, two measures are adopted to avoid excessive detours. One can lead the algorithm to "hop on" a better shortcut and the other can help the algorithm "hop off" the shortcut more smoothly.

4.1   Bidirectional Partitioning

For a 2D layout of the graph, a common way is grid partition, where nodes in the same grid are divided into a partition. Figure 2(a) shows an example of grid partition, which can partition a graph into different regions fast in an easy way. However, this method ignores other properties like the density of nodes. Another partition method is based on the K-Means clustering algorithm, which divides the sample set into k clusters according to the distance. The criterion of K-means is to reduce the distance between nodes within a cluster while increasing the distance between clusters. Figure 2(b) shows an example of the K-Means partition. However, the K-Means partition is not very suitable for road networks. First, longitude and latitude, used in distance calculations, can not represent the actual distance between two nodes in a road network. As the nodes are linked by several road segments, which have different speed limits and lengths. Second, the road network can be seen as a directed graph. For example, a car may go through different road segments when it goes from node a to node b and node b to node a.

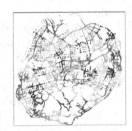

(a) Grid partition   (b) K-Means partition

Fig. 2. Two partition methods of Xiamen island

To generate the partitions considering the bidirectional distances between nodes, we process as follows:

1. First, we select core nodes based on K-means in two steps: 1) Obtain K partitions by the K-Means clustering algorithm; 2) the central node of each partition is identified as the core node, which has the shortest distance sum to other nodes in the same region. Then, we adopt the Distance-First Partitioning on graph G to assign nodes to suitable partitions in turn, whose pseudocode is shown in Algorithm 1. In the first part of the algorithm, the cluster centers(core nodes) are generated by K-Means algorithm (line 1). Then, the *candidateSet* is initialized to a set of all nodes except the core nodes (line 2). Queues are created for each core node to store the neighbor nodes in ascending order of distance to the core node (line 3–6). In the second part, we select partitions for each node in turn. For each partition, we extract a node from the queue and add it into the partition if it is in the candidate set. Then, we add the neighbor nodes of the node to the queue in order (line 14–18). Each partition performs the same steps in turn.

2. We also adapt the *Distance-First Partitioning* algorithm on the reversed graph[1] G^{-1} to represent the distance relationship between nodes and core nodes more comprehensively. The partition and core node in G^{-1} are denoted by P_m^{-1} and C_m^{-1} ($1 \leq m \leq k$) respectively.

---

[1] G^{-1} has the same vertex set as G but all edges reversed.

Algorithm 1: DistanceFirstPartition(G, k)

---

   input : A graph G, number of clusters k
   output: A partitioned graph

1 Obtain the core nodes N_{core} of K partitions according to the K-Means clustering algorithm;
2 Initialize the candidate set S_c as the node in the graph except the core nodes;
3 Initialize empty queues Q for each partition;
4 **for** i in k **do**
5   Otain the neighbor nodes of $N_{core}[i]$;
6   Add the sorted neighbor nodes into $Q[i]$ by distance in ascending order;

7 **while** S_c is not $empty$ **do**
8   **for** i in k **do**
9   **while** $Q[i]$ is not $empty$ **do**
10   currentNode = $Q[i]$.pop();
11   **if** $currentNode$ in S_c **then**
12   Add the currentNode into the partition of core node $N_{core}[i]$;
13   Remove the currentNode from the candidate set S_c;
14   Otain the neighbor nodes N_{cur} of the currentNode;
15   **for** $node$ in N_{cur} **do**
16   **if** $node$ in S_c **then**
17   Calculate the distance from the node to the core node;
18   Add the node to $Q[i]$ and sort $Q[i]$;

19   break;

20 **return** G;

We call this algorithm *Bidirectional Partitioning* because it considers the bidirectional distances between nodes and obtained two partitioning schemes according to the directions of edges.

4.2 Add Shortcuts

To reduce the complexity of searching the shortest path, we created a shortcut for each pair of core nodes: additional edges with time-dependent weight equal to the original shortest path between their endpoints. And we use $sc(u, v)$ to denote the shortcut from node u to node v. Then, we divide a day evenly into x time slices for that the time-dependent weight of the path is dynamic. Then we calculate the shortcut between each core node pair in each time slice and store them in the memory. It is obvious that the accuracy and storage space are increase with the time slices x.

5 Time-Dependent A^* with Shortcuts

In this section, we introduce a fast approach for estimating the shortest paths of a node pair. Our algorithm can reduce the search time significantly while

---

Algorithm 2: TDAWS(G, o, d, t_0)

---

    input : A preprocessed graph G, the origin node o, the destination node d, the
              start time t_0
    output: A approximate shortest path from o to d

1 **if** $G.C_o^{-1} == G.C_d$ **then**
2 | $p = TDRA(G, o, d, t_0)$;
3 | **return** p ;
4 **else**
5 | $p_1 = TDRA(G, o, C_o^{-1}, t_0)$;
6 | $p_2 = C_o^{-1}.shortcut(C_d, t_0 + w(p_1))$;
7 | $p_3 = TDRA(G, C_d, d, t_0 + w(p_1) + w(p_2))$;
8 | **return** $p_1 + p_2 + p_3$;

---

the weight of the result is nearly optimal. The main idea is to use the precomputed information, partitions and shortcuts, to narrow the search and omit the calculation.

Given a graph $G = (V, E)$ that has been processed by *Bidirectional Partitioning* algorithm and source and destination vertices $o, d \in V$, the algorithm for estimating the shortest time-dependent path works as follows:

(a) If $C_o^{-1} = C_d$, then start a restrained time-dependent $A*$ search from o on G and the search scope of nodes is restrained in $V_{P_o^{-1}} \cup V_{P_d}$.

(b) If $C_o^{-1} \neq C_d$, the process of estimating shortest time-dependent path from o to d can be decomposed into four steps:

    step 1. A Time-Dependent Restrained $A*$(TDRA) occurs on G from o to C_o^{-1} and the search scope of nodes is restrained in $V_{P_o^{-1}}$. The path obtained in this step is denoted by p_1. TDRA is a Time-Dependent $A*$(TDA) with limited search scope.

    step 2. The shortcut from C_o^{-1} to C_d provides the shortest time-dependent path p_2 from C_o^{-1} to C_d.

    step 3. A TDRA occurs on G like step 1 while the source and target are C_d and d and the search scope of nodes is restrained in V_{P_d}. The path obtained in this step is denoted by p_3.

    step 4. The final estimated shortest time-dependent path is the combination of p_1, p_2 and p_3.

We call this algorithm Time-Dependent A^* With Shortcuts (TDAWS). The Algorithm 2 presents the pseudocode of TDAWS.

6   Avoid Detours

Although TDAWS can effectively reduce the cost of computation time, it can also cause some unnecessary detours. This section describes two mechanisms to avoid detours: hops on the shortcut and hops off the shortcut.

6.1   Hop on Directionally

Given a graph $G = (V, E)$ that has been processed by *Bidirectional Partitioning* algorithm. The origin and destination nodes $(o, d \in V)$ are not in the same partition, i.e. $C_o^{-1} \neq C_d$. As shown in Fig. 3(a), m and n are the core nodes of o and d, respectively. According to TDAWS, the searching hops on the shortcut between m and n although there is a detour from o to m. Hence, we propose the Hop On Directionally (HOD) mechanism to avoid detours with the help of adjacent core node h of m. Hence, we propose the Hop On Directionally (HOD) mechanism to avoid detours with the help of adjacent core node k of m. Specifically, the HOD is described as follows:

1. Select X nodes from the adjacent core nodes of m by comparing the weight of shortcut to n as the candidate nodes.
2. Calculate the time cost from o to each candidate node. We chose the path with the lowest total time cost to replace the path obtained in Step 1 of TDAWS.
3. Then the TDAWS progresses as previously defined until the target is settled.

6.2   Hop Off Early

Given a graph $G = (V, E)$ that has been processed by *Bidirectional Partitioning* algorithm and source and destination vertices $o, d \in V$ and $C_o^{-1} \neq C_t$. As shown in Fig. 3(b), m is C_o^{-1}, n is C_d and h is a node on the shortcut. As we can see, the shortcut between m and n goes too "far" and the searching has to take a detour to get d. If the searching hops off the shortcut at k, the detour can be avoided. So we proposed a mechanism called *Hop Off Early(HOE)* to stop the TDAWS step 2 before it makes more detours. The HOE is as follows:

1. The TDAWS step 1 progresses as defined.
2. As the TDAWS progresses to step 2, the p_2 is obtained. Then traversal p_2 forward until it reaches the node that is in V_{P_d} and the node is denoted by h. The p_2 only keeps the path from the start point of p_2 to h and abandons the rest, which means the TDAWS hops off the shortcut early at node h.
3. A TDA occurs on G and the origin and destination are h and d. The path obtained in this step replaces the path obtained in TDAWS step 3 and we still denote it by p_3.
4. Then the TDAWS returns the combination of p_1, p_2 and p_3.

7   Experiments

We conduct experiments with real-world road network and taxi trajectory datasets to verify the performance of the proposed algorithm. The schemes are implemented in Java 1.8 and experiments are run on a desktop computer with AMD R9 3900XT CPU, 3.8 GHz, 64G RAM under Ubuntu 18.04.5 LTS.

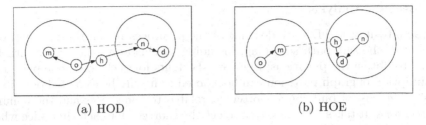

(a) HOD   (b) HOE

Fig. 3. Two mechanisms for avoiding detours, m is C_o^{-1}, n is C_d, h is a core node and the dotted lines are shortcuts

The road network of the Xiamen island is used for the simulation, which contains 24,750 road nodes and 3,234 road segments. The source file of map ([118.0660E,118.1980E] × [24.4240N,24.5600N]) is from OpenStreetMap[2] and the road network is based on the JGraphT[3] framework.

The default simulation settings are set as follows unless otherwise stated. The Xiamen Island is divided into 80 partitions by the K-Means clustering algorithm. And a day is divided into 24 time slices to represent the time-dependent properties of the road network.

7.1 Compared Algorithms

To study the performance, we compared the efficiency of algorithms that also use modified A^* algorithm on dynamic road network. We conduct the following algorithms:

- Time Dependent A*(TDA): the time-dependent case of $A*$, whose potential function uses Euclidean distance and an upper bound speed to estimate the weight between a node and the target. It serves as the baseline of the schemes.
- Time Dependent A* With Shortcuts (TDAWS): the modified time-dependent case of $A*$ using shortcuts to accelerate the searching process.
- Time Dependent A* With Shortcuts And Hop on Directionally (TDAWS+HOD): the TDAWS algorithm with Hop on Directionally mechanism.
- Time Dependent A* With Shortcuts And Hop off Early (TDAWS+HOE): the TDAWS algorithm with Hop off Early mechanism.
- Time Dependent A* With Shortcuts, Hop on Directionally And Hop off Early (TDAWS+HOD+HOE): the TDAWS algorithm with Hop on Directionally and Hop off Early mechanism.
- K Shortest Path Algorithm Based on Lifelong Planning A* Technique(KSP-LPA*): is adopted based on [1] , which formulates the deviation path calculation process as repeated one-to-one searches for the shortest path in a dynamic network.

---

[2] https://www.openstreetmap.org/.
[3] https://jgrapht.org/.

7.2 Result Analysis

Compared with the TDA, we do some offline preprocessing on the road network before the shortest path searching, including 1) clustering the graph with K-Means to obtain the partitions; 2) create shortcuts for each core node pair. The consumption of graph partition can be ignored as it only be executed once for a graph. The cost of building a shortcut is related to time slices and the number of partitions. It takes 24.562s to construct the shortcut for each time slice when the number of partitions is 80. And storing a day's shortcut consumes about 12MB when the number of time slices is 24.

Table 1. Overall performance of the schemes.

Schemes	Metrics			
	Mean search time (ms)	Standard deviation of search time	Shortcuts hit rate (%)	CR
TDA	4.272	32.235	–	1
TDAWS	0.123	0.503	87.4	1.44
TDAWS+HOD	0.150	0.450	83.7	1.33
TDAWS+HOE	0.263	0.726	87.4	1.29
TDAWS+HOD+ HOE	0.243	0.603	83.7	1.20
KSP-LPA*	2.44	1.681	–	3.28

Overall Performance. We evaluate the performances of TDA, TDAWS, TDAWS+HOD, TDAWS+HOE, TDAWS+HOD+HOE, and KSP-LPA* with 19,101 origin-destination pairs. We use a competitive ratio to evaluate the quality of an approximate time-dependent shortest path, which is defined as follows:

$$CR = \frac{w(p_a)}{w(p_{min})} \tag{1}$$

where p_a and p_{min} are the search path and the shortest path from the source node to the target node, respectively. When the $CR \in [1, \infty)$ is smaller, the search result is closer to the shortest path.

As shown in Table 1, the CR of TDA is the lowest (1.00) as its search result is the shortest path with the highest search time (4.272 ms) and standard deviation. The search time of TDAWS is the lowest (0.123 ms) with the cost of about 44% longer estimated path than TDA. As shown in the result of TDAWS+HOD and TDAWS+HOE, HOD and HOE mechanisms both can reduce the CR compared with TDAWS. However, the HOD mechanism will reduce the shortcut hit rate while the HOE mechanism will double the search time of TDAWS. When both HOD and HOE mechanisms are adopted, the estimated path quality (CR = 1.20) is further improved while it still costs more query time (0.243 ms) than TDAWS. The KSP-LPA* has about 43% of query timeless (2.44 ms) than TDA while its CR is 3.28, which means the estimated path weight is 3.28 times the shortest

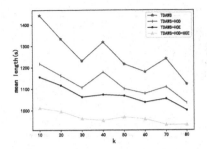

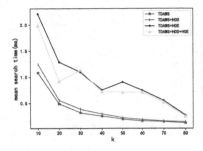

Fig. 4. Impact of the number of partitions on the mean path length

Fig. 5. Impact of the number of partitions on the mean search time

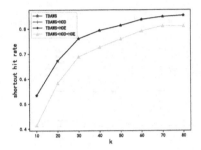

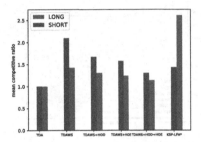

Fig. 6. Impact of the number of partitions on shortcut hit rate

Fig. 7. Impact of the distances of requests on the mean competitive ratio

path weight. As for the stability of the algorithms, the algorithms based on shortcuts have very small standard deviations, which means for any shortest path request, they can respond in a stable time.

Impact of the Number of Partitions. Figure 4 shows the experimental results of the mean path length with different numbers of partitions, k, from 10 to 80. As shown in Fig. 4, when the number of partitions increases, the mean path length of the results achieved by all the approaches shows a trend of downward. The reason is that when the road network is divided into more partitions, the distances between core nodes and other nodes are decreasing, and the estimated path contains fewer detours. When k is 40 and 70, the values of mean length of TDAWS and TDAWS+HOD rise because the locations of some core nodes may cause more detours, while the HOE can effectively correct the detours. The influence of the number of partitions on TDAWS+HOD+HOE is small, which shows that TDAWS+HOD+HOE can effectively avoid detours caused by the locations of core nodes. Figure 5 illustrates the impact of the number of partitions on mean search time. The mean search times of all the algorithms show a downward trend as k increases. While the TDAWS has the best result, TDAWS+HOE and TDAWS+HOD+HOE have close results.

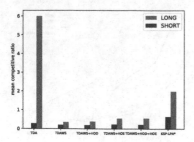

Fig. 8. Impact of the distances of requests on the mean search time

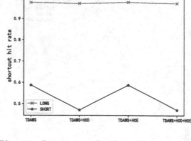

Fig. 9. Impact of the distances of requests on the shortcut hit rate

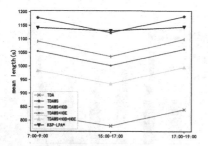

Fig. 10. Impact of traffic time on the mean path length

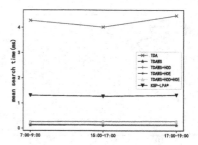

Fig. 11. Impact of traffic on the mean search time

From above, we can infer that the HOD in the AWS+HOD+HOE is not the the main factor for the time-consuming while the HOE is. As we can see from Fig. 6, the shortcut hit rates of all the algorithms decrease as k increases. The curves of TDAWS and TDAWS+HOE overlap, so as the TDAWS+HOD and TDAWS+HOD+HOE. This is because the HOD mechanism can affect the shortcut hit rate.

Impact of the Distances of Requests. To evaluate the performance of the proposed algorithms for different distance requests, We divided requests into two categories: the short-distance request and the long-distance request. Requests are classified according to the Euclidean distance between the origin and destination. If the distance is less than 3 km, it is called a *short-distance request*, otherwise, it is a *long-distance request*.

We conducted experiments with short-distance requests and long-distance requests, respectively. As shown in Fig. 7, The CR of KSP-LPA* increase sharply when the distance exceeds 3KM. In contrast, TDAWS and its deformations are not affected by the length of the distance, which takes advantage of the short-cut. Figure 8 illustrates the impact of the distances of requests on the mean search time. It can find that the search time of KSP-LPA* is significantly influenced while TDAWS and its deformations are stable when the distance increased.

This means that the algorithms based on shortcuts have stable search efficiency regardless of the distances of requests. This is because TDAWS has a higher shortcut hit rate in long-distance requests, which is also reflected in Fig. 9.

Impact of Traffic Time. We also verify the performance of the algorithms in different traffic periods, including morning peak time (7:00–9:00), evening peak time (17:00–19:00), and normal time (15:00–17:00). Figure 10 illustrates the impact of traffic time on the mean path length. It can be found that the estimated path weight in the peak period is higher, which is due to road congestion. As shown in Fig. 11, the traffic time has little impact on the algorithms that use shortcuts while the TDA and KSP-LPA* are more affected. This is because TDA and KSP-LPA require more resources to handle increased requests during peak times.

8   Conclusion

We have proposed an efficient algorithm for estimating the time-dependent shortest path based on the shortcut mechanism. The road network is preprocessed offline and partitioned into different regions. Each region has one core node and shortcuts between core nodes are constructed. We utilizes shortcuts to omit most of the searching process when searching a long-distance source-target pair. Besides, the HOD and HOE mechanisms are proposed to correct the detours of the approximated shortest paths. Experimental results show that the proposed algorithm can effectively reduce the searching time with an acceptable path length deviation.

References

1. Chen, B.Y., Chen, X.W., Chen, H.P., Lam, W.H.K., Talley, W.: Efficient algorithm for finding k shortest paths based on re-optimization technique. Transp. Res. Part E Logs Transp. Rev. **133**, 101819 (2020)
2. Chou, Y.L., Romeijn, H.E., Smith, R.L.: Approximating shortest paths in large-scale networks with an application to intelligent transportation systems. Inf. J. Comput. **10**(2), 163–179 (1998)
3. Delling, D., Nannicini, G.: Core routing on dynamic time-dependent road networks. Informs J. Comput. **24**(2), 187–201 (2012)
4. Delling, D., Sanders, P., Schultes, D., Wagner, D.: Engineering route planning algorithms. In: Lerner, J., Wagner, D., Zweig, K.A. (eds.) Algorithmics of Large and Complex Networks. LNCS, vol. 5515, pp. 117–139. Springer, Heidelberg (2009). https://doi.org/10.1007/978-3-642-02094-0_7
5. Dijkstra, E.W.: A note on two problems in connexion with graphs. Numerische Mathematik **1**, 269–271 (1959)
6. Dreyfus, S.E.: An appraisal of some shortest-path algorithms. Oper. Res. **17**(3), 395–412 (1967)
7. Geisberger, R., Sanders, P., Schultes, D., Vetter, C.: Exact routing in large road networks using contraction hierarchies. Transp. Sci. **46**(3), 388–404 (2012)

8. Goldberg, A.V., Kaplan, H., Werneck, R.F.: Reach for A*: efficient point-to-point shortest path algorithms. In: Proceedings of the Meeting on Algorithm Engineering & Expermiments, pp. 129–143. Society for Industrial and Applied Mathematics, USA (2006)
9. Goldberg, A.V., Kaplan, H., Werneck, R.F.: Better landmarks within reach. In: Demetrescu, C. (ed.) WEA 2007. LNCS, vol. 4525, pp. 38–51. Springer, Heidelberg (2007). https://doi.org/10.1007/978-3-540-72845-0_4
10. Gonzalez, H., Han, J., Li, X., Myslinska, M., Sondag, J.P.: Adaptive fastest path computation on a road network: a traffic mining approach. In: Proceedings of the 33rd International Conference on Very Large Data Bases, VLDB '07, VLDB Endowment, pp. 794–805 (2007)
11. Gutman, R.: Reach-based routing: a new approach to shortest path algorithms optimized for road networks, pp. 100–111 (2004)
12. Hart, P.E., Nilsson, N.J., Raphael, B.: A formal basis for the heuristic determination of minimum cost paths. IEEE Trans. Syst. Sci. Cybern. 4(2), 100–107 (1968)
13. Lai, Y., Yang, S., Xiong, A., Yang, F., Li, L., Zhou, X.: Utility-based matching of vehicles and hybrid requests on rider demand responsive systems. IEEE Trans. Intell. Transp. Syst., 1–15 (2020)
14. Lauther, U.: An extremely fast, exact algorithm for finding shortest paths in static networks with geographical background. In: Geoinformation und Mobilität - von der Forschung zur praktischen Anwendung (2004)
15. Lauther, U.: An experimental evaluation of point-to-point shortest path calculation on roadnetworks with precalculated edge-flags. In: DIMACS Book, vol. 74 (2009)
16. Li, L., Kim, J., Xu, J., Zhou, X.: Time-dependent route scheduling on road networks. SIGSPATIAL Spec. 10(1), 10–14 (2018)
17. Macqueen, J.B.: Some methods for classification and analysis of multivariate observations. In: Proceedings of the Fifth Berkeley Symposium on Mathematical Statistics and Probability 1967 (1967)
18. Möhring, R.H., Schilling, H., Schütz, B., Wagner, D., Willhalm, T.: Partitioning graphs to speed up Dijkstra's algorithm. In: Nikoletseas, S.E. (ed.) WEA 2005. LNCS, vol. 3503, pp. 189–202. Springer, Heidelberg (2005). https://doi.org/10.1007/11427186_18
19. Shapiro, J., Waxman, J., Nir, D.: Level graphs and approximate shortest path algorithms. Networks 22(7), 691–717 (2010)
20. Wagner, D., Willhalm, T.: Geometric speed-up techniques for finding shortest paths in large sparse graphs. In: Di Battista, G., Zwick, U. (eds.) ESA 2003. LNCS, vol. 2832, pp. 776–787. Springer, Heidelberg (2003). https://doi.org/10.1007/978-3-540-39658-1_69
21. Wang, Y., Li, G., Tang, N.: Querying shortest paths on time dependent road networks. Proc. VLDB Endowment 12(11), 1249–1261 (2019)
22. Zhang, D., Yang, D., Wang, Y., Tan, K.-L., Cao, J., Shen, H.T.: Distributed shortest path query processing on dynamic road networks. VLDB J. 26(3), 399–419 (2017). https://doi.org/10.1007/s00778-017-0457-6

Multi-level PWB and PWC for Reducing TLB Miss Overheads on GPUs

Yang Lin, Dunbo Zhang, Chaoyang Jia, Qiong Wang$^{(\boxtimes)}$, and Li Shen

National University of Defense Technology, Deya Road 109, Changsha, Hunan Province, China
wangqiong@nudt.edu.cn

Abstract. Nowadays, GPU is becoming popular across a broad range of domains. To provide virtual memory support for most applications at present, GPU introduces the address translation process. However, many applications show an irregular memory access pattern, i.e. accesses are poor structured and often data dependent, which makes performance worse especially with virtual-to-physical address translations. GPU memory management unit (MMU) adopts caching units, e.g. page walk buffer (PWB) and page walk cache (PWC), and schedule strategies to accelerate the address translations after TLB misses. However, limited by the linear table structure of traditional PWB and PWC, they hold too many redundant information, which further limits the performance of irregular applications. Although nonlinear structure can eliminate the redundancy, it requires sequential look-up on PWB and PWC, which brings greater performance loss. In this paper, we propose the multi-level PWB and PWC structure, which features the multi-level structure for eliminating the redundancy in traditional structure and the co-design of PWB and PWC for enabling parallel look-up. Besides, we design four corresponding address translation processes to ensure the efficiency of the new structure. We evaluate our design with real-world benchmarks under GPGPU-Sim simulator. Results show that our design achieves 42.6% IPC improvement with 35.1% less space overheads.

Keywords: GPU · Address translation · IOMMU · TLB · Page walk cache

1 Introduction

With better virtual memory support [18], GPU is becoming the top-class computing platforms with high productivity and programmability.

Memory virtualization is a powerful technology that automates data transmission between the main memory and the secondary storage, provides memory protection, and enables software modularity.

While the virtual memory benefits GPU a lot, it introduces the virtual-to-physical address translation process to GPU. GPU vendors accelerate address translation by using hardware translation look-aside buffers (TLBs) to buffer

Y. Lai et al. (Eds.): ICA3PP 2021, LNCS 13156, pp. 33–52, 2022.
https://doi.org/10.1007/978-3-030-95388-1_3

recently accessed page table entries (PTEs). When TLB misses, GPU has to look up the multi-level page tables in its global memory, incurring several memory accesses. Ideally, the overheads of these memory accesses can be hidden by the computation on GPU. However, the memory access patterns of many new applications demonstrate a large degree of irregularity, i.e. accesses are poor structured and often data dependent, which leads to insufficient computation for latency hiding. Consequently, these applications show poor spatial locality [11,12,17], which leads to a low TLB hit ratio. A study [25] shows that the TLB miss overheads on the GPU side can be 25x higher than that on the CPU side, and the divergent memory accesses could slow down an irregular GPU application by up to 4x owing to the TLB miss overheads alone. It also found that such irregularity could have greater impact on TLB than on cache. While a cache miss incurs one access to the main memory, a TLB miss will take up to four sequential memory accesses in the prevalent x86-64 or ARM architecture. Furthermore, accesses to cache cannot be issued until the address translation requests on TLB misses finish, as modern GPUs tend to employ physical caches.

Modern GPUs employ memory management unit (MMU) [20] caches, such as page walk buffer (PWB) and page walk cache (PWC), to accelerate the accesses to each level of page tables, which can also be called page walks. A hit in these caches enables GPU to skip one or more page walks. However, flaws exist in the current design of PWB and PWC in two aspects: 1) the space redundancy in PWB and PWC, which makes them hold less PTEs than they are designed to and leads to a low TLB hit ratio; 2) the lack of delay hiding in the current address translation mechanism, which introduces unnecessary time overheads.

This paper aims to reduce the TLB miss overheads for GPU workloads, especially for applications with irregular memory access patterns. Our work is based on two key observations. Firstly, compared with regular applications, the memory access patterns of irregular applications result in the variety of L2 tags of virtual addresses, which exceeds the capacity of traditional PWB and PWC. Secondly, address translation requests in traditional PWB are handled in a first-come-first-serve (FCFS) order. In this paper, we propose a multi-level PWB and PWC to make use of these two observations and improve the performance of irregular GPU applications. We also extend the mechanism of GPU MMU to ensure accuracy and efficiency of our design.

This paper has the following contributions.

First, we find the rule that the number of different L4 and L3 tags that appear during the execution of typical GPU workloads is no more than two. For irregular applications, the number of different L2 tags during execution ranges from tens to hundreds, while the corresponding L2 PTEs are continuous or segmented continuous in L2 page tables. That means a great number of L2 tags show good locality in terms of L2 PTEs.

Second, we propose a new multi-level structure of PWB and PWC, which rearranges the way data is stored in the PWB and PWC to remove the redundancy existing in traditional PWB and PWC structure and co-relates PWB and PWC for better cooperation in processing page walks. With such rearranging and co-relating, multi-level PWB and PWC achieves higher space utilization rate and enables parallel look-up of PWB and PWC, thus speeding up page walk processing. This contribution is the main innovation of this paper.

Third, we propose four new processes for our multi-level PWB and PWC to ensure the efficiency and accuracy of our design.

The rest of paper is organized as follows. Section 2 introduces related background knowledge. Section 3 introduces the structure of the multi-level PWB and PWC. Section 4 introduces the extended MMU mechanism. Section 5 evaluates the performance and overheads of our design and analyzes the experimental results. Section 6 introduces related works. Section 7 concludes this paper.

2   Background

2.1   GPU Architecture and Execution Model

The typical architecture of a GPU is shown in Fig. 1. Streaming multiprocessors (SMs) are the basic executional units of a GPU. Each SM consists of multiple Single-Instruction-Multiple-Data (SIMD) units, each having multiple lanes for execution. Each SM also includes a private L1 data cache and a scratchpad shared between the SIMD units within this SM. All SMs in a GPU share a larger L2 cache.

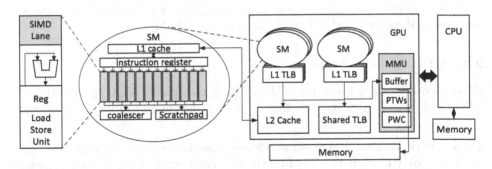

Fig. 1. The architecture of a typical GPU.

GPU applications use fine-grained multi-threading. A GPU application is made up of thousands of threads. These threads are clustered into thread blocks (also known as work groups), each consisting of multiple smaller bundles of threads that execute concurrently. Such thread bundle is known as a warp, or a wavefront [2,13,21,24,25]. Threads in the same warp execute the same instruction on the same SIMD unit with different data. A Single-Instruction-Multiple-Thread (SIMT) model is mapped to SIMD units using execution masks when GPU threads in the same warp follow different execution paths due to branches. Under SIMT, all threads in a warp execute in lockstep, where a warp stalls when any one of its threads stalls. This means that a warp is unable to proceed to the next instruction until the slowest thread in the warp completes the current instruction.

2.2 Virtual Memory Support in GPU

Hardware-supported virtual memory relies on address translation process to map each virtual memory address to a physical address in GPU memory. Address translation uses page-granularity virtual-to-physical mappings that are stored in multi-level page tables. Before the program is executed, GPU transfers all the required data and corresponding page tables from CPU to the GPU memory for initialization. To look up a mapping in multi-level page tables, GPU performs several page walks, where a page table walker (PTW) traverses through each level of the multi-level page tables to locate one PTE in the last level of the page tables. GPUs usually adopt translation look-aside buffers (TLBs), which cache PTEs, to speed up address translations. Since a TLB miss stalls multiple threads and degrade performance significantly, it becomes a critical path of execution.

Nowadays, many operating systems support 2MB large pages. In previous work [20], some researchers have adopted large page to reduce TLB miss overheads. However, for irregular applications, large page methods bring serious data transmission and page fault overheads. Besides, a large number of internal fragments exist within large pages and decrease the space utilization of GPU memory. Although it is possible to combine large page methods with small page transmission mechanism, each page walk still falls on the smallest base page in the end, making the overheads of TLB misses remain high.

2.3 GPU Memory Management Unit

GPU memory management unit (MMU) [3,4] uses caches including PWB and PWC and processing units including PTWs for the support of virtual memory.

Page Walk Buffer. PWB stores address translation requests until they are processed by PTWs. If PWB is full, the processor would have to stall to avoid generating new address translation requests. As shown in Fig. 2, traditional PWB adopts the linear table structure, while L1 to L4 tags are used to look up each corresponding level of page table. If the high-level tags have good locality, PWB will store many duplicated tags (i.e. redundancy), shown as the shadowed blocks in Fig. 2.

Page Walk Cache. PWC [9,14] stores the look-up results of each level of page tables, i.e. the physical base addresses of L3, L2, and L1 page tables (L3 to L1 shown PAs in Fig. 3) corresponding to L4, L3 and L2 tags separately. As is shown in Fig. 3, the shadowed blocks represent the redundancy. It should also be noticed that the redundant information of PWB and PWC overlaps in terms of high-level tags.

L4 tag	L3 tag	L2 tag	L1 tag	Offset
051	0a3	12b	133	fe1
051	0a3	12b	022	36c
051	0a3	12a	00e	62d
051	04e	151	0ef	112
051	04e	151	034	1a2

Fig. 2. The structure of traditional PWB.

L4 tag	L3 PA	L3 tag	L2 PA	L2 tag	L1 PA
051	51	0a3	43	12b	12
051	51	0a3	43	12a	34
051	51	04e	32	151	43
-	-	-	-	-	-

Fig. 3. The structure of traditional PWC.

Page Table Walker. PTWs are responsible for handling address translation requests stored in PWB and performing page walks. One PTW handles one request at a time. The number of PTW is generally set from 4 to 8, since too many PTWs will lead to severe contention of memory access ports and decrease in GPU performance.

2.4 Summary

Although the GPU memory capacity has been increasing, TLB capacity (i.e. the max number of PTEs TLB can hold) has not kept pace due to area constraint. As a result, address translation overheads have started to significantly increase, and the execution time of many large memory workloads has been increasing as well. GPU MMU adopts PWB, PWC and PTWs to accelerate address translation requests and reduce TLB miss overheads. However, as shown in Fig. 2 and Fig. 3, traditional PWB and PWC hold too much redundant information, thus lacking enough useful information. Therefore, we aim to redesign the structure. The linear table structure of traditional PWB and PWC is the main source of redundant information. Besides, we found that PWB and PWC have related functions, but they do not cooperate in actual work. The address translation causes not only the stalls in the PWB but also the overheads of looking up the PWC. To solve these problems, we propose the multi-level PWB and PWC to improve the efficiency of address translation.

3   The Multi-level PWB and PWC

The overall structure of the multi-level PWB and PWC is shown in Fig. 4, where blocks in the same color have the same information. Our design abandons the linear structure of traditional PWB and PWC, which is the main source of redundancy, and adopts the multi-level structure to reallocate the storage space for different levels of tags so as to achieve higher space utilization rate as well as faster PWB and PWC look-up. With our design, most address translation requests need only one page walk to the last level of page table for the physical address and most of the redundant information can be eliminated. There are three main components: the multi-level PWB, the multi-level PWC and the writeback table (WT).

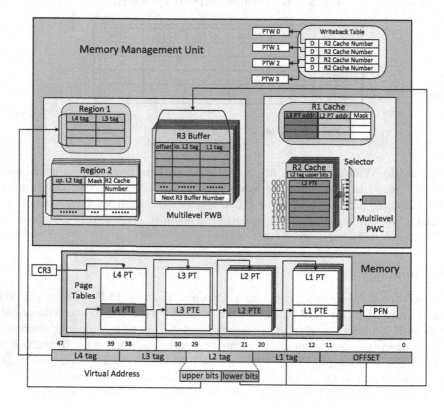

Fig. 4. The architecture of the multi-level PWB and PWC.

3.1   The Multi-level PWB

We redivide the multi-level PWB into three regions, with the tags of virtual addresses stored in these regions respectively, as shown in the left of MMU in Fig. 4. Region 1 has only one buffer, each entry of which stores L4 and L3 tags. Region 2 consists of several buffers, each entry of which stores the whole or only the upper bits of a L2 tag, depending on the actual needs, a mask field and a pointer pointing to a PWC Region 2 Cache, which is named R2 Cache number in this paper. The mask field indicates which Region 3 buffers (R3 buffers for abbr.) are allocated to this Region 2 entry(the benefit of applying mask field is explained in the third advantage in the next paragraph). Region 3 includes several buffers, each entry of which stores the rest of a virtual address, i.e. the lower bits of L2 tag(if Region 2 entries store only the upper bits of L2 tag, otherwise not), L1 tag and offset.

The multi-level PWB structure has three advantages over the traditional structure. First, it eliminates all the redundant information and minimize the storage space for L4 and L3 tags, i.e. the size of Region 1, as there are no more than two different L4 and L3 tags during execution according to our observation. Second, it is designed to keep as many active L2 tags as possible, which results from the elimination of redundant L4 and L3 tags, and to provide more space for L2 tags by dividing an L2 tag into upper bits and lower bits(stored in Region 2 and 3 respectively), which reduces the space for storing L2 tags by coalescing those with the same upper bits. Third, it adopts a flexible strategy for the assignment of R3 buffers to the Region 2 entries by mask fields. Since the number of L1 tags is too large for R3 buffers, this strategy helps R3 buffers to hold only L1 tags that belong to active L2 tags, improving the space utilization rate of R3 buffers. Moreover, with this strategy, several R3 buffers can be assigned to the same Region 2 entry, making it possible to hold all L1 tags belonging to the same active L2 tag. What's more, the structure of the multi-level PWB can easily support other optimization methods, such as Neighborhood [7], with almost no extra overheads. To implement Neighborhood, the upper 6 bits of L2 tags are stored in Region 2, which means that virtual addresses in the same Neighborhood reside in R3 buffers belonging to the same Region 2 entry.

3.2   The Multi-level PWC

We redivide the multi-level PWC into two Regions and add a selector, as shown in the right of MMU in Fig. 4. Region 1 contains only one Cache (R1 Cache for abbr.), each entry of which stores mask fields and the physical base addresses of L3 and L2 page tables, which correspond to L4 and L3 tags in the entries of **PWB** Region 1. In other words, the entries of PWB Region 1 and R1 cache lines are directly mapped. Region 2 contains several Caches(R2 Cache for abbr.), each of which stores the upper bits of one L2 tag and the corresponding L2 PTEs that have the same upper bits. Each L2 PTE contains the base address of one L1 page table. If one bit of the mask field of one R1 Cache line is set to 1, it means the corresponding R2 Cache is assigned to this line. As a result, the length of mask fields depends on the number of R2 Caches. The selector uses mask fields to find out R2 Caches assigned to each R1 Cache line.

With the structure of multi-level PWB and PWC, the information of L4 to L2 tags in multi-level PWB is associated with the information in multi-level PWC. Specifically, the direct mapping associates R1 Cache with L4 and L3 tags in PWB Region 1 and the R2 Cache number associates PWB Region 2 buffers with R2 Caches. Such association helps accelerate the process of looking up PWC by enabling parallel look-up, which is detailed in Fig. 5.

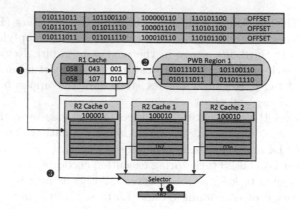

Fig. 5. The parallel look-up in the multi-level PWC.

When a PTW looks up the multi-level PWC, it looks up the R1 Cache by the L4 and L3 tags, compares the upper bits of L2 tag with that in the R2 Caches and indexes the entries of R2 Caches by the lower bits of L2 tag at the same time(❶). Due to the direct mapping between the PWB Region 1 and R1 Cache(❷), the PTW only needs to compare the L4 and L3 tags with that of PWB Region 1 entries to find the corresponding R1 Cache line. If that R1 Cache line is nonempty, its mask field is sent to the selector(❸). Otherwise, the entire PWC misses and the PTW has to perform all levels of page walks. Several R2 Caches could hit at the same time(R2 Cache 1 and R2 Cache 2 in this case). The selector picks out the right one by mask field sent previously(010 in this case, which selects R2 Cache 1 and filters out R2 Cache 2, ❹). If no R2 Cache hits, the PTW needs to perform page walks starting from L2 page table.

Most of the time, it is not necessary to look up the entire PWC, because a PTW can directly find a R2 Cache by the R2 Cache number in the PWB Region 2 and select the requested L2 PTE by the lower bits of L2 tag. Only when the R2 Cache number is empty, i.e. the request newly arrives and has not been assigned with an R2 Cache, will the PTW need to perform an entire PWC look-up.

3.3   The WT

The function of WT is to provide association information between PTWs and R2 Caches. Each entry of WT is linked to one PTW that is going to access L2 page table due to R2 Cache miss. Each entry of WT also stores a dirty bit and a R2 Cache number, which points to one empty R2 Cache. When a PTW finishes accessing L2 page table, it can directly update that R2 Cache with L2 page table walk results. After updating one R2 Cache by WT, the PTW will set the dirty bits of those WT entries that have the same R2 Cache number. That way, PTWs linked to those entries will have to skip updating. This could happen when there is no enough free R2 Caches.

4   MMU Mechanism

We extend the GPU MMU mechanism and propose four new processes to enable efficient address translations. In the following subsections, we introduce them in detail according to Fig. 4.

4.1   Process 1: Filling Requests

Process 1 first pre-classifies the address translation requests according to L4 tags, L3 tags, and the upper bits of L2 tags of virtual addresses. Then it performs the following steps: (1) Fill in the PWB Region 1 with L4 and L3 tags. Since the number of L4 and L3 tags is limited, this step only has two results: succeeding or finding an entry with the same tags, where step (1) can be skipped. (2) Fill in the PWB Region 2 with upper bits of L2 tag. This step has three results: succeeding, failing and skipping. If succeeding, a free R3 buffer will be assigned to this PWB Region 2 entry, while the mask bit of this entry is set. If failing, it means the PWB Region 2 is full and the processor must be stalled. If skipping, we can find R3 buffers that are already assigned to this PWB Region 2 entry by the mask field. (3) Fill the rest information, i.e. the lower bits of L2 tag, L1 tag, and offset, into the R3 buffers specified by step (2). If all R3 buffers are full, a new free R3 buffer will be assigned to the last of them as extension, which is recorded in the Next R3 Buffer Number of the last R3 buffer.

4.2   Process 2: Processing Requests

We design an adaptive schedule strategy (AD strategy) for requests in the PWB: PTWs process requests in one nonempty R3 buffer after another. This strategy is adaptive for two reasons: First, since the links between PWB Region 2 entries and R3 buffers and the states of R3 buffers both change dynamically, the process order of PTWs is dynamic. Second, PWB Region 2 entries assigned with more R3 buffers will be processed by more PTWs, which means that PTWs tend to process active PWB Region 2 entry first. Since requests in the same PWB Region 2 entry share the same R2 Cache, the AD strategy also maximizes the utilization of PTEs in R2 Caches.

After scheduling, PTWs start to process requests by looking up the multi-level PWC. The process of looking up the multi-level PWC is introduced in Sect. 3.2.

4.3   Process 3: Updating Information

Process 3 aims to reduce the update overheads of multi-level PWB and PWC and ensure the consistency among PWB, PWC, and WT. An update operation happens when: (1) A PTW finishes the accesses of L4 and L3 page tables, it needs to update the R1 Cache. (2) A PTW finishes the access of a L2 page table, it needs to update the R2 Cache indicated by the R2 Cache number in

WT and the dirty bits of WT entries with the same R2 Cache number. (3) A PTW fetches the last request of a R3 buffer, it needs to set the mask bit of the corresponding Region 2 entry as 0.

4.4 Process 4: Rearrangement

Process 4 is used to maximize the utilization of R3 buffers and R2 Caches. The three stages shown in Fig. 6 explain the rearrangement. In stage 1, R3 buffer 0 and 1 belong to the first and the second entries of PWB Region 2 respectively. R3 buffer 0 is full, R3 buffer 1 is empty, and R3 buffer 2 is free. The reason why R3 buffer 1 is empty is that its last request has just been processed (process 2). The first and the second entries of PWB Region 2 are assigned with R2 Cache 0 and 1 respectively. In stage 2, since R3 buffer 1 is empty, the second entry of PWB Region 2 is cleaned up and R3 buffer 1 becomes free. Although R2 Cache 1 becomes free, it would not be cleaned up. At the same time, two new requests arrive, waiting to be filled in the PWB (process 1). In stage 3, according to the tags of request 0, it is filled into R3 buffer 1. The R2 Cache 1 is reallocated to the second entry of PWB Region 2 and its entries are cleaned up. Request 1 has the same upper bits of L2 tag as the first entry of PWB Region 2, which is already assigned with R3 buffer 0. However, since R3 buffer 0 is full, a free R3 buffer 2 is assigned to this entry as extension to hold request 1.

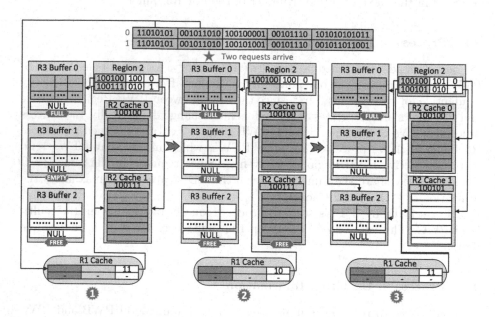

Fig. 6. An example of the rearrangement process.

5   Performance Analysis

5.1   Experiment Setting

We implement our design on GPGPU-Sim simulator [8]. The configuration of GPGPU-sim is listed in Table 1(BPE stands for base page entry and LPE stands for large page entry), the same as the Mosaic [5]. The configuration of our multi-level PWB and PWC is listed below:

- 1 4-entry PWB Region 1
- 1 64-entry PWB Region 2
- 16 16-entry R3 buffers
- 1 4-entry R1 Cache
- 16 8-entry R2 Cache
- 8 PTWs

Table 1. The configuration of GPGPU-Sim.

Unit	Configuration	
Shader	GTO warp scheduler [1]	30 SMs
L1 Cache	16 KB(4-way)	LRU
Shared L2 Config	2 MB(16-way)	LRU
L1 TLB	128 BPEs	16 LPEs
Shared L2 TLB	512 BPEs	256 LPEs

We selected 17 benchmarks from three benchmark suites: 6 from Rodinia 3.1 [13], 6 from Polybench GPU-1.0 [15] and 5 from ISPASS 2009, all of which have relatively low L2 TLB hit ratios. We ignored benchmarks whose L2 TLB hit ratios are higher than 90%, since high L2 TLB hit ratios mean too few address translation requests, which leaves little room for performance improvement. The L2 TLB hit ratios of selected benchmarks are shown in Fig. 7. The numbers of different L4 and L3 tags and L2 sets (8 consecutive PTEs in L2 page tables) generated by the benchmarks used in our work are listed in Table 2.

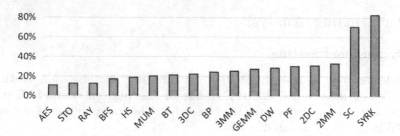

Fig. 7. L2 TLB hit ratio (128 entries).

Table 2. Benchmarks and the number of different L4 and L3 tags and L2 sets during the execution of each benchmark.

Applications	L4	L3	L2 set
2DC	1	1	15
2MM	1	1	9
3DC	1	1	14
3MM	1	1	9
BT	1	1	10
GEMM	1	1	9
BFS	1	1	9
MUM	1	1	18
SYRK	1	1	8
RAY	1	1	21
HS	1	2	10
PF	1	2	16
SC	1	2	11
BP	1	2	11
AES	1	2	37
STO	1	2	52
DW	2	3	23

5.2 Area Overheads

For the multi-level PWB, each entry of Region 1 takes 18 bits (9 bits for L4 tag and 9 bits for L3 tag). Thus, the total size of Region 1 is 9 bytes. As for Region 2, each entry takes 30 bits (6 bits for upper bits of L2 tag, 20 bits for mask field, and 4 bits for R2 Cache number). Thus, the total size of Region 2 is 240 bytes. As for Region 3, each R3 buffer entry takes 24 bits (3 bits for lower bits of L2 tag, 9 bits for L1 tag, and 12 bits for offset), while each R3 buffer consists of 16 entries and a 4-bit next R3 buffer number. Therefore, 16 R3 buffers together take 776 bytes. Eventually, the multi-level PWB totally takes 1025 bytes.

As for the multi-level PWC, each R1 Cache line takes 17 bytes (1 byte for mask field, 16 bytes for L3 and L2 page table base addresses). Thus, the 4-entry R1 Cache takes 68 bytes. Each R2 Cache takes 64 bytes for 8 L1 page table base addresses and 6 bits for upper bits of L2 tag. So 16 R2 Caches take 1036 bytes in total. Eventually, the multi-level PWC takes 1104 bytes altogether.

Since We use 8 PTWs, the WT has 8 entries. Each WT entry takes 4 bits (1 bit for dirty bit and 3 bits for R2 Cache number). Thus, the WT takes 4 bytes.

Overall, the multi-level PWB, the multi-level PWC and the WT take 2133 bytes (2.08KB) in total.

According to Table 2, the number of different L4 tags for any of the benchmarks is no more than 2 and that of L3 tags is no more than 3. Therefore, our configuration supports running one GPU kernel at a time. As for running multiple kernels concurrently, only increasing the number of entries of PWB Region 1, Region 2 and R1 Cache is needed. According to our test, additional two PWB Region 1 entries, two R1 Cache lines, and thirty-two PWB Region 2 entries (taking totally extra 74 bytes) can meet the requirements for two kernels to run simultaneously.

The area overheads of the traditional PWB and PWC can be calculated as below. Assume that the traditional PWB and PWC and the multi-level PWB and PWC record the same number of address translation requests and the corresponding page table base addresses. That way, the configuration of the traditional PWB and PWC is 324-entry and 128-entry respectively. As shown in Fig. 2, each entry of traditional PWB takes 6 bytes. Thus, a 256-entry traditional PWB takes 1536 bytes totally. As shown in Fig. 3, each entry of the traditional PWC includes a 27-bit tag field (L4, L3, and L2 tags) and 24 bytes for page table addresses (L3, L2, and L1). Thus, a 64-entry traditional PWC takes 1752 bytes. Overall, the traditional PWB and PWC take 3288 bytes (3.2KB). To summarize, the multi-level PWB and PWC can save 33.3% and 37.0% in terms of area overheads, respectively. With our design, the area overheads of GPU MMU can be reduced by 35.1%, as shown in Table 3.

Table 3. The comparison of spatial overheads between traditional PWB&PWC and multi-level PWB&PWC.

	PWB	PWC	WT	Total
Traditional	1536 bytes	1752 bytes	–	3288 bytes
Multi-level	1025 bytes	1104 bytes	4 bytes	2133 bytes
Reduction	33.3%	37.0%	–	35.1%

5.3 Performance Improvement

In order to analyze the performance of the multi-level PWB and PWC structure, we firstly evaluate the performance improvement. Then, in order to figure out what brings the performance improvement, we analyze the impact of update overheads and the page walk overheads of all benchmarks. The horizontal line in Fig. 8 represents the baseline performance of the traditional 256-entry PWB and 64-entry PWC. The average performance improvement of our design reaches 42.6%. Benchmark MUM has the least improvement which reaches 11.4%, while benchmark 2DC has the most improvement which reaches 62.4%. In order to analyze the difference of performance improvement between benchmarks, we record the update overheads, the page walk overheads, and the TLB hit ratios with different schedule strategies.

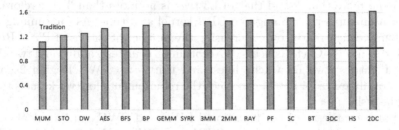

Fig. 8. Performance improvement (IPC).

The Update Overheads, After a PTW completes the access to the last level of page table, it will return a 64B addresses information. The traditional PWC structure will use 8B of the information to update itself, which will bring one cache look-up overheads and one cache write overheads. The update of the multi-level PWC can be orientated to a specific R2 Cache based on the R2 Cache number in the WT. If the corresponding dirty bit in the WT is 1, there is no need to update. If the corresponding R2 Cache already has the information, there is no need to update. If there is no information in the corresponding R2 Cache, only one write to it is needed. Through this method, the multi-level PWC structure can save 95% update operations.

The Page Walk Overheads. If no optimization technology is used to save the intermediate results of page walks (L3, L2 and L1 page table base addresses), each address translation request will walk through four levels of page tables one by one. What's more, the memory access overheads can be 100 times higher than the cache access overheads. Therefore, the overheads of page walks are an important indicator of the address translations overheads.

The horizontal line in Fig. 9 represents the page walk overheads of the traditional PWB and PWC structure. The yellow bars stand for the ideal situation that PWC has unlimited capacity. The page walk overheads of most benchmarks are reduced to the ideal situation, except for AES and STO, which is caused by the limited capacity of R2 Caches. The multi-level PWC can hold at most 16

L2 sets, while AES and STO will generate 37 and 52 L2 sets respectively during execution, as shown in Table 2. Thus, 16 R2 Caches are not enough for these two benchmarks. Only if the number of R2 Caches reaches over 20, can the page walk overheads of AES and STO be reduced to the ideal situation.

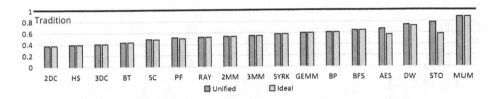

Fig. 9. Page walk overheads.

The Schedule Strategy. Fig. 10 shows the TLB hit ratios of FCFS strategy and AD strategy. With AD strategy, we can achieve an average improvement of TLB hit ratio of 12.5%. Due to spatial locality, requests falling in the same L2 sets are often generated concurrently. AD strategy gives priority to requests mapped to the same L2 set, i.e. in the same R3 buffer. By this way, TLBs can store more PTEs which are mapped to the same L2 set and the virtual addresses in this L2 set will have a greater hit probability. Thereby, AD strategy can improve the TLB hit ratios. The unsatisfying TLB hit ratios of MUM and DW explains why the performance improvement of these two benchmarks is not as good as other benchmarks even if their page walk overheads are close to the ideal situation.

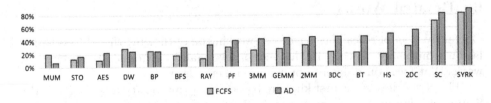

Fig. 10. TLB hit ratio of FCFS and AD schedule strategies.

5.4 Impact of Large Page

Many current works focus on large page, in the purpose of increasing L2 TLB hit ratio by enlarging page size. We select five of the benchmarks used in our experiment with relatively poor locality and test the L2 TLB hit ratios of each benchmark under different page sizes. From the results shown in Fig. 11, it is found that when page size is 2MB, compared to 4KB, L2 TLB hit ratios of all benchmarks have apparently increased. L2 TLB hit ratios of 2DC, MUM and RAY have almost reached 100%. According to the results, only when the page size is 2MB or 1MB, can L2 TLB hit ratios be improved, while other page sizes have limited impact on L2 TLB hit ratios.

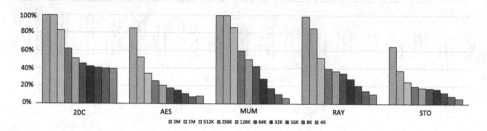

Fig. 11. L2 TLB hit ratio with large page.

However, the use of 2MB large page can cause a series of problems. Firstly, transferring large pages between CPU and GPU will lead to excessive resource overheads and transmission delay, resulting in reduced GPU performance. Besides, when using 2 MB large page, the replacement strategy for data blocks in memory also faces challenges. Since 2 MB page size is too large, a great amount of data will be swapped out of the memory every time one large page is replaced. Finally, if a 2 MB page is not fully utilized, memory fragments will exist within this page, reducing the space utilization of memory. Due to the low performance of 2MB large page, this paper adopts the multi-level PWB and PWC structure to obtain better performance.

6   Related Works

Currently, a lot of researches have been working on optimizing the address translation from many aspects. In this section, we mainly introduce three kinds of works that focus on different optimization methods.

The researches of the first kind are based on the optimization of the IOMMU. Seunghee Shin et al. [22] proposed a PWB scheduling strategy to reduce the overall execution time of a program by scheduling the service order of requests in the PWB. They have two key ideas: The first is to give processing priority to address translation requests that belong to the same warp over requests that belong to different warps, so as to reduce the total stall cycles of all warps, since one warp will move forward only if its address translation requests have all been processed. The second is to give priority to the instruction with the least address translation requests (i.e. the least amount of work), which is based on the shortest-job-first policy, to reduce overall execution time of instructions ("jobs"). However, with these two key ideas, Seunghee Shin's work only reduces the waiting time of warps, while our work focuses on eliminating redundant information in the PWB and PWC and reducing the number of memory accesses by structure designs. In our future work, we can adopt Seunghee Shin's schedule strategy to further decrease program execution time. Another work of Seunghee Shin is neighborhood-aware address translation [7]. In this work, they add 3 fields to each of the PWB entries to record useful information from previous page walks, so the address translation requests in the PWB can skip 1 to 3 page walks. To be specific, if any address translation request in the PWB will access the same level of page table as the one being processed, the base address of that page table will be stored in the corresponding PWB entry. When this address translation request is processed, the PTW can directly access the page table pointed by that base address, skipping accesses to the previous levels of page tables. However, this solution would bring two additional overheads: (1) Space overheads. Each PWB entry needs 8B additional space. The PWB size in this work can't be too small, either. (2) Update overheads. Whenever a page table walker finishes an access to one level of page table, it needs to update the additional information of every PWB entry that stores an address translation request.

Thomas W. Barr et al. proposed a PWC structure called TLB Path Cache (TPC) [9]. TPC is designed to record all the information of a complete address translation, including the base addresses of the L4, L3 and L2 page tables and the corresponding tags of the virtual address of this address translation request. When another address translation request misses in the TLB, it can look up the TPC for possible hits to skip accesses to the higher 3 levels of page tables.

The researches in the second category make efforts outside of IOMMU. Several studies [3,20,24,26,27] demonstrated that the address translation overheads of GPU have become a bottleneck in the execution of GPU applications. Rachata Ausavarungnirun et al. proposed a multi-granularity TLB and page table structure called Mosaic [5]. This structure can reduce TLB miss ratio and the overheads of transferring data from CPU main memory to GPU. Barr et al. proposed SpecTLB to accelerate program execution by predicting virtual to physical address translations [10], while the prediction accuracy is difficult to improve. Binh Pham et al. proposed a TLB structure called Clustered TLB [19], which improves the coverage of TLB by mapping multiple physical addresses to a single TLB entry, thereby increasing TLB hit ratios. Haria et al. proposed a technique for reducing the number of page table accesses by using the mapping relationship between the virtual memory and physical memory in GPU [6].

TLB prefetching is another promising way to increase TLB hit ratio and reduce address translation overheads. Most recently, Georgios Vavouliotis et al. has proposed a dynamic prefetch scheme named Sampling-Based Free TLB Prefetching (SBFP) [23] that exploits page table locality in the last level of page table, which is similar to the concept Neighborhood mentioned above, to reduce prefetch overheads and increase prefetch accuracy. Specifically, they found that each page walk to the last level of page table brings back one cache line containing 8 PTEs, while only one of them will be used. SBFP add counters for the unused PTEs to evaluate their usefulness and prefetches only those that are most possible to be accessed (useful). Besides, they also design an adaptive prefetcher called Agile TLB Prefetcher (ATP) that chooses the most appropriate prefetch strategy in run-time according to sampling results and disables prefetching when sampling results disapproves. ATP with SBFP together yields better performance for many workloads in comparison to traditional static prefetchers.

7   Conclusion

With the support of virtual memory, GPU programming becomes convenient. However, it also introduces the address translation overheads to the GPU side. As the locality of the virtual addresses continues to deteriorate, the address translations overheads of GPU are getting more and more expensive. GPU MMU is designed to reduce the overheads of address translation. However, the traditional PWB and PWC structure have a lot of redundant information which wastes the spatial resources. What's more, the traditional PWB and PWC cannot cooperate with each other. To solve these problems, we propose the multi-level PWB and PWC to eliminate the redundant information and improve the efficiency of page walks. The multi-level PWB and PWC structure abandon the traditional linear table structure for more flexible space allocation. Based on our multi-level structure, we also design four processes to ensure the correctness and efficiency of address translations. With the multi-level PWB and PWC structure, the average GPU performance can be improved by 42.6% with 35.1% less area overheads.

In the future, we plan to analyze the area overheads and energy consumption using professional tools like CACTI [16] to estimate whether the performance gains of our design are greater than the overheads it brings, as well as to validate our area overheads reduction under simulation close to realistic situation.

Acknowledgment. This work is supported by National Nature Science Foundation of China (Grant No. 62032001 and 61972407).

References

1. Rogers, T.G., O'Connor, M., Aamodt, T.M.: Cache-conscious wavefront scheduling. IEEE (2013)
2. Rossbach, C.J., Yu, Y., Currey, J., Martin, J.P., Fetterly, D.: Dandelion: a compiler and runtime for heterogeneous systems. In: Proceedings of the Twenty-Fourth ACM Symposium on Operating Systems Principles (2013)
3. Pichai, B., Hsu, L., Bhattacharjee, A.: Architectural support for address translation on gpus designing memory management units for CPU/GPUS with unified address spaces. In: Proceedings of the 19th International Conference on Architectural Support for Programming Languages and Operating Systems (2014)
4. Wang, B., Yu, W., Sun, X.H., Wang, X.: Dacache: memory divergence-aware GPU cache management. ACM (2015)
5. Ausavarungnirun, R., et al.: Mosaic: a GPU memory manager with application-transparent support for multiple page sizes. In: the 50th Annual IEEE/ACM International Symposium (2017)

6. Haria, S., Hill, M.D., Swift, M.M: Devirtualizing memory in heterogeneous systems. ACM SIGPLAN Notices (2018)
7. Shin, S., LeBeane, M., Solihin, Y., Basu, A.: Neighborhood-aware address translation for irregular GPU applications. In: 2018 51st Annual IEEE/ACM International Symposium on Microarchitecture (MICRO) (2018)
8. Bakhoda, A., Yuan, G.L., Fung, W., Wong, H., Aamodt, T.M.: Analyzing cuda workloads using a detailed GPU simulator. In: 2009 IEEE International Symposium on Performance Analysis of Systems and Software (2009)
9. Barr, T.W., Cox, A.L., Rixner, S.: Translation caching: skip, don't walk (the page table). Comput. Arch. News **38**(3), 48–59 (2010)
10. Barr, T.W., Cox, A.L., Rixner, S.: Spectlb: a mechanism for speculative address translation. In: International Symposium on Computer Architecture (2011)
11. Burtscher, M., Nasre, R., Pingali, K.: A quantitative study of irregular programs on GPUs (2012)
12. Chatterjee, N., O'Connor, M., Loh, G.H., Jayasena, N., Balasubramonian, R.: Managing dram latency divergence in irregular gpgpu applications. In: International Conference for High Performance Computing, Networking, Storage & Analysis (2014)
13. Che, S., et al.: Rodinia: a benchmark suite for heterogeneous computing. In: 2009 IEEE International Symposium on Workload Characterization (IISWC), pp. 44–54 (2009). https://doi.org/10.1109/IISWC.2009.5306797
14. Esteve, A., Gómez, M.E., Robles, A.: Exploiting parallelization on address translation: shared page walk cache. In: an Mey, D., et al. (eds.) Euro-Par 2013. LNCS, vol. 8374, pp. 433–443. Springer, Heidelberg (2014). https://doi.org/10.1007/978-3-642-54420-0_43
15. Karimov, J., Rabl, T., Markl, V.: PolyBench: the first benchmark for polystores. In: Nambiar, R., Poess, M. (eds.) TPCTC 2018. LNCS, vol. 11135, pp. 24–41. Springer, Cham (2019). https://doi.org/10.1007/978-3-030-11404-6_3
16. Li, S., Chen, K., Ahn, J.H., Brockman, J.B., Jouppi, N.P.: Cacti-p: architecture-level modeling for sram-based structures with advanced leakage reduction techniques. IEEE (2011)
17. Meng, J., Tarjan, D., Skadron, K.: Dynamic warp subdivision for integrated branch and memory divergence tolerance. ACM Sigarch Comput. Arch. News **38**(3), 235–246 (2010)
18. Nvidia, C.: nvidia's next generation cuda compute architecture: Fermi (2009)
19. Pham, B., Bhattacharjee, A., Eckert, Y., Loh, G.H.: Increasing TLB reach by exploiting clustering in page translations. In: IEEE International Symposium on High Performance Computer Architecture (2014)
20. Power, J., Hill, M., Wood, D.A.: Supporting x86–64 address translation for 100s of GPU lanes. In: IEEE International Symposium on High Performance Computer Architecture (2014)
21. Sartori, J., Kumar, R.: Branch and data herding: reducing control and memory divergence for error-tolerant GPU applications. IEEE Trans. Multimedia **15**, 279–290 (2013)
22. Shin, S., et al.: Scheduling page table walks for irregular GPU applications. IEEE Computer Society (2018)
23. Vavouliotis, G., et al.: Exploiting page table locality for agile TLB prefetching, pp. 85–98. IEEE (2021)

24. Vesely, J., Basu, A., Oskin, M., Loh, G.H., Bhattacharjee, A.: Observations and opportunities in architecting shared virtual memory for heterogeneous systems. In: 2016 IEEE International Symposium on Performance Analysis of Systems and Software (ISPASS) (2016)
25. Wang, B.: Mitigating GPU memory divergence for data-intensive applications (2015)
26. Zhang, S., Qin, Z., Yang, Y., Shen, L., Wang, Z.: Improving the efficiency of GPGPU work-queue through data awareness. ACM Trans. Archit. Code Optim. **14**(4), 1–22 (2017)
27. Zhang, S., Qin, Z., Yang, Y., Shen, L., Wang, Z.: Transparent partial page migration between CPU and GPU. Front. Comput. Sci. **14**(3), 1–13 (2020)

Hybrid GA-SVR: An Effective Way to Predict Short-Term Traffic Flow

Guanru Tan[1], Shiqiang Zheng[1], Boyu Huang[1], Zhihan Cui[1], Haowen Dou[1], Xi Yang[2(✉)], and Teng Zhou[1,3]

[1] Department of Computer Science, Shantou University, Shantou 515041, China
[2] School of Information Science and Technology, Guangdong University of Foreign Studies, Guangzhou 510006, China
yangxisunny@163.com
[3] Key Laboratory of Intelligent Manufacturing Technology (Shantou University), Ministry of Education, Shantou 515063, China

Abstract. Establishing an accurate short-term traffic flow prediction model is an important part of the intelligent transportation system (ITS). However, due to the nonlinear and stochastic dynamics of the traffic flow, building an effective predictive model remains a challenge. Support vector regression (SVR), a model that is widely used to solve non-linear regression problems, has good predictive performance for time series data such as traffic flow. But the hyperparameters of support vector machines affect their predictive performance. This paper presents a prediction model using a genetic algorithm (GA) to determine the combination of hyperparameters for the SVR model, called a hybrid GA-SVR model. Experiments on real-world traffic flow data have shown that the hybrid GA-SVR model has superior predictive performance than several state-of-the-art prediction algorithms.

Keywords: Intelligent transportation system · Short-term traffic flow · Genetic algorithm · Parameter optimization · Forecasting

1 Introduction

With the booming development of the intelligent system, the intelligent transportation management and control system has become popular research [24]. The key to realizing intelligent transportation system (ITS) is accurate prediction and

This work was supported by the Guangzhou Scientific and Technological Plan Project (No.202102021098), National Natural Science Foundation of China (No. 61902232), the STU Incubation Project for the Research of Digital Humanities and New Liberal Arts (No. 2021DH-3), the 2020 Li Ka Shing Foundation Cross-Disciplinary Research Grant (No. 2020LKSFG05D), the STU Scientific Research Foundation for Talents (No. NTF18006), the Natural Science Foundation of Guangdong Province (No. 2018A030313291), and the Education Science Planning Project of Guangdong Province (No. 2018GXJK048).

Y. Lai et al. (Eds.): ICA3PP 2021, LNCS 13156, pp. 53–62, 2022.
https://doi.org/10.1007/978-3-030-95388-1_4

evaluation of short-term traffic flow [9]. On the one hand, an effective short-term traffic flow forecasting model can help drivers reduce travel time and economic losses by avoiding congestion [6]. On the other hand, it will not only reduce carbon emissions caused by traffic congestion but also improve the efficiency of traffic operations. Besides, this technology is applied in many applications related to traffic, including traffic scene detection [12,16,27], vehicle network optimization [8,13,34], and geographic economics [15,22,23]. However, building an accurate and robust forecasting model remains a challenging task. Because of the randomness and nonlinear features of traffic flow data and the other interference of external factors, like unexpected traffic incidents and traffic control, it is hard to predict the flow.

In the past decades, researchers have proposed different methods and theories for traffic flow prediction. Traffic flow forecasting methods can be divided into three categories: statistical methods models, machine learning models [9,36], and deep learning models [3,28,29]. Statistical methods including auto-regressive integrated moving average (ARIMA) and Kalman filter (KF) [5]. Zhang et al. [35] designed a Kalman filter for denoising traffic flow data to getter lower RMSE. Zhou et al. [40] proposed a hybrid dual Kalman filtering model for short-term traffic flow prediction. Traditional machine learning models including k-nearest neighbor (kNN), decision tree, and ensemble learning. Cai et al. [4] presented a sample-rebalanced and outlier-rejected kNN regression model to forecast short-term traffic flow.

Recently, the deep learning method has been widely used in many domains and achieved good results, such as medical image analysis [30,31,37], disease diagnosis [17,25,26], and etc. Besides, deep learning has been applied in the complex nonlinear short-tern traffic flow prediction. Zhou et al. [39] trained the stacked autoencoders with an adaptive boosting scheme to improve the accuracy of traffic flow forecasting. Zhou et al. [38] proposed a deep learning ensemble method to select the most suitable forecasting model every time interval for accurate traffic flow forecasting. Lu et al. [29] used attentive diffusion convolution and bidirectional diffusion convolution and a stacked LSTM to learn the spatial-temporal dependencies of intricate traffic data. Fang et al. [11] proposed a stacked long short-term memory network with attention mechanism (AM-LSTM) for traffic flow forecasting. However, the deep learning model is easy to fall into local minimum value when it lacks sufficient data with high quality. Moreover, a well-trained neural network requires a lot of time and high computational complexity.

Support vector machine (SVM) is an effective prediction model to avoid the problem above and has superior advantages in dealing with complex problems [33]. Instead of determined by the weight of neurons determined by the adjustment of a large number of training data like the neural network-based methods, the decision of SVM is determined by the support vector determined during training, which makes SVM have a better performance on small and medium-sized data sets [7]. Theoretically, the support vector machine regression (SVR) is the regression version of SVM, which can obtain the optimal solutions in the global scope. SVR can also use kernel tricks to deal with non-linear data sets, avoiding the curse of dimensional phenomenon. The traffic flow prediction task concerned in this paper is a typical nonlinear time series prediction task, and the SVR model achieves superior performance when performing similar regression prediction tasks. Therefore, the SVR is good for small to medium-sized complex data sets and is suitable for short-time traffic flow forecasting. And some researchers applied the SVR to this task [2]. However, the prediction performance of SVR usually is limited by the inappropriate setting of its parameters, like kernel parameter γ and penalty factor C.

To solve this problem we use a genetic algorithm (GA), a method of finding the optimal solution by simulating the natural evolutionary process, as a way of selecting the appropriate parameters. The proposed method is termed GA-SVR. This method guarantees higher accuracy and real-time forecasting of short-time traffic flows. We have also compared this method with other state-of-the-art traffic flow forecasting methods through extensive experiments. The results show that GA-SVR has better performance in traffic flow prediction.

The remaining sections of the paper are organized as follows. The methodology is detailed in Sect. 2, and Sect. 3 is an empirical study of data from the real world. Conclusions are then drawn in Sect. 4.

2   Methodology

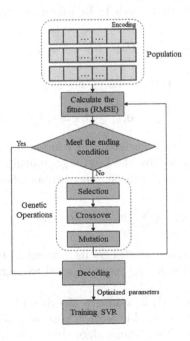

Fig. 1. The flowchart of the proposed GA-SVR

In this section, we first introduce the short-term traffic flow prediction model based on the SVR. This model uses the genetic algorithm to determine the hyperparameters combination of the SVR model, which can fully exploit the potential of the SVR model.

2.1 Support Vector Regression and Genetic Algorithm

Support vector machine (SVM) is an algorithm proposed by Vapnik, which can perform classification and regression tasks on linear or non-linear datasets. The theory of SVR is similar to that of SVM, which is trained by adjusting the feature weight vector of the model so that the objective function is minimized. The objective function is defined as follows,

$$\min_{\omega,b,\xi_i,\hat{\xi}_i} \frac{1}{2}||\omega||^2 + C\sum_{i=1}^{N} l_\varepsilon(y_i, f(x_i)), \tag{1}$$

where $\frac{1}{2}||\omega||^2$ is the regularization term, which minimizes the L2 norm of the feature weight vector ω of the SVR model; and the second term is to minimize training loss.

The $l_\varepsilon(y_i, f(x_i)$ is named ε-insensitive loss function, it can be defined as follows

$$l_\varepsilon(y_i, f(x_i)) = \begin{cases} |y_i - f(x_i)| - \varepsilon & otherwise \\ 0 & if|y_i - f(x_i)| \le \varepsilon \end{cases}, \tag{2}$$

The objective function that needs to be minimized in training turn into

$$\min_{\omega,b,\xi_i,\hat{\xi}_i} \frac{1}{2}||\omega||^2 + C\sum_{i=1}^{N}(\xi_i + \hat{\xi}_i),$$

$$s.t. \quad \begin{cases} f(x_i) - y_i \le \varepsilon + \hat{\xi}_i \\ y_i - f(x_i) \le \varepsilon + \xi_i \\ \xi_i \ge 0, \hat{\xi}_i \ge 0, i = 1,2,\cdots,m \end{cases} \tag{3}$$

where $\hat{\xi}_i$ and ξ_i are the slack variable. The minimization of the SVR objective function can be obtained by the Lagrange multiplier method. Finally, the regression equation of the SVR can be expressed as follows

$$f(x_i) = \sum_{i=1}^{N}(a_i^* - a_i)K(x_i, x) + b, \tag{4}$$

where a_i^* and a_i are Lagrange multipliers introduced by the Lagrange multiplier method, and $K(x_i, x)$ is the kernel function used to map nonlinearly separable feature vectors.

Genetic algorithm (GA) [1] is a swarm algorithm for searching the optimal solution by simulating the natural evolution process based on Charles Darwin's theory of natural selection. The swarm algorithms can automatically obtain the optimized search space and dynamically adjust the search direction without determining the rules [10].

2.2   GA-SVR for Traffic Flow Forecasting

GA for parameter optimization related to chromosome design, fitness function building. Firstly, we initialize the parameters C, ϵ, and γ to create a population, followed by calculating the fitness. Secondly, creating the next generation through genetic operations and add them to the population. Repeat this step until a certain amount of iteration or meet the termination criteria, we can get the optimized parameters C, ϵ, and γ. The flow chart of the Hybrid GA-SVR traffic flow prediction model can be seen as Fig. 1, and its pseudocode implementation is detailed in Algorithm 1.

Algorithm 1: Hybrid GA-SVR

Data: max iteration I_{max}, population size P_{size}, crossover rate r_c, mutation rate r_m
Result: optimized parameters C, ϵ, γ and a trained SVR model
1 Iteration $I = 0$;
2 Initialize popularion $P(I)$;
3 **repeat**
4 | Calculate the fitness of each individual: $F(I) = RMSE$
5 | **repeat**
6 | | Select two individuals from pop population by tournament selection algorithm according to fitness
7 | | **if** $random(0,1) \leq r_c$ **then**
8 | | | Perform single point crossover operation according to the crossover probability r_c ;
9 | | **end**
10 | | **if** $random(0,1) \leq r_m$ **then**
11 | | | Perform mutation operation according to the mutation probability r_m ;
12 | | **end**
13 | | Add new individual to the population;
14 | **until** *Traversed all individuals*;
15 | $I = I + 1$
16 **until** $I = I_{max}$;
17 Use optimized parameters C, ϵ, γ to train SVR model;

---

3   Experiments

In this section, the traffic flow data collected on four highways A1, A2, A4 and A8 connecting Amsterdam Ring Road (A10 Expressway) are used to evaluate our proposed GA-SVR model.

3.1   Data Description

In this section, we use four widely used benchmark datasets to evaluate the performance of the GA-SVR model in traffic flow prediction. The datasets containing the traffic flow data on the four motorways in Amsterdam, namely A1, A2, A4, and A8. These four roads end on the Ring Road of Amsterdam (A10). All the data were collected by MONICA loop detectors from May 20, 2010, to June 24, 2010, at 1-min intervals, representing the number of vehicles per minute. The four measurement points are located near the intersection of A10.

3.2   Evaluation Metrics

In this study, we use Root Mean Square Error (RMSE) and Mean Absolute Percentage Error (MAPE) as measures of the generalization performance of the proposed model. The two evaluation metrics are defined as follows:

$$RMSE = \sqrt{\frac{1}{N}\sum_{i=1}^{N}(\hat{y}_i - y_i)^2}, \tag{5}$$

$$MAPE = \frac{1}{N}\sum_{i=1}^{N}\left|\frac{\hat{y}_i - y_i}{y_i}\right| \times 100\%, \tag{6}$$

where N is the number of test samples, $\hat{y}_i$ and y_i represent the predicted value and the ground-truth of the ith sample, respectively. So the smaller the RMSE and MAPE, the better the performance of the prediction model.

3.3   Experimental Results

The original data contains some missing values because of the hardware failures, we use a statistical learning method motivated by Li *et al.* [21] to estimate the incorrect data. Then, we add up the raw data every 10 min to produce a traffic flow dataset at 10-min intervals of 5,040 items for each of the four roads. Each dataset contains 5 weeks of traffic flow data, corresponding to 1008 samples per week. The first four weeks of data are used as the training set and the last week of data as the test set. As a rule of thumb, we set the time lag to 12. The RMSE stabilizes after around 20 iterations of the genetic algorithm on the four test sets. Therefore, we set the maximum number of iterations to a smaller value (30) to save time. In this study, the RBF is selected as the kernel function. The initial setting of the GA is shown in Table 1.

Table 1. The initial setting of GA used

GA parameters	Setting
C	$[0, 100]$
ϵ	$[0, 50]$
γ	$[0, 25]$
Population size	100
Total iteration	30
Selection type	Tournament selection
Crossover type	Single-point crossover
Crossover rate	0.9
Mutation rate	0.02

In order to evaluate the performance of the proposed GA-SVR model, we compared it with several traffic flow prediction models commonly used in ITS. Table 2 demonstrates the results on four benchmark datasets. Obviously, our model achieved the best performance among several other ones.

Table 2. The RMSE and MAPE of different models.

Model	A1	A2 RMSE	A4 (veh/h)	A8	A1	A2 MAPE	A4 (%)	A8
SARIMA	308.44	221.08	228.36	169.36	12.81	11.25	12.05	12.44
GM	347.94	261.36	275.35	189.57	12.49	10.90	13.22	12.89
KF	332.03	239.87	250.51	187.48	12.46	10.72	12.62	12.63
DT	316.57	224.79	243.19	238.35	12.08	10.86	12.34	13.62
AR	301.44	214.22	226.12	166.71	13.57	11.59	12.70	12.71
ES	315.82	226.40	237.76	174.67	11.94	10.75	11.97	12.00
ANN	299.64	212.95	225.86	166.50	12.61	10.89	12.49	12.53
SVR	329.09	259.74	253.66	190.30	14.34	12.22	12.23	12.48
GA-SVR	**280.94**	**201.96**	**224.73**	**165.07**	**11.71**	**10.55**	**11.10**	**12.17**

Figure 2 shows the predicted values of the GA-SVR model compared to the true values under the conditions of using the hyperparameters set in Table 1, the orange line and the blue one represent the true values and the predicted values of our proposed model, respectively. The figure shows that in most cases, the predicted values of the model fit the true values very well.

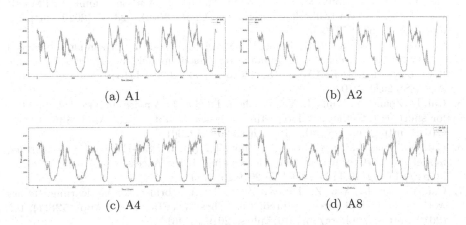

(a) A1   (b) A2

(c) A4   (d) A8

Fig. 2. Comparison of model predictions with the true values of the test set

4 Conclusion

In this paper, an support vector machine regression (SVR) model based on the genetic algorithm (GA) to determine the combination of hyperparameters is proposed for short-term traffic flow prediction. GA can quickly determine the best combination of hyperparameters of the SVR model under the guidance of no special hyperparameters, fully mining the predictive power of the SVR regression model, so that the GA-SVR model has excellent generalization ability. The method not only performs better than the SVR model optimized by other algorithms, such as PSO-SVR but superior to the deep learning neural network prediction model such as LSTM. Through experimental comparison, it has proved that the SVR regression model optimized by the GA algorithm has excellent prediction performance in short-term traffic flow prediction. In the future, we plan to extend the GA-SVR model to other applications, such as emotion prediction [14, 18, 32], and image enhancement [19, 20].

Conflict of Interest. The authors declare that they have no conflict of interest.

References

1. Banzhaf, W., Nordin, P., Keller, R.E., Francone, F.D.: Genetic Programming: An Introduction on the Automatic Evolution of Computer Programs and its Applications. Morgan Kaufmann Publishers Inc., Burlington (1998)
2. Cai, L., Chen, Q., Cai, W., Xu, X., Zhou, T., Qin, J.: Svrgsa: a hybrid learning based model for short-term traffic flow forecasting. IET Intell. Transp. Syst. **13**(9), 1348–1355 (2019). https://doi.org/10.1049/iet-its.2018.5315
3. Cai, L., Lei, M., Zhang, S., Yu, Y., Zhou, T., Qin, J.: A noise-immune LSTM network for short-term traffic flow forecasting. Chaos **30**(2), 023135 (2020). https://doi.org/10.1063/1.5120502
4. Cai, L., Yu, Y., Zhang, S., Song, Y., Xiong, Z., Zhou, T.: A sample-rebalanced outlier-rejected k-nearest neighbour regression model for short-term traffic flow forecasting. IEEE Access **8**, 22686–22696 (2020). https://doi.org/10.1109/ACCESS.2020.2970250
5. Cai, L., Zhang, Z., Yang, J., Yu, Y., Zhou, T., Qin, J.: A noise-immune kalman filter for short-term traffic flow forecasting. Physica A Stat. Mech. Appl. **536**, 122601 (2019). https://doi.org/10.1016/j.physa.2019.122601
6. Cai, W., Yang, J., Yu, Y., Song, Y., Zhou, T., Qin, J.: PSO-ELM: a hybrid learning model for short-term traffic flow forecasting. IEEE Access **8**, 6505–6514 (2020). https://doi.org/10.1109/ACCESS.2019.2963784
7. Cai, W., Yu, D., Wu, Z., Du, X., Zhou, T.: A hybrid ensemble learning framework for basketball outcomes prediction. Physica A Stat. Mech. Appl. **528**(1), 1–8 (2019). https://doi.org/10.1016/j.physa.2019.121461
8. Chen, M., Wang, T., Ota, K., Dong, M., Zhao, M., Liu, A.: Intelligent resource allocation management for vehicles network: an a3c learning approach. Comput. Commun. **151**, 485–494 (2020)
9. Cui, Z., Huang, B., Dou, H., Tan, G., Zheng, S., Zhou, T.: GSA-ELM: a hybrid learning model for short-term traffic flow forecasting. IET Intell. Transp. Syst. (2021). https://doi.org/10.1049/itr2.12127

10. Dou, H., Ji, J., Wei, H., Wang, F., Wang, J., Zhou, T.: Transfer inhibitory potency prediction to binary classification: a model only needs a small training set. Comput. Methods Prog. Biomed. (2022)
11. Fang, W., Zhuo, W., Yan, J., Song, Y., Jiang, D., Zhou, T.: Attention meets long short-term memory: a deep learning network for traffic flow forecasting. Physica A Stat. Mech. Appl. (2022). https://doi.org/10.1016/j.physa.2021.126485
12. Ge, Z., Li, Y., Liang, C., Song, Y., Zhou, T., Qin, J.: Acsnet: adaptive cross-scale network with feature maps refusion for vehicle density detection. In: 2021 IEEE International Conference on Multimedia and Expo (ICME), pp. 1–6. IEEE, Shenzhen (2021). https://doi.org/10.1109/ICME51207.2021.9428454
13. Hu, L., Liu, A., Xie, M., Wang, T.: UAVs joint vehicles as data mules for fast codes dissemination for edge networking in smart city. Peer-to-Peer Netw. Appl **12**(6), 1550–1574 (2019)
14. Huang, D., Chen, S., Liu, C., Zheng, L., Tian, Z., Jiang, D.: Differences first in asymmetric brain: a bi-hemisphere discrepancy convolutional neural network for EEG emotion recognition. Neurocomputing **448**, 140–151 (2021)
15. Huang, Z., Li, S., Gao, F., Wang, F., Lin, J., Tan, Z.: Evaluating the performance of LBSM data to estimate the gross domestic product of china at multiple scales: a comparison with NPP-VIIRS nighttime light data. Journal of Cleaner Production **328**, 129558 (2021)
16. Jiang, D., et al.: An audio data representation for traffic acoustic scene recognition. IEEE Access **8**, 177863–177873 (2020). https://doi.org/10.1109/ACCESS.2020.3027474
17. Jiang, D., et al.: A hybrid intelligent model for acute hypotensive episode prediction with large-scale data. Inf. Sci. **546**, 787–802 (2020). https://doi.org/10.1016/j.ins.2020.08.033
18. Jiang, D., et al.: A probability and integrated learning based classification algorithm for high-level human emotion recognition problems. Measurement **150**, 107049 (2019). https://doi.org/10.1016/j.measurement.2019.107049
19. Li, C., Tang, S., Kwan, H.K., Yan, J., Zhou, T.: Color correction based on CFA and enhancement based on retinex with dense pixels for underwater images. IEEE Access **8**, 155732–155741 (2020). https://doi.org/10.1109/ACCESS.2020.3019354
20. Li, C., Tang, S., Yan, J., Zhou, T.: Low-light image enhancement based on quasi-symmetric correction functions by fusion. Symmetry **12**(9), 1561 (2020). https://doi.org/10.3390/sym12091561
21. Li, L., Du, B., Wang, Y., Qin, L., Tan, H.: Estimation of missing values in heterogeneous traffic data: application of multimodal deep learning model. Knowl.-Based Syst. **194**, 105592 (2020)
22. Li, S., et al.: Spatially varying impacts of built environment factors on rail transit ridership at station level: a case study in Guangzhou, China. J. Transp. Geogr. **82**, 102631 (2020)
23. Li, S., et al.: The varying patterns of rail transit ridership and their relationships with fine-scale built environment factors: Big data analytics from Guangzhou. Cities **99**, 102580 (2020)
24. Li, S., Zhuang, C., Tan, Z., Gao, F., Lai, Z., Wu, Z.: Inferring the trip purposes and uncovering spatio-temporal activity patterns from dockless shared bike dataset in Shenzhen, China. J. Transp. Geogr. **91**, 102974 (2021)
25. Li, X., Bai, L., Ge, Z., Lin, Z., Yang, X., Zhou, T.: Early diagnosis of neuropsychiatric systemic lupus erythematosus by deep learning enhanced magnetic resonance spectroscopy. J. Med. Imaging Health Inf. **11**, 1341–1347 (2021). https://doi.org/10.1166/jmihi.2021.3378

26. Li, Y., Ge, Z., Zhiyan, Z., Shen, Z., Wang, Y., Zhou, T., Wu, R.: Broad learning enhanced 1h-mrs for early diagnosis of neuropsychiatric systemic lupus erythematosus. Comput. Mathe. Methods Med. **2020**, 1–13 (2020). https://doi.org/10.1155/2020/8874521, https://www.hindawi.com/journals/cmmm/2020/8874521/
27. Lin, Y., Li, L., Jing, H., Ran, B., Sun, D.: Automated traffic incident detection with a smaller dataset based on generative adversarial networks. Accid. Anal. Prev. **144**, 105628 (2020)
28. Lu, H., Ge, Z., Song, Y., Jiang, D., Zhou, T., Qin, J.: A temporal-aware LSTM enhanced by loss-switch mechanism for traffic flow forccasting. Neurocomputing **427**, 169–178 (2021). https://doi.org/10.1016/j.neucom.2020.11.026
29. Lu, H., Huang, D., Youyi, S., Jiang, D., Zhou, T., Qin, J.: St-trafficnet: a spatial-temporal deep learning network for traffic forecasting. Electronics **9**(9), 1–17 (2020). https://doi.org/10.3390/electronics9091474
30. Song, Y., et al.: Learning 3D features with 2D CNNs via surface projection for CT volume segmentation. In: Martel, A.L., et al. (eds.) MICCAI 2020. LNCS, vol. 12264, pp. 176–186. Springer, Cham (2020). https://doi.org/10.1007/978-3-030-59719-1_18
31. Song, Y., Zhou, T., Teoh, J.Y.-C., Zhang, J., Qin, J.: Unsupervised learning for CT image segmentation via adversarial redrawing. In: Martel, A.L., et al. (eds.) MICCAI 2020. LNCS, vol. 12264, pp. 309–320. Springer, Cham (2020). https://doi.org/10.1007/978-3-030-59719-1_31
32. Tu, G., Wen, J., Liu, H., Chen, S., Zheng, L., Jiang, D.: Exploration meets exploitation: Multitask learning for emotion recognition based on discrete and dimensional models. Knowl.-Based Syst., 107598 (2021). https://doi.org/10.1016/j.knosys.2021.107598
33. Vapnik, V., Guyon, I., Hastie, T.: Support vector machines. Mach. Learn. **20**(3), 273–297 (1995)
34. Wang, T., Wang, P., Cai, S., Ma, Y., Liu, A., Xie, M.: A unified trustworthy environment establishment based on edge computing in industrial iot. IEEE Trans. Ind. Inf. **16**(9), 6083–6091 (2019)
35. Zhang, S., Song, Y., Jiang, D., Zhou, T., Qin, J.: Noise-identified kalman filter for short-term traffic flow forecasting. In: 2019 15th International Conference on Mobile Ad-Hoc and Sensor Networks (MSN), pp. 462–466. IEEE (2019). https://doi.org/10.1109/MSN48538.2019.00093
36. Zheng, S., Zhang, S., Song, Y., Lin, Z., Dazhi, J., Zhou, T.: A noise-immune boosting framework for short-term traffic flow forecasting. Complexity (2021). https://doi.org/10.1155/2021/5582974
37. Zhou, T., et al.: Quantitative analysis of patients with celiac disease by video capsule endoscopy: a deep learning method. Comput. Biol. Med. **85**(2), 1–6 (2017). https://doi.org/10.1016/j.compbiomed.2017.03.031
38. Zhou, T., Han, G., Xu, X., Han, C., Huang, Y., Qin, J.: A learning-based multi-model integrated framework for dynamic traffic flow forecasting. Neural Process. Lett. **49**(1), 407–430 (2018). https://doi.org/10.1007/s11063-018-9804-x
39. Zhou, T., et al.: δ-agree adaboost stacked autoencoder for short-term traffic flow forecasting. Neurocomputing **247**(4), 31–38 (2017). https://doi.org/10.1016/j.neucom.2017.03.049
40. Zhou, T., Jiang, D., Lin, Z., Han, G., Xu, X., Qin, J.: Hybrid dual kalman filtering model for short-term traffic flow forecasting. IET Intell. Transp. Syst. **13**(6), 1023–1032 (2019). https://doi.org/10.1049/iet-its.2018.5385

Parallel and Distributed Algorithms and Applications

MobiTrack: Mobile Crowdsensing-Based Object Tracking with Min-Region and Max-Utility

Wenqiang Li[1,2], Jun Tao[1,2,3(✉)], Zuyan Wang[1,2], YiFan Xu[1,2], Xiaolei Tang[1,2], and YiChao Dong[1,2]

[1] School of Cyber Science and Engineering, Southeast University, Nanjing, China
{wqli,juntao,zuyan92,xyf,xiaoleitang,ycdong}@seu.edu.cn
[2] Key Lab of CNII, MOE, Southeast University, Nanjing, China
[3] Purple Mountain Laboratories for Network and Communication Security, Nanjing, China

Abstract. Exploiting *mobile* cameras embedded on the widely-used smartphones to serve object tracking offers a new dimension to reduce the deployment cost of the stationary cameras and shorten the tracking latency, but brings the challenges in efficient task assignment and cooperations among workers due to the requirement of Mobile Crowdsensing (MCS) system. Most existing effort in the literature focuses on object tracking with MCS where the workers capture the moving object photos at pre-calculated sites. However, the contradiction between the tracking coverage and the system cost in these MCS-based tracking solutions is sharpened when tracking scenarios and worker number vary. In this paper, we investigate the tracking region to conduct the task assignment among *top-k* most probable sensing locations, which can achieve maximal tracking utility. Specifically, we construct a N-Gram prediction model to determine the k tracking locations and formulate the task assignment problem solved by the Kuhn-Munkras algorithm, respectively, laying a theoretical foundation. The prediction model soundness is verified statistically and the task assignment effectiveness is evaluated via large scale real-world data simulations.

Keywords: Mobile Crowdsensing · Object tracking · Trajectory prediction · Task assignment

1 Introduction

With the prevalence of portable devices, Mobile CrowdSensing (MCS) has become a promising paradigm for various sensing tasks [18], e.g., the monitoring of air quality [19], traffic [17], and urban infrastructure [1]. Exploiting MCS to conduct object tracking has been attracting increasing research attentions [4,5,21]. Different from the traditional object tracking approaches which mainly relied on the stationary cameras pre-deployed in the urban area, MCS-based tracking systems outsource tracking tasks to the real-world participants

© Springer Nature Switzerland AG 2022
Y. Lai et al. (Eds.): ICA3PP 2021, LNCS 13156, pp. 65–80, 2022.
https://doi.org/10.1007/978-3-030-95388-1_5

(e.g., citizens). A real-life example of MCS-based tracking system is deployed on Alipay APP in China, which encourages users to participate the missing children finding as soon as possible.

Many early researches on MCS-based object tracking usually demand special devices [8], e.g., low-power BLE peripheral [16] and unique Bluetooth tags [21], to serve the tracking tasks. With the rapid development of mobile networks and the wide usage of sensor-enhanced smartphones, employing the cameras on smartphones to build crowd tracking systems has become a popular paradigm to perform object tracking [4,12]. The limitations of conventional stationary camera-based schemes, which include how to determine the proper density of deployed cameras to achieve the tradeoff between the tracking cost and the size of the tracking region, and how to identify the same moving object precisely through various camera cooperations [22], can be remedied by the wide distribution of tracking workers.

However, existing MCS-based tracking systems may suffer from two problems: 1) to avoid tracking miss, the predicted arrival region is often large so plenty of users should be recruited to guarantee tracking coverage, means a high cost; 2) users select their tracking locations randomly due to the non-cooperative behaviors among users, leads to a low benefit. Thus, the critical issues for object tracking are to scale down the tracking task by limiting the tracking region and determine an optimal assignment to maximize the system utility from a global perspective.

Targeting at the issues mentioned above, we propose a Minimum tracking Region and Maximun system Utility (MRMU) algorithm to develop MobiTrack, a MCS-based system that recruits an optimal set of workers to collaboratively take photographs to track the object in the city. The main contributions of this paper are as follows.

- We propose a variant of the k-means clustering algorithm to learn significant places as sensing locations from GPS data. A N-Gram model is constructed for object trajectory prediction and minimal sensing location number determination.
- We formulate the object tracking problem as an optimal task assignment problem through a novel system utility, the Maximum Utility Task Assignment (MUTA) algorithm is conducted to solve it in polynomial time, aims to achieve the maximal system utility.
- We conduct extensive experiments on real-world taxi trajectory datasets to evaluate the performance of MobiTrack. The results demonstrate that the proposed algorithm outperforms the other existing algorithms for movement prediction and system utility achievement.

The rest of this paper is organized as follows. Section 2 discusses the related work. The system model and problem statement are presented in Sect. 3. Section 4 introduces the proposed solution to vehicle movement prediction and tracking task assignment. The datasets and experiment results are presented in Sect. 5 and 6. Finally, we conclude the paper in Sect. 7.

2   Related Work

This paper is mainly related to two areas of research: 1) trajectory prediction of object; 2) task allocation in MCS.

2.1   Trajectory Prediction of Object

Observing the importance of trajectory prediction (e.g., narrow the tracking scope) in object tracking, much effort has been made to explore it [10,13,23, 25]. From the perspective of data used, the literature of trajectory prediction problem can be classified into two categories: individual oriented and general oriented. Several previous works on the destination prediction problem made use of personal trip data. For example, [25] proposed an approach that uses personal and social factors to estimate pedestrian destination and social relationships. [10] utilized trip durations to build Bayesian model, which serves to limit geographic extent of candidate destinations. Some other works [13,23], including ours, uses anonymous crowd trip data that contains no traveler information.

Most existing trajectory prediction methods focus on probabilistic models, in which the historical trajectories are used to train various Markov Chain (MC) and the *top-k* most probable destinations are returned. One typical approach is to partition the map into the grid cells [12], or roads into segments [4], and trip is decomposed into a sequence of transitions between cells or segments to build the model. Another point-cluster-based MC prediction algorithm was proposed in [2], in which GPS data was automatically clustered into meaningful locations and then used as the states of the Markov process. [23] introduced a new data-driven nonprobabilistic framework, which directly operates on the trajectories and makes the prediction.

In this paper, we adopt a probabilistic N-Gram model [7], which calculates the next probable movement of the object by all previous positions, with cluster-level granularity, to learn semantic information (e.g., home, school and intersection).

2.2   Task Assignment in MCS

Task assignment becomes a critical issue in MCS-powered tracking systems when trajectory prediction phase returns an arrival region, e.g., a grid, a road segment, *top-k* clusters etc., which requires many workers to finish the tracking task collectively. Many researches have been made in this MCS-based applications [11,20,24]. For example, Guo et al. investigated the multitask-oriented worker selection problem for large-scale MCS platforms, with the objective of optimizing task allocation under the situation of the time-sensitive tasks and delay-tolerant tasks, respectively in [9]. Huang et al. proposed an efficient task allocation algorithm called OPTA for maximizing the sensing capacity of each mobile user in time dependent crowdsensing systems [11]. Yucel et al. introduced a task assignment strategy in [28], with the consideration of each user's preference and reliability. The prediction-based task allocation algorithm (PBTA) was proposed in [15], with the objective of deriving the maximum overall system utility. Most of these existing effort focuses on the offline task assignment, which selects workers for tasks with given location contexts. However, [24] proposed a two-stage resource allocation process, including an offline phase and another sequential online phase.

Intuitively, object tracking can be viewed as online task, the sensing location of which changes over time. Therefore, our task assignment strategy applies an online model.

3   System Model and Problem Statement

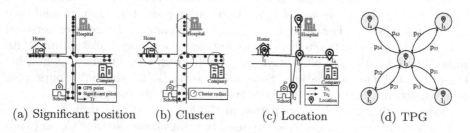

(a) Significant position   (b) Cluster   (c) Location   (d) TPG

Fig. 1. A scenario of location learning and transition probability graph (*TPG*) constructing.

3.1   System Model

We consider a MCS System that consists of a crowd of mobile users. Suppose that there is a user in the system, called the *requester*, who has some object tracking task. Other users in this system, called the *responders*, (hereafter, we use the term *worker* to denote *responders*), denoted by $W = \{w_1, w_2, \ldots, w_n\}$, are assumed to be willing to participate in these tasks due to some incentive mechanisms, such as [6], which are not our focus in this paper.

Without loss of generality, let $L = \{l_1, l_2, \ldots, l_m\}$ be the set of sensing locations in the system. The ongoing trip of the object at time slot t is denoted by $f(t)$. Suppose that the system maintains a large scale crowdsourced historical trajectory dataset D. Once the *requester* published a task T, the object's probable arrival region, denoted by $\hat{R}$, which consists of the *top-k* most probable arrival locations, can be approximated by some prediction methods according to D and the observed ongoing trip of the tracking target $f(t)$. Thus, the expected tracking region at time slot $t + 1$ is given by

$$\hat{R}(t + 1) = \mathcal{P}(f(t))$$
$$= \{\hat{l}_1, \hat{l}_2, \ldots, \hat{l}_k\}, \quad \forall \hat{l}_j \in L, \tag{1}$$

where $\mathcal{P}$ is the prediction method and $\hat{l}_i$ is *ith* probable arrival location.

Therefore, the origin tracking task T is decomposed as k concurrent subtasks, denoted by $T = \{s_1, s_2, \ldots, s_k\}$, i.e., one subtask for one sensing location.

Let $B(w_i, l_j, t)$ be the benefit of the system when assigning a subtask to worker w_i at time slot t to move to location l_j before time slot $t + 1$ for tracking. We assume that the benefit is proportional to the arrival probability, denoted by $B(w_i, l_j, t) = M(t)p(l_j|f(t))$. $M(t)$ is the total benefit of the task and $p(l_j|f(t))$ means the probability the target move to l_j at time slot t. Meanwhile, a cost $C(w_i, l_j)$ will incur for the purpose of rewarding worker w_i to execute the subtask. Suppose that the cost is equal to the distance powered to γ between the position of worker w_i and location l_j, namely $c(w_i, l_j) = d(w_i, l_j)^\gamma$. Thus, the utility of the subtask is defined as

$$u(w_i, l_j, t) = M(t)p(l_j|f(t))/d(w_i, l_j)^\gamma. \tag{2}$$

In addition, we use ϕ to denote a task assignment decision in a set Φ of all available assignment options, where

$$\phi(w_i, l_j) = \begin{cases} 1, & \text{if } w_i \text{ is assigned to } l_j \\ 0, & \text{otherwise} \end{cases}. \tag{3}$$

Therefore, the system utility to execute task T at time slot t is as follows:

$$U(T, t) = \sum_{w_i \in W} \sum_{l_j \in \hat{R}} u(w_i, l_j, t) \cdot \phi(w_i, l_j). \tag{4}$$

Suppose that the target is sensed passes $\hat{l}_1$ at next time slot $t + 1$, then new tracking region $\hat{R}(t + 2)$ generates according to $f(t + 1)$ (i.e., $f(t) \cup \hat{l}_1$). This process repeats until the task finished.

3.2   Problem Statement

In this paper, we focus on the movement prediction and task assignment problem in object tracking task. Specifically, we utilize the large-scale crowdsourced vehicle trajectory data to predict future arrival region of the target vehicle, and assign workers to the region to take photos if the target passes.

Before the problem definition, we define some basic concepts as follows:

Definition 1 (Vehicle Trajectory). *A vehicle trajectory Tr is a sequence of GPS points $\{g_1, g_2, \ldots, g_e\}$ corresponding to a vehicle's historical trip $g_1 \rightarrow g_2 \rightarrow \ldots \rightarrow g_e$. Each GPS point $g_i = (t_i, lon_i, lat_i)$ consists of a timestamp t_i, a longitude lon_i, and a latitude lat_i.*

Definition 2 (Significant Position (SP)). *A significant position is a GPS point at which vehicles stay beyond a time threshold $\mathbb{T}$.*

Definition 3 (Location). *A location marks a cluster of significant positions.*

Since SP are usually distributed around meaningful places, e.g., home, school and intersection etc., the locations learned from SP clustering can be exploited as sensing locations.

Definition 4 (Tracking Rate). *Tracking rate P_ζ means the probability that the object would move to predicted region $\hat{R}(t+1)$. MCS system sets it to determines the minimal k sensing locations that fits (5).*

$$\sum_{j=1}^{k} p(l_j|f(t)) > P_\zeta. \tag{5}$$

Based on the above definitions, we state and formalize our problems as follows:

- **Movement prediction:** this problem can be decomposed to two subproblems, 1) learning the locations from raw historical trajectory dataset D; 2) predict the minimal probable arrival region $\hat{R}(t+1)$ at each time slot t under the tracking rate P_ζ.
- **Task assignment:** determine an optimal assignment ϕ_{opt} to maximize the system utility $U(T,t)$:

4 Minimum Region Tracking And Maximum Utility Assignment

In this section, we propose a Minimum tracking Region and Maximum system Utility (MRMU) scheme, which consists of two phases, to tackle the object tracking problem in Sect. 3.2. First, *Offline object movement prediction* leverages the historical dataset D trains the offline Clustering representation-based N-Gram (N-Gram-C) movement prediction model. Second, *Online tracking task assignment* formulate the optimal decision problem as a maximum weighted bipartite matching (MWBM) problem, and Kuhn-Munkres (KM) algorithm is utilized to solve the MWBM problem.

4.1 Offline Object Movement Prediction

We employ a variant of the k-means clustering algorithm to learn locations from D like [2]. As Fig. 1(a)–(c) depicts, the key idea is to cluster all SP to belonged circles, the circle center is the mean of all SP within the circle. Finally, we collect a set of means, namely locations, and each GPS-based trajectory representation Tr can be transformed to location-based representation, e.g., $Tr_1 = \{l_2, l_3, l_1\}$. We omit the timestamp for the GPS-collection interval is often fixed (i.e., a time slot).

The core idea of N-Gram is to split each trajectory to a sequence of n-size grams. For example, for trajectory Tr_1 and a 2-Gram model, after decomposition, it will be denoted as $\{(l_2, l_3), (l_3, l_1)\}$.

Then the frequency of every gram is counted by

$$p(l_{i-n+1}, \ldots, l_i) = \frac{count(l_{i-n+1}, \ldots, l_i)}{count(Allgram)}. \tag{6}$$

Next, for a trajectory $Tr_i = \{l_{i1}, l_{i2}, \ldots, l_{ie}\}$, its probability according to the chain rule is given by

$$P(Tr_i) = p(l_{i1}) * p(l_{i2}|l_{i1}) \cdots p(l_{ie}|l_{i1}, \ldots, l_{i(e-1)}). \tag{7}$$

Applying the Markov Assumption and we can get

$$P(Tr_i) = \prod_{j=1}^{e} P(l_{ij}|l_{i(j-n+1)}, \ldots, l_{i(j-1)}). \tag{8}$$

$P(l_{ij}|l_{i(j-n+1)}, \ldots, l_{i(j-1)})$ (denoted by $P_M(l_{ij})$) can be obtained with maximum likelihood estimation as follows:

$$P_M(l_{ij}) = \frac{count(l_{ij}|l_{i(j-n+1)}, \ldots, l_{ij})}{count(l_{ij}|l_{i(j-n+1)}, \ldots, l_{i(j-1)})}. \tag{9}$$

All grams' conditional probability will be produced with (9), and a transition probability graph (TPG) would be formed, namely, the N-Gram model has been constructed. Figure 1(d) shows TPG in the scenario of Fig. 1(a) with a 2-gram model.

Once the ongoing trip of the object is updated by workers, and the tracking rate P_ζ is set, The minimized sensing region can be derived from (8), i.e., determines the minimal k most probable future trips.

4.2 Online Tracking Task Assignment

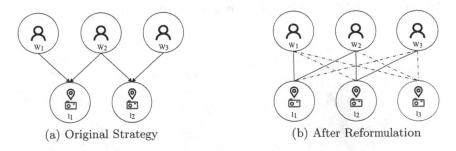

(a) Original Strategy   (b) After Reformulation

Fig. 2. An example of task assignment.

According to the prediction result, we define k concurrent subtasks for a tracking task T as $T = \{s_1, s_2, \ldots, s_k\}$. Each subtask requires a worker to take photos under the time constraint given by

$$\frac{dist(w_i, \hat{l})}{v_w} < \frac{dist(l_j, \hat{l})}{v_c}, \tag{10}$$

where $dist(w_i, \hat{l})$ is the distance that workers need to move to sensing location $\hat{l}$, $dist(l_j, \hat{l})$ is the distance between the object and $\hat{l}$. v_w and v_c are the average speed of workers and the object, respectively. (10) depicts an available assignment must meet the requirement that workers should arrive at the sensing locations before the target.

To simplify the expressions, we define a bipartite graph $G=<W,\hat{R},E>$, where E denotes the set of possible assignment. According to the definition of the optimal decision problem in Sect. 3, one location requires one worker, but there may be no worker fit the time constraint to be assigned for a certain location, or too many workers but fewer locations, as Fig. 2(a) depicts. Thus, we add dummy workers or locations to ensure $|W| = |\hat{R}|$, and dummy impossible assignment, which gains no utility, are added then. In this way, the original bipartite graph G can be extended to a balanced and complete bipartite graph $G'=<\mathcal{W},\mathcal{L},\mathcal{E}>$, which is shown in Fig. 2(b). Finally, the optimal decision problem (4) is formulated as a maximum weighted bipartite matching problem in G' as follows:

$$\max_{\phi} \sum_{(w_i,l_j)\in\mathcal{E}} u(w_i,l_j)\cdot\phi(w_i,l_j),$$

$$\text{s.t.} \sum_{l_j}\phi(w_i,l_j)=1, \forall l_j\in\mathcal{L}, \tag{11}$$

$$\sum_{w_i}\phi(w_i,l_j)=1, \forall w_i\in\mathcal{W},$$

$$\phi(w_i,l_j)\in\{0,1\}, \forall w_i\in\mathcal{W}, l_j\in\mathcal{L}.$$

In this paper, we conduct KM algorithm, which was proposed by Kuhn et al. [14], can efficiently solve the MWBM problem in $O(n^3)$, where n is the number of vertices in the bipartite graph, to achieve our Maximum Utility Task Assignment (MUTA) algorithm, and search an optimal task assignment (OTA) strategy.

The overall MRMU algorithm is shown in Algorithm 1.

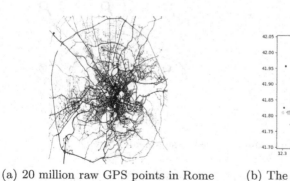

(a) 20 million raw GPS points in Rome   (b) The Density of Check-ins in Rome

Fig. 3. The experimental datasets.

5   Evaluation

In this section, we evaluate the effectiveness of the proposed MobiTrack on real-world datasets. We implement the mechanism in Python and make comparisons about its performance with various benchmarks.

Algorithm 1. Minimum Region Maximum Utility Algorithm

Require: $f(t), D, W, P_\zeta$.
Ensure: Determine the minimum sensing region $\hat{R}$, and find an optimal assignment
ϕ_{opt} to maximize $U(T, t)$.
Phase1: *Offline movement prediction*
1: Initialize $L = \emptyset$, set $\mathbb{T}, r, n$;
2: Filter out SP set S from D according to $\mathbb{T}$;
3: **while** S is not empty **do**
4:     Take a significant position g from S, $g_m = (g.lat, g.lon)$;
5:     **while** True **do**
6:         Collect SP set S' within circle (g_m, r);
7:         **if** $g_m = (mean(S'.lat), mean(S'.lon))$ **then**
8:             Break the current loop;
9:         **else**
10:             $g_m \leftarrow (mean(S'.lat), mean(S'.lon))$;
11:         **end if**
12:     **end while**
13:     $L \leftarrow L \cup g_m$;
14:     $S \leftarrow S \backslash S'$;
15: **end while**
16: Construct N-Gram model;
Phase2: *Online Task Assignment*
17: Initialize $p = 0, \hat{R} = \emptyset$, set P_ζ;
18: **while** $p < P_\zeta$ **do**
19:     Predict the most probable arrival location $\hat{l}$ in $L \backslash \hat{R}$;
20:     $p \leftarrow p + p(\hat{l}|f(t))$;
21:     $\hat{R} \leftarrow \hat{R} \cup \hat{l}$;
22: **end while**
23: Formulate $G =< W, \hat{R}, E >$ to $G' =< \mathcal{W}, \mathcal{L}, \mathcal{E} >$;
24: Conduct KM algorithm to find ϕ;
25: **return** ϕ.

5.1   Dataset Overview

Two datasets used in experiments will be described briefly in the chapter.

Rome Taxi Dataset: the experimental data for movement prediction we used
were collected from real-world mobility traces of taxi cabs in Rome, Italy [3].
The roma taxi dataset contains about 20 million GPS points of approximately
320 taxis collected over 30 days (as shown in Fig. 3(a)). Each GPS point consists
of a taxi ID, a timestamp, a longitude and a latitude, collected every 15 s.

Rome Check-ins Dataset: we use the Rome check-ins dataset extracted from
Foursquare in [26,27], which includes long-term (about 18 months) global-scale
check-in data in 415 cities in 77 countries from April 2012 to September 2013, to
evaluate the task assignment performance of the proposed mechanism. The data
of Rome contains 42574 check-ins and The density of check-ins in 18 months

is shown in Fig. 3(b). Obviously, most of the check-ins are distributed in the central urban area, i.e., within longitude (12.447, 12.512) and latitude (41.8957, 41.9112). Thus, we create the tasks in these areas and check-in users in these areas can be seen as the workers.

5.2   Simulation Setup

Movement Prediction: As the GPS points of different vehicles in Rome Taxi Dataset are mixed, we apply an aggregation algorithm by using the attributes *taxi ID* and *timestamp* to aggregate sequences of GPS points for each taxi. Considering that the stay time indicates whether a trip is terminated or not, we use the GPS points that vehicles stay beyond 120 s to split the data into trajectories. Therefore, we obtain a trajectory dataset, 10,000 trajectories are randomly picked from this dataset as the testing set, the remains is used as training set to construct the N-Gram model.

Two metrics are utilized to evaluate the effectiveness of the proposed movement prediction mechanism: the prediction accuracy (Acc) and tracking coverage (TC).

1) Acc: For each trajectory $Tr_i = \{l_{i1}, l_{i2}, \cdots\}$ in the testing set, there are $|Tr_i|$ locations, and for each location in Tr_i except the last one, we can predict the most probable movement with the constructed N-Gram model. The Acc is the total number of predictions divided by the number of correct predictions.
2) TC: given the number of sensing locations k, the ratio of the number of successfully tracked tasks that satisfy a certain tracking rate (see Definition 4) to the number of total tasks.

In order to evaluate the effectiveness of N-Gram-C, we compare our method with existing movement prediction algorithms. Particularly, another grid-based MMC prediction algorithm, i.e., N'-MPRE [12], which employs a grid representation of the data space including the urban space and incorporates $n' - 1$ previous visited grids of the object for next movement prediction, is used as the baseline. We set the side length of the grid as 100 m.

Task Assignment: We set the positions of tasks based on the locations learned by a variant of the k-means clustering algorithm (see Sect. 4.1), and the positions of workers are set based on the leisure places, e.g., hotel, rest and coffee, of users in the Rome Check-ins Dataset. There are 447 learned locations and 1125 checked-in leisure places in the central urban area of Rome.

In the experiments, we randomly select a certain number of learned locations as the position of tasks and leisure places as the position of workers. Specifically, to scale down the task assignment problem, the number of tasks is set as 50, and the number of workers is set from 10 to 100. For the calculation of the system utility in Eq. 2, we set the tracking task benefit M to 100, the exponent γ to 1, and the movement probability $p(l|f)$ is set according to the belonged ongoing trip f of l and N-Gram-C prediction model. Furthermore, To meet the time constraint, we assume that the average moving speed of a worker is 200 m/min and the average speed of a vehicle is 30 km/h.

For comparison, three performance metrics, including the system cost, system benefit and system utility, are adopted, which are defined in Sect. 3.1.

In order to simulate workers' behaviors in real world, we use the following benchmarks.

- **People-Centric Selection (PCS)** [12]. Each worker randomly selects a sensing task within the time constraint, to conduct the tracking task without considering any system performance.
- **Most Probable Location First (MPLF).** MPLF is a greedy strategy to select the most probable location that the object will move next for each worker, which MCS systems would like to adopt since they want to get the highest profit.
- **Nearest Location First (NLF).** NLF is a greedy strategy to select the closest sensing location for each worker, which aims to minimize the system cost while ignoring the system benefit.

6   Experimental Results and Analysis

6.1   Effectiveness of Movement Prediction

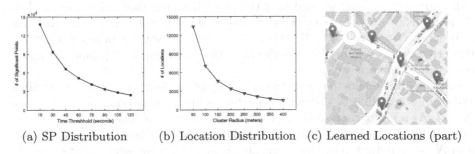

(a) SP Distribution   (b) Location Distribution   (c) Learned Locations (part)

Fig. 4. Simulations of location learning.

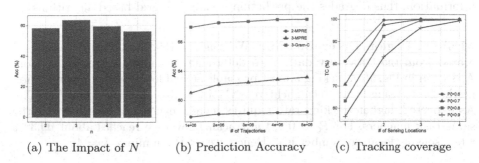

(a) The Impact of N (b) Prediction Accuracy   (c) Tracking coverage

Fig. 5. Simulations of movement prediction.

Location Learning: When analyzing the 30 days of GPS data, we discovered that the number of significant points and the time threshold $\mathbb{T}$ followed a nearly quadratic relationship (shown in Fig. 4(a)). The knee in the graph happens at $\mathbb{T}_k = 60$ s, where 51,5629 significant points were found. For the reason that the knee signifies the time just before the number of significant points begins to converge, we determined to take $60s$ as the final time threshold.

Figure 4(b) shows the number of locations found as cluster radius changes after we keep time threshold as $\mathbb{T}_k$. As the radius r approaches zero, the number of locations grows rapidly. When $r > 150$ m, a linear relationship between radius and the number of locations emerged. Considering that locations clustered from a large radius possibly contain multiple meaningful places, while a small radius would split one place to several locations, we apply $r = 100$ m to extract locations (at $r = 100$ m, 7,049 locations were learned). Figure 4(c) shows partial learned locations. As expected, meaningful places, e.g., intersection, community and bus stop are marked as locations by using our method.

Prediction Accuracy: First of all, a suitable N needs to be decided for our training dataset. We conduct an extensive experimental study to evaluate the performance of our N-Gram-C algorithm under different value of N. Note that N means the size of the gram. Figure 5(a) shows the results obtained by Gram-C with n ranging from 2 to 5. The number of trajectories is set to 1,000,000. With the n increasing, we find that the prediction accuracy is increasing when N is from 2 to 3, while its value decreases slightly when n is above 3. This is because $N = 3$ rolls the direction information to help for movement prediction. However, N-Gram-C may suffer from the "data sparsity" problem when N increases. Therefore, we set N as 3.

Figure 5(b) depicts the prediction accuracy of the 3-Gram-C and the baseline. We can observe that N'-MPRE also achieves higher prediction accuracy when $N = 3$. As a comparison, 3-Gram-C still outperforms the baseline, which shows around 10.03% and 8.515% on average under the experiment settings of $N' = 2$ and $N' = 3$, respectively. One possible reason is that the same location would be divided to different grids in N'-MPRE without the consideration of semantic information, thus degrades the prediction accuracy of grid-based algorithms.

Minimal Region Determination: We conduct 100,000 tracking tasks generated from the trajectory dataset to determine the minimal tracking region. As shown in Fig. 5(c), picking a most probable arrival location by our prediction method as sensing location can achieve 81.17% tracking coverage when $P_\zeta = 0.6$. As expected, higher tracking rate requires more sensing locations to cover the same task numbers. For $P_\zeta = 0.9$, the tracking coverage reaches about 99.38% when sensing location number is 4. Hence, we set the minimal $k = 4$.

6.2   Performance of Task Assignment Strategies

Figure 6(a) depicts the system cost of the four strategies. It is clear that PCS achieves an extremely high system cost, followed by MPLF. As expected, NLF achieves the lowest system cost because the workers always select the closest task to check in. We can also observe that the cost of all schemes rises dramatically when the number of workers is not larger than 50. Note that the number of tracking tasks are 50. The reason is that, more tasks would be allocated as workers arrive in the system continually. However, the cost of MUTA drops while costs of other schemes keep a subtle increasement when there are over 50 workers. This phenomenon indicates that MCS-based tasks can be better completed with more collaborative users roll in.

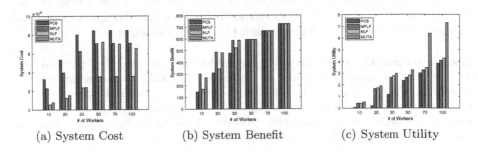

(a) System Cost   (b) System Benefit   (c) System Utility

Fig. 6. Simulations of different task assignment strategies.

The system benefit of the schemes is shown in Fig. 6(b). Apparently, when the number of workers is under 50, MPLF achieves the higheast system benefit, followed by MUTA. Both PCS and NLF have a poor performance in terms of system benefit when compared to our scheme, around 53.9% and 36.59% less on average, respectively. This is because they are not designed to assign the beneficial tracking tasks to workers. We can see that when the number of workers is larger than the number of tasks, four schemes achieve nearly the same benefit. Since the benefit reflects the allocated tasks to workers, the same benefit indicates that the same task set would be allocated by different strategies, as enough workers engaged in.

Figure 6(c) shows the system utility, which is the most important metric. For all schemes, the system utility increases with more workers participating in tracking. However, PCS achieves the lowest system utility since it cannot really help the system with the random selection. On the other hand, although MPLF and NLF achieve a good performance in terms of the system cost or the system benefit, neither of them performs well regarding to the system utility, especially when there are over 50 workers. Recall that our scheme cannot get the lowest cost or the highest benefit, whereas an extremely high system utility is achieved eventually, which shows around 789.21%, 84.82% and 72.62% improvement on average over PCS, MPLF and NLF, respectively. Therefore the performance results show that our task assignment strategy is indeed effective.

7 Conclusion and Future Work

In this paper, we have analytically investigate the object tracking in MCS. Two stage approach, namely a cluster representation based N-Gram model and the MUTA, have been exploited to predict the object movement offline and make optimal task assignment decision online, successively. System measures of the approach, e.g., the movement prediction accuracy, the number of sensing location, cost, benefit and utility have been explored. Extensive experiments on the real-world datasets confirm that our proposed MobiTrack can help the system achieve maximum utility on object tracking compared with other classical benchmarks, i.e., PCS, MPLF and NLF. Our future work will focus on the location learning process. We will further investigate whether the settings of the time threshold and the radius for clustering would influence the movement prediction accuracy, and determine a more reasonable time threshold and radius and possibly employ deep learning approach to solve this problem.

Acknowledgments. This work was supported by the Cyberspace International Governance Research Institute in Southeast University, the CERNET Southeastern China (North) Regional Network Center, the National Key Research and Development Program of China under Grant 2018YFB1800205 and the Industry-Academia-Research Innovation Fund of Chinese University (Alibaba Cloud Digital Innovation Project for University) under Grant 2021ALA03006.

References

1. Aly, H., Basalamah, A., Youssef, M.: Automatic rich map semantics identification through smartphone-based crowd-sensing. IEEE Trans. Mob. Comput. **16**(10), 2712–2725 (2016)
2. Ashbrook, D., Starner, T.: Learning significant locations and predicting user movement with GPS. In: Proceedings Sixth International Symposium on Wearable Computers, pp. 101–108 (2002)
3. Bracciale, L., et al.: Crawdad dataset roma/taxi (v. 2014-07-17) (2014). https://doi.org/10.15783/C7QC7M, https://crawdad.org/roma/taxi/20140717
4. Chen, H., Guo, B., Yu, Z., Han, Q.: Crowdtracking: real-time vehicle tracking through mobile crowdsensing. IEEE Internet Things J. **6**(5), 7570–7583 (2019)
5. Chen, Z., Yang, P., Xiong, J., Feng, Y., Li, X.Y.: Tagray: contactless sensing and tracking of mobile objects using cots RFID devices. In: IEEE INFOCOM, pp. 307–316 (2020)
6. Dai, M., Su, Z., Xu, Q., Wang, Y., Lu, N.: A trust-driven contract incentive scheme for mobile crowd-sensing networks. IEEE Trans. Veh. Technol. (2021)
7. Damashek, M.: Gauging similarity with n-grams: language-independent categorization of text. Science **267**(5199), 843–848 (1995)
8. Guo, B., Liu, Y., Wang, L., Li, V.O., Lam, J.C., Yu, Z.: Task allocation in spatial crowdsourcing: current state and future directions. IEEE Internet Things J. **5**(3), 1749–1764 (2018)

9. Guo, B., Liu, Y., Wu, W., Yu, Z., Han, Q.: Activecrowd: a framework for optimized multitask allocation in mobile crowdsensing systems. IEEE Trans. Hum.-Mach. Syst. **47**(3), 392–403 (2016)
10. Horvitz, E., Krumm, J.: Some help on the way: opportunistic routing under uncertainty. In: The 2012 ACM Conference on Ubiquitous Computing, Ubicomp '12, Pittsburgh, PA, USA, 5–8 September 2012, pp. 371–380 (2012)
11. Huang, Y., et al.: OPAT: optimized allocation of time dependent tasks for mobile crowdsensing. IEEE Trans. Ind. Inf. **18**, 2476–2485 (2021)
12. Jing, Y., Guo, B., Wang, Z., Li, V.O., Lam, J.C., Yu, Z.: Crowdtracker: optimized urban moving object tracking using mobile crowd sensing. IEEE Internet Things J. **5**(5), 3452–3463 (2017)
13. Khezerlou, A.V., Zhou, X., Tong, L., Li, Y., Luo, J.: Forecasting gathering events through trajectory destination prediction: a dynamic hybrid model. IEEE Trans. Knowl. Data Eng. **33**(3), 991–1004 (2019)
14. Kuhn, H.W.: The Hungarian method for the assignment problem. Naval Res. Logist. Q. **31**(1–2), 83–97 (1955)
15. Li, D., Zhu, J., Cui, Y.: Prediction-based task allocation in mobile crowdsensing. In: 2019 15th International Conference on Mobile Ad-Hoc and Sensor Networks (MSN), pp. 89–94 (2019)
16. Liu, K., Li, X.: Finding nemo: finding your lost child in crowds via mobile crowd sensing. In: 2014 IEEE 11th International Conference on Mobile Ad Hoc and Sensor Systems, pp. 1–9. IEEE (2014)
17. Liu, Z., Jiang, S., Zhou, P., Li, M.: A participatory urban traffic monitoring system: the power of bus riders. IEEE Trans. Intell. Transp. Syst. **18**(10), 2851–2864 (2017)
18. Nguyen, T.N., Zeadally, S.: Mobile crowd-sensing applications: data redundancies, challenges, and solutions. ACM Trans. Internet Technol. (TOIT) **22**(2), 1–15 (2021)
19. Pan, Z., Yu, H., Miao, C., Leung, C.: Crowdsensing air quality with camera-enabled mobile devices. In: AAAI, pp. 4728–4733 (2017)
20. Qian, Y., Ma, Y., Chen, J., Wu, D., Tian, D., Hwang, K.: Optimal location privacy preserving and service quality guaranteed task allocation in vehicle-based crowdsensing networks. IEEE Trans. Intell. Transp. Syst. **22**, 4367–4375 (2021)
21. Sun, J., Zhang, R., Jin, X., Zhang, Y.: Securefind: secure and privacy-preserving object finding via mobile crowdsourcing. IEEE Trans. Wirel. Commun **15**(3), 1716–1728 (2015)
22. Wang, G., Luo, C., Xiong, Z., Zeng, W.: SPM-tracker: series-parallel matching for real-time visual object tracking. In: Proceedings of the IEEE/CVF Conference on Computer Vision and Pattern Recognition, pp. 3643–3652 (2019)
23. Xu, M., Wang, D., Li, J.: Destpre: a data-driven approach to destination prediction for taxi rides. In: Proceedings of the 2016 ACM International Joint Conference on Pervasive and Ubiquitous Computing, pp. 729–739 (2016)
24. Xu, Y., Xu, P., Pan, J., Tao, J.: A unified model for the two-stage offline-then-online resource allocation. In: Bessiere, C. (ed.) Proceedings of the Twenty-Ninth International Joint Conference on Artificial Intelligence, IJCAI 2020, pp. 4206–4212 (2020)
25. Yamaguchi, K., Berg, A.C., Ortiz, L.E., Berg, T.L.: Who are you with and where are you going? In: CVPR 2011, pp. 1345–1352 (2011)
26. Yang, D., Zhang, D., Chen, L., Qu, B.: Nationtelescope: monitoring and visualizing large-scale collective behavior in LBSNS. J. Netw. Comput. Appl. **55**, 170–180 (2015)

27. Yang, D., Zhang, D., Qu, B.: Participatory cultural mapping based on collective behavior in location based social networks. ACM Trans. Intell. Syst. Technol. **7**, 1–23 (2015)
28. Yucel, F., Yuksel, M., Bulut, E.: Coverage-aware stable task assignment in opportunistic mobile crowdsensing. IEEE Trans. Veh. Technol. **70**(4), 3831–3845 (2021)

Faulty Processor Identification for a Multiprocessor System Under the PMC Model Using a Binary Grey Wolf Optimizer

Fulai Pan[1] and Weixia Gui[2(✉)]

[1] School of Computer and Electronics Information, Guangxi University,
Nanning 530004, China
1913301026@st.gxu.edu.cn
[2] College of Information and Statistics,
Guangxi University of Finance and Economics, Nanning 530003, China
wxgui@126.com

Abstract. With the increasing demand for computing power, multiprocessor systems composed of numerous processors are still deployed in various fields. Binary grey wolf optimizer cannot directly tackle system-level fault diagnosis in spite of considerable success in feature selection, set-union knapsack problem, and uncapacitated facility location problem. In this study, we proposed a binary grey wolf optimizer for system-level fault diagnosis (BGWOFD). BGWOFD employed Boolean algebra to mimic the social hierarchy of grey wolf according to the rank-based dominance weight. To balance the convergence and mutation, a new competitive mechanism is adopted. Furthermore, the mutation strategy designed for the PMC model can effectively improve diagnostic efficiency and population diversity. Experimental results demonstrate the advantage of the proposed algorithm in diagnostic accuracy and diagnostic time.

Keywords: Binary grey wolf optimizer · Multiprocessor system · PMC model · Reliability computing · System-level fault diagnosis

1 Introduction

Nowadays, popular applications like the Internet of Things and virtual reality demand stronger computing power [1]. Distributed and parallel systems mostly use interconnection networks to connect thousands of processors or computing nodes to increase computing power, so both are multiprocessor systems. However, the increment in the number of processors not only has a negative impact on reliability but also increases the difficulty in diagnosing faulty processors. The goal of system-level fault diagnosis is to locate the faulty processors in a large-scale multiprocessor system. When the faulty processors are found in the system, they can be

This work was supported by the National Natural Science Foundation of China (Grant No. 61862003, 61862004).

Y. Lai et al. (Eds.): ICA3PP 2021, LNCS 13156, pp. 81–95, 2022.
https://doi.org/10.1007/978-3-030-95388-1_6

isolated, repaired and replaced to avoid system downtime. The diagnosis strategies of system-level fault diagnosis can be categorized into precise diagnostic strategies and imprecise diagnostic strategies. Precise diagnostic strategies include one-step t-diagnosable system [2], *(t,k)*-diagnosable system [3], and more. Imprecise diagnostic strategies include t/k-diagnosable system [4], t/s-diagnosable system [5], and so on. Because in the actual network, the processor can test the processors that are not directly adjacent through routing, and there is no restriction on the location of the faulty processors, the one-step t-diagnosable system has always been a research hotspot among scholars. Although graph theory is the initial theoretical basis for designing fault diagnosis algorithms, with the increase of the number of processors in the system, it is difficult for such algorithms to meet the diagnostic demands in time. Metaheuristic algorithms have become an important tool to study one-step t-diagnosable system due to their advantages such as easy code implementation and few parameters. Many fault diagnosis algorithms based on metaheuristic algorithms have been proposed, such as genetic algorithm (GAFD) [6–8], bat algorithm (BAFD) [9], and fireworks algorithm (FWAFD) [10–12].

Nature-inspired metaheuristics have been used to tackle various combinatorial optimization problems, and their inspiration can be divided into evolutionary, swarm intelligence, physics phenomenon, and human beings. Swarm intelligence algorithm is the highest proportion in metaheuristics [13]. The grey wolf optimizer (GWO) [14], a novel swarm intelligence algorithm, has been applied successfully in many continuous-domain optimization problems. Since the position update of the grey wolf depends on the three dominant wolves at the same time, its ability to avoid local optima is relatively stronger. In recent years, scholars have proposed many versions of binary gray wolf algorithm, and achieved remarkable success in feature selection [15–17] and fault location in distribution network [18]. Although the GWO could be seen as a variant of existing particle swarm optimizer algorithms in the continuous domain [19], the performances of these binary grey wolf optimizers are better than any other widespread binary optimizer algorithm. To map the real-valued solution to binary vector, it is very common that apply the sigmoid functions to binary grey wolf optimizer. However, the transfer functions will lead to spatial disconnect [20]. Gölcük et al. proposed two binary grey wolf optimizers (BGWO$_{fbd}$ and BGWO$_{rbd}$) without transfer functions, and adopt multi-parent crossover to mimic the position update under the leadership hierarchy of grey wolves [21]. These two algorithms reduce some parameters in the canonical GWO and employ multi-parent crossover to manipulate the binary solution directly. The performances of them are validated in set-union knapsack problem (SUKP) and uncapacitated facility location problem (UFLP).

System-level fault diagnosis can be regarded as a binary optimization problem, because the state of a processor is only faulty or fault-free. Although the binary grey wolf optimizer has been used to solve many binary optimization problems, as far as we know, its application to system-level fault diagnosis for large-scale multiprocessor systems has not been studied yet. The fault diagnosis algorithm based on swarm intelligence algorithm usually employs the transfer function to achieve the mapping from continuous domain to binary space. Elhadef et al. think that the historical data of a multiprocessor system, such as MTTF and MTBF, can be used to deduce some fault-free units [6]. Then, the status of other units in the system is deduced by using a fault-free unit and target symptom. Deng et al. improved this method and named it as specifying a fault-free node generation (SFNG) method [7]. In fact, the theory of this method is similar to graph traversal in data structure. The SFNG method to generate correct individuals depends on the fault diagnosis model and whether the first selected node is fault-free or faulty. If the selected fault-free unit is fault-free in target fault mode, this method can accurately infer the states of many units. With the increase of faulty units, the probability of fault-free units being selected is also decreasing. Although the time complexity of generating an individual is so high (best case: $O\left(n^2\right)$, worst case: $O\left(n^{2.5}\right)$), lots of fault diagnosis algorithms still employ this method, such as GAFD [7,8], BAFD [9], and FWAFD [10–12]. Using this method to initialize a population can narrow down the search space, but it will consume more time in the phase of population initialization. Employing a random initial population may perform better in diagnostic time when the diagnostic algorithm converges well in the binary space.

The main contribution of this paper include: (1) We design a new competitive mechanism to balance the search agents to perform convergence or mutation. And the mechanism employs strategy of differentiated position update to prevent degradation of individual fitness value. (2) Based on the social hierarchy of grey wolf and the rank-based dominant weights, we propose a Boolean algebra for convergence of grey wolf that enables individuals to converge to dominant wolves quickly and efficiently. (3) Using the testing properties of the PMC model, we design a new mutation strategy that are effective in increasing population diversity and avoiding local optima. (4) We propose a binary grey wolf optimizer for system-level fault diagnosis (BGWOFD), which employs random initial population and does not require transfer function. The experimental results validate that the proposed algorithm significantly outperform others on diagnostic accuracy and time.

The rest of the paper is organized as follows: the PMC model and standard grey wolf optimizer are briefly introduced in Sect. 2. The detailed explanations of the proposed algorithm are given in Sect. 3. Experimental results are demonstrated in Sect. 4. The conclusion of the study is given in Sect. 5.

2 Preparation Knowledge

2.1 PMC Model

System-level fault diagnosis is based on the fault diagnosis model. In 1976, Preparata et al. proposed first fault diagnosis model called PMC model [2], which is still the focus of scholars' research. The main idea of the PMC models is to assign a test set to each processor. When performing fault diagnosis, each processor tests the processors in its own test set. The diagnostic center then combines the test results with the network topology to generate fault symptom and uses the fault diagnosis algorithm to calculate the status of each processor.

In system-level fault diagnosis, the state of processor is described by binary code, either 1 or 0. The bit 1 usually indicates a faulty processor, and bit 0 represents the fault-free processor. In a multiprocessor system with n processors, the status of processors can be described a binary string. For example, $X = \{0, 0, 1, 0, 1\}$, this indicates the third and fifth processors are faulty processors, and the others are fault-free processors. In PMC model, the fault-free processor can correctly identify arbitrary status of processors. However, the test result of faulty processor to any processor are random 0 or 1. The relationship of the PMC model is shown in Table 1.

Table 1. PMC model

State of test processor	State of tested processor	Test result
0	0	0
0	1	1
1	0	0/1
1	1	0/1

Preparata et al. also proposed the optimal design $D_{\delta,t}$ for one-step t-diagnosable systems [2]. In a system containing n processors, multiple test graph can be obtained by adjusting δ and t. Moreover, since the number of processors tested by each node is the same, the test load of each node is balanced. Therefore, $D_{\delta,t}$ networks are often used to verify the performance of fault diagnosis algorithms. In a multiprocessor system with n processors, a test link from unit u_i to unit u_j satisfy Eq. (1) and Eq. (2).

$$j - i = \delta m \bmod n \tag{1}$$

$$(\delta, n) = 1 \tag{2}$$

where m is a positive integer from 1 to t, and δ is prime to n.

In a one-step t-diagnosable system, each processor is tested by at least t processors. We employ a n-by-n array S to represent the fault symptom, and the entry in row i and column j denotes the test result of unit u_i to unit u_j. If there is not test link from unit u_i to unit u_j, the entry $S_{i,j}$ is defined as ∞.

2.2   Grey Wolf Optimizer

Grey wolves are gregarious animals with an average population size of 5–12. In the hierarchy of grey wolves, the alpha wolf is the most powerful wolf in the swarm, followed by beta wolf and delta wolf. The rest are the omega wolves. As the animal at the top of the food chain, the omega grey wolves track, surround, and attack their prey under the guidance of alpha, beta, and delta wolves. Grey wolf optimizer (GWO) was proposed by Mirjalili et al. and inspired by the strict social hierarchy of grey wolf [14]. In GWO, alpha wolf, beta wolf and delta wolf correspond to the top 3 ranked optimal solutions. Mathematically, the distance between dominant wolf and candidate solution $\overrightarrow{X}$ is denoted as $\overrightarrow{D}$, which can be calculated as follows:

$$\overrightarrow{D}_\alpha = \left| \overrightarrow{C}_1 \times \overrightarrow{X}_\alpha(t) - \overrightarrow{X}(t) \right|, \tag{3}$$

$$\overrightarrow{D}_\beta = \left| \overrightarrow{C}_2 \times \overrightarrow{X}_\beta(t) - \overrightarrow{X}(t) \right|, \tag{4}$$

$$\overrightarrow{D}_\delta = \left| \overrightarrow{C}_3 \times \overrightarrow{X}_\delta(t) - \overrightarrow{X}(t) \right|, \tag{5}$$

where $\overrightarrow{C}$ is a coefficient vector, $\overrightarrow{X}_\alpha$, $\overrightarrow{X}_\beta$, and $\overrightarrow{X}_\delta$ indicate the positions of alpha, beta, and delta wolves, respectively.

The position $\overrightarrow{X}$ of grey wolf individual at time step $t + 1$ is calculated as follows:

$$\overrightarrow{X}_1(t+1) = \overrightarrow{X}_\alpha(t) + \overrightarrow{A}_1 \times \overrightarrow{D}_\alpha, \tag{6}$$

$$\overrightarrow{X}_2(t+1) = \overrightarrow{X}_\beta(t) + \overrightarrow{A}_2 \times \overrightarrow{D}_\beta, \tag{7}$$

$$\overrightarrow{X}_3(t+1) = \overrightarrow{X}_\delta(t) + \overrightarrow{A}_3 \times \overrightarrow{D}_\delta, \tag{8}$$

$$\overrightarrow{X}(t+1) = \frac{\overrightarrow{X}_1 + \overrightarrow{X}_2 + \overrightarrow{X}_3}{3}, \tag{9}$$

where $\overrightarrow{A}$ denotes a coefficient vector.
And the vectors $\overrightarrow{A}$ and $\overrightarrow{C}$ can be calculated as follows:

$$\overrightarrow{A} = 2\overrightarrow{a} \times \overrightarrow{r_1} - \overrightarrow{a}, \tag{10}$$

$$\overrightarrow{C} = 2\overrightarrow{r_2}, \tag{11}$$

where $\overrightarrow{r_1}$ and $\overrightarrow{r_2}$ are generated randomly between 0 and 1, and $\overrightarrow{a}$ is a value that decreases linearly from 2 to 0 as the number of iterations increases.

The parameter $\overrightarrow{C}$ strengthen or weaken the distance between the dominant wolves and the current position of a grey wolf. The parameter $\overrightarrow{A}$ with random value can drive the grey wolf to approach the dominant wolves or to search far away from the dominant wolves.

3   Details of the Proposed Algorithm

3.1   Population Initialization

In this paper, we employ random initial population to raise population diversity and decrease the time complexity. Let a *popsize* $\times n$ array X be a population position, where *popsize* denotes population size. Therefore, the entries of X in row i represent the individual position of X_i, and the entry $X_{i,j}$ of X in row i and column j indicates a possible state of unit j. Since a t-system containing n processors can only identify at most t faulty processors, the initial population consist of individuals containing t faulty processors. Algorithm 1 shows the pseudocode of the process of population initialization.

Algorithm 1: Pseudocode of population initialization method

Input: *popsize* and *n*.

Output: The position X of wolves.

1 $t = \lfloor \frac{n-1}{2} \rfloor$;

2 **for** $i = 1 : popsize$ **do**

3 $\quad$ $faults = 0$;

4 $\quad$ $faultfree = 0$;

5 $\quad$ **for** $j = 1 : n$ **do**

6 $\quad\quad$ **if** *(rand < 0.5 and faults < t) or faultfree == n − t* **then**

7 $\quad\quad\quad$ $X_{i,j} = 1$;

8 $\quad\quad\quad$ $faults = faults + 1$;

9 $\quad\quad$ **else**

10 $\quad\quad\quad$ $X_{i,j} = 0$;

11 $\quad\quad\quad$ $faultfree = faultfree + 1$;

12 $\quad\quad$ **end**

13 $\quad$ **end**

14 **end**

3.2 Fitness Function

Because the test results created by faulty processors under the PMC model are random, either 0 or 1, the same potential solution may generate different symptoms. Even if the potential solution is equal to the target solution, the fault symptoms that generated by combining the potential solution with the network topology may not be exactly the same as the fault symptom S to be solved. Therefore, the fitness function in this paper relies on the fact that the test results of fault-free processors under PMC model are always correct. Algorithm 2 shows the process of calculating the fitness function for $D_{\delta,t}$ systems.

3.3 New Competitive Mechanism

The competitive binary grey wolf optimizer (CBGWO) [16] employs a competitive mechanism proposed by Cheng et al. [22]. The core of the competitive mechanism is that the pairwise individuals randomly selected from swarm compare their fitness values, the winner does not perform position update and directly passes to the swarm of next iteration, while the loser update its position according to the information attained from winner. After updating the positions of all the losers, CBGWO will reorder to update alpha, beta, and delta wolves, and the ruling wolves will perform leader enhancement to avoid local optima.

In our study, BGWOFD retrenched a lot of parameters of GWO like BGWO$_{fbd}$ and BGWO$_{rbd}$, which make it difficult to dynamically balance convergence and mutation. So, BGWOFD employs a new competitive mechanism. The first step in this mechanism is to select randomly two individuals from a wolf pack. The fitness values of pairwise individuals will be compared. The better wolf is called the winner, while the worse wolf is the loser. The winner will perform a

---

Algorithm 2: Fitness function.

Input: S, n, and X_i.
Output: $fv(X_i) = [fv(X_{i,1}), fv(X_{i,2}), \cdots, fv(X_{i,n})]$ and $FT(X_i)$.

1   **for** $j = 1 : n$ **do**
2      $CorrectTests = 0$;
3   **if** $X_{i,j} == 0$ **then**
4   **foreach** *processor* k *in* $\Gamma(u_j)$ **do**
            /* $\Gamma(u_j)$ represents the processors set which unit u_i need
              to test.   */
5   **if** $S_{j,k} == X_{i,j}$ **then**
6            $\vert$ $CorrectTests = CorrectTests + 1$;
7   **end**
8   **end**
9        $fv(X_{i,j}) = \frac{CorrectTests}{\vert\Gamma(u_j)\vert}$;
10   **else**
11   **foreach** *fault-free processor* k *in* $\Gamma(u_j)^{-1}$ **do**
            /* $\Gamma(u_j)^{-1}$ represents the processors set that test u_i.   */
12   **if** $S_{k,j} == 1$ **then**
13            $\vert$ $CorrectTests = CorrectTests + 1$;
14   **end**
15   **end**
16        $fv(X_{i,j}) = \frac{CorrectTests}{\left\vert \text{Fault-free processors in } \Gamma(u_j)^{-1}\right\vert}$;
17   **end**
18 **end**
19 $FT = \frac{\sum_{j=1}^{n} fv(X_{i,j})}{n}$;

---

mutation strategy for local optima avoidance, and the loser will converge to the dominant wolves for improving its fitness values. Note that each individual in the swarm can be selected once at each iteration. Figure 1 shows the framework of the new competitive mechanism.

The proposed mechanism employs strategy of differentiated position update, as shown in Eq. (12), in which the individual position with improving fitness value can be preserved to the population, but those with worse fitness value are discarded.

$$X_i(t+1) = \begin{cases} X_i(t+1) & , \text{if } FT(X_i(t+1)) > FT(X_i(t)) \\ X_i(t) & , \text{otherwise} \end{cases}. \qquad (12)$$

where $X_i(t+1)$ indicates the position of the i-th wolf at time step $t+1$.

Compared with the competition mechanism in CBGWO, the winner can perform mutation strategy to search instead of being stationary. Another advantage is that the loser can obtain information from the winner, such as different states in the same dimension.

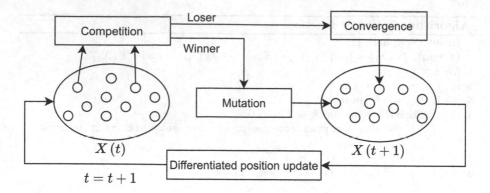

Fig. 1. Illustration of the new competitive mechanism.

3.4   Convergence Strategy

In binary weighted superposition attraction algorithm [23] and BGWO$_{rbd}$ [21], the weight of artificial agents is calculated as follow:

$$weight\,(i) = i^{-\tau}, \tag{13}$$

where i is the ranking of search agent and $\tau \in (0,1]$. Since the social hierarchy of the gray wolf contains only alpha, beta, delta and omega wolves, $i \in \{1,2,3,4\}$.

To mimic the strict social hierarchy of grey wolves, the convergence equation of the proposed algorithm utilizes the rank-based domination weight that can be calculated according to Eq. (13). Let's assume that the output is determined by the larger weight sum of the binary values of the three dominant wolves and a omega wolf. Suppose $\tau = 0.65$, the corresponding weights of the top three dominant wolves and the omega wolf are equal to 1, 0.64, 0.48, and 0.41, respectively. The binary values of alpha wolf, beta wolf, delta wolf and delta wolf in the same dimension are 0, 1, 1, 1 in that order. The weights sum of bit 0 is equal to 1, and the weights sum of bit 1 equals 1.53. So, the output will be updated to 1. Boolean algebra is a powerful tool for describing and designing binary logic circuits. We use Boolean algebra to express the relationship between outputs and input combinations.

$$
\begin{aligned}
X_{i,j}^{t+1} = {}& X_{\alpha,j}^{t} \cdot X_{\beta,j}^{t} + \bar{X}_{\alpha,j}^{t} \cdot X_{\beta,j}^{t} \cdot X_{\delta,j}^{t} \cdot X_{i,j}^{t} \\
& + X_{\alpha,j}^{t} \cdot \bar{X}_{\beta,j}^{t} \cdot X_{\delta,j}^{t} + X_{\alpha,j}^{t} \cdot \bar{X}_{\beta,j}^{t} \cdot \bar{X}_{\delta,j}^{t} \cdot X_{i,j}^{t}
\end{aligned}
\tag{14}
$$

where $\cdot$, $+$, and $^-$ denote logic operation AND, OR, NOT, respectively, $X_{\alpha,j}^{t}$, $X_{\beta,j}^{t}$, $X_{\delta,j}^{t}$, and $X_{i,j}^{t}$ denote status of j-th processor at in position vectors of alpha, beta, delta, and X_i wolves at time step t, respectively.

In fact, when $\tau \in (0,1]$ in Eq. (13), Eq. (14) is mostly established. In the proposed algorithm, the binary values of the loser inconsistent with that of the winner are updated by using Eq. (14) with the updating probability p_u.

3.5   Mutation Operator

Mutation operator is an important strategy to avoid local optima, which can improve population diversity. The fault-free unit in PMC model can correctly diagnose the status of the units within their own test set. So, we will select randomly a fault-free unit u_i from the potential solution X_i. Assume that the unit is also the fault-free node of the target fault mode. Then the test results of the processors in $\Gamma(u_i)$ are assigned to the potential solution with updating probability p_u.

The mutation operator has two remarkable advantages:

(1) With the increase of the number of iterations, it is easier to select a fault-free processor from potential solution that is also fault-free in target solution. If the selected processor u_i is also fault-free in the target solution, part of the processor states in $\Gamma(u_i)$ of the potential solution will be updated correctly, which is helpful to improve the fitness value of individual.
(2) Even if the selected processor is faulty in the target solution, as long as the updated solution has a better fitness value, it also can be saved in the swarm to improve the population diversity.

To sum up, the pseudocode for BGWOFD is given in Algorithm 3.

3.6   The Time Complexity of BGWOFD

The worst-case time complexity of proposed BGWOFD in $D_{\delta,t}$ is given as follows. At the beginning, BGWOFD needs to initialize a population, the complexity of population initialization is $O(popsize \times n)$. In the phase of position update, the time complexity for a loser to perform the position update is $O(n)$, and the time complexity for a winner to perform mutation operator is $O(t)$. In each iteration, the dominant wolves need to be updated, the time complexity is $O(popsize)$. For each individual, the fitness value needs to be computed once at each iteration. The time complexity of calculating fitness value is $O(n \times t)$. To sum up, the complexity of the proposed algorithm is $O(I \times posize \times n \times t)$, where I denotes the iteration times, and t is the maximum number of faulty units that can be identified.

4   Experiment

The parameters need to be calibrated based on their influence on performance before algorithm comparison. The experiments were carried on Matlab R2020a using the workstation with a processor Intel Xeon E5-1620 3.6 GHz and 8 GB RAM. With the same number of faulty nodes, 100 fault symptoms were randomly generated. To evaluate the performance of the proposed algorithm, the statistical parameters for comparison include diagnostic accuracy and average diagnostic time.

Algorithm 3: the Proposed BGWOFD algorithm.

Input: p_u, n. $popsize$, $MaxIter$, and S
Output: A solution compatible with S.

1 $t = 1$, $half popsize = popsize/2$;
    /* where t denotes iteration and $popsize$ is an even number.   */
2 Initialize population by running Algorithm 1;
3 Evaluate fitness values of wolves by running Algorithm 2;
4 **while** $t < MaxIter$ **do**
5   Update the dominant wolves of pack;
6   **for** $i = 1 : half popsize$ **do**
7   Compare the fitness values of X_i and $X_{i+half popsize}$;
8   **if** $FT(X_i) > FT(X_{i+half popsize})$ **then**
9 | $winner = i$, $loser = i + half popsize$;
10   **else**
11 | $winner = i + half popsize$, $loser = i$;
12   **end**
13   **for** $j = 1 : n$ **do**
14   **if** $X_{loser,j} \neq X_{winner,j}$ and $rand < p_u$ **then**
             /* $rand$ is a random number in $[0,1]$.   */
15   Update $X_{loser,j}$ according to Eq. (14);
16   **end**
17   **end**
18   Select randomly a fault-free unit u_i from X_{winner};
19   **foreach** $unit\ u_j\ in\ \Gamma(u_i)$ **do**
20   **if** $rand < p_u$ **then**
21 | $x_{winner,j} = S_{i,j}$;
22   **end**
23   **end**
24   **end**
25   **for** $i = 1 : popsize$ **do**
26   Evaluate the fitness value of X_i by running Algorithm 2;
27   **if** $FT(X_i) == 1$ **then**
28 | Return X_i;
29   **end**
30   Determine X_i at time step $t + 1$ by using Eq. (12);
31   **end**
32     $t = t + 1$;
33   Randomize the swarm;
34 **end**
35 Return the optimal solution;

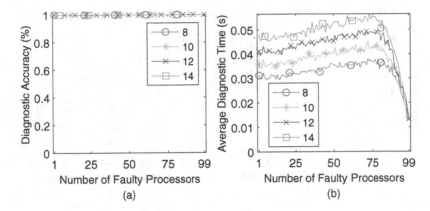

Fig. 2. The influence of population size on BGWOFD in $D_{7,99}$ system. (a) Diagnostic Accuracy; (b) Average Diagnostic Time.

4.1 Influence of Parameters on the Performance

Population Size. To explore the influence of different population sizes on the diagnostic performance, we set $popsize \in \{8, 10, 12, 14\}$, $MaxIter = 200$ and p_u is fixed to 0.9. Figure 2 demonstrates the effect of population size on the performance of the proposed algorithm in $D_{7,99}$ system.

From the simulation results, the different population sizes had no negative impact on the diagnostic accuracy. 100% diagnostic accuracy can be maintained for any population size. As the number of faulty processors approached 99, the average diagnostic time of the proposed algorithm greatly decreased at various population size, and the performance differences of average diagnostic time at different population sizes also reduced. Therefore, the population size of BGWOFD was set to 8 in the subsequent experiments.

Updating Probability p_u. Updating probability indicates the probability of whether the bit will be updated or not, which has a significant influence on random walks of the wolf. Obviously, the position of the grey wolf may remain stagnant when the updating probability is too small. A set of different levels for p_u ($\{0.5, 0.6, 0.7, 0.8, 0.9\}$) was examined, and the results were shown in Fig. 3.

Although different updating probabilities did not affect the diagnostic accuracy, it had negative impact on the average diagnostic time. When the updating probability was 0.9, the average diagnostic time was significantly less than other probability values. In subsequent comparison experiments, the updating probability was set to 0.9.

4.2 Empirical Comparison

The compared algorithms include GAFD [7], BAFD [9], and FWAFD [10]. All algorithms diagnosed 100 fault symptoms that randomly generated under the same number of faulty processors in $D_{7,74}$ and $D_{7,149}$ system. The parameters

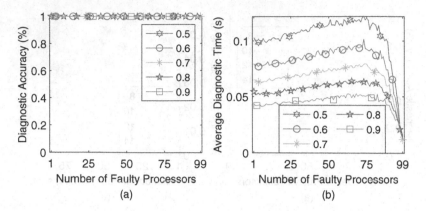

Fig. 3. The influence of p_u on BGWOFD in $D_{7,99}$ system. (a) Diagnostic Accuracy; (b) Average Diagnostic Time.

given in the corresponding paper were used as far as possible for the comparison experiment, as follows: In GAFD, the population was generated by SFNG method whose size was 7, $p_m = 0.5$, $p_c = 0.7$. The BAFD employs dual population, the small population size was 10, and it was initialized by SFNG method, and the large population initialize randomly and the size was 20, $v_{max} = 3$, $v_{min} = -3$. The population size of FWAFD was 10, and each individual was generated randomly. For fairness of the experiment, the maximum iteration number was fixed to 200. Figure 4 and Fig. 5 showed the fit curve of diagnostic accuracy and average diagnostic time, demonstrating the variation in performance of several diagnostic algorithms as the number of faulty processors increases.

The experimental results indicate that BGWOFD and GAFD superior to other compared algorithms in diagnostic accuracy and average diagnostic time. BAFD had a overall diagnostic accuracy of 98.25% and 69.58% for $D_{7,74}$ and $D_{7,149}$ systems respectively. The overall diagnostic accuracy of FWAFD was 99.30% and 98.91% in $D_{7,74}$ and $D_{7,149}$ systems respectively. The diagnostic accuracy of FWAFD and BAFD decreased as the number of faulty processors increased, and then increased again as the number approached maximum number of faulty processors can be identified in the system. In $D_{7,74}$, all diagnostic algorithm maintained a diagnostic accuracy of over 90% for each number of faulty processors. However, the diagnostic accuracy of BAFD dropped below 20% when the faulty number of processors was between 120 and 130 in $D_{7,149}$ system. Although the diagnostic accuracy of FWAFD was better than BAFD, FWAFD did not completely outperform BAFD in terms of the average diagnostic time. The overall average diagnostic time during diagnosing $D_{7,74}$ system was 0.3743 seconds for FWAFD compared to 0.2493 seconds for BAFD. However, FWAFD outperformed GAFD in average diagnostic time when the number of faulty processors was close to the maximum number that the system can recognize. In $D_{7,74}$ and $D_{7,149}$ system, the diagnostic accuracy of both BGWOFD and GAFD was maintained at 100%, but BGWOFD took less diagnostic time.

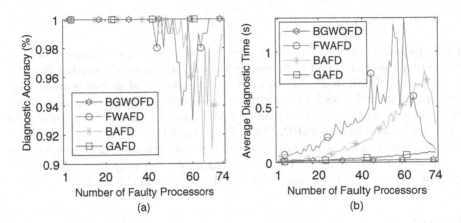

Fig. 4. The performance comparison of several diagnosis algorithms in $D_{7,74}$ system. (a) Diagnostic Accuracy; (b) Average Diagnostic Time.

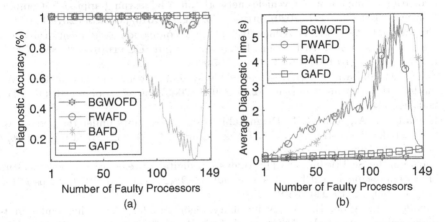

Fig. 5. The performance comparison of several diagnosis algorithms in $D_{7,149}$ system. (a) Diagnostic Accuracy; (b) Average Diagnostic Time.

As transfer functions are used in both BAFD and FWAFD to implement the conversion of continuous domain value to binary value, their convergence speed is relatively slow. In addition, the explosion operator and Gaussian mutation operator of FWAFD produce a large number of individuals at each iteration, resulting in a substantial increase in diagnostic time. The performance of GAFD is better than BAFD and FWAFD because the chromosome of genetic algorithm can express directly the state of each unit in the system, and the selection, crossover, and mutation operation can directly manipulate the binary values. The proposed algorithm employs a new competitive mechanism to balance convergence and mutation. The Boolean algebra preserve the grey wolf's original social hierarchy as well as avoiding the transfer functions which often used in binary optimization algorithms. Therefore, BGWOFD outperforms the other three diagnosis algorithms.

5   Conclusion

In this paper, we propose a binary grey wolf optimizer for t-diagnosable systems under the PMC model. According to the rank-based domination weight, we designed a Boolean algebra to imitate the progress of wolves searching for prey under the strict social hierarchy. We also designed a new mutation strategy according to the characteristic of PMC model. And the performance of BGWOFD is superior to BAFD, FWAFD and GAFD in the $D_{\delta,t}$ systems based on PMC model. This is the first attempt to apply the grey wolf algorithm to system-level fault diagnosis. We will try to apply the proposed algorithm to different fault diagnosis models and network topology in the future.

References

1. Chen, M., Wang, T., Ota, K., Dong, M., Zhao, M., Liu, A.: Intelligent resource allocation management for vehicles network: an A3C learning approach. Comput. Commun. **151**, 485–494 (2020). https://doi.org/10.1016/j.comcom.2019.12.054
2. Preparata, F.P., Metze, G., Chien, R.T.: On the connection assignment problem of diagnosable systems. IEEE Trans. Electron. Comput. **EC–16**(6), 848–854 (1967). https://doi.org/10.1109/PGEC.1967.264748
3. Araki, T., Shibata, Y.: (t, k)-diagnosable system: a generalization of the PMC models. IEEE Trans. Comput. **52**, 972–976 (2003). https://doi.org/10.1109/TC.2003.1214345
4. Kavianpour, A., Kim, K.H.: Diagnosabilities of hypercubes under the pessimistic one-step diagnosis strategy. IEEE Trans. Comput. **40**(2), 232–237 (1991). https://doi.org/10.1109/12.73595
5. Karunanithi, S., Friedman, A.D.: Analysis of digital systems using a new measure of system diagnosis. IEEE Trans. Comput. **C–28**(2), 121–133 (1979). https://doi.org/10.1109/TC.1979.1675301
6. Elhadef, M., Ayeb, B.: An evolutionary algorithm for identifying faults in t-diagnosable systems. In: Proceedings 19th IEEE Symposium on Reliable Distributed Systems SRDS-2000, pp. 74–83 (2000). https://doi.org/10.1109/RELDI.2000.885395
7. Deng, W., Yang, X., Wu, Z.: An efficient genetic algorithm for system- level diagnosis. Chin. J. Comput. **30**(07), 1115–1124 (2007). https://doi.org/10.3321/j.issn:0254-4164.2007.07.008
8. Gui, W., Liu, C.: System-level diagnosis algorithm based on Malek model. Comput. Eng. Appl. **53**(13), 78–82 (2019). https://doi.org/10.3778/j.issn.1002-8331.1607-0130
9. Xuan, H., Miao, C., Zhao, D.: System-level fault diagnosis based on bat algorithm. Comput. Eng. Sci. **38**(4), 640–647 (2016). https://doi.org/10.3969/j.issn.1007-130X.2016.04.004
10. Gui, W., Lu, Q.: System-level fault diagnosis fireworks algorithm based on PMC model. J. Chin. Comput. Syst. **39**(9), 1944–1950 (2018). https://doi.org/10.3969/j.issn.1000-1220.2018.09.010
11. Gui, W., Lan, T., Lu, Q.: Fireworks algorithm for system-level fault diagnosis based on Malek model. J. Chin. Comput. Syst. **40**(07), 46–51 (2019). http://xwxt.sict.ac.cn/CN/Y2019/V40/I7/1404

12. Lu, Q., Gui, W., Su, M.: A fireworks algorithm for the system-level fault diagnosis based on MM* model. IEEE ACCESS **7**, 136975–136985 (2019). https://doi.org/10.1109/ACCESS.2019.2942336

13. Mohamed, A.W., Hadi, A.A., Mohamed, A.K.: Gaining-sharing knowledge based algorithm for solving optimization problems: a novel nature-inspired algorithm. Int. J. Mach. Learn. Cybern. **11**(7), 1501–1529 (2019). https://doi.org/10.1007/s13042-019-01053-x

14. Mirjalili, S., Mirjalili, S.M., Lewis, A.: Grey wolf optimizer. Adv. Eng. Softw **69**(3), 46–61 (2014). https://doi.org/10.1016/j.advengsoft.2013.12.007

15. Emary, E., Zawbaa, H.M., Hassanien, A.E.: Binary grey wolf optimization approaches for feature selection. Neurocomputing **172**(8), 371–381 (2016). https://doi.org/10.1016/j.neucom.2015.06.083

16. Too, J., Abdullah, A.R., Mohd Saad, N., Ali, N., Tee, W.H.: A new competitive binary grey wolf optimizer to solve the feature selection problem in EMG signals classification. J. Comput. **7**(4), 58 (2018). https://doi.org/10.3390/computers7040058

17. Al-Tashi, Q., Abdul Kadir, S.J., Rais, H.M., Mirjalili, S., Alhussian, H.: Binary optimization using hybrid grey wolf optimization for feature selection. IEEE Access **7**, 39496–39508 (2019). https://doi.org/10.1109/ACCESS.2019.2906757

18. Chen, L., Zhan, Y., Tian, Q.: Fault location of distribution network based on improved binary grey wolf optimization algorithm. Electron. Meas. Technol. **42**(01), 1–5 (2019). https://doi.org/10.19651/j.cnki.emt.1802075

19. Camacho Villalón, C.L., Stützle, T., Dorigo, M.: Grey wolf, firefly and bat algorithms: three widespread algorithms that do not contain any novelty. In: Dorigo, M., et al. (eds.) ANTS 2020. LNCS, vol. 12421, pp. 121–133. Springer, Cham (2020). https://doi.org/10.1007/978-3-030-60376-2_10

20. Leonard, B.J., Engelbrecht, A.P., Cleghorn, C.W.: Critical considerations on angle modulated particle swarm optimisers. Swarm Intell. **9**(4), 291–314 (2015). https://doi.org/10.1007/s11721-015-0114-x

21. Gölcük, O., Ozsoydan, F.B.: Evolutionary and adaptive inheritance enhanced Grey Wolf Optimization algorithm for binary domains. Knowl.-Based Syst. **194**, 105586 (2020). https://doi.org/10.1016/j.knosys.2020.105586

22. Cheng, R., Jin, Y.: A competitive swarm optimizer for large scale optimization. IEEE Trans. Cybern. **45**(2), 191–204 (2015). https://doi.org/10.1109/TCYB.2014.2322602

23. Baykasoğlu, A., Ozsoydan, F.B., Senol, M.E.: Weighted superposition attraction algorithm for binary optimization problems. Oper. Res. **20**(4), 2555–2581 (2018). https://doi.org/10.1007/s12351-018-0427-9

Fast On-Road Object Detector on ROS-Based Mobile Robot

Gang Wang, Qiudi Song, Tao Li, and Min Li[(✉)]

Nankai University, Tianjin 300071, China
limintj@nankai.edu.cn

Abstract. The application environment of mobile robot is gradually expanding from indoor to outdoor. Vision-based detection, which acquires traffic information through the camera, is a state-of-the-art auxiliary technology. In this paper, a robotic middleware Robot Operating System (ROS) is applied to detect object and control application based on embedded processor. And, we present an effective On-road object detector which is suitable for embedded GPU by improving the performance of Single Shot MultiBox Detector (SSD). Our approach is to construct detection network by using depth-wise separable convolution for saving computing resource and present multi-category clustering to adjust the generated default boxes for optimizing accuracy. Experiments on KITTI dataset show that the proposed network runs 2.1 times faster than original SSD network on embedded GPU and maintains 71% mean average precision. Finally, a mobile robot is designed based on the detector and controller to demonstrate On-road assisted driving intuitively.

Keywords: ROS · Embedded GPU · Convolutional neural network · On-road object detection · Mobile robot

1 Introduction

Object detection is the premise of many robot behaviors and plays an important role in the field of robotics such as driverless car. Using cameras to obtain visual data is becoming a common method due to its low consumption and application cost, and other sensors can play a supporting role if necessary. Recently, deep learning has merged as powerful learning methods for object detection. Compared with traditional approached, deep learning based method is more suitable for tasks such as object detection and trajectory tracking in complex scenes due to the strong expressive ability of convolutional neural network. As an excellent deep learning detection method, SSD algorithm [1] achieves better performance by borrowing the anchor frame mechanism in Faster R-CNN [2] and generating default boxes on different feature graphs of multiple scales.

© Springer Nature Switzerland AG 2022
Y. Lai et al. (Eds.): ICA3PP 2021, LNCS 13156, pp. 96–107, 2022.
https://doi.org/10.1007/978-3-030-95388-1_7

If mobile robots can be integrated with object detection based on deep learning, more interesting features could be generated. Robot Operating System (ROS) is a linux-based open source middleware framework for robot applications [3]. ROS transforms the results of algorithms into robot's instructions smoothly, which gives robots cognitive abilities. At present, detection packages that come with ROS are mainly based on local feature description methods such as SIFT (Scale Invariant Feature Transform), which has poor robustness in complex scenarios [4, 5]. Thus, it's great significance to use deep learning methods to achieve fast and accurate detection algorithm on ROS platform.

In this paper, a mobile robot is developed to integrate detection and control applications based on Embedded processor NVIDIA Jetson TK1 and other electronic components. ROS middleware combines On-road detection algorithms with mobile robots and Arduino platform addresses the control of ROS-based robot. In the detection part, images captured by camera are used to locate and classify objects by SSD algorithms and embedded GPU. In the process of testing, SSD with the input size of 300*300 achieves 45.02 FPS on NVIDIA Titan V while achieving only 1.33 FPS on NVIDIA Jetson TK1. This phenomenon confirms portable embedded GPU which are common processors in robots are difficult to run the detection network quickly. High-speed response and high accuracy are the basic requirements of object detection method for robots. To obtain a small and efficient network, MobileNet [6] constructed by depth-wise separable convolution is used to replace VGG network in SSD for faster detection speed. And, we present a multi-category clustering method to adjust the generated default boxes to optimize detection accuracy. After adjustment, we obtain a better detection performance that provides an effective method for embedded GPU.

2 Proposed System

In this paper, NVIDIA Jetson TK1 was selected as core processor of the entire system. Table 1 describes the basic configuration of Jetson TK1 [7]. Apart from this, other sensors such as Arduino Mega2560 microcontroller panel, MC33926 two-wheel motor control panel, motor and camera play a supporting role. As is shown in Fig. 1, the system architecture of robot can be mainly divided into two modules: object detection and message communication. Object detection module is responsible for outputting the object category and position in the video [8]. In the process of detection, the method based on deep learning is used to process the image information of each frame in the video to obtain the position and category of each object. In message communication module, we have created a new ROS detection package for converting object category into moving direction.

ROS contains large number of nodes that subscribe to topics to receive information, control sensors and perform computations. Each node represents a task and they can publish messages to topics for other nodes. Publishing messages to topics is the primary method of passing data between nodes. The system takes different functional stages as ROS nodes respectively, and the processing results of each node are transmitted to the corresponding node by message [9].

Table 1. The configuration of NVIDIA Jetson TK1

Hardware	Configuration
CPU	32-bit ARM Cortex-A15
GPU	192-core CUDA Chip
Memory	2 GB
Storage	16 GB
Frequency	2.3 GHz

When the system starts up, Arduino node (/arduino) first opens the communication interface and requests a session from the direction node (/direction). After receiving the request, session requests are submitted layer by layer. The messaging relationships between nodes are shown in Fig. 2. Camera node (/camera) sends a session to detection node (/image_detect) to provide video for the detection algorithm. The detection algorithm processes each frame of image in video to obtain the position and category information of each object. To display the detection results intuitively, detection node sends a session to image node (/image_show) for displaying the position and category of object in the display box, and sends a session to direction node to provide the category information. The direction node sends a session to Arduino node to provide direction information.

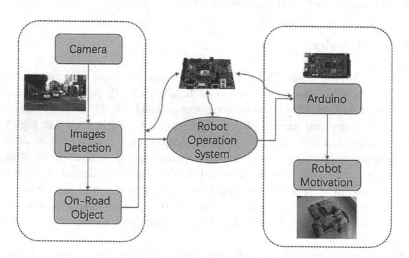

Fig. 1. System architecture of robot

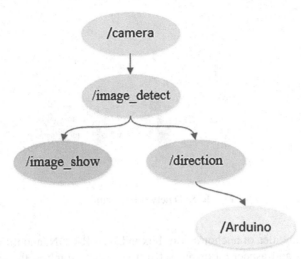

Fig. 2. Status diagram for system running node

3 Object Detector

In this section, we firstly introduce series of general method for object detection and choose SSD framework as the base method in this work. To accommodate embedded GPU, light weight network MobileNet is used to replace the feature layers in SSD. And, we propose a multi-category clustering method for optimizing accuracy for specific road dataset.

3.1 Basic Algorithm

Vision-Based methods can be divided into two categories: manual design features-based or deep learning-based. The method of manually designing features such as HOG, LBP and STFT is suitable for detecting a certain kind of object but not robust enough to detect multiple objects. Deep neural network learns natural features from dataset autonomously and is less affected by professional knowledge. Detection networks such as R-CNN [10], Fast R-CNN [11], YOLOv2 [12], YOLOv3 [13], YOLOv4 [14] and SSD [1] have been widely used in various research and application fields.

SSD is a regressive object detection algorithm, which uses different convolution kernel to construct multi-scale feature graph for improving the accuracy of object detection. The network structure of SSD is shown in Fig. 3. SSD network adopts high-quality convolutional network VGG16 [15] as the basic network for object detection. It retains the convolutional layer for feature extraction, removes the back-end classification function, and converts two full connection layers fc6 and fc7 before the classification function into two convolution layers.

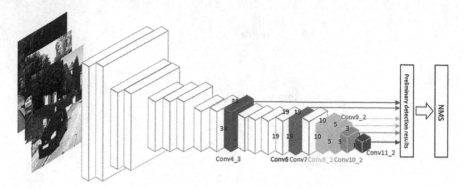

Fig. 3. SSD network structure

SSD refers to the idea of anchor's prior box in Faster R-CNN, and the default boxes of different scales and aspect ratios are set in the feature graph at the center of each grid cell. The default box is used as the benchmark for precision conversion between bounding box and ground-truth box. Default boxes generated on different feature maps are different on the scale and aspect ratio. With the deepening of convolutional neural network layer, the scale of feature maps become smaller, and the scale of default boxes increase linearly. The generation of default box can be calculated as follows:

$$S_k = S_{\min} + \frac{S_{\max} - S_{\min}}{m - 1} S_{\min} + \frac{S_{\max} - S_{\min}}{m - 1}(k - 1), k \in [1, m] \tag{1}$$

S_{max} is the highest maximum default box proportion to be predicted in the feature map and S_{min} is the minimum default box scale. Each feature map produces multiple default boxes, which are set according to different aspect ratio. The default aspect ratio is selected from $a_r\{1, 2, 3, 1/2, 1/3\}$, so the width and height of default box can be calculated by the following formula:

$$w_k^a = S_k \sqrt{a_r} \tag{2}$$

$$h_k^a = \frac{S_k}{\sqrt{a_r}} \tag{3}$$

When the default box's aspect ratio is 1, the algorithm will add a scale $S_k' = \sqrt{S_k S_{k+1}}$. In practice, Con4_3, Con10_2 and Con11_2 only use the default box whose aspect ratio is in {1, 1', 2, 1/2}.

3.2 Optimization for SSD

As an end-to-end detection framework, SSD can satisfy the requirements of detection in real-time on desktop devices. However, the GPU of embedded devices with limited computing power and memory cannot run large number of convolution operations quickly. It is an important problem for deep learning task to reduce the computational cost while maintaining high detection accuracy.

MobileNet-SSD. MobileNet network was proposed for improving computing efficiency under limited hardware conditions. It can reduce the model's size and improve running speed on the premise of guaranteeing the performance of model. The network uses depth-wise separable convolution to decompose the convolution operation into depth-wise convolution and point-wise convolution [6]. Figure 4 shows the separation process of the convolution operation. The network first convolves different channels with depth-wise convolution, and then the channels are integrated with point-wise convolution in a convolution operation.

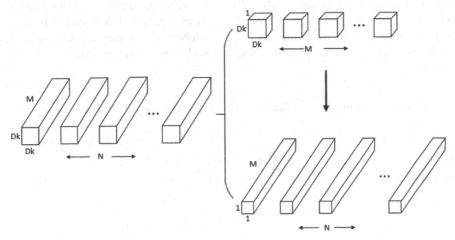

Fig. 4. MobileNet network decomposed convolution operation

In this paper, we set up MobileNet-SSD network with MobileNet as the basic network. In the network, Conv0 layer to Conv13 layer were consistent with MobileNet, excepting that average pooling layer, fully connected layer and softmax layer were removed. After the final convolutional layer, 8 convolution layers such as "Con14_1_depthwise" and "Con14_2_pointwise" were added and 6 feature layers were selected to extract features. Figure 5 shows the network structure of MobileNet-SSD.

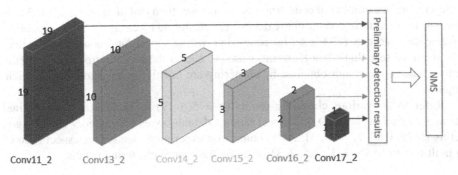

Fig. 5. MobileNet-SSD network structure

In Fig. 4, M is the number of input channels, Dk is the width and height of the convolution kernel, and N is the number of output layers. When the width and height of the input feature layer are DF, the computing cost of the original convolution operation is $D_k D_k N M D_F D_F$. In the MobileNet network, the computing cost calculated in the way of depth-wise separable convolution is $D_k D_k M D_F D_F + N M D_F D_F$. By dividing the two values, the computing costs of convolution calculation for MobileNet network is $\frac{1}{N} + \frac{1}{D_k^2}$ of original network, and the number of parameters will be compressed with the same ratio.

Table 2 shows the number of default boxes of SSD and MobileNet-SSD network when the pixels of input image is 300 × 300. The size of the shallowest feature map in SSD is 38 × 38, and that of the shallowest feature map in MobileNet-SSD is 19 × 19. Due to the size of extracted feature map in MobileNet-SSD is smaller, the number of default boxes generated in MobileNet-SSD network is much smaller than that in SSD network.

Table 2. The number of default boxes for SSD and MobileNet-SSD networks

	Input	1	2	3	4	5	6	Sum
SSD	300	8664	2166	600	150	24	6	11640
RM-SSD	300	2166	600	150	54	24	6	3000

Optimization for MobileNet-SSD. MobileNet-SSD network predict detection results by optimizing the regression relationship between default box and ground-truth box. In the network, default boxes are set subjectively according to human's experience, and the number and shape of default boxes set up in MobileNet-SSD network may not be applicable to specific dataset. Therefore, the default box in the network should be set according to the object's distribution of the dataset for fitting object position accurately.

The aspect ratio of ground-truth box annotated in the dataset can effectively visualize the division of output space. To make the generated default box more like the size and shape of ground box, K-means clustering method [16] is used to analyze the aspect ratio of object. The aspect ratio of vehicles and pedestrians in the road dataset is greatly different, and the number of pedestrians is much lower than that of vehicles. Table 3 lists the results of clustering on the entire dataset and clustering by category. When clustering by category, a center (C1) is set for pedestrian, whose aspect ratio is usually less than 0.3. It can be seen that when K-means is used to cluster the aspect ratio of object in the entire dataset, the center obtained by clustering are mostly inclined to that of vehicle objects.

Refer to the various clustering results (k = 5, 6, 7) in Table 3 and the original settings of MobileNet-SSD, the aspect ratio of default boxes for category clustering is set as {0.25, 0.48, 1, 1', 2, 3}. As a comparison experiment, we set the aspect ratio of default box to {0.45, 1, 1', 1.5, 2, 3} based on the overall clustering results.

Table 3. The aspect ratio of boxes in different clusters

Method	K	C1	C2	C3	C4	C5	C6	C7
Entire	5	0.45	1.14	1.59	2.18	2.85	\	\
	6	0.44	1.09	1.45	1.91	2.41	2.99	\
	7	0.43	1.03	1.34	1.68	2.08	2.52	3.05
Category	5	0.25	0.49	1.24	1.88	2.69	\	\
	6	0.25	0.47	1.13	1.57	2.17	2.81	\
	7	0.25	0.46	1.07	1.43	1.87	2.38	2.97

4 Evaluation

4.1 Detection Performance

This section evaluates the performance of the object detection module. In details, we evaluate this module from different aspects, including speed and accuracy mainly. We verify the experimental speed of SSD and MobileNet-SSD networks on NVIDIA Jetson TK1 firstly. And, we use KITTI, a publicly available dataset of self-driving, to train object detection network. Based on the accuracy of network, we consider improving accuracy by adjusting the input size and analyzing the characteristics of dataset while maintaining a high speed.

The speed of SSD and MobileNet-SSD networks was tested based on Caffe framework. Training was performed in server with Titan V graphics card, and the testing was conducted on Jetson TK1 board. We test the forward propagation time of network using the time tool in Caffe. As shown in Table 4, due to hardware limitations, M-SSD model constructed by lightweight network has not yet met the requirements for real-time detection richly on NVIDIA Jetson TK1, but MobileNet-SSD's detection speed is twice faster than that of original SSD model.

Table 4. Comparison of forward propagation time between M-SSD and VGG-SSD

Platform	Example	Input	Time(ms)
Jetson TK1	SSD	300	751.597
	M-SSD	300	313.391

KITTI dataset includes real data of different scenarios such as urban, rural and expressway [17]. There are 7481 images in the dataset, with a maximum of 15 vehicles and 30 pedestrians captured in each image. According to the number of objects in each category and appearance similarity, the objects are divided into 'Vehicle' and 'Pedestrian' categories. Among them, 'Var', 'Tram', 'Truck' are classified as 'Car', 'Person_sitting' and 'Cyclist' are incorporated into 'Pedestrian', 'Misc' and 'DontCare' are ignored. During the training process, the configured network loads initial model pretrained on the VOC dataset. Gamma and weight decay were set to 0.9 and 0.0005 respectively, learning rate was reduced from 10^{-3} to 10^{-5} by 10^{-1} when the iterations were 40,000 and 60,000 [18]. We evaluate the performance of SSD and M-SSD by mean average precision (mAP). Table 5 shows that the performance of M-SSD is lower than that of SSD due to the scale of feature map extracted by M-SSD being smaller than SSD.

Table 5. Detection results on KITTI dataset

Method	Input	mAP (%)	Car (%)	Pedestrian (%)
SSD	300	66.3	84.2	48.3
MobileNet-SSD	300	62.8	81.2	44.4

As shown in Table 6, compared to MobileNet-SSD with the input size of 300300, MobileNet-SSD with the input size of 416416 improves accuracy by 7.4% which achieves 70.2% mAP. In particular, increasing the size of image plays an important role to pedestrian target detection. At the same time, there is still a 48.7% improvement in speed with 416 × 416 M-SSD model compared to the 300 × 300 SSD model on Jetson TK1 board. Therefore, we consider appropriately increasing the size of the input image to improve detection performance.

Table 6. Detection results for different input sizes

Method	Input	mAP (%)	Car (%)	Pedestrian (%)	Time(ms)
SSD	300	66.3	84.2	48.3	751.597
MobileNet-SSD	300	62.8	81.2	44.4	313.391
	416	70.2	84.5	55.7	385.979

Based on the analysis of Table 3, we compare the detection accuracy of MobileNet-SSD, RM1-SSD and RM2-SSD. The mAP of RM1-SSD indicates that overall clustering on the aspect ratio of objects in KITTI dataset will reduce the accuracy of detection. This phenomenon proves that for dataset with unbalanced number of categories, overall clustering will cause objects in small categories to be easily ignored, while objects in large categories to be paid too much attention. Therefore, we adjust default box through the method of clustering by multi-category. It can be seen from Table 7, the detection result of RM2-SSD model is improved, especially for pedestrian detection that achieves 1.5% improvement in accuracy. Comparing the forward propagation times of RM2-SSD and MobileNet-SSD networks, the result shows that the improved RM2-SSD network only has little impact on the speed. Therefore, we choose RM2-SSD network with 416 × 416 to train the detection model, which can reach 2.6 FPS and 71% mAP on Jetson TK1 board.

Table 7. Detection results of three models

Method	Input	mAP (%)	Car (%)	Pedestrian (%)	Time(ms)
MobileNet-SSD	416	70.2	84.5	55.7	810.124
RM1-SSD	416	69.7	84.4	55.0	385.979
RM2-SSD	416	71.0	85.0	57.2	386.201

4.2 System Experiment

The experimental setup and running process is shown in Fig. 6. When experiment starts, communication interface is opened and Arduino requests session information to direction function package. After the communication interface is successfully started, Jetson TK1 can transfer information to Arduino Mega 2560. Requests are initiated by Arduino and are passed to detection function package level by level. Detection package starts the node, reads the actual scene information through camera, and confirms the position and category of objects. To show the experimental results clearly, the video resolution is adjusted to 640 × 640. The category of objects is converted into direction by ROS as shown in the right screen. After receiving the direction information, Arduino sends a signal to the stepper motor controller through pin.

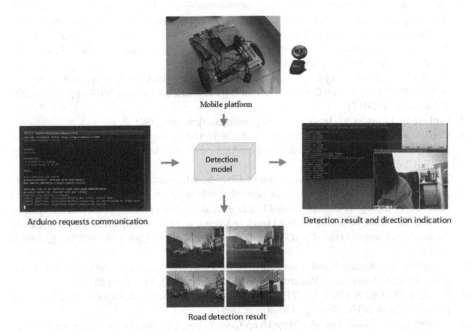

Fig. 6. Overview of the process for the function of mobile platform

5 Conclusions

This paper presents a new feature package of On-road object detection for Robot Operation System and constructs a mobile robot. We firstly develop MobileNet-SSD, a lightweight single depth neural network for object detection which is based on depth wise separable convolutions. To adapt to the road scene, we use K-means method to cluster the aspect ratio of objects in KITTI dataset by category, and an improved network is proposed for more accurate object detection by adjusting the aspect ratio of default boxes. Adjusted network model runs 2.1 times faster than original SSD network and improves accuracy. Experiment results prove the feasibility and superiority of the system we proposed.

References

1. Liu, W., et al.: SSD: single shot multibox detector. In: Leibe, B., Matas, J., Sebe, N., Welling, M. (eds.) ECCV 2016. LNCS, vol. 9905, pp. 21–37. Springer, Cham (2016). https://doi.org/10.1007/978-3-319-46448-0_2
2. Ren, S., He, K.: Faster R-CNN: towards real-time object detection with region proposal networks. In: Cortes, C., Lee, D.D. (eds.) International Conference on Neural Information Processing Systems, vol. 1, pp. 91–99. MIT Press, Montreal (2015)
3. Quigley, M., Gerkey, B., Smart, W.D.: Programming Robots with ROS: A Practical Introduction to the Robot Operating System, 1st edn. O'Reilly Media, Sebastopol (2015)
4. He, K., Ma, X.: Real-time monitoring for the mining robot based on an improved SIFT matching algorithm. In: 2017 10th International Congress on Image and Signal Processing, BioMedical Engineering and Informatics (CISP-BMEI), pp. 1–5. IEEE, Shanghai (2015)
5. Wang, X.: Autonomous Mobile Robot Visual SLAM Based on Improved CNN Method. IOP Conf. Ser. Mater. Sci. Eng. **466**(1), 012114 (2018)
6. Chollet F.: Xception: Deep Learning with Depthwise Separable Convolutions. In: Proceedings of the IEEE Conference on Computer Vision and Pattern Recognition (CVPR), pp.1251–1258, IEEE, Hawaii (2017)
7. Embedded Linux Wiki. Jetson TK1, http://elinux.org/Jetson_TK1
8. Chang, Y., Chung, P.: Deep learning for object identification in ROS-based mobile robots. In: 2018 IEEE International Conference on Applied System Innovation (ICASI), pp. 66–69. IEEE, Chiba (2018)
9. Zhang, Y., Bi, S.: The implementation of CNN-based object detector on ARM embedded platforms. In: 2018 IEEE 16th International Conference on Dependable, Autonomic and Secure Computing, 16th International Conference on Pervasive Intelligence and Computing, 4th International Conference on Big Data Intelligence and Computing and Cyber Science and Technology Congress (DASC/PiCom/DataCom/CyberSciTech), pp. 379–382. IEEE, Athens (2018)
10. Girshick, R.: Region-based convolutional networks for accurate object detection and segmentation. IEEE Trans. Pattern Anal. Mach. Intell. **38**(1), 142–158 (2016)
11. Girshick, R.: Fast R-CNN. In: IEEE International Conference on Computer Vision (ICCV), pp. 1440–1448, IEEE, Santiago (2015)
12. Simonyan, K., Zisserman, A.: Very Deep Convolutional Networks for Large-Scale Image Recognition. In: Neural Information Processing Systems (NIPS), Montréal (2015)
13. Xianbao, C., Guihua, Q., Yu, J., Zhaomin, Z.: An improved small object detection method based on Yolo V3. Pattern Anal. Appl. **24**(3), 1347–1355 (2021). https://doi.org/10.1007/s10044-021-00989-7

14. Yang, W., Zhang, W.: Real-time Traffic Signs Detection Based on YOLO Network Model. In: 2020 International Conference on Cyber-Enabled Distributed Computing and Knowledge Discovery (CyberC), pp. 354–357, IEEE, Chongqing (2020)
15. Xie, X., Han, X.: Visualization and Pruning of SSD with the base network VGG16. In: International Conference on Deep Learning Technologies. ACM, Chengdu (2017)
16. Urtasun, R., Lenz, P.: Are we ready for autonomous driving? The KITTI vision benchmark suite. In: IEEE Conference on Computer Vision & Pattern Recognition, pp. 3354–3361, IEEE, Providence (2012)
17. Hartigan, J.A.: Algorithm AS 136: a K-means clustering algorithm. J. Roy. Stat. Soc. **28**(1), 100–108 (1979)
18. Zhang, F.: Vehicle detection in urban traffic surveillance images based on convolutional neural networks with feature concatenation. Sensors **19**(3), 594 (2019)

A Lightweight Asynchronous I/O System for Non-volatile Memory

Jiebin Luo[1], Weijie Zhang[1], Dingding Li[1(✉)] (iD), Haoyu Luo[1], and Deze Zeng[2]

[1] School of Computer Science, South China Normal University, Guangzhou 510631, Guangdong, China
dingly@m.scnu.edu.cn
[2] School of Computer Science, China University of Geosciences, Wuhan 430074, Hubei, China
deze@cug.edu.cn

Abstract. Non-volatile memory, also called persistent memory (PM), has the features of byte addressing, non-volatility and the similar performance with traditional DRAM, but still shows obvious latency in several common scenarios which adopt the synchronous (sync) I/O, such as the application transferring large PM data or accessing the remote PM data in a NUMA architecture. These problems motivate the asynchronous (async) I/O of a PM file system. In this paper, we first investigate the efficiency of the combination of PM and IO_uring, which is a novel and highly-efficient async I/O system proposed recently. We find IO_uring on PM still incurs a serial of performance issues: (1) pseudo-async I/O path; (2) low efficiency memory allocation of I/O data and (3) unnecessary CPU overhead on user polling. Then we introduce LWAIO, a lightweight async I/O system to relieve the above issues. It mainly contains three techniques: (1) kernel-level threading; (2) dynamic memory pool and (3) kernel pushing. We implement LWAIO in NOVA, a well-known PM file system and conduct extensive experiments to verify its advantages on a real PM platform. The experimental results show that LWAIO brings up to 13% IOPS benefit when dealing with random write I/O operation, as well as 45% IOPS improvement when dealing with the random reads.

Keywords: Operating system · File system · Persistent memory · Asynchronous I/O · IO_uring

1 Introduction

The development of science and technology is getting faster [1]. Persistent memory (PM) is a new and practical storage technology that uses `load`/`store`-like CPU instructions to access the non-volatile data directly with byte granularity. According to the investigation of a real PM device, Intel Optane data center persistent memory module (DCPMM) [2], the read (`load`) latency of DCPMM is only 2–3× higher than the DRAM one while the write (`store`) latency is almost the same with DRAM.

Due to the matched performance with DRAM, it is often considered that an application should adopt the *sync* I/O mode to access the PM data, namely the application can deliver the next I/O request only if the prior sent one was served. In addition, the *sync* I/O path is simple, not spending too many CPU cycles on the I/O execution [3]. This characteristic makes the *sync* I/O suitable for high-performance storage devices, such as PCIe-SSD or PM. However, several typical common scenarios may trap the *sync* I/O into the performance pitfalls of PM. First, when transferring large data of PM, the waiting time of the application would be long, even forming blocking phenomenon to the user. Second, the local CPU node accessing the remote PM in a NUMA architecture also hurts the latency. Third, these scenarios can be overlapped, such as transferring large PM data from/to a remote node, which further punishes the PM performance [4].

To bypass the abnormal PM latency of *sync* I/O and support a responsiveness server, which often needs to handle massive I/O requests simultaneously, one cost-effective solution is using *async* I/O mode [5] to return the received I/O requests immediately, then group and marshal them in a buffer, finally send them to the underlying storage in a batch. When the requests are executed, the application can select a suitable time to pick up the associated results, instead of handling and waiting for them one by one. However, applying *async* I/O into PM is neither a trivial nor a drop-in procedure. Since the PM performance is much superior to the traditional block device, any unnecessary CPU cycles of an *async* I/O system would hurt the performance obviously.

Recently (in 2019), the Linux community proposes IO_uring [6], a new feature-rich, efficient, and scalable *async* I/O system. Compared with the conventional Kernel-AIO, IO_uring refines the performance substantially with the sub-optimizations of zero-copying on I/O data, system calls reduction and initiative kernel service. These benefits allow IO_uring to be the complete replacement (highly possible) for Kernel-AIO, especially on high-performance traditional disk devices. Consequently, it seems that IO_uring is the reasonable *async* option for PM I/O.

In this paper, we try to combine the two novel technologies, namely PM and IO_uring, in a practical system with DCPMM. As far as we are concerned, this is the first work to investigate the novel one-two combo. We find that running IO_uring on DCPMM still walks the *sync* I/O path, due to the reduction of the traditional storage stack on DCPMM: both (1) block layer and (2) scheduling layer are eliminated, thus showing the *pseudo-async* style. This deficiency violates the motive of IO_uring and AIO, trapping the system into the same performance pitfalls of *sync* I/O (discussed earlier). To relieve this issue, we then propose LWAIO, an effective *async* I/O system for PM, not only creating a lightweight kernel-level thread pool to asynchronize the I/O request, but also improving the efficiency of I/O buffer allocation and reducing the CPU consumption of user polling the AIO results. We implement LWAIO on the NOVA file system, a well-known and popular-deployed PM file system. The experimental results show that LWAIO brings up to 13% IOPS benefit when dealing with random write I/O operation, as well as 45% improvement on the read. In addition, with devising a dedicated log-structure for LWAIO, the consistency is maintained.

In summary, this paper makes the following contributions:

1. Investigating and analyzing the novel combination of IO_uring and PM, revealing its performance issue brought by the *pseudo-async* I/O path;
2. Designing LWAIO, a lightweight AIO system to relieve the above issue, while improving the efficiency of I/O buffer allocation and the CPU consumption of the user polling;
3. Implementing LWAIO on NOVA file system;
4. Conducting extensive experiments to verify the performance benefits of LWAIO on a real PM platform.

2   Background and Motivation

2.1   PM File Systems

PM has brought opportunities and challenges to revolutionize the conventional computer storage system, but the traditional file system for the slow storage devices is inefficient on PM. Therefore, the tailor-made file system, namely PM file system, attracts a lot of concerns. Some kernel-level PM file systems have been proposed, such as PMFS [7], EXT4-DAX [8] and NOVA [9]. PMFS improves and reduces the traditional I/O stack, and only maintains the VFS layer, thereby reducing the software overhead of the original I/O stack. EXT4-DAX supports user-mode software to directly access the files stored on PM, and the user-mode software does not need to copy file data to the page cache. NOVA uses lightweight atomic operations and logs to achieve metadata consistency. It also allocates log resources to each CPU so that metadata can be modified concurrently while improving the holistic performance of the multi-core system. All kernel-level PM file systems show the *pseudo-async* issue when dealing with the AIO requests, like Fig. 1(b) illustration. An I/O engine named PM-AIO [4] was designed to achieve an effective *async* I/O path on PM file systems based on Linux Kernel-AIO. However, it introduces significant overhead that cannot be ignored, especially when accessing small chunks of data. The overhead on the data path [10] cannot be ignored either.

On the other side, the user-level PM file systems have also been researched, such as Strata [11] and SplitFS [12]. These kinds of systems move the procedure of I/O data transferring from the kernel to the user space, thus refine both the performance and reliability, but the generality is traded. Note that all user-level PM file systems also have the same problem of *pseudo-async*. We leave the user-level PM file systems as our future work.

In this paper, LWAIO is built on a popular kernel-level file system, namely NOVA.

2.2 IO_uring

With the advent of the high-performance storage device, such as PCIe-SSD, traditional widely-used AIO system, namely Kernel-AIO (also called Lib-AIO), magnifies its innate running overhead, which accounts for a large proportion of the total cost on one I/O execution. To relieve this overhead, IO_uring was developed by Jens Axboe in 2019. It adopts the technologies of complete zero copying on I/O buffer, improved system calls and kernel-side submission, to boost the AIO performance effectively. According to the performance reported by Intel [13], IO_uring improves the latency by about 60% against Kernel-AIO on Intel Optane P4800X SSD.

The structure of IO_uring is shown in Fig. 1(a). When the application submits an I/O request, the application adds a submission queue entry (SQE) to the end of the submission queue, and the kernel asynchronously consumes and processes the SQE from the ring head of the submission queue, which is organized as the circular queue. After an I/O request is processed, the kernel will output the corresponding results into a completion queue entry (CQE). When the application extracts a CQE (or the kernel pushes the result to user actively), it will update the ring head of the completion queue correspondingly. Both SQE and CQE are the shared memory between user and kernel space.

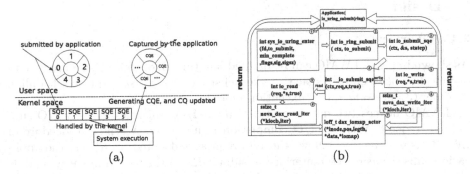

(a)   (b)

Fig. 1. (a) Description of IO_uring structure; (b) Code snippet of IO_uring, which is based on the Linux version 5.1.0, showing *pseudo-async* style.

2.3 Motivation

Although IO_uring improves the performance of Kernel-AIO, it still has the following issues on DCPMM:

1. **Showing *pseudo-async* style on PM.** As shown in Fig. 1(b), IO_uring is designed to the traditional I/O protocol stack. After both block layer and scheduling layer are eliminated, the capability of AIO on PM file system is disabled, thus presenting the *pseudo-async* (namely *sync*) style.
2. **Low efficiency on I/O buffer allocation.** IO_uring applies for memory by calling the `malloc()` routine, which is prone to produce memory fragmentation, thereby reducing the utilization of memory and leading to sub-optimal performance.

3 **Polling consumes many CPU cycles.** IO_uring provides the polling mode to user to inquiry the results in a spin. This manner reduces the overhead of interrupt mode, especially on accessing the high-performance storage device. Users are allowed to switch the modes between polling and interrupt. It exposes performance hazards such as polling overhead when few I/O requests are submitted.

To improve above issues, we propose LWAIO, a lightweight AIO system for PM. It includes the following sub-optimizations:

1. **A highly-efficient kernel-level thread pool** to asynchronize the AIO requests on DCPMM.
2. **A novel memory allocation for I/O buffer** based on shared memory to reduce the overhead of metadata replication, as well as the number of system calls and memory fragmentation.
3. **A self-adaptive I/O request submission strategy** based on both modes of polling and interrupt, to eliminate the overhead caused by system calls of conventional request submission, achieving a balance of efficiency, consistency and lightweight design.

3   Design

3.1   Overview

As shown in Fig. 2, LWAIO can be divided into three modules: (1) a shared memory module between user space and kernel space; (2) an *async* queue scheduling module; (3) an *async* queue execution module.

LWAIO defines two data structures about I/O semantics, namely I/O submission request (SR) and I/O completion result (CR). A typical procedure of LWAIO is described as follows (an I/O request is denoted by R): (1) the application calls the *async* I/O interface to submit R; (2) the shared memory module allocates the ring buffer queue of the producer and consumer for it, and fills R into the corresponding submission ring buffer (SRB); (3) the kernel extracts R from the SRB, and adds the file accessed by R to the corresponding conflict queue according to Algorithm 2; (4) the *async* execution module allocates R in the conflict queue to the corresponding CPU core for memory copying or data transferring; (5) after R is completed, the result will be returned to the completion ring buffer (CRB), and the application can directly extract the result of R from the buffer queue.

3.2   A Highly-Efficient Kernel-Level Thread Pool

LWAIO introduced a kernel-level thread pool technology to asynchronize the AIO requests from the upper applications. The thread pool we designed consists of two parts in the LWAIO system architecture, namely *async* scheduling queue and *async* execution module.

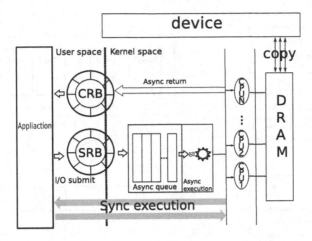

Fig. 2. LWAIO system architecture, containing the *async* execution path and the *sync* execution path.

The *async* scheduling queues are divided into a waiting queue and multiple conflict queues. The I/O requests are first submitted to the waiting queue. Then the system will detect the data block accessed by the I/O requests. If different I/O requests access the same data block, these I/O requests will be merged and added to the same conflict queue. When sending these I/O requests, a conflict queue corresponds to an I/O thread and other I/O requests in the waiting queue correspond to other I/O threads. When the asynchronous execution module is initialized, a fixed number of threads are created. The number of threads initialized by the thread pool is determined by the following formula:

$$N_{thread} = \begin{cases} N_{core} * 2, & N_{require} \leq N_{exit} \\ N_{core} * 2 + \ln N_{core}, & N_{exit} < N_{require} \end{cases} \quad (3.2)$$

N_{thread} refers to the number of I/O threads in the thread pool and N_{core} refers to the number of CPU cores. After repeated experiments, when the number of threads is insufficient to meet the requirements of the application, LWAIO increases the number of threads via Formula 3.2 to deal with the arrivals of the intensive I/O requests. On the basis of the thread pool, the *async* execution of I/O requests is realized by introducing a concurrent management work queue mechanism.

3.3   A Novel Memory Allocation for I/O Buffer

In essence, `malloc()` for memory allocation is a complicated invocation procedure. Figure 3(a) shows the working process of `malloc()`. When the application is constantly making I/O requests, a large number of calls to `malloc()` introduce the overhead of context switch from user to kernel, as well as the overhead of copying metadata.

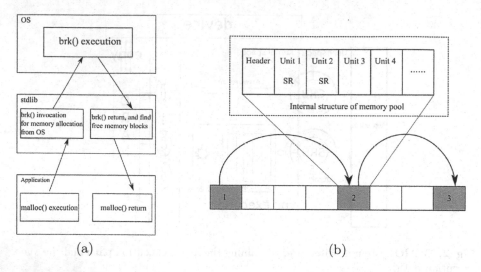

Fig. 3. (a) `malloc()` execution process, (b) a shared memory pool structure pre-allocated by LWAIO.

In LWAIO, we designed a shared memory pool to alleviate the aforesaid overhead. An appropriate size of memory is allocated as a memory pool in advance via the memory allocation system call. After that, the memory pool can be used to allocate and release the memory directly. The memory allocation system call will not be invoked until the memory pool is exhausted to support the need of the application. Otherwise, all operations on memory are controlled by the application.

By default, the memory pool has been first initialized with a capacity of 256 I/O requests, and the head pointer of the memory pool is returned. When an application submits an I/O request, a memory unit, whose size is equal to SR, from the memory pool is allocated for data transmission. LWAIO locates the memory pool that contains the empty units by traversing the header information of all memory pools. According to the header information of the located memory pool, the first empty unit is found, whose address is returned. At the same time, the next free one is also marked. Figure 3(b) depicts a memory pool structure, which contains 3 memory blocks, showing that the system has allocated 3 memory blocks. In the second block, there are 256 SR-sized units and each of them stores the header information of the memory pool respectively. Among the first four units shown, unit 1 and unit 2 have been allocated, while unit 3 and unit 4 are free (empty). When an I/O request is successfully handled and its memory is released, the unit can be directly marked as a free unit in the corresponding header information. When the number of the I/O requests submitted by the application exceeds the range that the memory pool can accommodate, LWAIO needs to apply for a new memory pool from the system and use a pointer to link the new memory pool and the existing one. When the memory pool needs to expand, LWAIO will expand the memory pool based on the previous expansion. M represents the block capacity of the new application, M' represents the block capacity of the previous application, V represents the memory block capacity applied during initialization, and n indicates the number of times for applying for memory blocks, then yields:

$$M = M' + V = nV \tag{3.3}$$

Note that the size of M cannot increase infinitely. When it reaches the specified maximum, the capacity of new blocks will remain the same as that of the previous blocks.

3.4   A Self-adaptive I/O Request Submission Strategy

In the traditional *async* I/O interface, a system call is required to submit an I/O request. The overhead of context switching caused by the system calls affects the performance of an *async* I/O system. If we can group multiple I/O submissions, we can reduce the CPU consumption.

IO_uring provides polling mode for users. Users can select polling mode to reduce the overhead of system calls. However, we have observed that on PM the CPU resources allocated to users are consumed heavily when few I/O requests are submitting. This case would produce serious performance hit when the system is overloaded.

In order to improve the resource consumption problem of IO_uring on PM, LWAIO proposes a self-adaptive strategy based on polling for I/O commitment, which is shown in Fig. 4. This strategy sets a threshold value α in the current system and then automatically starts or stops the kernel polling (KP) threads according to the system situation, so as to solve the CPU resource waste problem when the submitted I/O requests are few. In addition, a CPU load detection mechanism is provided to assign kernel threads to a CPU core according to the real-time status of the CPU to achieve load balancing.

However, there is a cost to start the KP thread. To take into account efficiency, sub-file parallelism, consistency and lightweight simultaneously, α is used to strike a balance. We show this trade-off as the following formula:

$$\alpha = 2E/L \tag{3.4}$$

Where E is the number of SRs initialized by the application and L is the size of the SRB allocated by the kernel. If $\alpha < 1$, the current number of SRs is small, thus the benefits of starting KP threads are not enough to offset the overhead caused by the system calls. When $\alpha > 1$, it means that there are plenty of I/O requests. Therefore, the KP threads are started so that the number of invoking system calls can be reduced.

In this strategy, LWAIO also provides a CPU load detection mechanism. It reaps load balancing by assigning kernel threads to a CPU core according to the real-time condition of all the CPU cores. Firstly, the system architecture is determined according to the *cpuinfo* file in *proc* file system. If it is SMP, the CPU load-measuring module only needs to return the CPU core with the lowest load value; if it is detected as a NUMA architecture, the destination address and the source address of the I/O requests will be checked respectively. If two

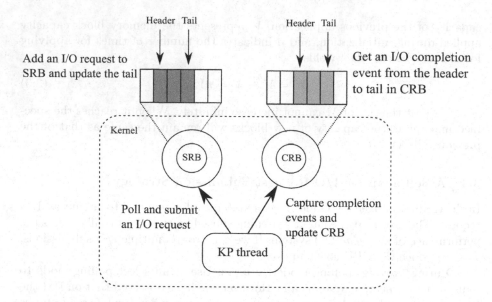

Fig. 4. KP thread polls SRB actively. If the application updates SRB and fills a new SR, SRB thread will submit automatically. That means the kernel can consume SRs in SRB independently and update its tail pointer without invoking a system call to submit an I/O request. The KP thread also captures I/O completion events and updates CRB independently.

addresses belong to the same CPU module, this CPU module will be returned. Otherwise, the CPU load-measuring module returns the CPU core with the lowest load in the CPU module to which the source address belonged. The load value calculation algorithm of each CPU core is described as Algorithm 1.

LWAIO does not need system calls during the completed I/O events reap, even when the KP thread has been started, because the user mode only needs to traverse the CRB to know whether there are completed I/O events. Note that the header and tail pointers of the shared memory need to use rmb()/wmb() memory barrier operations to ensure the correct order.

4   Implementation

We implement LWAIO on NOVA file system and IO_uring based on Linux Kernel 5.1.0. The details are described as follows, which present the important modifications to the original system.

io_init() initializes an *async* I/O session. After the application submits an I/O request, a shared memory pool that can hold 256 I/O requests(an I/O request is 512 bytes) will be immediately initialized. After that, io_init() allocates memory resources according to the number of I/O requests submitted by the application. To avoid the situation of running out of memory resources, io_init() sets the threshold of the memory resources allocation. Once the allocation exceeds the threshold, the system will throw an exception and interrupt the execution of the application. io_init() will return a file descriptor fd to perform subsequent I/O operations after it runs normally successfully.

Algorithm 1. Calculating the load on each CPU core.

Output:
  load_1[i]:cpu(i) average load in the current 1 minute
  load_5[i]:cpu(i) average load in the current 5 minute
  load_15[i]:cpu(i) average load in the current 15 minute

1: EXP_1:1884 ← 1 minute in a period of five seconds
2: EXP_5:2014 ← 5 minute in a period of five seconds
3: EXP_15:2037 ← 15 minute in a period of five seconds
4: f(load,exp,n)=[load * exp * 2 + n * ((1 ≪ 11)-exp)]≫11
   /* A formula for calculating the average number of processes in a given time */
5: **for** _each_online_cpu(i) **do**
6:     nr_active ← acctive_threads
7:     nr_uninterruptible ← uninterruptible_threads
8:     **if** $nr\_uninterruptible > 0$ **then**
9:         sum $=nr\_active + nr\_uninterruptible$
10:    **end if**
11:    avenrun[n] ← put EXP_n and nr_active into the formula
   /* Average number of processes in n minute */
12:    load_n[i]← Calculates the load average of the current core in n minute
13: **end for**

In io_queue_submit(), the KP thread is started according to the I/O request submitted by the application, which can sleep automatically if there is no I/O request submitted after a certain time threshold named kp_idle. When the application calls the io_queue_submit(), it will set the parameter, namely $min\_complete$. This parameter indicates that if the number of completed I/O requests is equal to $min\_complete$, the kernel will generate the corresponding CRs for these I/O requests. io_queue_submit() captures the completed I/O request and puts the CRs into the CRB queue. By traversing this queue, the user application can obtain and process CRs.

Secondly, an $async$ I/O path for PM is established using the module called $nova\_direct\_io$, and we maintain the original $sync$ I/O routine for compatibility. LWAIO implements two $async$ scheduling queues: a waiting queue and a conflict queue. When the application submits an I/O request, LWAIO will add the request to the $async$ scheduling queue according to Algorithm 2. LWAIO traverses the waiting queue to find out whether there are I/O requests overlapped with each other in the I/O range. If it exists, the new I/O request will join the conflict queue with the request itself as the chain header. Otherwise, the new I/O request will be inserted into the corresponding position of the waiting queue, so as to maintain an orderly waiting queue.

To refine the efficiency of the system and reduce unnecessary resource consumption, we have introduced the waiting bitmap and the execution bitmap respectively. LWAIO maintains the waiting bitmap for indicating the accessing status of the target file while the execution bitmap referring to the status of a data block.

Algorithm 2. Async I/O requests en-queuing algorithm
___

Input:
  request,
  offset,

1: first ← offset / blk_size;
2: nrblk ← size / blk_size;
3: QueueIter(head,tail,Areq)
4: **if** (Areq->firstblk+Areq->nrblk)>firstblk && Areq->firstblk<(firstblk+nrblk) **then**
5:     NextAreq = Areq.next;
6:     **if** (NextAreq->firstblk+NextAreq->nrblk)> firstblk && NextAreq->firstblk < (firstblk+brblk) **then**
7:         delFromQueue(Areq);
8:         LinkToConflictRequest(Areq,NextAreq);
9:     **else**
10:        LinkToConflictRequest(request,Areq);
11:    **end if**
12: **else**
13:    Enqueue(Areq,request);
14: **end if**

---

5   Evaluation

5.1   Experimental Setup

The experiments are conducted on a Dell R740 Server, which is equipped with two Intel(R) Xeon(R) Gold 5218 (2.30 GHz) processors with 16 physical cores. Each processor has one local 32 GB DDR4-DRAM and 128 GB Intel Optane DC persistent memory module (PMM). We deploy the server as Ubuntu server 16.04.6 with Linux kernel version 5.1.0. Besides, we turned off the hyper-threading of the server and set CPU power consumption to performance mode.

5.2   Bandwidth and Latency

We use FIO to simulate I/O workload. On the PM device, We pre-allocated a 32 GB file and sent 256 I/O operations which sizes are 128 KB. We set the measurement time as 120 s.

Figure 5(a) shows the bandwidth comparison. LWAIO has the highest bandwidth in random read evaluation compared with other I/O models. In random writing, LWAIO has the best bandwidth and is 1.87× and 1.12× versus Kernel-AIO and PM-AIO respectively. Compared with SYNC, POSIX-AIO, and Kernel-AIO, LWAIO improves performance because it solves the problem of *pseudo-async* on PM. Besides, LWAIO alleviates the defects of Kernel-AIO. Since PM-AIO is based on Kernel-AIO, this leads its performance to be inferior to LWAIO.

In Fig. 5(b), among these four *async* non-blocking I/O models, the read-write latency of LWAIO is the lowest. The *sync* blocking I/O model has the lowest latency because it only submits one I/O request at a time, which is different from the batch submission of the four *async* systems.

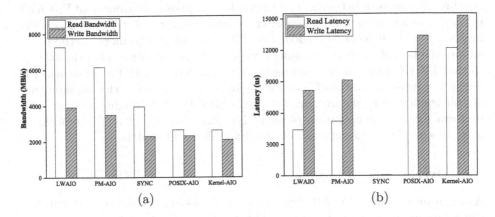

Fig. 5. (a) Bandwidth with random read/write (128 KB I/O size); (b) Averaged latency values with random read/write (128 KB).

5.3   IOPS

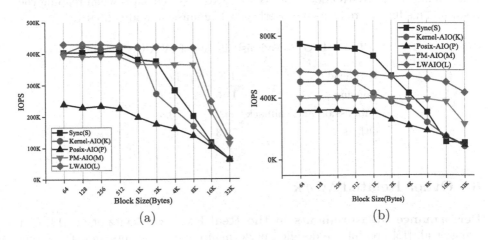

Fig. 6. IOPS with different I/O sizes: (a) random write; (b) random read.

As shown in Fig. 6(a), compared with SYNC, POSIX-AIO, Kernel-AIO, and PM-AIO, LWAIO delivers 1.42×, 2.19×, 1.53×, and 1.13× random write performance, respectively. In Fig. 6(b), compared with PM-AIO, IOPS on LWAIO is up to 45% higher in random read. Moreover, LWAIO is 3.1× comparing with the POSIX-AIO.

The IOPS of LWAIO performs best in the cases of small I/O sizes, the performance of PM-AIO is insufficient in these scenarios, and the performance of synchronization is in between. The reason for the poor performance of PM-AIO is that in order to ensure data consistency and concurrency, the operation performance of small block is traded. LWAIO uses a shared memory method and adopts the idea of producer-consumer, which reduces the overhead of the system so that LWAIO can poll the submission and completion of I/O requests according to the real-time status of the system. It can not only meet the requirements of consistency and concurrency, but also realize the lightweight, and can also perform well in the operation of small I/O sizes. As shown in Fig. 6, even in large blocks, the performance is better than other I/O models.

5.4 Overhead Distribution

As mentioned above, PM-AIO with *async* non-blocking model on PM still has some limitations and shortcomings. The overhead of data copy accounts for a large proportion of the whole process of PM-AIO handling I/O requests. Therefore, in order to reduce the cost, LWAIO proposes a shared memory metadata transfer mechanism to reduce the data copy between user space and kernel space. As shown in Table 1, thanks to the improved allocation of shared memory, data copy overhead of LWAIO is reduced by 63% and 44% respectively, compared with PM-AIO when handling 4 KB and 128 KB with the random read workload. In addition, LWAIO does not need to invoke system calls when reaping the results. This further reduces the overhead of submission and callback.

Table 1. Overhead distribution of LWAIO.

Overhead	4 KB(%)	128 KB(%)
Copying	11.5	51.7
Submission and callback	9.2	0.6
Others	79.3	47.7

6 Other Related Work

Performance Measurements of the Real PM. Izraelevitz et al. [14] and Yang et al. [15] present the detailed performance measurements and the empirical usage guides of DCPMM. They expose the complexities and idiosyncrasies of real PM and indicate that the performance of real PM is quite different from the simulated devices [16]. Meanwhile, Yang's work directly shows the AIO performance of PM is inferior to the *sync* one, but without further investigation. Instead, our work proposes LWAIO, which verifies the performance issues and improves them with a serial of techniques.

Async I/O Systems. Lee et al. propose AIOS [17], a novel I/O stack to asynchronize the original I/O path of the slow storage device, by overlapping I/O related CPU operations with the device I/O. But AIOS targets on traditional storage device such as ultra-low latency SSDs, while LWAIO focuses on the PM, which has a quite different I/O stack.

7   Conclusion

In this paper, we investigated the novel combination of PM and IO_uring, and found that the *pseudo-async* (namely *sync*) pattern of AIO execution on PM devices may trap the application into a performance dilemma, which is easily misunderstood and hard to amend with a handy configuration. Mainly to improve this issue, we then proposed LWAIO, establishing a lightweight thread pool to asynchronize the AIO requests effectively, along with an efficient memory allocation mechanism for I/O buffers and a self-adaptive strategy for reaping the AIO results, which further improves the CPU cycles. We implemented LWAIO on NOVA file system and tested its performance on a real PM system. The experimental results verify both the effectiveness and efficiency of LWAIO. In the near future, we plan to implement LWAIO on other PM file systems such as SplitFS and Strata.

LWAIO is publicly available at: https://gitlab.com/dingdly/pmaio.

Acknowledgment. This work was funded by the Key-Area Research and Development Program of Guangdong Province under grant number 2020B0101650001, by the National Natural Science Foundation of China under grant number 61972164, by the Guangdong Basic and Applied Basic Research Foundation under grant number 2019A1515011160, by the Guangzhou Key Laboratory of Big Data and Intelligent Education under grant number 201905010009.

References

1. Hu, L., Liu, A., Xie, M., Wang, T.: UAVs joint vehicles as data mules for fast codes dissemination for edge networking in smart city. Peer-to-Peer Netw. Appl. (2019). https://doi.org/10.1007/s12083-019-00752-0
2. Vučinić, D., et al.: DC express: shortest latency protocol for reading phase change memory over PCI express. In: 12th USENIX Conference on File and Storage Technologies (FAST 14), pp. 309–315. USENIX Association (2014)
3. Wang, T., Wang, P., Cai, S., Ma, Y., Liu, A., Xie, M.: A unified trustworthy environment establishment based on edge computing in industrial IoT. IEEE Trans. Ind. Inf. **16**(9), 6083–6091 (2020). https://doi.org/10.1109/TII.2019.2955152

4. Li, D., Zhang, N., Dong, M., Chen, H., Ota, K., Tang, Y.: PM-AIO: an effective asynchronous i/o system for persistent memory. IEEE Trans. Emerg. Topics Comput., 1 (2021). https://doi.org/10.1109/TETC.2021.3109047
5. Chen, Z., Li, D., Wang, Z., Liu, H., Tang, Y.: RAMCI: a novel asynchronous memory copying mechanism based on I/OAT. CCF Trans. High Perf. Comput. **3**(2), 129–143 (2021). https://doi.org/10.1007/s42514-021-00063-y
6. Jens, A.: Efficient io with io_uring (2019). https://kernel.dk/io_uring.pdf
7. Dulloor, S.R., et al.: System software for persistent memory. In: Proceedings of the Ninth European Conference on Computer Systems, EuroSys '14. Association for Computing Machinery (2014). https://doi.org/10.1145/2592798.2592814
8. Corbet, J.: Dax, mmap(), and a "go faster" flag (2016). https://lwn.net/Articles/684828/
9. Xu, J., Swanson, S.: NOVA: a log-structured file system for hybrid volatile/nonvolatile main memories. In: 14th USENIX Conference on File and Storage Technologies (FAST 16), pp. 323–338. USENIX Association, Santa Clara (2016)
10. Huang, M., Liu, A., Wang, T., Huang, C.: Green data gathering under delay differentiated services constraint for internet of things. Wirel. Commun. Mobi. Comput. (2018). https://doi.org/10.1155/2018/9715428
11. Kwon, Y., Fingler, H., Hunt, T., Peter, S., Witchel, E., Anderson, T.: Strata: a cross media file system. In: Proceedings of the 26th Symposium on Operating Systems Principles, SOSP '17, pp. 460–477. Association for Computing Machinery, New York (2017). https://doi.org/10.1145/3132747.3132770
12. Kadekodi, R., Lee, S.K., Kashyap, S., Kim, T., Kolli, A., Chidambaram, V.: Splitfs: reducing software overhead in file systems for persistent memory. In: Proceedings of the 27th ACM Symposium on Operating Systems Principles, SOSP '19, pp. 494–508. Association for Computing Machinery (2019). https://doi.org/10.1145/3341301.3359631
13. Vishal, V., John, K.: Improved storage performance using the new linux kernel i/o interface (2019). https://www.snia.org/educational-library/improved-storage-performance-using-new-linux-kernel-io-interface-2019
14. Izraelevitz, J., et al.: Basic performance measurements of the intel optane dc persistent memory module (2019). https://arxiv.org/abs/1903.05714
15. Yang, J., Kim, J., Hoseinzadeh, M., Izraelevitz, J., Swanson, S.: An empirical guide to the behavior and use of scalable persistent memory. In: 18th USENIX Conference on File and Storage Technologies (FAST 20), pp. 169–182. USENIX Association, Santa Clara (2020)
16. Volos, H., Magalhaes, G., Cherkasova, L., Li, J.: Quartz: a lightweight performance emulator for persistent memory software. In: Proceedings of the 16th Annual Middleware Conference, Middleware '15, pp. 37–49. Association for Computing Machinery (2015)
17. Lee, G., Shin, S., Song, W., Ham, T.J., Lee, J.W., Jeong, J.: Asynchronous i/o stack: A low-latency kernel i/o stack for ultra-low latency SSDs. In: 2019 USENIX Annual Technical Conference (USENIX ATC 19), Renton, WA, pp. 603–616 (2019)

The Case for Disjoint Job Mapping on High-Radix Networked Parallel Computers

Yao Hu$^{(\boxtimes)}$ and Michihiro Koibuchi

Information Systems Architecture Science Research Division, National Institute
of Informatics, 2-1-2 Hitotsubashi, Chiyoda-ku, Tokyo101-8430, Japan
{huyao,koibuchi}@nii.ac.jp

Abstract. Onboard optics and co-packaged optics (CPO) will enable
to build an ultra high-radix switching ASIC. Ultra high-radix interconnection networks, which take a low diameter, lead to a marginal impact
of intra-job network topology on the performance of job mapping, i.e.,
placement of message passing interface (MPI) ranks onto compute nodes.
In this context, we investigate the impact of job mapping algorithms on
job scheduling performance, which have different trade-offs between the
resource utilization and the constraint of intra-job network topology. Our
simulation results show that a simple disjoint job mapping policy (e.g.,
a topology-oblivious job mapping algorithm) surprisingly outperforms a
complicated joint one (e.g., a topology-aware job mapping algorithm)
for its substantially better job scheduling performance at the cost of a
larger network diameter, especially when dealing with an exceedingly
large workload on high-radix networked parallel computers.

Keywords: Interconnection network · Parallel computer · High-radix
switch · Job mapping.

1 Introduction

In parallel computers, the role of inter-process communication in performance
calls for strategies to reduce communication latency by ensuring data locality.
Job mapping, i.e., the process of placing the message passing interface (MPI)
ranks of a parallel program onto the compute nodes designated by the system
software, can effectively improve the access locality. Application runtime reduction by selecting an appropriate job mapping policy can result in both higher
resource utilization and lower energy consumption.

The adoption of job mapping policy usually depends on the network topology.
A well-known network topology for parallel computers is Fat-tree. A typical Fat-
tree configuration consists of some director chassis switches, e.g., 648 ports, and
a large number of ToR switches, e.g., 48 ports [1]. Since a director switch cabinet
is expensive and power-hungry, the number of director switches is limited on such

© Springer Nature Switzerland AG 2022
Y. Lai et al. (Eds.): ICA3PP 2021, LNCS 13156, pp. 123–143, 2022.
https://doi.org/10.1007/978-3-030-95388-1_9

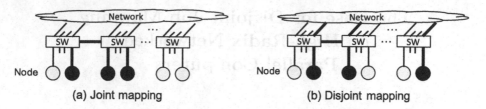

Fig. 1. An example of joint mapping and disjoint mapping on high-radix interconnection networks.

a Fat-tree topology. It achieves a good trade-off between cost and performance. A job mapping policy assigns each job to a subset of the Fat-tree topology. Another typical network topology for parallel computers is k-ary n-cube. A typical job mapping policy assigns each job to its subset [2]. Users should optimize their parallel-program codes for the network topology. The optimization sometimes requires a serious effort from users because they may reconstruct their design at the algorithm level so that the communication patterns fit with the given network topology.

Ultra high-radix switching ASICs enabled by the optical technology would drastically change the design of interconnection networks, which may reexamine job mapping and parallel programming optimization. Co-packaged optics (CPO), i.e., optical technology integration to chip package, is a promising technology for switching ASICs. Hyperscale datacenters highly demand top-of-rack high-radix high-throughput single-chip switches. BroadCom releases the Ethernet switching ASIC design, Tomahawk 3 (12.8 Tbps) in 2018 and Tomahawk 4 (25.6 Tbps) in 2019. It is expected that a switching ASIC will reach 51.2 Tbps in the first half of the 2020s. In current switches, the electric serializer-deserializer (SerDes) conversion consumes significant power, and the broad area of aggregate I/O pluggable ports increases the onboard wire length. To mitigate the both problems, the optical technology should be tightly coupled with a switching ASIC. In this context, onboard optics are needed to support up to 40 Tbps switching ASIC, and CPO becomes commercially mature before 51.2 Tbps switching ASIC is deployed. Currently, Cray builds up large systems using the Dragonfly topology for the Slingshot interconnects [3]. The Slingshot switches are based on 64-port 200Gbps Tomahawk 3 switches. For the largest-scale system, a switch is connected to 16 endpoints, leaving 48 ports for inter-networking, all using a diameter of three switch-switch hops. In other words, any hop from any switch to any other switch is a maximum of three hops.

These ultra high-radix interconnection networks would change a primary performance factor of a job mapping algorithm because the network diameter is extremely small and the network bandwidth can be increased by using multiple rails which can significantly reduce the impact of inter-job interference. Therefore, high node utilization would be preferred rather than topology-aware mapping which usually minimizes the path hops of intra-job communication. In this context, we investigate the impact of joint mapping and disjoint mapping (see Fig. 1) on such ultra high-radix interconnection networks. In general, a joint mapping policy, corresponding to a topology-aware mapping algorithm, involves a small number of intermediate switches to reduce the communication overhead between compute nodes while increasing the wait time for a right set of compute nodes. Comparatively, a disjoint mapping policy, corresponding to a topology-oblivious mapping algorithm, leads to high node utilization, and it can reduce the wait time of a job to be dispatched although this may impair the compactness of its topology embedding [4]. More specifically, we experiment with four job mapping algorithms, i.e., *In-order*, *Random*, *No-brige-switch (NBS)* and *Best-effort*, through simulations of large-scale high-radix supercomputer systems.

Our main contributions in this work are as follows:

- We design and evaluate four job mapping algorithms, i.e., *In-order*, *Random*, *NBS (No-bridge-switch)* and *Best-effort*, which demonstrate different trade-offs between node utilization and intra-job path hops, on ultra high-radix interconnection networks.
- With diverse workload traces, we show that a simple disjoint job mapping policy surprisingly outperforms a complicated joint one for its substantially better job scheduling performance at the cost of a large network diameter, especially when dealing with an exceedingly large workload.

The rest of this work is organized as follows. Background information and related works are discussed in Sect. 2. Section 3 presents job mapping algorithms on ultra high-radix interconnection networks. Section 4 shows evaluation methodology and results. Section 5 concludes with a summary of our findings in this work.

2   Background Information and Related Works

2.1   Co-packaged Optical Switch

Co-packaged optics (CPO) [5,6] is designed to place the optics with the ASIC in the same package. Placing the optics next to the switch chip simplifies the design of the high-speed serializer-deserializer (SerDes) and the circuit that gets data on and off the chip. The SerDes converter does not have to drive very high-speed signals all the way to the front panel's pluggables. This simplifies the printed circuit board (PCB) design, constrains the switching chip's power consumption, and reduces the die area that the SerDes converter consumes.

The CPO technology will continue the scalability for at least two more generations of switching ASICs: 25.6 terabits (400 Gbps × 64 ports) and 51.2 terabits (400 Gbps × 128 ports) [7]. We expect to obtain a further high-radix switching ASIC in the near future, which will change the effective and efficient design of network topology and job mapping. In this study, we assume 64-port and 128-port switching ASIC on the interconnection networks.

2.2   High-Radix Network Topology

The best-known indirect topology is Fat-tree [8,9]. A popular option is (p, q, r) in a Fat-tree, with a degree of $p + q$, where p is the number of upward connections, q is the number of downward connections, and r is the number of tree levels.

Recently, the two-layer Fat-trees consisting of director and edge switches are used in Top10 supercomputers [1], as described in Sect. 1. In another trend of a Fat-tree, each host has multiple links to connect different edge switches. This trend can be generalized in the design framework [10]. The technology-driven approach to use multiple host links to connect different switches, instead of link aggregation, can be optimized to theoretically minimize the diameter and the average shortest path length (ASPL) of interconnection networks.

The Dragonfly network [11] is proposed to use a group of routers as a virtual router to connect a large number of compute nodes. The connections distinguish inter- and intra-group networks. The study [11] recommended a configuration of $a \geq 2h$ and $2p \geq 2h$, where the parameters a, h and p are the number of routers in each group, the number of channels within each router used to connect to other groups and the number of end points connected to each router, respectively.

In this study, we follow the recommendation in [10]. We target a network topology in which each host connects multiple disjoint subnetworks to obtain a small diameter/ASPL and a high bandwidth using multiple rails to eliminate the impact of link contention and job interference. The detail of the network configurations will be explained in Sect. 4.1.

2.3   Job Mapping on Interconnection Networks

Job mapping algorithms have been extensively researched on existing high-performance computing (HPC) systems for many years. Early works focused on the 3-D Torus BlueGene/L system [2,12]. They assumed that nodes allocated for a job must be rectangular and contiguous. However, systems that implement such approaches suffer from potentially low utilization. The works [13–15] extended the traditional rectangular mapping to use node ordering to make contiguous allocations. These linear approaches have the advantage of fast allocations from their ordered list of free nodes. There are also some works [16,17] to take extensive calculations to evaluate numerous possible non-contiguous allocations with certain limitations. Other approaches [12,18–20] take into account the application communication pattern when using embedding techniques like folding to allocate nodes. However, such approaches require to have explicit knowledge of, or have prior application runs to detect their communication patterns beforehand.

The Fat-tree topology is one of the most commonly used network topologies in HPC systems, e.g., Sierra at Lawrence Livermore National Laboratory (LLNL) [21] and Summit at Oak Ridge National Laboratory [22]. The works [23] [24] studied the impact of simple linear node mapping on the performance of mini applications on different Fat-tree configuration systems. Similar to that in Torus, node ordering [25] is applied to the Fat-tree topology for job allocation. The works [26,27] implemented a topology-aware node allocation policy that allocates isolated partitions to jobs in order to eliminate inter-job interference on a Fat-tree network. The results obtained for production workloads indicate that a topology-aware node allocation can provide interference-free execution without negatively impacting the quality of service. Besides, the HyperX topology [28] was proposed and compared to the Fat-tree topology, where a simple random node mapping is used because a topology-/routing-aware mapping scheme is impractical in production environments due to limited availability of idle resources. The disadvantage of this approach is an increased latency for small messages.

Job mapping is also considered for the Dragonfly topology [11]. The work [29] analyzed Cartesian multi-dimensional nearest neighbor exchanges and showed that random job mapping with direct routing is consistently outperformed by Cartesian job mapping with indirect routing. The work [30] showed that the impact of task mapping is minimal by using small-scale experiments (up to 256 nodes) on a Cray XC30 system. Comparatively, a recent study [31] demonstrated that the impact of task mapping on communication overhead becomes significant on a large-scale Dragonfly system. The work [32] compared Torus, Fat-tree and Dragonfly by using linear and random job mapping schemes. It showed that different mapping schemes lead to similar performance for single job executions on all networks. For multi-job workloads with a few large jobs, the Torus network consistently achieves the best performance with the Fat-tree network performance slightly worse. The Dragonfly network is more likely to show higher performance variability when multiple jobs are executed on it using randomized job placement.

To the best of our knowledge, the work presented in this paper is the first trial to investigate the impact of job mapping policies on emerging low-diameter ultra-high-radix interconnection networks enabled by the adoption of the onboard optics and CPO technology.

3   Job Mapping on Ultra High-Radix Networks

In this work, we evaluate the job scheduling performance on ultra high-radix network systems by applying different custom joint and disjoint job mapping schemes. In general, there are three components to comprise the design of job scheduling on a target HPC system.

Queuing creates an ordering list of arrived jobs in the queue according to a policy based on inputs such as arrival timing, user priority, historical usage and job size (number or time of occupied compute nodes). A simple queuing policy is FCFS (First Come First Served), where scheduling stops at the first job for which resources are currently not available.

Reservation determines whether to allocate compute nodes now or to reserve compute nodes in the future for a given job set. Various backfilling policies have been proposed and implemented for resource reservation in production schedulers [33]. When backfilling is enabled, resources can be tentatively reserved for jobs that cannot be currently executed, and subsequent jobs can be scheduled if resources are available for them. There are two common approaches to backfilling: EASY backfilling (EASY) [34] and conservative backfilling (CBF) [35]. In EASY backfilling, reservation is made only for one job (the first job) in the queue, while in CBF, reservation is made for every job in the order they appear. In our evaluation, we order jobs based on their submission time and schedule jobs with EASY backfilling as it is common in many supercomputing centers.

Algorithm 1. The Random job mapping.

Require: Node count n
Ensure: Allocated node set S
1: **function** MAP_RANDOM(n)
2:     initiate $S := \{null\}$
3:     **for** each node i in the network **do**
4:         **if** i is idle **then**
5:             append i to S
6:         **end if**
7:     **end for**
8:     **if** node_count(S) $\geq n$ **then**
9:         randomly retain n elements and delete others in S
10:        return S
11:    **end if**
12:    return null
13: **end function**

Allocation judges if enough compute nodes exist to satisfy the requirements of a job, and then selects the exact number of compute nodes to allocate to or reserve for the job. This is where the job mapping policy resides. Generally, a disjoint job mapping with a large diameter/ASPL can reduce job queue time (wait time) but may increase the possibility of network bandwidth competition due to multi-job interference. Contrarily, a joint job mapping with a small diameter/ASPL can increase job queue time (wait time) but may avoid competing for network bandwidth with other jobs.

In light of this trade-off between the node utilization and the quality of service (QoS), we evaluate the job scheduling performance on ultra high-radix networks by adopting the following four job mapping approaches.

– *In-order:* allocates a job to the numbered compute nodes in numerical (ascending) order if available. All compute nodes are placed from lowest (first) to highest (last) within and across racks. A job is thus mapped onto the compute nodes either within a single rack or across multiple adjacent racks, which may lead to different communication path hops (latency). This algorithm is used as the *baseline* method in this work.
– *Random::* randomly assigns a job to the available compute nodes without considering whether they are adjacent or not. In this case, a job can be immediately dispatched to the system only if the number of available compute nodes is enough. If a job is mapped onto distant compute nodes, it may tamper with the compactness of node allocation, i.e., increasing the diameter/ASPL of topology embedding.
– *NBS (No-bridge-switch):* allocates a job to the available compute nodes whose attached switches are directly connected, so that there is no bridge switch connecting only other switches in the embedded topology. In this case, the end-to-end hop count can be reduced, which leads to a compact low-diameter/ASPL embedded topology for job execution. Due to the rigid restriction on node

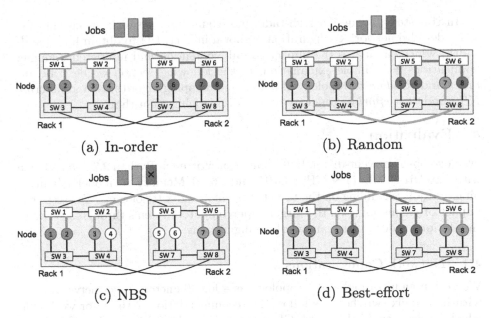

Fig. 2. The job mapping algorithms: (a) In-order (baseline), (b) Random, (c) NBS and (d) Best-effort.

allocation, the wait time (queue time) may increase for the releasing of near occupied compute nodes.

- *Best-effort*: makes every endeavor to assign a job to the near available compute nodes if they exist. Concretely, an *NBS* mapping is first applied if the corresponding available compute nodes are found. If the available compute nodes are not enough to satisfy the *NBS* restriction on the current system, a job mapping with a diameter of maximum two switch-to-switch hops is acceptable. Therefore, the restriction of node allocation is more relaxed when compared to that of *NBS*.

Figure 2 depicts an example of the four job mapping approaches on a simple target network. In general, the mapping of *In-order* or *Random* obtains a high node utilization without taking into account the diameter or ASPL of embedded topologies. As a result, the wait time (queue time) of a job can be minimized at the cost of an increased execution time due to a large diameter/ASPL of topology embedding. In this example, the *NBS* mapping cannot dispatch all the jobs due to its rigid mapping restriction to trade for compact node allocation. Comparatively, the *Best-effort* mapping makes a trade-off to pursue a low-diameter/ASPL embedding while keeping relatively high resource utilization by relaxing the restriction of node allocation. The pseudo-code of the job mapping algorithms of *Random*, *NBS* and *Best-effort* is described in Algorithms 1 to 3.

In this study, we design high-radix interconnection networks using multiple rails (detailed network configuration is shown in Sect. 4.1) to obtain high bandwidth, which eliminates the impact of link contention and interference among applications. For simple explanation, in the following section we describe *In-order* and *Random* as topology-oblivious job mapping algorithms, and describe *NBS* and *Best-effort* as topology-aware job mapping algorithms.

4   Evaluation

We developed an event-driven HPC simulator written in Python 2.7 in a machine with Intel i7-8550U (1.80 GHz) CPU and 16GB Memory to model job mapping and job scheduling on the target ultra high-radix topologies. We assess the impact of job mapping on the target supercomputer systems through a series of simulations under different network configurations.

4.1   Network Configurations

We design an ultra high-radix topology as a low-diameter, direct network to fit with high-radix switches. We follow the recommendation of the prior work [10], which will be enabled by the CPO technology. The primary benefit of our design is that it can fit to various combinations of switches/rack, ports/switch, nodes/rack and racks. The interconnection networks enable multiple rails to a compute node, which eliminates the impact of link contention and inter-job interference.

We assume that the number of switches/rack, ports/switch, nodes/rack and racks is s, p, n and r, respectively. Basically, we use half of the switch ports, i.e., $p/2$ ports for intra-rack switch-to-node connections and the other half for inter-rack switch-to-switch connections. Obviously, if the number of the switch ports is large enough, e.g., $p/2 \geq n$, each switch can connect all the compute nodes in the same rack. If the switch ports cannot cover all the compute nodes in the same rack, i.e., $p/2 < n$, multiple switches are required to connect different compute nodes. Similarly, for inter-rack switch-to-switch connections, multiple switches are required to connect the counterparts in all other racks if $p/2 < r$.

For simple explanation, we divide each entity type (rack, switch and compute node) into multiple groups according to their mutual connections. The group characteristic of each entity type is described as follows.

- *rack_group*: a group of racks, each consisting of groups of switches and groups of compute nodes. The number of racks in one rack group is dependent on the number of switch ports, i.e., p. To connect all other racks in the same rack group, the number of racks in one rack group is $\leq p/2$.
- *sw_group*: a group of switches which use half of switch ports to connect inter-rack switches and use the other half of switch ports to connect intra-rack compute nodes. To connect all other racks, the number of switch groups is equal to that of rack groups, and *sw_group* #i in *rack_group* #j connects *sw_group* #j in *rack_group* #i. The switches in each switch group connect all the compute nodes in the same rack.

Algorithm 2. The NBS job mapping.

Require: Node count n
Ensure: Allocated node set S
```
 1: function MAP_NBS(n)
 2:     for each switch j in the network do
 3:         initiate S := {null}
 4:         initiate linked switch set L := {j}
 5:         for each switch k ∈ L do
 6:             I := attached_idle_nodes(k)
 7:             if I = null then
 8:                 break
 9:             else
10:                 for each node i ∈ I do
11:                     append i to S
12:                     if node_count(S) = n then
13:                         return S
14:                     end if
15:                 end for
16:                 append linked switches of k to L
17:             end if
18:         end for
19:     end for
20:     return null
21: end function
```

- *node_group*: a group of compute nodes which connect the switches in the same rack. The number of compute nodes in one node group is $\leq p/2$ so that they can be connected by the same switch. If the number of switches in the same rack, i.e., s, is large enough, multiple switches can be used to connect the compute nodes in the same node group to multiply communication bandwidth and to avoid inter-job interference.

An example of such interconnection network is depicted in Fig. 3, where $s = 4$, $p = 4$, $n = 4$, $r = 4$. In this example, four racks are divided into two rack groups, four switches per rack are divided into two switch groups, and four compute nodes per rack are divided into two node groups. In *sw_group #1* of *rack_group #1* and *sw_group #2* of *rack_group #2*, the switches are connected to each other in the same rack group. In *sw_group #2* of *rack_group #1* and *sw_group #1* of *rack_group #2*, the switches are connected to the counterparts in the other rack group. Since there are four switch ports, basically each switch uses two ports to connect the compute nodes and uses the other two ports to connect the switches in other racks. However, for the switches (such as 1, 2, 5, 6, 11, 12, 15 and 16) that have switch-to-switch links in the same rack group, they retain one unused port since they do not have to connect themselves. The redundant unused ports can be used for establishing shortcut switch-to-switch connections within or across racks to keep interference-free routing.

Algorithm 3. The Best-effort job mapping.

Require: Node count n
Ensure: Allocated node set S
 1: **function** MAP_BEST_EFFORT(n)
 2:    **if** Map_NBS(n) != null **then**   ▷ Algorithm 2
 3:       **return** S := Map_NBS(n)
 4:    **else**
 5:       **for** each switch j in the network **do**
 6:          initiate switch_hop := 0
 7:          **while** switch_hop $\leq$ 2 **do**
 8:             I := attached_idle_nodes(j)
 9:             **if** I != null **then**
10:                **for** each node $i \in I$ **do**
11:                   append i to S
12:                   **if** node_count(S) = n **then**
13:                      **return** S
14:                   **end if**
15:                **end for**
16:             **end if**
17:             j := linked_switch(j)
18:             switch_hop++
19:          **end while**
20:       **end for**
21:    **end if**
22:    **return** null
23: **end function**

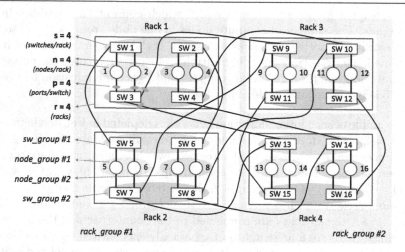

Fig. 3. An illustration of our design of interconnection network ($s = 4$, $p = 4$, $n = 4$, $r = 4$).

Table 1. Network configurations for ultra high-radix topologies in the evaluation (S: Switch, N: Node, R: Rack).

Network configuration	Nodes	Diameter	S-S(N) Ports	R/S/N groups
s4_p64_n32_r64	2,048	5	32	2/2/1
s4_p64_n32_r128	4,096	5	32	4/4/1
s4_p64_n64_r64	4,096	6	32	2/2/2
s2_p128_n64_r128	8,192	5	64	2/2/1
s4_p128_n64_r128	8,192	5	64	2/2/1

In the evaluation, we use 64-port ($p = 64$) and 128-port ($p = 128$) switches to compose the interconnection networks, respectively. The simulation parameters including the network configurations are described in Table 1. For instance, s4_p64_n32_r128 represents that a rack has 4 switches, and a switch has 64 ports, and a rack has 32 compute nodes and 128 racks in total are in the topology ($s = 4$, $p = 64$, $n = 32$, $r = 128$).

4.2 Workloads

Real-World Supercomputer Traces. We use real-world supercomputer workload traces of user jobs by employing the parallel workloads archive (PWA) datasets [36]. The datasets are portable and easy to parse since the same format is used for all the models and logs. Each archive in the PWA datasets uses a standard workload format [36], which concerns the arrivals of jobs and their basic resource requirements, namely the number of compute nodes and the processing time. More detailed information about the PWA datasets can be found in [37].

In the evaluation, we exemplarily use the following three of the PWA datasets which have different average job sizes (the requested number of compute nodes).

- *UniLu-Gaia:* contains 3 months worth of data from the Gaia cluster at the University of Luxemburg. It is used mainly by biologists working with large data problems and engineering people working with physical simulations. Each job takes 11 nodes on average for its execution. We mark the size of the node count requests as *small (S)*.
- *CEA-Curie:* contains more than 20 months worth of data from the Curie supercomputer operated by CEA (a French government-funded technological research organization). Each job takes 130 nodes on average for its execution. We mark the size of the node count requests as *medium (M)*.
- *ANL-Intrepid:* contains several months worth of accounting records from a large Blue Gene/P system called Intrepid, which is a 557 TF, 40-rack Blue Gene/P system deployed at Argonne Leadership Computing Facility (ALCF) at Argonne National Laboratory. Each job takes 1,106 nodes on average for its execution. We mark the size of the node count requests as *large (L)*.

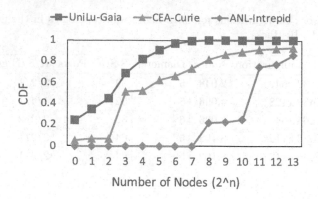

Fig. 4. Cumulative distribution function (CDF) of the requested number of compute nodes in the three PWA trace logs (UniLu-Gaia, CEA-Curie and ANL-Intrepid).

For each trace log file, we mainly use the data fields of *Number of Allocated Processors*, *Submit Time* and *Run Time* to model job mapping in the evaluation. Because the real times found in the trace log files are exceedingly large for our simulation, for realistic simulation time and fair comparison, we use the first 10,000 jobs in each workload log and divide both the *Submit Time* and the *Run Time* by 1,000. As observed in Fig. 4, the job sizes in each workload log are quite different, but their distributions are approximately log-uniform. Notice that, in *CEA-Curie* and *ANL-Intrepid* we discard the extremely large jobs whose requested numbers of compute nodes are larger than the network size (e.g., $2^{13} = 8,096$ nodes).

NPB Applications. We use an event-driven simulator SimGrid [38] to simulate the executions of Matrix Multiplication (MM) and NAS Parallel Benchmarks (NPB) applications [39], which include Block Tri (BT), Conjugate Gradient (CG), Fast Fourier (FT), Integer Sort (IS), Multi-Grid (MG) and Scalar Penta (SP) [40]. The computation power of each compute node is set to 100GFlops. The switch latency is set to 60ns and the switch bandwidth is set to 10Pbps. The cable bandwidth is set to 400Gbps. For the above applications, we obtain a series of simulation results of execution times on different-diameter/ASPL guest topologies, which are used for the estimation of runtimes during job scheduling. We use Class A as the problem size of FT, and use Class B as the problem size of BT, CG, LU, MG and SP. Generally, a larger-diameter/ASPL topology embedding brings a larger application runtime. Note that the order of execution time of the benchmark applications is from 5 ms to 5 s.

The host network is assumed to be a 4,096-node ($N = 4,096$) high-radix topology (s4_p64_n64_r64). We assume that each application occupies a fixed number of compute nodes during runtime by applying a common approach to model parallel "rigid" jobs [41]. We use different workload sizes by changing the number of jobs in a workload to assess the impact on the four job mapping algorithms. We evaluate the compactness of jobs and job scheduling performance by varying the workload size (the number of jobs) from $1K$ to $10K$ in the evaluation. We thus generate $c = [1K, 10K]$ jobs as a workload with random arrival timings for a *Poisson* process with $\lambda = \frac{c}{100}$. A larger value of workload size indicates a more intensive job process on the target system. The workload is composed of the above NPB applications, and each job randomly specifies the number (4, 16, 64, 256 or 1024) of required compute nodes.

4.3   Metrics for Comparison

We compare different job mapping policies using various metrics. The first metric, average shortest path length (ASPL), estimates the compactness of jobs under different mapping policies and is an indicator of the expected improvement in communication time between embedded compute nodes. The remaining metrics, queue time (QT) and makespan (MS), are used to measure the job scheduling performance.

Average Shortest Path Length (ASPL) quantifies the compactness of compute nodes allocated to a job by calculating the number of links which messages travel through between pairs of nodes within a job. In an ultra high-radix network topology T, we calculate the shortest path hop count $H_T(a, b)$ between a pair of compute nodes, node a and node b, which covers one node-to-switch hop, one or more switch-to-switch hops and one switch-to-node hop. For example, if node a and node b are in the same rack but connected by different switches, then the shortest hop count is three ($H_T(a, b) = 3$), which consists of one node-to-switch hop, one switch-to-switch hop and one switch-to-node hop. Notice that the hop count between two compute nodes necessarily includes one node-to-switch hop and one switch-to-node hop. We compute the average shortest hop count across all pairs of compute nodes within a job. For a job j that is assigned to N_j compute nodes, we calculate its ASPL and measure the average ASPL of all the dispatched jobs J as follows.

$$ASPL(J) = \frac{\sum\limits_{j \in J} \frac{\sum\limits_{a,b \in j, a \neq b} H_T(a,b)}{N_j(N_j - 1)}}{|J|} \qquad (1)$$

Queue Time (QT) measures the time interval between when a job is submitted and when it starts running. Let T_j^d denote the time when job j is dispatched and begins execution, and let T_j^s denote the time when job j is submitted to the scheduler. Node utilization and job queue time can be correlated, i.e., increasing node utilization typically decreases job queue time. There also exists a potential trade-off between these metrics and ASPL. On the one hand, delaying the execution of a job to wait for a node allocation with a lower ASPL can increase its queue time. On the other hand, quick node allocations can increase the node utilization, but may increase the ASPL. For job users, it is better to get lower queue time under any circumstances. We measure the average queue time of all the dispatched jobs J as follows.

$$QT(J) = \frac{\sum_{j \in J} (T_j^d - T_j^s)}{|J|} \tag{2}$$

Makespan (MS) defines the time interval from when the first job is submitted to the completion of all the dispatched jobs J, i.e.,

$$MS(J) = \max_{j \in J} T_j^c - \min_{j \in J} T_j^s \tag{3}$$

where T_j^c is the time when job j is completed and T_j^s is the time when job j is submitted to the scheduler. This is a way to quantify the compactness and efficiency of the whole system. The job scheduler usually aims to run a given number of jobs within a minimal makespan. When a significantly large number of compute nodes are requested, this metric reflects the efficiency of a job mapping scheme, especially for a set of intensively arriving jobs during a short period.

4.4   Results

Real-World Supercomputer Traces. Figures 5, 6, 7, 8 and 9 show the evaluation results under different network configurations by using the real-world trace logs which have distinct scales of job sizes (node count). As expected, compared to the topology-oblivious mapping algorithms (*In-order* and *Random*), the topology-aware mapping algorithms (*NBS* and *Best-effort*) reduce the ASPL of the embedded topologies. However, this does not necessarily bring better job scheduling performance accordingly in terms of queue time and makespan. When the job sizes are small (e.g., in *UniLu-Gaia*), there is subtle difference between the two types of job mapping policies. However, when the job sizes become larger (e.g., in *CEA-Curie* and *ANL-Intrepid*), the topology-aware algorithms, especially *NBS*, even increase the queue time and the makespan due to their rigid mapping conditions on compactness. For instance, in the case of s4_p64_n64_r64 (4 switches/rack, 64 ports/switch, 64 nodes/rack and 64 racks), compared to *Random*, *NBS* reduces the ASPL by 26%, while increasing the queue time by 490% and the makespan by 408% on the workload of *CEA-Curie*. *Best-effort* performs better than *NBS* due to its relaxed mapping restriction on compactness, which trades increased queue time for slightly better job scheduling performance. *Random* keeps a reasonable performance similar to the *baseline* mapping algorithm, *In-order*, in any case.

In the case of 64-port interconnection networks ($p = 64$), if one rack contains 32 compute nodes, i.e., $p : n = 2 : 1$, as shown in Fig. 5, the topology-aware mapping algorithms are slightly inferior to the topology-oblivious ones. This is because each switch connects all the compute nodes within one rack, and in this case 64 racks ($r = 64$) are divided into only two rack groups. When the

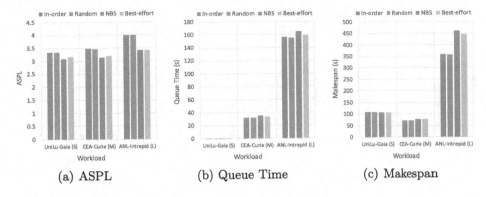

(a) ASPL   (b) Queue Time   (c) Makespan

Fig. 5. Performance of four job mapping algorithms (PWA traces on s4_p64_n32_r64).

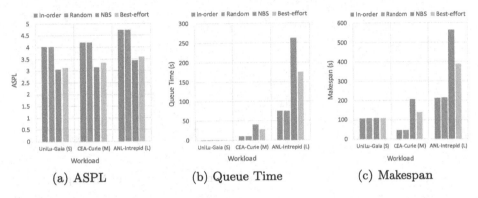

(a) ASPL   (b) Queue Time   (c) Makespan

Fig. 6. Performance of four job mapping algorithms (PWA traces on s4_p64_n32_r128).

number of racks increases to 128 ($r = 128$) under the same condition, as shown in Fig. 6, the topology-oblivious mapping algorithms substantially outperforms the topology-aware ones in terms of queue time and makespan. In this case, 128 racks are divided into 4 rack groups, which leads to the performance degradation of the topology-aware mapping algorithms. We thus conclude that, the ratio of the switch ports to the number of racks, i.e., $p : r$, is important for the job scheduling performance of the topology-aware mapping algorithms. When the ratio of $p : r$ becomes small, the performance of the topology-aware job mapping policies deteriorates dramatically.

The *Best-effort* mapping algorithm gains a larger ASPL compared to *NBS* because it allows to relax the compactness of the topology embedding if an *NBS* mapping cannot be found. However, *Best-effort* still restricts the diameter of each embedded topology, thus it obtains a smaller ASPL than the topology-oblivious mapping algorithms, i.e., *In-order* and *Random*. As a result, *Best-effort* makes a trade-off between a compact node mapping and a random node allocation in

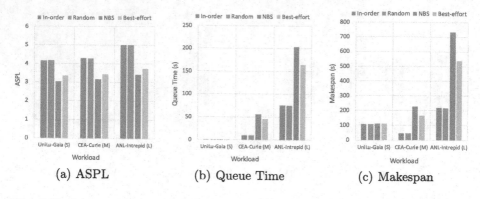

Fig. 7. Performance of four job mapping algorithms (PWA traces on s4_p64_n64_r64).

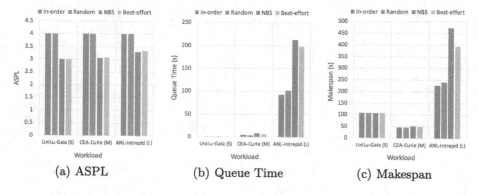

Fig. 8. Performance of four job mapping algorithms (PWA traces on s2_p128_n64_r128).

terms of job scheduling performance, performing better than *NBS* but yet falling behind *In-order* or *Random*.

Another observation is that, increasing the number of switches per rack, i.e., *s*, can slightly improve the performance of job mapping and job scheduling by using any of the four mapping algorithms on the target ultra high-radix networks. However, as shown in Figs. 8 and 9, it does not substantially change the performance tendency especially for *NBS*.

Overall, a complicated topology-aware job mapping algorithm performs poorly when dealing with the workloads of large job sizes, although it has a good performance when applying to the workloads of small job sizes. Comparatively, a simple topology-oblivious job mapping algorithm such as *Random* performs well and steadily using workloads of distinct scales of job sizes.

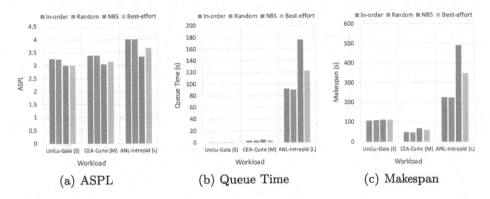

Fig. 9. Performance of four job mapping algorithms (PWA traces on s4_p128_n64_r128).

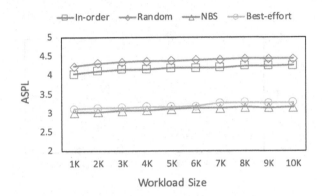

Fig. 10. ASPL of four job mapping algorithms (NPB applications on s4_p64_n64_r64).

NPB Applications. Figure 10 shows the evaluation of ASPL by using the four job mapping algorithms. As expected, the topology-aware mapping policies, i.e., *NBS* and *Best-effort*, obtain lower ASPLs than the topology-oblivious mapping policies, i.e., *In-order* and *Random*. However, this does not bring the benefit of the job scheduling performance in terms of average queue time and makespan, as depicted in Figs. 11 and 12, respectively. Because a compact job mapping enables a shorter execution time, the topology-aware mapping policies present a subtle advantage over the topology-oblivious mapping policies when the workload size is small, e.g., $\leq 6K$. When the workload size becomes larger than $6K$, the performance of the topology-oblivious mapping policies remains stable or gets slightly worse. Comparatively, the topology-aware mapping policies perform sharply worse when processing an intensively incoming workload. This indicates that, a topology-oblivious job mapping algorithm is preferred to deal with intensively incoming jobs during a short period, while a topology-aware one is slightly beneficial to a not busy system.

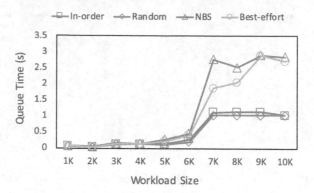

Fig. 11. Average queue time of four job mapping algorithms (NPB applications on s4_p64_n64_r64).

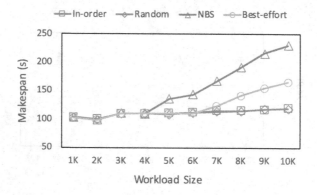

Fig. 12. Makespan of four job mapping algorithms (NPB applications on s4_p64_n64_r64).

Overall, on an ultra high-radix topology, a complicated topology-aware job mapping algorithm presents a tiny advantage when the workload size is not large. In comparison, a simple topology-oblivious job mapping algorithm, such as *Random*, is recommended for its uncompromising job scheduling performance at the cost of a large diameter/ASPL, especially when dealing with an exceedingly large workload.

5   Conclusion

High-radix interconnection networks, integrated with the co-packaged optics (CPO) technology, are being explored to cope with the scarcity of network resources. Most resource schedulers allocate compute nodes to jobs using topology-aware policies that assign isolated partitions to jobs for low inter-node communication overhead. In this context, we implemented several topology-oblivious and topology-aware job mapping algorithms, and compared their impacts on the job scheduling performance using different types of job trace logs on target ultra high-radix networks.

Through a series of evaluations with diverse workloads, the general perception is that locality is less important for job mapping on ultra high-radix interconnection networks. Specifically, a traditional topology-aware mapping algorithm severely impacts the performance of job scheduling when dealing with a large workload in terms of job size or job count, although it presents a limited advantage for a small workload. Comparatively, a disjoint job mapping policy, e.g., a topology-oblivious job mapping algorithm, can improve the QoS metrics of job scheduling such as queue time and makespan. In other words, the negative impact of a simple disjoint topology-oblivious mapping algorithm on the compactness of topology embedding is neutralized on ultra high-radix interconnection networks. Overall, our results suggest that a simple topology-oblivious job mapping algorithm provides better QoS by more than 4x in comparison to a complicated topology-aware one for dealing with large workloads on target ultra high-radix interconnection networks.

Acknowledgment. This work was supported by JSPS KAKENHI Grant Number 19H01106.

References

1. Top 500 Supercomputer Sites. http://www.top500.org/
2. Krevat, E., Castaños, J., Moreira, J.: Job scheduling for the bluegene/l system, pp. 38–54, November 2002
3. Sensi, D.D., Girolamo, S.D., McMahon, K.H., Roweth, D., Hoefler, T.: An in-depth analysis of the slingshot interconnect (2020)
4. Hu, Y.: Topology mapping of parallel applications onto random allocations. In: The 21st International Conferences on High Performance Computing and Communications (HPCC-2019), pp. 1437–1444. China, Zhangjiajie, August 2019
5. Fathololoumi, S., et al.: 1.6tbps silicon photonics integrated circuit for co-packaged optical-io switch applications. In: Optical Fiber Communication Conference (OFC) 2020. Optical Society of America, 2020, p. T3H.1. http://www.osapublishing.org/abstract.cfm?URI=OFC-2020-T3H.1
6. Minkenberg, C., Krishnaswamy, R., Zilkie, A., Nelson, D.: Co-packaged datacenter optics: opportunities and challenges. IET Optoelectronics **15**(2), 77–91 (2021). https://ietresearch.onlinelibrary.wiley.com/doi/abs/10.1049/ote2.12020
7. Maniotis, P., Schares, L., Lee, B.G., Taubenblatt, M.A., Kuchta, D.M.: Scaling hpc networks with co-packaged optics. In: Optical Fiber Communication Conference (OFC) 2020. Optical Society of America, 2020, p. T3K.7. http://www.osapublishing.org/abstract.cfm?URI=OFC-2020-T3K.7
8. Leiserson, C.E.: Fat-trees: universal networks for hardware-efficient supercomputing. IEEE Trans. Comput. **34**(10), 892–901 (1985)
9. Al-Fares, M., Loukissas, A., Vahdat, A.: A scalable, commodity data center network architecture. In: Proceedings of the ACM SIGCOMM 2008 Conference on Data Communication, pp. 63–74 (2008)

10. Yasudo, R., Nakano, K., Koibuchi, M., Matsutani, H., Amano, H.: Designing low-diameter interconnection networks with multi-ported host-switch graphs. Concurrency Computation Practice and Experience (2020)
11. Kim, J., Dally, W.J., Scott, S., Abts, D.: Technology-driven, highly-scalable dragonfly topology. In: Proceedings of the International Symposium on Computer Architecture (ISCA), pp. 77–88 (2008)
12. Agarwal, T., Sharma, A., Laxmikant, A., Kale, L.V.: Topology-aware task mapping for reducing communication contention on large parallel machines. In: Proceedings 20th IEEE International Parallel Distributed Processing Symposium, p. 10, April 2006
13. Leung, V.J. et al.: Processor allocation on cplant: achieving general processor locality using one-dimensional allocation strategies. In: Proceedings of the IEEE International Conference on Cluster Computing, pp. 296–304 (2002)
14. Albing, C., Troullier, N., Whalen, S., Olson, R., Glenski, J., Pritchard, H., Mills, H.: Scalable node allocation for improved performance in regular and anisotropic 3D torus supercomputers. In: Cotronis, Y., Danalis, A., Nikolopoulos, D.S., Dongarra, J. (eds.) EuroMPI 2011. LNCS, vol. 6960, pp. 61–70. Springer, Heidelberg (2011). https://doi.org/10.1007/978-3-642-24449-0_9
15. Albing, C.: Characterizing node orderings for improved performance. In: Proceedings of the 6th International Workshop on Performance Modeling, Benchmarking, and Simulation of High Performance Computing Systems, pp. 1–11, November 2015
16. Lo, V., Windisch, K.J., Liu, W., Nitzberg, B.: Noncontiguous processor allocation algorithms for mesh-connected multicomputers. IEEE Trans. Parallel Distrib. Syst. 8(7), 712–726 (1997)
17. Bender, M.A., Bunde, D.P., Demaine, E.D., Fekete, S.P., Leung, V.J., Meijer, H., Phillips, C.A.: Communication-aware processor allocation for supercomputers. In: Dehne, F., López-Ortiz, A., Sack, J.-R. (eds.) WADS 2005. LNCS, vol. 3608, pp. 169–181. Springer, Heidelberg (2005). https://doi.org/10.1007/11534273_16
18. Yu, H., Chung, I., Moreira, J.: Topology mapping for blue gene/l supercomputer. In: SC '06: Proceedings of the 2006 ACM/IEEE Conference on Supercomputing, pp. 52–52 (2006)
19. Bhatele, A., Kalé, L.V.: Application-specific topology-aware mapping for three dimensional topologies. In: 2008 IEEE International Symposium on Parallel and Distributed Processing, pp. 1–8 (2008)
20. Tuncer, O., Leung, V.J., Coskun, A.K.: Pacmap: topology mapping of unstructured communication patterns onto non-contiguous allocations. In: Proceedings of the 29th ACM on International Conference on Supercomputing, pp. 37–46 (2015)
21. The sierra advanced technology system (2017). http://computation.llnl.gov/computers/sierra-advanced-technology-system
22. Summit (olcf) (2017). http://www.olcf.ornl.gov/summit
23. Michelogiannakis, G., Ibrahim, K.Z., Shalf, J., Wilke, J.J., Knight, S., Kenny, J.P.: Aphid: hierarchical task placement to enable a tapered fat tree topology for lower power and cost in hpc networks. In: 17th IEEE/ACM International Symposium on Cluster. Cloud and Grid Computing (CCGRID) 2017, pp. 228–237 (2017)
24. Jain, N., et al.: Predicting the performance impact of different fat-tree configurations, pp. 1–13, November 2017
25. Zahavi, E.: Fat-trees routing and node ordering providing contention free traffic for mpi global collectives. In: IEEE International Symposium on Parallel and Distributed Processing Workshops and Phd Forum 2011, pp. 761–770 (2011)

26. Jain, N., Bhatele, A., Ni, X., Gamblin, T., Kale, L.V.: Partitioning low-diameter networks to eliminate inter-job interference. In. IEEE International Parallel and Distributed Processing Symposium (IPDPS) 2017, pp. 439–448 (2017)

27. Pollard, S.D., Jain, N., Herbein, S., Bhatele, A.: Evaluation of an interference-free node allocation policy on fat-tree clusters. In: SC18: International Conference for High Performance Computing, pp. 333–345. Storage and Analysis, Networking (2018)

28. Domke, J., et al.: Hyperx topology: first at-scale implementation and comparison to the fat-tree, pp. 1–23, November 2019

29. Prisacari, B., Rodriguez, G., Heidelberger, P., Chen, D., Minkenberg, C., Hoefler, T.: Efficient task placement and routing of nearest neighbor exchanges in dragonfly networks. In: HPDC 2014 - Proceedings of the 23rd International Symposium on High-Performance Parallel and Distributed Computing, June 2014

30. Budiardja, R., Crosby, L., You, H.: Effect of rank placement on cray xc 30 communication cost. In: The Cray User Group Meeting (2013)

31. Tuncer, O., Zhang, Y., Leung, V., Coskun, A.: Task mapping on a dragonfly super-computer. In: IEEE High Performance Extreme Computing Conference (HPEC) (2017)

32. Jain, N., Bhatele, A., White, S., Gamblin, T., Kale, L.V.: Evaluating hpc networks via simulation of parallel workloads. In: SC '16: Proceedings of the International Conference for High Performance Computing, Networking, Storage and Analysis, pp. 154–165 (2016)

33. Lifka, D.A.: The ANL/IBM SP scheduling system. In: Feitelson, D.G., Rudolph, L. (eds.) JSSPP 1995. LNCS, vol. 949, pp. 295–303. Springer, Heidelberg (1995). https://doi.org/10.1007/3-540-60153-8_35

34. Skovira, J., Chan, W., Zhou, H., Lifka, D.: The easy - loadleveler api project. In: Workshop on Job Scheduling Strategies for Parallel Processing, pp. 41–47 (1996)

35. Mu'alem, A.W., Feitelson, D.G.: Utilization, predictability, workloads, and user runtime estimates in scheduling the ibm sp2 with backfilling. IEEE Trans. Parallel Distrib. Comput. **12**, 529–543 (2001)

36. Parallel workloads archive. http://www.cs.huji.ac.il/labs/parallel/workload/

37. Dror G. Feitelsona, D.K., Tsafrirb, D.: Experience with using the Parallel Workloads Archive. J. Parallel Distrib. Comput. **74**(10), 2967–2982 (2014)

38. Casanova, H., Giersch, A., Legrand, A., Quinson, M., Suter, F.: Versatile, scalable, and accurate simulation of distributed applications and platforms. J. Parallel Distrib. Comput. **74**(10), 2899–2917 (2014). http://hal.inria.fr/hal-01017319

39. The NAS Parallel Benchmarks. http://www.nas.nasa.gov/Software/NPB/

40. Bailey, D., et al.: The NAS parallel benchmarks (1994). https://www.nas.nasa.gov/assets/pdf/techreports/1994/rnr-94-007.pdf

41. Feitelson, D.G.: Workload Modeling for Computer Systems Performance Evaluation. Cambridge University Press, Cambridge (2015)

FastCache: A Client-Side Cache with Variable-Position Merging Schema in Network Storage System

Lin Qian[1], BaoLiu Ye[1]([✉]), XiaoLiang Wang[1], Zhihao Qu[2], Weiguo Duan[3], and Ming Zhao[3]

[1] National Key Laboratory for Novel Software Technology, Nanjing University, Nanjing, China
dg1633014@smail.nju.edu.cn, {yebl,waxili}@nju.edu.cn
[2] School of Computer and Information, Hohai University, Nanjing, China
quzhihao@hhu.edu.cn
[3] CSG, Englewood, USA
duanwg@csg.cn, zhaoming@szcomtop.com

Abstract. Cache plays an important role in providing high throughput and low latency network storage service for I/O intensive applications. One major challenge is that performance of storage degrades significantly even with cache at backend while facing microwrite workload. A straightforward approach is to use cache at client to merge microwrites into sequential write. However, we notice that direct merging within block causes severe fragments problem. Specifically, simple cache update policy pollutes cache which leads to I/O performance degradation. In this paper, we introduce FastCache, a two level of cache based on hash table and linked list to store data slice and variable-position merging schema to convert random microwrites into sequential write. To avoid cache pollution, we design a new cache update policy based on measurable threshold to control flushing and Poisson distribution sampling to find the most suitable entries to be evicted. We implement FastCache in FastCFS and conduct extensive evaluations under benchmark FIO and real workload. We show that FastCache outperforms LRU and HCCache in terms of IOPS and access latency. The experimental results demonstrate that IOPS can be improved by up to $10\times$, and the access latency with FastCache decreases by 50%–90%.

Keywords: Network storage system · Client cache · Variable-position merging · Poisson distribution sampling · Microwrite

1 Introduction

Cache has been widely introduced in network storage systems to provides high throughput and low latency for I/O intensive applications [7,28,36,40]. Usually, it applies high-speed memory/SSD as backend-side cache in storage server

© Springer Nature Switzerland AG 2022
Y. Lai et al. (Eds.): ICA3PP 2021, LNCS 13156, pp. 144–160, 2022.
https://doi.org/10.1007/978-3-030-95388-1_10

to response I/O request from application as soon as possible. Great performance gains have been demonstrated by using cache in multiple network storage systems, e.g. ZFS [27] and Ceph [35], etc.

The Internet-of-things (IoT) and database On-Line Transaction Processing (OLTP) applications [3,26,41] generate random microwrite requests with block sizes of 4KB, 8KB, and 64KB. Fileserver creations, permission changes and timestamps involved in metadata updates are pervasive random microwrite operations in the file system [17]. It is notable that the workload of random microwrite takes a large proportion of major applications, e.g. 90% of Facebook messages file is smaller than 15MB and the I/O feature performs highly random microwrite [12].

Unfortunately, random microwrite may lead to severe I/O performance degradation. Specifically, for the backend cache using NVMe SSD or NVRAM, though it provides lower latency and potential uniform random-access speed to alleviate the poor random microwrite performance [19,25], it degrades the speed due to the requirement of $128\times$ written volume. It happens because the write amplification problem of SSD [6]. Blocks are erased 512KB first and write 4KB new data. Besides the lifetime of SSD can be dramatically reduced due to random writes [10].

An alternative solution is to deploy cache at the client to achieve effective I/O capability [5,14]. Take Ceph, one of the most remarkable network storage systems, as an example, it leverages client cache with a certain tree structure [30]. However, the time complexity of locating the block container is $O(\log n)$ where n is the number of blocks, and the write speed is confined because of the large searching space.

A new network storage system named FastCFS has been published recently [1]. It adopts key-value structure to identify and write data block in cache and the complexity is only $o(1)$ to complete the writing.

The experiments have demonstrated that FastCFS outperforms 1.43–$2.38\times$ faster than Ceph under different number of 4KB write threads. As depicts in Table 1.

Table 1. FastCFS vs. Ceph.

Jobs	FastCFS	Ceph	Ratio
4	6,374	4,454	1.43x
8	11,264	6,400	1.76x
16	16,870	7,091	2.38x

However, we notice that data blocks can not be easily merged exactly into one block due to the variance I/O size and write position. Therefore the write operation will generate fragments in cache. To address this problem, one straightforward approach is enlarging the cache capacity to store more blocks. Data stays in cache for longer time, which makes random write to sequential write. However, there exists a huge gap between applications with PB-level data and commercial SSD with only TB-level storage. The cache performance increases at the beginning stage but degrades more seriously when flushing to backend because of existing random microwrite I/O feature.

Another issue is the update policy when cache is fulfilled. Prior works have been proposed using the traditional FIFO, LRU etc. [32,38] based on various metric like accessing time. Furthermore, HCCache [21] distinguishes the caching scheme for small and large files, and the small data in HCCache are managed in the LRU list. But it judges hot certainty with only time criterion (LRU), and evicts improper data which will be written with high probability in future.

In this paper, we design and implement a novel client cache system, Fast-Cache, to efficiently convert random microwrites into sequential write with variable-position merging schema. FastCache updates cache based on measurable threshold and Poisson Distribution Sampling (PDS) to evict cold data [18]. FastCache consists of four components: 1) API Interceptor is responsible for intercepting I/O requests from applications for convenient cache accessing. 2) Memory Cache Entry (MCE) Manager creates a two level of cache based on hash table and linked list to store data slice and design variable-position merging schema to overcome fragmentation issue in the cache. 3) Flush Controller updates cache in MCE with measurable threshold and PDS policy to prevent cache pollution. FastCache redesigns FastCFS client architecture with above four modules and works with FUSE operations smoothly for applications.

In summury, this paper makes the following contributions:

- We design FastCache, a novel client-side caching schema with variable-position block to convert microwrites into sequential writes.
- We define a measurable threshold to release capacity of cache and introduce a new updating policy of Poisson distribution sampling which selects proper data to write backend storage to get rid of cache pollution.
- We have implemented FastCache in FastCFS which gains effective I/O ability. We have conducted extensive evaluations in realistic storage scenarios. The experimental results demonstrate that FastCFS IOPS increases by 4.5–14.7× and latency is reduced by 51.4%–93.5%, respectively. The new system also outperforms the well-known Ceph client system.

2   Background and Motivation

2.1   Background

Network Storage System. Modern applications generate huge volume of data. However, the server usually equips with limited capacity of disks. Network storage system [23] provides various API to access to remote storage resources [22] and extends to high-performance SSDs like NVMe SSD for meeting I/O intensive demand. The architecture of Network storage system generally consists of two parts: 1) Backend-side provides data storage service with storage software like ZFS, Ceph etc., where server disks or disk array are clustered into storage resource pool; 2) Client-side responses for translating operations and forwarding data to backend through common API provided by Lustre, Ceph or FastCFS, etc. [13] Therefore, I/O performance of network storage system depends on both components.

Client-Side Interface. To deploy with application more conveniently, our client-side cache is implemented in common API named FUSE, which is an interface for userspace programs to export a filesystem to the Linux kernel. The FUSE project consists of two components: the fuse kernel module and the libfuse userspace library [33]. Currently, at least 100 FUSE-based file systems are readily available on the Web. The metadata and data operations of FUSE are also implemented by userspace processes and can be accessed by kernel file system. The introduction of FUSE greatly facilitates the development and debugging of the file system. Users can mount it by themselves. Compared with the complex kernel file system, there is no needs to write any kernel code and recompile the kernel. Therefore, open-source file systems usually use FUSE to support Portable Operating System Interface (POSIX) protocol [20], such as CephFS, GlusterFS, FastCFS, ZFS etc.

Cache Structure and Update Policy. Cache layer in I/O stack is a core module to speedup storage system. In cache layer, data are organized in memory with certain structure and updated periodically with a given policy. Cache in backend constructs a cache tier [39] module to store data with linked list. Since writing operation has to search all blocks in the linked list with complexity $O(n)$ and execute insert operation, LSM-tree [37] is widely used to maintain a balanced tree to organize these blocks with key-value index and simplifies index difficulty to $O(logn)$. Hash table with fixed-length block maps data with hash function to blocks and only wastes $o(1)$ time to locate block to write.

When cache is fulfilled with data and hard to insert more data, the flush process is running to write data back and maintains enough space in cache to accelerate new writing processes. Accordingly, many studies have proposed to select data in cache to evict and get rid of cache pollution. Traditional flash-cache [31] provides three evicting policy: FIFO, LRU, LFU to flush based on time or frequency, and ZFS uses ARC [24] which takes the two dimensions into consideration to fit for workload changing. It works well for locality characteristics when an application accesses a storage subsystem. There are two basic types of reference locality - temporal and spatial locality. Temporal locality refers to the reuse of specific data and/or resources within a relatively small time duration. Spatial locality (also termed data locality) refers to the use of data elements within relatively close storage locations.

2.2 Motivation

FastCache is motivated by the low random access performance of network storage system. A straightforward approach is merging microwrites into larger sequential writes and caching hot items like FastCache to provide I/O performance guarantee for network storage system.

Fragmentation Caused by Microwrites. Network storage system has been widely studied in academia and applied in industry. The high random I/O is one of the main performance bottlenecks. The performance of random write is much worse than that of sequential write. Even in SSD, the difference between random write and sequential write bandwidth is more than ten times [9].

When the file system performs a large number of random write operations, the performance of HDD is unpredictable due to the seek delay caused by the hardware structure. Since the SSD is a purely electronic device with no mechanical parts, and thus can provide lower access latency, lower power consumption, lack of shock resistance and potential uniform random access speed. Therefore, many high-performance servers use SSD as the backend storage device to alleviate the poor random write performance. However, random writes can cause internal fragmentation of SSD and thus lead to higher frequency of expensive erase operations [4]. Besides performance degradation, the lifetime of SSD can also be dramatically reduced by random writes.

Unaligned Merging and Simple Flush. In order to address the above challenges on performance, many data are merged into fixed number of blocks which are constructed at the beginning of cache initialization. New arriving data and existing data are merged exactly right into a block for random data size and write position of microwrite workloads. Poor merging quality causes more fragments and tries more blocks to merge. Another issue affecting the cache performance is that cache has to be updated and release space for other write threads. There are two key points in this issue. On one hand, hot data which is frequently accessed by application should be stay in cache for a long time. In simple update policy, hot data is defined based on time (LRU) and frequency (LFU), or write back directly based on FIFO policy. In reality, hot data performance is also related to the write position and can be easily merged to sequential write. On the other hand, update threshold is usually defined by system manager and its efficiency depends on the experience which needs to be carefully tuned. So these problems motivate us to design suitable update policy and more reasonable threshold.

3   FastCache Design

In this section, we explain FastCache design. We start with an overview of FastCache system in Sect. 3.1, followed by a detailed description of each module. Finally, we explain the implementation details.

3.1   Overview

As shown in Fig. 1, we design a new client-cache framework, FastCache. User applications generate I/O operations and the API interceptor module of FastCache intercepts the I/O requests. Memory Cache Entry (MCE) manager module merges the random I/O requests into sequential I/O requests with variable-position merging schema. At the same time, the cold cache data is flushed to backend-side storage with measurable threshold and Poisson distribution sampling from client cache.

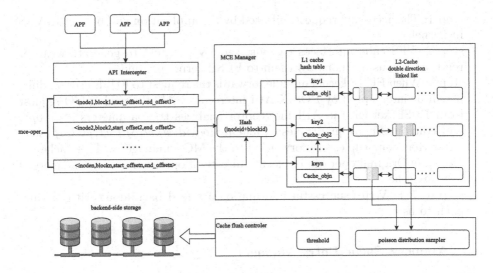

Fig. 1. Overview of FastCache.

3.2 API Interceptor

One of the goals of FastCache is to make complicated storage service transparent to application and not increase the user's burden. Therefore, API interceptor should be compatible with FUSE interface that support interaction between kernel VFS and non-privileged user space [34]. We take log operation as example to explain the design of API interceptor in Fig. 2.

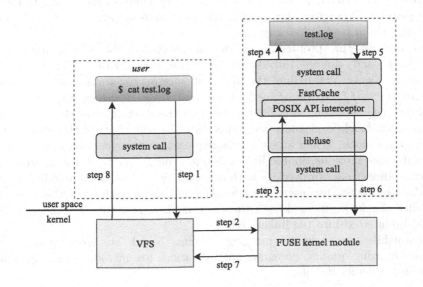

Fig. 2. API interceptor

- step 1: The accessing request initiated by the application will be sent to VFS in kernel.
- step 2: VFS calls interfaces e.g. vfs_read() vfs_write() to generate write or read operations and forward them to FUSE kernel module.
- step 3: When FUSE kernel module forwards the request to FUSE user module, it will be intercepted by POSIX API interceptor. After receiving I/O request from FUSE kernel, the API interceptor analyzes the parameters of io_oper and translates it to quadruples, $\langle inodeid, blockid, start\_offset, end\_offset \rangle$. After that, four tuples are forwarded to the MCE manager in FastCache.
- step 4, 5: Original operations execute directly if operation can not be merged in FastCache.
- step 6, 7, 8: Write successful information are feed back along with original path to user.

3.3 Memory Cache Entry Manager

MCE manager is the key component of FastCache. It creates the data block entries in cache with key-value structure and adopts a hash table to organize these blocks to ensure O(1) time complexity of cache data reading and writing. When I/O request hits mce_table, the request is processed directly by FastCache. While the missed requests are forwarded to the server. In traditional cache system, cache is divided into blocks of fixed length, which simplifies implementation. By doing so, data with different keys can be mapped into same block through hash function and realize sequential I/O operation. However, it causes the problem that these write operations can not be merged perfectly in a block when applications generate a large number of irregular write requests of different sizes. Most write requests have to search many times in hash table to locate write position. Therefore, large proportion of requests can not hit cache and write directly to backend storage.

To address the problem, our design constructs block container with hash table and double linked list to write data with larger space, as shown in Fig. 1. We define the data of mce_oper as data slice, $\langle inode, block\_id, start\_offset, end\_offset \rangle$. Inode and $block\_id$ specify the data block of this slicing operation, $start\_offset$ represents the start offset of this slice in the current data block, and end_offset represents the end offset of this slice in the current data block. When a new access request hits a cache entry and inserts a new data slice into the double linked list, it is necessary to judge whether the new data slice crosses or overlaps with the existing slice in the double-linked list. If it does not exist, we insert the new slice into the linked list. Otherwise, the new slice should be merged with the existing slice, and then the merged slice should be inserted into the linked list.

Meanwhile, we propose merging schema based on write position to increase merging quality. Four merging operations are introduced in Fig. 3 and Algorithm 1 depict details.

- **Left overlap merge:** as shown in Fig. 3(a), when the data of the left part of slice A intersects with the data of the right part of slice B, the merged slice C consists of the unique part on the left side of slice B and slice A;
- **Right overlap merge:** as shown in Fig. 3(b), when the data on the right side of slice A crosses the data on the left side of slice B, the merged slice C consists of slice A and the unique part on the right side of slice B;
- **Cover merge:** as shown in Fig. 3(c), slice A is completely covered by slice B, and the merged slice C consists of three parts: the unique part on the left side of slice B, slice A, and unique part on the right side of slice B. As shown in Fig. 3(d), slice A completely covers slice B, and the data in slice B can be directly discarded, so slice C is only composed of slice A.

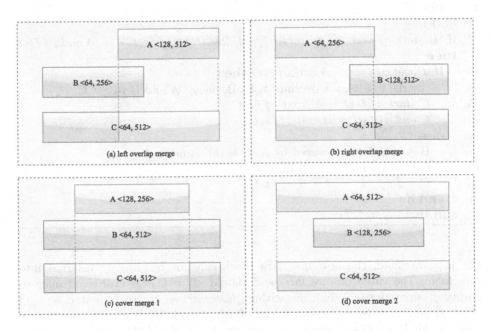

Fig. 3. Slice merge: the picture depicts the four conditions of slice merging.

3.4   Cache Flush Controller

The cache flush controller is primarily responsible for the second phase, the cache update of the writing process. It updates the cache entries in MCE to flushing work queue and waits for FastCache to call the native write function to send the data in the entries to server. There are two key problems to define, update opportunity and criterion of cold data.

Update Opportunity: The controller collects the access count of the missed entries from *miss_counter* in MCE and then compares it with the entries already in *mce_table*. When the number of cache entries stored in *mce_table* reaches

---

Algorithm 1. sliceMerge(slice A, slice B)

- slice C: a new slice which is merged by A and B

1: **if** $A.start\_offset > B.start\_offset$ && $A.start\_offset <= B.end\_offset$
    then
2:    **if** $A.end\_offset > B.end\_offset$ **then**
3:        the left side of A overlaps with B, merge A and B to get C
4:        $C.start\_offset = B.start\_offset$
5:        $C.end\_offset = A.end\_offsct$
6:    **else**
7:        A is completely covered by B, merge A and B to get C
8:        $C.start\_offset = B.start\_offset$
9:        $C.end\_offset = B.end\_offset$
10:    **end if**
11: **end if**
12: **if** $B.start\_offset > A.start\_offset$ && $.start\_offset <= A.end\_offset$
    then
13:    **if** $B.end\_offset > A.end\_offset$ **then**
14:        the right side of A overlaps with B, merge A and B to get C
15:        $C.start\_offset = A.start\_offset$
16:        $C.end\_offset = B.end\_offset$
17:    **else**
18:        B is completely covered by A, C is the same as A
19:        $C.start\_offset = A.start\_offset$
20:        $C.end\_offset = A.end\_offset$
21:    **end if**
22: **end if**

---

the *mce_threshold*, the new hot data block can not be directly inserted into *mce_table*. The value of *mce_threshold* should allow Cache flush controller to empty *flush_work_queue* in time within *flush_interval*. In the worst case, I/O requests generated by an application in a flushing cycle hit every entry *mce_table*, and the MCE manager inserts the number of *mce_threshold* cache entries into *flush_work_queue*. Before the next periodic flushing comes, *flush_thread* must be able to call the native write function to update the data in these cache entries to the server, so as to avoid head-of-line blocking. We denote the size of the cache block as *fastcache_block_size*. The throughput when the native write function updates the data of this size to server can be regarded as the average throughput, average_throughput, after FastCache optimization. Then the average number of cache entries that the client can send per second can be calculated as *average_throughput/fast_cache_block_size*. To sum up, we can get the formula for calculating *mce_threshold* of *mce_table*:

$$mce\_threshold = flush\_interval \times \frac{average\_throughput}{fastcache\_block\_size} \tag{1}$$

Criterion of Cold Data Based on Poisson Distribution. If real hot data are evicted, it may lead to cache pollution, which becomes the performance bottleneck of the FastCache design. LRU, LFU, ARC algorithm in traditional cache only judge cold data with simple criterion like time and frequency. However, application access requests satisfy the locality principle. So we need to propose a new criterion to use this feature.

From the point of view of data access, the essence of the locality principle is data distribution, and there is a greater correlation between data that are close in space. For example, the memory space adjacent to the currently accessed memory has a higher probability of being accessed in the next operation than non-adjacent memory space. Therefore, we use Poisson distribution model to identify the probability of a data block being accessed next time,

$$P(X = k) = \frac{e^{-\lambda} \lambda^k}{k!} \tag{2}$$

where λ is a workload-related constant, indicating the average distance between the next access cache block and the current access cache block. If $X = k$ is defined, it means an event that the cache block with k distance away from the current cache block is accessed again. Then, when k is smaller, the probability $P(X = k)$ of this event is higher, and we should try our best to keep this block in the cache. On the contrary, when k is larger, $P(X = k)$ is lower, i.e., the larger the distance from the currently accessed cache block, the lower probability that this cache block will be accessed again. Using this probability model, we can sample a few cache blocks with a low probability of being accessed again.

Cache Update Algorithm. Considering that when the number of cache entries has reached *mce_threshold*, and it is observed from *miss_counter* that the number of accesses to one data block that is not in *mce_table* exceeds *miss_threshold*. This data block will become an alternate hot data block, we call it *alternate_item*, and this *alternate_item* should be inserted into *mce_table*. At this time, a cache entry should be removed from *mce_table* by adopting the eviction flushing policy. However, if cache flush controller traverses all the entries, finding out the eligible entries, by comparison, will lock *mce_table* for a long time, which may lead to the decrease of concurrency performance. Therefore, according to the probability model of Poisson distribution, we only sample a few entries from *mce_table* and evict the coldest entry with the smallest *last_hit_time_ms* value. The pseudo-code of cache update algorithm is given in Algorithm 2.

Algorithm 2. Cache item eviction
- key: inode and block_id
- *mce_table*: in-memory key-value cache
- counters: in-memory access times

1: **if** $mce\_table.hit(key) == false$ & $mce\_table.size() >= mce\_threshold$ **then**
2:    **if** $counters.miss\_counter(key) > miss\_threshold$ **then**
3:       mark this key-value block as a *alternate_item*
4:       sample few items from *mce_table*
5:       $coldest\_item = items[0]$
6:       **for** index from 1 to sizeof(items) **do**
7:          $item = items[index]$
8:          **if** $coldest\_item.last\_hit\_time\_ms > item.last\_hit\_time\_ms$ **then**
9:             $coldest\_item = item$
10:         **end if**
11:      **end for**
12:      evict coldest_item from *mce_table*
13:   **end if**
14: **end if**

4 Implementation

We have implemented a prototype of FastCache over FastCFS file system [1]. Since we can obtain all the data and control variables carried in the user I/O request in fused module, it is a good choice to implement FastCache caching structure on fused module. Fused module is independent of other modules of FastCFS. Thus, other modules of FastCFS do not require to be modified.

API Interceptor. In order to intercept I/O requests sent by applications on FastCFS, we modified the functions *fs_do_write*, *fs_do_read* and *fs_do_fsync* on fuse_wrapper.c. The requests are parsed into quadruples $\langle inodeid, blockid, start\_offset, end\_offset \rangle$, and then forwarded to MCE manager.

MCE Manager. We implemented functions such as *do_cache_write* and *do_cache_read* in fcfs_api_file.c file, received the request quadruple forwarded by API interceptor, and converted these requests into access request quintuples $\langle inodeid, blockid, start\_offset, end\_offset \rangle$ to cache *mce_table*. The *inode* and *block_id* in quintuple are combined into *key_info*, which is used to query *mce_table* and counters in MCE. If the *key_info* hits *mce_table*, then the hot data slice is stored in buffer_list. We will insert the data slice of the access request into the *buffer_list*. If a slice in the *buffer_list* crosses or overlaps with the new slice, it will be merged with the new slice.

Flush Controller. When I/O requests initiated by applications arrive, we expect that each request can hit *cached_obj* in *mce_table*, and complete its processing in memory. However, there are always some requests that do not hit *mce_table*. In these cases, we will call the original function of FastCFS to directly establish a connection between client and server to transmit data. Because C language does not support functions with the same name, we modified some original function names. Taking the writing function as an example, we renamed the fs_do_write function to raw_fs_do_write. When the cache entries in *mce_table* meet the flushing policy, the Cache flush controller will insert them into the flush work queue, and then start flush_thread to continuously send data in the flush work queue to server.

5 Evaluation

5.1 Experiment Setup

Testbed. We implemented the FastCache caching framework based on FastCFS with the latest version V1.2.1. Specifically, we refer to the original client as FastCFS, and the client deployed with FastCache as FastCache for short. We tested the performance of FastCFS and FastCache under different workloads in the cluster, which applies one client node and three server nodes, each node contains four 2.10GHz processors, with model Xeon(R) E5-2620 v2. There are 24 cores, 32GB of memory in total, and the nodes are equipped with 10 Gigabit network interface cards for data transmission.

Workloads. FIO [11] and Filebench [2] are widely used to evaluate the performance of the general file system. FIO allows specify the type of I/O, such as read/write, sequential/random, I/O block size and the number of worker threads. Filebench is an automatic tool for testing file system performance. By simulating the scene of the real application server, the following two kinds of workloads are generated to measure the throughput, IOPS, and latency.

- FIO workload emulates the frequent write operations of an application to a single large file.
- FileServer workload, generated by Filebench tool, emulates the usage scenario of file server. During this workload, multiple threads will create, delete, append, read and write files in 20 directories of a directory tree. In particular, the ratios of reading operations to writing operations are 1:2.

5.2 Performance Improvement by FastCache

In our experiment, we adopt two metrics, IOPS and latency to evaluate the performance of FastCFS and FastCache. The experimental results under FIO and FileServer workloads are shown in Fig. 4. Compared with FastCFS, the IOPS of FastCache are increased by 2.1–14.6×, 4.0–11.6×, 4.1–8.6×, and 5.6–6.9× when the I/O block size is 4 KB, 8 KB, 16 KB, and 64 KB, respectively. The average latency is reduced by 51.4–93.5%, 75.2–91.7%, 75.4–88.8% and 82.3–85.9%, respectively. FastCache decreases fragments in cache and gains higher microwrite performance.

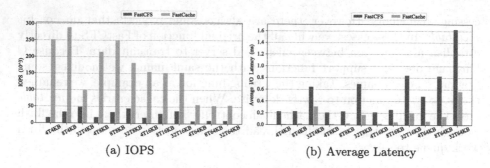

(a) IOPS   (b) Average Latency

Fig. 4. FIO workload.

The performance evaluation of the FileServer workload is illustrated in Fig. 5. Compared with FastCFS, the IOPS of FastCache increases by 12.9–14.7×, 10.5–11.3×, 5.7–6.3×, and 4.5–4.9× when I/O block sizes are 4 KB, 8 KB, 16 KB, and 64 KB, respectively. The average latency is reduced by 90.5–91.9%, 90–90.5%, 83–87.5% and 75.5–76% respectively. In addition to the average latency, we also record the maximum latency of all requests. As shown in Fig. 5(c), the ratio of the maximum latency decreases approximately the same as the average latency, which indicates that FastCache not only dramatically improves the read and write speed and the average response speed, but also effectively shortens the maximum response time of applications which represent probable most terrible poor I/O feeling for applications.

5.3   Comparison with Existing Client-Side Cache Algorithm

We conduct experiments to compare FastCache with the widely used LRU algorithm and HCCache algorithm under above two types of workloads. In these experiments, the write request has files of size ranging from 4 KB to 64 KB and the number of threads is set to 8. In particular, in order to verify that HCCache adopts different caching policies for files of different sizes.

The results under FIO workload and FileServer workload are illustrated in Fig. 6, respectively. The FastCache performs much better than LRU and HCCache in IOPS and latency, because FastCache is based on variable-position cache blocks, and only a few cache entries are sampled according to the Poisson distribution model when evicting cache, which reduces cache pollution. When the workload data block is large, the requested data block is large, the occupied space of the linked list in the cache entry is closer to the size of the whole cache block.

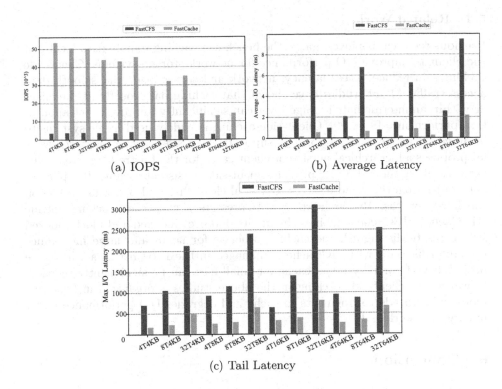

(a) IOPS

(b) Average Latency

(c) Tail Latency

Fig. 5. Fileserver workload.

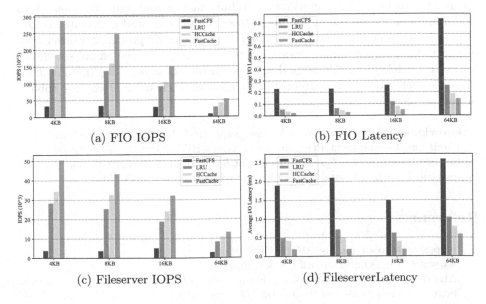

(a) FIO IOPS

(b) FIO Latency

(c) Fileserver IOPS

(d) FileserverLatency

Fig. 6. Cache policy comparison.

5.4   Related Work

Previous research has investigated the benefits of caching remote data locally at the client to improve I/O performance for network storage systems. Client-side caching can reduce access latency, network and server load, and smooth data access traffic. Many studies have shown that caching data locally at the client or within an intermediate storage layer can significantly improve client application performance [8,16,29]. Client-side caching is widely used in file systems to improve IO performance. Ceph [35] supports client-side caching, research work [5] proposes a hierarchical persistent client cache for the Lustre file system. The network file system AFS [15] provides client-side persistent caching. It replicates entire files from the remote server to a local client disk and performs all I/O on the local replicas. Research work [21] presents a client-side caching scheme (HCCache), HCCache combines the merits of object-indexed and block-indexed structures to distinguish the caching schemes for small and large files. Since the small file data with HCCache is managed in the LRU list as a whole, the probability of partially hit in cache for small files can be significantly reduced. However, the client-side caching in the above studies is organized in fixed-size block, which leads to fragments in cache and degrades I/O performance under micorwrites workload.

6   Conclusion

We present FastCache, a client-side caching design for network storage system that improves cache efficiency. FastCache adopts variable-position merging scheme to combine I/O operations with different size and write position. With this method, microwrites are merged into sequntial write and gains directly I/O improvement under microwrite workload. Meanwhile, we proposed a novel flush policy with measurable flush threshold and eviction data based on poisson distribution probability. FastCache is developed within common FUSE module from Linux kernel and can be extent to other network client as cache for solving performance problem.

Acknowledgement. This research was supported by Jiangsu Provincial Key Research and Development Program under Grant BE2020001-3, the National Natural Science Foundation of China under Grant 61832005 and 6217220, China Southern Power Grid Shenzhen Digital Power Grid Research Institute CGY21001.

References

1. https://gitee.com/fastdfs100/FastCFS
2. www.solarisinternals.com/wiki/index.php/FileBench
3. Atzori, L., Iera, A., Morabito, G.: From "smart objects" to "social objects": the next evolutionary step of the internet of things. IEEE Commun. Mag. **52**(1), 97–105 (2014)

4. Bouganim, L., Jónsson, B., Bonnet, P.: uFLIP: understanding ash IO patterns. In: arXiv preprint arXiv:0909.1780 (2009)
5. Cheng, W., et al.: NVMM-oriented hierarchical persistent client caching for lustre. In: ACM Trans. Storage (TOS) **17**(1), 1–22 (2021)
6. Desnoyers, P.: Analytic models of SSD write performance. ACM Trans. Storage (TOS) **10**(2), 1–25 (2014)
7. Eisenman, A., et al.: Flashield: a hybrid key-value cache that controls ash write amplification. In: 16th USENIX Symposium on Networked Systems Design and Implementation, pp. 65–78 (2019)
8. Eshel, M., et al.: Panache: a parallel file system cache for global file access. In: FAST, vol. 10, pp. 1–14 (2010)
9. Esmet, J., et al.: The TokuFS streaming file system. In: HotStorage (2012)
10. Fareed, I., et al.: Leveraging intra-page update diversity for mitigating write amplification in SSDs. In: Proceedings of the 34th ACM International Conference on Supercomputing, pp. 1–12 (2020)
11. fio. http://freecode.com/projects/fio
12. Harter, T., et al.: Analysis of HDFS under HBase: a Facebook messages case study. In: 12th Conference on File and Storage Technologies, pp. 199–212 (2014)
13. Hatzieleftheriou, A., Anastasiadis, S.: Host-side filesystem journaling for durable shared storage. In: 13th USENIX Conference on File and Storage Technologies, pp. 59–66 (2015)
14. Hou, B., Chen, F.: GDS-LC: a latency-and cost-aware client caching scheme for cloud storage. ACM Trans. Storage (TOS) **13**(4), 1–33 (2017)
15. Howard, J.H., et al.: Scale and performance in a distributed file system. ACM Trans. Comput. Syst. (TOCS) **6**(1), 51–81 (1988)
16. Howells, D., et al.: Fs-cache: a network filesystem caching facility. In: Proceedings of the Linux Symposium, vol. 1, pp. 427–440. Citeseer (2006)
17. Jannen, W., et al.: BetrFS: a right-optimized write-optimized file system. In: 13th USENIX Conference on File and Storage Technologies, pp. 301–315 (2015)
18. Joukar, A., Ramezani, M., MirMostafaee, S.M.T.K.: Parameter estimation for the exponential-Poisson distribution based on ranked set samples. In: Commun. Stat.-Theory Methods **50**(3), 560–581 (2021)
19. Kang, S., et al.: Performance trade-offs in using NVRAM write buffer for ash memory-based storage devices. IEEE Trans. Comput. **58**(6), 744–758 (2008)
20. Koopman, P., DeVale, J.: The exception handling effectiveness of POSIX operating systems. IEEE Trans. Softw. Eng. **26**(9), 837–848 (2000)
21. Li, X., et al.: HCCache: a hybrid client-side cache management scheme for I/O-intensive workloads in network-based file systems. In: 2012 13th International Conference on Parallel and Distributed Computing, Applications and Technologies (PDCAT) (2013)
22. Li, X., Qian, L.: A hybrid disaster-tolerant model with DDF technology for MooseFS open-source distributed file system. J. Supercomput. **73**(5), 2052–2068 (2016). https://doi.org/10.1007/s11227-016-1902-9
23. Luo, L., et al.: Envirostore: a cooperative storage system for disconnected operation in sensor networks. In: IEEE INFOCOM 2007–26th IEEE International Conference on Computer Communications, pp. 1802–1810. IEEE (2007)
24. Megiddo, N., Modha, D.S.: ARC: a self-tuning, low overhead replacement cache. Fast 3, 115–130 (2003)
25. Peng, B., et al.: MDev-NVMe: a NVMe storage virtualization solution with mediated pass-through. In: 2018 USENIX Annual Technical Conference, pp. 665–676 (2018)

26. Qian, L., et al.: Stabilizing and boosting I/O performance for file systems with journaling on NVMe SSD. Sci. China Inf. Sci. **65**(3), 1–15 (2022)
27. Šenolt, J.: Advanced File Systems, ZFS (2021)
28. Shen, Z., et al.: Didacache: an integration of device and application for ash-based key-value caching. ACM Trans. Storage (TOS) **14**(3), 1–32 (2018)
29. Shi, L., Liu, Z., Xu, L.: Bwcc: a fs-cache based cooperative caching system for network storage system. In: 2012 IEEE International Conference on Cluster Computing, pp. 546–550. IEEE (2012)
30. Sim, H., et al.: An integrated indexing and search service for distributed file systems. IEEE Trans. Parallel Distrib. Syst. **31**(10), 2375–2391 (2020)
31. Srinivasan, M., Saab, P., Tkachenko, V.: Flashcache. In: Facebook (2010)
32. Sung, H.: BBOS: efficient HPC storage management via burst buffer over-subscription. In: et al.: 20th IEEE/ACM International Symposium on Cluster, Cloud and Internet Computing (CCGRID), pp. 142–151. IEEE (2020)
33. Thompson, L., Clarke, J., Sheehan, R.: eduFUSE a visualizer for user-space file systems. In: Proceedings of the 2020 ACM Conference on Innovation and Technology in Computer Science Education, pp. 549–550 (2020)
34. Vangoor, B.K.R., Tarasov, V., Zadok, E.: To FUSE or not to FUSE: performance of user-space file systems. In: 15th USENIX Conference on File and Storage Technologies, pp. 59–72 (2017)
35. Sage A Weil et al. "Ceph: A scalable, high-performance distributed file system". In: Proceedings of the 7th symposium on Operating systems design and implementation. 2006, pp. 307–320
36. Wu, K., et al.: The storage hierarchy is not a hierarchy: optimizing caching on modern storage devices with orthus. In: 19th USENIX Conference on File and Storage Technologies, pp. 307–323 (2021)
37. Wu, X., et al.: LSM-trie: an LSM-tree-based ultra-large key-value store for small data items. In: 2015 USENIX Annual Technical Conference, pp. 71–82 (2015)
38. Yang, J., Yue, Y., Rashmi, K.V.: A large scale analysis of hundreds of in-memory cache clusters at Twitter. In: 14th USENIX Symposium on Operating Systems Design and Implementation, pp. 191–208 (2020)
39. Yang, Z., et al.: Cache placement in two-tier HetNets with limited storage capacity: cache or buffer? IEEE Trans. Commun. **66**(11), 5415–5429 (2018)
40. Zhang, J., et al.: Storage performance virtualization via throughput and latency control. In: ACM Trans. Storage (TOS) **2**(3), 283–308 (2006)
41. Zhang, Y., et al.: Smart contract-based access control for the internet of things. IEEE Internet Things J. **6**(2), 1594–1605 (2018)

An Efficient Parallelization Model for Sparse Non-negative Matrix Factorization Using cuSPARSE Library on Multi-GPU Platform

Hatem Moumni[1]([✉]) and Olfa Hamdi-Larbi[1,2]

[1] Faculty of Sciences of Tunis, LIPSIC-FST Laboratory,
University of Tunis El Manar, Manar II, 2092, Tunis, Tunisia
`moumnihatem@gmail.com`, `olfa.hamdi@utm.tn`
[2] College of Business Madinah, Taibah University, Medina, Kingdom of Saudi Arabia

Abstract. Positive or Non-negative Matrix Factorization (NMF) is an effective technique and has been widely used for Big Data representation. It aims to find two non-negative matrices W and H whose product provides an optimal approximation to the original input data matrix A, such that $A \approx W * H$. Although, NMF plays an important role in several applications, such as machine learning, data analysis and biomedical applications. Due to the sparsity that is caused by missing information in many high-dimension scenes (e.g., social networks, recommender systems and DNA gene expressions), the NMF method cannot mine a more accurate representation from the explicit information. Therefore, the Sparse Non-negative Matrix Factorization (SNMF) can incorporate the intrinsic geometry of the data, which is combined with implicit information. Thus, SNMF can realize a more compact representation for the sparse data. In this paper, we study the Sparse Non-negative Matrix Factorization (SNMF). We use Multiplicative Update Algorithm (MUA) that computes the factorization by applying update on both matrices W and H. Accordingly, to address these issue, we propose a two models to implement a parallel version of SNMF on GPUs using NVIDIA CUDA framework. To optimize SNMF, we use cuSPARSE optimized library to compute the algebraic operations in MUA where sparse matrices A, W and H are stored in Compressed Sparse Row (CSR) format. At last, our contribution is validated through a series of experiments achieved on two input sets i.e. a set of randomly generated matrices and a set of benchmark matrices from real applications with different sizes and densities. We show that our algorithms allow performance improvements compared to baseline implementations. The speedup on multi-GPU platform can exceed $11\times$ as well as the Ratio can exceed 91%.

Keywords: SNMF · Unsupervised learning algorithm · Multiplicative update algorithm · Sparse matrix · Compressed formats · Optimization

© Springer Nature Switzerland AG 2022
Y. Lai et al. (Eds.): ICA3PP 2021, LNCS 13156, pp. 161–177, 2022.
https://doi.org/10.1007/978-3-030-95388-1_11

1   Introduction

Many real-life data, such as gene expressions, health data, image pixels, electronic books, online documents, are known increasingly to be non-negative [10]. They can be arranged in to a matrix which is often called a non-negative matrix. Accordingly, generalized computational methods are required for extracting informations [28]. Although, great success has been achieved by various matrix factorization methods, such as Principal Component Analysis (PCA) [15], Singular Value Decomposition (SVD) [6], Independent Component Analysis (ICA) [5] and Network Component Analysis (NCA) [22]. The general factorizations of non-negative matrices by PCA, ICA, SVD and NCA contain negative information entries and thus have difficulties for interpretation and representation [10]. Therefore, Non-negative Matrix Factorization (NMF) has advantages over the other dimension reduction methods (e.g., SVD) since NMF allows only non-subtractive combinations of non-negative components. This non-negative constraint eventually leads to the parts-based representation of NMF [18].

Recently, the NMF has become a very popular machine learning method [3]. Technically, NMF seeks to identify a product of two non-negative matrices that provides a good approximation to the original matrix (e.g., $A \approx W * H$). This results in a reduced representation of the original data that can be seen either as a feature extraction or as a dimensionality reduction technique. NMF has successfully been applied in several applications of science including machine learning applications [32], biomedical applications [7], data clustering [12], etc.

From another viewpoint, the most of these applications using NMF method for a large data matrix making this method computationally space-time consuming. Therefore, several algorithms of NMF have been proposed. Among them, the basic NMF does not impose sparseness on the decomposition process. The NMF gives a holistic representation, instead of independent blocks information on some datasets. For this issue, in many applications, the constraint of sparseness can give better representation, revealing the local features or latent structures information in the data. Thus, many methods that use additional constraints to enforce the sparse decomposition have been proposed, such as local NMF [21], fisher NMF [14], and sparse NMF [8].

In this study, we will use Sparse Non-negative Matrix Factorization (SNMF) with sparseness constraints which is widely used in many datasets applications such as bioinformatics [8], image processing [13], data clustering [25], etc. Most of these applications using a sparse data matrix representation (e.g., bioinformatics). We notes that a matrix is called sparse if it has a large (resp. weak) number of zero (resp. non-zero) [26]. From the viewpoint of optimization, we propose a parallel model for parallelizing the SNMF on a GPU platform using Multiplicative Update Algorithm (MUA). We use the cuSPARSE optimized library to compute the algebraic operations in MUA where sparse matrices A, W and H are stored in Compressed Sparse Row (CSR) format, since it is the most used format in the literature [26]. In order to optimize computational performance, we propose another optimized parallel model for parallelizing the SNMF version on a multi-GPU platform. Afterwards, we implement a parallel version of the

SNMF on two GPUs using the NVIDIA CUDA framework. The structure of this paper is organized as follows:

Section 2 gives the related work, Sect. 3 introduces the general concepts of the NMF and the SNMF methods, Sect. 4 devoted to the proposed optimization methods for the SNMF technique, implemented versions and discussions are shown in Sect. 5. Finally, the conclusion of the paper is presented in the Sect. 6.

2   Related Work

Non-negative Matrix Factorization (NMF) was first presented by Lee et al. in 1999. It is a subspace method [18]. The NMF refers to the set of problems on approximating non-negative matrix as the product of several non-negative matrices dimensionally lower than the input matrix [19]. Owing to its innate interpretability and good performance in practice, NMF has been successfully applied to a broad range of important various applications in areas including computer vision, community detection in social networks, visualization, recommender systems, bioinformatics, etc. Lee et al. [18] proposed the basic NMF method which is used to learn parts of faces and semantic features of text. Wang et al. [31] proposed a novel supervised NMF method in neural networks, by exploring the class label information and using it to constrain the learning of coefficient vectors of the data samples. Kannan et al. [17] used NMF methods to address the anomaly detection in the underlying data. Trigeorgis et al. [29] proposed a deep semi-NMF method which has a close relation to k-means clustering with machine learning algorithms for images clustering. In other domains, Vilamala et al. [30] proposed the NMF method for the classification of human brain tumors. These methods acquire good results with different types of tumors. The most of these applications used NMF method for a large data matrix. This latter, make NMF method computationally poor with big datasets analysis. Therefore, several works have been proposed to improve NMF performances by adding sparseness constraints to NMF algorithms. Hoyer et al. [11] used Sparse Non-negative Matrix Factorization (SNMF) and proved that the adding sparseness constraint explicitly allows them to discover parts-based representations that are qualitatively better than those given by the basic NMF. Chen et al. [4] proposed SNMF method for ultrasound factor analysis and showed that the method works well in comparison to the truth in computer simulations. Guo et al. [9] applied the SNMF method in face image processing and recognition, the reconstructed faces by the proposed method with the SNMF are clearer and more recognizable and the recognition rate is three percentage points higher by comparison. The SNMF has an important role in cancer discovery and classification. X Yang et al. [33] presented an integrated tumor classification framework with the SNMF method by exploiting information in existing available samples.

There are some studies on accelerating the NMF as well as the SNMF in parallel and distributed platforms. Platoš et al. [27] developed the NMF method on a GPU platform by using the CUDA framework with small dense matrices. Kannan et al. [16] presented a parallel implementation of the NMF algorithm using (i) tools from the field of High-Performance Computing (HPC),

(ii) Message Passing Interface (MPI) standard to organize interprocessor communication. Mejía-Roa et al. [24] used the NMF approach on multi-GPUs systems in bioinformatics. For the SNMF, Liu et al. [23] used these latter to solve Dyadic Data Analysis problem on a cloud platform using MapReduce. Li et al. [20] presented the SNMF on a multi-GPUs platform for recommender systems. To address the problem of limited memory on a single GPU in [20], authors proposed a multi-GPU CuSNMF approach with low communication overhead between multi-GPUs.

In all studies, we observe that (i) the communication overhead between multi-GPUs, CPU-GPU consume a relevant percentage of computation running time, (ii) space-limited memory on a single GPU owing to high dimension intermediate matrices, (iii) the spatio-temporal complexity of the NMF and the SNMF algorithms has a very important role in the effectiveness of the studies.

3   General Concepts

3.1   Non-negative Matrix Factorization

The NMF method is applied to minimize the dimensionality of data with a representation learning technique. It aims to learn two low rank factors $W \in \mathbb{R}_+^{m \times k}$ and $H \in \mathbb{R}_+^{k \times n}$ to approximate a given input non-negative data matrix $A \in \mathbb{R}_+^{m \times n}$, such that $A \approx W * H$. Here, $\mathbb{R}_+^{m \times n}$ denotes the set of data $m \times n$ matrices with non-negative entries [18,19]. The product $W.H$ is an approximate factorization. An appropriate decision on the value of k is critical in practice, but the choice of k is very often problem dependent. In most cases, however, k is usually chosen such that $k << \min\{m,n\}$ in which case $W.H$ can be thought of as a compressed form of the data in the matrix A. There is a vast literature on algorithms for NMF and their convergence properties. The most existing NMF algorithms in the literature can be classified to one of three general algorithms: Multiplicative Update Algorithm (MUA), Alternating Least Squares (ALS) and Gradient Descent (GD) algorithms [2]. The general structure of all NMF algorithms is given in Algorithm 1 where W and H are initialized with random non-negative values before the iteration starts.

Algorithm 1: General NMF Algorithm

---

1 Given a data matrix $A \in \mathbb{R}_+^{m \times n}$ and $k << \min\{m,n\}$;
2 $W = \text{rand}\ (m,k)$ initialize W as random dense matrix;
3 $H = \text{rand}\ (k,n)$ initialize H as random dense matrix;
4 **for** $i = 1$ *to maxiter* **do**
5 | Update W and H ;
6 | Check termination criterions;
7 **end**

The variable of maxiter specifies the maximum number of iterations for the complete algorithm with both randomly initialized non-negative matrices W

and H. Hence, the NMF update steps are processed iteratively until a maximum number of iterations is reached. Formally, Lee et al. [19] proposed the original method of the NMF algorithm which is also known as Multiplicative Update Algorithm (MUA). Due to their status as the first well-known NMF algorithms, the MUA have become a baseline NMF algorithm against others algorithms (i.e. ALS and GD). A solution to the NMF problem can be obtained by solving the following optimization object function:

$$\min_{W,H} = \|A - W.H\|_F^2 \qquad (1)$$

The $\|.\|_F^2$ is the Frobenius norm where the entries elements of both matrices W and H need to be non-negative. The minimum in (1) is typically non-zero. If the approximation error of the algorithm drops below a predefined threshold, or if the change between two successive iterations is very small, the algorithm may terminate before maximum iterations are processed. Therefore, the algorithm has converged to a limit point in the interior of the feasible region; this point is a stationary point. This latter may be a local minimum at the end. The NMF with MUA is given in Algorithm 2.

Algorithm 2: The MUA for NMF method

---

1   Given a data matrix $A \in \mathbb{R}_+^{m \times n}$ and $k << \min\{m, n\}$;
2   $W = \text{rand } (m, k)$ initialize W as random dense matrix;
3   $H = \text{rand } (k, n)$ initialize H as random dense matrix;
4   **for** $i = 1$ to $maxiter$ **do**
5   $\quad$ (MUA) $H = H \otimes (W^T A) \oslash ((W^T W H) + \epsilon)$;
6   $\quad$ (MUA) $W = W \otimes (A H^T) \oslash ((W H H^T) + \epsilon)$;
7   $\quad$ Check termination criterions;
8   **end**

Where ϵ is a constant equal to 10^{-9} added in each update rule to avoid division by zero, W^T and H^T represent respectively the transposition of matrix W and H, the symbol $\otimes$ denotes the Hadamard product (element-wise multiplication) and $\oslash$ denotes the Hadamard division (element-wise division). Lee et al. [19] proved two main properties of this algorithm. First, the objective function (1) is non-increasing with each iteration. Second, W and H become constant, if and only if they represent a stationary point or a maximum number of iterations are reached.

3.2   Sparse Non-negative Matrix Factorization

The SNMF is a special case of the NMF method, the algorithms for general NMF cannot be directly applied to solve the SNMF issues. Further, the NMF has no control over the sparseness constraints of the decomposition with sparse data matrix i.e. $A \approx W * H$. Actually, a few works have been proposed to add sparseness constraints to the basic NMF method [8,11,13]. Moreover, their SNMF algorithms are notoriously fast to converge. They require a small number of iterations compared to the basic NMF algorithms.

In this paper, we study the Sparse Non-negative Matrix Factorization (SNMF) where W and H are enforced to be sparse. Therefore, we use two sparseness constraints (also called regularization parameters) $\alpha, \beta \in [0 ; 1]$. To this end, we presented a modified SNMF algorithm described in the Algorithm 3, where α is the sparseness constraint of the data matrix W, and β is the sparseness constraint of the data matrix H. Given initial matrices $W0 \in \mathbb{R}_+^{m \times k}$ and $H0 \in \mathbb{R}_+^{k \times n}$ with random entries, the SNMF algorithm consists of an iterative application of the following two steps:

$$H_{i,j}^{t+1} = H_{i,j}^t \otimes (W^T A)_{i,j} \oslash ((W^T W H^t + \beta H^t)_{i,j} + \epsilon) \qquad (2)$$

$$W_{i,j}^{t+1} = W_{i,j}^t \otimes (A H^T)_{i,j} \oslash ((W^t H H^T + \alpha W^t)_{i,j} + \epsilon) \qquad (3)$$

Here $(\cdot)_{i,j}$ refers to the entry in row "i" and column "j" of the data matrix in parentheses and "t" denotes the iteration index.

Algorithm 3: The SNMF Algorithm with Sparseness Constraints

---

1 Given a data matrix $A \in \mathbb{R}_+^{m \times n}$ and $k << \min\{m, n\}$;
2 $W = \text{rand} (m, k)$ initialize W as random dense matrix;
3 $H = \text{rand} (k, n)$ initialize H as random dense matrix;
4 **for** $i = 1$ to maxiter **do**
5   (2) $H = H \otimes (W^T A) \oslash ((W^T W H + \beta H) + \epsilon)$;
6   (3) $W = W \otimes (A H^T) \oslash ((W H H^T + \alpha W) + \epsilon)$;
7   Check termination criterions;
8 **end**

---

4   Proposed Optimization Methods for SNMF Technique

Our aim in this work is (i) to study the optimization of the SNMF method using the Multiplicative Update Algorithm (MUA), (ii) to propose two parallel optimized models for the SNMF method with low communication overhead, (iii) To reduce space-time complexity of the SNMF algorithm.

4.1   Single GPU Computation Model

In this section, we present a parallel model for parallelizing the SNMF method on a single GPU platform (Fig. 1). We use different intermediate matrices to compute several algebraic operations in MUA such that matrix-matrix product, matrix-matrix addition, Hadamard product and Hadamard division, etc.

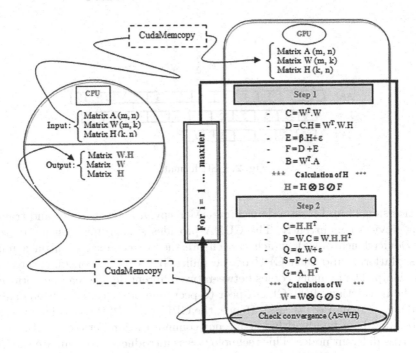

Fig. 1. Parallel Model on a Single GPU Platform.

Moreover, to reduce the spatio-temporal complexity, we use a Sparse Compressed Formats (CSF) [26]. We use the Compressed Sparse Row (CSR) format where all matrices in MUA are acceded row-wise, since CSR is the most used format in the literature, it provides a best performance and improves data locality. From there, to store a given input data matrix $A(m, n)$ having NNZ_A non-zero element values (see Fig. 2), CSR format uses a data-structure of three arrays denoted: AA, of size NNZ_A, to store the non-zero elements of A on a row-wise (from row 1 to row m), JA, of size NNZ_A, to store column indices of each stored element in AA and IA, of size $m + 1$, to store pointers on the head of each row in arrays AA and JA with $IA(m) = NNZ_A$. At last, our contribution with a single GPU model is implemented using the CUDA framework with the cuSPARSE optimized library that contains a set of basic linear algebra sub-routines used for handling sparse matrices operations.

4.2 Multi-GPUs Computation Model

In this section, we present a multi-GPUs parallel model for parallelizing the SNMF method (Fig. 3). The model of computation on a multi-GPUs platform is presented where two GPUs are connected to the host by Peripheral Communication Interconnect express (PCIe). Therefore, the CUDA framework can perform computation on the device and data transfers between the device and the host concurrently. Moreover, it has two or more copy engines, which can operate

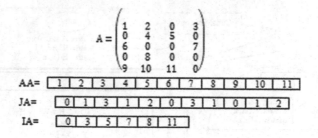

Fig. 2. CSR format.

data transfers to and from a device (cudaMemcpyDeviceToDevice) and transfer among devices concurrently. The CUDA provides synchronization instructions (cudaDeviceSynchronize), which can ensure the correct execution on a multi-GPUs platform, and each GPU of the multi-GPUs has a consumer/producer relationship. The memory copies between two different devices can be performed after the instruction of the CUDA peer-to-peer memory access has been enabled (cudaDeviceEnablePeerAccess). Hence, the GPUDirect P2P technology was created to allow high-bandwidth, low-latency communication between GPUs within and across different nodes. This technology was introduced to eliminate the CPU overheads when one GPU needs to communicate with another. GPUDirect P2P technology depends on both source and destination device being on the same PCIe fabric.

5   Experimental Study and Analysis

A series of experimentations have been achieved in order to evaluate the practical performance of the parallel SNMF versions and to validate our approach with both parallel SNMF models (see Fig. 1 and Fig. 3). For this purpose, we use two input datasets i.e. (i) randomly generated input data matrices (see Table 1), (ii) a set of benchmark data matrices from real applications with different sizes and densities (see Table 2) [1]. The input data matrix $A \in \mathbb{R}_+^{m \times n}$, the data matrix $W \in \mathbb{R}_+^{m \times k}$ and the data matrix $H \in \mathbb{R}_+^{k \times n}$. We denote by "$d$" the density of data matrix with $n * m$ dimension such that $d = 100 * NNZ/(n * m)$ where NNZ denotes nonzero elements. As previously mentioned, the choice value of k is critical in practice and it is very often problem dependent. However, in our study, k is chosen randomly in the range [5 .. 100] such that $k << \min\{m, n\}$.

5.1   Environment

We use a machine from the "gemini" cluster on the Grid'5000 platform which is equipped with two "Intel Xeon E5-2698 v4" processors of 2.20 GHz where each one contains 20 cores. The machine contains 8 GPUs. Therefore, each one of these GPUs is an NVIDIA Tesla V100 SXM2 of 32 GB operating at a frequency

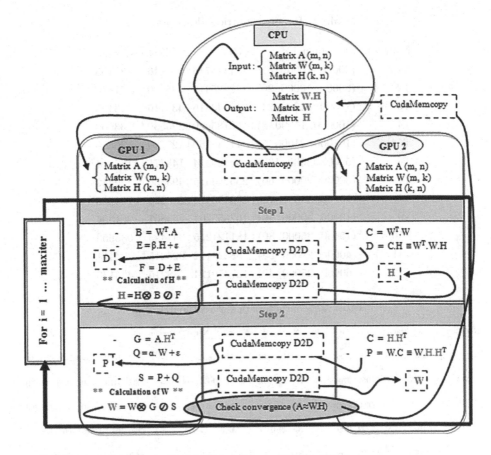

Fig. 3. Parallel Model on a 2GPUs Platform.

of 1290 MHz. Furthermore, the GPUs platform is equipped with the latest CUDA framework. Hence, the multi-GPUs platform with two GPUs is used to implement and evaluate our approach. Let us mention that our tests are performed on the UNIX operating system (Ubuntu version 17.10) and the algorithms of the SNMF are coded in the C programming language. The running time correspond to the mean of several runs.

5.2 Performance Evaluation on Single GPU Platform

In order to prove the efficiency of both SNMF models, a baseline implementation of the NMF on CPU is done. We use the BLAS (Basic Linear Algebra Subprograms) optimized library and the LAPACK (Linear Algebra Package) library to compute several algebraic operations. The experimental study shows that the baseline implementation of the NMF-CPU provides a large running time. Hence, it requires much iteration that provides a slow convergence to a stationary point. Thus, the NMF algorithm has a poor quality on the CPU essentially when we have a big data analysis with important density. Table 3, Table 4, Fig. 4

Table 1. Random matrices description

Notation	Size (m, n, k)	NNZ_A	NNZ_W	NNZ_H
T1	(90000, 7000, 16)	171143716	165116	32103
T2	(80000, 10000, 20)	178225413	325420	77810
T3	(70000, 12000, 24)	212143416	435116	123103
T4	(100000, 15000, 8)	460185420	225530	33606
T5	(101000, 21000, 5)	517248350	127720	26856
T6	(5000, 43000, 100)	52123344	145371	1133214
T7	(30000, 20000, 60)	235243615	493856	529442
T8	(20000, 30000, 70)	203156374	533224	754215
T9	(10000, 40000, 90)	162655703	263801	1231304
T10	(15000, 35000, 80)	181121215	341423	985653
T11	(40000, 22000, 55)	88224112	623215	324111
T12	(60000, 25000, 40)	127350124	788215	423170

Table 2. Characteristics of real matrices

Notation	Name	Structure	m	n	k	NNZ	d	Notation	Name	Structure	m	n	k	NNZ	d
M1	lp_osa_07		1118	25067	25	144812	0.51	M2	c8_mat11		4562	5721	100	2462970	9.43
M3	landmark		71952	2704	8	1151232	0.59	M4	lp_osa_14		2337	54797	10	317097	0.24
M5	TF15		6334	7742	90	80057	0.16	M6	IG5-14		6735	7621	80	173337	0.33
M7	ak2010		45292	45292	5	108549	0.005	M8	lp_osa_30		4350	104374	15	604488	0.13
M9	IG5-15		11369	11987	70	323509	0.23	M10	IG5-16		18846	18485	50	588326	0.16
M11	TF16		15437	19321	60	216173	0.07	M12	mat-2005		40421	40421	20	175693	0.01
M13	IG5-17		30162	27944	40	1035008	0.12	M14	TF17		38132	48630	30	586218	0.01

and Fig. 6 illustrate a comparison of the running time for different implementations. For this issue, the constraint of sparseness can give better performance. So, we use an additional sparseness constraints (α and β) to enforce the sparse decomposition of both matrices W and H. Thereby, we get a sparse version of the NMF method (SNMF-CPU). We note that the SNMF-CPU gives the lowest number of iterations compared to the NMF-CPU. It gives an effective data representation. Table 3 summarizes the obtained results for computation time of the NMF-CPU and the SNMF-CPU. In order to optimize the SNMF algorithm, we propose an optimized parallel model for parallelizing the SNMF algorithm on a GPU platform using the CUDA parallel programming framework (see Fig. 1). Afterward, to optimize the SNMF-GPU, we use the CUDA Sparse Matrix cuSPARSE optimized library to compute the several algebraic operations in MUA.

Moreover, to reduce the space-time complexity, we use the CSR format to store all matrices in MUA (see Algorithm 3).

Results Using Random Matrices. Using a set of random matrices, the experimental results show that the SNMF-GPU version gives the best performance (Fig. 4 and Table 3). Therefore, it gives the lowest time complexity compared to other versions i.e. the NMF-CPU and the SNMF-CPU. We used the following Ratio defined by:

$$Ratio = (1 - [run\_opt/run\_v]) * 100 \qquad (4)$$

Where run_opt is the running time of the best version (the SNMF-GPU in this case) and run_v is the running time of the NMF-CPU version. It is necessary to highlight that the performance evaluation considers not only the computation time but also the communication time between CPU-GPU and they consume a relevant percentage of the running time. It is very relevant, especially for a big data matrix with high values of n, m and NNZ (see Table 3). The speedup is graphically illustrated in Fig. 5. We notice that the SNMF-GPU has an average speedup that can reach 2× compared to the SNMF-CPU, as well as it gives an average ratio that can reach 48% compared to the NMF-CPU.

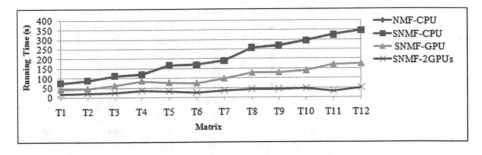

Fig. 4. Comparison of running time for random matrices.

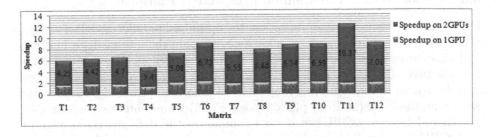

Fig. 5. Improvement speedup for random matrices.

Results Using Benchmark Matrices. When we use a set of benchmark matrices (see Table 2), the experimental results show that the SNMF-GPU version allows the performance improvements compared to the NMF-CPU and the SNMF-CPU implementations. It gives the lowest time complexity compared to other methods. The efficiency of the SNMF-GPU is essentially due to the reduced number of accesses to all matrices in Algorithm 3 by using CSR format, the cuSPARSE optimized library, the CUDA framework and the GPU platform. Hence, the SNMF-GPU gives a fast convergence to a stationary point; it requires a few iterations number compared to the basic NMF-CPU and the SNMF-CPU. Table 4 and Fig. 6 illustrate the comparison of the running time for different implementations with benchmark matrices. The SNMF-GPU provides a good performance essentially when we have a large data analysis. Further, the average speedup can reach 2× compared to the SNMF-CPU, as well as the average ratio can reach 44% compared to the NMF-CPU.

Table 3. Summary table of running time, improvement ratio (%) and speedup for random matrices

Notation	NMF-CPU (s)	SNMF-CPU (s)	SNMF-GPU (s)	SNMF-2GPUs (s)	Ratio-GPU	Speedup-GPU	Ratio-2GPUs	Speedup-2GPUs
T1	72.50	72.44	41.71	17.04	42.46	1.73	76.49	4.25
T2	86.45	86.32	45.09	19.51	47.84	1.91	77.45	4.42
T3	110.17	109.36	61.13	23.25	44.51	1.78	78.89	4.70
T4	119.26	118.61	84.50	34.85	29.14	1.40	70.77	3.40
T5	166.31	166.09	77.36	32.67	53.48	2.14	80.35	5.08
T6	169.84	167.48	73.64	24.94	56.64	2.27	85.31	6.72
T7	189.71	188.16	97.12	33.89	48.80	1.93	82.13	5.55
T8	256.26	255.53	126.46	43.57	50.65	2.02	82.99	5.86
T9	268.56	266.01	127.22	40.67	52.62	2.09	84.85	6.54
T10	293.13	291.52	136.61	44.22	53.39	2.13	84.91	6.56
T11	323.38	322.43	168.22	31.07	47.98	1.91	90.39	10.37
T12	344.97	344.72	172.82	49.11	49.90	1.99	85.76	7.01

5.3   Performance Evaluation on Multi-GPU Platform

From another viewpoint of optimization, the optimized parallel model on a single GPU platform requires many memory space to store the intermediate matrices and this causes a problem on the GPU memory as well as the communication times between CPU-GPU consume a relevant percentage of running time. Hence, in order to solve these issues, we propose to use another optimized parallel model with a multi-GPUs (2GPUs) platform (see Fig. 3) whose intermediate matrices are shared between 2GPUs in order to minimize the data matrix storage on each GPU memory. This model can reduce the communication times by using GPUDirect P2P access/transfers technique between the GPU1 and the GPU2 without returns to the CPU on each operation.

Results Using Random Matrices. The experimental results show that the SNMF-2GPUs gives the lowest time complexity compared to other methods. This efficiency is essentially due to the fast convergence to a stationary point in a few iterations number. Table 3 and Fig. 4 illustrate the efficiency of the SNMF-2GPUs using a set of random matrices. As previously mentioned, we use the ratio defined in (4) where run_opt in this case is the running time of the SNMF-2GPUs and run_v is the running time of the NMF-CPU. The speedup is graphically presented in Fig. 5. We notice that the SNMF-2GPUs gives an average speedup that can reach 5× compared to the SNMF-CPU, as well as it gives an average ratio that can reach 81% (Table 3 and Fig. 5).

Table 4. Summary table of improvement running time, ratio (%) and speedup for benchmark matrices

Notation	NMF-CPU (s)	SNMF-CPU (s)	SNMF-GPU (s)	SNMF-2GPUs (s)	Ratio-GPU	Speedup-GPU	Ratio-2GPUs	Speedup-2GPUs
M1	44.96	41.28	30.30	10.28	32.60	1.36	77.13	4.01
M2	49.28	48.18	20.84	7.56	57.71	2.31	84.65	6.37
M3	56.57	55.41	24.35	16.23	56.95	2.27	71.30	3.41
M4	57.04	53.24	38.29	16.70	32.87	1.39	70.72	3.18
M5	93.54	92.50	41.57	10.69	55.55	2.22	88.57	8.65
M6	89.05	87.77	38.93	10.60	56.28	2.25	88.09	8.28
M7	275.15	272.46	163.26	52.61	40.66	1.66	80.87	5.17
M8	359.81	353.72	202.01	55.89	43.85	1.75	84.46	6.32
M9	404.56	402.83	184.73	36.17	54.33	2.18	91.05	11.13
M10	410.65	404.05	215.89	61.08	47.42	1.87	85.12	6.61
M11	509.78	506.95	250.65	82.23	50.83	2.02	83.86	6.16
M12	689.12	685.09	330.54	96.91	52.03	2.07	85.93	7.06
M13	1187.83	1167.54	543.96	108.78	54.20	2.14	90.84	10.73
M14	1689.06	1681.06	1118.23	362.42	33.79	1.50	78.54	6.63

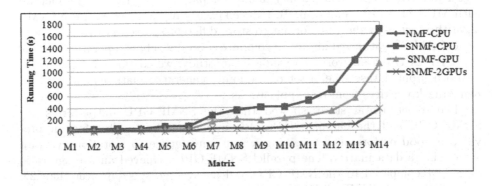

Fig. 6. Comparison of running time for benchmark matrices.

Results Using Benchmark Matrices. As a matter of fact, with the benchmark input matrices, the SNMF-2GPUs allows performance improvements compared to the remaining implementations methods. Table 4, Fig. 6 illustrates a comparison of the running time of the SNMF-2GPUs using a set of benchmark matrices. The speedup of the SNMF-2GPUs is illustrated in Table 4 and Fig. 7. Therefore, the SNMF-2GPUs gives an average ratio that can reach 82% and an average speedup that can reach 6× compared to the SNMF-CPU. The speedup on a multi-GPUs platform can exceed 11× as well as the ratio can exceed 98%. We can conclude that our approach with 2GPUs is the best using method among the remaining implementations.

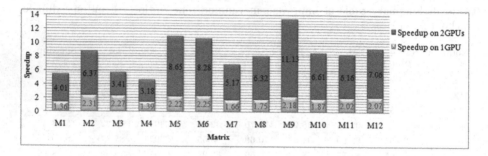

Fig. 7. Improvement speedup for benchmark matrices.

6   Conclusion and Future Work

In this paper, we have studied the optimization of Sparse Non-negative Matrix Factorization (SNMF) method with Multiplicative Update Algorithm (MUA). We enforced both matrices W and H to be sparse when two sparseness constraints α, $\beta \in [0; 1]$ are used with Non-negative Matrix Factorization (NMF) algorithm. We proposed a parallel model for parallelizing the SNMF method with MUA on a GPU platform. To reduce space-time complexity of the SNMF algorithm, we used the CSR format to store different sparse matrices. We used the cuSPARSE optimized library to compute several algebraic operations on the NVIDIA CUDA framework. To validate our study, we conducted experiments on both input datasets i.e. a set of randomly generated matrices and a set of benchmark matrices from real applications.

The experimental study showed that the SNMF-GPU outperforms the SNMF-CPU and the baseline NMF-CPU implementations. Therefore, it provided a good performance by giving a fast convergence to a stationary point with a large data matrix. The parallel SNMF-GPU achieved an average ratio over 44% compared to the NMF-CPU and an average speedup over than 2× compared to the SNMF-CPU. According to the previous results, we concluded that the communication times between CPU-GPU and the space-limited GPU memory are played an important role in the performance of our approach. For these reasons, we proposed another parallel model for parallelizing the SNMF algorithm on a multi-GPU platform especially on 2GPUs. Therefore, the SNMF-2GPUs improved the performance by provided a minimum number of iterations with MUA. It rapidly converged very well to a stationary point. Thence, the SNMF-2GPUs reduced the space-time complexity by shared intermediate matrices between 2GPUs and it optimized the communication times between host / device by used GPUDirect peer-to-peer (P2P) technology. Furthermore, the SNMF-2GPUs achieved an average ratio over 82% compared to the NMF-CPU and an average speedup 6× compared to SNMF-CPU. To conclude, we can say that our work arises some interesting points constituting our near future work.

We may cite (i) achieving a series of experiments in other programming environments to establish more extensive comparisons, (ii) to optimize the SNMF-2GPUs, sparse matrix fragmentation algorithms with load balancing can be applied, (iii) to optimize the communication times, a new model on nGPUs platform will be developed.

References

1. Tim Davis Matrix Collection. http://sparse.tamu.edu/
2. Berry, M.W., Browne, M., Langville, A.N., Pauca, V.P., Plemmons, R.J.: Algorithms and applications for approximate nonnegative matrix factorization. Comput. Stat. Data Anal. **52**(1), 155–173 (2007)
3. Bisot, V., Serizel, R., Essid, S., Richard, G.: Supervised nonnegative matrix factorization for acoustic scene classification. IEEE AASP Challenge on Detection and Classification of Acoustic Scenes and Events (DCASE), pp. 62–69 (2016)
4. Chen, X., Wu, K., Ding, M., Sang, N.: Sparse non-negative matrix factorizations for ultrasound factor analysis. Optik **124**(23), 5891–5897 (2013)
5. Comon, P., Jutten, C.: Handbook of Blind Source Separation: Independent component analysis and applications. Academic press (2010)
6. De Lathauwer, L., De Moor, B., Vandewalle, J.: A multilinear singular value decomposition. SIAM J. Matrix Anal. Appl. **21**(4), 1253–1278 (2000)
7. Devarajan, K.: Nonnegative matrix factorization: an analytical and interpretive tool in computational biology. PLoS Comput. Biol. **4**(7) (2008)
8. Gao, Y., Church, G.: Improving molecular cancer class discovery through sparse non-negative matrix factorization. Bioinformatics **21**(21), 3970–3975 (2005)
9. Guo, Z., Zhang, Y.: A sparse corruption non-negative matrix factorization method and application in face image processing & recognition. Measurement **136**, 429–437 (2019)
10. He, P., Xu, X., Ding, J., Fan, B.: Low-rank nonnegative matrix factorization on stiefel manifold. Inf. Sci. **514**, 131–148 (2020)
11. Hoyer, P.O.: Non-negative matrix factorization with sparseness constraints. J. Mach. Learn. Res. **5**, 1457–1469 (2004)
12. Huang, S., Wang, H., Li, T., Li, T., Xu, Z.: Robust graph regularized nonnegative matrix factorization for clustering. Data Min. Knowl. Disc. **32**(2), 483–503 (2017). https://doi.org/10.1007/s10618-017-0543-9
13. Inuganti, S., Gampala, V.: Image compression using constrained non-negative matrix factorization. Int. J. **3**(10) (2013)

14. Jia, Y.W.Y., Turk, C.H.M.: Fisher non-negative matrix factorization for learning local features. In: Proceedings of the Asian Conference on Computer Vision, pp. 27–30. Citeseer (2004)
15. Jolliffe, I.T., Cadima, J.: Principal component analysis: a review and recent developments. Philosophical Trans. Roy. Soc. A: Math. Phys. Eng. Sci. 374(2065), 20150202 (2016)
16. Kannan, R., Ballard, G., Park, H.: A high-performance parallel algorithm for non-negative matrix factorization. ACM SIGPLAN Notices 51(8), 1–11 (2016)
17. Kannan, R., Woo, H., Aggarwal, C.C., Park, H.: Outlier detection for text data: An extended version. arXiv preprint arXiv:1701.01325 (2017)
18. Lee, D.D., Seung, H.S.: Learning the parts of objects by non-negative matrix factorization. Nature 401(6755), 788–791 (1999)
19. Lee, D.D., Seung, H.S.: Algorithms for non-negative matrix factorization. In: Advances in Neural Information Processing Systems, pp. 556–562 (2001)
20. Li, H., Li, K., Peng, J., Hu, J., Li, K.: An efficient parallelization approach for large-scale sparse non-negative matrix factorization using kullback-leibler divergence on multi-gpu. In: 2017 IEEE International Symposium on Parallel and Distributed Processing with Applications and 2017 IEEE International Conference on Ubiquitous Computing and Communications (ISPA/IUCC), pp. 511–518. IEEE (2017)
21. Li, S.Z., Hou, X.W., Zhang, H.J., Cheng, Q.S.: Learning spatially localized, parts-based representation. In: Proceedings of the 2001 IEEE Computer Society Conference on Computer Vision and Pattern Recognition, CVPR 2001, vol. 1, p. I. IEEE (2001)
22. Liao, J.C., Boscolo, R., Yang, Y.L., Tran, L.M., Sabatti, C., Roychowdhury, V.P.: Network component analysis: reconstruction of regulatory signals in biological systems. Proc. Natl. Acad. Sci. 100(26), 15522–15527 (2003)
23. Liu, C., Yang, H.C., Fan, J., He, L.W., Wang, Y.M.: Distributed nonnegative matrix factorization for web-scale dyadic data analysis on mapreduce. In: Proceedings of the 19th International Conference on World Wide Web, pp. 681–690 (2010)
24. Mejía-Roa, E., et al.: Biclustering and classification analysis in gene expression using nonnegative matrix factorization on multi-gpu systems. In: 2011 11th International Conference on Intelligent Systems Design and Applications, pp. 882–887. IEEE (2011)
25. Meng, Y., Shang, R., Jiao, L., Zhang, W., Yuan, Y., Yang, S.: Feature selection based dual-graph sparse non-negative matrix factorization for local discriminative clustering. Neurocomputing 290, 87–99 (2018)
26. Moumni, H., Hamdi, O., Ezouaoui, S.: Algorithms and performance evaluation for sparse matrix product on grid'5000 intel xeon processor. In: 2018 IEEE/ACS 15th International Conference on Computer Systems and Applications (AICCSA), pp. 1–7. IEEE (2018)
27. Platoš, J., Gajdoš, P., Krömer, P., Snášel, V.: Non-negative matrix factorization on GPU. In: Zavoral, F., Yaghob, J., Pichappan, P., El-Qawasmeh, E. (eds.) NDT 2010. CCIS, vol. 87, pp. 21–30. Springer, Heidelberg (2010). https://doi.org/10.1007/978-3-642-14292-5_4
28. Tian, L.P., Luo, P., Wang, H., Zheng, H., Wu, F.X.: CASNMF: a converged algorithm for symmetrical nonnegative matrix factorization. Neurocomputing 275, 2031–2040 (2018)
29. Trigeorgis, G., Bousmalis, K., Zafeiriou, S., Schuller, B.W.: A deep matrix factorization method for learning attribute representations. IEEE Trans. Pattern Anal. Mach. Intell. 39(3), 417–429 (2016)

30. Vilamala, A., Lisboa, P.J., Ortega-Martorell, S., Vellido, A.: Discriminant convex non-negative matrix factorization for the classification of human brain tumours. Pattern Recogn. Lett. **34**(14), 1734–1747 (2013)
31. Wang, J.J.Y., Gao, X.: Max-min distance nonnegative matrix factorization. Neural Netw. **61**, 75–84 (2015)
32. Wang, S., Deng, C., Lin, W., Huang, G.B., Zhao, B.: NMF-based image quality assessment using extreme learning machine. IEEE Trans. Cybern. **47**(1), 232–243 (2016)
33. Yang, X., et al.: An integrated inverse space sparse representation framework for tumor classification. Pattern Recogn. **93**, 293–311 (2019)

HaDPA: A Data-Partition Algorithm for Data Parallel Applications on Heterogeneous HPC Platforms

Jingbo Li, Li Han, Yuqi Qu, and Xingjun Zhang[(✉)]

School of Computer Science and Technology,
Xi'an Jiaotong University, Xi'an 710049, Shaanxi, China
xjzhang@xjtu.edu.cn

Abstract. As the heterogeneity of the high-performance computing platform and the scale of data-parallel applications increased significantly, data partition becomes a key issue. Recent works use computation performance model to optimize the data partition algorithm generally. However, these methods cannot take the communication overhead into account, resulting in incompatibility for the applications with high communication ratio or unbalanced communication topology. In this paper, a new heterogeneous-aware data partition algorithm, HaDPA, is proposed. Firstly, the computation and communication overhead are predicted by suitable computation and communication performance models given a partition topology. Then, the search tree is constructed, and the hierarchical deep first search with branch and bound is designed to obtain the optimal solution, which makes up the whole HaDPA process with the constructing of optimizing model. Finally, to verify the performance of the algorithm, Matrix multiplication and axial compressor rotor applications are tested on TianHe-2A supercomputer. Experimental results show that HaDPA can effectively reduce the execution time of data parallel applications. What's more, the impact factors of performance improvement are analyzed and explained. Regression model proofs that the communication to computation ratio matters more to the data-partition on heterogeneous HPC platforms. Besides, compared with HPOPTA, the HaDPA improvement ratio increases with a higher communication ratio and a lower heterogeneity of hardware platform.

Keywords: Data parallel · Performance model · Heterogeneous computing · Data partition algorithm · Load balance

1 Introduction

As the continuous development of chip technology and the tight integration of multicore processors and accelerators like GPU, high performance computing (HPC) platforms become more and more highly heterogeneous [1]. There are 140 supercomputers with GPU of Nvidia as accelerator and many other supercomputers with AMD GPU and Intel Xeon Phi on the latest Top500 ranking [2].

© Springer Nature Switzerland AG 2022
Y. Lai et al. (Eds.): ICA3PP 2021, LNCS 13156, pp. 178–192, 2022.
https://doi.org/10.1007/978-3-030-95388-1_12

The TianHe-2A, a cluster on heterogeneous nodes which has been the number one for many years, uses the tight integrated multicore processor Matrix-2000 as accelerator. However, the tight integration results in many problems such as the access competition for shared resource like shared memory and PCIe link and the Non-uniform Memory Access (NUMA) [3].

Parallel applications own larger scales and more complex logic. Taking Computational Fluid Dynamics program (CFD) as an example, it aims to model the actual scenarios of physical fluid systems, perform decomposition of fluid regions to achieve parallel computing and solve complex fluid dynamics control equations. The scale of meshes in CFD is often tens of billions and the communication relation is also extremely complicated [4].

The trends of the isomerization of HPC platforms and the complication of parallel applications challenge the execution and optimization of the large-scale parallel applications on modern heterogeneous HPC platforms, especially the load balance between the heterogeneous processors to utilize the resource of each processor fully, which greatly influences the performance of applications [5]. Data-partition algorithm, a kind of algorithm that distributes all data units among all the processors according to a certain strategy, balances the load in the data-parallel applications to achieve the optimal performance [6].

Recent works [3,7] adopt the computation performance models to predict computation cost and design the data-partition algorithm to minimize the overall cost generally on both homogeneous (CPUs) and heterogeneous (CPUs + accelerators) platforms. However, without considering the overhead of communication, these algorithms cannot be applied in practice. Modern HPC platforms have become highly heterogeneous. Therefore, the heterogeneous-aware data partition algorithm, HaDPA, is proposed. The main contributions are as follows. 1) A data-partition algorithm with comprehensively considering the overhead of computation and communication is proposed and explained. 2) To verify the algorithm, the most representative data-parallel applications, matrix multiplication and axial compressor rotor model are implemented. Results show that our algorithm can effectively reduce the execution time. 3) By Constructing the random forest and exploiting the explainable machine learning tool, the impact factors of performance improvement are analyzed and explained.

2   Related Work

The researches on load-balancing algorithm could be divided into two types: static and dynamic algorithms. Static algorithms aiming to determine the mapping topology between application and platform by using the prior information of application and platform. Marrakchi S et al. [8] propose a approach for solving triangular band linear systems to balance the load and obtain a high degree of parallelism. Khaleghzadeh H et al. [9] are committed to exploit cache resources with affinity-aware thread mapping to maximize data reuse. Dynamic algorithms migrate the loads according to the runtime performance of processor during the execution of parallel application [10]. Song F et al. [6] propose a cyclic distribution algorithm to reduce the communication cost and achieve load balance maximally on heterogeneous multi-core and multi-GPU system.

The migration of data is necessary in dynamic algorithm and the strategy of migration could be used to distinguish between centralized and non-centralized algorithm. Centralized algorithm migrates the loads based on the global load information and usually has a higher convergence speed and a higher communication cost. It could be divided into task-queue and predicting-the-future algorithms. Task-queue algorithms use queue structure to distribute the independent tasks on shared memory platforms [11]. They are not suitable for the distributed platforms or iterative applications. Obviously, predicting-the-future algorithms depends on an accurate performance model extremely. Performance model includes computation and communication performance model.

In terms of computation performance model, Constant Performance Model (CPM), a positive constant to characterize the speed of an application running on processor, was proposed firstly. Subsequently, Functional Performance Model (FPM) are proposed which uses a continuous function satisfying some assumptions of problem size [12].

As for the communication performance model, there are two classifications: hardware model and software model. Hardware models describe the communication procedure using parameters relative to hardware. Most of them are derived from LogP model [13]. LogP model uses the network delay L, the overhead of CPU o, the minimum time interval for message passing g and the number of processes P to model the communication procedure. Moreover, Alexandrov et al. [14] propose LogGP using the reciprocal of network bandwidth for a long message G to extend LogP model. Other parameters are supplemented to LogGP to generate new models called LogGPH [15], LogGPO [16], lognP [17] and mlognP [18]. τ-Lop which describes the communication cost under different channels such as network and RDMA accurately [19].

Data-partition algorithms for data-parallel application belong to the static/dynamic centralized predicting-the-future load-balancing algorithms [7]. A model-based data-partition algorithm was proposed which reduces the execution time and energy consumption maximally at the same time. The recent research shows that speed function in FPM no longer satisfies the origin assumption because of the competition for shared resources and NUMA. Furthermore, as the amount of data increases, the limited memory and acceleration effect of CPU makes it a performance bottleneck. To solve these problems, a discrete data-partition algorithm on heterogeneous platforms was proposed based on FPM to minimize the calculation time of application [3]. However, this algorithm is not suitable for applications with a high communication to computation ratio due to the lack of consideration of communication performance.

In summary, there is not a data-partition algorithm that takes computation and communication cost into account for general data-parallel applications running on the large scale heterogeneous platforms.

3 HaDPA: Heterogeneous Aware Data-Partition Algorithm

A data-parallel application with N data units is executed on HPC platform with P heterogeneous processors. Distributing balanced data units to these processors to achieve the optimal performance is the primary target of HaDPA.

3.1 Framework of HaDPA

As shown in Fig. 1, HaDPA takes the information of the data-parallel application and the heterogeneous HPC platform as input and the optimal data-partition topology as output, consisting of four modules called computation characterization, communication characterization, model building and model solving module.

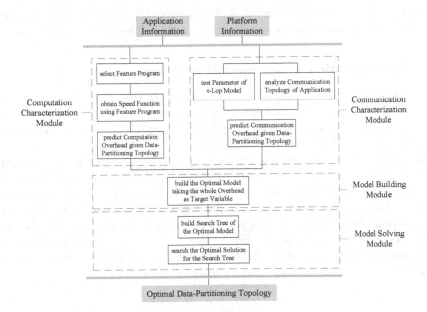

Fig. 1. The framework of HaDPA.

In this framework, computation characterization and communication characterization module predict the computation and communication cost under a given data-partition topology. The model building module builds the optimal model by taking overall cost as target variable and data-partition topology as decision variable. The optimal model is solved by our propose search tree.

3.2 Computation Characterization Module

Computation Characterization Module takes information of application and platform as input and executes three steps: selecting feature program, testing speed function and building FPM to predict computation cost under a given data-partition topology.

The feature program is defined as the program owning the shortest execution time and same computation characteristics and memory access characteristics as the original program. The selected feature program is executed on target HPC platform to obtain the speed function of heterogeneous processors. And then, FPM is built to predict the computation cost, shown as Eq. 1.

The n independent data units is distributed between p heterogeneous processors whose speed functions are represented by $S = s_1(x), s_2(x), \ldots, s_p(x)$ where the value collection SET of independent variable x consists of M nonnegative integer. The data-partition topology is defined as $D = \{n_1, n_2, \ldots, n_p\}$.

$$t_{comp}^D = max \frac{n_i}{s_i(n_i)} \qquad i = \{1, 2, \ldots, p\} \qquad (1)$$

where, $n_1 + n_2 + \ldots + n_p = n$ and $n_i \in SET$, $len(SET) = M$. The computation cost of target application is the maximum of that of all heterogeneous processors.

3.3 Communication Characterization Module

Communication Characterization Module also takes the information of application and platform as input and executes three steps: analyzing communication topology, testing model parameter, building τ-Lop to predict communication cost under a given data-partition topology.

The communication topology of target application is represented by multiple quadruples (sender, receiver, channel, message length). The channel in quadruple is not only three types but any numbers of types that don't have shared resource. And then, τ-Lop model is built after obtaining the model parameters and analyzing the communication topology of application to predict the communication cost t_{comm}^D, shown as Eq. 2. The jth data unit of ith processor has a transmission with $m_{i,j}$ length through channel $c_{i,j}$ with other processor. This symbol "||" represents the concurrent communication.

$$t_{comm}^D = \frac{\sum_{i=1}^{p}(\|_{j \in n_i} T^{c_{i,j}}(m_{i,j}))}{p} \qquad (2)$$

which is subject to $n_1 + n_2 + \ldots + n_p = n$. This shows that the communication cost of target application is the average of that of all processes.

3.4 Solving Hetergeneous-Aware Data-Partition Problem Based on the Computation and Communication Module

The overall cost of a data-parallel application is the sum of the computation and communication cost of this application. Considering about the dependency of computation and communication, computation relies on the receiving of intermediate computation results from other processors. The computation time includes the time of dependencies between two sub-data blocks.

Accordingly, the heterogeneous-aware data-partition problem (HaDP) is defined as Eq. 3 which is an integer nonlinear programming problem to search an optimal data-partition $D_{opt} = \{n_1, n_2, \ldots, n_p\}$ to minimize the overall cost.

$$t_{opt} = \min_{D} \max_{i\in[1,p]} \frac{n_i}{s_i(n_i)} + \frac{\sum_{i=1}^{p}(\|_{j\in n_i} T^{c_{i,j}}(m_{i,j}))}{p} \tag{3}$$

which is subject to $n_1 + n_2 + \ldots + n_p = n$, $n_i \in SET, len(SET) = M, i = 0, \ldots, p-1$, besides, $p, m, c, n \in Z^+$ and $s_i(x) \in R^+$.

With the help of integer nonlinear optimal model, the HaDPA which is based on the deep first search (DFS) with branch and bound is introduced and explained. Assuming that there are 4 processors, the speed functions are shown as Fig. 2(a). The number of data units to be allocated is 32. The partial structure of the search tree according to the speed functions is shown as Fig. 2(b). In this search tree, each node is a data-partition state represented by a structure $< size, isLeaf, dp, t_{comp}, t_{comm} >$. The $size$ means numbers of data units to be allocated. The $isLeaf$ is a judgement mark whether current node is leaf, and the dp refers to the current data-partition topology. The corresponding computation and communication cost are t_{comp} and t_{comm}. Each edge refers to a data-partition operation where the corresponding processor of current level is allocated a certain number of data units.

size	0	1	2	3	4	5	6	7	8	9	10	11	12	13	14	15
$T_0(x)$	0	8	5	4	5	8	7	7	2	7	7	4	6	2	1	1
$T_1(x)$	0	8	1	2	12	7	3	4	8	6	9	8	5	4	1	3
$T_2(x)$	0	7	9	4	7	5	5	7	6	6	6	7	2	4	7	3
$T_3(x)$	0	5	1	8	10	11	9	4	4	14	7	10	2	1	9	7

(a) Speed functions

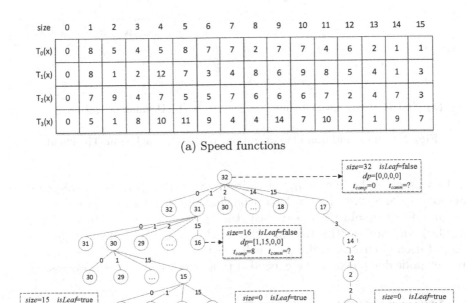

(b) Partial structure of search tree

Fig. 2. Example of partial structure of search tree.

Obviously, the feasible solution is that the *size* equals 0 and the *isLeaf* is true. The global optimal solution is selected from these feasible solutions according to the sum of t_{comp} and t_{comm}. The t_{comp} is decided by the maximum of that of all processors so that each node has its own t_{comp}. Nevertheless, the t_{comm} is calculated by using the complete dp, which makes that t_{comm} is an unknow value in the node representing the unfeasible solution. It is precisely because of this feature that using the classical branch and bound method to reduce the time complex is infeasible.

To solver this issue, the pruning method is designed based on the DFS to reduce the overhead of search process. The main idea is to set a optimal time threshold opt_{time} and initialize it as corresponding overall cost of the optimal solution using load-balancing algorithm based CPM. The opt_{time} is updated when a feasible solution whose overall cost is smaller than opt_{time} is searched. When the *isLeaf* of current node is false and t_{comp} of current node is larger than opt_{time}, current node could be pruned and its all children will not be considered due to the feature of this search tree that the computation cost increases along the order from parent to child.

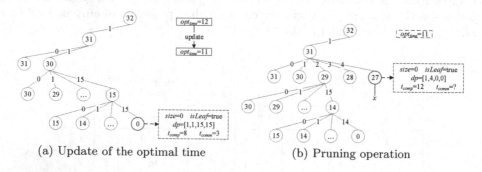

(a) Update of the optimal time   (b) Pruning operation

Fig. 3. Update and prunning operations of the Optimal Time Threshold.

In this example, the opt_{time} is initialized as 12 where the data-partition topology is [8, 8, 8, 8] by the load-balancing algorithm based on CPM. When the first feasible solution is searched, the opt_{time} is updated to 11 shown in Fig. 3(a). In the Fig. 3(b), the time threshold opt_{time} equals 11 and the cost of computation of current node t_{comp} is larger than opt_{time}. Thus, the children of current node don't need to be expanded to accelerate the search process.

4   Using HaDPA for Data Partition

For the cluster of heterogeneous nodes, the hierarchical data-partition algorithm HaDPA (HiHaDPA) is able to reduce the time complexity efficiently. HiHaDPA minimizes the parallel execution time of data-parallel applications on clusters heterogeneous multi-accelerator nodes.

The application is expressed as *App* with n independent data units. The heterogeneous cluster contains p_1 same nodes $ND_1 - ND_{p_1}$, and each node has $p2$ heterogeneous processors called $P_1 - P_{p_2}$. The speed functions of nodes are represented by $s_{nd}(x)$ where the value collection $SET1$ of independent variable x consists of $M1$ nonnegative integer. The speed functions of processors are represented by $S = s_1(x), s_2(x), \ldots, s_{p_2}(x)$ where the value collection $SET2$ of independent variable x consists of $M2$ nonnegative integer. Assuming that k^{th} data unit of jth processor in i^{th} node has a transmission with $m_{i,j,k}$ length through channel $c_{i,j,k}$ with other process under a topology D. Finding the optimal data-partition topology $D_{opt} = (n_{ij})$ to minimize the overall cost of the target application is the goal of the HiHaDPA.

As shown in Fig. 4, the whole partition process of n data units in this platform is divided into two layers. The decision target of each layer is the sum of the computation and communication cost of current layer. In the first layer, the n data units are distributed between $p1$ nodes by the Eq. 4.

$$D_{1,x}^{opt} = \min_{D_1} \max_{i \in [1,p_1]} \frac{n_i}{s_{nd}(n_i)} + \frac{\sum_{i=1}^{p_1}(\|k \in n_i \ T_{internode}^{c_{i,k}}(m_{i,k}))}{p_1} \qquad (4)$$

In the second layer, the n_i data units are distributed between p_2 heterogeneous processors in node i by the Eq. 5.

$$D_{2,x}^{opt} = \min_{D_{2,i}} \max_{i \in [1,p_2]} \frac{n_{i,j}}{s_j(n_{i,j})} + \frac{\sum_{j=1}^{p_2}(\|k \in n_j \ T_{intranode}^{c_{i,j,k}}(m_{i,j,k}))}{p_2} \qquad (5)$$

which shows that the speed functions of the heterogeneous processors are used in computation characterization module and the intranode communication cost is only taken into account in communication characterization module. Finally, the D_{opt} is a combination of D_1^{opt} and $D_{2,i}^{opt}$, the optimal topologies of these two layers.

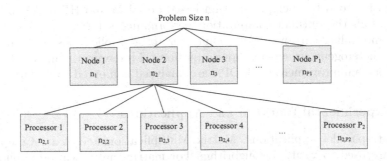

Fig. 4. The situation of HiHaDPA.

Shown as Algorithm 1, the optimal topology $D_{2,x}^{opt}$ and overall cost $t_{2,x}^{opt}$ are calculated using the 2nd layer HaDPA. All the pairs $(x, t_{2,x}^{opt})$ make up the speed function $s_{nd}(x)$. Then, $s_{nd}(x)$ is used to obtain the optimal topology D_1^{opt} using the 1st layer HaDPA. Finally, the optimal topology D_{opt} is a combination of the optimal topologies of two layers. It is worth mentioning that the speed function of the whole single node $s_{nd}(x)$ is defined as the overall cost of the D_{opt} for the application with x data units on the single node. Besides, the solution of HaDPA could be guaranteed to be the global optimal while the solution of HiHaDPA could not.

Algorithm 1. HiHaDPA

Require: num of data units, n;   speed functions, $S = \{s_1(x), s_2(x), ..., s_{p_2}(x)\}$; value collection of independent variable of speed function, SET_1, SET_2

Ensure: the optimal data-partition topology, D_{opt}

1: **initialize:** set s_{nd} = empty dict
2:             set D_{opt} = empty dict
3: **for** x in SET_1 **do**
4:     $D_{2,i}^{opt}, t_{2,i}^{opt}$ = HaDPA(x,p_2,S)
5:     $s_{nd}[x] = t_{2,i}^{opt}$
6: **end for**
7: D_1^{opt}, t_1^{opt} = HaDPA(n,p_1,s_{nd})
8: **for** $i = 1, ..., p_1$ **do**
9:     **for** $j = 1, ..., p_2$ **do**
10:         $D_{opt}[i \times p_2 + j] = D_{2,i}^{opt}[D_1^{opt}]$
11:     **end for**
12: **end for**
13: **return** D_{opt}

---

5   Experimental Analysis of HaDPA

In this section, the overall performance optimization of HaDPA is verified compared to the load-balancing algorithm based on CPM and HPOPTA [3] which could obtain the optimal computation performance solution at present using matrix multiplication and axial compressor rotor applications on TianHe-2A which is heterogeneous supercomputer platform. Moreover, the impact factor of performance improvement of HaDPA are analyzed compared to HPOPTA.

5.1   Experimental Platform and Applications

Two data-parallel applications, Matrix Multiplication and Axial Compressor Rotor are used to verify our algorithm. For matrix multiplication application, $2 N*N$ square matrices A and B are multiplied to obtain a $N*N$ square matrix C. Each matrix is divided into p submatrices by column-based method [1]. Each processor only owns the corresponding submatrices of A and B to calculate the corresponding submatrix of C. The solving target of the axial compressor rotor is a Rotor35 model with 36 channels. As shown in Fig. 5(a), each single channel is decomposed into 12 regions. There are 36 * 12 = 432 data units that needs to be partitioned. The whole calculation process of each single region is performed by Full Multi-Grid Method (FMG) containing three levels called coarse mesh, medium mesh and fine mesh. It's worth mentioning that the computation process is implemented by using openblas [1] and the communication process is implemented by using MPI and SCIF which is a communication library suitable to coprocessor in TianHe-2A.

TianHe-2A is a supercomputing platform including 17792 compute nodes. As shown in Fig. 5(b), each node contains two Intel Ivy Bridge CPUs and two Matrix-2000 accelerators. Data need to be transferred through PCI-E link between them. A Matrix-2000 is divided into four super-node (SNs) which are the basic unit of job assignment so that one node could be regarded as ten heterogeneous processors.

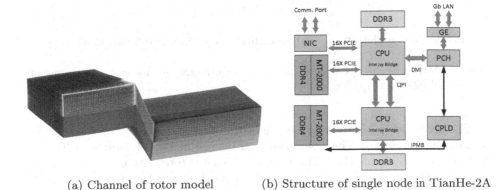

(a) Channel of rotor model   (b) Structure of single node in TianHe-2A

Fig. 5. Experimental platform and applications.

5.2 Verification of HaDPA's Overall Performance Optimization

The first step of our proposed algorithm is to analyze the feature program and obtain the speed function. Due to the fact that the matrix multiplication application is implemented using openblas library, the application itself is selected to obtain the speed functions as the feature program. In this experiment, 4 processors in single node are used to be the platform for matrix multiplication application. Three SNs with 32 computing cores and their dedicated core form 3 abstract processors, named AP_SN0, AP_SN1 and AP_SN2 where the dedicated core is used to communicate with CPU. The remaining nine CPU cores form an abstract processor called AP_CPU, shown as Fig. 6(a). Besides, the $SET1$ is a set composed of several triples (M, N, K) where M, N or K are element of {64, 128, ..., 4096}. The triple (M, N, K) means the situation that the M*K matrix A and the K*N matrix B are multiplied to obtain the M*N matrix C. The speed is calculated by $S = 2MNK/(T * 10^6)$ where the T is the computation cost measured in a running application on the corresponding processor. As the competition for shared resource such as the shared memory on CPU and the PCIe link between CPU and accelerators, the speed functions of four heterogeneous processors should be measured simultaneously. The speed functions is shown in Fig. 6(b). It is worth noting that the lines of origin data are transparent and processed into the solid trendlines using the sliding window idea.

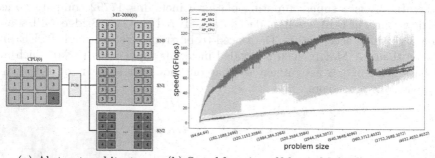

(a) Abstract architecture   (b) Speed function of Matrix Multiplication

Fig. 6. Abstract architecture description for TianHe-2A and its speed functions of matrix multiplication application.

The second step of our proposed algorithm is to measure τ-Lop parameters as mentioned in Sect. 3. Their parameters are shown in Table 1. Besides, $o^0(m) = 0.52$, $o^1(m) = 1.62$, $L^2(64) = 21.30149$, in which c = 0 refer to intranode shared memory channel, c = 1 means internode network channel and c=2 is RDMA channel between CPU and accelerators.

Table 1. The parameters of τ-Lop Model on TianHe-2A (ms).

τ	2	3	4	5	6	7	8	9	10	11	12
$L^0_{(64,\tau)}$	0.0086	0.0088	0.0077	0.00813	0.0079	0.00805	0.0075	0.0148	0.008	0.012	0.0138
$L^1_{(64,\tau)}$	0.0214	0.6912	0.0423	0.472	0.422	0.123	1.288	0.430	0.127	0.378	0.711

The improvement rate is defined as $ImprRate_X = \min\left(\frac{t_{CPM}-t_X}{\max{(t_X,\delta)}}, 1\right) \times 100\%$, where X represents HaDPA and HPOPTA and δ is the interactive threshold aiming to avoid the excessive proportion because of the bitty base.

As shown in figure Fig. 7(a), the theoretical values predicted by our proposed optimal model are same as the measured values of HaDPA and HPOPTA, which means that our proposed model is able to predict the execution time of data-parallel applications running on the heterogeneous platforms. Due to the consideration of communication cost based on the FPM, it is inevitable that the performance optimization effect of HaDPA is better than the effect of HPOPTA. As shown in Fig. 7(b), $ImprRate_{HPOPTA}$ reaches the maximum value 77.09%

when N is 256 and $ImprRate_{HaDPA}$ reaches the maximum value 81.33% at the same time. The average of $ImprRate_{HPOPTA}$ is 65.49% while the average of $ImprRate_{HaDPA}$ is 65.90%.

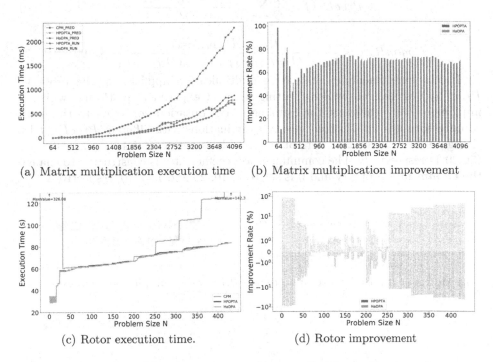

(a) Matrix multiplication execution time   (b) Matrix multiplication improvement

(c) Rotor execution time.   (d) Rotor improvement

Fig. 7. Comparison of the performance optimization effect for applications when using HaDPA, HPOPTA and the Load-Balancing Algorithm based on CPM.

For the axial compressor rotor, as shown in Fig. 7(c), the performance optimization effect of HaDPA is always better than the load-balancing algorithm based on CPM. Nevertheless, the effect of HaDPA is worse than the HPOPTA in some data points. The effect of performance improvement of HaDPA is obvious under larger problem size, which results from the larger processor difference and communication to computation ratio under a larger problem size. As shown in Fig. 7(d), $ImprRate_{HPOPTA}$ and $ImprRate_{HaDPA}$ reaches the maximum value 91.11% when N is 6. The average of $ImprRate_{HPOPTA}$ is 17.50% while the average of $ImprRate_{HaDPA}$ is 18.00%.

To analysis the impact factor of performance of HaDPA relative to HPOPTA, two factors, $ProcDiff$ and $CommRate$, described as Eqs. 6 and 7, are introduced. $ProcDiff$ is defined as the mean standard deviation of speed functions samples of heterogeneous processors, represents the computation performance difference between processors, in which d_{ij} is the speed of ith sample of jth processor and $i = 1, \ldots, C$ and $j = 1, \ldots, P$. $CommRate$ stands for the proportion of communication cost in the overall cost. The problem size is not selected as the impact factor as the problem size affect the performance improvement by changing $ProcDiff$ and $CommRate$.

$$ProcDiff = \frac{1}{C} \sum_{i=1}^{C} \sqrt{\frac{\sum_{j=1}^{P} (d_{ij} - \overline{d_i})^2}{P}}$$ (6)

$$CommRate = \frac{t_{comm}(D_{HPOPTA})}{t_{comm}(D_{HPOPTA}) + t_{comp}(D_{HPOPTA})} \times 100$$ (7)

In the experiment about matrix multiplication application, the property $ProcDiff$ is changed by constructing different experiment platforms, which is implemented by changing the number of computation cores. As to the axial compressor rotor application, several examinations with different $ProcDiff$ by changing iter_count. The iter_count variable is set to (5,5,10), (1,20,50) and (50,20,1) respectively. The communication coefficient η is constructed to change the $CommRate$ property and η is set to 1, 10, 20 and 1, 5, 10, respectively.

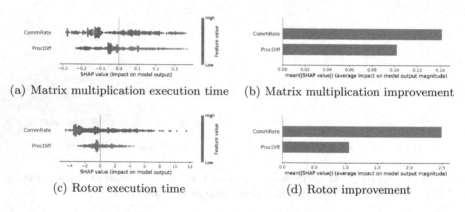

(a) Matrix multiplication execution time   (b) Matrix multiplication improvement

(c) Rotor execution time   (d) Rotor improvement

Fig. 8. Comparison of the performance optimization effect for matrix multiplication application using HaDPA, HPOPTA and the Load-Balancing Algorithm based on CPM.

To analyze the influencing factors, a dataset containing triples ($ProcDiff$, $CommRate$, $ImprRate$) is constructed. The regression relation between $ImprRate$ and other two properties is learned by random forest regression. The learned regression model is analyzed using SHapley Additive exPlanation (SHAP) [20], a explainable machine learning python library.

For the two applicaitons, the mean accuracy of trained regression model is 81.19% and 91.29%, which shows a strong regression relation between $ImprRate$ and other two properties. As shown in Fig. 8(a, c), the larger ImprRate results from larger CommRate and smaller ProcDiff. It makes sense because the HaDPA is an expansion with communication cost of HPOPTA that could reach the optimal computation performance. Figure 8(b, d) shows that the property $CommRate$ matters more to the data-partition on heterogeneous HPC platforms.

6   Conclusion

As the stronger isomerism of modern HPC platforms and the larger parallel scale of applications, the data-partition algorithm for data-parallel applications is necessary. However, without considering the overhead of communication, the state-of-the-art algorithms are not suitable for the applications with high communication to computation ratio.

In this paper, a heterogeneous-aware data-partition algorithm, HaDPA, is proposed based on the DFS with branch and bound. Moreover, a hierarchical data-partition algorithm for the cluster on heterogeneous nodes using HaDPA to reduce the time complexity is introduced and explained. To verify the algorithm, the most representative data-parallel applications, matrix multiplication and axial compressor rotor model are used. Compared with HPOTPA and the load-balancing algorithm based on CPM, results shows that our algorithm can get a higher performance improvement. In addition, the analysis about the impact factor of performance improvement of HaDPA relative to HPOPTA is performed. According to the explanation of regression analysis, a higher communication to computation ratio results in a higher performance improvement.

In the future, to reduce the prior information, a dynamic centralized future prediction algorithm will be designed, which is divided according to the computation and communication load of the current program.

Acknowledgment. The work was funded by the National Key Research and Development Program of China (2016YFB0200902).

References

1. Li, J., Zhang, X., Han, L., Ji, Z., Dong, X., Hu, C.: OKCM: improving parallel task scheduling in high-performance computing systems using online learning. J. Supercomput. **77**(6), 5960–5983 (2020). https://doi.org/10.1007/s11227-020-03506-5
2. Top500 (2020). https://www.top500.org/lists/top500/2020/11. Accessed 16 June 2021
3. Khaleghzadeh, H., Manumachu, R.R., Lastovetsky, A.L.: A novel data-partitioning algorithm for performance optimization of data-parallel applications on heterogeneous HPC platforms. IEEE Trans. Parallel Distrib. Syst. **29**(10), 2176–2190 (2018)
4. Li, J., Zhang, X., Zhou, J., Dong, X., Zhang, C.: swHPFM: refactoring and optimizing the structured grid fluid mechanical algorithm on the sunway taihulight supercomputer. Appl. Sci. **10**(1), 72–93 (2020)
5. Martínez, J.A., Garzón, E.M., Plaza, A., García, I.: Automatic tuning of iterative computation on heterogeneous multiprocessors with ADITHE. J. Supercomput. **58**(2), 151–159 (2011)
6. Song, F., Tomov, S., Dongarra, J.J.: Enabling and scaling matrix computations on heterogeneous multi-core and multi-gpu systems. In: International Conference on Supercomputing, ICS 2012, Venice, Italy, June 25–29, 2012, pp. 365–376. ACM (2012)

7. Lastovetsky, A.L., Manumachu, R.R.: New model-based methods and algorithms for performance and energy optimization of data parallel applications on homogeneous multicore clusters. IEEE Trans. Parallel Distrib. Syst. **28**(4), 1119–1133 (2017)
8. Marrakchi, S., Jemni, M.: Static scheduling with load balancing for solving triangular band linear systems on multicore processors. Fundam. Informaticae **179**(1), 35–58 (2021)
9. Khaleghzadeh, H., Deldari, H., Reddy, R., Lastovetsky, A.: Hierarchical multicore thread mapping via estimation of remote communication. J. Supercomput. **74**(3), 1321–1340 (2017). https://doi.org/10.1007/s11227-017-2176-6
10. Giordano, A., Rango, A.D., Rongo, R., D'Ambrosio, D., Spataro, W.: Dynamic load balancing in parallel execution of cellular automata. IEEE Trans. Parallel Distributed Syst. **32**(2), 470–484 (2021)
11. Li, M., Chen, C., Zhu, G., Savaria, Y.: Local queueing-based data-driven task scheduling for multicore systems. In: IEEE 61st International Midwest Symposium on Circuits and Systems, MWSCAS 2018, Windsor, ON, Canada, 5–8 August, 2018, pp. 897–900. IEEE (2018)
12. Lastovetsky, A.L., Reddy, R.: Data partitioning with a functional performance model of heterogeneous processors. Int. J. High Perform. Comput. Appl. **21**(1), 76–90 (2007)
13. Culler, D.E., Karp, R.M., Patterson, D.A., and A.S.: Logp: Towards a realistic model of parallel computation. In: Proceedings of the Fourth ACM SIGPLAN Symposium on Principles & Practice of Parallel Programming (PPOPP), San Diego, California, USA, 19–22 May, 1993, pp. 1–12. ACM (1993)
14. Alexandrov, A.D., Ionescu, M.F., Schauser, K.E., Scheiman, C.J.: Loggp: incorporating long messages into the logp model for parallel computation. J. Parallel Distributed Comput. **44**(1), 71–79 (1997)
15. Yuan, L., Zhang, Y., Tang, Y., Rao, L., Sun, X.: Loggph: a parallel computational model with hierarchical communication awareness. In: 13th IEEE International Conference on Computational Science and Engineering, CSE 2010, Hong Kong, China, 11–13 December, 2010. pp. 268–274. IEEE Computer Society (2010)
16. Chen, W., Zhai, J., Zhang, J., Zheng, W.: Loggpo: an accurate communication model for performance prediction of MPI programs. Sci. China Ser. F Inf. Sci. **52**(10), 1785–1791 (2009)
17. Cameron, K.W., Ge, R., Sun, X.: $\log_n p$ and $\log_3 p$: accurate analytical models of point-to-point communication in distributed systems. IEEE Trans. Comput. **56**(3), 314–327 (2007)
18. Tu, B., Fan, J., Zhan, J., Zhao, X.: Performance analysis and optimization of MPI collective operations on multi-core clusters. J. Supercomput. **60**(1), 141–162 (2012)
19. Rico-Gallego, J., Martín, J.C.D.: τ-lop: modeling performance of shared memory MPI. Parallel Comput. **46**, 14–31 (2015)
20. Lundberg, S.M., Lee, S.I.: A unified approach to interpreting model predictions. In: Advances in Neural Information Processing Systems 30, pp. 4765–4774. Curran Associates, Inc. (2017)

A NUMA-Aware Parallel Truss Decomposition Algorithm for Large Scale Graphs

Zhebin Mou, Nong Xiao, and Zhiguang Chen[✉]

School of Computer Science and Engineering, Sun Yat-sen University,
Guangzhou, China
mouzhb3@mail2.sysu.edu.cn, {xiaon6,chenzhg29}@mail.sysu.edu.cn

Abstract. Truss decomposition algorithm is to decompose a graph into
a hierarchical subgraph structure. A k-truss ($k \geq 2$) is a subgraph that
each edge is in at least $k - 2$ triangles. The existing algorithm is to
first compute the number of triangles for each edge, and then iteratively
increase k to peel off the edges that are not in the $(k + 1)$-truss. Due to
the scale of the data and the intensity of computations, truss decomposition algorithm on the billion-side graph may take more than hours on a
commodity server. In addition, today, more servers adopt NUMA architecture, which also affects the scalability of the algorithm. Therefore, we
propose a NUMA-aware shared-memory parallel algorithm to accelerate
the truss decomposition for NUMA systems by (1) computing different
levels of k-truss between each NUMA nodes (2) dividing the range of k
heuristically to ensure load balance (3) optimizing data structure and triangle counting method to reduce remote memory access, data contention
and data skew. Our experiments show that on real-world datasets our
OpenMP implementation can accelerate truss decomposition effectively
on NUMA systems.

Keywords: Truss decomposition · Triangle counting · NUMA ·
Multithread · Graph analysis

1 Introduction

Graphs are everywhere, such as social networks [33], molecular structure [26], and
many more. Any group of interactive entities can be abstracted as a graph, with
entities as vertices and interactions as edges. To better understand the graph, it
is often useful to find cohesive subgraphs in the graph. Cohesive subgraphs have
many well-known types, such as maximal clique, n-clique [16], k-plex [25], quasi-
clique [21] and so on. Because most of the formulas of clique-based problems are
NP-complete, exactly computation is computationally intensive for large graphs.

As a kind of cohesive subgraph, k-truss [8] is very useful. Because it can be
computed accurately in a polynomial time. The density of truss depends on the
support of each edge in the subgraph, i.e. the number of triangles in the subgraph

© Springer Nature Switzerland AG 2022
Y. Lai et al. (Eds.): ICA3PP 2021, LNCS 13156, pp. 193–212, 2022.
https://doi.org/10.1007/978-3-030-95388-1_13

formed by the edge. A k-truss ($k \geq 2$) is defined as follows, in graph G, there is a subgraph in which the support of all edges is not less than $k - 2$. Figure 1 is an example, showing the support value of each edge in its *class*: if an edge is in a k-truss, the edge is in class k, but not in a $(k + 1)$ truss. Truss decomposition is to find the k-class of each edge [31]. Truss decomposition has many applications [4,11,24] in graph mining and social networks, such as community search and personalized recommendation.

At first, the existing algorithms compute the support of each edge and then peel the edge iteratively [13,22,31]. In the support initialization stage, compute the support by counting the common neighborhood of vertexes of each edge in graph G. After that, increasing k ($k \geq 2$) in each edge peeling stage, and iteratively peeling the edges whose support degree is not larger than $k - 2$. In k iteration, the removed edges are added to class k and updating the support degree of all remaining edges in the triangle containing these removed edges. The decomposition will end when all edges in G are removed.

The time complexity depends on the triangle number in G [22]. For each peeled edge $e(u, v)$, the triangle enumeration can find all triangles of $\triangle uvw$ from the other edges in G. For each triangle $\triangle uvw$ support update is performed on the edges of $e(u, w)$ and $e(v, w)$. Triangle enumeration is very expensive due to intensive triangle existence checking and supporting updates will lead to massive random memory access. For this reason, truss decomposition is time-consuming, and researchers propose parallelization algorithms to speed up.

Due to the intensity computation, truss decomposition takes much time on large graphs [22,31]. To accelerate truss decomposition, many researchers [23] have optimized the algorithm for different devices, such as [5,17,19] for GPU. But few pay attention to the system based on NUMA architecture. NUMA, i.e. non-uniform memory access architecture. In NUMA system, each CPU has a shorter time to access local memory than remote memory [14]. Therefore, we study how to accelerate truss decomposition algorithm in NUMA.

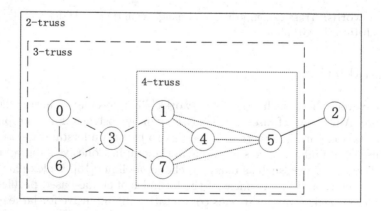

Fig. 1. An example graph G

In summary, we make the following contributions:

- We design a parallel truss decomposition method for parallel computing different levels of trussness between NUMA nodes. And we propose a heuristic k partition method based on the number of edges.
- We design an optimize data structure for NUMA characteristics. Maintain a compressed local graph topology between each NUMA node.
- We optimize the triangle enumeration for data skew. Especially, dynamically select method skipping binary search or sequential merge to enumerate triangles.
- We evaluate the optimization of each part of truss decomposition and show that our implementation achieves effective acceleration compared with an in-memory algorithm, PKT, on NUMA.

2 Background and Motivation

In this section, we describe the definition of truss decomposition, introduce the existing algorithm, and show the motivation for our work.

Table 1. Notations

Notation	Description
G	An undirected graph
V, E and $\triangle$	Vertex, edge, and triangle sets of G
$N(u)$	Neighbor set of a vertex u in G
Φ_k	The k-class of G
Rs, Adj	Compressed Sparse Row (CSR) format of G
El	An edge list array of G
Eid	An edge mapping array, associated with adj
Sup	An array of support for each edge, ordered by id
$sup(e), sup(e, G)$	Support value of an edge e in G
SI, IEP	Support initialization and iterative edge peeling

2.1 Preliminaries

Given an undirected graph G, we denote the edge, vertex and triangle sets by E_G, V_G and $\triangle_G$ respectively. Given a vertex $u \in V_G$, $N_G(u)$ is the neighbor vertex set of u, $d_G(u)$ represents the degree of u in G, $d_G(u) = |N_G(u)|$. $\triangle uvw$ represents a triangle formed by vertexes u, v, w $(u, v, w \in V_G)$.

Definition 1. (Support) The support of an edge $e(u, v) \in E_G$, denoted by $sup(e, G)$, is defined as $|\{\triangle uvw | w \in V_G\}|$, which can be computed by $|N_G(u) \cap N_G(v)|$.

Definition 2. (k-Truss) The k-truss of G ($k \geq 2$), denoted by T_k, is defined as the largest subgraph of G such that $\forall e \in E_{T_k}$ $sup(e, T_k) \geq (k-2)$. The trussness (truss number) of an edge $e \in E$, denoted by $\phi(e)$, is defined as the maximum k of the k-truss that the edge e is in.

Definition 3. (k-Class) The k-class of G denoted by Φ_k is defined as $\{e | e \in E \land \phi(e) = k\}$. All k-classes of G form a hierarchy. A k-truss of G can be computed by a union of all the i-classes ($i \geq k$).

Truss decomposition of graph G is to find all k-classes $\Phi_k (k \geq 2)$ of G [31]. And the common notations are shown in Table 1.

2.2 Related Work

In this chapter, we will introduce several representative algorithms. We mainly take PKT [13], one of the cutting-edge parallel algorithms with the lowest theoretical complexity, as an example.

Algorithm 1. Truss Decomposition

Input: an undirected graph $G_0 = (V_{G_0}, E_{G_0})$
Output: Φ_i of G_0, ($i \geq 2$)
1: **for all** $e(u, v) \in E$ **do**
2:     $sup(e(u, v)) \leftarrow |\triangle_{uvw}|$
3: **end for**
4: $k \leftarrow 2$
5: **while** $|E| \neq 0$ **do**
6:     $E_{remove} \leftarrow \{e | e \in E \land sup(e) = k - 2\}$
7:     **while** $|E_{remove}| \neq 0$ **do**
8:         $\Phi_k \leftarrow \Phi_k \cup E_{remove}$
9:         **for all** $e \in E_{remove}$ **do**
10:             **for all** $\triangle_{uvw}, e \in \triangle_{uvw}$ **do**
11:                 **for all** $e' \in \triangle_{uvw}, e' \neq e$ **do**
12:                     $sup(e') \leftarrow max(k - 2, sup(e') - 1)$
13:                 **end for**
14:             **end for**
15:             $E \leftarrow E \setminus \{e\}$
16:         **end for**
17:         $E_{remove} \leftarrow \{e | e \in E \land sup(e) = k - 2\}$
18:     **end while**
19:     $k \leftarrow k + 1$
20: **end while**

Sequential Truss Decomposition. As Algorithm 1 shown, there are two main steps in state-of-art algorithms. The support initialization (Line 1–3) is to compute each edges' support, and the peeling phases (Lines 5–20) proceed level by level and find a $k-class(k \geq 2)$ at each level. In each k corresponding level, edges with the support $k - 2$ are filtered (Lines 6 and 17), which triggers the peeling of triangles containing these edges. And then update support of the edges in these triangles in turn. Each triangle is peeled off exactly once for correctness, which is ensured by removing the edge $e(u, v)$ (Line 17) after completing the enumeration of $\triangle_{uvw}$ and support update of $e(v, w)$ and $e(u, w)$ (Lines 10–13). Different from the above algorithm, [31] present an effective sequential algorithm. Inspired from [6], by using an edge array ordered by support, it can find the edge to be peeled (Line 6 and 17) and update support (Line 12) in a constant time, and construction of the array only need linear time. Although has low theoretical complexity in time and space, its practical performance is hard to compare with parallel algorithms.

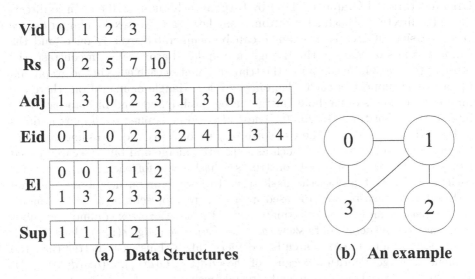

(a) **Data Structures**   (b) **An example**

Fig. 2. An example graph and its data structure

Parallel Truss Decomposition. PKT [12,13] is a representative and effective parallel algorithm for computing in memory. In IEP, it achieves efficient parallelism by parallelizing each edge peeling iteration and synchronizing among iterations. PKT adopts the CSR format and introduces a boolean array to indicate the edge removals. As shown in Fig. 2, the data structure mainly consists of adjacency lists, edges, support, and mappings from the vertexes to the edges. The adjacency lists are represented in a CSR, i.e., Compressed Sparse Row format [13,17], which consists of each row starting position and adjacency arrays denoted by Rs and Adj, respectively. For triangle enumeration, each adjacency list is sorted and used for merge operations [13,18,27]. Edges (denoted by El) are represented as a list of source and destination vertex pairs, and each edge is associated with a support value denoted by $sup(e)$. To find a triangle enumeration result (three location index in the Adj array) into edge indexes, an Eid array is introduced and associated with Adj [35].

Another frontier method MSP [27] is similar. But they differ in the design of adjacency representation, support update, and so on. MSP maintains array-based doubly-linked lists and dynamically updates them upon edge removals. For support update, PKT uses atomic operations, whereas MSP expands all the edges in the peeled-off triangles and groups these edges by the source vertex for lock-free computation. It maintains the bucket index during IEP in $O(|\triangle|)$ time and space. Obviously, in most cases, PKT is better than MSP in its space utilization.

Support Initialization and Triangle Enumeration. The SI counts the number of triangles that each edge is in (Line 2 of Algorithm 1). There are two approaches to parallelizing SI. The first approach [20,30,32] creates a Degree Oriented Directed Graph (DODG) by turning each undirected edge into directing. The direction of each edge is from a smaller degree vertex to a larger degree vertex. Using DODG, each triangle can be enumerated exactly once, and the support values of edges in the triangle are updated atomically. In contrast, the other approach [34,35] computes the triangle count of each edge in the graph and updates the support of each edge once. As for triangle enumeration, there are mainly three kinds of methods, merge-based, hash-based, and bitmap-based set intersection algorithms [10,29,30]. These also can be applied to support updates in IEP. Merge-based scan the two sorted arrays of $N(u)$ and $N(v)$ and compare the elements to find matches, such as sequential merge and binary-search-based merge [10,34,36]. Hash-based constructs a hash table for each $N(u)$. Then for each $w \in N(v)$, it probes the hash table to find common neighbors of u and v. Similar to hash-based, [13] used a bitmap to represent $N(u)$ and dynamically construct and clear the bitmap during the edge's vertex common neighbor counting. When there is data skew ($d(u) \gg d(v)$, given edge $e(u,v)$), hash-based, bitmap-based and binary-search-based merge algorithms work better than the sequential merge algorithm because of the $O(d(v))$, $O(d(v))$, $O(log(d(u)) \cdot d(v))$, and $O(d(u) + d(v))$ time complexity, respectively.

Other Works. Besides, we focus not only on Methods on the CPU in memory. [5] presented a scalable multi-GPU implementation in which each GPU handles a different k value, which plays an enlightening role in our work. Recently, truss maintenance on dynamic graphs also has been studied. Specifically, Zhang et al. [37] have studied how to track the trusses given edge insertions and deletions. But, for edge insertion cases, these algorithms do not have a polynomial time complexity bound. Diab et al. [9] surveys the optimizations to truss decomposition on GPUs showing that the best optimizations combination highly depends on the graph of choice, and then presents a framework, KTRUSSEXPLORER. About work on NUMA, there are many graph analysis frameworks for NUMA architecture. Taking Polymer [14] as an example, it mainly improves the computational performance of general graph analysis algorithms by allocating and placing data according to memory access and reducing random access as much as possible.

2.3   Motivation

In order to study the performance bottleneck of truss decomposition on the NUMA architecture, we evaluated the bandwidth of different memory access and the parallel algorithm PKT[13] on multiple real graphs in a NUMA server.

Table 2. The bandwidth (MB/s) of memory access on the distance.

Access	0-hop	1-hop	2-hop
Sequential	9870	8056	4756
Random	401	207	342

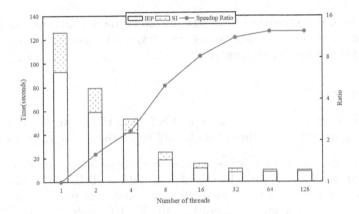

Fig. 3. Time and speedup ratio of PKT on soc-LiveJournal

We used the same hardware as in Sect. 5, and PKT implementation from [13]. In Table 2, hop-0, hop-1, and hop-3 represent access to local memory, the memory on the same socket but different dies, and the memory on different sockets, respectively. In Fig. 3, when the number of threads is no more than 32, PKT is executed on the same NUMA node. The left and right coordinate axes respectively represent the speedup ratio (compared with 1 thread), and the abscissa axis is the number of threads.

Through preliminary experiments, as shown in Table 2 and Fig. 3, we have verified or found the following problems in NUMA system:

- The memory access performance is that local memory access is better than remote memory access, and sequential memory access is better than remote memory access.
- The most time-consuming stage is the IEP, and the second time-consuming is SI.

- When the number of threads reaches a certain threshold, as the number of threads increases, the performance improvement gradually slows down.

After analysis, we find that the improvement of PKT performance on NUMA node is limited, which may be due to the following reasons:

- Because the calculation depends on the overall graph topology, there are a large number of random or remote memory access.
- Due to atomic operations in the algorithm, when there are too many threads and the data size is too small, many data contentions may arise.
- Data skew affects triangle counting in SI and triangle enumeration in IEP, resulting in unbalanced load among threads.

3   NUMA-Aware Parallel Truss Decomposition

In this section, we introduce our design, including data structure, SI, IEP, and heuristic k partition, and analyze its complexity. At the same time, we also explained the reasons for our design.

3.1   Overview

In order to improve the performance of PKT on NUMA, we have carried out the following design and optimization according to the problems we found.

- To avoid data contention, we adopt the design of reducing atomic operations and multi-level parallelism. In the SI, the data is divided according to the vertices, and the triangles of each edge are counted in parallel between processes to reduce the atomic operation. In the IEP, multi-level parallelism is adopted to perform truss decomposition in different ranges among NUMA nodes to avoid data contention by reducing the number of threads.
- In order to reduce remote and random memory access, we redesigned the data structure. A set of compressed graph topology is maintained on each NUMA node, which also ensures space utilization.
- For the data skew problem, we adopt the method of traversing by vertices and dynamically selecting the intersection according to the two vertices' neighbor set size. Further, we optimize the binary-search-based merging.
- More importantly, for the multi-level parallelism in IEP, because the size of the k range and the calculation of each level are unknown, how to divide the k-range of NUMA nodes is also an important problem. We propose a heuristic k-partition method between NUMA nodes to ensure the compute load balancing.

Next, we will introduce our design from the data structure, SI, IEP, and heuristic k partition.

3.2   Data Structure

The data structure of PKT used is shown in Fig. 2, and this is also the data structure (See data structure of any node from Fig. 4) on a single NUMA node in our method. In addition to the compressed sparse row representation (Es, Adj), four arrays are used. The array Eid with a size of $2 \times |E|$ is used to store the edge ID corresponding to each neighbor of the vertex. The array sup of size $|E|$ is used to store the support of each edge. Finally, an array El of size $|E|$ is used to store the edge list, that is, the vertices corresponding to each edge. Therefore, assuming a 4-byte integer, the main space requirement is $(|V|+2 \times |E|+2 \times |E|+2 \times |E|) \times 4$ bytes$= 24 \times |E| + |V|$ bytes.

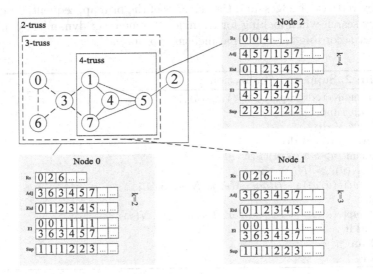

Fig. 4. An example for our method

Different from the PKT, in order to reduce the remote memory access and the contention of shared variables, each NUMA node maintains a set of graph topology data separately, Its size is taken as the minimum k of its calculation. Section 3.4 below will describe how to compress the graph before each NUMA node formally executes IEP. Note that a complete set of graphs needs to be maintained to calculate the minimum k node. Combined with the heuristic partition method of k, the maximum local data size of each node shall not exceed $|V|+8 \times |E|$(In the extreme case of only two nodes) Therefore, with the increase of NUMA nodes, the memory space will continue to increase, but will not exceed n times(denote the number of NUMA nodes as n) the original size.

We also show a simple example in Fig. 4. In the figure, node 0, node 1 and node 2 calculate $k = 2$, $k = 3$ and $k = 4$ respectively. Node 0 (calculate the minimum k) needs a complete set of the graph, and the data size of other nodes is smaller than the node calculating the k range with little upper bound, i.e., the data size of the node calculating $k = 4$ is smaller than the node calculating $k = 3$. Actually, each node will not be divided into only one k, but into a consecutive k range.

3.3 Support Initialization

We use the method of counting each edge directly to avoid atomic operation. The original PKT adopts the bitmap-based method. Traverse by vertexes in parallel, and then find the emitted edge of each vertex to participate in forming a triangle, and update the support of each edge atomic.

Among them, frequent atomic operations make it perform poorly on dense graphs and large-scale graphs. We compare the current mainstream parallel schemes by vertices or edges, and the schemes of the bitmap, sequential merging, and binary search when looking for triangles. A scheme of dynamically initializing support according to vertex parallelism is proposed.

Algorithm 2. Support Initialization

Input: an undirected graph $G_0 = (V_{G_0}, E_{G_0})$
Output: sup, support array
 1: **for all** $v \in V$ **do**
 2:    **for all** $u \in N(v)$ **do**
 3:       assume $u > v \wedge |N(u)| > |N(v)|$
 4:       **if** $|N(u)| \gg |N(v)|$ **then**
 5:          $sup(e(u,v)) \leftarrow BinaryMerge(N(u), N(v))$
 6:       **else**
 7:          $sup(e(u,v)) \leftarrow SequentialMerge(N(u), N(v))$
 8:       **end if**
 9:    **end for**
10: **end for**

As Algorithm 2 shown, first, parallel computing by vertexes. When taking the intersection of the edge composed of the current vertex and the neighbor vertex, compare the neighbor set size between them, i.e., the vertex degree. When it is too skewed, choose the binary search to take the set intersection. When the scale of the two is similar, the basic merging is adopted. In the SI, the parallel method of data division by vertex is adopted between processes. Because it will be used many times after taking the current vertex neighbor set data once, it makes more full use of the cache. In the IEP, because of the method of edge peeling, the parallel of data division by vertex is required between processes. Both data division by vertex or edge, the part from Algorithm 2 Line 3 to Line 8 is applicable.

We observe that there is a certain optimization space for merging based on binary search. Specifically, when taking the intersection of two sets, each binary search is independent of the other. However, we can find that the results of each binary search can be applied to the next binary search, reduce the range of the next search, and further optimize the efficiency of taking the intersection.

3.4   Iterative Edge Peeling

Except for some differences in the algorithm, as Algorithm 3 shown, this part has heuristic k range division before IEP, local preprocessing of NUMA nodes, and write back global array after IEP.

The purpose of the heuristic k partition is to balance the load among NUMA nodes as much as possible. After observing and analyzing the experimental data, we find that the calculation time is related to the number of edges and triangles. Section 3.5 will explain the specific design and methods.

Algorithm 3. Iterative Edge Peeling

Input: an undirected graph $G_0 = (V_{G_0}, E_{G_0})$, a support array sup, a target range $[k_l, k_r]$

Output: $\Phi_k(k \in [k_l, k_r])$, target k-classes of G

1: $G \leftarrow FilterCompressed(G, sup)$
2: $sup \leftarrow SI(G)$
3: $k \leftarrow k_l$
4: **while** $|E| \neq 0 \wedge k \leftarrow k_l$ **do**
5:     $E_{remove} \leftarrow \{e|e \in E \wedge sup(e) = k - 2\}$
6:     **while** $|E_{remove}| \neq 0$ **do**
7:        $\Phi_k \leftarrow \Phi_k \cup E_{remove}$
8:        **for all** $e \in E_{remove}$ **do**
9:           **for all** $\triangle_{uvw}, e \in \triangle_{uvw}$ **do**
10:              **for all** $e' \in \triangle_{uvw}, e' \neq e$ **do**
11:                 $sup(e') \leftarrow max(k - 2, sup(e') - 1)$
12:              **end for**
13:           **end for**
14:           $E \leftarrow E \setminus \{e\}$
15:        **end for**
16:        $E_{remove} \leftarrow \{e|e \in E \wedge sup(e) = k - 2\}$
17:     **end while**
18:     $k \leftarrow k + 1$
19: **end while**

Local preprocessing of NUMA nodes this step is only performed on NUMA nodes when the range starting value is not 2, that is, $k \neq 2$. Firstly, copy a support array to the local area, and then mark all edges less than the minimum value of the interval, which is regarded as removed from the graph. Then, according to the remaining graphs, rebuild a set of graph topology locally, and re-initialize the support. On this basis, carry out the IEP in the range. The process here is the same as the IEP of PKT.

Write back the global array. After the calculation of each NUMA node is completed, the local support array on each node is only a partial solution, which needs to be written back to the global support array. Before writing back, you need to set the global support to zero, and all nodes should complete the calculation of the IEP stage. During writeback, each NUMA node needs to traverse the local k-value array and update the global k-value array. The updated principle is that if the k of the corresponding edge of the local k-value array is within the local k range, the k corresponding to the position of the global k array is updated.

3.5   Heuristic Partition of k

Before each NUMA node performs IEP, we need to determine the range of k calculated by each node. According to PKT, each iteration (i.e. decomposing of one level) needs to complete $|E_k|$ times triangle enumeration. Further, from our experiments, it is found that there is a certain relationship between the peeled edge of each k-level and the corresponding edge with $k - 2$ support.

In addition, when the lower bound of the partition range is not 0, the overhead of filtering, compressing, and reconstructing the graph before calculating the range needs to be considered. This part of the calculation is mainly to initialize the support of a part of the graph. Based on the triangle counting algorithm, the amount of calculation is positively correlated with the edges in the graph.

Therefore, we design a heuristic k partition method based on the number of edges. Specifically, first, complete the calculation of the edge number distribution of each support degree for the whole graph. Next, based on the edge distribution, make the calculation amount of each NUMA node closely (i.e., the number of edges processed closely).

Besides, we found that when the graph size is large enough, the performance improvement caused by increasing threads (on the same socket) is less affected by memory access latency or data contention. So we also adjust the unit when dividing k range based on the graph scale, mainly the number of edges. So, for large graph, we use two NUMA nodes on the same socket as a task execution unit. Compared with taking each NUMA node as a task execution unit, the space occupation is reduced.

3.6   Algorithm Analysis

This section will analyze the algorithm from the time and memory complexity.

Time Complexity. As described in PKT [13] SI cost is mainly determined by triangle counting. As described in Sect. 3.3 the time complexity of each $|N(u) \cup N(v)|$ calculation is $O(min(d(u), d(v)))$ or $O(log(d(u)) \cdot d(v))$. The time complexity of the above two cases is $O(|e|^{1.5})$, as demonstrated by the previous triangle listing work [28]. IEP cost includes triangle enumeration (TE), $O(|\triangle|)$ support update, and $O(|\triangle|)$ edge filtering. We use binary-based merging for TE with a time complexity of $O(min(d(u), d(v)))$ (as demonstrated in Sect. 2). Considering the complexity of $O(min(d(u), d(v)))$, TE is $O(|e|^{1.5})$ time [31]. This is because the overall time complexity limit of TE is in $\sum_{e \in E} min(d(u), d(v)) = O(\alpha \cdot |E|)$, ($\alpha$ is representing the arboricity of the graph [7]). In the worst case, this bound is $O(|e|^{1.5})$, because

$\alpha \leq p \cdot |E|$. Therefore, the total time complexity of our algorithm is $O(|e|^{1.5})$. Although the time complexity limit is the same as the previous work [13], our optimization significantly reduces the actual workload.

Memory Complexity. The input graph Es and adj arrays in CSR format are in $O(|E| + |V|)$ space. Auxiliary arrays for preprocessing and graphics compression are in $O(|V|)$ space. The edge list, edge mapping, support values, and processing flag arrays El, Eid, sup, and P are all in the $O(|E|)$ space. There may be other auxiliary arrays, but they are generally in $O(|E|)$ or $O(|V|)$. The array used for the heuristic k partition may be a special one, its size is sup_{max}. Generally, this value will not exceed $O(|E|)$ or $O(|V|)$. Therefore, the total memory complexity of our algorithm is $O(|E| + |V|)$.

4 Implementation

Our parallelism is implemented by OpenMP [3]. And we do different parallels at different levels. In the SI, we divide the vertex individual as the smallest data division unit (In practice, we set 10 as a scheduling unit) to each thread and complete the support calculation of its outgoing edge in parallel. In the IEP, k is divided into several ranges by the heuristic method according to the number of NUMA nodes and then executed on different NUMA nodes at the same time. On a NUMA node, parallel processing is performed in each iteration, and the edges to be peeled are divided into each thread.

In order to handle concurrent updates and partial array maintenance, we use GCC's built-in atomic primitive [1]. Specifically, we use the atomic comparison and exchange (CAS) primitive. At first, it compares the value in the memory address with the target value, then it exchanges the value in the memory with the new value only when the comparison value and the target value are equal. We also use atomic fetch and addition, acquisition, and subtraction primitives. Each primitive combines the read, modify, and write steps into an atomic operation.

Furthermore, in order to avoid the overhead caused by remote memory access and thread migration, we use NUMA interface [2]. Specifically, we bind each thread to a unique core and further bind it to the local memory of the core. In IEP, except for the start and end phases, the remaining main memory access behaviors occur locally. As for the size of the execution unit in the heuristic method, we take 10^8 as the boundary. When the edges' number is greater than, two NUMA nodes are taken as a unit. For data skew in triangle enumeration, we take 10 as the boundary. If the ratio of the two sets size is greater than 10, it is considered that there is data skew.

5 Evaluation

In this chapter, we mainly compare the performance improvement of our method and the PKT on NUMA devices. At the same time, we also evaluate the scalability performance on different data sets and compared the optimized initialization support with that without optimization.

5.1   Experimental Setup

The evaluation was carried out on a dual-socket Huawei shared memory server with 256 GB memory. The server contains two 2.6 GHz Kunpeng 920 7260 processors. Each processor has 64 cores distributed on 2 dies, 64 MB L3 cache, i.e., there are 4 NUMA nodes distributed on two sockets, and each socket has 2 NUMA nodes.

All the codes are compiled using the GNU C/C++ compiler with −O3 optimization. And for parallelization, we use OpenMP and enable environment variable OMP_PROC_BIND.

For the dataset, we selected several real-world graphs of different sizes. These datasets are picked from the Stanford Network Analysis Project [15] and are listed in Table 3. The cit-Patents is the U.S. patent citation network spanning almost 30 years. The wiki-topcat is a web graph of Wikipedia hyperlinks collected in September 2011. Besides, the soc-pokec, soc-LiveJournal, com-orkut and com-friendster are social networks from different regions or fields. Before the experiment, we make a preliminary arrangement of the data, such as transforming a directed graph into an undirected graph, deleting duplicate edges, and so on. Besides we also list the number of triangles, vertexes and maximum degree, maximum trussness for them, respectively. Most of the graphs we used are snapshots of social networks. We repeat each experiment more than 5 times and take other values except the maximum and minimum values to take the mean value, to reduce the experimental error.

Table 3. Statistics of datasets and Performance

Graph	$|E|(\times 10^6)$	$|V|(\times 10^6)$	$|\triangle|(\times 10^9)$	d_{max}	t_{max}	SI			IEP			Total		
						PKT	NKT	S_p	PKT	NKT	S_p	PKT	NKT	S_p
cit-Patents	16.52	3.77	0.01	793	36	0.87	0.54	1.61	1.15	1.14	1.01	2.04	1.70	1.20
wiki-topcat	28.51	1.79	0.05	100029	39	4.11	0.53	7.75	4.70	2.55	1.84	8.97	3.11	2.88
soc-pokec	30.62	1.63	0.03	14854	29	0.42	0.29	1.45	2.20	1.62	1.36	2.70	1.93	1.40
soc-LiveJournal	68.99	4.85	0.29	20333	362	1.30	0.53	2.45	8.55	3.30	2.59	9.89	3.85	2.57
com-orkut	117.19	3.07	0.63	33313	78	7.29	3.39	2.15	23.70	15.10	1.57	31.00	18.5	1.68
com-friendster	1806.07	65.61	4.17	5214	129	150.55	71.30	2.11	346.20	245.71	1.41	497.25	317.89	1.56

5.2   Evaluation of Comparing with PKT

We compare SI, IEP, and the whole truss decomposition of our method with PKT.

Support Initialization. We record our method in this paper as NKT (i.e. An optimized parallel k−truss decomposition for NUMA). In the SI column of Table 3, PKT and NKT record the time-consuming of SI phase of the two methods when 128 threads are used in parallel, in seconds, accurate to two decimal places. The S_p represents the speedup ratio, it is the ratio of PKT to NKT. The same applies to the column of IEP and Total of Table 3. As the SI column of Table 3 shown, NKT is about twice as fast as PKT. The speedup ratio of wiki-topcat graph is up to nearly 8 times. The possible reason is that there are many data skews in the graph, as the highest vertex d_{max} is shown in Table 3.

Iterative Edge Peeling. We also compare IEP with PKT, this is the most time-consuming part of algorithm, in most cases. As the IEP column of Table 3 shown, our method can achieve an average speedup of 1.6, excluding the best dataset, soc-LiveJournal, and the worst, cit-Patents. The limited improvement on cit-Patents may be due to the small size of its data set. When too many threads are used, the performance improvement is limited due to the high proportion of data contention.

Truss Decomposition. We compare the truss decomposition algorithm with PKT as a whole. Through experiments, as the Total column of Table 3 shown, we found that on the same 128 core server, compared with PKT, we can achieve an average speedup of nearly 1.9. Careful observation shows that the total time is not equal to the sum of the value in SI and IEP. The time recorded by Total here is from the beginning of SI to the end of obtaining the last k-class array, which also includes operations such as k division and writing back to the global array. However, it accounts for a low proportion of the total time, so it is not listed separately.

5.3   Evaluation of Scalability

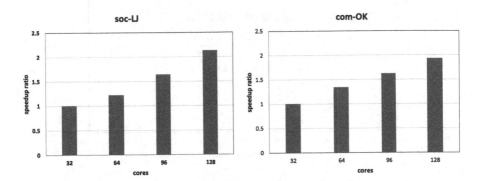

Fig. 5. Parallel relative scaling

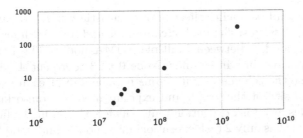

Fig. 6. Dataset size scaling

Scalability of Parallel Threads. We report the relative parallel acceleration of multithreaded execution in Fig. 5. As shown in Fig. 5, We show the parallel scalability on soc-LiveJournal and com-orkut. The vertical axis represents the speedup ratio and the horizontal axis represents the number of cores used (one NUMA node is added each time, i.e. 32). Note that we use the runtime of a single NUMA node as the baseline. On medium and large-scale data sets, we can achieve a nearly linear speedup ratio.

Scalability of Data Set Size. From the data set size and running time of our experiment, we draw a figure about the scalability of the data set size, as shown in the Fig. 6. The vertical axis represents the calculation time in seconds, and the horizontal axis represents the number of data set edges, both in the form of logarithm with the bottom of 10. It is not difficult to see from the figure that our method has near-linear scalability in data set size. Here are the results obtained by using our implement in the case of 128 threads in parallel.

5.4   Evaluation of Heuristic k Partition

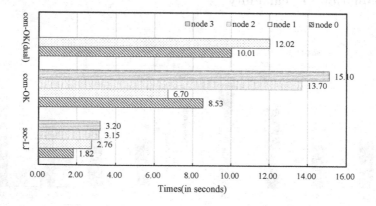

Fig. 7. IEP time of each NUMA node

We evaluate the load balancing effect of our heuristic k partition among nodes. As shown in Fig. 7, we test the load of com-orkut and soc-LiveJournal, denoting as com-OK and soc-LJ, between Multiple NUMA nodes. The horizontal axis represents computing time in seconds. Node 0 to 3 represent 4 NUMA nodes. And we also test the scheme of auto-adjusting the size of each execution unit according to the size of the graph and experimented on com-orkut by taking two NUMA nodes as a task execution unit, which is shown in the figure as com-OK(dual). Since it has only 2 task execution units, node 0 and node 1 refer to the calculation time of the 2 units respectively. It is not difficult to see from the chart that there is a certain load imbalance during node execution. This is because we must divide at the truss level, but the number of edges in each range cannot be divided evenly. In order to quickly complete the division with low computational cost, we adopt a relatively simple traversal method and set an error interval of 30%, so there may be a certain load imbalance. By comparing com-OK with com-OK(dual), when the graph scale is relatively large, using more NUMA nodes(i.e. the number of threads) as a task execution unit is better. It also proves that when the graph scale is large, the negative impact of data conflict and remote memory access is smaller.

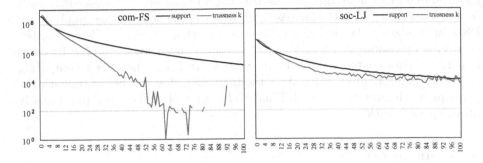

Fig. 8. Edge distribution at different levels of k-truss and support

In addition, we count the number of edges contained in each k-truss level and corresponding support (as shown in Fig. 8). In the figure, the vertical axis is the number of edges (expressed by the logarithm with the base of 10), and the horizontal axis is trussness (actually $k - 2$) or support. Note that here, because soc-LiveJournal and com-orkut are too large and dense, we only show the distribution of their partial edges up to $k - 2 = 100$. We can observe that there is a certain correlation between the two, although there may be a large deviation with the increase of support and trussness k.

5.5   Evaluation of Triangle Enumeration Optimization

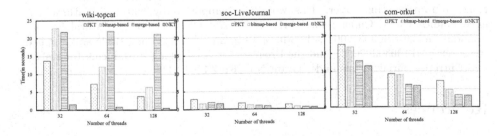

Fig. 9. Comparison of triangle enumeration

We evaluate four methods of triangle enumeration with the different number of threads on three graphs. In Fig. 9, the vertical and horizontal axis represents computing time, in seconds, and the number of threads used, i.e., the number of NUMA nodes used, respectively. The three charts are the results on wiki-topcat, soc-Liverjournal, and com-orkut. PKT represents the original triangle enumeration. Bitmap-based represents using bitmap calculation for each edge without atomic update. Merge-based represents using the merging method for each edge, and NKT represents our optimized method. It can be seen that the merge-based takes more time on the wiki-topcat because the dataset may have serious data skew. With the increase of graph size, the performance gap between PKT and others is becoming smaller. Because that there are a large number of atomic operations in PKT. When the ratio of data size to threads becomes larger, the data contention can be alleviated. NKT has the fastest computing speed on data sets of all sizes. With the increase of the number of threads, the performance improvement of PKT method is limited, while NKT has a nearly linear speedup ratio.

6   Conclusion

We design a multi-level parallel truss decomposition algorithm for NUMA shared memory multi-core platform. And for the characteristics of NUMA, the algorithm proposes a method of parallel computing k in different ranges between NUMA nodes, which avoids the delay caused by remote memory access and data contention to a certain extent. On a 128 core NUMA system, we demonstrate that our algorithm reaches a mean speedup of nearly 2× compared with the original method PKT, by experimenting on a group of real world graph instances.

The future work related to this algorithm includes more fine-grained scheduling with thread as the unit (at present, NUMA node is the smallest unit) and the method of extending to distributed systems. In addition, this idea can also be applied to multi-level cohesive subgraph isomorphism algorithms other than truss decomposition, such as core decomposition.

Acknowledgments. We are grateful to our anonymous reviewers for their suggestions to improve this paper. This work was supported by National Natural Science Foundation of China (No. U1811461, 61872392), Guangdong Natural Science Foundation (2018B030312002), the Major Program of Guangdong Basic and Applied Research (2019B030302002), and the Program for Guangdong Introducing Innovative and Entrepreneurial Teams under Grant No. 2016ZT06D211.

References

1. Gcc atomic built-ins. https://gcc.gnu.org/onlinedocs/gcc-4.1.1/gcc/Atomic-Builtins.html. Accessed 2021
2. Numactl documentation. https://github.com/numactl/numactl. Accessed 2021

3. Openmp documentation. https://www.openmp.org/. Accessed 2021
4. Akbas, E., Peixiang, Z.: Truss-based community search: a truss-equivalence based indexing approach. Proc. VLDB Endowment **10**(11), 1298–1309 (2017)
5. Almasri, M., Anjum, O., Pearson, C., Qureshi, Z., Hwu, W.M.: Update on k-truss decomposition on GPU. In: 2019 IEEE High Performance Extreme Computing Conference (HPEC) (2019)
6. Batagelj, V., Zaveršnik, M.: An o(m) algorithm for cores decomposition of networks. Comput. Sci. **1**(6), 34–37 (2003)
7. Chiba, N., Nishizeki, T.: Arboricity and subgraph listing algorithms. SIAM J. Comput. **14**(1), 210–223 (1985)
8. Cohen, J.: Trusses: Cohesive subgraphs for social network analysis. National security agency technical report 16(3.1) (2008)
9. Diab, S., Olabi, M.G., Hajj, I.E.: Ktrussexplorer: exploring the design space of k-truss decomposition optimizations on GPUs. In: 2020 IEEE High Performance Extreme Computing Conference, HPEC 2020, Waltham, MA, USA, 22–24 September, 2020, pp. 1–8. IEEE (2020)
10. Gui, C., Zheng, L., Yao, P., Liao, X., Jin, H.: Fast triangle counting on GPU. In: 2019 IEEE High Performance Extreme Computing Conference, HPEC 2019, Waltham, MA, USA, 24–26 September, 2019, pp. 1–7. IEEE (2019)
11. Huang, X., Cheng, H., Qin, L., Tian, W., Yu, J.X.: Querying k-truss community in large and dynamic graphs. In: Dyreson, C.E., Li, F., Özsu, M.T. (eds.) International Conference on Management of Data, SIGMOD 2014, Snowbird, UT, USA, 22–27 June, 2014, pp. 1311–1322. ACM (2014)
12. Kabir, H., Madduri, K.: Parallel k-truss decomposition on multicore systems. In: 2017 IEEE High Performance Extreme Computing Conference (HPEC) (2017)
13. Kabir, H., Madduri, K.: Shared-memory graph truss decomposition. In: 2017 IEEE 24th International Conference on High Performance Computing (HiPC), pp. 13–22 (2017)
14. Kaiyuan, Z., Haibo, C.: Numa-aware graph-structured analytics. Acm Sigplan Notices A Monthly Publication of the Special Interest Group on Programming Languages (2015)
15. Leskovec, J., Krevl, A.: Snap datasets: Stanford large network dataset collection, June 2014. http://snap.stanford.edu/data. Accessed 2021
16. Luce, R.D.: Connectivity and generalized cliques in sociometric group structure. Psychometrika **15**(2), 169 (1950)
17. Mailthody, V.S., Date, K., Qureshi, Z., Pearson, C., Hwu, W.M.: Collaborative (cpu + gpu) algorithms for triangle counting and truss decomposition. In: 2018 IEEE High Performance extreme Computing Conference (HPEC) (2018)
18. Matthieu, L.: Main-memory triangle computations for very large (sparse (power-law)) graphs. Theoret. Comput. Sci. **407**(1), 458–473 (2008)
19. Ouyang, Z., Wu, S., Zhao, T., Yue, D., Zhang, T.: Memory-efficient GPU-based exact and parallel triangle counting in large graphs, pp. 2195–2199, August 2019
20. Pearce, R.: Triangle counting for scale-free graphs at scale in distributed memory. In: 2017 IEEE High Performance Extreme Computing Conference (HPEC) (2017)
21. Pei, J., Jiang, D., Zhang, A.: On mining cross-graph quasi-cliques. In: Proceedings of the Eleventh ACM SIGKDD International Conference on Knowledge Discovery in Data Mining, pp. 228–238 (2005)
22. Rossi, R.A.: Fast triangle core decomposition for mining large graphs. In: Pacific-asia Conference on Knowledge Discovery & Data Mining (2014)
23. Samsi, S., et al.: Static graph challenge: subgraph isomorphism, pp. 1–6, September 2017

24. Sariyuce, A.E., Seshadhri, C., Pinar, A., Catalyurek, U.V.: Finding the hierar-
    chy of dense subgraphs using nucleus decompositions. In: Proceedings of the 24th
    International Conference on World Wide Web, pp. 927–937 (2015)
25. Seidman, S., Foster, B.: A graph-theoretic generalization of the clique concept*. J.
    Math. Sociol. **6**(1), 139–154 (1978)
26. Shang, H., Tao, Y., Gao, Y., Zhang, C., Wang, X.: An improved invariant for
    matching molecular graphs based on vf2 algorithm. IEEE Trans. Syst. Man
    Cybern. Syst. **45**, 122–128 (2015)
27. Smith, S., Xing, L., Ahmed, N.K., Tom, A.S., Karypis, G.: Truss decomposition
    on shared-memory parallel systems. In: 2017 IEEE High Performance Extreme
    Computing Conference (HPEC) (2017)
28. Suri, S., Vassilvitskii, S.: Counting triangles and the curse of the last reducer. In:
    Proceedings of the 20th International Conference on World Wide Web, WWW
    2011, Hyderabad, India, 28 March–1 April, 2011, pp. 607–614. ACM (2011)
29. Tom, A.S., Sundaram, N., Ahmed, N.K., Smith, S., Karypis, G.: Exploring opti-
    mizations on shared-memory platforms for parallel triangle counting algorithms.
    In: High Performance Extreme Computing Conference (2017)
30. Voegele, C., Lu, Y.S., Pai, S., Pingali, K.: Parallel triangle counting and k-
    truss identification using graph-centric methods. In: 2017 IEEE High Performance
    Extreme Computing Conference (HPEC) (2017)
31. Wang, J., Cheng, J.: Truss decomposition in massive networks. Proc. VLDB
    Endow. **5**(9), 812–823 (2012)
32. Wu, J., Goshulak, A., Srinivasan, V., Thomo, A.: K-truss decomposition of large
    networks on a single consumer-grade machine. In: IEEE/ACM 2018 International
    Conference on Advances in Social Networks Analysis and Mining, ASONAM 2018,
    Barcelona, Spain, 28–31 August, 2018 (2018)
33. Yang, L., Hao, F., Li, S., Min, G., Kim, H.C., Yau, S.: An efficient approach to gen-
    erating location-sensitive recommendations in ad-hoc social network environments.
    IEEE Trans. Serv. Comput. **8**, 1 (2015)
34. Yulin, C., Zhuohang, L., Shixuan, S., Qiong, L., Yue, W.: Accelerating all-edge
    common neighbor counting on three processors. In: Proceedings of the 48th Interna-
    tional Conference on Parallel Processing, ICPP 2019, Kyoto, Japan, 05–08 August,
    2019, pp. 42:1–42:10. ACM (2019)
35. Yulin, C., Zhuohang, L., Shixuan, S., Yue, W., Qiong, L.: Accelerating truss decom-
    position on heterogeneous processors. Proc. VLDB Endow. **13**(10), 1751–1764
    (2020)
36. Zhang, J., Spampinato, D., McMillan, S., Franchetti, F.: Preliminary exploration
    of large-scale triangle counting on shared-memory multicore system. In: IEEE High
    Performance Extreme Computing Conference (2018)
37. Zhang, Y., Yu, J.X.: Unboundedness and efficiency of truss maintenance in evolving
    graphs. In: Proceedings of the 2019 International Conference on Management of
    Data, SIGMOD Conference 2019, Amsterdam, The Netherlands, 30 June–5 July,
    2019, pp. 1024–1041. ACM (2019)

Large-Scale Parallel Alignment Algorithm for SMRT Reads

Zeyu Xia, Yingbo Cui[✉], Ang Zhang, Peng Zhang, Sifan Long, Tao Tang, Lin Peng, Chun Huang, Canqun Yang, and Xiangke Liao

National University of Defense Technology, Changsha 410073, Hunan, China
yingbocui@nudt.edu.cn

Abstract. Single Molecule Real-Time (SMRT) sequencing is one of the popular issues in third-generation sequencing technology. Compared with next-generation sequencing technology, SMRT can detect single molecules and has much longer read lengths, which also leads to a huge increase in the amount of data. As the performance of a single CPU has reached its bottleneck, single-node computing is far from meeting the SMRT sequencing requirements. An alternative solution is parallel computing. It makes the alignment algorithm run on multiple computing nodes, thus greatly decreases the running time. The Regional Hashing-based Alignment Tool (rHAT) is a novel approach developed especially for SMRT sequencing. It has better sensitivity, improved correctness compared with existing sequence alignment tools. However, the original rHAT source can only run on a single node, which dramatically limits its performance. In this article, we developed PrHAT, a parallel sequence alignment version of rHAT. We test PrHAT on simulated and real datasets which the original rHAT used. Our results show that PrHAT reduces the computing wall-time from nearly an hour to several minutes. In the process of increasing the number of nodes from 2 to 16 on aligning large-scale datasets, PrHAT achieves speedups of 1.94–14.87x. The parallel efficiency decreases from 97% to 93%; moreover, its weak scaling remains almost unchanged. Based on PrHAT, we developed OpenPrHAT. It has a similar performance towards PrHAT, but can run on other computing devices like GPU in the platform. We expect that the implementation of PrHAT will promote the development of SMRT in third-generation sequencing technology.

Keywords: Third-generation sequencing · SMRT · MPI · OpenCL · Parallel sequence alignment

1 Introduction

As sequencing technology continues to develop, the amount of measured DNA sequence data is proliferating rapidly, which has promoted the in-depth development of related research directions in bioinformatics. As a crucial element of bioinformatics, sequence alignment has achieved significant progress since it first emerged. The first generation of sequencing technology, specifically Sanger sequencing [1] technology, has been widely applied in the Human Genome Project. However, due to its limitations (including low sequencing coverage, long sequencing cycle, and high cost), Sanger sequencing technology is not suitable for datasets with large amounts. The second-generation sequencing technology, also known as next-generation sequencing technology (NGS) [2], has brought revolutionary improvements to the field of sequencing technology. Compared with the Sanger sequencing technology, next-generation sequencing technology has several characteristics that make it superior, including its high throughput and high sequence data coverage, making it suitable for large-scale and high-throughput sequence data processing [3].

The birth of single molecular real-time sequencing technology (SMRT) has in turn promoted the development of third-generation sequencing technology [4]. Both PacBio and Oxford Nanopore have exploited SMRT. This approach can measure DNA sequence fragments with an average length of 10000 bp. The problem with SMRT is that the measurement of sequence data has a high error rate [5], as high as 15%. However, this kind of long read is still of great significance to specific genomic problems.

Regional Hashing-based Alignment Tool (rHAT) [6] is a novel third-generation sequence alignment approach designed to process noisy long reads. It consists of three key phases: (i) constructing the index of each window's k-mers; (ii) generating and prioritizing the k-mers of each seed; (iii) analyzing and manipulating the candidate windows [6]. Compared with other state-of-the-art aligners, such as BWA-SW [7], BLASR [8], and BWA-MEM [9]. rHAT is robust when aligning reads with a high error rate and can align SMRT reads with high efficiency. Meanwhile, the throughput of rHAT is reasonably high among these aligners.

The original rHAT source program implements thread-level parallel to speed up the sequence alignment. Therefore, it can run only on a single node. Nowadays, due to the explosive growth of data and the performance of a single node encounters a bottleneck, thread-level parallelism in one node is far from meeting the actual needs. One feasible way of optimizing the program is parallel programming, which makes the algorithm run on multiple nodes. And with the implementation of heterogeneous parallel, the alignment can be computed by other processing units like GPU, FPGA, Xeon Phi, etc. in a node.

In this paper, we propose PrHAT, a parallel version of rHAT. It dramatically decreases the time required for matching large-scale sequencing fragments to a reference genome. Based on PrHAT, we use OpenCL to accelerate the alignment matrix and propose OpenPrHAT. The main contributions of this paper can be listed as follows:

1. We develop the primary version of PrHAT, PrHAT-ND, by distributing the read file with the number.
2. By considering Load Balance and hash table transmission, we optimize PrHAT-ND to PrHAT-PD and PrHAT-PDBc by distributing read files with pointer and utilizing *MPI-Bcast*.
3. We test the three versions of PrHAT on real and simulated datasets and verify each version's speedup, parallel efficiency, and weak scaling efficiency.
4. Based on PrHAT, we use OpenCL to call the GPU and accelerate the alignment.

The remainder of this paper is organized as follows. Section 2 introduces the specific way of paralleling rHAT. Section 3 presents the experimental results of each version on both simulated and real datasets. Finally, Sect. 4 concludes the discussion of different versions of rHAT we developed and outlines some avenues for future work.

2 Parallel of rHAT

2.1 Sequence Distribution

Since distributed memory systems share neither variables nor RAM, each process in PrHAT needs to apply for address space and read in the index file. After loading the index, PrHAT initializes the alignment. PrHAT obtains most of its parallel acceleration by distributing sequences across different processes. There are typically two strategies used to implement sequence distribution.

The first of these strategies is to distribute the read sequences by their number. The FASTQ file uses four lines to record each sequence [10]. We can obtain the number of reads in the FASTQ file N. Each process processes N/p pieces of sequence alignment, where p is the number of processes.

Considering that the length of each sequence is uneven, distributing the FASTQ file by its number would cause each process to manage a diverse volume of the read sequences; this leads to load imbalance, resulting in uneven processing time. An alternative strategy is to distribute the read sequences by their pointer. According to this strategy, each process processes a volume of sequence alignments fileSize/p, where fileSize is the size of the FASTQ file [11].

2.2 MPI Version of rHAT

Message-Passing Interface (MPI) is a commonly used tool for implementing parallel programming in distributed memory systems. Message passing refers to a process in which each process executed in parallel has its own independent stack and code segment. The independent programs explicitly call the communication function to complete the information interaction between processes.

The Primary Version of PrHAT. Based on the first sequence distribution strategy, we develop the primary version of PrHAT, PrHAT-ND. Figure 1 presents an overview of PrHAT-ND. Generally speaking, PrHAT-ND consists of three main phases:

Initialization. This phase is the initialization of the MPI environment and some additional variables. First, we initialize the environment MPI. Then in the second step, we use the structure pointer address *read_rank_Pos* and *read_rank_endPos* to store the start and end position that each process needs to process. The remaining steps are to load the exiting hash table and open the read sequences from the FASTQ file path for each process.

Sequence Distribution. In this phase, process 0 will calculate the number of read sequences N, after which it will broadcast the number N to process $1 \sim p-1$. After receiving the number N, each process sets its *read_rank_Pos* to $i*(N/p)$, where p is the number of processes and i is the rank of each process.

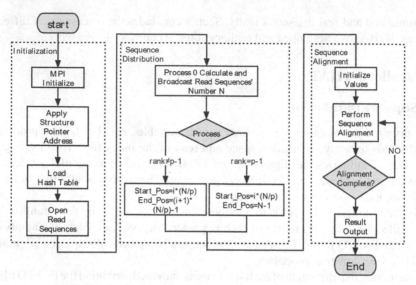

Fig. 1. An overview of PrHAT-ND for sequence alignment

Sequence Alignment. Following sequence distribution, each process obtains the start and end position of the read sequences it needs to process. When processing the sequence alignment, each process moves the pointer to the position to be processed according to *read_rank_Pos*. It then determines whether the pointer's position exceeds the value of *read_rank_endPos* after aligning each piece of the read sequences. If the pointer's position exceeds the value of *read_rank_endPos*, the process will exit the sequence alignment loop.

The Advanced Version of PrHAT. PrHAT-PD distributes the FASTQ file with reference to the pointers of the read sequences rather than the number. Figure 2 illustrates the process of PrHAT-PD for sequence distribution. The general process consists of two key parts, as outlined below:

Simple Distribution. We apply the same structure pointer used in PrHAT-ND to store the FASTQ file's pointer, start position, and end position of each process. The key difference is that the integer variables *read_rank_Pos* and *read_rank_endPos* are used to store the position of the pointers, not the order position.

Precise Distribution. Once Simple Distribution is complete, each process obtains its *read_rank_Pos* and *read_rank_endPos*. However, Simple Distribution only ensures that each process will process an even volume of data. The file pointer of each process may not point to each read's head, which will result in the program's failure. Therefore, in Precise Distribution, we relocate the pointer to the head of each read sequence.

PrHAT with MPI_Bcast. Each process obtains the hash table by loading the existing hash file In PrHAT-PD. An alternate strategy for each process to get the hash table is to use *MPI_Bcast*.

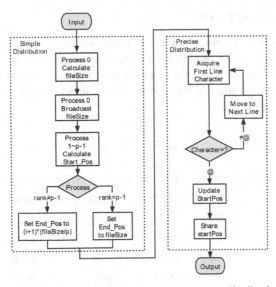

Fig. 2. The process of PrHAT-PD for sequence distribution.

In MPI programming, it is inefficient to send data from one particular process to all other processes with *MPI_Send* and *MPI_Recv*. Therefore, *MPI_Bcast* was developed to facilitate more efficient broadcasting. One of the most common and efficient approaches is protocol tree broadcasting [12], in which all processes receiving broadcast data participate in the data broadcasting process. Using this approach reduces the complexity of broadcasting from $O(n)$ to $O(log\ n)$. Figure 3 illustrates the structure of protocol tree broadcasting.

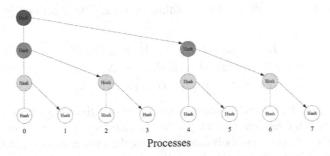

Fig. 3. The structure of protocol tree broadcasting.

Based on PrHAT-PD, we utilize *MPI_Bcast* to broadcast the hash table and develop the third version of PrHAT PrHAT-PDBc. In PrHAT-PDBc, process *0* is responsible for loading the hash table from the hash index directory. Once the hash table has been loaded, process *0* broadcasts it to process *1 ~ p−1* via *MPI_Bcast*. After the hash file is obtained, each process performs the sequence alignment, as in PrHAT- PD.

2.3 OpenCL Version of PrHAT

At the stage of alignment, rHAT mainly contains two voids: void *proCans* and void *conductAlign*. The first void is used to extend the candidate windows. And the other one is responsible for the calculation of alignment matrix. The time computing the alignment matrix is over 60% at the stage of alignment. Table 1 lists ten random runs at the stage of alignment.

Table 1. Ten random runs at the stage of alignment.

Total time(ns)	proCans	Percentage	conductAlign	Percentage
4784	1965	**41.07**	2720	**56.85**
3557	1324	**37.22**	2209	**62.10**
6450	2044	**31.68**	4377	**67.86**
3801	1185	**31.17**	2580	**67.87**
4243	1725	**40.65**	2487	**58.61**
4758	1793	**37.68**	2932	**61.62**
8715	2425	**27.82**	6229	**71.47**
5567	2765	**49.66**	2764	**49.64**
4506	1790	**39.72**	2676	**59.38**
4408	2888	**65.51**	1466	**33.25**

The Smith-Waterman Algorithm. rHAT uses the Smith-Waterman algorithm [13] to calculate the best subsequence match between the given sequences in the void *conductAlign*. Gotoh [14] modified the algorithm in 1982. The algorithm is defined as follows:

$$H_{i,j} = \max\{H_{i-1,j-1} + M, E_{i,j}, F_{i,j}, 0\}$$
$$E_{i,j} = \max\{(E_{i,j-1}, H_{i,j-1} - \Delta) - \delta\}$$
$$F_{i,j} = \max\{(F_{i-1,j}, H_{i-1,j} - \Delta) - \delta\}$$

Where $H_{i-1,j-1} + M$ is the alignment score of the two given sequences. $E_{i,j}$ and $F_{i,j}$ are used to denote the influence of the previous column and row on the current score, respectively. Δ and δ are the symbols used to indicate the gap open and extension penalty, respectively. M is the scoring matrix. It usually contains the match and mismatch scores between the two sequences. Additionally, $H_{i,j}$, $E_{i,j}$, and $F_{i,j}$ are set to 0, when $i < 1$ or $j < 1$. We define the two sequences with the length of m and n, the computational complexity of the algorithm is $O(mn)$, and the space complexity is $O(m)$ [15].

OpenCL. OpenCL (Open Computing Language) is first proposed by Apple company. It aims to provide a general open API, which can call computing units like GPU, FPGA, and Xeon Phi, etc., in a node. Compared with other programming languages, the main advantage of OpenCL is that it has good portability.

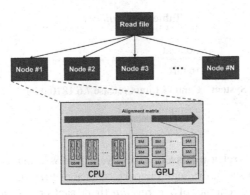

Fig. 4. The flow of OpenPrHAT

OpenPrHAT. Based on PrHAT-PD, we developed the OpenCL version of PrHAT, OpenPrHAT. It can also run on multiple nodes like PrHAT. Moreover, OpenPrHAT can choose different computing devices at the alignment stage. Figure 4 illustrates the flow of OpenPrHAT. The read file is divided into different nodes evenly. And in each node, it uses thread-level parallel as the original rHAT source to do the alignment. When coming to the alignment stage, we call GPU in the platform and calculate the alignment matrix.

Thus far, we have developed three versions of PrHAT. PrHAT-ND is the primary version we utilize to parallel rHAT. In this version, we distribute the datasets with reference to the number of the read sequences. Considering load balancing, we further developed the advanced version of PrHAT PrHAT-PD, which distributes the read sequences by pointer. PrHAT-PDBc follows the idea of PrHAT-PD, but it utilizes *MPI_Bcast* to broadcast the hash table rather than loading the hash table by each processer. Based on PrHAT, we developed OpenPrHAT. It can choose computing devices like GPU in each node to calculate the alignment matrix. In the following section, we test the three versions of PrHAT and OpenPrHAT on simulated and real SMRT datasets to determine their performance.

3 Results

We utilize the HPCL Cluster Server to test the performance of each version of PrHAT. HPCL Cluster Server has hundreds of nodes, the single node configuration of which is listed in Table 2 [16].

Table 2. The single node configuration of HPCL cluster server.

Items	Content
CPU	Intel(R) Xeon(R) CPU E5–2620 v2 @ 2.10 GHz
Cores	6
Threads	12

(continued)

Table 2. (*continued*)

Items	Content
Memory	16 GB
Operating System	CentOS Linux release 7.6.1810 (Core)
MPI	openmpi-2.1.6

Three SMRT P5/C3 release datasets respectively from *S. cerevisiae*, *D. melanogaster*, and *H. sapiens* were used to evaluate the performance of PrHAT. The three reads were aligned to the reference genomes of *S. cerevisiae* (build sacCer3), *D. melanogaster* (build DM6), and *H. sapiens* (build hg19), respectively. These SMRT datasets are the same datasets that the original rHAT uses to test. And they represent small, medium-sized, and large datasets respectively. By opting to test these datasets, we can determine the performance of each version on datasets of various scales (Table 3).

Table 3. The real and simulated datasets for the test.

Name	Size of reads	Size of bases	Reference
H. sapiens	931.99 MB	2.98 GB	hg19
S. cerevisiae-sim	23.21 MB	11.83 MB	sacCer3
D. melanogaster-sim	247.76 MB	164.14 MB	DM6
D. melanogaster-sim-2	1.04 GB	164.14 MB	DM6
H. sapiens-sim	5.33 GB	2.98 GB	hg19

In each node, PrHAT runs with the same default settings as rHAT. By selecting various threads, we discover that when the number of threads *t* is set to 12, each node achieves optimal performance. We implement three versions of PrHAT on datasets with different numbers of nodes. The program is run four times in each test. We choose the node with the longest running time as the benchmark and calculate the average value. The testing results are presented in Table 4.

Table 4. Results of parallel alignment on various SMRT databases.

Databases	Versions	Time(s)					
		1 Node	2 Nodes	4 Nodes	8 Nodes	16 Nodes	32 Nodes
S. cerevisiae-sim	ND	2.85	1.89	1.29	0.92	0.87	0.82
	PD	2.88	1.79	1.20	0.95	0.82	0.68

(*continued*)

Table 4. (*continued*)

Databases	Versions	Time(s)					
		1 Node	2 Nodes	4 Nodes	8 Nodes	16 Nodes	32 Nodes
	PDBc	2.75	3.28	2.91	2.53	2.49	2.50
D. melanogaster-sim	ND	29.12	22.10	12.29	9.67	6.94	6.33
	PD	28.82	21.56	11.48	8.89	6.75	5.63
	PDBc	28.69	23.91	15.05	12.18	8.56	7.79
D. melanogaster-sim-2	ND	123.17	91.02	47.93	26.81	16.17	10.90
	PD	123.41	88.22	45.85	23.92	12.93	8.12
	PDBc	122.79	92.13	47.95	26.09	15.92	10.16

From the table, we can observe that as the number of nodes increases, the elapsed time for each version decreases to some degree. Another significant observation is that the decrease in total processing time is more distinct with the larger input dataset.

3.1 Performance of PrHAT

Speedup. For a given application, speedup refers to the times that the execution speed of a parallel algorithm (or parallel program) is faster than that of a serial algorithm (or serial program). It is thus a measure of the relative benefits of the process of parallel acceleration [12, 17]. The formula for speedup is as follows:

$$S_p = \frac{T_1}{T_p}$$

Here, p is the number of processors. T_1 is the execution time of a serial program, and T_p is that of a parallel program.

Figure 5 plots the speedup of PrHAT-ND and PrHAT-PD on different scales of datasets. As the results show, the advanced version PrHAT-PD achieves a better speedup. The reason for this is PrHAT-ND's uneven distribution of sequences. It leads to the different running time on each node. As the dataset volume increases, the amount of data each node needs to process becomes more distinct. Another phenomenon we can observe from the figure is that when the dataset is small, the speedup ratio increases linearly with the number of nodes; with the increase of dataset volume, it is closer to exponential growth.

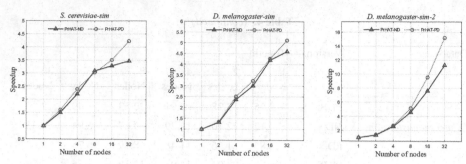

Fig. 5. The speedup of PrHAT-ND and PrHAT-PD

To verify the impact of hash table broadcasting on PrHAT, we compare the results of PrHAT-PD and PrHAT-PDBc. Figure 6 shows the speedup of the two versions. As we can see from the figure, the performance of PrHAT-PDBc is poor when the dataset is small, then improves with the increase of dataset volume. However, because hash table broadcasting consumes more time in communication overhead than loading hash tables from existing files, the performance of PrHAT-PDBc still lags behind that of PrHAT-PD.

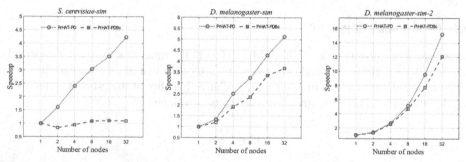

Fig. 6. The speedup of PrHAT-PD and PrHAT-PDBc

Parallel Efficiency. The ideal speedup ratio of a parallel computer with p processors is p. However, due to communication and other overhead, it is impractical for each processor to use 100% of its computing power. Parallel efficiency (E) derives from speedup. This is a parameter used to measure each processor's effective utilization time and is defined as the ratio of speedup to the number of processors [12, 17]. The formula of efficiency is as follows:

$$E = \frac{S_p}{p}$$

Here, S_p is the abbreviation for speedup, while p is the number of processes.

Figure 7 shows that the efficiency of PrHAT-ND and PrHAT-PD decreases to a certain extent as the number of nodes increases. When the dataset volume is small, the efficiency of the two versions does not vary significantly. However, between the two versions, PrHAT-PD exhibits a smaller decline when using larger datasets, which indicates that PrHAT-PD achieves better performance than PrHAT-ND.

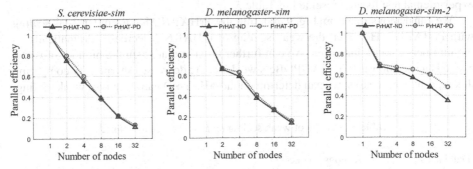

Fig. 7. The parallel efficiency of PrHAT-ND and PrHAT-PD

We further test the impact of hash table broadcasting on efficiency. Figure 8 illustrates the parallel efficiency of PrHAT-PD with and without hash table broadcasting. The experimental results show that PrHAT-PD achieves better efficiency than PrHAT-PDBc, which further indicates that hash table broadcasting results in increased communication overhead.

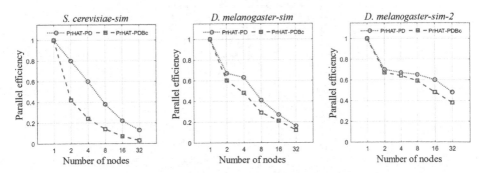

Fig. 8. The parallel efficiency of PrHAT-PD and PrHAT-PDBc

Weak Scaling. In addition to speedup and efficiency, the weak scaling of a parallel program is also a crucial index for evaluating parallel computing performance. This index is used to describe whether the parallel program can effectively utilize the ability of scalable processes. Weak scaling is a function of the number of nodes p [12, 18]. The formula is defined as follows:

$$Weak\ Scaling = \frac{T_{seq}}{T_{par}}$$

Here, T_{seq} is the running time of a single node, while T_{par} is the running time of the program when the problem size and the number of nodes increase p times. We utilize

224   Z. Xia et al.

the moderately sized dataset *D. melanogaster-sim-2* to verify the weak scaling of each version. In each test, we keep the reference sequences' size unchanged and increase the size of the read sequences synchronously according to the number of nodes. The experimental results are presented in Table 5.

We can demonstrate from Fig. 9 that, initially, PrHAT-ND has a similar weak scaling with PrHAT-PD. However, the weak scaling of PrHAT-ND decreases dramatically as the number of nodes increases. We can further observe that when the number of nodes exceeds a specific value, PrHAT-PDBc's weak scaling decreases sharply. By comparing the experimental results, we can determine that PrHAT-PD gains the best weak scaling.

Table 5. Results of weak scaling on *D. melanogaster-sim-2*.

Databases	Versions	Time(s)					
		1 Node	2 Nodes	4 Nodes	8 Nodes	16 Nodes	32 Nodes
D. melanogaster-sim-2	ND	33.52	34.35	35.77	38.83	53.08	85.72
	PD	33.28	33.47	33.65	33.60	33.55	33.58
	PDBc	33.28	36.74	37.11	37.43	37.89	49.18

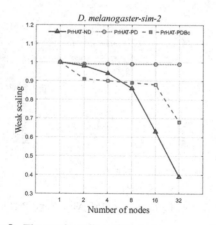

Fig. 9. The weak scaling of *D. melanogaster-sim-2*

We implement further experiments on the large datasets *H. sapiens-sim* and *H. sapiens*. The hash table of these two datasets approaches 11 GB in size. Considering that the H. sapiens FASTQ file size is too large, we employ only its first SMRT cells, for a total size of 0.93 GB.

From Table 6 and Fig. 10, it is not difficult to observe that the parallel acceleration performance of rHAT is more evident for large datasets. The speedup is closer to the exponential growth, and the parallel efficiency decreases slowly. The advanced version of PrHAT PrHAT-PD has still achieved better results.

Table 6. Results of parallel alignment on *H. sapiens-sim* and *H. sapiens* datasets.

Databases	Versions	Time(s)				
		1 Node	2 Nodes	4 Nodes	8 Nodes	16Nodes
H. sapiens-sim	ND	2972.29	1530.42	785.41	408.69	213.37
	PD	2957.78	1518.97	765.54	393.30	198.93
H. sapiens	ND	1169.00	612.09	332.59	184.85	102.86
	PD	1167.60	605.26	313.75	167.70	92.75

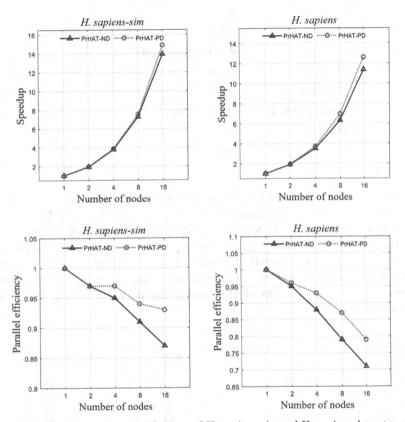

Fig. 10. The speedup and efficiency of *H. sapiens-sim* and *H. sapiens* datasets

3.2 Accelerate PrHAT with GPU

To verify the performance of OpenPrHAT, we test it on our personal laptop and MATGEN cluster server. The configuration of them is listed in Table 7.

Table 7. The configuration of the laptop and MATGEN cluster server's single node

Platform	Items	Content
Laptop	CPU	Intel(R) Core (TM) CPU i7-9750H @ 2.60 GGHz
	Cores	6
	Threads	12
	Memory	16 GB
MATGEN	CPU	Intel(R) Xeon (R) CPU Gold 6132 @ 2.60GGHz
	Cores	14
	Threads	28
	Memory	64 GB
	GPU	NVIDIA Tesla V100
	GPU Memory	16 GB
	CUDA cores	5120
	Operating System	Ubuntu 18.04
	OpenCL	3.0
	MPI	openmpi-2.1.6

We first test the OpenPrHAT and PrHAT-PD on SMRT databases *S. cerevisiae-sim*, *D. melanogaster-sim*. The threads we choose are 1, 2, 4, and 8. Figure 11 (A) and (B) are the results on the laptop, (C) and (D) are that on MATGEN cluster server. Generally speaking, OpenPrHAT gains similar performance compared to PrHAT. By comparing the results of OpenPrHAT between Fig. 11 (A) and (B), it is not hard to find that the performance improves as the size of the database increases. Additionally, the performance gap between OpenPrHAT and PrHAT-PD is also getting smaller when using more threads.

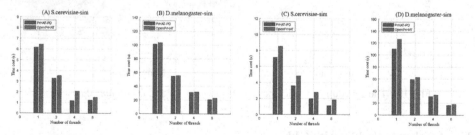

Fig. 11. The running of OpenPrHAT and PrHAT-PD on laptop and MATGEN.

The main aspect that leads to the difference between OpenPrHAT and PrHAT is the communication overhead between the host and devices in OpenCL. Every time OpenPrHAT calls GPU to do the computation, it needs to send data from the host side (CPU) to the device side (GPU). After the device side finishes computation, the host side retrieves the results from it. This will result in an increase in the running time of the program. However, as the size of the database and threads increase, the time proportion of communication overhead is reduced, which improves the performance of OpenPrHAT.

We further test the performance of OpenPrHAT on multiple nodes with large datasets. The number of nodes we choose is 1, 2, and 4. The number of threads is set to 12 in the test. We compare the results with PrHAT, and the results are illustrated in Fig. 12. From the figure, we can find that OpenPrHAT can also run well on multiple nodes, and the running time almost keeps the same.

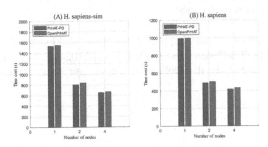

Fig. 12. The performance of OpenPrHAT on multiple nodes

From the results of the test above, we verify the performance of OpenPrHAT. Generally, it has a similar performance towards PrHAT, which means that OpenPrHAT has good portability. Compared with PrHAT, OpenPrHAT can run on different computing devices with the implementation of OpenCL. Users can choose specific computing devices on the platform.

4 Conclusion

In this paper, we developed PrHAT, a parallel version of rHAT. Then based on PrHAT, we developed OpenPrHAT. With the implementation of OpenCL, it can call different computing devices in the platform. By testing each version of PrHAT on datasets of various scales, we determine that the version PrHAT-PD gains the best performance. First, PrHAT-PD realizes the parallel alignment of rHAT and dramatically cuts down the sequence alignment time. Benefiting from the use of cluster servers, PrHAT-PD reduces the computing time from nearly one hour to several minutes for large reference datasets. Second, compared with PrHAT-ND, PrHAT-PD achieves better load balancing by distributing the pointers rather than the number of read sequences. This ensures that each node's processing time is closer, thus reducing the running time of sequence alignment. Third, PrHAT-PD has improved the utilization of computing resources relative to PrHAT-PDBc. PrHAT-PDBc utilizes *MPI_Bcast* to broadcast the hash table. However, PrHAT-PD loads the hash table directly from the existing file. Using *MPI_Bcast* to broadcast the hash table results in increased communication overhead and longer running time. Finally, OpenPrHAT provides the researchers with the opportunity of choosing specific computing devices in the platform. And the performance of it keeps the same as PrHAT-PD.

Future works will focus on three aspects. The first of these is better load balancing. In our tests, it could be readily determined that even if we divide the data evenly, each node's running time still varies to some extent. Therefore, the next work we need to consider is how to better divide the processing performance of each node. The second aspect is enhanced scalability. The experimental results show that the weak scaling is good. However, the number of nodes we use is not very large. Considering that cluster servers or supercomputers have hundreds of nodes, it is crucial to control the system's scalability. Last is the modification of OpenPrHAT. We hope to develop a version that can use different computing devices for co-processing, advancing the performance and running faster than the current version.

Acknowledgments. This work was supported by National Key R&D Program of China 2020YFA0709803, 2018YFB0204301 and NSFC Grants 62102427. The funding bodies did not influence the design of the study, data collection, analysis, or interpretation, or writing of the manuscript.

Appendix

All source codes of PrHAT can be found on:
    https://drive.google.com/drive/folders/1OLjYANWXHz6b22sfdf7Mqv6vm1zil
B69?usp=sharing.

References

1. Sanger, F., Coulson, A.R., Barrell, B., Smith, A., Roe, B.: Cloning in single-stranded bacteriophage as an aid to rapid DNA sequencing. J. Mol. Biol. **143**(2), 161–178 (1980)
2. Roberts, R.J., Carneiro, M.O., Schatz, M.C.: The advantages of SMRT sequencing. Genome Biol. **14**(6), 405 (2013)
3. Mary, Q., Yang, B., Athey, H., Arabnia, A.: High-throughput next-generation sequencing technologies foster new cutting-edge computing techniques in bioinformatics. BMC Genomics **10**(Suppl 1), 11 (2009)
4. Korlach, J., Bjornson, K.P., Chaudhuri, B.P., Cicero, R.L., Turner, S.W.: Real-time DNA sequencing from single polymerase molecules. Methods Enzymol. **472**, 431–455 (2010)
5. Carneiro, M.O., Russ, C., Ross, M.G., Gabriel, S.B., Nusbaum, C., Depristo, M.A.: Pacific biosciences sequencing technology for genotyping and variation discovery in human data. BMC Genomics **13**, 375 (2012)
6. Bo, L., Dengfeng, G., Mingxiang, T., Yadong, W.: rHAT: fast alignment of noisy long reads with regional hashing. Bioinformatics **32**(11), 1625–1631 (2015)
7. Li, H., Durbin, R.: Fast and accurate long-read alignment with Burrows-Wheeler transform. Bioinformatics **26**(5), 589–595 (2010)
8. Chaisson, M.J., Tesler, G.: Mapping single molecule sequencing reads using basic local alignment with successive refinement (BLASR): application and theory. BMC Bioinf. **13**(1), 238 (2012)
9. Li, H.: Aligning sequence reads, clone sequences and assembly contigs with BWA-MEM (2013). arXiv preprint arXiv:13033997

10. Peter, J.A.C., Christopher, J.: The Sanger FASTQ file format for sequences with quality scores, and the Solexa/Illumina FASTQ variant. Nuclelic Acids Res. **38**(6), 1767–1771 (2010)
11. Peters, D., Luo, X., Qiu, K., Liang, P.: Speeding up large-scale next generation sequencing data analysis with pBWA. J Biocomput **1**(2), 1–6 (2012)
12. Brawer, S.: Preface - an introduction to parallel programming. Introduction Parallel Program. **5**(4), 361–370 (2011)
13. Smith, T.F., Waterman, M.S.: Identification of common molecular subsequences. J. Mol. Biol. **147**(1), 195–197 (1981)
14. Gotoh, O.: An improved algorithm for matching biological sequences. J. Mol. Biol. **162**(3), 705–708 (1982)
15. Kucherov, G.: Evolution of biosequence search algorithms: a brief survey. Bioinformatics **35**(19), 3547–3552 (2019)
16. Xing, Y., Wu, C., Yang, X., Wang, W., Yin, J.: ParaBTM: a parallel processing framework for biomedical text mining on supercomputers. Molecules **23**(5), 1028 (2018)
17. Patterson, D.A., Hennessy, J.L., Goldberg, D.: Computer Architecture: A Quantitative Approach, vol. 2. Morgan Kaufmann, San Mateo, CA (1990)
18. Bondi, A.B.: Characteristics of scalability and their impact on performance. In: Proceedings of the 2nd International Workshop on Software and Performance, pp. 195–203 (2000)

Square Fractional Repetition Codes for Distributed Storage Systems

Bing Zhu[1](✉), Shigeng Zhang[1,2], and Weiping Wang[1]

[1] School of Computer Science and Engineering,
Central South University, Changsha, China
{zhubing,sgzhang,wpwang}@csu.edu.cn
[2] State Key Laboratory of Information Security,
Institute of Information Engineering, Chinese Academy of Sciences, Beijing, China

Abstract. Fractional repetition (FR) codes have been proposed for distributed storage systems to achieve low-complexity repair of failed nodes, i.e., each contacted helper node in the repair process simply transfers a portion of stored data to the replacement node without arithmetic operations. In this paper, we propose square fractional repetition (SFR) codes, which have the key feature that a failed storage node can be repaired by two helper nodes, thus achieving the smallest non-trivial repair degree. Moreover, we show that determining the supported file size of SFR codes is equivalent to solving an integer partition problem, and an algorithm is then presented.

Keywords: Distributed storage · Erasure codes · Fractional repetition codes · Storage capacity · Integer partition

1 Introduction

A distributed storage system usually consists of a large number of physical storage devices which are connected by networks. In these systems, a user can access the required data object by contacting neighboring devices and downloading data from them. When the contacted storage nodes are out of service (e.g., network congestion or power failure), it is desirable to introduce replacement nodes to fulfill the functionality of those failed nodes. The data stored in the replacement nodes can be generated with the help of other surviving nodes in the system, of which the process is called *node repair*. To ensure successful node repairs, storage systems need to insert data redundancy by adopting replication or erasure codes. For the same redundancy level, erasure codes can achieve higher data reliability than the replication scheme, which increases the popularity of large-scale implementations of erasure-coded distributed storage systems [1–4].

Maximum distance separable (MDS) codes can achieve the optimal trade-off between data redundancy and reliability. An $[n, k]$ MDS code encodes a data file of k packets into n coded packets such that any k out of the n coded packets are eligible to reconstruct the source data. If the n coded packets are stored in

Y. Lai et al. (Eds.): ICA3PP 2021, LNCS 13156, pp. 230–239, 2022.
https://doi.org/10.1007/978-3-030-95388-1_15

n nodes, the corresponding system can tolerate up to $n - k$ node failures. When a storage node fails, it can be recovered by downloading data from k surviving nodes. However, this node repair method requires a large consumption of network traffic. Regenerating codes are introduced in [5] with the capability to minimize the repair bandwidth. An $[n, k, d]$ regenerating code preserves the MDS property, yet the repair process is different from conventional MDS codes in that each failed node can be recovered by contacting $d > k$ surviving nodes. The amount of data transferred by the d helper nodes can be minimized to be precisely the size of lost data, and in this case, the code is called a *minimum-bandwidth regenerating (MBR) code.*

In addition to repair bandwidth, the operational complexity involved in the repair process is also a crucial metric that needs to be taken into full consideration. Traditional MDS codes and regenerating codes usually need to perform a sufficient number of linear combinations over the packets in the helper nodes and replacement nodes, which inevitably increases the node repair complexity. To address this issue, a novel repair framework is presented in [6], in which each helper node simply transfers a portion of stored data and the replacement node stores exactly the transferred data. This repair technique is basically the same as that of data replication, and is called *repair-by-transfer* [6]. The construction is later generalized to a new family of codes in [7], which support a wider range of parameters. These codes are built on the concatenation of an outer MDS code and an inner repetition code called *fractional repetition (FR) code*. The data is first encoded by an MDS code with predetermined parameters, and then the coded packets will be replicated and distributed across the storage nodes in the system according to the FR code. The MDS code in the outer layer is employed for data reconstruction, and the inner FR code is devised to ensure the repair-by-transfer property of failed nodes.

Contributions: In this paper, we introduce *square* FR codes, which are a special class of FR codes with the number of nodes being a square number. In an SFR code, any failed node can be repaired by contacting only two surviving nodes. Furthermore, by establishing a connection with the integer partition problem, we present an algorithm for computing the supported file size of SFR codes.

Organization: The remainder of this paper is organized as follows. Section 2 provides the necessary backgrounds on FR codes. Section 3 proposes SFR codes and discusses their properties. Finally, we conclude in Sect. 4.

2   Background and Related Work

2.1   Fractional Repetition Codes

The original data of an FR code is first encoded by an outer MDS code, and then these coded packets are equally replicated a certain number of times. All the coded packets are distributed across the storage nodes in the system according to the inner FR code, which elaborately determines the exact placement of coded packets. The efficiency of such a concatenated encoding scheme is evaluated in practical peer-to-peer environments [8], where the authors showed that the combined scheme achieves better features than each of the methods separately.

Specifically, consider a data object of size M that needs to be stored. We first encode this file by using a $[\theta, M]$ MDS code and assume that the θ outputted packets are indexed by $1, 2, \ldots, \theta$. An $(n, \alpha, \theta, \rho)$ *fractional repetition code* C is a collection of n subsets $W_1, W_2, \ldots, W_n$ of $\Omega := \{1, 2, \ldots, \theta\}$, satisfying the requirements that the cardinality of each subset is α and each point of Ω belongs to ρ sets in C. These parameters follow the basic relation that

$$n\alpha = \theta\rho. \tag{1}$$

The defined FR code C can be implemented in a distributed storage system with n nodes of capacity α each, i.e., each node corresponds to a certain subset in C and contains the packets indexed by the points in this set. Therefore, each node stores α coded packets, and every packet is replicated ρ times, wherein ρ is called the *repetition degree*. As a consequence, each failed node can be repaired by simple data transfers, and on the other hand, the source file can be retrieved by contacting a sufficient number of storage nodes in the system. The smallest number of nodes that are guaranteed to cover M distinct packets, is called the *reconstruction degree*. Equivalently, the *supported file size* of an FR code with reconstruction degree k, denoted by $M(k)$, is defined as follows:

$$M(k) := \min_{K \subset \{1, 2, \ldots, n\}, |K| = k} \left| \cup_{i \in K} W_i \right|.$$

By definition, any set of k nodes contain at least $M(k)$ distinct packets. Thus if we set $M = M(k)$, then a data collector can reconstruct the stored file by connecting to any k storage nodes in the FR code based system.

2.2 Related Work

Due to the appealing repair property, FR codes have recently attracted much attention and many explicit constructions have been proposed. In the pioneer work [7], the authors introduced constructions of FR codes based on regular graphs and Steiner systems. Scalable constructions from bipartite cage graphs are proposed in [9], wherein the corresponding storage system can be expanded in a simple manner. Optimal FR codes supporting the maximum possible file size are presented in [10], which are derived from extremal graphs and transversal designs. Flexible FR codes with varying repetition degrees are considered in [11], which are constructed from resolvable combinatorial designs. FR codes based on partially ordered sets are presented in [12], which can store larger files as compared to MBR codes. Recent developments have included some additional properties of FR codes. For example, the authors in [13] and [14] discussed the construction of FR codes for distributed systems with dynamic parameters. Constructions of FR codes with the fewest number of nodes for data reconstruction are studied in [15]. Moreover, FR codes having the load-balancing property for multiple node repairs or access-balancing property for multiple data requests are studied in [16] and [17], respectively.

Despite the various constructions of FR codes, determining the supported file size of resulting codes remains a challenging problem. Among the constructions in the literature, only a few (e.g., [10] and [11]) have determined the file size of designed FR codes for certain parameter ranges.

3   Square Fractional Repetition Codes

In this section, we introduce a special family of codes called *square fractional repetition (SFR) codes*. The design rationale of SFR codes is to partition the storage nodes into clusters and arrange the coded packets on the nodes of different clusters in a sophisticated manner. We show that determining the file size of SFR codes is equivalent to an integer partition problem, and present an algorithm for computing the supported file size.

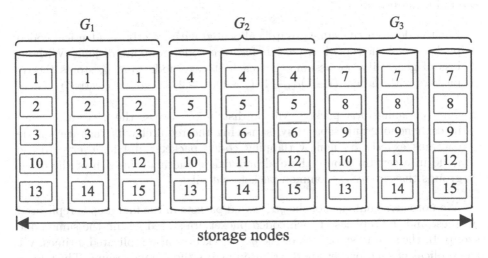

Fig. 1. An explicit SFR code with parameters $(n, \alpha, \theta, \rho) = (9, 5, 15, 3)$. The storage nodes are partitioned into three groups $\mathcal{G}_1, \mathcal{G}_2, \mathcal{G}_3$, and the points in the blocks are the indices of coded packets stored in the node.

3.1   An Illustrative Example

Consider a distributed storage system with parameters $n = 9$ and $\alpha = 5$. We partition these nodes into 3 groups $\mathcal{G}_1, \mathcal{G}_2, \mathcal{G}_3$, as shown in Fig. 1. A data object consisting of $M = 12$ packets is first encoded by a $[15, 12]$ MDS code, and each coded packet is then equally replicated three times. All these coded packets are distributed across the 9 storage nodes according to the FR code shown in Fig. 1. We observe that any collection of $k = 5$ nodes contain at least 12 distinct coded packets, which can be used to retrieve the original data. Moreover, the coded packets can be viewed as two parts based on whether or not the replicas of each packet are stored within the same group. For example, the packets with indices $1, 2, 3$ and their replicas are stored in the nodes in $\mathcal{G}_1$ while those packets with indices $10, 11, \ldots, 15$ and their replicas are spread across the 3 groups. This special placement ensures that upon failure of a storage node, we can recover the lost packets by contacting only two helper nodes.

3.2   Code Construction

Let $g \geq 2$ be a positive integer. Consider now a distributed storage system consisting of g^2 nodes, where each node stores α packets. We first divide these g^2 storage nodes into g groups, denoted by $\mathcal{G}_1, \mathcal{G}_2, \ldots, \mathcal{G}_g$, where each group contains g nodes. Moreover, for each storage node, we divide the α packets into two disjoint parts of size α_1 and α_2, i.e., $\alpha = \alpha_1 + \alpha_2$. Suppose that we now have $g\alpha = g\alpha_1 + g\alpha_2$ coded packets (indexed by $1, 2, \ldots, g\alpha$) generated by an MDS code. We can distribute the coded packets across g^2 nodes according to the following two steps:

1. Each node from the same group is allocated with exactly α_1 identical coded packets, and the sets of α_1 packets for each node group are disjoint. Without loss of generality, we assume that each storage node from $\mathcal{G}_i$ stores the α_1 packets with indices $(i-1)\alpha_1 + 1$, $(i-1)\alpha_1 + 2, \ldots, i\alpha_1$ respectively, where $1 \leq i \leq g$.
2. The remaining $g\alpha_2$ packets will be distributed across the g storage nodes in each node group separately, satisfying the requirements that each node contains exactly α_2 non-overlapping coded packets, and for every storage node in a certain group, there always exists one node in each of the other groups that shares α_2 common packets with it.

We note here that each of the $g\alpha_1$ coded packets in the first step is replicated g times, and the replicas of each coded packet are stored within the same node group. In the second step, each of the $g\alpha_2$ packets is also replicated g times, yet the replicas of each packet are distributed across the g node groups. Thus, for a triplet (g, α_1, α_2), we can obtain an FR code with parameters $(g^2, \alpha_1 + \alpha_2, g(\alpha_1 + \alpha_2), g)$ based on the two procedures above. Since the number of nodes in the resulting FR codes is a square number, we refer to the constructed codes as *square* FR codes. For example, with $g = 3, \alpha_1 = 3$, and $\alpha_2 = 2$, we can generate the SFR code shown in Fig. 1.

According to the construction of SFR codes, we observe that each failed node can be repaired by contacting only two helper nodes, i.e., one from the same group of the failed storage node contributing α_1 coded packets, and another one from any other node groups contributing α_2 packets. Therefore, one appealing benefit of SFR codes is that the number of surviving nodes that need to be contacted for node repair is 2, which is independent of other code parameters. Notice that since we do not consider the trivial case where two storage nodes contain the same set of packets, SFR codes have the minimum possible repair degree.

3.3   Supported File Size

We consider now the file size of proposed SFR codes. Recall that for a given reconstruction degree k, the supported file size $M(k)$ essentially refers to the number of distinct coded packets in any collection of k nodes. In particular, the storage nodes in SFR codes are partitioned into groups and the intersection size of two nodes can be different depending on which group they belong to. We should take this neat property into consideration when computing the supported file size of SFR codes.

Let $\mathcal{C} = \{W_1, \ldots, W_{g^2}\}$ be an SFR code based on the triplet (g, α_1, α_2) with $\alpha_1 \geq \alpha_2$.[1] According to the construction, we have that there are g node groups in $\mathcal{C}$, i.e., $\mathcal{G}_1, \ldots, \mathcal{G}_g$. Without loss of generality, assume that the storage nodes in $\mathcal{G}_i$ are given as $W_{(i-1)g+1}, \ldots, W_{ig}$, where $i = 1, \ldots, g$. Clearly, we have

$$|W_{(i-1)g+j} \cap W_{(i-1)g+j'}| = \alpha_1, \tag{2}$$

and

$$W_{(i-1)g+j} \cap W_{(i-1)g+j'} = W_{(i-1)g+j} \cap W_{(i-1)g+j''}, \tag{3}$$

where $1 \leq j \neq j' \neq j'' \leq g$.

Let S_i denote the set of α_1 common packets shared by the g storage nodes in $\mathcal{G}_i$, i.e., $S_i := W_{(i-1)g+j} \cap W_{(i-1)g+j'}$. For $1 \leq i \neq i' \leq g$, we have

$$S_i \cap S_{i'} = \varnothing. \tag{4}$$

Furthermore, based on the packet placement of SFR codes, we can assume that the ℓ-th node of each group has the following α_2 coded packets in common, i.e.,

$$W_{(i-1)g+\ell} - S_i = W_{(i'-1)g+\ell} - S_{i'}, \tag{5}$$

where $1 \leq \ell \leq g$.

Our objective is to figure out the smallest number of distinct packets in any k out of the g^2 storage nodes. Suppose that we have k nodes taken from $h \leq g$ node groups $\mathcal{G}_{i_1}, \mathcal{G}_{i_2}, \ldots, \mathcal{G}_{i_h}$, where $|\mathcal{G}_{i_u}| := \xi_{i_u} \leq g$ and $\sum_{u=1}^{h} \xi_{i_u} = k$. We further assume that the h chosen groups are listed in a non-decreasing order of the number of contained nodes, i.e., $\xi_{i_1} \leq \xi_{i_2} \leq \cdots \leq \xi_{i_h}$. We call $\mathbf{k} := [\xi_{i_1}, \xi_{i_2}, \ldots, \xi_{i_h}]$ the *group selection vector*.

We consider now the number of distinct packets contributed by the h node groups one by one. According to (2) and (3), the number of distinct packets covered by the ξ_{i_h} nodes of $\mathcal{G}_{i_h}$ is

$$\alpha_1 + \alpha_2 \xi_{i_h}.$$

In addition to the $\alpha_1 + \alpha_2 \xi_{i_h}$ packets above, the $\xi_{i_{h-1}}$ nodes of $\mathcal{G}_{i_{h-1}}$ can contribute a minimum number of α_1 distinct packets according to (4) and (5). Similarly, we have that the minimum number of distinct packets contributed by

---

[1] If $\alpha_1 < \alpha_2$, we can rearrange the g storage nodes that contain α_2 common packets into groups, and interchange α_1 and α_2.

the nodes from each of the remaining $h-2$ groups is also α_1. Based on the analysis above, we thus obtain that the number of distinct coded packets contained in the k storage nodes is

$$\alpha_1 h + \alpha_2 \xi_{i_h}.$$

For a given group selection vector $\mathbf{k}$, the minimum number of distinct packets covered by the k nodes is determined by the length and the maximum cardinality of $\mathbf{k}$. Thus, the supported file size $M(k)$ can be obtained by considering all the possible $\mathbf{k}$'s. Formally, the supported file size $M(k)$ of SFR codes can be stated as follows:

$$M(k) = \min_{\mathbf{k}} \alpha_1 h + \alpha_2 \xi_{i_h}, \tag{6}$$

subject to

$$1 \le h \le g, \tag{7}$$

$$1 \le \xi_{i_u} \le g, \forall u = 1, 2, \ldots, h, \tag{8}$$

$$\sum_{u=1}^{h} \xi_{i_u} = k. \tag{9}$$

We notice that the optimization can be viewed as an *integer partition problem* [18,19]. A *partition* of a positive integer x is a representation of x as a sum of positive integers, which are not necessarily distinct. For example, $2+2+3+4$ is a partition of 11. In the literature, the summands of a partition are called *parts*, and we assume by default that the collection of parts are ordered in a non-decreasing order.

By definition, each group selection vector $\mathbf{k}$ is equivalent to a partition of k since the sum of the elements in $\mathbf{k}$ is k. Thus, to compute the file size $M(k)$ of SFR codes, we need to consider those partitions of k satisfying the requirements that each part is smaller than or equal to g and the number of parts is smaller than or equal to g. With the number of parts and the maximum part of each valid partition, we then obtain $M(k)$ in (6).

Let x be a positive integer. We apply $N[i][x][j]$ to denote the number of partitions of x satisfying the requirements that the number of parts is i and the maximum part is j. In particular, for these partitions, if we remove the maximum part j, then it remains to count the number of partitions of $x - j$ such that the number of parts is $i - 1$ and the maximum part is smaller than or equal to j. Hence, we have

$$N[i][x][j] = \sum_{l=0}^{j} N[i-1][x-j][l]. \tag{10}$$

In our formulation, we have $x = k$ and only need to consider $N[i][k][j]$ with $1 \le i, j \le g$. For each valid $N[i][k][j]$, we use $M_{i,j}^k$ to denote the number of distinct packets contained by k storage nodes. Clearly, we have

$$M_{i,j}^k = i\alpha_1 + j\alpha_2. \tag{11}$$

Algorithm 1. Algorithm for computing $M(k)$ of SFR codes

Input: code parameters: g, α_1, α_2; reconstruction degree: k.
Output: $M(k)$.
1: Initialize all $N[i][x][j] = 0$.
2: Set $N[0][0][0] = 1$.
3: **for** $i = 1$ to g **do**
4:   **for** $x = i$ to k **do**
5:     **for** $j = 1$ to x **do**
6:       **for** $l = 0$ to j **do**
7:         $N[i][x][j]+ = N[i-1][x-j][l]$.
8:       **end for**
9:       **while** $j \leq g$ and $N[i][k][j] > 0$ **do**
10:         $M_{i,j}^k \leftarrow i\alpha_1 + j\alpha_2$.
11:       **end while**
12:     **end for**
13:   **end for**
14: **end for**
15: Return $M(k) = \min\limits_{i,j} M_{i,j}^k$.

Based on the discussion above, the supported file size $M(k)$ of SFR codes can be obtained as

$$M(k) = \min_{1 \leq i,j \leq g} M_{i,j}^k. \tag{12}$$

We formally state our method for computing the supported file size $M(k)$ of SFR codes as Algorithm 1. The computation complexity of the proposed algorithm is $O(gk^3)$. As a concrete example, the file size $M(k)$ of the SFR code in Fig. 1 is given in Table 1, where we also list the optimal partitions of k such that the number of distinct packets covered by k storage nodes reaches the minimum.

Table 1. Supported File Size $M(k)$ of the SFR Code in Fig. 1 for $2 \leq k \leq 8$

k	Optimal Partition	$N[i][k][j]$	$M(k)$
2	2	$N[1][2][2] = 1$	$1 \times 3 + 2 \times 2 = 7$
3	3	$N[1][3][3] = 1$	$1 \times 3 + 3 \times 2 = 9$
4	$2+2$	$N[2][4][2] = 1$	$2 \times 3 + 2 \times 2 = 10$
5	$2+3$	$N[2][5][3] = 1$	$2 \times 3 + 3 \times 2 = 12$
6	$3+3$	$N[2][6][3] = 1$	$2 \times 3 + 3 \times 2 = 12$
7	$1+3+3$ or $2+2+3$	$N[3][7][3] = 2$	$3 \times 3 + 3 \times 2 = 15$
8	$2+3+3$	$N[3][8][3] = 1$	$3 \times 3 + 3 \times 2 = 15$

Remark. Note that the proposed algorithm can also be extended to the heterogeneous storage environments, in which the repetition degree of each packet may be different [20]. For example, if we remove the three nodes containing packets with indices 10 and 13 in Fig. 1, then the remaining coded packets will have a repetition degree of 2 or 3. In this scenario, we can still utilize Algorithm 1 by adjusting the constraint conditions slightly, i.e., the maximum part in the partition of k is smaller than or equal to $g - 1$.

4   Conclusion

In this paper, we introduce square fractional repetition codes, which are a simple class of FR codes with small repair degree. Moreover, we analyze and present an algorithm for computing the supported file size of proposed SFR codes.

Acknowledgment. This work was supported in part by the National Natural Science Foundation of China under Grants No. 61901529 and 61772559, and in part by the Natural Science Foundation of Hunan under Grant No. 2020JJ5776.

References

1. Huang, C., et al.: Erasure coding in windows azure storage. In: Proceedings of the USENIX Annual Technical Conference, pp. 15–26, June 2012
2. Sathiamoorthy, M., et al.: XORing elephants: novel erasure codes for big data. Proc. VLDB Endowment **6**(5), 325–336 (2013)
3. Rashmi, K.V., Shah, N.B., Gu, D., Kuang, H., Borthakur, D., Ramchandran, K.: A "Hitchhiker's" guide to fast and efficient data reconstruction in erasure-coded data centers. In: Proceedings of the ACM SIGCOMM, pp. 331–342, August 2014
4. Rashmi, K.V., Nakkiran, P., Wang, J., Shah, N.B., Ramchandran, K.: Having your cake and eating it too: jointly optimal erasure codes for I/O, storage, and network-bandwidth. In: Proceedings 13th USENIX Conference File Storage Technology (FAST), pp. 81–94, February 2015
5. Dimakis, A.G., Godfrey, P.B., Wu, Y., Wainwright, M., Ramchandran, K.: Network coding for distributed storage systems. IEEE Trans. Inf. Theory **56**(9), 4539–4551 (2010)
6. Rashmi, K.V., Shah, N.B., Kumar, P.V., Ramchandran, K.: Explicit construction of optimal exact regenerating codes for distributed storage. In: Proceedings 47th Annual Allerton Conference Communication, Control, Computing, pp. 1243–1249, September 2009
7. El Rouayheb, S., Ramchandran, K.: Fractional repetition codes for repair in distributed storage systems. In: Proceedings of 48th Annual Allerton Conference Communication, Control, Computing, pp. 1510–1517, October 2010
8. Friedman, R., Kantor, Y., Kantor, A.: Replicated erasure codes for storage and repair-traffic efficiency. In: Proceedings of 14th IEEE International Conference on Peer-to-Peer Computing, pp. 1–10, September 2014
9. Koo, J., Gill, J.: Scalable constructions of fractional repetition codes in distributed storage systems. In: Proceedings of 49th Annual Allerton Conference Communication, Control, Computing, pp. 1366–1373, September 2011

10. Silberstein, N., Etzion, T.: Optimal fractional repetition codes based on graphs and designs. IEEE Trans. Inf. Theory **61**(8), 4164–4180 (2015)
11. Olmez, O., Ramamoorthy, A.: Fractional repetition codes with flexible repair from combinatorial designs. IEEE Trans. Inf. Theory **62**(4), 1565–1591 (2016)
12. Aydinian, H., Boche, H.: Fractional repetition codes based on partially ordered sets. In: Proceedings of IEEE Information Theory Workshop (ITW), pp. 51–55, November 2017
13. Zhu, B., Li, H.: Adaptive fractional repetition codes for dynamic storage systems. IEEE Commun. Lett. **19**(12), 2078–2081 (2015)
14. Su, Y.-S.: Pliable fractional repetition codes for distributed storage systems: design and analysis. IEEE Trans. Commun. **66**(6), 2359–2375 (2018)
15. Zhu, B., Shum, K.W., Li, H.: Fractional repetition codes with optimal reconstruction degree. IEEE Trans. Inf. Theory **66**(2), 983–994 (2020)
16. Porter, A., Silas, S., Wootters, M.: Load-balanced fractional repetition codes. In: Proceedings of the IEEE International Symposium Information Theory (ISIT), pp. 2072–2076, June 2018
17. Yu, W., Zhang, X., Ge, G.: Optimal fraction repetition codes for access-balancing in distributed storage. IEEE Trans. Inf. Theory **67**(3), 1630–1640 (2021)
18. van Lint, J.H., Wilson, R.M.: A Course in Combinatorics, 2nd edn. Cambridge Univ. Press, Cambridge (2001)
19. Andrews, G.E., Eriksson, K.: Integer Partitions. Cambridge Univ. Press, Cambridge (2004)
20. Zhu, B., Li, H., Shum, K.W., Li, S.-Y.R.: HFR code: a flexible replication scheme for cloud storage systems. IET Commun. **9**(17), 2095–2100 (2015)

An Anti-forensic Method Based on RS Coding and Distributed Storage

Xuhang Jiang[1], Yujue Wang[1], Yong Ding[1,2(✉)], Hai Liang[1], Huiyong Wang[3], and Zhenyu Li[1]

[1] Guangxi Key Laboratory of Cryptography and Information Security,
School of Computer Science and Information Security,
Guilin University of Electronic Technology, Guilin, China
[2] Cyberspace Security Research Center, Pengcheng Laboratory, Shenzhen, China
[3] School of Mathematics and Computing Science,
Guilin University of Electronic Technology, Guilin, China

Abstract. The anti-forensics (AF) technology has become a new field of cybercrime. The problems of existing forensic technologies should be considered from criminals' perspective, so as to make improvement to existing AF technologies. There are two types of AF methods, namely, data hiding and destruction, where most AF tools are primarily based on data hiding. If the data can be intercepted by investigators during the AF process, the remaining data may be destroyed by the criminal, which would make investigators obtain nothing about data information. To address this issue, this paper proposes an AF scheme with multi-device storage based on Reed-Solomon codes by combining data hiding and data destruction. The data is divided into multiple out-of-order data blocks and parity blocks, where these blocks are stored separately in different devices. This method can reduce the storage cost and protect the privacy of data. Even if the data is destroyed, it allows AF investigators to recover the data. Security analysis showed that this AF method can prevent malicious, erroneous or invalid files while acquired and ensure data security in data stolen. Theoretical analysis indicated that this method was difficult for investigators but easy for AFer in files recovery. Experimental results demonstrated that the proposed method is effective and has practical efficiency.

Keywords: Anti-forensics · Digital forensics · Encryption · Computer crime · Distributed storage · Erasure coding

1 Introduction

Evidence has traditionally been used as a criterion for the judge's determination of guilt or innocence and is of the nature of Relevance, Materiality and Facts-in-issue and Admissibility [23]. In [15], Garber mentioned that computer forensics is the process of analyzing various types of storage media to discover evidence of the crime. e.g., Microsoft's toolkit COFEE [27], Volatile Systems' open source

© Springer Nature Switzerland AG 2022
Y. Lai et al. (Eds.): ICA3PP 2021, LNCS 13156, pp. 240–254, 2022.
https://doi.org/10.1007/978-3-030-95388-1_16

memory forensics framework Volatility [35], AccessData's hard drive scanning software FTK [1], etc. There are also some operating systems that can be used for forensics, such as Kali Linux [5], CAINE Linux [2], etc.

The opposite area of research to forensics, anti-forensics, refers to the removal or concealment of evidence during the forensic investigation phase, thereby reducing the data validity [18]. Rogers proposed AF methods in [33], but the tools or algorithms available were divided into two main areas, data hiding, and data destruction. Data hiding includes methods such as encryption and steganography, with some standard tools such as Invisible Secrets[3], software with steganography and file encryption released by East-Tec, and strongSwan [10], a multi-platform IPsec implementation that provides encryption and authentication for servers and clients. The earliest erase algorithms were filled with zeros through one pass. Nowadays, most erase algorithms write different Zeros, Ones, and Random Characters to the sector, e.g., [8,9,19,25,34]. The algorithms can be viewed in [6], and the anti-forensic toolset was classified in more detail and made publicly available in [13]. Other methods such as trace obfuscation Timestomp (a component of the Metasploit Framework) [7], and attacks on computer forensics can also reduce data validity.

1.1 Our Contributions

However, simple data hiding and data destruction do not reduce the validity of the data and make it more difficult for the anti-forensicser (AFer) to obtain the data again after it was erased or destroyed. The problems of effectively hiding data while ensuring the integrity of the data and how to reduce the difficulty of the recovery process if an AFer needs to recover a file after some of the data has been destroyed have not been well addressed. This paper proposes a data hiding method with EC codes to address the above issues. With the proposed method, data are stored in chunks on different storage media, which hides the original data format, and keeps only the actual data part, while the AFer encodes the chunked data to save the parity blocks. This method is not focus on the process of attack, but on how to keep secure of the obtained files after attack. The main contributions of this paper are summarized as follows:

- A new anti-forensic method is proposed, which on the one hand, hides and obfuscates the AFer data files, ensuring the confidentiality of the data. On the other hand, it supports the AFer in recovering the destroyed data, ensuring the integrity of the data throughout the process.
- The proposed method can rewrite the file header signatures of different files and remove the trailing signatures of some files, allowing AFer to manage large numbers of files efficiently while further increasing the concealment of the original files.
- By breaking up the data stream into chunks and encoding it with Reed-Solomon codes, it can be ensured that AFer can recover and review the data later in the process if a certain amount of data blocks were erased, destroyed, or lost.

1.2   Related Works

Data hiding is one of the earliest AF technology [37]. As the oldest data hiding tool, StegFS [28], uses the steganography and encrypted file systems to make data and files system contents indistinguishable via modified ext2 kernel driver. Piper et al. [31] presented further discussion of different data hiding techniques for ext2 and ext3. Göbel and Baier [16] have analyzed and evaluated different hiding methods in the ext4 file system. Later, with the ext4 data hiding technique based on the nanoseconds part of the timestamp [29], Göbel and Baier [17] improved the secrecy of hidden data and reduced the threshold of users. Besides hiding data in the file system, data can be hidden in other types of files. Kakde, Gonnade and Dahiwale [22] proposed an audio steganography method to hiding secret text information in the video file based on Discrete Wavelet Transform and Singular Value Decomposition and random Least Significant Bit. Kumar, Kansal and Singh [26] proposed JPEG AF technique by hiding the artifacts of compression in Discrete Cosine Transform domain, so as to trick the forensic detectors.

Trail obfuscation is a dangerous anti-forensic technology by obfuscating and distracting the forensics investigators [37]. In [14], Cristea and Groza found that the Android platform did not mask ICMP timestamp requests by default, which was used to distinguish smartphone remotely by calculating the clock skew of ICMP packets. By exploiting a bug in IEEE 802.11, Banakh and Piskozub [11] intercepted the location identification via WIFI metadata. Through different machine learning algorithms, Perez, Musolesi and Stringhini [30] analyzed the atomic fields in the metadata to be used in identifying the user. Beside the above mentioned methods for forging data or modifying file metadata, there also exists spoofing related techniques. Jeitner and Shulman [21] has found that encoding malicious payloads into DNS records can launch string injection attacks. Chandramouli et al. [12] found that if the mailing script failed to check the presence of e-mail header in user input, e-mail header injection might occur in the built-in mail functionality in mainstream programming languages such as PHP and Python. Hitefield, Fowler and Clancy [20] found that buffer overflow vulnerabilities can be used to launch denial-of-service attacks and modify the behaviour of the executing waveform remotely through shellcode injection in software defined radios. Wang et al. [36] also has established a trustworthy environment that can filter and detect unreal information.

1.3   Paper Organization

The remainder of the paper is organized as follows. Section 2 describes some preliminaries of the file header signatures and Reed-Solomon codes. Section 3 introduces the system architecture and design goals. Section 4 presents the technical details. The proposed method is analysed in Sect. 5 and Sect. 6 concludes the paper.

2 Preliminaries

2.1 File Header Signatures

File header is also known as file signatures or magic numbers[24], which is contained in the first few bytes of a file. File header is fixed for many types of files and can be used to indicate the format of a file or protocol. For example, the first few bytes of a jpg file are 0xFFD8FFE10018457869660000, where 0xFFD8 denotes the start-of-image (SOI) marker and the corresponding end-of-file 0xFFD9 is the end-of-image (EOI) marker. The two bytes following the SOI 0xFFE1 indicate that the file is a JPEG file with the Exif metadata standard, which is also known in images as the Application Marker Segment 1 (APP1) Marker and 0x0018 refers to the length outside the APP1 segment. 0x457869660000 is the ASCII code for "Exif" and is terminated by a null byte. The two bytes after the SOI 0xFFEx, $x = 0, \cdots ,$ F indicate the different segment tags that contain application-specific information.

   File signatures are not equivalent or similar to ASCII codes. For example, in some files, they can represent the birthday, name, or even the initials of the developer of the file format. For some files, file signatures are insufficient to identify the file type, where most typically are plain text files, including txt, HTML, XHTML, XML files, and source code. It is usually possible to analyze such files according to the beginning of the text, e.g., $< html >$ for HTML files.

2.2 Reed-Solomon Codes

Erasure Coding was first applied to communication processes to check and correct errors in transmitted data and was later introduced to storage systems to address data volume inflation and high storage costs.

   Reed-Solomon (RS) [32] code is one of the erasure coding technologies, evolved from BCH codes, which is a system based on bytes rather than individual zeros and ones, and has gradually become one of the most commonly used types of censoring codes. If less than m blocks are damaged or lost, the original data can be recovered by RS codes as long as $k + m$ blocks are available.

   During the encoding stage, the data is divided into k blocks in bytes and formed into a matrix

$$\mathbf{D} = (D_1, D_2, \cdots , D_k)^{\mathrm{T}}$$

A matrix $\mathbf{B}$ can be constructed as follows

$$\mathbf{B} = (\mathbf{I}_k, \mathbf{V})^{\mathrm{T}}$$

from the unit matrix $\mathbf{I}_k$ and the Vandermonde matrix $\mathbf{V}$. Then, the coded vector $\mathbf{R}$ can be computed as follows

$$\mathbf{R} = \mathbf{B} \cdot \mathbf{D} = (D_1, D_2, \cdots , D_k, C_1, C_2, \cdots C_m)^{\mathrm{T}}$$

where C_a $(a = 1, 2, \cdots , m)$ are the parity blocks.

In the decoding stage, suppose there are less than n $(n<m)$ blocks missing, any k blocks can be selected from $\mathbf{R}$ to form the matrix $\mathbf{R}'$ for recovering the data. The corresponding rows in matrix $\mathbf{B}$ can be chosen to form a new matrix $\mathbf{B}'$, which is used to calculate

$$\mathbf{D} = (\mathbf{B}')^{-1} \cdot \mathbf{R}'$$

to recover the original data.

3 System Architecture and Design Goals

3.1 System Architecture

An AFer program can be planted on the target computer or server to access the operation through Virus, Web Proxy, Autorun. inf, etc. To not be detected by the victim, the AFer can forge a digital signature to ensure that the program seems legitimate. The AFer can either wait for the victim to access the file or select the desired file itself and send it to a cloud server for processing. The main reason for choosing to process in the cloud is to prevent information such as the AFer's IP address from being compromised.

The system consists of three main processes, namely, chunking, storage, and merging, as shown in Fig. 1.

- Chunk: In the chunking phase, the AFer processes the acquired files in the cloud server. The data is then divided into chunks and generates a hash for each chunk. A parity block is generated using Reed-Solomon codes. A new file header is generated for each chunk, which is then encrypted. The encrypted file header is concatenated with the data chunk for storage.
- Storage: In the storage phase, the AFer needs to randomly place the new data blocks which have been generated in the chunking phase in storage device, such as a mobile storage device or a cloud server. The AFer creates a database that stores the index field of each file, the extension name of the file, the file's hash, each data block's hash and the location of the parity blocks. Except for the device that stores the data block, the AFer should have a more secure storage device to store the database files and parity blocks.
- Merge: The merging phase allows the AFer to recover the needed data. The AFer selects the file it needs to recover in the database, retrieves the corresponding data blocks, checks whether the file is complete through the hash value. If not, the AFer recovers the damaged or missing data block from the parity codes, then decrypts the file header. The data blocks are concatenated to form the original file, so that the original file header can be added via the expanded name of that file.

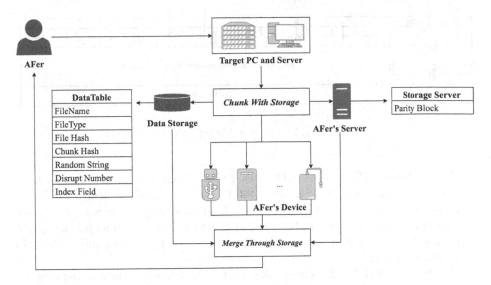

Fig. 1. System architecture

3.2 Design Goals

During the file process after an AFer obtained the file, he/she must prevent the erroneous file and ensure the security of the data file. For the AFer, if the data file needs to be recovered, it is easy for him/her but difficult for a third party. Also, for accidental destruction or lost data file, the AFer should also have the ability to recover the destroyed part in order to read the content. Therefore, this method should be designed with the following objectives:

– This method needs to ensure that common file types can be processed, their existing identifiers can be removed, and that the read data stream can be disrupted and chunked to prevent unsafe software on the victim's device from compromising the AFer's device.
– This method needs to strengthen the data security to ensure that any third party cannot read the real content even if it has access to the data revised by the AFer.
– This method needs to ensure that the AFer can recover the contents of corrupted data in exceptional cases while reducing the storage costs.
– This method needs to ensure that the recovering process of a file is easy for an AFer, while it is difficult or even impossible for a third party such as an investigator.

4 System Design

4.1 A New File Signature

As shown in Fig. 2, the new file header has 16 bits and supports dynamic expansion to 80 bits.

Offsets	Octet	0								1							
Octet	Bit	7	6	5	4	3	2	1	0	7	6	5	4	3	2	1	0
0	0	HL		BN				ECI	CST	Reserved (0 0 0 0 0 0 0 0)							
2	16	Index (The index length depends on first two bits)															
4	32																
6	48																
8	64																
...	...	Data segments															

Fig. 2. The new file signature

- Header Length (HL): This field takes 2 bits, which denotes the length of the new file header. This field is set to 00 by default, which indicates the Index field has 16 bits and the length of new file header is $16 + 16 \times 1$ bits. When this field is not 00, it indicates the Index field has $16 \times n$ bits and the length of new file header is $16 + 16 \times n$ bits, where $n = 2, 3, 4$ correspond to the field values $01, 10, 11$.
- Block Number (BN): This field takes 4 bits, which denotes the number of serial numbers after division, and determines the concatenation order of blocks in data recovering. It starts counting from 0 and can support up to 2^4 chunks.
- EC-Identification (ECI): This field takes 1 bit, which indicates the type of erase code that AFer has selected. The field value 1 means that the Reed-Solomon code is selected.
- CheckSum Type (CST): This field takes 1 bit, which indicates the type of checksum, where 0 denotes the CRC checksum and 1 represents the Hash function. The default value is 1.
- Reserved (ReS): The field is 8 bits long and is reserved for other uses, which is set to 0 if not used.
- Index (InD): The length of this field is determined by the HL field, which takes 16 bits by default and can support up to 64 bits. This field is unique, which means different files should have different Index values. With this field, AFer is able to search for file types, Hash values, and the generated parity blocks. Also, this field can be used by the AFer to find the data blocks with the same Index value, so as to avoid using the blocks of other files in achieving data recovery.

4.2   CSM Scheme

4.2.1   Chunk with Storage

Once AFer has obtained the file, he/she reads the file byte stream $File\_Buf$ according to the file's storage path. Based on the first few bytes of the byte stream, $getFileType()$ can identify the file type, and the ext function can get the current file's extension, such as jpg, png, doc, etc. If the file type by the byte stream does not match the extension name, the byte stream is discarded and the next file is read. If matched, the AFer removes the file header and file tailer of the file in byte stream by using $DeleteSign()$ and calculates the hash value H_0 of the remaining data stream $Data\_Buf$. For some files without file signature, the AFer can generate the file hash value H_0 directly. Furthermore, AFer generates a random byte stream string $RandByte$ to encrypt the new file header, and a random number $DisruptNum$ that allows AFer to make the data stream arranged in a pseudo-random order after being chunked. Before each operation on the file, the $getMaxIndex()$ function is invoked to obtain the current maximum value of Index field.

In the chunking step, the AFer generates a new $NewHeader$ based on the current block number n and the largest $index$ field, which is then XOR-ed with $RandByte$ to obtain $encNewHeader$ using one-time pad encryption. The AFer then chunks the data stream according to the pre-defined number of chunks and the $DisruptNum$ mentioned above, generates hash value H_n for each chunk $Chunk\_n$ and fills the beginning of each chunk with the encrypted header file. Finally, the AFer uses RS codes to generate the parity block $Parity\_m$ for this data stream. Note that, since the AFer also needs to guarantee the security of its data and storage device after acquiring the file, the block number should not be as many as possible. The AFer should keep the number of chunks it needs to a maximum that it can afford.

Algorithm 1. Separate Files

Input: File_Path, Block_Number, RSCodes_Number
Output: Chunk_1, $\cdots$, Chunk_N, Parity_1, $\cdots$, Parity_M
 1: **Set** $N \leftarrow$ Block_Number, $M \leftarrow$ RSCodes_Number
 2: **for** Files $\in$ File_Path **do**
 3:    File_Buf $\leftarrow$ readFile(File_Path)
 4:    Ext $\leftarrow$ ext(Files.Name())
 5:    StreamExt, HeaderLens $\leftarrow$ getFileType(File_Buf)
 6:    **if** Ext != StreamExt **then**
 7:      **Discard** File_buf
 8:    **else**
 9:      Data_Buf $\leftarrow$ DeleteSign(File_Buf)
10:      $H_0 \leftarrow$ getHash(Data_Buf)
11:      **for** $n \in N$ **do**
12:        NewHeader $\leftarrow$ GetNewFileHeader(n)
13:        encNewHeader = NewHeader $\oplus$ RandByte
14:        Chunk_$n \leftarrow$ disruptDataBuf(Data_Buf, n, DisruptNum)
15:        $H_n \leftarrow$ getHash(Chunk_n)
16:        Chunk_$n \leftarrow$ Append(encNewHeader, Chunk_n)
17:      **end for**
18:      Parity_1, $\cdots$, Parity_M $\leftarrow$ Encode(Chunk_1, $\cdots$, Chunk_N)
19:    **end if**
20: **end for**

Before the data blocks are merged, the AFer needs to create a private database as described in Sect. 3.1. It stores some of the data files generated during the chunk phase, including the file name, extension name, the hash H_0 of data stream, the hash H_n of each data block, a random byte stream $RandByte$, a random number $DisruptNum$, the $Index$ field of the new header, and the location of the parity block to which it points.

4.2.2   Merge Through Storage

In order to merge the data blocks, the AFer can select a file based on the information stored in the database or general information, and obtain the block header $encNewHeader$ based on the $RandByte$ of the same length, which are then XOR-ed for decryption. The decrypted $Index$ field is compared with that in the database. If they are the same, the current data block header is removed. The blocks are concatenated using the $Append()$ function in the order of the BN field in the block header.

After each block has been concatenated into a data stream, the AFer examines the current data stream. If the hash value does not match that in the database, the AFer should re-hash each data block for comparison. Suppose the hash value of a block matches the one in database, the AFer can discard the current incorrect block and use the $Decode()$ function to recover the incorrect block from the correct data blocks and the parity blocks. The recovered block is put into its original position in the data stream. Then the AFer restores the order of the data stream based on $DisruptNum$ and the original file header, and updates the matched extension name.

The AFer cannot ensure that every storage device is secure. If a device is unsafe, the AFer must discard the device or the data blocks on it. However, since the erasure coding is used, even if some part of data is lost, the data can be recovered by the AFer. When the number of discarded blocks n is less than the number of parity blocks m, the data can be recovered from the locally stored parity blocks. In contrast, when $n>m$, it would be difficult for the AFer to recover the original data.

5   Analysis

This section analyzes the security and performance of the proposed method.

5.1   Security and Theoretical Analysis

This method is designed to allow the AFer to store the acquired files in a new way to avoid investigation. This section analyzes the possible forensic threats to the AFer in the proposed scheme according to the design goals mentioned in Sect. 3.2.

Theorem 1. *The proposed method can effectively prevent acquiring malicious, erroneous or invalid files and thus can guarantee the security of AFer's other data.*

Proof. In the proposed method, after the AFer acquired one or more files, it first goes through the first few bytes of the file stream and checks whether it matches the byte stream identified by the current extension name. If not matched, the

---

Algorithm 2. Merge Blocks

Input: RandByte, Index, DisruptNum
Output: File
1: **for** $n \in N$ **do**
2:    **for** Chunk_$n \in$ Chunk_Path **do**
3:       decNewHeader = encNewHeader $\oplus$ RandByte
4:       **if** decNewHeader.Index == Index **then**
5:          Chunk_n = DeleteHeader(Chunk_n)
6:          Data_Buf = Append(Data_Buf, Chunk_n)
7:       **end if**
8:    **end for**
9: **end for**
10: **if** getHash(Data_Buf) != H_0 **then**
11:    **for** $n \in N$ **do**
12:       **if** getHash(Chunk_n) != H_n **then**
13:          **Discard** this Chunk_i
14:       **end if**
15:    **end for**
16:    Chunk_$i \leftarrow$ Decode(Chunk_1, $\cdots$, Chunk_N, Parity_1, $\cdots$, Parity_M)
17:    Put the new Chunk_i into original place
18: **else**
19:    File_Buf $\leftarrow$ reDisrupt(Data_Buf, DisruptNum)
20:    File $\leftarrow$ getOriginalSign(File_Buf)
21: **end if**

---

acquired files are classified as error ones and discarded. For the files have not been identified in the first step, the subsequent disruption of the data stream and chunking also prevent some erroneous files from contaminating the storage device or exposing the location of the AFer, who can then delete all information about the malicious files when these files are detected.

Theorem 2. *After the data is stolen, this method can prevent third party from reading the real content of the data.*

Proof. Once the AFer has acquired the file, it is not stored locally but rather in the cloud server. When the data is separated, it is stored in different storage devices, which also avoids exposing the AFer's file information in a single storage environment. The scheme also removes the file header information from the file and disrupts the data stream by pseudo-random number, making it more difficult for others to recover the file after accessing the chunk and impossible for them to access the current file's information. The file content can only be obtained by running the merge process by the AFer.

Theorem 3. *In forensics, the proposed method can make it difficult for investigators to recover data files.*

Proof. When an investigator does not obtain all data blocks of a file, such file cannot be merged entirely. Also, the new file header is encrypted, so that the investigator cannot detect the exact number of chunks in the current file, making it more difficult for the investigator to merge blocks. If the investigator obtains all of the data blocks, although he/she can delete the header file and merge these chunks, the data flow is disrupted by $DisruptNum$. Thus, the current file cannot be opened correctly even if the original header identifier or tail identifier was added. The forensic case is also difficult for the AFer to recover the data if the unique data table in this method was destroyed. As mentioned earlier, the data stream is randomly disrupted, and the encrypted file header of each block is also a random string.

Theorem 4. *Even if part of data is lost or destroyed, the AFer can also recover data blocks.*

Proof. The AFer uses RS codes to ensure the recoverability of data blocks. If any number of blocks within the recoverable range are in error during the recovery process, the AFer can recover the corrupted data blocks based on the parity block information stored in the data table. After the investigator has obtained all data blocks, the parity blocks and data tables need to be stored securely in an effective way or can be destroyed physically.

5.2   Performance Analysis

In experiments, the number of data was set to 5 and the number of parity blocks was set to 3. Our simulation experiments were run on a machine with an Intel i7-6700 HQ and 16 GB of RAM. Since the method is also related to I/O speed, our experiments were run on a 7200 RPM mechanical hard drive.

We randomly selected a file with a size of 333 KB. As shown in Fig. 3, the time taken for several essential stages are illustrated, where $Chunk()$ and $Merge()$ denote the two overall stages of file chunking and merging. The $Chunk()$ includes the $GetNewfileHeader()$, $disruptDatabuf()$ and $Encode()$ stages. It can be seen that very little time was spent in the operations of generating a new header file and disrupting the data stream, and less than 0.1 s were taken by the entire chunking process.

The efficiency of the program for different file sizes was also tested. To prevent excessive errors, the file sizes were basically between 30 KB and 350 KB. Figure 4 showed that as the number of files increases in the chunking process, the running time does not increase exponentially but takes more than twice the current time. The reason for this problem is that the files are not uniform in size, that is, the efficiency is determined by the size of the processed files.

To further demonstrate the validity of the proposed method, a randomly selected image was analyzed using the analysis tool Hex Workshop [4]. This tool was used to open file as hexadecimal format, where a standard jpg file with a hexadecimal beginning is marked in red in Fig. 5.

By running the proposed program, the image file was split into five data blocks and three parity blocks. Two random blocks are opened, which are shown in Fig. 6. The data block starts with an encrypted random string marked in red,

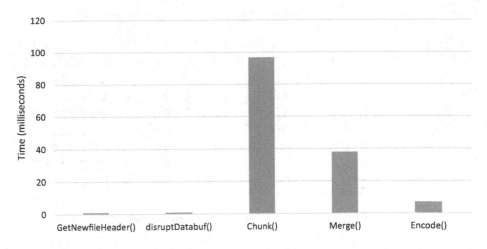

Fig. 3. Time cost of each stage

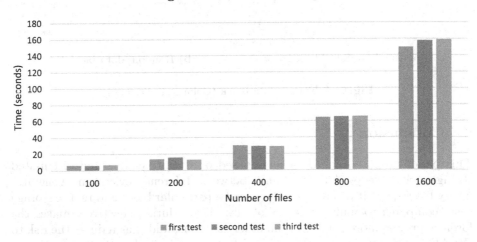

Fig. 4. Time cost of the chunking process for different file numbers

and the followed bytes do not show the exact contents of the file and its primary format. Without knowing $DisruptNum$ that randomly generated for this file stream, it is impossible to be recovered even if several data blocks with similar header files are deleted. The random nature of the encrypted string could lead to two different files corresponding to the same file header, which makes forensics even more difficult.

	0	1	2	3	4	5	6	7	8	012345678
00000000	FF	D8	FF	E0	00	10	4A	46	49	??.☐JFI.
00000009	46	00	01	01	01	00	F0	00	F0	F.☐☐☐.?.?
00000012	00	00	FF	ED	33	6A	50	68	6F	.. ?jPho.
0000001B	74	6F	73	68	6F	70	20	33	2E	toshop 3.
00000024	30	00	38	42	49	4D	03	ED	00	0.8BIM☐?.
0000002D	00	00	00	00	10	00	F0	00	00	....☐.?..
00000036	00	01	00	01	00	F0	00	00	00	.☐.☐.?...
0000003F	01	00	01	38	42	49	4D	04	04	☐.☐8BIM☐☐
00000048	00	00	00	00	00	A4	1C	01	5A	|.....?☐Z.

Fig. 5. Initial file format (Color figure online)

	0	1	2	3	4	5	6	7	01234567
00000000	41	47	73	37	01	F0	33	74	AGs7☐?t.
00000008	70	00	03	00	00	01	00	42	p.☐..☐.B
00000010	00	A4	03	02	04	08	30	02	.?☐☐☐☐.
00000018	36	2B	1C	32	37	3F	34	02	6+ 27?4☐
00000020	72	65	00	65	64	1C	44	63	re.ed Dc
00000028	64	29	65	74	70	68	6D	20	d)etphm

(a) Random data block 1

	0	1	2	3	4	5	6	7	01234567
00000000	49	47	73	37	00	00	50	73	IGs7..Ps
00000008	33	42	00	10	00	F0	00	4D	3B.☐.?.M
00000010	00	01	25	00	02	30	31	00	.☐%.☐01.
00000018	36	30	3E	31	30	06	35	00	60>10☐5.
00000020	61	1C	42	6E	02	65	75	6C	a Bn☐eul
00000028	02	64	50	73	4C	72	36	4D	☐dPsLr6M

(b) Random data block 2

Fig. 6. Arbitrary data block (Color figure online)

6   Conclusion

This paper proposed an AF scheme based on erasure coding and distributed storage, which keeps data in chunks between different devices and generates parity blocks, i.e., it can tolerate the loss of a particular block and reduce storage costs compared to multiple copies of files. This solution effectively makes the forensic process more complex than other solutions, and thus reduces the risk to the AFer in preserving the files. Theoretical and empirical analysis showed that the proposed method is effective in hiding data without encrypting it.

Acknowledgments. This article is supported in part by the National Key R&D Program of China under project 2020YFB1006004, the National Natural Science Foundation of China under projects 61772150, 61862012 and 61962012, the Guangxi Natural Science Foundation under grants 2018GXNSFDA281054, 2019GXNSFFA245015 and 2019GXNSFGA245004, the Guangxi Young Teachers' Basic Ability Improvement Program 2021KY0214, the Peng Cheng Laboratory Project of Guangdong Province PCL2018KP004, and the open program of Guangxi Key Laboratory of Cryptography and Information Security under grant GCIS201930.

References

1. AccessData. https://accessdata.com/product-download/ftk-tools-7-4-2. Accessed 14 Aug 2021

2. CAINE Linux. https://www.caine-live.net/. Accessed 15 Aug 2021
3. east-tec InvisibleSecrets. https://www.east-tec.com/invisiblesecrets/. Accessed 16 Aug 2021
4. Hex workshop. http://www.hexworkshop.com/. Accessed 14 Aug 2021
5. Kali Linux. https://www.kali.org/. Accessed 15 Aug 2021
6. Killdisk User Manual. https://www.killdisk.com/manual/index.html#erase-methods.html. Accessed 15 Aug 2021
7. Metasploit. https://github.com/rapid7/metasploit-framework/. Accessed 16 Aug 2021
8. U.S. Air Force System Security Instruction 5020 (September 2000). https://cryptome.org/afssi5020.htm. Accessed 16 Aug 2021
9. DoD 5220.22-M National Industry Security Program Operating Manual (NISPOM) (May 2016). https://www.esd.whs.mil/portals/54/documents/dd/issuances/dodm/522022m.pdf. Accessed 16 Aug 2021
10. Andreas, S.: strongSwan. https://github.com/strongswan/strongswan. Accessed 14 Aug 2021
11. Banakh, R., Piskozub, A.: Attackers' wi-fi devices metadata interception for their location identification. In: 2018 IEEE 4th International Symposium on Wireless Systems within the International Conferences on Intelligent Data Acquisition and Advanced Computing Systems (IDAACS-SWS), pp. 112–116 (2018). https://doi.org/10.1109/IDAACS-SWS.2018.8525538
12. Chandramouli, S.P., et al.: Measuring e-mail header injections on the world wide web. In: Proceedings of the 33rd Annual ACM Symposium on Applied Computing, SAC 2018, pp. 1647–1656. Association for Computing Machinery, New York (2018). https://doi.org/10.1145/3167132.3167308
13. Conlan, K., Baggili, I., Breitinger, F.: Anti-forensics: furthering digital forensic science through a new extended, granular taxonomy. Digital Invest. 18, S66–S75 (2016). https://doi.org/10.1016/j.diin.2016.04.006
14. Cristea, M., Groza, B.: Fingerprinting smartphones remotely via ICMP timestamps. IEEE Commun. Lett. 17(6), 1081–1083 (2013). https://doi.org/10.1109/LCOMM.2013.040913.130419
15. Garber, L.: Computer Forensics: high-tech law enforcement. Computer 34(01), 22–27 (2001). https://doi.org/10.1109/MC.2001.10008
16. Göbel, T., Baier, H.: Anti-forensic capacity and detection rating of hidden data in the ext4 filesystem. In: DigitalForensics 2018. IAICT, vol. 532, pp. 87–110. Springer, Cham (2018). https://doi.org/10.1007/978-3-319-99277-8_6
17. Göbel, T., Baier, H.: Anti-forensics in ext4: on secrecy and usability of timestamp-based data hiding. Digital Invest. 24, S111–S120 (2018). https://doi.org/10.1016/j.diin.2018.01.014
18. Grugq, T.: Defeating forensic analysis on unix. Phrack Mag. 11(58) (2002). http://phrack.org/issues/59/6.html
19. Gutmann, P.: Secure deletion of data from magnetic and solid-state memory. In: 6th USENIX Security Symposium (USENIX Security 96). USENIX Association, San Jose, CA (July 1996)
20. Hitefield, S.D., Fowler, M., Clancy, T.C.: Exploiting buffer overflow vulnerabilities in software defined radios. In: 2018 IEEE International Conference on Internet of Things (iThings) and IEEE Green Computing and Communications (GreenCom) and IEEE Cyber, Physical and Social Computing (CPSCom) and IEEE Smart Data (SmartData), pp. 1921–1927 (2018). https://doi.org/10.1109/Cybermatics_2018.2018.00318

21. Jeitner, P., Shulman, H.: Injection attacks reloaded: tunnelling malicious payloads over DNS. In: 30th USENIX Security Symposium (USENIX Security 21), pp. 3165–3182. USENIX Association (August 2021)
22. Kakde, Y., Gonnade, P., Dahiwale, P.: Audio-video steganography. In: 2015 International Conference on Innovations in Information, Embedded and Communication Systems (ICIIECS), pp. 1–6 (2015). https://doi.org/10.1109/ICIIECS.2015.7192885
23. Karagiannis, C., Vergidis, K.: Digital evidence and cloud forensics: contemporary legal challenges and the power of disposal. Information **12**(5), 181 (2021)
24. Kessler, G.C.: GCK'S File Signatures Table (June 2021). https://www.garykessler.net/library/file_sigs.html. Accessed 15 Aug 2021
25. Kissel, R., Regenscheid, A., Scholl, M., Stine, K.: NIST Special Publication 800–88 Revision 1: sGuidelines for Media Sanitization (December 2014). https://nvlpubs.nist.gov/nistpubs/SpecialPublications/NIST.SP.800-88r1.pdf. Accessed 16 Aug 2021
26. Kumar, A., Kansal, A., Singh, K.: An improved anti-forensic technique for jpeg compression. Multimedia Tools Appl. **78**(18), 25427–25453 (2019)
27. Mansfield-Devine, S.: Fighting forensics. Comput. Fraud Secur. **2010**(1), 17–20 (2010). https://doi.org/10.1016/S1361-3723(10)70112-3
28. McDonald, A.D., Kuhn, M.G.: StegFS: a steganographic file system for Linux. In: Pfitzmann, A. (ed.) IH 1999. LNCS, vol. 1768, pp. 463–477. Springer, Heidelberg (2000). https://doi.org/10.1007/10719724_32
29. Neuner, S., Voyiatzis, A.G., Schmiedecker, M., Brunthaler, S., Katzenbeisser, S., Weippl, E.R.: Time is on my side: steganography in filesystem metadata. Digital Invest. **18**, S76–S86 (2016). https://doi.org/10.1016/j.diin.2016.04.010
30. Perez, B., Musolesi, M., Stringhini, G.: You are your metadata: identification and obfuscation of social media users using metadata information. In: Proceedings of the 12th International Conference on Web and Social Media, ICWSM 2018, Stanford, California, USA, 25–28 June 2018. pp. 241–250. AAAI Press (2018)
31. Piper, S., Davis, M., Manes, G., Shenoi, S.: Detecting hidden data in Ext2/Ext3 file systems. In: Pollitt, M., Shenoi, S. (eds.) DigitalForensics 2005. ITIFIP, vol. 194, pp. 245–256. Springer, Boston, MA (2006). https://doi.org/10.1007/0-387-31163-7_20
32. Reed, I.S., Solomon, G.: Polynomial codes over certain finite fields. J. Soc. Ind. Appl. Math. **8**(2), 300–304 (1960)
33. Rogers, M.: Anti-forensics (September 2005). https://www.researchgate.net/profile/Marcus-Rogers-2/publication/268290676_Anti-Forensics_Anti-Forensics/links/575969a908aec91374a3656c/Anti-Forensics-Anti-Forensics.pdf
34. Schneier, B., Kelsey, J.: Secure audit logs to support computer forensics. ACM Trans. Inf. Syst. Secur. **2**(2), 159–176 (1999). https://doi.org/10.1145/317087.317089
35. Walters, A.: Volatility Foundation. https://www.volatilityfoundation.org/. Accessed 14 Aug 2021
36. Wang, T., Wang, P., Cai, S., Ma, Y., Liu, A., Xie, M.: A unified trustworthy environment establishment based on edge computing in industrial IoT. IEEE Trans. Ind. Inf. **16**(9), 6083–6091 (2020). https://doi.org/10.1109/TII.2019.2955152
37. Wani, M.A., AlZahrani, A., Bhat, W.A.: File system anti-forensics - types, techniques and tools. Comput. Fraud Secur. **2020**(3), 14–19 (2020). https://doi.org/10.1016/S1361-3723(20)30030-0

Data Science

Predicting Consumers' Coupon-usage in E-commerce with Capsule Network

Wenjun Jiang[1]($\boxtimes$)(iD), Zhenqiong Tan[1](iD), Jiawei He[1], Jifeng Zhang[1], Tian Wang[2], and Shuhong Chen[2,3]

[1] College of Computer Science and Electronic Engineering, Hunan University,
Chang'sha 410082, China
jiangwenjun@hnu.edu.cn
[2] BNU-UIC Institute of Artificial Intelligence and Future Networks,
Beijing Normal University (BNU Zhuhai), Zhuhai, Guangdong, China
[3] School of Computer Science and Cyber Engineering, Guangzhou University,
Guangzhou 510006, China

Abstract. In e-commerce, merchants usually increase their profit by issuing coupons to potential customers. If merchants don't develop a suitable coupon strategy, or randomly issue coupons, they may not take effects and thus waste the budget. Therefore, it is very important for merchants to issue coupons to customers who are more likely to purchase, leading to the necessity of predicting consumer's coupon usage. However, existing methods such as questionnaires cannot get enough data and traditional deep learning cannot solve the complex features of coupon usage prediction. To this end, this paper proposes a novel model for predicting customer's coupon usage behavior with capsule network. It classifies coupon features into multiple groups of capsules, and designs two capsule network structures for predicting coupon usage behavior. Meanwhile, we intensively compare the proposed model with multi-layer perception (MLP), convolutional neural network (CNN) and recurrent neural network (RNN). The experimental results show that the proposed model has significantly better prediction accuracy (e.g. AUC).

Keywords: E-commerce · Coupon usage behavior · Capsule network

1 Introduction

E-coupon plays an indispensable role in e-commerce. By issuing e-coupons to users, merchants can increase the exposure of the store, increase the sales of products and obtain greater profits. Meanwhile, it can also meet customer's needs and help them reduce the economic cost of product payment. The change of consumption intention and behavior can directly affect the economic benefits. If merchants can estimate the probability of consumers coupon usage when issuing

Supported by NSFC grant 62172149, 61632009, 62172159, the Natural Science Foundation of Hunan Province of China (2021JJ30137).

e-coupons, it will bring great convenience and benefits. Therefore, it is of great importance to predict user's coupon-usage behaviors.

According to the theory of consumer motivation, consumers will have both utilitarian and hedonic motivation in the whole shopping process [1]. The former means that consumers want to buy the goods efficiently, cheaply and on time. The latter refers to consumers' desire to acquire hedonic components in the process of shopping [2]. Acquiring the emotional and social value in the process of purchasing products helps satisfy these motivations [3].

According to valassis's annual survey[1], there are significantly more consumers who often use coupons in recent years, as shown in Fig. 1. Meanwhile, people are eager to find more suitable coupons online. According to "millennial shopping report 2019"[2], people are willing to spend more time looking for discounts. For instance more than half of people (56%) spending three minutes or longer searching the Internet for coupons. More details can be seen in Fig. 2.

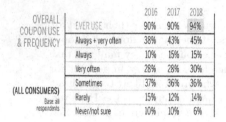

Fig. 1. Overall coupon usage and frequency.

Fig. 2. Duration of searching coupons.

The coupon usage behavior refers to that of receiving and using coupons. Existing researches usually use questionnaires to study such behaviors. However, the form of questionnaire usually needs a huge amount of work and only obtains a small amount of data. Some researchers study the usage behaviors of some specific coupons. These models usually focus on specific types of coupons, so they may not be suitable for general coupons. Some existing researches explore the features of coupon itself. These researches mainly focus on the issue of coupon forwarding or coupon duration, neglecting the coupon usage. Some other researches study other aspects of coupon usage. Lu et al. [4] predict the usage of internet coupons and rank the importance of factors. Shi et al. [5] propose an O2O coupon usage prediction model based on XGBoost.

Our Motivation. Keeping the coupon usage prediction task in mind, our motivations are threefold. (1) Fully understanding all aspects of the coupons usage behaviors and identifing all the key features. (2) Selecting a suitable calculation model and exploiting these features to make predictions. The model should be

---

[1] CouponIntelligenceReport: http://www.199it.com/archives/711270.html.
[2] https://couponfollow.com/research/millennial-shopping-report.

able to handle large amount of data and have good interpretability. (3) Verifing the effect of the calculation model on real data set and comparing with common deep leaning models.

In this paper, we try to promote the deep learning technique in the coupon usage prediction task and improve the accuracy and intepretability. We propose a coupon usage prediction model with capsule network. The capsule network has good interpretability, and the pattern of vector in-vector out allows us to cover various aspects of the coupon usage behaviors. As far as we know, there is no research on applying capsule networks to coupon usage prediction yet.

Our contributions are threefold: (1) **Coupon-usage feature extraction.** In order to better analyze coupon related data, we extract five types of features related to coupon usage predictions. We obtain a total of 71 features, which will be used to construct capsules for prediction model. (2) **Coupon-usage prediction with capsule network.** We propose two coupon usage prediction models with capsule network. This is the first work that applying capsule network into coupon usage prediction. **Experiment at evaluation.** We conduct intensive comparative experiments to verify the effectiveness. We also test the components of the capsule network. The results validate the effectiveness of our work and verify the effects of each part of the model.

2   Related Work

In this section, we briefly review the related work.

Researches on User Purchase Behaviors. The purpose of user purchase behavior analysis is to predict the purchase tendency of specific users for specific products within a given time range, and to predict whether users will purchase during the next visit to the e-commerce platform [6]. Thanks to the massive purchase behavior data retained by e-commerce platforms [7], researchers can mine user features in the data and build a machine learning model to predict the purchase behavior. Wu et al. [8] analyzed users'purchase behavior in the online market. Li et al. [9] constructed feature engineering from seven aspects: user feature, commodity feature, position feature and combination feature. Researchers also tried to apply deeping learning methods in the area of user purchase behaviors [10]. Our work also explore the features of the customer's purchase behavior, and we use the coupon behavior data of the customer in the real scene to understand the data from the three objects: user, coupon and merchant.

Researches on Coupon Usage Behaviors. Researchers found that e-coupons can bring consumers functional values[11], emotional values [12] and social value [13]. Specifically, electronic coupons usage can help consumers reduce the economic cost of product payment [11]. Consumers can query, obtain, store and use them anytime and anywhere [14]. The form of e-coupon allows consumers to carry out independent search on the Internet [15]. As the e-coupon is an innovative consumption mode, the use of e-coupon will make consumers feel more fashionable than those who do not use e-coupon [13]. It can be seen that deep learning is rarely used in coupon usage behavior, and the commonly used deep learning algorithms are not well explained. Therefore, we study and select the capsule network model which has better interpretability. We also consider many factors related to the coupons usage behaviors.

3   Problem Statement and Preliminaries

In this section, we formulate the coupon usage prediction problem, and introduce the capsule network model we use in this paper.

Coupon Usage Prediction Problem. Given a set of users in e-commerce, $\{u_1, u_2, u_3, \ldots, u_z\}$, and their purchase histories and coupon usage records, a set of items, $\{i_1, i_2, i_3, \ldots, i_x\}$ and a set of coupons, $\{c_1, c_2, c_3, \ldots, c_y\}$. The coupon usage prediction problem is trying to effectively predict whether a target user will use some specific coupon. We consider this problem as a binary classification problem. The input is a user's purchase and coupon usage records, and the output is a binary value, where 0 means that the target user will not use coupon and 1 is to use the coupon.

Solution Overview. We try to comprehensively exploit coupon related features and build a coupon usage prediction model with capsule network. Our solution has three main steps: (1) Feature extraction; (2) Model construction; (3) Probability prediction. The solution overview is shown in Fig. 3.

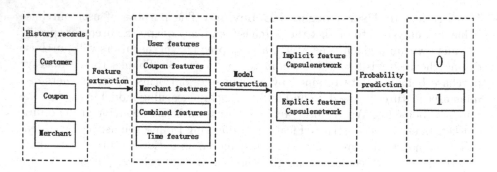

Fig. 3. Solution overview.

We first study three types of objects related to coupons usage, including customers, coupons and merchants. Then we extract five sets of features from these three objects. Finally, we build the prediction model with two kinds of capsule networks, i.e., implicit and explicit feature capsule network.

Preliminary of Capsule Network. Capsule network is a new deep learning network proposed by Hinton [16]. It can model the hierarchical relationship of knowledge representation inside the neural network better. The information transmission between the upper and lower layers of the capsule network is implemented by a dynamic routing algorithm. Each of the upper and lower capsule connections contains a weight matrix for extracting the underlying capsule information. The values of matrices are all parameters that can be trained by the capsule network. The lower capsule does not directly transmit itself to the upper layer, but uses a copy of the feature to convey the information. Next, we must use feature copies for dynamic routing between capsules.

Dynamic Routing for Coupon Usage Prediction. Wang et al. [17] pointed out the shortcomings of the original dynamic routing. They proposed an improved dynamic routing algorithm, which revealed the relationship between dynamic routing and clustering algorithm. We exploit the dymatic routing algorithm in [17] for coupon usage prediction. In order to use dynamic routing with capsule network, we need to fully understand all aspects of the coupon usage behavior and identify all the features. Details are in the following.

4   Data Processing and Feature Engineering

This section describes the construction process of coupon features. We extract five types of features from three kinds of entity objects, including customers, coupons and merchants. In next section, we will construct capsules for the capsule network, each original capsule is a vector that represents multiple features of a certain aspect of the coupon usage behavior. We design many fine-grained features with a large amount of real behavior data. The feature engineering carried out in this section can serve as a reference for e-commerce data processing.

4.1   Data Processing

We use the coupon consumption data released by Ant Financial Services Group in the O2O scenario[3]. The O2O industry naturally connects hundreds of millions of consumers, where all kinds of applications record more than 10 billion users' behavior and location records everyday.The original dataset provides information about customers with real online and offline consumption behavior between January 1, 2016 and June 30, 2016. In order to protect the privacy of users and businesses, all the datas are processed anonymously.

The data is divided into the training set and the test set. The former includes online scenarios and offline scenarios in the first five months. While the latter includes only the data for offline scenarios in the last month. We aim to predict the use of coupons online and offline by combining the data of online and offline scenarios, mining laws and predicting the behavior of offline coupons. In the original dataset, if both *Date* and *Coupon_id* are not null, then it indicates that the customer uses the coupons to purchase goods, and we regard it as a positive sample. If *Date* is null, and *Coupon_id* is not null, which means the customer does not use coupons and we regard it as a negative sample.

---

[3] https://tianchi.aliyun.com/competition/entrance/231593/information.

4.2 Feature Engineering

User features can describe the user's purchasing preference and usage of coupons. These habits can have an impact on the coupon usage behavior of users in the future. We extract a total of 18 user offline features and 8 online features, which are partially described in detail in Table 1.

Coupon Features. We extract coupon features that will affect the usage tendency of users, such as discount ratio, preferential form, distribution breadth and so on. The description of coupons in the original data has only one Discount_rate field, indicating its discount rate, which is far from enough. Therefore, we extract a total of 11 coupon features, some of which are shown as in Table 2.

Table 1. Detailed description of user features

Feature	Explanation
$N_{user\_purchase}$	The total number of historical goods purchased by a user
$N_{user\_coupon\ recipt}$	The total number of historical coupons received by a user
$N_{user\_coupon\ verification}$	The total number of a user receiving and using a coupon
$N_{user\_purchase\ without\ coupons}$	The total number of historical purchases without coupons
$N_{user\_full\ discount}$	the total number of coupon for a user using $x : y$ as a discount
$N_{user\_common\ discount}$	The total number of coupon history for a user using a normal discount, that is, a non-full discount
$R_{user\_purchase\ by\ coupons}$	The ratio of $N_{user\_coupon\ verification}$ over $N_{user\_purchase}$
$R_{user\_coupon\ discount}$	The ratio of $N_{user\_common\ discount}$ over $N_{user\_coupon\ verification}$
$N_{user\_behavior}^{online}$	The total number of times a user clicks, buys, or receives coupons online
$N_{user\_click/buy/receive}^{online}$	Number of times a user clicks/buys/receives coupons online
$R_{user\_click/buy/receive}^{online}$	The proportion of online click/buy/receive coupons by a user to all online behaviors
$N_{user\_verification}^{online}$	Number of user coupons verification in a user's online scenario
$R_{user\_verification}^{online}$	Verification rate of user coupons in a user's online scenario
$O_{user\_verification}^{allline}$	Count the number of coupons verification in online and offline scenarios
$P_{user\_using\ coupon}^{online}$	A ratio to measure the preference of a user's online coupons
$P_{user\_using\ coupon}^{offline}$	A ratio to measure the preference of a user's offline coupons

Table 2. Detailed description of some coupon features

Feature	Explanation
$N_{coupon\ publish}$	Total number of historical coupons that has been published
$N_{coupon\ verification}$	The total number that a coupon has been verified by the user
$R_{coupon\ verification}$	Measure the rate at which a coupon is verified by a user
$R_{coupon\ abandon}$	Measure the rate at which a coupon is abandoned
$N_{coupon\ reuse}$	The number of behaviors that a coupon is used at least twice by same user

Merchant Features. We extract merchant features. The strategy of issuing coupons plays an important role in the verification of coupons. Therefore, it is very important to extract the features of merchants and digitize the methods and strategies of issuing coupons. We extract a total of 15 merchant features, some of which are shown as in Table 3.

Table 3. Detailed description of some merchant features

Feature	Explanation
$N_{mer\_coupon\ publish}$	The total number of historical coupons issued from a merchant
$N_{mer\_coupon\ verification}$	The total number of historical coupons issued by a merchant and having been successfully verified
$N_{mer\_repeat\ rc}$	The number of times that the same user is receiving the same coupon for more than two times at a certain merchant
$N_{mer\_use\ repeat\ rc}$	The number of times the same user who receives the same coupon twice at a merchant and has at least one consumption behavior
$N_{mer\_purchase}$	The total number of historical purchases that have occurred in the past by a merchant
$R_{mer\_purchase\ by\ coupon}$	Measure the rate of purchase of coupons in the historical purchase behavior of a merchant

Combined Features. By combining the features of users with that of the merchants, as well as that of the users and the coupons, the combined features can specific performances. Therefore, the combined features are of great importance to the prediction of coupon usage behavior. We extract a total of 12 combined features, some of which are shown as in Table 4.

Table 4. Detailed description of some combined features

Feature	Explanation
$N_{u,m}^{purchase}$	The total number of purchases by a user u in a particular merchant m
$N_{u,m}^{receive}$	The total number of times a user u has received coupons in a merchant m
$N_{u,m}^{verification}$	The total number of times a user u has received and verified coupons in a particular merchant m
$R_{u,m}^{verification}$	Verification rate of a user u receiving coupons from a merchant m

Time Features. The influence of time on consumer behavior is great, which has been studied in the prediction of purchase behavior. We find that the time features also have a certain impact on the collection and verification of coupons. Figure 4 shows the statistics on coupons received from January to May 2016.

Table 5. Detailed description of some time features

Feature	Explanation
$T_{fm}^{receipt}$	The receipt of coupons occurs in the first few days of the month
T_{fm}^{use}	The use of coupons occurs in the first few days of the month
$T_{fw}^{receipt}$	The receipt of coupons occurs in the first few days of the week
T_{fw}^{use}	The use of coupons occurs in the first few days of the week
$T_{isholiday}$	0 is a non-holiday, and 1 is a holiday
$T_m^{receipt}$	Coupon receipt occurs in the early, middle, or late part of the month. 0 means the first ten days, 1 means the middle ten days, and 2 means the last ten days
T_m^{use}	The use of coupon usage behavior occurs in early, middle, or late part of the month. Among them, 0 means the first ten days, 1 means the middle ten days, 2 represents the last ten days

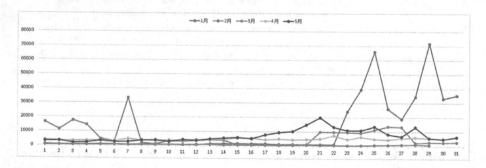

Fig. 4. Statistical of coupons received from January to May, 2016

In general, it shows more coupons are received by users later in a month. This may be because many users are always paid in the later days. Meanwhile, it can be seen that in February, users received far more coupons in the first ten days of February than that in late February. Therefore, the time factor also has an important impact on the prediction of coupon usage behavior. The digital features of the time factors that affect the coupon usage behavior are constructed, and the detailed descriptions of 7 time features is given in Table 5.

5   Coupon Usage Prediction with Capsule Network

This section will build the coupon usage prediction model based on capsule network. The features that we process in Sect. 4 are scalar, but the input of capsule network should be a vector. Therefore, we need to construct the input vector. In this section, we propose two types of prediction models with explicit feature capsule network and implicit feature capsule network, respectively.

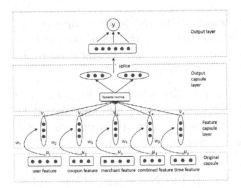

Fig. 5. Explicit feature capsule network.

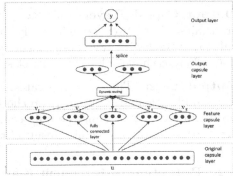

Fig. 6. Implicit feature capsule network.

5.1   Prediction with Explicit Feature Capsule Network (ECapsNet)

In this section, we introduce the coupon usage prediction model based on explicit feature capsule network structure and describe the composition of its layers. We encapsulate five features: user features, coupon features, merchant features, combination features and time features into five original capsules: user feature capsule, coupon feature capsule, merchant feature capsule, combination feature capsule and time feature capsule. Because the original capsule is constructed by its explicit feature group, this network is called the "explicit feature" capsule network (ECapsNet for short).

The above five original capsules have inconsisity, which makes them unable to be treated directly by the capsule network. Therefore, we need to unify the dimensions of the features, and it is set to be 16 dimensions. Then we introduce five weight matrices $[W_1, W_2, W_3, W_4, W_5]$, and $W_1 \in R^{26*16}$, $W_2 \in R^{11*16}$, $W_3 \in R^{15*16}$, $W_4 \in R^{12*16}$, $W_5 \in R^{7*16}$. Using thse five weight matrices, the five capsules are mapped to the 16-dimensional feature space. In this way, we unify the input dimensions of the capsule network.

Figure 5 shows the structure of the explicit feature capsule network. There are four layers in ECapsNet: the original capsule layer, the feature capsule layer, the output capsule layer and the output layer. Details are as follows.

Original Capsule Layer: The user feature, coupon feature, merchant feature, combination feature and time feature are packaged respectively. They are the inputs obtained directly by the model, and their dimensions are not uniform, so they cannot be directly used by the dynamic paths of the capsule network.

Feature Capsule Layer: This layer has five sets of weight matrices. The five capsules are set up as: v_1, v_2, v_3, v_4, v_5, respectively. In this layer, the weight matrix is used to map it to the feature space of dimension unity. We define u_i as the ith capsule in the original capsule layer. The feature capsule after conversion v_i is calculated as follows:

$$v_i = W_i \times u_i \tag{1}$$

Output Capsule Layer: This layer is connected to the feature capsule and transmits information through the dynamic routing algorithm. The output capsule layer is set with two capsules, corresponding to the two classification problem, where each capsule contains a class of information.

Output Layer: This layer generates the probability result. In order to solve the sample imbalance problem, we choose to splice the capsule and map it to probability output y using the fully connected neural network layer, where $y \in R^2$, represents the probability result of the binary classification.

5.2   Prediction with Implicit Feature Capsule Network (ICapsNet)

In this section, we introduce the coupon usage prediction model based on the implicit capsule network structure (ICapsNet for short), as well as its similarities with and differences from *ECapsNet*.

The implicit feature capsule network is also divided into four layers, and its structure is similar to that of the explicit feature capsule network, as shown in Fig. 6. The difference lies in the treatment of the original capsule layer and the construction of the feature capsule layer. Details are as follows.

Original Capsule Layer: The original capsule layer of ICapsNet does not separate the capsule, but directly inputs all 93 dimensional features constructed by the feature engineering in Sect. 4 (Note that the feature engineering extracted a total of 71 types of features, which contain more than one statistic. Thus, the data finally reaches 93 dimensions after all features were expended). Therefore, the input feature of this layer is $u \in R^{93}$.

Feature Capsule Layer: We define v_i as the ith capsule of the feature capsule layer. In Fig. 6, there is a connection between the original capsule layer and the capsule of each feature capsule layer, which represents a fully connected neural network between the original capsule u and each feature capsule v_i, and its structure is shown in Sect. 5.3. Here we use a two-layer fully connected neural network. Each feature capsule v_i can be calculated as follows:

$$h_i = W_{i1}u + b_{i1} \tag{2}$$

$$v_i = W_{i2}h_i + b_{i2} \tag{3}$$

where W_{i1} and W_{i2} are the parameters of a two-layer fully connected neural network; b_{i1} and b_{i2} are their bias. In particular, the number of capsules contained in the feature capsule layer is not limited and can be set freely. Because the fully connected neural network is used to implicitly extract the feature information from the original capsule layer, it is called "implicit feature" capsule network.

5.3   Sample Imbalance Processing

In this section, Focal loss function [18] is introduced to deal with sample imbalanced data, so as to make the capsule network be suitable for coupon usage prediction. It is originally used to deal with the few-shot problem in target detection task, that is, the number of samples from some analogies is very small, which is easy to be ignored by the model [17]. Focal loss is introduced into two kinds of capsule networks. We define y_t as the tth probability output of the capsule network. Then, the Focal loss function is calculated as follows:

$$FL(y_t) = -\alpha_t(1 - y_t)^{\gamma}log(y_t) \tag{4}$$

In Eq. (4), α_t controls the impact of positive and negative samples to the weight of the loss function. We set parameter $\alpha \in (0,1)$. When the sample is a positive one, we let $\alpha_t=\alpha$. When the sample is a negative one, $\alpha_t=1-\alpha$. Thus, when $\alpha > 0.5$, we can reduce the impact of negative samples, so that the model can pay more attention to the positive samples. Meanwhile, $(1-y_t)^{\gamma}$ is the modulation coefficient. If y_t is close to 0.5, it is more difficult to classify the sample. The higher the modulation coefficient is, the higher the loss contribution is, so that the model can pay more attention to samples that are difficult to judge.

5.4   Coupon Usage Prediction

In this section, we introduce the integrated process of coupon usage prediction. Firstly, user features, coupon features, merchant features, combination features and time features are taken as the input of capsule network. Then, according to whether the original capsule layer is divided into multiple capsules, two forms of capsule networks are formed for processing separately (the capsule network needs to be segmented as the explicit feature capsule network; the capsule network that is directly input all the features as the implicit feature capsule network). After transforming the original capsule layer into the feature capsule layer, the dynamic routing algorithm is used to transmit information to form the output capsule layer. The output capsule layer is set with two capsules, corresponding to the two classification problems, where each capsule contains a class of information. Finally, the capsules are spliced and mapped to the probability output y using the fully connected neural network layer.

6   Experiments

In order to verify the effectiveness of the proposed model, we study the effects of the parameters, and conduct comparative experiments with three most commonly used neural network models. Finally, we conduct the ablation experiments to test the components of the capsule network structure.

Evaluation Metrics. AUC scores are used to evaluate such probability classification. AUC is the area under the ROC curve, and the higher AUC scores represent better classification results. AUC is calculated as follows:

$$AUC = \frac{\sum_{i \in positiveClass} rank_i - \frac{M(1+M)}{2}}{M * N} \tag{5}$$

in Eq. 5, M is the number of positive samples, N is the number of negative samples, $rank$ is the probability that the classifiers rate a sample and how likely it is to be a positive sample.

Baseline Models. In order to verify the effectiveness of our work, we set up several sets of control models as the baselines, all of them are network models based on deep learning, as follows:

- **MLP:** In order to make a fair comparison with the two kinds of capsule networks, we use a multi-layer perceptual network with two hidden layers. The input layer is 93 dimensions, the hidden layers dimensions are 80 and 32, the hidden layer uses relu as the activation function, the output layer uses softmax as the activation function, and the loss function uses cross entropy.
- **MLP-FL:** It is the same as that of the multi-layer perceptual machine, but the loss function uses the Focal loss.
- **SVM-Bagging:** Support vector machine model with 5-fold cross-validation and 7 under-sampling, integrated with Bagging.
- **RF-Bagging:** Random forest model with 5-fold cross-validation and 7 under-sampling, integrated with Bagging.
- **CNN:** Convolution network with an input layer of 93 dimensions, using 64*5 one-dimensional filters, and the step size is 1. Then, the mean-pooling operation with 4 is used to get the second layer. In the third layer, we use 32 one-dimensional filters and use mean-pooling to get 32-dimensional vectors. Finally, we use the full connection layer and softmax activation function to get the output, and uses cross entropy loss as the loss function.
- **CNN-FL:** It is the same as the convolution network, but uses the Focal loss as the loss function.
- **RNN:** The initial input layer of recurrent neural network is five groups of features with a total of 93 dimensions. We use the same original feature structure as that of the explicit feature capsule network to obtain five 16-dimensional feature vectors respectively. Then we use the two-layer RNN structure and connect the full connection layer with the softmax activation function, and also uses cross entropy as the loss function.
- **RNN-FL:** It is the same as that of recurrent neural network, but uses Focal loss as the loss function.

6.1   Parameter Sensitivity

This section studies the effects of model parameters, including the number of feature capsules in implicit capsule network and the number of iterations.

The Effects of Number of Feature Capsules: For the implicit feature capsule network, we check the effect of the number of capsules in feature capsule layer. Table 6 shows results. It shows that the performance of the capsule network reaches the best when the number of feature capsules is 8. When there are fewer feature capsules, the feature types represented by the capsule layer are fewer, which makes the feature information in each capsule too complex. Therefore, the performance of the capsule network is weakened.

Table 6. The effect of the number of capsules on $ICapsNet$

Number of feature capsules	Online (AUC)	Offline (AUC)
2	0.75	0.73
5	0.78	0.79
8	0.80	0.90
10	0.79	0.78
15	0.78	0.76
20	0.75	0.76
25	0.72	0.73
30	0.65	0.68

When the number of feature capsules is too large, the performance of capsule network also decreases. As shown in Table 6, when the number of capsules is more than 8, the performance of implicit feature capsule network shows a downward trend. It indicates that when there are more feature capsules, the hidden feature categories are too fine, so that each feature capsule contains too little information and makes the capsule network perform worse.

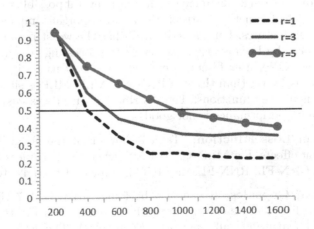

Fig. 7. Effects of iteration number on the performance

Therefore, it is important to select the appropriate number of feature capsules. In the following experiments, we set the number of feature capsules to 8. It is worth noting that the optimal number may be different for each data.

The Effects of the Number of Iterations: The dynamic routing algorithm involves another parameter, i.e., the number of iterations. Figure 7 shows the effect of iterations r in dynamic routing. The loss function trained when iterations $r=3$ decreases the fastest and the convergence value is lower. Therefore, we set the number of iterations as 3 in the following experiments.

6.2   Comparative Experiments

We compare our work with 8 baseline models : MLP, MLP-FL, SVM-Bagging, RF-Bagging, CFF, CFF-FL, RNN and RNN-FL.

In our prediction model, the dimensions of capsules are set to 16 dimensions. Both the explicit feature capsule network and the implicit feature capsule network configuration are configured with only two layers of capsule layers. We use the dynamic routing algorithm as the dynamic routing mechanism for transferring information between two layers of capsule. In the implicit feature capsule network, we set the feature capsule layer as a multi-layer sensor network with one hidden layer and its output layer as the feature capsule. The number of capsules in the capsule layer is set to 5. $\alpha =0.75$, $\gamma=2$ in our Focal loss function.

The Results: The experimental results are shown in Table 7. It can be seen that our explicit feature capsule network has better performance than the traditional deep learning model MLP, CNN, RNN, and also better than the implicit feature capsule network. This shows that the dynamic routing algorithm of capsule network, which uses fuzzy clustering to transfer information between capsule layers, can effectively obtain the hidden relations and factors in the features, and mine the relationships between the features.

The Effects of Network Structure: There are several possible reasons for the results. First of all, the network structure has an important impact on extracting coupon usage features. For example, RNN has the worst performance in all models. This may be because RNN is better at processing serialized information. Meanwhile, CNN uses filters to extract implicit features in parallel, and its performance is better than those of RNN and MLP. MLP is simulated by its simple use of nonlinear functions. The distribution of data is easy to produce over-fitting, so its performance is not good.

The Effects of Loss Function: Table 7 shows that the Focal loss function takes significant effects. For MLP, CNN, RNN, when the Focal loss is exploited, i.e., MLP-FL, CNN-FL, RNN-FL, the AUC is improved from 4% to 15%.

The Effects of Capsules: It can also be found from Table 7 that the performance of implicit feature capsule network ($ICapsNet$) is slightly lower than that of explicit feature capsule network ($ECapsNet$). The $ECapsNet$ explicitly corresponds to five groups of features extracted from Sect. 4, which is more interpretable. Different from the explicit feature capsule network, the number of feature capsule layer capsules in the implicit feature capsule network is variable.

Table 7. Comparative results on AUC

Model	Online	Offline
MLP	0.61	0.58
MLP-FL	0.68	0.67
SVM-Bagging	0.70	0.63
RF-Bagging	0.73	0.77
CNN	0.75	0.73
CNN-FL	0.78	0.78
RNN	0.55	0.59
RNN-FL	0.61	0.63
ECapsNet	**0.79**	**0.81**
ICapsNet	**0.78**	**0.79**

Table 8. Ablation experiment on AUC

Ablation model	Online	Offline
ECapsNet-NO-1	0.76	0.74
ICapsNet-NO-1	0.71	0.73
ECapsNet-NO-RT	0.77	0.78
ICapsNet-NO-RT	0.75	0.72
ECapsNet-NO-FL	0.78	0.79
ICapsNet-NO-FL	0.76	0.76
ECapsNet	**0.79**	**0.81**
ICapsNet	**0.78**	**0.79**

6.3 Ablation Study

In this part, we test the effectiveness of each components in our model. We remove different parts of the model to carry out ablation experiments. We remove it separately and supplement the general alternative mechanism as a control. The results of ablation experiments are shown in Table 8. Overall, the performance of capsule network with partial structure removed decreased more or less.

The variant models we construct are as follows:

ECapsNet-NO-1: The variant of the explicit feature capsule network, where the feature mapping layer is removed, and the original feature layer is directly used as the feature capsule.

ICapsNet-NO-1: The variant of feature mapping layer, which is different from the explicit feature capsule network. The implicit feature capsule network divides the 93-dimensional feature vector into 5 parts on average, and for each portion, the excess 16-dimensional part is removed as the feature capsule.

ECapsNet-NO-RT: The variant of removing dynamic routing in explicit feature capsule networks. A multi-layer perceptual machine containing 2 hidden layers is used to connect between each feature capsule and the output capsule.

ICapsNet-NO-RT: The variant of removing dynamic routing in implicit feature capsule networks, with the same approach as **ECapsNet-NO-RT**.

ECapsNet-NO-FL: The variant of removing Focal loss function in explicit feature capsule networks. The Focal loss function is changed into the cross entropy loss function, and the rest is unchanged.

ICapsNet-NO-FL: The variant of removing Focal loss function in implicit feature capsule networks, with the same approach as **ECapsNet-NO-FL**.

7   Conclusion and Future Work

This paper studies coupon usage prediction in e-commerce. In order to better improve the performance of prediction and make the model more interpretable, we propose a capsule network-based coupon usage prediction model, and the coupon related data is preprocessed as the input. We compare the designed capsule network with multi-layer perceptual machine, convolution neural network and recurrent neural network. The experimental results show that the capsule network structure designed in this paper has significant advantages. To the best of our knowledge, we are the first to apply capsule network to coupon usage prediction. In future work, we will test our model with more coupon usage data in other e-commerce platforms, and compare our model with more other works.

References

1. Holbrook, M.B.: The experiential aspects of consumption: consumer fantasies, feelings, and fun. J. Consum. Res. **9**(2), 132–140 (1982)
2. Hsia, T.-L.: Omnichannel retailing: the role of situational involvement in facilitating consumer experiences. Inf. Manage. **57**(8), 103390 (2020)
3. Zhu, Y.-Q.: No trespassing: exploring privacy boundaries in personalized advertisement and its effects on ad attitude and purchase intentions on social media. Inf. Manage. **58**, 103314 (2020)
4. Ping, L.U., Xiao-Tian, C.: Prediction of internet coupon usage based on gradient boosting decision tree model. Sci. Technol. Eng. **19**(18), 234–238 (2019)
5. Qiongyu, S.: Prediction of o2o coupon usage based on xgboost model. In: Proceedings of ICEME, pp. 33–36 (2020)
6. Jannach, D.: Finding preferred query relaxations in content-based recommenders. In: International IEEE Conference Intelligent Systems, p. 355 (2006)
7. Huang, M., Liu, A., Wang, T., Huang, C., Liu, Z.: Green data gathering under delay differentiated services constraint for internet of things. Wirel. Commun. Mob. Comput. **3**, 1–23 (2018)
8. Yi, W.: How does scarcity promotion lead to impulse purchase in the online market? a field experiment. Inf. Manage. **58**(1), 103283 (2021)
9. Dong, Y., Jiang, W.: Brand purchase prediction based on time-evolving userbehaviors in e-commerce. Concurrency Comput. Pract. Experience **31**(1), e4882.1–e4882.15 (2019)
10. Wang, T., Wang, P., Cai, S., Ma, Y., Liu, A., Xie, M.: A unified trustworthy environment establishment based on edge computing in industrial IoT. IEEE Trans. Ind. Inf. **16**(9), 6083–6091 (2020)
11. Li, L., Li, X., Qi, W., Zhang, Y., Yang, W.: Targeted reminders of electronic coupons: using predictive analytics to facilitate coupon marketing. Electron. Commer. Res. 1–30 (2020)
12. Song, J., Koo, C., Kim, Y.: Investigating antecedents of behavioral intentions in mobile commerce. J. Internet Commer. **6**(1), 13–34 (2008)

13. Yang, S., Yaobin, L., Cao, Y.: From the cross-environment perspective. Sci. Res. Manage. Mob. Payment Serv. Adoption **32**(10), 79–88 (2011)
14. Banerjee, S., Yancey, S.: Enhancing mobile coupon redemption in fast food campaigns. J. Res. Interact. Market. **4**(2), 97–110 (2012)
15. Tian, W., et al.: Propagation modeling and defending of a mobile sensor worm in wireless sensor and actuator networks. Sensors **17**(1), 139 (2017)
16. Hinton, G.E., Krizhevsky, A., Wang, S.D.: Transforming auto-encoders. In: Honkela, T., Duch, W., Girolami, M., Kaski, S. (eds.) ICANN 2011. LNCS, vol. 6791, pp. 44–51. Springer, Heidelberg (2011). https://doi.org/10.1007/978-3-642-21735-7_6
17. Wang, D., Liu, Q.: An optimization view on dynamic routing between capsules. In: Workshop Track ICLR (2018)
18. Lin, Y.T., Goyal, P.: Focal loss for dense object detection. In: Proceedings of ICCV, pp. 2999–3007 (2017)

A High-Availability K-modes Clustering Method Based on Differential Privacy

Shaobo Zhang[1,2,3(✉)], Liujie Yuan[1,2], Yuxing Li[1,2], Wenli Chen[1,2], and Yifei Ding[1,2]

[1] School of Computer Science and Engineering, Hunan University of Science and Technology, Xiangtan 411201, China
shaobozhang@hnust.edu.cn
[2] Hunan Key Laboratory of Service Computing and New Software Service Technology, Xiangtan 411201, China
[3] Key Laboratory of Software Engineering for Complex Systems, College of Computer, National University of Defense Technology, Changsha 410073, China

Abstract. In categorical data mining, the K-modes algorithm is a classic algorithm that has been widely used. However, the data analyzed by the K-modes algorithm usually contains sensitive user information. If these data are leaked, it will seriously threaten the privacy of users. In response to this problem, the existing method that combines differential privacy with the K-modes algorithm can effectively prevent privacy leakage. Nevertheless, differential privacy adds noise to the data while protecting data privacy, which will reduce the availability of clustering results. In this paper, we propose a high-availability K-modes clustering mechanism based on differential privacy(HAKC). In this mechanism, based on the use of differential privacy to protect data privacy, we select the initial centroid of the clustering by calculation, and improve the calculation method of the distance between the data point and the centroid in the iterative process.

Keywords: Privacy protection · Categorical data mining · Differential privacy · K-modes clustering

1 Introduction

With the rapid development of information technology, mankind has entered an era of explosive growth of data, and a large amount of data is generated at all times. These massive data contain great values which provide unprecedented space for people to gain deeper insights. For various fields, if the potential value in the data can be obtained, which will gain a huge competitive advantage [1–4]. Clustering is a commonly-used data analysis technique, which divides the data set into different clusters according to a certain standard, making the data in the same cluster more similar [5]. After years of research, there are a variety of clustering algorithms. Among them, K-means algorithm is a classical algorithm

Y. Lai et al. (Eds.): ICA3PP 2021, LNCS 13156, pp. 274–283, 2022.
https://doi.org/10.1007/978-3-030-95388-1_18

for numerical data clustering [6], and K-modes algorithm extended from K-means algorithm is a classical algorithm for categorical data clustering [7]. In the era of big data, the application of data analysis technology is developing rapidly. As an important data analysis technology, cluster analysis plays an important role in data mining, service recommendation and other fields. For example, in business activities, with the rapid development of information technology, the complexity and scale of each customer's data continue to increase, and the total amount of data for the entire customer group is even greater. Massive customer data makes the traditional method of analyzing data based on experience useless, and cluster analysis can solve this problem well. By using cluster analysis, huge customer data can be divided into different categories, and the corresponding characteristics of different customer groups can be portrayed. Merchants can further analyze the behavior patterns of different types of customer groups based on the results of the classification, in order to provide targeted services or guide future business decisions. Although cluster analysis can effectively mine valuable information in data, the data it analyzed usually contains a large amount of sensitive information. If this information is used maliciously, it will seriously threaten the privacy of users. For example, the attacker can infer the user's home address or work location from the location information, and infer the user's hobbies from the social network data [8–10]. Therefore, when using clustering for data analysis, there is an urgent need to protect the privacy of user data [11].

Differential privacy [12] is a privacy protection model with strict mathematical definition. It can quantify the degree of user privacy protection and resist background knowledge attacks and synthetic attacks launched by attackers [13,14]. Since Dwork first proposed the differential privacy protection model in 2006, with its strong privacy protection ability, differential privacy has been widely used of privacy protection in data mining, data publishing, location services and other fields [15–17]. Similarly, in terms of cluster analysis data privacy protection, differential privacy has obvious advantages over traditional privacy protection technologies such as random disturbance and data exchange [18,19]. Differential privacy is widely used in the protection of clustered data privacy, but most of the research focuses on the combination of K-means algorithm and differential privacy, and there are few studies on K-modes algorithm. Moreover, the current K-modes algorithm based on differential privacy protects user privacy while adding a certain amount of noise to the data, which will reduce the availability of data. The goal of our research is to improve the availability of clustering results while protecting data privacy. The main contributions of this paper are as follows.

- We propose a high-availability K-modes clustering mechanism based on differential privacy. On the basis of using differential privacy to protect data privacy, we select the initial cluster centroid through calculation to reduce the influence of random initial centroid on the availability of clustering results and improve the quality of the clustering results.
- We improve the calculation method of the distance between data points and centroid in the iterative process. According to the compactness of data points

in each cluster, the corresponding weight is given, and then the corresponding weight is added when calculating the distance between data points and centroid, so as to further improve the availability of clustering results.

2   Related Work

Different from previous privacy protection technologies, differential privacy adopts a mathematical model with strict mathematical definitions. It not only has strong privacy protection capabilities, but also can quantify the degree of privacy protection, so it has become a research hotspot in the field of privacy protection. Hardt et al. [20] narrowed the response error boundary of the online query system by adding weights. Mohan et al. [21] reduced the privacy budget on the premise of ensuring data privacy security according to the sensitivity and timeliness of different data. Blum et al. [22] proposed a distributed differential privacy algorithm in combination with interval query and half space query in order to further improve the degree of privacy protection. Li et al. [23] proposed the PrivBasis algorithm for the frequent item mining problem of high-dimensional data sets. It improves the availability of mining results under the premise of protecting data privacy by reducing the dimensionality of the dataset. Aiming at the problem that the direct use of differential privacy in batch queries will cause excessive noise in the query results, Xiao et al. [24] used wavelet transform to map the frequency statistical matrix to the wavelet transform matrix, and then added noise to each wavelet transform coefficient. In terms of clustering data privacy protection, differential privacy has obvious advantages over previous methods, so it has been widely used. Blum et al. [25] implemented the K-means algorithm based on differential privacy on the SuLQ platform. Dwork [26] further studied on this basis and proposed two privacy budget allocation schemes in the iterative process. Ni et al. [27] aimed at the problem that the random selection of the initial centroid in the differential privacy DBSCAN clustering method seriously affects the quality of the clustering results, and proposed a differential privacy DBSCAN method that optimizes the initial centroid selection, which improves the quality of the clustering results. Su et al. [28] proposed a differential privacy K-means algorithm for interactive and non-interactive scenes by analyzing the error boundary of K-means under differential privacy. Nguycn [29] further researched on this basis and proposed different Differential privacy K-modes algorithm under the scene.

3   Preliminaries

Differential Privacy. Differential privacy is different from traditional privacy protection methods. It uses strict mathematical definition of security model, which can quantify the degree of privacy protection. The definition of differential privacy is as follows.

Definition 1. Suppose there are two arbitrary datasets D and D', and they differ by at most one record. Give the algorithm M and all possible outputs

$Ran(M)$ on D and D'. S is any subset of $Ran(M)$. If formula (1) is satisfied, then the algorithm M satisfies the definition of differential privacy.

$$Pr[M(D) \in S] \leqslant e^{\varepsilon} \times Pr[M(D') \in S] \tag{1}$$

The ε in definition 1 is called the privacy budget, representing the privacy protection strength of user's data, and its value is greater than zero. Therefore, in specific practice, two aspects of data privacy and availability should be weighed to determine the value of ε.

Laplce mechanism is a classic mechanism of differential privacy, which is defined as follows: Given a function $f : D \rightarrow R^d$, if the output result of a random algorithm S satisfies formula (2), then S satisfies the definition of differential privacy.

$$S(D) = f(D) + Laplace(\Delta f/\varepsilon)^d \tag{2}$$

where d represents the dimension of the data set, and Δf represents the global sensitivity, which is defined as follows: Given a function $f : D \rightarrow R^d$, the output of any input data set is a d-dimensional real variable. For two adjacent data sets D and D', the global sensitivity Δf is:

$$\Delta f = \max_{D,D'} \|f(D) - f(D')\|_1 \tag{3}$$

The size of Δf is independent of the data set and is only determined by function f. When ε is unchanged, the larger Δf is, the more noise will be added to the query results. The Laplace mechanism is a classic mechanism for numerical query, and for the case where the function return value is an integer, Ghosh et al. [30] proposed a geometric mechanism by extending the Laplace mechanism. The noise Δ added by it is generated by the bilateral geometric distribution, i.e. $Gem(\alpha) : Pr[\Delta = \delta|\alpha] = \frac{1-\alpha}{1+\alpha}\alpha^{|\delta|}$, where $\alpha = e^{-\varepsilon}$. In this paper, we use geometric mechanism to noise the data.

Differential privacy has two characteristics: sequence composition and parallel composition [31]. Sequence composition emphasizes that privacy budget ε can be allocated in different steps of differential privacy, while parallel composition ensures the privacy of the algorithm satisfying differential privacy on the disjoint subset of its dataset.

Theorem 1 (Sequence Composition). *Suppose there is a dataset and n differential privacy algorithms $M = \{M_1, \cdots, M_n\}$. If these algorithms all meet the definition of differential privacy, then the combination of these differential privacy algorithms on the dataset also meets the definition, where $\varepsilon = \sum_{i=1}^{n} \varepsilon_i$.*

Theorem 2 (Parallel Combination). *Suppose there is a dataset N and divide it into n disjoint subsets $N = \{N_1, \cdots, N_n\}$. If there is an algorithm that satisfies the definition of differential privacy for the dataset N, then the algorithm satisfies the definition of differential privacy on all n subsets.*

4   Our Proposed Scheme

4.1   Overview

Assume that there are data set $U = \{u_1, \cdots, u_n\}$ and attribute set $M = \{A_1, \cdots, A_d\}$. Each data point $u_i(1 \leqslant i \leqslant n)$ has a d-dimensional attribute tuple $m_i = \{a_1, \cdots, a_d\}$, and $a_{jr}(1 \leqslant j \leqslant d, 1 \leqslant r \leqslant |A_j|)$ is a certain attribute value of A_j. The goal of the K-modes algorithm is to divide the data set into k clusters $C = \{c_1, \cdots, c_k\}$, and the clustering process usually contains some sensitive user information. The use of differential privacy can provide protection for user privacy, but the existing research does not consider the impact of the initial centroid. It will lead to a decrease in the accuracy of the clustering results.

4.2   Program Description

In order to improve the availability of the clustering results of the differential privacy K-modes algorithm, we introduce the K-modes cluster centroid initialization mechanism of Bai et al. [32], and improve the method of calculating the distance between the data point and the centroid in the iteration process, and propose a high-availability data clustering mechanism based on differential privacy, the specific process is as follows.

The initial centroid selection is usually based on the density of the data point, and the density depends on the total distance between the data point and all data points, so we define the density of each data point as follows.

$$Dens(x) = -\frac{1}{|U|} \sum_{y \in U} d(x, y) \tag{4}$$

where x and y are the data points of dataset U, and $d(x,y)$ represents the distance between x and y. According to formula (4), $|A| \leqslant Dens(x) \leqslant 0$. Formula (4) needs to calculate the distance between each data point and all data points. When the data set U is large, the time complexity will be very high. In order to improve efficiency, formula (4) is optimized. The K-modes algorithm uses Hamming distance to measure the distance between two points, i.e. $d(x, y) = \sum_{a \in A} \gamma_a(x, y)$, where $\gamma_a(x, y)$ is defined as follows.

$$\gamma_a(x, y) = \begin{cases} 1 & if f(x, a) \neq f(y, a) \\ 0 & if f(x, a) = f(y, a) \end{cases} \tag{5}$$

where $f(x, a)$ represents the attribute value of data point x in attribute A. It can be obtained by formula (4) and formula (5).

Algorithm 1. Calculate CZ_k

Input: Dataset U, x.

Output: CZ_k.

1: Define set $S_i = \{y|d(x,y) = i, y \in U\} = \varnothing$, $Q_i = \{y|d(x,y) = i, y \in U\} = \varnothing$,
 $CZ_k = \varnothing$, $1 \leqslant i \leqslant |A|$.

2: **for** each y in U **do**

3:    $i = d(x,y)$.

4:    $S_i = S_i \bigcup y$

5: **end for**

6: **for** $i = 1$ to $|A|$ **do**

7:    **if** $i = 1$ **then**

8:       $Q_i = S_i$

9:    **end if**

10:   **if** $i \neq 1$ **then**

11:      $Q_i = Q_{i-1} + S_i$

12:   **end if**

13: **end for**

14: **for** each Q_i **do**

15:   Calculate the frequency of all attribute values in Q_i.

16:   Calculate the $Dens$ of the data point in Q_i, and $pc_i = Max(Dens)$.

17:   $CZ_k = pc_i \bigcup CZ_k$

18: **end for**

$$
\begin{aligned}
Dens(x) &= -\frac{1}{|U|} \sum_{y \in U} d(x,y) \\
&= -\frac{1}{|U|} \sum_{y \in U} \sum_{a \in A} \gamma_a(x,y) \\
&= -\frac{1}{|U|} \sum_{a \in A} (|U| - |\{y \in U|f(x,a) = f(y,a)\}|) \\
&= \sum_{a \in A} (\frac{|\{y \in U|f(x,a) = f(y,a)\}|}{|U|} - 1)
\end{aligned}
\tag{6}
$$

where $|\{y \in U|f(x,a) = f(y,a)\}|$ represents the frequency of attribute values. After calculating the density of all data points, select the data point with the largest density value as the center point, i.e. $Dens(z) = Max_{x \in U} Dens(x)$. Then, considering the density of data points and the distance between data points and center point z, define $PosExe_{c_i}(x) = Dens(x) + d(x,y)$, and take the data point with the maximum value of $PosExe_{c_i}(x)$ as the centroid example point of cluster C_1. Then calculate the candidate initial centroid set $CZ_k = \{pc_1, \cdots, pc_{|A|}\}$ of cluster C_k, the specific process is shown in Algorithm 1.

After obtaining the initial set of centroids, define $Center_{c_k}(y) = Dens(y) + d(y,z) - d(y,x)$, where y is the data point in CZ_k, and use the data point with the maximum value of $Center_{c_k}(y)$ as the centroid. After the above process is completed, the centroid of the first cluster C_1 can be obtained, and the centroids of other clusters are solved by defining $PosExec_{c_{l+1}}(x) = Dens(x) + Min_{i \in l}d(x, z_i)$ and $Center_{c_{l+1}}(x) = Dens(x) + Min_{i \in l}d(x, z_i) - d(y, x)$. Where $1 \leqslant l \leqslant k - 1$, z_i are the centroids that have been solved. The entire initial centroid solution process is shown in Algorithm 2.

After obtaining the initial centroid set, we can divide the dataset U into k initial clusters $IniClu_k = \{ic_1, \cdots, ic_k\}$. The similarity of data points in each cluster is different. Some clusters have higher similarity of data points, and the whole cluster is closer, while some clusters are looser. The traditional K-modes algorithm does not consider that the similarity of data points in each cluster may be different during each iteration, which affects the quality of the clustering results. Our scheme first calculates the similarity of each cluster in the iterative process, and then when calculating the distance between the data point and the centroid, the corresponding weight is given according to the similarity of the cluster. In this paper, we measure the similarity of clusters by calculating the variance between data points and centroid in clusters. The larger the variance is, the lower the similarity of the data points in the cluster is and the looser the whole cluster is. Therefore, a lower weight is given when calculating the distance between the data points and the centroid. The smaller the variance, the higher the similarity of the cluster and the closer the whole cluster. Therefore, a higher weight is given when calculating the distance. In summary, the weight can be expressed as the reciprocal of the variance, which is defined as follows.

$$w_i = \frac{1}{Var_i} = \frac{|c_i|}{\sum\limits_{x \in c_i} d^2(x, z_i)} \tag{7}$$

where z_i is the centroid of cluster c_i, so the distance calculation formula in the iteration process is as follows.

$$ReDis(x, z_i) = w_i * d(x, z_i) \tag{8}$$

In each iteration, the relative distance between the data point and the centroid is calculated and divided into the centroid with the closest distance. In this process, differential privacy is used to protect data privacy. The specific process is shown in Algorithm 3.

4.3 Privacy Analysis

As can be seen from Algorithm 3, our proposed scheme adds noise $Gem(\alpha)$ when counting the frequency of each attribute value in the cluster, where $\alpha = e^{\frac{-\varepsilon}{|M|*T}}$. In other words, the privacy budget ε obtained for each attribute value in each iteration depends on the attribute set size of the dataset U and the number of iterations. Therefore, according to the sequence composition of differential privacy, our scheme meets the definition of differential privacy.

Algorithm 2. Calculate the initial centroid

Input: Dataset U, number of clusters k.
Output: Initial centroid set $Centers$.
1: Calculate the frequency of each attribute value in dataset U.
2: Definition $Centers = \varnothing$.
3: Calculate the density $Dens(x)$ of each $x \in U$, and use the data point of $Max_{x \in U} Dens(x)$ as z.
4: **for** $i = 1$ to k **do**
5:　　$PosExe_{c_i}(x_{c_i}) = Max_{y \in U}(PosExe_{c_i}(y))$
6:　　Use algorithm 1 to calculate $CZ_k = \{pc_1, \cdots, pc_{|A|}\}$.
7:　　**for** $j = 1$ to $|A|$ **do**
8:　　　　Calculate $Dens(pc_j)$
9:　　**end for**
10:　　$Center_{c_i}(z_i) = Max_{pc_j \in CZ_i}(Center_{c_i}(pc_j))$
11:　　$Centers = Centers \bigcup \{z_i\}$
12: **end for**
13: Return $Centers$

Algorithm 3. Data clustering

Input: Dataset U, number of clusters k, initial clusters $IniClu$, initial centroids $Centers$, privacy budget ε, number of iterations T, attribute set size $|M|$.
Output: Clustering result.
1: $\alpha = e^{\frac{-\varepsilon}{|M| * T}}$
2: **for** 1 to T **do**
3:　　Calculate the weight w of each cluster.
4:　　**for** each x in U **do**
5:　　　　Calculate $ReDis(x, z)$
6:　　　　Divide x to the nearest centroid.
7:　　**end for**
8:　　**for** 1 to k **do**
9:　　　　Count the frequency sum_a of each attribute value in each cluster.
10:　　　　$sum'_a = sum_a + Gem(\alpha)$
11:　　　　Update the centroid of clusters.
12:　　**end for**
13: **end for**
14: Return Clustering result.

5　Conclusion

Aiming at the privacy protection problem of user sensitive information in categorical data, the K-modes algorithm based on differential privacy can effectively prevent the leakage of user privacy. However, differential privacy needs to add noise to the data while protecting data privacy, which will reduce the quality of the clustering results. In this paper, we propose a high-availability data clustering mechanism based on differential privacy. Based on the use of differential privacy technology to protect data privacy, this mechanism improves the quality of the clustering results by calculating the initial centroid and improving the calculation method of the distance between the data point and the centroid in the iteration process.

Acknowledgments. This work was supported in part by the Hunan Provincial Education Department of China under Grant number 21A0318, and the Research project on Teaching Reform of Ordinary Colleges and Universities in Hunan Province under Grant Number HNJG-2021-0651.

References

1. Wang, T., Jia., W., Xing, G., Li, M.: Exploiting statistical mobility models for efficient Wi-Fi deployment. IEEE Trans. Veh. Technol. **62**(1), 360–373 (2012)
2. Chen, M., Wang, T., Ota, K., Dong, M., et al.: Intelligent resource allocation management for vehicles network: an A3C learning approach. Comput. Commun. **151**, 485–494 (2020)
3. Zhang, S., Mao, X., Choo, K., Peng, T., et al.: A trajectory privacy-preserving scheme based on a dual-K mechanism for continuous location-based services. Inf. Sci. **527**, 406–419 (2020)
4. Zhang, S., Li, X., Tan, Z., Peng, T., et al.: A caching and spatial k-anonymity driven privacy enhancement scheme in continuous location-based services. Future Gener. Comput. Syst. **94**, 40–50 (2019)
5. Cao, W., Wu, S., Yu, Z., Wong, H.: Exploring correlations among tasks, clusters, and features for multitask clustering. IEEE Trans. Neural Netw. Learn. Syst. **30**(2), 355–368 (2019)
6. Wang, S., Sun, Y., Bao, Z.: On the efficiency of K-means clustering: evaluation, optimization, and algorithm selection. Proc. VLDB Endowment **14**(2), 163–175 (2020)
7. Huang, Z.: Extensions to the k-means algorithm for clustering large data sets with categorical values. Data Min. Knowl. Disc. **2**(3), 283–304 (1998)
8. Zhang, S., Wang, G., Alam, B., Liu, Q.: A dual privacy preserving scheme in continuous location-based services. IEEE Internet Things J. **5**(5), 4191–4200 (2018)
9. Liu, Q., Peng, Y., Wu, J., Wang, T., et al.: Secure multi-keyword fuzzy searches with enhanced service quality in cloud computing. IEEE Trans. Netw. Serv. Manage. (2020). https://doi.org/10.1109/TNSM.2020.3045467
10. Wang, T., Cao, Z., Wang, S., Wang, J., et al.: Privacy-enhanced data collection based on deep learning for internet of vehicles. IEEE Trans. Ind. Inf. **16**(10), 6663–6672 (2019)
11. Yuan, L., Zhang, S., Zhu, G., Alinani, K., Peng.: privacy-preserving mechanism for mixed data clustering with local differential privacy. Concurrency Comput. Pract. Experience (2021). https://doi.org/10.1002/cpe.6503
12. Dwork, C.: Differential privacy. In: 33th International Conference on Automata, Languages and Programming - Volume Part II, pp. 1–19. Springer, Germany (2006)
13. Dewri, R., Thurimella, R.: Exploiting service similarity for privacy in location-based search queries. IEEE Trans. Parallel Distrib. Syst. **25**(2), 374–383 (2014)
14. Jana, M.: Composition attack against social network data. Comput. Secur. **5**, 115–129 (2018)
15. Zhao, B., Yang, K., Wang, Z., Li, H., et al.: Anonymous and privacy-preserving federated learning with industrial big data. IEEE Trans. Ind. Inf. **17**(9), 6314–6323 (2021)

16. Jung, W., Kwon, S., Shim, K.: TIDY: publishing a time interval dataset with differential privacy. IEEE Trans. Knowl. Data Eng. **33**(5), 2280–2294 (2021)
17. Takagi, S., Cao, Y., Asano, Y., Yoshikawa, M.: Geo-graph-indistinguishability: protecting location privacy for LBS over road networks. In: Foley, S.N. (ed.) DBSec 2019. LNCS, vol. 11559, pp. 143–163. Springer, Cham (2019). https://doi.org/10. 1007/978-3-030-22479-0_8
18. Xiao, X., Tao, Y., Chen, M.: Optimal random perturbation at multiple privacy levels. Proc. VLDB Endowment **2**(1), 814–825 (2010)
19. Kifer, D.: On estimating the swapping rate for categorical data. In: 21th ACM SIGKDD International Conference on Knowledge Discovery and Data Mining, pp. 557–566. ACM, USA (2015)
20. Hardt, M., Rothblum, G.: multiplicative weights mechanism for privacy-preserving data analysis. In: 51th Annual Symposium on Foundations of Computer Science, pp. 61–70. IEEE, USA (2010)
21. Mohan, P., Thakurta, A., Shi, E.: GUPT: privacy preserving data analysis made easy. In: 18th ACM SIGKDD International Conference on Knowledge Discovery and Data Mining, pp. 349–360. ACM, USA (2012)
22. Blum, A., Ligett, K., Roth, A.: A learning theory approach to non-interactive database privacy. J. ACM **60**(2), 1–25 (2013)
23. Li, N., Qardaji, W., Su, D., Cao, J.: PrivBasis: frequent itemset mining with differential privacy. Proc. VLDB Endowment **5**(11), 1340–1351 (2012)
24. Xiao, X., Wang, G., Gehrke, K.: Differential privacy via wavelet transforms. IEEE Trans. Knowl. Data Eng. **23**(8), 1200–1214 (2010)
25. Blum, B., Dwork, C., McSherry, F., Nissim, K.: Practical privacy: the SuLQ framework. In: 24th ACM SIGMOD-SIGACT-SIGART Symposium on Principles of Database Systems, pp. 128–138. ACM, USA (2005)
26. Dwork, C.: A firm foundation for private data analysis. Commun. ACM **54**(1), 86–95 (2011)
27. Ni, L., Li, C., Wang, X., Jiang, H., et al.: DP-MCDBSCAN: differential privacy preserving multi-Core DBSCAN clustering for network user data. IEEE Access **6**, 21053–21063 (2018)
28. Su, D., Cao, J., Li, N., Bertino, E.: Differentially private k-means clustering and a hybrid approach to private optimization. ACM Trans. Priv. Secur. **20**(4), 1–33 (2017)
29. Nguyen, H.: Privacy-preserving mechanisms for K-modes clustering. Comput. Secur. **78**, 60–75 (2018)
30. Ghosh, A., Rougharden, M., Sundararajan, M.: Universally utility maximizing privacy mechanisms. SIAM J. Comput. **41**(6), 1673–1693 (2012)
31. Mcsherry, F.: Privacy integrated queries: an extensible platform for privacy-preserving data analysis. In: 15th ACM SIGMOD International Conference on Management of Data, pp. 19–30. ACM, USA (2009)
32. Bhatt, K., Dalal, P., Panwar, P.: A cluster centres initialization method for clustering categorical data using genetic algorithm. Int. J. Digital Appl. Contemp. Res. **2**(1), 1–8 (2013)

A Strategy-based Optimization Algorithm to Design Codes for DNA Data Storage System

Abdur Rasool[1,2], Qiang Qu[1]([✉]), Qingshan Jiang[1], and Yang Wang[1]

[1] Shenzhen Key Laboratory for High Performance Data Mining, Shenzhen Institute of Advanced Technology, Chinese Academy of Sciences, Shenzhen 518055, China
{rasool,qiang}@siat.ac.cn
[2] Shenzhen College of Advanced Technology, University of Chinese Academy of Sciences, Beijing 100049, China

Abstract. The exponential increase of big data volumes demands a large capacity and high-density storage. Deoxyribonucleic acid (DNA) has recently emerged as a new research trend for data storage in various studies due to its high capacity and durability, where primers and address sequences played a vital role. However, it is a critical biocomputing task to design DNA strands without errors. In the DNA synthesis and sequencing process, each nucleotide is repeated, which is prone to errors during the hybridization reactions. It decreases the lower bounds of DNA coding sets which causes the data storage stability. This study proposes a metaheuristic algorithm to improve the lower bounds of DNA data storage. The proposed algorithm is inspired by a moth-flame optimizer (MFO), which has exploration and exploitation capability in one dimension, and it is enhanced by opposition-based learning (OBL) strategy with three-dimension search space for the optimal solution; hereafter, it is MFOL algorithm. This algorithm is programmed to construct the DNA storage codes by reducing the error rates of DNA coding sets with GC-content, Hamming distance, and No-runlength constraints. In experiments, 13 benchmark functions and Wilcoxon rank-sum test are implemented, and performances are compared with the original MFO and three other algorithms. The generated DNA codewords by MFOL are compared with a state-of-the-art Altruistic algorithm and KMVO algorithm. The proposed algorithm improved 30% DNA coding rates with shorter sequences, reducing errors during DNA synthesis and sequencing.

Keywords: DNA data storage · Biocomputing · DNA coding sets · Opposition-based learning · MFO algorithm

1 Introduction

International Data Corporation estimated that the digital data would exponentially grow from 33 ZB to 175 ZB (2.5 EB/day) during 2018–2025 due to

Supported by The National Key Research and Development Program of China under grant number 2020YFA0909100.

extensive usage of IoT worldwide [1]. Meanwhile, the limitation of storage density and longevity in the existing storage media demands the development of the latest technology. DNA is a step-forward molecular-based solution due to primers that play a vital role in its density and long-lasting stability. It comprises four nucleotides - adenine (A), thymine (T), cytosine (C), and guanine (G). The A and T nucleotides are integrated by dual Hydrogen bonds while C and G with triple H-bond and form a double helix with the pairing of complementary bases known as hybridization. In DNA synthesis, primers are added into the strands during the data writing which is utilized in polymerase chain reaction (PCR) amplification for particular required data during the data reading process. As DNA molecules lack particular spatial organization, the encoded strands should have a specific address to recognize their location in the data stream [2]. Each DNA strand is divided into blocks to encode a big amount of data, as presented in Fig. 1. DNA has the capability to store 4.2×1021 bits binary data per gram of single-strand, which is 420 billion times high-performance bio-computing than existing electromagnetic media [3]. DNA data storage technology can be defined by following three fundamental steps [3–5]: (1) Digital data is converted into binary form and encoded into DNA strands (A, T, C, or G strings) with a particular coding scheme. These stings are called DNA codes or codewords. (2) The encoded DNA strands are synthesized into oligonucleotides by a DNA synthesizer, and data is stored. This process is called data writing on DNA. (3) DNA strands are decoded by DNA sequencing to retrieve the original digital data, which is called data reading from DNA.

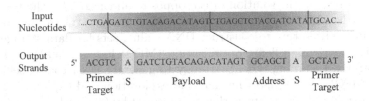

Fig. 1. DNA strand structure with primers, payload, sense (s) and address.

A plethora of studies have shown the novel tracks for its developments. For instance, Church [4] encoded 5.27 MB files into DNA chemical molecules and efficiently decoded those files by DNA sequencing. Goldman [5] proposed a scalable method to store the 739 kilobytes of digital information. Bornholt [3] delivered random access features by XOR encoding scheme and synthesized DNA of 151 KB dataset. The author has developed an end-to-end DNA data storage system to overcome the challenges of high risks in data loss [6]. It proposed a self-contained DNA storage system with three different methods, which thoroughly reduce the data redundancy and improve the DNA coding sets. The reported results indicate the significance of DNA sequence codes. All the above-mentioned studies found that DNA coding sets directly affect DNA synthesis and sequences efficiency. Thus, it is strongly required to develop robust DNA coding sets that must satisfy the DNA coding constraints. It is compulsory to detect the error source to avoid the insertion, substitution, and deletion errors that occur during the development of DNA codes. For example, a DNA code: ACAGGGTACT, G has been consecutively repeated, which will be considered a single G for the reading process and caused the lowest convergence rate for the DNA reading and writing. Thus, GC content and homopolymer length constraints are deemed initially in the DNA Fountain code [2].

Song [7] proposed a coding method that satisfied No-runlength and GC-content constraints, but still, it generated errors during the encoding and decoding and reduced the DNA codes. Therefore, DNA codewords have been significantly improved with the constraints and stochastic search algorithm recently. Metaheuristic algorithms, i.e., moth-flame optimization (MFO) [8], firefly optimization algorithm (FOA) [9], grey wolf optimizer (GWO) [10], harris hawks optimization (HHO) [11], and mean-variance optimization (MVO) [12], have been efficiently used in various aspects of computation engineering. For example, KMVO [13] has been adopted for DNA coding sets for DNA-based data storage by using MVO. Their results stated that the proposed algorithm attained a bunch of sequences that satisfy the energy-free constraint at a particular melting temperature. The motivations of this paper are KMVO and Altruistic algorithms [14]. KMVO algorithm attained the 1.5 times higher DNA coding set than Altruistic algorithm with the same purpose. However, authors [13,14] suggested it further can be improved by mutation strategy. In biocomputing, A mutation strategy enables the alteration in the nucleotides sequence to generate high-quality codes-for example, the opposition-based learning (OBL) strategy focuses on exploring the solution in the opposite dimension. To the best of our knowledge, the MFO algorithm with the OBL mutation strategy has not been reported in the literature to construct DNA coding sets for data storage.

In this paper, moth-flame optimization (MFO) has been enhanced by the opposition-based learning (OBL) strategy to generate DNA coding sets - hereafter, its MFOL. MFO algorithm has the exploration and exploitation ability in one dimension of search space that is improved by OBL; which considers the opposite solution of the concerned solution in three dimensions to boost the local search capability. The experiments are conducted on 13 benchmark functions, including unimodal and multimodal functions. As a result, the MFOL algorithm efficiently enhanced the global exploration and exploitation abilities to improve the convergence rates. The results are compared with 4 different well-known optimizers. MFOL algorithm is applied to design DNA codes for DNA-based data storage systems. To overcome the critical issue of error occurrence during the DNA synthesis, the MFOL algorithm is utilized with GC-content, Hamming distance, No-runlength constraints. The results are compared with the state-of-the-art Altruistic algorithm and KMVO. The overall mechanism of the MFOL algorithm with the opposition-based learning strategy and existing constraints reported the high quality of large DNA coding sets with improved lower bounds to construct a dense-based DNA storage system. The significant contributions are as follows:

- A novel algorithm (MFOL) is proposed based on a moth-flame optimizer which synergy by opposition-based learning mutation strategy for faster convergence and stronger exploration and exploitation capabilities.
- The proposed algorithm is applied to construct DNA codewords. It contributes to improving the lower bounds of DNA coding sets, and it is validated by computing the temperature variance.
- The MFOL algorithm satisfies the DNA coding constraints to avoid the non-specific hybridization for storing larger digital data files in the shorter sequence of DNA to deliver a stable data storage system.

The structure of the rest article is as follows; Sect. 2 introduces the existing DNA constraints, Sect. 3 elaborates the proposed algorithm, Sect. 4 explains the experiments and results, Sect. 5 concludes the work.

2   DNA Code Constraints

The critical aspect of DNA storage is to design DNA strands with the least errors during its vital processes; synthesis and sequencing. The existing state-of-the-art constraints (GC-content, Hamming distance, and No-runlength) are used to design the DNA codes with C(n, M, d), wherein n is the length of the sequence and d presents Hamming distance and M is a symbol to indicate GC-content with $\lfloor n/2 \rfloor$ parameters.

The GC-content constraint in C(n, M, d) set is the ratio of the sum of bases content (G and C) to the total number of bases. It can be defined for s sequence length as [7]:

$$GC(s) = \frac{|G+C|}{|s|} \times 100\% \tag{1}$$

Similarly, the No-runlength constraint is to avoid the existence of homopolymers in a sequence, and for a DNA sequence S with n bases $(S_1, S_2, S_3, \ldots, S_n)$ can be presented as [11]:

$$S_i \neq S_{i+1}, i \in [1, n-1] \tag{2}$$

Meanwhile, the Hamming distance H between 2 sequences $(\alpha \ \& \ \beta)$ of the same length in C(n, M, d) set can be computed by the sum of different base elements by satisfying the $H(\alpha, \beta) \geq d$, where, d is threshold [15]:

$$H(\alpha, \beta) = \sum_{i=1}^{n} h(\alpha_i, \beta_i), h(\alpha_i, \beta_i) = \begin{cases} 0, \alpha_i = \beta_i \\ 1, \alpha_i = \beta_i \end{cases} \tag{3}$$

In Hamming distance, H determines the similarity between 2 DNA sequences by calculating the d. The greater H shows the greater distance and less similarity among the particular sequences, which avoids non-specific hybridization. Overall, these constraints aim to develop feasible DNA codes with different lengths.

3 Proposed Algorithm - MFOL

The proposed algorithm leverages the moth-flame optimizer (MFO) [8], where the moth uses a transverse orientation (TO) navigation mechanism. The TO method enables a moth to fly by adjusting a fixed angle by the moon's focal point. Meanwhile, the moth collided with artificial lights and lost its destination. However, the moth persists in maintaining the same angle, which causes its deadly spiral path. This concept provides a mathematical optimizer algorithm that supports the convergence of an object or moth. MFO algorithm has two candidate solutions; Moths (M) and Flame (F). In a population-based algorithm, there can assume another array of fitness (f) values for all solutions. Both candidate solutions can be considered in the following matrices.

$$M = \begin{bmatrix} m_{1,1} & m_{1,2} & \cdots & m_{1,d} \\ m_{2,1} & m_{2,2} & \cdots & m_{2,d} \\ \vdots & \vdots & \vdots & \vdots \\ m_{n,1} & m_{n,2} & \cdots & m_{n,d} \end{bmatrix}, \quad Mf = \begin{bmatrix} Mf_1 \\ Mf_2 \\ \vdots \\ Mf_n \end{bmatrix} \tag{4}$$

$$F = \begin{bmatrix} F_{1,1} & F_{1,2} & \cdots & F_{1,d} \\ F_{2,1} & F_{2,2} & \cdots & F_{2,d} \\ \vdots & \vdots & \vdots & \vdots \\ F_{n,1} & F_{n,2} & \cdots & F_{n,d} \end{bmatrix}, \quad Ff = \begin{bmatrix} Ff_1 \\ Ff_2 \\ \vdots \\ Ff_n \end{bmatrix} \tag{5}$$

where n shows the candidate solution number and d is the dimension variable.

The only difference between both solutions is the system how we deal with them in the iteration process. The moth flies in the search space and acts as a search agent, while the flame is the optimal solution for the moth to achieve it as a destination in the search space. Thus, a moth flies around the search space by focusing the destination (flame) on finding a globally optimal solution. In this paper, the parameters have been chosen as given in the original work of MFO. As the motivation of this optimizer is TO, the moth updates its position corresponding to the flame with the following mathematically model:

$$M_i = S\left(M_i, F_j\right) = D_i \cdot e^{bt} \cdot \cos(2\pi t) + F_j \tag{6}$$

where M_i represents the i-th moth, S indicates the spiral function, F_j presents the j-th flame, Di shows the distance of i-th moth for the j-th flame, b is a constant for spiral function, and t is a random number $[-1, 1]$.

Equation (6) adjust the moth's spiral path, which allows a moth to fly around a flame. The spiral function is a key component of MFO which decides the moth movement with respect to flames. Thus, it enables the MFO algorithm to attain the ability of exploration and exploitation in the search space. The logarithmic spiral, position with different t curves and space around the flame are illustrated in Fig. 2.

Apart from these spiral functions of the MFO algorithm, the following variable-based array is also considered as lower bounds for MFO:

$$ub = [ub_1, ub_2, ub_3, \ldots, ub_{n-1}, ub_n] \tag{7}$$

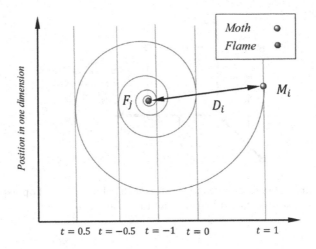

Fig. 2. Logarithmic spiral, position concerning t and space around the flame [8].

$$lb = [lb_1, lb_2, lb_3, \ldots, lb_{n-1}, lb_n] \tag{8}$$

where ub and lb indicate the upper bounds and lower bounds with n number of moths, respectively.

These bounds decide the search space limit of the moth after the initialization. The optimization of this mechanism enables the moth to acquire the best position in the search space. However, a problem can occur due to one dimension search space that causes MFO to fall into local optima and affects searchability. In order to maintain the balance between exploitation and exploration and find the best optimal solution, this paper utilized the following mutation strategy.

3.1   Opposition-based Learning Strategy

In optimizing any problem, solution Z is estimated as $\check{Z}$, which is not the exact solution. It is not a best practice to consider the initial guess as to the best result. Practically, for all the optimal solutions, the optimized system should focus on all dimensions or aspects, more specifically toward the opposite direction/dimension [16]. Tishoosh et al. (2005) reported opposition-based learning (OBL) mutation strategy for computational intelligence [17]. The OBL strategy tackles the moth solution Z in three dimensions (3D) if its searching is advantageous in the opposite direction with opposite moth solution $\check{Z}$. In which, considering the 3D interval (a, b, c), the solution for the concern problem can be observed in moth Z. The $\check{Z}$ will be generated at the opposite interval (a', b', c') of initial moth Z, as illustrated in Fig. 3. It will prior search the opposite moth solution $\check{Z}$ according to the following definitions.

Definition 1. *Let $Z \in \mathbb{R}$ is a real number for a particular interval; $Z \in [a, b, c]$. The opposite number $\check{Z}$ can be defined as follows:*

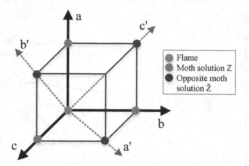

Fig. 3. Three-dimension search space for the moth solution Z and opposite moth solution $\check{Z}$ for the Opposition-based learning mutation strategy.

$$\check{Z} = a + b + c - Z \qquad (9)$$

For $a + b = 0$ and $c = 1$, or vice versa, then,

$$\check{Z} = 1 - Z \qquad (10)$$

Meanwhile, this behavior of opposite number for multiple dimensions can be defined as follows:

Definition 2. *let $Z(a_1, a_2, \ldots, a_n)$ is a location in n-dimensional search space for the coordinate system with $a_i \in [x_i, y_i]$ and $i \in 1, 2, \ldots, n$. The opposite location or area $\check{Z}_i = (a_1', a_2', \ldots, a_n')$ is defined as follows:*

$$\check{Z}_i = a_1' + a_2' + a_n' - Z_i \quad i = 1, 2, \ldots, n. \qquad (11)$$

Based on Eq. (11), the moth Z or opposite moth $\check{Z}$ are close to a solution with respect to the flame. The 3-dimension interval can recursively optimize until either moth or opposite moth come close enough to the targeted solution. These characteristics furnish the opportunity for the MFOL algorithm to access the global optima solution by balancing between exploitation and exploration abilities. The computation time complexity of MFOL is also same as the MFO algorithm $(O(MFOL) = O(tn^2 + tnd))$, where d is the number of variables and t is the maximum number of iterations [8]. The pseudo-code of the MFOL algorithm is presented in Algorithm 1. The architecture of MFOL is illustrated in Fig. 4.

4   Experiments and Results Evaluation

The experiments were executed in an integrated environment; for instance, all algorithms performed on MacBook 2.4 GHz, 8 GB DDR3, Python with 3.7.10v, platform Google's Colab, and 3D convergence plots into MATLAB R2018b. To

---

Algorithm 1: Pseudocode of proposed MFOL algorithm

Input: The population size N for two candidate solutions (M, F), Location of moth (L), FitnessFunction of moth M_f, Fitness Function of flame N_f.
Output: Global best individual solution X_m.
1: Initialize random population X_i
2: **for** (each moth X_i) **do**
3: Calculate fitness of M_f and F_f population using Eq. (4) and (5);
4: **if** (population N converge) **then**
5 :   Update the moths' position L for lb using Eq. (8);
6 :   Compute global optimal L with opposition-based learning strategies
   (Eq. 11); **else**
7 :   **while** (not converge) **do**
8 :   **for** $i = 1 : n$;
9 :   update candidate solutions (M, F) with Eq. (6)
10 :   **end for**
11 :   **end while end if**
12 : **end for**
Return: Global optimal solution X_m.

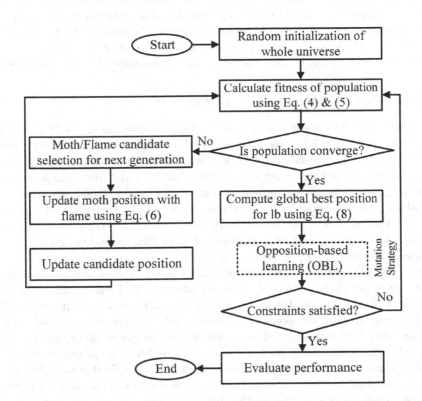

Fig. 4. An architecture of the proposed MFOL algorithm is presented based on the MFO algorithm and opposition-based learning mutation strategy.

construct DNA codewords, DNA bases (A, T, C, and G) are mapped with the quarterly number (A-0, T-1, C-2, and G-3). It employed 13 mainstream functions (mathematically defined in [8]) to demonstrate the optimization performance of MFOL. A set of different parameters have been implemented. However, the significant results presented in this paper are based on these parameters; the number of moths or population size: 50, and the number of iterations for each function: 500. If an algorithm performs for n times will yield average or standard deviation (SD) with the best solution. The following mechanism is utilized to report the optimal solution for average and SD values.

- The lowest the average value, the highest the algorithm' performance.
- The minimum the SD value, the maximum the stability of the algorithm.

Additionally, the proposed algorithm MFOL is compared with the original MFO [8] and the other three algorithms; FOA [9], GWO [10], and HHO [11]. A non-parametric Wilcoxon Rank-sum test [18,19] is accompanied to validate the result's originality of MFOL algorithms and compare with MFO [8]. Furthermore, the MFOL algorithm is trained with available DNA coding constraints, i.e., GC-content, Hamming distance, etc., to overcome the occurrence of the error of sequences for the DNA storage effectiveness. The lower bounds values are compared with the state-of-the-art Altruistic algorithm [14]. Eventually, a thermodynamic analysis is performed on existing constraints to validate the generated sequences by computing the temperature variance of DNA coding sets.

4.1 Benchmark Functions' Evaluation

This study used 2 types of benchmark functions; Unimodal (F1–F7) and Multimodal Functions (F8–F13), to test the MFOL performance. Unimodal functions have the exploitation capability, deal only with 1 global optimal score, and do not consider the local optimal values. In contrast, multimodal functions have exploration ability due to having numerous numbers of local optimal solutions [8].

Tables 1 and 2 indicate the average and standard deviation of unimodal and multimodal functions, respectively. In Table 1, a general trend presents the improved performance of our proposed algorithm in various functions. For instance, the functions F2–F5 achieved the best convergence in both matrices of average and SD. However, the score of MFOL with F6 lags behind the original MFO due to probably larger optimization intervals. In Table 2, MFOL exhibits superior performance with the lowest average and SD scores as compared to MFO [8]. The average and SD scores of F8 and F10–F12 secured the global optimal solution after 500 iterations, demonstrating the proposed algorithm jumping-out performance from the local optimum. Meanwhile, the proposed algorithm failed to attain the maximum global optimal solution for F9 due to high variance values as compared to the rest of the other algorithms. This insufficient result may be appeared due to the moth's large interval for optimization in search

Table 1. Comparison of different algorithms with MFOL for unimodal functions.

Functions	Metrics	MFO [8]	FOA [9]	GWO [10]	**HHO** [11]	MFOL
F1	AVG	8.63E+03	3.61E+03	6.29E+02	1.51E+04	**1.49E+02**
	SD	**1.48E+04**	9.78E+03	4.80E+03	2.14E+04	3.80E+03
F2	AVG	-7.61E+03	-3.55E+03	-4.18E+03	**-1.22E+04**	0.00E+00
	SD	1.26E+03	2.22E+02	**1.91E-02**	1.02E+03	0.00E+00
F3	AVG	3.50E+04	1.75E+04	3.24E+03	4.77E+04	0.00E+00
	SD	1.65E+04	2.52E+04	1.28E+04	3.53E+04	0.00E+00
F4	AVG	6.44E+00	1.38E+01	**3.51E+00**	5.62E+01	0.00E+00
	SD	6.55E+00	2.26E+01	1.29E+01	9.36E+00	0.00E+00
F5	AVG	2.01E+07	7.58E+06	1.63E+06	9.15E+07	0.00E+00
	SD	4.94E+07	2.76E+07	1.60E+07	1.04E+08	0.00E+00
F6	AVG	**3.44E+01**	5.04E+04	5.59E+04	2.36E+04	5.27E+01
	SD	1.26E+04	5.10E+03	2.64E+03	6.78E+03	3.05E+03
F7	AVG	1.55E+01	4.75E+00	**7.31E-01**	3.57E+01	1.17E+00
	SD	2.04E+01	1.41E+01	7.04E+00	4.50E+01	**4.10E-01**

Table 2. Comparison of different algorithms with MFOL for multimodal functions.

Functions	Metrics	MFO [8]	FOA [9]	GWO [10]	HHO [11]	MFOL
F8	AVG	**1.09E+04**	3.33E+10	2.81E+10	8.32E+09	**0.00E+00**
	SD	1.18E+11	7.43E+11	6.28E+11	1.82E+11	**0.00E+00**
F9	AVG	1.92E+02	1.64E+02	**1.50E+02**	1.60E+02	2.42E+02
	SD	6.75E+01	9.48E+01	8.45E+01	**1.26E+02**	5.93E+01
F10	AVG	1.69E+01	8.56E+00	1.65E+01	1.19E+01	**6.16E-01**
	SD	1.70E+00	3.99E+00	2.75E+00	2.88E+00	**8.28E-01**
F11	AVG	9.18E+01	**1.12E+00**	5.71E+00	1.40E+02	1.05E+00
	SD	1.34E+02	8.87E+01	4.35E+01	2.02E+02	**1.19E+00**
F12	AVG	3.50E+07	1.34E+07	3.43E+06	2.57E+08	**2.61E+00**
	SD	1.01E+08	5.70E+07	3.56E+07	2.76E+08	**3.99E+00**
F13	AVG	1.00E+08	2.88E+07	7.02E+06	4.23E+08	**2.38E+04**
	SD	1.98E+08	1.16E+08	7.09E+07	4.89E+08	7.37E+08

space. As compared to the remaining three optimizers, the proposed optimizer competitively jumps out of the local optimum and secures itself in the global optimum solution with minimum magnitude and variances. These significant results indicate the demand and importance of the OBL strategy.

4.2 Convergence Efficiency

The convergence curve is a vital criterion to assess the algorithm convergence speed and capability to jump out from the local optima [8]. The convergence curves with 3D representation are depicted in Fig. 5. This paper considers only one function's outcome from each unimodal and multimodal function due to their significant convergence efficiency and paper page limit. In the unimodal F5 function, MFOL converges speedily than MFO and other algorithms to attain the global optimal solution. In contrast, in the multimodal F12 function, the proposed algorithm achieved optimal solution at 50 iterations, while MFO fell into the local optima. In summary, the MFOL convergence curves are experimentally guaranteed by quantitative and qualitative metrics that exhibit the competitive results over the state-of-the-art algorithms by establishing a balanced nature between exploration and exploitation.

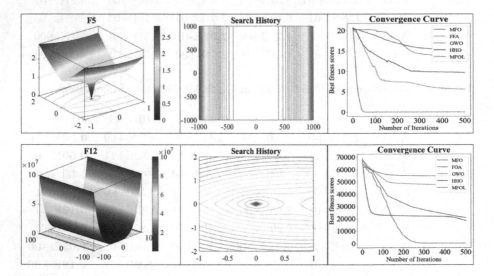

Fig. 5. A 3D representation and convergence efficiency of unimodal function F5 and multimodal function F12 is illustrated separately. Each function has its particular search space, search history, and convergence curves indicating the highest performance for the MFOL algorithm.

4.3 Wilcoxon Rank-sum Test

The results of benchmark functions indicate the algorithm's general performance, while the statistical test, Wilcoxon Rank-sum Test, proves the algorithm's statistical significance [19]. According to the Wilcoxon test's hypothesis, an algorithm is considered statistically significant if the $P - value$ is greater than 0.05. This study compared the statistical significance between MFO and MFOL by ranking any 2 samples of the 30 iterations from unimodal and multimodal functions.

In Fig. 6, the results met the criteria in most cases which present the optimum results of the proposed algorithm.

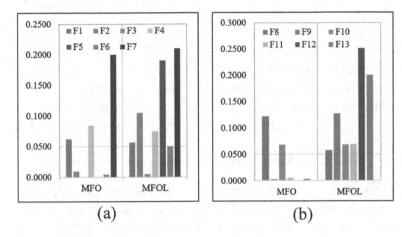

Fig. 6. Compersion of wilcoxon rank-sum test for MFO [8] and MFOL with (a) Unimodal functions and (b) Multimodal functions. A dotted line at the $P-value$ of 0.0500 indicates the threshold level for this rank-sum test.

4.4   Bounds on DNA Storage Constraints Coding

MFOL algorithm is trained and practically applied to improve the lower bounds of DNA storage coding sets with GC-content, No-runlength, and Hamming distance constraints $C^{GC,NL}(n, M, d)$, where n indicates sequence length, d presents the Hamming distance, and M shows the GC-content with $\lfloor n/2 \rfloor$ parameters. The Altruistic [14] and KMVO [13] algorithms used $4 \leq n \leq 10$ and $3 \leq d \leq n$ bounds to satisfy the constraints $C^{GC,NL}(n, M, d)$. In Table 3, the values in parenthesis with superscripts 'a' and 'k' indicate the Altruistic and KMVO's lower bounds, respectively. In contrast, the bold black values are outperformed the bounds values of the MFOL algorithm. A plethora of lower bounds delivered by the MFOL algorithm are better than the existing algorithm. For instance, at n = 10 and d = 5, the size of our DNA coding set is 25% better than the KMVO algorithm. In all sequences with d = 4, new DNA codes are 37% higher than the Altruistic algorithm and 30% better than the KMVO algorithm. Overall, MFOL enhanced 30% and 17% DNA coding sets in the given boundary compared to the Altruistic and the KMVO algorithm, respectively. These significant improvements are due to the consideration of the OBL mutation strategy with MFO, which empowers the exploration and optimization ability of the MFOL algorithm. In addition, Table 4 presents the DNA coding sets satisfying the $C^{GC,NL}(n, M, d)$ constraints when n = 10 and d = 7.

Furthermore, these improvements of lower bounds for the given sequence length are directly advantageous to the improvements of DNA coding rates.

Table 3. Comparison of lower bounds of MFOL algorithm with Altruistic and KMVO algorithms for $C^{GC,NL}(n, M, d)$.

n	d = 3	d = 4	d = 5	d = 6	d = 7	d = 8	d = 9
4	11 (11ª)						
5	24 (20ᵏ)	8 (7ª)					
6	58 (44ª)	26 (16ª)	7 (6ª)				
7	148 (127ᵏ)	49 (36ª)	19 (11ª)	6 (4ª)			
8	328 (289ª)	114 (94ᵏ)	35 (32ᵏ)	11 (9ª)	6 (4ᵏ)		
9	906 (680ᵏ)	281 (202ᵏ)	83 (65ᵏ)	30 (23ᵏ)	9 (8ª)	4 (4ª)	
10	2254 (2081ᵏ)	721 (547ᵏ)	189 (151ᵏ)	79 (54ᵏ)	17 (7ª)	5 (5ª)	5 (4ª)

Table 4. DNA storage coding sets when n = 10 and d = 7.

GACACTATAG	CTATACAGTG	AGCACATGAC	TATGCTACAT
ATCACACAGT	ATACAGCGAT	GAGTATACAT	ATAGCACATC
CTACTGACTA	CAGCATGATC	ATAGCAGATG	TACACGATAC
GTCACGTACT	CAGTAGAGCA	GACGATGCTG	ATGCATCGAT
TCTAGCATCA			

The coding rate (R) defines as; $R = \log_4 K/n$, where K is the number of DNA coding sets, and n is the number of sequence lengths [13]. The analysis of Table 5 indicates that the improved MFOL algorithm attained the same coding rate with shorter sequence lengths in 89% coding sets. For instance, the Altruistic algorithm achieved the coding rate R = $\log_4 86/8$ = 0.4016 when n = 8 and d=4. In contrast, the proposed algorithm reported a 0.4010 coding rate when n = 7 and d = 4. Similarly, the KMVO algorithm attained a 0.5227 coding rate when n = 9 and d = 3. In comparison, the MFOL algorithm has a 0.5223 coding rate when n = 8 and d = 3. Thus, it analytically proved that shorter sequences can also accomplish the same DNA storage performance as longer sequences. It indicates that shorter sequences are less expensive and easier to synthesize with more stable conditions, which shows the improved lower bounds effectiveness for the further deployment of the DNA data storage system.

4.5   Temperature Variance of DNA Codes

The validity of DNA coding constraints is empirically computed by the temperature variance of DNA coding sets. In the coding of DNA storage, the melting temperature (Tm) is a certain temperature when half of the double-strand DNAs convert into single-strand DNAs during the denaturation process [20]. Tm depends on GC content, which affects the reaction rates of DNA molecules: the higher GC content presents, the higher Tm. In PCR amplification, sufficiently lower Tm can be more effective in binding the forward and reverse primers. Thus, both primers must be having similar Tm that can avoid the non-specific hybridization possibility. The non-specific hybridization is associated with oligonucleotides structure and its thermodynamic properties. Therefore, each DNA sequence should be with the same Tm to construct the DNA coding sets. The temperature variances are utilized to distinguish the sequence quality; the smaller the temperature variance, the more stable the Tm of the DNA coding set [21].

Table 5. Comparison of $C^{GC,NL}$ for Tm variance of DNA codes with $5 < n < 10$ and $2 < d < 9$.

n/d	Constraints	d = 3	d = 4	d = 5	d = 6	d = 7	d = 8
6	$C^{GC,NL}$	3.6311	4.2734	4.0246			
7	$C^{GC,NL}$	5.3691	4.1368	3.6814	4.7168		
8	$C^{GC,NL}$	3.9812	3.2451	3.1931	3.0161	4.364	
9	$C^{GC,NL}$	4.6841	5.3017	5.8054	2.8972	3.9218	2.7204

As the primary focus of this study was to construct the DNA codes with shorter sequences, an empirical thermodynamic test is conducted to validate the DNA sequences. For the temperature variance, the empirical values of primer concentration are set at 200 nM while the salt concentration is set at 50 nM. For example, based on these concentrations, a primer (TATGTAGTAC) with sequence length 10 delivers the 30% GC-content, and nucleotides degeneration is allowed at Tm = 26°C. The coding sets with the proposed MFOL algorithm are analyzed with existing constraints for its correlated Tm values. Table 12 compared the Tm variances with $C^{GC,NL}$ constraints for $5 < n < 10$ and $2 < d < 9$ lower bounds. The results present the significantly lowest Tm variance for the $C^{GC,NL}$. This analysis signifies the practical implication and necessity of the MFOL algorithm with the OBL strategy for DNA coding sets. These smaller Tm variances of DNA coding set advantageous the more stable PCR reaction due to reduction of non-specific hybridization.

5   Conclusion and Future Work

This paper proposed a novel MFOL algorithm based on MFO that is synergized by the OBL strategy to construct the DNA coding sets. In experiments, the MFOL's exploration and exploitation capabilities are compared with 4 different state-of-the-art optimization algorithms. Based on MFOL's competent results (Tables 1 and 2 and Fig. 5), MFOL is applied in practical problems to generate DNA codewords with GC-content, Hamming distance, No-runlength constraints. It improved 30% and 17% lower bounds DNA coding sets compared to the Altruistic and the KMVO algorithms, respectively (Table 3). Meanwhile, the temperature variance with $C^{GC,NL}$ constraints for the given lower bounds also reported practical implications and the necessity of the MFOL algorithm for DNA data storage (Table 5). It is concluded that improved lower bounds can avoid further non-specific hybridization, and the shorter sequences can reduce more errors during the DNA synthesis and sequencing.

In the future, the DNA sequences generated by the MFOL algorithm will be assessed by the combinatory constraints of GC and RC. As the OBL strategy significantly improved the proposed algorithm capabilities, this work can be further extended by testing Levy flight or Cauchy mutation strategies with more benchmark functions (F1–F19). The effective efficiency of this stochastic algorithm will support the generation of the DNA codewords for a DNA-based data storage system.

References

1. David Reinsel, J.G.: John Rydning, Data Age 2025: The Digitization of the World From Edge to Core, in An IDC White Paper. IDC, November 2018
2. Erlich, Y., Zielinski, D.: DNA fountain enables a robust and efficient storage architecture. Science **355**(6328), 950–953 (2017)
3. Bornholt, J., et al.: Toward a DNA-based archival storage system. IEEE Micro **37**(3), 98–104 (2017)
4. Church, G.M., Gao, Y., Kosuri, S.: Next-generation digital information storage in DNA. Science **337**(6102), 1628–1628 (2012)
5. Goldman, N., et al.: Towards practical, high-capacity, low-maintenance information storage in synthesized DNA. Nature **494**(7435), 77–80 (2013)
6. Li, M., et al.: A self-contained and self-explanatory DNA storage system. Sci. Rep. **11**(1), 18063 (2021)
7. Song, W., et al.: Codes with run-length and GC-content constraints for DNA-based data storage. IEEE Commun. Lett. **22**(10), 2004–2007 (2018)
8. Mirjalili, S.: Moth-flame optimization algorithm: a novel nature-inspired heuristic paradigm. Knowl.-Based Syst. **89**, 228–249 (2015)
9. Emary, E., et al.: Firefly optimization algorithm for feature selection. In: Proceedings of the 7th Balkan Conference on Informatics Conference, Association for Computing Machinery: Craiova, Romania. p. Article 26 (2015)
10. Mirjalili, S., Mirjalili, S.M., Lewis, A.: Grey wolf optimizer. Adv. Eng. Softw. **69**, 46–61 (2014)
11. Heidari, A.A., et al.: Harris hawks optimization: algorithm and applications. Future Gener. Comput. Syst. **97**, 849–872 (2019)
12. Mirjalili, S., Mirjalili, S.M., Hatamlou, A.: Multi-verse optimizer: a nature-inspired algorithm for global optimization. Neural Comput. Appl. **27**(2), 495–513 (2015). https://doi.org/10.1007/s00521-015-1870-7
13. Cao, B., et al.: K-means multi-verse optimizer (KMVO) algorithm to construct DNA storage codes. IEEE Access **8**, 29547–29556 (2020)
14. Limbachiya, D., Gupta, M.K., Aggarwal, V.: Family of constrained codes for archival DNA data storage. IEEE Commun. Letters **22**(10), 1972–1975 (2018)
15. Aboluion, N., Smith, D.H., Perkins, S.: Linear and nonlinear constructions of DNA codes with hamming distance d, constant GC-content and a reverse-complement constraint. Discrete Math. **312**(5), 1062–1075 (2012)
16. Abualigah, L., et al.: The arithmetic optimization algorithm. Comput. Methods Appl. Mech. Eng. **376**, 113609 (2021)

17. Tizhoosh, H.R.: Opposition-based learning: a new scheme for machine intelligence. In: International Conference on Computational Intelligence for Modelling, Control and Automation and International Conference on Intelligent Agents, Web Technologies and Internet Commerce (CIMCA-IAWTIC 2006) (2005)
18. Rasool, A., et al.: GAWA-a feature selection method for hybrid sentiment classification. IEEE Access 8, 191850–191861 (2020)
19. Kim, D.H., Kim, Y.C.: Wilcoxon signed rank test using ranked-set sample. Korean J. Comput. Appl. Math. 3(2), 235–243 (1996)
20. Chee, Y.M., Ling, S.: Improved lower bounds for constant GC-content DNA codes. IEEE Trans. Inf. Theory 54, 391–394 (2008)
21. Sager, J., Stefanovic, D.: Designing nucleotide sequences for computation: a survey of constraints. In: Carbone, A., Pierce, N.A. (eds.) DNA 2005. LNCS, vol. 3892, pp. 275–289. Springer, Heidelberg (2006). https://doi.org/10.1007/11753681_22

Multi-Relational Hierarchical Attention for Top-k Recommendation

Shiwen Yang, Jinghua Zhu$^{(\boxtimes)}$, and Heran XI$^{(\boxtimes)}$

Heilongjiang University, Harbin, Heilongjiang, China
{zhujinghua,xiheran}@hlju.edu.cn

Abstract. As one of the critical application directions in the Recommendation Systems domain, the top-k recommendation model is to rank all candidate items through non-explicit feedback (e.g., some implicit interact behavior, like clicking, collecting, or viewing) from users. In this ranking, the rank shows the users' satisfaction with recommended items or the relevance of the target item. Although previous methods all improve the performance of the final recommended ranking, they suffer from several limitations. To overcome these limitations, we propose a Multi-Relational Hierarchical Attention within Graph Neural Network (GNN)-attention-Deep Neural Network (DNN) architecture for the top-k recommendation, named MRHA for brevity. In our proposed method, we combine the GNN's ability to learn the local item representation of graph-structure data and attention-DNN architecture's ability to learn the user's preference. For processing the multi-relational data that occurs in the real application scenarios, we propose a novel hierarchical attention mechanism based on the GNN-attention-DNN architecture. The comparative experiments conducted on two real-world representative datasets show the effectiveness of the proposed method.

Keywords: Top-k recommendation · Hierarchical attention · Multi-relational graph

1 Introduction

As one of the two major recommendation systems' application scenarios (rating prediction and top-k recommendation), the top-k ranking recommendation is to predict the ranking of users' preferences for candidate items. In the deep learning phase, the major method is learning user's approximate preference by many item representations. So top-k recommendation model's problem becomes how to learn sufficiently representative item representations and user's approximate preference. Inspired by Skip-gram [1] and Deep-walk model [2], the top-k recommendation model uses GNN to learn item representations instead of previous embedding mechanisms, which lack the ability of learning item-to-item relationships. We name the feature information of the GNN's neighbor node as the local

This work was supported by National Key R&D Program of China under Grant No. 2020YFB1710200

Y. Lai et al. (Eds.): ICA3PP 2021, LNCS 13156, pp. 300–313, 2022.
https://doi.org/10.1007/978-3-030-95388-1_20

information, and the item representation, including the local information as the local representation. But the item representation cannot be used to predict the ranking directly as the user's preference. Meanwhile, GNN-only model cannot learn users' preference from the item representation and use them to predict ranking. Based on the attention-DNN architecture, the recommendation model [3] can effectively learn the item representation that is closest to the user's preference in the features space. Although these methods using GNN or attention-DNN architecture improve the performance of recommendation models, they still have some limitations. First, methods based on GNN or attention-DNN architecture have their own problems in practice. For GNN-based models [4,5], they overlook the learning of the user's preference. On the other hand, the model using the attention-DNN architecture [6] normally is difficult to model graph-structure data and learn the item representation, including the local information. Second, inspired by the research [7], we assume that there are multiple interact behaviors in the actual application scenario of the recommendation model, which can be divided by the relevant degree with the predicted target into two parts, the target interact behavior (high relevant behavior as clicking, adding to cart, buying) and the auxiliary interact behavior (low relevant behavior as viewing, collecting, liking). For multi-relational data (multiple interact behavior), previous works [8,9] and works in other recommendation systems' application scenarios [10,11] propose GNN as the method of extracting the multi-relational data's local information. However, the model lack the effective learning ability for the user's preference. To overcome these limitations, we propose a Multi-Relational Hierarchical Attention within GNN-attention-DNN architecture for top-k recommendation, named MRHA for brevity. Based on the multi-relational GNN, we combine it with our proposed hierarchical attention mechanism and finally perform ranking prediction by DNN.

The main contribution of this work are as follows:

1. In multi-relational top-k items recommendation task, we propose the GNN-attention-DNN architecture based on the promising performance of GNN's learning the local representation and attention-DNN architecture's learning the user's preference. In the proposed method, the multi-relational GNN module adequately extracts multi-relational local information from graph-structure data. Based on multi-relational GNN, the attention-DNN architecture learns the user's preference and predicts ranking.
2. For learning the users' preference more effectively, we propose a novel hierarchical attention strategy in the GNN-attention-DNN architecture. The hierarchical attention mechanism on two different layers uses the attention of single interact behavior and multiple interact behavior to emphasize separately important features of different layers in the local representation.

2 Related Work

2.1 Graph Neural Networks

The GNN method is a updating method of node's hidden status (or node's representation)originally in the graph based on the immobile point theory [5].

In this paper, the updating function of node's hidden status named briefly as the local transfer function. So the neighbor information learned by GNN named as the local information in our research. Subsequent GNN's relevant researches are all based on this function. Early, the GNN method were mainly applied to solve problems in the direction of the graph theory. Subsequently, the convolutional method [12] was proposed based on the spatial-domain GNN and the spectral-domain Fourier transforming for the Graph Signal Processing. Because the spatial-domain GNN method in the direction of representation learning for graph has the promising performance. Inspired by the word2vec model [1] and DeepWalk model [2], the graph representation learning method is proposed and becomes the major development direction of GNN. In the RS, inspired by the multi-relational research [7], the MGNN-SPred model [8] can learn multi-relational local representation due to add of the information sources constituting the graph.

2.2 Attention Mechanisms

Firstly, the RAM model [13] proposes the architecture combining RNN(Recurrent Neural Network) model and attention mechanism in the image classification tasks. The attention mechanism can extract and emphasize parts of the whole image that need to be processed urgently. In the Natural Language Process, the seq-to-seq research [14] proposes that the attention mechanism can process concurrently translation and alignment operations in the machine translation task. Because of the advantage, the attention mechanism is widely used in various RNN-based models and gradually replaces RNN. Due to the parallel emphasis capability of the attention mechanism, it is also used to emphasize the important information of CNN(Convolutional Neural Network)'s convolutional kernel. Subsequently, the Transformer model [15] uses the self-attention mechanism to replace RNN or CNN for learning the text representation in the machine translation task. In RS, AFM [16] firstly utilizes the attention mechanism to emphasize important decomposition vectors. Then, a large amount of RS's researches gradually start to use widely and improve the attention mechanism. It can be divided into the single-layer attention and the multi-layer attention based on the its' structure. Based on computational approach of the attention score, it can be divided into the local attention and the global attention. Among many single-layer attention approaches, the global attention approach [17] learns the attention score matrix of item representations by the adaptive learning. The local attention approach gains the attention scores by computing the sum [18] or the product [3] of weighted item representations. Among many multi-layer attention approaches, there are some models that compute an attentive score once at each layer [19], and others models that gain the attention score of different attended degree by emphasizing different information at each layer [20].

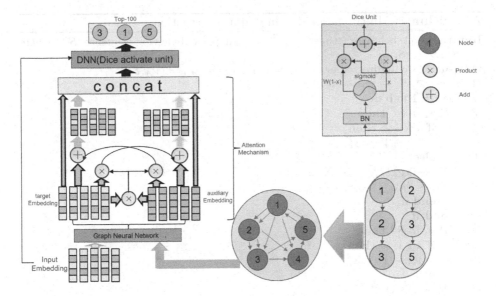

Fig. 1. Network Architecture. The left section is our proposed MRHA model including three parts. 1) Input Embedding, the lower right part and Graph Neural Network: construct graph and learn item status;2)Attention Mechanism; 3) DNN. The upper right part illustrates the Dice activation unit of the DNN module.

3 The Proposed Method

3.1 Symbolic Description

In our top-k recommendation model, let $S = \{s_1^T, s_2^A, s_3^{T,A}, ..., s_i, ..., s_n^T, ..., s_o^A, ..., s_m\}$ denote the set including all items. The item with the superscript denotes the item interacted by the user's target behavior or auxiliary behavior. So we name the history sequence of target interactive behaviors as the target sequence, and the history sequence of auxiliary interactive behaviors as the auxiliary sequence. In the target sequence $S^T = \{s_1^T, s_3^T, ..., s_i^T, ..., s_n^T\}$, s_i^T represents a target item(a clicked item or an add-to-cart item in this paper). Similarly, in the auxiliary sequence $S^A = \{s_2^A, s_3^A, ..., s_i^A, ..., s_o^A\}$ ordered by timestamp, s_i^A represents an auxiliary item(a clicked item or an add-to-cart item in this paper). In our proposed model, $\hat{y} = \{\hat{y}_{s_1}, \hat{y}_{s_2}, ..., \hat{y}_{s_i}, ..., \hat{y}_{s_m}\}$ denote the probability set for all candidate items that interact with the user's target behavior.

3.2 Constructing Multi-Relational Graphs

For the multi-relational GNN, we can use the target sequence S^T and the auxiliary sequence S^A to construct two undirected graphs by the Algorithm 1. We name the undirected graph constructed by the target sequence G^T as the target undirected graph $\mathcal{G}_T = (\mathcal{V}_T, \mathcal{E}_T)$. In the target directed graph, each node $s_i^T \in \mathcal{V}_T$ represents an item that interacted by user's target behavior, and each

---

Algorithm 1. Multi-relational item graph construction

Input: target behavior sequence S^T and auxiliary behavior sequence S^A, where $S^T, S^A \subset S$;

Output: Two undirected graph $\mathcal{G}_T = (\mathcal{V}_T, \mathcal{E}_T)$ and $\mathcal{G}_A = (\mathcal{V}_A, \mathcal{E}_A)$

1: $\mathcal{V}_T \leftarrow \varnothing, \mathcal{E}_T \leftarrow \varnothing, \mathcal{V}_A \leftarrow \varnothing, \mathcal{E}_A \leftarrow \varnothing$
2: **for** $i = 1$ to b **do**
3:     **if** s_i in S^T **then**
4:       **if** $\mathcal{V}_T$ is $\varnothing$ **then**
5:         $\mathcal{V}_T \leftarrow \mathcal{V}_T \cup s_i^T$
6:       **else**
7:         $\mathcal{V}_T \leftarrow \mathcal{V}_T \cup s_i^T$
8:         $\mathcal{E}_T \leftarrow \mathcal{E}_T \cup (s_{i-1}^T, s_i^T)$
9:       **end if**
10:    **end if**
11:    **if** s_i in S^A **then**
12:      **if** $\mathcal{V}_A$ is $\varnothing$ **then**
13:        $\mathcal{V}_A \leftarrow \mathcal{V}_A \cup s_i^A$
14:      **else**
15:        $\mathcal{V}_A \leftarrow \mathcal{V}_A \cup s_i^A$
16:        $\mathcal{E}_A \leftarrow \mathcal{E}_A \cup (s_{i-1}^A, s_i^A)$
17:      **end if**
18:    **end if**
19: **end for**

---

edge $(s_{i-1}^T, s_i^T) \in \mathcal{E}_T$ represents that there is the sequential relation of time between two nodes s_i^T and s_{i-1}^T. The undirected graph constructed by the auxiliary sequence G^A (the auxiliary undirected graph $\mathcal{G}_A = (\mathcal{V}_A, \mathcal{E}_A)$) is similar to the target undirected graph $\mathcal{G}_T$. In the lower right part of Fig. 1, the target undirected graph $\mathcal{G}_T$ and the auxiliary undirected graph $\mathcal{G}_A$ form together the multi-relational graph. We use the embedding e_{s_i} of each item s_i in the embedding space of all items $E \in \mathbb{R}^{|S| \times dim}$ to represent embedding of the node, which denotes the initial status of the node representation. Due to encoding uniformly of items, the node for the item such as the item $s_3^{T,A}$ exists in both the target undirected graph $\mathcal{G}_T$ and the auxiliary undirected graph $\mathcal{G}_A$. Meanwhile, the node representation e_{s_i} for the node is also consistent.

3.3 Learning the Status of Item Nodes on Multi-Relational Graphs

After constructing the multi-relational graph, we present how to learn the status of node $e_{s_i^{T or A}}$ (the node s_i exists in the target undirected graph or auxiliary undirected graph or both the two undirected graph as the node s_3) by multi-relational GNN. Inspired by the spatial-domain approach [12], we use the mean-pooling method for the set of node s_i's neighbor nodes to update the status of node s_i. We formally demonstrate the updating process of node s_i in graphs $\mathcal{G}_T$ and $\mathcal{G}_A$ as follows.

$$\mathcal{E}_{\mathbf{Neigh}}^{T,dep}(s_i^T) = \{e_{s_{i-1}^T}^{dep} | (s_{i-1}^T, s_i^T) \in \mathcal{E}_T\}$$

$$\mathcal{E}_{\mathbf{Neigh}}^{A,dep}(s_i^A) = \{e_{s_{i-1}^A}^{dep} | (s_{i-1}^A, s_i^A) \in \mathcal{E}_A\} \tag{1}$$

cted gra For node s_i^{TorA}'s sets of neighbor nodes $\mathcal{E}_{\mathbf{Neigh}}^{TorA,dep}(s_i^{TorA})$ in the target undirected graph or the auxiliary undirected graph, we use the multi-relational GNN to obtain the node s_i^{TorA} 's representation $e_{s_i^{TorA}}^k$. The superscript $TorA$ in s_i^{TorA} denotes the node s_i may exist in the target undirect graph $\mathcal{G}_T$ or the auxiliary undirect graph $\mathcal{G}_A$ or both two graphs. And the superscript dep in $e_{s_i^{TorA}}^d ep$ denotes the node s_i's representation through dep layers' computation of the multi-relational GNN.

$$Agg^{TorA,dep}(\mathcal{E}_{\mathbf{Neigh}}^{TorA,dep}(s_i^{TorA})) = \begin{cases} \mathcal{E}_{\mathbf{Neigh}}^{TorA,dep}(s_i^{TorA}) & if dep \leq 0, \\ Agg^{T,dep-1}(\mathcal{E}_{\mathbf{Neigh}}^{T,dep}(\mathcal{E}_{\mathbf{Neigh}}^{T,dep-1}(s_i^T))) \\ +Agg^{A,dep-1}(\mathcal{E}_{\mathbf{Neigh}}^{A,dep}(\mathcal{E}_{\mathbf{Neigh}}^{A,dep-1}(s_i^A))) & if dep > 0. \end{cases} \tag{2}$$

$$Agg^{TorA,dep}(s_i^{TorA}) = \frac{Agg^{TorA,dep}(\mathcal{E}_{\mathbf{Neigh}}^{TorA,dep}(s_i^{TorA})) +}{|\mathcal{E}_{\mathbf{Neigh}}^{TorA,dep}(s_i^{TorA})|} \tag{3}$$

$$e_{s_i^{TorA}}^{dep} = Agg^{TorA,dep}(s_i^{TorA}) + e_{s_i^{TorA}}^{dep} \tag{4}$$

After the multi-relational GNN of Fig. 1 aggregate the neighbor nodes' set k times, we gain the local representation $e_{s_i^{TorA}} \in \mathcal{E}_{LocaRep}^{TorA}(s_i^{TorA})$ containing the feature of node , the status of node s_i's neighbor nodes $Agg^{TorA,dep}(s_i^{TorA})$ and the sequential feature of edges connected with neighbor nodes. The node s_i's status of neighbor nodes and the sequential feature of edges connected with neighbor nodes are our proposed local information.

3.4   Hierarchical Attention Model

Inspired by these researches [3,19], for ranking candidate items more accurately, we plan to obtain the inner-relationships among the feature of the local representation by the attention mechanism. Through learning the inner-relationships of all local representations' feature globally, we can approximately gain the representation of user's preference combining local representations' feature. Inspired by the design of multi-layer attention mechanism [20], we propose the multi-layer parallel hierarchical attention mechanism as follows.

$$Att_T(s_i^{TorA}) = W_T\mathcal{E}_{LocaRep}^T(s_i^{TorA}) \quad Att_A(s_i^{TorA}) = W_A\mathcal{E}_{LocaRep}^A(s_i^{TorA})$$

$$W_T, W_A \in \mathbb{R}^{dim \times dim} \quad \mathcal{E}_{LocaRep}^T(s_i^{TorA}), \mathcal{E}_{LocaRep}^A(s_i^{TorA}) \in \mathbb{R}^{|S| \times dim} \tag{5}$$

where W_T and W_A are attention weights matrixs. In the single behavior phase, two weighted local representation $Att_T(s_i^{TorA})$ and $Att_A(s_i^{TorA})$ can emphasize separately the respective features of the target and auxiliary behavior related to the user preference. In the multi-behavior phase, the attention mechanism uses the attention score for learning features combinations $\alpha_T(s_i^{TorA})$ and $\alpha_T(s_i^{TorA})$ to emphasize weights of local representations' important features.

$$\alpha_{TA}(s_i^{TorA}) = Att_T Att_A^T \tag{6}$$

$$\alpha_T(s_i^{TorA}) = \alpha_{TA} \mathcal{E}_{LocaRep}^T + S_A \qquad \alpha_A(s_i^{TorA}) = \alpha_{TA} \mathcal{E}_{LocaRep}^A + S_T \tag{7}$$

In the comparative experiment of Sect. 4.4, we compared several attention mechanisms proposed in Sect. 2.2. In the multi-behavior phase, we use the previous computation results Att_T and Att_A as the input to avoid possible information loss during the computation.

$$\mathcal{UP}(s_i^{TorA}) = Linear([\alpha_T, \alpha_A, \mathcal{E}_{LocaRep}^T, \mathcal{E}_{LocaRep}^T]) \tag{8}$$

where Linear denotes the linear computation degenerated by one-layer MLP.

3.5 Making Recommendation and Model Training

Through inputting the user preference and the local representation of items, we use DNN to predict the ranking of items. DNN fits high-level nonlinear computation to learn the relationships of the user preference and all local representations through multiple layers of linear computations. The relationships learned by DNN improve the ranking performance of our proposed MRHA model.

$$Rank(s_i^{TorA}) = DNN([\mathcal{UP}(s_i^{TorA}), \mathcal{E}_{LocaRep}^T(s_i^{TorA}), \mathcal{E}_{LocaRep}^A(s_i^{TorA})]) \tag{9}$$

where $Rank(s_i^{TorA})$ denote the ranking of item s_i^{TorA} in the ranking of items set S. We learn the ranking by concatenating user preference and local representations. During DNN computation process, we adopt the Dice activation function in the [3] work to fit the different distribution of user preference reflected by user behaviors of different time periods. For MRHA model, we use cross-entropy loss function to train.

$$loss = - \sum_{i=1}^{batch} y_i \log(\hat{y}_i) + (1 - y_i) \log(1 - \hat{y}_i) \tag{10}$$

where $\hat{y}_i$ simply denote $Rank(s_i^{TorA})$.

4 Experiment

4.1 Datasets and Data Preparation

For fitting the actual recommendation scenarios as closely as possible, we exclude datasets that not contain multiply interactive behaviors. And for the experiments' reproducibility, we exclude hard-to-get and not widely used datasets from multi-relational datasets. Combining needs of all aspects,

Table 1. Basic statistics of the datasets.

Data	Yoochoose	Retailrocket
Item	52,740	36,968
Time duration	2014/04/01–09/30	06/09–10/24
Edge of target	225,879	69,332
Edge of auxiliary	3,277,411	2,664,312
Training data	163,005	433,648
Validation data	12,985	40,342
Test data	25,971	15,132

Table 2. Evaluation results of all methods.

Methods	Yoochoose			1/64 Yoochoose			Retailrocket		
	H@100	M@100	N@100	H@100	M@100	N@100	H@100	M@100	N@100
Pop	6.095	0.2529	1.2231	6.714	1.1247	2.3785	0.0644	0.0032	0.0066
Item-KNN	15.286	1.9415	4.4040	51.609	4.362	13.4224	0.1933	0.0155	0.0268
GRU4Rec	19.114	2.5292	5.5830	60.641	4.5782	16.1025	0.732	0.0156	0.0265
NARM	18.775	2.5819	5.5813	68.322	5.7266	18.3805	0.852	0.1490	0.1283
STAMP	20.361	2.3487	5.6879	68.741	5.9345	18.2852	1.0648	0.1870	0.1281
SR-GNN	21.262	2.6892	6.1232	70.575	6.1883	18.6437	2.0404	0.2109	0.2165
MGNN-SPred	28.632	3.6564	8.2722	68.767	9.9210	21.2084	**6.040**	0.8821	1.7741
MRHA	**34.110**	**5.8707**	**11.3311**	**75.342**	**12.9710**	**25.1053**	5.774	**1.3038**	**2.1351**

we chose two real world datasets, Yoochoose[1] and Retailrocket[2] as shown in Table 1. Yoochoose dataset contains all users on the e-commerce website of clicking and buying event stream for items during 6 months. In the Yoochoose dataset, we use the buying behavior as the target behavior, and the clicking behavior as the auxiliary behavior. Retailrocket dataset contains all users on the e-commerce website of all interactive behaviors(view, click, add to cart and purchase)' event stream for items during 4.5 months. Considering that too few interactive behaviors cannot be used to learn local representation, we merged the purchase behavior into the add-to-cart behavior as the target behavior. Also, in order to fit the Yoochoose's rate between target and auxiliary behavior to construct different datasets' comparison, we chose the viewing behavior having more interactive times than the auiliary behavior. When processing the original datasets, we screened out events of item that occur too infrequently or have only a single interacitve behavior to ensure that constructed multi-relational graph architecture would not degenerate into a tree architecture. In the Table 2 evaluation results of all methods, we use 1/64 Yoochoose dataset as one of comparative datasets to compare the effect of dataset size on the experimental results.

---

[1] https://www.kaggle.com/chadgostopp/recsys-challenge-2015.
[2] https://www.kaggle.com/retailrocket/ecommerce-dataset.

4.2   Model Comparison

As shown in Table 2, the above comparative methods have many shortcomings compared to our model MRHA. We use three evaluative metrics in this comparative experiment. **H@100**(Hit Ratio in top-100) calculating the proportion that 'hits' how many positive ranked items sample the user has in the total number of 100 candidate samples. **MRR@100** (Mean Reciprocal Rank) is a way for evaluating the average where reciprocal ranks list of the possible recommended items list. The smaller MRR value, the more items predicted failure before the first successful prediction item in the predicted ranking list of candidate items. **NDCG@100** (Normalized Discounted Cumulative Gain) measures the accuracy of model's predicting recommend ranking through calculating the score rate of the predicted ranking position score and correct ranking position score. **Pop** method is an early representative recommendation method. But the most popular item only indicates that the item fits the preference of major users rather than matches the preference of the target user. **Item-KNN** [21] model is used to screen top-k items. It is an early top-k recommendation method that simplifies the computation process of item-to-item relation to the computation process of item-to-item distance. The recommendation method still not considers self-features of items and item-to-item associated features. **GRU4Rec**'s work [22] used multi-GRU(RNN) to extract the possible sequential relations among items. But in the aspect of combining low-level features, the Transformer [15] proposes that attention is more efficient and outperform about the extracting features of CNN and the learning sequential relations of RNN. **NARM** model [23] uses parallel module of combining multi-RNN and GRU-attention for extracting item-to-item sequential relation. However, compared with the attention mechanism, RNN is more easily to forget long sequential information [24], even occurs easily the problem of the gradient explosion and gradient disappearance. The **STAMP** [6] model fully defines the embedding-attention-DNN architecture. It uses the attention mechanism to learn the combination of low-level features and to extract sequential relations, firstly. And in **STAMP** [6], the embedding-attention-DNN architecure is fully defined and only use the attention mechanism to learn the combination of low-level features and extract sequential relations. And learning items' features representation only by embedding mechanism is shifting the task of learning item-to-item relation and items' local information to the attention mechanism and DNN. **SR-GNN** [18] uses GNN for replacing embedding mechanism to capture item-to-item sequential relations and extract local information based on the architecture of embedding learns representation-attention learns combination of low level feaures-DNN fits high-level computation. However, in the actual recommendation scenarios of having multiple interactive behaviors, **MGNN-SPred** model [8] uses the multi-relational GNN that can extract the relation of multiple interactive behaviors for top-k recommendation. But the top-k recommendation model not only learns item-to-item relation consisting by multiple relations and items' local information, but also needs to use the module like the attention mechanism to combine low-level features and DNN to fit high-level computation.

Table 3. Results of not using auxiliary behavior sequences in Yoochoose.

Methods	Without auxiliary			With auxiliary		
	H@100	M@100	N@100	H@100	M@100	N@100
GRU4Rec	14.817	1.6032	4.0012	19.114	2.5292	5.5830
NARM	14.443	1.5540	3.8900	18.775	2.5819	5.5813
SR-GNN	15.302	1.5782	4.0852	21.262	2.6892	6.1232
MGNN-SPred	21.089	2.3798	5.8221	28.632	3.6564	8.2722
MRHA	**30.434**	**4.2086**	**9.1328**	**34.110**	**5.8707**	**11.3311**

4.3 Comparison with and Without Auxiliary Behavior Sequence

As the Sect. 2.1 and Sect. 1 of our paper shown, we have clarified the superiority of GNN in the top-k recommendation. And whether GNN needs the auxiliary behavior sequence, how much improvement multi-relational GNN have than other GNNs, we will compare detailed in the Table 3. In the Table 3, we use several models that can model interactive behavior sequences to compare. Through the horizontal comparison, we can find that **SR-GNN**'s and **MGNN-SPred**'s constructing graph process outperform than **GRU4Rec**'s and **NARM**'s sequential process to interactive historical sequence. And compared with **SR-GNN**, our proposed model uses auxiliary behavior sequence and the novel attention mechanism. Compared with **MGNN-SPred**, our proposed model use GNN-attention-DNN architecure and the novel attention mechanism. Thus, compared with all comparative models, our proposed **MRGD-HA** outperforms. Then through the longitudinal comparison, we can observe that the performance of models with the auxiliary behavior sequence outperforms than the performance of models without the auxiliary behavior sequence. According to these, we can conclude that the auxiliary behavior contains the auxiliary information that can assist the recommendation.

4.4 Comparison with Different Variants of Attention Mechanism

In this subsection, we will verify the one of the main innovation hierarchical attention mechanism in this paper. As the Fig. 2(a) shown, we compare four different MRHA variants, MRHA without the attention mechanism(MRHA_WOA), MRHA with traditional attention mechanism(MRHA_TA), MRHA with self-attention mechanism(MRHA_SA) and MRHA. In our experiments, we found that the metric values of 1/64 Yoochoose dataset are larger among three datasets. The characteristics facilitate us to enlarge experimental results and highlight the difference among results. Meanwhile, for showing different performance among different attention mechanism, we will use the graph to show. **H@100** metric is more representative so selected as the comparison metric in the graph. As Fig. 2(a) shown, MRHA_TA as the traditional attention mechanism [18] and MRHA_SA as the self-attention mechanism [3] have worse

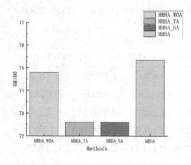
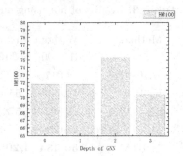

(a) Comparison results of using different attention mechanism in 1/64 Yoochoose

(b) Results of our model with different depths of GNN in 1/64 Yoochoose

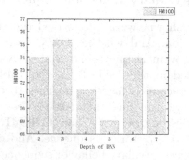
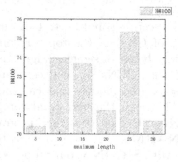

(c) Results of our model with different depths of DNN in Yoochoose 1/64

(d) Results for different maximum nodes number in Yoochoose 1/64

Fig. 2. All comparison

performance than MRHA_WOA and MRHA. It is because traditional attention mechanism and self-attention mechanism do not have the hierarchical method consisting of multiple layers, which can compute attention scores by the target information and the auxiliary information. So the adding auxiliary information inversely reduces the computational efficiency. Compared to MRHA_WOA shifting the task of learning low-level features combination to DNN, MRHA's multi-layers way of learning and prediction achieves better results. From the comparison, we can conclude that hierarchical attention has enough innovation than previous attention mechanisms indeed.

4.5   Comparison with Different GNN Depth

In the comparison, we research the impact of different GNN' learning depth on the model's performance. The learning depth of GNN denotes the aggregated range of GNN on the nearest-neighbor(NN) item nodes set. We can observe from the Fig. 2(b) that the GNN lacking enough NN item nodes leads to the model's performance worse when $dep = 0$'s GNN degenerate to embedding and $dep = 1$'s

GNN only aggregate One-hop item node set. When GNN's depth $dep = 2$, it can aggregate one-hop and two-hop item nodes set, and the model's performance is optimal. Then when the GNN's aggregated range reaches three hop($dep = 3$), because GNN samples too many distant NN nodes, the model's performance will decrease. In the experiment, we find that there are problems of the model's performance decreasing and frequent model's gradient explosion once GNN's learning depth is over 3. Thus, we only show the comparison results of GNN's learning depth from 0 to 3.

4.6   Comparison with Different DNN Depth

In this subsection, we find that the change of DNN's layers number(actually DNN's hidden layers number) will affect the DNN's ability of fitting high-level non-linear computation and model training efficiency, which show on the effect of model performance. DNN comprises one inputting layer, multiple hidden layers and one outputting layer. Because DNN with less than two layers(inputting and outputting layer) cannot construct a basic DNN for basic linear computing, we compare by the model performance of two layers' DNN. From Fig. 2(c), we can observe that DNN with 3 layers has the best performance. Although the model performance has a noticeable improvement when DNN's layers changed from 5 to 6, the model performance still decreases as the numbers increase of DNN's hidden layers. In the comparison experiment, the model performance will decrease further and the model occurs the gradient explosion problem frequently while DNN's layers have over 7 layers. Thus, we only compare the effect of DNN's layer from 2 to 7 layers. The 3 layers' DNN structure(one inputting layer, one hidden layer and one outputting layer) combines two advantages of fitting ability of high-level computation and model training efficiency.

4.7   Comparison with Different Maximum Nodes Number

In the GNN learning item representation process, for improving the efficiency of GNN training and simplifying the computation of **Equation** 3, we set a fixed maximum numbers of item nodes for each-hop set of item nodes per aggregation, named the maximum nodes number. For avoiding the poor model performance caused by too few item nodes and frequent problem of model gradient explosion caused by too many item nodes, we chose 6 different maximum nodes number in the range from 5 to 30 for comparison. As the comparison experiment of Fig. 2(d) shown, nodes number 5 and 30 lead to poor model performance, respectively because of the too few nodes number and difficult convergence caused by too many nodes number. And the model with the maximum nodes number of 25 combines learning sufficient NN nodes number and model training efficiency to obtain the best model performance.

5   Conclusions

In this paper, we present a Multi-Relational Hierarchical Attention within GNN-attention-DNN architecture for top-k recommendation. It is a novel architecture for top-k items sequence recommendation that incorporates the aggregated method GNN for the multi-relational graph and the hierarchical attention mechanism and DNN into predicting top-k recommend items. Comprehensive experimental analysis verified that our proposed model MRHA can consistently achieve the best performance than other state-of-art methods.

References

1. Mikolov, T., Sutskever, I., Chen, K., Corrado, G., Dean, J.: Distributed representations of words and phrases and their compositionality. arXiv preprint arXiv:1310.4546 (2013)
2. Perozzi, B., Al-Rfou, R., Skiena, S.: Deepwalk: online learning of social representations. In: the 20th ACM SIGKDD on KDDM, pp. 701–710. KDD 2014, Association for Computing Machinery, New York (2014). https://doi.org/10.1145/2623330.2623732
3. Zhou, G., et al.: Deep interest network for click-through rate prediction. In: the 24th ACM SIGKDD on KDDM, KDD 2018, pp. 1059–1068. Association for Computing Machinery, New York (2018). https://doi.org/10.1145/3219819.3219823
4. Kipf, T.N., Welling, M.: Semi-Supervised Classification with Graph Convolutional Networks. arXiv e-prints arXiv:1609.02907 (September 2016)
5. Scarselli, F., Gori, M., Tsoi, A.C., Hagenbuchner, M., Monfardini, G.: The graph neural network model. IEEE Trans. Neural Netw. **20**(1), 61–80 (2009). https://doi.org/10.1109/TNN.2008.2005605
6. Liu, Q., Zeng, Y., Mokhosi, R., Zhang, H.: STAMP: short-term attention/Memory priority model for session-based recommendation, pp. 1831–1839. Association for Computing Machinery, New York (2018), https://doi.org/10.1145/3219819.3219950
7. Krohn-Grimberghe, A., Drumond, L., Freudenthaler, C., Schmidt-Thieme, L.: Multi-relational matrix factorization using bayesian personalized ranking for social network data. In: the Fifth ACM on WSDM, WSDM 2012, pp. 173–182. Association for Computing Machinery, New York (2012). https://doi.org/10.1145/2124295.2124317
8. Wang, W., et al.: Beyond clicks: modeling multi-relational item graph for session-based target behavior prediction, pp. 3056–3062. Association for Computing Machinery, New York (2020). https://doi.org/10.1145/3366423.3380077
9. Wu, Z., Pan, S., Chen, F., Long, G., Zhang, C., Yu, P.S.: A comprehensive survey on graph neural networks. CoRR abs/1901.00596 (2019). http://arxiv.org/abs/1901.00596
10. Chang, B., Jang, G., Kim, S., Kang, J.: Learning graph-based geographical latent representation for point-of-interest recommendation. In: Proceedings of the 29th ACM International Conference on Information & Knowledge Management, CIKM 2020, pp. 135–144. Association for Computing Machinery, New York (2020). https://doi.org/10.1145/3340531.3411905
11. He, Z., Chow, C.Y., Zhang, J.D.: Game: learning graphical and attentive multiview embeddings for occasional group recommendation. Association for Computing Machinery, New York (2020). https://doi.org/10.1145/3397271.3401064
12. Bruna, J., Zaremba, W., Szlam, A., LeCun, Y.: Spectral networks and locally connected networks on graphs. arXiv e-prints arXiv:1312.6203 (December 2013)

13. Mnih, V., Heess, N., Graves, A., Kavukcuoglu, K.: Recurrent models of visual attention. In: the 27th NIPS, NIPS 2014, pp. 2204–2212. MIT Press, Cambridge, MA, USA (2014)
14. Bahdanau, D., Cho, K., Bengio, Y.: Neural Machine Translation by Jointly Learning to Align and Translate. arXiv e-prints arXiv:1409.0473 (September 2014)
15. Vaswani, A., et al.: Attention is all you need. CoRR abs/1706.03762 (2017). http://arxiv.org/abs/1706.03762
16. Xiao, J., Ye, H., He, X., Zhang, H., Wu, F., Chua, T.S.: Attentional factorization machines: learning the weight of feature interactions via attention networks. In: Proceedings of the Twenty-Sixth International Joint Conference on Artificial Intelligence, IJCAI-17, pp. 3119–3125 (2017). https://doi.org/10.24963/ijcai.2017/435
17. Wang, S., Hu, L., Cao, L., Huang, X., Lian, D., Liu, W.: Attention-based transactional context embedding for next-item recommendation. In: Thirty-Second AAAI 2018, pp. 2532–2539. Association for the Advancement of Artificial Intelligence, United States (2018)
18. Wu, S., Tang, Y., Zhu, Y., Wang, L., Xie, X., Tan, T.: Session-based recommendation with graph neural networks. In: the AAAI Conference on Artificial Intelligence, vol. 33, no. 01, pp. 346–353 (July 2019). https://doi.org/10.1609/aaai.v33i01.3301346, https://ojs.aaai.org/index.php/AAAI/article/view/3804
19. Zhou, C., et al.: Atrank: an attention-based user behavior modeling framework for recommendation. In: Proceedings of the AAAI Conference on Artificial Intelligence, vol. 32, no. 1, April 2018. https://ojs.aaai.org/index.php/AAAI/article/view/11618
20. Lu, J., Yang, J., Batra, D., Parikh, D.: Hierarchical question-image co-attention for visual question answering. CoRR abs/1606.00061 (2016), http://arxiv.org/abs/1606.00061
21. Sarwar, B., Karypis, G., Konstan, J., Riedl, J.: Item-based collaborative filtering recommendation algorithms. In: the 10th WWW, WWW 2001, pp. 285–295. Association for Computing Machinery, New York (2001). https://doi.org/10.1145/371920.372071
22. Hidasi, B., Karatzoglou, A., Baltrunas, L., Tikk, D.: Session-based Recommendations with Recurrent Neural Networks. arXiv e-prints arXiv:1511.06939 (November 2015)
23. Li, J., Ren, P., Chen, Z., Ren, Z., Lian, T., Ma, J.: Neural attentive session-based recommendation, pp. 1419–1428. Association for Computing Machinery, New York (2017). https://doi.org/10.1145/3132847.3132926
24. Khandelwal, U., He, H., Qi, P., Jurafsky, D.: Sharp nearby, fuzzy far away: how neural language models use context. In: Proceedings of the 56th Annual Meeting of the Association for Computational Linguistics (Volume 1: Long Papers), pp. 284–294. Association for Computational Linguistics, Melbourne, Australia, July 2018. https://doi.org/10.18653/v1/P18-1027, https://www.aclweb.org/anthology/P18-1027

Edge Computing and Edge Intelligence

EdgeSP: Scalable Multi-device Parallel DNN Inference on Heterogeneous Edge Clusters

Zhipeng Gao[1]([✉]), Shan Sun[1]([✉]), Yinghan Zhang[2], Zijia Mo[1], and Chen Zhao[1]

[1] State Key Laboratory of Networking and Switching Technology, Beijing University of Posts and Telecommunications, Beijing 100876, China
{gaozhipeng,sunshan,mozijia,zc_zhaochen}@bupt.edu.cn
[2] China International Engineering Consulting Corporation, Ltd., Beijing, China
zyh@ciecc.com.cn

Abstract. Edge computing has emerged as a promising line of research for processing large-scale data and providing low-latency services. Unfortunately, deploying deep neural networks (DNNs) on resource-limited edge devices presents unacceptable latency, hindering artificial intelligence from empowering edge devices. Prior solutions attempted to address this issue by offloading workload to the remote cloud. However, the cloud-assisted approach ignores that devices in the edge environment tend to exist as clusters. In this paper, we propose EdgeSP, a scalable multi-device parallel DNN inference framework that maximizes resource utilization of heterogeneous edge device clusters. We design a multiple fused-layer blocks parallelization strategy to reduce inter-device communication during parallel inference. Further, we add early exit branches to DNNs, empowering the device to trade-off latency and accuracy for a variety of sophisticated tasks. Experimental results show that EdgeSP enables inference latency acceleration of $2.3 \times - 3.7 \times$ for DNN inference tasks of various scales and outperforms the existing naive parallel inference method. Additionally, EdgeSP can provide high accuracy inference services under various latency requirements.

Keywords: Edge computing · Edge intelligence · Parallel inference · Deep neural networks · Early-exit · Internet of Things

1 Introduction

Deep neural networks (DNNs) have become indispensable for handling complex tasks in computer vision, natural language processing, and other fields [1]. While DNNs provide intelligent services with high accuracy, they place higher demands on the computing resources of the devices. At the same time, the number of Internet of Things (IoT) devices has grown exponentially in recent years, and edge computing has emerged to cope with the resulting massive amounts of data and tasks. Edge computing aims to provide low-latency services by performing tasks close to the edge of the network where data is generated, such as end devices

© Springer Nature Switzerland AG 2022
Y. Lai et al. (Eds.): ICA3PP 2021, LNCS 13156, pp. 317–333, 2022.
https://doi.org/10.1007/978-3-030-95388-1_21

or edge servers [2]. It is rewarding to equip DNNs on edge devices, enabling the edge to provide a wide range of intelligent services.

Enable resource-limited edge devices to rapidly execute large DNNs to meet the demands of real-time tasks has attracted extensive research. A common approach is for edge devices to perform DNNs inference tasks collaboratively with the edge server or cloud [3,4]. In addition, neural networks with early exit branches are receiving more and more attention because of their effectiveness and flexibility [5]. This kind of neural network reduces redundant calculations by allowing simple samples to exit from the shallow layer of the network, thereby significantly reducing inference latency. A triple-partition network with multiple exit branches is proposed [6] based on the early exit mechanism, as shown in Fig. 1. However, this server-assisted approach is critically hampered by the quality of the device's network connection to the remote servers. When the network connection degenerates, the DNN inference time also increases sharply. In addition, transferring local data to edge servers or cloud servers may result in privacy disclosure.

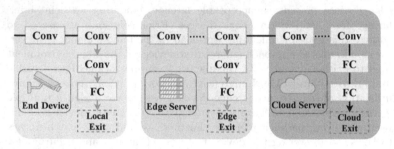

Fig. 1. A sketch of the triple-partition network architecture: simple input samples can be inferred at the DNN branch at the end device, while complex samples require further computation at the edge server and cloud.

Another prospective way to accelerate DNN inference is to perform tasks in parallel by multiple devices, as edge devices typically appear in the form of clusters [7–10]. Some previous work explored the parallel execution of DNN inference on multiple devices [11–13]. However, it is non-trivial to distribute the inference of DNNs on multiple devices. Parallel inference presents data dependency problems since DNNs are inherently tightly coupled [7]. Due to the data dependency problems, existing DNN parallel inference methods incur frequent inter-device communication [14] or substantial overlapping computation [15]. Moreover, none of the above methods can dynamically adjust the inference latency, yet the tasks in edge computing scenarios typically have different requirements. Taking traffic cameras as an example, the task of detecting traffic jams requires low latency but not high accuracy; the task of identifying license plate numbers requires high accuracy, but a moderate amount of latency is acceptable [16]. Therefore, it is indispensable to provide different services according to the application requirements.

To tackle the aforementioned problems, we propose EdgeSP, a scalable multi-device parallel DNN inference framework that leverages the computational resources of heterogeneous edge devices in IoT environments. Multi-device synergy enables fast execution of DNN inference on devices with scarce computing resources. Unlike the server-assisted approaches, EdgeSP resides data on the local trusted devices, avoiding performance instability and privacy disclosure caused by sending data to remote servers. Furthermore, EdgeSP can trade-off between dynamic response time and accuracy to adapt to the needs of different tasks in the IoT environment.

Concretely, our contributions are summarized as follows:

- We propose EdgeSP, a scalable parallel DNN inference framework for heterogeneous edge devices, which accelerates DNN inference and improves the utilization of computational resources in edge clusters.
- We propose a multiple fused-layer blocks (MFLB) parallelization strategy to minimize inter-device communication and overlapping computation overhead, and we further design an adaptive fused-layer workload partition algorithm based on the compute capabilities of heterogeneous devices and dynamic network bandwidth.
- We propose a stepwise method for determining the confidence threshold of exit branches based on task latency requirements so that edge devices can complete the inference task within the specified time.
- We implement EdgeSP on a cluster of heterogeneous edge devices and evaluate its performance on three different scales of DNNs. Experimental results show that EdgeSP is effective in minimizing the inference latency and outperforms prior works.

The rest of this paper is organized as follows. Section 2 provides background information. Section 3 overviews the design of EdgeSP, followed by the description of technical details. Section 4 evaluates the performance of EdgeSP, and Sect. 5 concludes.

2   Related Work

To enable resource-limited edge devices to perform large DNNs, some researchers focus on refining neural network structures to reduce computation. Model pruning is dedicated to removing nonsignificant weights in the DNNs model to reduce calculation [17]. Weight quantization reduces the number of model parameters and calculations by replacing the floating-point number parameters in the original DNN network with low-bit parameters [18]. However, the above methods will degrade the accuracy of the model. The early exit mechanism takes advantage of the variability between samples by adding branches to the shallow layers of the neural network to allow simple samples to complete their inference in advance [5,19]. Although the early exit mechanism can reduce computation, its acceleration of DNNs inference for edge devices is insufficient [20].

Some researchers are inclined to offload compute-intensive tasks from edge devices to powerful servers. Neurosurgeon [3] proposes to accelerate DNNs inference on edge devices with the help of the cloud. The edge device performs the front part of the DNNs and sends the intermediate data to the cloud, which subsequently performs the rest of the computation. Edgent [21] proposes an end device and edge co-inference method with two early exit points by combining BranchyNet and Neurosurgeon. The Triple-partition Network [6] adds three exit points to traditional DNNs and deploys them to end devices, the edge, and the cloud. However, this server-assisted approach is highly dependent on the quality of the network connection. Worse still, sending local data to edge or cloud servers may result in privacy disclosure.

Another rising star, multi-device parallel inference, has attracted increasing attention. MoDNN [14] first put forward to allocate DNN inference tasks to multiple devices for parallel execution, but its method will cause additional communication overhead. DeCNN [22] reduces frequent inter-device communication during parallel inference by modifying the network structure. Deepthings [15] fuses the first few layers of the DNN network to reduce the communication overhead, which will generate extensive overlapping computations when the number of fused layers is too large. None of the parallel inference architectures mentioned above are scalable, i.e., they cannot provide the flexibility to adjust DNN inference response times according to task requirements.

3   EdgeSP Framework

Our work aims to accelerate DNN inference by leveraging heterogeneous edge device clusters and provide edge devices with the ability to trade-off latency and accuracy to accommodate the varied needs of real-time applications. To do this, we need to address the following issues: (1) how to optimize the impact of data dependency problems caused by parallel inference; (2) how to adaptively distribute tasks to heterogeneous devices in a dynamic network environment; (3) how to empower devices with scalable DNN inference capabilities. Our research focuses on convolutional neural networks (CNNs) as they are widely used in broad-spectrum intelligent services [11].

3.1   Framework Overview

We design a framework, EdgeSP, that can adaptively distribute CNN inference tasks to heterogeneous devices in a dynamic network environment. In order to enable the device to adapt to tasks with different response time requirements, EdgeSP adds several early exit branches to the original CNN network. EdgeSP includes the preparation phase and inference phase. In the preparation phase, we first train CNNs with branching structure and subsequently train the compute capability models of the heterogeneous devices to quantify their performance. As the compute capability of the devices is invariant, each device only needs to be trained once. Each edge device will then broadcast the trained compute

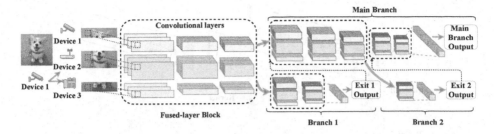

Fig. 2. An example of the inference workflow of EdgeSP. In addition to the main branch, two early exit branches are added to the DNN, namely Branch 1 and Branch 2. An input sample is distributed to three heterogeneous devices, and they execute the DNN in parallel using a multiple fused-layer blocks approach.

capability model to the other devices involved in parallel inference. Eventually, each device will be aware of the compute capabilities of the other devices.

Figure 2 illustrates an instance of the EdgeSP inference workflow. Three devices execute a CNN with two branches in parallel. The inference workflow is as follows:

- Device **1**, which initiates the CNN inference task, runs the adaptive fused layer workload partition algorithm that assigns different workloads to Device **2** and Device **3** based on network bandwidth and devices' compute capability.
- The three devices perform successive multilayers in a multiple fused layer blocks manner, which will be discussed in Sect. 3.2. The fused layer blocks are followed by synchronization points where the devices will recombine the feature maps.
- When the neural network executes to Branch **1**, each device will save the feature maps computed in the main branch at this point and initiates a new fused layer block. When executing to the fully connected layer, each device sends the computed feature map to the device with the most powerful compute capability in the entire cluster, i.e., Device **2**.
- Then Device **2** will execute the fully connected layer and determine whether to exit the inference in advance at this branch. The details of the early exit mechanism will be elucidated in Sect. 3.4. If Device **2** determines to quit the inference at this point, it will send the result to the task initiating device. Otherwise, Device **2** will send the command to continue execution to Device **1** and Device **3**, and the edge cluster will restore the feature map just retained and continue to execute the main branch.
- When the execution reaches the later branches, the cluster will repeat the above process and determine whether to exit the inference until the whole CNN network is executed.

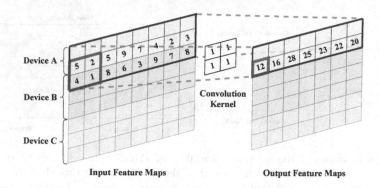

Fig. 3. Schematic diagram of the data dependency problem arising from parallel inference. Device A needs data from device B to compute the output feature map.

3.2 Multiple Fused-Layer Blocks Parallelization Strategy

According to [13], convolutional operations account for more than 70% of the
overall execution time of CNN networks, so accelerating the execution of the
convolutional layer has become a hot research topic. Since the structure of the
convolutional neural network is tightly coupled, distributing the convolution
operation to multiple devices incurs data dependency problem. In this section,
we present the details of the data dependency problem and the corresponding
solutions.

In a convolutional neural network, the convolutional layer extracts massive
features from the input samples and passes the results to subsequent convolutional layers to extract higher-level features. For a convolution layer with feature
map $\mathbf{M}\{Ch_M, H, W\}$ and convolution kernel $\mathbf{K}\{Ch_K, F, F\}$, the convolution
operation can be expressed as follows [23]:

$$\mathbf{M} \otimes \mathbf{K} = \sum_{i=0}^{F-1} \sum_{j=0}^{F-1} \mathbf{M}[Sx + i][Sy + j] \times \mathbf{K}[i][j]$$

$$0 \leq x < \frac{H - F + S}{S}, 0 \leq y < \frac{W - F + S}{S}$$

(1)

where H, W, and Ch_M denote the height, width, and number of input channels
of the feature map, F, S, and Ch_K denote the size, stride, and number of output
channels of the convolution kernel, respectively.

From Eq. 1, it can be derived that a neuron in the output of the convolution is
only relevant to the partial data in the input feature map. This characteristic of
the convolution operation provides the possibility of distributing the CNN task
to multiple devices for parallel execution. But this characteristic also indicates
that the CNN structure is highly coupled, which incurs the data dependency
problem. Figure 3 presents an instance of the data dependency problem. In Fig. 3,
the input feature map is assigned to three devices. Calculating the data in the
red box in the output feature map requires the contents of a 2×2 size matrix in

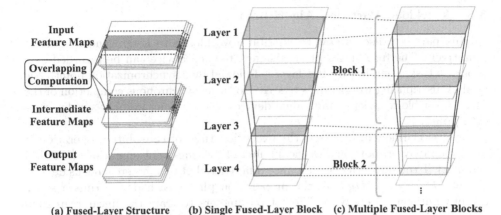

(a) Fused-Layer Structure   (b) Single Fused-Layer Block   (c) Multiple Fused-Layer Blocks

Fig. 4. Comparison of overlap computation caused by fused layer. (a) Schematic diagram of overlap computation caused by fused layer. Variation of computation area size for (b) a single fused layer block and (c) multiple fused layer blocks.

the input data, but these data are stored in two different devices. Generally, for a convolution kernel of $F \times F$, each device needs its allocated feature map partition to extend $\lfloor F/2 \rfloor$ along the edges to contain the data required for convolution.

To resolve the data dependency problem, some researchers have adopted a layer-wise approach [11,12,14], where each device exchange overlapping data before performing each layer of convolution. This layer-wise approach will undoubtedly incur frequent inter-device communications [13]. We propose a multiple fused-layer blocks (MFLB) parallelization strategy. Each device performs multiple consecutive convolutional layers without exchanging overlapping data during this period, thus avoiding frequent inter-device communication. For workload assignment, we first divide the last layer of the block according to the device compute capability and network bandwidth, and then each workload feature map is extended $\lfloor F/2 \rfloor$ along the edge and recursively to the first layer of the block layer by layer.

As shown in Fig. 4(a), the fused-layer method removes data dependencies by introducing overlapping computations. As the number of fusion layers increases, redundant computations also increase layer by layer. Therefore, we trade off the communication overhead and overlapping computation and adopt multiple fused-layer blocks to reduce the overlapping computation caused by too many fusion layers, as shown in Fig. 4(c). We divide the entire CNN network into blocks, where each device performs the workload within a block consecutively. Each fused block is followed by a synchronization point where each device aggregates and redistributes the feature maps. Figure 4(b) and Fig. 4(c) are sketches of the naive fused layer method and the MFLB method. In order to calculate Layer 4, the computation amount of the single fused layer block is more than that of multiple fused layer blocks. How to determine the size of each fusion block will be elucidated in Sect. 3.3.

3.3   Workload Partition Algorithms

In this part, we discuss how to distribute workloads to heterogeneous devices adaptively. The fused-layer block assigned to each device can be regarded as a separate task. Each block's last layer is followed by a synchronization point. The goal of distributing workloads is to strive for near-synchronous completion of the fused-layer block tasks by individual devices to avoid long waits at synchronization points.

It was clarified in [24] that the execution time of convolution operation is approximately proportional to the number of floating-point operations (FLOPs) required. To quantify the performance differences between heterogeneous devices $D_k = \{D_1, D_2, \cdots, D_K\}$, in the preparation phase, each device runs a series of convolutional layers with different parameters to train the linear regression model of its compute capability. For a convolutional layer L with feature map $\mathbf{M}\{Ch_M, H, W\}$ and convolutional kernel $\mathbf{K}\{Ch_K, F, F\}$, the FLOPs required can be expressed as follows [25]:

$$FLOPs = 2HW\left(Ch_M F^2 + 1\right)Ch_K \tag{2}$$

The linear regression model of the compute capability of the device D_k is denoted as C_k. Then the execution time for the device D_k to run convolutional layer L can be predicted, which is $C_k(L)$.

Data transmission delay is another factor that affects the execution time of each individual fused-layer block. Edge devices are typically under the same network, so we focus on edge clusters under the same LAN in this work. We use B to denote the network bandwidth. We take a bottom-up approach to analyze the size of the communication data, i.e., we first calculate the size of the last layer of the fused layer block. For device D_k, assuming that the size of the feature map matrix for the last layer of the block is W_{end}, the amount of data required to transmit the last layer is $4W_{end}$ bytes since the size of the floating-point number is 4 bytes. The size of the first layer of the fused layer block, denoted as W_{first}, can be obtained by expanding $\lfloor F/2 \rfloor$ layer by layer along the edge of the W_{end} and recursively to the first layer. Then the total time for device D_k to execute a fused layer block with N layers can be expressed as follows:

$$T_k = \sum_{i=1}^{N} C_k(L_i) + \frac{4\left(W_{first} + W_{end}\right)}{B} \tag{3}$$

We perform one-dimensional workload partitioning of the feature map because one-dimensional partitioning has better performance than two-dimensional partitioning [8].

We propose an adaptive fused-layer workload partition algorithm, as shown in Algorithm 1. This algorithm continuously fine-tunes each device's workload based on its compute capability and network bandwidth until the execution

---

Algorithm 1. Adaptive Fused-Layer Workload Partition Algorithm

---

Input:

  $\{D_k | k = 1, ..., K\}$: K available devices

  $\{C_k | k = 1, ..., K\}$: computation capabilities of K devices

  $\{L_{start}, L_{end}\}$: the start and end layer of the block

  ζ: waiting time factor

Output:

  $\mathcal{S}\{W_k\}$: workload partition strategy

1: **Procedure**

2: **for** D_k $(k = 1, ..., M)$ **do**

3:    $W_{k_{end}} \leftarrow L_{end} \times \frac{C_k}{\sum_{k=1}^{M} C_k}$, $W_{k_{first}} \leftarrow W_{k_{end}}$

4:    compute T_k from Eq. 3

5: **end for**

6: $T_{avg} \leftarrow \frac{1}{M} \times \sum_{k=1}^{M} T_k$

7: $T_k^{diff} \leftarrow abs\left(T_{avg} - T_k\right)$

8: **if** $max\ T_k^{diff} > \zeta \cdot T_{avg}$ **then**

9:    $W_{argmin(T_k)}$ expands by one pixel

10:   $W_{argmax(T_k)}$ decreases by one pixel

11:   Goto Step 6

12: **else**

13:   **return** $\mathcal{S}\{W_k\}$

14: **end if**

---

time of each device differs by no more than ζ, where ζ is a hyperparameter that adjusts the tolerable wait time of the synchronization point. For example, when ζ is set to 10%, the maximum tolerable wait time at the sync point is 10% of the total execution time of the current fusion layer block.

With the workload partition strategy $\mathcal{S}$, we can further determine the size of each fused-layer block. As mentioned above, the MFLB parallelization strategy reduces inter-device communication overhead while also introducing overlapping computation. The amount of overlapping computation W_{oc} can be obtained by extending $\lfloor F/2 \rfloor$ layer by layer along W_k in $\mathcal{S}$. We design a multiple fused-layer blocks strategy search algorithm that greedily expands the fused-layer block layer by layer until the maximum overlap computation delay is greater than the reduced communication delay or an early exit branch is encountered, as shown in Algorithm 2. This greedy algorithm can select the size of each fused-layer block based on the CNN structure and network bandwidth to minimize the total latency.

3.4 Early Exit Mechanism

To meet the needs of different real-time tasks, we leverage the early exit mechanism to provide devices with the ability to trade-off latency and accuracy. The early exit mechanism adds branches to the original CNN, allowing simple input samples to

---

Algorithm 2. Multiple Fused-Layer Blocks Strategy Search Algorithm

---

Input:

$\{C_k | k = 1, ..., K\}$: computation capabilities of K devices

$\{L_i | i = 1, ..., N\}$: CNN model with N layers

E: set of early exit branches

B: network bandwidth

W_{oc}: overlapping feature map

Output:

$\mathcal{F}$: multi fused layer strategy

1: **Procedure**

2: $L_{start} \leftarrow L_1$, $L_{end} \leftarrow L_{start}$

3: **if** $L_{end+1} \neq L_N$ **and** $L_{end+1} \notin E$ **then**

4:     $L_{end} \leftarrow L_{end+1}$

5:     execute Algorithm 1 with $\{L_{start}, L_{end}\}$

6:     **if** $max\ C_k\ (W_{oc}) > max \sum_{i=first+1}^{end-1} 4Wi/B$ **then**

7:         add $\{L_{start}, L_{end}\}$ to $\mathcal{F}$

8:         $L_{start} \leftarrow L_{end+1}, L_{end} \leftarrow L_{start}$

9:     **end if**

10:    goto Step 3

11: **else if** $L_{end+1} \in E$ **then**

12:    goto Step 7

13: **else**

14:    add $\{L_{start}, L_{end}\}$ to $\mathcal{F}$

15: **end if**

16: **return** $\mathcal{F}$

---

be inferred in a shallow layer of the CNN. Here entropy is used to evaluate how confident the branch is about the input sample. Entropy is defined as:

$$entropy\ (y) = \sum_{c \in \mathcal{C}} y_c \log y_c \tag{4}$$

where y is a vector containing computed probabilities for all possible class labels and $\mathcal{C}$ is a set of all possible labels [5]. It is worth noting that EdgeSP has multiple synchronization points, which are well adapted to the added branches.

The confidence threshold for each exit branch needs to be dynamically scaled according to the task latency requirements. For each branch $n \in \{1, 2, \cdots, N\}$, the probability that a sample exits at this branch is P_n ($P_n \in [0, 1]$), where N is the main branch. We can predict the execution time T_n for each branch based on Eq. 3. Then for a given task time threshold T_{th}, P_n should satisfy the following constraints:

$$\sum_{n=1}^{N} P_n \times T_n \leq T_{th},\ \sum_{n=1}^{N} P_n = 1 \tag{5}$$

We propose a stepwise method for determining branches confidence thresholds with the following procedure:

- In the training phase, we record a list of entropy values for the entire training set samples at each exit branch, denoted as $\mathcal{L}_n$
- In the inference phase, a set of eligible P_n values is generated based on the delay requirement T_{th}, and the set with the highest percentage of posterior exit branches is selected to obtain higher accuracy.
- The entropy value at P_1 of the entropy list $\mathcal{L}_1$ is chosen as the confidence threshold of the first branch.
- Subsequently, the first $\sum_{i=1}^{n-1} P_i$ values are eliminated from the entropy list $\mathcal{L}_n$, and then we choose the entropy value at $\frac{P_n}{1-\sum_{i=1}^{n-1} P_i}$ as the confidence threshold for exit branch n.

We note that adding too many exit branches is inadvisable since complex samples need to go through each branch without being able to exit inference earlier. Therefore, increasing the number of branches, while providing a more fine-grained service, also leads to an increase in the average inference latency. The exit branch at the shallow level of the CNN fails to give high confidence results due to the insufficient features extracted. Therefore the exit branch should not be positioned too close to the front of the models. Previous work has demonstrated that branches added at 1/2 and 3/4 of the CNNs can achieve the satisfactory speedup without excessive loss of accuracy [26]. In this work, for comparison with the server-assisted architecture, we added exit branches at 1/2 and 3/4 of the original CNNs to simulate the exit branches at the edge server and the cloud, respectively.

4   Evaluation

We implement EdgeSP in a cluster of heterogeneous edge devices and evaluate its performance under different device counts and network bandwidths. Moreover, we further test the average inference accuracy of EdgeSP under different latency requirements.

Table 1. Heterogeneous edge devices used in experiments

Device	CPU frequency	Memory
Raspberry Pi 4B × 2	1.5 GHz	4 GB
Virtual machine × 2	1000 MHz	4 GB
Virtual machine × 2	800 MHz	4 GB

4.1   Experiment Settings

We simulate edge device clusters with heterogeneous computing capabilities with the devices in Table 1. We increase the number of devices in the edge cluster from 1 to 6 in the order shown in Table 1. For comparison with the Edgent [21] and

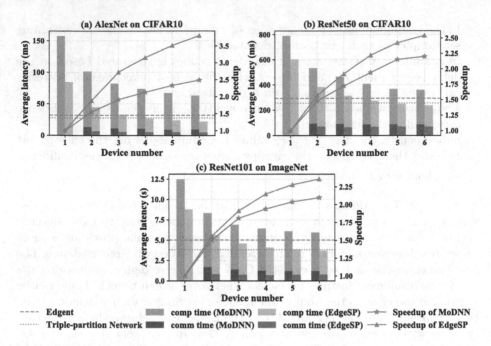

Fig. 5. The performance of EdgeSP at different device counts. Its average latency is compared with MoDNN, Edgent, and Triple-partition Network.

Triple-partition Network [6], we use a PC with an i5-8400 CPU to simulate the edge server and a server with four GTX3090 GPUs to simulate the cloud. We implement EdgeSP on AlexNet [27], ResNet50 [1], and ResNet101 [1] as they represent CNN models with different depths. The CIFAR10 [28] and ImageNet [29] datasets are employed to evaluate the performance of EdgeSP in tasks of varying difficulty. We use the WonderShaper [21] tool to adjust the available bandwidth between devices.

4.2   Performance Comparison

The variation of the average inference delay for each CNN model with an exit rate of $P_n = [40\%, 40\%, 20\%]$ and network bandwidth of 100 Mbps are shown in Fig. 5. It's a representative case as the entire inference workflow described in Sect. 3.1 is executed at this exit rate, and different CNN models can achieve satisfactory acceleration performance. Our framework achieves desired performance in CNN inference tasks of three different sizes and difficulties. We can observe that the average latency of CNN tasks decreases as the number of devices increases. Benefiting from the early exit mechanism, the average latency of EdgeSP is significantly lower than MoDNN in all three CNN tasks. Moreover, a lower communication latency than MoDNN is achieved thanks to the MFBL parallelization strategy. When the number of devices exceeds five, EdgeSP can complete the inference task faster than Edgent and Triple-partition Network.

Although they speed up the inference with the help of edge servers and the cloud, tasks that reside on end devices cannot be accelerated. Furthermore, EdgeSP does not involve uploading data to third-party servers, thus avoiding the risk of privacy disclosure.

As the number of devices increases, the acceleration ratio curves of EdgeSP and MoDNN flatten out, but EdgeSP consistently achieves a higher acceleration ratio than MoDNN. This trend is due to the increase in overlapping computation and communication overhead, which suggests that involving too many devices in parallel inference is not justifiable. Previous work [13] has demonstrated that when the number of devices exceeds six, the additional overhead significantly diminishes the acceleration effect.

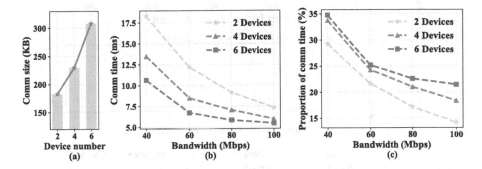

Fig. 6. AlexNet communication overhead at different bandwidths. (a) Variation of total communication data size with the number of devices. (b) Variation of communication time with bandwidth. (c) Variation of communication time as a percentage of total time with bandwidth.

4.3   Analysis of the Communication Overhead

Figure 6 shows the impact of network bandwidth on the performance of EdgeSP using AlexNet as an example. As the number of devices increases in Fig. 6(a), the workload is divided into smaller areas, but the overlap of tasks between devices increases. Therefore, the amount of data to be transferred also increase. The smaller the number of devices, the smaller the total communication size, but the more workload is allocated to each device. Therefore, the communication time is higher with fewer devices, as shown in Fig. 6(b). Combining Fig. 6(b) and Fig. 6(c), we can see that the communication time gradually decreases as the network bandwidth increases. The more devices there are, the faster the computing task will be completed, so the communication time occupies a higher percentage when there are more devices. On the other hand, multi-device can complete the task faster, which means that EdgeSP can mitigate the impact of bandwidth reduction to some extent.

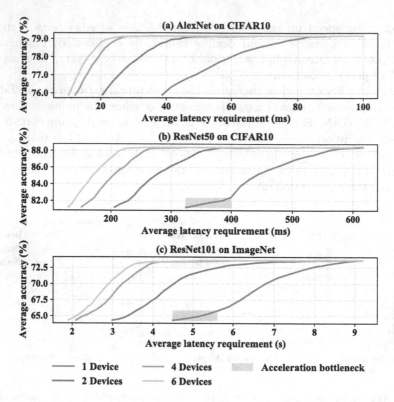

Fig. 7. Variation of the average accuracy of the three CNNs for different task latency requirements.

4.4 Performance Under Different Latency Requirements

EdgeSP is capable of adjusting the inference time according to the task latency requirements. Taking AlexNet in Fig. 7(a) as an example, when the latency requirement is 59 ms, the inference accuracy of a single device can only reach 77.9%, while the inference accuracy of multiple devices can reach 79.2%, and a single device cannot complete the task within 38 ms. As the number of devices increases, EdgeSP can achieve higher accuracy with a specified latency requirement. For example, when the latency requirement is 24 ms, the inference accuracy of two devices is 76.6%, while the inference accuracy of six devices can be as high as 79%. Due to the complexity of ImageNet, the accuracy of early exit branches is not as high as on CIFAR10, so the average accuracy in Fig. 7(c) will have more attenuation than in Fig. 7(b), but is still within an acceptable range. In Fig. 7(b) and Fig. 7(c), ResNet with multiple exit points running on a single device suffers from the acceleration bottleneck phenomenon due to its complex architecture. The acceleration bottleneck arises because the accuracy of the preceding exit branch is unsatisfactory, and the later branches require a longer execution time. Most input samples can only exit from the preceding branches with lower accuracy to meet the latency requirement. However, multi-device parallelism effectively suppresses the impact of acceleration bottlenecks. In a word, the multi-device parallelism and early exit mechanism complement each other, thus enabling EdgeSP to provide scalable and fast DNN inference capability for edge devices.

5 Conclusion

In this paper, we propose EdgeSP, a scalable multi-device parallel DNN inference framework, which substantially reduces the latency of DNN execution by resource-limited edge devices. We design a multiple fused-layer blocks parallelization strategy to minimize the communication overhead incurred by parallel inference. In addition, we add early exit branches to the original DNNs and propose a stepwise confidence threshold determination method, which empowers the device to trade-off latency and accuracy. Experimental evaluations show that EdgeSP achieves lower latency than server-assisted approaches and naive parallel inference in tasks of different scales. Furthermore, EdgeSP enables scalable inference for edge devices to provide high-accuracy services under various latency requirements. In future work, we plan to explore multi-device parallel execution of fully connected layers to accelerate DNN inference further.

Acknowledgments. This work was supported in part by the General Program of National Natural Science Foundation of China under Grant 62072049, and in part by the National Key Research and Development Project of China under Grant 2019YFB2103202 and Grant 2019YFB2103200.

References

1. He, K., Zhang, X., Ren, S., Sun, J.: Deep residual learning for image recognition. In: 2016 IEEE Conference on Computer Vision and Pattern Recognition (CVPR), pp. 770–778 (2016). https://doi.org/10.1109/CVPR.2016.90
2. Xiao, K., Gao, Z., Shi, W., Qiu, X., Yang, Y., Rui, L.: EdgeABC: an architecture for task offloading and resource allocation in the Internet of Things. Future Gener. Comput. Syst. **107**, 498–508 (2020). https://doi.org/10.1016/j.future.2020.02.026
3. Kang, Y., et al.: Neurosurgeon: collaborative intelligence between the cloud and mobile edge. SIGARCH Comput. Archit. News **45**(1), 615–629 (2017). https://doi.org/10.1145/3093337.3037698
4. Teerapittayanon, S., McDanel, B., Kung, H.: Distributed deep neural networks over the cloud, the edge and end devices. In: 2017 IEEE 37th International Conference on Distributed Computing Systems (ICDCS), pp. 328–339 (2017). https://doi.org/10.1109/ICDCS.2017.226
5. Teerapittayanon, S., McDanel, B., Kung, H.T.: BranchyNet: fast inference via early exiting from deep neural networks. CoRR abs/1709.01686 (2017). http://arxiv.org/abs/1709.01686
6. Gao, Z., Miao, D., Zhao, L., Mo, Z., Qi, G., Yan, L.: Triple-partition network: collaborative neural network based on the 'end device-edge-cloud'. In: 2021 IEEE Wireless Communications and Networking Conference (WCNC), pp. 1–7 (2021). https://doi.org/10.1109/WCNC49053.2021.9417243

7. Du, J., Shen, M., Du, Y.: A distributed in-situ CNN inference system for IoT applications. In: 2020 IEEE 38th International Conference on Computer Design (ICCD), pp. 279–287 (2020). https://doi.org/10.1109/ICCD50377.2020.00055
8. Zhang, S., Zhang, S., Qian, Z., Wu, J., Jin, Y., Lu, S.: DeepSlicing: collaborative and adaptive CNN inference with low latency. IEEE Trans. Parallel Distrib. Syst. **32**(9), 2175–2187 (2021)
9. Mohammed, T., Joe-Wong, C., Babbar, R., Francesco, M.D.: Distributed inference acceleration with adaptive DNN partitioning and offloading. In: IEEE INFOCOM 2020 - IEEE Conference on Computer Communications, pp. 854–863 (2020). https://doi.org/10.1109/INFOCOM41043.2020.9155237
10. Xue, F., Fang, W., Xu, W., Wang, Q., Ma, X., Ding, Y.: EdgeLD: locally distributed deep learning inference on edge device clusters. In: 2020 IEEE 22nd International Conference on High Performance Computing and Communications; IEEE 18th International Conference on Smart City; IEEE 6th International Conference on Data Science and Systems (HPCC/SmartCity/DSS), pp. 613–619 (2020). https://doi.org/10.1109/HPCC-SmartCity-DSS50907.2020.00078
11. Zeng, L., Chen, X., Zhou, Z., Yang, L., Zhang, J.: CoEdge: cooperative DNN inference with adaptive workload partitioning over heterogeneous edge devices. IEEE/ACM Trans. Netw. **29**(2), 595–608 (2021). https://doi.org/10.1109/TNET.2020.3042320
12. Mao, J., et al.: MeDNN: a distributed mobile system with enhanced partition and deployment for large-scale DNNs. In: 2017 IEEE/ACM International Conference on Computer-Aided Design (ICCAD), pp. 751–756. IEEE (2017)
13. Zhou, L., Samavatian, M.H., Bacha, A., Majumdar, S., Teodorescu, R.: Adaptive parallel execution of deep neural networks on heterogeneous edge devices. In: Proceedings of the 4th ACM/IEEE Symposium on Edge Computing, SEC 2019, pp. 195–208. Association for Computing Machinery, New York (2019). https://doi.org/10.1145/3318216.3363312
14. Mao, J., Chen, X., Nixon, K.W., Krieger, C., Chen, Y.: MoDNN: local distributed mobile computing system for deep neural network. In: Design, Automation Test in Europe Conference Exhibition (DATE) 2017, pp. 1396–1401 (2017). https://doi.org/10.23919/DATE.2017.7927211
15. Zhao, Z., Barijough, K.M., Gerstlauer, A.: DeepThings: distributed adaptive deep learning inference on resource-constrained IoT edge clusters. IEEE Trans. Comput. Aided Des. Integr. Circuits Syst. **37**(11), 2348–2359 (2018)
16. Fang, B., Zeng, X., Zhang, M.: NestDNN: resource-aware multi-tenant on-device deep learning for continuous mobile vision. In: Proceedings of the 24th Annual International Conference on Mobile Computing and Networking, MobiCom 2018, pp. 115–127. Association for Computing Machinery, New York (2018). https://doi.org/10.1145/3241539.3241559
17. Xu, Z., Yut, F., Liu, C., Chen, X.: ReForm: static and dynamic resource-aware DNN reconfiguration framework for mobile device. In: 2019 56th ACM/IEEE Design Automation Conference (DAC), pp. 1–6 (2019)
18. Oh, Y.H., et al.: A portable, automatic data quantizer for deep neural networks. In: Proceedings of the 27th International Conference on Parallel Architectures and Compilation Techniques, PACT 2018. Association for Computing Machinery, New York (2018). https://doi.org/10.1145/3243176.3243180
19. Tan, X., Li, H., Wang, L., Huang, X., Xu, Z.: Empowering adaptive early-exit inference with latency awareness. In: Proceedings of the AAAI Conference on Artificial Intelligence, vol. 35, no. 11, pp. 9825–9833, May 2021. https://ojs.aaai.org/index.php/AAAI/article/view/17181

20. Laskaridis, S., Venieris, S.I., Almeida, M., Leontiadis, I., Lane, N.D.: SPINN: synergistic progressive inference of neural networks over device and cloud. In: Proceedings of the 26th Annual International Conference on Mobile Computing and Networking, MobiCom 2020. Association for Computing Machinery, New York (2020). https://doi.org/10.1145/3372224.3419194

21. Li, E., Zeng, L., Zhou, Z., Chen, X.: Edge AI: on-demand accelerating deep neural network inference via edge computing. IEEE Trans. Wireless Commun. **19**(1), 447–457 (2020). https://doi.org/10.1109/TWC.2019.2946140

22. Du, J., et al.: Model parallelism optimization for distributed inference via decoupled CNN structure. IEEE Trans. Parallel Distrib. Syst. **32**(7), 1665–1676 (2021). https://doi.org/10.1109/TPDS.2020.3041474

23. Zhao, K., et al.: FT-CNN: algorithm-based fault tolerance for convolutional neural networks. IEEE Trans. Parallel Distrib. Syst. **32**(7), 1677–1689 (2021). https://doi.org/10.1109/TPDS.2020.3043449

24. Ma, N., Zhang, X., Zheng, H.-T., Sun, J.: ShuffleNet V2: practical guidelines for efficient CNN architecture design. In: Ferrari, V., Hebert, M., Sminchisescu, C., Weiss, Y. (eds.) Computer Vision – ECCV 2018. LNCS, vol. 11218, pp. 122–138. Springer, Cham (2018). https://doi.org/10.1007/978-3-030-01264-9_8

25. Molchanov, P., Tyree, S., Karras, T., Aila, T., Kautz, J.: Pruning convolutional neural networks for resource efficient transfer learning. arXiv preprint arXiv:1611.06440 3 (2016)

26. Zhang, L., Tan, Z., Song, J., Chen, J., Bao, C., Ma, K.: SCAN: a scalable neural networks framework towards compact and efficient models. arXiv preprint arXiv:1906.03951 (2019)

27. Krizhevsky, A., Sutskever, I., Hinton, G.E.: ImageNet classification with deep convolutional neural networks. Adv. Neural. Inf. Process. Syst. **25**, 1097–1105 (2012)

28. Krizhevsky, A.: Learning multiple layers of features from tiny images, pp. 32–33 (2009). https://www.cs.toronto.edu/~kriz/learning-features-2009-TR.pdf

29. Deng, J., Dong, W., Socher, R., Li, L.J., Li, K., Fei-Fei, L.: ImageNet: a large-scale hierarchical image database. In: 2009 IEEE Conference on Computer Vision and Pattern Recognition, pp. 248–255 (2009). https://doi.org/10.1109/CVPR.2009.5206848

An Efficient Computation Offloading Strategy in Wireless Powered Mobile-Edge Computing Networks

Xiaobao Zhou, Jianqiang Hu[✉], Mingfeng Liang, and Yang Liu

School of Computer and Information Engineering,
Xiamen University of Technology, Xiamen 361024, China
jqhucn@xmut.edu.cn

Abstract. The emergence of mobile edge computing (MEC) has improved the data processing capabilities of devices with limited computing resources. However, some tasks that require higher latency and energy consumption are still facing huge challenges. In this paper, for the time-varying wireless channel conditions, we proposed an effective method to perform offloading calculations on the computing tasks of wireless devices, that is, to distribute the tasks to the local of offload to the edge server under the premise of satisfying time delay and energy consumption. Based on this, we adopt the parallel calculation model of Deep Reinforcement Learning Optimal Stopping Theory (DRLOST), which is composed of two parts: offloading decision generation and deep reinforcement learning. The model uses a parallel deep neural network (DNN) to generate offloading decisions, and stores the generated offloading decisions in the memory according to the optimal stopping theory model parameters to further train the model. The simulation results show that the proposed algorithm can minimize delay time, and can respond quickly to tasks even in a fast-fading environment.

Keywords: Mobile edge computing · Offloading decision · Parallel computing · Optimal stopping theory

1 Introduction

In 5G era, the pace towards the Internet of Everything is getting faster and faster. The storage capacity, battery power consumption, and the delay constraint problems brought by IoT devices are enormous challenges we need to face. If we only rely on local devices to process computing, we cannot meet the computing requirements of some tasks under the delay constraint and the energy consumption. In recent years, even with the rapid development of wireless communication technology and data calculation scheduling methods, the communication transmission distance between mobile wireless devices and remote servers is long, which has a huge impact on transmission rate and energy consumption, and data security cannot be obtained. The proposal of MEC [1] can effectively solve the above problems.

© Springer Nature Switzerland AG 2022
Y. Lai et al. (Eds.): ICA3PP 2021, LNCS 13156, pp. 334–344, 2022.
https://doi.org/10.1007/978-3-030-95388-1_22

The MEC decentralizes computing resources to the edge of the network, and deploys small-capacity edge servers at base stations close to users. This has great advantages for computing tasks that require the large delay constraint and energy consumption, such as environmental detection [2], cloud Games [3], AR applications [4], and it can also be an intermediate data processing layer to provide resources for mobile node data offloading. The MEC server is sometimes used by a large number of users at the same time, and only a few users are using it at other times [5], so the key to the mobile device is to solve the problem of offloading decision.

In the field of wireless communication, the amplitude of the received signal changes randomly due to the change of the channel. Therefore, we need to make real-time decision-making in the fast fading channel. The main problems faced by the multi-user scenario are the selection of calculation methods and the resource allocation of joint optimization. In order to reduce the complexity of calculation, Chen et al. [6] uses heuristic local methods, and Alghamdi et al. [7] proposes convex optimization methods. However, they need to perform multiple iterations to find a local optimal solution, and they are not suitable for the time-varying wireless channel conditions.

In this paper, we study an MEC network of multiple users and an edge server, and each user decides to run or offloading computing tasks. The calculation data all obey the binary offloading decision, and the optimal offloading decision is determined according to the time delay and energy consumption. We propose an optimal stopping theory method based on deep reinforcement learning, which maximizes the user's data processing rate by quickly determining the offloading decision. Compared with existing methods, our contributions are:

1) In the environment where multi-user wireless channel transmission is rapidly attenuating, we propose an efficient the algorithm framework can quickly select offloading decisions.
2) Aiming at the problem of making optimal choices for offloading decisions of exponential order, we use preprocessing to optimize the number of offloading decisions, and then quickly select offloading decisions based on the optimal stopping theory.
3) We propose an optimal stopping theory model based on deep learning to judge the offloading decision. The purpose is to determine the offloading decision in the shortest time. Through the memory, it can learn and optimize from the past experience.

2   Related Work

What the task offloading strategy focuses on is whether the data is calculated locally or offloaded to the edge server, and the optimal offloading strategy is determined according to the execution delay and energy consumption. Zhan et al. [8] proposed an optimal stopping theoretical model with continuous time optimization to minimize the expected processing time. Pan et al. [9] uses the optimal stopping theory principle of three continuous-time optimization decision models to solve the problem of task offloading. The proposed optimal stopping time model for house sales can be effectively used in wireless users and actual data. Alghamdi et al. [10] uses the principle of optimal stopping theory to solve the problem of offloading decision-making, aiming to select the best server under the best load and optimize the service quality of mobile users. It is proposed to adopt sequential decision-making method to minimize delay. For the multi-decision problem, Hekmati et al. [11] proposed a Markov process to solve the offloading shunt decision problem with offloading time constraints on the wireless channel, and used the online energy optimal calculation shunt algorithm to verify the effectiveness of the Markov stopping theory. Kuang et al. [12] studied the optimal task offloading strategy and resource allocation, minimizes the weighted sum of wireless device energy consumption and delay, and proposes a binary search method to obtain the optimal solution, and then obtains the optimal solution according to the Gibbs sampling algorithm Optimal offloading decision.

Most research uses deep learning to generate offloading decisions. Bozorgchenani et al. [13] minimizes the energy consumption and task processing delay of mobile devices, model task offloading in MEC as a constrained multi-objective optimization problem (CMOP). Mukherjee et al. [14] studied a distributed deep learning offloading algorithm, which generates a near-optimal offloading decision for a single edge server and multi edge server computing network. Alfakih et al. [15] proposed a deep reinforcement learning offloading scheme, which considers making the best offloading decision for users in the temporary mobile cloud, uses the Markov decision process to solve the offloading decision problem. Huang et al. [16] proposed an online shunting framework for deep reinforcement learning. The training data does not need to be labeled. It generates an offloading decision storage database online based on the training data and then performs training.

3   System Model and Computing Method

3.1   System Model

In this paper, we consider an MEC network with an edge server and N wireless devices (WDs), shown in Fig. 1. The mutual interference between our wireless power supply system and transmission time stamp users is negligible. Each WD is equipped with a rechargeable battery and can independently choose whether to perform tasks locally or send an offload request. There is a connection between the edge server and the user. For the communication line, since the computing power of the edge server is higher than that of the wireless device, the wireless device can choose to offload tasks to the edge server. In order to avoid the interference caused by the wireless power transmission system to the communication, each device adopts a time division multiplexing (TDD) circuit [17].

In RF-enabled wireless energy transfer (WET) provides energy for the wireless device [18]. Since the thermal noise power and user transmit power are far less than the transmit power of the electric base station, their influence can be ignored. According to the law of conservation of energy, get the energy received by the i-th user, i.e.

$$E_i^H = \sigma p_i h_i \tau_0 \tag{1}$$

During the transmission time τ_0, the channel transmission power p_i, where $\sigma \in (0, 1]$ represents the energy conversion efficiency, and hi represents the channel gain between the power base station and the i-th user.

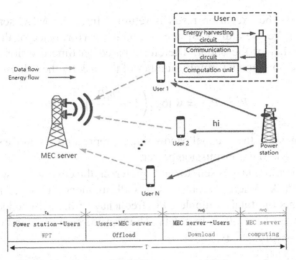

Fig. 1. The DRLOST model involving a P-MEC server, a set of N user and system time allocation.

Through the harvested energy, the data collected by wireless devices need to be calculated within a limited time frame. In order to simplify the calculation, we assume that there is no difference in the computing power of each wireless device. The decision whether to split is mainly based on the size of its own load and the data. The number of bits, the user chooses the calculation method, set $a_i \in \{0, 1\}$ represents the offloading decision, where $a_i = 0$ indicates that the task is performed locally, $a_i = 1$ indicates that the task is offloaded to the edge server.

3.2 Computing Method

There are two calculation methods: local computing and computation offloading.

Local calculation mode: each user can perform local calculations in the entire time frame and local calculations can be performed at the same time when energy is collected, for example, [19–21]. Assume that f_i represents the CPU frequency, and C represents the total number of CPU cycles required to complete the task. Therefore, the amount of data processed locally by the i-th user is expressed as $D_i = t_i f_i / C$, and the energy consumption is $e_i^l = t_i \gamma_c f_i^3$, γ_c represents the effective capacitance of the processor chip on the user side the coefficient, f_i represents the energy efficiency coefficient calculated by the user terminal. The local computing time [22] as:

$$t_i^l(f_i) = \frac{C}{f_i} \tag{2}$$

User computing energy consumption subjects to $E_i^C \leq E_i^H$, i.e.

$$t_i \gamma_c f_i^3 =\leq \sigma Ph_i \tau_0, \forall i \in N \tag{3}$$

The computation offloading is divided into three stages: 1) the data to be offloading is transferred from the user to the MEC server, 2) the MEC server calculates the remotely input data, and 3) the execution result is returned from the MEC server to the user. As mentioned in the literature [23], the computing performance of the edge server is far greater than that of the client. Therefore, based on time division multiple access According to the Shannon's formula, number of the task by the i-th user, i.e.

$$R(\hat{w}, P_i) = \hat{w} \log_2\left(1 + \frac{h_i P_i}{\sigma^2}\right), i \in N \tag{4}$$

where $\hat{w}$ represents the channel bandwidth, σ^2 represents the noise spectral density, P_i represents offload the transmission power.

After the offloading task is sent to the edge server, the edge server will allocate CPU to the offloading task. Where f_0 represents the CPU frequency allocated to the offloading task, F_0 represents the total available CPU frequency of the MEC edge server, and D_i represents the size of the offloading data. The transmission time and calculation time consumption are expressed as:

$$t_i^{ex}(f_0) = \frac{C}{f_0} \tag{5}$$

$$t_i^{ex}(\hat{w}) = \frac{D_i}{R(\hat{w}, P_i)}$$

$$subject\ to\ \sum_{i \in N} a_i f_i \leq F_0 \tag{6}$$

The total time delay of UEi can be formulated as:

$$t_i^0(\hat{w}, f_i) = t_i^{tx}(\hat{w}) + t_i^{ex}(f_0) \tag{7}$$

The total energy computation of UEi is divided into transmission energy consumption and calculation energy consumption. In this paper ignores the energy consumed during the MEC calculation task, and $e_i^0(w)$ represents the total energy consumed.

$$e_i^0(\hat{w}) = p_i t_i^{tx}(\hat{w}) \tag{8}$$

4 Problem Formulation and Problem Solving

4.1 Problem Formulation

When processing task data, the main factors that affect user experience are execution delay and user-side energy consumption.

$$t_i = a_i t_i^0(\hat{w}, f_i) + (1 - a_i)t_i^1 \tag{9}$$

$$e_i = a_i e_i^0(\hat{w}) + (1 - a_i)e_i^1 \tag{10}$$

Based on the paper [24], we designed a practical function based on user service quality to detect the effectiveness of the computing offloading scheme. Compared with local computation, the time and energy spent on offloading tasks to the edge for computing is significantly reduced. Therefore, we define the trade-off between energy consumption and latency, i.e.

$$Q(a_i, \hat{w}, f_i) \triangleq \sum_{i=1}^{N} \eta_i^T \left(\frac{t_i^l - t_i}{t_i^l} \right) + \eta_i^E \left(\frac{e_i^l - e_i}{e_i^l} \right) \tag{11}$$

Where $\eta_i^T \in [0, 1]$ and $\eta_i^E \in [0, 1]$ indicate the proportion of the weight required by the task computation when the user performs the task. We define $\eta_i^T + \eta_i^E = 1$. Assuming that the task does not impose constraints on energy consumption and requires relatively high time delay, we can increase the time weight parameter. The opposite is also true.

4.2 Problem Solving

Offloading Optimization Problem. We first decompose the evaluation user service quality function into two sub-problems for solving, namely, the offloading decision problem (P1) and the resource allocation problem (P2). The key to solving the P1 problem is the integer optimization problem. Real-time optimization of traditional solving algorithms is impossible in a rapidly changing environment. In order to solve this problem, we use the deep reinforcement learning and obtain the offloading decision a_i, which can quickly generate offloading decisions.

$$t_i^{ex}(f_0) = \frac{C}{f_0} \tag{12}$$

$$P1: \quad \max Q(a_i, \hat{w}, f_i)$$

$$s.t: \quad a_i \in \{0, 1\}$$

$$f_i > 0, \forall i \in N, a_i = 1,$$

$$t_i \leq d_i, \forall i \in N, \tag{13}$$

In Eq. (13), the i-th user is in the local computing mode, and the user service quality function $Q(a_i, \hat{w}, f_i) = 0$ is evaluated. Where d_i represents the maximum time delay total time delay.

After the offloading decision a_i is obtained, the convex optimization P2 problem can be effectively solved. A certain amount of resources must be allocated to offloaded tasks. We assume that the computing cycle of the edge computing server is much greater than the computing request resources.

$$P2: \quad \min Q(1, \hat{w}, f_i)$$

$$s.t: \quad \sum_{i \in N} a_i f_i \leq F_0,$$

$$f_i > 0, \forall i \in N, a_i = 1, \tag{14}$$

The key to solving the P1 problem is the size of the offloading solution, which depends on the number of mobile users in the MEC system. Since each task has 2^N candidate modes, it is obvious that the amount of calculation is very large. In order to control the number of offloading decisions, we have learned from the literature [15].

Deep learning can iteratively learn from optimal offloading decisions and output better offloading decisions over time. However, in a rapidly decayed wireless channel, we hope that on the premise of meeting time delay and energy consumption, offloading decisions can be generated faster for data processing. To address the above challenge, the detailed description of DRLOST algorithm is provided in Algorithm 1.

Algorithm 1: DRLOST

1: Randomly initialize the local parameter and empty memory

2: Initialize the inputs

3: For i=1 to iteration.size do

4:    The amount of data processed D_i is input to K DNNs

5:    In a distributed manner, a candidate offloading decision a_n is generated from each DNN

6:    Select and save the offloading decision that minimizes (P2) in the previous $a_r - 1$

7:    Among $a_n - a_r + 1$, select the candidate offloading decision that minimizes (P2), $q_i^* = \arg min \, Q\left(1, \hat{w}, f_i\right)$

8:    Save (D_i, q_i^*) to the memory

9:    Select k training data from the memory and train the DNN

10:    Update parameter using the Adan algorithm

11: End

Optimal Stopping Theory Heading. In each time frame, after obtaining the offloading decision, the user decides the selected offloading decision that satisfies the conditions, and then offloads the computing task. In response to this problem, we use the optimal stopping theory model to solve the processing problem of the offloading solution, that is, the resource allocation problem, in order to minimize the expected processing time.

First, the user knows in advance the number of offloading decisions a_n, that are candidates for task offloading. Our goal is to select the best offloading decision as much as possible for task offloading. The best strategy is to reject the top $a_r - 1$, $a_r \in [2, a_n]$ candidate offloading decisions, and then judge the remaining $a_n - a_r + 1$ offloading decisions and choose the best offloading compared to the previous a_r Decision, we select the probability model of the optimal offloading decision [24], i.e.

$$P(a_r) = \frac{a_r - 1}{a_n} \sum_{k=a_r}^{a_n} \frac{1}{k - 1} \tag{15}$$

In this paper, we assume that the computing resources of the edge server are large enough. When $a_n \to \infty$, we get the familiar secretary solution problem, where the optimal probability is $e^{-1} = 0.368$, which is the optimal offloading decision probability for us. Figure 2 shows the influence of the number of offloading decisions on the optimal decision For example, when $a_n = 20$, we have a 38.4% probability that the optimal offloading strategy will be selected.

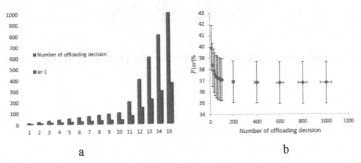

a   b

Fig. 2. The value of $a_r - 1$ for different numbers of offloading decision (a) and the probability of offloading to the best (b).

5 Simulation Results

Table 1. The simulation experiment parameters.

Parameter	Value
The CPU frequency of the UEi(cycle/s)	0.6×10^9
The CPU frequency of the edge server(cycle/s)	10×10^9
h_i	0.2×10^{-6}
σ/mW	3.423×10^{-8}
F_0/CPU cycle/s	1×10^3
η_i^T, η_i^E	0.6, 04
$\hat{w}$/MHz	20

In this section, we compare the DROO algorithm with our proposed DRLOST algorithm. There are ten edge servers in the experimental simulation, and at the same time, each user may offload tasks to the edge. Considering the limited performance of the computer used in the experiment, we set the number of algorithm iterations to 10. The simulation experiment parameters are listed in Table 1.

Figure 3 compares the total time delay by the two algorithms for task processing with different numbers of users. It can be observed that when the number of users is small, the total time consumed by our proposed algorithm is much lower than that of the DROO algorithm. For example, when the number of users n = 20, our proposed algorithm saves half of the time than the DROO algorithm.

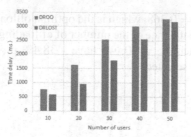

Fig. 3. The total time delay by the two algorithms for task processing with different numbers of users.

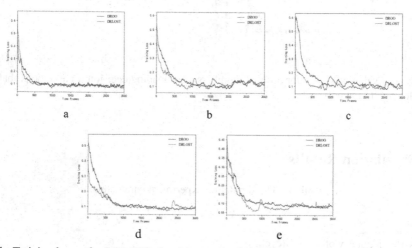

Fig. 4. Training losses for DRLOST algorithm under the different user, a: $n = 10$, b: n = 20, c: n = 30, d: n = 40, e: n = 50.

In Fig. 4, we studied the impact of different user numbers on the two algorithms, where we set the number of iterations to 10 and the learning rate to 0.01. As shown in the figure, the training loss utility function of our proposed algorithm converges quickly and then tends to a stable value. Figure 4 (b)-(e) appear jitter after converging to a stable value because when selecting the best offloading decision, the optimal decision is included in the top 37%, but the final offloading decision is saved in the memory.

6 Conclusion

In this paper, we propose a parallel computing model of the deep reinforcement learning optimal stopping theory for the rapidly attenuating wireless channel. While considering the average delay and average energy demand, the distributed parallel processing data is used to generate the offloading decision. The number of offloading decisions is controlled within a reasonable range. The optimal offloading decision is selected based on the optimal stopping theory. Finally, we study the convergence and time delay performance of DRLOST through simulation. The results show that the algorithm can quickly determine the optimal offloading decision for task calculation within the controllable range of energy consumption.

In the future work, we will consider the cloud server and cloud-side collaboration structure, and further consider making further improvements in the mobile user group. In addition, we will continue to study the cloud-side collaborative inference calculation model and apply it to the heart sound detection model based on this. This is also one of our purposes for designing efficient computation offloading.

Funding. This research has been supported in part by the new generation information technology innovation project of China University Industry-University-Research In novation Fund under Grant No. 2020ITA03015, Fujian Provincial Natural Science Foundation of China under Grant No. 2019J01856, and the science and technology innovation program for graduate student of Xiamen University of Technology.

References

1. Merluzzi, M., Di Lorenzo, P., Barbarossa, S., Frascolla, V.: Dynamic computation offloading in multi-access edge computing via ultra-reliable and low-latency communications. IEEE Trans. Signal Inform. Process. Over Netw. **6**, 342–356 (2020)
2. Saffari, P., Basaligheh, A., Sieben, V., Moez, K.: An RF-powered wireless temperature sensor for harsh environment monitoring with non-intermittent operation. IEEE Trans. Circ. Syst. I Regul. Pap. **65**, 1529–1542 (2018)
3. Philip, S., Sharma, Y.: Cloud gaming: future of computer games. IITM J. Manage. IT **12**(1), 4–11 (2021)
4. Wen, F., Sun, Z., He, T., et al.: Machine learning glove using self-powered conductive super-hydrophobic triboelectric textile for gesture recognition in VR/AR applications. Adv. Sci. **7**(14), 2000261 (2020)
5. Zaw, C.W., Tran, N.H., Saad, W., Han, Z., Hong, C.S.: Generalized nash equilibrium game for radio and computing resource allocation in co-located MEC. In: ICC 2020–2020 IEEE International Conference on Communications (ICC), pp. 1–6 (2020)
6. Cheng, N., et al.: Space/aerial-assisted computing offloading for IoT applications: a learning-based approach. IEEE J. Sel. Areas Commun. **37**(5), 1117–1129 (2019)
7. Alghamdi, I., Anagnostopoulos, C., Pezaros, D.P.: On the optimality of task offloading in mobile edge computing environments. In: 2019 IEEE Global Communications Conference (GLOBECOM), pp. 1–6. IEEE (2019, December)
8. Zhan, Y., Guo, S., Li, P., Zhang, J.: A deep reinforcement learning based offloading game in edge computing. IEEE Trans. Comput. **69**(6), 883–893 (2020)
9. Pan, S., Zhang, Z., Zhang, Z., Zeng, D.: Dependency-aware computation offloading in mobile edge computing: a reinforcement learning approach. IEEE Access **7**, 134742–134753 (2019)
10. Alghamdi, I., Anagnostopoulos, C., Pezaros, D.P.: Delay-tolerant sequential decision making for task offloading in mobile edge computing environments. Information **10**(10), 312 (2019)
11. Hekmati, A., Teymoori, P., Todd, T.D., Zhao, D., Karakostasy, G.: Optimal multi-decision mobile computation offloading with hard task deadlines. In: 2019 IEEE Symposium on Computers and Communications (ISCC), pp. 1–8. IEEE (2019, June)
12. Kuang, L., Gong, T., OuYang, S., et al.: Offloading decision methods for multiple users with structured tasks in edge computing for smart cities. Futur. Gener. Comput. Syst. **105**, 717–729 (2020)

13. Bozorgchenani, A., Mashhadi, F., Tarchi, D., Monroy, S.S.: Multi-objective computation sharing in energy and delay constrained mobile edge computing environments. IEEE Trans. Mobile Comput. **20**(10), 2992–3005 (2020)
14. Mukherjee, M., Kumar, V., Lat, A., et al.: Distributed deep learning-based task offloading for UAV-enabled mobile edge computing. In: IEEE INFOCOM 2020-IEEE Conference on Computer Communications Workshops (INFOCOM WKSHPS), pp. 1208–1212. IEEE (2020)
15. Alfakih, T., Hassan, M.M., Gumaei, A., et al.: Task offloading and resource allocation for mobile edge computing by deep reinforcement learning based on SARSA[J]. IEEE Access **8**, 54074–54084 (2020)
16. Huang, L., Bi, S., Zhang, Y.J.A.: Deep reinforcement learning for online computation offloading in wireless powered mobile-edge computing networks. IEEE Trans. Mob. Comput. **19**(11), 2581–2593 (2019)
17. Guo, W., Tian, W., Ye, Y., et al.: Cloud resource scheduling with deep reinforcement learning and imitation learning. IEEE Internet Things J. **8**(5), 3576–3586 (2020)
18. Khayyat, M., Elgendy, I.A., Muthanna, A., et al.: Advanced deep learning-based computational offloading for multilevel vehicular edge-cloud computing networks. IEEE Access **8**, 137052–137062 (2020)
19. Jeong, C., Son, H.: Cooperative transmission of energy-constrained IoT devices in wireless-powered communication networks. IEEE Internet Things J. **8**(5), 3972–3982 (2020)
20. Nguyen, P.X., et al.: Backscatter-assisted data offloading in OFDMA-based wireless-powered mobile edge computing for IoT networks. IEEE Internet Things J. **8**(11), 9233–9243 (2021)
21. Hu, X., Wong, K.K., Yang, K.: Wireless powered cooperation-assisted mobile edge computing. IEEE Trans. Wireless Commun. **17**(4), 2375–2388 (2018)
22. Shi, H., Luo, R., Gui, G.: Joint offloading and energy optimization for wireless powered mobile edge computing under nonlinear EH Model. Peer-to-Peer Networking Appl. **14**, 1–14 (2021)
23. Zhou, S., Jadoon, W.: Jointly optimizing offloading decision and bandwidth allocation with energy constraint in mobile edge computing environment. Computing **103**, 1–27 (2021)
24. Zhang, Y., Dong, X., Zhao, Y.: Decentralized computation offloading over wireless-powered mobile-edge computing networks. In: 2020 IEEE International Conference on Artificial Intelligence and Information Systems (ICAIIS), pp. 137–140. IEEE (2020)

WiRD: Real-Time and Cross Domain Detection System on Edge Device

Qing Yang[1] , Tianzhang Xing[1(✉)] , Zhiping Jiang[2] , Junfeng Wang[1] ,
and Jingyi He[1]

[1] School of Information Science and Technology, Northwest University, Xi'an, China
xtz@nwu.edu.cn
[2] School Computer Science and Technology, Xidian University, Xi'an, China

Abstract. WiFi-based perception systems can realize various gesture recognition in theory, but they cannot realize large-scale applications in practice. Later, some work solved the problem of cross-domain identification of the WiFi system, and promoted the possibility of the practical application of WiFi perception. However, the existing cross-domain recognition work requires a large number of calculations to extract motion features and recognition through a complex network, which determines that it cannot be deployed directly on edge devices. In addition, some hardware limitations of edge devices (for example, the network card is a single antenna), the amount of data we obtain is far less than that of the general network card. If the original data is not calibrated, the error information carried by the data will have a huge impact on the recognition result. Therefore, in order to solve the above problems, we propose WiRD, a system that can accurately calibrate the amplitude and phase in the case of a single antenna, and can be deployed on edge devices to achieve real-time detection. Experimental results show that WiRD is comparable to existing methods for gesture and body recognition within the domain, and has 87% accuracy for gesture recognition cross the domain, but the overall system processing time is reduced by 9× and the model inference time is reduced by 50×.

Keywords: Wi-Fi sensing · Deep learning · Routing node · Edge computing · Convolutional neural network

1 Introduction

IOT research is now divided into two main directions, one is the transmission and protection of sensing data [15, 17], and the other is the research of sensing applications. With the development of artificial intelligence, sensing technology has been newly developed, among which the technology represented by gestures recognition has been widely used in related fields, such as smart city [16], virtual reality and mobile games. The earliest gesture recognition relied heavily on specialized hardware devices, which not only brought additional overhead to the user but also seriously affected the user experience. Later, with the development of deep learning, computer vision-based action recognition became mainstream [4, 10]. However, accurate image recognition relies heavily on internal chip computing power

© Springer Nature Switzerland AG 2022
Y. Lai et al. (Eds.): ICA3PP 2021, LNCS 13156, pp. 345–360, 2022.
https://doi.org/10.1007/978-3-030-95388-1_23

and has privacy leakage problems. The device-free recognition technologies has attracted a lot of attention, and they can not only solve the privacy problem, but also work in NLOS scenarios. Initially people have chosen to use RSS for their research because it is easily accessible on the existing wireless infrastructure [1]. Later, with the successful extraction of CSI [22], it triggered extensive research on commodity Wi-Fi based sensing solutions.

Because the signal in the cross-domain recognition will lead to a significant decrease in accuracy, infinite perception has not been able to achieve widespread use. In order to solve the above problems, Widar3.0 [23], WiHF [9] extract the motion features independent of the domain, and achieved good results by using the CNN-GRU network for recognition. However, the above work requires a lot of calculations to extract motion features, and because the neural network model is too complex, its model reasoning also requires very high computing power. The above requirements limit the deployment of its system on edge devices, and it must require the participation of a high computing power platform, which brings a lot of inconvenience to actual deployment and use.

In this paper, we propose WiRD, a deployed end-to-end WiFi action recognition system at the routing node. First of all, due to the limitation of the edge device network card, only one antenna can be used for signal acquisition, which not only results in fewer features, but also cannot use multiple signal calibration methods such as phase difference calculation between multiple antennas and conjugate multiplication, which brings difficulties for us to obtain accurate CSI. Therefore, in view of the current actual situation, we propose a single-antenna CSI enhancement method, which achieves calibration for amplitude and phase. Then considering the weak computing power of edge devices, we need to extract gesture features through some uncomplicated calculations for subsequent recognition. Finally, by using the redundancy of convolution operations, we designed a neural network specifically for edge devices, which improved the model's inference speed while ensuring accuracy.

Design Challenges: the design of such a WiFi gesture recognition system on edge device involves the following challenges.

Necessity of Single Antenna CSI Calibration. Due to the limitation of the number of antennas of the edge device's network card, the amount of data that can be obtained is far less than that of the commonly used network card. If the CSI is not calibrated, the error information contained in the original CSI will have a great impact on subsequent recognition, especially the recognition of fine-grained actions. How to achieve accurate CSI correction in the case of a single antenna is the primary challenge we face.

Timeliness of Feature Extraction. Although widar3.0 achieves high-precision recognition by extracting cross-domain features, the amount of calculation for feature extraction is too large, the calculation time is too long, and it does not meet the real-time requirements. Therefore, how to extract rich features while ensuring low extraction calculations will be our biggest challenge.

Rapidity of Mini Network Model Inference. Because of the computational power limitation of the edge devices, we cannot deploy more complex neural networks on them. It will be an important challenge to design a lightweight neural network that can extract as many features as possible with as little computation as possible while ensuring accurate gesture recognition, and can guarantee real-time inference on mobile.

WiRD offers efficient countermeasures to solve the challenges mentioned above. First, we separately enhance the amplitude and phase of the signal. We manually turn off the AGC to stabilize the amplitude data and eliminate additional interference. As far as we know, this is the first time that AGC jitter has been eliminated for amplitude. Regarding the phase, we eliminated the distortion and related linearity errors caused by the baseband through fitting, and achieved the stability of the phase. Secondly, we analyze the power of motion to get the relationship between power and motion speed, and then through orthogonal decomposition and principal component fusion, we can extract the motion features. Third, using the feature redundancy of convolutional extraction, each channel data feature is extracted separately. Then the features are expanded using linear variation, which substantially reduces the computation of the neural network.

We implemented the real-time inference of the neural network model on the Raspberry Pi 4B and conducted experiments to evaluate its performance in various scenarios. Experimental results show that WiRD is comparable to existing methods for gesture and body recognition within the domain, and has 87% accuracy for gesture recognition cross the domain, but the overall system processing time is reduced by 9× and the model inference time is reduced by 50×.

In summary, the main contributions of this work are as follows:

- For the first time, we realized the real-time reasoning of the model on the edge device on the cross-domain recognition, which satisfies the real-time condition.
- Under the condition of the network card based on the edge device, we realized for the first time to eliminate the influence of AGC on the amplitude, and we enhanced the phase part, so as to realize the accurate calibration of the information under the premise of fewer features.
- By analyzing the relationship between power and motion speed in a certain time interval, we orthogonally decompose and fuse the power, thereby extracting fine-grained motion features under the premise of low computational complexity.

2   Preliminaries

As we all know, the CSI in the frequency domain returned by every router is given by a complex-valued matrix H of dimension $R \times S$, where R is the total number of antenna ports of the device and S is the number of subcarriers used. The elements of H are given by

$$h_{r,s} = |h_{r,s}| \exp(j\angle h_{r,s}) \tag{1}$$

in which r is the antenna index, k is the subcarrier index and $\angle h_{r,s}$ refers to the angle of the complex channel coefficient $h_{r,s}$. The channel between a transmitter and receiver, which is estimated in a typical propagation environment, can be modeled as a multipath channel

$$h_{r,s} = \sum_{n=0}^{N} a_n \cdot e^{-j2\pi f_k \tau_n} \qquad (2)$$

where N is the total number of paths, a_n is the attenuation and τ_n is the time of flight of the respective path n.

In a standard WiFi setup, every transceiver derives' LO and sampling clocks from its own crystal oscillators. This results in a number of impairments to the CSI, especially on the phase of $h_{r,s}$. The estimated phase $\angle \overline{h_{r,s}}$ is given as

$$\angle \overline{h_{r,s}} = \angle h_{r,s} + (\lambda_{PDD} + \lambda_{SFO}) \cdot k + \lambda_{CFO} + \alpha + \beta \qquad (3)$$

where $\angle h_{r,s}$ is the real phase, $\angle \overline{h_{r,s}}$ is the phase which we get, λ_{PDD} is the phase slope caused by the PDD, λ_{SFO} is the phase slope caused by the SFO and λ_{CFO} is an additive phase offset caused by the CFO, α is a constant system phase offset, and β is the measurement noise [3,20,21]. α is a time-invariant phase offset as long as the PLL is locked. α contains phase offsets due to different cable lengths and the PLL locking points. As long as we ensure that the router is not rebooted or the WiFi channel is not switched we can ensure that α is constant so that we can disregard the impact it brings. And we can use the filter to eliminate the β. So we need to solve the remaining unknown quantities in order to get a stable phase. In the existing work, we use multiple antennas to do phase difference or by calculating conjugate multiplication to get an approximation of the real data. But in our edge devices, it is difficult to meet the conditions of multiple antennas (such as the Raspberry Pi has only one antenna), so how to achieve phase calibration on a single-antenna device is something we need to solve.

3   System Overview

It is a well-known knowledge that the raw CSI measurement contains multiple errors [7], if only the neural network is used to eliminate these errors, it not only requires a lot of computing resources but also easily affects the overall recognition accuracy. And because the existing edge devices have a single antenna on the NIC, this makes some common methods in calibrating the phase unusable. Firstly, we need to calibrate the CSI to ensure that we can use the stable amplitude and phase information for gesture recognition. Secondly, we need to extract the power change of the signal as a feature, and ensure that there can be no excessive calculation amount. Finally, we propose a lightweight network to ensure real-time inference on edge devices. The whole flow of our system is shown in the Fig. 1.

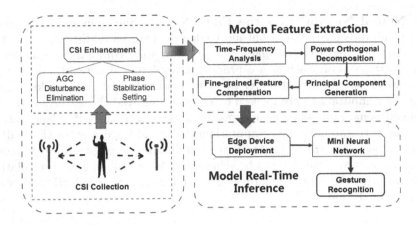

Fig. 1. System overview

CSI Enhancement on the Single Antenna. The CSI we acquire directly is an inaccurate data, and existing work generally eliminates errors by conjugate multiplication with multiple antennas, but here we need to get a stable phase data on a single antenna of edge devices. First, By shutdown the AGC and specifying the Rx gain manually, we obtain continuous and smooth CSI measurement across packets. Then, in order to eliminate the CSI distortion caused by the baseband, we collect the CSI measurement value between the two nodes as the baseband distortion profile. Then subtract the distortion profile from the collected data to get the distortion-free CSI. Finally, we use two consecutive packets to removed the linear fit of CSI phase response for first packet to obtain modified phase response.

Motion Feature Extraction on the Domain We know that human behavioral actions affect CSI, specifically in the frequency domain, by influencing the amplitude and phase of the signal. However, it also contains a lot of relevant information in the time domain. Also we know that the phase is much more sensitive to the gesture than the amplitude information, so the high responsiveness of the system can be improved by using an accurate phase. This ensures that we can accurately track more fine-grained movements (e.g., finger movements). Here we make the assumption that when a person performs an action we can consider the action as a combination of several atomic actions and decompose the action. The frequency of the atomic action and the power of the energy generated are considered to be constant for a certain period of time. So we filter the obtained raw data and then perform Short Time Fourier Transform (STFT) to divide it through the window to obtain the spectrogram in the time-frequency domain. Meanwhile, since we know that the power distribution of the spectrogram is related to the velocity of motion and the reflected area, but trying to extract it requires complex calculations [9,23]. So we want to create a new feature more representative of the motion velocity and reflected area to describe the motion, and to achieve accurate recognition of the pose by extracting this motion feature.

Mini Neural Networks on the Edge Nodes. Since our entire system is
deployed all directly on the front-most edge devices, no additional computing
devices are required to participate, but this limits the computing requirements
of the entire system. So here we propose a mini neural network architecture
for the weak computational power of edge devices. In neural networks, a large
number of computations are focused on convolution. And the features extracted
by convolutional operations have certain redundancy. If the redundant features
can be used reasonably, the computational effort of feature extraction will be
greatly reduced. We transform the extracted features through a linear function,
so that the feature expansion can be achieved with a small amount of calculation.
Compared with the conventional network, we can achieve a reduction of nearly
50% in computation.

4   System Design

4.1   CSI Enhancement on the Single Antenna

The raw CSI measurement contains multiple errors, including but not limited to
the carrier frequency offset (CFO), sampling frequency offset (SFO), sampling
time offset (STO), phase ambiguity, etc. It requires considerable modelling and
computation efforts to isolate and remove these measurement errors even by
human researchers [7]. In order to achieve the accuracy of fine-grained action
recognition, we propose an efficient three-step CSI stabilization method.

Step 1: removing AGC caused amplitude disturbance. COTS Wi-Fi
NICs employ automatic gain control (AGC) algorithm to perform the per-packet
Rx Gain control. AGC algorithm scales the input signal to a proper size to
maximally utilize the ADC range, which improves the signal noise ratio (SNR).
However, AGC calculates the amplification ratio in per-packet fashion, resulting
in non-smoothed CSI amplitude measurement even in stationary environment.
This amplitude variance inevitably introduces additional burden to the neural
network training and inference.

To address this issues, we analyzed AR9300's open-source driver and confirmed that AR9300 NIC has three stages of signal amplification in the analog frontend, which provide up to 66 dB amplification all-together. We modify
the QCA9300's driver and integrated the Rx gain control into PicoScenes platform [7]. By shutdown the AGC and specifying the Rx gain manually, we obtain
continuous and smooth CSI measurement across packets, as shown in Fig. 2.

To the best of our knowledge, this is the first platform that offer manual Rx
gain control for the COTS Wi-Fi NICs.

Step 2: removing the baseband-caused phase distortion. To remove
the magnitude and phase distortion, we follow Jiang [7] approach to eliminate
the baseband introduced distortion. We collected the mean phase and magnitude
CSI measurement between two nodes, which were later used as the baseband
distortion profile. Then, for each raw CSI measurement, the distortion profile is
then subtracted. In this way, we obtain the distortion-free CSI measurement.

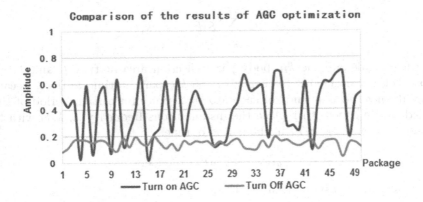

Fig. 2. The influence of AGC on amplitude

Step 3: linear phase error correction by phase sanitization. For CFO, SFO and STO, we use the phase sanitization scheme [8] to remove the linear error terms. It is worth noting that, this scheme removes not only the linear error terms, but also the phase slope value caused by propagation distance.

4.2 Motion Feature Extraction on the Domain.

We consider that each action can be divided into multiple atomic actions that cannot be further subdivided within a certain time period. And in each process we consider that the direction and speed of the finger movement remain constant. We then used the short-time fourier transform to obtain a spectral map of the action by using a window function to segment the action in the time domain.

$$X(n,\varpi) = \sum_{m=-\infty}^{\infty} x(m)\varpi(n-m)e^{-j\varpi m} \tag{4}$$

where $x(m)$ is the input signal, $\varpi(m)$ is a window function that is inverted in time and has an offset of n samples, and $X(n,\varpi)$ is a two-dimensional function of time and frequency, which links the time and frequency domains of a signal and allows us to perform time-frequency analysis of the signal.

And in previous studies [18] we know that the power distribution of the spectrogram is related to the velocity of the motion and the reflection region. If we want to extract the motion information from spectrogram we still need to face several challenges. First, spectrogram only shows the power value of a specific velocity component over time. Due to the superposition of velocity components at the receiver side, it cannot provide accurate fine-grained motion information. Secondly, the spectrogram contains too much redundant information, which can unnecessarily interfere with the results. Therefore, we define the power P by propagating the proportional loss factor C, which describes the connection between the velocity of motion, the reflected area and the spectrogram.

$$P(t) = C \cdot \sum_{k=1}^{K} S(k,t) \cdot f_d(k,t) \tag{5}$$

where $S(k,t)$ denote the k_{th} body part reflection area at time t, and $f_d(k,t)$ denote the instantaneous frequency of the k_{th} part at time t. Here, because we think that the frequency of each atomic action in a certain period of time is fixed, so we choose to replace the instantaneous frequency $f_d(k,t)$ with the average frequency $f_D(k,T)$ in the period of time,

$$f_d(k,t) \approx f_D(k,T), t \in T \tag{6}$$

So, our formula can be written like this,

$$P(T) \approx C \cdot \sum_{k=1}^{K} S(k,T) \cdot f_D(k,T) \tag{7}$$

At the same time, f_d and v are related in the following way [11, 12].

$$v = f_d \times \frac{\lambda}{2} \tag{8}$$

By observing the above formula, we find that there is actually a direct relationship between the power and the speed of the moving part of the body, $P \propto (S, v)$. However, since there is frame overlap in the process of using STFT, it is difficult for us to directly extract the direct relationship between power, body reflective area and motion speed. Although the existing work chooses to further calculate the acceleration, that brings a huge amount of computation and does not match the actual situation of edge devices. So we want to construct a new feature that can accurately describe the variation of power.

Here we use PCA to construct new features. The advantages of using PCA here are mainly the following three points. First, because the covariance matrix obtained in the PCA process is symmetric, the principal components are orthogonal, so they are not related to each other, thereby eliminating the mutual influence of the original data due to frame stacking. Second, it is possible to extract features that can better describe the reflection area and movement speed of the body from the spectrogram, and reconstruct some new and more representative attributes. Third, replace most indicators with a few indicators to reduce the amount of calculations.

When we get the principal components by PCA, we find from the Fig. 3 that the same gestures have similar features in power distribution in different people and environments. So we can use the extracted principal component power distribution as the main feature to identify the gesture.

Fine-Grained Feature Compensation. Different principal components will have different granularity of features. so they need to compensate each other for fine-grained features. As we know, the principal components are orthogonal, not related to each other, and the contribution rate of each principal component

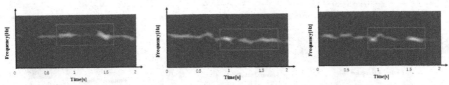

(a) Person1 do the same ges-(b) Person2 do the same ges-(c) Person3 do the same gesture in environment A   ture in environment A   ture in environment B

Fig. 3. Power distribution of different people in different environments

is gradually decreasing. Therefore, when we fuse multiple principal component features, we need to proceed according to their contribution.

$$\begin{cases} PCA = \alpha \cdot V_1 \cdot pca[1] + \beta \cdot V_2 \cdot pca[1] + \cdots + \lambda \cdot V_n \cdot pca[n] \\ s.t. \qquad \alpha + \beta + \cdots \lambda = 1 \end{cases} \tag{9}$$

where V_i is the eigenvalues of the diagonal matrix by diagonalizing the covariance matrix, and α, β etc. are scale factors. In this way, we can ensure that while extracting the motion features, some fine-grained features are also fused to ensure the accuracy of the features.

4.3 Mini Neural Network Design on the Edge Nodes

Due to the limitation of computational power on edge devices, we seek faster inference speed and fewer computational operations. Here we design a kind of miniature network module suitable for weak computing power devices. When faced with multi-channel inputs, most people use full-channel convolution (General Convolution). We use convolution with feature extraction on each channel. In fact, the operation of generating an arbitrary convolutional layer of feature maps can be expressed as:

$$Y = X * f + b \tag{10}$$

Here $*$ is the convolution operation, x is the input data of size $n \times h \times w$, f is the corresponding weight, b is the bias. However, the ordinary convolution operation produces a large number of redundant features and wastes computing power. In order to make rational use of computing resources, we will make good use of the redundancy of the existing feature maps [5]. Similarly, to obtain the feature maps for $2n$ feature channels, we first use depthwise convolution on n of the channels to obtain the feature maps on the respective channels. Then we perform cheap linear operations on the obtained n feature maps and obtain similar feature maps by linear transformation, which are generated by using redundancy. Specifically expressed as follows:

$$Y' = \emptyset_i(Y_i), \forall i = 1, ..., n \tag{11}$$

Here Y_i is the i-th original feature map in Y, $\emptyset_i$ is the i-th linear operations, which used to generate the i-th redundant feature map.

$$N = Y \oplus Y' \tag{12}$$

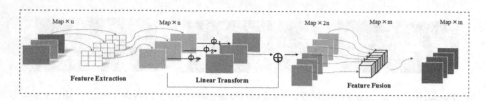

Fig. 4. Mini network block

Finally, we connect the feature maps obtained twice as the input for the next operation. However, all the feature maps we get here are extracted from a single channel and there is no exchange of information between each channel, which will generate feature barriers as the depth of the network deepens. To solve this problem, we will fuse the features of different channels by used $1 * 1$ convolution to obtain m feature maps ($m \leq 2n$). The framework of the whole neural network is shown in Fig. 4.

5   Implement and Evaluation

Data Collection Platform. We use the PicoScenes platform [7] for CSI collection, and achieve CSI enhancement on a single antenna.

Hardware. Here we are using Raspberry Pi 4B as a routing node. The Raspberry Pi 4B is chosen here for three main reasons. Raspberry Pi is cheap, which can meet the large-scale deployment. The Raspberry Pi has a wireless network card, which can realize the function of sending and receiving WiFi signals and can be used as a router. The performance of the Raspberry Pi is moderate among edge devices and can be used as a representative of most edge devices.

Data Sets. Before conducting all experiments, we first collected data in three environments and collected data for 7 body actions. The 7 actions are *Standing Up, Sitting Down, Walking, Falling, Lying, Getting Up, Picking Up*. Also, to verify the fine-grained, 7 sets of hand gestures were captured. The 7 hand gestures are *Draw Rectangle, Draw Triangle, Drawing Circles, Draw X, Draw Z, Waving left and right, Waving up and down*.

5.1   PCA Feature Construction Analysis

We use PCA for power analysis to construct new power-related features from the time-frequency diagram. We mainly analyzed the first five principal components, because the subsequent principal components contain less obvious features and are less effective for practical use. Through the Fig. 5 we find that the first principal component is a feature extraction of the whole action process and some redundant information is removed. And the subsequent principal component features mainly extract the most obvious features. It can be seen from the figure

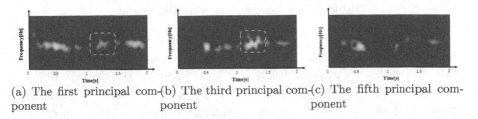

(a) The first principal com-(b) The third principal com-(c) The fifth principal component ponent ponent

Fig. 5. This is the spectrogram for the Z gesture, we found that PCA can extract the most concentrated features in the entire process, such as the content circled in the red box. At the same time, multiple principal components can complement each other with some fine-grained features, such as the content circled in blue. (Color figure online)

that they are mainly concerned with the part with greater power, that is, the time period during which the speed reaches the highest speed.

So we can learn that by using PCA we can eliminate the mutual influence of the original data due to frame stacking and also separate the gesture features from the surrounding environment, thus achieving a more fine-grained feature representation. Therefore, feature fusion of the obtained principal component features can ensure that the features are rich in information. As the part circled in red box in the Fig. 5, it is the most obvious part of the whole feature, which is the fastest part of the whole motion process, so multiple principal components have this part. The blue box is the complement of the remaining principal components to the fine-grained features to ensure the comprehensiveness of the features.

5.2 Fine-Grained Hand Gestures Recognition

Gesture recognition is a fine-grained action recognition, and to ensure the accuracy of the recognition, here we achieve the phase calibration by borrowing only a single antenna. Since the phase information is highly responsive, it is more sensitive to small action changes. By comparison, From the Fig. 6 we find that accurate phase information helps the recognition of small movements. Meanwhile, we put the gesture information of different volunteers together for recognition and found that our method is still effective.

5.3 Recognition of Body Actions in Different Environments

We tested the accuracy of body action recognition in different environments. From Fig. 7, we found our miniature neural network can achieve high recognition accuracy in different environments. Compared with an ordinary convolutional neural network, our accuracy is comparable to it. So this proves that our miniature neural network has excellent results. Table 1 shows the recognition accuracy of each body movement. From the table, we can see that the recognition of falling movements is the most accurate but the recognition of getting up is inaccurate.

Table 1. Confusion matrix of related actions

	Lie down	Fall	Pick up	Walk	Sit down	Stand up	Get up
Lie down	**92.46%**	0.15%	1.23%	1.92%	1.12%	2.15%	0.96%
Fall	0.45%	**97.60%**	0.91%	0	0.86%	0.13%	0.10%
Pick up	0.65%	0.24%	**95.89%**	0.21%	1.75%	0.64%	0.62%
Walk	1.84%	0.44%	1.92%	**91.22%**	3.06%	0.71%	0.82%
Sit down	0.25%	0.27%	1.92%	0.4%	**96.58%**	0.31%	0.27%
Stand up	4.75%	0.5%	0.70%	1.05%	0.5%	**89.25%**	3.25%
Get up	1.00%	0.33%	1.00%	0.75%	1.30%	6.83%	**88.33%**

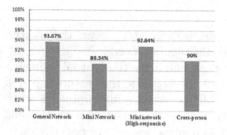

Fig. 6. Fine-grained hand gestures recognition.

Fig. 7. Recognition of body actions in different environments and cross domain.

At the same time, we also conduct cross-domain experiments. The experimental results show that the accuracy is substantially reduced. We analyzed the results that body actions have a larger area of motion compared to hand gestures, making the power distribution somewhat affected by body size, which leads to a decrease in accuracy. And hand gestures are less affected by the reflected area and are therefore more accurate. Also to ensure low computing, we did not extract more complex features, such as BVP. However, by extracting the features of power variation, it still reflects good results on the cross domain. In other words, this is a balanced solution in terms of computation and accuracy.

5.4   Comparison of Gesture Recognition Approaches

We compared CARM [18], Widar3.0 [23], and WiHF [9], where the latter two are feasible for cross-domain recognition. Specifically, CARM directly uses the DFS configuration file as a learning feature without further processing and it also adopts HMM model. Widar3.0 realizes cross-domain detection by extracting domain-independent BVP features. WIHF calculates the derivative of the DFS configuration file to obtain the relationship between power and acceleration, and uses the derivative result as a feature for detection, which also achieves cross-domain. However, none of them consider the feature extraction time and model

Table 2. Comparison of gesture recognition approaches

	CRAM	Widar3.0	WiHF	WiRD
Accuracy	80%	92.4%	92.07%	87%
Feature extraction	0.38 s	52.80 s	1.10 s	0.70 s
Model types	HMM	CNN+GRU	CNN+GRU	CNN
Model Inference (Raspberry Pi 4B)	–	6.57 s	6.55 s	**0.13 s**
Total time	–	59.37 s	7.65 s	**0.83 s**
Gesture duration	1.86 s	1.62 s	1.62 s	1.86 s

inference speed, so this determines that their models cannot be implemented for deployment on edge devices. Here we have performed a comprehensive test of the above methods, and from the Table 2 we can find that our system can achieve real-time detection on edge devices. Our model inference is 50X faster than the fastest, and our feature extraction also takes very little time.

6   Related Work

6.1   RSSI Based

RSSI-based human activity recognition systems exploit the signal intensity changes caused by human activity [13]. This approach can only perform coarse-grained activity recognition, such as standing up, sitting down, etc. Accurate recognition of fine-grained activities such as finger movements is often not possible. Sigg et al. improved the granularity of RSSI thus achieving an accuracy of 72% for gesture recognition [14]. Therefore, in the follow-up wireless sensing research, almost no one continues to choose to use RSSI.

6.2   Radar Based

Similarly, human activity detection can be performed using radar technology. Adib et al. [2] used a specially designed FM carrier wave (FMCW) signal with broad bandwidth from 5.56 GHz to 7.25 GHz for indoor positioning with an error of almost 8 cm. In addition, this system has good synchronization and can calculate the time of flight (ToF) of electromagnetic waves through transmission, refraction and reflection before reception. On the other hand, the bandwidth available for radar signals is much larger compared to WIFI signals.

6.3   CSI Based

Existing work is based on Intel 5300 or Atheros 9300 NICs to extract CSI and perform conjugate multiplication operations with multiple antennas to achieve data calibration. E-eyes [19] utilizes statistical distribution and time series characteristics for walking and in-place activities recognition. CARM calculates the power distribution of DFS components as a learning feature of the HMM model. However, most signal recognition cannot do gesture detection across domains. Widar 3.0 extracted domain-independent features BVP from CSI, and Jiang et al. [6] extracted 3DVP to achieve 3D pose reconstruction. In contrast, WiHF found that the derivative of the power gives the relationship between body motion acceleration and power, thus also enabling cross-domain identification.

7 Conclusion

In this paper, We propose the WiRD system to achieve CSI enhancement under the condition of conforming to the single antenna of the edge device, and to achieve real-time body and hand gesture detection that can be achieved on the edge device. Firstly, in order to ensure the accuracy of subsequent detection, we achieve the enhancement of CSI in compliance with the premise that the edge device has only a single antenna, eliminating the disturbance caused by AGC and solving the problem of phase instability. We then propose a mini neural network, implement it for deployment on edge devices, and test it on two datasets. Experimental results show that WiRD is comparable to existing methods for gesture and body recognition within the domain, and has 87% accuracy for gesture recognition cross the domain, but the overall system processing time is reduced by 9× and the model inference time is reduced by 50×. As far as we know, we are the first to fully consider the deployment of the system on the edge device and implement real-time inference of the model on the edge device.

Acknowledgment. This work was supported in part by International Cooperation Project of Shaanxi Province (No. 2020KW-004), the China Postdoctoral Science Foundation (No. 2017M613187), and the Shaanxi Science and Technology Innovation Team Support Project under grant agreement (No. 2018TD-026).

References

1. Abdelnasser, H., Youssef, M., Harras, K.A.: WiGest: a ubiquitous WiFi-based gesture recognition system. In: 2015 IEEE Conference on Computer Communications (INFOCOM), pp. 1472–1480 (2015)
2. Adib, F., Kabelac, Z., Katabi, D., Miller, R.C.: 3D tracking via body radio reflections. In: Proceedings of the 11th USENIX Conference on Networked Systems Design and Implementation, NSDI 2014, pp. 317–329. USENIX Association, USA (2014)
3. Chen, Y., Su, X., Hu, Y., Zeng, B.: Residual carrier frequency offset estimation and compensation for commodity WiFi. IEEE Trans. Mob. Comput. **19**(12), 2891–2902 (2020)
4. Gkioxari, G., Girshick, R., Dollár, P., He, K.: Detecting and recognizing human-object interactions. In: 2018 IEEE/CVF Conference on Computer Vision and Pattern Recognition, pp. 8359–8367 (2018)

5. Han, K., Wang, Y., Tian, Q., Guo, J., Xu, C., Xu, C.: GhostNet: more features from cheap operations. In: 2020 IEEE/CVF Conference on Computer Vision and Pattern Recognition (CVPR), pp. 1577–1586 (2020)
6. Jiang, W., et al.: Towards 3D human pose construction using WiFi. In: Proceedings of the 26th Annual International Conference on Mobile Computing and Networking, MobiCom 2020. Association for Computing Machinery, New York (2020)
7. Jiang, Z., et al.: Eliminating the barriers: demystifying Wi-Fi baseband design and introducing the PicoScenes Wi-Fi sensing platform. IEEE Internet Things J. 1 (2021). https://doi.org/10.1109/JIOT.2021.3104666
8. Kotaru, M., Joshi, K., Bharadia, D., Katti, S.: SpotFi: decimeter level localization using WiFi. ACM SIGCOMM Comput. Commun. Rev. **45**(4), 269–282 (2015)
9. Li, C., Liu, M., Cao, Z.: WiHF: enable user identified gesture recognition with WiFi. In: IEEE INFOCOM 2020 - IEEE Conference on Computer Communications, pp. 586–595 (2020)
10. Li, X., Li, D.: GPFS: a graph-based human pose forecasting system for smart home with online learning. ACM Trans. Sens. Netw. **17**(3), 1–19 (2021)
11. Qian, K., Wu, C., Yang, Z., Liu, Y., Jamieson, K.: Widar: decimeter-level passive tracking via velocity monitoring with commodity Wi-Fi. In: Proceedings of the 18th ACM International Symposium on Mobile Ad Hoc Networking and Computing, Mobihoc 2017. Association for Computing Machinery, New York (2017)
12. Qian, K., Wu, C., Zhang, Y., Zhang, G., Yang, Z., Liu, Y.: Widar2.0: passive human tracking with a single Wi-Fi link. In: Proceedings of the 16th Annual International Conference on Mobile Systems, Applications, and Services, MobiSys 2018, pp. 350–361. Association for Computing Machinery, New York (2018)
13. Sigg, S., Blanke, U., Tröster, G.: The telepathic phone: frictionless activity recognition from WiFi-RSSI. In: 2014 IEEE International Conference on Pervasive Computing and Communications (PerCom), pp. 148–155 (2014)
14. Sigg, S., Scholz, M., Shi, S., Ji, Y., Beigl, M.: RF-sensing of activities from non-cooperative subjects in device-free recognition systems using ambient and local signals. IEEE Trans. Mob. Comput. **13**(4), 907–920 (2014)
15. Wang, T., Bhuiyan, M.Z.A., Wang, G., Qi, L., Wu, J., Hayajneh, T.: Preserving balance between privacy and data integrity in edge-assisted Internet of Things. IEEE Internet Things J. **7**(4), 2679–2689 (2020)
16. Wang, T., Luo, H., Zeng, X., Yu, Z., Liu, A., Sangaiah, A.K.: Mobility based trust evaluation for heterogeneous electric vehicles network in smart cities. IEEE Trans. Intell. Transp. Syst. **22**(3), 1797–1806 (2021)
17. Wang, T., et al.: Propagation modeling and defending of a mobile sensor worm in wireless sensor and actuator networks. Sensors **17**(1), 139 (2017)
18. Wang, W., Liu, A.X., Shahzad, M., Ling, K., Lu, S.: Device-free human activity recognition using commercial WiFi devices. IEEE J. Sel. Areas Commun. **35**(5), 1118–1131 (2017)
19. Wang, Y., Liu, J., Chen, Y., Gruteser, M., Yang, J., Liu, H.: E-eyes: device-free location-oriented activity identification using fine-grained WiFi signatures. In: Proceedings of the 20th Annual International Conference on Mobile Computing and Networking, MobiCom 2014, pp. 617–628. Association for Computing Machinery, New York (2014)
20. Xie, Y., Li, Z., Li, M.: Precise power delay profiling with commodity WiFi. In: Proceedings of the 21st Annual International Conference on Mobile Computing and Networking, MobiCom 2015, pp. 53–64. Association for Computing Machinery, New York (2015)

21. Zhang, D., Hu, Y., Chen, Y., Zeng, B.: Calibrating phase offsets for commodity WiFi. IEEE Syst. J. **14**(1), 661–664 (2020)
22. Zhang, Y., Zheng, Y., Zhang, G., Qian, K., Qian, C., Yang, Z.: GaitSense: towards ubiquitous gait-based human identification with Wi-Fi. ACM Trans. Sen. Netw. **18**(1), 1–24 (2021)
23. Zheng, Y., et al.: Zero-effort cross-domain gesture recognition with Wi-Fi. In: Proceedings of the 17th Annual International Conference on Mobile Systems, Applications, and Services, MobiSys 2019, pp. 313–325. Association for Computing Machinery, New York (2019)

Deep Learning with Enhanced Convergence and Its Application in MEC Task Offloading

Zheng Wan[1], Xiaogang Dong[1,2]($\boxtimes$), and Changshou Deng[2]

[1] School of Information Management, Jiangxi University of Finance and Economics, Nanchang 330013, China
dxg110@aliyun.com
[2] School of Computer and Big Data Science, Jiujiang University, Jiujiang 332005, China

Abstract. As an emerging computing paradigm, the mobile edge computing (MEC) has become the top topic in various research fields. Nevertheless, task offloading, as a key issue in MEC environment, is still an immense challenge because it is often NP-hard. Currently, many researchers adopt deep learning frameworks to solve task offloading problem of MEC. Unfortunately, most of these works directly use various deep learning frameworks. It is insufficient consideration that how to improve the convergence performance of deep learning in solving MEC task offloading problem. To cope with this issue, we propose two methods to enhance the convergence of deep learning in this paper, which are named as uniform design method (UDM) and hadamard matrix method (HMM), respectively. UDM and HMM can enhance exploiting ability of the space near the specific offloading decision, benefiting to improve the convergence performance of deep learning algorithms. An improved deep learning algorithm is built by integrating UDM or HMM. The validity of our proposed algorithm is verified through extensive simulation experiments. The results show that our proposed algorithm can achieve better convergence performance than the benchmark algorithm under different learning rates and memory sizes.

Keywords: Mobile edge computing · Task offloading · Deep learning · Uniform design · Hadamard matrix

1 Introduction

With the sustained development of mobile networks and communication technologies over the past several years, a good deal of intelligence applications (e.g., automatic navigation, face recognition, unmanned driving, virtual reality, augmented reality, etc.) are gaining growing popularity. This kind of applications usually have high requirements for response time and stable execution. It poses tremendous challenges to resources constrained mobile devices.

© Springer Nature Switzerland AG 2022
Y. Lai et al. (Eds.): ICA3PP 2021, LNCS 13156, pp. 361–375, 2022.
https://doi.org/10.1007/978-3-030-95388-1_24

Mobile edge computing (MEC) [1,2], a supplement to cloud computing, has been considered as a promising computing paradigm. The architecture of MEC was firstly proposed by European Telecommunications Standards Institute in 2014, enabling the provision of resources close to users via radio access network. In MEC network environment, mobile devices can offload the computation-intensive and time-sensitive tasks to edge servers for execution. This helps mobile devices with saving power consumption as well as significantly reduce the response time of application, making mobile user can enjoy higher quality of experience (QoE).

However, MEC still faces many of application challenges, such as, more efficient edge server deploy [3] and task offloading solution. Among these challenges, the task offloading problem is widely concerned. Task offloading problem is usually NP-hard [4], since at least combination optimization of communication and computing resources along with the contention of edge devices is required [5]. Therefore, the efficient and effective task offloading scheme has received great attention from many of researchers.

Deep learning (DL) that uses deep neural network (DNN) constituting of multiple processing layers has achieved many breakthroughs in different areas [6], such as natural language process [7], game [8], computer vision [9]. Inspired by these successful applications in these fields, DL has received great attention from researchers of wireless communications field in recent years, e.g., some works have adopted DL to solving the task offloading problem in MEC environment [10–13]. But, these works often directly use existing deep learning framework to solve the task offloading problem, and cannot adequately consider how to speed up the convergence of deep learning algorithm, thus failing to effectively improve the response speed of offloading solution, which affects the improvement of user's QoE.

To fill this gap, we design two schemes to speed up the convergence of deep learning algorithm, and propose an improved deep learning algorithm (I-DDLO) for MEC task offloading by integrating them into existing DDLO algorithm. Simulation results prove the effectiveness of our scheme. The major contributions of this paper are summarized as follows.

- We propose an enhancing convergence method for DL based on uniform design (UDM). The method uses advanced uniform experimental design to search specific local space. In the case of a small increase in computing overhead, the better offloading action can be found as soon as possible. Therefore, it is beneficial to speed up the convergence of DL.
- Another enhancing convergence method for DL based on hadamard matrix (HMM) was constructed. HMM takes full advantage of the row orthogonality of hadamard matrix to search the better offloading action. Consequently, HMM can also speed up the convergence of DL.
- We construct a modified deep learning algorithm with enhancing convergence based on UDM or HMM. Extensive simulation experiments are conducted to evaluate the performance of the two methods. The results show that they

can significantly improve the convergence rate of deep learning algorithm in solving the task offloading problem.

2   Related Works

There are many of works about computation task offloading in MEC environment. In these works, one direction is to use various classical optimal algorithms to solve the task offloading problem. Li et al. [14] considered an ultra-dense networks constituted of different macro base stations and small-cell base stations. They proposed a cuckoo search algorithm aided green communication and computation offloading scheme. The global convergence analysis and simulation results show that the scheme could achieve a satisfying performance. Zhao et al. [15] studied how to efficiently offload dependent tasks to edge nodes with limited service caching. An efficient convex programming based algorithm was proposed for the sake of solving this problem. Simulation results show that this algorithm can significantly reduce task completion time by about 27–51% compared with other alternatives. Ma et al. [16] developed an iterative algorithm based on Gibbs sampling for solving the problem of cooperative service caching and task scheduling in mobile edge computing. The algorithm can jointly reduce the service response time and the outsourcing traffics compared with the benchmark algorithms.

Furthermore, duo to DL technology has achieved remarkable success in various fields, making use of deep learning to obtain the optimal offloading policy draw researcher's extensive attention. Mukherjee et al. [17] studied the task offloading strategy in unmanned aerial vehicle-enabled MEC systems. A distributed DNN was used to find the optimal offloading decision of end-users. In this algorithm, multiple DNNs were trained by the same training instance, the DNN that gives the least training loss was selected finally. Simulation results show that the algorithm can achieve near-optimal performance with numerous system parameter settings. Ali et al. [18] proposed a novel energy-efficient deep learning based offloading scheme. The scheme can select an optimal offloading set of application components through considering multiple factors synthetically, such as remaining energy of user, energy consumption by application components, network conditions, computational load, amount of data transfer, and communication delay. Huang et al. [6] investigated a mobile edge computing network with single access point and multiple wireless devices. To conserve energy and maintain quality of service for WDs, a mixed integer programming problem was formulated. They proposed a distributed deep learning algorithm which used multiple parallel deep neural networks for sake of solving the problem. The algorithm can achieve better convergence performance when the number of DNN is greater than 1. Other more advanced deep learning algorithms, such as, Deep Reinforcement Learning [19–21], Recurrent Neural Network [22,23], Convolutional Neural Network[24], were also been applied to the task offloading problem in MEC environment. To save space, the details of these tasks are omitted here.

3   Network Model and Optimization Problem

In MEC network environment, task offloading decision means that determining whether the task is to be executed locally or offloaded to the edge server for execution. Generally speaking, there is different network model for the different application scenario. In this work, we focus on how to speed up the convergence of deep learning algorithm in solving task offloading problem. So, we use the network model of literature [6], because their experimental results show that the distributed deep learning algorithm (DDLO) proposed by them can not converge when one DNN is used. The following is a brief description of the model and DDLO.

This model includes one edge server, one wireless access point and n wireless devices (WDs). Each WDs has m independent task needing to execute. All WDs's tasks constitute a set of system task $\mathcal{M}$. The $|\mathcal{M}|$ is $n \times m$. d_{nm} denotes the workload of mth task of nth wireless devices. x_{nm} denotes the offloading decision. $x_{nm} = 1$ represents that the wireless device n decides to offload its mth task to the edge server. Otherwise, $x_{nm} = 0$ represents that the wireless device n decides to execute its mth task locally.

Based on this model, they constructed the energy and delay model of edge computing and local computing. Next, the system utility function $Q(\mathbf{d}, \mathbf{x}, \mathbf{c})$ was defined as the weighted sum of energy consumption and task completion delay.

$$Q(\mathbf{d}, \mathbf{x}, \mathbf{c}) = \sum_{n=1}^{N}(\sum_{m=1}^{M}(E_{nm}^l(1 - x_{nm}) + E_{nm}^c x_{nm}) + \beta max(T_n^l, T_n^c)) \quad (1)$$

where E_{nm}^l, E_{nm}^c are the energy model of local and offloading execution. T_n^l, T_n^c are delay model of local and offloading execution. β denotes the weight of energy consumption and task completion. Aimed to minimize $Q(\mathbf{d}, \mathbf{x}, \mathbf{c})$, an optimization problem $P1$ was formulated as follows.

$$P1 : Q^*(d) = \underset{\mathbf{x}, \mathbf{c}}{\text{minimize}} \quad Q(\boldsymbol{d}, \boldsymbol{x}, \boldsymbol{c}) \quad (2)$$

$$\text{subject to :}$$

$$\sum_{n=1}^{N} c_n < C \quad (2a)$$

$$c_n \geq 0, \forall n \in \mathcal{N} \quad (2b)$$

$$x_{nm} \in \{0, 1\} \quad (2c)$$

The more details of $E_{nm}^l, E_{nm}^c, T_n^l, T_n^c, Q(\mathbf{d}, \mathbf{x}, \mathbf{c})$ and $P1$ see the literature [6]. To address problem $P1$, DDLO algorithm was proposed. The experiments show that DDLO cannot achieve good convergence (the convergence accuracy is less than 88%) when only one DNN is used. Therefore, DDLO uses multiple parallel neural networks to achieve good convergence performance. But, the change from "single DNN" to "multiple DNNs" not only complicates algorithm structure but also leads to a doubling of training complexity.

To address the issue, we propose two methods (UDM and HMM) to enhance the convergence of deep learning algorithms when only one DNN, and introduce a modified DDLO algorithm based on them.

4   Two Methods of Enhancing Convergence

4.1   Uniform Design Based Enhancing Convergence Method

Uniform design (UD) is one of powerful and high quality experimental design tools, which is proposed by Wang and Fang [25]. The number of experiments of uniform design is far less than other popular experimental design tools(e.g., orthogonal design). For instance, for an experiment with k factors that each one has q levels, the experiment's number of orthogonal design and uniform design are q^2 and q, respectively. More details about the uniform design can be found in [25]. Because of this advantages, UD has been applied to many of areas including computer experiments.

Generally speaking, uniform design is used to obtain the optimal parameter setting, to achieve robust performance with low development and manufacturing cost. Inspired by this, we introduce uniform design based enhancing convergence method (UDM) for deep learning. The major idea of UDM is to find better offloading decision via uniform design after the neural network generates an offloading decision.

The general steps for using of uniform design were given in [26]. Thereinto, determining appropriate uniform design table is the most critical step. Normally, the notation $U_n(n^s)$ represents an uniform design table, which has n rows and s columns. The numbers of row mean that the times of experiments to be executed, yet the numbers of column means that maximum factors to be chosen. There are a lot of uniform design tables for user to utilize conveniently. Table 1 gives an example of uniform design table $U_7(7^6)$. The uniform design table $U_6(6^6)$ can be constructed from $U_7(7^6)$ by deleting the last row [27]. The reason is that the last row of $U_7(7^6)$ represents the original offloading action in our UDM. In our work, we choose $U_6(6^6)$ to arrange experimental plan.

To illustrate specific process of the UDM, we given a simple example by Fig. 1, in which of x1 and x2 are two offloading decisions. One factor of $x1$ and $x2$ was split into six levels, noted $L1, ..., L6$ with red forecolor, and $L1, ..., L6$ with green forecolor, respectively. The six circles with yellow forecolor are six new values about this factor produced by mixed $x1$ and $x2$ based on the first and second column of $U_6(6^6)$. Obviously, a better offloading decision is more likely to be found between these six new values.

Algorithm 1 describes the details of UDM. There are two offloading decisions as input parameters. One comes from the output of DNN. The other is an auxiliary offloading decision generated by a random way at near the former. Owing to offloading decision is a binary string consisting of 0 and 1, splitting the level is inconvenient. Hence, we divide offloading decision into k (k is not greater than

Table 1. Uniform design table $U_7(7^6)$

No	1	2	3	4	5	6
1	1	2	3	4	5	6
2	2	4	6	1	3	5
3	3	6	2	5	1	4
4	4	1	5	2	6	3
5	5	3	1	6	4	2
6	6	5	4	3	2	1
7	7	7	7	7	7	7

the number of factors) segments (as factors) and convert them to corresponding decimal number. This operation facilitates splitting and combination of levels. In addition, the **discrete operations** in step 2 means that calculate the difference between $x1$ and $x2$ on each segment, and split to six parts uniformly (as levels).

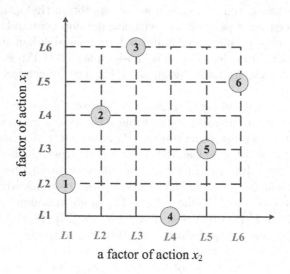

Fig. 1. An example of UDM method

4.2 Hadamard Matrix Based Enhancing Convergence Method

A hadamard matrix is a square matrix whose entries are $+1$ or -1, and rows are mutually orthogonal. The earliest construction method of Hadamard matrix was proposed by James Joseph Sylvester [28]. Specifically, assuming H_n is a n-order hadamard matrix, then the partitioned matrix as Eq. (3) is a $2n$-order hadamard matrix.

Algorithm 1. Uniform design based method, UDM

Require: input two offloading decisions $x1$ and $x2$.
Ensure: a set of six offloading decisions ux.
1: divide $x1$ and $x2$ into k segments and convert to decimal number.
2: for each segment(factor),perform *discrete operations* and produce 6 levels.
3: for each segment, according to $U_6(6^6)$, produce 6 new values by mixed $x1$ and $x2$.
4: performs a rounding operation and converts to binary string.
5: produces 6 new offloading decisions by combining the six values on each segment.
6: add each new offloading decision into ux.

$$\begin{bmatrix} H_n & H_n \\ H_n & -H_n \end{bmatrix} \tag{3}$$

Consequently, giving the 1-order hadamard matrix $H_1 = [1]$, we can obtain the 2-order and 4-order hadamard matrix as Eq. (4) and (5), respectively.

$$H_2 = \begin{bmatrix} 1 & 1 \\ 1 & -1 \end{bmatrix} \tag{4}$$

$$H_4 = \begin{bmatrix} 1 & 1 & 1 & 1 \\ 1 & -1 & 1 & -1 \\ 1 & 1 & -1 & -1 \\ 1 & -1 & -1 & 1 \end{bmatrix} \tag{5}$$

And so on, other higher order hadamard matrix can be obtained. It is worth noting that the order of hadamard matrix must be 1, 2, or a multiple of 2 [29]. So, the hadamard matrix with 2^k order H_{2^k} can obtained through Eq. (6).

$$H_{2^k} = \begin{bmatrix} H_{2^{k-1}} & H_{2^{k-1}} \\ H_{2^{k-1}} & -H_{2^{k-1}} \end{bmatrix} = H_2 \otimes H_{2^{k-1}} \tag{6}$$

Where, $\otimes$ denotes the Kronecker product, k is a non-negative integer, and $k \geq 2$. The hadamard matrix has a significant character as Property 1.

Property 1. *for a n-order Hadamard matrix H_n,*

$$H_n * H_n^T = nI \tag{7}$$

where H_n^T is the transpose matrix of H_n, I is an identity matrix, respectively.

In geometric terms, this means that each pair of rows in the hadamard matrix represents two perpendicular vectors [30], and they are orthogonal to each other. This is the most important property of hadamard matrix. Inspired by this property, we propose a novel method for constructing multiple offloading decisions in near space of the given decision, named hadamard matrix based method HMM. These offloading decisions constructed by HMM distribute in the local space of the specified decision, and meet the characteristics of vertical and orthogonal. It is beneficial to improve the probability of finding better offloading decision.

Algorithm 2 is the details of HMM. Noted that notation "¬" in step 12 represents reverse operation. Because of offloading decision is a vector consisting of 0 or 1, so the reverse operation refers to 0 transform to 1, 1 transform to 0 in HMM.

Algorithm 2. Hadamard matrix based method, HMM

Require: Input a offloading action x.
Ensure: a set of multiple offloading actions mx.
 1: **Initialization:**
 2:    Initializes a n-order hadamard matrix H_n.
 3:    computes the size of offloading x,and stores to the variate b.
 4:    divide x into n segments through $n-1$ random number.
 5: **For** i=1,2,...,n do
 6:    reads the ith row of H_n,and stores to vector e.
 7:    defines a null vector t with the same size of x, and divides it into the same
       n segments.
 8:    **For** j=1,2,...,n do
 9:      **if** e[i]==1
10:        sets each element of t's jth segment to be equal to each element of x's
           jth segment.
11:      **else**
12:        each element of t's jth segment $= \neg$ [each element of x's jth segment].
13:      **end if**
14:    **end for**
15:    adds offloading decision t into mx.
16: **end for**

4.3   Improving the DDLO Algorithm

Our idea is that searching the local space around the offloading decision which is generated by DNN. Therefore, UDM and HMM are executed timely after the neural network produces output. To simply and specifically describe the effectiveness of UDM and HMM, we construct the improve DDLO algorithm (I-DDLO) via incorporating UDM or HMM into DDLO algorithm. The difference between I-DDLO and DDLO includes two aspects. One is that I-DDLO only has one DNN. The other is that the UDM or HDM were used to generate multiple candidate offloading decisions after the neural network produces output. Algorithm 3 gives the pseudo-code of I-DDLO. In the step 12, the gradient descent algorithm is used for training, and the loss function is the cross-entropy loss.

5   Performance Evaluation

In this section, we evaluate the performance of two methods (UDM and HMM). We choose the DDLO as comparison algorithm in the process of simulation. In order to make a fair comparison, the neural network structure and the parameter settings of the simulation experiment are consistent with those in [6]. For distinguishing UDM and HMM, the I-DDLO algorithm that incorporates these two methods are named I-DDLO-UDM and I-DDLO-HMM, respectively. Uniform design table $U_6(6^6)$ is used in algorithm I-DDLO-UDM, and I-DDLO-HMM uses the 4-order hadamard matrix H_4. The objective of UDM and HMM is to speed up the convergence of deep learning algorithm. Therefore, our simulation

Algorithm 3. Improved DDLO(I-DDLO)

Require: Inputs workloads d_t of all user's task at time t.
Ensure: Optimal offloading action.
1: **Initialization:**
2:    **initializes one DNN with random parameters** θ_t.
3:    empties the memory structure.
4: **For t=1,2,...,G do**
5:    inputs all workloads to DNN.
6:    generates one offloading action x from DNN with θ_t.
7:    **uses the UDM or HMM to exploit action space, and generates multiple**
     candidate offloading actions set $\{x_k\}$ **from** x.
8:    solves bandwidth allocation optimization problem.
9:    selects the best offloading decision as the output.
10:   stores the best action and corresponding workload into the memory structure.
11:   randomly samples one batch of training data from the memory structure.
12:   trains the DNN and update θ_t.
13: **end for**

---

experiments mainly focus on the verification of convergence. Similar to [6], we use *Gain ratio* as the measurement of convergence. The definition of *Gain ratio* is Eq. 8. In order to maintain fairness, parameters setting of I-DDLO-UDM and I-DDLO-HMM are same to DDLO.

$$Gain \quad ratio = \frac{Q(d,x)}{Q^*(d,x')} \tag{8}$$

where x' is the optimal offloading decision obtained by a greedy method, $Q^*(d,x')$ is the system utility of x'.

Figure 2, 3, and 4 show the convergence curves of three algorithms in solving $P1$ under three learning rates (0.1, 0.01, 0.001) and fixed memory size (1024). From these three convergence curves, we can clearly find the following fact. I-DDLO-UDM and IDDLO-HMM all achieve better convergence than DDLO under three learning rates. Although, the convergence performance of I-DDLO-HMM less than 90% under 0.1 learning rate, it is still higher at least 5% than DDLO. Yet, I-DDLO-HMM can obtain close to 95% convergence performance under 0.01 and 0.001 learning rate, it is far higher than DDLO. Especially at the 0.001 learning rate, I-DDLO-HMM significantly better than DDLO. Furthermore, I-DDLO-UDM is clearly better than DDLO at three learning rates 0.1, 0.01 and 0.001. I-DDLO-UDM can rapidly converge at above 95% (within 5000 steps) under learning rates 0.01 and 0.001. For three different learning rates, the convergence performance of I-DDLO-UDM and I-DDLO-HMM is the best at learning rate 0.001. Consequently, we can draw a conclusion that UDM and HDM can effectively improve the convergence performance of the deep learning at different learning rate in solving task offloading problem $P1$.

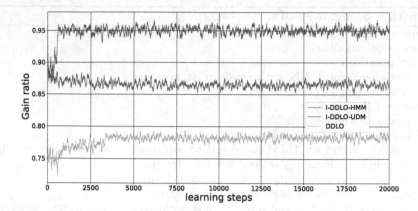

Fig. 2. Convergence curve of 0.1 learning rate.

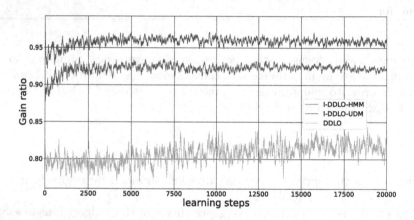

Fig. 3. Convergence curve of 0.01 learning rate.

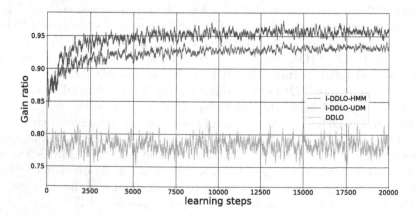

Fig. 4. Convergence curve of 0.001 learning rate.

Figure 5, 6 and 7 show the convergence curves of three algorithms in solving $P1$ under three memory sizes (512, 2048, 4096) and fixed learning rate (0.001). Three convergence curves show that I-DDLO-UDM and I-DDLO-HMM can all acquire a good convergence performance. When the memory size is 512, their convergence performance is the best. The convergence performance of DDLO algorithm is far lower than IDDLO-UDM and I-DDLO-HMM at three sizes of memory. In consequence, UDM and HMM can also significantly improve the convergence at different memory size in solving task offloading problem P1.

To better verify the performance of UDM and HMM, we additionally compare the convergence performance of two proposed algorithms (I-DDLO-UDM and I-DDLO-HMM) and DDLO algorithm with two DNNs (learning rates is 0.001, and memory size is 1024). The simulation results are shown in Fig. 8. In this simulation, DDLO with two DNNs get a good convergence performance than DDLO with one DNN. The result is consistent with literature [6]. At the same time, the simulation results also show two things. On the one hand, the final convergence accuracy of I-DDLO-UDM and I-DDLO HMM is higher than DDLO. On the other hand, the convergence rate of I-DDLO-UDM and I-DDLO HMM is faster than DDIO. Hence, we can also conclude that UDM and HMM effectively enhance the convergence of deep learning algorithm in solving task offloading problem $P1$

In a word, I-DDLO-UDM and I-DDLO-HMM are superior to DDLO in terms of convergence performance. This proves that UDM and HMM can effectively enhance the convergence performance for deep learning algorithm when it is used to address task offloading problem. In addition, the performance of UDM is slightly better than HDM.

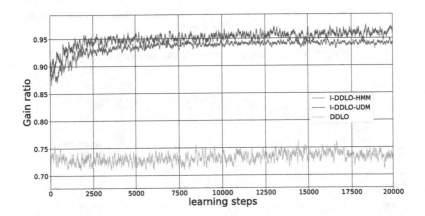

Fig. 5. Convergence curve of 512 memory size.

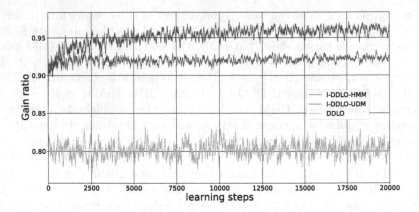

Fig. 6. Convergence curve of 2048 memory size.

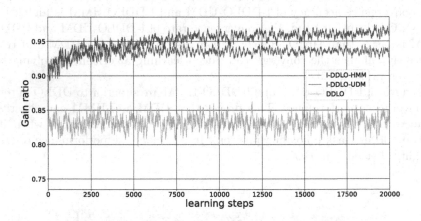

Fig. 7. Convergence curve of 4096 memory size.

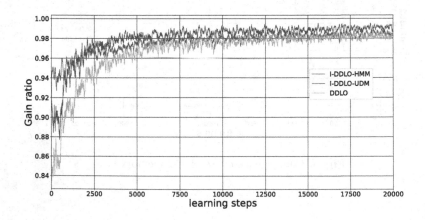

Fig. 8. Convergence curve of 2 DNNs.

6 Conclusion

In this work, we proposed two novel methods to enhance the convergence of deep learning algorithm. They are constructed based on uniform design method and hadamard matrix, respectively. Then, two modified deep learning algorithms I-DDLO-UDM and I-DDLO-HMM was constructed by integrating these two methods into advanced distributed deep learning algorithm DDLO. These two new algorithms show the preferable convergent performance than original DDLO algorithm in the simulation experiments of solving task offloading. This proves the effectiveness of UDM and HDM, as well as the superiority of I-DDLO-UDM and I-DDLO-HMM.

In the future work, we will further study the application of UDM and HMM for other deep learning algorithms, and extend them to more complex task offloading problem, such as the task offloading problem for wireless powered MEC networks with multiple edge devices.

Acknowledgments. This work was supported by the National Natural Science Foundation of China (No. 61961021), the Science and Technology Project of Jiangxi Education Department (No. GJJ180251), and the Natural Science Foundation of Jiangxi Province (Nos. 20202BABL202036, 20202BABL202019).

References

1. Taleb, T., Dutta, S., Ksentini, A., Iqbal, M., Flinck, H.: Mobile edge computing potential in making cities smarter. IEEE Commun. Mag. **55**(3), 38–43 (2017)
2. ETSI MEC: Mobile edge computing (MEC); framework and reference architecture. ETSI, DGS MEC 3 (2016)
3. Chen, Y., Lin, Y., Zheng, Z., Yu, P., Shen, J., Guo, M.: Preference-aware edge server placement in the Internet of Things. IEEE Internet Things J. **9**, 1289–1299 (2021)
4. Chen, X., Jiao, L., Li, W., Fu, X.: Efficient multi-user computation offloading for mobile-edge cloud computing. IEEE/ACM Trans. Netw. **24**(5), 2795–2808 (2016)
5. Wang, X., Han, Y., Leung, V.C.M., Niyato, D., Yan, X., Chen, X.: Convergence of edge computing and deep learning: a comprehensive survey. IEEE Commun. Surv. Tutorials **22**(2), 869–904 (2020)
6. Huang, L., Feng, X., Feng, A., Huang, Y., Qian, L.P.: Distributed deep learning-based offloading for mobile edge computing networks. Mob. Netw. Appl. 1–8 (2018)
7. Sharma, A.R., Kaushik, P.: Literature survey of statistical, deep and reinforcement learning in natural language processing. In: 2017 International Conference on Computing, Communication and Automation (ICCCA), pp. 350–354. IEEE (2017)
8. Mnih, V., et al.: Human-level control through deep reinforcement learning. Nature **518**(7540), 529–533 (2015)
9. Tassinari, P., et al.: A computer vision approach based on deep learning for the detection of dairy cows in free stall barn. Comput. Electron. Agric. **182**, 106030 (2021)
10. He, Y., Yu, F.R., Zhao, N., Leung, V.C.M., Yin, H.: Software-defined networks with mobile edge computing and caching for smart cities: a big data deep reinforcement learning approach. IEEE Commun. Mag. **55**(12), 31–37 (2017)

11. Min, M., Xiao, L., Chen, Y., Cheng, P., Wu, D., Zhuang, W.: Learning-based computation offloading for IoT devices with energy harvesting. IEEE Trans. Veh. Technol. **68**(2), 1930–1941 (2019)
12. Chen, X., Zhang, H., Wu, C., Mao, S., Ji, Y., Bennis, M.: Performance optimization in mobile-edge computing via deep reinforcement learning. In: 88th IEEE Vehicular Technology Conference, VTC Fall 2018, Chicago, IL, USA, 27–30 August 2018, pp. 1–6. IEEE (2018)
13. Huang, L., Feng, X., Qian, L., Wu, Y.: Deep reinforcement learning-based task offloading and resource allocation for mobile edge computing. In: Meng, L., Zhang, Y. (eds.) MLICOM 2018. LNICSSITE, vol. 251, pp. 33–42. Springer, Cham (2018). https://doi.org/10.1007/978-3-030-00557-3_4
14. Li, F., Yao, H., Du, J., Jiang, C., Yu, F.R.: Green communication and computation offloading in ultra-dense networks. In: 2019 IEEE Global Communications Conference, GLOBECOM 2019, Waikoloa, HI, USA, 9–13 December 2019, pp. 1–6. IEEE (2019)
15. Zhao, G., Xu, H., Zhao, Y., Qiao, C., Huang, L.: Offloading dependent tasks in mobile edge computing with service caching. In: 39th IEEE Conference on Computer Communications, INFOCOM 2020, Toronto, ON, Canada, 6–9 July 2020, pp. 1997–2006. IEEE (2020)
16. Ma, X., Zhou, A., Zhang, S., Wang, S.: Cooperative service caching and workload scheduling in mobile edge computing. In: 39th IEEE Conference on Computer Communications, INFOCOM 2020, Toronto, ON, Canada, 6–9 July 2020, pp. 2076–2085. IEEE (2020)
17. Mukherjee, M., Kumar, V., Lat, A., Guo, M., Matam, R., Lv, Y.: Distributed deep learning-based task offloading for uav-enabled mobile edge computing. In: 39th IEEE Conference on Computer Communications, INFOCOM Workshops 2020, Toronto, ON, Canada, July 6–9, 2020. pp. 1208–1212. IEEE (2020)
18. Ali, Z., Jiao, L., Baker, T., Abbas, G., Abbas, Z.H., Khaf, S.: A deep learning approach for energy efficient computational offloading in mobile edge computing. IEEE Access **7**, 149623–149633 (2019)
19. He, X., Lu, H., Huang, H., Mao, Y., Wang, K., Guo, S.: QoE-based cooperative task offloading with deep reinforcement learning in mobile edge networks. IEEE Wirel. Commun. **27**(3), 111–117 (2020)
20. Chen, J., Chen, S., Luo, S., Wang, Q., Cao, B., Li, X.: An intelligent task offloading algorithm (iTOA) for UAV edge computing network. Digital Commun. Netw. **6**(4), 433–443 (2020)
21. Yan, P., Choudhury, S.: Optimizing mobile edge computing multi-level task offloading via deep reinforcement learning. In: 2020 IEEE International Conference on Communications, ICC 2020, Dublin, Ireland, 7–11 June 2020, pp. 1–7. IEEE (2020)
22. Baek, J., Kaddoum, G.: Heterogeneous task offloading and resource allocations via deep recurrent reinforcement learning in partial observable multifog networks. IEEE Internet Things J. **8**(2), 1041–1056 (2021)
23. Li, Z., Hu, H., Hu, H., Huang, B., Ge, J., Chang, V.: Security and energy-aware collaborative task offloading in D2D communication. Future Gener. Comput. Syst. **118**, 358–373 (2021)
24. Yang, Q., Luo, X., Li, P., Miyazaki, T., Wang, X.: Computation offloading for fast CNN inference in edge computing. In: Proceedings of the Conference on Research in Adaptive and Convergent Systems, RACS 2019, Chongqing, China, 24–27 September 2019, pp. 101–106. ACM (2019)
25. Wang, Y., Kaitai, F.: A note on uniform distribution and experimental design. Kexue Tongbao (Chinese) **6**, 485–489 (1981)

26. Fang, K., Lin, D.K.J., Winker, P., Zhang, Y.: Uniform design: theory and application. Technometrics **42**(3), 237–248 (2000)
27. Peng, H., Wu, Z., Deng, C.: Enhancing differential evolution with commensal learning and uniform local search. Chin. J. Electron. **26**(4), 725–733 (2017)
28. Sylvester, J.J.: Lx. Thoughts on inverse orthogonal matrices, simultaneous sign-successions, and tessellated pavements in two or more colours, with applications to newton's rule, ornamental tile-work, and the theory of numbers. Philos. Mag. **34**, 461–475 (1867)
29. Kimura, H.: New Hadamard matrix of order 24. Graphs Comb. **5**(1), 235–242 (1989)
30. En.wikipedia.org: Hadamard   matrix.   https://en.wikipedia.org/wiki/Hadamardmatrix

Dynamic Offloading and Frequency Allocation for Internet of Vehicles with Energy Harvesting

Teng Ma[1], Xin Chen[2(✉)], Yan Liang[2], and Ying Chen[2]

[1] School of Automation, Beijing Information Science and Technology University, Beijing 100192, China
mateng@bistu.edu.cn
[2] School of Computer Science, Beijing Information Science and Technology University, Beijing 100101, China
{chenxin,liangyan,chenying}@bistu.edu.cn

Abstract. The emerging vehicle services need more stable and efficient communication environments. Furthermore, fast-developing in-vehicle applications increase power consumption, and bring new challenges to the endurance of electric vehicles (EVs). In this paper, taking a vehicular network with energy harvesting as the background, we propose a joint online algorithm based on vehicle mobility to minimize the energy consumption of electric vehicles. Specifically, we determine the relationship between MEC computing power allocation and vehicle information (position and driving speed), and minimize vehicles' energy consumption while ensuring the completion rate of offloading task calculations. This problem is NP-hard, and we use the Lyapunov optimization to transform the original problem into a deterministic optimization problem, which has a coupling between the local calculation amount and the MEC calculation frequency allocation decision. Toward this end, we apply the Lagrangian duality method to decouple the problem, and propose a Joint Local Computing and CPU-cycle Frequency Allocation (JLCCFA) algorithm to obtain the approximate optimal solution of the original problem. The simulation experiment results show that JLCCFA can effectively reduce the energy consumption of vehicle users and maintain a small task queue backlog.

Keywords: Task offloading · Frequency allocation · Lyapunov optimization · Energy harvesting · Internet of Vehicles

1 Introduction

The gradual popularization of 5G networks has promoted the rapid development of the Internet of Vehicles (IoV) [1]. A large number of in-vehicle applications emerge to meet the needs of users, which put forward more stringent requirements for task processing efficiency and power consumption [2]. Furthermore, the rapid increase in information interaction bring huge challenges to the endurance of electric vehicles (EVs). Compared with the traditional remote cloud, users can

© Springer Nature Switzerland AG 2022
Y. Lai et al. (Eds.): ICA3PP 2021, LNCS 13156, pp. 376–390, 2022.
https://doi.org/10.1007/978-3-030-95388-1_25

choose to offload the computing tasks to the edge server for processing, which can improve the computing efficiency of the tasks [?]. In addition, with the development of energy harvesting technology, especially for EVs, using energy harvesting technology to capture green energy to ensure battery power is a very promising solution, which is in line with the concept of green communication.

As an energy harvesting technology, photovoltaic power generation directly converts solar radiation energy into electric energy by using the photovoltaic effect of semiconductor materials of solar cells [3]. The photovoltaic intelligent road uses this technology, which aims to provide energy for EVs in motion, and has been tested in Jinan, China [4]. The photovoltaic pavement can convert collected solar energy into electrical energy. Electromagnetic induction coils are reserved on the pavement to continuously charge the driving vehicles. Information collection ports are usually reserved under photovoltaic roads to collect traffic big data such as vehicle driving information, road safety information and road congestion information, which is one of the important development directions of smart cities [5].

The related vehicular network communication has gradually become the research focus of scholars. Yang *et al.* [6] propose a network resource management scheme based on Deep Reinforcement Learning (DRL), which effectively responded to the dynamics and unknowns of the IoV network environment, and guarantee the low latency and high stability of vehicle communication. A branch-and-bound solution with imitative learning ability is proposed in [7], which combines offloading and caching technology to reduce the task completion delay of vehicle users. In addition, Wang *et al.* [8] study the task scheduling problem in Road-Side-Unit (RSU) powered by green energy to optimal the energy consumption for communication, and ensure the network persistence. In the actual network service scenario, the stay time of high-speed vehicles in the service range of edge nodes is limited, and it is necessary to switch links frequently, which is one of the difficult problems in vehicle network optimization [9]. In addition, the ever-increasing complex computing tasks put pressure on the computational efficiency and energy sustainability of vehicles. The existing in-vehicle network design solutions mainly focus on spectrum allocation and communication efficiency, and seldom consider the mobility of the vehicle and the energy efficiency of the vehicle [7].

In order to meet the above challenges, we investigate the joint offloading and frequency allocation scheme with energy harvesting. The scheme performs intelligent local computing, offloading and MEC server's CPU-cycle frequency scaling decision based on the vehicle's battery power reserve information, driving information (position, direction and speed, etc.), and task queue backlog. The main aim of this scheme is to efficiently use the green energy collected to process the computing tasks, and to reduce the energy consumption on the premise of satisfying the quality of service (QoS) of vehicle users. Specifically, the contributions of this paper can be summarized as follows.

– We formulate a dynamic offloading and frequency allocation problem for a IoV system with energy harvesting. Considering the limited communication time of vehicles in each RSU's service range, we maximize the time average energy consumption utility subject to the constraints of queue stability and remaining battery power.

- In order to solve the problem, a Joint Local Computing and CPU-cycle Frequency Allocation (JLCCFA) algorithm is designed. Firstly, we use stochastic optimization techniques to transform the original problem into a stochastic optimization problem. Then, we decompose the problem into three subproblems and solve them in parallel, which greatly reduces the complexity of the algorithm.
- For the proposed scheme, we perform simulation experiment performance analysis, which prove that the online algorithm has low time complexity, and can converge to the optimal average energy consumption under the premise of guaranteeing the stability of the average task queue.

2   System Model

2.1   Scene Model

An heterogeneous IoV system with energy harvesting is considered in Fig. 1, which consists of a MBS, R RSUs and N EVs. Let $\mathcal{R} = \{1, 2, ..., R\}$ and $\mathcal{N} = \{1, 2, ..., N\}$ denote the index set of RSUs and EVs, respectively. In this system, the photovoltaic highway provide green energy for EVs, and RSUs equipped with MEC server can process tasks offloaded by vehicle users. Each vehicle stores the green energy in the battery that supports information interaction, and uses the energy for local computing and task offloading. A time-slotted model $\mathcal{T} = \{1, 2, ..., T\}$ is adopted, and the length of each time slot t is τ.

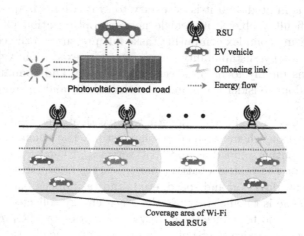

Fig. 1. Schematic diagram of JLCCFA in vehicular network.

2.2 Vehicle Mobility Model

In our mobile scene, it is assumed that any vehicle n driving on a photovoltaic highway with a constant speed v_n. Due to the limitation of the service range of RSU, the vehicle n needs to perform task offloading to multiple RSUs in a time slot. Let d_{rsu} represent the service range of the RSU in the horizontal direction. And vehicle n with a random actual position can pass through the service area of two RSUs at most in any time slot, which means $v_n \cdot \tau \leqslant d_{rsu}$.

Figure 2 depicts the moving scenario of vehicle n in a time slot. $x_n^{start}(t)$ represents the horizontal position of vehicle n at the beginning of time slot t. Let $x_{rsu}^{start}(t)$ and $x_{rsu}^{end}(t)$ respectively denote the start position and the end position of the current RSU horizontal service range. Thus, the driving time that vehicle n stay in the current RSU service range within the time slot t is,

$$t_{rsu}^n(t) = \frac{x_{rsu}^{end}(t) - x_n^{start}(t)}{v_n}, \tag{1}$$

and the driving time of vehicle n in the service range of next RSU is $\tau - t_{rsu}^n(t)$.

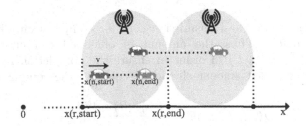

Fig. 2. Schematic diagram of vehicle mobility.

2.3 Task Model

In each time slot t, $A_n(t)$ (in bits) represents the amount of computation tasks arrived in the vehicle n. The vehicle can compute the arrival task locally and offload the task to the RSUs in a parallel way. Note that this model does not require any prior statistic information about $A_n(t)$ (in bits), which is more extensive and applicable than other related literature.

Local Computing: Let $D_n^l(t)$ represent the amount of computation tasks processed locally in time slot t. As the energy harvesting unit and computing unit are independent, the vehicle can operate the energy harvesting and local computing simultaneously. Due to the limitation of vehicle computing power, the allocated local computation task cannot exceed the maximum compute capacity of vehicle n,

$$D_n^l(t) \leqslant \frac{f_n^{max}\tau}{\eta_n}, \forall n \in \mathcal{N}, \tag{2}$$

where f_n^{max} is the maximum CPU-cycle frequency of vehicle n, and η_n is the number of CPU-cycles required to compute the unit bit task.

Computation Offloading: In each time slot t, the wireless transmission rate between vehicle n and the nearby RSU can be obtained by Shannon Formula,

$$R_{v2r}^n = B_{r,n} \log_2(1 + \frac{p_r h_r d_{r,n}^{-\alpha}}{\sigma^2}), \tag{3}$$

where $B_{r,n}$ is the communication bandwidth, p_r is the transmission power, h_r is the channel gain, and $d_{r,n}$ is the distance between EV and RSU. α and σ^2 represent the path loss exponent and noise power, respectively. Due to the mobility of the vehicle, $d_{r,n}$ is constantly changing. Let $f(d)$ represent the probability density function of $d_{r,n}$, and the average offloading rate of vehicle n is $\overline{R_{v2r}^n} = \int_{d_0}^d f(d) \cdot R_{v2r}^n \mathrm{d}d$ [9]. (x_0, y_0) represents the coordinates when the vehicle just enters the RSU service area, and (x_r, y_r) represents the coordinates of the RSU. The process of a vehicle passing through a complete RSU service area is considered, the average offloading rate of vehicle n is,

$$\overline{R_{v2r}^n} = \frac{\int_{x_r-x_0}^0 B_{r,n} \log_2(1 + \frac{p_r h_r \sqrt{(y_n-y_0)^2+d^2}^{-\alpha}}{B_n \sigma^2}))\mathrm{d}d}{x_r - x_0}. \tag{4}$$

Let $t_{n \to r}^{tr}(t)$ denote the transmission time for computation offloading from vehicle n to RSU_r. Thus, the amount of offloaded computation tasks is $D_{n \to r}^0(t) = \overline{R_{v2r}^n} \cdot t_{n \to r}^{tr}(t)$. In order to ensure the completion rate of offloading tasks, the offloaded amount should be equal to the computed amount of RSU_r,

$$\overline{R_{v2r}^n} \cdot t_{n \to r}^{tr}(t) = \frac{f_r^n(t_{rsu}^n(t) - t_{n \to r}^{tr}(t))}{\eta_r}, \tag{5}$$

where variable f_r^n is the CPU-cycle frequency allocated to vehicle n by RSU_r, and η_{rsu} is the number of CPU-cycles required to compute the unit bit task. According to Eq. (4), the amount of offloaded computation tasks of vehicle n to RSU_r is $D_{n \to r}^0(t) = \frac{f_r^n(t)t_{rsu}^n(t)}{\eta_r \overline{R_{v2r}^n}+f_r^n(t)} \overline{R_{v2r}^n}$. Similarly, the amount of offloaded computation tasks of vehicle n to next $RSU_{r'}$ is $D_{n \to r'}^0(t) = \frac{f_{r'}^n(t)(\tau - t_{rsu}^n(t))}{\eta_{r'} \overline{R_{v2r}^n}+f_{r'}^n(t)} \overline{R_{v2r}^n}$. Due to the mobility of vehicles, the number of vehicles in the service range of RSU_r and $RSU_{r'}$ is different in each time slot. Therefore, RSU_r and $RSU_{r'}$ only allocate computing power to their service vehicles,

$$f_r^n(t) = \begin{cases} f_r^n(t), & \text{vehicle } n \text{ is served by } RSU_r \\ 0, & \text{otherwise} \end{cases}, \tag{6}$$

and

$$f_{r'}^n(t) = \begin{cases} f_{r'}^n(t), & \text{vehicle } n \text{ is served by } RSU_{r'} \\ 0, & \text{otherwise} \end{cases}, \tag{7}$$

$f_r^n(t)$ and $f_{r'}^n(t)$ should satisfy $\sum_{n=1}^N f_r^n(t) \leqslant f_r^{max}$ and $\sum_{n=1}^N f_{r'}^n(t) \leqslant f_{r'}^{max}$, where f_r^{max} and $f_{r'}^{max}$ represent the maximum CPU-cycle frequency of RSU_r and $RSU_{r'}$, respectively.

Task Queue: Let $D_n(t) = D_n^l(t) + D_{n \to r}^0(t) + D_{n \to r'}^0(t)$ represent task completion amount of vehicle n in time slot t. The unprocessed tasks would be stored in the task queue sequentially and processed preferentially in the next time slot. Let $Q_n(t)$ denote the queue backlog of the unaccomplished tasks in time slot t. Thus, the queue backlog in time slot $t + 1$ is,

$$Q_n(t + 1) = max\{Q_n(t) - D_n(t), 0\} + A_n(t). \tag{8}$$

Notice that the task queuing delay is proportional to its queue backlog. Due to the high delay sensitivity of computing tasks in IoV, this paper tries to constrain the average queue backlog l_n^Q to reduce the average queuing delay of tasks,

$$l_n^Q = \lim_{T \to \infty} \frac{1}{T} \sum_{t=0}^{T-1} E\{Q_n(t)\} < \varepsilon, \exists \varepsilon \in \mathbb{R}^+, \tag{9}$$

where ε is the constraint value of the average queue backlog.

2.4 Energy Harvesting and Consumption Model

For each vehicle, the energy consumption for task processing consists of two parts, which are the local computing energy and transmission energy for computation offloading. When too many computing tasks arrive or the energy harvesting efficiency becomes poor, the renewable energy would not be able to support the operation of the vehicle task processing module. In this case, the vehicle uses local driving energy to support task processing, which would reduce the endurance of the vehicle.

Energy Harvesting: The green energy is mainly obtained from photovoltaic highways through electromagnetic induction coils. Without loss of generality, the harvested energy obeys an independent and identically distributed Poisson process. Let $e_n^h(t)$ denote the amount of energy harvested in time slot t, which can be expressed as $e_n^h(t) \sim Poisson(\mu\tau)$, where μ is the energy harvesting intensity, representing the energy collected per second.

Energy Consumption: For each vehicle, we consider two parts of energy consumption, which are local computing energy and transmission energy for task offloading. Denote $e_n^l(t)$ as the local computing energy consumption of vehicle n, which can be given by,

$$e_n^l(t) = \varphi_n f_n^2(t) D_n^l(t), \tag{10}$$

where φ_n is the energy factor, and f_n is the actual local computing power of vehicle n.

Due to the limitation of vehicle speed v_n and time slot length τ, the vehicle can offload tasks to the current and the next RSU for computing during the driving process. Let $e_{n \to r}^{tr}$ and $e_{n \to r'}^{tr}$ denote the transmission energy consumption of vehicle n in the service area of RSU_r and $RSU_{r'}$,

$$e_{n \to r}^{tr}(t) = p_n t_{n \to r}^{tr}(t), \tag{11}$$

and

$$e_{n \to r'}^{tr}(t) = p_n(\tau - t_{n \to r}^{tr}(t)), \tag{12}$$

where p_n is the transmission power of vehicle n.

Vehicle Energy Consumption: The battery energy $Q_n^E(t)$ and renewable energy $e_n^h(t)$ in the current time slot provide all the energy for computing and offloading tasks, and the remaining energy in each time slot is stored in the energy buffer for task processing in the next time slot. Devote $e_n^c(t) = e_n^l(t) + e_{n \to r}^{tr}(t) + e_{n \to r'}^{tr}(t)$ is the total energy for computing and offloading tasks, and $Q_n^E(t+1)$ is the battery queue backlog for the next time slot,

$$Q_n^E(t+1) = max\left\{Q_n^E(t) + e_n^h(t) - e_n^c(t), 0\right\}. \tag{13}$$

2.5 Problem Formulation

This paper attempts to reduce the average energy consumption of EVs. By reducing the amount of local computation and the offloading time, the corresponding energy consumption of the vehicle can be reduced. In order to ensure that the vehicle receives the offloading computation result before leaving the current RSU's service range, we define that the offloading amount is equal to the computable amount of RSU, and the offloading time is expressed by the CPU-cycle frequency allocated to the vehicle by RSU. However, these solutions can also lead to the queue backlog become very large and unstable. Thus, this paper studies the problem of joint local computing and MEC's CPU-cycle frequency allocation, which can optimize the average energy consumption of vehicles while guaranteeing the stability of the task queue. let $\overline{E_v} = \lim_{T \to \infty} \frac{1}{T} \sum_{t=0}^{T-1} \mathrm{E}\left\{e_n^c(t)\right\}$ represent the long-term average energy consumption of vehicle n. The optimization problem is,

$$\textbf{P1:} \quad \min_{D_n^l(t), f_r^n(t), f_{r'}^n(t)} \overline{E_v}$$

$$s.t. \quad C1: D_n^l(t) \leqslant \frac{f_n^{max}\tau}{\eta_n}, \forall n \in \mathcal{N},$$

$$C2: \sum_{n=1}^N f_r^n(t) \leq f_r^{max}, \forall n \in \mathcal{N},$$

$$C3: \sum_{n=1}^N f_{r'}^n(t) \leq f_{r'}^{max}, \forall n \in \mathcal{N}, \tag{14}$$

$$C4: e_n^c(t) \leq Q_n^E(t) + e_n^h(t), \forall n \in \mathcal{N},$$

$$C5: \lim_{T \to \infty} \frac{1}{T} \sum_{t=0}^{T-1} \mathrm{E}\left\{Q_n(t)\right\} < \varepsilon, \exists \varepsilon \in \mathbb{R}^+, n \in \mathcal{N},$$

where $C1$ to $C5$ are the constraints of **P1**. $C1$ guarantees that the local computation allocated can be completed. $C2$ and $C3$ indicate that the CPU-cycle frequency allocated by MEC server to all vehicles cannot exceed their maximum computing capacity. $C4$ constraints the energy consumption of vehicles, which means that the energy consumption of vehicles for local calculation and unloading cannot exceed the available electricity. And $C5$ stabilizes the vehicles' task queue.

P1 has two-fold challenges. Firstly, **P1** is a stochastic optimization problem, due to the randomness of vehicle mobility, task arrival and channel state. These random factors change over time, and it is difficult to obtain accurate forecast information. Offline solutions are difficult to deal with this problem. How to make local computing and CPU-cycle frequency allocation decisions in response to dynamic changes in IoV is a huge challenge. Secondly, as the increasing number of vehicles would increase the complexity of problem solving, the traditional optimization algorithm is difficult to satisfy the response requirements of delay-sensitive tasks.

3   Algorithm Design

In order to solve this stochastic optimization problem, a Joint Local Computing and CPU-cycle Frequency Allocation algorithm called JLCCFA is designed in this section. **P1** is transformed into a deterministic problem through the Lyapunov method, and then divided into a series of sub-problems to reduce the complexity of the algorithm. JLCCFA does not require any prior knowledge of vehicle mobility, task arrival, and channel status when making decisions, which are also difficult to obtain or predict in actual scenarios.

3.1   Problem Transformation

By using the Lyapunov optimization method to transform the original problem, **P1** with long-term constraints is decomposed into each time slot for optimization. Let $\Theta(t) = \{Q_1(t), Q_2(t), ..., Q_N(t)\}$ represent the task queue backlog of all vehicles in time slot t, and define the Lyapunov function is,

$$L(\Theta(t)) = \frac{1}{2} \sum_{n=1}^{N} Q_n^2(t). \tag{15}$$

Specifically, $L(\Theta(t))$ represents the queue backlog state of the IoV system with energy harvesting. When the value of $L(\Theta(t))$ is large, it means that there exists at least one EV with the large queue length. Next, the conditional Lyapunov drift $\Delta(\Theta(t))$ is expressed in,

$$\Delta(\Theta(t)) = \mathrm{E}\left[L(\Theta(t+1)) - L(\Theta(t))|\Theta(t)\right], \tag{16}$$

which reflects the increase in the task queue of all vehicles in the system from time slot t to time slot $t+1$.

To combine the queue backlog and vehicle energy consumption, the drift plus energy consumption is defined,

$$\Delta_V(\Theta(t)) = \Delta(\Theta(t)) + V \cdot \mathrm{E}\{e_n^c(t)\}, \tag{17}$$

where V represents the trade-off factor between the task queue and vehicle energy consumption in the system, which is a non-negative number. Then, its upper bound is derived by Theorem 1.

Theorem 1. *In any time slot t, with any local task and CPU-cycle frequency allocation strategy, given that $A_n(t) \leq A_n^{max}$, $f_n(t) \leq f_n^{max}$ and $\overline{R_{v2r}^n} \leq \overline{R_{v2r}^{max}}$, $\Delta_V(\Theta(t))$ would be upper bounded by,*

$$\Delta_V(\Theta(t)) \leq C + \sum_{n=1}^{N} Q_n(t)\mathrm{E}\{A_n(t) - D_n(t)|\Theta(t)\}$$
$$+ V \cdot \sum_{n=1}^{N} \mathrm{E}\{\varphi_n f_n^2(t)D_n^l(t) + p_n t_{n \to r}^{tr}(t) + p_n t_{n \to r'}^{tr}(t)|\Theta(t)\}, \tag{18}$$

where $C = \frac{1}{2}\sum_{n=1}^{N}[(A_n^{max})^2 + (\frac{f_n^{max}\tau}{\eta_n} + \overline{R_{v2r}^{max}}t_{n \to r}^{tr}(t)) + \overline{R_{v2r}^{max}}t_{n \to r'}^{tr}(t))^2]$ is a constant.

3.2   Optimal Algorithm Design

According to the Lyapunov optimization theory, by minimizing the $\Delta_V(\Theta(t))$'s upper bound of a under each discrete time slot, a near-optimal solution to the original stochastic optimization problem can be obtained, effectively reducing the average energy consumption of the vehicle, and keeping the cumulative task queue length of vehicles low. The problem of local computing and MEC's CPU-cycle frequency allocation in each time slot is a deterministic optimization problem. As C and $A_n(t)$ are the constant in each slot, the following problem is formulated,

$$\mathbf{P2:} \quad \min_{\mathbf{D}^l, \mathbf{f}_r, \mathbf{f}_{r'}} \sum_{n=1}^{N} (V \cdot \varphi_n f_n^2(t) - Q_n(t))D_n^l(t)$$
$$+ \sum_{n=1}^{N} (V \cdot P_{n,r}(t) - \overline{R_{v2r}^{r,n}}(t)Q_n(t))t_{n \to r}^{tr}(t) \tag{19}$$
$$+ \sum_{n=1}^{N} (V \cdot P_{n,r'}(t) - \overline{R_{v2r}^{r',n}}(t)Q_n(t))t_{n \to r'}^{tr}(t),$$
$$s.t. \quad C1 - C4.$$

The optimization objective and all constraints in **P2** can be proved to be convex functions, and **P2** is a convex optimization problem. Due to the variable coupling in **P2**, the problem cannot be solved directly. This paper first uses the Lagrangian dual method to decouple the convex optimization problem, then decomposes the problem into a series of sub-problems, and finally solves the optimal solutions of the three sub-problems separately.

Denote λ_r, $\lambda_{r'}$ and $\omega = \{\omega_1, \omega_2, ..., \omega_N\}$ are the Lagrange multipliers to relax the constraints $C2$ to $C4$. Let $\mathcal{L}(D^l(t), f_r(t), f_{r'}(t), \lambda_r, \lambda_{r'}, \omega)$ denote the Lagrangian function. Thus, the dual problem of **P2** is,

$$\max_{\lambda_r, \lambda_{r'}, \omega} \min_{D^l(t), f_r(t), f_{r'}(t)} \mathcal{L}(D^l(t), f_r(t), f_{r'}(t), \lambda_r, \lambda_{r'}, \omega)$$

$$s.t. \quad C1 : D_n^l(t) \leqslant \frac{f_n^{max}\tau}{\eta_n}, \forall n \in \mathcal{N}, \tag{20}$$

For the given Lagrangian multiplier, an iterative-based method solves the following problems to get the optimal $\hat{D^l}(t)$, $\hat{f_r}(t)$ and $\hat{f_{r'}}(t)$,

$$
\begin{aligned}
min \sum_{n=1}^{N} & \left[(V + \omega_n) \cdot \varphi_n f_n^2(t)\xi_n - Q_n(t) \right] D_n^l(t) \\
+ \sum_{n=1}^{N} & \left[(V + \omega_n)p_{n,r} - \overline{R_{v2r}^{r,n}}(t)Q_n(t) \right] t_{n,r}^{tr}(t) + \lambda_r f_r^n(t) \\
+ \sum_{n=1}^{N} & \left[(V + \omega_n)p_{n,r'} - \overline{R_{v2r}^{r',n}}(t)Q_n(t) \right] t_{n,r'}^{tr}(t) + \lambda_{r'} f_r^n(t).
\end{aligned}
\tag{21}
$$

Obviously, problem (24) can be decoupled into three independent subproblems: Local Computation Control (LCC), CPU-cycle Frequency Control in Current RSU (FCCR) and CPU-cycle Frequency Control in Next RSU (FCNR).

Local Computation Control (LCC):

$$\sum_{n=1}^{N} \left[(V + \omega_n) \cdot \varphi_n f_n^2(t)\xi_n - Q_n(t) \right] D_n^l(t)$$

$$s.t. \quad D_n^l(t) \leqslant \frac{f_n^{max}\tau}{\eta_n}, \forall n \in \mathcal{N}. \tag{22}$$

This problem is a basic one-time problem, and its optimal solution $\hat{D_n^l}(t)$ is,

$$D_n^{\hat{l}}(t) = \begin{cases} \frac{f_n^{max}\tau}{\eta_n}, & \left[(V + \omega_n) \cdot \varphi_n f_n^2(t)\xi_n - Q_n(t) \right] < 0 \\ 0 & otherwise. \end{cases} \tag{23}$$

CPU-Cycle Frequency Control in Current RSU (FCCR):

$$\sum_{n=1}^{N} \left[(V + \omega_n)p_{n,r} - \overline{R_{v2r}^{r,n}}(t)Q_n(t) \right] t_{n,r}^{tr}(t) + \lambda_r f_r^n(t)$$

$$s.t. \quad 0 \leq f_r^n(t) \leq f_r^{max}, \tag{24}$$

Since $t_{n,r}^{tr}(t) = \frac{f_r^n(t)t_{rsu}^n(t)}{\eta_r R_{v2r}^n + f_r^n(t)}$ and $f_r^n(t)$ of the variable $f_r^n(t)$ are monotonically increasing, the problem of FCCR can be divided into the following two situations for classification discussion,

1) $\left[(V + \omega_n)p_{n,r} - \overline{R_{v2r}^{r,n}}(t)Q_n(t))\right] > 0$ and the optimal solution $f_r^{\hat{n}}(t) = 0$.

2) $\left[(V + \omega_n)p_{n,r} - \overline{R_{v2r}^{r,n}}(t)Q_n(t))\right] < 0$ and the optimal decision $f_r^{\hat{n}}(t)$ is,

$$f_r^{\hat{n}}(t) = \begin{cases} x, & f_r^{max} \geq x, \\ f_r^{max}, & otherwise, \end{cases} \qquad (25)$$

where $x = \frac{\sqrt{-\left[(V+\omega_n)p_{n,r}-\overline{R_{v2r}^{r,n}}(t)Q_n(t)\right]t_{rsu}^n(t)\eta_r \overline{R_{v2r}^n}\lambda_r} - R_{v2r}^n \lambda_r}{\lambda_r}$ is the positive point of (27).

CPU-Cycle Frequency Control in Next RSU (FCNR): Similar to FCCR, the optimal solution is,

1) $\left[(V + \omega_n)p_{n,r} - R_{v2r}^{r',n}(t)Q_n(t))\right] > 0$ and the optimal solution $f_{r'}^{\hat{n}}(t) = 0$.

2) $\left[(V + \omega_n)p_{n,r'} - \overline{R_{v2r}^{r',n}}(t)Q_n(t))\right] < 0$ and the optimal decision $f_{r'}^{\hat{n}}(t)$ is,

$$f_{r'}^{\hat{n}}(t) = \begin{cases} x, & f_{r'}^{max} \geq x, \\ f_{r'}^{max}, & otherwise, \end{cases} \qquad (26)$$

where

$$x = \frac{\sqrt{-\left[(V+\omega_n)p_{n,r'}-\overline{R_{v2r}^{r',n}}(t)Q_n(t)\right]t_{rsu}^n(t)\eta_{r'} \overline{R_{v2r}^n}\lambda_{r'}} - R_{v2r}^n \lambda_{r'}}{\lambda_{r'}}.$$

After obtaining the optimal $D^{\hat{i}}(t)$, $f_r^{\hat{}}(t)$ and $f_{r'}^{\hat{}}(t)$, the dual problem of **P2** is transformed into (30),

$$\max_{\lambda_r,\lambda_{r'},\omega} \mathcal{L}(D^{\hat{i}}(t), f_r^{\hat{}}(t), f_{r'}^{\hat{}}(t), \lambda_r, \lambda_{r'}, \omega). \qquad (27)$$

The optimal Lagrangian multipliers $\hat{\lambda}_r$, $\hat{\lambda}_{r'}$ and $\hat{\omega}$ can be obtained by the gradient method,

$$\lambda_r(k+1, t) = \left[\lambda_r(k,t) + \iota_k(\sum_{n=1}^{N} f_r^n(\hat{k}, t) - f_r^{max})\right]^+, \qquad (28)$$

$$\lambda_{r'}(k+1, t) = \left[\lambda_{r'}(k,t) + \iota_k(\sum_{n=1}^{N} f_{r'}^n(\hat{k}, t) - f_{r'}^{max})\right]^+, \qquad (29)$$

$$\omega_n(k+1,t) = [\omega_n(k,t) + \iota_k(\varepsilon_n f_n^2(t)\varphi_n \hat{D}^l(t)$$
$$+ p_{n,r}(t)\hat{t_{n,r}^{tr}}(t) + p_{n,r'}(t)\hat{t_{n,r'}^{tr}}(t)$$
$$- Q_n^E(t) - e_n^h(t))]^+, \tag{30}$$

where k is the number of iterations, and ι_k is the step size. In the process of iteration, the values of Lagrange multipliers in Eq. (28), Eq. (29) and Eq. (30) would converge to the optimum by continuously deceasing the value of ι_k.

For clarity, the detail of Joint Local Computing and CPU-cycle Frequency Allocation (JLCCFA) is given by Algorithm 1.

Algorithm 1: JLCCFA Algorithm

1: Input: Task queue length and battery queue length of each vehicle $Q_n(t)$ and $Q_n^E(t)$;
2: Output: Decision variables $D^l(t)$, $f_r(t)$ and $f_{r'}(t)$;
3: Initialize Decision variables $D^l(t) = 0$, $f_r(t) = 0$ and $f_{r'}(t) = 0$;
4: Choose the appropriate Lagrangian multiplier λ_r, $\lambda_{r'}$, ω and update the step size ι_k;
5: **while** The accuracy does not meet the requirements **do**
6:     Obtain the optimal solution $\hat{D_n^l}(t)$ of LCC;
7:     Obtain the optimal solution $\hat{f_r^n}(t)$ of FCCR ;
8:     Obtain the optimal solution $\hat{f_{r'}^n}(t)$ of FCNR;
9:     Update the Lagrangian multiplier λ_r, $\lambda_{r'}$, ω with Eq. (31), Eq. (32) and Eq. (33);
10:     Decease the value of ι_k appropriately;
11: **end while**
12: **return** $\{D_1^l(t), D_2^l(t), ..., D_N^l(t)\}$, $\{f_r^1(t), f_r^2(t), ..., f_r^N(t)\}$ and $\{f_{r'}^1(t), f_{r'}^2(t), ..., f_{r'}^N(t)\}$

---

4 Simulation

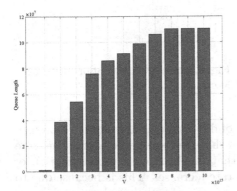

Fig. 3. Queue length with the four algorithms

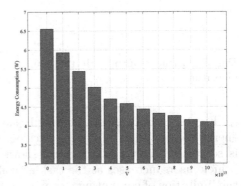

Fig. 4. Energy consumption with different V

In this section, we evaluate the performance of JLCCFA through extensive simulations on Matlab. We consider that all vehicles are randomly distributed on the road and travel in the same direction at a certain speed. In addition, the amount of tasks generated by each vehicle at the beginning of each time slot obeys a uniform distribution with $[A_n^{min}, A_n^{max}]$. In fact, JLCCFA does not need any statistical information about the task arrival and vehicle speed. In the simulation scenario, we consider the RSU with 500 m coverage and 30 m/s vehicle speed. Beside, the bandwidth of RSU is 1 MHz, $f_r^{max} = 1010$ GHz, $p_r = 2$ W, $p_n(t) \sim U [0.03, 0.05]$ W, $f_n^{max} = 1$ GHz, $\eta_n \sim U [1000, 2000]$ cycles/bit and φ_n.

Figure 3 and Fig. 4 describes the impact of different parameter V on user energy consumption and queue backlog. Figure 3 shows that the queue backlog increases as the parameter V increases. Note that the queue backlog has an upper bound, which proves that JLCCFA can maintain the stability of the queue. Figure 4 shows that the energy consumption of vehicle users decreases as V increases. This is because V represents the proportion of energy consumption, and JLCCFA would adaptively adjust the output decision to reduce energy consumption. It can be seen from Fig. 3 and Fig. 4 that when V is large enough, JLCCFA can obtain the minimum energy consumption while maintaining the stability of the queue. In addition, by adjusting V, JLCCFA can arbitrarily compromise between queue backlog and energy consumption.

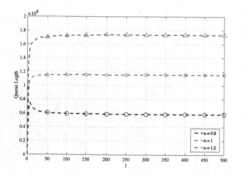

Fig. 5. Queue length with the four algorithms

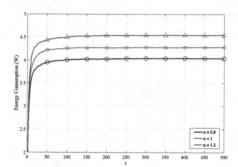

Fig. 6. Energy consumption with different V

Figure 5 and Fig. 6 depicts the impact of different task arrival rate α on user energy consumption and queue backlog. In the experiment, the task arrival rate is set to 0.8, 1 and 1.2. Figure 5 shows that the local energy consumption of vehicle users increases as the task arrival rate increases. This is because due to the limitation of computing resources, the increase of task arrival rate may cause more tasks need to be processed locally and offloaded to the RSU to ensure the stability of the task queue, resulting in increased energy consumption for local processing and data transmission. As shown in Fig. 6, the task queue backlog increases as the task arrival rate increases and gradually stabilized. Combining

Fig. 5 and Fig. 6, we can draw a conclusion that JLCCFA can adapt to different task arrival rate, always stabilize the task queue fast and minimize energy consumption.

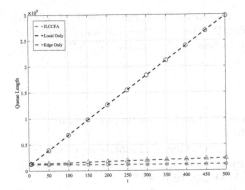

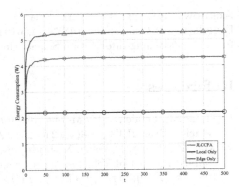

Fig. 7. Queue length with the four algorithms

Fig. 8. Energy consumption with different V

Figure 7 and Fig. 8 depicts the impact of different algorithm on user energy consumption and queue backlog. The Only Local algorithm has the lowest energy consumption, but the queue backlog shows a linear increasing trend. This is because all tasks are only processed locally, which means that there is no offloading energy consumption. Due to the limitation of computing power, the EVs cannot handle the continuously arriving tasks, resulting in a serious backlog of task queues. From the Only Edge algorithm, it can be seen that just offloading all tasks to MEC server for processing can improve task processing efficiency and stabilize the task backlog queue, but the energy consumption under this strategy is the highest. The experiment shows that the effect of JLCCFA is the best, which can effectively reduce vehicle energy consumption and stabilize the task queue at a small value. This is because JLCCFA can dynamically adjust the amount of local calculations and the allocation of CPU-cycle frequencies based on the status of this time slot, including vehicle driving status, channel status, and task queue backlog status.

5 Conclusion

A dynamic offloading and frequency allocation problem for IoV with Energy Harvesting is studied in our paper, and the objective is to optimal the EVs' energy consumption while providing task queue stability guarantees. We analyze the influence of vehicle mobility on the system, and design a distributed online algorithm JLCCFA to solve this problem. Specifically, JLCCFA requires no prior statistical knowledge about the task arrival and wireless channel, and solves the three sub-problems in parallel, which effectively improves the efficiency of the algorithm. The simulation experiments prove that JLCCFA can make the arbitrary trade-off between vehicle energy consumption and task queue length, and effectively reduce vehicle energy consumption on the premise of guaranteeing queue stability.

Acknowledgment. This work is partly supported by the National Natural Science Foundation of China (Nos. 61872044, 61902029), The Key Research and Cultivation Projects at Beijing Information Science and Technology University (No. 5211910958).

References

1. Zhang, J., Letaief, K.B.: Mobile edge intelligence and computing for the internet of vehicles. Proc. IEEE **108**(2), 246–261 (2019)
2. Ning, Z., Huang, J., Wang, X., Rodrigues, J.J.P.C., Guo, L.: Mobile edge computing-enabled Internet of Vehicles: toward energy-efficient scheduling. IEEE Netw. **33**(5), 198–205 (2019). https://doi.org/10.1109/MNET.2019.1800309
3. Zhang, S., Wang, J., Liu, H., et al.: Prediction of energy photovoltaic power generation based on artificial intelligence algorithm. Neural Comput. Appl. **33**(3), 821–835 (2021)
4. Sun, L., Zhao, H., Tu, H., et al.: The smart road: practice and concept. Engineering **4**(4), 436–437 (2018)
5. Khan, L.U., Yaqoob, I., Tran, N.H., Kazmi, S.M.A., Dang, T.N., Hong, C.S.: Edge-computing-enabled smart cities: a comprehensive survey. IEEE Internet Things J. **7**(10), 10200–10232 (2020). https://doi.org/10.1109/JIOT.2020.2987070
6. Yang, H., Xie, X., Kadoch, M.: Intelligent resource management based on reinforcement learning for ultra-reliable and low-latency IoV communication networks. IEEE Trans. Veh. Technol. **68**(5), 4157–4169 (2019). https://doi.org/10.1109/TVT.2018.2890686
7. Ning, Z., et al.: Intelligent edge computing in Internet of Vehicles: a joint computation offloading and caching solution. IEEE Trans. Intell. Transp. Syst. **22**(4), 2212–2225 (2021). https://doi.org/10.1109/TITS.2020.2997832
8. Wang, C., Li, J., Cheng, X., He, Y., Sun, L., Xiao, K.: LSTM-based communication scheduling mechanism for energy harvesting RSUs in IoVs. In: 2020 IEEE 92nd Vehicular Technology Conference (VTC 2020-Fall) 2020, pp. 1–5 (2020). https://doi.org/10.1109/VTC2020-Fall49728.2020.9348859
9. Ma, T., Chen, X., Ma, Z., Jiao, L.: Deep reinforcement learning based dynamic content placement and bandwidth allocation in Internet of Vehicles. In: Liu, Z., Wu, F., Das, S.K. (eds.) WASA 2021. LNCS, vol. 12939, pp. 244–253. Springer, Cham (2021). https://doi.org/10.1007/978-3-030-86137-7_27

SPACE: Sparsity Propagation Based DCNN Training Accelerator on Edge

Miao Wang[1], Zhen Chen[2], Chuxi Li[1], Zhao Yang[1], Lei Li[2], Meng Zhang[1(✉)], and Shengbing Zhang[1(✉)]

[1] Northwestern Polytechnical University, Xi'an 710129, China
{zhangm,zhangsb}@nwpu.edu.cn
[2] National and Local Joint Engineering Research Center for Reliability Technology of Energy Internet Intelligent Terminal Core Chip, Beijing Smart-Chip Microelectronics Technology Co., Ltd., Beijing 100192, China

Abstract. On-edge learning enables edge devices to continually adapt to the new data of AI applications. However, much more computing capacity and memory space are needed to achieve the batch backward propagation oriented training, in which the system power budget is limited by the edge circumstance. As the operands are propagated during the training, useless zero values are inevitably propagated, which will cause unnecessary waste of memory accesses and computations. This paper conducted a thorough analysis of the origin of sparsity in all three phases of the training based on sparse propagation and gives three insights about the absolute sparsity and the nonabsolute sparsity found for efficient deployment of the training process. An efficient training accelerator named SPACE which can not only reduce memory footprint but also delete a massive amount of computations by exploiting the nonabsolute sparsity and the absolute sparsity is proposed. SPACE can improve performance and energy efficiency by a factor of 3.2x and 2.8x, respectively, compared with dense training architecture.

Keywords: Sparsity propagation · On-edge learning · Sparse training accelerator

1 Introduction

In smart edge computing circumstances, deep convolution neural networks (DCNN) are widely deployed for inference such as image classification [1], object recognition [2]. However, the inference accuracy of the pre-trained model will decrease due to the unfamiliar data collected on the smart edge devices. Compared with the straightforward solution which transfers newly collected data to the remote server and tunes the model on it, and then transfers the new model

Supported by The Laboratory Open Fund of Beijing Smart-chip Microelectronics Technology Co., Ltd. grant number SGTYHT/20-JS-221.

Y. Lai et al. (Eds.): ICA3PP 2021, LNCS 13156, pp. 391–405, 2022.
https://doi.org/10.1007/978-3-030-95388-1_26

back to the edge devices, on-edge learning keeps the sensitive user data and fine-tunes the pre-trained model locally to avoid communication round trips and the sacrificing of privacy.

The training process consists of three phases: forward propagation (FP) which is the overlapped procedure of inference, backward propagation (BP), and weight gradient computation and update (WU). Compared with inference, the neural network training processes are more computation and memory intensive, which require additional computing elements and memory resources to processing gradient backward propagation and parameter update in the batched inputs. The deploying of the training process has a more energy efficiency impact on edge devices that have limited energy and memory resources than deploying inference.

However, not all memory footprint and computation contribute to the training results. Computation in which at least one of the two operands is zero not only fails to improve performance but also increases energy consumption. The ubiquitous sparsity of neural networks provides great potentials concerning enhancing the energy efficiency of neural network hardware. Some work mitigates deployment difficulties by eliminating redundant parameters through manual construction [4] or automated neural network architecture search [5] to obtain compact models. There have been some explorations of sparsity in network inference [3,9,10,12] and training [6–8,14]. [6] and [8] only pay attention to the training rules of the ReLU layer to optimize memory or computation; [7] uses the compression method to fine-tune only the fully connected layer sparsely; [14] is dedicated to introducing a scheduler for improving the data reuse rate and PE utilization of the sparse training architecture. Although the use of sparsity has been accelerated, all of them ignore the correlation of the sparsity between the three phases, and the lack of a systematic discussion on the sparsity of the entire training process has led to insufficient use of sparsity.

First, as the operands are propagated during the three training phases, the zero value of related data has corresponding propagation characteristics due to the layer correlation and operand dependence. Furthermore, the origin of the sparsity in the training process can be targeted by analyzing the dataflow from input activations to updated weights. This paper does not only focus on the individual phase but considering the entire training process of the network to analyzes the mutual influence between the three phases, and proposes insights into the deployment of the sparse training process on edge devices. The contributions of this paper are as follows:

(1) A thorough analysis of the origin of sparsity in all three phases of the training based on sparse propagation and some insights into the energy efficiency deploying training process on edge devices.
(2) A reconfigurable sparse training accelerator named SPACE with a compression method for delivering sparsity, deletes useless computations and extra memory for more energy efficiency.
(3) The workflow of SPACE about sparsity propagation handles various sparsity in the training process efficiently and flexibly.

The rest of this paper is organized as follows. Section 2 summarizes the background of DCNN training and motivation. Section 3 analyzes the origin of sparsity based on sparsity propagation and proposes three insights for training process. Section 4 presents the dedicated SPACE that aims to exploit sparsity to obtain energy efficiency deployment of the training process. Section 5 describes the dataflow of PE array and workflow of SPACE. Section 6 shows experiments to manifest the benefits of both the compression method and the SPACE. Section 7 summarizes the full paper.

2 Background and Motivation

2.1 DCNN Training

During the training process, features of activation from the input image are extracted by the FP phase of convolutional layers and pass through some non-linear and fully connected layers finally. Then, the final loss is computed after the classification step to be propagated back for the WU phase. Subsequently, the gradient of the loss are propagated back to produce weight gradient of each layer for the WU.

Equation (1) (2) and (3) summarizes the three phases of DCNN training.

$$FP: O_i^l = \sigma(\sum_{j=0}^{N} O_j^{l-1} * W_{i,j}^l + b_i^l) \tag{1}$$

Where O_i^l is the output activations of i-th channel and O_j^{l-1} is the input activations of j-th channel in layer l. Each convolution kernel of j-th channel in i-th filter $W_{i,j}$ is a 2-D tensor with the size of K × K, and vector b is the bias. N and M are the corresponding input channels and output channels, respectively. Non-linear activation function ReLU applies point-wise function $\sigma(x) = max(0, x)$ on all activations.

$$BP: \delta X_j^l = \sigma' \odot (\sum_{i=0}^{M} \delta O_i^{l+1} * W_{i,j}^{l+1}) \tag{2}$$

Where δX_j^l is the loss gradients of j-th channel in layer l and σ' refers to the derivative of the activation function ReLU. $\odot$ is Hadamard Product, used to multiply the corresponding elements of the matrices.

$$WU: \delta W_{i,j}^l = \delta X_i^l * O_j^{l-1} \tag{3}$$

Where $\delta W_{i,j}^l$ is the weight gradients of j-th channel in i-th filter on layer l. Normally, a batch of samples is used to update the weight. Then the weight gradients are computed by averaging the batch of gradients. Finally, the weights are updated according to a learning rate α.

Compared with the inference, the training process not only requires additional computations of loss gradients and weight gradients but also needs to allocate additional memory for repeated use in the BP phase and the WU phase.

2.2 Exploring Sparsity Throughout Training

We collected the memory footprint during inference and training on AlexNet and VGGNet, respectively. As shown in Fig. 1(a), the memory footprint is increased several times comparing to the inference, which reaches the giga-byte level. As the limitation of physical size and power budget on edge circumstances, the memory consumption of DCNN training is more critical than inference.

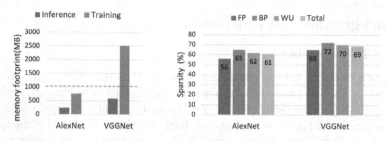

(a) Memory footprint comparison. (b) The sparsity in three training phases.

Fig. 1. (a) The memory footprint required for training and inference under batch size 8. (b) Sparsity during training.

As shown in Fig. 1(b), the sparsity of AlexNet and VGGNet with 1000 random images was collected in the three phases, in which the sparsity not only exists in the FP phase but also in the BP phase and WU phase. In general, the sparsity of the BP phase is higher than that of the FP phase and the WU phase. Leveraging the sparsity in BP would get more benefits in reducing memory and computation footprint. In this process, a huge amount of memory and processing elements are utilized to handle zeros, therefore about 60% energy is wasted in zero-data storage, communication, and computing.

Therefore, it is necessary and potential to analyze sparsity during the whole training process to relieve the memory and computation pressure of training.

3 Sparsity Characteristics Analysis

3.1 Origin of Sparsity

A large number of zeros naturally exist in the activations and gradients during the training. To explore the origin of sparsity, a sparse index matrix (SIM) is introduced to express the sparsity (equals the number of the zero value divided by the number of the total) of the operands. In Fig. 2(a), the activations are taken as an example to illustrate the set rules of the SIM that sets the nonzero position of the original matrix to 1, and the zero position to 0. The more zeros in the SIM, the sparser the activations.

Figure 2(b) shows the three phases based on the SIM for analyzing sparsity propagation and the origin of sparsity. The sparsity of the input activations carried by the SIM can propagate the sparsity to the SIM corresponding to the loss gradients and activations through the data transfer and the computation of various hidden layers.

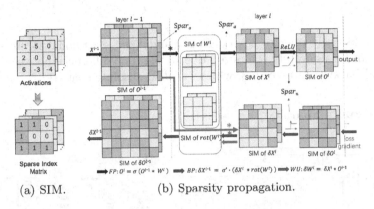

(a) SIM.   (b) Sparsity propagation.

Fig. 2. (a) SIM is introduced to represent the sparsity of different operands. (b) The sparsity is propagated based on SIM.

For each layer of the DCNN, the origin of sparsity includes the sparsity from the input operands marked $Spar_o$, the sparsity obtained by the accumulation marked $Spar_a$ and the sparsity achieved by the nonlinear layer and the pooling layer marked $Spar_n$.

Where $Spar_o$ means the sparsity propagated from the other layers to the layer l through the operands because of the layer correlation and operand dependency as shown in Table 1. The $Spar_o$ of the FP of layer l is provided by the FP of layer $l-1$, and the BP of layer l is dependent on the BP of layer $l+1$. Specifically, the input activations O^{l-1} with a certain sparsity (SIM of O^{l-1}) bring the initial sparsity to the layer l. However, $Spar_o$ cannot be evaluated accurately since the sparsity of the input operand is dynamically changing.

Where $Spar_a$ is the sparsity derived by the accumulation operation of the convolutional layer or the fully connected layer. The SIM that is featured with the sparseness, can obtain a certain degree of sparseness through multiplication. After the accumulation of multiple channels, the occurrence of zero loses its certainty and turns into a relatively accidental behavior. Therefore, although $Spar_a$ is associated with a convolution operation, it cannot be accurately computed.

Where $Spar_n$ is the sparsity derived by the nonlinear layer or pooling layer. And $Spar_{nf}$ is for FP and $Spar_{nb}$ is for BP, Specifically. After X^l has passed the ReLU function and the pooling layer with certain rules, the SIM of the output activation still cannot be accurately evaluated due to the uncertainty sparsity of X^l. Therefore $Spar_{nf}$ cannot be accurately computed.

Table 1. The operand dependence and layer correlation of the three phases of DCNN.

Training phase	Input	Weight	Output	Layer correlation
FP	O^{l-1}	W^l	O^l	FP^{l-1}
BP	δX^{l+1}	$(W^{l+1})^T$	δX^l	BP^{l+1}
WU	O^{l-1}	δX^l	δW^l	FP^{l-1}, BP^l

We collectively refer to $Spar_o$, $Spar_a$ and $Spar_{nf}$ as nonabsolute sparsity. $Spar_{nb}$ can be accurately computed due to the time difference between the forward and backward processing, which is called absolute sparsity.

3.2   Absolute Sparsity

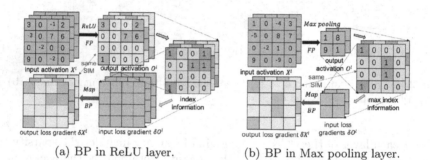

(a) BP in ReLU layer.   (b) BP in Max pooling layer.

Fig. 3. (a) The output loss gradients (δX^l) and the output activations (O^l) of the ReLU layer have the same SIM; (b) The sparsity of the output loss gradients (δX^l) is same as the max index information of the pooling layer in the FP.

Figure 3(a) shows the FP and BP methods of the ReLU in the DCNN, and the bottom of Fig. 2(b) displays the processing rules of the loss gradient backward mapping. σ' refers to the derivative of the activation function ReLU. Then, it is learned from observation that the pixel positions whose value is less than or equal to zero in the activations (O^l) are not necessary to propagate the input loss gradients (δO^l) of these positions to the output loss gradients (δX^l) when performing loss gradient propagation. Instead, only these positions need to be mapped to zero. In short, the output activations (O^l) and the input loss gradients (δX^l) can share the same SIM. The absolute sparsity indicates that the SIM of δX^l can be obtained in advance in the FP, which can be exploited for further optimization in memory and computation. Figure 3(b) shows the same phenomenon also appears in the pooling layer, but the max index information (mark the position of the maximum) of the max-pooling layer and the SIM of the output loss gradients (δX^l) are the same.

In addition, if the activation gradient is approximately computed, there is also a similar absolute sparsity for other activation functions. But this paper only focuses on ReLU, and the corresponding research on other activation functions will be shown in future research.

3.3 Sparse Training Insights

Naturally, the absolute and nonabsolute sparsity can be employed to reduce the footprint of memory and computation. Thus, some sparsity training insights for optimizing the training process on edge devices were put forward.

(1) For the nonabsolute sparsity, exploit the sparsity of activation and loss gradient in FP phase and BP phase is considered respectively and targets sparsity in loss gradient for the WU phase. First of all, the weight exhibits negligible sparsity unless the training method incorporates pruning, while the activation and the output gradient are featured with considerable sparsity. Secondly, to maintain the control logic overhead, loss gradient with a slightly larger sparsity are selected for exploitation.
(2) For the absolute sparsity, the pixel positions in the input loss gradient that are destined to be zero after the backward mapping does not need to be computed. Therefore, all convolution computations corresponding to these zero pixels can be deleted to reduce the computation cycles.
(3) As the loss gradient and the output activation have the same SIM, the two should have the same encoding information due to the absolute sparsity when a compression method is adopted for relieving memory pressure. Therefore, it is efficient to share the encoding information during training.

4 Architecture of the SPACE

4.1 The Architecture Overview

Figure 4 shows the architecture of the proposed SPACE which consists of a PE array, the activation/loss gradient/weight/output global buffer (see blocks named AG GBuffer, Weight GBuffer et al.), SIM Buffer, Selectors for selection of nonzero data pairs for a PE Unit, a post-processing engine for ReLU and pooling, a weight gradient Psum control logic, a weight update engine and a global controller. The proposed accelerator can use three different data processing modes according to the training process, and then the global controller is adopted to reconfigure the dataflow (black for FP, red for BP, green for WU) for acquiring, distributing and collecting data to adapt to the corresponding computation behavior.

4.2 Compression Method

Leverage the sparsity propagation in training, the data compression should deliver the sparsity layer by layer. The SIM can not only be used to select nonzero pairs for nonabsolute sparsity but also to characterize absolute sparsity

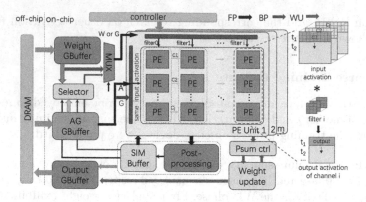

Fig. 4. An illustration of the architecture of proposed SPACE. (Color figure online)

for computing deletion operations without cost. Neither CSR nor RLC commonly used in sparse computing can characterize the sparsity of operands and propagate sparsity without cost show in Fig. 5. Furthermore, they two need more coding information than SIM and are more sensitive to different sparsity.

Therefore, SPACE uses the SIM-based compression (SIMC) method to compress operands and propagate sparsity naturally. Figure 6 shows an example of how to compress the activations using the proposed SIMC method that mainly includes two different fields: (1) the SIM field and (2) the nonzero value field. To be specific, the SIM field is a mask for the original data as encoding information that need extra store, and carries the sparsity of the original data. In addition, the nonzero value field is the nonzero value in the original data, and the size of the field is related to the sparse ratio in the original data.

Note that in the actual memory architecture, the SIM filed and the nonzero value field are decoupled and stored in the SIM Buffer and the corresponding GBuffer respectively. This is for easy address computation in the BP phase.

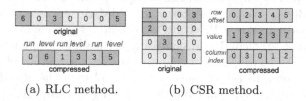

(a) RLC method.   (b) CSR method.

Fig. 5. Commonly used compression method in other sparsity architectures.

4.3   Block Details

PE Array. A PE Array consists of m PE Units, each of which is composed of $n \times n$ PEs connected via simple interconnections. Besides, each PE includes a MAC unit, which performs multiplication and accumulation operations in the training process.

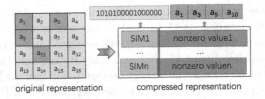

Fig. 6. An example of how to compress activation using proposed SIMC method.

Post-processing and Weight Update. The final results are sent to the post-processing engine to operate ReLU and pooling in FP. A weight gradient Psum control logic is set to arrange the computed partial sums of weight gradient within a batch, and the final weight gradient is sent to the weight update engine for the update.

Index Selector. The index selectors select nonzero data pairs for the data to be distributed to the PE array according to the corresponding training phase, which will not only skip invalid computation cycles but also save energy consumption for data movement.

SIM Buffer. The SIM buffer stores the SIM field of activation and loss gradient and is multiplexed for different situations in different layers. For ReLU layers with absolute sparsity, the SIM of O^l generated in the FP phase is stored in the SIM buffer for reuse in the BP phase and WU phase to eliminate extra memory accesses and skip useless computation cycles, thanks to the sparsity of the output loss gradient that can be predicted in advance. For convolutional operation with absolute sparsity, the SIM field of activation or loss gradient is used to select nonzero data pairs.

Optimization of SIM. To reduce the number of off-chip memory accesses as much as possible for reducing the energy consumption of data movement, we force the SIM during the training process to always reside in the on-chip SIM Buffer. The efficient SIMC method provides the possibility for this optimization.

5 Workflow of SPACE

5.1 Dataflow of PE Array

SPACE accelerates MAC operations for the FP, BP, and WU based on the output stationary dataflow, where the same positions on multiple output channels are computed at once.

The right of Fig. 4 shows the dataflow of a PE unit. Specifically, each PE column shares the same filter, and each PE row shares the an input channel activation with the same sparsity because only the sparsity of activation is exploited in FP. Each PE row is employed to compute the partial result of same position on multiple output channels at t1 (a time to execute a step). Each PE column is employed to compute some positions (dark orange) on a single channel at t1. M PE units process the output of m groups output channels in parallel for high parallelism. In order to reduce the energy consumption caused by the movement of data as much as possible, the filter is reused vertically in a PE unit, while the activation is reused horizontally in the PE unit. Similar reuse methods are also adopted in the BP phase and WU phase.

5.2 Workflow of Nonabsolute Sparsity

Take the FP in layer l as an example to illustrate the nonabsolute sparsity workflow.

(1) Input activations O^{l-1} and weights W^l are loaded from the corresponding GBuffer.
(2) The SIM of O^{l-1} is loaded from the SIM buffer as the indication information for the selector to select nonzero data pairs and distribute them to different PE Units.
(3) Parallel computations according to the internal dataflow of the PE array.
(4) Perform post-processing, and store the SIM information of O^l to the SIM buffer, as the selector indication information of the next layer.

5.3 Workflow of Absolute Sparsity

Take the absolute sparsity in layer l as an example to illustrate the absolute sparsity workflow in BP.

(1) Input gradients δX^{l+1} and weights W^{l+1} are loaded from the corresponding GBuffer.
(2) Based on the PE internal dataflow, obtain the SIM information of O^l from the SIM buffer as the indication information to delete the computations on the PE array. As shown in Fig. 7, the sparsity of the loss gradients δX^l in ReLU layer can be obtained in advance, which is the SIM of output activations O^l stored in the SIM buffer in FP, and then the useless convolution computation of the pixels corresponding to the zero-valued can be deleted safely, thus eliminates a huge amount of computation. Note that there is no need to store the SIM information of δX^l because it is the same as that of O^l.

Once the computation on the pixels is required to be deleted, the cycles of the corresponding PE columns are skipped to execute the next sliding window in the shared input activation. This will prevent the PE from being idle, thus speeding up the entire training process. Nevertheless, different PE columns still have different numbers of necessary MAC operations in the same computation step. Next, we use a load balancing method similar to [15] to schedule a considerable amount of workload to a single PE unit. Specifically, computing blocks with close execution times are scheduled to the same PE unit by adjusting the order of filters, which can alleviate load imbalance due to irregular sparsity distribution.

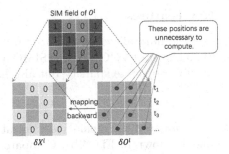

Fig. 7. The pixels of red dots in input loss gradients (δO^l) are meaningless, so the computation on the PEs corresponding to the pixels can be deleted in advance without affecting the result. (Color figure online)

6   Evaluation

Methodology. We adopted a validated synthetic evaluation model [11] for model the accelerated architectures and evaluate the latency and energy quickly and flexibility instead of actual deployment as a more elegant method, and verified the evaluation model against the corresponding RTL implementation to ensure its correctness. Specifically, the gate-level netlist is generated based on a commercial 28 nm technology using the Synopsys Design Compiler. We refer to [13] for the unit energy of DRAM accesses and the unit energy costs for computation and SRAM accesses. Two typical networks (AlexNet [1] and VGGNet [16]) are used for the evaluation and ImageNet as the dataset, but the optimization method is adapted to any network with a convolutional + ReLU layer structure. Exploiting absolute sparsity and nonabsolute sparsity in the network simply skips redundant computations in this paper, which have no impact on the final accuracy.

Architecture Configuration. (1) By deleting the sparse processing components in SPACE, a dense training accelerator is constructed for Baseline. And a PE array contains a total of 512 PEs. (2) We add a few modifications to a sparse inference accelerator [9] as a sparse training accelerator marked as SparTrain. (3) A training accelerator based on the DianNao architecture to only accelerate BP by selective computation of gradients marked as DianNao-S [8]. (4) In order to evaluate the nonabsolute and absolute sparsity proposed in this paper flexibly, we consider the three SPACE configurations shown in the Table 2 for evaluation.

Table 2. Three SPACE variants participated in the evaluation.

Architecture	Nonabsolute	Absolute	Optimization of SIM
Baseline	Not support	Not support	Not support
ACE+N	Support	Not support	Not support
ACE+NA	Support	Support	Not support
SPACE	Support	Support	Support

6.1 Evaluation on Key Features

SIMC. Figure 8(a) shows the normalized extra encoding information of RLC and CSR in the convolutional layer of VGGNet over SIMC. Compared with RLC and CSR, SIMC can not only propagate sparsity but also has stronger stability and efficiency.

Memory Footprint. We evaluated the memory optimization of three SPACE variants based on Baseline as shown in Fig. 8(b). Compared with the Baseline, ACE+N which uses the SIMC method to compress the activation and loss gradient reduces the memory footprint by 1.09x and 1.45x on AlexNet and VGGNet. On the basis of ACE+N, ACE+NA which considers the absolute sparsity based on sparsity propagation reduces the memory footprint by 1.12x and 1.89x compared with baseline. ACE+N and ACE+NA have a better speedup on VGGNet than on AlexNet because VGGNet has higher sparsity than AlexNet. Compared with ACE+NA, SPACE reduces the energy consumption of data movement without affecting memory footprint and reducing the amount of computation.

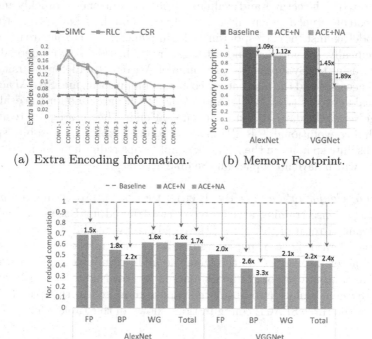

(a) Extra Encoding Information.   (b) Memory Footprint.

(c) Reduced Computation.

Fig. 8. (a) The normalized extra encoding information over proposed SIMC on VGGNet. The normalized reduced of memory footprint (b) and computation (c) over baseline required for training achieved by SPACE under batch size 8.

Reduced Computation. We evaluated the reduced computation of three SPACE architectures based on baseline as shown in Fig. 8(c). ACE+N reduces the amount of computation by 1.6x and 2.2x, and the benefit mainly comes from the cycles of zero-product skipped in the three training phases. On the basis of ACE+N, considering the absolute sparsity caused by sparsity propagation, the massive amount of convolution operation deleted makes ACE+NA reduce the computation amount by 1.7x and 2.4x compared with the Baseline. Note that unlike the reduction of the computation amount in the BP, ACE+NA which considers absolute sparsity does not reduce the amount of computation in the FP and WU compared to ACE+N.

6.2 Performance Evaluation

We benchmark the three SPACE variants with two architecture: DianNao-S [8] and SparTrain [9] mentioned above. For a fairer comparison, the computation resources for the accelerators may be different from their original papers, the bandwidth settings are configured accordingly based on their papers' design. All of the accelerators employ the same number of multipliers (512) and the same size of on-chip memory (2 MB) so that we can compare the performance of the accelerators with the same computational resources.

Latency Speedup. Fig. 9(a) shows the normalized speedup of the three SPACE variants and the two previous accelerators. Experiments show that SPACE has achieved the best performance under the two DCNNs, and realized the speedup from 2.3x and 3.2x, which verified the effectiveness of SPACE which supports the nonabsolute and absolute sparsity and optimization of SIM. Compared with DianNao-S, the benefits come from the exploit of nonabsolute sparsity in three training phases and optimization of SIM. Compared with SparTrain, the benefits are mainly derived from the computation cycles deleted due to absolute sparsity, optimization of SIM.

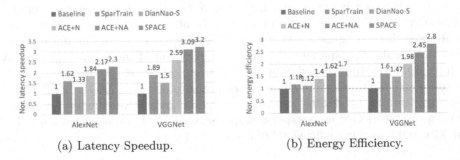

(a) Latency Speedup.   (b) Energy Efficiency.

Fig. 9. The normalized latency speedup (a) and energy efficiency (b) over baseline achieved by SPACE variants under batch size 8.

Energy Efficiency. Figure 9(b) shows the normalized energy efficiency of the three SPACE variants and the two previous training accelerators. The results show that SPACE achieves an energy efficiency improvement of 1.7x on AlexNet, 2.8x on VGGNet compared with baseline. The reason for its high energy efficiency is that on the one hand, it comes from the reduction of unnecessary computing energy consumption obtained, on the other hand, it comes from the reduction of energy consumption of data movement achieved by the SIMC method, the share of SIM and optimization of SIM, which benefits from the fit of SIMC and SPACE architecture.

6.3   Power Breakdown

We analyze the power breakdown and area of SPACE as shown in the Fig. 10. Due to the high memory footprint in the propagation, power consumption mostly comes from them (69.8% for memory), where Weight GBuffer and AG GBuffer are 15.5% and 31.6%. In addition, SIM buffer also accounts for a larger proportion which is 22.7%. Overall, the SPACE accelerator consumes 10% more power when executing the same dense workloads. Both are a small price to pay for the 2.8× energy savings offered by SPACE.

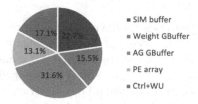

Fig. 10. Power breakdown of the proposed SPACE architecture.

7   Summary and Conclusions

Based on the sparsity propagation process of training, this paper conducted a thorough analysis of the origin of sparsity in all three phases of the training, and gives three insights about found absolute sparsity of the nonlinear layer and the nonabsolute sparsity for efficient deployment of the training process. A training architecture named SPACE was proposed, which propagates sparsity based on SIMC to alleviate the memory pressure and computation pressure of on-edge learning by skiping useless computation and extra memory. Compared with accelerators that ignore sparse propagation, SPACE has achieved a speedup of 3.2x and an energy efficiency improvement of 2.8x.

References

1. Krizhevsky, A., Sutskever, I., Hinton, G.: ImageNet classification with deep convolutional neural networks. In: NIPS (2012)

2. Amodei, D., Ananthanarayanan, S., Anubhai, R., Bai, J., Zhu, Z.: Deep Speech 2: end-to-end speech recognition in English and Mandarin. Computer Science (2015)
3. Parashar, A., et al.: SCNN: an accelerator for compressed-sparse convolutional neural networks. In: International Symposium (2017)
4. Howard, A.G., et al.: MobileNets: efficient convolutional neural networks for mobile vision applications. arXiv:1704.04861 (2017)
5. Liu, H., Simonyan, K., Yang, Y.: DARTS: differentiable architecture search. arXiv:1806.09055 (2018)
6. Choi, S., Sim, J., Kang, M., et al.: An energy-efficient deep convolutional neural network training accelerator for in situ personalization on smart devices. IEEE J. Solid-State Circuits **55**, 2691–2702 (2020)
7. Zhe, Y., Yue, J., Yang, H., et al.: Sticker: a 0.41-62.1 TOPS/W 8bit neural network processor with multi-sparsity compatible convolution arrays and online tuning acceleration for fully connected layers. In: 2018 IEEE Symposium on VLSI Circuits. IEEE (2018)
8. Lee, G., et al.: Acceleration of DNN backward propagation by selective computation of gradients. In: DAC 2019. ACM (2019)
9. Wang, M., Fan, X., Zhang, W., et al.: Balancing memory-accessing and computing over sparse DNN accelerator via efficient data packaging. J. Syst. Architect. **117**(1), 102094 (2021)
10. Chen, Y.H., Emer, J., Sze, V.: Eyeriss: a spatial architecture for energy-efficient dataflow for convolutional neural networks (2016)
11. Li, C., Fan, X., Geng, Y., et al.: ENAS oriented layer adaptive data scheduling strategy for resource limited hardware. Neurocomputing **381**(1), 29–39 (2019)
12. Zhao, Y., Chen, X., Wang, Y., Li, C., Lin, Y.: SmartExchange: trading higher-cost memory storage/access for lower-cost computation. In: 2020 ACM/IEEE 47th Annual International Symposium on Computer Architecture (ISCA) (2020)
13. Yang, X., et al.: Interstellar: Using Halide's scheduling language to analyze DNN accelerators. In: Larus, J.R., Ceze, L., Strauss, K. (eds.) ASPLOS 2020: Architectural Support for Programming Languages and Operating Systems, Lausanne, Switzerland, 16–20 March 2020. ACM (2020)
14. Mahmoud, M., Edo, I., Zadeh, A.H., et al.: TensorDash: exploiting sparsity to accelerate deep neural network training and inference (2020)
15. Liu, L., et al.: DUET: boosting deep neural network efficiency on dual-module architecture. In: MICRO 2020, pp. 738–750 (2020)
16. Simonyan, K., Zisserman, A.: Very deep convolutional networks for large-scale image recognition. arXiv preprint arXiv:1409.1556 (2014)

Worker Recruitment Based on Edge-Cloud Collaboration in Mobile Crowdsensing System

Jinghua Zhu, Yuanjing Li, Anqi Lu, and Heran Xi[✉]

Heilongjiang University, Harbin, China
xiheran@hlju.edu.cn

Abstract. In recent years, with the rapid development of mobile Internet and smart sensor technology, mobile crowdsensing (MCS) computing model has attracted wide concern in academia, industry and business circles. MCS utilizes the sensing and computing capabilities of smart devices carried by workers to cooperate through the mobile Internet to fulfill complex tasks. Worker recruitment is a core and common research problem in MCS, which is a combinatorial optimization problem that considers tasks, workers additionally other factors to satisfy various optimization objectives and constraints. The existing methods are not suitable for large-scale and real-time sensing tasks. Thus, this paper proposes a multi-layers worker recruitment framework based on edge-cloud collaboration. At the cloud computing layer, the whole sensing area is partitioned into small grids according to task position. At the edge computing layer, real-time data processing and aggregation are performed and then a mathematical model is constructed to make decision on worker recruitment by considering a variety of factors from the perspective of workers. Experimental results on real data prove that, compared with existing methods, our method can achieve good performance in terms of spatial coverage and running time under task cost and time constraint.

Keywords: Mobile crowdsensing · Worker recruitment · Edge-cloud collaboration · Spatial coverage · Cost constraint

1 Introduction

In recent years, with the popularization of smart mobile devices and embedded sensors, people can obtain a variety of sensor data in daily life. Moreover, the continuous progress of wireless network technology promotes the vigorous development of MCS.

The traditional MCS as shown in Fig. 1(a) is a kind of cloud-based centralized model which is convenient for overall scheduling [1]. However, due to concurrent

This work was supported by National Key R&D Program of China under Grant No. 2020YFB1710200.

Y. Lai et al. (Eds.): ICA3PP 2021, LNCS 13156, pp. 406–420, 2022.
https://doi.org/10.1007/978-3-030-95388-1_27

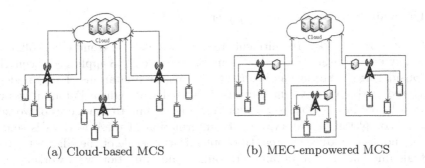

(a) Cloud-based MCS   (b) MEC-empowered MCS

Fig. 1. MCS architecture.

communication with a large number of terminal devices, cloud-based central-ized service platforms will encounter unpredictable network delays which is not suitable for real-time and large-scale MCS applications. Specifically, to ensure that the proper workers are recruited, the worker recruitment in MCS needs to track worker real-time information obtained by the communication between the platform and the worker which leads to both large amount of communication and serious network delay. To solve this problem, some studies have proposed new MCS architecture empowered with mobile edge computing (MEC) [2,3], as shown in Fig. 1(b). Edge nodes (such as base stations) usually have certain stor-age and computing capabilities. Thus, the MCS platform can extend services to the edge of the network, and workers' real-time information updates can occur near mobile devices, in this way, the overall propagation and calculation delay can be reduced greatly.

However, the recruitment of workers either in the cloud or at the edge nodes is inadequate. On the one hand, recruiting workers in the cloud will inevitably overload the system as the complexity of sensing tasks continue to grow, which will affect the scale and real-time of MCS; on the other hand, due to the lack of localized logs at the edge nodes, it is difficult to update worker scores locally and thus greatly reduce the effectiveness of worker recruitment. It is necessary and important to design a worker recruitment method combining the advan-tages of both cloud computing and edge computing. In this paper, we propose a worker recruitment framework based on edge-cloud collaboration named ECRe-cruitment which aims to reduce the communication delay for real-time and large-scale MCS tasks while ensuring overall scheduling. Our goal is to maximize the spatial coverage of tasks under task cost and time constraints. Especially, when obtaining the real-time information by communicating with workers at the edge nodes, we consider much more factors of workers such as the sensing ability of the worker's device, the worker's bid for the sensing task, the maximum number of tasks assigned to the worker and etc. all. A mathematical model is built based on these factors to determine whether the worker can be recruited by edge nodes. In brief, the recruitment of workers in the ECRecruitment framework is based on the score evaluated according to the historical performance of the workers which is a kind of real-time dynamic information.

408   J. Zhu et al.

The main contributions of this paper are as follows:

- We propose a worker recruitment framework based on cloud edge collaboration, which is suitable for real-time and large-scale MCS application scenarios. Considering the storage and computing capacity limitations of edge nodes, a layered worker recruitment framework is further designed. Potential workers are selected in the cloud service platform according to the scores of workers' tasks completed in history, and the information of these workers is sent to edge nodes to reduce the real-time optimization scale of the edge network;
- Real-time information obtained through communication with workers when recruiting workers at the edge nodes, some recruitment factors such as the sensor configuration of the worker's sensing device, the worker's bid for the sensing task, and the maximum number of tasks assigned to the worker are considered from the worker's perspective. This paper builds a model to judge whether workers can be recruited, which is more in line with actual MCS applications;
- Experiments results show that the proposed worker recruitment framework has good performance in terms of spatial coverage and running time under the time and cost constraints.

2   Related Work

The traditional MCS platform is usually based on a centralized architecture. Sherchan et al. [4] propose a framework CAROMM that provides an efficient and extensible method for MCS data collection, enabling end workers to upload different types of sensed data to the cloud. Messaoud et al. [5] design an end-to-end common MCS platform Sensarena that recruits suitable workers based on the preferences of workers and requirement of tasks.

Recently, distributed MCS gradually attracted attention. Sahni et al. [6] study a new computing paradigm, named Edge Mesh, which distributes decision-making tasks among edge devices in the network instead of sending all data to a centralized server. Marjanović et al. [7] propose an edge-computing architecture that satisfies large-scale MCS services, which significantly improves performance, reduces privacy threats, and allows workers to control the flow of contributed sensed data. Roy et al. [8] propose a MCS architecture for music creation, the music components of singing and instrumental are provided by the edge layer of the music MCS framework, in this way, they can improve computing efficiency and reduce the data flow of information processing and storage in cloud services. Zhou et al. [9] study a context-aware worker recruitment framework for MCS in edge computing scenarios, using tree-based context online learning algorithms and clustering of participants to achieve efficient Reputation management realizes the privacy protection of participants, the privacy protection of task requesters and task-oriented reputation management of participants. Wu et al. [10] propose PETA, which uses powerful edge servers deployed between users and platforms to achieve privacy-preserving task assignment.

The above research can not take advantages of both the cloud and edge. Thus, in this paper, we propose a worker recruitment framework based on cloud-edge collaboration which is a common MCS model suitable for edge computing environments. The layered architecture can not only perform data analysis but also meet the demand of the edge network, which is suitable for large-scale extensible MCS services.

3 System Model and Problem Formulation

3.1 System Model

The system model of the worker recruitment framework ECRecruitment consists of three layers, as shown in Fig. 2.

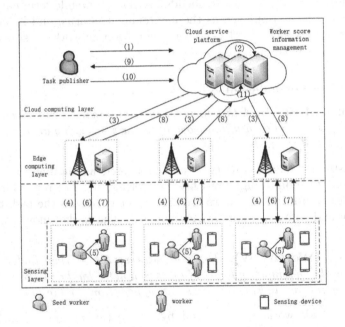

Fig. 2. ECRecruitment system model.

1) Cloud computing layer. This layer provides resources for complex data analysis and long-term storage, and also enables service interactions with multiple edge nodes. The task publisher submits the requirements of the sensing task to the cloud service platform. The cloud server divides the whole task into several sub-tasks according to the region scope specified by the sensing task. The cloud service platform also has a worker score information management module, which can select the candidate seed worker sets based on the worker's historical scores, then it sends the sub-tasks and the index of the selected candidate seed workers to the corresponding ME server. Finally, the summarized sensed results are sent to the task requester, and the worker's score is updated in time according to the requester's feedback after the task is completed.

2) Edge computing layer. It is located near the workers, between sensing devices and the cloud. The ME server forwards the content of the sub-task to the candidate seed workers selected from the cloud service platform according to their index, and then tracks their real-time information. Workers who receive the task content communicate with the ME server and upload their real-time information. The ME server establishes a mathematical model based on the real-time information to determine whether the worker can be recruited. Then the recruited workers upload the sensed data to the corresponding ME server after completing the sensing task. Finally, all the ME servers transmit the received sensed data to the cloud service platform.

3) Sensing layer. Workers use embedded sensors in mobile terminal devices to sense various information such as the environment, status, and behavior. Seed workers can use social networks and communication networks to spread tasks to their friends and neighbors.

3.2   Problem Formulation

Definition 1 (Task T). *A task includes information such as task content, sensor types required for the task, the scope of the task's sensing area, effective time and the reward of the task.*

The tasks can have a variety of contents, such as air quality monitoring, traffic conditions monitoring, forest fire monitoring, etc. The reward for the task also includes an additional reward for the worker to spread the task to a friend or neighbor and compensation for each kilometer the worker moves to complete the task.

Definition 2 (Worker W). *The attributes of the worker include check-in information, the maximum number of tasks completed by the worker, the sensing device configuration, and the worker's bid information for the task.*

The set of all workers is denoted by $W = \{w_1, w_2, \cdots, w_{m+n}\}$. Among them, the set of workers recorded in the cloud service platform is represented by $CW = \{cw_1, cw_2, \cdots, cw_m\}$, and the set of workers not recorded is denoted by $EW = \{ew_1, ew_2, \cdots, ew_n\}$. Specifically, we use $W = < w.id, w.t, (w.x_t, w.y_t), w.block >$ to represent a check-in record of the worker. This paper assumes that every worker involved in the sensing task is honest and the sensed data they upload is true. In addition, the situation in which workers outside the sensing area of task requirements move into the sensing area is not considered.

Definition 3 (Spatial Coverage). *If a subarea obtains at least one sensed data, it is considered to be covered. Spatial coverage is related to the sensing area covered by workers.*

The sensing task released by the task publisher has a certain range of sensing area $T.region$, which is subdivided into small sensing subareas according to a certain scale. These sensing subareas constitute the task target sensing region set $R = \{r_1, r_2, \cdots, r_k\}$, that is, there are k subareas in total, and each subarea has a unique identifier called a block number. Let $W_{recruited} \subseteq W$ denote all recruited workers. In our model, there are two kinds of recruited workers $CW_{recruited} \subseteq CW$ and $EW_{recruited} \subseteq EW$. The set of sensing areas covered by these workers is expressed as $Covered(CW_{recruited} + EW_{recruited})$, therefore, the spatial coverage rate can be expressed as:

$$SC\left(CW_{recruited}, EW_{recruited}\right) = \frac{\left|Covered\left(CW_{recruited} + EW_{recruited}\right)\right|}{|R|} \quad (1)$$

Definition 4 (Worker Recruitment Problem). *The problem of worker recruitment is to solve the following optimization problem:*

$$Maximize\left(SC\left(CW_{recruited}, EW_{recruited}\right)\right) \quad (2)$$

$$s.t.$$
$$1)\ Cost_{CW} + Cost_{EW} \leq T.cost \quad (3)$$
$$2)\ \forall cw_i \in CW_{recruited}, cw_i.t \in T.validTime \quad (4)$$
$$3)\ \forall ew_i \in EW_{recruited}, ew_i.t \in T.validTime \quad (5)$$

where $Cost_{CW}$ and $Cost_{EW}$ represent the total cost of recruiting workers. The ultimate goal is to maximize the spatial coverage under the constraints of the total cost and effective time of the task.

The worker recruitment problem proposed in this paper is a combinatorial optimization problem that satisfies the constraints and optimization goals. According to the above definition of tasks and workers, there are a total of $(m + n)$ workers and k sensing subareas for pairing, so the time complexity required for this idea is $O((m + n) \times k)$. It is necessary to design a greedy or heuristic algorithm to obtain the approximate optimal solution of the problem.

4 Edge-Cloud Collaborative Worker Recruitment

4.1 Recruitment Factors for Workers

Before recruiting workers, we first establish a mathematical model to determine whether workers can be recruited based on the real-time information obtained when the edge node communicates with the workers. This paper considers the following factors affecting the recruitment of workers from the perspective of workers [11]:

1) The sensing device configuration

The edge node can judge whether the worker can be recruited based on the matching between the sensor configuration of the sensing device carried by the worker and the sensor required for the task.

$$isRecruited_1(w) = \begin{cases} 1, T.sensorSet \subseteq w.sensorSet \\ 0, else \end{cases} \tag{6}$$

2) Worker's bid for tasks

When the worker communicates with the edge node in real-time, the worker will inform the price they need to complete the sensing task. The relationship between the worker's price and the maximum reward limit of the task is one of the judging factors.

$$isRecruited_2(w) = \begin{cases} 1, T.maxReward \geq w.bid \\ 0, T.maxReward < w.bid \end{cases} \tag{7}$$

3) The maximum number of tasks assigned to workers

If workers need to complete too many tasks, it will affect the quality of their tasks. This paper predefines the maximum number of tasks assigned to each worker, $w.num$ represents the number of tasks the worker currently has to complete.

$$isRecruited_3(w) = \begin{cases} 1, w.num \leq w.maxTaskNum \\ 0, w.num > w.maxTaskNum \end{cases} \tag{8}$$

4) Availability of workers

Workers who are willing to accept tasks in the sensing area mean that workers are available. This paper assumes that each worker can have a spatial subarea where they are unwilling to perform sensing tasks. When the MCS platform recruits workers and assigns them sensing tasks, it will bring the risk of interference and privacy leakage to workers. For example, some workers may consider the privacy of their location and refuse to accept tasks when they are at home. Specifically, this paper defines an availability list l_w for each worker in the sensing subarea. When $l_w[r] = 1$, it means that worker w is willing to accept the task in the rth sensing subarea.

$$isRecruited_4(w) = \begin{cases} 1, l_w[r] = 1 \\ 0, l_w[r] = 0 \end{cases} \tag{9}$$

5) Possibility of completion of tasks

This paper assumes that each worker has a probability of completing a task, which can be learned from the historical situation of completing the task, and p_w represents the probability of completing the task by worker w. For workers with a record of completing tasks, the possibility of completing a worker's task is expressed as

$$p(w) = \frac{completeCount(w)}{receiveCount(w)} \tag{10}$$

For workers who have not completed the task record, we set p_w as the average of the task completion probability of other workers within the control range of their edge nodes. In this paper, a threshold of task completion probability p_{thr} is set in advance. If $p_w \geq p_{thr}$, it is considered that worker w can be recruited.

$$isRecruited_5(w) = \begin{cases} 1 & , p_w \geq p_{thr} \\ 0 & , p_w < p_{thr} \end{cases} \tag{11}$$

Combining the above five factors that affect recruitment from the perspective of workers, when the edge node communicates with worker, the mathematical modeling of the recruitment of worker can be expressed as

$$isRecruited(w) = \prod_{k=1}^{5} isRecruited_k(w) \tag{12}$$

Where, $isRecruited(w) = 1$ indicates that worker w can be recruited, and 0 means not.

4.2 Worker Recruitment Algorithm for ECRecruitment

This paper proposes a worker recruitment framework ECRecruitment based on cloud-edge collaboration, which uses a layered worker recruitment design concept. The algorithm at the edge computing layer is shown in Algorithm 1.

In the edge computing layer, the edge node forwards the task content to candidate seed workers and communicates with them in real time. In lines 3–8, seed workers are recruited according to the heuristic function $seedHeurFunc(cw)$ until the number of seed worker sets recruited reaches a limit, where the heuristic function can be expressed as

$$seedHeurFunc(cw) = [\beta \times seedInfluence(cw, CW_{cand}) + (1 - \beta) \\ \times (Covered(W_{recruited} \cup \{cw\}) - Covered(W_{recruited}))]/cw.bid \tag{13}$$

Among them, $seedInfluence(cw, CW_{cand})$ function is used to measure the size of influence of seed workers (related to the number of seed workers' spreading task), $(Covered(W_{recruited} \cup \{cw\}) - Covered(W_{recruited}))$ represents the increase of spatial coverage by adding seed workers cw into the recruited worker set $W_{recruited}$, and β is a parameter used to balance the size of influence and the utility of spatial coverage. In lines 11–20, workers are recruited according to the heuristic function $heurFunc(ew)$.

$$heurFunc(ew) = \frac{Covered(ew)}{ew.bid} \tag{14}$$

In 22–36 line, if there are uncovered sensing subareas and remaining task budget, first cluster the remaining sensing subareas set R to form cluster RC, then pair the candidate worker set EW_{cand} and the subarea cluster RC to form a worker-cluster WRC, last based on the utility function to recruit workers.

$$Utility(ew, rc) = \frac{Num(rc)}{distFunc(ew, CP(rc)) \times ew.bid} \tag{15}$$

414   J. Zhu et al.

Algorithm 1. ECRecruitment algorithm

Require: $CW_{initCand}$: The initial set of candidate seed workers from the cloud computing layer; $MaxSeedWorker$: Maximum number of seed workers; $cw.bid and ew.bid$: Worker's bid; $T.rewardProp$: Reward for spread tasks; $T.comKM$: Compensation per kilometer of movement; $T.cost$: Task cost constraint; R_l: The target sensing area set of the lth partition

Ensure: $W_{recruited}$: The set of workers recruited

1: $CW_{cand} = isRecruited(CW_{initCand})$
2: set $W_{recruited} = \emptyset$
3: **while** $|W_{recruited}| \leq MaxSeedWorker$ **do**
4:      Select cw from CW_{cand} with maximum $seedHeurFunc(cw)$
5:      $W_{recruited} = W_{recruited} \cup \{cw\}$
6:      $CW_{cand} = CW_{cand} - \{w\}$
7:      $T.cost = T.cost - cw.bid - T.rewardProp \times friendNum(cw)$
8: **end while**
9: $EW_{initCand} = networkPropagate(W_{recruited})$
10: $EW_{cand} = isRecruited(EW_{initCand})$
11: **while** $T.cost \geq 0$ **do**
12:      select ew from $EW_{recruited}$ with maximum $heuristicFunc(ew)$
13:      **if** $Covered(W_{recruited} \cup \{ew\}) - Covered(W_{recruited}) = \emptyset$ **then**
14:          Continue
15:      **else**
16:          $W_{recruited} = W_{recruited} \cup \{ew\}$
17:          $EW_{cand} = EW_{cand} - \{ew\}$
18:          $T.cost = T.cost - ew.bid$
19:      **end if**
20: **end while**
21: $R_l = R_l - Covered(W_{recruited})$
22: **if** $R_l! = \emptyset$ and $T.cost \geq 0$ **then**
23:      Cluster R_l into sensing area cluster set RC
24:      From $|EW_{cand}| \times |RC|$ worker-cluster set WRC
25:      **for** worker-cluster $wrc \in WRC$ **do**
26:          Select wrc with maximum $Utility(ew, rc)$
27:          **if** $R_l! = \emptyset$ and $T.cost \leq 0$ **then**
28:              Break
29:          **else**
30:              $T.cost = T.cost - T.comKM \times disFunc(ew, CP(rc))$
31:              $W_{recruited} = W_{recruited} \cup \{ew\}$
32:              $EW_{cand} = EW_{cand} - \{ew\}$
33:              $R_l = R_l - rc$
34:          **end if**
35:      **end for**
36: **end if**
37: Return $W_{recruited}$

Among them, the $Num(rc)$ function counts the number of subarea of cluster rc, the $CP(rc)$ function obtains the central position of cluster rc, and the

$distFunc(ew, CP(rc))$ function calculates the distance between worker ew and the center of cluster rc.

5 Experiment and Result Analysis

5.1 Experimental Dataset

Similar to documents [12,13], this paper uses real-world location-based social network data sets Brightkite and Gowalla. We assume that the users in the Brightkite and Gowalla datasets are workers participating in MCS, and each check-in site is considered to be the place where workers perform sensing tasks. The details of the relevant data set are shown in Table 1.

Table 1. Datasets summary

	Brightkite	Gowalla
Number of workers	111	583
Number of friendship edges	782	3774
Number of neighbor edges	8592	210156
Number of check-in records	6876	23320
Average number of check-in records	61.946	40

The given task demand sensing area is a rectangular area of 240 km × 240 km, We divide it into 480 equal virtual subareas. Since the ocean area does not require sensed data, this paper finally needs to consider 344 virtual subareas. Suppose that the cloud service platform divides the whole rectangular area into four small areas, each of which is equipped with a ME host. ME node 1 involves 92 subareas, ME node 2 involves 66 subareas, ME node 3 involves 92 subareas, and ME node 4 involves 94 subareas. The divided target sensing area is shown in Fig. 3.

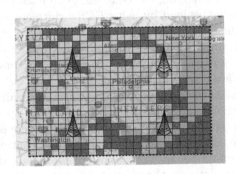

Fig. 3. The divided target sensing region (irrespective subareas are removed).

5.2 Experimental Setup

The parameter settings are shown in Table 2. The longitude information in the check-in record is mapped to two-dimensional coordinates during the experiment.

Table 2. Parameter settings

Parameter	Parameter value
$maxSeedWorker$	Brightkite:5, Gowalla:10
β	Brightkite:0.64, Gowalla:0.56
$w.maxTaskNum$	5
$T.cost$	1500\$–4000\$
$T.maxReward$	10\$
$T.rewardProp$	\$0.1 per person
$T.comKM$	1\$/km
p_{thr}	0.5

Table 3. Task cost settings

Total cost	R_1	R_2	R_3	R_4
1500\$	401\$	288\$	401\$	410\$
2000\$	535\$	384\$	535\$	546\$
2500\$	668\$	480\$	668\$	684\$
3000\$	802\$	576\$	802\$	820\$
3500\$	936\$	672\$	936\$	956\$
4000\$	1070\$	767\$	1070\$	1093\$

In order to evaluate the effect of the constraint of the total cost on the spatial coverage performance of the worker recruitment algorithm, the total cost is set from \$1500 to \$4000. Assume that the upper limit of the incentive amount paid to each worker is \$10. An additional \$0.10 per worker is paid to seed workers for the spread task; A compensation of \$1 per kilometer is given to workers who move to a specific location to perform sensing tasks. According to the number of sensing subareas involved in each ME node, the total cost is allocated proportionally. The specific set of task costs assigned to the four ME nodes is shown in Table 3.

5.3 Analysis of Results

In the two data sets, by changing the constraint conditions of the total cost, the spatial coverage results obtained by using ECRecruitment framework to recruit workers in four ME nodes are shown in Fig. 4.

Due to the constrained budget of changing the total cost, the running time results for the ECRecruitment framework to recruit workers on the edge nodes for the two datasets are shown in Fig. 5.

The results of spatial coverage of workers recruited by all ME nodes summarized by the cloud service platform are shown in Fig. 6.

Figure 4, Fig. 6 show that as the total cost budget increases, the ECRecruitment framework's spatial coverage on both datasets continues to increase. In addition, because the number of workers in the Gowalla dataset is larger than that of the Brightkite dataset, the spatial coverage in the Gowalla dataset is larger.

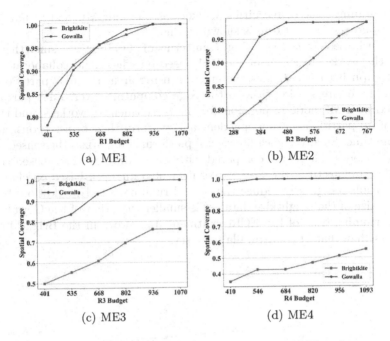

Fig. 4. Spatial coverage obtained by different 4 ME nodes.

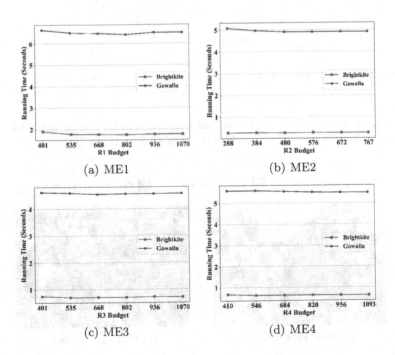

Fig. 5. Running time of different ME nodes.

The running time of recruiting workers on the four ME nodes summarized by the cloud service platform is shown in Fig. 7.

As can be seen from Fig. 5, Fig. 7, in terms of running time, since this paper adopts the worker recruitment method based on edge cloud collaboration, the cloud computing layer divides the entire sensing area into four partitions and offloads the entire sensing task to the edge computing layer. Each partition is managed by a ME node responsible for the recruitment of workers, and the ME nodes of all partitions are independent and perform their own responsibility at the same time. Finally, the cloud service platform summarizes the sensed results of all ME nodes. Therefore, compared with the traditional cloud-based centralized MCS architecture, the worker recruitment framework based on cloud-edge collaboration can greatly reduce the overall running time. In addition, because the data size of the Brightkite data set is smaller than that of the Gowalla data set, the running time of the ECRecruitment framework in the Brightkite data set is less than that of the Gowalla data set.

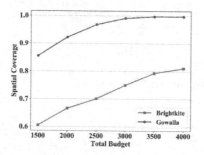

Fig. 6. ECRecruitment's spatial coverage.

Fig. 7. ECRecruitment's running time.

Under the setting of a total cost constraint of $4000, the intuitive display of the sensing subareas covered by the two data sets is shown in Fig. 8.

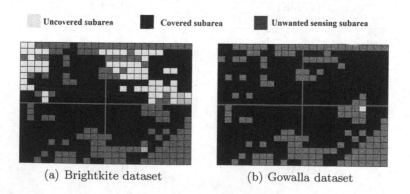

(a) Brightkite dataset

(b) Gowalla dataset

Fig. 8. The results of covered sensing subareas.

The performance comparison results of the ECRecruitment framework proposed in this paper and the comparison algorithm under the same setting (i.e., the fixed total cost budget is $4000) of spatial coverage and running time are shown in Table 4.

Table 4 shows that for the two datasets of Brightkite and Gowalla, the ECRecruitment framework can achieve high spatial coverage in a short running time, even the Gowalla data set can cover almost the entire sensing area within 8 s of running time. In general, the ECRecruitment framework is superior to the comparison methods of MaxDegree [14], MacCov [15], HG [14], NaïveFast [14], Fast-Selector [14], H-GWR [16] and HySelector [5] in terms of spatial coverage and running time.

Table 4. The results of spatial coverage and running time comparison

Algorithm	Brightkite		Gowalla	
	Spatial coverage	Running time	Spatial coverage	Running time
ECRecruitment	**0.811**	**3**	**0.997**	**8**
MaxDegree	0.65(−0.161)	22(+19)	0.65(−0.347)	22(+14)
MacCov	0.68(−0.131)	24(+21)	0.68(−0.317)	26(+18)
HG	0.67(−0.141)	23(+20)	0.64(−0.357)	25(+17)
NaïveFast	0.69(−0.121)	280(+277)	0.73(−0.267)	270(+262)
Fast-Selector	0.8(−0.011)	720(+717)	0.73(−0.267)	860(+852)
H-GWR	0.75(−0.061)	44(+41)	0.78(−0.217)	45(+37)
HySelector	0.8(−0.011)	7(+4)	0.98(−0.017)	25(+17)

6   Conclusion and Future Work

This paper proposes a worker recruitment framework ECRecruitment based on edge-cloud collaboration for large-scale and real-time tasks in MCS whose goal is to maximize the spatial coverage of tasks under time and cost constraints of sensing tasks. ECRecruitment is a layered framework consisting of cloud-end, edge-end and sensing-end. The decision of worker recruitment is made on the edge-end by collecting workers' real-time information. The experimental results prove that the worker recruitment framework proposed in this paper has good performance in terms of spatial coverage while ensuring task time and cost constraints. Besides, since all edge nodes recruit workers in parallel, the time complexity of overall worker recruitment can be greatly reduced.

Privacy protection worker recruitment algorithm is one of our future work. Sensing tasks in MCS are usually location-based and workers are required to move to the task-specific location to collect sensing data. When the sensing data is uploaded, the workers' location privacy information will be leaked. We will focus on how to protect worker privacy during the recruitment process.

References

1. Antonić, A., Marjanović, M., Pripužić, K., et al.: A mobile crowd sensing ecosystem enabled by CUPUS: cloud-based publish/subscribe middleware for the internet of things. Futur. Gener. Comput. Syst. **56**, 607–622 (2016)
2. Ma, L., Liu, X., Pei, Q., Yong, X.: Privacy-preserving reputation management for edge computing enhanced mobile crowdsensing. IEEE Trans. Serv. Comput. **12**, 786–799 (2018)
3. Hu, Y., Shen, H., Bai, G., Wang, T.: P2TA: privacy-preserving task allocation for edge computing enhanced mobile crowdsensing. In: Algorithms and Architectures for Parallel Processing, ICA3PP 2018, pp. 431–446 (2018)
4. Sherchan, W., Jayaraman, P.P., Krishnaswamy, S., et al.: Using on-the-move mining for mobile crowdsensing. In: 2012 IEEE 13th International Conference on Mobile Data Management, pp. 115–124. IEEE (2012)
5. Messaoud, R.B., Rejiba, Z., Ghamri-Doudane, Y.: An Energy-aware end-to-end crowdsensing platform: sensarena. In: 2016 13th IEEE Annual Consumer Communications & Networking Conference (CCNC), pp. 284–285. IEEE (2016)
6. Sahni, Y., Cao, J., Zhang, S., et al.: Edge Mesh: a new paradigm to enable distributed intelligence in Internet of Things. IEEE Access **5**, 16441–16458 (2017)
7. Marjanović, M., Antonić, A., Žarko, I.P.: Edge computing architecture for mobile crowdsensing. IEEE Access **6**, 10662–10674 (2018)
8. Roy, S., Sarkar, D., Hati, S., et al.: Internet of Music Things: an edge computing paradigm for opportunistic crowdsensing. J. Supercomput. **74**(11), 6069–6101 (2018)
9. Zhou, P., Chen, W., Ji, S., et al.: Privacy-preserving online task allocation in edge-computing-enabled massive crowdsensing. IEEE Internet Things J. **6**(5), 7773–7787 (2019)
10. Wu, D., Yang, Z., Yang, B., Wang, R., Zhang, P.: From centralized management to edge collaboration: a privacy-preserving task assignment framework for mobile crowdsensing. IEEE IoT J. **8**, 4579–4589 (2020)
11. Wang, J., Wang, F., Wang, Y., et al.: Allocating heterogeneous tasks in participatory sensing with diverse participant-side factors. IEEE Trans. Mob. Comput. **18**(9), 1979–1991 (2018)
12. Zheng, L., Chen, L.: Maximizing acceptance in rejection-aware spatial crowdsourcing. IEEE Trans. Knowl. Data Eng. **29**(9), 1943–1956 (2017)
13. née Müller, S.K., Tekin, C., van der Schaar, M., et al.: Context-aware hierarchical online learning for performance maximization in mobile crowdsourcing. IEEE/ACM Trans. Netw. **26**(3): 1334–1347 (2018)
14. Wang, J., Wang, F., Wang, Y., et al.: Social-network-assisted worker recruitment in mobile crowd sensing. IEEE Trans. Mob. Comput. **18**(7), 1661–1673 (2018)
15. Zhang, D., Xiong, H., Wang, L., et al.: CrowdRecruiter: selecting participants for piggyback crowdsensing under probabilistic coverage constraint. In: Proceedings of the 2014 ACM International Joint Conference on Pervasive and Ubiquitous Computing, pp. 703–714 (2014)
16. Lu, A., Zhu, J.: Hybrid network assisted dynamic worker recruitment algorithm. In: 2019 IEEE International Conference on Smart Internet of Things (SmartIoT), pp. 254–261. IEEE (2019)

Energy Efficient Deployment and Task Offloading for UAV-Assisted Mobile Edge Computing

Yangguang Lu, Xin Chen$^{(\boxtimes)}$, Fengjun Zhao⑩, and Ying Chen⑩

School of Computer Science, Beijing Information Science and Technology University, Beijing, China
chenxin@bistu.edu.cn

Abstract. With the popularization of mobile wireless networks and Internet of Things (IoT) technologies, energy-hungry and delay-intensive applications continue to surge. Due to the limited computing power and battery capacity, mobile terminals rarely satisfy the increasing demands of application services. Mobile Edge Computing (MEC) deploys communication and computing resources near the network edge closing to the user side, which effectively reduces devices' energy consumption and enhances system performance. However, the application of MEC needs infrastructures that can deploy edge services, and is limited by the geographical environment. UAV-assisted MEC has better flexibility and communication Line-of-Sight (LoS), which expands service scope while improving the versatility of MEC. Meanwhile, the dynamic task arrival rate, channel condition, and environmental factors pose challenges for task offloading and resources allocation strategy. In this paper, we jointly optimize UAV deployment, frequency scaling, and task scheduling to minimize energy consumption for devices while ensuring system stability in the long term. Due to the dynamic and randomness of task arrival rate and wireless channel, the original problem is defined as a stochastic optimization problem. The Drone Placement and Online Task oFFloading (DPOTFF) algorithm is designed to decouple the original problem into several sub-problems and solve them within a limited time complexity. It is also proved theoretically that the DPOTFF can obtain close-to-optimal energy consumption while ensuring system stability. The effectiveness and reliability of the algorithm are also verified by simulation and comparative experiments.

Keywords: Mobile Edge Computing · Energy efficiency · Resources allocation · Task offloading · UAV deployment

1 Introduction

With the in-depth research of wireless mobile technologies, the complexity of smart applications continues to increase. The limited computing power and battery capacity of mobile devices (MDs) can no longer guarantee the quality of

© Springer Nature Switzerland AG 2022
Y. Lai et al. (Eds.): ICA3PP 2021, LNCS 13156, pp. 421–435, 2022.
https://doi.org/10.1007/978-3-030-95388-1_28

application services. MEC transfers resources to the edge of network closing devices, which relieves the computation load and prolongs the time life of MDs [1]. There exist some challenges: (1) In the remote areas where there are not enough terrestrial infrastructures that can deploy edge servers. (2) According to complex terrains in the actual situation, it is impractical to have the suitable areas to deploy BSs for communication and providing services anytime [2]. Therefore, how to deploy the UAV in an appropriate location to achieve flexible coverage for providing efficient wireless communication and computation offloading services is worth researching.

The UAV-assisted MEC, as a promising paradigm, is advanced to tackle the challenges. The task arrival rate of each application and wireless channel state is stochastic and dynamic over time, which are not only affected by the actual complex environment but also by the actual complex environment [3]. In addition, the offloading strategy needs to consider the current task queue state and wireless channel condition. Impertinent computation allocation would lead to extra energy consumption and a large queue backlog. As a result, how to formulate an efficient task offloading and resources allocation scheme that adapts to the highly dynamic and stochastic scenario is a hot and difficult spot.

Some works in the UAV-assisted MEC have received wide attention. Messous et al. [4] applied game theory to the UAV-assisted MEC to balance UAV energy consumption and task processing delay. Dinh et al. [5] took the minimum system energy consumption while ensuring task execution delay as the goal to design a task scheduling and CPU-cycle frequency allocation strategy. Sun et al. [6] designed a user-oriented management strategy to minimize time delay following the constraints in energy consumption. Besides, considering the practical offloading process, some works have studied the stochastic optimization problem for a long-term task scheduling problem. Jiang et al. [7] considered multi-core mobile devices and proposed an energy-efficient cloud offloading scheme. Mao et al. [8] jointly considered processing latency and energy consumption of MDs to design task offloading and resources allocation scheme. Liu et al. [9] taken into account system latency and reliability with multiple users and MEC servers to minimize transmit and computing power. Although there have been many works in the field of UAV-assisted MEC, most of them considered the task offloading decision in a short period. In actual situations, the computation offloading and task execution process are a continuous cycle. Meanwhile, the tasks arrival rate and channel condition are both stochastic and dynamic, which cannot be accurately obtained.

In this paper, we consider the dynamics and randomness in the real environment, following the system's long-term performance and stability. The main contributions are as follows:

- We jointly optimize the UAV deployment, frequency scaling and task offloading. The goal is to minimize energy consumption while ensuring long-term performance and system stability.

- Based on Lyapunov optimization methods, the Drone Placement and Online Task Offloading (DPOTFF) algorithm are formulated to decouple and solve the original stochastic optimization problem.
- The algorithm efficiency is evaluated through comparative experiment analysis, and the results prove the DPOTFF algorithm can reduce energy consumption effectively.

The remaining is as follows: Section 2 develops relevant models and puts forward optimization problem. In Sect. 3, the DPOTFF is proposed and proved its feasibility. Section 4 conducts simulation experiments. The summary of the paper is made in Sect. 5.

2   System Model

A UAV-assisted MEC system is considered, where the UAV configured with a MEC server provides offloading and communication services for the MD that contains n different applications. The set of applications is denoted as $N = \{1, 2, ..., n\}$. Each application has a certain number of computation tasks and the MD can partially or completely offload application tasks to the UAV. The time-slotted system is introduced and indexed by $t \in \{0, 1, 2, ..., T - 1\}$, where the length of slot is τ.

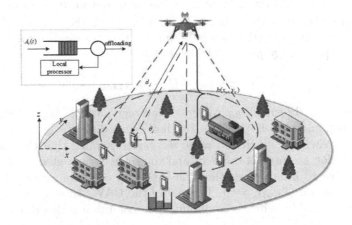

Fig. 1. UAV-assisted MEC network

2.1   Communication Model

For generality, a 3-D Cartesian coordinate is constructed, the UAV hovers over the area at the altitude $h(x_u, y_u)$, mapping coordinate in the horizontal plane is (x_u, y_u). The location of MD j at time slot t is $(x_j(t), y_j(t), 0)$. As illustrated in Fig. 1, the actual space and horizontal distances between MD j and the UAV can express as

$$d_j = \sqrt{(x_u - x_j(t))^2 + (y_u - y_j(t))^2 + h(x_u, y_u)^2}, \tag{1}$$

$$l_j = \sqrt{(x_u - x_j(t))^2 + (y_u - y_j(t))^2}. \tag{2}$$

The wireless channel between MD and the UAV is represented as a probabilistic Line-of-Sight (LoS) link. Define the pathloss in LoS and NLoS as η_{LoS} and η_{NLoS}, respectively. As mentioned in [12], η_{LoS} and η_{NLoS} denote as

$$\eta_{LoS} = 20 \log(\frac{4\pi f_c d_j}{c}) + \xi_{LoS}, \tag{3}$$

$$\eta_{NLoS} = 20 \log(\frac{4\pi f_c d_j}{c}) + \xi_{NLoS}, \tag{4}$$

where ξ_{LoS} and ξ_{NLoS} represent the average value of the LoS and NLoS excessive pathloss. c is the light speed and f_c means carrier frequency.

The probability that the transmission link is LoS express as

$$\rho = \frac{1}{1 + be^{-\beta(\theta_j - b)}}, \tag{5}$$

where b and β are constants related to actual environment. $\theta_j = \arcsin(\frac{h(x_u, y_u)}{d_j})$ is the elevation angle of MD j. It can be seen that with the increase of the UAV hovering height, the elevation angle becomes larger, resulting in a higher LoS probability. The average pathloss is denoted as

$$\bar{\eta}_j = \rho \eta_{LoS} + (1 - \rho)\eta_{NLoS}. \tag{6}$$

There exists a threshold η_{th}. When the average pathloss is greater than η_{th}, wireless communication is possible, the horizontal distance between the UAV and MD will reach the maximum when $\bar{\eta} = \eta_{th}$. Assuming that the positions of MD at each slot are pre-determined, and the set is represented as J. a_j is the binary variable to indicate whether the UAV can communication with MD j, (i.e., $a_j = 1$) or not (i.e., $a_j = 0$). The size of the UAV's coverage is represented by the sum of a_j. The wireless communication condition is described as

$$a_j(\bar{\eta}_j - \eta_{th}) \le 0, \forall j \in J. \tag{7}$$

Consider the actual flight performance of UAV, the altitude meets

$$h(x_u, y_u)_{min} \le h(x_u, y_u) \le h(x_u, y_u)_{max}, \tag{8}$$

where $h(x_u, y_u)_{min}$ restricts the minimum feasible altitude, and $h(x_u, y_u)_{max}$ is the maximum altitude that the UAV can achieve.

When the horizontal distance is maximum between the UAV and MD, the optimal elevation angle is obtained. Taking the derivative of the Eq. (6), the optimal elevation angle θ^* can obtain, which is obtained from

$$\frac{\pi}{9\ln(10)}\tan\theta^* + \frac{b\beta(\eta_{LoS}+\eta_{NLoS})e^{(-\beta(\theta^*-b))}}{be^{(-\beta(\theta^*-b))}+1} = 0. \tag{9}$$

Besides, the optimal altitude of the UAV is the altitude when the horizontal distance reaches the maximum. By solving Eq. (9), we can get the optimal elevation angle θ^* when the horizontal distance is maximum. The maximum horizontal distance l_{max} is easy to obtain. Then, the optimal altitude of the UAV can express as $h(x_u,y_u)^* = l_{max}\tan\theta^*$.

2.2 Energy Consumption Model

In time slot t, $A_i(t)$ denotes the number of tasks generated by application i. $D_i^l(t)$ represents the amount of tasks locally executed. ρ_i indicates the number of CPU cycles/bit in local execution, and $f(t)$ indicates the computation ability of MD, which has an upper bound f_{max}, there is

$$0 \le f(t) \le f_{max}. \tag{10}$$

For a known frequency $f(t)$, the amount of tasks processed locally satisfies

$$\sum_{i\in N} \rho_i D_i^l(t) \le f(t)\tau. \tag{11}$$

The energy consumption of total local execution $E_l(t)$ describes as

$$E_l(t) = \zeta f^2(t)\sum_{i\in N}\rho_i D_i^l(t), \tag{12}$$

where ζ denotes the effective capacitance, depending on the CPU hardware architecture. $D_i^r(t)$ means the number of tasks offloading to the UAV. The amount of computation tasks offloaded is $\sum_{i=1}^{n} D_i^r(t)$. The transmission rate can obtain from

$$R(t) = B\log_2(1 + P\frac{10^{-\bar{\eta}/10}}{\sigma^2}), \tag{13}$$

where B is the wireless channel bandwidth, P is the transmission power, and σ^2 denotes the noise power. The number of tasks offloaded and transmission rate follows

$$\sum_{i\in N} D_i^r(t) \le R(t)\tau. \tag{14}$$

$E_r(t)$ expresses the energy consumption of data transmission, which can be derived by

$$E_r(t) = P\sum_{i\in N}\frac{D_i^r(t)}{R(t)}. \tag{15}$$

The energy consumption of MD $E_t(t)$ including local processing and offloading energy consumption, given by

$$E_t(t) = \zeta f^2(t) \sum_{i \in N} \rho_i D_i^l(t) + P \sum_{i \in N} \frac{D_i^r(t)}{R(t)}. \tag{16}$$

We pay more attention to average energy consumption on the long-term as follows

$$\bar{E} = \lim_{T \to \infty} \frac{\sum_{t=0}^{T-1} \mathbb{E}(E_t(t))}{T}. \tag{17}$$

2.3   Task Queueing Model

For each application, the task queue is denoted as $Q_i(t)$ in time slot t, and the queue $Q_i(t+1)$ in next slot is

$$Q_i(t+1) = max(Q_i(t) - D_i^l - D_i^r, 0) + A_i(t). \tag{18}$$

According to *Little's Law* [10], the queue delay and the average queue backlog are related. We minimize the long-term queue backlog, which is denoted as

$$q_i = \lim_{T \to \infty} \frac{\sum_{t=0}^{T-1} \mathbb{E}(Q_i(t))}{T} < \xi, \exists \, \xi \in \mathbb{R}^+. \tag{19}$$

2.4   Optimization Problem

In order to ensure system stability and avoid excessive queue backlog, the optimization goal denotes as

$$\min_X \bar{E} = \lim_{T \to \infty} \frac{\sum_{t=0}^{T-1} \mathbb{E}\{E_t(t)\}}{T}, \tag{20}$$
$$\text{s.t}\quad (7), (8), (10), (11), (14), (19).$$

where $\mathbf{X}$ denotes the variables set composed of $\{x_u, y_u, h(x_u, y_u), \mathbf{D^r(t)}, \mathbf{D^l(t)}, f(t)\}$. Because task arrival rate and channel state are stochastic and dynamic, the objective function (20) is a stochastic optimization problem.

3   Algorithm Design

The DPOTFF algorithm is formulated to decouple and tackle the stochastic optimization problem. We decompose the original problem into two sub-problems 1) initialize the UAV deployment problem 2) frequency scaling and task offloading problem. The DPOTFF can approximate minimum energy consumption and maximum coverage while ensuring queue stability in low time complexity.

3.1   Initialize UAV Deployment Problem

Divide the area into multiple blocks of the same size. The set of blocks is defined as M. When the UAV is placed at position m, it would try to communicate with MDs in the area. The goal is to obtain the UAV position where the UAV covers the most MDs. We iteratively place the UAV in each block and record the number of MDs. Specific steps are as follows:

- Selecting location m and place UAV over each block. According to Eq. (9), the optimal elevation angle θ^* and optimal altitude $h(x_u, y_u)^*$ can obtain. In order to meet constraint (8), $h(x_u, y_u)^* = h(x_u, y_u)_{max}$, if $h(x_u, y_u)^* > h(x_u, y_u)_{max}$ and $h(x_u, y_u)^* = h(x_u, y_u)_{min}$, if $h(x_u, y_u)^* < h(x_u, y_u)_{min}$.
- Obtaining the average pathloss and recording the number of MDs covered. K_m as the set of MDs covered when the UAV is deployed at m, i.e., $K_m = \{j \in J | \bar{\eta}_j > \eta_{th}\}$.
- The optimal position can be obtained according to the value of $|K_m|$, $m^* = \text{argmax}\{|K_m| | m \in M\}$.

3.2   Frequency Scaling and Task Offloading Problem

According to Lyapunov optimization methods, the applications queue backlog matrix $\mathbf{Q}(t)$ is defined. The Lyapunov function defines as

$$L(\mathbf{Q}(t)) = \frac{1}{2} \sum_{i \in N} Q_i^2(t), \tag{21}$$

where $L(\mathbf{Q}(t))$ represents the queue backlog status. When $L(\mathbf{Q}(t))$ is large, it means at least one application is large. Therefore, we have to reduce $L(\mathbf{Q}(t))$ as possible to ensure queue stability. We define the *conditional Lyapunov drift* function as follows

$$\Delta(\mathbf{Q}(t)) = \mathbb{E}\{L(\mathbf{Q}(t+1)) - L(\mathbf{Q}(t)) | \mathbf{Q}(t)\}. \tag{22}$$

To minimize energy consumption while stabilizing application queues, the *drift plus energy consumption* function $\Delta_V(\mathbf{Q}(t))$ is defined, which expressed as

$$\Delta_V(\mathbf{Q}(t)) = \Delta(\mathbf{Q}(t)) + V\mathbb{E}\{E_t(t) | \mathbf{Q}(t)\}, \tag{23}$$

where V is the penalty coefficient that used to balance the queue backlog and energy consumption, which is non-negative. A larger value of V is more inclined to optimize energy consumption, but it is easier to generate the queue backlog. The upper bound of *drift plus energy consumption* function is proved in Theorem 1.

Theorem 1. *In each time slot t, if $A_i(t)$ and $R(t)$ have upper bounds $A_i^{max}(t)$ and R_{max}, the drift plus energy consumption of any strategies would satisfy*

$$\Delta(\mathbf{Q}(t)) + V\mathbb{E}\{E_t(t) | \mathbf{Q}(t)\} \leq C + \sum_{i \in N} Q_i(t)\mathbb{E}\{A_i(t) - D_i(t) | \mathbf{Q}(t)\}$$

$$+ V\zeta\mathbb{E}\{f^2(t) \sum_{i \in N} \rho_i D_i^l(t) | \mathbf{Q}(t)\} + VP\mathbb{E}\{\sum_{i \in N} \frac{D_i^r(t)}{R(t)} | \mathbf{Q}(t)\}, \tag{24}$$

where $C = \frac{1}{2}\sum_{i=1}^{n}[(A_i^{max})^2 + (\frac{f_{max}\tau}{\rho_i} + R_{max}\tau)^2]$ is a constant.

Proof (Theorem 1). Define $D_i(t) = D_i^l(t) + D_i^r(t)$. Taking square on (18), obtain

$$Q_i^2(t+1) \leq Q_i^2(t) + D_i^2(t) + A_i(t) - 2Q_i(t)D_i(t) + 2A_i(t)\max[Q_i(t) - D_i(t), 0]. \quad (25)$$

Define $\bar{D}_i(t)$ as the number of tasks actually processed, which is non-negative. Summing up applications in (25) with conditional expectation expresses as

$$\Delta(\mathbf{Q}(t)) \leq \frac{1}{2}\sum_{i \in N}\mathbb{E}\{A_i^2(t) + D_i^2(t)|\mathbf{Q}(t)\} + \sum_{i \in N}Q_i(t)\mathbb{E}\{A_i(t) - D_i(t)|\mathbf{Q}(t)\}. \quad (26)$$

For any $i \in n$, existing $D_i^l(t) \leq \frac{f(t)\tau}{\rho_i}$ and $D_i^r(t) \leq R_{max}\tau$. Applying $A_i(t) \leq A_i^{max}(t)$, we have

$$\sum_{i \in N}\mathbb{E}\{A_i^2(t) + D_i^2(t)|\mathbf{Q}(t)\} \leq \sum_{i \in N}[(A_i^{max})^2 + (\frac{f_{max}\tau}{\rho_i} + R_{max}\tau)^2]. \quad (27)$$

Add $V\mathbb{E}\{E_t(t)|\mathbf{Q}(t)\}$ to (27) while making C equals to $\frac{1}{2}\sum_{i=1}^{n}[(A_i^{max})^2 + (\frac{f_{max}\tau}{\rho_i} + R_{max}\tau)^2]$. We get (24).

3.3 The DPOTFF Algorithm

To minimize the upper bound of *drift plus energy consumption* function, we rewrite the objective function as

$$\min_{\mathbf{D^r}(t), \mathbf{D^l}(t), f(t)} \{\sum_{i=1}^{n}[V\zeta f^2(t)\rho_i D_i^l(t) - Q_i(t)D_i(t)] + \sum_{i=1}^{n}[\frac{VP}{R(t)} - Q_i(t)]D_i^r(t)\},$$

s.t (10), (11), (14).

$$(28)$$

Because the variables are uncoupled, we firstly simplify (28) by determining the CPU-cycle frequency, and propose the Lemma 1.

Lemma 1. *When the CPU cycle required for local computation $\sum_{i=1}^{n}\rho_i D_i^l(t)$ is known, the optimal cycle frequency $f^*(t) = \frac{\sum_{i=1}^{n}\rho_i D_i^l(t)}{\tau}$.*

Proof (Lemma 1). Given known $\sum_{i=1}^{n}\rho_i D_i^l(t)$, the function (28) with $f(t)$ as independent variable is non-decreasing. The value of optimal solution $f^*(t) = \frac{\sum_{i=1}^{n}\rho_i D_i^l(t)}{\tau}$.

Based on Lemma 1, constraint (10) can transform into

$$\sum_{i=1}^{n}\rho_i D_i^l(t) \leq f_{max}\tau. \quad (29)$$

The function (28) can equivalently transformed into

$$\min_{\mathbf{D^r}(t),\mathbf{D^l}(t)} \left\{ \frac{V\zeta}{\tau^2} \sum_{i=1}^{n}[\rho_i D_i^l(t)]^3 - \sum_{i=1}^{n} Q_i(t)D_i^l(t) + \sum_{i=1}^{n}[\frac{VP}{R(t)} - Q_i(t)]D_i^r(t) \right\}. \quad (30)$$

s.t (14), (29).

Because $\mathbf{D^l}(t)$ and $\mathbf{D^r}(t)$ are uncoupled, we convert (30) into two sub-optimization problems.

Local Task Allocation. Consider the terms containing the variable $D_i^l(t)$ in (30).

$$\min_{\mathbf{D^l}(t)} \frac{V\zeta}{\tau^2} \sum_{i=1}^{n}[\rho_i D_i^l(t)]^3 - \sum_{i=1}^{n} Q_i(t)D_i^l(t), \qquad s.t \quad (29). \quad (31)$$

We assume that the term $\sum_{i=1}^{n} \rho_i D_i^l(t)$ is known, then (31) is simplified to

$$\min_{\mathbf{D^l}(t)} - \sum_{i=1}^{n} \frac{Q_i(t)}{\rho_i}\rho_i D_i^l(t). \quad (32)$$

It is obvious that (32) is a generalized min-weight problem. Local computation CPU cycle $\rho_i D_i^l(t)$ is weight by the value of $-\frac{Q_i(t)}{\rho_i}$. The optimal solution is obtained as

$$D_i^l(t) = \begin{cases} \frac{\sum_{i=1}^{n} \rho_i Q_i(t)}{\rho_i}, & i = i^*, \\ 0, & \text{otherwise,} \end{cases} \quad (33)$$

where $i^* \in \text{argmax} \frac{Q_i(t)}{\rho_i}$ for $i \in \{1, 2, ..., n\}$. However, we can't get the value of $\sum_{i=1}^{n} \rho_i D_i^l(t)$. So, we make X equal to $\sum_{i=1}^{n} \rho_i D_i^l(t)$, function (31) is transformed into

$$\min_{X} \frac{V\zeta}{\tau^2} \sum_{i=1}^{n} X^3 - \sum_{i=1}^{n} \frac{Q_{i^*}(t)X}{\rho_i}, \quad s.t \ 0 \le X \le f_{max}\tau. \quad (34)$$

Problem (34) is a convex optimization problem. The optimal solution X is easy to obtain within a limited time complexity.

Offloading Task Allocation. Consider the remaining terms in (30) that contains the variable $D_i^r(t)$.

$$\min_{\mathbf{D^r}(t)} \sum_{i=1}^{n}[\frac{VP}{R(t)} - Q_i(t)]D_i^r(t), \qquad s.t \quad (14). \quad (35)$$

Problem (35) is min-weight problem, which is weight by the value of $(\frac{VP}{R(t)} - Q_i(t))$. The optimal solution can get as

$$D_i^r(t) = \begin{cases} R(t)\tau, & i = i^*, \\ 0, & \text{otherwise,} \end{cases} \quad (36)$$

where $i^* \in \text{argmin}\{\frac{VP}{R(t)} - Q_i(t)\}$ for $i \in \{1, 2, ..., n\}$ is the optimal solution. Based on the above, the optimal solutions of independent variables $f(t)$, $\mathbf{D^l(t)}$ and $\mathbf{D^r(t)}$ are determined. According to the variables, we iteratively update each application queue backlog.

Algorithm 1. DPOTFF

1: Divide the area into blocks of the same size.
2: **for** $i = 1$ to m **do**
3:    Obtain the optimal altitude $h(x_u, y_u)^*$ of UAV in each location.
4:    Record the number of MDs that can be covered $|K_m|$.
5: **end for**
6: Calculate the optimal location of UAV, $m^* = \text{argmax}\{|K_m|| m \in M\}$.
7: Observe current queue backlog for each application $Q(t)$.
8: Get $\sum_{i=1}^{n} \rho_i D_i^l(t)$ by solving (34).
9: **for** $i = 1$ to n **do**
10:    Calculate the value of $\frac{D_i^l(t)}{\rho_i}$ for each application.
11: **end for**
12: **for** $i = 1$ to n **do**
13:    Find the index i^* corresponding to the application of the maximum $\frac{D_i^l(t)}{\rho_i}$.
14: **end for**
15: Obtain the value of $D_i^l(t)$.
16: Obtain the value of $f(t)$.
17: **for** $i = 1$ to n **do**
18:    Calculate the value of $\frac{VP}{R(t)} - Q_i(t)$ for each application.
19: **end for**
20: **for** $i = 1$ to n **do**
21:    Find the index i^* corresponding to the application of the minimum $\frac{VP}{R(t)} - Q_i(t)$.
22: **end for**
23: Obtain the value of $D_i^r(t)$ according to (36).

---

4   Algorithm Analysis

We conduct mathematical analysis to theoretically show the algorithm's performance. Define $\bar{Q}$ as the queue backlog in the average time, which expresses as

$$\bar{Q} = \lim_{T \to \infty} \frac{1}{T} \sum_{t=0}^{T-1} \sum_{i=1}^{n} \mathbb{E}\{Q_i(t)\}. \tag{37}$$

Theorem 2. *The applications satisfy the Poisson distribution, corresponding to the arrival rates $\lambda = \{\lambda_1, \lambda_2, ..., \lambda_n\}$. For any value of V, if there is $\epsilon > 0$ that satisfies $\sum_{i=1}^{n}(\lambda_i + \epsilon) \in \Lambda$, there is an upper bound on the average energy consumption, expressed as*

$$\bar{E} = e^* + \frac{C}{V}, \tag{38}$$

in addition, there is also an upper bound on the queue backlog of the online algorithm in the average time, expressed as

$$\bar{Q} \le \frac{V(\hat{E}) - \check{E} + C}{\epsilon}, \tag{39}$$

where C is defined in Theorem 1, and e^* is the optimal minimum average energy consumption.

Proof (Theorem 2). We propose an optimal task offloading strategy that is not affected by the queue backlog, which can scale computation offloading and CPU frequency allocation with a fixed distribution, and optimize energy consumption. Described in *Lemma 2*.

Lemma 2. *Application arrival rate λ_i meets $\sum_{i=1}^{n} \lambda_i \in \Lambda$, there exists the optimal strategy $\pi^* = \{D_i^{l^*}(t), D_i^{r^*}(t), f^*(t)\}$, which satisfies the following*

$$\mathbb{E}\{\bar{E}^{\pi^*(t)}\} = e^*(\lambda), \tag{40}$$

$$\mathbb{E}\{A_i(t)\} \le \mathbb{E}\{D_i^{l^*}(t) + D_i^{r^*}(t)\}, \tag{41}$$

where $e^*(\lambda)$ denotes the optimal energy consumption under λ_i and Λ is the system capacity .

Proof (Lemma 2). Caratheodory's theorem is used to prove *Lemma 2* [11], we will not give detailed proof.

The task $A_i(t)$ has the upper bound A_i^{max}, there is also an upper bound $\hat{E}$ and a lower bound $\check{E}$ for energy consumption. According to the *Lemma 2*, for $\sum_{i=1}^{n}(\lambda_i + \epsilon) \in \Lambda$, where $\epsilon > 0$, there is an optimal strategy π^* satisfies

$$\mathbb{E}\{\bar{E}^{\pi^*(t)}\} = e^*(\lambda + \epsilon), \tag{42}$$

$$\mathbb{E}\{A_i(t)\} \le \mathbb{E}\{D_i^{l^*}(t) + D_i^{r^*}(t)\} - \epsilon. \tag{43}$$

For the strategy π^*, we can obtain that

$$\Delta(\mathbf{Q}(t)) + V\mathbb{E}\{E_t(t)|\mathbf{Q}(t)\} \le C + V\mathbb{E}\{e^{\pi^*}(t)|\mathbf{Q}(t)\} + \sum_{i=1}^{n} Q_i(t)\mathbb{E}\{A_i(t) - D_i^{l^*}(t) - D_i^{r^*}(t)|\mathbf{Q}\}. \tag{44}$$

According to (42), (43), taking iterative expectation on (44) and adding up time slots, we can obtain

$$\mathbb{E}\{L(\mathbf{Q}(t))\} - \mathbb{E}\{L(\mathbf{Q}(0))\} + V\sum_{i=1}^{n}\mathbb{E}\{\bar{E}(t)\}$$
$$\le CT + VTe^*(\lambda + \epsilon) - \epsilon\sum_{t=0}^{T-1}\sum_{i=1}^{n}\mathbb{E}\{Q_i(t)\}. \tag{45}$$

Because $Q_i(T)$ and $\mathbb{E}\{L(\mathbf{Q}(t))\}$ are both non-negative terms, (45) can be equivalently transformed into

$$\frac{1}{T}\sum_{t=0}^{T-1}\mathbb{E}\{\bar{E}(t)\} \le \frac{C}{V} + e^*(\lambda + \epsilon). \tag{46}$$

Assuming $T \to \infty$ and $\epsilon \to 0$, (38) is obtained. According to (45), combining the upper bound $\hat{E}$ and the lower bound $\check{E}$ of energy consumption mentioned above, we can get

$$\frac{1}{T}\sum_{t=0}^{T-1}\sum_{i=1}^{n}\mathbb{E}\{Q_i(t)\} \le \frac{C + V(\hat{E} - \check{E})}{\epsilon}. \tag{47}$$

Let $T \to \infty$, we get (39).

5   Evaluation

The size of the horizontal area is 2×2 km, which further divides into multiple 20×20 m small areas [12]. We set up 4 types of heterogeneous applications, and the task amount of each application follows a fixed distribution. The number of CPU cycle is distributed from 1000 to 2500 cycles/bit [13], carrier frequency $f_c = 2$ GHz. The environment parameters b and β are 9.61 and 0.16, respectively [14]. The average excessive pathloss ξ_{LoS} and ξ_{NLoS} are 1 dB and 20 dB [15]. Besides, the time slot length $\tau = 1$ s, $B = 1$ MHz, $P = 1.6$ W, $\sigma^2 = 10^{-6}$ W [16], $f_{max} = 1$ GHz, $\zeta = 10^{-27}$.

5.1   Parameter Analysis

The Influence Analysis of Weight Factor V. In Fig. 2, with the increase of V, energy consumption decreases. Because of the greater V, the greater weight on optimizing energy consumption. It means that the distribution strategy is more to reduce energy consumption. In Fig. 3, the increase of V leads to an increase in queue backlog, but there is still an upper bound. Combined with Fig. 2 and 3, the DPOTFF can tradeoff energy consumption with queue backlog. Additionally, when V reaches a certain value, the minimum energy consumption can achieve while ensuring the system stability.

The Influence Analysis of Arrival Rate. We set respectively different application arrival rates $\alpha = 0.3, 0.5$ and 1.0. Figure 4 shows that the larger application arrival rate, the more energy consumption. Because the increase of application arrival rate means that there are more computation tasks that need to be processed, thereby increasing energy consumption. In Fig. 5, when the tasks arrival rate increases, the queue backlog would be longer. Jointly considering Fig. 4 and Fig. 5, it is obvious that the DPOTFF algorithm can make energy consumption and queue length for applications stable quickly in different cases of application arrival rates.

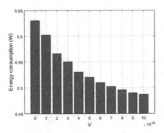

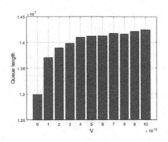

Fig. 2. Energy consumption with different values of V

Fig. 3. Queue length with different values of V

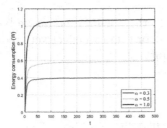

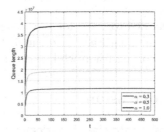

Fig. 4. Energy consumption with different arrival rates

Fig. 5. Queue length with different arrival rates

5.2 Comparison Experiments

To further verify the performance of the DPOTFF, the other two other types of algorithms in [17] and Task Scheduling (TS) algorithm mentioned are used to compare with the DPOTFF:

- Round-Local Execution in Turn (RLET): Computation tasks are processed locally, and tasks of applications are processed in turn.
- Round-UAV Execution in Turn (RUET): Offload computation tasks to the UAV for processing, and application tasks are processed in turn.

Compared to the other three algorithms, the DPOTFF has lower energy consumption than the other algorithms in Fig. 6, which reduces by about 57% compared to the RUET. Comparing to the RLET and TS, energy consumption are respectively reduced by about 30% and 20%. The DPOTFF dynamically offloads computation tasks and allocates CPU frequency according to the scheduling situation in each time slot, to adjust to the dynamics and randomness for channel condition and task arrival rates. In Fig. 7, the RLET shows a linear growth. Because the computation ability of MD is limited to processing the tasks arrived in each slot, resulting in remaining tasks are backlogged in queues, which causes system instability. The queue lengths under the DPOTFF, TS, and RUET algorithms are relatively small and tend to be stable. Because computation tasks are

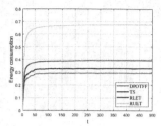

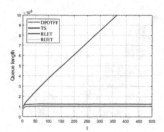

Fig. 6. Energy consumption of different algorithms

Fig. 7. Queue length of different algorithms

all offloaded to UAV for processing in the RUET, there will be no queue backlog. Combining Fig. 6 and Fig. 7, the DPOTFF algorithm can effectively reduce energy consumption while ensuring system stability.

6   Conclusion

We investigate the UAV deployment and task offloading problem. The goal is to minimize MD energy consumption while ensuring system queue stability. To reduce solution complexity, we separately solve 1) initialize UAV deployment problem 2) frequency scaling and task offloading problem. By introducing Lyapunov optimization methods to convert the original stochastic optimization problem into deterministic sub-problems. The DPOTFF algorithm is designed to solve them. And it is proved theoretically that they can obtain close-to-optimal energy consumption while ensuring system stability. Simulation and comparative experiments are given to verify the effectiveness of the DPOTFF algorithm.

References

1. Jeong, S., Simeone, O., Kang, J.: Mobile edge computing via a UAV-mounted cloudlet: optimization of bit allocation and path planning. IEEE Trans. Veh. Technol. **67**(3), 2049–2063 (2018). https://doi.org/10.1109/TVT.2017.2706308
2. Hu, Q., Cai, Y., Yu, G., Qin, Z., Zhao, M., Li, G.Y.: Joint offloading and trajectory design for UAV-enabled mobile edge computing systems. IEEE Internet Things J. **6**(2), 1879–1892 (2019). https://doi.org/10.1109/JIOT.2018.2878876
3. Yang, J., Yang, Q., Kwak, K.S., Rao, R.R.: Power-delay tradeoff in wireless powered communication networks. IEEE Trans. Veh. Technol. **66**(4), 3280–3292 (2017). https://doi.org/10.1109/TVT.2016.2587101
4. Messous, M.-A., Sedjelmaci, H., Houari, N., Senouci, S.-M.: Computation offloading game for an UAV network in mobile edge computing. In: IEEE International Conference on Communications (ICC), vol. 2017, pp. 1–6 (2017). https://doi.org/10.1109/ICC.2017.7996483
5. Dinh, T.Q., Tang, J., La, Q.D., Quek, T.Q.S.: Offloading in mobile edge computing: task allocation and computational frequency scaling. IEEE Trans. Commun. **65**(8), 3571–3584 (2017). https://doi.org/10.1109/TCOMM.2017.2699660

6. Sun, Y., Zhou, S., Xu, J.: EMM: energy-aware mobility management for mobile edge computing in ultra dense networks. IEEE J. Sel. Areas Commun. **35**(11), 2637–2646 (2017). https://doi.org/10.1109/JSAC.2017.2760160

7. Jiang, Z., Mao, S.: Energy delay tradeoff in cloud offloading for multi-core mobile devices. IEEE Access **3**, 2306–2316 (2015). https://doi.org/10.1109/ACCESS.2015.2499300

8. Mao, Y., Zhang, J., Letaief, K.B.: Joint task offloading scheduling and transmit power allocation for mobile-edge computing systems. In: IEEE Wireless Communications and Networking Conference (WCNC), vol. 2017, pp. 1–6 (2017). https://doi.org/10.1109/WCNC.2017.7925615

9. Liu, C., Bennis, M., Poor, H.V.: Latency and reliability-aware task offloading and resource allocation for mobile edge computing. In: IEEE Globecom Workshops (GC Wkshps), vol. 2017, pp. 1–7 (2017). https://doi.org/10.1109/GLOCOMW.2017.8269175

10. Little, J.D.C., Graves, S.C.: Little's law. In: Chhajed, D., Lowe, T.J. (eds.) Building Intuition. International Series in Operations Research & Management Science, vol. 115 (2008). Springer, Boston. https://doi.org/10.1007/978-0-387-73699-0_5

11. Neely, M.: Stochastic Network Optimization with Application to Communication and Queueing Systems, Morgan & Claypool (2010)

12. Wu, D., Sun, X., Ansari, N.: An FSO-based drone assisted mobile access network for emergency communications. IEEE Trans. Netw. Sci. Eng. **7**(3), 1597–1606 (2020). https://doi.org/10.1109/TNSE.2019.2942266

13. You, C., Huang, K., Chae, H., Kim, B.: Energy-efficient resource allocation for mobile-edge computation offloading. IEEE Trans. Wirel. Commun. **16**(3), 1397–1411 (2017). https://doi.org/10.1109/TWC.2016.2633522

14. Shi, W., et al.: Multiple drone-cell deployment analyses and optimization in drone assisted radio access networks. IEEE Access **6**, 12518–12529 (2018). https://doi.org/10.1109/ACCESS.2018.2803788

15. Zhou, F., Wu, Y., Sun, H., Chu, Z.: UAV-enabled mobile edge computing: offloading optimization and trajectory design. In: IEEE International Conference on Communications (ICC), vol. 2018, pp. 1–6 (2018). https://doi.org/10.1109/ICC.2018.8422277

16. Mao, Y., Zhang, J., Letaief, K.B.: Dynamic computation offloading for mobile-edge computing with energy harvesting devices. IEEE J. Sel. Areas Commun. **34**(12), 3590–3605 (2016). https://doi.org/10.1109/JSAC.2016.2611964

17. Bi, S., Zhang, Y.J.: Computation rate maximization for wireless powered mobile-edge computing with binary computation offloading. IEEE Trans. Wirel. Commun. **17**(6), 4177–4190 (2018). https://doi.org/10.1109/TWC.2018.2821664

18. Wang, T., et al.: Mobile edge-enabled trust evaluation for the Internet of Things. Inf. Fusion **75**, 90–100 (2021)

19. Wang, T., Wang, P., Cai, S., Ma, Y., Liu, A., Xie, M.: A unified trustworthy environment establishment based on edge computing in industrial IoT. IEEE Trans. Ind. Inf. **16**(9), 6083–6091 (2020). https://doi.org/10.1109/TII.2019.2955152

Blockchain Systems

Research on Authentication and Key Agreement Protocol of Smart Medical Systems Based on Blockchain Technology

Xiaohe Wu[1,2], Jianbo Xu[1,2(✉)], W. Liang[1,2], and W. Jian[1,2]

[1] Hunan University of Science and Technology, Xiangtan 411201, China
{jbxu,wliang}@hnust.edu.cn
[2] Hunan Key Laboratory of Service Computing and New Software Service Technology, Xiangtan, China

Abstract. The wireless body area network in the smart medical systems uses wearable devices to remotely monitor the patient's physiological information and transmits the information to the medical center through an open channel. To prevent security issues such as privacy leakage and malicious attacks in the wireless body area network, anonymous authentication and key negotiation are required between the sensor and the server. The protocol must not only satisfy confidentiality and security but also provide anonymity and untraceability for sensor nodes. In response to this problem, this paper proposes an authentication and key agreement protocol for sensors and servers based on blockchain technology in the wireless body area network, with the help of session keys for subsequent access and data transmission. The safety of our scheme was evaluated through an informal safety analysis. In addition, our scheme was also simulated by using ProVerif. The experimental results showed that the scheme is safe.

Keywords: WBAN · Key agreement · Mutual authentication · Blockchain

1 Introduction

The development of the Internet of Things makes concepts such as smart cities, smart transportation, smart homes, and smart healthcare become a part of people's lives [1, 2]. The smart medical system collects information that needs to be monitored in real-time through various sensors and sensors and other equipment and technologies and transmits it to local nodes through various networks. Wireless Body Area Networks (WBANs) are a kind of wearable devices that can be implanted in the human body or attached to the surface of the human body to remotely monitor the physical health of patients, and transmit this real-time traffic to the medical health center for observation the patient's physiological state [3]. WBANs bring convenience to patients and the medical service industry. Doctors can use WBANs to remotely monitor the physical health of patients and provide timely treatment to patients. At the same time, wearable sensor devices also improve the comfort of patients.

© Springer Nature Switzerland AG 2022
Y. Lai et al. (Eds.): ICA3PP 2021, LNCS 13156, pp. 439–452, 2022.
https://doi.org/10.1007/978-3-030-95388-1_29

The architecture of WBANs is shown in Fig. 1. The terminal equipment is exposed, and the user's identity information and transmitted content are transmitted through open channels. Since terminal equipment uses public open channels to transmit real-time data, any malicious node can initiate security against it. Attacks, loss of information, or tampering by adversaries may lead to irreparable consequences. The leakage of this sensitive and confidential information will threaten the privacy of users. How to ensure that both parties in communication are legitimate users and encrypt the transmitted information is a problem that needs to be resolved at present [4]. For this architecture, the following two main challenges need to be solved: (1) To ensure that both parties are legitimate users in the WBANs environment, both parties need to perform identity authentication before communicating. (2) Given the characteristics of wireless body area network terminal equipment transmitting in the open channel, both parties negotiate a secure session key for subsequent communication.

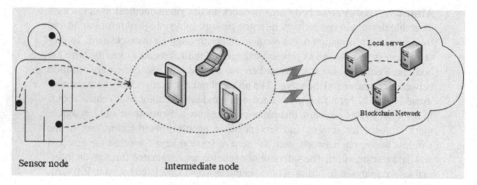

Fig. 1. An authentication model of blockchain-based in WBANs environment.

In WBANs, due to the mobility of sensor nodes and the characteristics of data communication in public channels, their security is low. It is particularly important to ensure that the data collected by sensor nodes is not captured by malicious attackers. Therefore, authentication schemes are required to ensure security in WBANs. To solve these problems, domestic and foreign scholars have proposed some authentication schemes to solve the security problems in the WBANs [5–14]. The proposed schemes should be able to resist various types of security attacks. Provide users with privacy protection, and the amount of calculation and communication should be as low as possible.

2   Related Work

Due to the increasing demand for medical services, the development of the WBAN has gradually attracted the attention of researchers. At present, domestic and foreign scholars have proposed some authentication schemes to solve the security problems in WBAN. Sensor nodes in WBAN are wearable devices with limited resources, so lightweight and security are two challenges that need to be solved urgently in WBAN.

In 2018, the scheme [8] proposed an anonymous mutual authentication key agreement scheme. The author believes that the compromise of the hub node or the intermediate node will not lead to the compromise of the entire system. But in this architecture, attackers may abuse intermediate nodes by using relay services. Scheme [9] designed a robust and efficient WBAN mutual authentication and untraceable key agreement scheme, which has anonymity and untraceability. The principle used to achieve untraceability in the proposed scheme can also be used to improve the scheme of Kaya et al. [10].

An authentication scheme based on physiological signals has gradually become a popular authentication scheme. Physiological signals refer to unique and non-replicable personal physiological characteristics and signals such as iris, fingerprints, and electrocardiogram. Scheme [10] proposed a hybrid anonymous authentication and key agreement scheme using physiological signals to improve the imitation attack of sensor nodes and greatly enhance the security features. The scheme also provides additional security features to resist the camouflage attack and key escrow problem of the central node. However, the limitation of this solution is that if the static biometrics are stolen, they cannot be replaced, and during the physiological data recording process, the features may change significantly or become unusable, which has high calculation and communication costs. The scheme [11] analyzed the existing centralized two-hop WBAN lightweight anonymous mutual authentication and key agreement scheme and found that the protocol has defects in the untraceability and forward secrecy of the session key. A new anonymous mutual authentication and key agreement scheme was proposed, which has untraceability and forward secrecy of session keys.

Since Satoshi Nakamoto proposed the concept of blockchain in 2008, blockchain technology has been applied in many fields. Blockchain can be regarded as a kind of ledger. Due to the distributed consistency of blockchain, immutability, traceability, many researchers combine blockchain and cryptography to improve the security and privacy of authentication [12–14]. Xu et al. [13] proposed an authentication and key agreement scheme based on blockchain technology, which is anonymous and can realize cross-region authentication of sensor nodes. According to the monitoring application type of physiological data in WBAN, the scheme is divided into two protocols. In protocol-1, the sensor node sends out an authentication request to realize mutual authentication with the local node. In protocol-2, the local node sends out an authentication request to realize mutual authentication with the sensor node.

In order to solve the above-mentioned problems and challenges in WBANs, this paper proposes an authentication and key agreement protocol based on blockchain technology in the wireless body area network, with the help of the session key for subsequent access and data transmission.

The main contributions of this paper are summarized as follows:

- A sensor and server authentication and key agreement protocol based on blockchain technology is proposed.
- Use BAN logic to prove the establishment of the secure session key of this protocol and the ability to recover from various known attacks.
- A simulation experiment was carried using ProVerif, and the experimental result shows that the scheme is safe.

The rest of the paper is structured as follows. Section 3 is the system model including network model and threat model, Sect. 4 proposes improved anonymity and key agreement protocol, and Sect. 5 is about the protocol simulation experiment results and BAN logic, Sect. 6 is a summary of this article.

3 Related Work

3.1 System Model

The network model is shown in Fig. 2. The architecture consists of three components, which are sensor nodes, super nodes (Intermediate node), and server nodes in the blockchain. Sensor nodes are implanted in the human body or attached to the surface of the human body with limited resources. Wearable devices, its main function is to collect sensitive data such as physiological information of patients, and the collected data is forwarded to the cloud server via super nodes (smart devices, etc.)

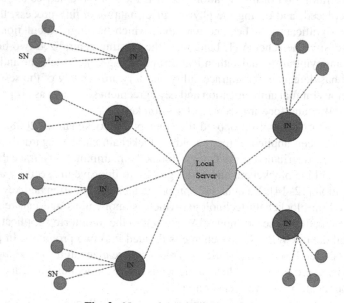

Fig. 2. Network model for WBANs.

In this network model, all local servers form a blockchain-based network, and these local servers can be considered miners in the blockchain network. Miners generate new blocks through certain consensus mechanisms (we will not discuss the time complexity of the consensus algorithm used for block verification and addition in the blockchain in detail).

The sensor node needs to mutually authenticate with the server to determine that both parties are legal identities. After authentication, a secret session key is negotiated. Due to the limited resources of sensor nodes, data needs to be forwarded through super nodes with strong communication capabilities. The data collected by the sensor node is stored and processed by the blockchain, and users can realize access control to the data stored in the blockchain by authorization. Due to the addition of the blockchain, the privacy protection of users and the security of data are greatly enhanced.

3.2 Threat Model

In order to evaluate the security features of the proposed scheme, we define the adversarial model as follows.

1. The adversary can eavesdrop, modify and replay any message transmitted on the open communication channel.
2. The adversary can capture any sensor node in some way, and further obtain the secret data stored in the capture node, and capture any sensor node will not affect the communication of other sensor nodes. (This aims to capture the capabilities of mutual authentication.
3. All *LN* are semi-trusted parties, which means they may have bad behaviors, but they will not collude with other *LN*.
4. We use the well-known threat model Dolev-Yao [14], that is, all entities participating in communication transmit messages through open channels. We use this model to analyze and simulation the security of this protocol.

3.3 Blockchain Consensus Mechanism

Blockchain is a distributed database system, and the generation of blocks is jointly produced by each participating member. The blockchain-based WBANs system guarantees the safety.

Blockchain is a distributed database system, and the generation of blocks is jointly generated by each participating member. The blockchain-based WBAN system guarantees the safety and privacy of users. The block structure is mainly composed of block header and block body. The block header saves information about itself and another block, mainly including: the block version number (used to quickly comply with the verification rules in this area), the hash address of the previous block of the block, and the transaction information in the block, the hash value of the root of the Merkle tree, the timestamp of the block creation, the difficulty target of the proof-of- work algorithm, and the random number set to meet the target. The block body includes all transaction records generated during the block creation process that have been verified for the current block. These records generate a unique Merkle root through the hashing process of the Merkle tree and record it in the block header. Checking whether there is a certain transaction in the block can be done through the Merkel tree. The Merkel tree needs to hash the hash nodes recursively, and insert the newly generated hash node into the Merkel tree until there is only one hash node, which is the root of the Merkel tree. Through this structure, one of the transactions can be quickly located [15, 16].

Algorithm 1	Consensus for block verification and addition in block

Input: All Server nodes LN in cloud servers,a full block

Output: Commitment for block addition.

1: The initiator generates a timestep T.

2: **for** each peer cloud server node LN **do**

3: The initiator encrypts the parameters and sends a block verification message to other server nodes.

4: **end for**

5: Initialize n=0, where n represents the number of valid votes.

6: **for** each follower node LN in the blockchain network **do**

7: Record the time T' when the message was received.

8: LN checks validity of T by the condition: $|T'-T| \leq \Delta T$.

9: **if** timestep is valid **then**

10: Verify that the parameters are valid

11: **if** all the verifications by LN are successful **then**

12: The server node sends a status verification message to the initiator.

13:    **end if**

14: **end if**

15: **end for**

16: **for** each status verification message from the follower peer nodes LN **do**

17: The initiator verifies that the message.

18: **if** the message is correct **then**

19: n=n+1.

20:   **end if**

21: **end for**

22: **if** $n>2f+1$, where f is the fault nodes number **then**

23: Add the block to the blockchain.

24: Broadcast commitment messages to the **P2P** cloud servers' network.

25:   **end if**

Smart contracts are programs that are stored on the blockchain and executed automatically. Consensus algorithms include Proof of Work (PoW), Proof of Stake (PoS), Delegated Proof of Stake (DPoS), Proof of Activity (PoA), Practical Byzantine Fault Tolerance (PBFT), Delegated BFT. Blockchain traceability can easily track malicious users and protect user privacy.

In this protocol, the local server node mines new blocks based on the PBFT consensus algorithm. PBFT realizes the BFT in the case of a limited number of nodes, has $3f + 1$ fault tolerance, and at the same time guarantees certain performance. Algorithm 1 shows the process of generating new blocks, as shown in Algorithm 1.

4 Proposed Scheme

This section proposes an improved anonymous authentication and key agreement protocol based on blockchain technology for WBANs. Table 1 shows the list of symbols required in the protocol. The protocol consists of an initialization phase, registration phase, and mutual authentication phase. The initialization phase is the operation of the system administrator on the sensor node, and the registration phase is the operation of the system administrator on the sensor node and the super node. These two parts are performed off-chain to avoid generating new blocks during the identity verification phase and reduce computational consumption. In the mutual authentication phase, the sensor node and the server node mutually authenticate their identities and conduct key agreement, and the negotiated session key will be used for subsequent communication. The specific process is as follows.

Table 1. Notations are used in this protocol

Symbol	Description
SA	System administrator
SN	Sensor node requesting authentication
LN	Local server
IN	Intermediate nod
id_N	The real identity of the sensor node
id_{IN}	Identity of the intermediate node
tid_N	Temporary secret parameter
k_{LN}	Master secret paraments
k_N	Master key of the sensor node
k^+, r^+	Temporary secret parameter
a_N, b_N	Authen1tication parameter
r_N	Random number generated by the sensor node
t_1	A timestamp generated by the sensor node
x_N	Auxiliary parameters required for authentication
α, β, γ, H	Authentication parameters
k_S	Session key to be agreed on
$h(\cdot)$	The secure one-way hash function
(a, b)	Concatenation of data a and data b
$\oplus$	XOR operation

4.1 Initialization Phase

The steps for the system administrator to initialize the local server are as follows.

Step 1: The SA selects a master key k_{LN} for the LN.

Step 2: Send the master key k_{LN} to the LN for storage through a secure channel.

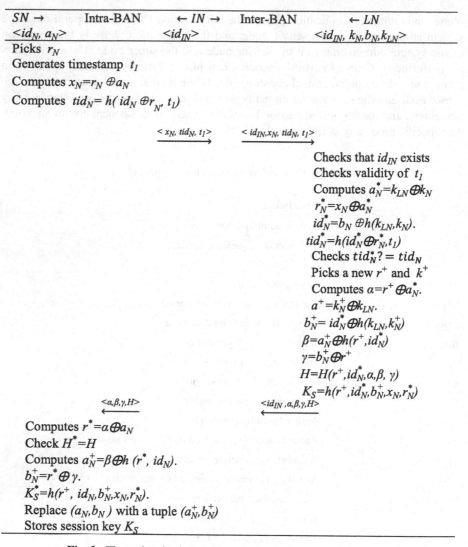

Fig. 3. The authentication and key agreement phase of our scheme.

4.2 Registration Phase

The steps SA to register the SN and the LN as follows.

Step 1: The SA selects a unique secret identity id_N for SN.

Step 2: SA selects a master key k_N for SN.

Step 3: SA chooses a unique secret identity id_{IN} for IN.

Step 4: Calculate the parameters $a_N = k_N \oplus k_{LN}$, $b_N = id_N \oplus h(k_{LN}, k_N)$.

Step 5: Store $< k_N, b_N >$ in the memory of the SN, store $< id_{IN} >$ in the LN, and store $< k_N, b_N >$.

Step 6: The blockchain stores the registration information of all sensor nodes and intermediate nodes, and then the server uses a certain consensus mechanism to package this registration information into blocks. After verification by all local servers, these blocks can become valid blocks and allow links to the blockchain.

4.3 Authentication Phase

Figure 3 shows the authentication phase. The authentication phase of SN and LN is as follows:

Step 1: $SN \rightarrow IN$: $< x_N, tid_N, t_1 >$, SN performs the following operations:

- SN generates a random number r_N and timestamp t_1.
- SN calculates the parameters $x_N = r_N \oplus a_N$, $tid_N = h(id_N \oplus r_N, t_1)$.
- Send the message $< x_N, tid_N, t_1 >$ to the IN.

Step 2: $IN \rightarrow LN$: $< x_N, tid_N, t_1, id_{IN} >$

- The intermediate node forwards the message tuple from SN, and sends it to LN with its own identity.

Step 3: $LN \rightarrow IN$: $< \alpha, \beta, \gamma, H >$, LN performs the following operations:

- In the ledger of the blockchain, we can think that there is a pointer or block identifier P, P points to the block, and any server node can quickly find the corresponding information from the blockchain through P [17]. LN receives the request message from IN, first finds IN identity information according to the P identifier, and checks whether IN id exists in the blockchain. If not, terminate this authentication. If id_{IN} is found in the blockchain, perform the following operations.
- Check the validity of the timestamp t_1, check the condition $\Delta t \geq |t^* - t_1|$, where t^* is the time when the LN receives the tuple message, if the conditions are not met, the key agreement will be terminated, and if the conditions are met, continue to proceed as follows.
- Calculate $a_N^* = k_{LN} \oplus k_N$.
- $r_N^* = x_N \oplus a_N^*$.
- $id_N^* = b_N \oplus h(k_{LN}, k_N)$
- Calculate $tid_N^* = h(id_N^* \oplus r_N^*, t_1)$, check $id_N^*? = tid_N$, if not equal, terminate this authentication, otherwise proceed as follows.
- Regenerate a random num r^+.
- Calculate the parameter $\alpha = r^+ \oplus a_N^*$.
- Reselect a k_N^+.
- $a^+ = k_N^+ \oplus k_{LN}$.
- $b_N^+ = id_N^* \oplus h(k_{LN}, k_N^+)$.
- Calculate the parameter $\beta = a_N^+ \oplus h(r^+, id_N^*)$.
- Calculate the parameter $\gamma = b_N^+ \oplus r^+$.
- Calculate the parameters $H = H(r^+, id_N^*, \alpha, \beta, \gamma)$.
- Calculate the session key $K_S = h(r^+, id_N^*, b_N^+, x_N, r_N^*)$.

Step 4: $IN \rightarrow SN :< \alpha, \beta, \gamma, H >$

- The intermediate node removes its own identity id_{IN} from the message and forwards send to the sensor node.

Step 5: SN receives the message tuple $< \alpha, \beta, \gamma, H >$, SN performs the following operations.

- Calculate $r^* = \alpha \oplus a_N$.
- Calculate $H^* = h(r^*, id_N, \alpha, \beta, \gamma)$.
- Check $H^* = H$, if they are not equal, terminate this authentication, if they are equal, proceed as follows.
- $a_N^+ = \beta \oplus h(r^*, id_N)$.
- $b_N^+ = r^* \oplus \gamma$.
- Calculate the session key $K_S^* = h(r^+, id_N, b_N^+, x_N, r_N^*)$.
- Store the session key K_S and replace (a_N, b_N) with a tuple (a_N^+, b_N^+).

5 Safety Analysis

5.1 Simulation Verification Based on ProVerif

ProVerif is a cryptographic protocol validator widely used by researchers at present [18]. It is used to specify and analyze the security of the authentication key negotiation protocol. In this section, we use the validator to formally verify the proposed scheme, analyze the safety of the scheme, and the simulation results are given in Fig. 4.

```
Verification summary:

Query not attacker(idN[]) is true.

Query not attacker(k_LN[]) is true.

Query not attacker(k_N[]) is true.

Query not attacker(ks[]) is true.

Query inj-event(BeginAuth(id)) ==> inj-event(EndAuth(id)) is true.
```

Fig. 4. Simulation results using ProVerif.

5.2 Security Proof Based on BAN Logic

This section describes the safety analysis of the proposed scheme using Burrows- Abadi-Needham (BAN) logic [19]. The following basic logical symbols are used to analyze our plan: (where A and B are participants).

- $A| \equiv X$: A believes the statement X.
- $A \Delta X$: A sees the statement X.
- $A| \sim X$: A once said the statement X.
- $A| =\gg X$: A has jurisdiction over the statement X.
- $\#(X)$: X is fresh.
- (X, Y): X or Y is one part of the formula.
- $< X > Y$: X combined with Y.
- $A \overset{k}{\leftrightarrow} B$: A is the secret parameter shared (X, Y) (to be shared) between A and B.
- $A \leftrightarrow B$: x is a secret parameter known only A to B or a third party they trust.
- $\frac{A}{B}$: If A is true, then B is true.

1) Inference rules
• Message meaning rule

$$\frac{A|A \overset{Y}{\leftrightarrow} B, A \triangleleft < X > Y}{A| \equiv B|X}$$

• Nonce-verification rule

$$\frac{A| \equiv \# < X >, A| \equiv B - X}{A| \equiv B| \equiv X}$$

• Jurisdiction rule

$$\frac{A| \equiv B| \Rightarrow X, A| \equiv B| \equiv X}{A| \equiv X}$$

• Freshness rule

$$\frac{A| \equiv \#(X)}{A| \equiv \#(X, Y)}$$

• Belief rule

$$\frac{A| \equiv B| \equiv (X, Y)}{A| \equiv B| \equiv X}$$

2) Goals:
• Goal 1: $LN| \equiv (SN \overset{b_N}{\leftrightarrow} LN)$.
• Goal 2: $LN| \equiv SN| \equiv (SN \overset{b_N}{\leftrightarrow} LN)$.
• Goal 3: $SN| \equiv LN| \equiv (SN \overset{k_S}{\leftrightarrow} LN)$.
• Goal 4: $SN| \equiv (SN \overset{k_S}{\leftrightarrow} LN)$.

3) Idealization

- $M_1 : SN \rightarrow LN :< SN \overset{b_n}{\leftrightarrow} LN, r_N, t_N >_{SN \overset{id_N}{\leftrightarrow} LN}$

- $M_2 : LN \rightarrow SN :< SN \overset{b_n}{\leftrightarrow} LN, r_N, r^+, k^+, SN \overset{k_S}{\leftrightarrow} LN >_{SN \overset{id_N}{\leftrightarrow} LN}$

4) Initial assumptions:

- A1: $LN| \equiv (SN \overset{id_N}{\leftrightarrow} LN).$
- A2: $LN| \equiv \#(t_N).$
- A3: $LN| \equiv SN| => (SN \overset{b_N}{\leftrightarrow} LN).$
- A4: $SN| \equiv (SN \overset{id_N}{\leftrightarrow} LN).$
- A5: $SN| \equiv \#(r_N).$
- A6: $SN| \equiv LN| \Rightarrow (SN \overset{k_S}{\leftrightarrow} LN).$

5) Formal verification

D1 From M1, A1 by applying Message meaning rule, we deduce:

$$\frac{LN| \equiv \left(SN \overset{id_N}{\leftrightarrow} LN \right), LN \triangleleft < SN \overset{b_n}{\leftrightarrow} LN, r_N, t_N >_{SN \overset{id_N}{\leftrightarrow} LN}}{LN| \equiv SN| \sim (SN \overset{b_N}{\leftrightarrow} LN, r_N, t_N)}$$

D2 From A2 and by applying Freshness rule, we can deduce:

$$\frac{LN| \equiv \#(t_N)}{LN| \equiv \#(SN \overset{b_N}{\leftrightarrow} LN, r_N, t_N)}$$

D3 From D1, D2 and by applying Nonce-verification rule, we can deduce:

$$\frac{LN| \equiv \#\left(SN \overset{b_N}{\leftrightarrow} LN, r_N, t_N \right), LN| \equiv SN| \sim (SN \overset{b_N}{\leftrightarrow} LN, r_N, t_N)}{LN| \equiv SN| \equiv (SN \overset{b_N}{\leftrightarrow} LN, r_N, t_N)}$$

D4 From D3 and by applying Belief rule, we can deduce:

$$\frac{LN| \equiv SN| \equiv \left(SN \overset{b_N}{\leftrightarrow} LN, r_N, t_N \right)}{LN| \equiv SN| \equiv (SN \overset{b_N}{\leftrightarrow} LN)} \quad \text{(Goal 2)}$$

D5 From D4, A3 and by applying Jurisdiction rule, we can deduce:

$$\frac{LN| \equiv SN| \equiv \left(SN \overset{b_N}{\leftrightarrow} LN \right), LN| \equiv SN| \equiv (SN \overset{b_N}{\leftrightarrow} LN)}{LN \equiv (SN \overset{b_N}{\leftrightarrow} LN)} \quad \text{(Goal 1)}$$

D6 From M2, A4 and by applying Message meaning rule, we can deduce:

$$\frac{SN| \equiv \#\left(SN \overset{id_N}{\leftrightarrow} LN \right), SN \triangleleft < r_N, r^+, k^+, SN \overset{k_S}{\leftrightarrow} LN >_{SN \overset{id_N}{\leftrightarrow} LN}}{SN| \equiv LN| \sim < r_N, r^+, k^+, SN \overset{k_S}{\leftrightarrow} LN >}$$

D7 From A5 and by applying Freshness rule, we can deduce:

$$\frac{SN \mid \equiv \#(\, r_N)}{SN \mid \equiv \#(r_N, r^+, k^+, SN \overset{k_S}{\leftrightarrow} LN)}$$

D8 From D6 and D7 and by applying Nonce-verification rule, we can deduce:

$$\frac{SN| \equiv \#\left(r_N, r^+, k^+, SN \overset{k_S}{\leftrightarrow} LN\right), SN| \equiv LN| \sim (r_N, r^+, k^+, SN \overset{k_S}{\leftrightarrow} LN)}{SN| \equiv LN| \equiv < r_N, r^+, k^+, SN \overset{k_S}{\leftrightarrow} LN >}$$

D9 From D8 and using Belief rule, we can draw the following inference:

$$\frac{SN| \equiv LN| \sim < r_N, r^+, k^+, SN \overset{k_S}{\leftrightarrow} LN >}{SN| \equiv LN| \equiv < SN \overset{k_S}{\leftrightarrow} LN >} \quad \text{(Goal 3)}$$

D10 From A6, D9 and by applying Jurisdiction rule, we can deduce:

$$\frac{SN| \equiv LN| \equiv \left(SN \overset{k_S}{\leftrightarrow} LN\right), SN| \equiv LN| \equiv (r_N, r^+, k^+, SN \overset{k_S}{\leftrightarrow} LN)}{SN| \equiv < SN \overset{k_S}{\leftrightarrow} LN >} \quad \text{(Goal 4)}$$

Therefore, in our proposed scheme, mutual authentication and key agreement between sensor nodes and hub nodes are realized.

6 Conclusions

This paper proposes an authentication and key agreement protocol based on blockchain technology, which fixes some vulnerabilities in existing solutions. The proposed scheme implements mutual authentication and session key negotiation between the terminal device and the server. The attacker cannot track the future session key based on the existing key, which provides anonymity and unlinkability for the terminal device. Finally, through the use of ProVerif tools and informal security analysis, the security of the proposed protocol is simulated and verified. The experimental results show that the scheme is secure.

References

1. Surantha, N., Atmaja, P., David, W.M.: A review of wearable internet-of-things device for healthcare. Procedia Comput. Sci. **179**, 936–943 (2021)
2. Wei, L.A., Zn, B., Sx, A., et al.: Secure fusion approach for the internet of things in smart autonomous multi-robot systems. Inform. Sci. **579**(1), 468–482 (2021)
3. Liang, W., Huang, W., Long, J., Zhang, K., Li, K., Zhang, D.: Deep reinforcement learning for resource protection and real-time detection in IoT environment. IEEE Internet Things J. **7**(7), 6392–6401 (2020). https://doi.org/10.1109/JIOT.2020.2974281

4. Narwal, B., Mohapatra, A.K.: A survey on security and authentication in wireless body area networks. J. Syst. Architect. **113**, 101883 (2020)
5. Odelu, V., Saha, S., Prasath, R., Sadineni, L., Conti, M., Jo, M.: Efficient privacy preserving device authentication in WBAN for industrial e-health applications. Comput. Secur. **83**, 312 (2019)
6. Xie, Y., Zhang, S., Li, X., Li, Y., Chai, Y., Zhang, M.: CasCP: efficient and secure certificateless authentication scheme for wireless body area networks with conditional privacy-preserving. Secur. Commun. Networks **2019**, 1–13 (2019)
7. Xu, Z., Liang, W., Li, K.C., et al.: A blockchain-based Roadside Unit- assisted authentication and key agreement protocol for Internet of Vehicles. J. Parallel Distrib. Comput. **149**(6), 29–39 (2021)
8. Chen, C.-M., Xiang, B., Wu, T.-Y., Wang, K.-H.: An anonymous mutual authenticated key agreement scheme for wearable sensors in wireless body area networks. Appl. Sci. **8**(7), 1074 (2018)
9. Kompara, M., Hafizul Islam, S.K., Hölbl, M.: A robust and efficient mutual authentication and key agreement scheme with untraceability for WBAN. Comput. Networks **148**, 196–213 (2019)
10. Koya, A.M., Deepthi, P.P.: Anonymous hybrid mutual authentication and key agreement scheme for wireless body area network. Comput. Networks **140**, 138–151 (2018)
11. Meng, X., Xu, J., Liang, W., Li, K.-C.: An anonymous mutual authentication and key agreement scheme in WBAN. In: 2019 IEEE 5th International Conference on Big Data Security on Cloud (BigDataSecurity), IEEE International Conference on High Performance and Smart Computing, (HPSC) and IEEE International Conference on Intelligent Data and Security (IDS), Washington, DC, USA, pp. 31–36 (2019). https://doi.org/10.1109/BigDataSecurity-HPSCIDS.2019.00017
12. Mwitende, G., Ye, Y., Ali, I., Li, F.: Certificateless authenticated key agreement for blockchain-based WBAN. J. Syst. Archit. **110**, 101777 (2020)
13. Xu, J., Meng, X., Liang, W., et al.: A secure mutual authentication scheme of blockchain-based in WBAN. China Commun. **17**(9), 34–49 (2020)
14. Liang, W., Zhang, D., Lei, X., Tang, M., Zomaya, Y.: Circuit copyright blockchain: block chainbased homomorphic encryption for IP circuit protection. IEEE Trans. Emerg. Topics Comput. **9**(3), 1414–1420 (2020). https://doi.org/10.1109/TETC.2020.2993032
15. Liang, W., Zhang, D., Lei, X., et al.: Circuit copyright blockchain: blockchain-based homomorphic encryption for IP circuit protection. IEEE Trans. Emerg. Topics Comput. **99**, 1–1 (2020)
16. Liang, W., Xiao, L., Zhang, K., et al.: Data fusion approach for collaborative anomaly intrusion detection in blockchain-based systems. IEEE Internet Things J. **99**, 1–1 (2021)
17. Zisang, X., Wei, L., Ching, L.K., Jianbo, X., Hai, J.: A blockchain-based roadside unit-assisted authentication and key agreement protocol for internet of vehicles. J. Parallel Distrib. Comput. **149**, 29–39 (2021)
18. Blanchet, B.: ProVerif Automatic Cryptographic Protocol Verifier User Manual. Departement dInformatique, Ecole Normale Superieure, CNRS, Paris, France (2005)
19. Burrows, M., Abadi, M., Needham, R.M., et al.: A logic of authentication. ACM Trans. Comput. Syst. **8**(1), 18–36 (1990)

CRchain: An Efficient Certificate Revocation Scheme Based on Blockchain

Xiaoxue Ge[1,2], Liming Wang[1(✉)], Wei An[1], Xiaojun Zhou[1], and Benyu Li[1,2]

[1] Institute of Information Engineering, Chinese Academy of Sciences, Beijing, China
{gexiaoxue,wangliming,anwei,libenyu}@iie.ac.cn
[2] School of Cyber Security, University of Chinese Academy of Sciences,
Beijing, China

Abstract. One of essential parts of public key infrastructure is the ability to efficiently check the certificate status and quickly distribute certificates revocation information. The existing certificate revocation schemes generally suffer from a time-consuming process of certificate status verification as well as a long interval of revocation information updating. To address aforementioned issues, this paper proposes a blockchain-based certificate revocation mechanism, namely CRchain, which can efficiently check certificate status and revoke the certificate. Specifically, to achieve efficient certificate status queries, revokedCertCF and valid-CertCF cuckoo filters are constructed for storing the revoked and valid certificates, respectively. And then, the co-controlled key published on CRchain is presented for shortening the certificate revocation process and abridging the authority of certificate authorities. Finally, we implement and evaluate CRchain on Hyperledger Fabric with smart contract. The theoretical analysis and experimental results show that CRchain achieves better performance in latency and exchanged data size than existing reference methods in the duration of the certificate status checking.

Keywords: Certificate revocation · Blockchain · Smart contract · Cuckoo filter

1 Introduction

Nowadays, Transport Layer Security (TLS) is the cornerstone of the Internet to protect sensitive exchanged data and users' privacy. TLS is based on the X.509 Public Key Infrastructure (PKI) to authenticate identity. In PKI, Certificate Authorities (CA) digitally signs each certificate to declare the binding with subject identity. In practice, some certificates may be unavailable in the validity due to the certificate's private key exposure, the change of subject, or other reasons [17]. The traditional certificate revocation mechanisms, such as Certificate Revocation List (CRL) [7] and Online Certificate Status Protocol (OCSP) [20],

---

Supported by National Research and Development Program of China (No. 2019YFB1005200).

Y. Lai et al. (Eds.): ICA3PP 2021, LNCS 13156, pp. 453–472, 2022.
https://doi.org/10.1007/978-3-030-95388-1_30

are proposed to provide certificate status checking service. However, CRL and CRLite [14] have a long update cycle. With the development of cloud computing and the Internet of things, the scope of CRL overgrows with the blooming of certificates, which results in the communication overhead and latency increasing. Besides, CRL and OCSP are fragile to the single point of failures and denial of service (DoS) attacks. A failed node of CRL and OCSP will undermine the availability of certificate verification service. Moreover, misbehaved CA has been reported to cause many security issues recently [6,9,22,25] due to the exposure to internal and external threats. The absolute authority of CA might hinder the certificate revocation from timely distribution.

The emergence of blockchain technology provides a new method for decentralized certificate revocation schemes. As the core supporting technology of Bitcoin [21], blockchain technology has attracted wide attention since 2008, due to its advantages of decentralization, immutability, openness and transparency [8,16,27,29]. Many researchers have combined blockchain technology with certificate revocation by establishing an open and transparent certificate revocation information sharing platform to solve the security issues posed by the centralized schemes [3,18,28]. Despite the existing blockchain-based certificate revocation schemes [12,13,15,23] have solved the single-point failures of conventional schemes as well as other defects to a certain extent, several issues still need to be addressed:

- **Time-consuming checking certificate status.** The retrieval of related transactions with the certificate status on the blockchain is time-consuming owing to the traversal retrieval mechanism of the blockchain;
- **Long updating certificate status interval.** The majority of the existing approaches are based on the CRL, hence they have the same update period as CRL. Besides, the revocation generally relies on arbitrary CA and misbehaved CA may delay issuing the certificate revocation information.

To address these aforementioned issues, we propose an efficient **C**ertificate **R**evocation scheme based block**chain** (CRchain), which makes certificate revocation and verification more efficient and transparent. The main contributions of this work are as follows:

- To improve the efficiency of certificate status checking, we design double cuckoo filters named validCertCF and revokedCertCF to store valid/ revoked certificates' fingerprints. Besides, validCertCF and revokedCertCF support deleting elements dynamically, thus CRchain can delete expired certificates periodically from double cuckoo filters to improve scalability.
- To simplify the revocation process and shorten the latency of publishing revocation information, we propose a server and CA co-controlled certificate revocation method. A new data structure called CertInfo is defined, stored in blocks to record the operations on the certificate for timely publication. With the co-controlled key CPK stored in CertInfo, the server can revoke its compromised certificate without the issuer.

- CRchain is implemented on Hyperledger Fabric [2] with smart contract. We make the theoretical analyses and evaluate the performance of CRchain in aspects of time cost and communication overhead. The results show that CRchain is superior to the existing methods, while ensures the correctness and availability of certificate status services.

2 Related Work

2.1 Traditional Certificate Revocation Mechanisms

CRL: CRL is signed by CA and updated periodically [7], which includes the certificate serial numbers of revoked certificates. The user can verify the certificate by checking whether the certificate serial number is in CRL or not. Delay on the update of CRL is a common issue of conventional PKI, which causes the inconsistency between the actual state and the CRL state. It severely affects the quality of PKI service and increases security threats. The scale of CRL is proportional to the number of terminal entities in the CA domain. With the number of issued certificates increasing, the size of the CRL grows much larger, resulting in that the user consumes much more bandwidth when checking the certificate status.

OCSP: The OCSP server conducts as an online responder for querying whether a certificate has been revoked [20]. OCSP reduces the threat of the CRL update delay. However, the clients query the OCSP server online and block the subsequent process before getting the query results during the TLS handshake. It causes a long time of blank page when the network is insufficient, reduces TLS performance and seriously affects the user's experience.

2.2 Blockchain-Based Certificate Service

With the development of blockchain technology, some schemes based on blockchain have been proposed recently to improve certificate revocation service.

Improve Certificate Transparency. The schemes using the openness of blockchain have been proposed to make certificates revocation transparent. The certificate information on the blockchain can be audited public, and the malicious behavior of CA can be monitored. Wang et al. [26] propose a blockchain-based certificate and revocation transparency scheme. The scheme relies on the certificate revocation information published by CAs on the blockchain to provide revocation transparency. However, a private-key-stolen or failed CA cannot issue a CRL or OCSP response to the user within the specified time. Meanwhile, the client needs to check all the blocks behind the block that the server claimed to contain the certificate transaction, which increases the latency of certificate verification. Certcoin [12] uses Namecoin to build a distributed PKI system with a consistent offering of identity retention. Every operation on the certificate is packaged as a transaction on the blockchain. Kubilay et al. [13] propose CertLedger, in which the CA stores the status updates of the certificates on the blockchain such that all TLS clients can verify the certificate using the preagreed status hash tree in the block header. The management of the state object of the trusted CA is responsible by the Certledger board of directors, and the private key of the account state object is the threshold key. Matsumoto et al. [18] propose IKP, which can respond automatically to unauthorized certificates and provides incentives or penalties for positive or malicious behaviors of CAs. However, this scheme does not offer a certificate revocation status checking service.

Enhance PKI. Chen et al. [5] propose a blockchain-based, public and efficient certificate audit scheme, Certchain, which utilizes double counting bloom filters to reduce false positives and realizes the economic space and efficient query for certificate revocation. SCRaaPS [19] utilizes cuckoo filter and blockchain to provide a quick response service for certificate revocation status queries with no false negatives. However, they design a single cuckooo filter to store the revoked certificate, thus more potential revocations indicated by cuckoo filter need to be backed up by complex and rigorous service queries than double cuckoo filter. And they update the coefficients of cuckoo filter periodically rather than in real time, which opens a window of opportunity for attackers to work with revoked certificates. Adja et al. [1] employ the extension field of the X.509 certificate's structure to introduce a field that describes to which distribution point the certificate will belong if revoked. Each distribution point is represented by a bloom filter filled with revoked certificates. Besides, they propose the data structure of RSI to implement additional validation when the bloom filter provides a positive response. However, the time consumption in the positive response scenario is very high, even higher than CRL and OCSP. Yakubov et al. [28] also utilizes X.509 extension fields to embed blockchain metadata, which makes X.509 certificate compatible with the blockchain-based PKI scheme. Cecoin [23] implements a distributed Certificate Library with the modified Merkle Patricia tree. However, the large storage overhead of Cecoin is unacceptable for a lightweight client.

The majority of the existing blockchain-based certificate revocation schemes necessitate clients to retrieve the related original transactions that record the certificate operation in the blockchain during certificate verification, which has a high delay or communication overhead. Besides, the revocation depends on arbitrary CAs in most schemes, and certificate owners are less involved in the revocation process. Some schemes design specialized blockchain architecture which means that they are unable to take advantage of security assurances of existing established blockchain platforms.

3 Preliminaries

3.1 Blockchain

Blockchain serves on a decentralized and immutable database maintained by multiple entities relying on a peer-to-peer network [21,29,30]. Blockchain utilizes consensus mechanism to verify and confirm transactions, and the data of ledgers across blockchain nodes are synchronized and replicated.

A blockchain consists of a continuous sequence of blocks that chronologically record all valid transactions. The block header contains the previous block's hash value, the timestamp, the random number $Nonce$, and the Merkle root calculated in the consensus process. Except for the genesis block (the first block), each block is chained by keeping the previous block's information in the block header, hence the transactions on blockchain are immutable and traceable.

Blockchain offers the potential to improve the openness and integrity of certificate revocation information. The blockchain is transparent on account of all the data on the blockchain is available. The distributed and replicable features of blockchain make it possible to avoid the need for a third party.

3.2 Cuckoo Filter

The cuckoo filter [10] is a data structure for set representation and membership testing. Compared with the classic bloom filter [4], cuckoo filter has the following advantages: (1) support dynamically adding and deleting elements; (2) support more efficient storage and query. The cuckoo filter can improve the efficiency and scalability of the certificate revocation scheme because it can quickly detect whether the certificate is a member of revoked certificate set or not and remove the certificate from the set.

The cuckoo filter uses partial key cuckoo hashing to insert new items dynamically, and indexes are determined as follows:

$$h_1(x) = hash(x) \tag{1}$$

$$h_2(x) = h_1(x) \oplus hash(x\text{'}sfingerprint) \tag{2}$$

Each item maps two optional locations with two hash functions. If both locations are empty, the item selects a location to insert its fingerprint arbitrarily. However, if both optional locations are occupied, the item will remove the original fingerprint from the randomly selected one of the two locations and then insert its fingerprint.

4 CRchain Overview

This section provides a high-level overview of the CRchain scheme, composed of the design goals and the system model.

4.1 Design Goals

Many reasons can cause certificate revocation prior to expiration, such as user's identity change, private key leakage, etc. And delayed or fake certificate revocation information can cause massive damages. Because after checking the certificate status during the TLS handshake, the client may still establish the connection with the attacker having a revoked certificate. To promptly provide available certificate revocation information, CRchain should satisfy the basic functions of the certificate revocation mechanism as well as achieve the following goals.

- **Streamline the process of revocation:** In the X.509 PKI, only the CA can alter the status of certificate, the compromised CA may delay the revocation information update, resulting in the abuse of compromised certificates. CRchain should be able to shorten the time needed to revoke a certificate, distribute revocation information quickly and decentralize the authority of the CA.
- **Improve the efficiency of validation:** To amend the users' experience and reduce the latency and communication overhead of checking certificate status in the duration of TLS handshake, CRchain is expected to efficiently verify certificates without false positives.
- **Enhance security:** To improve the security of certificate revocation mechanism, CRchain should be reliably decentralized to avoid the risk under centralization. CRchain is supposed to guarantee consistency with the actual statuses of certificates to provide the correct certificate status.

4.2 System Model

To meet the goals mentioned above, we propose a blockchain-based certificate revocation scheme, namely CRcahin, to provide efficient certificate status checking service during the TLS handshake. CRchain contains four entities: **CA**, **server**, **client** and **peer node**, as shown in Fig. 1. CA submits the certificate registration transactions to blockchain. When the certificate needs to be revoked, both authorized CA and server can submit the revocation transactions. During the TLS handshake, client checks the certificate status with CRchain before establishing the connection with server.

- **CA:** The CA is the entity that can register and revoke certificates. In CRchain, CA publishes the certificate status with peer nodes submitting transactions to the blockchain.
- **Client:** The client is the entity that intends to launch a TLS connection with the server. The client checks the certificate status by sending a query request to the peer node before establishing the connection with the server.
- **Server:** The server, for example, a web server, is authenticated by the client with the certificate signed by CA in the duration of TLS communication. If the server's certificate requires to be revoked, the server can perform revocation with the assistance of peer nodes instead of sending a revocation request to the CA in X.509 PKI.

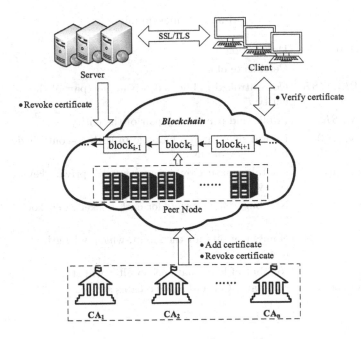

Fig. 1. The proposed CRchain model

- **Peer Node:** The peer node maintains the blockchain recorded the operations on certificates and responds to the certificate status queries from clients. The operations on certificates are kept in the form of transactions with an immutable and distributed certificate ledger. The statuses of certificates are stored on blockchain with the double cuckoo filters, called validCertCF and revokedCertCF. Readers can refer to Sect. 5.4 for the details of validCertCF and revokedCertCF.

5   CRchain Design

This section describes the components and functions of CRchain implemented with the smart contract [24]. The key components contain the CertInfo, Block, co-controlled certificate scheme, and double certificate cuckoo filters. The main notations used in this paper are listed in Table 1.

Table 1. Main symbols

Notation	Description
$cert_{sub}$	Certificate of server
CPK_i, CSK_i	Co-controlled public and private key pair of the entity i^*
PK_i, SK_i	Public and private key pair of the entity i
$\sigma_{CSK_i}(m)$	Digital signature on message m with co-controlled private key of entity i
$\sigma_{SK_i}(m)$	Digital signature on message m with private key of entity i
b	Number of fingerprints for each bucket in cuckoo filter
f	Number of bits for each item, which is length of fingerprint
n	Number of keys that cuckoo filter will store

* For entity i, ca indicates CA and sub indicates server.

5.1 CertInfo

CertInfo is a new defined data structure to record the information of certificate on CRchain. CertInfo contains the following fields:

- ID_{cert}: certificate serial number, the unique identifier of certificate.
- $Validity$: the end time of validity of the certificate.
- $Hash_{cert}$: hash of the certificate.
- CA: the name of a CA who issues this certificate.
- CPK_{ca}: co-controlled public key of above CA.
- $Subject$: the name of server that is certificate's owner.
- CPK_{sub}: co-controlled public key of above certificate's owner.
- $OperCode$: certificate operation type, 0 for registration, 1 for revocation.

Besides CertInfo, two other data structures named validCertCF and revoked-CertCF are defined for storing the fingerprints of valid/revoked certificates, respectively. The cascade structure of double cuckoo filters support efficient retrieval of certificate status.

5.2 The Storage Structure—*Block*

As shown in Fig. 2, the storage structure of blockchain in CRchain is a sequence of blocks. A block $block_i$ contains the header, *data* and *metadata*. The block header includes the number of transactions in $block_i$ m, the hash of previous block header $PreHash$ and the hash of previous block data $PreDataHash \in \{0,1\}^*$. *Metadata* is associated with the current block that describes key information about *data*. The *data* contains m number of transactions (Tx), which contains CertInfo, validCertCF and revokedCertCF. The *MerkleRoot* ensures that Txs cannot be modified.

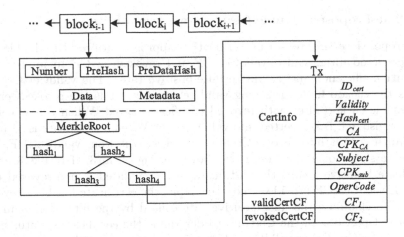

Fig. 2. The storage structure of CRchain

5.3 The Proposed Co-controlled Certificate Scheme

To enable the certificate revocation information distributed in a timely manner and balance the absolute authority of CA, we propose a co-controlled certificate service, which allows authenticated CA or server to register/revoke a certificate with co-controlled key. Different from CA's key and certificate key, the co-controlled key is served for the CA and server to manage certificates together, which supports the identity verification during certificate registration and revocation. The proposed co-controlled certificate scheme includes the following functions:

- $Gen(1^\lambda)$: With the input of the security parameter λ, the key generation function $Gen()$ outputs a pair public-private keys (CPK_i, CSK_i).
- $Sign(CSK_i, m)$: With the inputs of private key CSK_i and message m, the signing function $Sign()$ outputs signature $\sigma_{CSK_i}(m)$.
- $Verify(CPK_i, m, \sigma)$: With the inputs of the public key CPK_i, message m and the signature σ, the signature verification function $Verify()$ outputs that 1 indicates σ is valid and vice versa.

We store the co-controlled keys as CPK_{ca} and CPK_{sub} for CA and server, respectively, in CertInfo. When CA publishes a certificate registration transaction on blockchain, $\sigma_{CSK_{ca}}(hash_{cert})$ and $\sigma_{CSK_{sub}}(hash_{cert})$ are checked whether they are valid or not. It means that each valid certificate on CRchain is published with permission from the server. When CA or server revokes a certificate, it should send the request consists of ID_{cert} and $\sigma_{CSK_i}(hash_{cert})$.

In the case of a hacked CA, the candidate certificate for revocation cannot be revoked by CA in a timely manner, which will lead to the abuse of the certificate to be revoked. In the co-controlled certificate revocation scheme CRchain, certificate owners are involved in certificate revocation, and CRchain can shorten the certificate revocation time.

5.4   The Proposed Double Certificate Cuckoo Filters

The proposed certificate status verification approach utilizes the double certificate cuckoo filters called validCertCF and revokedCertCF to improve the verification efficiency and eliminate false-positive rates. The validCertCF represents the cuckoo filter for saving valid certificates, while the revokedCertCF denotes the cuckoo filter with revoked certificates saved. When a new certificate is registered, it is inserted into validCertCF. When a certificate is revoked, CRchain inserts it into revokedCertCF and deletes it from validCertCF. The certificate status query process is as shown in Algorithm 3. If revokedCertCF provides a negative result, the certificate to be validated is non-revoked definitely. If validCertCF provides a negative reply, the certificate has been revoked indeed. To eliminate the false positive rate caused by the filter, CRchain will check the OperCode in the CertInfo to determine the certificate's status when either revokedCertCF or validCertCF provides a positive result.

Compared with the DCBF designed in Certchain [5], the validCertCF and revokedCertCF have the advantages concerning more economical space and efficient query. CRchain removes expired certificates from validCertCF and revokedCertCF to spare some space for the subsequent certificates. Within a specific certificate scale, CRchain continuously inserts new certificates into the original filters without reconstructing the new filters. The operation functions of the validCertCF and revokedCertCF are described as follows:

- $CreatFilter(XCertCF, b, f, n)$: $CreatFilter()$ is implemented to create a cuckoo filter called $XCertCF$ to store certificates. The inputs of $CreatFilter()$ is the name of the cuckoo filter to be created $XCertCF$, the number b of fingerprints stored in each bucket of $XCertCF$, the length of fingerprints f, the maximum capacity n of $XCertCF$ for storing certificates, and $CreatFilter()$ outputs a cuckoo filter.
- $Insert(XCertCF, hash_{cert})$: $Insert()$ function inserts the hash of certificate into the validCertCF or revokedCertCF. With the inputs of $hash_{cert}$ and $XCertCF$, $Insert()$ calculates the fingerprint of the certificate, then selects the mapped location in the $XCertCF$ to store the $hash_{cert}$. When the insertion fails due to no position for the $hash_{cert}$, $Insert()$ outputs 0, and vice versa.
- $Delete(XCertCF, hash_{cert})$: CRchain employs $Delete()$ to delete the certificate from validCertCF or revokedCertCF. Deleting $hash_{cert}$ from $XCertCF$ by removing corresponding fingerprints from $XCertCF$. The deletion process begins with checking both candidate buckets for $hash_{cert}$: if the fingerprint of $XCertCF$ is found in any bucket, one copy of that matched fingerprint is removed from the bucket.
- $Query(XCertCF, hash_{cert})$: $Query()$ is used to query whether the $XCertCF$ contains the certificate. With the inputs of $hash_{cert}$ and $XCertCF$, $Query()$ outputs 0 if the certificate is not in the $XCertCF$, and outputs 1 if the certificate might be in the $cuckoo filter$ with false positive.

5.5   System Operation

This section describes the main oprerations of CRchain including blockchain initialization, certificate registration, certificate revocation, certificate verification and expired certificate deletion.

Blockchain Initialization: CRchain utilizes $Gen(1^\lambda)$ to generate key pairs (CPK_i, CSK_i) and distributes them to authenticated CAs and servers (the subjects of certificates to be registered). Then it initializes the validCertCF and revokedCertCF through the smart contract with $CreatFilter()$.

Certificate Registration: In addition to the parameters required to register a certificate in traditional X.509 PKI, the server needs to send CPK_{sub} to the CA during the certificate registration request. The procedure of certificate registration is as shown in Fig. 3 and Algorithm 1. The issuance of certificates is required signatures of the CA and server to the certificate to reduce the absolute authority of CA. As shown in Algorithm 1, CA invokes smart contract with checking the $validity$ and σ of the certificate. In the case of certificate registration, CRchain saves the CertInfo and inserts $hash_{cert}$ into the validCertCF before publishing the certificate.

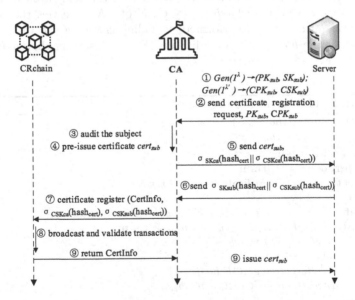

Fig. 3. Certificate registration process

Algorithm 1. TLS certificate registration

Input: $CertInfo, \sigma'_{CSK_{ca}}(hash_{cert}), \sigma'_{CSK_{sub}}(hash_{cert})$
Output: *success* or *error*

1: $CPK_{ca} \leftarrow CertInfo.CPK_{ca}$, $CPK_{sub} \leftarrow CertInfo.CPK_{sub}$, $hash_{cert} \leftarrow CertInfo.hash_{cert}$
2: **if** $CertInfo.validity < currenttime$ **then**
3:     **return** error
4: **else**
5:     **if** $CertInfo.ID_{cert}$ exists **then**
6:         **return** error
7:     **else**
8:         **if** $Verify(CPK_{ca}, hash_{cert}, \sigma'_{CSK_{ca}}(hash_{cert})$ &
   $Verify(CPK_{sub}, hash_{cert}, \sigma'_{CSK_{sub}}(hash_{cert})$ **then**
9:             save $CertInfo$
10:             $Insert(validCertCF, hash_{cert})$
11:             **return** success
12:         **else**
13:             **return** error

Certificate Revocation: The certificate revocation is performed either by the CA or server. As shown in Algorithm 2, the smart contract checks the value of OperCode if it has been revoked. If the certificate is non-revoked, when the σ is verified to be signed to $hash_{cert}$ by CSK of CA or server, the certificate revocation operation can be performed, including changing the value of Oper-Code, deleting the $hash_{cert}$ from validCertCF, and inserting the $hash_{cert}$ into revokedCertCF.

Algorithm 2. TLS certificate revocation

Input: ID_{cert}, $\sigma_{CSK_i}(hash_{cert})$
Output: *success* or *error*

1: **if** ID_{cert} exists **then**
2:     **if** operCode == 1 **then**
3:         **return** error("certificate has been revoked!")
4:     **else**
5:         **if** $Verify(CPK_{ca}, hash_{cert}, \sigma_{CSK_i}(hash_{cert}))$ ||
   $Verify(CPK_{sub}, hash_{cert}, \sigma_{CSK_i}(hash_{cert}))$ **then**
6:             $CertInfo.OperCode \leftarrow 1$
7:             save $CertInfo$
8:             $Delete(validCertCF, hash_{cert})$
9:             $Insert(revokedCertCF, hash_{cert})$
10:         **else**
11:             **return** error("Signature error, no permissions!")
12: **else**
13:     **return** error("certificate doesn't exist!")
14: **return** success

Algorithm 3. TLS certificate revoked status checking

Input: ID_{cert}, $hash_{cert}$
Output: *valid* or *revoked*
1: **if** $Query(revokedCertCF, hash_{cert}) == 1$ **then**
2:    **if** $Query(validCertCF, hash_{cert}) == 1$ **then**
3:       query the record of ID_{cert} from ledger
4:       **if** $CertInfo.OperCode == 1$ **then**
5:          **return** revoked
6:       **else if** $CertInfo.OperCode == 0$ **then**
7:          **return** valid
8:    **else**
9:       **return** revoked
10: **else**
11:    **return** valid

Certificate Verification: CRchain records the whole certificates revocation information as transactions in blocks. The process of certificate status query is shown in Algorithm 3. Firstly, CRchain queries $hash_{cert}$ in the revokedCertCF, if it receives a negative response, the certificate is valid. Otherwise, it continues to query $hash_{cert}$ in the validCertCF. If it receives a negative response from validCertCF, the certificate is revoked. If not, it queries the CertInfo of the certificate. For a certificate that cuckoo filters provide a positive response, the status can be ascertained by the value of OperCode in CertInfo, our method eliminates the false positive rate resulting from the cuckoo filters.

Certificate Expired: To save storage space and improve query efficiency, CRchain deletes expired certificates periodically. As shown in Algorithm 4, deleting a certificate from CRchain involves two steps: (a) remove the $hash_{cert}$ from the validCertCF; (b) remove the $hash_{cert}$ from the revokedCertCF. The period to delete expired certificates is determined by the capacity of the validCertCF and revokedCertCF. If the capacity is higher than the number of storing certificates, it needs to extend the period properly, and vice versa.

Algorithm 4. TLS certificate deletion

Input: ID_{cert}
Output: *success* or *error*
1: **if** ID_{cert} exists **then**
2:    **if** $CertInfo.validity < currenttime$ **then**
3:       $Delete(validCertCF, hash_{cert})$
4:       $Delete(revokedCertCF, hash_{cert})$
5:    **else**
6:       **return** error("Certificate is not expired!")
7: **else**
8:    **return** error("Certificate does not exist!")
9: **return** success

---

6 Efficiency and Security Analysis

This section mainly focuses on the efficiency analysis of CRchain in the aspect of certificate verification in theory and security analysis in terms of correctness and availability of CRchain under some security threat.

6.1 Efficiency Analysis

Assuming that the time to lookup an element in the validCertCF or revoked-CertCF, which refers the step line1 and line2 in the Algorithm 1 is T_f, and the time to check the certificate status through CertInfo, which refers to the step line3 in the Algorithm 1 is T_b. The lookup throughput of validCertCF and revokedCertCF is higher than the blockchain, thus the $T_f < T_b$.

CRchain firstly checks whether the revokedCertCF contains the certificate's hash $hash_{cert}$. For a non-revoked certificate, the revokedCertCF provides a negative response with the possibility of $(1-\epsilon)$, which is the final result for certificate status; the revokedCertCF provides a positive response with the possibility of ϵ, under the circumstances, CRchain needs to lookup $hash_{cert}$ in the validCertCF and checks the $CertInfo.OperCode$ in the blockchain. The total time T_n for the non-revoked certificate status checking is as shown in Eq. (3). For a revoked certificate, the revokedCertCF provides a positive response, then CRchain executes $Query(hash_{cert}, validCertCF)$. The validCertCF offers a negative response with the possibility of ϵ, and CRchain completes the certificate status check; The validCertCF returns a positive response with the possibility of $(1-\epsilon)$, CRchain then checks the $CertInfo.OperCode$ to ascertain the certificate status, the total time T for checking a revoked certificate is as shown in Eq. (4). The Certchain [5] designs the dual counting bloom filter (DCBF) storing certificate status to offer certificate validation.

Compared to the DCBF, T_f of revokedCertCF and validCertCF is smaller, as a consequence, both T_n and T become smaller. Hence, it can be concluded that using revokedCertCF and validCertCF is more efficient in certificate verification than DCBF with the same blockchain platform.

$$T_n = \epsilon \cdot (2 \cdot T_f + T_b) + (1 - \epsilon) \cdot T_f = T_f + \epsilon \cdot T_f + \epsilon \cdot T_b \qquad (3)$$

$$T = \epsilon \cdot (2 \cdot T_f + T_b) + (1 - \epsilon) \cdot 2 \cdot T_f = 2 \cdot T_f + \epsilon \cdot T_b \qquad (4)$$

When the bloom filter is selected to store certificates in the certificate revocation scheme, the bloom filter for saving valid certificates cannot be generated because the bloom filter doesn't support deleting revoked certificates from the bloom filter for containing registered certificates. If the bloom filter saving the revoked certificates provides a positive reply, the client must perform additional operations to ensure whether the certificate status is a false positive or not [1]. Suppose the aforementioned further operations to confirm the certificate status is querying the certificate record on the blockchain. For the non-revoked certificate, the total time T'_n of the validation process is as shown in Eq. (5), and for the revoked certificate, the total time T_n is as shown in Eq. (6). Apparently,

$T_b < T_f$, hence $T < T'$. When the T_b gets larger, ϵ gets smaller, $T_n < T'_n$. It takes a longer time with bloom filters than cuckoo filters for certificate verification.

$$T'_n = \epsilon \cdot (T_f + T_b) + (1 - \epsilon) \cdot T_f = T_f + \epsilon \cdot T_b \tag{5}$$

$$T' = T_f + T_b \tag{6}$$

Based on the above analysis, certificate verification with cuckoo filter is more efficient than it with bloom filter or counting bloom filter. Consequently, cuckoo filter is more suitable for certificate verification.

6.2 Security Analysis

Property 1: CRchain ensures the integrity of certificate revocation information and the correctness of certificate state verification service.

CRchain records all historical operations corresponding with a given certificate. Suppose a malicious node wants to modify the certificate status information on the blockchain, thus continuing to exploit the revoked certificate to trick the attacked client into communicating. In that case, it needs to change the information of all subsequent blocks to make the Merkle root value consistent. However, it is challenging because it needs to unite 51% of the CAs in the CRchain for illegal transactions to be recorded on the blockchain. The consensus mechanism can supervise CAs' behaviors and prevent adversaries and malicious peers from colluding and issuing forged certificate information. The operations in the system, such as initiating transactions and endorsements, are verified by digital signatures, which can trace malicious operations effectively. Although the cuckoo filter has false positives during the certificate state check, we reduce the false positives by cascading cuckoo filters and finally determine the states of certificates that generate false positives by querying the original records on the blockchain. Hence we eliminate the false positives and provide the correct revocation status for each certificate using CRchain.

Property 2: The latency in updating the certificate revoke information is low, and consequently, the window of opportunity for an attacker to make use of a revoked certificate reduces substantially.

The CRchain nodes will broadcast the certificate revocation transaction immediately when receiving the revocation request. Afterward, the revocation information will be recorded on the blockchain after confirmation of the transaction. Hence CRchain can provide a more current certificate revocation status for the clients timely. However, the existing schemes, such as CRL, [19], and [1], update revoked certificates periodically. With the co-controlled key, the server can revoke the certificate timely. A misbehaved or hacked CA may issue wrong certificates and can not process a certificate revocation request timely. In our scheme, CertInfo contains the co-controlled keys of the CA and the certificate owner, which allows the certificate owner to revoke the compromised certificate in a timely manner, even if the CA cannot provide revocation service due to the hacker's attack. It overcomes the problem that the traditional certificate revocation mechanism only grants the right to the CA and cannot revoke the compromised certificates promptly when the CA is damaged. It effectively saves the time of the certificate owner and protects the user from the loss caused by the damage of the certificate in time. Consequently, CRchain is capable of reducing the window of opportunity for an attacker to exploit a revoked certificate.

Property 3: CRchain is able to tolerate DoS attacks.

Attacker may conduct a DoS attack on a server, which will make the certificate status verification and revocation service unavailable and decrease the accuracy of certificate verification. Compared with traditional PKI such as CRL and OCSP, peers that provide certificate status verification service in CRchain are parallel, meaning they are the same in terms of storage and computing services. Even if multiple peers cannot communicate or are offline, CRchain can continue operating and verifying transactions. When the interrupted peers resume work, they will get the latest data from the peers not being attacked. Our scheme can provide stable services, resist DoS attacks, and avoid the security threat of a single point of failure.

7 Experiment and Evaluation

7.1 Implementation

This section implements CRchain on Hyperledger Fabric blockchain network [2]. Hyperledger Fabric is a permissioned distributed ledger technology platform that only permits authorized nodes to participate. The smart contract is implemented with the golang language. The CRchain runs in the environment of Inter Core i7-8700 CPU @3.20 GHz × 2, 4G RAM and Ubuntu 20.04.1 LTS 64bit operation system. Both CAs and certificate owners to be authenticated in the revocation transaction rely on the ECDSA signature algorithm.

Assuming that the number of certificates is one million, and the revoked certificates account for 5%. The size of revokedCertCF and validCertCF are 2048 KB and 128 KB with false-positive rate $\epsilon = 0.0001$, respectively. A single CertInfo is about 250 bytes in size, and the size of T_x is about 2.5 MB. Under the same false-positive rate, the DCBF [5] is about 8.9 MB. When the false-positive rate decreases, the space cost of revokedCertCF and validCertCF increases. The false-positive rates of revokedCertCF and validCertCF can be modified based on the size of the block on blockchain to balance the storage space and validation efficiency.

In our implementation, the parameters of revokedCertCF and validCertCF are set to the optimal solution for the number of items $n = 20000$. According to [10], number of entries per bucket b affects the load factor α, which represent the maximum space utilization of the filter. There is an optimal b for different target false positive rate ϵ. Larger b requires longer fingerprint size f to retain. The space-optimal bucket size depends on ϵ: when ϵ decreases to $0.00001 < \epsilon \leq 0.002$, four entries per bucket minimizes space. The minimal f required is approximately as shown in Eq. (7). Thus we set $\epsilon = 0.0001$, $b = 4$, $f = 16$.

$$f \geq \lceil \log_2(2 \cdot b/\epsilon) \rceil = \lceil \log_2(1/\epsilon) + \log_2(2 \cdot b) \rceil \quad bits \quad (7)$$

7.2 Performance Evaluation

This prototype mainly focuses on evaluating performance in terms of communication overhead and certificate validation latency. The server runs in the same environment as the client. Based on [17], the revoked certificates are for approximately 5.3% of all issued certificates, thus we conduct six sets of experiments, the number of revoked certificates is [20,100,250,500,750,1000] and the number of issued certificates is [377,1887,4717, 9434,14151,18868] correspondingly according to this ratio. The number of certificates in our experiments is consistent with comparison scheme RSI [1].

Firstly, we compare CRchain with two other schemes - CRL and RSI in the aspect of transmitted data size and time consumption during the process of checking the status of the certificates. Secondly, We compare the performance of different filters employed in CRchain, including cuckoo filter, bloom filter, and counting bloom filter [11] which is the method used in CertChain [5]. Each of the results we presented was obtained from 100,000 certificate status validation experiments.

Comparison of Transmitted Data Size. Figure 4 shows the size of transmitted data when verifying the certificate status. Since CRchain depends on the request/response mechanism, the size of data needed is constant, including 206 bytes for revoked certificates and 208 bytes for non-revoked certificates regardless of the number of revoked certificates. Since the CRL contains revocation status information for all certificates, the entire CRL file must be cached by the client, even if the dependent party only needs to verify a handful of certificates. The size of the CRL file is proportional to the number of revoked certificates. According to [17], the average size of entry in CRL is 38 bytes. For RSI, when the certificate is non-revoked, the filter provides a negative response. Hence their approach only needs a request with one response that contains the RSI structure (520 bytes). However, when the certificate is revoked, additional verification using all LRSI is needed, and each LRSI is 170 bytes. Therefore, CRchain requires fewer data exchanged than the CRL and RSI to ensure the revocation status verification.

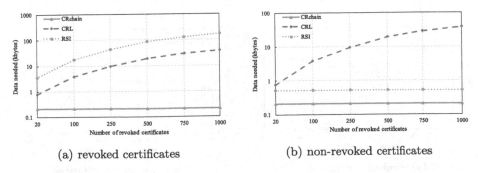

(a) revoked certificates   (b) non-revoked certificates

Fig. 4. The size of data needed to exchange in the duration of certificate verification

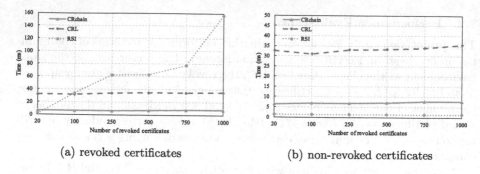

(a) revoked certificates   (b) non-revoked certificates

Fig. 5. The time required to verify certificate status with different schemes

Comparison of Time Consumption. Figure 5 shows the consumed time CRchain required to verify the certificate status compared with CRL and RSI. For revoked certificates, CRchain's consumed time is 7 ms to 9 ms. The CRL scheme requires 30 ms to 38 ms. However, the time needed by the RSI scheme increases largely with the number of revoked certificates. When the number of revoked certificates is 1000, the consumed time is 157 ms. CRchain improves performance by approximately 94.2% over RSI. As the number of revoked certificates grows, the amount of time RSI consumed grows faster than CRchain. For non-revoked certificates, CRchain's consumed time is 6.3 ms to 8 ms, which takes less time than the scenario where the certificate is revoked. The result is significantly lower than that of CRL, though slightly higher than that of RSI. According to the above analysis of the experimental results, CRchain has relatively excellent performance compared with CRL and RSI.

Figure 6 shows the consumed time CRchain required to verify the certificate status compared with different filters, including bloom filter (BFchain) and counting filter (DCBFchain). For three different filters, we set the same number of items $n = 20000$ and false positive rates $\epsilon = 0.0001$, other parameters are optimal as well. CRchain consumes less time and has better performance than the other two schemes.

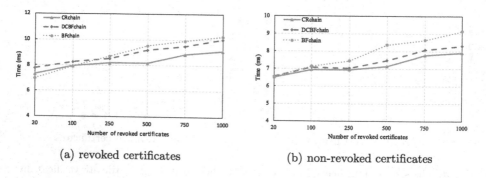

(a) revoked certificates   (b) non-revoked certificates

Fig. 6. The time required to verify certificate status with different filters

8 Conclusion

In this paper, we propose an efficient certificate revocation scheme based on blockchain, namely CRchain. CRchain provides efficient and correct online certificate status checking with double cuckoo filters. And a co-controlled certificate revocation method is presented to support the server revoking its certificate without the issuer. We implement and evaluate CRchain on Hyperledger Fabric, and theoretical analysis and experimental results show that CRchain has excellent performance and is resistant to some security threats. In future work, we will focus on the structure of cuckoo filters for storing certificates to provide a much more responsive certificate service and support mass certificate storage.

References

1. Adja, Y.C.E., Hammi, B., Serhrouchni, A., Zeadally, S.: A blockchain-based certificate revocation management and status verification system. Comput. Secur. **104**, 102209 (2021)
2. Androulaki, E., Manevich, Y., Muralidharan, S., Murthy, C., Laventman, G.: Hyperledger fabric: a distributed operating system for permissioned blockchains. In: The 13th EuroSys Conference (2018)
3. Axon, L., Goldsmith, M.: PB-PKI: a privacy-aware blockchain-based PKI (2016)
4. Bloom, B.H.: Space/time trade-offs in hash coding with allowable errors. Commun. ACM **13**(7), 422–426 (1970)
5. Chen, J., Yao, S., Yuan, Q., He, K., Ji, S., Du, R.: CertChain: public and efficient certificate audit based on blockchain for TLS connections. In: IEEE Conference on Computer Communications, IEEE INFOCOM 2018, pp. 2060–2068. IEEE (2018)
6. Comodo CA Ltd.: Comodo report of incident-comodo detected and thwarted an intrusion on 26-mar-2011. Technical report (March 2011)
7. Cooper, D., Santesson, S., Farrell, S., Boeyen, S., Housley, R., Polk, W.T., et al.: Internet x.509 public key infrastructure certificate and certificate revocation list (CRL) profile. RFC 5280, pp. 1–151 (2008)
8. Dinh, T.T.A., Liu, R., Zhang, M., Chen, G., Ooi, B.C., Wang, J.: Untangling blockchain: a data processing view of blockchain systems. IEEE Trans. Knowl. Data Eng. **30**(7), 1366–1385 (2018)
9. Ducklin, P.: The TURKTRUST SSL certificate fiasco-what really happened, and what happens next. Naked Security. SOPHOS (8 January 2013)
10. Fan, B., Andersen, D.G., Kaminsky, M., Mitzenmacher, M.D.: Cuckoo filter: practically better than bloom. In: Proceedings of the 10th ACM International on Conference on Emerging Networking Experiments and Technologies, pp. 75–88 (2014)
11. Fan, L., Cao, P., Almeida, J., Broder, A.Z.: Summary cache: a scalable wide-area web cache sharing protocol. IEEE/ACM Trans. Netw. **8**(3), 281–293 (2000)
12. Fromknecht, C., Velicanu, D., Yakoubov, S.: A decentralized public key infrastructure with identity retention. IACR Cryptol. ePrint Arch. **2014**, 803 (2014)
13. Kubilay, M.Y., Kiraz, M.S., Mantar, H.A.: CertLedger: a new PKI model with certificate transparency based on blockchain. Comput. Secur. **85**, 333–352 (2019)
14. Larisch, J., Choffnes, D., Levin, D., Maggs, B.M., Wilson, C.: CRLite: a scalable system for pushing all TLS revocations to all browsers. In: Security & Privacy (2017)

15. Leiding, B., Cap, C.H., Mundt, T., Rashidibajgan, S.: Authcoin: validation and authentication in decentralized networks. arXiv preprint arXiv:1609.04955 (2016)
16. Li, X., Jiang, P., Chen, T., Luo, X., Wen, Q.: A survey on the security of blockchain systems. Fut. Gener. Comput. Syst. **107**, 841–853 (2020)
17. Liu, Y., et al.: An end-to-end measurement of certificate revocation in the web's PKI. In: Proceedings of the 2015 Internet Measurement Conference, pp. 183–196 (2015)
18. Matsumoto, S., Reischuk, R.M.: IKP: turning a PKI around with decentralized automated incentives. In: 2017 IEEE Symposium on Security and Privacy (SP), pp. 410–426. IEEE (2017)
19. Medury, S., Skjellum, A., Brooks, R.R., Yu, L.: SCRaaPS: X.509 certificate revocation using the blockchain-based Scrybe secure provenance system. In: 2018 13th International Conference on Malicious and Unwanted Software (MALWARE), pp. 145–152. IEEE (2018)
20. Myers, M., Ankney, R., Malpani, A., Galperin, S., Adams, C.: X.509 internet public key infrastructure online certificate status protocol-OCSP (1999)
21. Nakamoto, S., Bitcoin, A.: A peer-to-peer electronic cash system. Bitcoin (April 2008). https://bitcoin.org/bitcoin.pdf
22. Prins, J.R., Cybercrime (BU): Diginotar certificate authority breach "operation black tulip". Fox-IT, p. 18 (November 2011)
23. Qin, B., Huang, J., Wang, Q., Luo, X., Liang, B., Shi, W.: Cecoin: a decentralized PKI mitigating MitM attacks. Fut. Gener. Comput. Syst. **107**, 805–815 (2020)
24. Szabo, N.: The idea of smart contracts (1997). http://szabo.best.vwh.net/smart_contracts_idea.html
25. Tung, L.: Mozilla to China's WoSign: we'll kill Firefox trust in you after mis-issued GitHub certs. ZDNet (27 September 2016)
26. Wang, Z., Lin, J., Cai, Q., Wang, Q., Zha, D., Jing, J.: Blockchain-based certificate transparency and revocation transparency. IEEE Trans. Dependable Secure Comput. **19**, 681–697 (2020)
27. Yaga, D., Mell, P., Roby, N., Scarfone, K.: Blockchain technology overview. arXiv preprint arXiv:1906.11078 (2019)
28. Yakubov, A., Shbair, W., Wallbom, A., Sanda, D., et al.: A blockchain-based PKI management framework. In: The 1st IEEE/IFIP International Workshop on Managing and Managed by Blockchain (Man2Block) colocated with IEEE/IFIP NOMS 2018, Tapei, Tawain, 23–27 April 2018 (2018)
29. Zheng, Z., Xie, S., Dai, H.N., Chen, X., Wang, H.: Blockchain challenges and opportunities: a survey. Int. J. Web Grid Serv. **14**(4), 352–375 (2018)
30. Zheng, Z., Xie, S., Dai, H., Chen, X., Wang, H.: An overview of blockchain technology: architecture, consensus, and future trends. In: 2017 IEEE International Congress on Big Data (BigData Congress), pp. 557–564 (2017). https://doi.org/10.1109/BigDataCongress.2017.85

Anonymous Authentication Scheme Based on Trust and Blockchain in VANETs

Li Zhang[1] and Jianbo Xu[2]([✉])

[1] School of Computer Science and Engineering, Hunan University of Science
and Technology, Xiangtan 411201, China
[2] Hunan Key Laboratory of Service Computing and New Software Service
Technology, Xiangtan 411201, China
jbxu@hnust.edu.cn

Abstract. Vehicular ad-hoc network (VANET) has been applied in intelligent transportation systems due to its tremendous potential to improve vehicle and road safety, traffic efficiency, and promote convenience as well as comfort to both drivers and passengers. However, the dynamic wireless network environment and the high mobility of vehicles bring huge challenges to the security of VANETs. A trust-based certificateless anonymous authentication scheme for VANETs has been proposed in this paper. In this scheme, bilinear pairing operations and elliptic curve cryptographic algorithm are utilized to achieve anonymous authentication. Blockchain technology is introduced to store the trust value of vehicles, realizing the identity tracking of malicious vehicles. Practicability and reliability have been improved through the combination of trust, traditional authentication and blockchain, which also realize privacy-preserving. Simulation results have proved that the proposed scheme outperforms baseline schemes in computational cost and communication cost.

Keywords: Blockchain · Anonymous authentication · Certificateless signature · VANETs

1 Introduction

For decades, with the development of the economy and technology, the number of vehicles has increased year by year. Intelligent transportation systems (ITS) are playing an increasingly important role in transportation networks. Vehicular ad-hoc network (VANET) has emerged under the broad application of vehicle-mounted wireless communication equipment, which will facilitate the communication among vehicles, and also between vehicles and roadside units (RSU), so as to conveniently spread traffic information, such as traffic jams, traffic accidents, and road conditions.

Although the VANET has many advantages and can bring great convenience to traffic management, the dynamic wireless network environment and the high

© Springer Nature Switzerland AG 2022
Y. Lai et al. (Eds.): ICA3PP 2021, LNCS 13156, pp. 473–488, 2022.
https://doi.org/10.1007/978-3-030-95388-1_31

mobility of vehicles bring huge challenges to the safe transmission of traffic information and the privacy protection of vehicles. Adversaries can easily launch various attacks through wireless networks, such as tampering with the emergency level of traffic accidents, tracking the trajectory of vehicles, etc.

In order to ensure the information security of VANET, a variety of security mechanisms have been developed, such as the message authentication scheme based on public key infrastructure (PKI), the identity-based encryption scheme, and the certificateless encryption scheme. These schemes enable to satisfy different security requirements to a certain extent. In the PKI-based schemes, the certificate authority (CA) needs to manage a large number of public key certificates, which brings a great burden to the CA. At the same time, RSU also needs to consume a lot of computing power and storage capacity to verify these certificates of traffic messages sender. In order to reduce the overhead caused by public key certificate management, identity-based authentication has been proposed. In this authentication process, the user's public key is generated from identity information such as email addresses, phone numbers, etc. However, private keys of all users are generated by a certain key generation center (KGC), KGC may forge user signatures, causing key escrow problems.

Although traditional authentication can ensure that the message comes from a legitimate sender, and ensure the integrity and confidentiality of the message during transmission, these mechanisms still have certain limitations and cannot effectively prevent malicious attackers from pretending to be a legitimate sender and maliciously spreading fake or wrong messages to other vehicles.

The main contributions of this paper are listed as follows:

(1) Bilinear pairing operations and elliptic curve cryptographic algorithm are utilized to achieve anonymous authentication of messages, and support aggregated signature verification to improve verification efficiency.
(2) A blockchain scheme is proposed to store the trust value of nodes and public information. In this scheme, node pseudo-identity and related public information are regarded as transactions to provide authentication credentials for RSUs. For those nodes with too low trust values, they can be inserted into the revocation blockchain. An anonymous authentication mechanism can be combined to realize the identity tracking.
(3) A trust value calculation method based on the message feedback model is proposed. The location certificate is used to prove the geographical location of the message sender at the time of the traffic event, so as to determine whether the event message sent is valid and reliable, which provides evidence for the receiver to give the follow-up message feedback.

2   Related Work

The authentication and privacy for VANETs are broad terms related to different security requirements. The authentication process comprises two major phases (signing and verifying), by which only traffic-related messages sent by authorized entities are accepted. The sender signs messages and the receiver verifies the signed ones. The authentication process helps to guard an early attack known as a masquerade attack and is considered as the first stage of defense from attackers.

PKI-based authentication is a simple and effective solution proposed earlier to implement security for VANETs. However, it needs to consume large computational and storage resources to manage certificates in the PKI mechanism, which probably makes a bottleneck in performance. In order to overcome the defects of the PKI mechanism, identity-based public key cryptography (ID-PKC) [11] is proposed, which has been widely applied for secure authentication in VANETs. The biggest advantage of identity-based signature is that the public key of an entity could be derived from its public identity information, such as name, e-mail address, etc., which avoids the use of certificates for public key verification in the conventional PKI scheme. Most existing algorithms of ID-PKC are based on the bilinear pairing in a discrete domain where the Discrete Logarithm Problem (DLP) in groups is difficult. Pairing-based cryptography is pairing elements of two additive cyclic groups to the third element of multiplicative cyclic group for constructing cryptographic system. In [8], Li et al. proposed a scheme that uses identity-based signature to authenticate vehicle-infrastructure communication.

Although ID-PKC mechanism exists without certificate management problem, it has other disadvantages. As a unique part responsible for generating private keys for all entities, KGC perhaps uses the private key to forge signature, which is known as the key escrow problem. To address the problem in ID-PKC, the concept of certificateless public key cryptography (CL-PKC) was introduced by Al-Riyami and Paterson in 2003 [1]. On this basis, many certificateless signature schemes have successively proposed [3,6,7,10,13]. Most of them use the bilinear pairing method to realize signature verification, and use different hash functions in the operations of signature, verification, and aggregation verification, with different computational cost.

Recently, blockchain has already been applied in many Internet of Things (IoTs) application. The development of blockchain techniques facilitate decentralized trust management in VANETs. Blockchain-assisted authentication has also become a popular research issue. The relevant privacy-preserving trust model for VANETs is proposed in [9]. Feng et al. proposed BPAS, a blockchain-assisted privacy-preserving authentication system for VANET [4]. In [12], Tan et al. proposed a secure authentication and key management scheme. In this scheme, consortium blockchain is employed for V2V group key construction, and real-time group membership arrangement has been realized with efficient group key updating. In order to detect malicious node and prevent misbehaving of legitimate vehicles from harming the VANET, Ghosh et al. proposed the misbehaving detection agency [5].

From the comparison of existing research work, the blockchain mainly acts as a database to store valid certificates or revoked vehicle certificates while ignoring reasonable calculations of vehicle trust values. In this paper, we propose a trust value calculation method based on the message feedback mode to detect malicious vehicles, and manage a revoke vehicle list in the blockchain. Furthermore, compared with existing certificateless public key cryptography, we design different signature operation, which outperforms them.

3   Proposed Scheme

3.1   System Model

In order to describe the proposed secure authentication scheme, this section describes the system model of the VANET, as shown in Fig. 1. It mainly includes three entities, namely, Trust Authority (TA), RoadSide Unit (RSU) and OnBoard Unit (OBU).

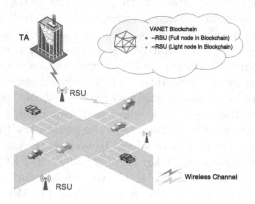

Fig. 1. Network architecture based on blockchain in VANET.

(1) **TA:** The highest authority in the VANET. It consists of two parts, the Key Generation Center (KGC) and the Trace Center (TRA). It is mainly responsible for system initialization and provides registration services for OBUs and RSUs. It can also perform identity management to each entity in VANET and track the vehicle's real identity. TA has enough computing power and storage capacity.

(2) **RSU:** It is widely distributed on roadsides or at crossroads, with stable computing power and a certain storage capacity, and can be regarded as a router between the trust organization and the vehicle node, or regarded as an edge node. It provides services such as accessing and message dissemination for vehicles. The blockchain proposed in our scheme is also composed of RSUs.

(3) **OBU:** It is installed inside the vehicle, the vehicle identity and some secret information needed by the authentication process are stored in the OBU's tamper-proof device (TPD). Compared with TA and RSU, OBU has limited computing power and storage capacity.

The VANET system model based on the consortium chain is shown in Fig. 1. The OBU of the driving vehicle is connected to the nearby RSU. All RSUs form a consortium chain network, and RSUs are used as ledger nodes to process the legal identity information of the vehicle with the public key and trust level, and record it in the blockchain to provide credentials for vehicles to realize anonymous authentication.

3.2 Construction of Trust Model

In this scheme, we use RSUs to form the consortium chain, which is also a trust manager to realize the calculation, storage and update of the trust value. When a vehicle encounters a specific traffic-related condition or event, it wants to broadcast a relevant message to surrounding vehicles or RSU. Before that, it needs to obtain a location certificate in advance to prove that the vehicle is near the place of occurrence.

After the vehicle obtains the location certificate, it can broadcast event or road condition messages to others. The message includes the sender's pseudo-identity, event ID, event type, direction, location, vehicle location certificate, and timestamp. When receivers obtain the message, it will verify the reliability of the message source. The verification content of the message includes the identity of the sender and the authenticity of the message. The authenticity of event can be verified according to the location of the event, the location certificate of the sender, the timestamp, or even the subsequent real experience of the receiver.

After executing the verification strategy, the receiver believes that the message is authentic and credible. It will give RSU positive feedback. If the receiver regards the message as fake and invalid, it will give negative feedback. After RSU receives the feedback, the trust value of the sender will be recalculated. Here, we assume that the number of feedbacks for authentic messages and fake messages are m and n, respectively, then the new trust value is calculated according to:

$$TR_{value} = \frac{(m + m_{pre})}{(m + n + m_{pre} + n_{pre})} \qquad (1)$$

where m_{pre} and n_{pre} represent the previous number of positive feedbacks and negative feedbacks in records of the message sender, respectively.

As time goes by, the number of feedbacks received by RSU will continue to update. The value of m will be increased by 1 when positive feedback is received, while the value of n will be increased by 1 when negative feedback is received. It can be easily seen that as the value of m and n changes, it will cause the trust value of the vehicle to change constantly. Considering that it is infeasible to execute a real-time update of trust value stored in the blockchain, the frequent calculation will bring massive overhead to the system. Therefore, we define a calculation interval. During each interval, RSU only calculates for one time, then records the new trust value and the new number of positive feedback and negative feedback in the blockchain.

3.3 Blockchain Construction

In our proposed scheme, different regional RSUs form a consortium chain network. There are two blockchains defined as follows:

- *Blockchain for pseudo-identities (PID-BC):* It works as the public database for all those pseudo-identities which have generated but have not been revoked by TRA.
- *Blockchain for revoked pseudo-identities (RID-BC):* It works as the public database for all those pseudo-identities which have been revoked by TRA.

Both PID-BC and RID-BC are analogous to the conventional blockchain in Bitcoin. The transaction about pseudo-identities and other public information of vehicles for authentication are stored chronologically. Due to massive computational consumption, the Proof-of-Work (PoW) consensus mechanism is not suitable for the needs of real-time and rapid authentication in VANET. In our solution, the Practical Byzantine Fault Tolerance (PBFT) consensus mechanism is utilized to shorten the block generation time to meet the needs of the VANET. Furthermore, PBFT can tolerate less than 1/3 invalid or malicious nodes, and transaction throughput under the PBFT consensus mechanism can reach 200–2000 transactions per second (TPS), achieving a millisecond confirmation time, and resistance to Sybil attacks.

A prototype system of the fast anonymous and message authentication for the VANET has been designed using open-source Hyperledger consortium chain. In this system, the blockchain is mainly used to store vehicle-related information. In our proposed scheme, we adopt Merkle Tree (MT) to store the vehicle's public information, which is packaged as a vehicle's tuple. The tuple comprises four parts: vehicle identity, vehicle public key, trust field, and timestamp. Vehicle identity is a pseudo-identity generated by TA, which is denoted as PID_i. Trust field includes TR_{value}, m_{pre} and n_{pre} which are described in Sect. 3.2. The timestamp represents the valid time of the vehicle tuple.

In order to instantly store vehicle tuple into the consortium chain, smart contract technology is utilized, which can be regarded as a computer program running on a distributed ledger to complete preset rules without the third party interferes. In our proposed solution, the smart contract will be invoked under the following circumstances:

(1) When the TA requests to store vehicle tuple in the consortium blockchain, the smart contract will be triggered to add the tuple to PID-BC; if the trust value of the vehicle changes, it will be triggered to add the new tuple to PID-BC.
(2) When the timestamp of tuple is expired, the smart contract will be triggered to add the pseudo-identity mentioned in this tuple to the revocation blockchain RID-BC; if TA requests to revoke the vehicle or vehicle's trust value is below the preset threshold, it will trigger the same revoking process.
(3) The behavior of the message receiver requesting the sender's tuple will trigger a smart contract to quickly retrieve the sender's pseudo-identity on RID-BC; if no record is found, it will search it in PID-BC.

4   Proposed Authentication Protocol

The proposed protocol in this paper implements certificateless signature based on pairing operation, and uses RSU to build a consortium blockchain. The distributed ledger stores the vehicle trust value, public key and other related information to provide a credential for message verification. In this protocol, it is assumed that the RSU has been registered by the TA at the early stage of deployment, so the registration process of RSU is not introduced in detail in this section. The detailed algorithm is described as follows:

Step 1: *System initialization.* As a trusted authority, TA is the executor of system initialization. TA is composed of two parts: Key Generation Center (KGC) and Trace Authority (TRA), assuming that both parties have sufficient computing power and storage capacity. In the system initialization phase, TA generates the necessary system parameters.

(1) First, a safety parameters l^k for $k \in N$ is taken as input, TA outputs G_1, G_2, e, where $(G_1, +)$ and $(G_2, \cdot)$ are a cyclic additive group and a cyclic multiplicative group based on elliptic curve discrete domain with the same prime order q, respectively, and $\hat{e} : G_1 \times G_1 \rightarrow G_2$ is a bilinear pairing. TA randomly selects a point $P \in G_1$ as the generator of the group G_1 and calculates $g = \hat{e}(P, P)$.
(2) TRA randomly selects a number $s \in Z_q^*$ as its master private key and calculates $P_{pub} = s \cdot P$ as its public key, keeping s secret.
(3) KGC randomly selects a number $k \in Z_q^*$ as its master private key and sets $P_k = (P_{k1}, P_{k2}) = ((\frac{1}{k})P, kP)$ as its public key, keeping k safe.
(4) TA chooses three different secure hash functions $H_1, H_2, H_3 : \{0,1\}^* \rightarrow Z_q^*$. After the steps mentioned above are completed, TA publishes the system public parameters: $\{p, q, G_1, G_2, \hat{e}, g, P, P_{pub}, P_k, H_1, H_2, H_3\}$.

Step 2: *Vehicle pseudo-identity registration.* The vehicle submits a registration request through a secure channel. For example, it performs an offline registration using the tamper-proof device (TPD).

(1) Vehicles V_i submits relevant credentials such as the owner's ID card and vehicle license. After verification by TRA, the real identity of the vehicle denoted as RID_i is generated according to certain rules such as hash-to-point operations, and then pseudo-identity is generated by computing the $PID_i = RID_i \oplus H_1(s, T_{reg})$, where T_{reg} represents the vehicle registration time.
(2) TRA will record (PID_i, T_{reg}) in the vehicle registration table, which is used to track the real identity of the vehicle, and (PID_i, T_{reg}) will also be sent back to the OBU and written into the vehicle's TPD.

Step 3: *Vehicle partial public and private key generation.* KGC selects a random number $b_i \in Z_q^*$, calculates $A_i = b_i \cdot P$, and $\alpha_i = H_2(PID_i, A_i)$, $\beta_i = b_i +$

$k\alpha_i$ mod q and $B_i = \beta_i \cdot P_{k2}$, where taking B_i as the vehicle's partial public key, β_i as the vehicle's partial private key. KGC will send (B_i, β_i) back to the vehicle and write it into the TPD through a secure channel.

Step 4: *Vehicle public and private key generation.* OBU selects a random number $x_i \in Z_q^*$, calculates $X_i = x_i \cdot P_{k2}$, sets the $PK_i = (B_i, X_i)$ and $SK_i = (\beta_i, x_i)$ as the public key and private key of the vehicle, respectively. The vehicle submits PK_i to TA, so that TA can record its identity information into the RSU blockchain.

Step 5: *Vehicle information storage to blockchain.* After TA receiving the PK_i, it initializes a trust value $TV_i = 1$ for the vehicle, and generates a tuple including pseudo-identity PID_i, public key PK_i, and original trust value TV_i, then requests the RSU to record the tuple in blockchain. After receiving the request, the smart contract is triggered and the tuple is recorded in the block. When each RSU reaches a consensus, the tuple is published to the blockchain.

Step 6: *Message signature generation.* After the relevant information of the vehicle is stored in the blockchain, the vehicle can communicate with RSU. If it encounters road condition and needs to publish the message M_i, the vehicle calculates $h_i = H_3(M_i, PID_i, PK_i, T_i)$ and generates the signature Sig_i according to the following Eq. (2), then send the $\sigma_i = (M_i, PID_i, Sig_i, T_i)$ to nearby RSU.

$$Sig_i = \left(\frac{1}{h_i \cdot x_i + \beta_i}\right) \cdot P_{k1} \tag{2}$$

Step 7: *Preliminary judgement of the message.* When the RSU receives the message, it first judges whether $T_c - T_i \leq \Delta T$, where T_c is the current time when the message is received, and ΔT is a reasonable time range. If the message expires, the message is directly discarded. Otherwise, it means that the message is still fresh. Then, the RSU searches PID_i in revocation chain RID-BC according to the pseudo-identity. If the identity is in RID-BC, it is considered that the message is untrustworthy or the sender's identity has already expired, and the subsequent verification is aborted. If it is not in the RID-BC, turn to retrieves in PID-BC and finds out the public key PK_i and the trust value TV_i of the sender, simultaneously, judges whether the value is reasonable. If the value is greater than the preset threshold, the next message signature verification process will be executed. Here, it is noteworthy that records in blockchain can not be modified. A new tuple about vehicle public information should be re-added into blockchain when the trust value update. Therefore, multiple records related to a certain vehicle are probably found. In this case, only the latest record should be used.

Step 8: *Message signature verification.* If the judgement in Step 7 is successful, RSU calculates $h_i = H_3(M_i, PID_i, PK_i, T_i)$ with σ_i and PK_i, then verifies whether the following equation holds.

$$\hat{e}(Sig_i, h_i X_i + B_i) = g \tag{3}$$

If Eq. (3) holds, RSU accepts the message, otherwise it rejects it. The proof of correctness is as follows:

$$
\begin{aligned}
&\hat{e}\left(Sig_i,\ h_iX_i + B_i\right) \\
&= \hat{e}\left(\left(\left(\frac{1}{h_i \cdot x_i + \beta_i}\right)P_{k1},\ h_iX_i + B_i\right)\right) \\
&= \hat{e}\left(\left(\left(\frac{1}{h_ix_i + \beta_i}\right)P_{k1},\ h_ix_iP_{k2} + \beta_iP_{k2}\right)\right) \\
&= \hat{e}\left(\left(\left(\frac{1}{h_ix_i + \beta_i}\right)\left(\frac{1}{k}\right)P,\ (h_ix_i + \beta_i)kP\right)\right) \\
&= \hat{e}(P,P)^{\left(\frac{1}{h_i x_i k + \beta_i k}\right)(h_i x_i k + \beta_i k)} \\
&= \hat{e}(P,P) \\
&= g
\end{aligned}
\tag{4}
$$

According to the proof mentioned above, the correctness of Eq. (3) indicates that the message digest h_i contained in sender signature Sig_i is equal with the one calculated by RSU, which verifies the integrity of the message. In addition, the authenticity of signature and non-repudiation of message are also guaranteed.

Step 9: *Aggregation verification.* As a message receiver, RSU probably receives multiple messages during a certain interval. It can search for the public key PK_i and trust value TV_i according to pseudo-identity set $\{E_i | i = 1, 2, ..., n\}$ of the multiple message senders. The concrete search and preliminary judgment are similar to those described in Step 7. Here, we will not elaborate on it, and we only discuss the multi-signature aggregation verification. The specific verification is as the following equation:

$$
\hat{e}\left(\sum_{i=1}^{n}(Sig_i,\ h_iX_i + B_i)\right) = g
\tag{5}
$$

If Eq. (5) holds, it indicates authenticity of the multi-signature and integrity of the messages. The proof of correctness is as follows:

$$
\begin{aligned}
&\hat{e}\left(\sum_{i=1}^{n}(Sig_i,\ h_iX_i + B_i)\right) \\
&= \hat{e}\left(\sum_{i=1}^{n}\left(\left(\frac{1}{h_i \cdot x_i + \beta_i}\right)P_{k1},\ h_iX_i + B_i\right)\right) \\
&= \hat{e}\left(\sum_{i=1}^{n}\left(\left(\frac{1}{h_i \cdot x_i + \beta_i}\right)P_{k1},\ h_ix_iP_{k2} + \beta_iP_{k2}\right)\right) \\
&= \hat{e}\left(\sum_{i=1}^{n}\left(\left(\frac{1}{h_i \cdot x_i + \beta_i}\right)\left(\frac{1}{k}\right)P,\ (h_ix_i + \beta_i)kP\right)\right) \\
&= \hat{e}(P,\ P)^{\sum_{i=1}^{n}\left(\frac{1}{h_i x_i k + \beta_i k}\right)(h_i x_i k + \beta_i k)} \\
&= \hat{e}(P,\ P) \\
&= g
\end{aligned}
\tag{6}
$$

5   Security Analysis

This section will focus on analyzing the protocol proposed in this paper and show that the protocol has satisfied security requirements.

(1) **Single-point registration:** According to the protocol, TA registers for vehicles in blockchain. Subsequently, communication between vehicle and RSU, or between different vehicles will be permitted. The consensus mechanism of the consortium blockchain eliminates the need for duplicate registration even in cross-domain communications.

(2) **Message integrity:** In the process of signing the message, the private key of vehicle (β_i, x_i) is used, and any malicious attackers cannot steal the private key. The hash function $H_3(M_i, PID_i, PK_i, T_i)$ takes information such as message and pseudo-identity as input, and any slight tampering in the input will cause the output change. Therefore, the strong collision resistance of the hash function makes adversary impossible to tamper messages without being detected in probability polynomial time.

(3) **Anonymity:** When registering, the formula $PID_i = RID_i \oplus H_1(s, T_{reg})$ is used by TRA to calculate pseudo-identity of vehicle. The formula takes the private key of the TRA and the real identity of the vehicle as inputs. Since the vehicle uses the pseudo-identity for signature and TRA's private key is absolutely safe, no adversary can speculate $H_1(s, T_{reg})$ because the hash function has a strong collision resistance characteristic. Therefore, except for TRA, no others can acquire the real identity of the vehicle.

(4) **Traceability:** When a legal vehicle is attacked and becomes a malicious vehicle, the release of malicious false information will cause the trust value to reduce. After the value is warned, the RSU node can report to TRA. TRA looks up the vehicle registration information table (PID_i, T_{reg}) and uses its own private key to track the real identity of the vehicle based on a reverse calculation $RID_i = PID_i \oplus H_1(s, T_{reg})$.

(5) **Revocability:** When a vehicle is considered as a malicious node, it can be added to the RID-BC. When it initiates communication again, RSU will determine whether the node's identity is in RID-BC, and if it exists, communication will be refused directly.

(6) **Resistance to replay attacks:** In our proposed protocol, we assume that traffic and road conditions are broadcasted in a public non-secure wireless channel. Therefore, attackers can completely eavesdrop on the messages. In order to prevent attackers from intercepting the messages and continuously replay them to other vehicles, which causes channel congestion, waste of resources, and even misleading vehicles, the signature tuple of message $\sigma_i = (M_i, PID_i, V_i, T_i)$ contains a timestamp. To prevent the timestamp from being maliciously modified, the hash function $H_3(M_i, PID_i, PK_i, T_i)$ in the signature also contains the timestamp. Therefore, even if the attacker replays the signed message, the receiver can verify whether the message has expired.

(7) **Resistance to impersonation attacks:** During the signing process, the sender uses its pseudo-identity and private key. The pseudo-identity and public key are stored in the distributed ledger of the blockchain. Any vehicles or entities can access RSU to obtain them. However, the private key is stored in the tamper-proof device of the vehicle. Even if an attacker obtains the pseudo-identity and public key from the RSU, he still cannot obtain the corresponding private key. According to the discrete logarithm problem of the elliptic curve, it is impossible for an attacker to forge a signature with a non-negligible advantage in probability polynomial time.

(8) **Resistance to internal attacks:** Before signature verification, RSU needs to judge the sender's trust value. Once a vehicle is maliciously attacked and disseminates fake messages, the trust value calculated according to feedback from other vehicles will inevitably decrease. When the trust value of the malicious vehicle is lower than a certain threshold, its identity will be recorded in the revocation blockchain. It can no longer communicate with other vehicles or RSUs as a legal node, which will benefit avoiding further attacks in VANET.

6 Performance Analysis

6.1 Blockchain Deployment

The Hyperledger Fabric 1.4 was used to deploy the authentication system to test the feasibility of the proposed scheme. Due to the limitations of the experimental environment, it is assumed that the registration of vehicles has been completed. In the experiments, we mainly complete the consensus establishment and rapid identity verification. Five virtual machines of Aliyun are deployed to implement different RSUs to build PID-BC and RID-BC. At the beginning of the experiment, the smart contract is invoked to simulate the registration process to blockchain. RSU packages Vehicle-related public information, and PBFT algorithm is used to reach a consensus. After a consensus authentication between the RSU nodes, a block is generated, then deposits to the blockchain.

In order to verify the feasibility of the PBFT consensus algorithm in this scheme, two scenarios with a query request rate of 100 and 200 TPS were configured to evaluate the respective consensus delays and obtain the maximum, average and minimum consensus delays of these two network environments. The experimental results show that when the request rate in Hyperledger Fabric does not exceed 200 TPS, the average delay can be around 40 ms, reaching a consensus speed of milliseconds, which meets the communication delay requirements for real-time authentication in VANET environment.

Using the automatic triggering mechanism of smart contracts in blockchain and the easy retrieval characteristic of the MPT block structure, it effectively shortens the time delay of identity authentication and message verification process. Experiments have verified the relationship between the number of different pseudonym requests and the delay. The results are shown in Fig. 2. Compared with the traditional PKI scheme by Zeng et al. [14] and the pseudonym authorized authentication scheme by Calandriello et al. [2], as the number of pseudonym requests increases, the anonymous identity authentication method of this scheme outperforms others, and it is more efficient and has the slowest increase in delay.

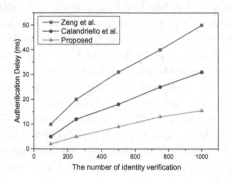

Fig. 2. Comparison of delay.

6.2 Performance Analysis

In order to analyze the computational performance of the proposed signature scheme, we compared the computational cost of this scheme with other certificateless signature schemes [3, 6, 7, 10, 13] in three aspects including signature, verification, and aggregation verification. All these schemes use the bilinear pairing method to realize signature verification. For the convenience of analysis, we use T_{bp} to represent the time of bilinear pairing operation, T_{sm} to denote the time of scalar multiplication operation on the addition group G_1, T_{pa} to denote the time of point addition operation on the addition group G_1, and T_{mtp} to represent the time of hash mapping to the point, while the calculation time of one-way hash function on Z_q^* is not considered in this analysis, because it is negligible compared with other operations.

In order to obtain the time cost of the above four basic operations, we built a simulation platform under the Linux Ubuntu 18.04 LTS system. The CPU processor is Intel Core i5-8250 with a CPU speed 1.66 GHz, and the memory is 2 GB. We use the PBC-0.5.14 cryptographic library and a more secure type A curve $y^2 = x^3 + x$ for simulation. We ran 100 times to obtain the average time of each operation. Table 1 shows the time cost of the four basic operations.

From Table 2, a signature generated by vehicle V_i in Malhi et al. [10] includes four scalar multiplication and two point addition operations; while for verifying, a receiver V_j needs three bilinear pairing, three scalar multiplication, and one point addition operations. In Table 2, the vehicle V_i in Malhi et al.'s scheme requires $4T_{sm} + 2T_{pa} \approx 8.948$ ms for message signing while for corresponding signature verifying, the receiver V_j requires $3T_{bp} + 3T_{sm} + 1T_{pa} \approx 19.6$ ms.

Table 1. Basic operation time.

Operation Type	T_{bp}	T_{sm}	T_{pa}	T_{mtp}
Runtime (ms)	4.298	2.232	0.010	0.003

Therefore, in message signing and signature verifying, the total computation cost is approximately 28.548 ms. Similarly, the receiver V_j needs to execute $3T_{bp} + 3nT_{sm} + nT_{pa} \approx 6.706n + 12.894$ ms for batch signature verification on n messages. In Horng et al.'s scheme [6], the vehicle V_i requires around 4.474 ms in message signing while for verifying the corresponding signature, the V_j needs around 15.139 ms. The total computational cost for message signing and verifying is approximately 19.613 ms. The V_j in Horng et al.'s scheme needs $3T_{bp} + nT_{sm} + nT_{pa} + nT_{mtp} \approx 2.245n + 12.894$ ms to verify n signatures. In Kumar et al.'s scheme [7], the total computational cost for message signing and verifying is approximately 32.842 ms. The V_j needs $4T_{bp} + 3nT_{sm} + (n+1)T_{mtp} \approx 6.699n + 17.195$ ms to verify n signatures. Similarly, we can also make an analysis to Xiong et al.'s scheme [13] and Cheng et al.'s scheme [3].

Table 2. Computation complexity comparison of signature scheme.

Scheme	Message-signing	Single-Sig verify	Aggregate-Sig verify
Malhi et al. [10]	$4T_{sm} + 2T_{pa}$	$3T_{bp} + 3T_{sm} + 1T_{pa}$	$3T_{bp} + 3nT_{sm} + nT_{pa}$
Horng et al. [6]	$2T_{sm} + 1T_{pa}$	$3T_{bp} + 1T_{sm} + 1T_{pa} + 1T_{mtp}$	$3T_{bp} + nT_{sm} + nT_{pa} + nT_{mtp}$
Kumar et al. [7]	$4T_{sm} + 2T_{pa} + 1T_{mtp}$	$4T_{bp} + 3T_{sm} + 1T_{mtp}$	$4T_{bp} + 3nT_{sm} + (n+1)T_{mtp}$
Xiong et al. [13]	$3T_{sm} + 2T_{pa}$	$3T_{bp} + 2T_{sm} + 1T_{pa} + 1T_{mtp}$	$3T_{bp} + 2nT_{sm} + 3nT_{pa} + nT_{mtp}$
Cheng et al. [3]	$4T_{sm} + 3T_{pa}$	$3T_{bp} + 2T_{sm} + 2T_{pa} + 1T_{mtp}$	$3T_{bp} + 2nT_{sm} + 4nT_{pa} + nT_{mtp}$
Proposed	$1T_{sm}$	$1T_{bp} + 1T_{sm} + 1T_{pa} + 1T_{mtp}$	$1T_{bp} + nT_{sm} + nT_{pa} + nT_{mtp}$

Table 3. The comparison of communication cost.

Scheme	Single-Msg. Transmission
Malhi et al. [10]	$4|G_1| + |Z_q| + |M_i| + |T_i|$
Horng et al. [6]	$4|G_1| + |Z_q| + |M_i| + |T_i|$
Kumar et al. [7]	$4|G_1| + |Z_q| + |M_i| + |T_i|$
Xiong et al. [13]	$3|G_1| + |ID| + |M_i|$
Cheng et al. [3]	$3|G_1| + |ID| + |M_i|$
Proposed	$|G_1| + |Z_q| + |M_i| + |T_i|$

In our proposed scheme, the vehicle V_i generates the signature on message with one scalar multiplication operation while the verification of the corresponding signature comprises one bilinear pairing, one scalar multiplication, one point

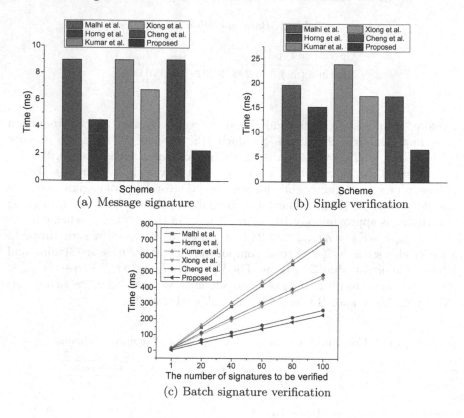

(a) Message signature

(b) Single verification

(c) Batch signature verification

Fig. 3. Computational cost comparison.

addition operations and one map-to-point hash operation. The vehicle V_i in our scheme requires $1T_{sm} \approx 2.232$ ms to sign the message while to verify the corresponding signature on the message, the V_j needs $1T_{bp} + 1T_{sm} + 1T_{pa} + 1T_{mtp} \approx 6.543$ ms. Thus, the total computational cost of our scheme in message signing and in signature verifying is approximately 8.775 ms, Similarly, the V_i in the proposed scheme needs $1T_{bp} + nT_{sm} + nT_{pa} + nT_{mtp} \approx 2.236n + 4.298$ ms to verify n signatures. Comparison results in the three aspects of signature, verification, and aggregation verification are presented by Fig. 3(a), (b), (c), respectively, which have proved that the proposed scheme outperforms baseline schemes in terms of computational cost.

As shown in Table 3, the comparison of communication costs is presented. The vehicle V_i in Malhi et al.'s [10] scheme broadcasts pseudo-identity $PID_i = (PID_{i,1} \in G_1, PID_{i,2} \in Z_q^*)$, public key $PK_i \in G_1$, timestamp T_i, and Signature $\sigma_i = (S_i, V_i) \in G_1$ to other vehicles nearby it. Therefore, the communication cost for the vehicle V_i in Malhi et al.'s scheme could be calculated. Similarly, in the schemes of Horng et al. [6] and Kumar et al. [7], the vehicle V_i broadcasts pseudo-identity $PID_i = (PID_{i,1} \in G_1, PID_{i,2} \in Z_q^*)$, public key $PK_i \in G_1$, timestamp T_i, and the signature $\sigma_i = (S_i, V_i) \in G_1$ to other vehicles. Therefore, the communication costs for the vehicle V_i is the same as Malhi et al.'s [10]. The vehicle V_i in Xiong et al.'s [13] scheme broadcasts pseudo-identity $ID_i \in \{0,1\}^*$, public key $PK_i \in G_1$, and signature $\sigma_i = (S_i, V_i) \in G_1$ to other vehicles. Therefore, the communication cost for the vehicle V_i in Xiong et al.'s [13] scheme is $3|G_1| + |ID| + |M_i|$. Cheng et al.'s [3] scheme is just an improvement on Xiong et al.'s [13] scheme, however, its communication cost is the same as Xiong et al.'s [13].

In our proposed scheme, the vehicle V_i broadcasts pseudo-identity $PID_i \in Z_q^*$, timestamp T_i and signature $Sig_i \in G_1$ to RSU, the communication cost for the vehicle V_i in the proposed scheme is $|G_1| + |Z_q| + |M_i| + |T_i|$. Considering that $|T_i|$ generally has only short bits, the proposed scheme has less communication cost compared with the other baseline schemes. Therefore, our proposed scheme is suitable for bandwidth-limited infrastructure, especially for VANETs, and can efficiently perform V2I communication.

7   Conclusion

In this paper, a trust-based certificateless anonymous identity authentication scheme for the VANET has been proposed. Bilinear pairing operations and elliptic curve cryptographic algorithm are utilized to achieve anonymous authentication of messages, and support aggregated signature verification to improve verification efficiency. Two blockchains, namely blockchain for pseudo-identities and blockchain for revoked pseudo-identities, have been proposed to store the trust value of the vehicle and public information. A trust value calculation method based on the message feedback mode is proposed to detect malicious vehicles and invalid vehicles. Simulation results have proved that the proposed scheme achieves efficient certificateless signature and authentication.

Acknowledgments. This work was supported by National Natural Science Foundation of China (No. 61872138), and Natural Science Foundation of Hunan Province (No. 2021JJ30278).

References

1. Al-Riyami, S.S., Paterson, K.G.: Certificateless public key cryptography. In: Laih, C.-S. (ed.) ASIACRYPT 2003. LNCS, vol. 2894, pp. 452–473. Springer, Heidelberg (2003). https://doi.org/10.1007/978-3-540-40061-5_29
2. Calandriello, G., Papadimitratos, P., Hubaux, J., Lioy, A.: Efficient and robust pseudonymous authentication in VANET. In: Proceedings of the 4th International Workshop on Vehicular Ad Hoc Networks, VANET 2007, Montréal, Québec, Canada, 10 September 2007, pp. 19–28. ACM (2007)
3. Cheng, L., Wen, Q., Jin, Z., Zhang, H., Zhou, L.: Cryptanalysis and improvement of a certificateless aggregate signature scheme. Inf. Sci. **295**, 337–346 (2015)
4. Feng, Q., He, D., Zeadally, S., Liang, K.: BPAS: blockchain-assisted privacy-preserving authentication system for vehicular ad hoc networks. IEEE Trans. Ind. Inf. **16**(6), 4146–4155 (2020)

5. Ghosh, M., Varghese, A., Gupta, A., Kherani, A.A., Muthaiah, S.N.: Detecting misbehaviors in VANET with integrated root-cause analysis. Ad Hoc Netw. **8**(7), 778–790 (2010)

6. Horng, S., Tzeng, S., Huang, P., Wang, X., Li, T., Khan, M.K.: An efficient certificateless aggregate signature with conditional privacy-preserving for vehicular sensor networks. Inf. Sci. **317**, 48–66 (2015)

7. Kumar, P., Kumari, S., Sharma, V., Li, X., Sangaiah, A.K., Islam, S.H.: Secure CLS and CL-AS schemes designed for VANETs. J. Supercomput. **75**(6), 3076–3098 (2019)

8. Li, J., Lu, H., Guizani, M.: ACPN: a novel authentication framework with conditional privacy-preservation and non-repudiation for VANETs. IEEE Trans. Parallel Distrib. Syst. **26**(4), 938–948 (2015)

9. Lu, Z., Liu, W., Wang, Q., Qu, G., Liu, Z.: A privacy-preserving trust model based on blockchain for VANETs. IEEE Access **6**, 45655–45664 (2018)

10. Malhi, A.K., Batra, S.: An efficient certificateless aggregate signature scheme for vehicular ad-hoc networks. Discret. Math. Theor. Comput. Sci. **17**(1), 317–338 (2015)

11. Shamir, A.: Identity-based cryptosystems and signature schemes. In: Blakley, G.R., Chaum, D. (eds.) CRYPTO 1984. LNCS, vol. 196, pp. 47–53. Springer, Heidelberg (1985). https://doi.org/10.1007/3-540-39568-7_5

12. Tan, H., Chung, I.: Secure authentication and key management with blockchain in VANETs. IEEE Access **8**, 2482–2498 (2020)

13. Xiong, H., Guan, Z., Chen, Z., Li, F.: An efficient certificateless aggregate signature with constant pairing computations. Inf. Sci. **219**, 225–235 (2013)

14. Zeng, K.: Pseudonymous PKI for ubiquitous computing. In: Atzeni, A.S., Lioy, A. (eds.) EuroPKI 2006. LNCS, vol. 4043, pp. 207–222. Springer, Heidelberg (2006). https://doi.org/10.1007/11774716_17

BIPP: Blockchain-Based Identity Privacy Protection Scheme in Internet of Vehicles for Remote Anonymous Communication

Hongyu Wu, Xiaoning Feng$^{(\boxtimes)}$, Guobin Kan, and Xiaoshu Jiang

Harbin Engineering University, Harbin 150001, China
fengxiaoning@hrbeu.edu.cn

Abstract. Aiming at the difficult problem of anonymous communication between vehicles and vehicles at long distances in Internet of Vehicles, we propose a identity privacy protection scheme based on blockchain (BIPP). In this scheme, the response value of the PUF function and the continuous timestamp are used as the basis of encryption, which is associated with the pseudonym of the user ID information to prevent adversaries from conducting forgery attacks. The pseudonym mechanism and the confusion mechanism between identity and message protect the privacy of vehicle users' identities. The information on the blockchain must pass reasonable judgment algorithms and meet the conditions for ending of the event. Blockchain technology can ensure the information received by the vehicles in the target area is credible. The scheme is proved to be secure and feasible through analysis, implementation and evaluation.

Keywords: Internet of Vehicles · Blockchain · Identity privacy · PUF · ECC · Anonymous communication

1 Introduction

In the Internet of Vehicles (IoV), it is difficult to achieve long-distance communication across regions under the limited communication range of RSUs and OBUs [14]. Due to the problem of unfamiliar identity, it is not easy to optimize the trust environment on the communication between vehicles. A single RSU does not have strong communication security measures, which makes RSU more vulnerable to various attacks [15]. Moreover, it is threatened for car owners to reveal their identity. In the face of untrusted RSUs, it is difficult for vehicles to actively upload information about incidents that occur around them while protecting their privacy.

Traditional remote anonymous communication based on the central cloud architecture relies on the security of the central cloud architecture. M. Garai et al. [4] proposed a typical vehicle-mounted cloud architecture in 2015: the bottom layer is the vehicle node layer; the second layer is called the roadside unit; the uppermost layer is the central cloud, which is the central cloud built on the roadside unit. Subsequently, many vehicle-to-cloud (V2C) communication schemes

© Springer Nature Switzerland AG 2022
Y. Lai et al. (Eds.): ICA3PP 2021, LNCS 13156, pp. 489–506, 2022.
https://doi.org/10.1007/978-3-030-95388-1_32

[13] based on the central cloud and vehicle-to-infrastructure (V2I) communication schemes [1] emerged. However, C.Quevedo et al. [10] pointed out that one of the most dangerous attacks in IoV is Sybil which forges false identities in the network to disrupt compromise the communication between the network nodes. Sybil attacks affect the service delivery related to road safety, traffic congestion, multimedia entertainment and others. In addition, IoV based on the central cloud architecture will have centralization problems such as high data security risks and excessive load on central nodes. This is far from meeting the requirements of long-distance cross-domain communication.

Recently, many scholars have actively introduced blockchain technology into the IoV. Blockchain [3] is a distributed storage technology based on technologies such as consensus algorithms, smart contracts, and encryption algorithms. It has excellent characteristics such as data immutability, collective maintenance of nodes, and data transparency, which can make the vehicle environment safer and more reliable. The blockchain-based Internet of Vehicles architecture has a higher quality of service (QoS) satisfaction than the traditional centralized architecture [6]. And the blockchain-based security framework can effectively cope with the data confidentiality challenge brought by the edge cloud [7]. PUF refers to inputting an stimulus to a physical entity, and outputting an unpredictable response using the inevitable physical difference of the physical entity [8]. The combination of blockchain and PUF can ensure the data source and data integrity in the Internet of Things network [9]. PUF is used to provide a unique hardware fingerprint for the data source. The blockchain-based system provides a decentralized digital ledger that can resist Sybil and tampering attacks.

In this context, it is significant to study the remote anonymous communication of the IoV based on the blockchain. The author was inspired by Coinshuffle's obfuscation mechanism [12] and combined with PUF and elliptic curve encryption (ECC) to established a blockchain-based identity privacy protection scheme (BIPP). The scheme first collects information in the area where the incident occurred. Then verify and store event information on the blockchain. Finally, the RSU in the target area broadcasts event messages and the vehicle group in the area responds to the event messages. The scheme can not only ensure that the long-distance communication message is credible, but also can guarantee the privacy of the identity of the vehicle node. By verifying the event message, the unforgeability of the message is guaranteed, and only events recognized by most vehicle nodes can be confirmed on the blockchain. Specifically, the main contributions of this article are as follows:

- Established the main architecture of the proposed BIPP scheme and the overall scheme process. The scheme describes 4 phase, including initialization phase, registration phase, event discovery and message sending phase and message verification and block updation phase.
- A security analysis of scheme was carried out. In the security analysis, the correctness (credibility), unlinkability, and unforgeability of the scheme were mainly proved in detail.

– The simulation was implemented on Ethereum. The scheme is evaluated in storage cost, calculate cost and communication cost. For storage sustainability, we calculate and observe the block size under multiple cumulative times.

Section 2 focuses on the BIPP scheme proposed in this paper. Section 3 provides relevant security analysis for this scheme. Section 4 is a implementation and evaluation of the BIPP scheme. The Sect. 5 provides a summary.

2   The Proposed BIPP Scheme

2.1   Architecture and Preliminaries

The architecture of BIPP system that includes three processes is shown in Fig. 1. The scheme mainly involves three parties that are trusted third party (TA), roadside unit (RSU) and vehicle Node (VN). A trusted third-party organization is used as authenticating the identity of vehicle nodes, including the identity authentication of ordinary nodes and priority vehicle nodes. Priority node vehicles refer to special vehicles such as police cars, fire trucks, emergency vehicles, cash transport vehicles, etc. It is generally believed that TA has high computing, storage and communication capabilities, and cannot be easily Breached. The blockchain full ledger information is stored in the RSU, and the vehicle generally selects the RSU that is relatively close to communicate to obtain the information of a specific road section. RSUs are distributed among different road

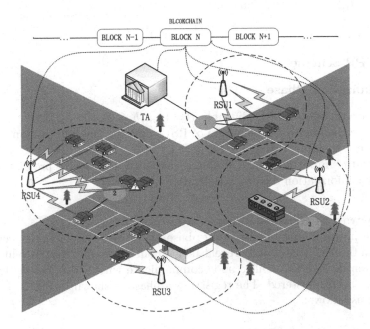

Fig. 1. The architecture of BIPP system that includes three processes.

sections. The hardware working principle of the IoV is realized by technologies such as DSPC technology of on-board units (OBUs) mounted on vehicle nodes and RFID of RSU. The figure shows the registration process of vehicles in the RSU1 area; A road segment event is found in the RSU4 area, and vehicles (adjacent to RSU4) sent event message to RSU2 through the blockchain; The vehicles in the RSU2 area are notified of event message. On the basis of this architecture, we describe in detail the four phases involved in the scheme.

The main symbols used in this paper are described in Table 1. And the system uses IAP variable to indicate whether the vehicle agrees with the message of this section. The PSN variable is used to indicate whether the vehicle is a priority node. The $\parallel$ is to represent the concatenation operator.

Table 1. Symbol description tables.

Symbol	Description of meaning
V_i, V_r	Vehicle node
RSU_i, RSU_r	Roadside unit node
Q, K	Public and private keys corresponding to the ECC
G	Selected ECC base points
PUF_{V_i, V_r}	The PUF function of V_i, V_r the node
ID_{V_i, V_r}	ID information of a vehicle node
C_i, R_i	Challenge and response values
$H(\Delta)$	Hash function

2.2 BIPP Scheme

A. Initialization Phase

1. Initialize the global ECC six-tuple $T = (p, a, b, G, n, h)$.
2. Initialize the identity information of RSUs and the key information of RSUs. TA stores them as $<RSU_X, PK_X> = \{<RSU_1, PK_1>, ..., <RSU_n, PK_n>\}$. Due to the importance of RSUs, it is necessary to directly preset the RSUs identity information during initialization.

B. Registration Phase

The main purpose of the registration phase is to provide the identity certificate of VNs on the blockchain and prevent illegal nodes from forging the vehicle node information. Before the vehicle node communicate with RSUs, the vehicle node must have been registered. The registration phase is shown in Fig. 2. The main steps are as follows:

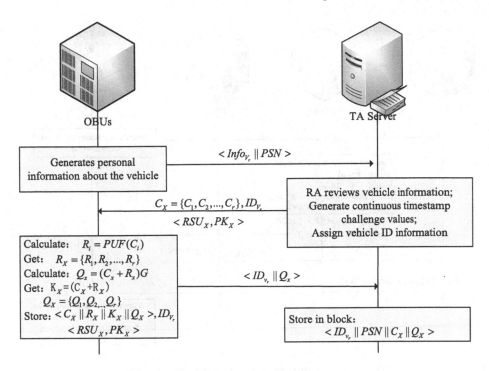

Fig. 2. Register phase.

1. The VN requests TA to start registration, and the vehicle owner generates and sends the identity information $<Info_{V_r}, PSN>$.

2. RA (TA's sub-organizations) conducts review online or offline. After passing the review, TA randomly selects consecutive time stamps $C_X = \{C_1, C_2, ..., C_r\}$ as the challenge value, and the challenge value can also be referred to as the valid window values of VN. Then TA sends challenge values, trusted RSUs public key list information $<RSU_X, PK_X>$ and an vehicle ID information to VN together.

3. VN calculate $R_i = PUF(C_i)$ and get $R_X = \{R_1, R_2, ..., R_r\}$. Then VN calculate $Q_x = (C_x + R_x)G$ and get $K_X = C_X + R_X$, $Q_X = \{Q_1, Q_2, ..., Q_r\}$. VN store $<C_X||R_X||K_X||Q_X>, <RSU_X, PK_X>, ID_{V_r}$ and send $<ID_{V_r}||Q_X>$ to TA.

4. TA performs data verification, package $<ID_{V_r}||PSN||C_X||Q_X>$ and store on the blockchain.

C. Event Discovery and Message Sending Phase

RSUs send time stamps C_i to nearby VNs in a fixed time period. The frequency of sending time stamps can be set according to factors such as the frequency of accidents on the road section, the flow of VNs, and whether the road section is a core hub section. The phase of event discovery and message sending is shown in

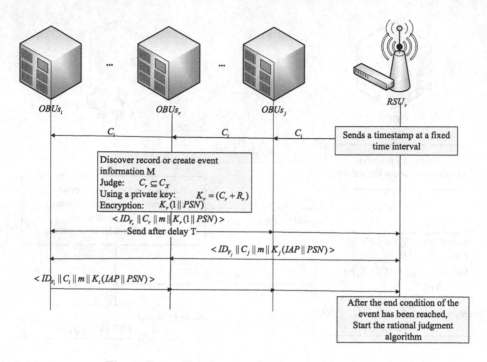

Fig. 3. Event discovery and message sending phase.

Fig. 3. After an incident occurred in the vehicle, the vehicle starts the following process:

1. V_r judges whether $C_r \subset C_X$. If yes, use $K_r = (C_r + R_r)$ as a private key to encrypt the message M, and send $<ID_{V_r}||C_r||m||K_r(1||PSN)>$ to other vehicles and adjacent RSU_r after a random delay of T.
2. After the adjacent vehicles receive the message, they will check the message M, and then send $<ID_{V_r}||C_r||m||K_r(IAP||PSN)>$ to other vehicles and adjacent RSU_r.
3. After RSU_r receiving the message, it starts to make a reasonable judgment algorithm.

D. Message Verification and Block Updation Phase

Before explaining the reasonable judgment algorithm, we first define the important RSUs internal data structure-recent event status information. This mainly includes $<M_{ID}, M_m, M_\alpha, M_\beta, M_\rho>$. ID is the tag of event message, m is the event message, α is the message recognition rate, β is the priority node rate, and ρ indicates whether the event is over.

The event message ID is the primary key of the recent event status information. It can generally be set as an auto-increment field and used to uniquely represent an event in the event table. When ρ is 1, it indicates that the event

M has been confirmed by the target area and there is no need to receive the event M in this area. In other words, only when ρ is 0, the event M in RSU_r is accepted. IAP1 indicates that the vehicle believes that the event message m is true; IAP0 indicates that the vehicle believes that the event message m is false. PSN1 indicates that the vehicle is a priority node and considers that the event message m is true. α and β is determined by the following formula:

$$\alpha = \frac{IAP1}{IAP0 + IAP1}, \beta = \frac{PSN1 * \alpha}{IAP1} \tag{1}$$

After RSU_r receiving the $<ID_{V_x}||C_x||m||K_x(IAP||PSN')>$ sent by the vehicle in the region (which means RSU_r does not know which vehicle initiated the incident), RSU_r starts to make a reasonable judgment algorithm. The flow chart of rational judgment algorithm is shown in Fig. 4 below. The reasonable judgment algorithm includes the following steps:

1. Determine M_ρ whether it is 0. If M_ρ is 0, it indicates that the event has been stored in block and other vehicles in the target area RSU_j are notified; Otherwise proceed to the next step.
2. Determine whether event m belong to M_m. If $m \notin M_m$, create an entry in M. Otherwise, go to the next step.
3. Through the registration phase information to search ID_{V_x} for getting $<C_X||Q_X||PSN>$.
4. Determine whether C_x belong to C_X, which is to judge whether the time challenge value of the registered vehicle has expired. If the time challenge value has expired, V_x should be notified immediately to restart the registration phase.
5. A reasonable judgment: judge C_x whether less than the current time C_{now}, if C_x more than the current time C_{now}, notify the vehicle sent the timestamp error; Otherwise proceed to the next step.
6. Decrypt received message $K_r(IAP||PSN')$ to obtain $<IAP||PSN'>$ using Q_x corresponding to C_x.
7. Determine whether the sent PSN' is consistent with PSN of the registration phase, if $PSN \neq PSN'$, inform the vehicle of PSN comparison failure; Otherwise proceed to the next step.
8. Determine whether PSN is 1 and IAP is 1. If PSN is 1, modify IAP1 and PSN1 variables; If PSN is not 1, modify the IAP0 variables.
9. Update message recognition rate α and priority node rate β.
10. Determine whether the message recognition rate α is greater than the set threshold value θ. If $\theta \leq \alpha$, it ends a reasonable judgment algorithm; if $\theta > \alpha$, it needs to notify the vehicles in the area that the event m is invalidated due to the low support rate. θ explained in Sect. 3.

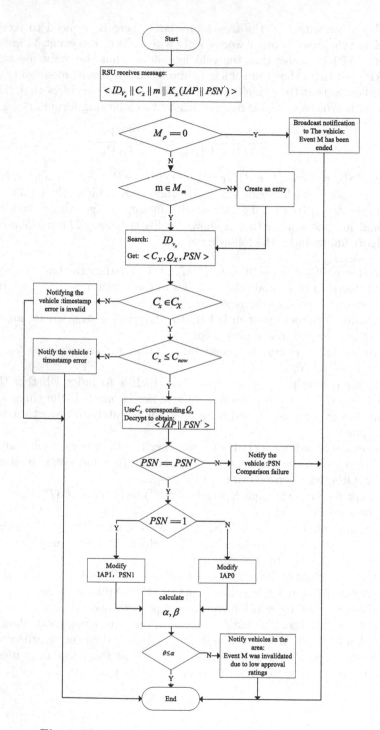

Fig. 4. The flow chart of rational judgment algorithm.

After the completion of a reasonable judgment algorithm, it is also necessary for RSU_r to judge:

1. Whether the value β is 1.
2. Whether the time of event collection T_L reaches the specified time, where T_L defined as $T_L = T_{now} - T_0$. T_{now} is the current time, and T_0 is the time when the event message is first received.

The above condition 1 can meet the requirements of priority vehicle nodes to send special events. If any of the above conditions are met, RSU_r ends reasonable judgment algorithms and the block updation phase is started. The block updation phase is shown in Fig. 5. The block updation phase mainly includes the following steps:

1. RSU_r sent $<RSU_r||m||RSU_j||\alpha||\beta||H_a>$ to RSU_x, $H_a = H(m||\alpha||\beta)$.
2. When $x \neq j$, RSU_x calculate $H_b = H(m||\alpha||\beta)$, if $H_a = H_b$, RSU_x will store it locally and sent it to other RSU nodes.

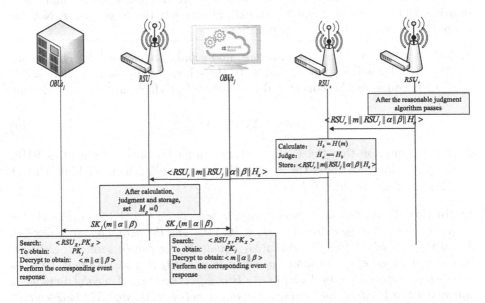

Fig. 5. Block updation and confirmation of target area message phase.

3. when $x = j$, RSU_j calculate, judge and store likely step two, then RSU_j will sent $SK_j(m||\alpha||\beta)$ to VNs in the region and set the corresponding event M_ρ to 0.
4. VNs search for the list of $<RSU_X, PK_X>$ to obtain the corresponding PK_j and decrypted $SK_j(m||\alpha||\beta)$ by using PK_j. And then VNs react to the incident.

3   Security Analysis

The proposed BIPP scheme builds the security model based on [5]. The main participants in this scheme are VN, RSU, TA, A. Adversary A can make the following probabilistic polynomial query on VN, RSU, TA:

1. $Execute(X, Y)$: This query simulates the passive eavesdropping ability of adversary A. Adversary A can intercept all information between the X and Y channels.
2. $Send(X, Y, m, n)$: This query simulates the active attack capability of adversary A. Adversary A can pretend to be X and then send a message m to the Y oracle. If the message meets the specification, the Y oracle will give feedback n according to the prediction; if the message does not meet the specification, then returns null.
3. $Reveal(X)$: Through this query, the adversary A can obtain the session key X for this time.

What needs to be noted is that adversary A can use *Execute* and *Send* multiple times during a complete attack, but can only use *Reveal* once. Now we make the following two safety assumptions:

1. RSU and TA are honest, non-honest nodes only appear in VN. This means RSU and TA will execute according to the scheme. Suppose that there are Σ Vehicle nodes and Σ_x honest nodes under RSU_x, which satisfies the following equation:

$$\theta \geq \frac{\Sigma_x}{\Sigma} \& \Sigma_x > \Sigma - \Sigma_x \tag{2}$$

2. The assumption that the PUF function cannot be cloned. Defined as PUF: $0, 1^{\{l_1\}} \to 0, 1^{\{l_1\}}$. Under the hypothetical game of [5], the probability that A wins the game is $Adv_A^{puf}(l_2) \leq \varepsilon$.

Definition 1. *During the communication between entity A and entity B, the actual message sent by entity A is $M_1 \in \{0,1\}^{l_1}$, and the actual message received by entity B is $M_2 \in \{0,1\}^{l_2}$. When M_1 equals M_2, it can be said that entity B can obtain the difference-free message sent from entity A, also said that the communication between entity A and entity B is difference-free. After the message is normalized to length l, the Hamming distance between M1 and M2 is calculated as η, it is said that entity A can obtain a relative η difference free message sent from entity B.*

Theorem 1. *In the process of communication between entity A and entity B, there are multiple communication anchors $\{\chi_1, \chi_2, ..., \chi_n\}$, in which χ_1 can be obtained the difference free message sent from entity A, χ_2 can be obtained the difference free message sent from entity χ_1, ..., χ_n can be obtained the difference free message sent from entity χ_{n-1}, entity B can get the difference free message sent from entity χ_n. So entity B can get the difference free message sent from entity A.*

Lemma 1. *RSU_r can obtain the relative C difference free messages sent by the vehicles V_r' in the region.*

Proof. A calls $Send(V_r', RSU_r, M_1, n|null)$ and $Execute(V_r', RSU_r)$ for a polynomial number of times. Suppose the message $M1$ sent by vehicle A in the area, the following four considerations are taken into account:

1. RSU_r will search for the ID of the registered vehicle. Unless the adversary is registered in the registration phase, it will not be found in the reasonable judgment algorithm, which will cause the sent content to be discarded; if A modify ID_{V_x} using himself ID_A, the subsequent fields will also change accordingly. That means A has become a new vehicle node and can not affect the reception of M_1 in RSU_r.
2. Considering the modification of C_x by A. Since A does not know the challenge value sent to the vehicle V_r' at registration phase, A can only change C_x in the form of guessing to make the verification that $C_x \in C_X$ can be passed. Of course, A has a certain probability of guessing truly. It assume that the number of digits of C_x is $C = |C_x|$.
3. If A changes m, RSU_r will think that this is a new event information because of $m \notin M_m$. So A can not affect RSU_r to accept $M1$.
4. The message $K_x(IAP||PSN')$ is in ciphertext form relative to A who intercepted the information. A must know about K_x before changing the message and decrypting the message. Obviously, $K_x = C_x + R_X, R_x = PUF(C_x)$, the adversary needs to know the response value R_x of the challenge value C_x in order to obtain K_x. According to the hypothesis that PUF function cannot be cloned, the possibility of PUF function being breached is negligible in the absence of physical devices.

To sum up, RSU_r can obtain the relative C no-difference message sent from V_r', where $C = |C_x|$. The lemma is also referred to as the unforgeability of message sending phase.

Lemma 2. *RSU_j can obtain the difference free message sent from RSU_r.*

Proof. A calls $Execute(RSU_j, RSU_r), Send(RSU_r, RSU_j, M_1, n|null)$ for a polynomial number of times. If the message sent by RSU_r is $M_1 = <RSU_r||m_1||RSU_j||\alpha_1||\beta_1, H_a>$ and the information synchronized by other nodes on the blockchain as $M_2 = <RSU_r||m_2||RSU_j||\alpha_2||\beta_2||H_2>$. It is obvious that:

$$Pr[M_1 = M_2] = Pr[\alpha_1 = \alpha_2 \& \beta_1 = \beta_2 | m_1 = m_2]$$
$$= \frac{Pr[\alpha_1 = \alpha_2 \& \beta_1 = \beta_2 \& m_1 = m_2]}{Pr[m_1 = m_2]} \tag{3}$$
$$= \frac{Pr[H_a = H_b]}{Pr[m_1 = m_2]}$$

Before each blockchain node synchronizes the information, it needs to verify whether H_a and H_b are equal or not. Only $H_a = H_b$, RSU will accept the message. And because of the avalanche effect and strong collision resistance of the hash function, it is impossible for A to find the existence of $H_a = H_b$ in $m1 \neq m2$.

Definition 2. *During the communication between multiple entities A and certain entity B, the actual message sent by entity A is $M_{Ai} \in \{0,1\}^{l_1}$, and the actual message received by entity B is $M_2 \in \{0,1\}^{l_2}$. If the message received by entity B is $M_2 = cal(M_{Ai})$, where cal() is a calculation function. It means that multiple sent messages M_{Ai} are calculated. It is said that entity B can obtain the cal() difference free message sent from the entity A, or said that the communication between entity B and entity A has cal() difference free.*

Theorem 2 (correctness). *The vehicles V_j' in the RSU_j can get the cal() difference free message sent by the vehicles V_r' in the RSU_r.*

Proof. RSU_r ends the reasonable judgment algorithm and send the message to others. Messages M_1 sent by vehicles V_r' in RSU_r are mainly sent through three logical links. First , M_1 from the vehicle V_r' is sent to RSU_r. Then, RSU_r ends the reasonable judgment algorithm and send the message to other RSU_x. Finally, RSU_j sends a message to V_j'. Each vehicle V_r' in the RSU_r will send a message $M_1 = <ID_{V_x}||C_x||m||K_x(IAP||PSN)>$, and the actual message is $M_2 = <m_2||\alpha_2||\beta_2>$ received by V_j'.

Using Lemma 1 many times, RSU_r can obtain the relative C difference free messages sent by the vehicles V_r' in the region. C_x do not appear in M_2. Therefore, RSU_r can obtain the difference free message sent from V_r' during the proof of this theorem. RSU_r uses $cal(m, IAP, PSN)$ and get $M_1' = <m_1||\alpha_1||\beta_1>$. Due to Lemma 2, RSU_j get the difference free message $M_2 = M_1'$ from RSU_r. In the process of RSU_j sends M_2 to V_j', the public and private keys allocated by TA in the initialization phase are used for encryption and decryption, so that the received information can be guaranteed correct in the insecure channel of the network of vehicles.

Finally, because of Theorem 1, the theorem is proved.

Theorem 3 (unforgeability). *Adversary A cannot forge an empty or fake message on RSU_r, nor can he forge A message sent by V_r and RSU_r.*

Proof. If the adversary A wants to forge an unavailable message on a road section, the adversary A first needs to go through the registration phase. The difficulty lies in bypassing the review of the RA, which is subjective. Now assume that adversary A has a legitimate identity ID_{Va} on the blockchain. Then adversary A forges an empty message that does not exist. The honest node will identify the actual condition of the road, and then make the right choice to give the IAP. Now suppose all of the honest nodes Σ_x make the right choice 0 and all the non-honest nodes $\Sigma - \Sigma_x$ make the wrong choice 1. Then the following inequality exists:

$$\theta \geq \frac{\Sigma_x}{\Sigma} > \frac{\Sigma - \Sigma_x}{\Sigma} = \alpha \tag{4}$$

because of $\theta \geq \alpha$, the algorithm must fail according to reasonable judgment. Therefore, adversary A cannot forge an empty message or fake message that does not exist on A road.

The adversary A forges the information of the event m, which can be modeled by the following game between the challenger C as a BIPP system and the adversary A:

1. C generates a bounded event generation, forming event unit E.
2. For each event generated, A calls Execute, Send and Reveal.
3. C randomly chooses m_x of E.
4. A make m_x' as a legitimate event.

According to the definition of the game, the probability of adversary A winning the game is $Adv_A^{forge}(E) = Pr[m_x = m_x']$. The adversary A cannot forge a message sent by V_r (by Lemma 1). In the block updation phase, according to the model of attack benefit and attack success rate established in the literature [11], there are the following equations:

$$Adv_A^{forge}(E) \leq \frac{\varepsilon}{v+\varepsilon}, \varepsilon = \frac{B}{K} \tag{5}$$

Where K is the number of blockchain nodes, and B is the miner's reward for a single block in the Bitcoin system and v is the event value. When $K \geq B^2$ can ensure the probability that the adversary forges the message sent by the RSU is negligible.

Theorem 4 (unlinkability). *The identity of the vehicle that initiated the event, the event information, and the calculation process of the message sending phase, are universally unlinkable.*

Proof. The practice of the adversary's link relationship, which can be modeled by the following game between the challenger C as a BIPP system and the adversary A:

1. C generates a bounded event generation, forming event unit E and $F_l = (f, g)$, where $f(m_i) = ID_{V_i}, g(m_i) = cal_i(\boldsymbol{m}, \boldsymbol{IAP}, \boldsymbol{PSN})$.
2. For each event generated, A calls Execute, Send and Reveal.
3. C randomly chooses m_x of E.
4. A predicts ID_{V_x} and cal_i.

According to the definition of the game, the probability of adversary A winning the game is $Adv_A^{link}(F_l) = Pr[f(m_x) = ID_{V_x} \& g(m_i) = cal_i]$.

V_r that initiated the event information starts sending after a random delay T, the identity of V_r is hidden among the vehicles in $\boldsymbol{V_r}$. Even if the adversary A and RSU_r obtain the information on the channel, they cannot know the identity of the specific V_r that initiated the event m. Only relying on the blind guessing method, the probability of identifying the corresponding relationship between the message m and the specific vehicle identity is $Pr[m \in V_r] = \frac{1}{V_{Ra}}$, where V_{Ra} is the number of vehicles in RSU_r.

So let's think about the corresponding relations between event M and cal_i. Assume that cal_i consists of all vehicles in the RSU_r. Adversary A uses $Reveal$ to obtain IAP and PSN during a communication between V_r and RSU_r. However, $Reveal$ cannot be challenged at the next time. And there is the difficult problem of discrete logarithm in ECC elliptic encryption algorithm, even if $Execute(X,Y)$ is used, the probability that the adversary A obtains the relationship between event M and cal_i is $Pr[\boldsymbol{IAP\&PSN} \in cal_i] = \frac{1}{V_{Ra}-1}$. Taking these two points together, $Adv_A^{link}(F_l) \leq \frac{1}{V_{Ra}^2-V_{Ra}}$. The theorem is proved.

4   Implementation and Evaluation

4.1   Implementation Details

We use Solidity language (0.7.0–0.9.0) to implement the proposed BIPP scheme in Ethereum and use Truffle to deploy&link Ganache (Ethereum node testing tool) for testing. The hardware used in our experimental evaluations included a PC with Ubuntu 16.04 64-bit OS, AMD A10-5450M CPU and 8G RAM.

Table 2. Experimental node setting.

Network information	Number	The way of simulation	Main contract
TA of BIPP	1	ACCOUNT ADDRESS	3, 9
RSU of BIPP	9	ACCOUNT ADDRESS	1, 2, 4, 5, 6, 10
VN of BIPP	900	Contract simulation	None
UTILS	1	Contract simulation	7, 8

The scheme is implemented on the main 10 smart contracts as shown in Table 3. TA and RSU can used such as 0xC5E05c75C. (39-bit hash address) for access and the vehicle nodes performs a random simulation on each RSU. And the permission authority is need to set for the smart contract. Table 2 shows the detailed node settings of the experiment. The main simulation and implementation details are shown in Algorithm 1.

Table 3. Main contract.

Number	1	2	3	4	5
Name	VNRandom	Calandstorge	Store	CiC	Createevent
	6	7	8	9	10
	Judge	Randomfromseed	MtoMh	Receiveinfo	Broadcast

Algorithm 1. Implementation Details

Require: Main contract
Define: Experimental volume(alias v), Number of regional vehicles(alias n), interval, seed

1: BIPPinit();
2: TAinit();
3: **for** $RSU_1, RSU_2, ..., RSU_9$ in $RSUs$ **do**
4:     VNs[] ← RSU_i.VNRandom(n)
5:     **for** VN_i in VNs **do**
6:         TAdistribution ← TA.receiveinfo(VN_i)
7:         RSU_i.calandstorge(TAdistribution)
8:         TA.store(TAdistribution, VN_i)
9: **for** $RSU_1, RSU_2, ..., RSU_9$ in $RSUs$ **do** RSU_i.CiC(interval)
10: **while** v-- **do**
11:     r,j ← UTILS.randomfromseed(seed)
12:     M ← RSU_r.Createevent()
13:     **if** RSU_r.judge(M) **then**
14:         Mh ← UTILS.MtoMh(M)
15:         RSU_j.Broadcast(Mh)

4.2   Evaluation

The cost variables related to performance evaluation used in this paper are shown in the following Table 4. C_t is the number of timestamps allocated for TA, n is the number of vehicle nodes in the area where the proposal is initiated, and m is the number of global RSUs. There is a calculation cost Table 5. The calculation cost is the maximum cost of the same node identity in the table. The size of

Table 4. Performance evaluation related concepts and explanations.

Symbol	Symbol meaning
$Phase - I$	The registration phase
$Phase - II$	Message sending & RSU verification phase
$Phase - III$	Block updation & target area broadcast phase
T_{puf}	Execution time using PUF
T_e	Execution time using ECC encryption
T_d	Execution time of ECC decryption
T_h	Execution time of hash algorithm
T_m	Execution time of searching for M_m
T_t	Execution time of searching for a valid timestamp
T	Cumulative time in system
T_B	Storage space occupied by an event in system
T_p	Occurrence frequency of the event

Table 5. Calculation cost table.

Phase \ Role	Phase − I	Phase − II	Phase − III
VN	$C_t * T_{puf}$	$T_t + T_e$	$m + T_d$
RSU		$n(mn + T_t + T_d) + T_m$	$T_h + nT_e$

Table 6. The size of variable table.

Phase	Data	Size
Phase − I	$C_X, Info_{V_r}, <RSU_X, PK_X>$	171 bytes
	R_X, K_X, Q_X	43 bytes
	PSN, ID_{V_r}	8 bytes
Phase − II	m	1024 bytes
	$K_r PSN, IAP, C_x$	8 bytes
Phase − III	$H(\Delta)$	128 bytes
	RSU_r, α, β	8 bytes
	$SK_j(m||\alpha||\beta)$	256 bytes

each variable is shown in the Table 6. The communication and storage costs of each stage are shown in the Fig. 6.

The literature [2] are very similar to our scheme. If $Phase − I$ are not calculated and assume $n = m = C_t$ & $T_t = T_m = T_{pg}$, where T_{pg} is the time of generating public and private key pairs in literature [2]. The scheme is at least $3T_{puf} + 3T_h + 4T_e$ superior in time. In our environment, the average time for T_h is 83 ms and T_e is 57 ms.

Considering the sustainability of scheme stored on the blockchain, we also conducted an analysis of the event and the size of the blockchain block. The size of event message stored on the blockchain is 1184 bytes and size of blockchain header information is 80 bytes. Assume that the RSU sends a timestamp at an interval of 60 s. In each timestamp, only one event occurs. The block size information generated in a single day is 1.73 MB. The block size of the blockchain has a strong correlation with the frequency and time of events. The block size of blockchain is defined as the following formula:

$$SizeOfBlockchain = T * T_p * T_B \tag{6}$$

Now the block size of the blockchain is calculated when the cumulative time is one month, three months, five months, seven months and one year, and the occurrence frequency of events is 5 s, 10 s, 20 s and 30 s, as shown in Fig. 7.

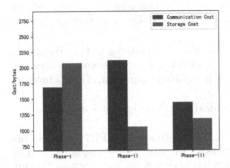

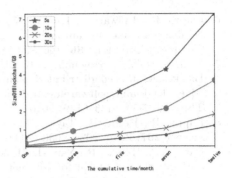

Fig. 6. Communication and storage costs.

Fig. 7. Blocks consume.

5 Conclusion and Future Work

In this paper, a new blockchain-based identity privacy protection scheme (BIPP) are proposed. The blockchain-based architecture establishes pre-domain trust, which can greatly enhance system trust. Through security analysis, the scheme in this paper guarantees the correctness, unlinkability and unforgeability under the hands of probabilistic polynomial adversaries. The implementation and evaluation prove the feasibility of the scheme in terms of time, communication and storage. In the future, we will consider developing a DAPP based on the proposed BIPP scheme so that passers-by can know the traffic information of the city at any time.

Acknowledgement. We are grateful to the editor and anonymous reviewers for their constructive comments. This work is supported by the National Nature Science Foundation of China through project 51979048.

References

1. Akhtar, A., et al.: Low latency scalable point cloud communication in VANETs using V2I communication. In: 2019 IEEE International Conference on Communications (ICC), ICC 2019, pp. 1–7. IEEE (2019)
2. Dwivedi, S.K., Amin, R., Vollala, S., Chaudhry, R.: Blockchain-based secured event-information sharing protocol in internet of vehicles for smart cities. Comput. Electr. Eng. **86**, 106719 (2020)
3. Gai, K., Guo, J., Zhu, L., Yu, S.: Blockchain meets cloud computing: a survey. IEEE Commun. Surv. Tutor. **22**(3), 2009–2030 (2020)
4. Garai, M., Rekhis, S., Boudriga, N.: Communication as a service for cloud VANETs. In: 2015 IEEE Symposium on Computers and Communication (ISCC), pp. 371–377. IEEE (2015)
5. Gope, P., Lee, J., Quek, T.Q.: Lightweight and practical anonymous authentication protocol for RFID systems using physically unclonable functions. IEEE Trans. Inf. Forensics Secur. **13**(11), 2831–2843 (2018)

6. Gupta, R., Tanwar, S., Kumar, N., Tyagi, S.: Blockchain-based security attack resilience schemes for autonomous vehicles in industry 4.0: a systematic review. Comput. Electr. Eng. **86**, 106717 (2020)
7. Medhane, D.V., Sangaiah, A.K., Hossain, M.S., Muhammad, G., Wang, J.: Blockchain-enabled distributed security framework for next-generation IoT: an edge cloud and software-defined network-integrated approach. IEEE Internet Things J. **7**(7), 6143–6149 (2020)
8. Pappu, R., Recht, B., Taylor, J., Gershenfeld, N.: Physical one-way functions. Science **297**(5589), 2026–2030 (2002)
9. Patil, A.S., Hamza, R., Yan, H., Hassan, A., Li, J.: Blockchain-PUF-based secure authentication protocol for Internet of Things. In: Wen, S., Zomaya, A., Yang, L.T. (eds.) ICA3PP 2019. LNCS, vol. 11945, pp. 331–338. Springer, Cham (2020). https://doi.org/10.1007/978-3-030-38961-1_29
10. Quevedo, C.H., Quevedo, A.M., Campos, G.A., Gomes, R.L., Celestino, J., Serrhrouchni, A.: An intelligent mechanism for Sybil attacks detection in VANETs. In: 2020 IEEE International Conference on Communications (ICC), ICC 2020, pp. 1–6. IEEE (2020)
11. Rosenfeld, M.: Analysis of hashrate-based double spending. arXiv preprint arXiv:1402.2009 (2014)
12. Ruffing, T., Moreno-Sanchez, P., Kate, A.: CoinShuffle: practical decentralized coin mixing for bitcoin. In: Kutyłowski, M., Vaidya, J. (eds.) ESORICS 2014. LNCS, vol. 8713, pp. 345–364. Springer, Cham (2014). https://doi.org/10.1007/978-3-319-11212-1_20
13. Safi, Q.G.K., Luo, S., Wei, C., Pan, L., Yan, G.: Cloud-based security and privacy-aware information dissemination over ubiquitous VANETs. Comput. Stand. Interfaces **56**, 107–115 (2018)
14. Wang, C., Li, J., Cheng, X., He, Y., Sun, L., Xiao, K.: LSTM-based communication scheduling mechanism for energy harvesting RSUs in IoVs. In: 2020 IEEE 92nd Vehicular Technology Conference (VTC2020-Fall), pp. 1–5. IEEE (2020)
15. Yang, Z., Yang, K., Lei, L., Zheng, K., Leung, V.C.: Blockchain-based decentralized trust management in vehicular networks. IEEE Internet Things J. **6**(2), 1495–1505 (2018)

Deep Learning Models and Applications

Self-adapted Frame Selection Module: Refine the Input Strategy for Video Saliency Detection

Shangrui Wu[1,2,3], Yang Wang[2(✉)], Tian Wang[1,3], Weijia Jia[1,3], and Ruitao Xie[4]

[1] BNU-UIC Institute of Artificial Intelligence and Future Networks, Beijing Normal University (BNU Zhuhai), Zhuhai, Guangdong, China
[2] Southwest Petroleum University, Chengdu, Sichuan, China
wangyang@swpu.edu.cn
[3] Guangdong Key Lab of AI and Multi-Modal Data Processing, BNU-HKBU United International College, Zhuhai, China
jiawj@uic.edu.cn
[4] Shenzhen University, Shenzhen, China

Abstract. Video saliency detection is intended to interpret the human visual system by modeling and predicting while observing a dynamic scene. This method is currently widely used in a variety of devices, including surveillance cameras and Internet-of-Things sensors. Traditionally, each video contains a large amount of redundancies in consecutive frames, while the common practices concentrate on extending the range of input frames to resist the uncertainty of input images. In order to overcome this problem, we propose Self-Adapted Frame Selection (SAFS) module that removes redundant information and selects frames that are highly informative. Furthermore, the module has high robustness and extensive application dealing with complex video contents, such as fast moving scene and images from different scenes. Since predicting the saliency map across multiple scenes is challenging, we establish a set of benchmarking videos for the scene change scenario. Specifically, our method combined with TASED-NET achieves significant improvements on the DHF1K dataset as well as the scene change dataset.

Keywords: Video saliency detection · Mobile edge computing · Deep learning · Refine input frames

The above work was supported in part by grants from The Natural Science Foundation of Fujian Province of China (No. 2020J06023), the National Natural Science Foundation of China (NSFC) under Grant No. 62172046, the Special Project of Guangdong Provincial Department of Education in Key Fields of Colleges and Universities (2021ZDZX1063); the joint project of Production, Teaching and Research of Zhuhai (ZH22017001210133PWC).

Y. Lai et al. (Eds.): ICA3PP 2021, LNCS 13156, pp. 509–516, 2022.
https://doi.org/10.1007/978-3-030-95388-1_33

1 Introduction

The perception of the Internet of things (IoT) connecting everything has opened an era of sharp increase in data, with the cutting-edge artificial intelligence (AI) algorithms and services [1], enabling communication network [2,3] and mobile edge computing [4,5] excavate invaluable resources from the massive data. In light of this trend, there is a pressing need to push the last iteration of AI technology to the edge computing in order to better applied in a number of practical applications [6,7] and analysis [8]. Specially, there are some mobility scenarios that need to locate critical areas in video clips, the technology behind it is known as video saliency detection. Previous research has demonstrated that video saliency detection is useful in a wide range of applications, such as human-robot interaction [9], video compression [10], etc.

Computer vision tasks have recently been greatly improved by deep learning, methods based on deep learning are gradually dominant in the field of video saliency detection. The large dataset of this field like DHF1K [11] that collecting human gaze data across diverse content of videos, encouraging models better imitate the complex function of human eyes. Previous state-of-art approaches on DHF1K that extract features from fixed frames (e.g., read 16 or 32 consecutive frames at a time) have demonstrated superior results. However, there will be a large number of highly similar frames in videos recorded on edge devices, particularly in slow-moving scenes. As a result of the temporal redundancy in the input, it is wasteful to read fixed input frames and the model's accuracy is reduced. More importantly, reading a fixed number of frames can only effectively be used to process a single video scene. The accuracy drops rapidly with increased use of images from the other scene when detecting saliency in a new scene.

Aiming at the problem that the existing video saliency detection technology does not effectively identify redundant frames and is not suitable for applied to multi-scene video, we proposed a novel self-adapted frame selection (SAFS) module for solving the problem. As opposed to the sliding window that reads the entire video frame-by-frame, with the SAFS module, a larger input frame search region, sense scene changes and redundant frames, and prioritize frames to achieve self-adapted frame selection.

The rest of the paper is organized as follows: In Sect. 2, we lay out the background and related works. In Sect. 3 details the architecture and process of our proposed module. Then in Sect. 4, several experiments have been conducted using video saliency datasets, the results of which are presented here. Finally, we conclude the paper and future works in Sect. 5

2 Related Work

Edge computing tends to be more efficient, more intelligent by deploying AI to devices at the edge where data is generated. Driven by AI and IoT, combining AI and edge computing cooperatively is essential to a variety domains, such as video surveillance, object detection, action detection, vehicle detection, etc.

DIVS [12] is one example of surveillance system with AI. DIVS is a distributed system using deep learning in edge computing, the multi-layer architecture providing edge devices distributed training efficiently. Hung et al. [13] propose VideoEdge which is an edge-based system for analyzing live video streams, maintaining high prediction accuracy while balancing the load across hierarchical architecture. ACDnet [14] is an action detection network, which incorporated with Single Shot MultiBox Detector (SSD) to explore the coherence of video for real-time detection on edge devices.

In the field of video saliency detection, as an alternative to manual features, models based on deep neural network have become ubiquitous. To obtain the salient region, He et al. [15] used a super-pixel method, which has fewer overheads and is more robust. However, this method is not able to provide accurate predictions given the difficulty in obtaining local features. Hou et al. [16] proposes a top-down model structure and introduces shortcut connections between different layers of the network, which connects spatial features of the upper layer with semantic features of the lower layer. TASED-NET [17] employs an encoder-decoder structure that can predict a full-resolution saliency map. The encoder extracts features with separable 3D convolutional neural networks (S3D), and the decoder uses auxiliary pooling in transposed layers to ensure temporal compatibility.

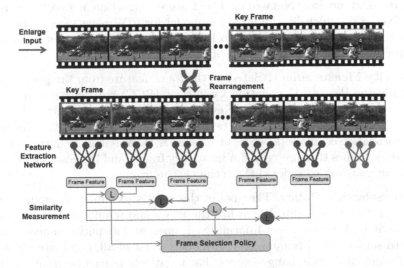

Fig. 1. An illustration of the overall flow of SAFS module. Expanding the search range to enlarge input frames of the model, then follow the steps below: (1) Frame Rearrangement, (2) Feature Extraction Network, (3) Similarity Measurement, (4) Frames Selection Policy.

3   Self-adapted Frame Selection

Eliminate redundant information on a fixed number of input frames [17] for video saliency detection, we represent the consecutive input frames as a series of high informative frames with correlations to the Key frame. This is accomplished by expanding the search scope of input clip and extracting spatiotemporal features from the enlarged input, and then comparing the similarity between the Key frame (i.e., current frame) and auxiliary frames (the frames in the input clip except the Key frame) to filter highly informative frames with closer the Key frame temporally.

Self-Adapted Frame Selection (SAFS) consists of (1) Frame Rearrangement, (2) Feature Extraction Network, (3) Similarity Measurement, (4) Frames Selection Policy. Figure 1 shows the overall process flow of our proposed module.

Frame Rearrangement. For the purpose of finding high-correlation images in the field of video compression, the codec uses information from adjacent frames that are temporally close in directions forward and backward (such as Bi-directional prediction). The proposed method continues this practice, we highlight the Key frame and put it as the first frame in the new sequence, and then, place the auxiliary frames in order of their temporal distances from the Key frame (see Fig. 1 - Frame Rearrangement).

Feature Extraction Network. The feature extraction network we used is GhostNet [18], which is a lightweight model for 2D image recognition. Compared to the prevalent neural network backbones, the design of efficient neural architectures minimizes the impact of introducing new module.

Similarity Measurement. Based on the frame feature from the previous step, we apply the Pearson Correlation Coefficient (PCC) with cheap cost to measure the differential between the Key frame and auxiliary frames. The procedure selects frames based on their temporal distances from the Key frame and their correlation coefficients, we regard frames with extremely high coefficients as redundant frames that are very similar to Key frame, and frames with extremely low coefficients are considered the scene change frame.

Frame Selection Policy. The goal of this step is to refine the group of input frames on the current clip. We utilize the PCCs and temporal distances among each auxiliary frame to select informative frames, and its performance is comparable to sophisticated frame selection models. First of all, eliminate the redundant frames and scene change frames that negatively impact accuracy, in accordance to PCCs. It is worth noting that the Key frame identifies which parts need to be removed when the scene changes, for example, if the scene change frame appears after the Key frame in the original sequence, then the frames immediately subsequent to the scene change frame need to be removed, and vice versa. Then, the general consideration of saliency detection should prioritize frames nearer to the Key frame, and therefore frames farther away from Key frame will only be selected if they have a lower PCC.

4   Experiments

4.1   Experiments Setup

We constitute TASED-SAFS by combining our SAFS module with TASED-NET [17]. Experiments are conducted on two large-scale datasets: DHF1K [11] and a scene change dataset. DHF1K consists of approximately 580,000 frames capturing 1000 annotated videos and classified into 7 main categories with 150 classes in total. The dataset is the largest published in the field of video saliency detection, hence we picked out the DHF1K dataset as our major benchmark. We produced the scene change dataset by merging single scene videos from UCFSports [19], the detail will be discussed in Sect. 4.3.

To evaluate the performance of our model, we follow the DHF1K [11] using the following evaluation metrics: (1) Normalized Scanpath Saliency (NSS), (2) Linear Correlation Coefficient (CC), (3) Similarity (SIM), (4) Area Under the Curve by Judd (AUC-J) and (5) Shuffled-AUC (s-AUC).

4.2   Evaluation on DHF1K

Since the ground-truth of test set was held by the DHF1K creators for fair comparisons, we tested the accuracy of our model in the validation set, and transferred the final results of test set that gained from the optimal model to the DHF1K creators for the unified examination. In this experiment, our module selects 32 frames from the amplification range of 48 frames, Table 1 shows the quantitative comparison with previous state-of-art models on DHF1K. TASED-SAFS outperforms all other models in the following metrics: NSS, CC, SIM, and AUC-J. Specifically, the most obvious improvement is the NSS, which is the average of the response values at human eye positions. This is showing that our SAFS module achieved considerable gains in predicting the correct eye movement.

Table 1. Comparison results of different video saliency detection models on the test set of DHF1K, TASED-SAFS significant improvement in multiply evaluation metrics.

Method	Metric				
	NSS	CC	SIM	AUC-J	s-AUC
SALICON [20]	1.901	0.327	0.232	0.857	0.590
OM-CNN [21]	1.911	0.344	0.256	0.856	0.583
SalGAN [22]	2.043	0.370	0.262	0.866	0.709
ACLNet [11]	2.354	0.434	0.315	0.890	0.601
TASED-NET [17]	2.667	0.470	0.361	0.895	0.712
TASED-SAFS	**2.848**	**0.501**	**0.396**	**0.898**	0.710

4.3   Performance on Scene Change Dataset

Early evaluation of TASED-NET on content of scene change revealed a remarkable degeneration within results after scene change, we visualize the sample frames of scene change in Fig. 2. We noticed that TASED-NET may introduce frames from another scene in a manner of fixed input, for example, if the scene change frame is in the middle of the input, half of it will be useless or even harming. Accordingly, We perform a scene change dataset, which consists ten classes that each video created by combining two or three videos that contain only single scene [19].

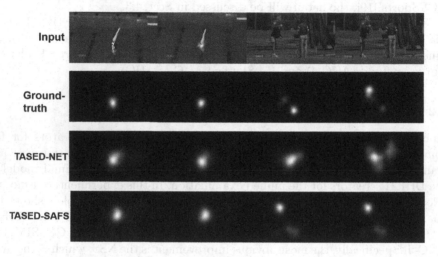

Fig. 2. An example of scene change content affects the accuracy of the results. The TASED-SAFS can cope better with scenes change, and saliency maps associated instantly with the input images in any given frame compared to the TASED-NET.

We compared the TASED-NET that sequential read frame with our module, the performance of SAFS to resist the particular effects of scene change in Table 2. According to the results, our module outperforms the TASED-NET on all evaluation metrics. Furthermore, the present results clearly indicate that video content in general contains a lot of misleading and redundant data, as with the data cleaning process for sieving information, it is worth to filter video information before the analytics.

Table 2. Comparison result on the scene change dataset, serial number in parentheses corresponding the classes of the dataset.

Method	Metric				
	NSS	CC	SIM	AUC-J	s-AUC
TASED-NET(1)	3.0342	0.5897	0.4452	0.9069	0.6769
TASED-SAFS(1)	3.3388	0.6489	0.4922	0.9102	0.7093
DTASED-NET(2)	3.1014	0.5782	0.4739	0.9102	0.7184
TASED-SAFS(2)	3.6391	0.6372	0.5013	0.9037	0.7307
TASED-NET(3)	2.2523	0.4520	0.3646	0.8667	0.6844
TASED-SAFS(3)	2.4507	0.4901	0.3947	0.8676	0.6909
...	...	...	...	...	...
TASED-NET(Avg)	2.7216	0.5487	0.4420	0.8901	0.6937
TASED-SAFS(Avg)	**2.9607**	**0.5806**	**0.4729**	**0.8967**	**0.7032**

5 Conclusion

In this research, we presented SAFS, a self-adapted frame selection module for enhancing the quality of the clip of the input frame. Our module according to the correlation between the Key frame and auxiliary frames, selecting the most informative frames from an enlarge input. Considering the general video content consists consecutive frames from the different scenes frequently, we built a scene change video benchmarking dataset that merging from single scene video and evaluated the performance of SAFS module. The experiment results showed that our SAFS module combined with TASED-NET has made a significant improvement.

Following this study, we will explore lighter deep neural network models that are better suited to edge computing. Future works can explore: (1) Filtering rogue data collected by edge nodes, the neural networks will be re-sized according to the complexity of the input to optimize efficiency; (2) Using the SAFS module for a broader variety of applications.

References

1. Wang, T., et al.: Privacy-enhanced data collection based on deep learning for internet of vehicles. IEEE Trans. Ind. Inf. **16**(10), 6663–6672 (2019)
2. Qu, Y., Xiong, N.: RFH: a resilient, fault-tolerant and high-efficient replication algorithm for distributed cloud storage. In: 2012 41st International Conference on Parallel Processing, pp. 520–529. IEEE (2012)
3. Yin, J., Lo, W., Deng, S., Li, Y., Zhaohui, W., Xiong, N.: Colbar: a collaborative location-based regularization framework for QoS prediction. Inf. Sci. **265**, 68–84 (2014)
4. Wang, T., Jia, W., Xing, G., Li, M.: Exploiting statistical mobility models for efficient Wi-Fi deployment. IEEE Trans. Veh. Technol. **62**(1), 360–373 (2012)

5. Fang, W., Yao, X., Zhao, X., Yin, J., Xiong, N.: A stochastic control approach to maximize profit on service provisioning for mobile cloudlet platforms. IEEE Trans. Syst. Man Cybern. Syst. **48**(4), 522–534 (2016)
6. Huang, M., Liu, A., Wang, T., Huang, C.: Green data gathering under delay differentiated services constraint for Internet of Things. Wirel. Commun. Mob. Comput. **2018**, 23 (2018)
7. Zeng, Y., Xiong, N., Park, J.H., Zheng, G.: An emergency-adaptive routing scheme for wireless sensor networks for building fire hazard monitoring. Sensors **10**(6), 6128–6148 (2010)
8. Li, H., Liu, J., Liu, R.W., Xiong, N., Wu, K., Kim, T.: A dimensionality reduction-based multi-step clustering method for robust vessel trajectory analysis. Sensors **17**(8), 1792 (2017)
9. Ferreira, J.F., Dias, J.: Attentional mechanisms for socially interactive robots - a survey. IEEE Trans. Auton. Ment. Dev. **6**(2), 110–125 (2014)
10. Hadizadeh, H., Bajić, I.V.: Saliency-aware video compression. IEEE Trans. Image Process. **23**(1), 19–33 (2013)
11. Wang, W., Shen, J., Guo, F., Cheng, M.-M., Borji, A.: Revisiting video saliency: a large-scale benchmark and a new model. In: Proceedings of the IEEE Conference on Computer Vision and Pattern Recognition, pp. 4894–4903 (2018)
12. Chen, J., Li, K., Deng, Q., Li, K., Philip, S.Y.: Distributed deep learning model for intelligent video surveillance systems with edge computing. IEEE Trans. Ind. Inf. (2019)
13. Hung, C.-C., et al.: Processing camera streams using hierarchical clusters. In: 2018 IEEE/ACM Symposium on Edge Computing (SEC), pp. 115–131 (2018)
14. Liu, Yu., Yang, F., Ginhac, D.: ACDnet: an action detection network for real-time edge computing based on flow-guided feature approximation and memory aggregation. Pattern Recogn. Lett. **145**, 118–126 (2021)
15. He, S., Lau, R.W.H., Liu, W., et al.: SuperCNN: a superpixelwise convolutional neural network for salient object detection. Int. J. Comput. Vis. **115**, 330–344 (2015). https://doi.org/10.1007/s11263-015-0822-0
16. Hou, Q., Cheng, M.-M., Hu, X., Borji, A., Tu, Z., Torr, P.H.S.: Deeply supervised salient object detection with short connections. In: Proceedings of the IEEE Conference on Computer Vision and Pattern Recognition, pp. 3203–3212 (2017)
17. Min, K., Corso, J.J.: TASED-Net: temporally-aggregating spatial encoder-decoder network for video saliency detection. In: Proceedings of the IEEE/CVF International Conference on Computer Vision, pp. 2394–2403 (2019)
18. Han, K., Wang, Y., Tian, Q., Guo, J., Xu, C., Xu, C.: GhostNet: more features from cheap operations. In: Proceedings of the IEEE/CVF Conference on Computer Vision and Pattern Recognition, pp. 1580–1589 (2020)
19. Soomro, K., Zamir, A.R.: Action recognition in realistic sports videos. In: Moeslund, T.B., Thomas, G., Hilton, A. (eds.) Computer Vision in Sports. ACVPR, pp. 181–208. Springer, Cham (2014). https://doi.org/10.1007/978-3-319-09396-3_9
20. Jiang, M., Huang, S., Duan, J., Zhao, Q.: SALICON: saliency in context. In: Proceedings of the IEEE Conference on Computer Vision and Pattern Recognition, pp. 1072–1080 (2015)
21. Jiang, L., Xu, M., Wang, Z.: Predicting video saliency with object-to-motion CNN and two-layer convolutional LSTM. arXiv preprint arXiv:1709.06316 (2017)
22. Pan, J., et al.: SalGAN: visual saliency prediction with generative adversarial networks. arXiv preprint arXiv:1701.01081 (2017)

Evolving Deep Parallel Neural Networks for Multi-Task Learning

Jie Wu and Yanan Sun[✉]

College of Computer Science, Sichuan University, Chengdu, China
ysun@scu.edu.cn

Abstract. Multi-Task Learning (MTL) can perform multiple tasks simultaneously with a single model, and can achieve competitive performance for each individual task. In recent years, the Deep Neural Networks (DNNs) based models have demonstrated their advantages in the field of MTL. Yet, most of such models are commonly manually designed with expertise through performing trial and error experiments, which is prohibitively ineffective. In view of this, we design a method based on evolutionary algorithm in this paper, named EVO-MTL, to automate the parallel DNN architectures for effectively addressing the MTL problems. Specifically, our main idea is to evolve the connections between the parallel task-specific backbone networks, and then leverage the useful information contained in the tasks by fusing the task-specific features. In order to verify the effectiveness of the proposed algorithm, the experiments are designed to compare with recent MTL methods including the manually designed and automatically designed. The experimental results demonstrate that the proposed algorithm can outperform the carefully hand-designed methods. In addition, the proposed algorithm can also attain promising competitive performance in balancing multi-task conflicts compared with the DNN architecture searched by state-of-the-art automated MTL method.

Keywords: Evolutionary computation · Multi-Task Learning · Neural architecture search · Computer vision · Deep Neural Networks

1 Introduction

During past years, great achievements have been made in computer vision tasks, such as object detection [8,13,25], semantic segmentation [12,17,21], surface normal estimation [11,23,34] and so on. Generally, these tasks are commonly single-task, i.e., only a single one objective is considered in the task. However, many real-world applications usually involve multiple tasks simultaneously. For example, automatic driving often needs to tackle object detection, semantic segmentation and surface normal prediction at the same time to provide an accurate driving decision [32]. Similarly, face detection in the noisy environment, often needs to perform multiple auxiliary tasks, such as head posture detection and face attribute judgment to improve its effect [36]. Multi-Task Learning

© Springer Nature Switzerland AG 2022
Y. Lai et al. (Eds.): ICA3PP 2021, LNCS 13156, pp. 517–531, 2022.
https://doi.org/10.1007/978-3-030-95388-1_34

(MTL) refers to performing such multiple tasks simultaneously by leveraging useful information contained in each task. Compared with learning the task individually, MTL has the potential to improve the generalization ability of all the tasks in a single model.

Recently, the Deep Neural Networks (DNNs) is widely used in MTL owing to its reasonably good ability of feature extraction and hierarchical representation [6]. As a result, the DNNs are also extensively used to address MTL tasks. Generally, the DNN based MTL algorithms can be divided into two categories: hard parameter sharing algorithms and soft parameter sharing algorithms, which are shown in Fig. 1.

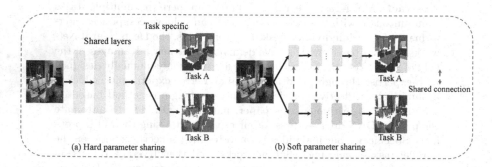

Fig. 1. Hard parameter sharing (a) and soft parameter sharing (b) for MTL.

Hard Parameter Sharing. In the hard parameter sharing methods, the multiple tasks share the same hidden layers in the early stage, and each individual task heads to its task-specific output layer, which can be observed from Fig. 1(a). Hard parameter sharing is the most commonly used approach in the early DNN based MTL. For example, Zhang et al. [36] proposed a tasks-constrained deep convolutional network that consists of a shared feature extractor and some auxiliary task-specific output heads, to help the landmark detection. Furthermore, Dai et al. [2] introduced a Multi-Task Network Cascades (MNCs) for instance-aware semantic segmentation. The MNCs also shares a feature extractor, while the output of each task-specific layer is appended as the input of the other task. These work is able to greatly reduce the risk of overfitting, because signals from different tasks are fully shared in the early feature extraction layers. However, interfaces between loosely related tasks will easily result in worse results than single task model [26]. In practice, most of the MTL tasks are often loosely related.

Soft Parameter Sharing. Different from the hard parameter sharing methods, each task in the soft parameter sharing has a task-specific network, sharing parameters or features between parallel tasks, as illustrated in Fig. 1(b). In recent years, most state-of-the-art MTL algorithms fall into this category [7,15,20]. Specifically, these work focuses on fusing the features from parallel task-specific backbone networks through an indirect transformation. For example, Misra et al. [20] introduced a linear combination unit in their designed Cross-Stitch

Network (CSN) to fuse the features from the same stage layers of different parallel task-specific backbone networks. These features are transformed by the linear combination, before feeding into the next layer in the task-specific network. Furthermore, Gao et al. [7] generalized the CSN by introducing the Neural Discriminative Dimensionality Reduction (NDDR) method into its proposed feature combination unit (named as NDDR-CNN). NDDR-CNN concatenates the features from each parallel task-specific network, and then uses the 1×1 convolution operation to reduce the dimension of the concatenated feature to satisfy the following layer. Recent years, most work regarding MTL is based on the soft parameter sharing.

Although existing work has improved the performance of MTL, especially some designs with the soft parameter sharing, the fusion operations are all simply performed, and their potentials have not been fully explored. For example, the NDDR-CNN unit is simply performed after each pooling layer of the task-specific VGG-16 [29] network. It may fuse some negative features, resulting in a decrease to the overall performance of the model. Consequently, a problem arises: *what features should be fused and where the feature fusion should be operated?* Clearly, it requires a lot of time and expertise to manually determine the features to be fused and locations to perform the fusion operation. For example, if we take VGG-16 as the parallel task-specific backbone network for two tasks, and each convolution layer is followed by a fusion point, it will produce $2^{13 \times 13}$ different network architectures. Obviously, it is exhaustive to find the proper architecture from the combinations with manual effort. As a result, it is natural to consider to automatically design the network architecture.

To achieve this, we propose a Genetic Algorithm (GA) based neural architecture search algorithm in this paper, to automatically design the soft parameter based optimal parallel DNN architecture, to solve the key issues discussed above. The contributions of the proposed algorithm are summarized as follows:

- **A novel genetic encoding strategy of GA is proposed to encode the individual neural network architecture in the process of evolution.** Different from the traditional linear encoding strategies used in the single-task learning, the proposed encoding strategy can well represent the variation of parallel MTL model topology during the evolution, and a population of such individuals can evolve a better model for MTL.
- **The effective genetic operators are designed to enhance the exploration and the exploitation search.** The proposed evolution operators include the crossover operator and the mutation operator, which can efficiently help the algorithm discover promising DNN architecture and prevent individuals from falling into the local optimum.
- **A balanced fitness function is designed to select promising individuals as offspring.** The weighted balanced metric is specially designed as the fitness of the individuals, which is helpful to find a high-performance model being able to balance different tasks.

- **The experiments are well designed to verify the effectiveness of the proposed algorithm.** The proposed algorithm is examined on a widely used MTL dataset, and the experimental results demonstrate the remarkable improvement on each individual task and a good performance against multi-task conflicts.

2   Background and Related Work

In this section, we first review some related Multi-Task Learning (MTL) algorithms to help the readers have a broad understanding of MTL. Then, some work regarding automatically designing network architectures will be introduced.

2.1   Multi-Task Learning (MTL) Algorithms

Before the Deep Neural Networks (DNNs) become popular among the machine learning community, most MTL algorithms are DNN-free [5,18,35]. These algorithms mainly focus on enforcing the sparsity or modeling the relationship between tasks [26]. However, they all assume that there are linear relationships between the data and the target labels, which greatly limits their application [31]. Recent work for MTL is mainly based on DNNs. For example, the work in [9,10] mainly shares a feature extraction layer for multiple tasks, and then designs different task-specific output layers. While in [7,27], the fixed backbone network of each task is designed and the features are shared between the backbone networks. In addition to the above work, some other new mechanisms have also been proposed. For example, Lu et al. [19] proposes a branch method which starts from a thin network and greedily groups similar tasks during the training process. Liu et al. [15] designed the task-specific attention modules to extract features from the backbone network. In general, DNN based MTL algorithms largely focus on how to fuse features and where to share features.

2.2   Neural Architecture Search (NAS)

NAS is widely used in automatically network architecture design by developing effective search strategies, including Reinforcement Learning (RL), gradient-based optimization, and Evolution Computation (EC) [16]. Specially, the RL-based NAS algorithms utilize the performance on the validation datasets as reward, and then guide its search for optimal network architecture [37,38]. The gradient-based NAS algorithms transform the discrete search space into a continuous representation first, and then utilize the gradient based optimization methods to search for the optimal DNN [14,22]. The EC-based NAS algorithms commonly follow the standard flow of evolution algorithms, but with well-designed core evolution steps, to explore the globally optimal DNN architectures [24,30]. Generally, the EC-based NAS algorithms often require less computing resource than RL-based algorithms do. Furthermore, the EC-based methods do not need to design a super network search space in advance, so it can avoid manual intervention as much as possible during the search process.

3 The Proposed Algorithm

In this section, we will first provide the overview of the proposed algorithm (named as EVO-MTL) in Subsect. 3.1 and then the main steps of EVO-MTL are elaborated from Subsects. 3.2 to 3.4.

3.1 Algorithm Overview

The framework of the proposed EVO-MTL algorithm is shown in Algorithm 1, where the contributions are highlighted in bold and italic. First, the population is initialized and each individual in the population is randomly generated with the proposed flexible gene encoding strategy (line 1). Then, the fitness of each individual in the initialized population is evaluated for the parent selection (line 2). After that, the evolution begins to take effect until the predefined stopping criterion is satisfied (lines 4–10). Finally, the best individual is selected from the final generation and decoded into the CNN model for the final training (line 11).

During the stage of evolution, the parent individuals are selected by using the binary tournament operation (line 5). Then, the selected parent individuals generate the offspring individuals by using the proposed genetic operations (line 6) and the offspring individuals are evaluated (line 7). Next, the environment selection is performed to select individuals from the combination of the current population and the new offspring (line 8), which serve as the parent individuals of the next generation.

Algorithm 1: Framework of EVO-MTL

---

1 $P_0 \leftarrow$ Initialize the population with *the proposed gene encoding strategy*;
2 Evaluate fitness of P_0;
3 $t \leftarrow 0$;
4 **while** *the stopping criterion is not satisfied* **do**
5 $\quad$ $S \leftarrow$ Select parent individuals by the binary tournament selection operation from P_t ;
6 $\quad$ $G_t \leftarrow$ Generate the offsprings with *the proposed novel genetic operations*;
7 $\quad$ Evaluate fitness of G_t;
8 $\quad$ $P_{t+1} \leftarrow$ Environment selection from $P_t \cup G_t$ by using the proposed strategy;
9 $\quad$ $t \leftarrow t + 1$;
10 **end**
11 **Return** P_t and decode the best individual from P_t to the corresponding CNN.

3.2 Gene Encoding Strategy

The fixed or variable-length linear encoding strategy is widely used to encode the CNN architectures in literature. However, such strategies are not suitable to the soft parameter sharing based MTL networks, which compose of multiple parallel task-specific backbone networks. In order to better represent the shared connection between different backbone networks, we design a matrix gene encoding strategy to encode the individuals in the proposed algorithm.

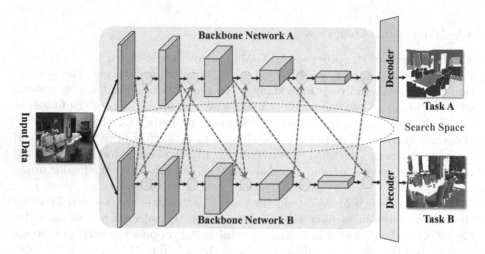

Fig. 2. An example of the individual. The blue dotted arrows between the backbone networks are the feature fusion edges to be searched, which are encoded by our proposed algorithm. The yellow circles denote the feature fusion points, where features from other backbones are concatenated and then, go through a 1×1 convolutional layer with batch normalization, following a non-linear activation. (Color figure online)

Considering a case of task A and task B with its task-specific backbone network, as shown in Fig. 2, the green and orange blocks denote each layer of task A and task B, respectively, while the blue dotted arrow denotes the connection between task-specific networks, and the yellow circle denotes the feature fusion point. An individual in the population, say D, can be encoded by matrices D_A and D_B. Specifically, the matrix D_A represents the connection from each layer in the backbone of task B. The i-th row of matrix D_A represents the i-th feature fusion point of task A. When the value of the element at the position (i, j) is 1, it means there is a connection from the j-th layer of task B to the i-th feature fusion point of task A, while 0 means there is no connection. Similarly, the matrix D_B represents the connection of task A. In this example, the matrix D_A and matrix D_B are formulated by Eq. (1).

$$D_A = \begin{bmatrix} 1 & 0 & 0 & 0 & 0 \\ 1 & 1 & 0 & 0 & 0 \\ 0 & 0 & 1 & 0 & 0 \\ 0 & 0 & 0 & 1 & 0 \\ 0 & 0 & 0 & 0 & 1 \end{bmatrix}, D_B = \begin{bmatrix} 1 & 0 & 0 & 0 & 0 \\ 0 & 1 & 0 & 0 & 0 \\ 0 & 1 & 1 & 0 & 0 \\ 0 & 0 & 1 & 0 & 0 \\ 0 & 0 & 0 & 1 & 0 \end{bmatrix} \tag{1}$$

The population is initializated by using the proposed genetic encoding strategy. Firstly, the size of an empty population (denoted as N) and the length of task-specific backbone (denoted as L) are predefined. Secondly, the individuals are created with random settings to fill in the population until the population reaches its predefined size N. Specifically for each individual, two $L \times L$ zero matrices are initialized first. Then a number r is randomly generated from (0, 1) before traversing each row of the two matrices. If $r < 0.5$, the value of this position is set as 1, indicating that there is a connection in between. Otherwise, there is no connection by setting the value as 0. Finally, an initialized population P_0 is returned. It should be noted that in order to prevent generating a directed closed-loop structure, we limit the connection from the other task within the same or earlier layers in the process of initializing individuals.

3.3 Offspring Generation

As mentioned in Subsect. 3.1, the parent individuals will be selected to generate offsprings by performing the proposed genetic operators. The genetic operators include crossover operation and mutation operation. The crossover operation has the potential to retain promising genes of parent individuals, and the mutation would make offspring more diverse. Both are the key factors deciding the performance of the EC-based algorithms, and playing the role of local search and global search, respectively. The specific steps of generating offspring are described as follows:

1. Select two parent individuals by binary tournament selection;
2. Perform crossover operation to generate the offspring by the selected parent individuals;
3. Perform mutation operation on the offspring;
4. Repeat the Steps 1–3 until the number of generated offspring reaches the population size.

Figure 3 illustrates an example of the crossover operation. In this example, the two parent individuals have three layers (denoted by rectangles) and each layer is followed by a feature fusion points (denoted by circles). Based on the proposed gene encoding strategy introduced in Subsect. 3.2, the fusion condition of the first parent individual can be represented by two matrices, say P_{1A} and P_{1B}, which are shown in Eq. (2).

$$P_{1A} = \begin{bmatrix} 1 & 0 & 0 \\ 0 & 0 & 0 \\ 0 & 1 & 0 \end{bmatrix}, P_{1B} = \begin{bmatrix} 1 & 0 & 0 \\ 0 & 1 & 0 \\ 0 & 0 & 1 \end{bmatrix} \tag{2}$$

Similarly, the matrix P_{2A} and matrix P_{2B} of the second parent individual are as given in Eq. (3).

$$P_{2A} = \begin{bmatrix} 0 & 0 & 0 \\ 1 & 1 & 0 \\ 0 & 0 & 1 \end{bmatrix}, P_{2B} = \begin{bmatrix} 1 & 0 & 0 \\ 0 & 0 & 0 \\ 0 & 1 & 1 \end{bmatrix} \tag{3}$$

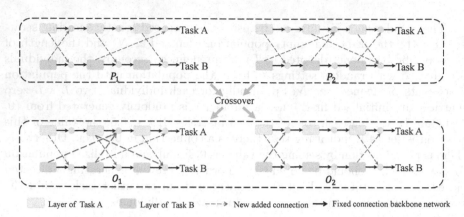

Fig. 3. An example of crossover. P_1 and P_2 are parent individuals, and after crossover, the offspring individuals O_1 and O_2 are generated.

Specifically, each individual has a predetermined crossover rate and a mutation rate, we randomly generate a floating number between 0 and 1. When the crossover rate of a feature fusion point is greater than the floating number, the corresponding feature fusion point in the task-specific backbone network will perform the crossover with each other, i.e., swapping a row of task-specific matrix. In Fig. 3, the first and second feature fusion point in task A of the two parent individuals (i.e., the first row in P_{1A} and the second row in P_{2A}) perform crossover with each other, and the third feature fusion point in task B of the two parent individuals (i.e., the third rows in P_{1B} and P_{2B}) perform crossover with each other.

After the crossover, the two corresponding offspring individuals can be expressed as O_{1A}, O_{1B}, O_{2A} and O_{2B}, as shown in Eqs. (4) and (5).

$$O_{1A} = \begin{bmatrix} 0 & 0 & 0 \\ 1 & 1 & 0 \\ 0 & 1 & 0 \end{bmatrix}, O_{1B} = \begin{bmatrix} 1 & 0 & 0 \\ 0 & 1 & 0 \\ 0 & 1 & 1 \end{bmatrix} \tag{4}$$

$$O_{2A} = \begin{bmatrix} 1 & 0 & 0 \\ 0 & 0 & 0 \\ 0 & 0 & 1 \end{bmatrix}, O_{2B} = \begin{bmatrix} 1 & 0 & 0 \\ 0 & 0 & 0 \\ 0 & 0 & 1 \end{bmatrix} \tag{5}$$

3.4   Environmental Selection

The environmental selection is to select a population of individuals surviving into the next generation, with the expectation that more promising offspring can be generated with these selected parent individuals. Commonly, the environmental selection should concern two aspects: convergence and diversity, which are achieved by different selection operations. In the proposed algorithm, the elite strategy [33] is used for maintaining the convergence and the binary tournament selection algorithm is adopted for improving the diversity.

Algorithm 2: Environment Selection

Input: The current parent population P_t, the generated offspring population G_o, and the elite ration r

Output: The next generation P_n

1 $G_r \leftarrow G_P \cup G_o$;

2 $G_r \leftarrow$ Sorted by individual fitness in G_r;

3 $n \leftarrow$ The number of G_r 2N multiply the elite rate r to get the number of elite individuals;

4 $P_n \leftarrow$ Select the first n individuals in G_r as elite individuals to the next generation;

5 $G_r \leftarrow$ Remove the selected elite individuals and randomly shuffle the remained individual;

6 **while** $|P_n| \leq N$ **do**

7 $\quad ind_s \leftarrow$ Use Binary Tournamen Selection to choose an individual from G_r;

8 $\quad$ **if** ind not in P_n **then**

9 $\quad\quad P_n \leftarrow$ Add the ind_s into the next generation;

10 $\quad$ **end**

11 **end**

12 **return** P_n

The details of the environmental selection are shown in Algorithm 2. First, the parent solutions and the offspring are combined, and sorted according to their fitness (lines 1–2). Then, according to the predefined elite ratio, a corresponding number of individuals are selected as elites to directly enter into the next generation to maintain the convergence (line 3–4). After that, in order to ensure the diversity of the population, we randomly shuffle the unselected individuals in the combined population, and reselect the individuals by the binary tournament algorithm until the predefined population size is reached (lines 5–11). Finally, the next generation P_n is returned (line 12).

4 Experiment Design

In order to verify the performance of the proposed EVO-MTL algorithm, the experiments are designed to compare with peer competitors on benchmark dataset. In the following, the experiment setup, which includes benchmark dataset, backbone network, loss function and evaluation metrics, are first introduced in Subsect. 4.1. Then, the peer competitors are provided in Subsect. 4.2. After that, the parameter settings and the training details are given in Subsects. 4.3 and 4.4, respectively.

4.1 Experimental Setup

Benchmark Dataset. We carry out the experiments on the widely used NYUD-v2 [28] dataset for MTL, which mainly concerns the indoor scenes, and contains 795 training images and 654 testing images. In this work, we mainly consider surface normal estimation and semantic segmentation tasks on these indoor scene images.

Backbone Network. We use Deeplab-VGG-16 [1], which is designed for the pixel-level tasks (e.g., semantic segmentation), as the task-specific backbone network. Specifically, the Deeplab-VGG-16 adopts dilated convolutional layers to improve the receptive field of the original VGG-16 [29] network.

Loss Function. The Softmax cross-entropy is used for semantic segmentation as the loss function, while for the surface normal estimation, we use the cosine loss, which indicates the angle difference to the ground truth. Since the loss of normal surface estimation is much smaller than the loss of semantic segmentation, in this work, we weight them at a ratio of 20:1 to balance the gap.

Evaluation Metrics. Based on the convention of the MTL community, the performance of the semantic segmentation is evaluated by the mean intersection over union (mIoU) and pixel accuracy (PAcc). For the surface normal estimation, we measure the mean and median error in angular distance. Besides, as suggested by [6], we also measure the percentage of pixels that are within the angles of 11.25° to the ground truth, in which a higher number indicates a better performance of the surface normal estimation.

4.2 Peer Competitors

The peer competitors used in this experiment can be divided into two categories, one is the manually designed including the fine-tuned single model for each task, i.e., Single model, and a typical hard parameter sharing model, i.e., Shared model, and the recent soft parameter sharing models, i.e., Cross Stitch Network [20] and NDDR-CNN [7]. While the other is the state-of-the-art NAS based multi-task network in most recent literature, i.e., MTL-NAS [6].

Specially, we use Deeplab-VGG-16 as the single task network to train semantic segmentation and surface normal estimation on the NYUD-v2 dataset. After that, we use the fine-tuned single task network as the pre-trained backbone network to initialize the backbone network for the proposed EVO-MTL algorithm and the peer competitors for a fair comparison. Please note that, in order to perform a fair comparison with MTL-NAS, we use the topology (the fusion connection) of the model searched by MTL-NAS for individual training and then compare it with the proposed algorithm.

4.3 Parameter Settings

The feature fusion points are set after each convolutional layer of Deeplab-VGG-16. Similar to [6], considering both the complexity and computation, we make the following operations: the output features in a task-specific backbone network can only be fused within three fusion points in the same stage of another backbone network.

All the parameter settings of the evolution stage are following the conventions of GA community [3]. Specifically, the population size and the total generation number are both set to be 20. The probabilities for crossover and mutation are specified as 0.9 and 0.2, respectively. In the environmental selection, the elitism rate is specified as 20% based on the Pareto principle [4]. In order to select an individual that can achieve better performance on both tasks as much as possible, we choose the weighted loss on the validation dataset as the fitness, i.e., 20:1, as mentioned in Subsect. 4.1.

4.4 Training Details

We use the stochastic gradient descent with the momentum of 0.9 and weight decay of 0.00025 to train the models. The initial learning rate is set as 0.0005 and the poly learning rate decay with a power of 0.9 is used for the Deeplab-VGG-16 backbone network. The batchsize is set as 3 on the NYUD-v2 dataset and 20,000 iterations are performed on the model selected by the proposed algorithm for the final training. As suggested by [6], in the fusion point, we set the initial weights of 1×1 convolution layer for semantic segmentation and normal surface estimation with the diagonal elements of 0.8 and 0.2, respectively. For a fair comparison, all the compared algorithms use the same training details and are conducted on a NVDIA 2080 Ti GPU card.

5 Experimental Results and Analysis

In this section, the experimental results are reported and analyzed. Specifically, the experimental results of the proposed EVO-MTL algorithm against with five peer competitors are shown in Subsect. 5.1. Then, the evolution trajectory of the proposed algorithm is given in Subsect. 5.2 to show the effectiveness of the proposed algorithm more intuitively.

5.1 Overall Results

The overall results of the five performance evaluation indicators are listed in Table 1, where the best result of each evaluation indicator is marked in bold. The peer competitors are grouped into two different blocks based on the algorithm category (i.e., Manually designed and Automatic).

For the peer competitors in the first category, which can be seen from the first block in Table 1, in terms of all the five indicators, the proposed algorithm surpasses all the carefully hand-designed methods, i.e., NDDR-CNN [7] and Cross Stitch Network [20], and the single-task methods. It demonstrates that the proposed method has good performance on generalizing ability and improving the performance of each individual task. Specifically, on the semantic segmentation task, the proposed EVO-MTL algorithm achieves the highest results regarding mIou and PAcc, and is the only algorithm with PAcc up to 66. Similarly, EVO-MTL attains the lowest value in the indicator of Mean, Median error, i.e., 15.92 and 12.31, respectively, and the highest value in 11.25° indicator of the Surface Normal task, i.e., 46.47, which shows that EVO-MTL successfully integrates extra useful features from semantic segmentation task.

Table 1. Comparisons between the proposed algorithm and the five peer competitors with respect to surface normal estimation and semantic segmentation on NYUD-v2 benchmark dataset. Note that all competitor algorithms are conducted locally and the training settings are the same as the proposed algorithm.

	Semantic Seg.		Surface normal estimation			Category of algorithms
	(%)(upper better)		Errors (lower better)		Within (upper better)	
	mIou	PAcc	Mean	Median	11.25°	
Single	34.4	64.4	17.04	14.72	36.59	Manually designed
Shared	34.6	64.6	16.46	13.07	44.05	
Cross stitch network	34.7	64.9	16.33	12.91	44.47	
NDDR-CNN	35.5	65.6	16.21	12.64	45.46	
MTL-NAS	34.8	65.1	**15.76**	12.32	46.37	Automatic
EVO-MTL (ours)	**35.7**	**66.0**	15.92	**12.31**	**46.47**	

For the peer competitors in the second category, i.e., the Automatic block in Table 1, it is obvious that the performance of the architecture searched by MTL-NAS [6] has task bias. The three indicators in terms of normal surface estimation task are better than other hand-designed models, but in semantic segmentation task, both metrics in terms of the segmentation are worse than manually designed NDDR-CNN [7], which demonstrates that the architecture searched by MTL-NAS is biased against semantic segmentation task. Instead, the model architecture searched by the proposed algorithm has better performance on balancing different tasks, and all the metrics are better than the manually designed models.

5.2 Evolution Trajectory

In order to show the effectiveness of the proposed algorithm more intuitively, the evolution trajectory of the proposed algorithm in terms of the chosen benchmark dataset is provided and analyzed. To achieve this, we collect the weighted loss of the elite individuals in each generation, and then plot the statistical results in Fig. 4.

As shown in Fig. 4, the horizontal axis represents the generation number, and the vertical axis denotes the weighted loss on the NYUD-v2 dataset. The red line denotes the mean weighted loss of the elite individuals in the same stage, while the green area is contoured by the weighted loss of the worst and best individual among the elite individuals. Specifically, the mean loss in each generation shows a downward trend in the evolution process, even from the eighth generation to the eighteenth generation where the best individual has not been replaced (as can be observed from the bottom line of the green area). This demonstrates that the individuals with better performance are continuously generated in the population by using the proposed evolution operators. As can be observed from the lower boundary of the green area, the best individual is gained in the 8-th generation and remains until the final best individual appears in the 19-th generation. As can be seen from the upper boundary of the green area, the worst loss sharply decreases from the first generation to the second generation, and then gradually decreases. Noting that, when approaching the termination

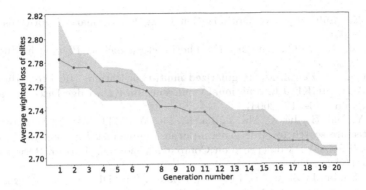

Fig. 4. Evolutionary trajectory of the proposed algorithm on the NYUD-v2.

of the proposed algorithm, the three lines get much closer, which indicates that the overall performance of the individuals has greatly been improved, and the proposed algorithm converges.

6 Conclusions

The objective of this paper is to propose an automatic architecture design algorithm for DNN based MTL by using GA (in short named EVO-MTL), which is capable of evolving the best parallel DNN architecture for performing the MTL tasks simultaneously, and improving the performance for each individual task reasonably. This goal has been successfully achieved by the proposed encoding strategy that flexibly encodes the feature fusion connections between different task-specific backbone networks, and the proposed crossover operator and mutation operator which provide the proposed algorithm with effective local search and global search ability. The proposed algorithm is examined on the NYUD-v2 dataset, against five recent peer competitors. The result shows that the proposed algorithm outperforms all the hand-crafted MTL algorithms in terms of the five chosen metrics, and the model evolved by the proposed algorithm gains better ability in balancing biases among different tasks than the state-of-the-art automatic algorithm. In the future, we will place efforts on developing effective feature fusion methods to significantly leverage the shared information between different tasks.

References

1. Chen, L.C., Papandreou, G., Kokkinos, I., Murphy, K., Yuille, A.L.: DeepLab: semantic image segmentation with deep convolutional nets, atrous convolution, and fully connected CRFs. IEEE Trans. Pattern Anal. Mach. Intell. **40**(4), 834–848 (2017)
2. Dai, J., He, K., Sun, J.: Instance-aware semantic segmentation via multi-task network cascades. In: Proceedings of the IEEE Conference on Computer Vision and Pattern Recognition, pp. 3150–3158 (2016)

3. Deb, K.: Multi-objective Optimization Using Evolutionary Algorithms, vol. 16. Wiley (2001)
4. Dunford, R., Su, Q., Tamang, E.: The Pareto principle. Plymouth Stud. Sci. **7**, 140–148 (2014)
5. Evgeniou, T., Pontil, M.: Regularized multi-task learning. In: Proceedings of the 10th ACM SIGKDD International Conference on Knowledge Discovery and Data Mining, pp. 109–117 (2004)
6. Gao, Y., Bai, H., Jie, Z., Ma, J., Jia, K., Liu, W.: MTL-NAS: task-agnostic neural architecture search towards general-purpose multi-task learning. In: Proceedings of the IEEE/CVF Conference on Computer Vision and Pattern Recognition, pp. 11543–11552 (2020)
7. Gao, Y., Ma, J., Zhao, M., Liu, W., Yuille, A.L.: NDDR-CNN: layerwise feature fusing in multi-task CNNs by neural discriminative dimensionality reduction. In: Proceedings of the IEEE Conference on Computer Vision and Pattern Recognition, pp. 3205–3214 (2019)
8. Hu, H., Gu, J., Zhang, Z., Dai, J., Wei, Y.: Relation networks for object detection. In: Proceedings of the IEEE Conference on Computer Vision and Pattern Recognition, pp. 3588–3597 (2018)
9. Kendall, A., Gal, Y., Cipolla, R.: Multi-task learning using uncertainty to weigh losses for scene geometry and semantics. In: Proceedings of the IEEE Conference on Computer Vision and Pattern Recognition, pp. 7482–7491 (2018)
10. Kokkinos, I.: UberNet: training a universal convolutional neural network for low-, mid-, and high-level vision using diverse datasets and limited memory. In: Proceedings of the IEEE Conference on Computer Vision and Pattern Recognition, pp. 6129–6138 (2017)
11. Li, B., Shen, C., Dai, Y., Van Den Hengel, A., He, M.: Depth and surface normal estimation from monocular images using regression on deep features and hierarchical CRFs. In: Proceedings of the IEEE Conference on Computer Vision and Pattern Recognition, pp. 1119–1127 (2015)
12. Lin, G., Milan, A., Shen, C., Reid, I.: RefineNet: multi-path refinement networks for high-resolution semantic segmentation. In: Proceedings of the IEEE Conference on Computer Vision and Pattern Recognition, pp. 1925–1934 (2017)
13. Lin, T.Y., Dollár, P., Girshick, R., He, K., Hariharan, B., Belongie, S.: Feature pyramid networks for object detection. In: Proceedings of the IEEE Conference on Computer Vision and Pattern Recognition, pp. 2117–2125 (2017)
14. Liu, H., Simonyan, K., Yang, Y.: DARTS: differentiable architecture search. arXiv preprint arXiv:1806.09055 (2018)
15. Liu, S., Johns, E., Davison, A.J.: End-to-end multi-task learning with attention. In: Proceedings of the IEEE Conference on Computer Vision and Pattern Recognition, pp. 1871–1880 (2019)
16. Liu, Y., Sun, Y., Xue, B., Zhang, M., Yen, G.: A survey on evolutionary neural architecture search. arXiv preprint arXiv:2008.10937 (2020)
17. Long, J., Shelhamer, E., Darrell, T.: Fully convolutional networks for semantic segmentation. In: Proceedings of the IEEE Conference on Computer Vision and Pattern Recognition, pp. 3431–3440 (2015)
18. Lounici, K., Pontil, M., Tsybakov, A.B., Van De Geer, S.: Taking advantage of sparsity in multi-task learning. arXiv preprint arXiv:0903.1468 (2009)
19. Lu, Y., Kumar, A., Zhai, S., Cheng, Y., Javidi, T., Feris, R.: Fully-adaptive feature sharing in multi-task networks with applications in person attribute classification. In: Proceedings of the IEEE Conference on Computer Vision and Pattern Recognition, pp. 5334–5343 (2017)

20. Misra, I., Shrivastava, A., Gupta, A., Hebert, M.: Cross-stitch networks for multitask learning. In: Proceedings of the IEEE Conference on Computer Vision and Pattern Recognition, pp. 3994–4003 (2016)
21. Noh, H., Hong, S., Han, B.: Learning deconvolution network for semantic segmentation. In: Proceedings of the IEEE International Conference on Computer Vision, pp. 1520–1528 (2015)
22. Pham, H., Guan, M.Y., Zoph, B., Le, Q.V., Dean, J.: Efficient neural architecture search via parameter sharing. arXiv preprint arXiv:1802.03268 (2018)
23. Qi, X., Liao, R., Liu, Z., Urtasun, R., Jia, J.: GeoNet: geometric neural network for joint depth and surface normal estimation. In: Proceedings of the IEEE Conference on Computer Vision and Pattern Recognition, pp. 283–291 (2018)
24. Real, E., et al.: Large-scale evolution of image classifiers. arXiv preprint arXiv:1703.01041 (2017)
25. Ren, S., He, K., Girshick, R., Sun, J.: Faster R-CNN: towards real-time object detection with region proposal networks. In: Advances in Neural Information Processing Systems, pp. 91–99 (2015)
26. Ruder, S.: An overview of multi-task learning in deep neural networks. arXiv preprint arXiv:1706.05098 (2017)
27. Ruder, S., Bingel, J., Augenstein, I., Søgaard, A.: Learning what to share between loosely related tasks. arXiv (2017)
28. Silberman, N., Hoiem, D., Kohli, P., Fergus, R.: Indoor segmentation and support inference from RGBD images. In: Fitzgibbon, A., Lazebnik, S., Perona, P., Sato, Y., Schmid, C. (eds.) ECCV 2012. LNCS, vol. 7576, pp. 746–760. Springer, Heidelberg (2012). https://doi.org/10.1007/978-3-642-33715-4_54
29. Simonyan, K., Zisserman, A.: Very deep convolutional networks for large-scale image recognition. arXiv preprint arXiv:1409.1556 (2014)
30. Sun, Y., Xue, B., Zhang, M., Yen, G.G., Lv, J.: Automatically designing CNN architectures using the genetic algorithm for image classification. IEEE Trans. Cybern. 50, 3840–3854 (2020)
31. Thung, K.-H., Wee, C.-Y.: A brief review on multi-task learning. Multimed. Tools Appli. 77(22), 29705–29725 (2018). https://doi.org/10.1007/s11042-018-6463-x
32. Vandenhende, S., Georgoulis, S., Proesmans, M., Dai, D., Van Gool, L.: Revisiting multi-task learning in the deep learning era. arXiv preprint arXiv:2004.13379 (2020)
33. Vasconcelos, J., Ramirez, J.A., Takahashi, R., Saldanha, R.: Improvements in genetic algorithms. IEEE Trans. Magn. 37(5), 3414–3417 (2001)
34. Wang, X., Fouhey, D., Gupta, A.: Designing deep networks for surface normal estimation. In: Proceedings of the IEEE Conference on Computer Vision and Pattern Recognition, pp. 539–547 (2015)
35. Zhang, C.H., Huang, J., et al.: The sparsity and bias of the lasso selection in high-dimensional linear regression. Ann. Stat. 36(4), 1567–1594 (2008)
36. Zhang, Z., Luo, P., Loy, C.C., Tang, X.: Facial landmark detection by deep multitask learning. In: Fleet, D., Pajdla, T., Schiele, B., Tuytelaars, T. (eds.) ECCV 2014. LNCS, vol. 8694, pp. 94–108. Springer, Cham (2014). https://doi.org/10.1007/978-3-319-10599-4_7
37. Zoph, B., Le, Q.V.: Neural architecture search with reinforcement learning. arXiv preprint arXiv:1611.01578 (2016)
38. Zoph, B., Vasudevan, V., Shlens, J., Le, Q.V.: Learning transferable architectures for scalable image recognition. In: Proceedings of the IEEE Conference on Computer Vision and Pattern Recognition, pp. 8697–8710 (2018)

An Embedding Carrier-Free Steganography Method Based on Wasserstein GAN

Xi Yu[1], Jianming Cui[1], and Ming Liu[2(✉)]

[1] Chang'an University, Xi'an 710064, Shaanxi, China
`cjianming@chd.edu.cn`
[2] National Computer Network Emergency Response Technical Team/Coordination Center of China, Beijing 100029, China
`liuming@cert.org.cn`

Abstract. Image has been widely studied as an effective carrier of information steganography, however, low steganographic capacity is a technical problem that has not been solved in non-embedded steganography methods. In this paper, we proposed a carrier-free steganography method based on Wasserstein GAN. We segmented the target information and input it into the trained Wasserstein GAN, and then generated the visual-real image. The core design is that the output results are converted into images in the trained network according to the mapping relationship between preset coding information and random noise. The experimental results indicated that the proposed method can effectively improve the ability of steganography. In addition, the results also testified that the proposed method does not depend on the complex neural network structure. On this basis, we further proved that by changing the length of noise and the mapping relationships between coding information and noise, the number of generated images can be reduced, and the steganography ability and efficiency of the algorithm can be improved.

Keywords: Information hiding · Wasserstein GAN · Steganographic algorithm · Steganographic capacity · Carrier-free steganography

1   Introduction

Information steganography has become one of the research fields that attracts lots of attention and develops rapidly at present. Since the image has abundant redundant space and learning-based related processing tools, image has become a popular carrier. The typical image-based information steganography approaches include spatial domain and transformation domain. The former one realizes steganography by directly changing some bits of the image pixels, such as Least

This work was supported in part by the National Natural Science Foundation of China under Grant U2003206 and 62106060; and in part by the Natural Science Base Research Plan in Shaanxi Province of China under Grant 2018JM6103.

Y. Lai et al. (Eds.): ICA3PP 2021, LNCS 13156, pp. 532–545, 2022.
https://doi.org/10.1007/978-3-030-95388-1_35

Significant Bit (LSB) [1], adaptive LSB [2], Spatial-UNIversal WAvelet Relative Distortion (S-UNIWARD) [3], Highly Undetectable steganography (HUGO) [4] and Wavelet Obtained Weights (WOW) [5], etc. Transform domain methods such as Discrete Fourier Transform (DFT) [6], Discrete Cosine Transform (DCT) [7] and Discrete Wavelet Transform (DWT) [8], etc. However, there are still some technical issues to be solved in the detection resistance and usable capacity.

A typical approach of carrier-free information steganography refers to the direct use of Generative Adversarial Networks (GAN) to re-encode specific information and generate normal images without using additional carriers [13]. Liu proposed a carrier-free information steganography method based on Auxiliary Classifier GAN (ACGAN), which took encoded information and noise as input to the generator and then generated camouflaged images [9]. Based on Deep Convolutional GAN (DCGAN), Hu mapped the specific information into noise and inputs it into the generator, and then generated the steganographic image [10]. Zhang attempted to improve the quality of steganographic image based on coding and decoding structure by using the Boundary Equilibrium GAN (BEGAN). It was the first time to evaluate the quality of steganographic image [11]. However, the disadvantages of the aforementioned methods are of the debased image quality and low steganographic capacity.

Spatial steganography is a method that directly in spatial domain, such as hiding specific information behind pixels of a normal image [18]. Transformational steganography is to perform overlay synthesis, such as using neural network as encoder and transform specific information into feature space for information hiding, and one of the main advantages is there almost has no image distortion of the outputs [9,10,18–21]. However, it should be noted that the quality of steganography image completely depends on the structure of neural network and corresponding optimization methods. Coverless image steganography is a updated version of transformational steganography. Bag of Words model (BOW) is a widely used coverless image steganography method, which defines a set of atomic meta images associated with specific information and implements information steganography according to the mapping relationship [22,23]. The limitation of this method is that the atomic meta images and the corresponding mapping relationship need to be defined in advance, so there are certain application restrictions. Other methods include robust image hashing based steganography [24], custom texture synthesis based steganography [25], reversible texture synthesis steganography [26], etc. However, there is still a big gap between the above methods and the traditional steganography methods in performance, and the low steganography capacity is one of the important problems. The capacity of carrier-based information steganography is shown in Table 1.

In this paper, we proposed an improved carrier-free information steganography method based on Wasserstein GAN [12]. First we established a mapping relationships between the specific information binary bit stream and the Gaussian noise and extended the mapping intervals from two to four. Therefore, the capacity of embedded information is increased by two times under the same length of noise input. Then, in the steganography process, the influence of input noise length on steganography capacity and steganography efficiency is analyzed

Table 1. Capacities of various carrier-based methods.

Reference	Image size	Absolute capacity	Relative capacity
[9]	32×32	0.375	3.70e$-$4
[10]	64×64	$\geq$37.5	9.16e$-$3
[18]	64×64	18.3–135.4	1.49e$-$3–1.10e$-$2
[22]	$\geq$512 $\times$ 512	3.72	1.42e$-$5
[23]	512×512	1.125	4.29e$-$6
[24]	512×512	2.25	8.58e$-$6
[25]	800×800	1.73	6.40e$-$3
[26]	1024×1024	1535–4300	1.46e$-$3–4.10e$-$3

by setting input noises of different lengths. Finally, the experimental results verified that the steganographic capacity can be effectively improved, and the number of steganographic images can be reduced by modifying the noise length of the generator and the mapping relationships.

2   WGAN-Based Information Steganography Method

The main framework of the improved WGAN-based information steganography method is shown in Fig. 1. In this framework, specific information s is transformed into noise z according to the predetermined mapping relationship. Then z is inputted into trained WGAN and the images Stegos that contain s are generated.

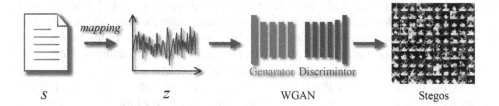

Fig. 1. WGAN-based Steganography process.

2.1   Wasserstein GAN

Gradient disappearance is a common problem in GAN training. In order to solve this problem, Arjovsky proposed Wasserstein GAN (WGAN) [12]. It adopted Wasserstein distance also named Earth-Mover (EM) distance instead of JS divergence to measure the distance between the distribution of the real sample and the generated sample. Wasserstein distance is expressed as follows:

$$W(P_r, P_g) = \inf_{\gamma \sim \Pi(P_r, P_g)} E_{(x,y) \sim \gamma} ||x - y|| \tag{1}$$

In a high-dimensional space, if the overlap between this two distributions can be neglected, KL and JS would lose efficacy. But the Wasserstein distance is smoother and can still reflect their distances, thereby providing meaningful gradients. Because $\inf_{\gamma \sim \Pi(P_r, P_g)}$ in the definition of Wasserstein distance Eq. 1 is difficult to calculate, it can be written as:

$$W(P_r, P_g) = \frac{1}{k} \sup_{||f||_L \leq k} E_{x \sim P_r}[f(x)] - E_{x \sim P_g}[f(x)] \tag{2}$$

First of all, Lipschitz continuity is to impose an additional restriction on a continuous function f, which requires the existence of a constant $K \geqslant 0$. And any two elements x_1 and x_2 in the domain should satisfy $| f(x_1) - f(x_2) | \leqslant K | x_1 - x_2 |$. In this case, the Lipschitz constant of function f is called K. Wasserstein distance actually needs to consider all 1-Lipschitz functions. If the K-Lipschitz function [14] is considered, the Wasserstein distance becomes K times the original. Generally, it can be assumed that the discriminator D of GAN is a K-Lipschitz function, and the optimized discriminator D is actually looking for a suitable function (parameters of is ω) on a certain K-Lipschitz function set $\{f_\omega\}_{\omega \in W}$ [15]. Equation 2 expresses that under the condition of Lipschitz constant $||f||_L$ of function f does not exceed K, for taking the upper bound of $E_{x \sim P_r}[f(x)] - E_{x \sim P_g}[f(x)]$ for all that may satisfy the condition, and then divide by K. In particular, a set of parameters ω can be used to define a series of possible functions f, where Eq. 2 can be approximately as shown in Eq. 3 below.

$$K \cdot W(P_r, P_g) = \max_{\omega:|f_\omega|_L \leq K} E_{x \sim P_r}[f_\omega(x)] - E_{x \sim P_g}[f_\omega(x)] \tag{3}$$

Therefore, a discriminator network f_ω with parameter ω and the last layer is not a nonlinear active layer can be constructed. Under the condition that the parameter does not exceed a certain range, Eq. 4 can be maximized as much as possible. Then, the Wasserstein distance can be approximated (ignoring the constant multiple K). Under this approximate optimal discriminator, reducing the Wasserstein distance to optimize the generator. This can effectively reduce the distribution of generated data and real data. The loss functions of generator G and discriminator D are shown in Eq. 5 and Eq. 6.

$$L = E_{x \sim P_r}[f_\omega(x)] - E_{x \sim P_g}[f_\omega(x)] \tag{4}$$

$$V_G(G, D) = -E_{x \sim P_g}[f - \omega(x)] \tag{5}$$

$$V_G(G, D) = E_{x \sim P_g}[f - \omega(x)] - E_{x \sim P_r}[f_\omega(x)] \tag{6}$$

2.2 Mapping Relationships

Reference [10] proposed for the first time the establishment of a mapping relationship. However, the paper does not give a specific interval for the mapping relationship. It is determined based on different information lengths. In addition,

Reference [10] does not analyze the influence of the mapping relationship and the length of the input noise on the steganographic capacity. In this paper, the mapping relationship between s and z is updated. The one to one relationship between the original binary information value and noise is updated to two to one, which makes the noise interval divided into four intervals. Under the same noise length, the corresponding information length is two times of the original method. Since the input of generator G is $(-1, 1)$ random noise, it is necessary to map binary specific information to $(-1, 1)$. The mapping relationship designed in this paper takes every two bits of binary data as a group and maps it to a random noise value. The mapping relation is shown in Table 2.

Table 2. Binary data and noise mapping relationship.

Binary data	Noise range
00	random$(-1, -0.5)$
01	random$(-0.5, 0)$
10	random$(0, 0.5)$
11	random$(0.5, 1)$

- If the mapping relationship between binary information value and noise value is many to one, it makes the noise interval partition more intensive, and it is difficult to guarantee the randomness of noise value.
- Without changing the length of information, the number of noise vectors will be reduced due to the many to one mapping relationship. At this time, the quality and authenticity of the image generated by this noise driven generator is very low. And it is easy to distinguish from the real image.
- With the increase of the amount of information corresponding to the noise value, it will be a difficult problem for the receiver to extract information, the computational complexity will increase, and the extraction accuracy will be greatly reduced.

The mapping process is shown in Fig. 2, the binary specific information s is segmented according to the specified number of bits. If the number of bits in the last segment is insufficient, the remaining number of bits is filled with '0' to obtain $s = \{s_1, s_2, ..., s_n\}$. Each piece of binary specific information s_i corresponds to the noise z_i on $(-1, 1)$ according to the mapping relationship in Table 2. Then, connecting all the noise fragments z_i to get the input noise z. The noise z is used as the input of the WGAN model generator G, and the image with steganographic information is output.

2.3   Network Building

As shown in Fig. 3(a), the network structure of generator G consists of a fully connected layer and four deconvolution layers. The input of the generator G is

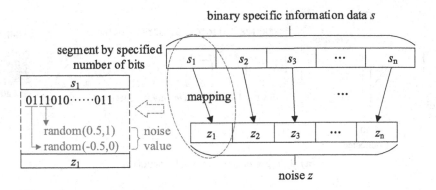

Fig. 2. Information stenographic mapping process.

random noise with a tensor of 1×128. The first layer is a fully connected layer, using the LeakyRelu activation function, and reshaping the shape to $8 \times 8 \times 256$. The size of the convolution kernel of the four deconvolution layers is 5×5. The first deconvolution stride is 1, and the other three layers are 2. The first three deconvolution layers use LeakyRelu as the activation function. The last deconvolution layer uses Tanh as the activation function. The output image shape is $64 \times 64 \times 3$.

As shown in Fig. 3(b), the network structure of the discriminator D consists of four convolutional layers and two fully connected layers. The input of the discriminator D is composed of real images and $64 \times 64 \times 3$ images generated by the generator G. The size of the convolution kernel of the four convolution layers are 5×5. The strides are 2. And the activation function of each layer is LeakyRelu. The $4 \times 4 \times 256$ tensor output by the four convolutional layers obtains 256 scalars through Global Average Pooling and enters the fully connected layer with 1024 neurons. After the fully connected layer, the BN (Batch Normalization) layer is added to speed up the convergence of the discriminator, and LeakyRelu is used as the activation function. Finally, '1' or '0' is output through the fully connected layer.

2.4 Carrier-Free Information Steganography

The processing of steganography is shown in Fig. 4. During the process of non-carrier image steganography, there are two stages: training carrier image generation model G and steganography. In the first stage, we need to train generator G of WGAN. When the parameter training of generator G is fixed, we can use generator G to convert the specific information into the steganographic image. In the second stage, specific information s is mapped to noise z. The noise z is used as the input of the generator G to generate a steganographic image.

The carrier-free image steganography method based on WGAN refers to the process of generating the steganographic image using the generator G of WGAN. The steganography algorithm is shown in Algorithm 1. The training stable

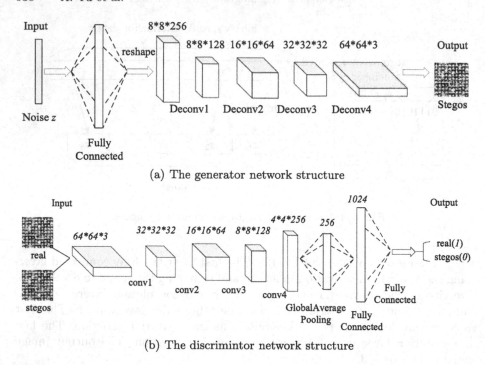

(a) The generator network structure

(b) The discrimintor network structure

Fig. 3. Instantiated WGAN network structure.

generation model G can generate the steganographic image *stego* driven by the specific information s. According to the segment number b, the specific information is divided into n segments $n = [length(s)/b]$, and $s\{s_1, s_2, ..., s_n\}$ is obtained. Depending on the mapping relationship defined in Table 2, every two bits of the specific information s_i are mapped into a noise value r. Then, $z\{z_1, z_2, ..., z_n\}$ is used as the input of the generating model to generate the steganographic image *stego* in turn. Finally, n steganographic images are generated according to the length of the specific information.

3   Experiments and Results

This experiment uses the Anime Faces cartoon avatar dataset as the real sample dataset, which contains a total of 21551 images. The input noise of WGAN generator G is 1×100. The output image size is 64×64. And the learning rate is $5e - 5$. The effect of 1000 rounds of WGAN model training is shown in Fig. 5. The 100th round of training gradually appeared cartoon head profile visible to the naked eye. And the 300th round began to output the overall effect of the image is better than before. There is no obvious change from the 500th to 1000th round images, but it can be seen that the latter is more detailed than former. The experimental platform is Google's deep learning platform Tensorflow v2.3.0. And the computing graphics card is NVIDIA Quadro P4000.

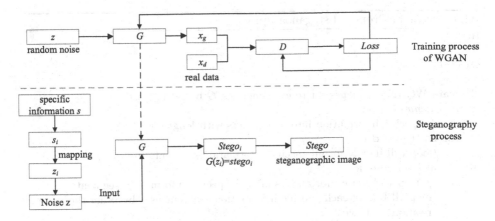

Fig. 4. The steganography process.

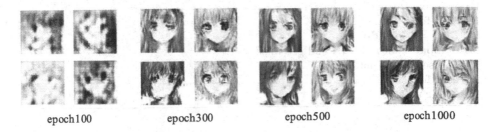

epoch100   epoch300   epoch500   epoch1000

Fig. 5. WGAN model training effect diagram.

As shown in Fig. 6, when the WGAN model is trained to 800 rounds, the loss functions of the generator and discriminator tend to be stable. When the WGAN model is trained to 1000 rounds, the loss functions of the generator and discriminator are basically stable, and there is no obvious difference in the visual image. Then the convergent WGAN model is used to input 100×100 noise vectors to test the training effect. And the result is shown in Fig. 7.

3.1 Steganographic Capacity

Steganography capacity refers to the size of specific information s that can be embedded into the generated image. This paper used the relationship between the size of the specific information contained in each image and the size of the steganographic image to measure the steganography capacity of different steganography algorithms. In Eq. 7, $capacity$ denotes the steganographic capacity of each steganographic image. B denotes the size of specific information contained in each steganographic image (unit: bit). And P denotes the size of each steganographic image (unit: piexl).

$$capacity = \frac{B}{P} \tag{7}$$

Algorithm 1. Propoesd steganography

Input:
  s, b;
Output:
  $stego$;
1: train WGAN on images set to get generator G by using Eq. 6;
2: $n = [length(s)/b]$;
3: divide specific information into n segments with length b;
4: **for** $i = 1$ to n **do**
5:    //loop will iterate for all specific information segments from i to n;
6:    **for** $j = 1$ to b **do**
7:       //loop will iterate for all bits of each specific information segment;
8:       map all bits of each specific information segment as r by using the mapping relation in Table 2;
9:       insert r to z_i;
10:    **end for**
11:    insert z_i to z;
12: **end for**
13: **for** $i = 1$ to n **do**
14:    input z_i into WGAN and get $stego_i = G(z_i)$;
15:    insert $stego_i$ into $stego$;
16: **end for**
17: **return** $stego$;

The steganography algorithm proposed in this paper was to generate a steganographic image with a size of 64×64 from the WGAN model. The input noise size of the generator was 1×100 and 1×128 . Since the model in this paper used every two bits of specific information to map a noise value, the specific information contained in each image generated by the generator was 200 bit and 256 bit. The steganographic capacity was 4.88×10^{-2} bit/pixel and 6.25×10^{-2} bit/pixel calculated according to Eq. 7.

As shown in Fig. 8(a), it describes the length of the secret information contained in the steganographic images corresponding to different methods. Figure 8(b) describes the steganographic capacity corresponding to different methods. The input noise length of the model DCGAN in Reference [10] is $1\,times\,100$. The input noise length of the model BEGAN in Reference [11] is $1\,times\,128$. WGAN-1 indicates that the input noise is 1×100. WGAN-2 indicates that the input noise is 1×128.

When the mapping relationship is consistent with the output image size, BEGAN has a higher steganographic capacity of 0.69×10^{-2} bit/pixel than DCGAN, and WGAN-2 has a higher steganographic capacity of 1.37×10^{-2} bit/pixel than WGAN-1. This proves that when the output image size is consistent with the mapping relationship, changing the input noise length can increase the steganography capacity of each dense image. When the input noise length is the same as the output image size, the steganographic capacity of WGAN-1 is 2.44×10^{-2} bit/pixel higher than that of DCGAN. The steganographic capacity of WGAN-2 is 3.12×10^{-2} bit/pixel higher than that of BEGAN. It can

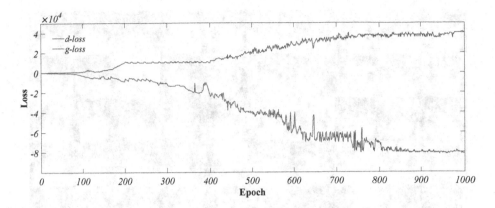

Fig. 6. The training loss of WGAN model.

be proved that when the output noise length is the same as the output image size, changing the mapping relationship between the hidden information and the noise can effectively increase the steganographic capacity. The steganographic capacity of WGAN-2 is 3.81×10^{-2} bit/pixel higher than that of DCGAN. This proves that when the size of the output steganographic image is the same, changing the input noise length of the model generator and the mapping relationship between specific information and noise greatly increase the size of the specific information contained in each steganographic image. In summary, changing the input noise length and the mapping relationship can increase the steganographic capacity.

3.2 Analysis of Indistinguishability

This experiment used the indistinguishability of the model [16] to measure the security of the model. For the security of steganography algorithm, Fridrich [17] takes the KL divergence between the carrier and the distribution of the steganographic image as the criterion to determine whether the carrier and the steganographic carrier are indistinguishable. In this paper, the classification accuracy between the steganographic image generated by generator G and the real sample image is used as the criterion to determine whether they are indistinguishable. The classified steganographic images generated by WGAN model and sample images are classified to analyze the classification accuracy.

This experiment tested the indistinguishability between the steganographic image and the real image data generated by different generator input noise. In this experiment, convolutional neural network was used for classification. The sample image generated by WGAN generator was used as the training set of the classifier for training. The steganographic image generated is used as the test set for testing. In the case of different input noise dimensions, the classification accuracy is shown in Fig. 9. When steps are 500, the classification accuracy of 1×100 and 1×128 noise dimensions is 19.67% and 29.97%. Therefore, it is difficult to distinguish the steganographic image in the sample image. The result proves

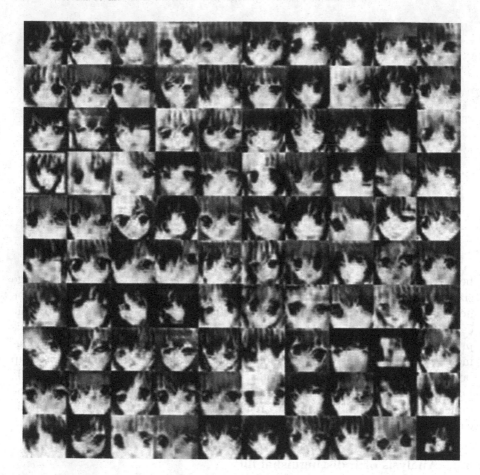

Fig. 7. The output image when WGAN converges.

that the steganographic image generated by this model is indistinguishable. In addition, in the same steps, the classification accuracy of the 1×100 noise dimension is lower than that of the 1×128 noise dimension, which indicates that the noise length will affect the classification accuracy of the steganographic image. The longer the noise length is, the higher the classification accuracy of the steganographic image is. Consequently, the smaller the size of the specific information contained in each steganographic image is, the more difficult it is to generate the steganographic image from the true image. It is proved that the proposed steganography model has the ability to resist steganography attacks and meets the security of steganography algorithm.

3.3 Time Analysis

In the steganography process, the binary specific information data with a length of 1000 bits was selected for steganography. As shown in Fig. 10(a) and Fig. 10(b),

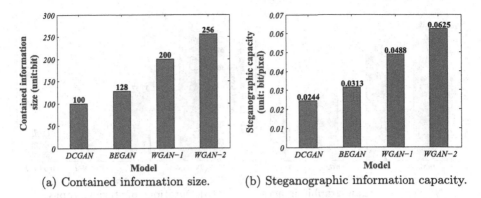

(a) Contained information size.   (b) Steganographic information capacity.

Fig. 8. Result comparisons of steganographic images.

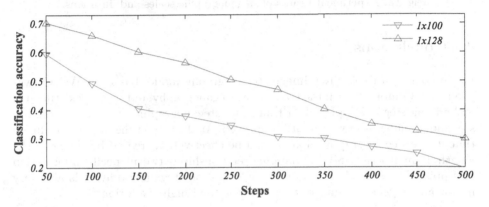

Fig. 9. Classification accuracy under different input noise size.

DCGAN steganography in Reference [10] needed to generate 10 secret images, and BEGAN in Reference [11] needed to generate 8 secret images. The steganographic times of the two models in Reference [10] and Reference [11] were 71.69 s and 37.47 s. In this paper, when the input noise length was 1×100, the steganography method generated 5 secret images and the steganography took 15.24 s. And when the input noise length was 1×128, it generated 4 secret images and the steganography took 13.67 s.

The steganography time of the steganography model in this paper was less than that of Reference [10] and Reference [11]. When the steganographic capacity of a single picture increases, the number of secret images embedded in the steganographic information will decrease, and the steganographic time required by the steganographic algorithm will decrease accordingly. So in terms of steganographic time complexity, the WGAN model proposed in this paper was better than the above two models.

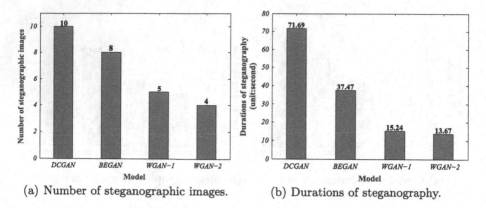

(a) Number of steganographic images.   (b) Durations of steganography.

Fig. 10. Experiment results of steganographic scales and durations.

4   Conclusions

In this paper, a carrier-free image steganography model based on WGAN was proposed. Compared with the traditional steganography and several existing non embedding steganography algorithms, the steganographic capacity of a single steganographic image was greatly improved. At the same time, it was concluded that image steganography capacity can be effectively increased by changing the length of input noise and the mapping relationship between specific information and noise. In the field of carrier-free information steganography, it is also very important to generate images with diversity and high resolution.

References

1. Tirkel, A.Z., et al.: Electronic watermark. In: Digital Image Computing, Technology and Applications, DICTA 1993, pp. 666–673 (1993)
2. Yang, C.-H., et al.: Adaptive data hiding in edge areas of images with spatial LSB domain systems. IEEE Trans. Inf. Forensics Secur. **3**(3), 488–497 (2008)
3. Holub, V., Fridrich, J., Denemark, T.: Universal distortion function for steganography in an arbitrary domain. EURASIP J. Inf. Secur. **2014**(1), 1–13 (2014). https:// doi.org/10.1186/1687-417X-2014-1
4. Pevný, T., Filler, T., Bas, P.: Using high-dimensional image models to perform highly undetectable steganography. In: Böhme, R., Fong, P.W.L., Safavi-Naini, R. (eds.) IH 2010. LNCS, vol. 6387, pp. 161–177. Springer, Heidelberg (2010). https:// doi.org/10.1007/978-3-642-16435-4_13
5. Holub, V., Fridrich, J.: Designing steganographic distortion using directional filters. In: 2012 IEEE International Workshop on Information Forensics and Security (WIFS). IEEE (2012)
6. Ruanaidh, J.J.K.O., Dowling, W.J., Boland, F.M.: Phase watermarking of digital images. In: Proceedings of 3rd IEEE International Conference on Image Processing, vol. 3. IEEE (1996)

7. Cox, I.J., et al.: Secure spread spectrum watermarking for multimedia. IEEE Trans. Image Process. **6**(12), 1673–1687 (1997)
8. Lin, W.-H., et al.: An efficient watermarking method based on significant difference of wavelet coefficient quantization. IEEE Trans. Multimedia **10**(5), 746–757 (2008)
9. Liu, M., et al.: Coverless information hiding based on generative adversarial networks. arXiv preprint arXiv:1712.06951 (2017)
10. Hu, D., et al.: A novel image steganography method via deep convolutional generative adversarial networks. IEEE Access **6**, 38303–38314 (2018)
11. Zhang, M., et al.: Generative steganography based on boundary equilibrium generative adversarial network. J. Zhengzhou Univ. Nat. Sci. Edn. **52**(3), 34–41 (2020)
12. Arjovsky, M., Chintala, S., Bottou, L.: Wasserstein generative adversarial networks. In: International Conference on Machine Learning. PMLR (2017)
13. Goodfellow, I.J., et al.: Generative adversarial networks. arXiv preprint arXiv:1406.2661 (2014)
14. Cui, S., Jiang, Y.: Effective Lipschitz constraint enforcement for Wasserstein GAN training. In: 2017 2nd IEEE International Conference on Computational Intelligence and Applications (ICCIA). IEEE (2017)
15. Wang, Y., Niu, K., Yang, X.: Image steganography scheme based on GANs. Netinfo Secur. **19**(5), 54 (2019)
16. Fridrich, J., Kodovsky, J.: Rich models for steganalysis of digital images. IEEE Trans. Inf. Forensics Secur. **7**(3), 868–882 (2012)
17. Fridrich, J.: Steganography in Digital Media: Principles, Algorithms, and Applications. Cambridge University Press (2009)
18. Zhang, Z., et al.: Generative steganography by sampling. IEEE Access **7**, 118586–118597 (2019)
19. Tancik, M., Mildenhall, B., Ng, R.: StegaStamp: invisible hyperlinks in physical photographs. In: Proceedings of the IEEE/CVF Conference on Computer Vision and Pattern Recognition (2020)
20. Hayes, J., Danezis, G.: Generating steganographic images via adversarial training. arXiv preprint arXiv:1703.00371 (2017)
21. Li, J., et al.: A generative steganography method based on WGAN-GP. In: Sun, X., Wang, J., Bertino, E. (eds.) ICAIS 2020. CCIS, vol. 1252, pp. 386–397. Springer, Singapore (2020). https://doi.org/10.1007/978-981-15-8083-3_34
22. Zhou, Z.L., Cao, Y., Sun, X.M.: Coverless information hiding based on bag-of-words model of image. J. Appl. Sci. **34**(5), 527–536 (2016)
23. Zhou, Z., Sun, H., Harit, R., Chen, X., Sun, X.: Coverless image steganography without embedding. In: Huang, Z., Sun, X., Luo, J., Wang, J. (eds.) ICCCS 2015. LNCS, vol. 9483, pp. 123–132. Springer, Cham (2015). https://doi.org/10.1007/978-3-319-27051-7_11
24. Zheng, S., Wang, L., Ling, B., Hu, D.: Coverless information hiding based on robust image hashing. In: Huang, D.-S., Hussain, A., Han, K., Gromiha, M.M. (eds.) ICIC 2017. LNCS (LNAI), vol. 10363, pp. 536–547. Springer, Cham (2017). https://doi.org/10.1007/978-3-319-63315-2_47
25. Xu, J., et al.: Hidden message in a deformation-based texture. Vis. Comput. **31**(12), 1653–1669 (2014). https://doi.org/10.1007/s00371-014-1045-z
26. Wu, K.-C., Wang, C.-M.: Steganography using reversible texture synthesis. IEEE Trans. Image Process. **24**(1), 130–139 (2014)

Design of Face Detection Algorithm Accelerator Based on Vitis

Jie Wang[1,2(✉)] ⓘD, Ao Gao[1,2], and Jingxin Li[1,2]

[1] School of Software Technology, Dalian University of Technology, Dalian, China
wang_jie@dlut.edu.cn
[2] Key Laboratory for Ubiquitous Network and Service Software of Liaoning Province, Dalian, China

Abstract. With the development of artificial intelligence, Machine learning based FPGA (Field Programmable Gate Array) is becoming more and more important, Compared with CPU and GPU, FPGA has the advantages of reconfigurability, low power consumption and high performance of parallel computing. Due to the complexity of FPGA development process. This can be said to be the biggest obstacle for FPGA to be widely used in the field of artificial intelligence. In this paper, the FPGA accelerator is designed by a concise computation framework. This development method shortens the development time. And the accelerator built in this paper detection speed is 9 times that of CPU. The detection power consumption is about 0.1 times that of GPU.

Keywords: Face detection · FPGA · Vitis · Deep learning · Hardware acceleration

1 Introduction

From the development history of CPU, we can know that it has always been a general processor to handle all tasks, so the efficiency of CPU in the field of artificial intelligence is very low. Although GPU has strong computing power, the huge power consumption of GPU makes it limited in some application scenarios. Therefore, FPGA plays an important role in some special scenarios. FPGA offer many advantages over traditional CPU/GPU acceleration, including a custom architecture capable of implementing any function that can run on a processor, resulting in better performance at lower power dissipation. In 2017, Aysegul Dundar et al. proposed an accelerator optimization technology, which can reach more than 240G-ops on the premise of power consumption less than 4 W [1].

In the past, due to the complexity of FPGA development process, it is very difficult for software scholars to study. And artificial intelligence is applied more and more in our daily life. Under the influence of the field of intelligent vehicles, emerging fields such as wireless rechargeable sensor networks [2–6] and secure big data [7] and embedded intelligence (EI) [8–10] are also booming.

This paper uses Vitis to simplify the hardware development process. The FPGA accelerator of RetinaFace [11] algorithm was soon designed. The experimental results show that the accelerator detection speed is about 9 times that of CPU. The detection power consumption is about 0.1 times that of GPU.

© Springer Nature Switzerland AG 2022
Y. Lai et al. (Eds.): ICA3PP 2021, LNCS 13156, pp. 546–554, 2022.
https://doi.org/10.1007/978-3-030-95388-1_36

2 Hardware Platform Construction

2.1 DPU (Deep Learning Processor Unit)

DPU is a programmable engine optimized for convolutional neural networks, which is applied to FPGA. It is composed of a high performance scheduler module, a hybrid computing array module, an instruction fetch unit module and a global memory pool module. The DPU uses a specialized instruction set, which allows for the efficient implementation of many convolutional neural networks. DPU Hardware Architecture is shown in the Fig. 1.

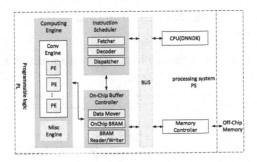

Fig. 1. DPU hardware architecture.

2.2 Vitis Hardware Image Construction

The Vitis unified software platform enables the development of embedded software and accelerated applications on heterogeneous Xilinx platforms including FPGAs, SoCs, and Versal ACAPs. It provides a unified programming model for accelerating Edge, Cloud, and Hybrid computing applications.

Design hardware platform through Vitis. Then build the hardware platform. This process takes about an hour. After successful build, a Vivado [12] project will be generated and also create the SD card image file. Figure 2 mainly shows the core structure design of Vivado. Zynq ultrascale+MPSoC is the core processing system. AXI Interconnect is the interface manager of AXI bus. It can connect one or more AXI memory mapping master devices and slave devices. Processor System Reset is a reset module used to generate a high reset valid signal and a low reset valid signal. Clocking Wizard is the clock manager. Its main function is to generate clock signals. AXI Verification is mainly used in the simulation phase. During simulation, it can be used to help the simulation of AXI4, AXI4-Lite, etc. AXI Register Slice is used to improve the timing and enable the bus to reach a higher frequency. However, each slice will introduce delay. Therefore, this IP module mainly makes a trade-off between the maximum operation frequency and the delay cycle.

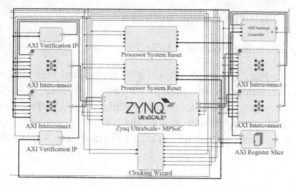

Fig. 2. Core hardware structure.

Three DPU structures are connected to the hardware structure in Fig. 3.

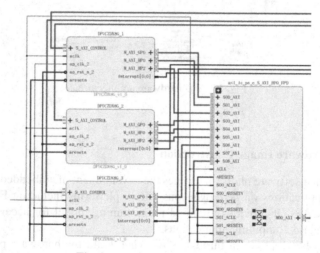

Fig. 3. DPU hardware connection.

3 DF-RetinaFace

RetinaFace is an efficient and high-precision face detection algorithm just published in May 2019.It is a face detection algorithm based on RetinaNet [13]. Compared with the traditional target classification and frame prediction face detection algorithms [14–18], RetinaFace adds two other parallel branch tasks. One of them is five human face key point (landmark) detection and the other is dense 3D face prediction.

Lin et al. [19] pointed out that in the process of extracting feature information from deep neural network, the shallow network is closer to the input picture data, so the detailed information is richer and the extracted location information is more accurate.

And the deep network is farther from the input picture data, which can extract more abstract semantic information, the resolution is better, but the detection position will deviate.

The improved method in this paper is to change the single FPN structure into double FPN. The original FPN network structure is from top to bottom, so that the shallow layer feature information and deep layer information are accumulated, and the shallow layer obtains more feature information. However, at this time, the overall FPN structure only includes the path from deep layer to shallow layer (as shown in Fig. 4a). The deep layer information is lost due to multiple down sampling and convolution operations, In order to make the deep layer contain more shallow feature information, this paper adds a reverse bottom-up FPN connection (as shown in Fig. 4b). This method was first proposed by Liu et al. [20] in 2018. After improvement, only the information of shallow C2 in the six-layer structure is transmitted to N5, which fully shortens the path, Compared with the 39 layers of the original structure, the path is shortened by 5.5 times, thus reducing the loss of location information.

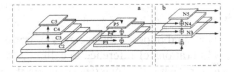

Fig. 4. The architecture of double feature pyramid network.

The data show that DF-RetinaFace in this paper has significantly improved the face detection effect of easy level and medium level in the WiderFace data set. Among them, the hard level AP value of MobileNetV1-0.25 backbone has increased by 0.16%, the medium level AP value has increased by 0.78% and the easy level AP value has increased by 1.56%. The hard level AP value of resnet50 backbone remains almost unchanged, the easy level AP value has increased by 0.89% and the medium level AP value has increased by 0.41% (See Table 1).

Table 1. The results of network structure optimization.

Network structure	Size	Easy	Medium	Hard
ResNet50+FPN+SSH	105 MB	94.19%	93.21%	83.53%
ResNet50+2FPN+SSH	119 MB	95.08%	93.62%	83.52%
MobileNetV1-0.25+FPN+SSH	2.02 MB	90.56%	87.96%	72.79%
MobileNetV1-0.25+2FPN+SSH	3.1 MB	92.12%	88.74%	72.95%

4   Transfer Model

4.1   Frozen Model

Freezing prevents the weights of a neural network layer from being modified during the backward pass of training. Ensure that the graph is the inference graph rather than the training graph before quantization.

4.2   Model Quantization

Generally, 32-bit floating-point weights and activation values are used when training neural networks. By converting the 32-bit floating-point weights and activations to 8-bit integer (INT8) format, the Vitis AI quantizer can reduce computing complexity without losing prediction accuracy. The fixed-point network model requires less memory bandwidth, thus providing faster speed and higher power efficiency than the floating-point model. The Vitis AI quantizer supports common layers in neural networks, including but not limited to, Convolution, Pooling, Fully Connected and BatchNorm.

4.3   Generation Model

To capture activation statistics and improve the accuracy of transfer model, the Vitis AI quantizer must run several iterations of inference to calibrate the activations. Vitis AI provides tensorflow quantizer. Using the quantizer requires the preparation of frozen models, calibration data sets, and a processing python script input_fn. Generally, the quantizer works well with 100–1000 calibration images. Because there is no need for back propagation, the un-labeled dataset is sufficient. After calibration, the quantized model is transformed into a DPU deployable model which follows the data format of the DPU. Finally, through VAI_C (Vitis AI Compiler) compiles the model to generate elf files that can run on DPU. The process is shown in Fig. 5 below.

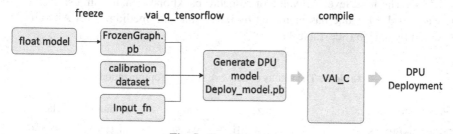

Fig. 5. Transfer process.

5   Deploy Model and Result Analysis

5.1   Deploy Model and Get Results

The FPGA used in this paper is Xilinx zynq ultrascale+MPSoC zcu102 board. Before deployment, burn the image into the SD card. Then Insert the SD card into the development board slot and connect the power supply and network cable, as shown in Fig. 6

Log in to the development board in SSH mode, and copy the transfer model to the development board. Finally, write a python script to run the model accelerator.

Fig. 6. Schematic diagram of FPGA connection.

The following is a picture of the detection results in the Fig. 7.

Fig. 7. Detection result.

5.2 Comparative Analysis of Experimental Results

Table 2 shows the performance of ResNet50 backbone model on different platforms.

Table 2. Results of different test platforms.

Platform	Detection speed	Power waste
CPU(Intel Core i5)	58.3 ms	20 W
GPU(Nvidia GTX 1060)	5.8 ms	65 W
FPGA(Xilinx ZCU 102)	6.6 ms	6 W

Table 3 shows the comparison between the work of this paper and that of others. The meanings of the parameters in Table 3 are as follows. FPGA: Model of development board. Frequency: Hardware operating frequency. Weight accuracy: Bit width of model weight. GOP: Detect the number of operations such as addition and multiplication of a picture. Accuracy loss: Accuracy loss range after acceleration. Speed: Time to detect a picture. GOPS: The number of operations such as addition and multiplication per second. DF-Reinaface1: The network with MobileNetV1-0.25 as the backbone. DF-Reinaface2: The network with ResNet50 as the backbone. The data show that the DF-RetinaFace model ensures that the prediction accuracy will not be reduced and the prediction speed will be improved under the condition of lower weight accuracy and less memory resources.

Table 3. Data comparison of different methods.

	DF-Reinaface1	DF-Reinaface2	ResNet50 [21]	ResNet50 [22]	MbleNetV1 [23]
FPGA	ZCU102	ZCU102	GX1150	GX2800	XCK325T
Frequency	300 MHz	300 MHz	200 MHz	300 MHz	200 MHz
Weight accuracy	8 bit	8 bit	16 bit	16 bit	8 bit
GOP	0.3	10	7.7	7.7	–
Accuracy loss	<1%	<1%	<2%	–	–
Speed	1.6 ms	6.6 ms	13 ms	11.85 ms	3.78 ms
GOPS	**187.5**	**1506.2**	611.4	651.5	147.9

6 Conclusion

In this paper, the model is trained with tensorflow2. Then use the official quantitative tools to quantify and fine tune the model. At the same time, Vitis is used to design and generate an image, and burn the image into the development board. Finally, deploy the model to the development board to run the accelerator. This computation framework has good scalability, if you want to replace the algorithm, you only need to change the transfer model.

FPGA has great potential in the field of artificial intelligence. There are still many optimization methods in hardware design, which will be studied in the future.

Acknowledgment. National Key Research and Development Project (Key Technologies and Applications of Security and Trusted Industrial Control System NO. 2020YFB2009500).

References

1. Dundar, A., Jin, J., Martini, B., et al.: Embedded streaming deep neural networks accelerator with applications. IEEE Trans. Neural Netw. Learn. Syst. **28**(7), 1572–1583 (2017)

2. Lin, C., Yang, Z., Dai, H., Cui, L., Wang, L., Guowei, W.: Minimizing charging delay for directional charging. IEEE/ACM Trans. Netw. **29**(6), 2478–2493 (2021)
3. Lin, C., Zhou, Y., Ma, F., et al.: Minimizing charging delay for directional charging in wireless rechargeable sensor networks. In: IEEE Conference on Computer Communications, IEEE INFOCOM 2019, pp. 1819–1827. IEEE (2019)
4. Lin, C., Zhou, J., Guo, C., et al.: TSCA: a temporal-spatial real-time charging scheduling algorithm for on-demand architecture in wireless rechargeable sensor networks. IEEE Trans. Mob. Comput. **17**(1), 211–224 (2017)
5. Lin. C., Wang, Z., Deng, J., et al.: mTS: temporal-and spatial-collaborative charging for wireless rechargeable sensor networks with multiple vehicles. In: IEEE Conference on Computer Communications, IEEE INFOCOM 2018, pp. 99–107. IEEE (2018)
6. Lin, C., Shang, Z., Du, W., et al.: CoDoC: a novel attack for wireless rechargeable sensor networks through denial of charge. In: IEEE Conference on Computer Communications, IEEE INFOCOM 2019, pp. 856–864. IEEE (2019)
7. Wu, Y., Huang, H., Wu, N., et al.: An incentive-based protection and recovery strategy for secure big data in social networks. Inf. Sci. **508**, 79–91 (2020)
8. Seng, K.P., Lee, P.J., Li, M.A.: Embedded intelligence on FPGA: survey, applications and challenges. Electronics **10**(8), 895 (2021)
9. Wang, T., et al.: Eihdp: edge-intelligent hierarchical dynamic pricing based on cloud-edge-client collaboration for IoT systems. IEEE Trans. Comput. **70**(8), 1285–1298 (2021). https://doi.org/10.1109/TC.2021.3060484
10. Wang, T., Liu, Y., Zheng, X., et al.: Edge-based communication optimization for distributed federated learning. IEEE Trans. Netw. Sci. Eng. (2021)
11. Deng, J., Guo, J., Zhou, Y., et al.: RetinaFace: single-stage dense face localisation in the wild (2019)
12. Windh, S., Ma, X., Halstead, R.J., et al.: High-level language tools for reconfigurable computing. Proc. IEEE **103**(3), 390–408 (2015)
13. Lin, T., Goyal, P., Girshick, R., et al.: Focal loss for dense object detection. In: 2017 IEEE International Conference on Computer Vision, Venice, pp. 2999–3007 (2017)
14. Kim, H.J., Rivera, E.D., Frahm, J.M.: Proceedings of the 2015 IEEE International Conference on Computer Vision, ICCV 2015. IEEE (2016)
15. Redmon, J., Farhadi, A.: YOLO9000: better, faster, stronger. In: IEEE Conference on Computer Vision & Pattern Recognition, pp. 6517–6525. IEEE (2017)
16. Liu, W., et al.: SSD: single shot multibox detector. In: Leibe, B., Matas, J., Sebe, N., Welling, M. (eds.) Computer Vision – ECCV 2016: 14th European Conference, Amsterdam, The Netherlands, October 11–14, 2016, Proceedings, Part I, pp. 21–37. Springer, Cham (2016). https://doi.org/10.1007/978-3-319-46448-0_2
17. Redmon, J., Divvala, S., Girshick, R., et al.: You only look once: unified, real-time object detection. In: Computer Vision & Pattern Recognition (2016)
18. Ren, S., He, K., Girshick, R., Sun, J.: Faster R-CNN: towards real-time object detection with region proposal networks. IEEE Trans. Pattern Anal. Mach. Intell. **39**(6), 1137–1149 (2017). https://doi.org/10.1109/TPAMI.2016.2577031
19. Lin, T., Dollar, P., Girshick, R., et al.: Feature pyramid networks for object detection. In: 2017 IEEE Conference on Computer Vision and Pattern Recognition, Honolulu, HI, pp. 936–944 (2017)
20. Liu, S., Qi, L., Qin, H., et al.: Path aggregation network for instance segmentation. In: 2018 IEEE/CVF Conference on Computer Vision and Pattern Recognition, Salt Lake City, UT, pp. 8759–8768 (2018)
21. Ma, Y.Y., Cao, S.V., Seo, J.-S.: Optimizing the convolution operation to accelerate deep neural networks on FPGA. IEEE Trans. Very Large Scale Integr. (VLSI) Syst. **26**(7), 1354–1367 (2018)

22. Ma, Y., Cao, Y., Vrudhula, S., et al.: Automatic compilation of diverse CNNs onto high-performance FPGA accelerators. IEEE Trans. Comput. Aided Des. Integr. Circ. Syst. **39**(2), 424–437 (2020)

23. Yu, Y., Zhao, T., Wang, K., et al.: Light-OPU: an FPGA-based overlay processor for lightweight convolutional neural networks. In: 2020 ACM/SIGDA International Symposium on Field-Programmable Gate Arrays, Seaside, CA, USA, pp. 122–132 (2020)

FSAFA-stacking2: An Effective Ensemble Learning Model for Intrusion Detection with Firefly Algorithm Based Feature Selection

Guo Chen, Junyao Zheng[✉], Shijun Yang, Jieying Zhou, and Weigang Wu

School of Computer Science and Engineering,
Sun Yat-sen University, Guangzhou, China
isszjy@mail.sysu.edu.cn

Abstract. This paper presents a two-layer ensemble learning model stacking2 based on the Stacking framework to deal with the problems of lack of generalization ability and low detection rate of single model intrusion detection system. The stacking2 uses SAMME, GBDT, and RF to generate the primary learner in the first layer and constructs the meta learner using the logistic regression algorithm in the second layer. The meta learner learns from the class probability outputs produced by the primary learner. In order to solve "the curse of dimensionality" of intrusion detection dataset, this paper proposes the feature selection approach based on firefly algorithm (FSAFA), which is used to select the optimal feature subsets. Based on the selected optimal feature subsets, the training set and test set are reconstructed and then applied to stacking2. As a result, a FSAFA based stacking2 intrusion detection model is proposed. The UNSW-NB15 and NSL-KDD datasets are chosen to verify the effectiveness of the proposed model. The experiment results show that the stacking2 intrusion detection model has better generalization ability than the individual learner based intrusion detection models. Compared with other typical algorithms, the FSAFA based stacking2 intrusion detection model has good performance in detection rate.

Keywords: Intrusion detection · Ensemble learning · Stacking · Feature selection · Firefly algorithm

1 Introduction

Both the industries and the public are increasingly concerned about the service provider's ability to ensure information security. Traditional Internet security technologies such as firewall and user authentication cannot cope with intrusions from within the network, cannot effectively deal with attacks that bypass the firewall, and cannot fully protect the network and system from increasingly complex attacks and malicious software [24].

© Springer Nature Switzerland AG 2022
Y. Lai et al. (Eds.): ICA3PP 2021, LNCS 13156, pp. 555–570, 2022.
https://doi.org/10.1007/978-3-030-95388-1_37

Intrusion detection technology [1] is a network security protection technology born after data encryption, firewall, and user authentication. It searches for suspicious activities and known threats and issues threat warnings when such situations are discovered. Different from firewall technology, intrusion detection can not only monitor malicious behaviors from outside the network, but also monitor malicious behaviors and unauthorized behaviors from inside the network. It can provide detection and response mechanisms for malicious behaviors in the network in real time, stop them before the network is seriously attacked, thereby ensuring the security of the network.

Traditional intrusion detection system (IDS) relies on manual extraction of intrusion rules, that is, the network security expert analyze the intrusion behaviors, extract the characteristic forming rules and compare them with the behavior to be inspected, then make the judgment. However, manually constructing detection rules is not only a time-consuming and laborious task, but will also greatly reduce the update efficiency of the IDS rule library. In face of this problem, machine learning has been introduced into the field of intrusion detection. In addition, one characteristic of the data to be processed in IDS is the high dimensionality of the feature, and it has a trend to increase. Among those features there are a lot of irrelevant ones, which will increase the workload of analysis and will seriously affect the real-time performance of IDS [8]. In order to deal with the curse of dimensionality, many researchers explore feature selection approaches, and combine them with machine learning technology to improve the timeliness of intrusion detection. Therefore, it is gradually becoming an important researching direction in IDS to improve the system's efficiency by applying machine learning and feature selection to it.

Current researches on intrusion detection technology have to deal with the following challenges: 1) The intrusion detection dataset is stale. 2) The dimension of the dataset is high. 3) The accuracy of intrusion detection is not ideal. With the aim of designing an intrusion detection model that has higher detection rate, higher timeliness, lower false positive rate and certain generalization ability, this paper makes the following contributions:

1. This paper designed a two-layer stacking2 intrusion detection model based on the Stacking framework of ensemble learning.
2. This paper proposes a wrapper based feature selection approach, the Feature Selection Approach based on Firefly Algorithm (FSAFA), for the high dimensionality characteristic of the intrusion detection dataset.

2   Related Work

The following analyzes the related works of intrusion detection from three aspects: single model machine learning algorithm, ensemble learning algorithm and feature selection algorithm.

2.1   Single Model Based Intrusion Detection

Early applications of machine learning in intrusion detection were based on a single model, where people train data and build model based on a single machine learning algorithm. Commonly used machine learning algorithms include decision tree, Bayesian network [22], support vector machine [7,18], neural network [5,6,16], etc. Shi-Jinn Horng proposed a support vector machine based IDS in 2011, which combines simple feature selection approach, hierarchical clustering algorithm and support vector machine technology [7]. Text [16] designed an deep neural network based accelerated IDS, which identifies different classes of attack by finding complex relationships in the input dataset. In 2018, Papamartzivanos et al. proposed a Dendron based IDS [15]. Dendron is a new approach that uses genetic algorithm to evolve decision tree classifiers, its purpose is to generate detection rules in the context of detection system misuse.

2.2   Ensemble Learning Based Intrusion Detection

Didaci et al. introduced the basic principles of ensemble learning and used ensemble learning methods to identify intrusion behaviors [4]. They compared the result with that of the single model classifier, which proved the effectiveness of ensemble learning in intrusion detection. Kevric J. combined the random tree with the sum rule scheme based NBTree algorithm and applied them in IDS [10]. Sornsuwit proposed an approach that uses Adaboost algorithm to integrate decision tree, Naive Bayes model, support vector machine and multi-layer perceptron [21]. In the IDS proposed by Fadi Salo, the learners that trained by support vector machine, k-nearest neighbor and multi-layer perceptron are combined first, then the prediction results of these three individual learners are combined by a voting method based on the average of probability (AOP) to produce the final result [17]. In 2018, Demir proposed an improved ensemble learning method and applied it to IDS [3]. This method draws on the idea of the random forest algorithm and uses the random feature selection approach to construct the primary classifier on the basis of the Stacking framework, and it improves the generalization ability of the model.

2.3   Feature Selection Based Intrusion Detection

The dataset of intrusion detection often comes with the characteristic of high dimensionality. Faced with this problem, researchers have begun to study feature selection algorithms and apply them alongside the machine learning algorithms to intrusion detection to improve the performance. In the IDS proposed by Shrivas, the artificial neural network and the Bayesian Network are first integrated, then the features are selected with respect to the gain ratio [20]. Wang W. applied a feature selection approach based on filtering and wrapper to IDS, selected the 10 most important features on the KDD CUP 99 dataset and detected on the Bayesian network and C4.5 classifier [23]. Mazini applied Artificial Bee Colony

(ABC) as a searching strategy for feature subset and used the Adaboost.M2 algorithm to evaluate the pros and cons of the feature subset, proposed a wrapper based feature selection algorithm and applied it to IDS [12].

3   The stacking2 Intrusion Detection Model

A two-layer stacking2 intrusion detection model is proposed in this paper. The first layer of this model uses SAMME (Stagewise Additive Modeling using a Multi-class Exponential loss function), GBDT (Gradient Boosting Decision Tree) and RF (Random Forest) to generate the primary learner. The second layer of the model uses the logistic regression algorithm to generate the meta learner. The input data of the meta learner is composed of the class probability output of the primary learner. The framework of stacking2 intrusion detection model is divided into training phase and prediction phase.

In the training phase, the original training set D containing m samples is divided into K groups of mutually exclusive data subsets of similar size. K = 5 in this paper. D_1, D_2,..., D_k represent datasets, where $D_i \cap D_j = \emptyset$. $D_{train\_k}(k = 1, 2, ..., K)$ represents the training set of the k-th fold , and D_{test_k} represents the test set of the k-th fold, where $D_{train\_k} = D \backslash D_{test\_k}$. $D = D_{train\_k} \cup D_{test\_k}$. In order to prevent over-fitting, SAMME, GBDT, and RF usually share cross-validated dataset, which shows as storing the index of the cross-validated dataset in the experiment. Each of the three learning algorithms ς_{SAMME}, ς_{GBDT} and ς_{RF} of the primary learner iteratates K times, that is, the algorithm ς_j is trained on each of $D_{train\_1}, D_{train\_2}, ..., D_{train\_k}$, obtaining $Model_j^{(1)}$, $Model_j^{(2)}$, ..., $Model_j^{(K)}$, where $Model_j^{(k)} = \varsigma_j(D_{train\_k})$. Then the trained $Model_j^{(k)}$ is used to predict D_{test_k}, which produces $Model_j^{(k)}(D_{test\_k})$. When the K-time iteration ends, the prediction results of the K models applied on D_{test_1}, D_{test_2}, ..., D_{test_K} are stacked together and denoted as P_j, $j\in\{$-SAMME, GBDT, RF$\}$. Because of the stacking, P_j refers to the class probability matrix output of the j-th individual learner in the first layer applied on the training set D, with a size of $m \times C$. When $K = 5$, the stacking result is shown in Fig. 1. When each algorithm in the first layer of stacking2 has finished the above operations, the secondary training set $D_{new} = \{(u_1, y_1), (u_2, y_2), ..., (u_m, y_m)\}$ is obtained, which has the same number of samples m of the original training set$((m/K) \times K = m)$. Then the D_{new} is trained on the meta learning algorithm ς_{LR} in the second layer of stacking2, which generates the meta learner $Model_{LR}$. The training process is expressed as $Model_{LR} = \varsigma_{LR}(D_{new})$. At this point, the training phase of the stacking2 model is over and the first layer of stacking2 has produced $3 \times K$ individual learners. These individual learners form the primary learner of stacking2, and together with meta learner constitute the entire stacking2 intrusion detection model.

In the prediction phase, the test set $D' = \{x_1', x_2', ..., x_n'\}$ of a total of n samples is inputted. Because each algorithm ς_j in the first layer of stacking2 generates K individual learners $Model_j^{(1)}$, $Model_j^{(2)}$, ..., $Model_j^{(K)}$ on the K-fold training set, the K results generated by these K individual learners on test set D' are

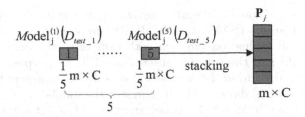

Fig. 1. $Model_j^{(k)}(D_{test\_k})$ stacking process

$Model_j^{(1)}(D')$, $Model_j^{(2)}(D')$, ..., $Model_j^{(K)}(D')$, $j \in \{SAMME, GBDT, RF\}$. The K test results are presented in the form of class probability. In order to obtain a secondary test set with the same number of samples as the original test set D', these K results are averaged, namely:

$$P_j' = \frac{\sum_{k=1}^{K} Model_j^{(k)}(D')}{K}, j \in \{SAMME, GBDT, RF\} \qquad (1)$$

P_j' refers to the class probability prediction matrix output of the j-th individual learner on the test set D', which has a size of $n \times C$. When $K = 5$, the average effect is shown in Fig. 2. Then the test set D' is predicted on each of the individual learners in the first layer, with the produced class probability matrix represented by P', which has a size of $n \times (C \times 3)$. Similar to the definition of the secondary training set, P' can be expressed as $P' = [P'_{SAMME}\ P'_{GBDT}\ P'_{RF}] = \{[u_1' ... u_n']\}^T$, of which every line corresponds to one sample of the secondary test set D'_{new}, whose size is $C \times 3$. In the end, a secondary test set of n samples is obtained $D'_{new} = \{u_1', u_2', ..., u_n'\}$. Finally, the secondary test set is inputted into $Model_{LR}$, which is the meta learner trained in the training phase of stacking2, and the prediction result $y'_{pred} = Model_{LR}(D'_{new})$ is obtained.

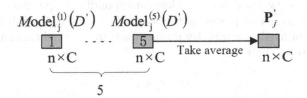

Fig. 2. $Model_j^{(k)}(D')$ average process

4 Feature Selection Approach Based on Firefly Algorithm (FSAFA)

A wrapper based feature selection approach is proposed in this paper, called the Feature Selection Approach based on Firefly Algorithm (FSAFA). This approach uses the firefly algorithm as the searching strategy of the feature subset and uses the individual learners (SAMME, GBDT, RF) in stacking2 as the classifiers. It reconstructs an evaluation function with respect to the detection rate, the false positive rate and the feature subset size, with the purpose of finding the optimal feature subset from the original features. Let F represent the number of features in the original dataset, and d represent the number of features selected by FSAFA. In the UNSW-NB15 dataset and the NSL-KDD dataset, F is equal to 42 and 41, respectively.

The brightness and attractiveness of fireflies show the characteristic of fluorescence, that it decays gradually due to the medium light absorption as it propagates. The brightness of the firefly is:

$$B(r) = B_0 e^{-\gamma r} \tag{2}$$

B_0 represents the initial brightness when $r = 0$, and γ represents the light absorption coefficient of the medium, which is a constant. r indicates the distance between any two fireflies. For two fireflies i and j, the cartesian distance between the two fireflies r_{ij} is:

$$r_{ij} = \boldsymbol{v}_i - \boldsymbol{v}_j = \sqrt{\sum_{f=1}^{F}(\boldsymbol{v}_{if} - \boldsymbol{v}_{jf})^2} \tag{3}$$

F represents the dimension of the features in the intrusion detection dataset, and $\boldsymbol{v}_i$ and $\boldsymbol{v}_j$ represent the F-dimension binary position vectors of firefly i and firefly j in the searching space, v_i is:

$$\boldsymbol{v}_i = (v_{i1}, v_{i2}, ..., v_{iF}), i = 1, 2, ..., p \tag{4}$$

The value of each element in v_i is either 0 or 1, which represents whether a feature in the original feature set is selected. If a feature is selected, the corresponding element in the position vector $\boldsymbol{v}_i$ has a value of 1, otherwise the value is 0. p represents the number of fireflies, corresponding to p points to search that are evenly and randomly placed in the searching space during initialization. The attractiveness of fireflies is directly proportional to the brightness and affects the location update of the fireflies:

$$A(r) = A_0 e^{-\gamma r^2} \tag{5}$$

The meaning of r and γ is the same as in the brightness formula (2), representing the distance between two fireflies and the medium light absorption coefficient respectively. A_0 represents the attractiveness of zero distance. As can be seen from the above function (5), the attractiveness between two fireflies will decrease as the distance between them increases.

In the searching space, the firefly with lower brightness will move towards the one with higher brightness. The brightness of the firefly is determined by an objective function. The stronger the brightness of the firefly, the larger the value of the objective function. The function is:

$$Function = \omega_1 \times DR + \omega_2 \times (1 - FPR) + \omega_3 \times size^{-1} \tag{6}$$

$\omega_1, \omega_2, \omega_3$ are random numbers in the range of [0,1] and satisfy $\omega_1 + \omega_2 + \omega_3 = 1$, which represent the weights of the detection rate, the false positive rate and the number of selected features in the objective function respectively. Specifically for the firefly algorithm, the objective function of firefly i's location v_i is:

$$Obj(v_i) = \omega_1 \times DR(v_i) + \omega_2 \times (1 - FPR(v_i)) + \omega_3 \times (\|v_i\|_0^{-1}) \tag{7}$$

Since v_i represents whether each of the F features is selected, $DR(v_i)$ represents the detection rate of classifier on the corresponding dataset. $FPR(v_i)$ represents the false positive rate on the corresponding dataset. In order to prevent over-fitting, part of the original training set are used with the cross-validation technique to obtain the detection rate and the false positive rate of the feature subset v_i. $\|v_i\|_0$ refers to the number of elements with value 1 in the position vector v_i, that is, the number of features in the corresponding feature subset.

Because the brightness of the firefly is proportional to the value of the objective function, the comparison of the brightness between the fireflies can be converted into the comparison of the values of the objective function, which corresponding to the position vector of the fireflies. In the implementation of the algorithm, the brightness of the firefly is replaced by the value of the objective function of its current position. In the searching space, a firefly with higher brightness will attract a firefly with lower brightness to move towards it, which leads to the update of position. The postion of firefly i after attracted by j becomes:

$$v_i^{t+1} = v_i^t + A_0 e^{-\gamma r^2}(v_j^t - v_i^t) + \alpha(R - 0.5) \tag{8}$$

v_i^{t+1} represents the position vector of the firefly i after the $t+1$-th iteration, that is, the updated firefly position vector. Similarly, v_i^t represents the position vector before the update. $A_0 e^{-\gamma r^2}$ is defined as in formula (5), which represents the attractiveness between firefly i and firefly j after the t-th iteration. α is a constant in the range of [0,1], called the step factor, and R is an uniform distributed random parameter in the range of [0,1]. $(R - 0.5)$, as a disturbance term, can prevent the firefly vector from entering the local optimum too early. In the iterative process, if the brightness of two fireflies is the same, then they make random movements respectively. Let v_* represent the current position vector of the brightest firefly. The brightest firefly also moves randomly, and the position vector is updated as:

$$v_*^{t+1} = v_*^t + (R - 0.5) \tag{9}$$

When the firefly algorithm is used to search for feature subset, the value of each element in the firefly position vector is either 0 or 1. However, the position vector updated by Eqs. (8) and (9) may not necessarily be a binary vector that consists only of 0 and 1. Thus, to get the real position vector of the firefly after the iteration, the following transformation is required [19]:

$$v_{if}^{t+1} = \begin{cases} 1, & p_{if} \geq rand \\ 0, & otherwise \end{cases} \tag{10}$$

$$p_{if} = \frac{1}{1 + e_{x_{if}}} \tag{11}$$

v_{if}^{t+1} represents the value of the f-th element in the position vector of the i-th firefly after the $t+1$-th iteration, $rand$ is an uniformly distributed random number in the range of $[0, 1]$. p_{if} means the probability that the f-th element in the position vector of the i-th firefly is 1, which is given by Eq. (11), where $x_{if} = A_0 e^{-\gamma r^2}(v_{jf} - v_{if}) + \alpha(R - 0.5)$, v_{jf} and v_{if} are determined by the status of fireflies i and j after the current iteration. Eventually, after the transformation of Eqs. (10) and (11), the updated firefly position vector is obtained.

5   FSAFA Based stacking2 Intrusion Detection Model

The FSAFA and the stacking2 are combined to build a FSAFA based intrusion detection model. As shown in Fig. 3, FSAFA selects feature subsets for each individual learner in stacking2. To be specific, SAMME, GBDT, and RF are used to generate classifiers to select the optimal feature subsets, and based on it, reconstruct the training set and the test set. Then they are applied to the corresponding algorithms in the first layer of stacking2. As stated above, the individual learners are generated by SAMME, GBDT and RF, and their class probability outputs on the training set form the input for the meta learner. Then the logistic regression algorithm is used to fit the input data to generate the meta learner. The selection approach of the classifiers in FSAFA has the following two characteristics: 1) By applying customized feature selection for different individual learners of the primary learner, irrelevant features can be removed and the ones with better representativeness can be found. 2) From another perspective, the fine-grained feature selection is also a way to increase difference in feature dimension of the primary learner.

In order to give a better illustration of the workflow of the FSAFA based stacking2 intrusion detection model, a flow chart is presented in Fig. 4. As shown by Figs. 3 and 4, this model has the following important steps.

First, data subsets are randomly sampled from the original training set D for the purpose of feature selection. To be specific, the 10%, 30%, 50%, and 70% data subsets are randomly selected from the original training set, and each subset is randomly divided into K parts of equal size using cross-validation technique (label 1 in Fig. 4). $K - 1$ of them are selected as the training sets and trained on SAMME, GBDT, and RF separately, while the remaining piece of data is used as the validation set for the evaluation of the following objective function. For each classification algorithm, this process repeats K times according to the selected validation set, and finally the subsets with the optimal performance are chosen.

Second, FSAFA is applied to the data subsets and classification algorithms in the first step. Initially p fireflies with random position are produced. The training sets for training the classifiers are constructed according to the position vectors of the p fireflies (label 2), and the trained classifier are used to predict the

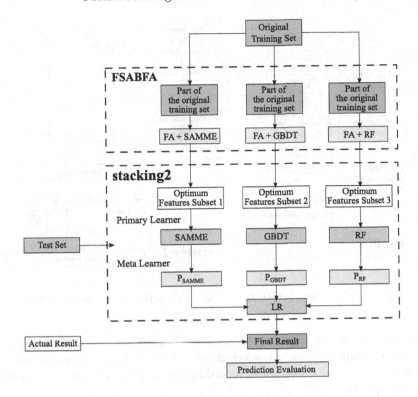

Fig. 3. FSAFA based stacking2 intrusion detection model structure diagram

validation set (label 3), thereby calculating the value of the objective function according to formula (7). The values are sorted from big to small. Then current iteration time is checked. If it doesn't reach the maximum $Tmax$, then each firefly needs to go through the following three steps:

1. Moving according to formula (8) based on its own objective function value, that is, the firefly with a smaller objective function value will move to the firefly with a larger value.
2. Update the value of its own attractiveness according to Eq. (5).
3. Update its position based on formula (10) and formula (11), and start the next iteration.

The above process is repeated until the maximum time of iteration is reached, then the position vector of the firefly with the maximum objective function value is outputted. This position vector represents the optimal feature subset selected with the corresponding data subset and classifier.

Third, new training set and test set are constructed from the original dataset according to the selected optimal feature subsets. This corresponds to label 4 and 5 in Fig. 4.

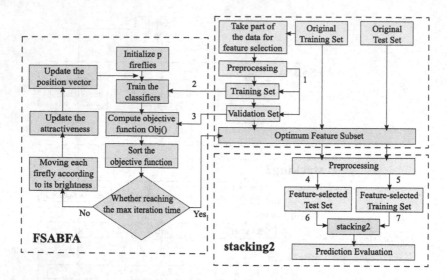

Fig. 4. FSAFA based stacking2 intrusion detection model flow diagram

Fourth, the feature-selected training set is trained on stacking2 (label 6). After the training, the feature-selected test set is used for prediction (label 7). The prediction result is evaluated according to the performance criterion of the intrusion detection.

6   Experiment

6.1   Dataset and Preprocessing

Considering the equipment requirements and time cost, the UNSW_NB15_training-set and the UNSW_NB15_testing-set provided by Nour Mousta [13,14] were chosen as the benchmark datasets of the proposed model. In order to improve the sample's representativeness, the stratified sampling method was applied, with 20% of the data randomly selected as the training set and the test set, denoted as UNSW_NB15_training-set 20% and UNSW_NB15_testing-set 20% respectively.

UNSW_NB15_training-set 20% and UNSW_NB15_testing-set 20% have a total of 44 features (Nour Mousta deleted 6 items from the original UNSW_NB15 and added the feature of rate). The symbolic features are digitized using one-hot code method and the method used in article [25]. Then the dataset is normalized.

6.2   Experiment and Result Analysis

The experiment used three intrusion detection evaluation indexes, the accuracy, the detection rate (DR) and the false positive rate (FPR). The experiment was divided into two stages: the first stage compared the plain stacking2 intrusion detection model with the individual learner based intrusion detection model.

Table 1. Experiment results of stacking2 and individual learners (%)

Classes	SAMME	GBDT	RF	LR	stacking2
Normal	80.81	78.9	77.34	61.92	**86.70**
Analysis	2.22	0.74	**4.44**	0	3.70
Backdoor	3.42	**5.98**	4.27	0	5.13
Dos	17.97	8.92	9.66	4.9	**29.10**
Exploit	78.48	86.16	88.5	75.47	**89.31**
Fuzzers	37.79	59.9	58.5	**73.35**	59.40
Generic	95.92	**96.58**	96	95.1	96.53
Reconnaissance	76.82	80.69	79.97	54.65	**81.69**
Shellcode	52.63	**67.11**	63.16	0	65.79
Worm	0	11.11	11.11	0	11.11
Accuracy	76.13	77.89	77.27	67.56	**82.83**
DR	72.31	77.06	77.21	72.18	**79.66**
FPR	19.19	21.09	22.66	38.08	**13.3**

The second stage used FSAFA to make feature selection for the stacking2 and compared this FSAFA based stacking2 model with plain stacking2 and other typical models.

Experiment on Stacking2. The experiment used 5-fold cross-validation on UNSW_NB15_training-set 20% and are combined with grid search method to determine the value of the parameters. Table 1 shows the prediction results of each intrusion detection model on the UNSW_NB15_testing-set 20% after being trained by UNSW_NB15_training-set 20%, with the upper half listing the DR to each class, and the lower half listing the indexes to the whole test set. The following analyzes the experimental results from two aspects.

1. The overall accuracy, DR and FPR: It can be seen from the table that all three performances of stacking2 are better than that of the other four individual classifiers, especially on FPR. Compared to the best-performing individual learner in terms of FPR (SAMME), this index of stacking2 is lowered by 5.89%. In terms of accuracy, stacking2 is 4.94% higher than the best-performing individual learner (GBDT). In terms of DR, stacking2 is 2.45% higher than the best-performing individual learner (RF).

2. DR on Each Class: As can be seen from Table 1, stacking2 has the highest DRs on Normal, DoS, Exploit, and Reconnaissance. In terms of Worm, stacking2 has the same DR as GBDT and RF. However, SAMME and LR did not detect Worm. This is because the Worm only constitutes 0.005% of the test set. For the remaining five attack classes, Analysis, Backdoor, Fuzzers, Generic, and Shell-code, although the DRs of stacking2 did not exceed that of the best-performing individual learners, they reached a relatively good level.

In summary, the stacking2 has a good performance in intrusion detection, and it can obtain better results than individual learners.

Experiment on FSAFA-stacking2. The 10%, 30%, 50%, and 70% samples are drawn from the training set UNSW_NB15_training-set 20% for four set of experiments. Each group of experiment used SAMME, GBDT, and RF as the classifiers and applied 5-fold cross-validation. Finally, for each classifier, the feature subset with the largest objective function value was selected. The parameters of FSAFA was set as the following: initial brightness $B_0 = 1$, medium light absorption coefficient $\gamma = 1$, number of fireflies $p = 10$, initial brightness $A_0 = 1$, the weights of DR, FPR and the feature subset size (No) in the objective function (Obj), ω_1, ω_2 and ω_3 were 0.6, 0.3, and 0.1 respectively, the step factor α in position update was 0.1, and the maximum number of iterations $Tmax = 100$.

After obtaining the optimal feature subsets, the experiment input the three subsets into the stacking2. As shown in Table 2, the performance of FSAFA-stacking2 (the FSAFA based stacking2 intrusion detection model) and the plain stacking2 were compared.

Table 2. Experimental results of intrusion detection model after feature selection (%)

Classes	Stacking2	FSAFA-stacking2
Normal	86.7	87.69
Analysis	**3.7**	2.97
Backdoor	5.13	**6.84**
Dos	29.1	**31.42**
Exploit	89.31	88.77
Fuzzers	59.4	60.64
Generic	96.53	96.98
Reconnaissance	81.69	82.26
Shellcode	65.79	**69.74**
Worm	11.11	11.11
Accuracy	82.83	83.55
DR	79.66	80.18
FPR	13.3	12.31
Training Time(s)	165.94	**98.19**
Test Time(s)	173.67	**103.99**

Table 3. Comparison between FSAFA-stacking2 and other algorithms on UNSW-NB15 (%)

Methods	Accuracy	DR	FPR
KNN	70.25	71.45	31.22
ANN	75.88	73.63	21.35
Dendron	**84.33**	63.2	**2.61**
GALR-DT	81.42	77.06	6.39
FSAFA-stacking2	83.55	**80.18**	12.31

The structure of Table 2 is similar to Table 1, the difference is that two rows of performance index—training time and test time—are added at the bottom. Training time is the time to build the model, they are the indexes that should be paid extra attention to. It can be seen from Table 2 that the training time and test time of FSAFA-stacking2 are obviously shorter than those of stacking2. In addition to the time indexes, FSAFA-stacking2 is also better than stacking2 in terms of the accuracy, the DR, and the FPR. Although all the improvements of FSAFA-stacking2 do not exceed 1%, which are not huge, they are achieved under the premise of reducing training and test time.

Table 3 shows the comparison between FSAFA-stacking2 and the intrusion detection models based on other typical algorithms. Dendron[15] uses genetic algorithm to evolve decision tree classifiers. Its accuracy rate on UNSW-NB15 is 0.78% higher than FSAFA-stacking2. However, it is 16.98% lower in terms of DR. It is worth noting that Dendron's FPR is only 2.61%, about 1/5 of the that of FSAFA-stacking2. The reason is that Dendron is a misuse detection technology. The mechanism of misuse detection technology is to compare the inspected behavior with a series of rules generated by attack records, thus the FPR is usually low for normal sample. However, its disadvantage is also obvious, that it cannot detect unknown attack classes, so the DR is low. GALR-DT [11] uses a logistic regression classifier based genetic algorithm to select the optimal feature subset on UNSW-NB15 and classifies using decision tree. Its accuracy rate is 2.31% lower than FSAFA-stacking2, and its DR is 3.12% lower. However, GALR-DT is better in terms of FPR, which is about 5.92% lower than FSAFA-stacking2. In addition to the above two models, FSAFA-stacking2 is also compared with two basic classification algorithms KNN (K Nearest Neighbor) and ANN (Artificial Neural Network). It can be seen from the table that all the accuracy, the DR and the FPR of KNN and ANN are not ideal. This shows that for complex datasets, a single basic machine learning algorithm can no longer achieve good prediction results.

As can be seen, FSAFA-stacking2 achieves the best result in DR among the experimented models. In terms of FPR, although FSAFA-stacking2 is not as good as Dendron and GALR-DT, it beats other algorithms. In terms of accuracy, FSAFA-stacking2 is only a slight 0.78% lower than Dendron and outperforms other models. In intrusion detection systems, the DR is usually more convincing than accuracy, which shows that the FSAFA based stacking2 intrusion detection model proposed in this paper has its advantage, with good performances in all the accuracy, DR and FPR.

Table 4. Comparison between FSAFA-stacking2 and other algorithms on NSL-KDD (%)

Methods	Accuracy	DR	FPR
KNN	74.04	59.86	7.22
ANN	75.9	62.66	6.32
STL	74.38	62.99	7.21
FSAFA-stacking2	**79.01**	**65.1**	**2.61**

Although the NSL-KDD dataset has some shortcomings [2], it is still a commonly used dataset in intrusion detection research. Therefore, this paper also experimented on it to further illustrate the generalization ability of the proposed model (STL [9], short for Self-Taught Learning, is a self-learning method that uses a large number of unlabeled samples and a small number of labeled samples to train the model). The results, shown in Table 4, verified once again the effectiveness of the proposed model.

7 Conclusion

In order to deal with the low detection rate and the weak generalization ability of single-model machine learning approaches, a two-layer ensemble learning model—the stacking2—is proposed in this paper. Besides, to deal with the high dimensionality characteristic of the intrusion detection dataset, a wrapper based feature selection approach—the FSAFA—is proposed and applied to stacking2, leads to a FSAFA based stacking2 intrusion detection model.

Experiments was conducted on the up-to-date intrusion detection dataset UNSW-NB15, where the model was compared with other typical algorithms, with a mainly focus on accuracy, detection rate and false positive rate. In order to further verify the generalization ability of the model, a similar experiment on the NSL-KDD dataset was also added. The results show that the FSAFA based stacking2 intrusion detection model has good performances on all the accuracy, detection rate and false positive rate, especially in detection rate.

References

1. Anderson, J.P.: Computer security threat monitoring and surveillance. Technical report, James P. Anderson Co., Fort Washington, PA (1980)

2. Brugger, T.: Kdd cup '99 dataset (network intrusion) considered harmful. Technical report, Department of Computer Science, UC Davis (2007). https://www.kdnuggets.com/news/2007/n18/4i.html
3. Demir, N., DALKILIÇ, G.: Modified stacking ensemble approach to detect network intrusion. Turkish J. Electr. Eng. Comput. Sci. **26**(1), 418–433 (2018)
4. Didaci, L., Giacinto, G., Roli, F.: Ensemble learning for intrusion detection in computer networks. In: Workshop Machine Learning Methods Applications, Siena, Italy (2002)
5. El Farissi, I., Saber, M., Chadli, S., Emharraf, M., Belkasmi, M.G.: The analysis performance of an intrusion detection systems based on neural network. In: 2016 4th IEEE International Colloquium on Information Science and Technology (CiSt), pp. 145–151. IEEE (2016)
6. Gautam, S.K., Om, H.: Computational neural network regression model for host based intrusion detection system. Perspectives in Science **8**, 93–95 (2016)
7. Horng, S.J., et al.: A novel intrusion detection system based on hierarchical clustering and support vector machines. Expert Syst. Appl. **38**(1), 306–313 (2011)
8. Idowu, R.K., Muniyandi, R.C., Lateef, U.O.: Tackling the menace of curse of dimensionality in intrusion detection systems: membrane computing approach. In: Proceedings of the 2nd Interdisciplinary conference of TASUED-UCC 2016, pp. 1539–1549 (2016)
9. Javaid, A., Niyaz, Q., Sun, W., Alam, M.: A deep learning approach for network intrusion detection system. In: Proceedings of the 9th EAI International Conference on Bio-inspired Information and Communications Technologies (formerly BIONETICS), pp. 21–26 (2016)
10. Kevric, J., Jukic, S., Subasi, A.: An effective combining classifier approach using tree algorithms for network intrusion detection. Neural Comput. Appl. **28**(1), 1051–1058 (2016). https://doi.org/10.1007/s00521-016-2418-1
11. Khammassi, C., Krichen, S.: A GA-LR wrapper approach for feature selection in network intrusion detection. Comput. Secur. **70**, 255–277 (2017)
12. Mazini, M., Shirazi, B., Mahdavi, I.: Anomaly network-based intrusion detection system using a reliable hybrid artificial bee colony and adaboost algorithms. J. King Saud Univ. Comput. Inf. Sci. **31**(4), 541–553 (2019)
13. Moustafa, N., Slay, J.: Unsw-nb15: a comprehensive data set for network intrusion detection systems (unsw-nb15 network data set). In: 2015 Military Communications and Information Systems Conference (MilCIS), pp. 1–6. IEEE (2015)
14. Moustafa, N., Slay, J.: The evaluation of network anomaly detection systems: statistical analysis of the unsw-nb15 data set and the comparison with the kdd99 data set. Inf. Secur. J. Global Perspect. **25**(1–3), 18–31 (2016)
15. Papamartzivanos, D., Mármol, F.G., Kambourakis, G.: Dendron: Genetic trees driven rule induction for network intrusion detection systems. Futur. Gener. Comput. Syst. **79**, 558–574 (2018)
16. Potluri, S., Diedrich, C.: Accelerated deep neural networks for enhanced intrusion detection system. In: 2016 IEEE 21st International Conference on Emerging Technologies and Factory Automation (ETFA), pp. 1–8. IEEE (2016)
17. Salo, F., Nassif, A.B., Essex, A.: Dimensionality reduction with IG-PCA and ensemble classifier for network intrusion detection. Comput. Netw. **148**, 164–175 (2019)
18. Saxena, H., Richariya, V.: Intrusion detection in kdd99 dataset using SVM-PSO and feature reduction with information gain. Int. J. Comput. Appl. **98**(6), 25–29 (2014)

19. Selvakumar, B., Muneeswaran, K.: Firefly algorithm based feature selection for network intrusion detection. Comput. Secur. **81**, 148–155 (2019)
20. Shrivas, A.K., Dewangan, A.K.: An ensemble model for classification of attacks with feature selection based on kdd99 and NSL-KDD data set. Int. J. Comput. Appl. **99**(15), 8–13 (2014)
21. Sornsuwit, P., Jaiyen, S.: Intrusion detection model based on ensemble learning for u2r and r2l attacks. In: 2015 7th International Conference on Information Technology and Electrical Engineering (ICITEE), pp. 354–359. IEEE (2015)
22. Sun, C., Xing, J.c., Yang, Q.l., Han, D.s.: Intrusion detection methods based on improved naive bayesian. Microcomputer Appl. **36**(01), 8–10 (2017)
23. Wang, W., He, Y., Liu, J., Gombault, S.: Constructing important features from massive network traffic for lightweight intrusion detection. IET Inf. Secur. **9**(6), 374–379 (2015)
24. Wu, S.X., Banzhaf, W.: The use of computational intelligence in intrusion detection systems: a review. Appl. Soft Comput. **10**(1), 1–35 (2010)
25. Zhi, H.: Research on intrusion detection model based on dimensional reduction and improved CS-WNN. Master's thesis, Lanzhou University (2018)

Attention-Based Cross-Domain Gesture Recognition Using WiFi Channel State Information

Hao Hong[1], Baoqi Huang[1(✉)], Yu Gu[2], and Bing Jia[1]

[1] Engineering Research Center of Ecological Big Data Ministry of Education,
Inner Mongolia Key Laboratory of Wireless Networking and Mobile Computing,
College of Computer Science, Inner Mongolia University, Hohhot 010021, China
cshbq@imu.edu.cn
[2] School of Computer and Information, Hefei University of Technology,
Hefei 230009, China
yugu.bruce@ieee.org

Abstract. Gesture recognition is an important step to realize ubiquitous WiFi-based human-computer interaction. However, most current WiFi-based gesture recognition systems rely on domain-specific training. To address this issue, we propose an attention-based cross-domain gesture recognition system using WiFi channel state information. In order to overcome the shortcoming of handcrafted feature extraction in state-of-the-art cross-domain models, our model uses the attention mechanism to automatically extract domain-independent gesture features from spatial and temporal dimensions. We implement the model and extensively evaluate its performance by using the Widar3 dataset involving 16 users and 6 gestures across 5 orientations and 5 positions in 3 different environments. The evaluation results show that, the average in-domain gesture recognition accuracy achieved by the model is 99.67% and the average cross-domain gesture recognition accuracies are 96.57%, 97.86% and 94.2%, respectively, in terms of rooms, positions and orientations. Its cross-domain gesture recognition accuracy significantly outperforms state-of-the-art methods.

Keywords: Cross-domain · Gesture recognition · Channel state information · Attention mechanism · Commodity WiFi

1 Introduction

As one of core technologies of human-computer interaction, human gesture recognition has a large number of applications such as smart home, robot control and virtual reality. Many existing gesture recognition approaches employ cameras [1–3], wearable devices and phones [4–6] or sonar [7–9] as sensing tools. However, these approaches suffer from several inherent drawbacks, including concern

Supported by organization Inner Mongolia University.

of privacy, needing to be worn on the body and smaller sensing range. The WiFi-based perception possesses several advantages, including privacy protection, more convenience, larger sensing scale, etc. Many excellent researchers in the field of perception leverage WiFi as a sensing tool such as [10–13]. Therefore, many advanced WiFi-based gesture recognition models have been proposed such as Wisign [14], WiFinger [15] and WIMU [16], and can be categorized as channel state information (CSI) based methods and received signal strength (RSS) based methods. Obviously, CSI-based methods receive particular interests recently due to adopting fine-grained channel information such as amplitude and phase. Early wireless sensing methods usually extract information such as amplitude, phase, Doppler frequency shifts, etc. from the original signal as recognition features. However, when these models are transferred from one domain to another, their performance is often very poor, due to the fact that the change of the domain will leads to recognition features variation. How to extract domain-independent features of human gestures across different domains is still a challenge.

Recent cross-domain gesture recognition works fail to fully resolve the challenge. For example, [30] translate features between domains through a translation function to recognize gestures. [31,33] inspired by transfer learning and adversarial learning, advanced learning methods are designed to improve cross-domain recognition performance. Although a certain degree of cross-domain recognition is achieved, when a new target domain is added to the recognition model, extra training efforts is performed in terms of data collection or model retraining. Widar3 [17] can extract gesture features which are independent on specific domains by using body-coordinate velocity profiles (BVP) and realize zero-effort cross-domain gesture recognition. Similarly, WiHF [18] is also a cross-domain gesture recognition system and aims to achieve "train once, use everywhere". It uses conjugate multiplication denoising to preprocess data, motion change pattern to extract features and a neural network for recognition. However, since gesture features are distributed in multiple subcarriers and the gesture features associated with each subcarrier may also be scattered, manually extracting features in Widar3 and WiHF will inevitably suffer from gesture features missing, limiting the performance of these works.

To overcome the drawback of handcrafted feature extraction, we propose a novel model to achieve both in-domain and cross-domain gesture recognition using off-the-shelf WiFi devices. The model can ignore environmental interference to realize gesture perception. When an ordinary person looks at a gesture, he or she will focus to the overall shape of the hand, intuitively separate it from surrounding environment, and then recognize the gesture type. Inspired by this observation, we design a neural network based on the well-known ResNet backbone and a dual attention module, namely a position attention module (PAM) and a channel attention module (CAM), to automatically focus on feature correlations from the spatial and temporal dimensions. ResNet has been widely recognized for enhancing correlation. The dual attention module assigns a weight to each pixel of the image to indicate how much it is valued, thereby forming an attention map that shows the distribution of the domain-independent features of gestures in the spatial and temporal dimensions. Our model assigns key features with large weights and interference features with small weights to eliminate the influence of environments, and finally obtains domain-independent gesture features for gesture recognition.

We train and evaluate the model using the publicly available Widar3 dataset [17]. In order to obtain a comprehensive result, we take into account all the 5 positions, 5 orientations and 3 environments provided in the dataset, and then evaluate the average performance, respectively. Since WiHF uses the HuFuM dataset collected using the original dataset from Widar3, our model is compared with Widar3 and WiHF [17, 18]. It is shown that our model is superior to the current best performance by 4.17%, 5.75%, 7.54%, and 11.6%, respectively, in terms of cross-environment, in-domain, cross-position and cross-orientation. Even with the HuFu dataset tailored based on Widar3, the recognition accuracy of WiHF is still inferior to our model by 2.02%, 5.79% and 11.82%, respectively, in terms of in-domain, cross-position and cross-orientation. Due to WiHF with the HuFu dataset of cross-environment performance is unknown, the corresponding comparison is not provided. As such, it can be concluded that our model outperforms its state-of-the-art counterparts.

The rest of this paper is organized as follows: The detailed description of the system design is presented in the Sect. 2. Its evaluation is reported in Sect. 3. Finally, Sect. 4 summarizes the paper.

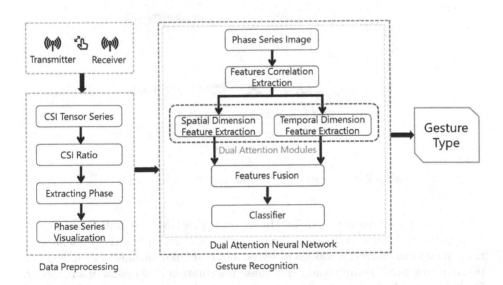

Fig. 1. System overview.

2 System Design

2.1 System Overview

In this section, we first present the cross-domain gesture recognition model based on WiFi CSI, and then introduce the model in detail. Figure 1 depicts the system architecture of the model, which mainly consists of two components: data pre-processing and gesture classification. The first component implements denoising and mapping raw CSI data into heatmaps, and the second component leverages a dual attention network to realize cross-domain gesture recognition.

2.2 Signal Model for Gesture Recognition

Supposing a person makes various gestures in a room where a pair of WiFi transmitter and receiver is set up, the propagation of indoor WiFi signals will inevitably be affected. For example, some WiFi signals are unavoidably absorbed, scattered, reflected and diffracted, resulting in specific changes in the amplitudes and phases of the received signals. Since the changed signals contain features that represent specific gesture, these features can be used to realize cross-domain gesture recognition.

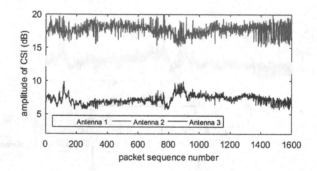

Fig. 2. CSI measurement value of the received signal.

Orthogonal Frequency Division Multiplexing (OFDM) is a multi-carrier modulation method. OFDM divides a single carrier into multiple orthogonal subcarriers, which can convert a wideband signal into many narrowband signal. 802.11n protocol can provide amplitude and phase information of 30 pairs of subcarrier. Each pair of information describes the status of the corresponding subcarrier.

Channel state information (CSI) presents the condition of the channel, which can show the effects of power, fading, and scattering along with signal propagation. CSI can be collected via off-the-shelf 802.11n wireless net card. Although the driver cannot obtain CSI directly, CSI can be obtained through some open

source tools such as Linux 802.11n CSI Tool [28]. The time sequence of the
CSI matrix can describe MIMO channel variations from the dimensions of space
(transceiver), frequency (subcarrier) and time (data packet). It is a 4-dimensional
tensor $H \in C^{N \times M \times K \times T}$, where N, M, K, and T represent the number of receiver
antennas, transmitter antennas, subcarriers, and packets, respectively. Figure 2
shows the CSI measurement values of the three antennas of a network interface
controller.

The CSI matrix of the received signal, denoted $H(f, t)$, can be expressed as
vector sum [19]:

$$H(f, t) = \sum_{i=1}^{L} A_i e^{-j2\pi d_i(t)/\lambda} \tag{1}$$

where L is the number of paths, A_i is the complex attenuation and $d_i(t)$ is the
propagation length of the ith path.

According to prior work [20], the propagation path of these signals can be
divided into static paths and dynamic paths. Thus, CSI can be reformulated as
[19]:

$$\begin{aligned} H(f, t) &= H_s(f, t) + H_d(f, t) \\ &= H_s(f, t) + A(f, t)e^{-j2\pi d(t)/\lambda} \end{aligned} \tag{2}$$

where $H_s(f, t)$ is the static component, $A(f, t)$, $e^{-j2\pi d(t)/\lambda}$ and $d(t)$ are the complex attenuation, phase shift and path length of dynamic component $H_d(f, t)$,
respectively.

When a person makes a gesture, the phase of the dynamic component will
be changed. Therefore, the phase variation of the receiver signal can be used for
gesture recognition.

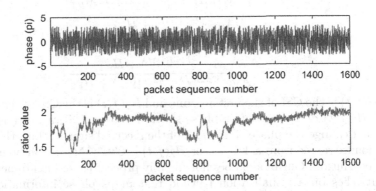

Fig. 3. Phase waveforms of received signal (top). Phase waveforms processed by CSI
ratio (bottom).

2.3 Data Processing

For commodity WiFi devices, there is a timing offset between the pair of WiFi transmitter and receiver. Such timing offset causes phase offset $e^{-j\theta_{offset}}$ in all CSI samples as follows:

$$H(f,t) = e^{-j\theta_{offset}}(H_s(f,t) + A(f,t)e^{-j2\pi d(t)/\lambda}) \tag{3}$$

where $A(f,t)$, $e^{-j2\pi d(t)/\lambda}$ and $d(t)$ denote the complex attenuation, phase shift and path length of dynamic components, respectively. However, since the presence of phase shift, the phase information of the received signal cannot be directly used for gesture recognition. Therefore, the random phase offset $e^{-j\theta_{offset}}$ must be removed. For commodity WiFi card such as the widely used Intel 5300, the time-varying phase offset is the same across different antennas on a WiFi card, due to the fact that different antennas share the same RF oscillator [21,22]. When the target makes a gesture, the difference between the two reflection path lengths of two close-range antennas $d_2(t) - d_1(t)$ can be considered as a constant Δd [23]. The CSI ratio of two antennas obtained is much more noise-free and sensitive compared to the original CSI reading from a single antenna when sensing subtle movements [19]. The top and bottom images in Fig. 3 respectively show the phase waveform of the received signal and the phase waveform of the ratio of the csi measurement values of the first antenna and the third antenna of the receiver. Obviously, the random phase offset is canceled out by the CSI ratio method:

$$
\begin{aligned}
H_r(f,t) &= \frac{H_1(f,t)}{H_2(f,t)} \\
&= \frac{e^{-j\theta_{offset}}(H_{s,1} + A_1 e^{-j2\pi d_1(t)/\lambda})}{e^{-j\theta_{offset}}(H_{s,2} + A_2 e^{-j2\pi d_2(t)/\lambda})} \\
&= \frac{A_1 e^{-j2\pi d_1(t)/\lambda} + H_{s,1}}{A_2 e^{-j2\pi(d_1(t)+\Delta d)/\lambda} + H_{s,2}} \\
&= \frac{A_1 e^{-j2\pi d_1(t)/\lambda} + H_{s,1}}{A_2 e^{-j2\pi\Delta d/\lambda} e^{-j2\pi d_1(t)/\lambda} + H_{s,2}}
\end{aligned}
\tag{4}
$$

where $H_1(f,t)$ is the CSI of the first antenna and $H_2(f,t)$ is the CSI of the second antenna. $H_r(f,t)$ does not contain phase shift. Moreover, CSI ratio transformation will not change the phase shift trend of the received signal. Thus, the phase information extracted from a 4-D tensor $H_r(f,t) \in C^{N \times M \times K \times T}$ can be used for gesture recognition. Our model does not directly process these high-dimensional data, but relies on a visualization method that maps phase information into a heatmap, which is fed into our model to effectively improve the recognition performance [24].

2.4 Classification Module

Gesture features included in CSI of the signal received by the WiFi receiver contain environmental features, human torso features and gesture features. However,

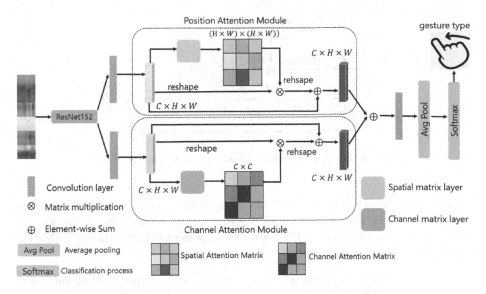

Fig. 4. The architecture of the adopted neural network.

the space occupied by the hand between the pair of transmitter and receiver is very small. Therefore, the influence of the hand on the signal propagation is also very small. Thus, the gesture features are not prominent compared to the trunk features and environmental features. Existing researches have shown that the attention mechanism can extract effective features and eliminate interference from irrelevant features [25,26]. Therefore, the attention mechanism can effectively extract gesture features. To overcome the drawback of handcrafted features extraction, we use the attention mechanism to automatically extract domain-independent gesture features.

According to [27], DANet model can effectively perform scene segmentation by the attention mechanism. Inspired by DANet, we designed the neural network shown in Fig. 4.

We adjust the size of the heatmaps containing gesture information to $3 \times 224 \times 224$ as the input of our model. First, the neural network uses ResNet152 as the backbone network to extract various features. These features are convolved to get the input A (see Fig. 5) with the size of $512 \times 7 \times 7$ for the position attention module and channel attention module. Then, the position attention module and channel attention module can extract ample domain-independent gesture features from A. Next, these extracted features will be fused as gesture recognition features. The last, these fused features go through the average pooling layer and the classification layer to predict the gesture type. The following describes the details of each attention module.

Position Attention Module (PAM) uses self-attention to focus on the importance of each pixel for gesture recognition, that is, domain-independent gestures feature pixels are given a large weight and interference feature pixels are

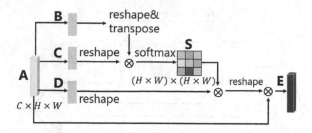

Fig. 5. Detailed structure of position attention module.

given a small weight. Therefore, PAM can transform the various spatial features information in the feature heatmaps into another space and only retains domain-independent gesture features. Figure 5 shows the detailed structure of PAM. The specific process is the following five steps:

1) A is convolved by 1×1 convolution kernel will obtain three new feature maps B, C and D. The sizes of B, C and D are $64 \times 7 \times 7$, $64 \times 7 \times 7$ and $512 \times 7 \times 7$ respectively.
2) The size of B, C and D are transformed into 49×64, 64×49 and 512×49.
3) The transpose of B is matrix multiplied by C. The result of the multiplication is entered into the softmax layer to get the spatial attention map S whose size is 49×49.
4) S is transposed and then multiplied by D. Then, the result of the multiplication is transformed into $512 \times 7 \times 7$.
5) The result of multiplying the output of the previous step with α is summed with A to obtain the final output E. The size of E is $512 \times 7 \times 7$.

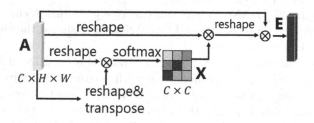

Fig. 6. Detailed structure of channel attention module.

Similar to PAM, Channel Attention Module (CAM) also employs self-attention to evaluate the value of each channel for gesture recognition. Finally, the domain-independent information in the high-value channel is extracted. Figure 6 describes the architecture of CAM in detail. The specific process is the following four steps:

1) The size of A is transformed into 512×49. Then, A and the transpose of A performs matrix multiplication.
2) The output of the first step is input into softmax to obtain channel attention map X size of 512×512.
3) The result size of matrix multiplication performed by the transpose of X and A is transformed into $512 \times 7 \times 7$.
4) The output of the third step is multiplied by β and then added with A to obtain the final output E whose size is $512 \times 7 \times 7$.

Table 1. Detailed introduction of the dataset adopted.

Room#	Users	Gestures	Orientation numbers	Position numbers	Sample numbers
1	user 5, 10, 11, 12, 13, 14, 15, 16, 17	1: Push& Pull; 2: Sweep; 3: Clap; 4: Slide; 5: Draw-O (Horizontal); 6: Draw- Zigzag (Horizontal);	5	5	6750
2	user 1, 2, 6	1: Push& Pull; 2: Sweep; 3: Clap; 4: Slide; 5: Draw-O (Horizontal); 6: Draw- Zigzag (Horizontal);	5	5	2250
3	user 3, 7, 8, 9	1: Push& Pull; 2: Sweep; 3: Clap; 4: Slide; 5: Draw-O (Horizontal); 6: Draw- Zigzag (Horizontal);	5	5	3000

3 Performance Evaluation

In this section, we first implement and evaluate our model through extensive experiments. The specific data division is as follows:

Dataset: Previous excellent gesture recognition work evaluated the performance of their proposed model on the data set collected by themselves such as WiGest [29], WiDraw [32], QGesture [34], Wikey [15,35,36], WiMu [16] and WiSign [14]. The purpose of constructing the public dataset Widar3 is to make a fair comparison between different models. There are already state-of-the-art models evaluated using Widar3 dataset [17,18]. Therefore, in order to compare with the state-of-the-art models, we also leverage Widar3 to evaluate our model. Widar3 dataset was collected by 16 users. All users made 9 gestures in 3 environments, 5 orientations and 5 positions. The detailed description of the dataset we adopted

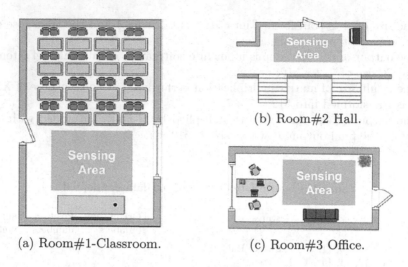

(a) Room#1-Classroom.   (b) Room#2 Hall.

(c) Room#3 Office.

Fig. 7. Experimental environment.

is shown in Table 1. When evaluating the cross-orientation, cross-position and in-domain performance of our model, we select 4500 samples (6 users × 6 gestures × 5 orientations × 5 positions × 5 instances) collected in Room 1, with 80 and 20% samples used for training and evaluating, respectively. 6 users are randomly selected from the 9 users samples. For cross-environments evaluation, we choose 12000 samples (16 users × 6 gestures × 5 orientations × 5 positions × 5 instances) collected from three Rooms. We use the data of two Rooms as the training samples and the remaining one Room data as the testing samples.

Experimental Setup for Dataset Collection: Two computers with Intel WiFi NIC5300 network cards are used as transmitters and receivers. The WiFi card works in 802.11n mode. The transmitter is equipped with an antenna to continuously transmit data packets. The receiver uses three antennas and the CSI tool in [28] to continuously collect and store CSI. The experimental collection environment and device deployment are shown in Fig. 7 and Fig. 8 respectively.

3.1 Overall Performance

Taking all domain factors into consideration, our model achieves on average the in-domain recognition accuracy of 99.67% and the gesture recognition accuracies of 96.57%, 97.86% and 94.2% in terms of environments, positions and orientations. Moreover, in order to obtain a comprehensive result, we take into account the 5 positions, 5 orientations and 3 environments and then evaluate the average performance, respectively. The detailed results are shown in Table 2. Obviously, the in-domain and cross-position performance of our model is very stable. For cross-orientation evaluation, our model has the lowest performance in the first orientation. The state-of-art models WiHF and Widar3 also encountered similar

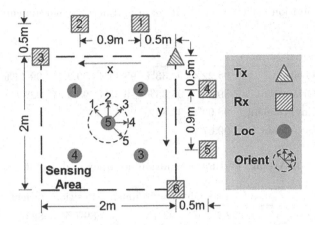

Fig. 8. Device deployment.

problems. The performance of our model exceeds Widar3 and WiHF equipped with HuFu dataset respectively is close to 10% and 18% in the first orientation. The reason for this phenomenon is when people are in the first orientation, the gesture may just be shadowed by the body.

3.2   Comparative Study

In this section, we compare with Widar3 [17] and WiHF [18]. The Widar3 process consists of the following three sections: 1) CSI data acquisition and denoising. 2) establishment of BVP. 3) using neural network to identify gesture types. The WiHF process is similar to Widar3, the difference is that the second step of WiHF generates motion change pattern. However, the methods these models extract features is manual. Since gesture features are likely to be scattered in space and channel dimensions, these models may lose some gesture features. Therefore, we use the neural network based on the dual attention module to automatically extract features, which not only avoids the complicated process of extracting features but also improves the recognition accuracy.

AS shown in Table 3, the performance of our model surpasses Widar3 and WiHF in both in-domain and cross-domain recognition, even for WiHF with the HuFu dataset (tailored from the WiDar3 dataset). When all models use the widar3 data set (WIHF with HuFuM), our model performance exceeds the current best solution by 5.75%, 4.17%, 7.54% and 82.6% in the domain, across environment, position, and orientation evaluation respectively. We think the reason for this phenomenon is that although the handcrafted features of Widar3 and WiHF are very brilliant they may not cover all the domain-independent features scattered on each subcarrier.

Table 2. Recognition accuracy in the domain and across environments, orientations and positions

Serial Number	1	2	3	4	5
Position	98.22%	94.33%	98.11%	99.22%	99.44%
Orientation	89%	95.33%	96.33%	98.33%	92%
Environment	98.09%	94.84%	96.57%		
In-domain	99.67%				

Table 3. Average gesture recognition accuracy of different models

	In-domain	Environment	Position	Orientation
Widar3	92.7%	92.4%	89.7%	82.6%
WiHF + HuFuM	93.92%	89.67%	90.32%	79.14%
WiHF + HuFu	97.65%	Unknown	92.07%	82.38%
Our Model	**99.67%**	**96.57%**	**97.86%**	**94.2%**

3.3 Impact of Gesture Numbers

To verify the stability and robustness of our model, we evaluate its performance with more gestures (the default number is 6). The evaluation results are shown in Table 4. The in-domain accuracy remains above 98.5% though the number of gestures is increased to 9. And cross-domain performance of our model not significantly affected by the number of gestures.

Table 4. Impact of gesture type numbers

Gesture numbers	6	7	8	9
In-domain	99.67%	99.71%	98.57%	98.89%
Position	97.86%	96.8%	94.42%	94.79%
Orientation	94.2%	95.16%	90.53%	91.33%

4 Conclusion

In this paper, we proposed a novel model to realize cross-domain gesture recognition using CSI. In order to overcome the shortcoming of manually extracting features, we used the attention mechanism to automatically extract domain-independent gesture features from spatial and channel dimensions. We built a model using the dual self-attention modules and evaluated its performance by using the publicly available Widar3 dataset. Our model achieves superior in-domain and across-domains compared to state-of-the-art methods.

Acknowledgements. This work is supported by the National Natural Science Foundation of China (Grant No. 41871363, 41761086, 61761035 and 62061036), the Key Science-Technology Project of Inner Mongolia Autonomous Region (Grant No. 2021GG0163), and the Natural Science Foundation of Inner Mongolia Autonomous Region of china (Grant No. 2021ZD13 and 2019MS06030).

References

1. Gkioxari, G., Girshick, R., Dollár, P., et al.: Detecting and recognizing human-object interactions. In: Proceedings of the IEEE Conference on Computer Vision and Pattern Recognition, pp. 8359–8367 (2018)
2. Li, T., Liu, Q., Zhou, X.: Practical human sensing in the light. In: Proceedings of the 14th Annual International Conference on Mobile Systems, Applications, and Services, pp. 71–84 (2016)
3. Wang, M., Ni, B., Yang, X.: Recurrent modeling of interaction context for collective activity recognition. In: Proceedings of the IEEE Conference on Computer Vision and Pattern Recognition, pp. 3048–3056 (2017)
4. Bulling, A., Blanke, U., Schiele, B.: A tutorial on human activity recognition using body-worn inertial sensors. ACM Comput. Surv. (CSUR) **46**(3), 1–33 (2014)
5. Guan, Y., Plötz, T.: Ensembles of deep LSTM learners for activity recognition using wearables. Proc. ACM Interact. Mob. Wearable Ubiquit. Technol. **1**(2), 1–28 (2017)
6. Shen, S., Wang, H., Roy Choudhury, R.: I am a smartwatch and i can track my user's arm. In: Proceedings of the 14th Annual International Conference on Mobile Systems, Applications, and Services, pp. 85–96 (2016)
7. Kalgaonkar, K., Raj, B.: One-handed gesture recognition using ultrasonic Doppler sonar. In: 2009 IEEE International Conference on Acoustics, Speech and Signal Processing, pp. 1889–1892. IEEE (2009)
8. Nandakumar, R., Takakuwa, A., Kohno, T., et al.: Covertband: Activity information leakage using music. Proc. ACM Interact. Mob. Wearable Ubiquitous Technol. **1**(3), 1–24 (2017)
9. Yatani, K., Truong, K.N.: Bodyscope: a wearable acoustic sensor for activity recognition. In: Proceedings of the ACM Conference on Ubiquitous Computing 2012, pp. 341–350 (2012)
10. Huang, B., Mao, G., Qin, Y., et al.: Pedestrian flow estimation through passive wifi sensing. IEEE Trans. Mob. Comput. (2019)
11. Tian, Y., Huang, B., Jia, B., et al.: Optimizing AP and Beacon Placement in WiFi and BLE hybrid localization. J. Netw. Comput. Appl. **164**, 102673 (2020)
12. Jia, B., Huang, B., Gao, H., et al.: Dimension reduction in radio maps based on the supervised kernel principal component analysis. Soft. Comput. **22**(23), 7697–7703 (2018)
13. Hao, L., et al.: DHCLoc: a device heterogeneity tolerant and channel adaptive passive WiFi localization method based on DNN. IEEE Internet Things J. (2021)
14. Zhang, L., Zhang, Y., Zheng, X.: Wisign: ubiquitous American sign language recognition using commercial wi-fi devices. ACM Trans. Intell. Syst. Technol. (TIST) **11**(3), 1–24 (2020)
15. Li, H., Yang, W., Wang, J., et al.: WiFinger: talk to your smart devices with finger-grained gesture. In: Proceedings of the ACM International Joint Conference on Pervasive and Ubiquitous Computing, pp. 250–261 (2016)

16. Venkatnarayan, R.H., Page, G., Shahzad, M.: Multi-user gesture recognition using WiFi. In: Proceedings of the 16th Annual International Conference on Mobile Systems, Applications, and Services, pp. 401–413 (2018)
17. Zheng, Y., Zhang, Y., Qian, K., et al.: Zero-effort cross-domain gesture recognition with Wi-Fi. In: Proceedings of the 17th Annual International Conference on Mobile Systems, Applications, and Services, pp. 313–325 (2019)
18. Li, C., Liu, M., Cao, Z.: WiHF: enable user identified gesture recognition with WiFi. In: IEEE INFOCOM 2020-IEEE Conference on Computer Communications. IEEE (2020)
19. Zeng, Y., Wu, D., Xiong, J., et al.: FarSense: pushing the range limit of WiFi-based respiration sensing with CSI ratio of two antennas. Proc. ACM Interact. Mob. Wearable Ubiquitous Technol. 3(3), 1–26 (2019)
20. Wang, W., Liu, A.X., Shahzad, M., et al.: Understanding and modeling of wifi signal based human activity recognition. In: Proceedings of the 21st Annual International Conference on Mobile Computing and Networking, pp. 65–76 (2015)
21. Kotaru, M., Joshi, K., Bharadia, D., et al.: Spotfi: decimeter level localization using wifi. In: Proceedings of the ACM Conference on Special Interest Group on Data Communication 2015, pp. 269–282 (2015)
22. Li, X., Li, S., Zhang, D., et al.: Dynamic-music: accurate device-free indoor localization. In: Proceedings of the ACM International Joint Conference on Pervasive and Ubiquitous Computing, pp. 196–207 (2016)
23. Zeng, Y., Wu, D., Gao, R., et al.: FullBreathe: full human respiration detection exploiting complementarity of CSI phase and amplitude of WiFi signals. Proc. ACM Interactive Mob. Wearable Ubiquitous Technol. 2(3), 1–19 (2018)
24. Gu, Y., Zhang, X.., Liu, Z., et al.: WiFE: WiFi and Vision based Intelligent Facial-Gesture Emotion Recognition. arXiv preprint arXiv:2004.09889 (2020)
25. Liu, N., Han, J., Yang, M.H.: Picanet: learning pixel-wise contextual attention for saliency detection. In: Proceedings of the IEEE Conference on Computer Vision and Pattern Recognition, pp. 3089–3098 (2018)
26. Wu, Z., Su, L., Huang, Q.: Cascaded partial decoder for fast and accurate salient object detection. In: Proceedings of the IEEE/CVF Conference on Computer Vision and Pattern Recognition, pp. 3907–3916 (2019)
27. Fu, J., Liu, J., Tian, H., et al.: Dual attention network for scene segmentation. In: Proceedings of the IEEE/CVF Conference on Computer Vision and Pattern Recognition, pp. 3146–3154 (2019)
28. Halperin, D., Hu, W., Sheth, A., et al.: Tool release: gathering 802.11 n traces with channel state information. ACM SIGCOMM Comput. Commun. Rev. 41(1), 53–53 (2011)
29. Abdelnasser, H., Youssef, M., Harras, K.A.: Wigest: a ubiquitous wifi-based gesture recognition system. In: 2015 IEEE Conference on Computer Communications (INFOCOM), pp. 1472–1480. IEEE (2015)
30. Virmani, A., Shahzad, M.: Position and orientation agnostic gesture recognition using WiFi. In: Proceedings of ACM MobiSys2 (2017)
31. Jiang, W., et al.: Towards environment independent device free human activity recognition. In: Proceedings of ACM MobiCom, New Delhi, India (2018)
32. Sun, L., Sen, S., Koutsonikolas, D., Kim, K.H.: Widraw: enabling hands-free drawing in the air on commodity wifi devices. In: Proceedings of the 21st Annual International Conference on Mobile Computing and Networking, pp. 77–89, September 2015

33. Zhang, J., Tang, Z., Li, M., et al.: CrossSense: towards cross-site and large-scale WiFi sensing. In: Proceedings of the 24th Annual International Conference on Mobile Computing and Networking, pp. 305–320 (2018)
34. Yu, N., Wang, W., Liu, A.X., Kong, L.: QGesture: quantifying gesture distance and direction with WiFi signals. Proc. ACM Interactive Mob. Wearable Ubiquitous Technol. **2**(1), 1–23 (2018)
35. Ali, K., Liu, A. X., Wang, W., Shahzad, M.: Keystroke recognition using wifi signals. In: Proceedings of the 21st Annual International Conference on Mobile Computing and Networking, pp. 90–102, September 2015
36. Tan, S., Yang, J.: WiFinger: Leveraging commodity WiFi for fine-grained finger gesture recognition. In: Proceedings of the 17th ACM International Symposium on Mobile ad hoc Networking and Computing, pp. 201–210, July 2016

Font Transfer Based on Parallel Auto-encoder for Glyph Perturbation via Strokes Moving

Chen Wang⑩, Yani Zhu, Zhangyi Shen, Dong Wang, Guohua Wu,
and Ye Yao$^{(\boxtimes)}$⑩

School of Cyberspace, Hangzhou Dianzi University, Hangzhou, China
{wchen,zyn,shenzhangyi,wangdong,wugh,yaoye}@hdu.edu.cn

Abstract. Glyph perturbation is an increasing subject in information embedding. It can be generated by moving strokes of Chinese characters to convey secret messages. However, the generation is limited by the large number and diverse fonts of Chinese characters. Several attempts have been made to generate Chinese characters in the font transfer based on deep learning, up to now no studies have investigated font transfer for glyph perturbation. We propose a font transfer method for glyph perturbation of Chinese characters named Glyph-Font, which focuses on the position of strokes while transferring fonts. More specifically, we first build an image dataset for glyph perturbation of Chinese characters through perturbing strokes. Secondly, the generator based on a parallel auto-encoder simultaneously generates four glyph perturbations for each character in target fonts. In addition, a discriminator is designed to optimize the network by calculating the difference between real and generated images of Chinese characters. Finally, perturbation loss and patch-pixel loss are defined to amend incorrectly generated pixels and distinguish position changes of strokes. Experimental results demonstrate that our proposed Glyph-Font has the potential to generate glyph perturbations of Chinese characters automatically in various fonts.

Keywords: Font transfer · Glyph perturbation · Chinese characters generation · Parallel auto-encoder

1 Introduction

Glyph perturbation conveying secret messages is becoming essential in information embedding. Glyph perturbation of Chinese characters can be generated by moving strokes. As shown in Fig. 1, the movements (up or down or left or right) of two strokes can produce four glyph perturbations accordingly. To be specific, the middle dot in the left part and the first horizontal stroke in the right part of the character '法' in FangSong moved down and up respectively, resulting in four glyph perturbations.

Supported by National Natural Science Foundation of China (62071267).

Y. Lai et al. (Eds.): ICA3PP 2021, LNCS 13156, pp. 586–602, 2022.
https://doi.org/10.1007/978-3-030-95388-1_39

Fig. 1. Glyph perturbations of Chinese character '法'.

Significantly, the difficulties are how extensive and various the Chinese characters library usually possesses. The number of Chinese characters is much larger than that of other languages such as English, French, and German. For example, the lowest standard coding for Chinese characters named GB2312-80 includes 6,763 characters commonly used. Moreover, the library has a wide variety of fonts, including typography designed by professional designers and calligraphy written by individuals. Therefore, the production of glyph perturbation is a laborious and time-consuming task.

Existing studies have recognized the critical role of font transfer for Chinese characters, that is to convert fonts from the perspective of images while remaining its content. It contributes to the generation of Chinese characters under the above difficulties. On the one hand, taking Chinese characters as a whole not only alleviates the work of dismemberment but also learns font features more comprehensively. On the other hand, font features of Chinese characters are comprised of contents and styles, which is consistent with the images. The images of Chinese characters generated by this attempt are generally satisfactory, but the generated strokes are blurred and disordered in some cases such as complex components.

Nevertheless, far too little attention has been paid to the font transfer for glyph perturbation of Chinese characters. To overcome the above problems, we propose a font transfer method for glyph perturbation of Chinese characters named Glyph-Font. Compared with the existing methods, it pays more attention to the position of strokes while transferring the font of Chinese characters and generates glyph perturbations from source to target fonts. In addition, normal Chinese characters can be replaced by generated glyph perturbations to convey secret information and be applied to information hiding.

In summary, our font transfer method for glyph perturbation of Chinese characters is proposed by analyzing font features. The main contributions are listed as follows:

i) We propose a feasible and effective model, Glyph-Font, exploiting four parallel auto-encoder branches, to transfer the font and generate glyph perturbations for each Chinese character.

ii) A difference discriminator for adversarial learning strategy is proposed to measure the difference between the real and generated images of Chinese characters, which is helpful to generate more realistic images in target fonts.

iii) To identify position changes of strokes for Chinese characters, perturbation loss and patch-pixel loss are proposed to compare extracted features and count white pixels in each fixed-size patch with the corresponding position.

iv) A new image dataset for glyph perturbation of Chinese characters is built containing 4 fonts and 995 characters with perturbing strokes.

v) Qualitative and quantitative results verify the effectiveness of our method in the font transfer for glyph perturbation of Chinese characters, which learns the position of strokes accurately and generates high-quality images.

2   Related Work

2.1   Font Transfer for Chinese Characters

The font transfer methods for Chinese characters are classified into strokes generation and Chinese characters generation according to whether characters are split or not. The former mainly generates desired strokes in target fonts and constitutes complete characters by a set of predefined rules. The latter generates images of Chinese characters by extracting and learning font features.

Strokes Generation. Lian et al. [1,2] established a relationship between target and reference characters through non-rigid point set registration, positioned critical points on strokes, and extracted writing track of the input characters. Zhang et al. [3] designed a conditional generation model with style encoding to draw recognizable Chinese characters. It automatically simulated three discrete pen states (pen down, pen up, or character end) to determine when and how to finish writing. Wen et al. [4] introduced stroke refinement, adaptation to pre-deformation, and online zoom-augmentation to convolutional neural networks. LSCGAN [5] generated strokes in the new font by fusing the styles of two existing fonts and optimizing the network using the least-squares loss. RD-GAN [6] generated unseen Chinese characters with a few samples, effectively utilizing radical extraction and rendering.

Chinese Characters Generation. To restore images more authentically, the encoder of auto-encoder needs to extract necessary features representing the input. That is, the auto-encoder has a powerful ability to extract the input's features. Therefore, many scholars have utilized it to design network architectures. SA-VAE [7] defined an informational rule to supplement the structural details of Chinese characters and encoded each character into 133-bits coding based on structure and strokes. Using the dependence between contents and styles of images, EMD [8,9] extracted common style and content features from a set of style-reference images (with the same style but different contents) and content-reference images (with the same content but different styles). The extracted features were fused by a bilinear model to generate Chinese characters with specified style and content.

Recent advances based on generated adversarial network (GAN) [10] have facilitated exploratory study in font transfer for Chinese characters. It can be divided into three categories according to the way of learning style features: self-learning style features, external style features, and extractive style features.

Self-learning Style Features. PEGAN [11] added a cascaded refinement connection to the encoder of Pix2Pix [12]. In addition, the pre-trained VGG19 was used to calculate perceived loss, which was weighted together with L_1 loss, font category loss, and adversarial loss to make up the objective optimization function. SAFont [13] used self-attention blocks to calculate the attention changes in features of Chinese characters before and after transferring and defined edge loss to make generated images with clearer edges of strokes. With the increase of layers in the transfer network, HAN [14,15] built a staged decoder to describe global and local strokes details using the feature maps of low and high levels and generated the corresponding images of middle layers, which were sent to the discriminator together with the generated images. In addition to the font transfer for printing fonts, CycleGAN [16] accomplished the transfer from printing to handwriting mutually. OFM-CycleGAN [17] applied an optimized feature matching algorithm in the former, effectively improving the quality of handwriting. StrokeGAN [18] introduced stroke encoding for the font transfer network to retain strokes details better and generate more realistic images.

External Style Features. Zi2Zi [19] connected the font category to the embedding layer of auto-encoder based on Pix2Pix [12] and added judgment for the font category. It is suitable for font transfer tasks aiming at Chinese and Korean characters. Chen et al. [20,21] generated a variety of Chinese characters in different fonts combining images with one-hot vectors of font labels. The losses of font category and semantic consistency were added to constrain the optimization of network parameters. CalliGAN [22] further divided the contents of Chinese characters into dictionary sequences and features extracted by encoders and concatenated them with one-hot vectors representing specified style.

Extractive Style Features. AEGN [23] is a calligraphy font transfer method composed of two auto-encoder networks. The supervision network provided a transfer network with strokes details of target characters. In the transfer network, residual modules connected the encoder and decoder to learn subtle differences in the spatial structure between the source and target images. DCFont [24] used VGG16 to extract high-level features (style features) of images, which were fused with content features extracted from the font transfer network and sent into the decoder. FontGAN [25] integrated stylization, de-stylization, and texture transfer of Chinese characters into a unified framework. The style consistency module (SCM) and content prior module (CPM) were introduced to alleviate the problems of multiple domains transformations and strokes missing. TET-GAN [26] extended artistic Chinese characters to the field of font transfer and designed a stylized and de-stylized network under the framework of auto-encoder. To separate style and content features of Chinese characters, AGIS-NET [27] extracted common style features from a reference image dataset with consistent style, fused content and style features, and generated shape and texture images at the same time using a cooperated-training decoder.

2.2   Glyph Perturbation Generation

FontCode [28] focused on embedding additional information in text documents. It assigned each English letter an integer and embedded this integer by perturbing the glyph of each letter according to a precomputed codebook. A simple CNN structure was proposed to recognize glyphs and systematically construct a codebook containing a set of perturbed glyphs for each character in commonly used fonts. However, it is also limited in some ways. Suppose a part of the text is completely occluded from the camera, contaminated by other inks, heavily crumpled, or attached to a highly curved surface. In that case, the embedded message will be lost. Furthermore, the letters in the document must have sufficient resolution and large font size for reliable message retrieval when extracting information from rasterized and printed text documents.

Up to now, there have been no studies in font transfer for glyph perturbation of Chinese characters. Our proposed Glyph-Font is competent to transfer font and generate satisfactory images for glyph perturbation of Chinese characters.

3   Method Description

Different from the natural images, the image generation of Chinese characters has higher requirements for the correctness of strokes and structures, which is of great importance to identify them. Our method aims to learn position changes of strokes and generate glyph perturbations in an expected font.

3.1   Data Preparation

An image dataset for glyph perturbation of Chinese characters including four fonts (skeleton, FangSong, KaiTi, and YouYuan) is built by font design software named high-logic Font Creator. It contains 995 Chinese characters used frequently in daily life and 3,980 glyph perturbations of Chinese characters in each font generated by perturbing strokes. Our purpose of preparation is to move strokes of Chinese characters while maintaining the overall vision feelings. For each Chinese character in four fonts, its glyph perturbations are produced through the same movements of two selected strokes. The preparation results of Chinese character '法' in four fonts are shown in Fig. 2.

3.2   Network Architecture

As shown in Fig. 3, the proposed model consists of a generator G and two discriminators: D and $D_{difference}$. G consists of four parallel auto-encoder networks.

Fig. 2. Glyph perturbations of Chinese character '法'.

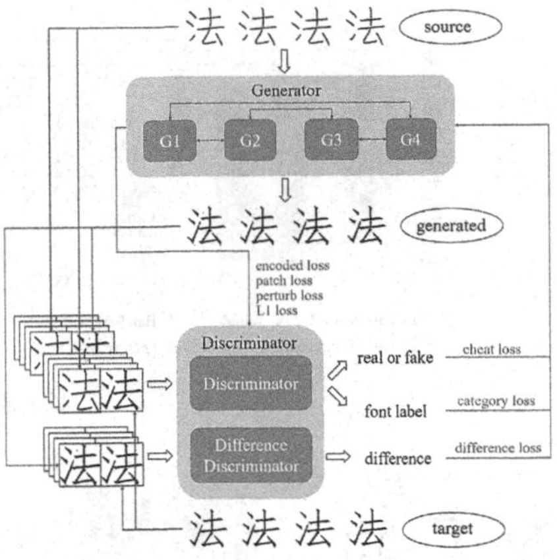

Fig. 3. The architecture of our model.

It extracts and restores the features representing glyph perturbations. Furthermore, two discriminators evaluate authenticity, font category, and difference of the inputs. For adversarial training, the generator learns the real samples' distribution and generates fake images to induce discriminators to make wrong decisions. The discriminators try to determine correctly whether the input data come from the real samples or the generator, and reduce the difference between real and generated images. Through the game confrontation, discriminators hardly distinguish the real from the fake images.

In the generator part, four generators (G1, G2, G3, and G4) output corresponding glyph perturbations simultaneously for each Chinese character. The encoder of each generator consists of a convolution layer and seven LeakyReLU-Conv-BN blocks whose normalization is omitted in the last block. The decoder of each generator consists of eight ReLU-Deconv-BN blocks which the last block replaces BN with Tanh activation function (see Fig. 4(a)). The features of Chinese characters extracted by the encoder of G and a label representing the font category are concatenated into the decoder to generate Chinese characters in specified fonts. These generated characters are consistent with its skeleton.

In the discriminator part, D consists of five Conv-BN-LeakyReLU blocks, except the last one without normalization and activation function (see Fig. 4(b)). $D_{difference}$ has two branches with a similar structure, including five Conv-Normalization-ReLU blocks and two convolution layers (see Fig. 4(c)). D makes the judgments of authenticity and font category on the input pairs with two full connection layers, and $D_{difference}$ calculates the difference between generated and real images.

During the training, the input data required by our method is paired. Specifically, the real and generated images of the target font are respectively paired with its corresponding skeleton for D. In addition, the real and generated images of the target font are paired as the inputs of $D_{difference}$.

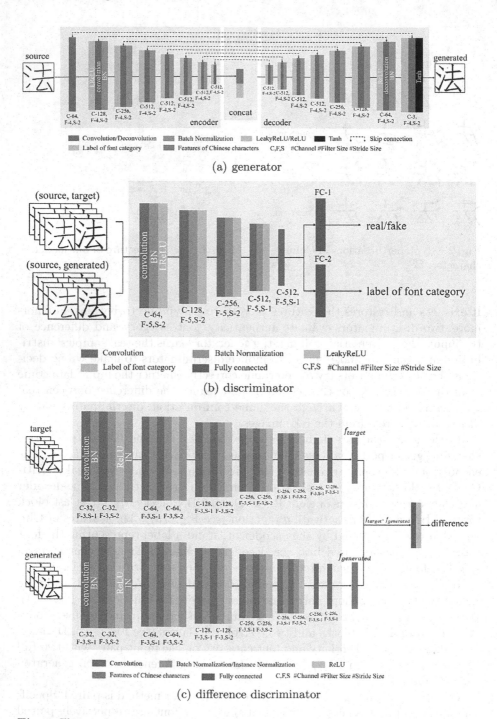

(a) generator

(b) discriminator

(c) difference discriminator

Fig. 4. Illustration of our model containing a generator, a discriminator, and a difference discriminator.

3.3   Loss Function

Our proposed Glyph-Font is trained by optimizing the loss functions, consisting of adversarial loss, encoded loss, perturbation loss, L_1 loss, and patch-pixel loss.

$$L_{total} = L_{adv} + L_{encoded} + L_{perturb} + L_1 + L_{patch} \tag{1}$$

Adversarial Loss. Our model containing G, D, and $D_{difference}$ is trained in an adversarial approach. The main purpose of G is to make the discriminators unable to distinguish the generated images from the real correctly, that is, to misjudge authenticity and font category of images and reduce the difference between the real and the generated images. D judges the authenticity and font category of input images, and $D_{difference}$ calculates the difference between generated and real images. The images generated by G mislead two discriminators, which constitute these loss functions:

$$L_{cheat} = \mathbb{E}_t[log(D_{r/f}(t))] + \mathbb{E}_s[1 - log(D_{r/f}(G(s)))] \tag{2}$$

$$L_{category} = \mathbb{E}_t[log(D_c(t))] + \mathbb{E}_s[1 - log(D_c(G(s)))] \tag{3}$$

$$L_{difference} = \mathbb{E}_{(s,t)}[\||1 - D_{difference}(G(s),t)\|_2] \tag{4}$$

$$L_{adv} = \lambda_{cheat}L_{cheat} + \lambda_{category}L_{category} + \lambda_{difference}L_{difference} \tag{5}$$

Where λ_{cheat}, $\lambda_{category}$ and $\lambda_{difference}$ control the weight of each item, 's' and 't' correspondingly denote real images of source and target fonts, and G(s) generates images of Chinese characters transferring font from the source to target. $D_{r/f}$, D_c and $D_{difference}$ denote the outputs representing authenticity, category, and difference, respectively.

Encoded Loss. The encoder of G can be regarded as a feature extractor in which the features of real and generated images can be extracted. To ensure that the generated images of Chinese characters fit their real images as much as possible, the encoded loss is defined for features extracted by the encoder of G:

$$L_{encoded} = \lambda_{encoded}\mathbb{E}_{(s,t)}[\||encoded_t - encoded_{G(s)}\|_2] \tag{6}$$

Where $\lambda_{encoded}$ is the weight for balancing, $encoded_t$ denotes features of the real images extracted by the encoder of G, and $encoded_{G(s)}$ denotes features of the generated images extracted by the same encoder.

Perturbation Loss. Fig. 5 provides four glyph perturbations of character '法' in source and target fonts, respectively. They are paired according to the position changes of strokes using green or yellow lines. From green lines in Fig. 5, the character '法' is perturbed by moving the first horizontal stroke up and down.

Also, it is apparent from yellow lines that the middle dot in the left part is moved up and down alternately.

$$L_{perturb\_g} = \sum_{img=s,G(s)} \mathbb{E}_{img}[\|encoded_{img_1} - encoded_{img_4}\|_2]$$
$$-\mathbb{E}_{img}[\|encoded_{img_2} - encoded_{img_3}\|_2] \tag{7}$$

$$L_{perturb\_y} = \sum_{img=s,G(s)} \mathbb{E}_{img}[\|encoded_{img_1} - encoded_{img_2}\|_2]$$
$$-\mathbb{E}_{img}[\|encoded_{img_3} - encoded_{img_4}\|_2] \tag{8}$$

$$L_{perturb} = \lambda_{perturb}[L_{perturb\_g} + L_{perturb\_y}] \tag{9}$$

Where $\lambda_{perturb}$ is the weight of perturbation loss, $L_{perturb\_g}$ and $L_{perturb\_y}$ are perturbation loss labeled green or yellow correspondingly, 'img' encompasses source and generated images of Chinese characters, and $Img = \{img_1, \ldots, img_4\}$ denote four corresponding glyph perturbations for each character.

L$_1$ Loss. The generated images of Chinese characters are obtained by G from skeleton images, which constitutes pixel-level loss with its real images. We set λ_1 as the weight of L_1 loss, and select L_1 distance instead of L_2 to alleviate blurry images and focus on regularizing the shape[12].

$$L_1 = \lambda_1 \mathbb{E}_{(s,t)}[\|t - G(s)\|_1] \tag{10}$$

Patch-pixel Loss. To learn the spatial information of strokes better, we divided the real and generated images of the target font into the small patch with the size 16×16 and calculated the number of white pixels in each patch to form two one-dimensional vectors. For example, the Chinese character '法' is split into patches by red dotted lines in Fig. 6, and one of the patches is explicitly shown on the right. The fitting degree of two vectors constitutes patch-pixel loss:

$$L_{patch} = \lambda_{patch} H(W_t, W_{G(s)}) = -\lambda_{patch} \sum_{k=1}^{K} w_t^k log(w_{G(s)}^k) \tag{11}$$

Where $W_t = \{w_t^1, \ldots, w_t^k, \ldots, w_t^K\}$ and $W_{G(s)} = \{w_{G(s)}^1, \ldots, w_{G(s)}^k, \ldots, w_{G(s)}^K\}$ denote white pixel vectors of real and generated images of target font, w_t^k and $w_{G(s)}^k$ mean the count of white pixels in the k-th patch, and K means the count of patches in each image.

Finally, the proposed model can be trained by playing the following maxi-min game:

$$\max_{D,D_{difference}} \min_{G} L_{adv} + L_{encoded} + L_{perturb} + L_1 + L_{patch} \tag{12}$$

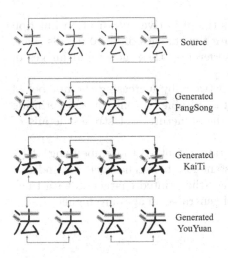

法 法 法 法 Source

法 法 法 法 Generated FangSong

法 法 法 法 Generated KaiTi

法 法 法 法 Generated YouYuan

Fig. 5. Illustration of perturbation loss.

Fig. 6. Illustration of patch-pixel loss.

4 Experiments

4.1 Experimental Setting

Dataset. We build a new image dataset of Chinese characters for experiments to verify our method's availability, which contains 995 Chinese characters and 3980 glyph perturbations in each font. It can be expanded by adding new characters and fonts in the data preparation above. In addition, our experiments adopt skeleton images [27] as source font and select three commonly used fonts of Chinese characters as the target: FangSong, KaiTi, and YouYuan. In the experiments, we take these glyph perturbations produced by 795 Chinese characters as a training dataset, and the remaining constituted test dataset.

Implementation Details. The generator G of our proposed Glyph-Font has seven convolution blocks and eight deconvolution blocks. Each block of the former contains convolution, Batch Normalization, and LeakyReLU. Each deconvolution block is made up of deconvolution, Batch Normalization, and ReLU. Following the structure of discriminator in ACGAN, D outputs the judgments of images' authenticity and font category, and $D_{difference}$ calculates the difference between the real and the generated images. All images of Chinese characters are in size 256×256. Weights in the loss functions are set as $\lambda_{category} = 10.0$, $\lambda_{cheat} = \lambda_{patch} = 1.0$, $\lambda_{difference} = \lambda_{encoded} = \lambda_{perturb} = 15.0$, $\lambda_1 = 100.0$. For Chinese characters in each font, we use the batch size 8 with 100 epochs for training.

4.2 Competitors

We compare our method with three font transfer methods for Chinese characters whose source codes are available online.

Rewrite2 [29] adopts adversarial loss as the objective optimization function based on ICGAN [30], which is used to learn the changes of facial details (hair, expression, et al.). Despite some noise interference, these generated images of Chinese characters are recognizable basically.

Unet-GAN [31] deepens the generator network by increasing the number of convolution layers based on Pix2Pix [12]. It is suitable for font transfer (printing and handwriting fonts) while preserving the structure and strokes details of Chinese characters.

Zi2Zi [19] connects label representing target font to the embedding of its generator based on Pix2Pix [12]. The constant loss between generated and real images is added to optimize the network. For the printed characters with thick strokes and clear structure, the qualities of generated images are higher.

4.3   Evaluation Metrics

Common indexes of quantitative evaluation in images include Mean Square Error (MSE), Root Mean Square Error (RMSE), Pixel-level Accuracy (Pix_acc), et al. In pixel level, MSE measures the pixel error of the corresponding position of two images. RMSE is the square root of MSE. Pix_acc calculates the proportion of pixels in the whole image whose pixel values are identical at the corresponding position of two images.

The performance of methods is measured by comparing the quality of generated images. Based on the fact that the images of Chinese characters are composed of black and white pixels. We selected RMSE and Pix_acc as evaluation indexes, which are defined as follows:

$$RMSE(t, G(s)) = \sqrt{\frac{1}{MN} \sum_{i=1}^{M} \sum_{j=1}^{N} (t_{i,j} - G(s)_{i,j})^2} \tag{13}$$

$$Pix\_acc = \frac{\sum_{i=1}^{M} \sum_{j=1}^{N} \mathbb{I}\{t_{i,j} = G(s)_{i,j}\}}{MN} \tag{14}$$

Where M and N represent the count of pixels for each image in two dimensions, $t_{i,j}$ and $G(s)_{i,j}$ denote the pixel values of the i-th row and j-th column in real and generated character images, respectively. The value of $\mathbb{I}\{\cdot\}$ is 1 when $t_{i,j}$ is equal to $G(s)_{i,j}$. Otherwise, it is 0. It is considered that the images of Chinese characters generated by the font transfer network are more realistic when RMSE is small, and Pix_acc is large.

4.4 Experiment Results

Qualitative Results. As shown in Fig. 7, we test our method on three fonts that are used in daily life and compare the generated images of Chinese character '法' with those generated by other existing methods: Rewrite2, Unet-GAN, and Zi2Zi. We can see that the strokes generated by Rewrite2 are disordered and unidentifiable, the images generated by Unet are blurry and terrible in the background, and the strokes generated by Zi2Zi are incomplete. Overall, those images generated by the methods we compared often have problems of blurry images, incomplete strokes, and low identifiability. Both Zi2Zi and Glyph-Font

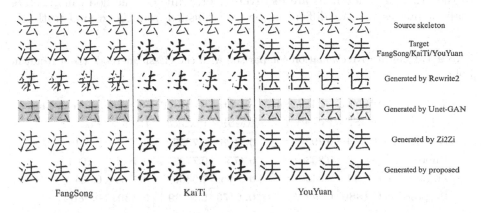

FangSong   KaiTi   YouYuan

Fig. 7. Comparison of generated images from skeleton to target fonts for Chinese character '法'.

FangSong   KaiTi   YouYuan

Fig. 8. Detailed comparison of generated images in target fonts (such as FangSong, KaiTi, and YouYuan).

are competent to the task of learning position changes of strokes and transferring font. Relatively speaking, our proposed Glyph-Font generates high-quality and realistic images of Chinese characters. Moreover, our method always outperforms other methods at the integrity and clarity of strokes, as depicted in Fig. 8.

Quantitative Results. The quantitative evaluations mentioned above measure the quality of generated images more directly. It is apparent that our proposed Glyph-Font obtains the lowest RMSE and the highest Pix_acc in Table 1. These quantitative results demonstrate that our method is superior to other methods, which is consistent with the above qualitative results. Overall, the performances of the other three methods are relatively poor, while our method can generate realistic images that are difficult to be distinguished from the ground truth.

Table 1. Quantitative evaluation comparison with the classic methods (Best result in bold).

Method	Skeleton → FangSong		Skeleton → KaiTi		Skeleton → YouYuan	
	RMSE	Pix_acc	RMSE	Pix_acc	RMSE	Pix_acc
Rewrite2	0.4544	0.7927	0.5128	0.7353	0.5351	0.7119
Unet-GAN	0.4412	0.8038	0.4754	0.7728	0.4871	0.7604
Zi2Zi	0.2314	0.9457	0.2496	0.9366	0.2538	0.9343
Proposed	**0.1380**	**0.9807**	**0.1373**	**0.9809**	**0.1391**	**0.9802**

Effects of Difference Discriminator. To validate the effects of the difference discriminator, we retrain our model without it. The quantitative results of the proposed Glyph-Font are similar to that without difference discriminator in RMSE and Pix_acc. From the generated results shown in Fig. 9, Chinese characters generated without and with the difference discriminator correspond to the first and second lines, respectively. Comparatively speaking, it can be seen that the use of difference loss further improves visual quality in the qualitative results, which is effective in generating strokes with high integrity.

办 办 办 办｜包 包 包 包｜费 费 费 费 Without difference loss

办 办 办 办｜包 包 包 包｜费 费 费 费 With difference loss

城 城 城 城｜动 动 动 动｜关 关 关 关 Without difference loss

城 城 城 城｜动 动 动 动｜关 关 关 关 With difference loss

动 动 动 动｜却 却 却 却｜觉 觉 觉 觉 Without difference loss

动 动 动 动｜却 却 却 却｜觉 觉 觉 觉 With difference loss

去 去 去 去｜势 势 势 势｜起 起 起 起 Without difference loss

去 去 去 去｜势 势 势 势｜起 起 起 起 With difference loss

准 准 准 准｜圳 圳 圳 圳｜输 输 输 输 Without difference loss

准 准 准 准｜圳 圳 圳 圳｜输 输 输 输 With difference loss

FangSong   KaiTi   YouYuan

Fig. 9. Detailed comparison of generated images with/without difference loss in target fonts (such as FangSong, KaiTi, and YouYuan).

5 Conclusion

In this paper, we propose the font transfer method named Glyph-Font for glyph perturbation of Chinese characters, which pays more attention to the position of strokes while transferring fonts. It is composed of a parallel generator and two discriminators under adversarial learning. The parallel generator learns strokes details and generates four glyph perturbations for each Chinese character simultaneously. Moreover, the discriminator is required to judge the images' authenticity and font category correctly. The proposed difference discriminator, perturbation loss, and patch-pixel loss improve strokes accuracy to some extent. We also build an image dataset for glyph perturbation of Chinese characters to provide support for subsequent work. Experiments on this dataset demonstrate that our method can transfer font and generate glyph perturbations of Chinese characters. At the same time, the generated dataset of Chinese characters can meet the needs for information hiding and be applied in IoT devices to protect privacy and data integrity [32–34].

It should be pointed out that we only collect glyph perturbations images of 995 Chinese characters in our dataset due to significant human intervention, which can be expanded further. In addition, it is found from experimental results that the method proposed is suitable for glyph perturbation generation automatically in information embedding, and more various fonts are needed in this field.

References

1. Lian, Z., Zhao, B., Xiao, J.: Automatic generation of large-scale handwriting fonts via style learning. In SIGGRAPH ASIA 2016 Technical Briefs, pp. 1–4. Association for Computing Machinery, New York (2016) https://doi.org/10.1145/3005358.3005371

2. Lian, Z., Zhao, B., Chen, X., Xiao, J.: EasyFont: a style learning-based system to easily build your large-scale handwriting fonts. ACM Trans. Graph. **38**(1), 1–18 (2018). https://doi.org/10.1145/3213767

3. Zhang, X.-Y., Yin, F., Zhang, Y.-M., Liu, C.-L., Bengio, Y.: Drawing and recognizing Chinese characters with recurrent neural network. IEEE Trans. Pattern Anal. Mach. Intell. **40**(4), 849–862 (2018). https://doi.org/10.1109/TPAMI.2017.2695539

4. Wen, C., et al.: Handwritten Chinese font generation with collaborative stroke refinement. arXiv preprint arXiv: 1904.13268 (2019)

5. Lin, X., Li, J., Zeng, H., Ji, R.: Font generation based on least squares conditional generative adversarial nets. Multimedia Tools Appl. **78**(1), 783–797 (2018). https://doi.org/10.1007/s11042-017-5457-4

6. Huang, Y., He, M., Jin, L., Wang, Y.: RD-GAN: few/zero-shot Chinese character style transfer via radical decomposition and rendering. In: Vedaldi, A., Bischof, H., Brox, T., Frahm, J.-M. (eds.) ECCV 2020. LNCS, vol. 12351, pp. 156–172. Springer, Cham (2020). https://doi.org/10.1007/978-3-030-58539-6_10

7. Sun, D., Ren, T., Li, C., Su, H., Zhu, J.: Learning to write stylized Chinese characters by reading a handful of examples. In: Proceedings of the 27th International Joint Conference on Artificial Intelligence, pp. 920–927. International Joint Conferences on Artificial Intelligence Organization, Stockholm (2018). https://doi.org/10.24963/ijcai.2018/128

8. Zhang, Y., Zhang, Y., Cai, W.: Separating style and content for generalized style transfer. In: Proceedings of the IEEE/CVF Conference on Computer Vision and Pattern Recognition, pp. 8447–8455. IEEE, Salt Lake City (2018). https://doi.org/10.1109/CVPR.2018.00881

9. Zhang, Y., Zhang, Y., Cai, W.: A unified framework for generalizable style transfer: style and content separation. IEEE Tran. Image Process. **29**, 4085–4098 (2020). https://doi.org/10.1109/TIP.2020.2969081

10. Goodfellow, I.J., et al.: Generative adversarial nets. In: Proceedings of the 27th International Conference on Neural Information Processing Systems, pp. 2672–2680. MIT Press, Cambridge (2014)

11. Sun, D., Zhang, Q., Yang, J.: Pyramid embedded generative adversarial network for automated font generation. In: 24th International Conference on Pattern Recognition, pp. 976–981. IEEE, Beijing (2018) https://doi.org/10.1109/ICPR.2018.8545701

12. Isola, P., Zhu, J.-Y., Zhou, T., Efros, A.A.: Image-to-image translation with conditional adversarial networks. In: 2017 IEEE Conference on Computer Vision and Pattern Recognition, pp. 5967–5976. IEEE, Honolulu (2017) https://doi.org/10.1109/CVPR.2017.632

13. Ren, C., Lyu, S., Zhan, H., Lu, Y.: SAFont: automatic font synthesis using self-attention mechanisms. Aust. J. Intell. Inf. Process. Syst. **16**(2), 19–25 (2019)

14. Chang, J., Gu, Y., Zhang, Y.: Chinese typeface transformation with hierarchical generative adversarial network. arXiv preprint arXiv: 1711.06448 (2017)

15. Chang, J., Gu, Y., Zhang, Y, Wang, Y.: Chinese handwriting imitation with hierarchical generative adversarial network. In: British Machine Vision Conference, pp. 1–12. BMVA Press, Newcastle (2018)
16. Chang, B., Zhang, Q., Pan, S., Meng, L.: Generating handwritten Chinese characters using CycleGAN. In: Proceedings of the 2018 IEEE Winter Conference on Applications of Computer Vision, pp. 199–207. IEEE, Lake Tahoe (2018) https://doi.org/10.1109/WACV.2018.00028
17. Zhang, Y.: Generating handwritten Chinese character with GANs. East China Normal University, Shanghai (2019). (张艺颖.: 基于生成对抗网络的手写体汉字生成. 华东师范大学, 上海 (2019))
18. Zeng, J., Chen, Q., Liu, Y., Wang, M., Yao, Y.: StrokeGAN: reducing mode collapse in Chinese font generation via stroke encoding. arXiv preprint arXiv: 2012.08687 (2020)
19. Tian, Y.: Zi2Zi. https://github.com/kaonashi-tyc/zi2zi/, Accessed 9 Aug 2019
20. Chen, J., Xu, X., Ji, Y., Chen, H.: Learning to create multi-stylized Chinese character fonts by generative adversarial networks. In: ACM TURC '19 Proceedings of the ACM Turing Celebration Conference, pp. 1–6. Association for Computing Machinery, Chengdu (2019) https://doi.org/10.1145/3321408.3322631
21. Chen, J., Chen, H., Xu, X., Ji, Y., Chen, L.: Learning to write multi-stylized Chinese characters by generative adversarial networks. J. Univ. Electron. Sci. Technol. China **48**(5), 674–678 (2019). (陈杰夫等.: 基于对抗生成网络的多风格化的汉字 电子科技大学学报. **48**(5), 674–678 (2019)) https://doi.org/10.3969/j.issn.1001-0548.2019.05.003
22. Wu, S.-J., Yang, C.-Y., Hsu, J.-Y.: CalliGAN: style and structure-aware Chinese calligraphy character generator. arXiv preprint arXiv: 2005.12500 (2020)
23. Lyu, P., Bai, X., Yao, C., Zhu, Z., Huang, T., Liu, W.: Auto-encoder guided GAN for Chinese calligraphy synthesis. In: Proceedings of the 14th IAPR International Conference on Document Analysis and Recognition, pp. 1095–1100. IEEE Computer Society, Kyoto (2017) https://doi.org/10.1109/ICDAR.2017.181
24. Jiang, Y., Lian, Z., Tang, Y., Xiao, J.: DCFont: an end-to-end deep Chinese font generation system. In: SIGGRAPH Asia 2017 Technical Briefs, pp. 1–4. Association for Computing Machinery, New York (2017) https://doi.org/10.1145/3145749.3149440
25. Liu, X., Meng, G., Chang, J., Hu, R., Xiang, S., Pan, C.: Decoupled representation learning for Character glyph synthesis. IEEE Trans. Multimedia., 1 (2021). https://doi.org/10.1109/TMM.2021.3072449
26. Yang, S., Liu, J., Wang, W., Guo, Z.: TET-GAN: text effects transfer via stylization and de-stylization. In: Proceedings of the 32nd AAAI Conference on Artificial Intelligence, pp. 1238–1245. AAAI Press, Hilton Hawaiian Village (2019) :https://doi.org/10.1609/aaai.v33i01.33011238
27. Gao, Y., Guo, Y., Lian, Z., Tang, Y., Xiao, J.: Artistic glyph image synthesis via one-stage few-shot learning. ACM Trans. Graph. **38**(6), 1–12 (2019). https://doi.org/10.1145/3355089.3356574
28. Xiao, C., Zhang, C., Zheng, C.: FontCode: embedding information in text documents using glyph perturbation. ACM Trans. Graph. **37**(2), 1–16 (2018). https://doi.org/10.1145/3152823
29. Chang, B., Zhang, Q.: Rewrite2: a GAN based Chinese font transfer algorithm. https://github.com/changebo/Rewrite2/, Accessed 18 Mar 2017
30. Perarnau, G., van de Weijer, J., Raducanu, B., Álvarez, J. M.: Invertible conditional gans for image editing. arXiv preprint arXiv: 1611.06355 (2016)

31. Chang, J., Gu, Y.: Chinese typography transfer. arXiv preprint arXiv: 1707.04904v1 (2017)
32. Wang, T., Liu, Y., Zheng, X., Dai, H.-N., Jia, W., Xie, M.: Edge-based communication optimization for distributed federated learning. IEEE Trans. Netw. Sci. Eng., 1 (2021) https://doi.org/10.1109/TNSE.2021.3083263
33. Wang, T., Lu, Y., Wang, J., Dai, H.-N., Zheng, X., Jia, W.: EIHDP: edge-intelligent hierarchical dynamic pricing based on cloud-edge-client collaboration for IoT systems. IEEE Trans. Comput. **70**(8), 1285–1298 (2021). https://doi.org/10.1109/TC.2021.3060484
34. Wang, T., Bhuiyan, M.Z.A., Wang, G., Qi, L., Wu, J., Hayajneh, T.: Preserving balance between privacy and data integrity in edge-assisted internet of things. IEEE Internet Things J. **7**(4), 2679–2689 (2020). https://doi.org/10.1109/JIOT.2019.2951687

A Novel GNN Model for Fraud Detection in Online Trading Activities

Jing Long[1,2] , Fei Fang[1(✉)], and Haibo Luo[3]

[1] College of Information Science and Engineering, Hunan Normal University,
Changsha 410081, China
{jlong,fangfei}@hunnu.edu.cn
[2] Guangxi Key Laboratory of Cryptography and Information Security,
Guilin University of Electronic Technology, Guilin 541004, China
[3] Fujian Provincial Key Laboratory of Information Processing and Intelligent
Control, Minjiang University, Fuzhou 350121, China
robhappy@qq.com

Abstract. The previous graph neural network-based fraud detection techniques were usually realized by clustering the neighbors with different relationships. However, the graph-based datasets face the issues of imbalanced features, classifications, and relationships, which directly decreases the detection performance. In this case, this work proposes a novel real-time GNN model to address this issue. Firstly, the features are measured to find the entities which have the highest similarity to the fraudster. The entities are sampled to identify the fraudsters in training. The fraudsters are far less than the normal nodes in the dataset. We then combine the Under-Sampling algorithm and the long-distance sampling algorithm to find the nodes that are similar to the neighbors. Finally, a reinforcement learning (RL)-based reward and punishment mechanism is proposed for sampling the weight between the relationships. It is effective to the issue of imbalanced relationships in the graph-based dataset. Experiments show that the proposed technique is superior to the comparative models on the real-world fraud dataset.

Keywords: GNN · Fraud detection · RL · Imbalance problem

1 Introduction

The widespread development of the Internet and mobile payment has greatly improved the convenience of people's daily life in the fields of finance [2], insurance [13,14,21,26], medical treatment [22], etc. Meanwhile, the cost of various fraud behaviors is also reduced in these fields. Similar to fraud detection in copyright protection [18] and intrusion detection [17], the fraudsters pretend to be the normal entities and bypass the anti-fraud system for its fraud. It will pose a great threat to the benefits of the users. There are many researchers who identify the fraudsters by utilizing the graph-based approaches [9,27,30]. Usually, the

© Springer Nature Switzerland AG 2022
Y. Lai et al. (Eds.): ICA3PP 2021, LNCS 13156, pp. 603–614, 2022.
https://doi.org/10.1007/978-3-030-95388-1_40

real-world entities are regarded as nodes and the relationships among these entities are denoted by the edges between each pair of nodes [6]. The feature of each entity is represented by the node feature and the relationship between two nodes is represented by the edge feature. Different relationships for two entities can be represented by weight [11]. Due to the effectiveness of the graph-based structure, it is widely used in fraud detection models for fields of finance, insurance, medical treatment, etc. However, most of the existing fraud detection models cannot deal with the imbalanced problems, which directly affects detection accuracy. In this case, this work aims to research an effective fraud detection model.

Our contribution is as follows, we designed a fraud detection model. First, the Under-sampling method is used to solve the problem of category imbalance in training. Secondly, a feature information extractor is designed. Finally, use reinforcement learning as a reward and punishment mechanism to obtain the sampling weight of each relationship, and perform high-order neighbor sampling on the entire graph according to the sampling weight. And did experiments on the dataset to prove the effectiveness of our proposed model.

2   Related Work

The existing fraud detection algorithms belong to the field of data mining. In [1], the authors utilized machine learning to address the fraud detection problem. The naive Bayes, K-nearest neighbor, and logistic regression are adopted to address the fraud of credit cards. The authors in [29] used the convolutional neural networks(CNN) in the proposed fraud detection model. In [8], the generative adversarial network (GAN) was utilized to generate a small number of class instances, which will combine with the original dataset and form an enhanced training dataset for better effectiveness of the classifier. These approaches usually use supervised learning for model training. However, supervised learning is less flexible when the node behavior changes or a new fraud occurs. In this case, the authors in [4] combined the supervised learning with unsupervised learning to improve the accuracy of fraud detection.

In recent years, graph neural network (GNN) has been widely applied in various fields, such as image identification [16], recommendation system [5] and fraud detection. For instance, the authors in [24] proposed a GAT- based semi-supervised graph neural network, called SemiGNN. It can realize fraud detection for the multi-view labeled data and the unlabeled data. In [15], a graph convolutional neural network-based model is proposed for large-scale spam review detection. In [19], a GEM model learned the importance of nodes with various types by utilizing the attention mechanism, whilst the hierarchical attention mechanism is used to set the model [12]. Besides, the authors in [28] designed the Player2Vec model by jointly utilizing the attention mechanism and GNN.

By analyzing the previous models, few of them focused on the imbalance issue of the dataset, which is closely related to the aggregation process of the GNN. Finally, the classifier will realize classification according to the result of aggregation. Therefore, it is critical to select an appropriate aggregation neighbor. The issue of data imbalance can be divided into three parts: category imbalance, feature imbalance, and relationship imbalance [3,7]. category imbalance means the number of fraudsters is far less than the number of the normal entities. On this basis of the category imbalance, the fraudsters can pretend to be normal, which will add noise or connect to several normal entities to make it similar to the normal entities. With the participation of the fraudsters, the GNN-based fraud detection model cannot reach a high detection accuracy. Practically, there are various relationships among entities. Each relationship has a different impact on the entities. So, the importance of the relationships should be considered, which reflects the relationship imbalance. To address the mentioned three problems, this work proposes a novel GNN-based fraud detection model. A neighbor sampler and the feature extractor are designed in this model. The Under-Sampling method is used to solve the issue of category imbalance. The distance scores are generated based on the features. With the deep reinforcement, the sampled weights for each relationship can be generated for high-order neighbor sampling. The performance of this work is evaluated on the public fraud detection dataset. The evaluation results show the effectiveness of the proposed model.

The remaining paper is organized as follows. Section 2 introduces and analyzes the previous techniques. Section 3 gives some preliminaries. Section 4 introduces the model framework and the proposed algorithm. The experiments are conducted and analyzed in Sect. 5. This paper is summarized in Sect. 6.

3   Preliminaries

Before presenting the detailed model, we provide some background knowledge on related techniques.

3.1   Multi-relation Graph

The multi-relation graph can be denoted by $\mathcal{G} = \{V, C, \{B_r\}|_{r=1}^{R}, Y\}$. Herein, $V = \{v_1, v_2, ..., v_n\}$ is the collection of n nodes in the graph. $C = \{c_1, c_2, ..., c_n\}$ is the feature of each node with the length of d. $B = \{B_1, B_2, ..., B_r\}$ represents the adjacent matrix of nodes for various relations. Herein, we have $r \in \{1, 2, ..., R\}$. $Y = \{y_1, y_2, ..., y_n\}$ denotes the label collection of all nodes.

3.2   Long-distance Sampling

The classes of graph-based data are generally imbalanced. For the binary classification problem, a small number of some classes will cause inaccurate classification results. If the sampling approach of classification or the selected evaluation metric is not suitable, the overall performance of the model cannot be objectively evaluated. Here, we adopt the Under-Sampling algorithm for sampling due to its. It performs sampling from the normal nodes without replacement. The number of samples is approached to the number of fraud nodes. In other words, it realizes under sampling for the majority classes to balance the sample number.

In this case, the model can better predict the fraud nodes. Here, the collection of sampled nodes for training is denoted by $\mathcal{N}_v$.

The fraud nodes can pretend to be normal and connect to the normal nodes. Here, long-distance sampling is utilized to predict the relations among nodes. The K-order neighbors of the sampled training nodes are used for the subsequent neighbor sampling. With the K-order neighbors, more nodes similar to the major node will be found. With (1), we can calculate the K-order neighbors under the relation r. The final K-order adjacent matrix for sampling can be calculated with (2).

$$T_{(k)}^{(r)} = B^{(r)k}. \tag{1}$$

$$B_{(k)}^{(r)} = \sum_{i=1}^{k} T_{(k)}^{(r)} + B^{(r)}. \tag{2}$$

Here, $T_{(k)}^{(r)}$ is the k-order adjacent matrix under relation r. $B_{(k)}^{(r)}$ represents the adjacent matrix of the 1-order to k-order neighbor, which will be used for subsequent neighbor sampling.

3.3 Neighbor Sampling

In the neighbor sampling, the multi-layer preceptor (MLP) is utilized as the feature extractor. The feature will be used for calculating the distance between neighbors and be the input of the subsequent GNN. With (3), the distance between the training node and the neighbor node can be calculated. Shorter distance represents higher similarity to the major node, which will be sampled with a high probability. The average distance score of each epoch can be calculated by (4).

$$\mathcal{D}_{(v,u)}^{l} = \sigma(\mathcal{M}_2(\mathcal{M}_1 h_v^{(l-1)} + b_1) + b_2) - \sigma(\mathcal{M}_2(\mathcal{M}_1 h_u^{(l-1)} + b_1) + b_2). \tag{3}$$

$$S_{(r)}^{(e)} = \frac{\sum_{v \in N_{(v)}} \mathcal{D}_{(r)}^{(e-1)}(Z_v, h_v^r)}{|N_{(v)}|}. \tag{4}$$

M is the weight matrix, the values in the matrix are the parameters learned by the model, and the b values are also the parameters learned by the model. $\mathcal{D}_{(r)}^{(e-1)}(Z_v, h_v^r)$ represents using (3) to calculate the distance between h_v^r of each node v under relation r after each epoch and Z_v after the aggregation of node v between relations. $|N_{(v)}|$ represents the number of training nodes, and $S_{(r)}^{(e)}$ represents the similarity degree of the features after all the training node relationships are aggregated in the final relationship.

This paper uses the most classic example of reinforcement learning K-armed Bandit [23] . In this paper, the reinforcement learning mechanism is embedded in the graph neural network to optimize the training of the graph neural network. We use the training data of the graph neural network to determine the number of neighbor samples under each relationship in the next training, initialize the proportion of training under each relationship to $O = o_1, o_2, ..., o_r$, and set two states, $S_1 : S_r^{(e)} - S_r^{(e-1)} \geq 0$, $S_1 : S_r^{(e)} - S_r^{(e-1)} < 0$, corresponding to two actions respectively, $a_{S_1} = 0.02$, $a_{S_2} = 0.03$, the reward function is defined as $f(s, a)$, as shown in (5), and finally, o is obtained according to the reward function $o^e = o^{e-1} + f^{(e)}(s, a)a_s$. This method is used to update the value of o^e under each relationship.

$$f(s, a) = \begin{cases} 1, S_1 \\ -1, S_2. \end{cases} \tag{5}$$

3.4 GNN Aggregation

In the model of HAN [25], the heterogeneous graphs are transformed into isomorphic graphs under different relations through the types of nodes and different relations, and the training is carried out separately. Finally, the data of each node under different relations. The features are merged to obtain the final feature of the node. The dataset used in this paper also uses this method for training. In [25], the node attention mechanism and semantic attention mechanism are utilized in node training and relationship training. Since we processed the samples in advance, the effect of using the attention mechanism is not obvious, and it will increase the amount of calculation and consume more time, so the attention mechanism is not used in our proposed method. We continue to use the Meta-path, divide the dataset into R relationships, select neighbors for training nodes under each relationship, we use (6) to calculate the aggregated features of the neighbor nodes of the training node, and use (7) to calculate the aggregated features of the training node and neighbor nodes.

$$h_{N_{(u)}}^{l+1} = AGG(\{MLP(h_u^l), \forall u \in N_{(u)}\}). \tag{6}$$

$$h_v^{l+1} = \sigma(\{CANCAT(h_v^l, h_{N_{(u)}}^{l+1}), \forall u \in N_{(v)}\}). \tag{7}$$

Among them, $h_{N_{(u)}}^{l+1}$ represents the aggregation of the neighboring nodes of node v, and h_v^{l+1} is the aggregation of the feature h_v^l of the neighboring node and the upper-level node v. AGG is an aggregate function.σ is the activation function. Then aggregate the features of each relationship of each node v, and we denote the final node v as z_v^l , as shown in (8).

$$z_v^l = \sigma(AGG(z_v^{l-1} \oplus \{o_r^{l-1} h_{v,r}^l\}|_{r=1}^R, \forall v \in N_{(v)})). \tag{8}$$

After graph neural network aggregation, we use the CrossEntropyLoss function to optimize, CrossEntropyLoss combines the LogSoftmax function and the NLLLoss function, as shown in (9).

$$Loss = - \sum_{v \in N_{(v)}} y_v[log(softmax(MLP(z_v)))]. \tag{9}$$

4   The Proposed Fraud Detection Model

The fraud detection problem is to distinguish the normal nodes and the fraud nodes in the multi-relationship graph. The nodes in the dataset are labeled with 0,1. 0 represents the normal node and 1 represents the fraud node. In this case, the problem belongs to the semi-supervised binary classification. The labeled nodes in the multi-relationship are used for model training, thus predicting the unlabeled nodes.

4.1   System Framework

The proposed model can be observed in Fig. 1. It consists of the neighbor sampler and the GNN. The neighbor sampler mainly includes two parts: long-distance sampling and neighbor sampling, which are illustrated concretely as follows.

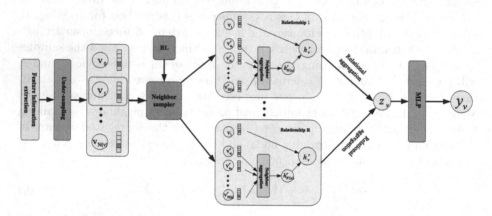

Fig. 1. The structure of the proposed model

Firstly, the feature information of the selected dataset is extracted. We then combine the Under-Sampling algorithm and the long-distance sampling algorithm to find the nodes that are similar to the neighbors. The RL-based reward/punishment mechanism is used for sampling the weight between the relationships. In thihs case, the relationships among the training nodes are aggregated into clusters.

4.2   Fraud Detection Algorithm

In this section, we describe the critical algorithm flow of this proposed model. Here, we focus on two algorithms, neighbor sampling and GNN aggregation.

Neighbor Sampling Algorithm. The neighbor sampling algorithm is to generate the final set of sampled neighbor nodes and the next neighbor sampling threshold. The inputs include $G = \{V,C,\{B_r\}_{r=1}^R,Y\},K,O^0,A$ collection of nodes for training obtained after Under-Sampling sampling N_v. The output is the final sampled neighbor node set N_u and the next neighbor sampling threshold O^e.The detailed flow is described as follows.

Step1: We set up an MLP as a feature extractor, which will be used to calculate feature similarity and used to select neighbors based on aggregation. It will be input to GNN as the feature of the node

Step2: Then we use (1) and (2) to perform long-distance sampling on the nodes under each relationship, that is, the high-order neighbors of the nodes, and finally obtain the high-order adjacency matrix B_k^r.

Step3: Perform neighbor sampling on this batch of nodes according to the O^{e-1} obtained from the previous neighbor sampling to obtain $N_{(u)}^e$.

Step4: According to (3), calculate the similarity between the different relations of each node, and combine the reinforcement learning to obtain the weight between the relations o^e.

Fraud Detection Algorithm. This algorithm is to generate the vector representation of each node. The inputs include $G=\{V,C,\{B_r\}|_{r=1}^R,Y\}$, K,O^0, Initialization parameters $O=\{o_1,...o_r\}$, the number of model layers L, the number of epochs E and a collection of nodes for training obtained after Under-Sampling sampling N_v.The output is the vector representation of each node v in $N_{(v)}$.

Step1: Calculate $N_{(u)}$ with the above neighbor sampling algorithm;

Step2: For each $v \in N_{(v)}$ and R, aggregate the neighbor $N_{(u)}$ sampled by the neighbor sampler to obtain $h_{N_{(u)}}^l$ with Eq. 6.

Step3: Aggregate the training node and the corresponding neighbor node to get h_v^l with Eq. 7. Repeat Step3 for each $u \in N_{(u)}$.

Step4: Aggregate each relationship of the training node to get z_v with Eq. 8.

With the above flow, the final vector representation of all nodes in $N_{(v)}$ can be generated.

5 Experiments and Analysis

5.1 Dataset

We use the Amazon review dataset to study fraudulent user detection tasks. The Amazon dataset includes product reviews under the Amazon musical instrument category. It marks more than 80% of users who help to vote as benign nodes and less than 20% of users who help to vote as fraudulent nodes. Each node contains 25 features.

The Amazon dataset regards users as nodes in the graph and divides the connections between nodes into three relationships: 1) U-P-U: Indicates that two connected users have viewed at least the same product. 2) U-S-U: Indicates that the two connected users have at least a one-star rating within a week. 3) U-V-U: It connects the top 5% of users with mutual evaluation text similarity (measured by TF-IDF) among all users. The specific distribution is shown in Table 1.

Table 1. The composition of graph-based Amazon dataset.

Nodes	Edge	Relation
11944	4398392	U-P-U 175608
		U-S-U 3566479
		U-V-U 1036737

5.2 Evaluation Metrics and Reference Models

For the problem of category imbalance, if the accuracy is used as the evaluation metric, when there are too many benign entities, even if the model predicts all nodes as benign nodes, the accuracy rate is as high as 80% or more. Therefore, we do not use accuracy as the evaluation metric. The AUC and Recall are utilized as evaluation metrics to measure the performance of all proposed models. AUC is the most commonly used evaluation index to measure the pros and cons of a two-class model, and the influencing factors of category imbalance have little effect on it. AUC is the area under the ROC curve, the abscissa of the ROC curve is as (10), the ordinate is TPR, and the definition of Recall is as in (11) .

$$FPR = \frac{FP}{TN + FP}.$$ (10)

$$Recall = \frac{TP}{TP + FN}.$$ (11)

We implement two GNN-based fraud detection models for performance comparison.

1. GraphSAGE [10]: Similar to the method proposed in this paper, the neighbors are sampled before neighbor aggregation. It uses a fixed number of neighbors sampling.
2. GraphConsis [20]: GraphConsis is a fraud detection model proposed for the problem of graph data inconsistency.

5.3 Evaluation Results

The proposed model is implemented in Pytorch 1.6.0 and Python3.7. All experiments are run on Ubuntu 18.04 server, which has 8 cores and 40GB memory. Since fraudsters account for a relatively small percentage in the Amazon dataset, we use the Under-Sampling algorithm for training set sampling and small batch training in order to improve training efficiency. The parameters in GNN are optimized using Adam, the learning rate is set to 0.005, Epoch = 50, batch_size = 256, dropout = 0.5, and O is initialized to $O = [0.6, 0.6, 0.6]$.

With the above parameters, we evaluate the performance of the proposed model and it compare to the reference models. The experiment utilizes the training ratio of 10%, 20% ,and 40% for evaluation. The results are listed in Table 2.

Table 2. The model performance under various training ratios

Model training ratio	AUC			Recall		
	10%	20%	40%	10%	20%	40%
GraphSAGE	0.6319	0.6973	0.8890	0.6049	0.6852	0.8438
GraphConsis	0.8594	0.8864	0.8836	0.8750	0.8784	0.8693
Our model	0.9430	0.9443	0.9451	0.8849	0.8847	0.8851

From the results in Table 2, the proposed model is superior to the reference models. With the growth of the training ratio, AUC and Recall keep stable relatively. It demonstrates the superiority of the semi-supervised GNN model, which is a good model that can be trained with less labeled data. GraphSAGE is a model that is trained in small batches on a large graph and has a fixed neighborhood size. For nodes with a relatively large neighborhood, the corresponding loss information will be relatively large. The model proposed in this paper also uses small batch training. We use reinforcement learning to train the sampling ratio to solve the problem of neighborhood sampling size and ensure that the loss of information for nodes with larger fields is reduced. GraphSAGE's AUC and Recall at 10% and 20% training percentages are not high. However, when the training percentage is 40%, the algorithm's AUC and Recall are higher, indicating that using GraphSAGE may require enough samples to train a better model. The model proposed in this paper performs better than the baseline model algorithm when the training ratio is 10% and 20%.

For better evaluation, we compare the proposed model with a single-relation model GraphSAGE and a multi-relation model GraphConsis. The experiment sets the training ratio as 40% and epoch = 50 for model training. We sample the results every four epochs from epoch = 6. The comparison results are observed from Fig. 2.

In Fig. 2(a), with the growth of epochs, AUC of GraphSAGE shows a relatively stable curve. Because there are fewer model parameters, the model can be trained rapidly but with lower AUC. The curves of our model and GraphConsis

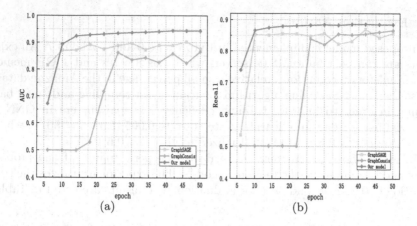

Fig. 2. Performance evaluation with various epochs. (a)*AUC*. (b)*Recall*

are similar with the growth of epochs, but the AUC of our model is higher than that of GraphConsis. In Fig. 2(b), three models show high Recall with the growth of epochs. The proposed model shows better performance in Recall than other reference models. When the epoch is 10, the Recall reaches a high and stable value. It demonstrates the proposed model has good performance in detection efficiency.

6   Conclusions

This work has investigated three data imbalance problems in fraud detection. Aiming at these problems, we propose a novel GNN-based fraud detection model in online trading activities. In this model, we design a neighbor sampler in combination with multiple samples and embed it in the GNN aggregation process to participate in training. We have conducted a series of experiments for performance evaluation. The experiments show the effectiveness of the proposed model. In our next work, we will further study the imbalance problems in graph-based data and enhance the generalization ability of the proposed model on multiple datasets.

Acknowledgements. This research is supported by the National Natural Science Foundation of China (Nos. 62072170,61902167,61872138), the Hunan Provincial Science & Technology Project Foundation (No. 2018TP1018), the Natural Science Foundation of Hunan Province, China (No. 2020JJ5369), the General Project of Education Department of Hunan Province, China (No. 19C1157), the Science Foundation of the Fujian Province, China (No. 2021J011015), Guangxi Key Laboratory of Cryptography and Information Security (No. GCIS201920) and Open Fund Project of Fujian Provincial Key Laboratory of Information Processing and Intelligent Control (Minjiang University) (No. MJUKF-IPIC202008).

References

1. Awoyemi, J.O., Adetunmbi, A.O., Oluwadare, S.A.: Credit card fraud detection using machine learning techniques: a comparative analysis. In: 2017 International Conference on Computing Networking and Informatics (ICCNI) (2017)
2. Bolton, R.J., Hand, D.J.: Statistical fraud detection: a review. Oper. Res. **17**, 235–255 (2004)
3. Buda, M., Maki, A., Mazurowski, M.A.: A systematic study of the class imbalance problem in convolutional neural networks. Neural Netw. **106**, 249–259 (2018)
4. Carcillo, F., Borgne, Y., Caelen, O., Kessaci, Y., Bontempi, G.: Combining unsupervised and supervised learning in credit card fraud detection. Inf. Sci. **557**, 317–331 (2019)
5. Chen, X., Liang, W., Xu, J., Wang, C., Li, K.C., Qiu, M.: An efficient service recommendation algorithm for cyber-physical-social systems. IEEE Trans. Netw. Sci. Eng. **1**, 1–11 (2021)
6. Dai, H., et al.: Adversarial attack on graph structured data. In: International Conference on Machine Learning, pp. 1115–1124. PMLR (2018)
7. Ebenuwa, S.H., Sharif, M.S., Alazab, M., Al-Nemrat, A.: Variance ranking attributes selection techniques for binary classification problem in imbalance data. IEEE Access **7**, 24649–24666 (2019)
8. Fiore, U., Santis, A., Perla, F., Zanetti, P., Palmieri, F.: Using generative adversarial networks for improving classification effectiveness in credit card fraud detection. Inf. Sci. **479**, 448–455 (2017)
9. Gidaris, S., Komodakis, N.: Generating classification weights with GNN denoising autoencoders for few-shot learning. In: Proceedings of the IEEE/CVF Conference on Computer Vision and Pattern Recognition, pp. 21–30 (2019)
10. Hamilton, W.L., Ying, R., Leskovec, J.: Inductive representation learning on large graphs. In: Proceedings of the 31st International Conference on Neural Information Processing Systems, pp. 1025–1035 (2017)
11. Hechtlinger, Y., Chakravarti, P., Qin, J.: A generalization of convolutional neural networks to graph-structured data. arXiv preprint arXiv:1704.08165 (2017)
12. Hu, B., Zhang, Z., Shi, C., Zhou, J., Qi, Y.: Cash-out user detection based on attributed heterogeneous information network with a hierarchical attention mechanism (2019)
13. Kabuye, F., Nkundabanyanga, S.K., Opiso, J., Nakabuye, Z.: Internal audit organisational status, competencies, activities and fraud management in the financial services sector. Manag. Audit. J. **32**(9), 924–944 (2018)
14. Karpoff, J.M.: The future of financial fraud. J. Corp. Finan. **66**, 101694 (2020)
15. Li, A., Qin, Z., Liu, R., Yang, Y., Li, D.: Spam review detection with graph convolutional networks. In: 28th ACM International Conference on Information and Knowledge Management, pp. 2703–2711 (2019)
16. Liang, W., Long, J., Li, K.C., Xu, J., Ma, N., Lei, X.: A fast defogging image recognition algorithm based on bilateral hybrid filtering. ACM Trans. Multimedia Comput. Commun. Appl. (TOMM) **17**(2), 1–16 (2021)
17. Liang, W., Xiao, L., Zhang, K., Tang, M., He, D., Li, K.C.: Data fusion approach for collaborative anomaly intrusion detection in blockchain-based systems. IEEE Internet Things J. **1**, 1–11 (2021)
18. Liang, W., Zhang, D., Lei, X., Tang, M., Li, K.C., Zomaya, A.: Circuit copyright blockchain: blockchain-based homomorphic encryption for IP circuit protection. IEEE Trans. Emerg. Topics Comput. **9**, 1410–1420 (2020)

19. Liu, Z., Chen, C., Yang, X., Zhou, J., Song, L.: Heterogeneous graph neural networks for malicious account detection (2020)
20. Liu, Z., Dou, Y., Yu, P., Deng, Y., Peng, H.: Alleviating the inconsistency problem of applying graph neural network to fraud detection (2020)
21. Reurink, A.: Financial fraud: a literature review. J. Econ. Surv. **16**(5), 1292–1325 (2016)
22. Waghade, S.S., Karandikar, A.M.: A comprehensive study of healthcare fraud detection based on machine learning. Int. J. Appl. Eng. Res. **13**, 4175–4178 (2018)
23. Vermorel, J., Mohri, M.: Multi-armed bandit algorithms and empirical evaluation. In: Gama, J., Camacho, R., Brazdil, P.B., Jorge, A.M., Torgo, L. (eds.) ECML 2005. LNCS (LNAI), vol. 3720, pp. 437–448. Springer, Heidelberg (2005). https://doi.org/10.1007/11564096_42
24. Wang, D., et al.: A semi-supervised graph attentive network for financial fraud detection. In: 2019 IEEE International Conference on Data Mining (ICDM) (2020)
25. Wang, X., et al.: Heterogeneous graph attention network. In: The World Wide Web Conference, pp. 2022–2032 (2019)
26. Wang, Y., Xu, W.: Leveraging deep learning with LDA-based text analytics to detect automobile insurance fraud. Decis. Supp. Syst. **105**(jan.), 87–95 (2018)
27. Yu, Y., Chen, J., Gao, T., Yu, M.: DAG-GNN: dag structure learning with graph neural networks. In: International Conference on Machine Learning, pp. 7154–7163. PMLR (2019)
28. Zhang, Y., Fan, Y., Ye, Y., Zhao, L., Shi, C.: Key player identification in underground forums over attributed heterogeneous information network embedding framework. In: the 28th ACM International Conference, pp. 549–558 (2019)
29. Zhang, Z., Zhou, X., Zhang, X., Wang, L., Wang, P.: A model based on convolutional neural network for online transaction fraud detection. Secur. Commun. Netw. **2018**, 1–9 (2018)
30. Zhou, K., Song, Q., Huang, X., Hu, X.: Auto-GNN: Neural architecture search of graph neural networks. arXiv preprint arXiv:1909.03184 (2019)

IoT

Non-interactive Zero Knowledge Proof Based Access Control in Information-Centric Internet of Things

Han Liu$^{(\boxtimes)}$ and Dezhi Han

College of Information Engineering, Shanghai Maritime University, Shanghai, China

Abstract. With the development of communication technology represented by 5G, the core business model of Internet of Things (IoT) has undergone great changes. The traditional host-centric network can no longer meet the needs of the IoT for throughput, privacy protection and interrupt tolerance. IC-IoT, the combination of ICN (Information Centric Networking) and IoT was put forward, which could provide scalable content distribution by using caching-router, multi-party communication, and the decoupling between senders and receivers. However, this paradigm still faces two major problems. First, the access control relationship established between publishers and subscribers requires additional maintenance of complex data structure and authentication process. Second, unencrypted named-data objects (NDO) lead to potential risks of privacy protection. To address those challenges, this paper proposes an algorithm called ZK-CP-ABE as an encryption means for distributed content distribution. Based on CP-ABE, it introduces the non-interactive zero knowledge proof protocol into the CP-ABE's secret-key existence proof to ensure user privacy and reduce invalid bandwidth consumption. On this basis, a system called DPS-IoT is proposed, which uses Hyperledger Fabric based blockchain system to store access policies and evidence for ZKP to prevent them from being tampered with. In addition, we use smart contract to implement ZK-CP-ABE based access control, so as to improve the robustness and throughput of the system. Finally, by comparing with the existing related works, it is proved that the method and system proposed in this paper have greater advantages in utilization of transmission bandwidth, and better performance in system throughput.

Keywords: IoT · ICN · ZKP · CP-ABE · Blockchain

1 Introduction

With the gradual expansion of IoT applications, such as smart home, smart city [15], smart transportation [5,6,23] and so on, the development of IoT has entered a new stage. According to the statistics and prediction of research institutions, the number of global IoT devices is expected to increase to more than 70 billion

© Springer Nature Switzerland AG 2022
Y. Lai et al. (Eds.): ICA3PP 2021, LNCS 13156, pp. 617–631, 2022.
https://doi.org/10.1007/978-3-030-95388-1_41

in 2025, and by this year, its output data will reach more than 40ZB. Traditionally, the data uploading/downloading in IoT is based on the named-host centered protocol(e.g. TCP/IP). While, with the proliferation of streaming services on it, such point-to-point packet exchange protocols are facing great challenges: 1) Single point of failure risk, which brings the problems of information redundancy and resource waste in the cluster environment; 2) Low throughput, limited by bandwidth and computing capability; 3) Weak data security, caused by lack of encryption. 4) Low interrupt tolerance, because of the instability of the network where devices are located. In addition, most IoT applications are content-oriented. Users mainly focus on how to request and consume the data in it, but do not care about which specific hosts or devices they communicate with [25].

Therefore, ICN (information centric Networking) is applied to the large-scale deployment of IoT. ICN uses named-data object (NDO), router-caching, replicated multiparty communication and the sender-receiver decoupling to distribute hotspot data more efficiently [1]. However, this approach requires additional maintenance of complex data structures and programs, and the NDOs themselves are not encrypted, exposing the privacy of the data owner. Attribute-based Encryption (ABE) [28] is a data encryption scheme that embeds attribute sets and policies into private keys and ciphertext respectively. According to the location of attribute and policy embedding, ABE can be divided into key policy attribute-based encryption (KP-ABE) [10] and ciphertext policy attribute-based encryption (CP-ABE) [3]. In CP-ABE, a user can decrypt the ciphertext only when the attributes in private key matches the access control policy embedded in the ciphertext. Compared with the traditional asymmetric encryption (e.g. RSA), the same data can be published to the network only after one encryption, instead of encrypting N times by N users' public keys respectively, which could greatly reduces the computing and bandwidth overhead. This characteristic make it especially suitable for the data content distribution of the IoT. Zero knowledge proof system [9] (also known as minimum leakage proof system) refers to that the prover makes verifier believe that a certain knowledge exists without disclosing any information about the knowledge itself. Non-interactive zero-knowledge proof [4] simplifies the interaction into one round, as a result, it is unidirectional and has higher convenience and applicability than interactive zero-knowledge proof. Hyperledger Fabric [2] is an open source project supported by the Linux foundation, which can be used to quickly build enterprise blockchain applications. Compared with other blockchain projects such as Bitcoin [24] or Ethereum [33], its biggest difference and advantage is that it supports a variety of consensus mechanisms like Raft, Kafka, and Practical Byzantine Fault Tolerance (PBFT), resulting in a high throughput to meet the basic needs of commercial applications.

In view of the advantages and disadvantages of ICN, CP-ABE and blockchain in the above analysis, this paper considers combining and improving these technologies to solve the security problems and meet the performance requirements in IoT environment. Firstly, we apply CP-ABE combined with ICN in IoT to achieve efficient distributed data sharing and fine-grained access control on the premise of ensuring user privacy. Then, we introduce non-interactive zero-knowledge proof protocol into CP-ABE's secret key existence proof to avoid the high bandwidth consumption caused by invalid access control requests. Finally, we use blockchain and smart contract as the implementation platform for data storage and access control. The main contributions of this paper are as follows:

1) We propose a lightweight non-interactive zero knowledge proof protocol to prove the existence of user attributes (private keys), the ciphertext can be transmitted only after successful verification, so as to solve the problem of high bandwidth occupation caused by illegal or invalid requests for encrypted data in traditional CP-ABE.
2) We put forward a system model called distributed publish-subscribe Internet of Things (DPS-IoT), it uses Pub/Sub paradigm to eliminate the dependence of participants on synchronous communication that enhance scalability, and adopts Information-Centric data distribution to reduce the waste of resources caused by repeated transmission in the network.
3) We adopt a blockchain system based on Hyperledger Fabric to store access policy copies, and use the smart contract (chain code) provided by it to implement the access control function based on ZK-CP-ABE.

The organization of this paper is arranged as follows: Sect. 2 is the introduction of related work; Sect. 3 introduces the system model; Sect. 4 details the proposed algorithm; Sect. 5 is experiment and analysis; Sect. 6 is the conclusion.

2   Related Work

IoT devices are often resource constrained (limited computing, power and storage), as a consequence, more and more IoT architectures outsource data processing and storage to the cloud. At present, some researches focus on applying CP-ABE and blockchain technologies to this field, and have achieved some achievements. In this section, we review the related works from two aspects: 1) the application of CP-ABE in IoT; 2) CP-ABE combined with blockchain;3) ICN with IoT.

Attribute-Based Encryption with IoT. Since CP-ABE was proposed, scholars have made many researches on efficiency (secret key length, access structure, algorithm complexity) and scalability (attribute revocation, computing outsourcing). Li [16] proposed a novel Distributed Publisher-Driven secure data sharing for ICIoT(DPD-ICOT) to solve the problem of high communication overhead caused by publishers retrieving attributes from centralized servers in CP-ABE. For big-data sharing in IC-IoT environment, Li [17] proposed a verifiable flexible data sharing (VFDS) mechanism, it uses CP-ABE for authorization, uses identity based signature (IBS) for distributed authentication, and get a lower bandwidth cost. Zhao [38] proposed an outsourced CP-ABE scheme to realize attribute revocation by using The Chinese residue theorem and keep the a fixed size of ciphertext and key. Lyes [29,30] proposed a kind of Batch-Based CP-ABE to solve the problem of difficulty in key management/attributes revocation in dynamic IoT environments. Xiao [34] put forward a multi-keyword ranked search based on mapping set matching in cloud ciphertext storage system. Vanga [26] proposed a RSA-based CP-ABE scheme with constant key and ciphertext size, and the time complexity of decryption and encryption is $O(1)$. pan [12] proposed a traceable and revocable CP-ABE scheme for privacy protection. Hao [14] proposed a garbled Bloom filter based CP-ABE that supports the expression access policy of full attribute hiding.

Access Control with Blockchain. Wang [31] proposed a framework combining Ethereum and ABE that realizes the supervision of the secret keys generation and the fine-grained access control of data. Fan [8] proposed using blockchain to record access policies and a policy hiding scheme to achieve user self-authentication and cloud non-repudiation. In [36], a new scheme combining blockchain and CP-ABE is proposed to solve the two major difficulties of blockchain regulation and privacy protection. Considering the integration of IoT and cloud computing, Zhang [37] combined the ABE with the blockchain, and uses Byzantine fault-tolerant mechanism (BFT) to replace PoW to improve the consensus speed. W. Liang proposed a series valuable methods in blockchain and security algorithm [18–22]. Zhu [13] proposed an ABAC based auditable access control model to support privacy in current IoT environments.

ICN with IoT. The ICN architecture improves the availability in IoT by using distributed data caching, and it also imposes a higher requirement for flexible authentication. Xue [35] analyzes the economic denial of Sustainability (EDOS) attack faced by the cloud side that encrypted with CP-ABE. EDOS is an attack that a malicious attacker downloads thousands of encrypted files, which is a huge drain on cloud resources at high cost to the cloud service provider. It is a kind of attack that malicious attackers request cloud resources by downloading thousands of encrypted files, resulting in cloud service providers bearing additional high bandwidth costs. To solve these problems, a black box method is proposed. Salvador [27] proposed a new architecture combining the flexibility of CP-ABE and the efficiency of symmetric key encryption technology to realize secure data exchange and privacy protection of participating entities. The above studies are related to this paper.

3   System Model

Combining the basic architecture of ICN and IoT, we design a new asynchronous distributed content distribution network named Distributed Publish-Subscribe Internet of Things (DPS-IoT). DPS-IoT involves five entities: Publisher, Rendezvous Node, Forwarding Node, Subscriber, and Blockchain. The comparison between ICN and DPS-IoT is shown in Fig. 1.

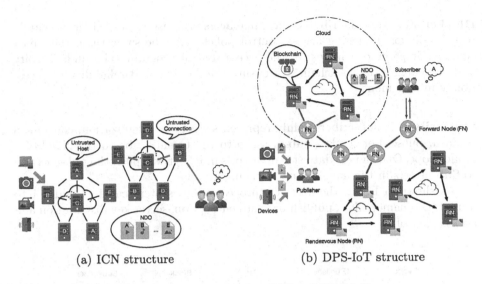

(a) ICN structure   (b) DPS-IoT structure

Fig. 1. Comparison between ICN and DPS-IoT

Device. A device refers to an independent IoT equipment or gateway, which is the producer of data. After the data is assigned a unique namespace, it becomes named data objects (NDO). NDO can be text, video, picture, audio, streaming media and interactive media, which is independent of transmission, location, storage method and application. The definition of NDO can be fine-grained, as small as packets. NDO can be replicated to multiple redundant nodes, and any RN holding an equivalent copy can provide same services to the requesters.

Publisher. A publisher represents the admin or device owner, the publisher of the data. Publisher is mainly responsible for namespace management of devices and customization of access control policies. Publisher uploads the NDO with access policies to RN based on a specific name scope.

RN (Rendezvous Node). RN implements rendezvous function, which is responsible for name resolution of received NDO. RN will cache the NDO locally, and encrypt it according to the access policy published by uploader. In our system, RN also acts as the working node of blockchain. This advantage is that RN can directly interact with blockchain locally to realize the management of access policy, which is efficient and secure. When the publisher wants to distribute the content, it sends a pub-message to other nearby RNs, which is forwarded by DHT route to other RNs with the corresponding ID of name scope.

FN (Forwarding Node). FN forwards the NDO to RN to realize the topology management function.

Blockchain. As a distributed data management cluster, blockchain is mainly responsible for managing access control policies. At the same time, the smart contract it provides can realize the access control program. The undeniability and traceability of blockchain can ensure the security and reliability of access policy management.

Subscriber. A subscriber mainly represents a user or organization, consumers of data. Subscriber sends a sub-message to RN to subscribe to the NDO of a name scope. Once a new data stream arrives in RN, it will push the pub-message to Subscribers in the name scope matching group.

As shown in Fig. 2, the overview process of our system can be divided into four stages, namely data publishing, data encryption, secret key distribution and access control.

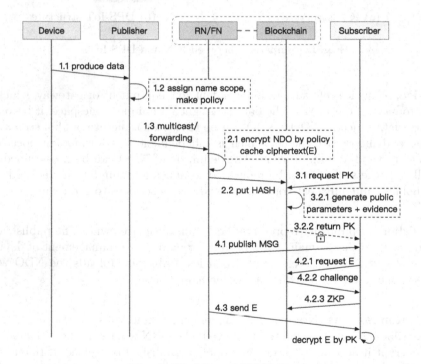

Fig. 2. Workflow of DPS-IoT

4   Proposed ZK-CP-ABE Scheme

Inspired by the non-interactive zero-knowledge proof, we propose a new zero-knowledge and ciphertext policy attribute based encryption (ZK-CP-ABE) algorithm, the core idea of which is to pre-authenticate the identity under the non-interactive zero-knowledge proof, so as to avoid public key exchange and private key disclosure. In addition, because the policy in CP-ABE is bound to the ciphertext, the user needs to download the full ciphertext before decryption. If the decryption fails (the private key is invalid), the consumption caused by the ciphertext transmission and decryption algorithm will be wasted. Our proposed algorithm can reduce the transmission bandwidth overhead caused by the transmission of invalid encrypted data in IoT environment, at the same time, ensure the data security and privacy of users. Firstly, the HASH of data is first encrypted by attributes, rather than directly encrypting the data itself. Secondly, an authentication step is added before the decryption step of the algorithm, which is achieved by the zero-knowledge proof protocol. The following is a detailed description of the algorithm.

$Setup(1^\lambda) \rightarrow \{PK, MK\}$. The Setup algorithm will random a big prime p, choose a bilinear group G_0 with prime order p, define bilinear pairing operations $e : G_0 \times G_0 \rightarrow G_1$, and select a generator g from it. Let's define a hash function $H : \{0,1\} \rightarrow G_0$ as a random prediction model, it can map any attribute (binary character) into the group. Next, choose 2 random numbers $\alpha, \beta \in Z_p(Z_p$ is a multiplicative group of module $p)$, and calculate $h = g^\beta, u = e(g,g)^\alpha$.

$$PK = \{G_0, g, h, u\}, MK = \{\alpha, \beta\} \tag{1}$$

$GenKey(Y, MK) \rightarrow \{SK, EV\}$. This algorithm has two main tasks: first is to generate the private key according to the parameters and user attributes initialized in the first step; second is to generate the public evidence for the private key for zero-knowledge proof. Suppose $Y = \{y_1, y_2, ..., y_m\}$ is a set of weighted attributes that will be used as decrypted attributes. The algorithm first randomly selects $r \in Z_p$, and randomly select $r_j \in Z_p$ for each attribute $y_j \in Y$ in Y Finally, SK is calculated.

$$SK = \Big\{ D = g^{(\alpha+r)/\beta}, \\ \forall y_j \in Y : \quad D_j = g^r \cdot H(y_j)^{r_j}, D'_j = g^{r_j} \Big\} \tag{2}$$

The following algorithm is to generate evidence for SK, where n is a big complex number, and $n = p * q$ is obtained from the product of two large prims, t is the bytes length of evidence EV, n and t depend on the security level required by the system.

$$X = |Hash256(SK)[0,...,t]|^2 \\ = |\{y_1, y_2, ..., y_t\}|^2 \\ = \{y_1^2, y_2^2, ..., y_t^2\} \\ = \{x_1, x_2, ..., x_t\} \\ EV = \{X, n = p * q\} \tag{3}$$

$Enc(M, A, PK) \rightarrow CT$. First, we use Hash algorithm to generate data summary M_{meta} for M. The advantage of doing this is to save storage space and transmission bandwidth. The main purpose of the encryption algorithm is to encrypt plaintext M by access tree T. It starts at the root R of the tree and recursively constructs a polynomial q_x for each child node x from top to bottom. For every node in the tree x, based on Lagrange interpolation principle $(f(x) = \sum_{i=1}^{d} f(x_i) (\prod_{j=1, j \neq i}^{d} \frac{x - x_j}{x_i - x_j}))$, the maximum number d_x of polynomial q_x is set to the node threshold value $k_x - 1$. Specifically, starting from the root node R, select a random $s \in Z_p$, and randomly select d_R nodes from $q_R(0) = s$, q_R. For other non-root nodes x, set $q_x(0) = q_{parent}(x)(index(x))$, and randomly select d_x other points to define q_x. When decrypting, the user only needs to bring the values of attributes in private key into the polynomial, then recover the plaintext message by calculation. Assuming that the leaf node set is L, the ciphertext CT is calculated as follows.

$$CT = \{T, \bar{C} = Me(g,g)^{\alpha s}, C = h^s$$
$$\forall l \in L: \quad C_l = g^{q_l(0)}, C'_l = H(att(l))^{q_l(0)}\} \tag{4}$$

$Proof(SK) \rightarrow true$. The $Proof$ algorithm mainly proves the exact existence of SK without providing it by using FFS protocol. The prover P (data request) first pre-proves his identity (SK) before directly requesting to download encrypted data from the storage server, which can avoid the bandwidth overhead caused by invalid transmission. The algorithm is mainly defined as follows: Prover P randomly generates the parameter $r, r \in (0, n)$ according to the preset public parameter n in EV, and calculates a according to r.

$$Setup(EV) = \{r, a | r \in (0, n), a \equiv r^2 \bmod n\} \tag{5}$$

The verifier V (data owner/storage service provider) generates a random verification sequence e based on the pre-reserved evidence EV of SK and initiates a challenge.

$$Challenge(EV) = Random(seed, t)$$
$$= \{e_1, e_2, ..., e_t\}, e_t \in \{0, 1\} \tag{6}$$

When the prover P receives the challenge, it computes an answer ANS based on private key and returns in a round.

$$ANS = r \prod_{i=1}^{t} y_i^{e_i} \bmod n \tag{7}$$

The verifier V checks the response ANS against EV and the public parameters.

$$Check(ANS, EV) = \begin{cases} 1, ANS^2 \equiv a\lambda \bmod n \\ 0, ANS^2 \neq a\lambda \bmod n \end{cases}$$
$$\lambda = \prod_{i=1}^{t} EV.x_i^{e_i} \bmod n \tag{8}$$

V can repeat the *Challenge* k times to meet the safety level required by the system. Once one challenge fails during a round, the *Proof* process will be canceled.

$Dec(CT, SK, PK) \rightarrow M_{meta}$. Decryption algorithm Dec is a recursive algorithm. Firstly, since the access policy adopted in the encryption phase is defined by the tree structure, for this type, we define a recursive algorithm to decrypt node $DecNode(CT, SK, x)$ layer by layer starting from the root of the tree. Its input parameters are ciphertext $CT = (T, \tilde{C}, C)$, private key SK associated with a set of attributes, and a node x from T. When x is a leaf node $i = att(x)$, the calculation definition is as follows:

$$
\begin{aligned}
DecNode(CT, SK, x) &= \frac{e(D_i, C_x)}{e(D_i', C_x')} \\
&= \frac{e(g^r \cdot H(i)^{r_i}, h^{q_x(0)})}{e(g^{r_i}, H(i)^{q_x(0)})} \\
&= e(g, g)^{rq_x(0)}
\end{aligned} \tag{9}
$$

When x is a non-leaf node, for its children z, run $DecNode$ separately to calculate F_z. Let Sx be a set of z with size k_x, if $k_x > 0$, then $F_z \neq 1$, otherwise $F_z = 1$. The expression of F_x is as follows:

$$
\begin{aligned}
F_x &= \prod_{z \in S_x} F_z^{\Delta k_r S_x'(0)} = \hat{e}(g, g)^{r\beta q_x(0)}, \\
k &= index(x), S_x' = \{index(z), z \in S_x\}
\end{aligned} \tag{10}
$$

Plaintext M can be decrypted by CK:

$$
\begin{aligned}
\tilde{C}/(e(C, D)/A) &= \tilde{C}/\left(e\left(h^s, g^{(\alpha+r)/\beta}\right)/e(g, g)^{rs}\right) \\
&= M|A = e(g, g)^{rqR(0)} = e(g, g)^{rs}
\end{aligned} \tag{11}
$$

5 Experiment and Result Analysis

In this part, we make a comprehensive comparison between the proposed research and related works. then design a large number of experiments to prove its effectiveness, and finally design experiments to prove the high throughput and low bandwidth occupation of the our work. Our experiments use two PCs (i7-7700 3.60 GHz, 8G RAM; i7-7500U 2.90 GHz, 16G RAM) and a raspberry pie (ARM A72 1.5 GHz, 4G RAM).

In order to verify the advantages of our proposed algorithm and system, we mainly make a comparative analysis from three aspects: algorithm performance evaluation, bandwidth occupation comparison and system throughput.

5.1   Algorithm Performance Evaluation

We compare our ZK-CP-ABE with the popular improved CP-ABE schemes. The existing research focuses on the following aspects: reducing the length of the secret key (Ref1) [11], optimizing the policy/access control structure (Ref2) [32], reducing the time complexity of encryption/decryption algorithm (Ref3) [7], issuing private keys by multiple CAs to improve system robustness and so on. However, as the Internet of things is gradually moving closer to the cloud, with the proliferation of video, audio and other streaming media services, the bandwidth cost of cloud servers is higher and higher, and the pressure of computing and storage is relatively small. In this case, we think it is unscientific to study how to improve the algorithm itself without considering the impact of the algorithm on the bandwidth. Therefore, instead of directly improving an algorithm in the basic CP-ABE, we introduce the step of zero knowledge proof as the intermediate link of encryption and decryption. This step can prove the existence of the user's private key without disclosing any other information of the user, avoiding the high bandwidth consumption caused by invalid access control requests. At the same time, through zero knowledge proof, we improve the asymmetric encryption model in CP-ABE to a secure symmetric encryption model to improve efficiency. In order to verify the advantages of our proposed algorithm in bandwidth consumption, we compare Ref1, Ref2 and Ref3. The designed experiments are as follows.

1) Set the number of different access policy attributes (the time consumption of most algorithms is directly proportional to the number of policy attributes), and count the time consumption of $GenKey()$, $Enc()$ and $Dec()$ in different algorithms under the different numbers of attributes for each access policy. The numbers of access policies here are set to $[10,20,...,90,100]$.
2) Set different sizes of plaintext data, and count the bandwidth consumption of ABE algorithm in each type of plaintext data.
3) Count the ratio between the time and transmission time of each CP-ABE algorithm. Here, we uniformly set the number of attributes of the access control policy to 50, and the size of the transmitted data as the independent variable. The range is $[2,4,...\ 512,1024](MB)$. Here is the definition of CP-ABE time cost and transmission time ratio: $f(x) = (T_{GenKey} + T_{Enc} + T_{Dec})/T_{Trans(x)}$.

The final statistics are shown in Fig. 3, Fig. 4. Our obvious advantages can be seen from the figure:

1) In terms of algorithm complexity, the performance of the three operations of $GenKey()$, $Enc()$ and $Dec()$ between the our and compared references is close, and the difference is very small in general, only within the range of serval milliseconds (MS).
2) In terms of bandwidth occupation, our algorithm has absolute advantages over other algorithms. It can be seen from the figure that with the increase of plaintext data size, the time consumed by other algorithms in transmitting data increases sharply (positively correlated). Because we adopt the method

based on zero knowledge verification that avoid directly transmitting the ciphertext data. Therefore, our bandwidth cost mainly lies in the challenges of zero knowledge proof, such as verifying the common parameters and evidence transmitted by the interaction. All of those functions are independent of the plaintext size, in that case, our results maintain a stable level.

3) As we can seen from the statistical chart of the "ratio of CP-ABE time consumption to Transmission time", with the increase of the size of plaintext data, the proportion of transmission time in the overall process surges to nearly 100%, while our algorithm remains stable.

To sum up, it can be concluded that the ZK-CP-ABE algorithm our proposed has extremely obvious advantages in bandwidth occupancy, and could meets the needs of IoT in the current big data environment.

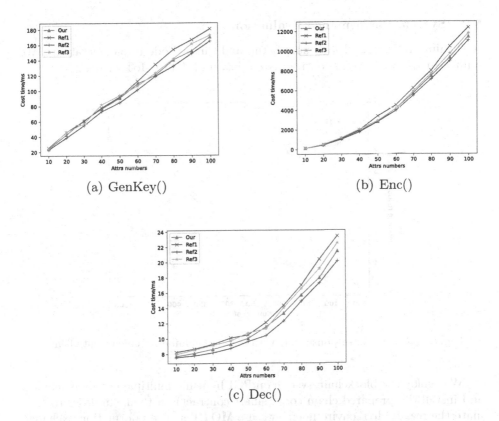

(a) GenKey()

(b) Enc()

(c) Dec()

Fig. 3. Time cost comparison of our and other references

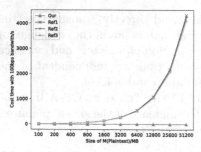
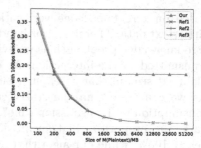

(a) Bandwidth consumption of algorithm running

(b) Ratio of CP-ABE time consumption to transmission time

Fig. 4. Bandwidth cost comparison of our and other references

5.2 System Performance Evaluation

According to Section "Blockchain Setup and Chain Code Implementation". We built a distributed access control system based on Fabric-IoT project.

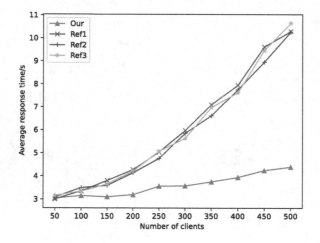

Fig. 5. The average response time with different number of concurrent clients

We deploy the blockchain system on PC1 by using multiple virtual machines, and install the prepared chain code (smart contract) on them. In order to simulate the real IC-IoT environment, we use MQTT as the information exchange protocol, the broker adopts EMQ and deployed to PC1 by docker container. On PC2, we implement the sub-client and pub-client, which communicate with each other through MQTT protocol, both of them could call the chain code that deployed in blockchain. On raspberry pie, we implemented a client to simulate device, which will upload data regularly and keep transmitting according to MQTT protocol.

In order to verify the throughput advantage of the system in distributed deployment, we designed experiments: simulate different numbers of sub/pub clients, conduct concurrent access to the blockchain system within a certain time, and test the average response time. The number of clients is set to [50,100,...,500]. For CP-ABE, we uniformly set the number of attributes for test to 50. The data block size is uniformly set to 512 KB. For comparison, we deployed Ref [1–3] based services on PC with the same configuration, and conducted concurrency tests with the same client and logic.

The final statistical results are shown in Fig. 5. It can be clearly seen from the figure that with the increase of the number of clients, the growth rate of average response time of our system is much slower than that of the compared references. It can be proved that the system proposed in this paper has obvious advantages in throughput.

6   Conclusion

More and more IoT architectures outsource data processing, storage and other functions to the third side, it has become a general trend for the IoT getting closer to the cloud. CP-ABE embeds the access policy into the ciphertext, binds attribute with user's identity, the decryption in which is only allowed when the attribute set matches the access policy, so as to realize a fine-grained and one-to-many access control. The purpose of ICN is to develop a network architecture more suitable for efficient access and distribution of content, and better deal with disconnection, interruption and group flash effect in communication services. Inspired by the above technologies, this paper applies CP-ABE and ICN model to IOT, and proposes an algorithm named ZK-CP-ABE with a system called DPS-IoT to provide scalable, high availability and fine-grained access control in IoT environment. Specifically, in the improved ZK-CP-ABE algorithm, a zero-knowledge proof protocol is designed to distribute the secret key containing user attributes, and a lightweight non-interactive zero-knowledge proof protocol is proposed to realize the existence proof of user attributes. In addition, based on the Fabric-IoT framework, the distributed data distribution and access control system for IoT is realized. Through experimental comparison and result analysis, it is proved that our research can effectively save the network bandwidth and maintain high throughput.

References

1. Ahlgren, B., Dannewitz, C., Imbrenda, C., Kutscher, D., Ohlman, B.: A survey of information-centric networking. IEEE Commun. Mag. **50**, 26–36 (2012)
2. Androulaki, E., et al.: Hyperledger fabric: a distributed operating system for permissioned blockchains. In: Proceedings of the Thirteenth EuroSys Conference (2018)
3. Bethencourt, J., Sahai, A., Waters, B.: Ciphertext-policy attribute-based encryption. In: 2007 IEEE Symposium on Security and Privacy (SP 2007), pp. 321–334 (2007)

4. Blum, M., Feldman, P., Micali, S.: Non-interactive zero-knowledge and its applications. In: STOC '88 (1988)
5. Cui, M., Han, D., Wang, J., Li, K.C., Chan, C.C.: ARFV: an efficient shared data auditing scheme supporting revocation for fog-assisted vehicular ad-hoc networks. IEEE Trans. Veh. Technol. **69**, 15815–15827 (2020)
6. Cui, M., Han, D., Wang, J.: An efficient and safe road condition monitoring authentication scheme based on fog computing. IEEE Internet Things J. **6**, 9076–9084 (2019)
7. Ding, S., Li, C., Li, H.: A novel efficient pairing-free CP-ABE based on elliptic curve cryptography for IoT. IEEE Access **6**, 27336–27345 (2018)
8. Fan, K., Wang, J., Wang, X., Li, H., Yang, Y.: A secure and verifiable outsourced access control scheme in fog-cloud computing. Sensors (Basel, Switzerland) **17**, 1695 (2017)
9. Goldwasser, S., Micali, S., Rackoff, C.: The knowledge complexity of interactive proof-systems. In: STOC '85 (1985)
10. Goyal, V., Pandey, O., Sahai, A., Waters, B.: Attribute-based encryption for fine-grained access control of encrypted data. IACR Cryptol. ePrint Arch. **2006**, 309 (2006)
11. Guo, F., Mu, Y., Susilo, W., Wong, D., Varadharajan, V.: CP-ABE with constant-size keys for lightweight devices. IEEE Trans. Inf. For. Secur. **9**, 763–771 (2014)
12. Han, D., Pan, N., Li, K.C.: A traceable and revocable ciphertext-policy attribute-based encryption scheme based on privacy protection. IEEE Trans. Depend. Secure Comput. **19**, 316–327 (2020)
13. Han, D., Zhu, Y., Li, D., Liang, W., Souri, A., Li, K.C.: A blockchain-based auditable access control system for private data in service-centric IoT environments. IEEE Trans. Ind. Inf., 1 (2021). https://doi.org/10.1109/TII.2021.3114621
14. Hao, J., Huang, C., Ni, J., Rong, H., Xian, M., Shen, X.: Fine-grained data access control with attribute-hiding policy for cloud-based IoT. Comput. Netw. **153**, 1–10 (2019)
15. Li, H., Han, D., Tang, M.: A privacy-preserving storage scheme for logistics data with assistance of blockchain. IEEE Internet Things J. (2021)
16. Li, R., Asaeda, H., Li, J.: A distributed publisher-driven secure data sharing scheme for information-centric IoT. IEEE Internet Things J. **4**, 791–803 (2017)
17. Li, R., Asaeda, H., Li, J., Fu, X.: A verifiable and flexible data sharing mechanism for information-centric IoT. In: 2017 IEEE International Conference on Communications (ICC), pp. 1–7 (2017)
18. Liang, W., Long, J., Li, K.C., Xu, J., Ma, N., Lei, X.: A fast defogging image recognition algorithm based on bilateral hybrid filtering. ACM Trans. Multimedia Comput. Commun. Appl. (TOMM) **17**, 1–16 (2021)
19. Liang, W., Ning, Z., Xie, S., Hu, Y., Lu, S., Zhang, D.: Secure fusion approach for the internet of things in smart autonomous multi-robot systems. Inf. Sci. **579**, 468–482 (2021)
20. Liang, W., Xiao, L., Zhang, K., Tang, M., He, D., Li, K.C.: Data fusion approach for collaborative anomaly intrusion detection in blockchain-based systems. IEEE Internet Things J., 1 (2021)
21. Liang, W., et al.: Deep neural network security collaborative filtering scheme for service recommendation in intelligent cyber-physical systems. IEEE Internet of Things J., 1 (2021)
22. Liang, W., Zhang, D., Lei, X., Tang, M., Li, K.C., Zomaya, A.: Circuit copyright blockchain: Blockchain-based homomorphic encryption for IP circuit protection. IEEE Trans. Emerg. Topics Comput. **9**, 1410–1420 (2021)

23. Liu, H., Han, D., Li, D.: Behavior analysis and blockchain based trust management in vanets. J. Para. Distrib. Comput. **151**, 61–69 (2021)
24. Nakamoto, S.: Bitcoin: a peer-to-peer electronic cash system (2009)
25. Nour, B., Sharif, K., Li, F., Biswas, S., Moungla, H., Guizani, M., Wang, Y.: A survey of internet of things communication using ICN: a use case perspective. Comput. Commun. **142–143**, 95–123 (2019)
26. Odelu, V., Das, A., Khan, M.K., Choo, K.K.R., Jo, M.: Expressive CP-ABE scheme for mobile devices in IoT satisfying constant-size keys and ciphertexts. IEEE Access **5**, 3273–3283 (2017)
27. Pérez, S., Rotondi, D., Pedone, D., Straniero, L., Nuñez, M., Gigante, F.: Towards the CP-ABE application for privacy-preserving secure data sharing in IoT contexts. In: IMIS (2017)
28. Sahai, A., Waters, B.: Fuzzy identity-based encryption. IACR Cryptol. ePrint Arch. **2004**, 86 (2005)
29. Touati, L., Challal, Y.: Batch-based CP-ABE with attribute revocation mechanism for the Internet of Things. In: 2015 International Conference on Computing, Networking and Communications (ICNC), pp. 1044–1049 (2015)
30. Touati, L., Challal, Y.: Efficient CP-ABE attribute/key management for IoT applications. 2015 IEEE International Conference on Computer and Information Technology; Ubiquitous Computing and Communications; Dependable, Autonomic and Secure Computing; Pervasive Intelligence and Computing, pp. 343–350 (2015)
31. Wang, S.R., Zhang, Y., Zhang, Y.: A blockchain-based framework for data sharing with fine-grained access control in decentralized storage systems. IEEE Access **6**, 38437–38450 (2018)
32. Wang, S., Wang, H., Li, J., Wang, H., Chaudhry, J., Alazab, M., Song, H.: A fast CP-ABE system for cyber-physical security and privacy in mobile healthcare network. IEEE Trans. Ind. Appl. **56**, 4467–4477 (2020)
33. Wood, D.D.: Ethereum: a secure decentralised generalised transaction ledger (2014)
34. Xiao, T., Han, D., He, J., Li, K.C., de Mello, R.F.: Multi-keyword ranked search based on mapping set matching in cloud ciphertext storage system. Connect. Sci. **33**, 95–112 (2021)
35. Xue, K., Chen, W., Li, W., Hong, J., Hong, P.: Combining data owner-side and cloud-side access control for encrypted cloud storage. IEEE Trans. Inf. For. Secur. **13**, 2062–2074 (2018)
36. Yuan, C., Xu, M., Si, X., Li, B.: Blockchain with accountable CP-ABE: how to effectively protect the electronic documents. In: 2017 IEEE 23rd International Conference on Parallel and Distributed Systems (ICPADS), pp. 800–803 (2017)
37. Zhang, Y., He, D., Choo, K.K.R.: Bads: blockchain-based architecture for data sharing with abs and CP-ABE in IoT. Wirel. Commun. Mob. Comput. **2018**, 2783658:1-2783658:9 (2018)
38. Zhao, Y., Ren, M., Jiang, S., Zhu, G., Xiong, H.: An efficient and revocable storage CP-ABE scheme in the cloud computing. Computing **101**, 1041–1065 (2018)

Simultaneous Charger Placement and Power Scheduling for On-Demand Provisioning of RF Wireless Charging Service

Huatong Jiang, Yanjun Li$^{(\boxtimes)}$ ⓘ, and Meihui Gao

School of Computer Science and Technology, Zhejiang University of Technology,
Hangzhou, China
{yjli,gaomeihui}@zjut.edu.cn

Abstract. To provision on-demand radio frequency (RF) charging service in a designated place, the problem of simultaneous charger placement and power scheduling is studied. Based on users' historic spatial and temporal distribution information, we formulate the problem as how to place a given number of chargers and how to adjust the chargers' power levels in each time interval so that the revenue of the charging service can be maximized, given the total power limitation constraint. The formulated problem is a mixed integer linear programming (MILP) problem and we propose a branch and bound (B&B) algorithm to solve it. Extensive simulations in both small-scale and large-scale networks, as well as simulations based on the real data set are conducted to validate the effectiveness of our proposed algorithm. The results show that, our proposed algorithm outperforms greedy algorithm, an algorithm that deals charger placement and power scheduling separately, in most of the simulation scenarios, and reaches the optimum in small-scale instances.

Keywords: RF charging · Charger placement · Power scheduling ·
Mixed integer linear programming

1 Introduction

Recent advances in wireless power transfer (WPT) technology have attracted the attention of both academia and industry [1–3]. One category of the WPT technology is to use tightly-coupled induction or loosely-coupled resonance to harness the power of magnetic fields. This technology requires the transmitter and receiver to be in direct or close contact. Examples of commercial uses for this type include smartphone charging pads and electrocars' wireless charging system. Another category of the WPT technology is radio frequency (RF) wireless

This work was supported in part by National Natural Science Foundation of China (61772472), Natural Science Foundation of Zhejiang Province (LZ21F020005, LQ21F020058) and the Fundamental Research Funds for the Provincial Universities of Zhejiang (RF-A2019002).

charging, which harnesses the power of waves in the radio spectrum and creates a charging zone similar to a Wi-Fi access point (AP). Compared with induction or resonance charging, RF charging works on far field and can be embedded in much smaller form factors, but it has lower power density and conversion efficiency [4,5]. It is thus more suitable for powering low power end-devices in the internet of things (IoT) [6]. RF power sources are ubiquitous, from cellular base stations, TV towers to Wi-Fi APs and RFID readers. There have been quite a few laboratory and commercial devices using RF power transfer, such as Wireless Identification and Sensing Platform (WISP) from Intel and University of Washington [7], Cota system from Ossia Incorporated [8], Powercaster transmitter and batteryless sensor tags from Powercast Corporation [9], etc.

The RF charging is achieved either by taking advantage of the ambient RF signals transmitted from nearby primary devices or by dedicated chargers that continuously transmit energy beacons. Typically, the power level of ambient RF signals in an indoor environment varies over time and is much lower compared to that from dedicated chargers. To provide continuous and stable RF wireless charging service in a designated indoor place, dedicated chargers are thus required to be deployed [4]. The chargers are plugged into the power outlet and thus they have unlimited power resources. The power of the chargers is adjustable and different power leads to different power consumptions. To provide dedicated RF wireless charging service for numerous devices, there are mainly three scenarios considered in the literature [4]: 1) Placing static chargers to recharge static devices; 2) Placing static chargers to recharge mobile devices; 3) Dispatching mobile charger(s) to recharge static devices. The third scenario is less relevant to our work since we consider static charger placement. There have been a few studies on charger placement and power scheduling under the first two scenarios. In [10], He et al. first investigate how to deploy least number of chargers to ensure that a static device placed in any position of the network receives a sufficient recharge rate for sustained operation. They also study how to exploit the potential mobility of devices to further reduce the number of required chargers. In [11], Li et al. adopt a new wireless recharge model considering phase shift of RF signals, and study how to deploy the chargers to ensure that the battery-free nodes maintain a designated duty cycle. In [12], Dai et al. raise the attention to the electromagnetic radiation (EMR) induced by chargers and propose approximation algorithms to find the charger placement that maximizes the overall charging utility subject to a EMR safety threshold. They further consider charger scheduling and power adjustment issues in [13] and [14], respectively. In [15], Zhang et al. jointly consider charger placement and power allocation problems to maximize the charging quality, subject to a power budget. They further extend this work in [16] to deal with mobile devices. In [17], Chiu et al. study charger deployment to achieve a maximum survival rate of mobile end-devices based on users's historical movement data. In [4], Li et al. study the charger placement problem based on specific mobility pattern of the users. Their work aims to find a charger placement to minimize the charging service budget, subject to the power non-outage probability requirement of the mobile devices.

634   H. Jiang et al.

In this paper, we consider the following scenario: A service provider decides to offer RF wireless charging service in an indoor area to avoid power outage of the devices. It is assumed that they can predict users' spatial and temporal distribution based on massive historical user localization data (devices are carried by users). Given the charger quantity budget and the total power limitation, the provider wants to maximize its revenue, which is defined as the service income minus the charger budget and the electricity cost. The problem is thus how to place a given number of chargers with appropriate power levels at a subset of the candidate locations, so that the revenue of the provider can be maximized. Our work differs from existing work in the following aspects. First, our work considers provisioning RF charging service for mobile devices. Second, the objective of our problem is to maximize the revenue of the charging service, which jointly considers the charging and advertising income, the charger budget and the electricity cost. Third, simultaneous charger placement and power scheduling are studied based on users' historic spatial and temporal distribution.

The contributions of this paper are two-fold:

- To provide on-demand RF charging service based on users' spatial and temporal distribution and obtain maximized revenue, we study the problem of simultaneous charger placement and power scheduling. The problem is formulated as a mixed integer linear programming (MILP) problem.
- We propose branch and bound (B&B) algorithm to solve the formulated problem. Extensive simulations in both small-scale and large-scale networks, as well as simulations based on the real data set are conducted to validate the effectiveness of our proposed algorithm. Simulation results show the superiority of our proposed algorithm over the greedy algorithm.

The remainder of the paper is organized as follows. In Sect. 2 and 3, basic models and assumptions are presented. We introduce and formulate the charger placement and power scheduling problem in Sect. 4. B&B algorithm is proposed in Sect. 5 to solve the problem. Extensive simulations are conducted in Sect. 6 to evaluate our algorithm. Section 7 concludes this paper.

2   System Model and Assumptions

We assume that a service provider would like to provide RF charging service in an indoor environment. There are I candidate locations on the ceilings for placing K chargers ($K < I$), as illustrated in Fig. 1. The chargers can only be placed at the candidate locations since the candidate locations are chosen based on the accessibility to the power outlets and user flow investigation. Users' spatial and temporal distribution profile can be characterized based on historical trajectory information of massive users (i.e., devices) during a period of time. We assume the trajectories are predefined, with the consideration that in practice the users' indoor trajectories are constrained by the rooms and corridors. For the sake of tractability, we discretize both the time and the trajectories. The time is divided into N equal intervals with length t, while the trajectories are divided into M segments with length Δl. We have the following notations and assumptions.

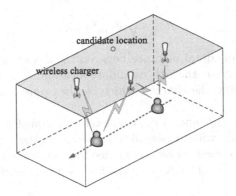

Fig. 1. Scenario of RF charging service provision in an indoor environment.

1. Users' spatial and temporal distribution profile is characterized by an $N \times M$ matrix $\mathbf{F} = \{f_{m,n}|m = 1, 2, ..., M; n = 1, 2, ..., N\}$, where $f_{m,n}$ represents the user flow volume of the m-th segment during the n-th interval.
2. Let $\mathbf{X} = \{x_i|i = 1, 2, ..., I\}$ be a boolean array, i.e., $x_i \in \{0, 1\}$, which represents whether a charger is placed at the i-th candidate location.
3. Suppose the charger's power level is linearly adjustable between 0 and the maximum power P_s. The same assumption has been made in [14] and [16]. Let $\mathbf{C} = \{c_{i,n}|i = 1, 2, ..., I; n = 1, 2, ..., N\}$, where $c_{i,n} \in [0, 1]$ represents the adjustable ratio of the charger placed at the i-th candidate location during the n-th interval.

3 Recharge Model

We assume that when a user moves along a segment, the recharge power of the device remains unchanged which equals to the recharge power at the midpoint of this segment. This assumption is reasonable if the length of the segment is small. The device captures RF energy transmitted by the wireless chargers, and then converts it into electrical energy with partial power loss. Based on the Friss transmission equation, an empirical recharge model for a wireless device on the m-th segment with a distance $d_{i,m}$ away from the charger placed at the i-th candidate location during the n-th interval is as follows [10]:

$$P_h^{(i,m,n)} = \begin{cases} c_{i,n}\eta\frac{G_sG_r}{L_p}\left(\frac{\lambda}{4\pi(d_{i,m}+\varepsilon)}\right)^2 P_s, & d_{i,m} \leq d_c \\ 0, & d_{i,m} > d_c \end{cases} \tag{1}$$

where η is the rectifier efficiency, G_s and G_r are the source and receiver antenna gains, λ is the wavelength, P_s is the charger's maximum transmit power, L_p represents the polarization loss, ε is a fixed small parameter ensuring that the associated recharge power is finite for short distance, d_c is the effective charging range. Further, $d_{i,m}$ is calculated by:

$$d_{i,m} = \sqrt{{d'_{i,m}}^2 + h^2},$$

(2)

where $d'_{i,m}$ is the horizontal distance between the device on the m-th segment and the charger placed at the i-th candidate location, h is the vertical distance between the device and the charger, which can be approximately regarded as a fixed value.

As evidenced by [10] and [11], a charger can transfer energy to multiple devices simultaneously without significantly reducing the received power at one device and the power received by one device from multiple chargers is additive. Thus the recharge power of a device on the m-th segment during the n-th interval can be calculated as:

$$P_h^{(m,n)} = \sum_{i=1}^{I} P_h^{(i,m,n)}.$$

(3)

4   Problem Statement

The revenue of the charging service is defined as the service income minus the charger budget and the electricity cost, where the service income consists of the user payment for the charging and the revenue from the advertising push during the service time, and the electricity cost is proportional to the adopted power of the chargers. Let the unit price of the charger be one, the unit price of charging, advertising push and electricity be p_1, p_2 and b units, respectively. In reality, the unit value can be determined by the service provider based on the market survey. Based on this, the revenue of the charging service in an area of M segments over a time of N intervals is as follows:

$$Q = (p_1 + p_2) \sum_{m=1}^{M} \sum_{n=1}^{N} \sum_{i=1}^{I} f_{m,n} P_h^{(i,m,n)} \frac{l_m}{\bar{v}}$$

$$- b \sum_{n=1}^{N} \sum_{i=1}^{I} c_{i,n} P_s t - \sum_{i}^{I} x_i,$$

(4)

where l_m is the length of the m-th segment and $\bar{v}$ is the average velocity of a user passing through a segment. The first part in (4) represents the service income, the second part is the electricity cost, and the third part is the charger budget.

The problem studied in this paper is:

Problem 1. *Given the users' spatial and temporal distribution profile F, I candidate locations for placing K chargers and a total power limitation B, how to place a given number of chargers and how to schedule the power of the chargers during a period of time, so that the revenue of the charging service is maximized.*

Problem 1 can be formulated as follows:

$$P_1 : \max \ Q(\mathbf{X}, \mathbf{C})$$

$$\text{s.t.} \ \sum_{i=1}^{I} x_i = K,$$

$$N x_i - \sum_{n=1}^{N} c_{i,n} \geq 0, i = 1, 2, ..., I,$$

$$\sum_{I=1}^{I} c_{i,n} P_s \leq B, n = 1, 2, ..., N,$$ (5)

$$x_i \in \{0, 1\},$$

$$0 \leq c_{i,n} \leq 1,$$

$$\text{w.r.t. } \mathbf{X} = \{x_i\}, \ \mathbf{C} = \{c_{i,n}\}.$$

The first constraint limits the total number of chargers. The second constraint ensures that for any candidate location i in the n-th time interval, the power level $c_{i,n}$ is non-zero if and only if $x_i = 1$, i.e., there is a charger placed at the i-th candidate location. The third constraint limits the total power of the K chargers in any time interval. The last two constraints scope the range of the variables.

5 Solutions

Obviously, Problem 1 is an MILP problem and is NP-hard. Explicit enumeration is normally impossible due to the exponentially increasing number of potential solutions. In the following, we will solve this problem by the well-known B&B method [18].

5.1 Initialization of the B&B Algorithm

For the B&B method, we first have to determine the initial upper and lower bounds of the objective function. We call this process initialization of the B&B algorithm. The pseudocode is shown in Algorithm 1. Specifically, we first replace the integer constraints $x_i \in \{0, 1\}$ by the bound constraints $x_i \in [0, 1]$, $i = 1, 2, ..., I$. The resulting LP problem denoted by $P_1' = \text{LP}(P_1)$ is called the LP relaxation of P_1. We then solve P_1' using CPLEX optimizer and obtain the solution $\overline{\mathbf{W}} = \{\overline{\mathbf{X}}, \overline{\mathbf{C}}\}$ with the objective function value $\overline{Q} = Q(\overline{\mathbf{W}})$, where $\overline{Q} = Q(\overline{\mathbf{W}})$ is the initial upper bound of the objective function of P_1. Next, we find the minimum non-zero element in $\overline{\mathbf{X}}$ and let it be 0 if it does not equal to 1. A new LP problem is thus formulated. We iteratively solve the new LP problem and let the minimum non-zero element in respective solution be 0 until the minimum non-zero element equals to 1. Finally, we obtain the solution $\underline{\mathbf{W}}$ with corresponding objective function value $\underline{Q} = Q(\underline{\mathbf{W}})$, where $\underline{Q}$ is the initial lower bound of P_1.

Algorithm 1. Initialization of the B&B algorithm

Input: $\mathbf{F}$, M, N, I, p_1, p_2, b, t, l_m, $\overline{v}$, parameters of
the recharge model.
Output: The initial upper bound and lower bound of
the objective function $\overline{Q}$ and $\underline{Q}$, and respective solu-
tions $\overline{\mathbf{W}} = \{\overline{\mathbf{X}}, \overline{\mathbf{C}}\}$ and $\underline{\mathbf{W}} = \{\underline{\mathbf{X}}, \underline{\mathbf{C}}\}$.
Relax all x_i from $x_i \in \{0, 1\}$ to $x_i \in [0, 1]$;
Let $P_1' = \text{LP}(P_1)$ be the LP relaxation of P_1, solve P_1',
obtain the solution $\overline{\mathbf{W}} = \{\overline{\mathbf{X}}, \overline{\mathbf{C}}\}$ and $\overline{Q} = Q(\overline{\mathbf{W}})$;
Let $\mathbf{U} = \overline{\mathbf{W}}$;
while $\mathbf{U} \neq \varnothing$ **do**
    Find the minimum non-zero element in $\overline{\mathbf{X}}$ and
denote it as x_a;
    if $x_a = 1$ **then**
        break;
    end
    Let $x_a = 0$, $\forall i \neq a$, let $x_i \in [0, 1]$ and update the
LP problem;
    Solve the updated LP problem and obtain the solu-
tion $\mathbf{W} = \{\mathbf{X}, \mathbf{C}\}$;
    Let $\mathbf{U} = \mathbf{W}$.
end
$\underline{\mathbf{W}} = \mathbf{U}$, $\underline{Q} = Q(\underline{\mathbf{W}})$;
Return $\overline{Q}$, $\underline{Q}$, $\overline{\mathbf{W}}$, $\underline{\mathbf{W}}$.

5.2 B&B Algorithm

Now we have obtained the initial upper and lower bounds of the objective function. In the following, we adopt B&B algorithm to obtain the optimal solution. The pseudocode is shown in Algorithm 2. We first construct a binary tree
with $P_1' = \text{LP}(P_1)$ as the root node. We start from P_1' and pick a variable x_j
($j = 1, 2, ..., I$) with the largest fractional part from $\overline{X}$ for branching. Then
we branch two ending nodes from P_1' corresponding to two new LP problems:
$P_2' := P_1' \wedge x_j = 0$ and $P_3' := P_1' \wedge x_j = 1$. We solve the two LP problems and
obtain solutions with respective objective function values, where the maximum
value is the new upper bound of the objective function of P_1. We further check
whether there are feasible (integer) solutions. If true, we denote the solution with
maximum objective function value by $W_{\max}'$ and the objective function by $Q_{\max}'$,
and compare $Q_{\max}'$ with current lower bound $\underline{Q}$. If $Q_{\max}' > \underline{Q}$, let $\underline{Q} = Q_{\max}'$,
$\underline{\mathbf{W}} = \mathbf{W}_{\max}'$. Otherwise we cut off branching nodes that are unsolvable or whose
objective function values are lower than or equal to current lower bound $\underline{Q}$. The
iteration terminates when all the nodes have been visited or $\overline{Q} - \underline{Q} \leq \epsilon$, where
ϵ is a small controllable error coefficient. Finally, we obtain the optimal solution
$\mathbf{W}^* = \underline{\mathbf{W}}$.

Algorithm 2. B&B algorithm

Input: $\overline{Q}$, $\underline{Q}$, $\mathbf{W} = \{\mathbf{X}, \mathbf{C}\}$ and $\underline{\mathbf{W}} = \{\underline{\mathbf{X}}, \underline{\mathbf{C}}\}$.
Output: The optimal solution $\mathbf{W}^* = \{\mathbf{X}^*, \mathbf{C}^*\}$.
Construct a binary tree with $P_1' = \mathrm{LP}(P_1)$ as the root
node;
while *there is node that has not been branched* **do**
    if $\overline{Q} - \underline{Q} \leq \epsilon$ **then**
        break;
    end
    Find the ending node P_z', $z \in \{$indices of all the end-
ing nodes$\}$ with current upper bound of the objective
function $\overline{Q}$;
    Select the variable x_j of P_z' with the largest frac-
tional part for branching;
    Creat two nodes: $P_{z+1}' := P_z' \wedge x_j = 0$ and $P_{z+2}' :=$
$P_z' \wedge x_j = 1$;
    Solve P_{z+1}' and P_{z+2}', obtain two solutions $\mathbf{W}_{z+1} =$
$\{\mathbf{X}_{z+1}, \mathbf{C}_{z+1}\}$, $\mathbf{W}_{z+2} = \{\mathbf{X}_{z+2}, \mathbf{C}_{z+2}\}$, and respective
objective functions Q_{z+1}, Q_{z+2};
    $\overline{Q} = \max\{Q_z\}$, $z \in \{$indices of all the ending
nodes$\}$;
    Find in $\mathbf{W}_z$ feasible solutions $\mathbf{W}_y$, $y \in \{$indices of all
the ending nodes whose solutions to $\mathbf{X}$ all take integer
values$\}$, with corresponding objective functions Q_y;
    $Q_{\max}' = \max\{Q_y\}$; $\mathbf{W}_{\max}' = \arg\max\{Q_y\}$;
    if $Q_{\max}' > \underline{Q}$ **then**
        $\underline{Q} = Q_{\max}'$; $\underline{\mathbf{W}} = \mathbf{W}_{\max}'$;
    end
    Cut off branches that are unsolvable or whose $Q \leq$
$\underline{Q}$;
end
$\mathbf{W}^* = \underline{\mathbf{W}}$;
Return $\mathbf{W}^*$.

Time Complexity: There are at most I iterations in Algorithm 1 and in each
iteration, we need to solve an LP problem. The time complexity of solving an
LP problem using interior point method is $O(d^{3.5})$ [19], where d is the number of variables. Since there are $I + IN$ variables in P_1, the time complexity of
Algorithm 1 is $O(I^{4.5}N^{3.5})$. For Algorithm 2, there are at most 2^I branches and
for each branch, we also need to solve an LP problem with $I + IN$ variables.
Therefore, the time complexity of Algorithm 2 is $O(2^I I^{3.5} N^{3.5})$. Finally, the
time complexity of solving P_1 is $O(I^{4.5}N^{3.5} + 2^I I^{3.5} N^{3.5})$, i.e., $O(2^I I^{3.5} N^{3.5})$.
Obviously, when the number of candidate locations is relatively large, the compu-
tation cost is unaffordable. However, in practice, the amount of branch pruning
is immerse, which can greatly reduce the time complexity of the algorithm.

6   Performance Evaluation

In this section, we first introduce baseline algorithms, then we present simulation setup and finally conduct both numerical and data-trace-driven simulations to evaluate the performance of our proposed algorithm.

6.1   Baseline Algorithms

Greedy Algorithm: It consists of two steps. In the first step, we separately place a charger at each candidate location and obtain the optimal power scheduling solution that maximizes the revenue by solving I LP problems. In the second step, we select K candidate locations that have the most revenue. We further check whether the total power of current solution exceeds the power budget B during any time period. If true, we reduce the power level of the charger placed at the candidate location that has the least revenue to satisfy the power budget constraint. The time complexity of the first step is $O(IN^{3.5})$, while the time complexity of the second step is $O(I \log I)$ for sorting I candidate locations in descending order of the revenue. Therefore, the time complexity of the greedy algorithm is $O(I(N^{3.5} + \log I))$.

Optimal Solution (OPT): First, exhaustive search is used to find all possible charger placement solutions. Then, for each placement solution, we obtain the power scheduling solution that maximizes the revenue by solving respective LP problem. Finally, the solution with most revenue is selected as the optimal solution. Due to its high time complexity $O((KN)^{3.5}(C_I^K)^2(\log(C_I^K)))$, OPT is only practical for small instances.

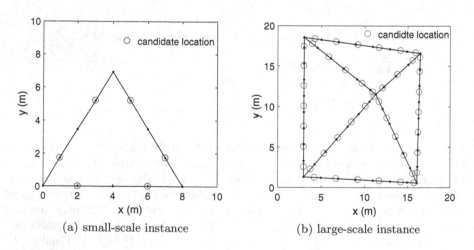

(a) small-scale instance   (b) large-scale instance

Fig. 2. Visualization of small-scale and large-scale instance.

6.2 Simulation Setup

For small-scale instances, three paths are divided into $M = 12$ segments with $\Delta l = 2$ m as shown in Fig. 2(a). We further set $N = 4$, $I = 6$.

For large scale instances, eight paths are divided into $M = 55$ segments with $\Delta l = 2$ m as shown in Fig. 2(b). We further set $N = 10$, $I = 45$.

In both small and large instances, user's spatial and temporal distribution profile $\mathbf{F}$ is an $N \times M$ matrix, whose elements are random integers ranging from [100, 500]. Other common simulation parameters are summarized in Table 1, where the recharge model related parameters follow the settings in [10] and the setting of charger's transmit power follows that of the TX91501 Powercaster transmitter [9]. Moreover, each result in the following simulation diagrams stands for the average value of 100 instances of the random user profile.

Table 1. Simulation parameters

Parameters	Values
Charger's maximum transmit power P_s (W)	3
Source antenna gain G_S (dBi)	8
Receiver antenna gain G_r (dBi)	2
Polarization loss L_p (dB)	3
Wavelength λ (m)	0.33
Adjusting parameter ε (m)	0.2316
Rectification efficiency ω	0.3
Effective charging range d_c (m)	15
Unit income of charging p_1 (unit/J)	3×10^{-4}
Unit income of advertising p_2 (unit/J)	0.1
Unit price of electricity b (unit/kWh)	0.5
Length of the time interval t (h)	1
User's average velocity $\bar{v}$ (m/s)	1
Vertical distance h (m)	2

6.3 Simulation in Small-Scale Instances

For small-scale instances, we compare the B&B algorithm with both the greedy algorithm and the optimal solution. In the first set of simulation, we set the total power constraint to $B = 10$ W, and vary the charger quantity K from 2 to 5. The results are shown in Fig. 3. As the charger quantity K increases, the revenue Q induced by all the three algorithms increases. This is because more chargers bring more charging and advertising income. Moreover, under our setting, large amount of users makes the increase in the charging and advertising income exceed the increase in the electricity and charger cost. When $K = 2$ and 3, the performances of all the three methods are exactly the same. This is because when the number of chargers is small, chargers are all set to the maximum power level to reach optimal performance without violating the total power constraint. In other words, the total power constraint does not take effect. When K increases to 4 and 5, the performance of B&B algorithm still reaches the optimum yet outperforms that of the greedy algorithm with an improvement of 6.85% at most and 2.25% on average.

In the second set of simulation, we set $K = 4$, and vary the total power constraint B from 6 W to 12 W. The results are shown in Fig. 4. As the total power constraint increases, more power can be allocated to all the chargers and thus the recharge power of the users also increases. Under our setting, large amount of users makes the increase in the charging and advertising income exceed the increase in the electricity cost. So the revenue Q induced by all the three algorithms increases. As expected, the performance of B&B algorithm reaches the optimum and outperforms the greedy algorithm with an improvement of 3.03% at most, 1.83% on average. The gap between B&B algorithm and the greedy algorithm decreases to 0 when B increases to 12 W, which is also because the total power constraint of 12 W is to loose and does not take effect.

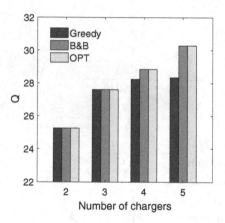

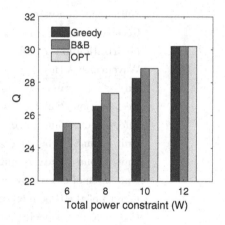

Fig. 3. The impact of the charger quantity K on the revenue Q for small-scale instance ($B = 10\,\text{W}$).

Fig. 4. The impact of total power constraint B on the revenue Q for small-scale instance ($K = 4$).

6.4   Simulation in Large-Scale Instances

For large-scale instances, we only compare the B&B algorithm with the greedy algorithm, since it is impractical to apply exhaustive search to large-scale instances. In the first set of simulation, we fix the total power constraint to $B = 50$ W, and vary the charger quantity K from 10 to 30. As shown in Fig. 5, the revenue Q of both solutions increases as K increases. When $K = 10$ and 15, both solutions have the same performance since the total power constraint is not violated when all the chargers are set to maximum power level. The performance of B&B algorithm starts to outperform the greedy algorithm when K increases from 20 to 30, with an improvement of 10.10% at most and 4.80% on average.

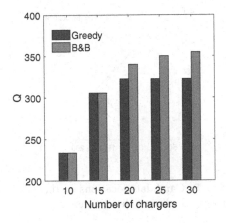

Fig. 5. The impact of the charger quantity K on the revenue Q for large-scale instance ($B = 50$ W).

Fig. 6. The impact of total power constraint B on the revenue Q for large-scale instance ($K = 20$).

In the second set of simulation, we set $K = 20$, and vary the total power constraint B from 20 W to 60 W. The results are shown in Fig. 6. As the total power constraint increases, more power can be allocated to all the chargers and thus the recharge power of the users also increases. Similar to the results in small-scale instances, the revenue Q induced by all the three algorithms increases. The performance of the B&B algorithm outperforms the greedy algorithm with an improvement of 13.76% at most and 7.27% on average when the total power constraint ranges from 20 W to 50 W. As the total power constraint further increases to $B = 60$ W, it has the same performance as the greedy algorithm, due to the fact that the total power constraint does not take effect.

6.5 Data-Set-Driven Simulation

We further conduct simulations using the real user location data collected by an indoor localization system deployed on a particular floor of a hospital. The floor plan is shown in Fig. 7.

To obtain users' indoor location information, the localization system adopts combined techniques of Bluetooth Low Power (BLE) and pedestrian dead reckoning (PDR), based on iBeacon tags and users' smartphones. iBeacon tags are deployed on the ceilings of 5 main galleries, as shown in Fig. 7. User's location information is estimated every 1 s. The data set records users' historic data of 3 months, from 8:00 a.m. to 6:00 p.m. each day. An instance of the data records

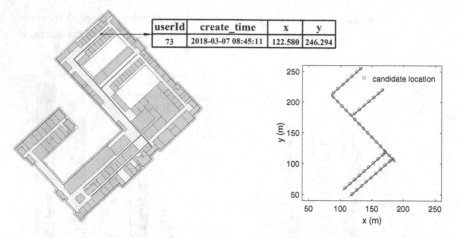

userId	create_time	x	y
73	2018-03-07 08:45:11	122.580	246.294

Fig. 7. Floor plan and instance of the data records.

Fig. 8. Candidate locations on the galleries for placing the chargers.

is shown in Fig. 7, where "userId" is the id of a specific user, "creat_time" is the generation time of this record, "x" and "y" stand for the location coordinates based on a custom coordinate system.

Suppose we would like to provide RF charging service for the users on this floor. A total of 49 candidate locations are selected for placing the chargers, as shown in Fig. 8. The paths along the 5 main galleries are divided into $M = 235$ segments with $\Delta l = 2$ m. Time in a day is divided into $N = 10$ intervals with the length of interval $t = 1$ h. A 235×10 matrix $\mathbf{F}$ is generated by counting the flow volume on the m-th segment in the n-th interval. Noting that if the same user continuously stays on the m-th segment within the n-th interval for T time and let $\gamma = \lfloor T\bar{v}/\Delta l \rfloor$, the flow volume $f_{m,n}$ will increase by γ instead of 1. The rationale of this processing method is that when a user simply walks through a segment with velocity $\bar{v}$, the flow volume will increase by 1, while if a user stays on a segment for a long time, it will be regarded as multiple people.

In the following, we first compare the performances of the B&B algorithm and the greedy algorithm under different charger quantity K with B fixed to 50 W. As shown in Fig. 9, the two algorithms have the same performance when $K = 10$ and $K = 15$, due to the fact that all the chargers are set to maximum power level. The B&B algorithm starts to outperform the greedy algorithm when K increase from 20 to 30, with an improvement of 11.83% at most, 5.86% on average.

Then we further compare the performance of the two algorithms under different total power constraint B with $K = 20$. The results are shown in Fig. 10. The performance of the B&B algorithm outperforms that of the greedy algorithm with an improvement of 26.19% at most and 12.62% on average when B grows from 20 W to 50 W. They present the same performance when $B = 60$ W.

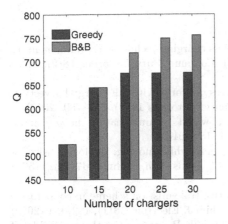

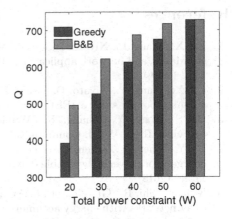

Fig. 9. The impact of the charger quantity K on the revenue Q for data-set-driven instance ($B = 50\,\text{W}$).

Fig. 10. The impact of total power constraint B on the revenue Q for data-set-driven instance ($K = 20$).

6.6 Discussions

Noting that though intuitively the time complexity of B&B algorithm is higher than that of the greedy algorithm, B&B algorithm is still preferred for its performance gain and the following reasons: first, the algorithm can be implemented in one move using high performance computer before real deployment and thus the complexity impacts will be small. Second, the operation of branch pruning in B&B algorithm will greatly reduce the practical computational cost.

7 Conclusion

In this paper, we study the problem of simultaneous charger placement and power scheduling based on users' spatial and temporal distribution information with total power constraint, aiming to maximize the revenue of the charging service. We formulate the problem as a mixed integer linear programming problem and propose a branch and bound algorithm to solve it. Extensive simulations demonstrate the following results: First, in small-scale network with less than 5 given chargers, our proposed algorithm can reach the optimum. Second, in large-scale network and the data-set-driven simulations, our proposed algorithm obtains the profit improvement over the greedy algorithm by 4.8% to 12.62% on average under different settings. Especially, when the given number of chargers increases, the provider's profits increase. Our work provides a preliminary solution for economic and effective deployment of wireless charging service. Future work aims to explore online power scheduling policies with users' spatial and temporal causal information a prior.

References

1. Lu, X., Wang, P., Niyato, D., et al.: Wireless charging technologies: fundamentals, standards, and network applications. IEEE Commun. Surv. Tutorials **18**(2), 1413–1452 (2016)
2. Lu, X., Wang, P., Niyato, D., et al.: Wireless networks with RF energy harvesting: a contemporary survey. IEEE Commun. Surv. Tutorials **17**(2), 757–789 (2017)
3. Bi, S., Zeng, Y., Zhang, R.: Wireless powered communication networks: an overview. IEEE Wirel. Commun. **23**(2), 10–18 (2016)
4. Li, Y., Chen, Y., Chen, C.S., et al.: Charging while moving: deploying wireless chargers for powering wearable devices. IEEE Trans. Veh. Technol. **67**(12), 11575–11586 (2018)
5. Kun, T., Shi, R., Guo, Y., et al.: An adaptive transmission scheme in cooperative relay networks with energy accumulation. Chin. J. Electron. **28**(1), 152–161 (2019)
6. Cid-Fuentes, R.G., Naderi, M.Y., Chowdhury, K.R., et al.: On the scalability of energy in wireless RF powered internet of things. IEEE Commun. Lett. **20**(12), 2554–2557 (2016)
7. Smith, J.R.: WISP. https://sensor.cs.washington.edu/WISP.html. 14 Mar 2019
8. Obeidat, M.: Cota. https://www.ossia.com/cota. 14 Mar 2019
9. Shearer, J.: Powercaster. https://www.powercastco.com. 14 Mar 2019
10. He, S., Chen, J., Jiang, F., et al.: Energy provisioning in wireless rechargeable sensor networks. IEEE Trans. Mob. Comput. **12**(10), 1931–1942 (2013)
11. Li, Y., Fu, L., Chen, M., et al.: RF-based charger placement for duty cycle guarantee in battery-free sensor networks. IEEE Commun. Lett. **19**(10), 1802–1805 (2015)
12. Dai, H., Liu, Y., Liu, X., et al.: Radiation constrained wireless charger placement. In: Proceedings of IEEE International Conference on Computer Communications (INFOCOM), San Francisco, California, USA, pp. 1–9 (2016)
13. Dai, H., Liu, Y., Chen, G., et al.: Safe charging for wireless power transfer. IEEE/ACM Trans. Netw. **25**(6), 3531–3544 (2017)
14. Dai, H., Liu, Y., Chen, G., et al.: SCAPE: safe charging with adjustable power. IEEE/ACM Trans. Netw. **26**(1), 520–533 (2018)
15. Zhang, S., Qian, Z., Kong, F., et al.: P^3: joint optimization of charger placement and power allocation for wireless power transfer. In: Proceedings of IEEE International Conference on Computer Communications (INFOCOM), Hong Kong, China, pp. 2344–2352 (2015)
16. Zhang, S., Qian, Z., Wu, J., et al.: Wireless charger placement and power allocation for maximizing charging quality. IEEE Trans. Mob. Comput. **17**(6), 1483–1496 (2018)
17. Chiu, T.-C., Shih, Y.-Y., Pang, A.-C., et al.: Mobility-aware charger deployment for wireless rechargeable sensor networks. In: Proceedings of 14th Asia-Pacific Network Operations and Management Symposium (APNOMS), Seoul, Korea, pp. 1–7 (2012)
18. Lawler, E.L., Wood, D.E.: Branch-and-bound methods: a survey. Oper. Res. **14**(4), 699–719 (1966)
19. Karmarkar, N.: A new polynomial-time algorithm for linear programming. In: Proceedings of 16th annual ACM symposium on Theory of computing (STOC), Washington, D.C., USA, pp. 302–311 (1984)

A Cross-domain Authentication Scheme Based on Zero-Knowledge Proof

Ruizhong Du[1,2], Xiaoya Li[1(✉)], and Yan Liu[3]

[1] School of Cyberspace Security and Computer Science, Hebei University,
Baoding 071002, Hebei, China
xiaoyali@hbu.edu.cn
[2] Hebei Key Laboratory of Highly Trusted Information System, Hebei University,
Baoding 071002, Hebei, China
drzh@hbu.edu.cn
[3] School of Systems Information Science, Future University Hakodate,
Hakodate 041-8655, Japan
g3220002@fun.ac.jp

Abstract. This paper proposes an anonymous, cross-domain authentication scheme based on zero-knowledge proof to combat the privacy leakage problem of cross-domain authentication when users in the heterogeneous domain access network services from different trust domains. First, we use the zero-knowledge proof algorithm to make the scheme independent of the trusted third party and realise secure data exchange between the device and the agent server (AS). The AS verifies the identity of the device through the proof that does not contain any private user information that can be reconstructed, which plays an effective role in protecting the privacy of the device. Second, the device submits the proof, which is generated from private device information and public parameter information. It has nothing to do with the trust domain authentication mechanism. Therefore, it can be used for mutual authentication between heterogeneous domains. Finally, we use the characteristics of decentralisation and tamper proof of blockchain technology to ensure the consistency of interdomain message storage and realise cross-domain authentication. Theoretical analysis shows that the scheme meets the security requirements of confidentiality, integrity and availability. The experimental results show that compared with the existing schemes, our scheme is feasible and effective.

Keywords: Internet of Things · Cross-domain authentication · Zero-knowledge proof · Blockchain · Privacy protection

1 Introduction

In the Internet of Things environment, especially in distributed network environments, such as the industrial internet, smart homes and smart medicine, it

Supported by organization National Natural Science Foundation of China (No. 61572170), Natural Science Foundation of Hebei Province (No. F2018201153) and Key Project of Natural Science Foundation of Hebei Province (F2019201290).

Y. Lai et al. (Eds.): ICA3PP 2021, LNCS 13156, pp. 647–664, 2022.
https://doi.org/10.1007/978-3-030-95388-1_43

is necessary to establish contacts between different trust domains for a cooperative production of devices, access to services or resources not available in one's own trust domain. It is easy to establish a connection through the widely used network infrastructure, but achieving secure communication is not as simple as we think. Due to people's incomplete research on device security in the Internet of Things environment [1], malicious attackers can use insecure cross-domain authentication to control devices and spread malicious code. Therefore, it is urgent to design a secure device cross-domain authentication scheme.

Traditional cross-domain authentication schemes are based on public key infrastructure (PKI) [2] systems and identity-based cryptography (IBC) [3] systems. The cross-domain authentication scheme based on PKI has several problems, such as a long trust path, complex topology, low efficiency of certificate verification and complex trust construction between domains. Cross-domain authentication technology based on IBC has a problem with key escrow, and its public key generally has a special meaning; thus, it cannot be revoked at will. The amount of calculation and communication is also relatively high. In addition, the two schemes have a problem because they rely on a trusted third party. Moreover, most cross-domain authentication schemes only study cross-domain authentication schemes between trust domains with the same authentication mechanism, and only a small part of the literature takes into account the mutual authentication of devices within heterogeneous domains. Therefore, research on cross-domain authentication is still incomplete [9–22].

Blockchain [4] has the advantages of decentralisation, as well as the characteristics of anti-tampering, unforgeability, traces throughout the entire process, traceability and a collective maintenance of data stored in the blockchain. Additionally, Blockchain has extensive research in the field of identity authentication. However, its open and transparent characteristics make it impossible to guarantee the privacy of a device, making user privacy face a major threat of leakage [5]. The zero-knowledge proof is a protocol in cryptography. On the one hand, it can protect the privacy of data and prove it without disclosing data. On the other hand, only a small amount of data can be generated to prove the large amount of data, which can play a substantial role in compressing the amount of data and improving the performance. Therefore, the combination of zero-knowledge proof and blockchain technology is currently the most reliable solution for data security and privacy protection issues. As a result, we propose an anonymous cross-domain authentication scheme for the current cross-domain authentication scheme in the IoT environment. The main contributions of this article are as follows:

(1) We propose a cross-domain authentication scheme suitable for heterogeneous domains with different authentication mechanisms. The device binds the self-generated public key (pk) and private keys (sk) with real identity information to calculate anonymous identity information. The credential provided during device authentication is only related to the authentication credential generated by using anonymous identity information and has nothing to do with the trusted domain authentication mechanism.

(2) We use zero-knowledge proof technology to protect the user's true identity information on their device. First, the public key is bound with the real identity information to calculate the anonymous information. The zero-knowledge proof algorithm is used to calculate the authentication certificate, which does not contain any information that can reconstruct the identity on the device. Finally, the zero-knowledge proof algorithm verification is used to verify the authenticity of the user's identity without disclosing any of the user's identity information.

(3) We put forward a cross-domain authentication scheme based on blockchain architecture. No centralised management servers, such as certificate centres and key management centres, are set in the trust domain. We take advantage of the decentralisation and tamper-proof characteristics of the blockchain to ensure the consistency of message storage between domains.

The remainder of the paper is organized as follows. In Sect. 2, we outline the related work of cross-domain authentication. The design of our scheme is described in Sect. 3. In Sect. 4, we introduces the system model. In Sect. 5, the cross-domain authentication scheme is introduced in detail. In Sect. 6, we analyzes the proposed scheme. Finally, Sect. 7 concludes the paper.

2   Related Work

Many schemes about device authentication [6–8] have been proposed by experts at home and abroad. However, with the popularisation and promotion of 5G communication technology, the services and resources of a single trust domain can no longer meet the basic needs of users, and cross-domain access will become increasingly frequent. According to the different technologies used, the traditional cross-domain authentication schemes can be divided into two categories: PKI-based and IBC-based cross-domain authentication schemes. Wang et al. [9] established a trust channel based on a trusted third party to realise authentication between PKI domains. Lu et al. [10] proposed a grid-based IBC multi-trust domain authentication model. These traditional schemes all have a series of problems, such as the complexity of interdomain trust construction brought by trusted third parties. With the rapid development of technology and the increasing number of users, these problems will be particularly prominent. To solve the above problems, many schemes [11–17] use blockchain technology to help improve the issues with trusted third parties.

For the cross-domain authentication problem of trust domains of different mechanisms, Ding et al. [18] proposed a certificate-based anonymous cross-domain authentication scheme that does not involve complex certificate management and has no key hosting or distribution issues. Ma et al. [19] realised the security authentication of information service entities between heterogeneous domains based on blockchain technology, but that did not solve the inherent problem of overhead waste caused by the storage data in the blockchain system. Zhang et al. [20] proposed a cross-domain authentication scheme based on a blockchain-based master-slave chain structure for cross-domain trusted authentication of power services. Wei et al. [21] proposed an efficient, secure, and privacy-protected IoT message authentication scheme, which supported IoT devices with different encryption configurations. This made the IoT composed of different types of smart devices have better practicability. Dong et al. [22] proposed a trust transfer model based on blockchain without a trusted third party. The model used a unified token to design a trust transfer method, which solved the problems with repeated construction and wasted resources. Dong et al. [23] proposed a blockchain-based cross-domain authentication strategy, which used the cosmos network model to greatly improve throughput.

With the increasing number of Internet of Things devices connected to the network and the open and transparent characteristics of the blockchain, protecting user privacy had also become an urgent problem to be solved. Some schemes used zero-knowledge proof technology to prevent user privacy from leaking. Zhu et al. [24] completed mutual authentication between users and medical data demanders under the condition of protecting users' privacy by using the zero-knowledge technology with succinct non-interactive arguments of knowledge (ZK-SNARK) [25]. Li et al. [26] introduced zero-knowledge proof [27] technology into the existing identity management model to protect the privacy of user identity information. To solve the problem with the lack of cryptocurrency auditing with strong privacy, Jiang et al. used zero-knowledge proof to propose an auditable confidential transaction (ACT) scheme [28] to ensure the privacy and correctness of transaction data. Therefore, zero-knowledge proof technology is an important means to protect users' privacy.

3   Preliminaries and Key Technology

3.1   Blockchain

Blockchain is a new type of decentralised protocol that can store transactions and data securely. The information cannot be forged or tampered with, and it does not need any centralised organisation's review. With the development of 5G technology, massive data and diverse services make traditional cross-domain authentication face security challenges. Therefore, the decentralised nature of blockchain can play a very important role in identity authentication.

3.2   Zero-Knowledge Proof

Zero-knowledge proof was proposed by S. Goldwasser, S. Micali and C. Rackoff in the early 1980s. It is essentially a series of steps taken by two or more parties to complete a task. One proves to the verifier and makes him believe that he knows or owns a certain message, but the authentication process cannot disclose any information about the proved message to the verifier. On centralised platforms such as Facebook, Amazon, and Google, some people profit by selling personal private data and attempt to manipulate our behaviour through advertising. All our activities are recorded and made public on the completely open blockchain network. The zero-knowledge proof provides a public and transparent crypto-graphic technology that can protect people from personal privacy infringements by snoopers in the digital age.

3.3 ZK-SNARK

ZK-SNARK refers to the zero-knowledge succinct non-interactive arguments of knowledge, which is a variant of zero-knowledge proof. It allows the prover to convince any verifier of the validity of a given assertion, which does not require an interaction between the prover and verifier. The classic algorithm Groth16 of ZK-SNARK [29] is used in this article.

4 System Model

The scheme architecture uses a layered design pattern, as shown in Fig. 1. There are multiple roles in the authentication mechanism, including roles for devices, AS and blockchain (BC). According to the different functions, they are divided into the entity layer, agent layer, blockchain layer and storage layer.

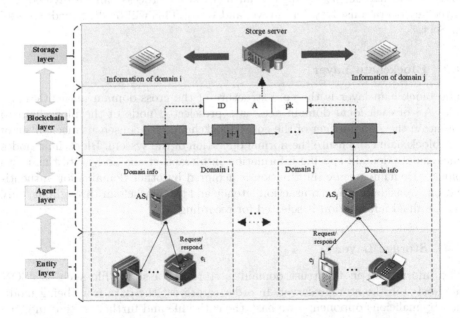

Fig. 1. Layered architecture of the cross-domain authentication mechanism.

4.1   Entity Layer

The entity layer includes IoT devices in the trust domain. It is assumed that the trusted platform module (TPM) is installed at the factory. The TPM has security functions, such as symmetric and asymmetric encryption, hashing, storage and management of data certificates. The entities can securely self-generate pk/sk pairs to communicate with the AS.

4.2   Agent Layer

The agent layer is composed of a semi-trusted identity authentication AS in each trust domain. The AS has two missions. On the one hand, it communicates with the device to process the authentication request and verification work from the trusted domain device. On the other hand, the AS assists with another AS in the blockchain to complete the cross-domain authentication action when the device requests cross-domain authentication. The AS only receives the information of the domain it belongs to from the device and writes it to the blockchain. The AS in the local domain uses the zero-knowledge proof algorithm for verification instead of traditional IBS technology and PKI technology. Therefore, the user's privacy will not be disclosed. The authentication process can be divided into three key operations: KeyGen, prove, and verify. This will be described in detail in Sect. 5.

4.3   Blockchain Layer

The blockchain layer is the core structure of the cross-domain authentication. The AS of each local domain acts as a preselected node of the blockchain to maintain the global ledger of the entire blockchain. The consensus mechanism of the blockchain can ensure the normal operation of the system. Blockchain nodes encapsulate domain-specific information into transactions and write them into blocks. Domain-specific information is acquired by other domains for authentication. Considering the transaction latency and the blockchain throughput, only the minimal information is selected for recording.

4.4   Storage Layer

The information in the trust domain is stored in a single file such as JSON file hosted in the storage server. In order to protect the data from being modified by malicious opponents, we hash the entire file and further write it into the blockchain. Therefore, the authenticity of the data can be easily verified by comparing the latest hash value maintained on the blockchain with the recalculated hash value on the actual file.

5   The Proposed Scheme of Cross-domain Authentication

This section describes in detail how to use zero-knowledge proof and blockchain technology to protect device privacy in the cross-domain authentication scheme. The scheme includes two stages: device registration and cross-domain authentication. The cross-domain authentication phase is also divided into two parts: local authentication and cross-domain authentication (Fig. 2). Table 1 describes the symbols used in our scheme.

Table 1. Symbol description.

Denotation	Implication
TPM	Trusted Platform Module
M_i	Message
ID_i	Identity Information
N_i	Random Number
T_i	Timestamps
PK	Proving Key
VK	Verification Key
S_{i1}	Set of Device Anonymous Identity
S_{i2}	Set of Device Real Identity
pk	Public Key
sk	Private Key
DN	Domain Name
A_i	Device Anonymous Identity

5.1   Device Registration

(1) $M_{1(e_i \rightarrow AS_i)} : En_{pk_{AS_i}}(T_1, N_1, pk_i, ID_i, A_i, sig_{sk_{e_i}}(pk_i \parallel ID_i), Request_1)$
Assuming that each device has a trusted platform module installed when it leaves the factory, the device can self-generate a public and private key pair to communicate securely with AS_i. The device selects a random number N_1 to calculate the anonymous identity $A_i = hash(pk_i \parallel ID_i \parallel N_1)$. Then, a registration request including N_1, pk_i, ID_i, A_i and $sig_{sk_{e_i}}(pk_i \parallel ID_i)$ is sent to AS_i at T_1.

(2) $M_{2(AS_i \rightarrow F)} : En_{pk_F}(T_2, ID_i, Request_2)$
After receiving M_1, the AS_i checks the validity of the timestamps T_1 and signature $sig_{sk_{e_i}}(pk_i \parallel ID_i,$ and then sends a verification request to manufacturer F according to ID_i at T_2 to check whether the device has been repeatedly registered. Manufacturer F is an AS in the trust domain of device production. Thus, the interaction between AS and F can be regarded as the query and verification operation between blockchain nodes.

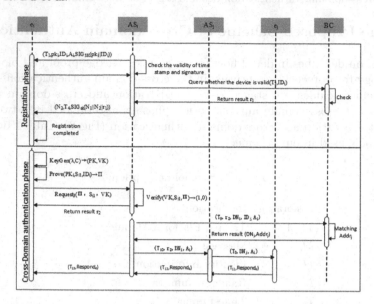

Fig. 2. Model flow chart.

(3) $M_{3(F \to AS_i)} : En_{pk_{AS_i}}(T_3, r_1, Respond_1)$
Manufacturer F decrypts the message from AS_i. The validity of the device is judged within the validity period of the timestamps T_2. If ID_i is valid, the response result r_1 is sent to AS_i at T_3.

(4) $M_{4(AS_i \to e_i)} : En_{pk_{e_i}}(T_4, N_2, sig_{pk_{e_i}}(N_1 \parallel N_2 \parallel r_1))$
AS_i receives message M_3 from manufacturer F. If the timestamp is valid, AS_i decrypts it and confirms whether the e_i is valid. If e_i is not registered repeatedly, AS_i will register it and store ID_i and A_i in the list $S_{i1} = (A_1, A_2, ..., A_n)$ and $S_{i2} = (ID_1, ID_2, ..., ID_n)$ of AS_i respectively. Then, AS_i selects a random number N_2 to sign the result and M_4 to e_i at T_4.

(5) $M_{5(e_i \to AS_i)} : En_{pk_{AS_i}}(T_5, Respond_2)$
When e_i receives message M_4, we check the timestamps T_4 and the signature $sig_{pk_{e_i}}(N_1 \parallel N_2 \parallel r_1)$ again to check if it is valid. If it is valid, e_i checks the registration result and completes the registration.

5.2 Cross-domain Authentication

Whether the device wants to access the services of the intradomain or the external domain, it needs to pass the authentication of the local domain first. We first use the hash function to anonymize the real identity of the device.

5.2.1 Local Authentication

(1) $KeyGen(\lambda, C) \to (PK, VK)$ According to the main logic of the $ZK-SNARK$ circuit, e_i selects the random number λ and writes the circuit file C. After that, the algorithm $KeyGen$ is used to generate PK and VK. The proof π is generated by PK, public parameters and private parameters,

which is used to prove the identity of the device. The VK is used to verify the validity of PK and π.

(2) $prove(PK, S_{i1}, AS_i) \rightarrow \pi$

The set of anonymous device identities S_{i1} in Domain i is a public parameter of the algorithm $prove$ and the device anonymous identity information A_i is the private input. Although A_i and the corresponding ID_i are already known and sent to the AS_i, the output π is the proof to prove the identity of e_i and it does not contain any information that can reconstruct the private input, nor will we know which device has sent an authentication request. So we can protect the privacy of the device.

(3) $M_{6(e_i \rightarrow AS_i)} : En_{pk_{AS_i}}(\pi, VK, T_6, A_i, Respond_3)$

After completing the above calculation tasks, e_i sends a request to the AS_i of the local domain at T_6. The parameters include identity authentication proof π, VK and anonymous identity information A_i.

(4) $verify(VK, \pi, A_i) \rightarrow (1, 0)$

AS_i decrypts message M_6 from e_i and checks the validity of the timestamp T_6. Then, it verifies whether the device is a legal device in its domain through the algorithm $verify$ and the parameters passed by e_i.

(5) $M_{7(AS_i \rightarrow e_i)} : En_{pk_{e_i}}(r_2, T_7, Respond_3)$

After AS_i successfully verifies e_i, it sends the result r_2 to e_i at T_7. Now the local authentication process is completed. Then, e_i can use the anonymous identity A_i as a legitimate user to interact with other devices.

5.2.2 Cross-domain Authentication

(1) $M_{8(e_i \rightarrow AS_i)} : En_{pk_{AS_i}}(DN_j, T_8, A_i, ID_j)$

e_i launches an authentication request using the anonymous identity A_i to interact with the device whose domain name is the DN_j domain at T_8. The parameters are the domain name of the target domain DN_j, the anonymous identity information of the subject device ID_j and the identity information of e_i, Additionally, the message is encrypted by pk_{AS_i}.

(2) $M_{9(AS_i \rightarrow AS_j)} : En_{pk_{AS_j}}(DN_i, T_9, A_i, ID_j, r_2, Request_4)$

AS_i always monitors various requests from its domain. Once it receives the cross-domain authentication request from the device if the timestamps is valid, the AS_i will query the domain table according to the passed domain name to obtain the blockchain account address $Addr_j$ of the target domain AS_j. Then the AS will send a cross-domain authentication request to this address. The parameters include the domain name DN_i of the trusted domain requested to be accessed, the anonymous information A_i of the requested access device, the device information ID_j of the target domain, and the authentication result r_2 of e_i in the local domain.

(3) $M_{10(AS_j \rightarrow e_j)} : En_{pk_{e_j}}(DN_i, T_{10}, A_i, r_2, Respond_4)$

AS_j listens to the cross-domain authentication request from AS_i and decrypts it if the timestamps is valid. It obtains the identity information of e_j and AS_i. Then, the result through the parameters transmitted by the event determines whether the verification is passed. Finally, it forwards the cross-domain authentication request and response result to e_j.

(4) $M_{11(e_j \rightarrow AS_j)} : En_{pk_{AS_j}}(T_{11}, Respond_4)$

   e_j receives the message from AS_j, and decrypts the message after checking the validity of the timestamps. After verifying the successful authentication result of the device, it responds to the authentication result at T_{11} and sends it to AS_j.

(5) $M_{12(AS_j \rightarrow AS_i)} : En_{pk_{AS_i}}(T_{12}, Respond_4)$

   AS_j receives the response sent by e_j and sends it to AS_i at T_{12}. At the same time, AS_j updates the history record that listened to the event.

(6) AS_i listens to the response from the target domain agent server AS_j. The AS_i decrypts the message from AS_j and sends a response to e_i requesting access at T_{13} if the timestamp is fresh.

(7) e_i decrypts the message from AS_i to check the corresponding result. After e_i passes the authentication, it can conduct cross-domain access with the device in an anonymous way.

6 Scheme Analysis

In this section, the proposed scheme will be compared and analysed with other existing schemes in terms of SVO certification, security attribute analysis and a performance evaluation of the protocol.

6.1 SVO Proof of the Protocol

SVO logic is a more reasonable semantic and axiomatic derivation system of theoretical models than BAN logic. The protocol is proven based on logical terms and axioms. There are three expected goals of the protocol:

1. $AS_i \mid\equiv F \ni e_i$;
2. $AS_i \mid\equiv AS_i \ni AS_i$;
3. $e_j \mid\equiv AS_i \ni e_i$;

(1) Initial assumption

   p_0 : All entities are equipped with TPM, which is used to generate pk/sk pairs, and then bind the pk/sk with their IDs;

   p_1 : Whether all timestamps are valid and can be verified;

   p_2 : $e_i \mid\equiv PK_{\Psi}(AS_i, pk_{AS_i})$;

   p_3 : $AS_i \mid\equiv PK_{\sigma}(e_i, pk_{e_i})$;

   p_4 : $AS_i \mid\equiv SV(sig_{sk_{e_i}}(pk_i \parallel ID_i), pk_{e_i}, e_i)$;

   p_5 : $AS_i \mid\equiv PK_{\Psi}(F, pk_F)$;

   p_6 : $AS_i \triangleleft M_3$;

   p_7 : The entities need to complete the calculation tasks required by themselves;

   p_8 : $AS_i \triangleleft M_6$;

   p_9 : $AS_i \mid\equiv PK_{\Psi}(AS_j, pk_{AS_j})$;

$p_{10} : AS_j \models PK_\Psi(AS_i, pk_{AS_i});$

$p_{11} : AS_j \triangleleft M_9;$

$p_{12} : AS_j \models PK_\Psi(e_j, pk_{e_j});$

$p_{13} : e_j \models PK_\Psi(AS_j, pk_{AS_j});$

P_2 denotes that e_i believes pk_{AS_i} is the public encryption key of AS_i. P_3 denotes that AS_i believes pk_{e_i} is the public encryption key of e_i. P_4 denotes that AS_i believes pk_{e_i} can verify $sig_{sk_{e_i}}(pk_i \parallel ID_i)$ is the signature of e_i. P_5 and P_9 denote that AS_i believes pk_F and pk_{AS_j} are the public encryption keys of F and AS_j, respectively. P_6 and P_8 denote that M_3 sees M_5. p_{10} and p_{12} denote AS_j believe that pk_{AS_i} and pk_{e_j} are the public encryption keys of AS_i and e_j, respectively. p_{11} denotes that AS_j sees M_9. p_{13} denotes that e_j believes pk_{AS_j} is the public encryption key of AS_j. Please note that PK_Ψ and pk_σ are symbols in the SVO logic system, which is different from the device's public key pk and the PK in the zero-knowledge proof system in this scheme.

(2) The proof of our protocol

1) Under the conditions of p_0 and p_1 and p_2, using the rules A_3 and A_{15}, we can obtain the result $R_1 : AS_i \models e_i \models \approx M_1$;

2) Under the conditions of p_3 and p_4, using the rules A_8, we can obtain the result $R_2 : e_i \models AS_i \ni pk_i, ID_i$;

3) Under the conditions of p_1 and p_5, using the rules A_4, we can obtain the result $R_3 : F \models AS_i \models \approx M_2$;

4) Under the conditions of p_0 and p_1, combining R_2 and R_3, using the rules A_8, we can obtain the result $R_4 : F \models AS_i \ni r_1$;

5) Under the conditions of p_1 and p_6, combining R_4, using the rules A_8, we can obtain the result $R_5 : AS_i \models F \ni e_i$;

Achieve the first expected goal;

6) Under the conditions of p_2 and p_7, using the rules A_{15}, we can get the result $R_6 : AS_i \models e_i \models \approx M_6$;

7) Under the conditions of p_7 and p_8, combining R_6, using the rules A_8 and A_{15}, we can obtain the result $R_7 : AS_i \models e_i \models \Rightarrow \pi, VK$;

8) Under the conditions of p_1 and p_7, combining R_7, using the rules A_8 and A_{13}, we can obtain the result $R_8 : AS_i \ni r_2$;

9) Under the conditions of p_1 and p_2, combining R_8, using the rules A_8 and A_{13}, we can obtain the result $R_9 : AS_i \models e_i \ni e_i$;

Achieve the second expected goal;

10) Under the conditions of p_1 and p_2 , using the rules A_4, we can obtain the result $R_{10} : AS_i \models e_i \models \approx M_8$;

11) Under the conditions of p_1 and p_9, combining R_{10}, we can obtain the result $R_{11} : AS_i \mid\equiv AS_j \propto DN_i, A_{i,ID_{j,r_2}}$;

12) Under the conditions of p_{10} and p_{11}, combining R_{10} and R_{11}, using the rules A_0 and A_3, we can obtain the result $R_{12} : AS_j \mid\equiv AS_i \mid\Rightarrow r_2$;

13) Under the conditions of p_1 and p_{12}, combining R_{12}, using the rules A_3, we can obtain the result $R_{13} : e_j \lhd M_{10}$;

14) Under the conditions of p_{13}, combining R_{12} and R_{13}, using the rules A_7 and A_8, we can obtain the result $R_7 : e_j \mid\equiv AS_j \mid\Rightarrow r_2$;

15) Under the conditions of p_1, combining R_{13} and R_{14} , we can obtain the result $R_{15} : e_j \mid\equiv AS_i \ni e_i$

Achieve the third expected goal

The above SVO logic proves that the cross-domain authentication protocol is complete and safe at each stage, and because the expected goals have a progressive relationship, it can ensure that the entire cross-domain authentication protocol meets the security requirements for integrity.

6.2 Security Attributes Analysis

This section will analyse the security attributes of the proposed scheme and compare it with other existing schemes, as shown in Table 2.

6.2.1 Analysis of the Anti-internal Attacks

This paper implements cross-domain authentication based on the blockchain model, which can ensure the consistency of data stored on the blockchain. System participants are equipped with TPM, which can generate pk/sk by themselves. The system does not set the system master key, which solves the problem of key escrow. The AS will use the timestamps and signature algorithm to verify the legality of the device before they interact with each other. Therefore, the proposed protocol can resist internal attacks effectively.

6.2.2 Analysis of the Anti-impersonation Attack

When the device is authenticated, first, it generates an authentication proof pi using the ZK-SNARK algorithm and then submits it to AS. After receiving pi, AS verifies that the device belongs to a legitimate member of the trust domain. If the certificate is being modified, then the authentication of the corresponding device will fail. Discovering this information is equivalent to cracking a difficult problem, making the attacker unable to obtain a temporary identity to complete the authentication. Therefore, it can effectively resist impersonation attacks.

6.2.3 Analysis of the Anti-replay Attack

The validity of the interactive messages in the scheme is guaranteed by the timestamps. After receiving the interactive message, the receiver first checks whether the message is in the validity period and then performs the next operations. The timestamps cannot be tampered with, and thus, if an attacker reuses the intercepted message, authentication will fail due to the invalidation of the timestamps; consequently, it can effectively prevent replay attacks.

6.2.4   Analysis of the Anti-middleman Attack

Our solution binds the device ID and pk. When a device wants to register, the AS will first check if it has been registered repeatedly and then check whether the device identity and public key match. The message sender signs the message with their own pk. If an attacker has tampered with the message, the signature message cannot be verified by the recipient. Therefore, it can effectively prevent middleman attacks.

6.2.5   Analysis of Privacy Protection

Before the registration phase, the AS must confirm that the device is not registered repeatedly. After that, the AS can complete the registration only if the ID and pk of the device can be matched. When the device requests authentication, the AS can only verify the device through the authentication proof pi, and pi cannot reconstruct any information related to the device identity. After authentication, the device interacts with the AS or other devices through anonymous identity and does not use its own real identity. Therefore, we can effectively protect the device user's privacy information.

6.2.6   Analysis of the Single Point of Failure

The decentralised structure of the blockchain composed of the AS of each trusted domain in the cross-domain authentication scheme takes the place of the trusted third party. A distributed system structure is adopted between heterogeneous domains, with dispersion, dynamic adjustment and fault tolerability to ensure the consistency of information storage and build interdomain trust. This effectively solves the single point of failure problem.

In addition, the proposed cross-domain authentication scheme based on zero-knowledge proof is compared with other existing cross-domain authentication schemes in many aspects, as shown in Table 2. The scheme proposed by Ma et al. [19] relied on the certificate issued by a trusted third party for authentication and did not protect the user's privacy. Li [13] and Dong [15] sent the user's address or identity directly to the server and did not protect user privacy. Gauhar's proposed scheme [16] relied on the trusted third-party BC Manager to release transactions, which was prone to the single point of fault problems. The scheme [22] proposed by Dong was an authentication scheme based on an IBC system, which had the problem of key escrow and was not suitable for systems with different authentication mechanisms. To protect user privacy, this paper uses blockchain technology and zero-knowledge proof technology to authenticate the device. The scheme does not rely on trusted third parties and is suitable for heterogeneous domains. The SVO logic proof proves the safety of the scheme. In conclusion, the scheme can ensure integrity and is superior to other schemes in terms of availability and confidentiality.

6.3   Performance Evaluation

This section will evaluate the performance of the proposed scheme from two aspects: computation overhead and storage overhead. To ensure the consistency

Table 2. Comparison between this scheme and other schemes.

References	No Trusted third party	Privacy Protection	Unforgettable	Anonymity	Generality
Ref. [13]	✓		✓		
Ref. [15]		✓	✓	✓	✓
Ref. [16]			✓		✓
Ref. [19]	✓				✓
Ref. [22]		✓	✓	✓	
Ours	✓	✓	✓	✓	✓

Table 3. Comparison of the time cost between Groth16, PGHR 13 and GM17.

Proof system	KeyGen time	Prove time	Verifier time	Prove time spent in FFTs
PGHR/BCTV14a	104.85 s	128.60 s	4.3 ms	7%
Groth16	72.53 s	84.01 s	1.3 ms	11%
GM17	100.41 s	116.42 s	2.3 ms	12%

of the conditions, we gradually increase the number of devices in the trust domain to 1,000. Then, we count the computational overhead and storage overhead of each phase of the cross-domain authentication and compare it with the existing scheme.

6.3.1 Computation Overhead

In this paper, an ubuntu 18.04 environment is built in a VMware 15.5 virtual machine on a Dell Inspiron 3670 (Intel Core i3-3217U, 2 cores 1.80 GHz, 6 GB) device to simulate the experiment. We combine zero-knowledge proof technology with blockchain architecture to achieve cross-domain authentication. Compared with the GHR13 algorithm and the GM17 algorithm, ZK-SNARK's Groth16 algorithm has certain time and space advantages. There are performance comparisons between different implementation methods of snarks in libsnarks, as shown in Tables 3 and 4. Therefore, we use the Groth16 algorithm to assist the experiment and complete the authentication process of the device.

The time overhead of KeyGen, prove and verify is shown in Fig. 3. As we can see, the time overhead of *KeyGen* and *prove* is relatively large and increases slowly as the number of users increases. When the number of devices increases

Table 4. Comparison of the storage cost between Groth16, PGHR13 and GM17.

Proof system	PK size MB	VK size bytes	Proof size bytes
PGHR/BCTV14	312	812	287
Groth16	201	558	127
GM17	385	605	127

to 1000, the time required for *KeyGen* and *prove* is approximately 48 s and 27 s, respectively, while *verify* time remains unchanged at 1.2 s. This is because the main calculation amount of the groth16 algorithm is composed of the Fourier transform (or inverse Fourier transform) and the addition of multiple scalars (MultiExp). The *prove* algorithm requires four inverse Fourier transforms and three Fourier transforms operations. The *KeyGen* and *prove* algorithm need many MultiExp. However, the computational complexity of the verification algorithm is relatively small. The two stages of *KeyGen* and *prove* are time-consuming, but the device only needs to generate PK/VK and zero-knowledge proof π during the first authentication. It can be used permanently in the future without repeated calculations. Therefore, the verification time is only needs to be calculate when performing the repeated authentication action.

As shown in Fig. 4, the experiment shows that the authentication time of this scheme is longer than that of BASA [17] at the first authentication. This is because the KeyGen and proven algorithms need more Fourier transform (or inverse Fourier transform) and multiple scalar addition (multiexp), which makes them take more time. The verification calculation is relatively small and is not affected by the number of devices, so the verification time remains the same. As mentioned above, the parameters generated in the two stages of KeyGen and proven can be reused once generated. However, in daily life scenarios, devices frequently access the same service. Therefore, this solution has considerable advantages when the device is repeatedly authenticated. The authentication time for the BASA scheme [17] also increases with the number of users. When the number of initial users is small, the authentication time required in this paper is longer than that of the BASA solution. However, the time is only approximately 1.2 s, which does not affect the user's experience. In addition, the verification time has not changed. With the gradual increase in the number of user devices, the advantages of this solution are more obvious and more practical.

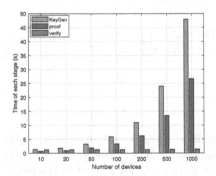

Fig. 3. Time required for each stage of this scheme.

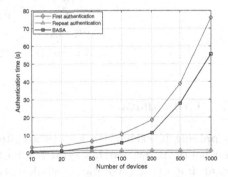

Fig. 4. Comparison of the authentication time with BASA.

6.3.2   Storage Overhead

During the simulation, as the number of devices increases, the sizes of the generated Proving Key, Verification Key and Proof are shown in Table 5. The size of the Proving Key increases from 337.9 kB to 3.2 MB. The size of the verification key increases from 21.0 kB to 185.7 kB. The size of the proof file is maintained at approximately 784 bytes. Under the same conditions, the comparison results between this paper and Huang et al.'s paper [24] are shown in Table 6. According to the comparison results, in terms of key generation time and verification time, Huang et al.'s scheme [24] requires less time. However, our proof generation time has been reduced by nearly 50%. The size of the proving key generated by the two schemes is almost the same, but the size of the verification key generated in this paper is only one-fifth of the scheme that Huang et al. proposed [24]. In summary, this scheme has certain practical value.

Table 5. The size of proving key, verification key and proof.

Device number	PK size	VK size	Proof size
100	337.9 kB	21.0 kB	783 bytes
250	795.4 kB	48.5 kB	785 bytes
500	1.6 MB	94.2 kB	784 bytes
750	2.6 MB	140.0 kB	784 bytes
1000	3.2 MB	185.7 kB	784 bytes

Table 6. Comparison between the proposed scheme and reference [24].

	Ref [24]	Our
KeyGen time	16.3 s	47.987 s
Prove time	52 s	26.665 s
Verify time	0.614 s	1.38 s
PK Size	15.3 MB	3.2 MB
VK Size	125.4 KB	185.7 kB

7   Conclusion

Applying blockchain to system architecture is a major trend in cross-domain authentication research. Cryptographic technology, such as zero-knowledge proof, is an important theoretical technique to protect the privacy stored in transparent blockchains. This paper proposes an anonymous cross-domain authentication scheme that combines zero-knowledge proof and blockchain technology to solve the problem of privacy leakage in cross-domain authentication. Our solution uses zero-knowledge proof technology to achieve anonymous authentication of user identities. Even if the attacker intercepts the message, it will not pose any threat to the system. The authentication certificate submitted by the device has nothing to do with the trusted domain authentication mechanism. Therefore, cross-domain authentication between heterogeneous domains is also applicable. Finally, the decentralised architecture of the plan is completed based on blockchain technology. Security analysis shows that the proposed scheme meets security requirements, such as integrity, availability and confidentiality. The experimental results show that compared with other typical schemes, this scheme achieves more satisfactory implementation efficiency in terms of time and storage costs. Therefore, this program has a wide range of application value.

This paper mainly studies a cross-domain authentication protocol in the Internet of things environment. The blockchain formed by all agent servers is simply considered to use the existing technology, which may be some ideal assumptions. Therefore, in the future, we will focus on the communication process between the agent servers, and add some blockchain experiments on the blockchain to improve this work.

References

1. Zhang, Y., Zhou, W., Peng, A.: Overview of internet of things security. Comput. Res. Dev. **54**(10), 2130–2143 (2017)
2. Myers, M., Ankney, R., Malpani, A., et al.: X.509 internet public key infrastructure: online certificate status protocol. RFC. **2459**, 1–129 (1999)
3. Shamir, A.: Identity-based cryptosystems and signature schemes. Adv. Cryptology **21**(2), 47–53 (1984)
4. Bitcoin: a peer-to-peer electronic cash system. https://bitcoin.org/bitcoin.pdf. Accessed 21 Aug 2020
5. Meng, X., Liu, L.X.: Data transparency based on blockchain: problems and challenges. Comput. Res. Dev. **58**(02), 237–252 (2021)
6. Wang, D., Wang, P.: Two birds with one stone: two-factor authentication with security beyond conventional bound. IEEE Trans. Dependable Secure Comput. **15**(4), 708–722 (2018)
7. Qiu, S., Wang, D., Xu G., et al.: Two birds with one stone: practical and provably secure three-factor authentication protocol based on extended chaotic-maps for mobile lightweight devices. IEEE Trans. Dependable Secure Comput. **17**, 1 (2020)
8. Wang, C., Wang, D., Tu, Y., et al.: Understanding node capture attacks in user authentication schemes for wireless sensor networks. IEEE Trans. Dependable Secure Comput. **19**, 1 (2020)
9. Zhang, W., Wang, X., Guo, W., et al.: Efficient cross-domain authentication scheme for virtual enterprises based on elliptic curve cryptosystem. Acta Electronica Sinica **42**(06), 1095–1102 (2014)
10. Lu, X., Feng, D.G.: Two birds with one stone: an identity based multi trust domain grid authentication model. Acta Electronica Sinica **2006**(04), 577–582 (2006)
11. Wang, W., Hu, N., Liu, X.: BlockCAM: a blockchain-based cross-domain authentication model. In: 2018 IEEE Third International Conference on Data Science in Cyberspace, pp. 896–901. IEEE, Guangzhou (2018)
12. Chen, Y., Dong, G., Bai, J., Hao, Y., et al.: Trust enhancement scheme for cross-domain authentication of PKI system. In: 2019 International Conference on Cyber-Enabled Distributed Computing and Knowledge Discovery, pp. 103–110. IEEE, Guilin (2019)

13. Li, C., Wu, Q., Li, H., Liu, J.: Trustroam: a novel blockchain-based cross-domain authentication scheme for Wi-Fi access. In: Biagioni, E.S., Zheng, Y., Cheng, S. (eds.) WASA 2019. LNCS, vol. 11604, pp. 149–161. Springer, Cham (2019). https://doi.org/10.1007/978-3-030-23597-0_12
14. Wierenga, K., Winter, S., Wolniewicz, T.: The Eduroam architecture for network roaming. Lect. Notes Comput. Sci. **7593**, 1–37 (2015)
15. Dong, G.S., Chen Y.X., Fan, J., et al.: Anonymous cross-domain authentication scheme for medical PKI system. In: Proceedings of the ACM Turing Celebration Conference, pp. 1–7. ACM, Chengdu (2019)
16. Gauhar, A., Ahmad, N., Cao, Y., et al.: xDBAuth: blockchain based cross-domain authentication and authorization framework for internet of things. IEEE Access **8**, 58800–58816 (2020)
17. Shen, M., Liu, H., Zhu, L., et al.: Blockchain-assisted secure device authentication for cross-domain industrial IoT. IEEE J. Sel. Areas Commun. **38**(5), 942–954 (2020)
18. Ding, Y., Li, L., Li, Z.H.: Certificate based anonymous cross-domain authentication scheme. J. Netw. Inf. Secur. **4**(05), 32–38 (2018)
19. Ma, X., Ma, W., Liu, X.X.: cross-domain authentication scheme based on blockchain technology. Acta Electronica Sinica **46**(11), 2571–2579 (2018)
20. Zhang, Z., Zhong C., et al.: A master-slave chain architecture model for cross-domain trusted and authentication of power services. In: The 7th International Conference on Information Technology: IoT and Smart City, pp. 483–487. IEEE, Shanghai (2019)
21. Wei J.N., Y, G.: An efficient privacy preserving message authentication scheme for internet-of-things. IEEE Trans. Ind. Inf. **17**(1), 617–626 (2021)
22. Dong, G., Chen, Y., Hao, Y., Zhang, Z., Zhang, P., Yu, S.: Tiger tally: cross-domain scheme for different authentication mechanism. In: Wen, S., Zomaya, A., Yang, L.T. (eds.) ICA3PP 2019. LNCS, vol. 11944, pp. 533–549. Springer, Cham (2020). https://doi.org/10.1007/978-3-030-38991-8_35
23. Dong, S., Yang, H., Y, J., et al.: Blockchain-based cross-domain authentication strategy for trusted access to mobile devices in the IoT. In: 2020 International Wireless Communications and Mobile Computing, pp. 1610–1612. IEEE, Limassol (2020)
24. Huang H., Zhu, P., X, F., et al.: A blockchain-based scheme for privacy-preserving and secure sharing of medical data. Comput. Secur. **99**, 102010 (2020)
25. Ben-Sasson, E., Chiesa, A., Genkin, D., Tromer, E., Virza, M.: SNARKs for c: verifying program executions succinctly and in zero knowledge. In: Canetti, R., Garay, J.A. (eds.) CRYPTO 2013. LNCS, vol. 8043, pp. 90–108. Springer, Heidelberg (2013). https://doi.org/10.1007/978-3-642-40084-1_6
26. Yang, X., Li, W.: A zero-knowledge-proof-based digital identity management scheme in blockchain. Comput. Secur. **99**, 102010 (2020)
27. Goldreich, O., Micali, S., Wigderson, A.: Proofs that yield nothing but their validity for all languages in NP have zero-knowledge proof systems. J. ACM **57**(10), 1610–1612 (1991)
28. Jiang, Y., Li, Y., Zhu, Y.: Act: an auditable confidential transaction scheme. Comput. Res. Dev. **57**(10), 2232–2240 (2020)
29. Groth, J.: On the size of pairing-based non-interactive arguments. In: Fischlin, M., Coron, J.-S. (eds.) EUROCRYPT 2016. LNCS, vol. 9666, pp. 305–326. Springer, Heidelberg (2016). https://doi.org/10.1007/978-3-662-49896-5_11

NBUFlow: A Dataflow Based Universal Task Orchestration and Offloading Platform for Low-Cost Development of IoT Systems with Cloud-Edge-Device Collaborative Computing

Lei Wang[1], Haiming Chen[1,2](✉) (iD), and Wei Qin[1]

[1] Faculty of Electrical Engineering and Computer Science, Ningbo University,
Ningbo 315211, Zhejiang, China
chenhaiming@nbu.edu.cn
[2] Zhejiang Provincial Key Laboratory of Mobile Network Application Technology,
Ningbo 315211, Zhejiang, China

Abstract. With the development of intelligent hardware technology, the heterogeneity of IoT devices in the edge and end layers, and diversity of application scenarios bring unprecedented challenges to the growth of IoT systems, mainly including a large amount of code be written for task construction in a cloud-edge-device collaborative environment, the inflexible configuration of offloading policies, and the high overhead in task scheduling/offloading. A dataflow based low-cost task orchestration and offloading platform, named as *NBUFlow*, is proposed to solve these problems. It is featured by defining tasks based on visualized dashboard of Node-RED to realize convenient and low-cost development of IoT systems, and multiple offload strategies of deployment and multi-task parallel processing based on dataflow migration. The performance of the platform in terms of complete time of task deployment are verified through experiments. Results show that the completion time of task offloading can be reduced by three times compared with the container migration-based offloading method.

Keywords: Internet of Things (IoT) · Edge computing · Node-RED

1 Introduction

Internet of Things (IoT) has continued to grow at a high rate globally over the past years. It has been used in various scenarios such as smart industry, cities, health, environment, and agriculture [1]. It is reported by GSMA in *The mobile economy 2020* that the total number of global IoT connections reached 12 billion in 2019 and is expected to reach 24.6 billion by 2025. With the massive growth of IoT connections, cloud servers need to process more data from physical devices, making the original centralized data processing model unsustainable.

© Springer Nature Switzerland AG 2022
Y. Lai et al. (Eds.): ICA3PP 2021, LNCS 13156, pp. 665–681, 2022.
https://doi.org/10.1007/978-3-030-95388-1_44

Distributed network devices need to be set up close to the data source for data processing and storage to improve the performance and reliability of application services and reduce the burden on the central server. This data processing and storage demand has given rise to edge computing [2,3]. In recent years, as a new computing model to meet the needs of IoT, edge computing gradually gains more and more attention.

With development of integrated computing environment involving cloud, edge and end devices, it is required to offload tasks in end devices to edge devices with higher computational power or the cloud for execution to achieve collaboration in the vertical direction. At the same time, tasks can also be offloaded to another edge node for horizontal collaboration to ensure load balance of tasks on the edge node [4]. However, the wide variety of IoT devices [5] and the different communication protocols used by the devices have posed significant challenges to manage IoT devices efficiently for meeting users' requirements, while migrate and deploy applications across devices flexibly.

Docker technology provides a very efficient and lightweight solution to this problem. It can manage virtualized processes and, therefore, deploy and manage cloud and edge applications distributed to clusters. However, as an IoT system developer, he still needs to know the internal details of task processing, to optimize task allocation to reduce latency and bandwidth consumption. It will increase the development cost and the overhead of resources in computation and communication. In order to reduce the development cost of applications, some platforms based on dataflow programming paradigms have emerged, such as WoTKit Processor [6], etc., but they are mainly oriented towards the construction of local tasks and do not consider the situation of task processing with cloud-edge-device collaborative computing.

There have been some systems based on distributed IoT infrastructure developed to provide FaaS services, such as the edge computing platform based on container virtualization technology proposed by Watanabe et al. in [7,8], FogFlow and Geelytics proposed by Cheng et al. in [9–11], and some NodeRED-based platforms proposed in [12–15]. The edge computing platform that can efficiently host large-scale IoT applications proposed by Simpkin et al. in [16], to some extent, can support collaborative IoT application development and scheduling deployment of tasks without the need to know internal network and node resource information. However, they still need to write many codes to construct and schedule tasks. Besides, most of the task scheduling is achieved through container migration, which leads to an increase in the total cost of task deployment. Secondly, the offload policy provided by most platforms is also fixed, and users cannot configure the scheduling/offloading policy flexibly.

In this regard, based on Node-RED, we designed and implemented a low-cost IoT task orchestration and offloading platform, named as *NBUFlow*, for cloud-edge-device collaboration. NBUFlow relieves the need to write many codes when building tasks, and reduce the overhead of task scheduling/offloading by solving problem of configuring offloading strategy flexibly, and realizes multi-task parallel processing in a single node. The main contributions of this article are embodied in the following aspects:

1. Based on the dataflow programming provided by Node-RED, NBUFlow realizes a rapid deployment model with a visual editor for defining tasks, which effectively reduces the development cost.
2. It provides task offloading decision modules in application layer for developers to integrate them when defining tasks, and also defining development rules of the module for other developers to extend the module and add their offloading policies, which improve the flexibility of configuring offloading policies.
3. Considering the inevitability of running multiple tasks in a single node and the possibility that task slices can be shared, we realize the non-repetitive parallel execution of multiple tasks on a single node through dataflow migration and interaction of Node-RED with K8s to reduce the overhead of task offloading.

The rest of the paper is organized as follows. Section 2 describes the characteristics of the relevant work on IoT orchestration and offloading platform. Section 3 describes the architecture of the platform and the functions of each module used. Section 4 presents the specific implementation of the platform. Section 5 presents our experimental evaluation of the platform. Section 6 summarizes the full paper and indicates our next steps.

2   Related Work

Many IoT applications are now built on commercial pay-per-service cloud platforms, such as Google Cloud IoT, Microsoft Azure IoT Suite, AWS Internet of Things, or as open-source IoT platforms, such as DeviceHive, Zetta, and DSA. These platforms provide APIs to link development boards such as Raspberry Pi, Arduino, and BeagleBone. Some of them, such as DeviceHive, also provides deployment options based on Docker and Kubernetes (K8s) to scale individual VMs to enterprise-class clusters and provide IoT services via REST API, WebSockets, or MQTT to connect to any end device or development board, even low-performance Wi-Fi devices like the ESP8266. IoT platforms are very well established, but they are still needed to be brought into the edge computing space for rapid task development and low-cost task offloading.

In addition, researchers have built some IoT platforms using serverless or microservice computing paradigms, primarily using Docker migration for task offloading. For example,

- The authors of [7,8] propose an edge computing platform based on container virtualization technology that can coordinate personal computing resources of devices, edge nodes, and clouds to modularize data processing instances and deploy them to the edge nodes that fulfill the users' requirements.
- In [9,10], the authors propose the FogFlow model to design and implement a new fog computing-based framework for an IoT smart city platform with a programming model that allows IoT service developers to write elastic IoT services on the cloud edge quickly. In addition, it supports standard interfaces for sharing and reusing contextual data across services.

Table 1. Comparison between different related studies.

Work reference	Task building	Multi-offload strategy	Migration method	Offloading/Scheduling overhead
[7,8]	Yaml	N/A	Docker	N/A
FogFlow [9,10]	Yaml	Two	Docker	Mild
Geelytics [11]	*Topology*[a]	N/A	Docker	Mild
NodeRED-based [15]	*Function modules*[b]	*One*[c]	Docker	Mild
NodeRED-VSA [16]	*Data flow graph*	N/A	*Vector Symbolic*	N/A

[a]Developers need to define scoped tasks with custom scope granularity first, and then reserve them in the repository. Task refactoring is executed as requirements arise.
[b]The Horizon dashboard allows users to define functions in blocks and compose complex workflows into pipelines that connect blocks.
[c]This scheduling policy is similar to the scheduling of K8s, with filtering by selectors.

- The authors of [11] designed and implemented a new system called Geelytics that enables on-demand edge analytics over a range of data sources through IoT-friendly interfaces with sensors and actuators.
- A system which provides FaaS services based on a distributed IoT infrastructure is presented in [15]. In addition, the authors provide a Node-RED-based dashboard that leverages the FaaS system on the back-end to enable users to conceive customized applications using resources (i.e., sensors and actuators) that IoT devices can host.
- In [16], the authors use a Vector Symbolic Architecture (VSA) to dynamically convert Node-RED workflows into decentralized workflows represented by a compact semantic vector, which encodes the service interfaces and the execution environment where they are to run in.

We used the following metrics for a comparative analysis of the platforms mentioned above:

- **Task Building**, to indicate how the platform or system builds tasks that meet user requirements, such as by coding or configuration files.
- **Multi-offload Strategy**, to indicate whether there are various offloading schemes for users to choose from, and whether they can be flexibly configured.
- **Migration Method**, to indicate the method of task offloading, such as file migration or container migration.
- **Offloading/Scheduling Overhead**, to indicate the bandwidth consumption, memory, and other resources incurred during offloading or scheduling tasks.

From Table 1, we can see that most of the IoT solutions build tasks in a way that still requires writing a lot of code, such as [15], which builds functions written into different modules for combination use during task construction, and although it can reduce the redundant writing of code to some extent, it still requires modifying the underlying function modules when the task requirements change. Most platforms also incur much overhead in offloading/scheduling. Whereas in [16], a dataflow approach is used for offloading, which effectively reduces the offloading overhead by automatically converting Node-RED IoT workflows into decentralized workflows by using a Vector Symbolic Architecture (VSA). However, it does not have multiple offloading schemes to support optional offloading in different scenarios. Finally, most of the schemes perform task offloading by container migration, which consumes considerable bandwidth resources and will fail to complete the task when deployed on devices in areas with poor network conditions.

3 Design

The overall architecture of NBUFlow is shown in Fig. 1, mainly using three technologies, Docker, Kubernetes, and Node-RED. First of all, we adopt Docker as the container engine technology, because it can build isolated standardized runtime environments, lightweight PaaS and continuous integration environments, where all applications can scale horizontally. The most apparent features of Docker are lightweight, small resource footprint, and fast startup compared to virtual machine technologies such as KVM. These features of Docker make it possible to run on some of the less computationally capable devices in the IoT field and support us to achieve rapid deployment of tasks.

Second, we use Kubernetes, which is an open-source system for automatic deployment, expansion, and management of containerized applications, to manage the container orchestration of our entire platform. Its flexible management capabilities provide a guarantee for the stable operation of our IoT platform. The master node on the cloud runs Kubernetes, and the Docker containing expanded Node-RED runs on each node to interact with it to achieve rapid task deployment.

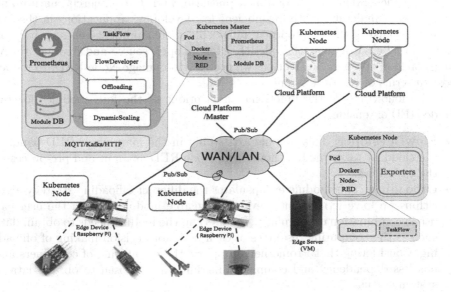

Fig. 1. Platform architecture of NBUFlow

Third, to facilitate capturing node information, we introduced the Prometheus system monitoring framework. It is written in Go language to obtain monitoring information, and provides a multidimensional data model and a flexible query interface using Pull. In terms of data collection, with the high concurrency of the Go language, Prometheus can collect monitoring data from hundreds of nodes, which provides good support for our platform to collect data. We put it on the cloud in the platform. In addition, the Exporter is a component of Prometheus, which is mainly used to collect data. Prometheus Server can access the monitoring data that needs to be collected by accessing the interface provided by the Exporter. It runs on each child node in the platform built.

Most notably, we take Node-RED as execution engine of dataflow defined task. Because Node-RED provides a JavaScript runtime based on the Node.js framework, it implements native support for building Node.js and JavaScript on browsers and servers in an asynchronous event-driven runtime [12]. The lightweight nature of Node.js and the simplicity of the Node-RED execution engine allows Node-RED dataflow to execute with good performance on edge devices (e.g., Raspberry Pi) [13], even on smart devices at the device layer. Besides, Node-RED provides a browser-based visual editor that defines tasks in the form of dataflow.

We extended Node-RED as a platform with fast offloading of task dataflow and distributed collaborative computing, making offloading and automatic deployment integral to rapid application development. Considering that task modules in Node-RED are defined in JSON, they can be exported and imported on other Node-RED to be ready to run. We automate importing of dataflow to realize automatic deployment of tasks. Although this idea is similar to that described by Sosa et al. in [14], the implementation of the self-deployment scheme is dependent on Heroku as a platform, and its commercial nature and high latency make it slightly insufficient for developing applications in the IoT domain. Unlike [14], our proposed auto-deployment approach relies entirely on the internal environment of Node-RED for its open source and free nature. As mentioned in the previous section, we use K8s to manage Node-RED, to reduce cost in terms of response latency.

The following are the functional descriptions of the four modules for the Node-RED extension:

- **FlowDeveloper:** This module exists only in the main Node-RED panel in the cloud. It takes the task flows from Node-RED as input and pre-processes the task flows.
- **Offloading:** This module encapsulates the different offloading strategy algorithms we have written into several draggable modules, which the user can use in combination or singularly. In addition, the module needs to obtain data such as the computing resources of each node for decision-making of offloading. Considering that Prometheus supports the monitoring of containers and has less dependency and complete functions, it is chosen to obtain data of system status.

- **DynamicScaling:** This module is in the main Node-RED in the cloud, and it ensures that at least one unloaded Node-RED is running on the child nodes to receive new tasks and achieve rapid deployment. Whenever a new task is issued, it first queries the Module DB for information about the Node-RED in the node that received the task, and creates a new Node-RED that does not conflict with the existing Node-RED (this Node-RED is used to receive the task for the next deployment) or does not create it if the node has insufficient resources. Furthermore, the information of the new Node-RED is stored in Module DB. When the task in a node is completed, it sends a message to the module for task deletion, and if it is not the last Node-RED, it deletes the container simultaneously.
- **Daemon:** This module is the daemon of our extended Node-RED and exists in all child Node-RED (all other Node-RED except the main Node-RED) to receive task dataflow sent from the main Node-RED and parse them for deployment to run in the local Node-RED.

In addition, we built the resource monitoring page of our platform through the Dashboard module of Node-RED to display the basic information of each node.

After the developer edits the task flow (TaskFlow) to be deployed in Node-RED, it imports the task into the specific module as JSON data. The arranged tasks are partitioned by the FlowDeveloper module, and the subtasks are processed. Then the Offloading module decides to offload each subtask to the specified node. Finally, the DynamicScaling module determines whether the subtask already exists on the specified node. If it does not exist, the K8s command will be called to create a new Docker containing Node-RED, and deploy it to the designated node. Each Node-RED loads the Daemon module by default so that after receiving the task dataflow, the deployed task will run automatically in the local Node-RED.

4   Implementation

This section will elaborate on the way to extend the dataflow-based task rapid deployment model provided by Node-RED to make it become a platform with rapid offloading of task flow and distributed collaborative computing capabilities.

4.1   Task Definition (FlowDeveloper) and Offloading Decisions (Offloading)

In order to achieve task definition and offloading, two modules need to be extended in Node-RED, namely FlowDeveloper and Offloading. In FlowDeveloper, after inputting the task in the form of a JSON stream into the module, the task is partitioned according to the Link module given by the user when building the task (as shown in Fig. 2). The cutting function is used to divide the task into several sub-tasks, and then call the Offloading module to make offloading

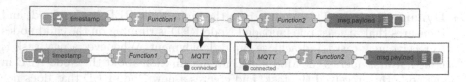

Fig. 2. Task flow division

decisions. When offloading is needed, the Link module will be converted to an MQTT module. The focus of this article is not to study the specific offloading strategy but to propose a method and interface module for the flexible configuration of the offloading strategy. The Offloading module raises the task offloading function to the application layer, allowing users to visually integrate offloading strategies while defining tasks, which improves the flexibility of configuring task offloading decision-making and scheduling.

For example, we currently provide two offloading schemes in the platform. One targets the minimum power consumption, and the other targets the shortest total delay. The specific implementations of these two offloading strategies are as follows:

Scheduling Based on Greedy Algorithm. The resources of all nodes in the current environment are obtained through Prometheus, including c for CPU resources, m for storage resources, t for upload bandwidth, and r for download bandwidth, and normalized to determine the weights of these four variables by the entropy value method, with α defined as the CPU resource weight, β defined as the storage resource weight, γ defined as the upload bandwidth weight, and δ defined as the download bandwidth weight, using Eq. (1):

$$\text{E} = \alpha c + \beta m + \gamma t + \delta r. \tag{1}$$

The score E of each node is calculated, and the node that makes the most significant E in the current environment is taken, and the cloud schedules the task to the node with the highest score, which performs the task.

Scheduling Based on Genetic Algorithm. We constructed the master node in the cloud task, and the task set represents a set of built with B, where B_i represents the size of task i, with X_i indicating whether the task i is scheduled when X_i equals 1 represents the task i has been scheduled while X_i equals 0 means task i is not scheduled. The set C represents the cloud node, and C_i represents the processing speed of the cloud node i. Similarly, E_i represents the processing speed of the edge node i and the processing speed D_i of the device node. The scheduling decision is modeled as a one-dimensional vector. $x_i(1, 0, 0)$ shows a node performs scheduling to the cloud. $x_i(0, 1, 0)$ shows a node performs scheduling to the edge. $x_i(0, 0, 1)$ means that the task is scheduled to be executed on the device node.

$$x_i = \begin{cases} (1,0,0), & cloud \\ (0,1,0), & edge \\ (0,0,1), & device \end{cases} \tag{2}$$

The transmission rate of task scheduling to the cloud node is μ_i, and the transmission delay of scheduling the task to the cloud node is:

$$Tr_i^{C_C} = B_i/\mu_i \tag{3}$$

The transmission rate for task scheduling to the edge node is v_i, and the transmission delay for task scheduling to the edge node is:

$$Tr_i^{C_E} = B_i/v_i \tag{4}$$

The transmission rate of the task scheduling to the device node is δ_i, and the transmission delay of the task scheduling to the device node is:

$$Tr_i^{C_D} = B_i/\delta_i \tag{5}$$

Therefore, the calculation delay for scheduling tasks to the cloud node is:

$$Cal_i^{C_C} = B_i/C_i \tag{6}$$

The calculation delay of task scheduling to the edge node is:

$$Cal_i^{C_E} = B_i/E_i \tag{7}$$

The calculation delay for scheduling tasks to the device side is:

$$Cal_i^{C_D} = B_i/D_i \tag{8}$$

Then the average delay T of task scheduling is composed of transmission delay and calculation delay:

$$T = \frac{1}{K} \sum_{i \in K} X_i \left\{ x_i \left[\left(Tr_i^{C_D} + Cal_i^{C_D}\right), \left(Tr_i^{C_E} + Cal_i^{C_E}\right), \left(Tr_i^{C_C} + Cal_i^{C_C}\right) \right]^T \right\} \tag{9}$$

Decisions are made through this scheme, and appropriate nodes are allocated to tasks to minimize the total delay of task deployment.

In addition, we have defined development rules for this module, and other developers can extend this module and add their offloading strategies. In order to join $NBUFlow$, the defined rules of the offloading module must be connected with the FlowDeveloper and DynamicScaling modules. The receiving end is the subtask array sent by the FlowDeveloper, and the sending end is the parameters to be received by DynamicScaling, which are node name $n.name$, task flow j, and node available resources r, respectively.

4.2 Task-Sharing Oriented Task Deployment and Multi-task Parallel Running Mechanism (DynamicScaling)

In order to avoid redundant deployment of tasks, when the subtask is determined to be offloading to the target node through the Offloading module, first, query the database to determine whether the target node has the subtask already running. If so, the subtask does not need to be deployed, and the output and input changes of the tasks connected before and after the subtask are connected to the input and output of the running task. For example, a subtask is to obtain data captured by a camera in a specific location, and there is no need to deploy the task again if the task is already running. After the coming subtask of the task is deployed, the camera data will be obtained from the node. This solution optimizes task offloading and scheduling, which reduces transmission costs and improves resource utilization.

In order to achieve the above functions, we use the MQTT protocol so that knowing the publishing topic of each subtask can receive the processing results of the subtask by subscribing to the same topic. For the topic, we set up a set of naming rules to divide the task sending and receiving as layer 0, receiving as /0, sending as /1. The distinction between the cloud edge side as the first layer, e.g. /cloud, /edge, /end. The IP is defined as the second layer, such as /1/cloud/192.168.0.1. The third layer is the port, because each Node-RED externally exposed port, such as /1/edge/192.168.0.2/1880. The following is an optional layer, which is the description label of the task, e.g. location or device. If you want to run the task of obtaining camera data, the sender subject of the task can be named as follows: /1/end/192.168.0.3/1880/CameraCapture. The names of these topics will also be stored in the cloud database.

If the target node does not have the task, the scheduling of the task is performed. In the use of this platform, we found that this architecture of a node running only one Node-RED can cause a lot of wasted resources, such as a Node-RED on a node with reasonable computing power is already running a task, at this time, when a new task needs to be deployed, this node cannot be used as a candidate node. Otherwise, it will overwrite the original task. Alternatively, it will need to consider the queuing situation, which will cause a lot of queuing delays and increase the overhead.

Considering the above, we add a dynamic expansion and contraction mechanism to Node-RED. Since our platform is deployed and managed through K8s, we need to deploy Node-RED as resources of K8s, so we expand Node-RED to call K8s commands in its internal runtime and interact with K8s to create new Node-RED on the specified nodes. In addition, to ensure that multiple Node-RED in a single node does not affect each other, they must use different mount paths, different exposed ports, different node names, etc. Therefore, we create a new Node-RED on the master node. Therefore, we added a database (Module DB) on the master node to store basic information (i.e., nodeIP, name, etc.) about the Node-RED on each node so that the new Node-RED will not conflict with existing ones when they join. For this, we added the DynamicScaling module, which is implemented as follows:

Algorithm 1. DynamicScaling: Expansion

Input: n: node names , j: json task flows , r: node resources
1: Initialize *red.tpoic* ← null and *red.id* ← null
2: *red* ← select (topic,id) from database where name = n & load = null
3: j.*topic* ← *red.topic*
4: j.*id* ← *red.id*
5: send j to this Node-RED
6: **if** r > resources occupied by a Node-RED **then**
7:      n.node-red++
8: **end if**
9: update changed information to the database

Expansion: When the task is published, this module receives the task flow sent by the Offloading module, the name of the target node, and the available resources of the current node, and then finds the information about the empty Node-RED in the node by querying the Module DB, through the topic of the MQTT module subscription in the Daemon of the node (Line 2 in Algorithm 1), and then pass the queried data information to the value corresponding to this field in the task flow (Line 3–4 in Algorithm 1), the primary purpose here is to modify the part of the Daemon module embedded in the task flow to ensure that it can communicate with the host normally after running on the specified node. Then the complete task stream is sent to the target node via the MQTT protocol. The Daemon module on the target node receives the task and completes the deployment. At the same time, the current node's resources are judged, and if the resources required to create a Node-RED are still met, then we interact with Kubernetes in the Node-RED to make it create a new Node-RED in that node (which is used to receive tasks for the next deployment). Finally, the information about the load situation of the Node-RED running the task and the basic information about the new Node-RED is updated and saved via Module DB.

Contraction: When the task is completed, we need to delete it to release the occupied resources and, at the same time to ensure the regular operation of other tasks on the node, so we set another receiving port of this module for receiving task completion information. The task completion is added by the user on the one hand when defining the task, such as getting the temperature record for 1 min continuously. On the other hand, it is up to the user to decide whether to end the task at the master node based on the quality of the task completion collected. For example, the camera of the target node is called to obtain a picture at an interval. After the master control node receives the picture, it decides whether to end the task according the users' judges on how much it meets the expected effect. In the first case, the module receives the node name and the current task Node-RED information from the task node, and this information can be used to locate the node in Module DB and find the number of Node-RED in the node. If the node has only one Node-RED, delete the task, otherwise delete the Node-RED (Line 3–7 in Algorithm 2). Finally, the changes are updated to Module

Algorithm 2. DynamicScaling: Contraction

Input: n.name , red: The task is done in the Node-RED(red) of this node(n)
1: Initialize n.number ← 0
2: n.number ← select number from database where name = n.name
3: **if** n.number == 1 **then**
4:     red.load ← null
5: **else**
6:     n.node-red−−
7: **end if**
8: update changed information to the database

DB. In the second case, the user can judge by himself and send the information to the module manually.

4.3   Task Automatic Loading (Daemon)

Through the analysis of Node-RED, it is found that the task flow on its panel is generated by reading *flow.json* file. Considering that the offloading subtask is not in the runtime environment of Node-RED, you need to receive the task flow sent from other Node-RED and write it into the *flow.json* file of the node, and then restart Node-RED to load the flow. json file to complete the task flow deployment. Therefore, we have extended the Daemon module. The main body of the module is shown in Fig. 3. When the container on each child node is created, it is loaded into the newly created Node-RED by default to complete the work of receiving task flow and restarting the container, and communicate with the master node through MQTT (also supports protocols such as HTTP and Kafka) to complete the resource management of the child nodes.

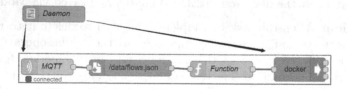

Fig. 3. Daemon module internal structure

Although the functionality of Daemon is similar to the idea described by Giang et al. in [13], the communication protocol used in the Daemon scheme by them is WebSocket, whose protocol overhead is too costly and not easy to implement such a protocol in devices with weak computing power. Moreover, the network conditions at some device ends are unstable, and there is a possibility that messages may not be received. Unlike [13], we have a different implementation method by using the MQTT protocol, which can better solve the above mentioned problems.

5   Performance Evaluation

This section first analyzes the platform characteristics concerning the four metrics presented in the related work.

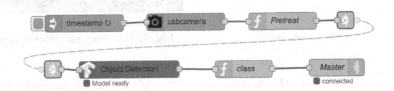

Fig. 4. Task flow construction

- **Task Building:** We use the Node-RED visual programming approach to build tasks. As shown in Fig. 4, we build a task stream that first controls the camera to capture images, pre-process them, and then sends the results to the Master node through the object detection module. This approach can effectively reduce the development cost compared to building tasks using Yaml configuration files or writing code.

Fig. 5. Multiple offload policy module

- **Multi-offload Strategy:** As shown in Fig. 5, we currently have two offload policy modules, and users can select different policies by connecting them, effectively improving the flexibility of configuring offload policies.
- **Migration Method:** NBUFlow inherits the methods of defining tasks in Node-RED in the form of dataflow. Compared with the migration method based on containers or execution files, dataflow is more convenient for modifying and extending tasks and effectively reducing the overhead in the migration process.
- **Offloading/Scheduling Overhead:** For the task in Fig. 5, we exported it as a JSON stream via the Export function of Node-RED, which is only 2.07 KB in size and transmitted via the MQTT protocol in the platform, while the task file built using the Docker container is 2.9 MB because it contains the packages needed for task execution. Experimentally, NBUFlow proves to be effective in reducing task offloading overhead.

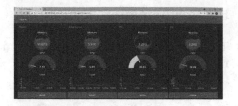

Fig. 6. Building dashboard   **Fig. 7.** Resource monitoring panel

In order to evaluate the performance of the platform, we use a desktop PC as the master of the platform (CPU: 4-core Intel(R) Core(TM) i5-7500 CPU @ 3.40 GHz, Memory: 16G, Storage capacity: 1T), and add the following two different types of equipment to *NBUFlow*, (1) 1 virtual machine as an Edge Server (CPU: 4-core Intel(R) Core(TM) i5-10500 CPU @ 3.10 GHz, Memory: 8G, Storage capacity: 60G), (2) 2 Raspberry Pi 4B as device layer nodes (CPU: 4-core ARMv7, Memory: 4G, Storage capacity: 16G) and use WiFi network to connect to the platform. We initialize each device to install node-exporter (a component of Prometheus, used to capture node information) and expanded Node-RED. In addition, we set up a dashboard monitoring panel in the Node-RED of the master node, as shown in Fig. 6, by triggering the HTTP node every 5 s to obtain the data captured by the node-exporter in each node integrated by Prometheus, and send the output to the function module, which analyzes, and finally imports the data into the Dashboard module. The result is shown in Fig. 7, where Memory represents the available storage resources, CPU represents the percentage of the current node's CPU usage, and Load represents the average load of the system within one minute.

In order to facilitate testing, we constructed a simple task flow for scheduling and calculated the time delay from publishing to the running of the task by using timestamps, that is, sending the timestamp to the master node when the task deployment is completed. We choose to schedule tasks based on a greedy algorithm (cloud is not considered in the experiment) for scheduling. Through the monitoring window, resources of Edge Server are most abundant among the child nodes so that the task will be deployed to the node. We use the program to execute the process repeatedly to collect multiple pieces of data. In order to compare with the container-based migration solution, we run the same task on Edge Server in the form of building an image and generating a container and collect data. Similarly, we use the designated scheduling method to deploy the task flow to the Raspberry Pi node and add the container migration plan for comparison. The experimental results are shown in Fig. 8. On different devices, the complete time of the task will be different. As shown in the figure, on Edge Server, the deployment completion time using Docker migration is 8 s, while NBUFlow only needs about 2 s. On the Raspberry Pi nodes, the deployment completion time using the Docker migration is about 16 s, and NBUFlow only takes 7 s. In general, NBUFlow can optimize by more than 50% compared to container migration-based methods. In addition, in the method based on the container

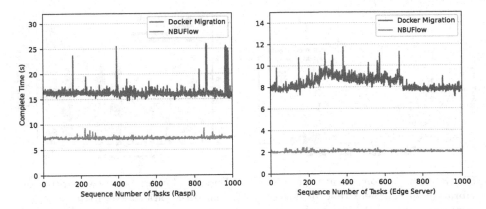

Fig. 8. Comparison of task deployment completion time of NBUFlow and docker container migration on different nodes

migration, the node needs to download the image. In the case of in-network congestion or network instability, the image is easily interrupted while being downloaded, resulting in increased delay. Figure 9 shows the variation range of the completion time of these two different task offloading methods. It can be seen that the completion time of migration tasks using Docker containers is unstable and fluctuates wildly. The dataflow-based migration method adopted by NBU-Flow dramatically reduces the amount of data that needs to be transmitted and can maintain a stable task offload completion time even when the link quality fluctuates.

In addition, to test the performance of multi-task parallel operation of our platform, we designed a task that consumes a lot of resources (the task only performs simple addition operations, but many loops are nested). Furthermore, we built this task on Node-RED and constructed an image to compare container migration methods. Then we chose to test on a Raspberry Pi with poor performance (CPU: 4 cores, memory: 4G). First, we use NBUFlow to schedule the constructed tasks on the master node to the Raspberry Pi. For each task, we conduct multiple experiments and take the average value. After completion, wait for the temperature of the Raspberry Pi CPU to cool down, and then do experiment to construct and offload tasks with container using the image. The experimental data were collected by Prometheus. The experimental results are shown in Fig. 10. The CPU consumption of NBUFlow and the container-based migration method is almost the same in the case of multi-task parallelism, but in terms of memory usage, the first few tasks of NBUFlow consume more memory than the container-based migration method. After the increase in the number of parallel tasks, NBUFlow can maintain good performance in comparison. Therefore, NBUFlow enables the edge devices to perform better in task-intensive scenarios.

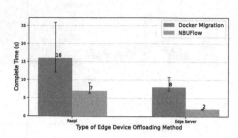
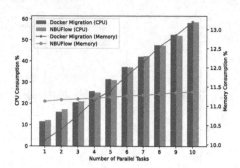

Fig. 9. Comparison of average and vibration of complete time of docker migration and NBUFlow with raspberry Pi and edge server

Fig. 10. Performance comparison of multi-task parallel execution

6 Conclusions

In this article, we propose a low-cost IoT task scheduling and offloading platform based on Node-RED. Developers can use the platform to define operations based on the visualized dataflow task, conveniently construct tasks with low-cost, and realize the deployment of multiple offloading strategies and parallel processing of multiple tasks based on dataflow migration and interaction of Node-RED with K8s and Docker. Experiment results show that the platform can significantly improve the efficiency of task scheduling. Compared with the method based on container migration, it can effectively reduce the completion time of task offloading.

We plan to fully develop the task sharing function and design an optimized algorithm for it as future work. In addition, for the task division module we will add an intelligent way to automatically divide the task. Finally, we will develop extension modules to transplant existing intelligent algorithms into NBUFlow, so that it can be applied in the field of intelligent computing.

Acknowledgement. Partial work of this paper is supported by the Zhejiang Provincial Natural Science Foundation of China (LY18F020011) and Ningbo Natural Science Foundation (2021J090).

References

1. Shafique, K., Khawaja, B.A., Sabir, F., Qazi, S., Mustaqim, M.: Internet of things (IoT) for next-generation smart systems: a review of current challenges, future trends and prospects for emerging 5G-IoT Scenarios. IEEE Access **8**, 23022–23040 (2020)
2. Yi, S., Li, C., Li, Q.: A survey of fog computing: concepts, applications and issues. In: Proceedings of the 2015 Workshop on Mobile Big Data, pp. 37–42 (2015)

3. Carvalho, G., Cabral, B., Pereira, V., Bernardino, J.: Edge computing: current trends, research challenges and future directions. Computing **103**(5), 993–1023 (2021). https://doi.org/10.1007/s00607-020-00896-5

4. Wang, K., Yin, H., Quan, W., Min, G.: Enabling collaborative edge computing for software defined vehicular networks. IEEE Netw. **32**, 112–117 (2018)

5. Mavromatis, A., et al.: A software-defined IoT device management framework for edge and cloud computing. IEEE Internet Things J. **7**, 1718–1735 (2020)

6. Blackstock, M., Lea, R.: Toward a distributed data flow platform for the Web of Things (Distributed Node-RED). In: Proceedings of the 5th International Workshop on Web of Things, pp. 34–39 (2014)

7. Kondo, T., Watanabe, H., Ohigashi, T.: Development of the edge computing platform based on functional modulation architecture. In: Proceedings of the International Computer Software and Applications Conference, vol. 2, pp. 284–285 (2017)

8. Watanabe, H., Kondo, T., Ohigashi, T.: Implementation of platform controller and process modules of the edge computing for IoT platform. In: Proceedings of the IEEE International Conference on Pervasive Computing and Communications, pp. 407–410 (2019). https://doi.org/10.1109/PERCOMW.2019.8730848

9. Cheng, B., et al.: FogFlow: easy programming of IoT services over cloud and edges for smart cities. IEEE Internet Things J. **5**, 696–707 (2018)

10. Cheng, B., et al.: FogFlow: orchestrating IoT services over cloud and edges. NEC Tech. J. **13**, 48–53 (2018)

11. Cheng, B., Papageorgiou, A., Bauer, M.: Geelytics: enabling on-demand edge analytics over scoped data sources. In: Proceedings of the 2016 IEEE International Congress on Big Data, pp. 101–108 (2016). https://doi.org/10.1109/BigDataCongress.2016.21

12. Blackstock, M., Lea, R.: FRED: a hosted data flow platform for the IoT. In: Proceedings of the 1st International Workshop Mashups Things APIs (WMTA), p. 4 (2016). https://doi.org/10.1145/3007203.3007214

13. Giang, N. K., Lea, R., Blackstock, M., Leung, V.C.M.: Fog at the edge: experiences building an edge computing platform. In: Proceedings of the IEEE International Conference on Edge Computing (EDGE), pp. 9–16 (2018)

14. Sosa, R., Kiraly, C., Parra Rodriguez, J.D.: Offloading execution from edge to cloud: a dynamic node-RED based approach. In: Proceedings of the International Conference on Cloud Computing Technology and Science, pp. 149–152 (2018)

15. Tricomi, G., et al.: A NodeRED-based dashboard to deploy pipelines on top of IoT infrastructure. In: Proceedings of the 2020 IEEE International Conference on Smart Computing (SMARTCOM), pp. 122–129 (2020). https://doi.org/10.1109/SMARTCOMP50058.2020.00036

16. Simpkin, C., et al.: Efficient orchestration of Node-RED IoT workflows using a vector symbolic architecture. Future Gener. Comput. Syst. **111**, 117–131 (2020)

IoT-GAN: Anomaly Detection for Time Series in IoT Based on Generative Adversarial Networks

Xiaofei Chen, Shuo Zhang, Qiao Jiang, Jiayuan Chen, Hejiao Huang[✉],
and Chonglin Gu

The Department of Computer Science and Technology,
Harbin Institute of Technology (Shenzhen), Shenzhen, China
huanghejiao@hit.edu.cn

Abstract. In order to monitor the behaviors of IoT devices, a large amount of time series data are collected by sensors embedded in them. To take timely action further to resolve the underlying issues of IoT devices, it is critical to detect anomalies among the time series. However, anomaly detection for time series in IoT is particularly challenging due to its complex temporal dependence and dynamics. In this paper, we propose an unsupervised anomaly detection method for time series based on generative adversarial networks (GANs), which can learn the normal patterns of time series data, and then use the reconstruction errors to recognize anomalies. To the best of our knowledge, we are the first to incorporate Gated Recurrent Unit with bi-directional generative adversarial network architecture to capture the complex temporal dependence and dynamics of time series in IoT. We also introduce cycle-consistent loss as a deterministic control to further improve the performance of anomaly detection and stabilize GANs training. Based on the trained model, any newly arrived observation can immediately be determined as anomalous or not without requiring an additional inference time. Extensive empirical studies on three real-world datasets demonstrate that the proposed IoT-GAN is effective and efficient in detecting anomalies of time series in IoT.

Keywords: Anomaly detection · Time series · Internet of Things · Generative Adversarial Networks · Gated Recurrent Unit

1 Introduction

Modern IoT consists of different kinds of devices. In order to monitor the behaviors of IoT devices, substantial amounts of time series data are collected by the sensors embedded in them. A critical task in managing IoT devices is to detect each device's behavioral anomalies such that the underlying issues can be resolved by taking timely actions.

In general, IoT data can mainly be divided into two categories: univariate time series data and multivariate time series data. Univariate data comprises a

© Springer Nature Switzerland AG 2022
Y. Lai et al. (Eds.): ICA3PP 2021, LNCS 13156, pp. 682–694, 2022.
https://doi.org/10.1007/978-3-030-95388-1_45

sequence of observations collected from one single sensor (e.g., the temperature of server machines [9,13]) and multivariate data comprises a sequence of observations from different sensors of the same device (e.g., the radiation and power of spacecrafts [8]). Thus, in this paper, we detect anomalies considering both univariate and multivariate data.

There are two major challenges for detecting anomalies of IoT data. *The first challenge* is how to model the complex behaviors of IoT devices. IoT devices are able to observe or interact with internal and external environments in a complex way [3]. As a result, their behaviors exhibit strong temporal dependence and dynamics. A previous work [17] has shown that modeling the behaviors of stocks should not only preserve temporal dynamics, but also introduce a deterministic control. Therefore, our work takes both temporal dynamics and deterministic control into consideration. However, despite the rich literature in IoT time series data anomaly detection [8–11], previous works either take deterministic control into consideration [8,9,11], or take temporal dynamics into consideration only [10].

The second challenge is how to train a model with few or even no anomaly label [19]. Supervised learning methods have made a significant progress in many areas (e.g., time series classification and speech recognition), but almost all the algorithms are depending on a large amount of labeled data [18], so it is not suitable for anomaly detection. Recently, some methods based on unsupervised learning are proposed to reduce the dependence on labeled data. Generative Adversarial Networks (GANs), as one of the most effective unsupervised learning algorithms, has been introduced in anomaly detection especially in image anomaly detection. However, there is few work that is related to time series anomaly detection. MAD-GAN [10] makes an early attempt in time series anomaly detection by replacing feed-forward network in vanilla GANs with LSTM, but it requires an additional inference time to search the optimal latent variable corresponding to the given sample.

The contributions of this paper are summarized as follows:

- We propose an unsupervised GAN-based anomaly detection method for time series in IoT that can capture strong temporal dynamics. As far as we know, we are the first to incorporate Gated Recurrent Unit [2] with bi-directional generative adversarial network (BiGAN) [4,5] architecture to capture the complex temporal dynamics of time series.
- We introduce the cycle-consistent loss to further improve the Encoder and Generator network and stabilize GAN training. Ablation studies show that this technique can improve the performance of anomaly detection.
- We design an efficient anomaly detection method which can detect anomalies from newly arrived observations independently. Moreover, our method does not require an additional inference time to detect anomalies.
- We conduct extensive empirical studies on three real-world datasets, including univariate and multivariate data. Our result demonstrates that the proposed IoT-GAN is effective and efficient in detecting anomalies of IoT.

The rest of this paper is organized as follows. Section 2 introduces the related work about anomaly detection of time series. Section 3 gives the problem formulation and overall structure. Section 4 describes the IoT-GAN in detail. Section 5 evaluates our proposed method. Section 6 summarizes the whole paper.

2   Related Work

As an active topic, unsupervised anomaly detection in time series has been studied for many years. During the past decades, the unsupervised solutions to time series anomaly detection in literature can be categorized into the following two types: traditional methods and deep learning methods.

Traditional unsupervised methods can be mainly divided into three categories: distance-based methods, classification-based methods and prediction-based methods. k-Nearest Neighbor (KNN) [7] is the most classical distance-based method in anomaly detection. In kNN, each data sample gets an anomaly score through averaging the distance to its k nearest neighbors. The samples with scores exceeding a certain threshold are considered to be anomalous. Due to the high time complexity of KNN, other methods such as Local Outlier Factor (LOF), Connectivity-based Outlier Factor (COF) and Cluster-Based Local Outlier Factor (CBLOF) are proposed to improve it. One-Class SVM [14] is a classification-based method for anomaly detection. It first models the density distribution of training data and then classifies the new data that can not fit this distribution as abnormal. Although these methods have demonstrated their effectiveness in various applications, they may not work well in time series because they cannot capture the temporal dependence appropriately. To address this problem, autoregressive integrated moving average (ARIMA) [12] was proposed to model temporal dependence through a prediction-based method and it performs better than the other traditional methods. However, ARIMA can not deal with the noise data and high-dimensional data.

Deep learning based unsupervised methods have achieved improved performance in time series anomaly detection compared to traditional algorithm. For instance, Long Short Term Recurrent Neural Networks (LSTM) [8] predicts future observations and flags large deviations from predictions. LSTM Autoencoder (LSTM-AE) [11] models time series temporal dependence by gated mechanism and achieves better generalization capability than traditional methods. Although LSTM and LSTM-AE can capture the temporal dependence of time series, they are unable to generate time series since they take only deterministic control into consideration, causing weak robustness. Recently, deep generative models have shown its high performance in many areas due to its generation capability. Generative Adversarial Networks (GANs), as one of the deep generative models, are also applied in time series anomaly detection. However, MAD-GAN proposed in [10] requires an additional inference time at the anomaly detection stage, where each latent state needs to be recovered by stochastic gradient descent. This process is computationally expensive as each test sample requires backpropagation through the generator network.

In this paper, we model the normal behaviors of IoT devices through GRU based BiGAN and introduce cycle-consistent loss to stabilize GAN training, so as to find the anomalies of IoT devices. Our anomaly detection method is efficient through adopting the encoder network of BiGAN and detecting anomalies for any newly arrived observation independently.

3 Problem Definition and Overall Structure

3.1 Problem Definition

Given one time series data $X = \{x_1, x_2, x_3, ..., x_T\}$, where T is the length of X, and an observation $x_t \in R^N$ is an N-dimensional vector at time t ($t = 1, 2, 3, ..., T$) (X is univariate data when $N = 1$, and X is multivariate data when $N > 1$), $X \in R^{T \times N}$.

The purpose of time series anomaly detection is to determine whether a timestamp x_t is anomalous or not. The difference between time series data and other types of data (e.g., image data and tabular data) is that we need to consider the temporal dependence of time series data. Given an observation x_t, we use a sequence of time series data $x_{M:t} = \{x_{t-M}, x_{t-M+1}, ..., x_t\}$ instead of a single observation x_t to determine whether it is anomalous or not. $M + 1$ denotes the length of the sequence of time series data (or sliding window size).

3.2 Overall Structure

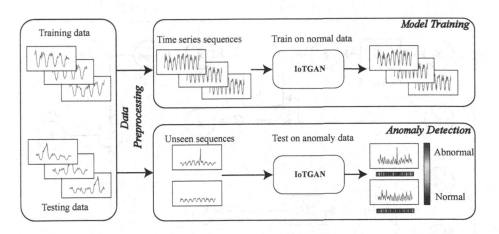

Fig. 1. Overall structure of IoT-GAN

As shown in Fig. 1, the overall structure of IoT-GAN consists of two parts: model training and anomaly detection. Both training data and testing data need to be preprocessed before model training and anomaly detection. In data preprocessing, time series data are normalized and then segmented into sequences through a sliding window [16] of length $M + 1$. In model training stage, the training time series which contain no anomaly are used in model training to capture the distribution of normal data. The model outputs an anomaly score for each observation. The threshold to judge whether an observation is anomalous or not is set according to the anomaly scores of training data. In anomaly detection stage, given an observation x_t, the anomaly detection module computes an anomaly score of x_t by trained model. If the anomaly score is above the threshold, x_t is declared as anomalous; otherwise, it is declared as normal.

4   Method

In this section, we first elaborate the network of IoT-GAN, including encoder, generator and discriminator. Then, we describe the proposed loss function, which is to further improve the Encoder and Generator network and stabilize GAN training. Finally, we show how to detect anomalies using reconstruction errors based on trained model, considering both temporal dependence and efficiency.

4.1   Network Architecture

IoT-GAN is a reconstruction-based method. The basic idea is to capture the patterns of normal data, then detect anomalies through evaluating how difference between a sample and its reconstruction. Normal data can be reconstructed well, while anomalous data are reconstructed poorly since anomaly related information will be lost during reconstruction.

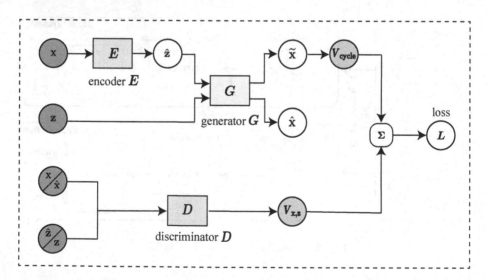

Fig. 2. Network architecture of IoT-GAN

As shown in Fig. 2, IoT-GAN network architecture consists of three parts: Encoder (E), Generator (G) and Discriminator (D). Firstly, Encoder is designed to get the precise latent representations $\hat{z}$ of real time series data x. Considering that standard GANs only contain Generator and Discriminator, we introduce an

Encoder to learn the mapping from observation space to latent space. Adding an Encoder not only supplies a way to get the latent representation for an observation x, but also improves the computational efficiency. Then, Generator produces generated time series data $\hat{x}$ using z that is sampled from normal distribution. At the same time, Generator takes $\hat{z}$ as input to reconstruct $\tilde{x}$. Finally, Discriminator takes x and $\hat{z}$ or $\hat{x}$ and z as inputs to distinguish which pair comes from Encoder and which pair comes from Generator. Discriminator learns to discriminate data by making x and $\hat{z}$ close to 1, and $\hat{x}$ and z close to 0, while Encoder and Generator work together to mislead Discriminator to assign 1 for data from Generator (i.e., $\hat{x}$ and z) and 0 for data from Encoder (i.e., x and $\hat{z}$). After sufficient training of the whole module, Encoder can correctly learn the latent representation of input and Generator can correctly model the distribution of data.

To capture the temporal dependence of time series data, we implement Encoder, Generator and Discriminator with GRU. RNNs are capable of capturing the temporal dependence of time series. Simple RNN could forget the long-term dependence of time series. GRU and LSTM, as RNN variants, were invented to address this problem through introducing gated mechanisms. In general, the performance of GRU and LSTM is similar, but GRU contains less parameter than LSTM, so GRU can prevent overfitting in a certain extent [2]. Therefore, we incorporate GRU with above architecture to model the distribution of time series data.

4.2 Adversarial Learning with Cycle Consistent Loss

In theory, we can update IoT-GAN parameters straightforwardly by optimizing Jensen-Shannon divergence to capture the patterns of normal data [5], considering both temporal dependence and dynamics. For convenience of notation, we use E, G and D to represent Encoder, Generator and Discriminator. The loss function can be formulated as:

$$\min_{E,G} \max_{D} V_{x,z}(E, G, D) \tag{1}$$

where:

$$V_{x,z}(E, G, D) = \mathbb{E}_{x \sim P_x}[log D(x, \hat{z})] + \mathbb{E}_{z \sim P_z}[log(1 - D(\hat{x}, z))] \tag{2}$$

and P_x is the distribution of time series x, P_z is a prior distribution, i.e. normal distribution.

In practice, training the model with the loss function above cannot guarantee mapping an input x to a desired output $\hat{z}$ which will be mapped back to x since adversarial learning is unstable. Training GANs requires finding a Nash equilibrium of a non-convex game with continuous, high dimensional parameters [15]. Actually, when training GANs using gradient descent, it is suggested to find a minimum value of a loss function rather than seek the Nash equilibrium of a game. If these algorithms are used to train GANs, they may fail to converge.

To lead GANs to seek the Nash equilibrium and improve the accuracy of reconstruction, we adopt cycle consistency loss as a deterministic control to time series reconstruction, which was first introduced by [20] for image translation tasks. We train the Encoder and Generator with the adapted cycle consistency loss by minimizing the L2 norm of the difference between the original and the reconstructed samples:

$$V_{cycle}(E, G) = \mathbb{E}_{x \sim P_x}[||(x - \tilde{x})||_2] \tag{3}$$

The full objective of IoT-GAN is:

$$L = \min_{E,G} \max_{D} V_{x,z}(E, G, D) + V_{cycle}(E, G) \tag{4}$$

Considering that our task is to detect anomalies, we use L2 norm instead of L1 norm that is used by [20] for the task of image translation to amplify the impact of abnormal points. Besides, we don't use the backward consistency loss ($\mathbb{E}_{z \sim P_z}[||(z - E(G(z))||_2]$) in IoT-GAN, since we just need an accuracy reconstruction of x to detect anomalies (*See Ablation Studies in Sect. 5.3*).

4.3 Reconstruction Errors Based Anomaly Detection

Now we can determine whether an observation at time step t is anomalous or not independently using the Encoder and Generator instead of considering multiple time windows concurrently. Compared with MAD-GAN [10], our GAN based anomaly detection method does not require an additional inference time in anomaly detection stage, making our anomaly detection method more efficient.

Note that, the input of IoT-GAN is a sequence data of length $M + 1$. Thus, we take the sequence $x_{t-M:t}$ ($x_{t-M}, x_{t-M+1}, ..., x_t$) as an input to reconstruct x_t. For any newly arrived observation, since all the observations preceding to it are already collected, we can use $x_{t-M:t}$ to detect anomalies independently. By doing this, not only can we efficiently detect anomalies, but also can capture the temporal dependence among x_t and $x_{t-M:t}$. Let s_t (namely anomaly score) denote the reconstruction error of x_t, it can be calculated as follows:

$$s_t = ||(x_t - G(E(x_t))||_2 \tag{5}$$

A low score means the input x_t can well be reconstructed. In model training stage, we could get all the scores of normal data. Then we can set a threshold according to those collected scores. One threshold selection way is first to obtain the maximum score of normal data, then multiply the maximum score by a constant α as the threshold (α is a hyper-parameters). Formally, x_t is marked as anomalous if s_t is higher than the threshold; otherwise, x_t is normal.

5 Evaluation

In this section, we first describe experimental datasets and performance metrics, including univariate dataset and multivariate dateset. Then, we give the setup in our experiment. Finally, we analyze the results of comparative experiment, ablation studies and the efficiency of anomaly detection.

5.1 Datasets and Performance Metrics

To demonstrate the effectiveness of IoT-GAN, we conduct experiments on three public real-world datasets for time series anomaly detection: Yahoo S5[1], SMAP (Soil Moisture Active Passive satellite) and MSL (Mars Science Laboratory rover) [8]. In particularly, Yahoo S5 is a univariate time series dataset, and the other two datasets are multivariate time series.

Yahoo S5 is provided by Yahoo Labs. It contains both real and synthetic time series with varying trend, noise and seasonality, representing the metrics of various Yahoo services. Moreover, it consist of four different parts: A1, A2, A3 and A4. A1 benchmark is the real data based on real production traffic to Yahoo computing system, and the other three benchmarks are synthetic data, we choose A1 benchmark to evaluate the anomaly detection methods. SMAP and MSL are released by NASA. Both datasets have a training and a testing subsets, and anomalies in both testing subsets have been labeled [8]. Among the three datasets, the first one is univariate time series dataset, and the other two are multivariate time series datasets. Table 1 shows the details of the datasets.

Table 1. Dataset Information.

Dataset name	Training set size	Testing set size	Anomaly ratio (%)
Yahoo	47433	47433	3.52
SMAP	135183	427617	13.13
MSL	58317	73729	10.72

We choose the commonly used metrics including Precision, Recall and F1-Score to measure the performance of different methods in our experiment. In practice, anomalous observations usually occur continuously to form contiguous anomaly segments. It is acceptable if an alert for anomalies is triggered within any subset of a ground truth anomaly segment [1]. Thus, we calculate those metrics based on the following rules: (1) If a predicted sequence of anomalies overlap with any ground truth anomaly sequence, a True Positive is recorded. (2) If a ground truth anomaly sequence does not overlap with any predicted sequence of anomalies, a False Negative is recorded. (3) If a predicted sequence of anomalies does not overlap any round truth anomaly sequence, a False Positive is recorded. This rules are also used in [8].

5.2 Experiment Setup

All the data in those three datasets are labeled. For Yahoo S5 with no splitting for training dataset and testing dataset, we divide it into two halves according to time stamp, corresponding to training and testing dataset, respectively. Then, those datasets are transformed by data standardization, and then it is segmented into sequences through sliding windows. Data preprocessing is a module shared by both model training and anomaly detection.

---

[1] https://webscope.sandbox.yahoo.com/catalog.php?datatype=s&did=70.

In our experiment, the length of sliding window is set to 10 for Yahoo S5, 100 for SMAP and MSL, and the dimension of latent state is 20. We implement the Encoder and Generator with 3-layer GRU, the Discriminator with 2-layer GRU for x inference, 1-layer GRU for z inference, and another 1-layer GRU for x concatenating z inference. All the GRU layers contain 60 hidden units in Yahoo and 100 in SMAP and MSL. Besides, drop out is used in Discriminator. We set batch size as 64 for training, and run 200 epochs with early stopping. We use Adam optimizer with an initial learning rate of 10^{-5} during model training. In anomaly detection stage, we need to decide the constant α that is related to threshold. We set α to 1.05 for Yahoo S5, 1 for SMAP and MSL. All the hyper-parameters are obtained through hyper-parameters search.

5.3 Result and Analysis

IoT-GAN vs Other Model. To demonstrate the effectiveness of IoT-GAN, we compare it with one classic unsupervised method and several state-of-the-art unsupervised time series anomaly detection methods: Autoregressive integrated moving average (ARIMA), Long Short-Term Memory with nonparametric dynamic thresholding (LSTM-NDT) [8], Long Short-Term Memory Auto Encoder (LSTM-AE) [11] and MAD-GAN [10]. LSTM-NDT is state-of-the-art prediction-based method, and MAD-GAN is state-of-the-art GAN-based method.

Table 2 shows the precision, recall, F1 of ARIMA, LSTM-NDT, LSTM-AE, MAD-GAN and IoT-GAN on three datasets. It can be found that IoT-GAN outperforms all the baseline methods under the three datasets, no matter it is univariate dataset or multivariate dataset.

Table 2. Performance of anomaly detection methods for three different datasets.

Datasets	Methods	Precision	Recall	F1
Yahoo	ARIMA	0.3770	0.7497	0.5017
	LSTM-NDT	0.7589	0.7403	0.7495
	LSTM-AE	0.7876	0.6602	0.7183
	MAD-GAN	0.7185	0.6721	0.6945
	IoT-GAN	**0.9089**	**0.8312**	**0.8684**
SMAP	LSTM-NDT	0.7105	0.8060	0.7552
	LSTM-AE	0.4962	1.0000	0.6633
	MAD-GAN	0.7714	0.7500	0.7606
	IoT-GAN	**0.7024**	**0.8806**	**0.7815**
MSL	LSTM-NDT	0.5862	0.9444	0.7234
	LSTM-AE	0.493	1.0000	0.6604
	MAD-GAN	0.6061	0.8955	0.7229
	IoT-GAN	**0.7805**	**0.8889**	**0.8312**

ARIMA is a statistical analysis model that learns the autocorrelations of time series. It predicts future value by modeling temporal dependence of time series. However, it only can capture linear temporal dependence of time series, while time series is usually non-linear. Besides, ARIMA cannot adapt to multivariable time series. IoT-GAN not only can model non-linear dependence, but also can deal with multivariate data. As a result, IoT-GAN performs better than ARIMA.

LSTM-NDT [8] is a deterministic model without leveraging stochastic information. A previous work [6] has shown that stochastic information can improve model performance since it can learn the inherent stochasticity of time series. IoT-GAN considers the stochastic information by adversarial learning, so IoT-GAN works better than LSTM-NDT.

LSTM-AE [11] is a sequence to sequence model that use the final state of Encoder as the initial state of Decoder to reconstruct input sample. It is hard for the final state of Encoder to remember all the information when the length or dimension is growing. In contrast, IoT-GAN utilizes all the state of Encoder to reconstruct input data. LSTM-AE is also a deterministic model as LSTM-NDT, which can only remember those data that have appeared in the training set. This deterministic nature may result in its inferior performance.

MAD-GAN [10] is a GAN-based method that considers temporal dynamics. But it uses the vanilla GAN adversarial loss, so it can not guarantee mapping input data to a desired state which can be further mapped back to input data. Besides, it need an additional time to search the optimal z_t that can appropriately reconstruct x_t. In IoT-GAN, we introduce cycle-consistent loss to guarantee the performance of reconstruction and joint train encoder, generator and discriminator, saving the time to search optimal z_t.

Overall, experimental results demonstrate the superiority of IoT-GAN compared with the baseline approaches and we can conclude that deterministic control and dynamic information is the key to predict or reconstruct time series. IoT-GAN captures the temporal dependence with GRU and includes dynamic information via adversarial learning. Besides, we introduce the cycle consistent loss as deterministic control to stabilize GAN training and improve the performance of anomaly detection.

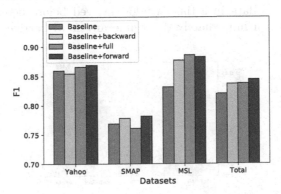

Fig. 3. Ablation Studies. Baseline means no cycle-consistent loss. Forward means reconstruct x. Backward means reconstruct z. Full means reconstruct x and z simultaneously.

Ablation Studies. Here we demonstrate the effect of cycle-consistent loss. In particular, cycle-consistent loss was first introduced by [20] in image translation area, and it is composed of two parts: forward consistent loss and backward consistent loss (i.e., $E_{x \sim P_x}[|||(x - E(G(x))|||]$ and $E_{z \sim P_z}[|||(z - E(G(z))|||]$). We adopt it by minimizing the L2 norm of the difference between the original and the reconstructed samples, as anomaly data is more important than normal data in anomaly detection.

The results in Fig. 3 show that adding the cycle-consistent loss can improve the performance of time series anomaly detection, and the forward consistent loss is the best choice. Cycle-consistent loss was first proposed to translate an image from a source domain X to a target domain Y with the inverse mapping that from target domain Y to a source domain X. In our architecture, x and z can be seen as two different domain. From Fig. 3, we can see that, F1 obtained through cycle-consistent loss is higher than baseline from a general perspective. However, backward and full consistent loss works worse than baseline in some dataset, that means they are unstable in some situation. In contrast, forward consistent loss performs better in all three datasets than baseline. Although forward consistent loss works worse than full consistent loss in MSL, its robustness is better than full consistent loss.

The reason is that we only need to reconstruct x to detect anomalies. It may cause instability of GAN training if we only reconstruct z or reconstruct x and z simultaneously.

Efficiency of Anomaly Detection. To demonstrate the efficiency of IoT-GAN in anomaly detection stage, we run the IoT-GAN, LSTM-NDT, LSTM-AE, MAD-GAN and ARIMA on a server with a GeForce GTX 1080Ti GPU, Intel(R) Xeon(R) E5-2640 v4 CPU under Yahoo dataset, and all algorithms are implemented in PyTorch. Figure 4 shows that IoT-GAN takes only 0.073 ms to determine an observation is anomalous or not. IoT-GAN performs better than other algorithms in terms of computational efficiency. MAD-GAN requires an additional inference time to search optimal latent variable corresponding to the given sample while IoT-GAN does not need it. LSTM-NDT and LSTM-AE require all the data in a time window arrived before detecting anomalies while IoT-GAN can immediately determine any newly arrived observation as

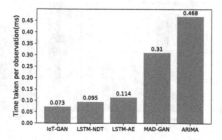

Fig. 4. Computation time of anomaly detection.

anomalous or not. ARIMA detects anomalies according to all the data in front of the newly arrived observation, which increases the computation as data volume grows, but IoT-GAN is not sensitive to data volume.

6 Conclusion

In this paper, we study anomaly detection of time series in IoT. We propose IoT-GAN, an unsupervised GAN-based anomaly detection method for time series data. We incorporate GRU with BiGAN architecture to capture the complex dynamics of time series and introduce cycle-consistent loss as a deterministic control to further improve the performance of anomaly detection and stabilize GAN training. Based on the trained model, any newly arrived observation can immediately be determined as anomalous or not. Extensive empirical studies on three real-world datasets demonstrate that the proposed IoT-GAN is effective and efficient in detecting anomalies of IoT.

Acknowledgements. This work is financially supported by Shenzhen Science and Technology Program under Grant No. JCYJ20210324132406016 and National Natural Science Foundation of China under Grant No. 61732022.

References

1. Audibert, J., Michiardi, P., Guyard, F., Marti, S., Zuluaga, M.A.: USAD: unsupervised anomaly detection on multivariate time series. In: Proceedings of the 26th ACM SIGKDD International Conference on Knowledge Discovery & Data Mining, pp. 3395–3404 (2020)
2. Chung, J., Gulcehre, C., Cho, K., Bengio, Y.: Empirical evaluation of gated recurrent neural networks on sequence modeling. arXiv preprint arXiv:1412.3555 (2014)
3. Cook, A., Mısırlı, G., Fan, Z.: Anomaly detection for IoT time-series data: a survey. IEEE Internet Things J. **7**, 6481–6494 (2019)
4. Donahue, J., Krähenbühl, P., Darrell, T.: Adversarial feature learning. arXiv preprint arXiv:1605.09782 (2016)
5. Dumoulin, V., et al.: Adversarially learned inference. arXiv preprint arXiv:1606.00704 (2016)
6. Fraccaro, M., Sønderby, S.K., Paquet, U., Winther, O.: Sequential neural models with stochastic layers. In: Advances in Neural Information Processing Systems, pp. 2199–2207 (2016)
7. Hautamaki, V., Karkkainen, I., Franti, P.: Outlier detection using k-nearest neighbour graph. In: Proceedings of the 17th International Conference on Pattern Recognition 2004, ICPR 2004, vol. 3, pp. 430–433. IEEE (2004)
8. Hundman, K., Constantinou, V., Laporte, C., Colwell, I., Soderstrom, T.: Detecting spacecraft anomalies using LSTMs and nonparametric dynamic thresholding. In: Proceedings of the 24th ACM SIGKDD International Conference on Knowledge Discovery & Data Mining, pp. 387–395 (2018)
9. Laptev, N., Amizadeh, S., Flint, I.: Generic and scalable framework for automated time-series anomaly detection. In: Proceedings of the 21th ACM SIGKDD International Conference on Knowledge Discovery and Data Mining, pp. 1939–1947 (2015)

10. Li, D., Chen, D., Jin, B., Shi, L., Goh, J., Ng, S.-K.: MAD-GAN: multivariate anomaly detection for time series data with generative adversarial networks. In: Tetko, I.V., Kůrková, V., Karpov, P., Theis, F. (eds.) ICANN 2019. LNCS, vol. 11730, pp. 703–716. Springer, Cham (2019). https://doi.org/10.1007/978-3-030-30490-4_56

11. Malhotra, P., Ramakrishnan, A., Anand, G., Vig, L., Agarwal, P., Shroff, G.: LSTM-based encoder-decoder for multi-sensor anomaly detection. arXiv preprint arXiv:1607.00148 (2016)

12. Zare Moayedi, H., Masnadi-Shirazi, M.A.: Arima model for network traffic prediction and anomaly detection. In: 2008 International Symposium on Information Technology, vol. 4, pp. 1–6. IEEE (2008)

13. Nair, V., et al.: Learning a hierarchical monitoring system for detecting and diagnosing service issues. In: Proceedings of the 21th ACM SIGKDD International Conference on Knowledge Discovery and Data Mining, pp. 2029–2038 (2015)

14. Perdisci, R., Gu, G., Lee, W.: Using an ensemble of one-class SVM classifiers to harden payload-based anomaly detection systems. In: Sixth International Conference on Data Mining (ICDM 2006), pp. 488–498. IEEE (2006)

15. Salimans, T., Goodfellow, I., Zaremba, W., Cheung, V., Radford, A., Chen, X.: Improved techniques for training GANs. In: Advances in Neural Information Processing Systems, pp. 2234–2242 (2016)

16. Su, Y., Zhao, Y., Niu, C., Liu, R., Sun, W., Pei, D.: Robust anomaly detection for multivariate time series through stochastic recurrent neural network. In: Proceedings of the 25th ACM SIGKDD International Conference on Knowledge Discovery & Data Mining, pp. 2828–2837 (2019)

17. Yoon, J., Jarrett, D., van der Schaar, M.: Time-series generative adversarial networks. In: Advances in Neural Information Processing Systems, pp. 5508–5518 (2019)

18. Yuille, A.L., Liu, C.: Deep nets: what have they ever done for vision? arXiv preprint arXiv:1805.04025 (2018)

19. Zhang, C., et al.: A deep neural network for unsupervised anomaly detection and diagnosis in multivariate time series data. In: Proceedings of the AAAI Conference on Artificial Intelligence, vol. 33, pp. 1409–1416 (2019)

20. Zhu, J.-Y., Park, T., Isola, P., Efros, A.A.: Unpaired image-to-image translation using cycle-consistent adversarial networks. In: Proceedings of the IEEE International Conference on Computer Vision, pp. 2223–2232 (2017)

Freshness and Power Balancing Scheduling for Cooperative Vehicle-Infrastructure System

Qian Qiu[1,2] , Liang Dai[1,2(✉)], and Guiping Wang[1,2]

[1] School of Electronics Control Engineering, Chang'an University, Xi'an, China
[2] Joint Laboratory for Internet of Vehicles Ministry of Education-China Mobile Communications Corporation, Xi'an, China

Abstract. Roadside units (RSUs) cache the sensed environment information in the buffer, and send them to the passing vehicles, which greatly improves the intelligence of the vehicle, and provides rich road information to the drivers. The age of information (AOI) can be used to describe the freshness of data accepted by the vehicles, which is defined as the elapsed time since the generation of the latest data received by the vehicles. The RSU transmits fused sensors' data, such as cameras, Lider, to the vehicles, which just enter the coverage of the RSU, and the distance between the vehicles and the RSU is relatively far, then the AOI of vehicles can be minimized. However, it lead to great amount of energy consumption due to the large transmission distance between the vehicles and the RSU. The RSU could reduce the transmission power according to the current data queue length of its buffer and the speed of current passing vehicle, and tend to transmit data when vehicles approaching the RSU. Then, the average energy consumption of the RSU can be minimized when the AOI of the vehicles does not exceed the threshold. A freshness and power balancing scheduling strategy (FPBS) in cooperative vehicle-infrastructure system was proposed in this paper. The simulation results show that the proposed strategy can effectively reduce the average energy consumption under the constraint of the average AOI of vehicles.

Keywords: Roadside units · Age of information · Cooperative vehicle-infrastructure system · Energy consumption

1 Introduction

Emerging vehicle networks provide vehicles with access points on the road, which will provide many benefits for intelligent driving, traffic safety [1,2]. End-to-end delay and energy consumption are the main issues discussed in V2X [3–6].

© Springer Nature Switzerland AG 2022
Y. Lai et al. (Eds.): ICA3PP 2021, LNCS 13156, pp. 695–708, 2022.
https://doi.org/10.1007/978-3-030-95388-1_46

AOI is used to describe the freshness of the information received from the remote system, which is formally defined as the time that has passed since the most recently received information was generated [7].

In existing research, [8] discussed the trade-off between service delay and AOI. They use regularly updated content to reduce service delay, and vehicles may receive outdated information from RSU. The research of [9] focused on the individuality of information, they designed an online task scheduling strategy to optimize the AOI of key information, but this sacrifices AOI of some low attention information. [10] considers the RSU detecting the vehicles entering the coverage of RSU, and decides to keep RSU work or sleep to save energy. [11] considers whether the RSU provides a transmission connection to the vehicle to meet the vehicles requests based on the vehicles location. To reduce the energy consumption, the RSU tends to provide services to vehicles approaching to the RSU, while maintaining the QoS threshold of vehicles on the road.

However, none of the above research consider the relationship between transmission power and the AOI of vehicles. Low-speed vehicles resides in low energy consumption zones for a long time, in order to save transmission energy consumption, the RSU reduces the transmission power and sends data to vehicles when the vehicles approaches the RSU, but it increases the delay of data received by vehicles. In order to solve the above problems, this paper proposed FPBS for power resource scheduling, which optimizes RSU energy consumption when the average AOI of vehicles passing through the RSU(AAVR) does not exceed the threshold. The simulation results show that the proposed FPBS can effectively reduce the average energy consumption while having a small impact on the AAVR.

2 System Model

A typical scenario of RSU data transmission in cooperative vehicle-infrastructure system is shown in Fig. 1. Road background information will be sensed and stored in the RSU, and the RSU will deliver the data to the vehicles within the communication coverage [12]. The RSU adaptively changes the transmission power according to the vehicle speed and the data queue length, when vehicle speed is small, its residence time around the RSU is long, the RSU reduces transmission power and delivering data to the vehicles when the vehicles approach the RSU can reduce its energy consumption.

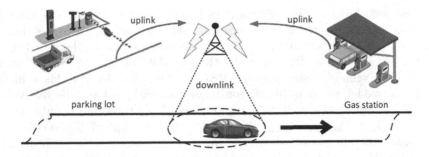

Fig. 1. Scenario of RSU data transmission in cooperative vehicle-infrastructure system.

2.1 Data Transmission Model

The data transmission model is shown in Fig. 2 [13]. Sensed data arrives at the RSU buffer randomly, and the AOI control center adjusts the transmission power $p[t]$ according to the data arrival status $a[t]$, the data queue length $q[t]$ and the vehicle speed state $s[t]$, and decides transmit data to the passing vehicles in which power state, if decides to transmit the data, $b[t] = 1$, otherwise, $b[t] = 0$.

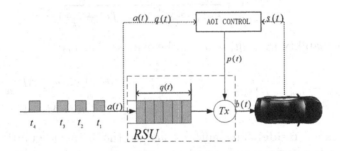

Fig. 2. Data transmission model.

(1) **vehicular traffic model.** According to the free flow traffic model of [14], the vehicle arriving at the RSU obeys the Poisson process of parameter. T_h represents the time headway, here refers to the time interval between two vehicles arriving at the RSU successively, the probability density function is:

$$f(t) = \begin{cases} \lambda e^{-\lambda(t)} & (t \geq 0) \\ 0 & (t < 0) \end{cases} \tag{1}$$

The length of the time slot is fixed, expressed by δ, the probability of (at least) one vehicle arriving at the RSU in the time slot is:

$$P_a = P(T_h \leq \delta) = 1 - e^{-\lambda\delta}(\delta > 0) \tag{2}$$

The probability of no vehicle arrives in a time slot is $1 - P_a$. The time slot is small enough, which can ensure that there is one vehicle passes through RSU in a time slot at most. Let $v[t]$ denotes $(v[t] > 0)$ the speed of the vehicle arriving at RSU in the t-th time slot. When $v[t] = 0$, it means that no vehicle passes through RSU in this time slot. In this vehicular traffic model, we quantify the continuous vehicle speed as a discrete vehicle speed state of $M + 1$. $V = [v_1, v_2, \cdots, v_{M+1}]$ is a threshold variable vector, $v_1 = V_{\max}, v_{M+1} = V_{\min}$, the smaller the subscript of the variable, the higher the speed. $s[t] = m(1 \leq m \leq M)$ represents $v[t] \in [v_m, v_{m+1}]$. $s[t] = M + 1$ means that no vehicle passes through RSU in the t-th time slot, that is, $v[t] = 0$.

The vehicle speed obeys a normal distribution with a mean value of $\bar{V}$ and a standard deviation of σ, when speed is v, the probability density function $f(v)^*$ is:

$$f(v)^* = \frac{1}{\sigma\sqrt{2\pi}}^{[-\left(\frac{v-\bar{V}}{\sigma\sqrt{2\pi}}\right)^2]} \tag{3}$$

When $v \in [V_{\min}, V_{\max}]$, then the truncated probability density function of the vehicle speed distribution is as follows:

$$f(v) = \frac{2f(v)^*}{erf(\frac{V_{\max}-\bar{V}}{\sigma\sqrt{2\pi}}) - erf(\frac{V_{\min}-\bar{V}}{\sigma\sqrt{2\pi}})} \tag{4}$$

The probability that $s[t] = m$ can be expressed as η_m:

$$\eta_m = P\{s[t] = m\} \begin{cases} P_a \int\limits_{v_{m+1}}^{v_m} f(v)dv ,1 \leq m \leq M \\ 1 - P_a \qquad , m = M + 1 \end{cases} \tag{5}$$

(2) **RSU cache model.** The buffer capacity of the RSU configuration is $Q(Q \in Z^+)$. At the beginning of the t-th time slot, the data queue length status is represented by $q[t]$, and the expression is as follows: $q[t] = \max\{\{\min\{q[t-1]+a[t-1], Q\}-b[t-1]\}, 0\}$. Among them, if there is sensed data generated, $a[t - 1] = 1$, otherwise, $a[t - 1] = 0$. If the buffer is full, $q[t - 1] = Q$, then the data arriving at the buffer in the (t-1)-th time slot will be discarded. Define the equivalent queue state of the t-th time slot as $x[t] = q[n] + a[t]$, we can get: $x[t + 1] = x[t] - s[t] + a[t + 1]$.

The arrival rate of sensed data is α, at most only one data is generated in each time slot, the probability function of $a[t]$ is expressed as:

$$P\{a[t] = 1\} = \alpha, P\{a[t] = 0\} = 1 - \alpha \tag{6}$$

(3) **Transmission power.** The transmission power state is discretized into $M + 1$ states. $L = \{L_1, L_2, \ldots, L_{M+1}\}$ is the transmission coverage range threshold variable, $P = \{p_1, p_2, \ldots, p_{M+1}\}$ is the transmission power variable vector correspondingly. The RSU transmission time is constant, to

ensure that the amount of data received by any vehicle is consistent, different speed vehicles correspond to different minimum transmission power. If the transmission power is lower than the minimum transmission, the vehicle AOI will not be updated effectively because the transmission time is insufficient. When $s[t] = m$, RSU can adaptively choose transmission power state $p[t] = k(k \in \{1, 2, \ldots, m\})$, $p[t] = k$ represents transmission range $L(t) \in [L_k, L_{k+1}]$ and transmission power is p_k. When $s[t] = M + 1$, $L_{M+1} = 0$, $p[t] = p_{M+1} = 0$, as shown in the Fig. 3. The probability that RSU transmission power state is k is $\rho_k = \frac{L_k - L_{k+1}}{L}$.

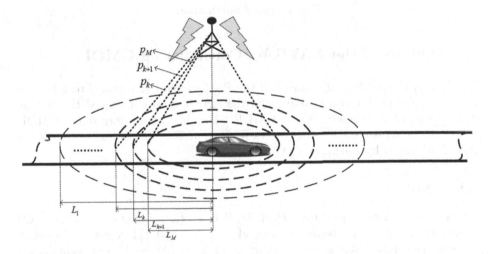

Fig. 3. Schematic diagram of transmission range and transmission power.

2.2 AAVR Definition

As shown in Fig. 4, it shows the change of vehicle AOI Δt, the vehicle AOI is a function of time t [15]. AOI can be obtained by $\Delta(t) = t - u(t)$, $u(t)$ is the birth time of the information received by vehicle, t is the current time. $T_i = t_i' - t_i$ defined as the sum of the queuing delay and the waiting time delay of i-th data transmitted by RSU, t_i' is the time when the i-th data was received by the vehicle, and t_i is the time i-th data was generated. The AAVR is the average AOI of data transmitted by RSU, which can be expressed as:

$$\Delta\Gamma = \frac{1}{n}\sum_{i=1}^{n}\Delta(t_i) = \frac{1}{n}\sum_{i=1}^{n}T_i = E(T_i) \tag{7}$$

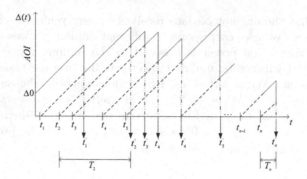

Fig. 4. Age of information.

3   Analysis of the AAVR by Constructing CMDP

This paper studies the adjustment of the RSU transmission power to minimize the average energy consumption when the AAVR does not exceed the threshold, this problem is modeled as a CMDP [16]. This section introduces CMDP, transmission scheduling strategy, Markov chain model, and the expression of the AAVR obtained by constructing CMDP.

3.1   CMDP

The frame consists of a 7-tuple $(D, A, M, P, B, P_{,.}(.,.), T)$. $D = \{0, 1, 2, \cdots, Q\}$ represents a set of the system status, $A = \{a | a \in \{0, 1\}\}$ represents a set of information arrival status, $s = \{m | m \in \{1, 2, \cdots, M + 1\}\}$ represents a set of vehicle speed status, $p = \{k | k \in \{1, 2, \cdots, M + 1\}\}$ represents a set of RSU transmission power status, $B = \{b | b \in \{0, 1\}\}$ represents a set of transmit status. $P_{m,k,s,a}(i, j) = P\{x[t] = j | x[t-1] = i, s[t-1] = m, p[t-1] = k, b[t-1] = s, a[t] = a\}$ represents the probability that the queue length changes from i to $i + 1$ when $x[t-1] = i, s[t-1] = m, p[t-1] = k, b[t-1] = s, a[t] = a$.

3.2   Transmission Scheduling Strategy

Assuming that RSU can perceive the vehicle speed [17–19], RSU decides whether to adjust the transmission power according to the current vehicle speed and the data queue length in the buffer according to the following strategy [20]. $b[t] = 1$ means that the RSU perceives the current vehicle speed $s[t]$ and the data queue state $x[t]$ in the buffer in the t-th time slot and decides to deliver the information to the vehicle under transmission power state $p[t] = k$, otherwise, $b[t] = 0$. The probability of $b[t]$ is expressed as $f^s_{i,m,k}$ ($f^s_{i,m,k} \in \{0, 1\}, s \in \{0, 1\}$), the expression is as follows:

$$P\{b[t] = s | q[t] = i, s[t] = m, p[t] = k\} = f^s_{i,m,k} \tag{8}$$

When there is no data queued in the RSU buffer, no data can be delivered, that is $i = 0$, $f^0_{0,m,k} = 0$, no vehicle arrives at the RSU in t-th time slot, and no vehicle can be delivered data, that is, $s[t] = M + 1$, $f^s_{i,M+1,k} = 0$.

3.3 Markov Chain Model

Markov chain is a discrete-time random process with Markov properties, which describes a sequence of states. The state of time slot t+1 in the system only depends on the state of time slot t, and has nothing to do with the previous system state. From time slot t to t+1, the one-step transition probability of the queue state in the buffer from i to j is represented by $x_{i,j} = \{x[t+1] = j|x[t] = i\} = \sum_m \sum_k \sum_s \sum_a P_{m,k,s,a}(i,j)$. $X = \{x_{i,j}\}$ represents the one-step transition probability matrix of the system. The one-step transition probability of the system state can be divided into the following three situations:

Case1: When i $= 0$, there is no data queued in the buffer. There are the following two situations, the one-step Markov chain of this state is shown in Fig. 5(a):

(1) The queue length transfers from 0 to 1, indicating that there is data arriving at the RSU, that is, $a = 1$, $b = 0$, for any vehicle speed state m, the length of the packet queue increases by 1, one-step transition probability is expressed as: $x_{0,1} = \alpha \sum_1^{M+1} \eta_m f^0_{0,m,k}$.

(2) The queue length in the buffer remains unchanged, that is, $x[t-1] = 0$, $x[t] = 0$, which means that there is no new generated data, that is, $a = 0$, $b = 0$, the one-step transition probability is expressed as: $x_{0,0} = 1 - \alpha \sum_1^{M+1} \eta_m f^0_{0,m,k}$.

The one-step transition probability when $i = 0$ is summarized as follows:

$$x_{i,j} = \begin{cases} \alpha \sum_1^{M+1} \eta_m f^0_{0,m,k} & ,j = 1 \\ 1 - \alpha \sum_1^{M+1} \eta_m f^0_{0,m,k} & ,j = 0 \end{cases} \qquad (9)$$

Case2: $i = n, 1 \le n \le Q - 1$, data queue length is n, and there are the following three situations. The Markov chain of one-step transition of this state is shown in Fig. 4(b):

(1) The data queue length transfers from i to $i+1$, that is, $a = 1$, $b = 0$, the one-step transition probability is: $x_{i,i+1} = \alpha \sum_1^{M+1} \eta_m f^0_{i,M+1,k}$.

(2) The data queue length transfers from i to i, that is, $a = 1$, $b = 1$. The corresponding one-step transition probability is: $x_{i,i} = \alpha \sum_1^{M+1} \eta_m f^1_{i,m,k}$.

(3) The data queue length transfers from i to $i-1$. It means that the RSU transmits data, but no new data arrives, that is, $a = 0$, $b = 1$. The corresponding one-step transition probability is: $x_{i,i-1} = (1-\alpha) \sum_1^{M+1} \eta_m f_{i,m,k}^1$.

The one-step transition probability when $i = n$ is summarized as follows:

$$
x_{i,j} = \begin{cases}
\alpha \sum_1^{M+1} \eta_m f_{i,M+1,k}^0 & ,j = i+1 \\
\alpha \sum_1^{M+1} \eta_m f_{i,m,k}^1 & ,j = i \\
(1-\alpha) \sum_1^{M+1} \eta_m f_{i,m,k}^1 & ,j = i-1
\end{cases}
\tag{10}
$$

Case3: $i = Q$, the queue length is Q, which means buffer is full. There are the following two situations. The Markov chain of one-step transition in this state is shown in Fig. 5(c):

(1) The queue length remains unchanged, that is, $x[t-1] = Q$, $x[t] = Q$. It means that RSU delivers data and new data arrives, that is, $b = 1$, $a = 1$. For any vehicle, the queue length does not change, the corresponding one-step transition probability is: $x_{Q,Q} = \alpha \sum_1^{M+1} \eta_m f_{i,m,k}^1$

(2) The queue length is transferred from Q to $Q-1$. It means that the RSU has not delivered data and no new data has arrived, that is, $a = 0$, $b = 1$. The corresponding one-step transition probability is: $x_{Q,Q-1} = (1 - \alpha) \sum_1^{M+1} \eta_m f_{i,m,k}^1$.

The one-step transition probability when $i = Q$ is summarized as follows:

$$
x_{Q,j} = \begin{cases}
\alpha \sum_1^{M+1} \eta_m f_{i,m,k}^1 & ,j = Q \\
(1-\alpha) \sum_1^{M+1} \eta_m f_{i,m,k}^1 & ,j = Q-1
\end{cases}
\tag{11}
$$

3.4   AAVR Formulation

The AAVR is the AOI of all data received by vehicles. The AOI of the data received by vehicles is the elapsed time since received data was generated, which including the queuing delay and waiting delay of the data.

(1) **Average queuing delay.** Queuing delay represents the delay between the data being cached to the RSU and the vehicle entering the maximum transmission range L_1, which can be obtained by Little's theorem. The average number of updated data in the buffer is: $L_s = \sum_{i=0}^{Q} i\pi_i(f_{i,m,k}^s)$, then the average queuing delay is:

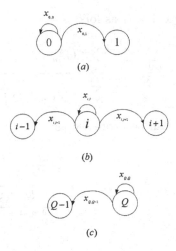

Fig. 5. Markov chain model.

$$T_q = \frac{L_s}{\alpha} = \alpha^{-1} \sum_{i=0}^{Q} i\pi_i(f_{i,m,k}^s) \tag{12}$$

(2) **Average waiting delay.** The waiting delay T_m^k represents the delay between the actual service time in the L_k and the service time in the maximum transmission range L_1 when $s[t] = m$ and the $p[t] = k$. T_m^k is divided into the following two cases.

Case1: $1 \le m \le M$, vehicle speed is the average speed in this speed state, and the average waiting delay is:

$$T_m^k = \frac{L_1 - L_k}{(v_m + v_{m+1})/2} + \frac{D}{\zeta} \tag{13}$$

Where D is the data size, ζ is the transmission time.

Case2: $m = M + 1$ means that no vehicle passes through RSU and no content is delivered, $T_{M+1}^k = 0$.

The average amount of information delivered by the RSU to the vehicle in each time slot, that is, the throughput is expressed by:

$$\gamma = \sum_{i=0}^{Q} \sum_{m=1}^{M+1} \sum_{k=1}^{M+1} \pi_i(f_{i,m,k}^s)\eta_m f_{i,m,k}^1 \tag{14}$$

The waiting delay of system in one time slot as follows:

$$\sum_{i=0}^{Q} \sum_{m=1}^{M+1} \sum_{k=1}^{M+1} \pi_i(f_{i,m,k}^s)\eta_m f_{i,m,k}^1 T_m^k \tag{15}$$

The average waiting delay T_t as follows:

$$T_t = \frac{\sum_{i=0}^{Q} \sum_{m=1}^{M+1} \sum_{k=1}^{M+1} \pi_i(f_{i,m,k}^s) \eta_m f_{i,m,k}^1 T_m^k}{\sum_{i=0}^{Q} \sum_{m=1}^{M+1} \sum_{k=1}^{M+1} \pi_i(f_{i,m,k}^s) \eta_m f_{i,m,k}^1} \tag{16}$$

(3) **AAVR.** The AAVR can be expressed as:

$$\Delta\Gamma = E(T_i) = T_q + T_t = \alpha^{-1} \sum_{i=0}^{Q} i\pi_i(f_{i,m,k}^s) + \frac{\sum_{i=0}^{Q} \sum_{m=1}^{M+1} \sum_{k=1}^{M+1} \pi_i(f_{i,m,k}^s) \eta_m f_{i,m,k}^1 T_m^k}{\sum_{i=0}^{Q} \sum_{m=1}^{M+1} \sum_{k=1}^{M+1} \pi_i(f_{i,m,k}^s) \eta_m f_{i,m,k}^1} \tag{17}$$

4 Trade-Off Between the AAVR and the Average Energy Consumption of the RSU

The AAVR and average energy consumption of the RSU are both determined by the steady-state probability of the queue length. Based on this, we will construct an optimization problem to describe the trade-off between AAVR and energy consumption. For a given AAVR threshold A, the optimization problem can be constructed as:

$$\min_{f_{i,m,k}^s} \sum_{s=1}^{1} \sum_{i=0}^{Q} \sum_{m=1}^{M+1} \sum_{k=1}^{M+1} \pi_i(f_{i,m,k}^s) \eta_m \rho_k f_{i,m,k}^s p_k \tag{18}$$

$$s.t. \ \Delta \leq A \tag{19}$$

$$\sum_{s=0}^{1} f_{i,m,k}^s = 1, 0 \leq i \leq Q, 1 \leq m \leq M+1, 1 \leq k \leq M+1 \tag{20}$$

$$f_{i,m,k}^s \in \{0,1\}, \forall i, m, k \tag{21}$$

In this optimization problem, the optimization goal is to minimize the average energy consumption, as shown in Eq. (18), where $\pi_i(f_{i,m,k}^s)$ represents the steady state probability of the length of the information queue, which is obtained by $\pi p = \pi$ and satisfies $\sum_{i=0}^{Q} \pi_i(f_{i,m,k}^s) = 1(\pi_i(f_{i,m,k}^s) \in [0,1])$, η_m represents the probability that the speed state is m, ρ_k represents the probability that the transmission power state is k, $f_{i,m,k}^s$ represents the transmission strategy, p_k represents the transmission power that the transmission power state is k. Formula (19) represents the AAVR constraint in the problem, formula (20), (21) is the scheduling variable constraint. This paper uses LINGO software to construct the optimization problem and obtains strategy $\{f_{i,m,k}^s\}$, and uses MATLAB software to model the system and conduct simulation experiments under FPBS, Q-Learning, greedy strategy (GS), the numerical results prove that FPBS can significantly reduce system energy consumption than other strategy.

5   Simulation Analysis

This section verifies the theoretical results through numerical analysis. When the RSU cache capacity is limited and the system is stable, the effectiveness of FPBS, GS and Q-Learning are analyzed according to different data generation rates. The simulation parameters are shown in the Table 1.

Table 1. Simulation parameters.

Parameter name	Symbol	Parameter value unit	Unit
RSU buffer capacity	Q	100	piece
Speed range	$[V_{\min}, V_{\max}]$	[22.22, 33.33]	m/s
Transmission power range	$[P_{\min}, P_{\max}]$	[10, 2]	w
Transmission coverage range	$[L_{\min}, L_{\max}]$	[300, 0]	m
Speed expectation	$\bar{V}$	25	m/s
Speed standard deviation	σ	5.56	–
Vehicle arrival rate	λ	0.8	$vehicles/s$

In the simulation process, take $\delta = 1\,\text{s}$, $M = 3$, the vehicle speed state is 3 states. When the vehicle speed state $M + 1 = 4$, RSU does not transmit data to the vehicle because there is no vehicle arriving or the transmission power is 0. To keep the system stable, take $\alpha \in [0.1, 0.7]$.

5.1   Analysis of Average Waiting Delay

As the data generation rate gradually increases, the queuing delay of GS and FPBS are roughly the same.

Since GS only considers the delivery of information within the maximum transmission range, its waiting delay is the smallest, and because the waiting delay under this scheme is nothing to do with the transmission range, the fluctuation is small under changing information generation rate. FPBS considers optimizing the average energy consumption of the system, it tends to choose slow vehicles to deliver information within the small transmission range, and waiting delay increases due to reduced transmission range. Compared with GS, the waiting delay of FPBS is slightly increased, which can be seen from the Fig. 6, that the increase time is about 2 s.

5.2   Analysis of the AAVR

As the data generation rate increases, the data queuing in the RSU waiting to be transmitted causes its queuing delay to increase, and the AAVR also increases. As shown in the Fig. 7.

706   Q. Qiu et al.

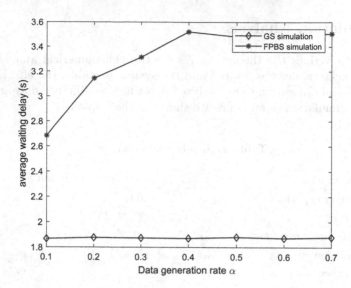

Fig. 6. The variation curve of the average waiting delay with the data generation rate α.

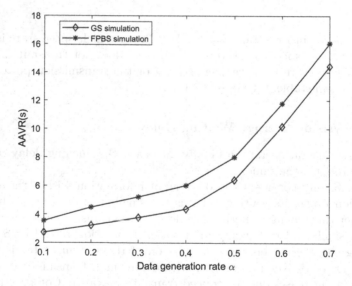

Fig. 7. The variation curve of the system average AOI with the data generation rate α.

5.3 Analysis of Average Energy Consumption

GS only considers the optimal AAVR, so the maximum transmission power is used to deliver data to all vehicles, resulting in a large average energy consumption. FPBS considers to minimizing the energy consumption of the RSU under the AAVR constraint, the energy consumption under this method is significantly smaller, as shown in Fig. 8. Although the AAVR of the FPBS is slightly higher than that of the GS, the sacrificed AOI is not worth mentioning compared to the reduced average energy consumption.

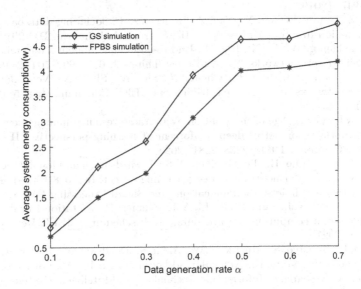

Fig. 8. The change curve of system energy consumption with the data generation rate α.

6 Conclusion

This article jointly considers the AAVR and energy consumption of the RSU. The purposed strategy is to minimize the average energy consumption of RSU without exceeding the threshold of the AAVR, constructing a Markov decision process to solve the problem, and RSU control center decides whether to adjust the transmission power according to the vehicle speed and data queue length. The simulation results show that, compared with the fixed transmission power, the method proposed in this paper can effectively reduce the average energy consumption while having little effect on the AAVR.

Acknowledgment. This paper is supported by the National Key Research and Development Program of China (2018YFB1600600).

References

1. Sun, Y., Sheng, Z., Jie, X.: Emm: energy-aware mobility management for mobile edge computing in ultra dense networks. IEEE J. Sel. Areas Commun. **PP**(99), 1 (2017)

2. Chen, J.Q., Mao, G.Q., Li, C.L., Zafar, A., Zomaya, A.Y.: Throughput of infrastructure-based cooperative vehicular networks. IEEE Trans. Intell. Transp. Syst. **18**(11), 2964–2979 (2017)
3. Abboud, K., Omar, H., Zhuang, W.: Interworking of DSRC and cellular network technologies for v2x communications: a survey. IEEE Trans. Veh. Technol. **65**, 9457–9470 (2016)
4. Zhou, Z., Gao, C., Chen, X., Yan, Z., Rodriguez, J.: Social big-data-based content dissemination in internet of vehicles. IEEE Trans. Ind. Inform. **PP**(99), 1 (2017)
5. Ye, Q., Zhuang, W., Li, X., Rao, J.: End-to-end delay modeling for embedded vnf chains in 5g core networks. IEEE Internet Things J. **6**(1), 692–704 (2019)
6. Zhang, S., Chen, J., Lyu, F., Cheng, N., Shi, W., Shen, X.: Vehicular communication networks in automated driving era. IEEE Commun. Mag. **56**(9), 26–32 (2018)
7. Chen, X.F., et al.: Age of information aware radio resource management in vehicular networks: a proactive deep reinforcement learning perspective. IEEE Trans. Wireless Commun. **19**(4), 2268–2281 (2020)
8. Shan, Z., Li, J., Luo, H., Jie, G., Shen, X.S.: Towards fresh and low-latency content delivery in vehicular networks: an edge caching aspect. In: 2018 10th International Conference on Wireless Communications and Signal Processing (WCSP) (2018)
9. Nie, L., Wang, X.J., Sun, W.T., Li, Y.K., Zhang, P.: Imitation-learning-enabled vehicular edge computing: toward online task scheduling. IEEE Network **35**(3), 102–108 (2021)
10. Adrian, R., Sulistyo, S., Mustika, I.W., Alam, S.: Roadside unit power saving using vehicle detection system in vehicular ad-hoc network. In: 2020 3rd International Seminar on Research of Information Technology and Intelligent Systems (ISRITI), pp. 198–202 (2020)
11. Atallah, R.F., Assi, C.M., Yu, J.Y.: A reinforcement learning technique for optimizing downlink scheduling in an energy-limited vehicular network. IEEE Trans. Veh. Technol. **66**(6), 4592–4601 (2017)
12. Nan, Z.J., Jia, Y.J., Ren, Z., Chen, Z.C., Liang, L.: Delay-aware content delivery with deep reinforcement learning in internet of vehicles. IEEE Trans. Intell. Transp. Syst., 1–12 (2021)
13. Al-Hilo, A., Ebrahimi, D., Sharafeddine, S., Assi, C.: Vehicle-assisted RSU caching using deep reinforcement learning. IEEE Trans. Emerging Topics Comput., 1 (2021)
14. Khabbaz, J.M., Fawaz, F.W., Assi, M.C.: A simple free-flow traffic model for vehicular intermittently connected networks. IEEE Trans. Intell. Transp. Syst. (2012)
15. Talak, R., Karaman, S., Modiano, E.: Optimizing age of information in wireless networks with perfect channel state information. IEEE (2018)
16. Huang, DH., Qiao, T.L., Cenk G, M.: Age-energy tradeoff optimization for packet delivery in fading channels. IEEE Trans. Wirel. Commun., 1 (2021)
17. Patra, M., Thakur, R., Murthy, Csr.: Improving delay and energy efficiency of vehicular networks using mobile femto access points. IEEE Trans. Vehicular Technol. **66**(2), 1496–1505 (2017)
18. Atallah, R., Khabbaz, M., Assi, C.: Multihop v2i communications: a feasibility study, modeling, and performance analysis. IEEE Trans. Veh. Technol. **66**(3), 2801–2810 (2017)
19. Hu, S.l., Chen, W.: Monitoring real-time status of analog sources: a cross-layer approach. IEEE J. Sel. Areas Commun. **39**(5), 1309–1324 (2021)
20. Wang, Y., Chen, W.: Adaptive power and rate control for real-time status updating over fading channels (2020)

A Low Energy Consumption and Low Delay MAC Protocol Based on Receiver Initiation and Capture Effect in 5G IoT

Hua-Mei Qi[ORCID], Jia-Qi Chen, Zheng-Yi Yuan, and Lin-Lin Fan[✉]

Central South University, 410000 Changsha, China

Abstract. The development of the fifth-generation (5G) network creates the possibility to deploy enormous sensors in the Internet of Things (IoT) network to transmit data with low delay. However, the traditional receiver-initiated MAC protocols used in IoT have the problems of high idle listening energy consumption and high transmission delay. A Low Energy Consumption and Low Delay MAC (Low-energy Low-latency MAC, LL-MAC) protocol based on receiver-initiated and captured effects is proposed. The proposed protocol realizes the fast matching between the senders and the receivers when the sending nodes have data to be sent. An improved greedy algorithm is proposed to allocate power to nodes, and a collision response mechanism is used for efficient data transmission.

Keywords: MAC Protocol · Capture effect · Receiver-initiated · 5G IoT · Low energy · Low latency

1 Introduction

With the ever-grow development of 5G technology, people's demand for "Internet of Everything" is increasing. Many applications require thousands of low-power nodes in IoT to conduct wireless communication for several kilometers. Most IoT sensor nodes are limited in battery capacity and costly in replacement. Therefore, energy saving is a key factor to be considered in the design of IoT protocol [1]. In addition, the emergency applications raise the higher real-time requirements. In IoT, the MAC layer is the main source of network energy consumption and directly controls the sending and receiving of data [2]. Therefore, in order to achieve a balance between network energy consumption and delay, to design a MAC protocol with low energy consumption and low delay is necessary.

In comparison with the sender MAC protocol in the asynchronous protocol, the receiver MAC protocol solves the problem that the preamble occupies too

This work has been sponsored by Natural Science Foundation of China (project number: 61803387). The work is also supported by Central South University of College students' free exploration project (project number: 2020105330184, 2020105330200, S2020105330857).

© Springer Nature Switzerland AG 2022
Y. Lai et al. (Eds.): ICA3PP 2021, LNCS 13156, pp. 709–723, 2022.
https://doi.org/10.1007/978-3-030-95388-1_47

long channel time in the transmission process. and the receiving node broadcasts the beacon frame to start data transmission, which has high energy utilization efficiency and network throughput efficiency [3]. In the receiver MAC protocol, how to effectively connect between two nodes and better avoid conflicts have become the focus. Among them, the PB-MAC protocol propose a predictive wake-up mechanism [4] which accurately predicts the wake-up time of node based on a random seed. Although it reduces the node's duty cycle, it increases the probability of collision. In the RI-MAC [5] protocol, after detecting a collision, the node will broadcast a beacon frame (Beacon) with a backoff window (BW), and multiple neighboring nodes will select the back-off time for retransmission. In a high-traffic scenario, the transmission efficiency is low.

Most MAC protocols adopt a conflict avoidance mechanism, when the network traffic increases suddenly, the nodes inevitably need to back off until the channel becomes idle, which cause huge transmission delays. But conflicts don't mean to the loss of data packets, the phenomenon that receiver can receive the data correctly is called capture effect [6]. In depth, scholars found that the receiver can receive frames with better power, even if it arrives after the receiver has locked the frame that arrived before [7]. In addition, M. Sha and G. Xing et al. [8] proposed that in concurrent transmission, the sum of the signal strengths of multiple interferences is equal to the sum of the signal strengths of each interference, and the SINR threshold is a fixed value, which will not increase with the increase of interference sources.

With the increase of sensor nodes in 5G IoT, the energy perception and interaction between devices also increase, which makes it more challenging to reduce energy consumption. Besides, emergency applications require lower latency. The following problems of receiver-initiated MAC protocol need to be further solved: the sending node only starts to send data after receiving the Beacon from the receiving node, which is not conducive to the timely delivery of data and produces a large idle listening energy consumption; using collision avoidance mechanism makes the node need to be retransmitted several times before finally arriving, which enlarge the delay and brings huge energy consumption.

Therefore, this paper proposes a low-energy low-latency MAC protocol based on receiver initiation and capture effect for the node's scheduling mode and collision response in data transmission, which reduce energy consumption and time delay.

The remainder of this paper is organized as follows. Sections 2 reviews the literature of existing MAC protocols with low energy consumption and low delay. Section 3 and 4 details the proposed protocol, consisting of node wake-up matching mechanism and implementation process of the collision response mechanism based on capture effect. Section 5 provides all the experimental results of this paper. Last, Sect. 6 concludes this paper.

2   Related Work

2.1   Asynchronous MAC Protocol

Asynchronous protocols are divided into initiated by the sender and initiated by the receiver according to the different initiators. In the MAC protocol initiated by the sender, the node needs to send a preamble to detect the working status of the receiver before sending data, and it can transmit data until the receiver wakes up. Buettner M and Yee G V et al. [9] used a shortened preamble method to retain the advantages of low-power listening, and embed the target address information in the preamble. Wu G and Ji P F et al. [10] used repeated transmission of short preamble packets to replace the long preamble, which improves energy efficiency. Amreel H and Jean D D [11] used the wake-up preamble technology. The preamble is sent before each data packet to remind the receiving node.

Based on the receiver's MAC protocol, the receiver sends a beacon frame when it wakes up and broadcasts itself. In the working state of the receiver, the sender sends data after receiving the receiver's Beacon, which prevents the sender from sending the pilot wave to detect the receiver's working status. Peron G and Brante G, et al. [12] proposed a passive mechanism in which the receiving node sends a beacon, the wake-up time carried in the beacon frame information, which reduced the energy consumption[16]. Zhou L Z [13] proposes a data transmission mechanism based on fast reply ACK, shortening the ACK reply time, which reduce the collision. Ma L and Gao H L et al. [14] dynamically changed the wake-up interval, and in order to reduce the energy black hole problem, the wake-up time of the node is adaptively changed according to the remaining energy of the node. JANG B and LIM J B et al. [15] propose an asynchronous wake-up scheduling mechanism through neighbor nodes to reduce eavesdropping and channel contention and waiting time.

2.2   Capture Effect

Stefanovic C and Momoda M et al. [17] proposed a technique which allows the capture of packets by detecting the preambles of the packet. Using capture effect, Wu H and Zeng Y extend the existing tag recognition Algorithm to capture environment, and propose a new anti-collision Algorithm to improve the efficiency of tag recognition [18]. Kosunalp S and Mitchell P D [19] introduced the capture coefficient, which is the reception rate of data packets in collision, which proves The capture effect improves the throughput of the ALOHA network. Zhou Li-Zhi [13] proposed a data transmission mechanism based on the capture effect, which uses a balanced greedy algorithm to allocate power to nodes, which reduces the data transmission delay and improves the channel utilization. Bankov D and Khorov E et al. developed a general model which can be used to evaluate performance of IoT in different scenarios, taking into account the capture effect [20]. López N A and Azurdia-Meza C A et al. [21] had verified through experimental simulation that the capture effect can still ensure the correct reception of several data packets in the presence of noise interference. Al Nahas B and Duquennoy S et al. proposed a network stack based on the capture effect [22], which achieved low power and low latency.

3   Wake-Up Matching Mechanism of LL-MAC Transceiver

All the devices deployed in the network share the medium in IoT and MAC protocol is responsible to provide the access to a shared medium among all the nodes. The LL-MAC protocol is receiver-initiated, and proposes a wake-up matching mechanism for both sender and receiver; in terms of data transmission collisions, a collision response mechanism is proposes based on the capture effect by allocating power to nodes through an improved greedy algorithm.

The IoT network constructed by the paper has the following conditions:

(1) M sensor nodes in the network are randomly distributed in a square area with a side length of L to continuously detect environmental events;
(2) All events in the network occur randomly and evenly distributed. Nodes at any location have the same probability of detecting the occurrence of the event, and the probability of generating data is also equal;
(3) The sink node is deployed in the network center, and each node independently wakes up and sleeps periodically, and immediately transmits the data packet to the sink node through the direct or forwarding node after detecting the event; and the transmission power of the node is adjustable.

3.1   Scheduling Strategy Design

In the LL-MAC protocol, nodes in the network have two scheduling modes: initial and follow-up. In the initial scheduling mode, each sensor node periodically wakes up and the node with data to be sent waits for the receiving node to send a beacon frame.

When the sending node S transmits a data frame with additional wake-up request information in the initial state, the receiving node R receives this data frame and learns the subsequent wake-up schedule of the sending node from the wake-up request information, then the receiving node enters the scheduling follow mode. The node uses the wake-up information to calculate the next wake-up time of the sending node, and adjusts its wake-up schedule to match it so that it is at the next wake-up time expected by the sending node S Wake up and receive data.

3.2   Wake-Up Time Calculation

LL-MAC adds two optional data frame fields T_{S_cur} and T_{S_wake} to the data frame. When the sending node needs to continue to transmit data, it can store the wake-up information by setting these two optional fields. To inform the receiving node.

Among them, T_{S_cur} is the current time of the sending node S, that is, the sending time at the time the data packet is sent, and T_{S_wake} is the wake-up interval of S; after receiving the wake-up information of the sending node S, the receiving node R calculates accurately The next wake-up time $T_{R\_nextwake}$ is shown, as shown in (1)(2).

$$T_{diff} = T_{R\_loc} - T_{S\_cur} \tag{1}$$

$$T_{R\_nextwake} = T_{R\_loc} - T_{diff} + T_{S\_wake} \tag{2}$$

Among them, T_{diff} is the clock deviation of the receiving node, and T_{R_loc} is the moment when the receiving node receives the data frame.

In addition, considering the error caused by clock drift, the receiving node wakes up in advance at T_d before the receiving node wakes up, as shown in (3). δ_{drift} is the clock frequency deviation.

$$T_d = T_{S\_wake} - \delta_{drift} \tag{3}$$

The receiving node uses the received wake-up information to calculate the next wake-up time, revises its wake-up schedule, and follows the receiving node to keep waking up the next time it sends data.

3.3   Data Frame Format

The data frame of the LL-MAC protocol is shown in Fig. 1, two optional fields T_{S_cur} and T_{S_wake} are located before the data packet.

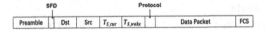

Fig. 1. Improved data frame structure

The sending node broadcasts data with T_{S_cur} and T_{S_wake} fields. In the LL-MAC protocol, when a node receives data whose destination is not the node during the listening process, it does not immediately ignore the data. When the node is on its path, the node can choose to receive the wake-up request T_{S_cur} and T_{S_wake} fields in the data, and adjust its next wake-up time to match it according to the wake-up information. As shown in Fig. 2, the LL-MAC protocol achieves the transmission of data at a specified time in this way.

4   LL-MAC Collision Response Mechanism

4.1   Conditions for the Capture Effect

There may be two situations when the sending node concurrently transmits data. As shown in Fig. 3, it can be seen that to meet the capture effect, two conditions

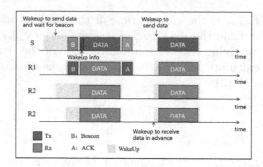

Fig. 2. Basic process of broadcast transmission

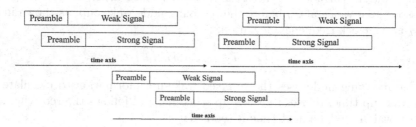

Fig. 3. Basic process of broadcast transmission

must be met: a) the time when the strong signal arrives at the receiver is no later than the synchronization word reception time of the weak signal; b) the signal strength difference between strong and weak signals needs to meet the SINR reception threshold.

However, the receiver can receive a frame with better power, even if it arrives after the frame that the receiver has already locked. And the SINR threshold is a fixed value and will not increase with the increase of interference sources. Therefore, the focus of the research on the capture effect is 1) the measurement of the capture effect threshold constant and 2) the design of a reasonable power allocation algorithm so that the neighboring nodes of the competing nodes meet the conditions for the capture effect.

4.2   Determination of the Threshold Constant

In the experiment, the nodes in the network are distributed. Sending nodes S1 and S2 reach receiver R equidistant. Set S1 to use a fixed transmission power for data transmission. Change the transmit power of S2. The two sending nodes send data immediately after receiving the Beacon sent by R, calculate the successful receiving rate. when the receiving rate rises to 90%, the power difference as the threshold constant obtained from the experiment.

4.3   Establishment of Power Allocation Target Model

Node Remaining Energy Ratio. Most of the energy consumption of wireless sensor network is generated by the sending and receiving of data. E_T represents the energy consumption of node sending, E_R represents the energy consumption of node receiving. The energy consumption formula of data sending and receiving is shown in formula (4)(5):

$$E_T = lE_e + lp_t d^2,   \tag{4}$$

$$E_R = lE_e.   \tag{5}$$

l is the length of the data packet, E_e is the energy consumption per bit of data sent or received, p_t is the transmission power, and d is the data transmission distance.

The total energy consumption of the node $E_t ot$ is expressed as equation (6).

$$E_{tot} = E_T + E_R + E_P   \tag{6}$$

$$E_P = e_p \times T_p   \tag{7}$$

E_p is the energy consumption of the node calculation, e_p is the energy consumption of the node in a unit time, T_p is the calculation time occupied, and E_{init} is the initial energy value, $E_{rest} = E_{init} - E_{tot}$ can be obtained. The remaining energy ratio of the node can be obtained as shown in equation (8).

$$\sigma_{rest} = \frac{E_{rest}}{E_{init}}   \tag{8}$$

Model Establishment. Take the ratio of the node's transmission power to the remaining energy as the power allocation standard. Suppose a receiving node x in the network has n neighbor nodes, and the set of neighbor nodes $N = \{N_i | i = 1, 2, 3, \ldots, n\}$ (i represents the number of the neighboring node), and build a model from this:

$$P = min \sum\nolimits_{i=1}^{n} \frac{p_t^i}{\sigma_{rest}^i}.   \tag{9}$$

p_t^i represents the transmit power of node i, σ_{rest}^i represents the remaining energy ratio of node i.

Constraints

$$\begin{cases} p_r^i > p_x & 1 \leq i \leq n \\ p_r^i > I_{i-1} & 1 \leq i \leq n \end{cases}   \tag{10}$$

p_x is the lowest power that the receiving node can receive and can work normally; and p_r^i is used to indicate when the data sent by node i arrives at the receiving node The power of, we get $p_r^i = c\frac{p_t^i}{d^\alpha}$, where c represents the antenna gain, α represents the path loss coefficient, and $\alpha \in [2, 4]$, enter the condition (1) to obtain $c\frac{p_t^i}{d^\alpha} > p_x$;

I_{i-1} is the total interference when i-1 neighboring nodes are sending data when node i is sending data, which is derived from the following relationship:

The selectable power set is $P_t = \{p_t^{min} \le p_t^i \le p_t^{max}\}$. The transmission distance and interference distance of the node are determined by the transmission power. When the node transmits with the maximum power p_t^{max}, the maximum transmission distance of the corresponding node is d_{max}. In the actual environment, transmission distance is: $d_{TR} = p_t^i \frac{d_{max}}{p_t^{max}}$, and the interference distance is generally twice the transmission distance, that is, $d_{IR} = 2d_{TR}$.

Assuming that node s is within the interference range, and the transmission power of node s is p_t^s, when node i and node s transmit data concurrently, node s becomes the interference node of node i. The signal-to-interference and noise ratio is used to describe the interference intensity of the link, as formula (11):

$$SINR_i = \frac{\lambda_{ix}p_t^i}{\sum_{d_{sx} \le d_{IR}} \lambda_{sx}p_t^s + N_0}. \tag{11}$$

Among them, $\lambda_{ix} = \frac{c}{d_{ix}^\alpha}$, $\lambda_{sj} = \frac{c}{d_{sj}^\alpha}$, N_0 represents the noise interference.

Then the current total interference intensity is shown in (12):

$$I_i = SINR_{Thr} + \sum_{t=1}^{i} SINR_i. \tag{12}$$

4.4   Algorithm Implementation

The design of power allocation needs to meet the two requirements: low time complexity and avoid falling into local optimum. In allocation process, if only consider the signal strength, the node with less available power will be allocated first, it is inevitable to allocate more power to the node with less remaining energy, but when some of the neighboring nodes with less remaining energy, we that they send data with little power to balance the energy of the entire network.

Therefore, when some of the neighboring nodes have less optional power, even if it is not the current optimal solution, priority should be given to adding these nodes to the result set, so that the result set can accommodate more nodes, that is, nodes with larger path fading are preferred, since these nodes are more likely to become nodes with fewer optional values. And nodes with less remaining energy tend to send data with less power to reduce energy consumption.

Before the power allocation, the Topsis model is used to weigh the node path fading and the remaining energy, establishes an optimal node selection model, and obtains the relative closeness of each node to the ideal optimal solution. Then using Greedy algorithm obtains the optimal power allocation result.

Specific steps:

Step 1. Initialization parameters: the number of neighboring nodes n; the set of candidate nodes A; the remaining energy of the node E; the path loss of node on the way to the receiving node Lose; the transmission power PT; the arrival power PR; the currently selected power value R, The current solution set C.

Step 2. Using node residual energy E and path loss *Loss* as indicators, establish a normalized matrix to standardize the data, That is:

$$Z_{ij} = \frac{X_{ij}}{\sqrt{\sum_{i=1}^{n} X_{ij}^2}} (i = 1, \cdots, n; j = 1, \cdots, m). \tag{13}$$

where i represents the number of neighboring nodes, j represents the number of indicators, and X_{ij} represents the jth indicator value of the ith node.

Step 3. From the Z matrix, obtain the optimal vector $Z_j^+ = \max_{1 \le i \le n} |Z_{ij}|$ and the worst vector $Z_j^- = \max_{1 \le i \le n} |Z_{ij}|$, calculate the distance $D^+ = \sqrt{\sum_{j=1}^{m} (Z_{ij} - Z_j^+)^2}$ between the neighboring node and the ideal optimal solution and the distance $D^- = \sqrt{\sum_{j=1}^{m} (Z_{ij} - Z_j^-)^2}$.

Step 4. Obtain the relative closeness of each node to the ideal optimal solution $W_i = \frac{D_i^-}{D_i^+ + D_i^-}$, as the set W.

Step 5. Calculate the sum of the interference intensity Sum(P) of the power selected by each node in the currently selected power value set to obtain the current power selection threshold $Thr = Sum(P) + SINR_{Thr}$.

Step 6. Compare the signal strength of the node corresponding to the maximum value of the set W with the current threshold Thr, find the minimum value of its reachable signal strength, and proceed to the next iteration.

Step 7. Update the current result set C, remove the selected node in A, and enter process 5.

Step 8. Repeat process 5–7 until the set of candidate nodes is empty. Take the current solution C as the allocation result set.

5   Experiment and Results

5.1   The Threshold Constant

Use the eight transmit power levels of the TELOSB node, as shown in Table 1. Experiment with the process described in Sect. 4.2. The successful receiving rate under different power difference as shown in Fig. 4, $SINR_{Thr} = 2dB$.

Table 1. TELOSB node transmit power level

Power levels	3	7	11	15	19	23	27	31
Sending power (dBm)	−25	−15	−10	−7	−5	−3	−1	0

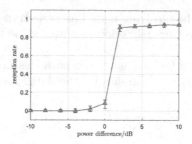

Fig. 4. Power difference-reception rate diagram

5.2   Examples of Power Allocation

Set the location of the receiving node in the network and its adjacent nodes to be fixed. Bring the path loss (in Table 2) and residual energy ratio of nodes (in Table 3) into the algorithm, and get the trade-off score W_{score} of nodes, as shown in Table 4.

Table 2. Node path loss

ID	1	2	3	4	5	6	7	8
Loss (dBm)	56.79	64.86	66.91	58.48	72.09	67.80	62.53	69.89

Table 3. Node residual energy ratio

ID	1	2	3	4	5	6	7	8
E_{rest}	0.78	0.56	0.85	0.91	0.89	0.65	0.47	0.71

The value of the received signal strength of the node arriving at the receiving node with different transmission power and the calculated trade-off score W_{score} are shown in Table 5.

Find the minimum reachable power of the node corresponding to the maximum value of W_{score}, and add it and its corresponding transmission power to the result set, namely $C = \{(2,3)\}$, add its corresponding signal strength to set P, and perform Sum(P) operation to calculate the current power selection threshold $Thr = Sum(P) + SINR_{Thr}$; remove the selected node from the set of candidate nodes, That is, set all signal strengths of this node to N/A, and then proceed to the next iteration, as shown in Figure VI, the highlighted in RED cell is the selected value, and the grey-out box is the removed value (Table 6).

Repeat the above process and get the result set after power allocation: $C = \{(2,3),(7,3),(6,7),(8,11),(5,23),(3,19),(1,11),(4,19)\}$.

Table 4. The calculated value of the trade-off coefficient

ID	Loss	E_{rest}	W_{score}
1	−56.79	0.78	0.056429
2	−64.86	0.56	0.179431
3	−66.91	0.85	0.104823
4	−58.48	0.91	0.018808
5	−72.09	0.89	0.127176
6	−67.80	0.65	0.172612
7	−62.53	0.47	0.177754
8	−69.89	0.71	0.162968

Table 5. Initial value of power distribution

Power	3	7	11	15	19	23	27	31
1	−56.8	−71.8	−66.8	−63.8	−61.8	−59.8	−57.8	−56.8
2	−64.9	−79.9	−74.9	−71.9	−69.9	−67.9	−65.9	−64.9
3	−66.9	−81.9	−76.9	−73.9	−71.9	−69.9	−67.9	−66.9
4	−58.5	−73.5	−68.5	−65.5	−63.5	−61.5	−59.5	−58.5
5	−72.1	−87.1	−82.1	−79.1	−77.1	−75.1	−73.1	−72.1
6	−67.8	−82.8	−77.8	−74.8	−72.8	−70.8	−68.8	−67.8
7	−62.5	−77.5	−72.5	−69.5	−67.5	−65.5	−63.5	−62.5
8	−69.9	−84.9	−79.9	−76.9	−74.9	−72.9	−70.9	−69.9

Table 6. The first traversal result

Power	3	7	11	15	19	23	27	31
1	−81.8	−71.8	−66.8	−63.8	−61.8	−59.8	−57.8	−56.8
2	−89.9	−79.9	−74.9	−71.9	−69.9	−67.9	−65.9	−64.9
3	−91.9	−81.9	−76.9	−73.9	−71.9	−69.9	−67.9	−66.9
4	−83.5	−73.5	−68.5	−65.5	−63.5	−61.5	−59.5	−58.5
5	−97.1	−87.1	−82.1	−79.1	−77.1	−75.1	−73.1	−72.1
6	−92.8	−82.8	−77.8	−74.8	−72.8	−70.8	−68.8	−67.8
7	−87.5	−77.5	−72.5	−69.5	−67.5	−65.5	−63.5	−62.5
8	−94.9	−84.9	−79.9	−76.9	−74.9	−72.9	−70.9	−69.9

5.3   Performance of LL-MAC Protocol

In order to verify the performance of the LL-MAC protocol, we used OMNET++ to simulate, and compared with the RI-MAC protocol and PB-MAC protocol in terms of network energy consumption, end-to-end transmission delay, and average duty cycle. A comparative analysis was carried out on this performance.

In order to ensure the comparability of several MAC protocols, the experiment set up relatively ideal environmental parameters while ignoring the interference of some other factors. Fifty wireless sensor nodes are randomly placed in a square area of 1000m×1000m, using a random event-related flow pattern, using a 200m sensing range, and triggering an event every 60s. The network simulation time is1000 s. The setting of network parameters is shown in Table 7.

Table 7. Network parameter settings

Parameter	Value	Parameter	Value
Packet length	50 Bytes	Listen consumption	0.344 W
Beacon length	6 Bytes	Send consumption	0.386 W
Transmission distance	200 m	Receive consumption	0.368 W
Environmental noise	−95 dBm	Sleep consumption	0.03 mW
Data burst	25	Transition consumption	0.05 W
Burst node ratio	1/3	Wake-up interval	1 s

The following indicators are tested in the simulation:
Network energy consumption:

$$E2ENC = \sum (E_T + E_R + E_L).\tag{14}$$

E_T and E_R are the energy consumption of node transmission and reception, E_L is the energy consumption of node idle listening.

Average end-to-end transmission delay:

$$E2ETD = \frac{\sum T_{datac}}{N_{datac}}.\tag{15}$$

T_{datac} represents the time when all successfully sent data packets are sent from the source node to the sink node, and N_{datac} represents the number of all successfully sent and received data packets.

Successful data delivery rate:

$$DDR = \frac{N_{datac}}{N_{data}}.\tag{16}$$

N_{data} represents the number of all data packets sent.

Set the initial period of RI-MAC, PB-MAC and LL-MAC to 10s, and the data packet sending interval of all protocols to 10s. Observe the energy consumption and transmission delay of LL-MAC, RI-MAC, and PB-MAC protocols as the network duration changes. The situation is shown in Fig. 5 and Fig. 6.

It can be seen from Fig. 5 that in terms of network energy consumption, the E2ENC of LL-MAC is generally low in the continuous network process. In comparison with RI-MAC and PB-MAC protocols, LL-MAC protocol saves network energy consumption by 24.35% and 17.33% 1000 s respectively and can always reach the best performance over a longer duration. In the initial stage of the network, LL-MAC and RI-MAC maintain the same initial scheduling, and their energy consumption is similar. After the initial stage of the network, RI-MAC still needs to continue to listen to the channel to wait for the receiving node to wake up, so it consumes too much energy; PB-MAC and LL-MAC adjust the node wake-up time for node scheduling matching, reducing idle listening time, Reduce network energy consumption. In addition, the collision response mechanism of LL-MAC reduces the probability of data retransmission to a certain extent, so the energy consumption is lower.

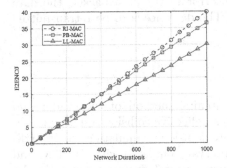

Fig. 5. Network energy consumption changes with network duration

Fig. 6. Transmission delay changes with network duration

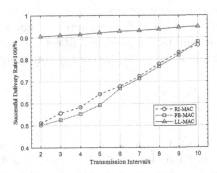

Fig. 7. Data successful delivery rate changes with data sending interval

It can be seen from Fig. 6 that in terms of network delay, the E2ETD of the LL-MAC protocol is continuously lower than RI-MAC and PB-MAC, 28.54% lower than RI-MAC, and 35.25% lower than PB-MAC. Since PB-MAC uses a fast dormant retransmission mechanism in the case of data packet loss, E2ETD is higher than RI-MAC.

In order to test the impact of the data stream size on the reliability of data transmission, set other conditions unchanged, gradually increase the data stream generation interval, and observe the changes in the data delivery rate of LL-MAC, RI-MAC and PB-MAC, as shown in Fig. 7.

It can be seen from Fig. 7 that as the data packet sending interval increases, that is, the amount of data decreases, the data delivery rate of nodes in the network gradually increases. Judging from the overall trend, the successful delivery rate of the LL-MAC protocol is maintained at more than 90% regardless of the amount of data or the high-traffic scenario, thus verifying that the collision response mechanism adopted by LL-MAC is stable Reliability. Because RI-MAC and PB-MAC are prone to collisions in data transmission in high-traffic scenarios, when a collision occurs or there is an error in the data packet, the data transmission will be declared as a failure. The data needs to be retransmitted several times to be successfully delivered.

6   Conclusion

In this paper, the wake-up scheduling matching method of the sender and receiver is improved. The protocol provides an effective collision response mechanism that uses the capture effect to tolerate collisions. Simulation results indicate that under the same packet sending interval, compared with RI-MAC and PB-MAC protocols, LL-MAC protocol reduces network energy consumption by 24.35% and 17.33%, respectively, and 28.54% and 35.25% in transmission delay reduction. In addition, it also verified the excellent performance and stable reliability of the collision response mechanism in the data delivery rate.

However, in this paper, the performance research of the proposed MAC protocol is only in the stage of experimental simulation, and there is still a deviation from the actual environment. And the background noise of actual scenario is often changeable, and its sudden increase will affect the performance of the conflict response mechanism and increase the energy consumption. So these will be the future work.

References

1. Arshad, R., Zahoor, S., Shah, M.A., et al.: Green IoT: an investigation on energy saving practices for 2020 and beyond. IEEE Access **5**, 15667–15681 (2017)
2. Shuo, Yu.: Summary of wireless sensor network technology development. Sci. Technol. Inf. **17**(05), 47–48 (2019)
3. Dash, L., Khuntia, M.: Energy efficient techniques for 5G mobile networks in WSN: a survey. In: 2020 International Conference on Computer Science, Engineering and Applications (ICCSEA), pp. 1–5. IEEE (2020)
4. Zhe-Tao, L., Geng-Ming, Z., Zhi-Qiang, W.: MAC protocol of asynchronous wireless sensor network with low duty cycle and low collision. J. Commun. **10**, 9–16 (2013)
5. Duan, R., Zhao, Q., Zhang, H., et al.: Modeling and performance analysis of RI-MAC under a star topology. Comput. Commun. **104**, 134–144 (2017)

6. Zanella, A., Zorzi, M.: Theoretical analysis of the capture probability in wireless systems with multiple packet reception capabilities. IEEE Trans. Commun. **4**, 1058–1071 (2012)
7. Halperin, D., Anderson, T., Wetherall, D.: Taking the sting out of carrier sense: interference cancellation for wireless lans. In: Proceedings of the 14th ACM International Conference on Mobile Computing and Networking, pp. 339–350 (2008)
8. Sha, M., Xing, G., Zhou, G., et al.: C-mac: model-driven concurrent medium access control for wireless sensor networks. In: IEEE INFOCOM. IEEE 2009, pp. 1845–1853 (2009)
9. Buettner, M., Yee, G.V., Anderson, E., et al.: X-MAC: a short preamble MAC protocol for duty-cycled wireless sensor networks. Sensys **14**(4), 307–320 (2015)
10. Ge, W., Peng-Fei, J., Zheng, Z., Jia-Pin, C., Kai, D.: MAC protocol of low-latency wireless sensor network based on asynchronous scheduling. Sensors Micro-systems **38**(06), 19–22 (2019)
11. Pande, H., Kharat, M.U., Saharan, K., et al.: Various ways to implement energy efficient WiseMAC protocol for wireless sensor network. In: 2013 IEEE International Conference on Systems, Man, and Cybernetics, pp. 22–25. IEEE (2013)
12. Peron, G., Brante, G., Souza, R.D., et al.: Physical and MAC cross-layer analysis of energy-efficient cooperative MIMO networks. IEEE Trans. Commun. **66**(5), 1940–1954 (2018)
13. Li-Zhi, Z.: Research on efficient data transmission mechanism based on receiver MAC protocol in wireless sensor networks. Xidian University (2018)
14. Li, M., Hong-Lei, G., Dong-Chao, M., Qing-Yuan, Q.: A wireless sensor network MAC protocol initiated by the receiving end. Data Acquisition Process. **31**(04), 719–727 (2016)
15. Jang, B., Lim, J.B., Sichitiu, M.L.: An asynchronous scheduled MAC protocol for wireless sensor networks. Comput. Netw. **57**(1), 85–98 (2013)
16. Yi, J., Lee, H.: Modeling and performance analysis for a receiver-initiated MAC protocol in wireless sensor networks. Comput. Networks **12**(11), 178–186 (2016)
17. Stefanović, Č., Momoda, M., Popovski, P.: Exploiting capture effect in frameless ALOHA for massive wireless random access. In: 2014 IEEE Wireless Communications and Networking Conference (WCNC), pp. 1762–1767. IEEE (2014)
18. Wu, H., Zeng, Y.: Passive RFID tag anticollision algorithm for capture effect. IEEE Sens. J. **15**(1), 218–226 (2014)
19. Kosunalp, S., Mitchell, P.D., Grace, D., et al.: Experimental study of capture effect for medium access control with ALOHA. ETRI J. **37**(2), 359–368 (2015)
20. Bankov, D., Khorov, E., Lyakhov, A.: Mathematical model of LoRaWAN channel access with capture effect. In: 2017 IEEE 28th Annual International Symposium on Personal, Indoor, and Mobile Radio Communications. IEEE, pp. 1–5 (2017)
21. López, N.A., Azurdia-Meza, C.A., Montejo-Sánchez, S., et al.: Experimental evaluation of capture effect in an IEEE 802.15.4 WSN based on unslotted-CSMA/CA. In: 2020 IEEE Latin-American Conference on Communications (LATINCOM). IEEE, pp. 1–6 (2020)
22. Al Nahas, B., Duquennoy, S., Landsiedel, O.: Network-wide consensus utilizing the capture effect in low-power wireless networks. In: Proceedings of the 15th ACM Conference on Embedded Network Sensor Systems, pp. 1–14 (2017)

Building Portable ECG Classification Model with Cross-Dimension Knowledge Distillation

Renjie Tang[1,2]([✉]), Junbo Qian[2], Jiahui Jin[1], and Junzhou Luo[1]

[1] School of Computer Science and Engineering, Southeast University, Nanjing, Jiangsu, China
tangrj@seu.edu.cn
[2] China Mobile Group Zhejiang Co., Ltd., Hangzhou, Zhejiang, China

Abstract. Portable electrocardiogram (ECG) devices are general tools for diagnosing and analyzing cardiovascular diseases. However, they are limited in computation and storage resources, and it is necessary to compress the model. For mismatched data dimension between the 12-leads ECG data and the single-lead portable devices, conventional compression techniques cannot be applied to ECG classification model directly. To solve this problem, a novel adaptive knowledge-distillation-based model compression method is proposed. First, two kinds of teacher models are trained, which applies single lead and 12 leads ECG data respectively. Then, a feature extension module is built. It compensates single lead ECG data into 12 leads ECG data through generative adversarial networks (GANs). Finally, a model distillation is performed via all teacher models. In this way, the proposed approach brings a deeper level of interaction between the single lead data and 12 leads data. Experiment results show it outperforms existing diagnostic methods on our collected dataset. The F1 metric increases from 49.54% to 79.3%, which demonstrates the effectiveness of our approach.

Keywords: ECG classification · Generative adversarial network · Knowledge distillation

1 Introduction

Electrocardiogram (ECG) classification is a common method for diagnosing and analyzing cardiovascular diseases, which determines the type of cardiovascular using a trained deep learning model. Portable ECG devices have been recognized as an important innovation in medical industry. It greatly help early detection of cardiovascular diseases, such as sinus rhythm, arrhythmia and sinus bradycardia.

Portable devices have limited computation and storage resources, so model compression techniques are needed. Knowledge distillation is an effective way for model compression, and it can distill the knowledge from a complex model to a simple model [1]. Hence the generalization ability of complex model can be inherited. In knowledge distillation, the small model is generally supervised by a large model [2, 3]. The complex model is called a teacher model, and the simple model is called a student model. The teacher model generates soft labels, and the student model learns the knowledge based

Y. Lai et al. (Eds.): ICA3PP 2021, LNCS 13156, pp. 724–737, 2022.
https://doi.org/10.1007/978-3-030-95388-1_48

on soft labels. The input data dimensions of the teacher model and the student model must be matched. However, ECG consists of 12 leads data, and portable devices only possess single lead data, which is shown in Fig. 1. Since their feature dimensions are not uniform, the traditional knowledge distillation cannot handle this cross-dimension case.

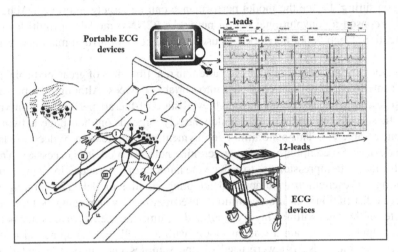

Fig. 1. ECG devices versus portable ECG devices

To solve the dimension mismatch problem, we propose a novel cross-dimension knowledge distillation method. The lacked 11 leads data for single lead are constructed via generative adversarial networks (GANs). The GANs model usually consists of two parts: a generator and a discriminator. With the iterative game between generator and discriminator, the generator can capture the distribution of real data. Single lead data with noise is regarded as the input of a generator. We take other lead data as the label of discriminator. Other 11 leads data are then simulated after GANs training. By this way, the feature dimensions between 12 leads ECG and single lead ECG in portable devices can be matched.

Our contributions are twofold: 1) we propose a novel adaptive model compression approach based on cross-dimension knowledge distillation, and 2) comprehensive experiments are conducted. The experimental results show this method can enhance the performance of the model for portable ECG data.

The rest of this paper is organized as follows: Sect. 2 introduces the related works. Section 3 describes the proposed adaptive model compression method. Experimental results are given in Sect. 4. Section 5 concludes this paper.

2 Related Works

In recent years, machine learning and statistics based methods are widely used in ECG analysis, such as Bayesian theory, k-nearest neighbor, decision tree and linear discriminator [4–6], etc. In ref. [7–9], support vector machines, least squares support vector machines and twin support vector machines were used for bioelectric signals classification. These methods were data-driven and concise, but they were limited by feature extraction and representation capabilities. With the explosive increase of data size and computing power, deep learning has become a dominant method for ECG classification. It can automatically represent complex feature of ECG signals via hierarchical non-linear fitting. Hence the model performance can be largely improved. Acharya U R [10] proposed a convolutional neural networks (CNNs) model for multi-lead ECG classification. Deep belief network was used to diagnosis of arrhythmia disease in ref. [11].

For better monitoring conditions of patient in real time, it is of great medical value to implant intelligent classification model into portable devices. Although the prevalence of deep learning, many models have achieved state-of-the-art performance in various fields, the success of current neural models largely depends on their huge network and abundant parameters. This state limits deployment and application of deep models on mobile devices. So compression of deep learning network models is necessary. The key issues for model compression are to reduce the number of parameters by using pruning, decreasing representation accuracy and adopting smaller model [12]. Among them, knowledge distillation is the most commonly used method. By increasing the temperature parameter of the final softmax layer output and minimizing the KL divergence between smooth outputs, it can train a student model with a small scale deep neural network. Counterattack methods [14] were used to find samples that support boundaries and designed an additional boundary loss function. It used samples that close to the boundary to guide student model training. Zagoruyko S [15] used a set of spatial feature maps to define attentions. It paid attentions to different parts of the network according to activation values of parameters. Tung F [16] proposed a binary similarity metric between the student model and the teacher model. It ensured that the similarity relationship is activated simultaneously. Lan X [17] proposed a single multi-branch neural network to combine multiple branches for stronger teacher model building.

Unfortunately, the traditional model compression methods cost great resources. In common knowledge distillation methods, classification performance of student model only inherits from knowledge of teacher models. Teacher models can't adapt to the change of local input dimension, and so does student model. In this research, a novel method is proposed to overcome the difference of cross-dimension between teacher model and student model. We designed an adaptive feature extension module to match the cross-dimension features. Hence, the personalized student model would achieve better generalization for Portable ECG data.

3   Cross-Dimension Knowledge Distillation

As shown in Fig. 2, the main architecture of the proposed ECG classification model with cross-dimension knowledge distillation is divided into three parts. First, teacher models construction. One global teacher model M_G^T is trained via 12 ECG lead data, and local teacher model M_P^T is trained with 1 lead ECG data from portable devices. Second, feature extension module construction. Simulated 12 lead ECG data is generated with Generative adversarial networks (GANs), which treats single lead ECG data as input feature and other 11 lead data are extended feature. Finally, cross-dimension knowledge distillation module construction. The knowledge in teacher models is distilled to the student model M_P^S based on the proposed feature extension module.

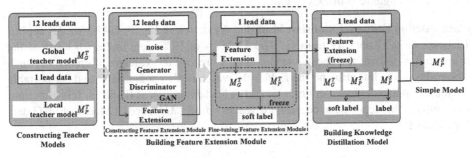

Fig. 2. Overview of cross-dimension knowledge distillation.

3.1 Constructing Teacher Models

The specific comparison results are given in Table 1. The back bone structure of teacher model M_G^T is tf_efficientnet_b8 [18]. It is trained by 12 leads of ECG data. The other teacher model M_P^T adopts dm_nfnet_f2 [19], which is trained with single-lead ECG data. Since 12-leads ECG data includes abundant pathogeny information, and we want to transfer this useful information to student model. Thus, we train two kinds of teacher model with different ECG feature extraction and representation. The differences can improve the performance of the student model.

Table 1. Overview table of teacher model.

Model	F_1	Param count	Leads
tf_efficientnet_b8	90.1%	193.78M	12
dm_nfnet_f2	86.3%	87.41M	1

3.2 Building Feature Extension Module

The teacher model M_G^T leverages 12 leads of ECG data. Most Portable devices are single lead. So the model trained through single lead of ECG data can't use knowledge of teacher model M_G^T. Therefore, it is necessary to extend dimension features. Generating 12-dimensional data via the feature extension module that supplements other 11 leads of ECG data except. The soft labels generated via the synthetic 12 dimensions data can be used to guide student model M_P^S training.

Building feature extension module is generally divided into two steps. First, training 11 generators that can simulate ECG data via GANs [13]. Generators simulate sufficiently real 11 leads of ECG data. Second, connecting feature extension module to teacher model and freezing parameters of model M_G^T and M_P^T. Train M_E preferably through the single lead of ECG data.

Constructing Feature Extension Module. As shown in Fig. 3, GANs model applies 12 leads of ECG data for training. The 12 leads of ECG data include 6 leads of the limbs and 6 leads of the chest. I lead is used to record the voltage difference between electrodes of the left arm and the right arm, which is also commonly used for portable devices. Portable devices can't measure other lead data, such as II and III. It is important to simulate other leads data, because the teacher model M_G^T needs 12 leads of ECG data for training.

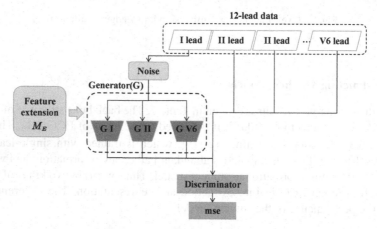

Fig. 3. The schematic diagram of feature extension module.

We construct 11 generators to simulate different leads data. I lead data is used as the input source data of all 11 generators. So I lead data with noise is regarded as the input of generator. Let d_I as I lead ECG data, and objective function is given as Eq. (1). It shows how to construct generator for II lead ECG data. $G_{II}()$ and $D_{II}()$ are generator and discriminator for II lead ECG data. In order to make $G_{II}()$ more robust, noise z is incorporated and $(z + d_I)$ is used as the input of $G_{II}()$.

$$\min_{G_{II}} \max_{D_{II}} V(D_{II}, G_{II}) = E_{x \sim p(x)}\big[logD_{II}(x)\big] + E_{z \sim p(z)}\big[log(1 - D_{II}(G_{II}(z + d_I)))\big]$$

(1)

In order to optimize this objective function, an iterative process is adopted. $D_{II}()$ is first optimized with $G_{II}()$ fixed, as shown in Eq. (2), then $G_{II}()$ is optimized with $D_{II}()$ fixed, as shown in Eq. (3). These two steps are alternatively executed, then $G_{II}()$ and $D_{II}()$ can both be trained in an adversarial mode. Generators of other 11 lead ECG data can be constructed in the same way.

$$\max_{D_{II}} V(D_{II}, G_{II}) = E_{x \sim p(x)}[logD_{II}(x)] + E_{z \sim p(z)}[log(1 - D_{II}(G_{II}(z + d_I)))] \quad (2)$$

$$\min_{G_{II}} V(D_{II}, G_{II}) = E_{z \sim p(z)}[log(1 - D_{II}(G_{II}(z + d_I)))] \qquad (3)$$

Fine-tuning Feature Extension Module. As shown in Fig. 4. The feature extension module is the prepositive input module of the teacher model M_G^T. Based on I lead data, the feature extension module is tuned by knowledge of teacher model M_P^T. M_G^T contains abundant ECG knowledge we want to capture. So in this work its parameters is frozen and only the feature extension module is fine-tuned. Optimizer and learning rate are the same as before. The loss function is given in Eq. (4). α is loss weight factor and T is distillation temperature.

$$L_{KD}(M_E) = \alpha T^2 \cdot KL(Q_S^\tau, Q_T^\tau) + (1 - \alpha) \cdot CE(Q_S, y_{true}) \qquad (4)$$

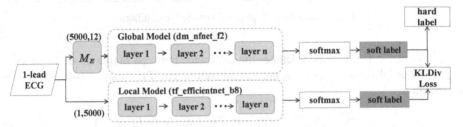

Fig. 4. Fine-tuning feature extension module.

3.3 Knowledge Distillation

As shown in Fig. 5, teacher model M_G^T, teacher model M_P^T and feature extension module M_E have been built. Student model M_P^S is trained under guidance of two teacher models.

Let D_p denotes a private data set, which is collected from portable devices.

$$D_p = \{D_{p_i} | 1 < i < N\} D_{p_i} = \{x_i, y_i\} \qquad (5)$$

As shown in Eq. (5), D_{p_i} is the i-th data tuple. x_i represents the i-th ECG data, and y_i indicates the type label. D_p is the input of teacher model M_G^T, teacher model M_P^T and student model M_P^S respectively. Three loss functions $loss_1$, $loss_2$ and $loss_3$ are defined as Eq. (6), where KL stands for KL divergence and CE stands for Cross Entropy loss.

$$loss_1 = KL\left(Q_{M_P}^\tau, Q_{M_G^T}^\tau\right)$$

$$loss_2 = KL\left(Q_{M_P}^\tau, Q_{M_P^T}^\tau\right) \qquad (6)$$

$$loss_3 = CE\left(Q_{M_P}^\tau, y_i\right)$$

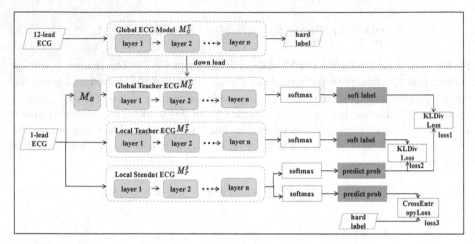

Fig. 5. Structure diagram of knowledge distillation.

As shown in Eq. (7) $loss_p$ denotes the difference between output of student model M_P^S and true label. ω_1, ω_2 and ω_3 are weight parameters. T_1, T_2 and T_3 are distillation temperature.

$$Loss_P = \omega_1 T_1^2 \cdot loss_1 + \omega_2 T_2^2 \cdot loss_2 + \omega_3 T_3^2 \cdot loss_3 \tag{7}$$

We transfer knowledge of teacher model to student model via distillation technology. To resolve the problem of different dimensions, a feature extension module is designed. Then two kinds of teacher models is used to ensure the performance of model distillation. Therefore, the trained personalized model achieves better generalization on Portable ECG data.

4 Experiments Evaluation

4.1 Datasets Description

We collect a clinical ECG dataset from primary medical institutions for experiment evaluation. ECG data generates from portable devices of the left and right limbs. Sampling time is 10 s. Sampling frequency is 500 Hz. Figure 6 shows samples of normal and abnormal ECG data. Abnormal ECG data exhibits more high frequency and low intensity shaking. There are totally 3518 samples. The specific cases distribution is shown in Table 2.

In addition, we collected part of 12-lead ECG data for GAN network training, and it is collected by GE facilities. Sampling frequency is 500 Hz. Sampling time is 10 s. Each lead contains 5000 measurement levels. There are about 100,000 samples. Batch size is set with 64. w_1, w_2 and w_3 are set with 0.3, 0.3 and 0.4. T_1, T_2 and T_3 are set with 0.9, 1 and 0.95. Learning rate is set with 1e-5. These parameters are optimal selected under various evaluations.

Table 2. Cases distribution in general hospitals and children's hospitals.

Case	General hospital
Sinus bradycardia	173
Sinus tachycardia	115
Sinus rhythm	1764
Sinus arrhythmia	72
Atrial flutter	39
Atrioventricular block	39
Atrial premature beats	57
Ventricular tachycardia	11
Ventricular premature beats	40
Normal electrocardiogram	1208

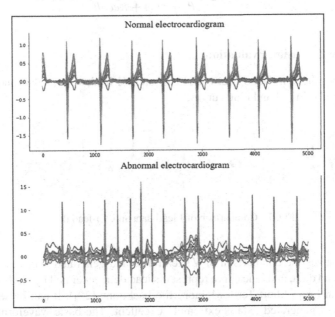

Fig. 6. ECG data samples.

4.2 Experimental Environment

Experiments are conducted on the Jiutian platform provided by China Mobile CMCC. It provides GPU cloud services with TeslaV100, E5-2640V4 CPU, 128GB DRAM memory. The deep framework are Tensorflow 2.3.1 and Keras 2.4.3.

4.3 Evaluation Criteria

We use standard accuracy, precision, recall and F_1 to evaluate the performance of the proposed method. As shown in Eq. (8), TP indicates the number of positive samples correctly classified. TN indicates the number of negative samples correctly classified. FP indicates the number of negative samples that are misclassified as positive samples. FN indicates the number of positive samples that are misclassified as negative samples.

$$Accuracy = \frac{TP + TN}{TP + TN + FP + FN}$$

$$Precision = \frac{TP}{TP + FP}$$

$$Recall = \frac{TP}{TP + FN} \tag{8}$$

$$F_1 = 2 * \frac{Precision * Recall}{Precision + Recall}$$

4.4 Feature Extension Evaluation

Figure 7 shows the comparison between I lead and V1 lead. V1 lead data and I lead data are demonstrated in red and blue curves.

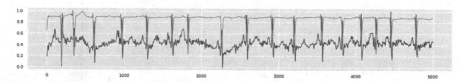

Fig. 7. Comparison of I lead data and V1 lead data.

Figure 8 gives the comparison of V1 lead data and generated lead data. Red curve denotes V1 lead data, and blue curve represents lead data generated by GANs (We adopt a bidirectional Long Short-Term Memory the backbone [20]). It can be seen that the performance of generated data is extremely excellent. The basic waveform rhythm is most similar. But there is still gaps in some graphic details. So it is necessary to be further improved by teacher models M_G^T and M_P^T.

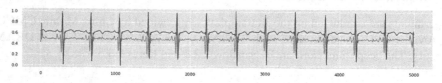

Fig. 8. Comparison of V1 lead data and generated lead data.

4.5 Comparative Experiment

Table 3 gives the evaluation results of different models. Table 4 shows the evaluation results of different models with adaptive distillation. There are 3519 samples from primary medical institutions. 519 samples are used for evaluating, and 3000 samples are used for training. efficientnet_lite0 and mobilenetv3 are adopted as simple models. The evaluation result of mobilenetv3 is better than efficientnet_lite0, and its accuracy, recall, precision and F1 reach 64.32%, 60.28%, 60.29% and 49.54%. We adopt efficientnet_b1_pruned as the model pruning method. Its accuracy, recall, precision and F1 can reach 71.14%, 73.36%, 70.18% and 68.22%. resnest200e, tf_efficientnet_b8, repvgg_b2 and gluon_senet154 are complex models. Their accuracy, recall, precision and F1 increase gradually. We add the adaptive distillation structure to above lightweight models.

Table 3. Comparison of evaluation results under different models.

Model	Best acc	Best recall	Best precision	Best F1	Param count
efficientnet_lite0	62.32%	61.58%	59.99%	48.29%	4.65
mobilenetv3	64.32%	60.28%	60.29%	49.54%	5.48
efficientnet_b1_pruned	71.14%	73.36%	70.18%	68.22%	6.33
resnest200e	80.35%	78.76%	79.28%	79.30%	70.2
tf_efficientnet_b8	82.15%	79.33%	80.98%	80.50%	87.41
repvgg_b2	83.11%	80.23%	81.15%	81.23%	89.02
gluon_senet154	85.33%	82.12%	83.21%	83.45%	115.09

Table 4. Comparison of results under different models with adaptive distillation.

Model	Best acc	Best recall	Best precision	Best F1	Param count
efficientnet_lite0 + adaptive distillation	65.35%	62.55%	60.93%	49.33%	4.65
mobilenetv3 + adaptive distillation	67.48%	61.38%	61.32%	50.56%	5.48
efficientnet_b1_pruned + adaptive distillation	81.24%	80.35%	79.16%	78.25%	6.33
gluon_senet154	85.33%	82.12%	83.21%	83.45%	115.09

As shown in Table 5, the proposed method is generally better than the models without adaptive distillation. Although efficientnet_b1_pruned is simple model, its performance is close to gluon_senet154. Its accuracy, recall, precision and F_1 can reach 81.24%, 80.35%, 79.16% and 78.25%. Correspondingly, the parameter count of gluon_senet154 is 115.09M. Its accuracy, recall, precision and F_1 can reach 85.33%, 2.12%, 83.21% and 83.45%. In consideration of parameter scale and performance of model, efficientnet_b1_pruned + adaptive distillation is preferred.

Table 5. Comparison with traditional methods.

Method	Best acc	Best recall	Best precision	Best F1
Lightweight schema	72.32%	70.53%	71.42%	70.78%
Model pruning	72.22%	74.98%	73.33%	75.69%
Model distillation	79.58%	78.97%	79.45%	79.23%
Adaptive model distillation	82.33%	81.12%	80.23%	81.11%

Table 5 shows the comparison results with some traditional methods. The lightweight scheme takes up less resources, but the performance is not good. Model pruning gets a little better than lightweight schema. Model distillation makes great progress, and its accuracy, recall, precision and F_1 can reach 79.58%, 78.97%, 79.45% and 79.23%. The proposed adaptive model distillation method achieves significant improvements. Its accuracy, recall, precision and F_1 can reach 82.33%, 81.12%, 79.23% and 79.11%.

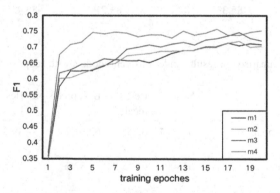

Fig. 9. Traditional methods versus the proposed method.

Figure 9 demonstrates the evaluation results with 4 traditional methods. x-axis represents the training epochs, and y-axis represents the F_1 value. m_1, m_2, m_3 and m_4 denote lightweight schema, model pruning, model distillation and adaptive model distillation. It shows that m_4 obtains optimal performance at about 16 epochs.

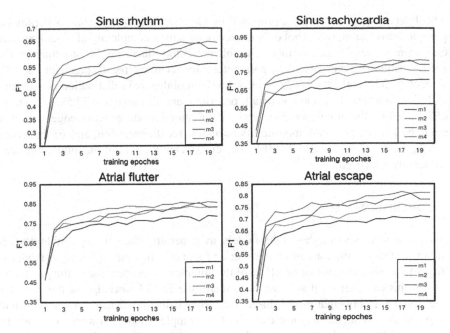

Fig. 10. Traditional method versus the proposed method in some symptoms.

Figure 10 shows the results of some symptoms, which display dissimilar distributions greatly. The x-axis represents the training epoch and the y-axis represents the F_1 value. m_1, m_2, m_3 and m_4 denote lightweight schema, model pruning, model distillation and adaptive model distillation degree. It can be seen that m_4 keeps more stable and smooth in training phase. At the same time, m_1 and m_2 show low efficiency. m_4 is faster and it obtains optimal performance at about 16 epochs. Above all, the proposed model knowledge distillation based method outperforms the referenced methods.

4.6 Ablation Study

As shown in Table 6. Ablation experiments are conducted on a variety of deployment modes, including mobilenetv3, mobilenetv3 + distillation and mobilenetv3 + adaptive distillation. The performances of model evaluation under different deployment modes.

Table 6. Comparison of model evaluation under different deployment modes.

Deployment mode	Avg acc	Avg recall	Avg precision	Avg F_1
mobilenetv3	64.32%	60.28%	60.29%	49.54%
mobilenetv3 + distillation	77.54%	71.55%	76.57%	74.33%
mobilenetv3 + adaptive distillation	80.35%	78.76%	79.28%	79.30%

Mobilenet is a mobile model proposed by Google. Its kernel module is depthwise separable convolution, which not only reduces calculation complexity of model but also greatly compresses the size of model. mobilenetv3 introduces the SE structure on the basis of mobilenet, and it has less parameters. Its accuracy, recall, precision, and F_1 can reach 64.32%, 60.28%, 60.29% and 49.54%. mobilenetv3+ distillation is a general distillation structure. Its accuracy, recall, precision, and F_1 can reach 77.54%, 71.55%, 76.57% and 74.33%. mobilenetv3+ adaptive distillation introduces knowledge of teacher models by feature extension module. Its accuracy, recall, precision, and F_1 can reach 80.35%, 78.76%, 79.28% and 79.30%. The classification effect of the model has been significantly improved.

5   Conclusions

Deployment schemes of lightweight models are generally adopted on portable devices to adapt to their limitations in computing and storage. But the lightweight model is difficult to achieve the evaluation effect of the complex model because of the parameter scale. In this case, an ideal solution is to distill the ECG knowledge of the complex model into the lightweight model through the knowledge distillation, so that the small model can also obtain the diagnostic effect of the complex model. However, because the data scale of the portable device is small, the diagnostic capability of the teacher model of the portable device still can't meet the requirements of initial diagnosis. Therefore, this paper proposes a novel adaptive model compression approach based on knowledge distillation. Single lead data can match the static ECG model via the feature extension module which simulates other lead data through generative adversarial network. To train the simple model, multi-level knowledge distillation mode is adopted, and the knowledge contained in the single lead of ECG model and 12 leads of complex model is distilled into the lightweight model. Experiment evaluations show that the performance of the proposed model can be significantly improved.

Acknowledgement. This work is supported by National Natural Science Foundation of China under Grants No. 61632008, 62072099, 61972085, 61872079, 61972083, Jiangsu Provincial Key Laboratory of Network and Information Security under Grant No. BM2003201, Key Laboratory of Computer Network and Information Integration of Ministry of Education of China under Grant No.93K-9, and partially supported by Collaborative Innovation Center of Novel Software Technology and Industrialization, Collaborative Innovation Center of Wireless Communications Technology, the Fundamental Research Funds for the Central Universities.

References

1. Hinton, G., Vinyals, O., Dean, J.: Distilling the knowledge in a neural network. CoRR abs/1503.02531 (2015)
2. Ba, J., Caruana, R.: Do deep nets really need to be deep? In: NIPS, pp. 2654–2662 (2014)
3. Urban, G., Geras, K.J., Kahou, S.E., et al.: Do deep convolutional nets really need to be deep and convolutional? In: ICLR 2017, Poster

4. Muirhead, R.J., Puff, R.D.: A Bayesian classification of heart rate variability data. Physica A **336**(3–4), 503–513 (2004)
5. Christov, I., Jekova, I., Bortolan, G.: Premature ventricular contraction classification by the Kth nearest-neighbours rule. Physiol. Meas. **26**(1), 123–130 (2005)
6. Jekova, I., Bortolan, G., Christov, I.: Pattern recognition and optimal parameter selection in premature ventricular contraction classification. In: IEEE Computers in Cardiology (2004)
7. Melgani, F., Bazi, Y.: Classification of electrocardiogram signals with support vector machines and particle swarm optimization. IEEE Trans. Technol. Biomed. **12**(5), 667–677 (2008)
8. Soman, S., Jayadeva, D.: High performance EEG signal classification using classifiability and the twin SVM. Appl. Soft Comput. **30**, 305–318 (2015)
9. She, Q., Ma, Y., Meng, M., Luo, Z.: Multiclass posterior probability twin SVM for motor imagery EEG classification. Comput. Intell. Neurosci. **251945**, 1–9 (2015)
10. Acharya, U.R., Oh, S.L., Hagiwara, Y., et al.: A deep convolutional neural network model to classify heartbeats. Comput. Biol. Med. **89**, 389–396 (2017)
11. Rahhal, M.M.A., Bazi, Y., Alhichri, H.S., et al.: Deep learning approach for active classification of electrocardiogram signals. Inf. Sci. **345**, 340–354 (2016)
12. Han, S., Mao, H., Dally, W.J.: Deep compression: Compressing deep neural networks with pruning, trained quantization and Huffman coding. Fiber **56**(4), 3–7 (2015)
13. Goodfellow, I., Pouget-Abadie, J., Mirza, M., et al.: Generative adversarial nets. In: NIPS, pp. 2672–2680 (2014)
14. Heo, B., Lee, M., Yun, S., Choi, J.Y.: Knowledge distillation with adversarial samples supporting decision boundary. In: IAAI, pp. 3771–3778 (2019)
15. Zagoruyko, S., Komodakis, N.: Paying more attention to attention: Improving the performance of convolutional neural networks via attention transfer. In: ICLR 2017, Poster
16. Tung, F., Mori, G.: Similarity-preserving knowledge distillation. In: ICCV, pp. 1365–1374 (2019)
17. Lan, X., Zhu, X., Gong, S.: Knowledge distillation by on-the-fly native ensemble. In: NIPS, pp. 7528–7538 (2018)
18. Ackermann, K., Angus, S.D.: A resource efficient big data analysis method for the social sciences: the case of global IP activity. Proceed. Int. Conf. Comput. Sci. **29**, 2360–2369 (2014)
19. Brock, A., De, S., Smith, S.L., Simonyan, K.: High-performance large-scale image recognition without normalization. In: ICML, pp. 1059–1071 (2021)
20. Zhang, Y., Zhao, Z., Deng, Y., Zhang, X., Zhang, Y.: Heart biometrics based on ECG signal by sparse coding and bidirectional long short-term memory. Multimedia Tools Appl. **80**(20), 30417–30438 (2020). https://doi.org/10.1007/s11042-020-09608-9

Author Index

An, Wei   II-453
An, Yunzhe   III-722
Andelfinger, Philipp   III-772

Bai, Hao   III-668
Bai, Xiangyu   I-147
Bian, Qingrong   III-540

Cai, Shangxuan   I-549
Cai, Wentong   III-772
Cai, Yuejin   I-354
Cai, Zhiping   I-162
Cao, Buqing   I-237
Cao, Jian   III-152, III-278
Cérin, Christophe   III-245
Chang, Kangkang   III-116
Chen, Bincai   III-432
Chen, Bolei   I-578
Chen, Chao   III-167
Chen, Cheng   III-479
Chen, Guo   II-555
Chen, Haiming   II-665
Chen, Jia-Qi   II-709
Chen, Jiayuan   II-682
Chen, Jie   I-645
Chen, Kai   III-754
Chen, Lijie   III-509
Chen, Shi   I-100
Chen, Shiping   I-743
Chen, Shuhong   II-257
Chen, Wenli   II-274
Chen, Xiaofei   II-682
Chen, Xin   II-376, II-421
Chen, Xu   I-460
Chen, Ying   II-376, II-421
Chen, Zhen   II-391
Chen, Zhichao   III-527
Chen, Zhiguang   II-193
Cheng, Baolei   III-540
Chu, Yan   I-85
Cui, Gang   I-115
Cui, Guangfan   I-50
Cui, Jianming   II-532
Cui, Jinhua   I-162

Cui, Yingbo   II-213
Cui, Yongzheng   I-578
Cui, Yuyang   III-397
Cui, Zhihan   II-53

Dai, Chenglong   I-445
Dai, Liang   II-695
Deng, Changshou   II-361
Deng, Liyu   I-726
Deng, Zhihong   III-376
Di, Xiaoqiang   I-402
Diao, Chunyan   I-3
Ding, Jianwen   I-193
Ding, Wei   I-129
Ding, Xuedong   I-65
Ding, Ye   III-462
Ding, Yepeng   I-693
Ding, Yifei   II-274
Ding, Yong   II-240
Dong, Dezun   III-668
Dong, Pusen   III-691
Dong, Xiaogang   II-361
Dong, Yangchen   I-790
Dong, YiChao   II-65
Dong, Yuzheng   I-422
Dou, Haowen   II-53
Dou, Wanchun   I-494
Du, Ruizhong   II-647
Du, Yang   I-743
Duan, Jirun   I-494
Duan, Keqiang   III-587
Duan, Weiguo   II-144

Eckhoff, David   III-772

Fan, Jianxi   III-540
Fan, Lin-Lin   II-709
Fan, Meng   III-196
Fan, Mingyuan   I-178
Fang, Fei   II-603
Fang, Juan   I-370
Fang, Peng   III-722
Feng, Guangsheng   III-214
Feng, Siqi   III-3

Feng, Xiaoning II-489
Fu, Jing I-564
Fu, Shaojing III-509
Fu, Siqing III-231
Fu, Xiangzheng III-620

Gan, Xinbiao III-668
Gao, Ao II-546, III-527
Gao, Guoju I-743
Gao, Haoyu III-527
Gao, Heran III-35
Gao, Jian III-432
Gao, Meihui II-632
Gao, Ming III-602
Gao, Peng III-67
Gao, Ruimin III-754
Gao, Ruixue I-354
Gao, Yonggang III-397
Gao, Yongqiang I-476, I-509
Gao, Yuanyuan III-346
Gao, Zhipeng II-317
Ge, Shuxin III-313
Ge, Xiaoxue II-453
Geng, Shichao III-707
Gong, Xiaorui III-101
Gu, Chonglin II-682
Gu, Yu II-571
Guan, Wei I-210
Gui, Weixia II-81
Guo, Qingli III-101
Guo, Suiming I-319
Guo, Wenzhong I-178

Hamdi-Larbi, Olfa II-161
Han, Dezhi II-617
Han, Jizhong I-790
Han, Li II-178
Han, Zhiheng I-115
Hao, Xinyu I-147
He, Jiawei II-257
He, Jingyi II-345
He, Juan I-422
Hong, Haibo I-676, I-710
Hong, Hao II-571
Hong, Haokai I-129, I-271
Hou, Gang III-527
Hou, Jun I-759
Hou, Qingzhi I-354
Hu, Guangwu III-494
Hu, Jianqiang II-334

Hu, Qinghua I-549
Hu, Shihong I-445
Hu, Songlin I-790, III-293
Hu, Wang II-3
Hu, Xingbo III-754
Hu, Yao II-123
Huang, Baoqi I-147, II-571
Huang, Boyu II-53
Huang, Chun II-213
Huang, He I-743
Huang, Hejiao II-682
Huang, Tao III-35
Huang, Tianyuan III-707
Huang, Weijia III-411
Huang, Yun III-214

Ji, Yanhui I-304
Jia, Bing II-571
Jia, Chaoyang II-33
Jia, Weijia II-509
Jia, YuLei I-222
Jia, Zhiping III-691
Jian, W. II-439
Jiang, Congfen III-293
Jiang, Congfeng III-245
Jiang, Di III-462
Jiang, Huatong II-632
Jiang, Man I-3
Jiang, Min I-129, I-271, II-18
Jiang, Qiao II-682
Jiang, Qingshan II-284
Jiang, Wenjun II-257
Jiang, Xiaoshu II-489
Jiang, Xikun III-691
Jiang, Xuhang II-240
Jiang, Zhiping II-345
Jin, Cheqing III-602
Jin, Fuqi III-3
Jin, Hang III-261
Jin, Jiahui II-724
Jin, Songchang III-35
Jin, Zuodong III-331

Kan, Guobin II-489
Kang, Guosheng I-237
Knoll, Alois III-772
Koibuchi, Michihiro II-123
Kong, Lanju III-3
Kuang, Li-Dan III-632

Lai, Yongxuan I-271, II-18
Lan, Yibing III-754
Lei, Yang III-362
Li, Benyu II-453
Li, Chengzhi III-35
Li, Chenxi I-445
Li, Chuxi II-391
Li, Dingding II-108
Li, Dong I-445
Li, Donghua III-707
Li, Donghui I-210
Li, Gaolei I-612
Li, Guanghui I-445
Li, Guoqing III-571
Li, Han I-33
Li, Haozhuang I-85
Li, Jianhua I-612
Li, Jingbo II-178
Li, Jingxin II-546
Li, Keqiu III-313
Li, Kuan-Ching I-3
Li, Lei II-391
Li, Min II-96
Li, Minglu III-152
Li, Ni III-620
Li, Pengfei III-527
Li, Qianmu I-759
Li, Ruixuan III-293
Li, Tao II-96
Li, Taoshen III-52
Li, Taotao III-376
Li, Tiejun III-231
Li, Wenjuan III-214
Li, Wenqiang II-65
Li, Wenquan III-3
Li, Xiang I-210
Li, Xiaoya II-647
Li, Yang I-759
Li, Yanjun II-632
Li, Yicong III-648
Li, Yike I-660
Li, Yu I-162
Li, Yuanjing II-406
Li, Yuxing II-274
Li, Zhaohui III-81
Li, Zhenyu II-240
Liang, Hai II-240
Liang, Jiayue III-261
Liang, Mingfeng II-334
Liang, Wei I-3, II-3, II-439, III-182, III-632

Liang, Yan II-376
Liang, Zhongyu I-402
Liao, Lei II-3
Liao, Linbo II-18
Liao, Qing III-462
Liao, Xiangke II-213
Liao, Zhengyu III-152
Lin, Chuangwei I-494
Lin, Fan I-193
Lin, Kai III-432
Lin, Liu III-509
Lin, Murao I-385
Lin, Yang II-33
Liu, Caizheng I-50
Liu, Dongdong III-376
Liu, Fang III-261
Liu, Han II-617
Liu, Jianxun I-237
Liu, Jingyu I-336
Liu, Jiqiang I-660
Liu, Lijin III-3
Liu, Ming II-532
Liu, Nan III-648
Liu, Pengbo III-313
Liu, Wantao III-293
Liu, Wei III-620
Liu, Xiaolei I-509
Liu, Ximeng I-178
Liu, Xu I-402
Liu, Yan II-647
Liu, Yang II-334, III-462
Liu, Yuan III-101
Liu, Yuting I-257
Liu, Yuzheng III-214
Liu, Zengguang III-278
Liu, Zhen I-402
Liu, Zhicheng I-549
Liu, Zhonglin I-257
Long, Hao I-597
Long, Jing II-603
Long, Sifan II-213
Lu, Anqi II-406
Lu, Haitang I-645
Lu, Kejie I-529, I-627
Lu, Pengqi III-133
Lu, Yangguang II-421
Lu, Yi III-346
Lu, Zhaobo I-529, I-627
Luo, Haibo II-603
Luo, Haoyu II-108

Luo, Jiebin II-108
Luo, Junzhou II-724
Luo, Meng I-18
Luo, Yuchuan III-509
Lv, Pin III-52
Lv, Shengbo I-193

Ma, Kefan III-231
Ma, Teng II-376
Meng, Dan III-196
Meng, Guozhu III-754
Meng, Kelong III-116
Meng, Shunmei I-759
Min, Xinping III-3
Mo, Zijia II-317
Mou, Zhebin II-193
Moumni, Hatem II-161
Muhammad, Adil III-432

Ni, Liang III-602
Ning, Hui I-85
Niu, Wenjia I-660

Ou, Dongyang III-245
Ouyang, Tao I-460

Pan, Fulai II-81
Pan, Yudong III-691
Pan, Zhiyong III-540
Pang, Zhengbin III-668
Peng, Li III-620
Peng, Lin II-213

Qi, Hua-Mei II-709
Qian, Junbo II-724
Qian, Lin II-144
Qian, Shiyou III-152
Qin, Guangjun I-257
Qin, Wei II-665
Qiu, Chao I-549
Qiu, Linling I-33
Qiu, Qian II-695
Qu, Peiqi I-18
Qu, Qiang II-284
Qu, Yuqi II-178
Qu, Zhihao II-144

Rao, Hongzhou III-447
Rasool, Abdur II-284

Ren, Gangsheng I-597
Ren, Ke I-494

Sato, Hiroyuki I-693
Sharif, Kashif III-447
Shen, Li I-336, II-33
Shen, Qianrong I-319
Shen, Zhangyi II-586
Shen, Zhaoyan III-691
Shen, Zhuowei III-67
Sheng, Yu I-578
shi, Jiamei I-370
Shi, Jianfeng III-35
Si, Jiaqi III-668
Song, Hanchen I-578
Song, Qiudi II-96
Song, Yuanfeng III-462
Su, Jinshu I-385
Sun, Bin III-691
Sun, Cheng I-18
Sun, Shan II-317
Sun, Weifeng III-116
Sun, Xun III-494
Sun, Yanan II-517
Sun, Yu-E I-743
Sun, Zhi I-50

Tan, Guanru II-53
Tan, Zhenqiong II-257
Tang, Mingdong III-182
Tang, Renjie II-724
Tang, Tao II-213
Tang, Wenyu III-182
Tang, Xiaolei II-65
Tang, Xuehai I-790
Tao, Dan III-331
Tao, Jun II-65
Tong, Endong I-660
Tong, Fei III-479
Tong, Guanghui I-612

Wan, Zheng II-361
Wang, Chen II-586
Wang, Chengyu I-162
Wang, Dong II-586
Wang, Gang II-96
Wang, Guiping II-695
Wang, Hailun III-19
Wang, Huiyong II-240
Wang, Jian I-660

Wang, Jianping   I-529, I-627
Wang, Jie   II-546, III-527
Wang, Jin   I-529, I-627, III-632
Wang, Jing   III-411
Wang, Jiwei   III-245
Wang, Junfeng   II-345
Wang, Lei   II-665
Wang, Liang   I-257
Wang, Liming   II-453
Wang, Lin   III-167, III-707
Wang, Lingfu   III-411
Wang, Lulu   III-346
Wang, Meihong   I-33
Wang, Meiying   III-648
Wang, Miao   II-391
Wang, Mingsheng   III-376
Wang, Qiong   I-336, II-33
Wang, Shuai   III-602
Wang, Tian   II-257, II-509, III-494
Wang, Wang   I-790
Wang, Wanliang   III-571
Wang, Weiping   II-230
Wang, Wenzhi   III-196
Wang, Xiaofei   I-549
Wang, XiaoLiang   II-144
Wang, Xiaoyu   I-743
Wang, Xinyu   III-691
Wang, Xuan   III-462
Wang, Yan   I-115, III-737
Wang, Yang   II-284, II-509
Wang, Yangqian   III-462
Wang, Yanping   I-476
Wang, Yilin   III-362
Wang, Yu   I-288
Wang, Yujue   II-240
Wang, Yule   III-571
Wang, Ziyue   I-422
Wang, Zuyan   II-65
Wei, Jianguo   I-354
Wei, Lifei   III-19
Wei, Qian   I-460
Wei, Ziling   I-385
Wen, Yiping   I-237
Wu, Guohua   II-586
Wu, Heng   III-35
Wu, Hongyu   II-489
Wu, Huaming   III-397
Wu, Jie   II-517
Wu, Jingjin   I-564
Wu, Jun   I-612

Wu, Shangrui   II-509
Wu, Sheng   I-100
Wu, Weigang   II-555
Wu, Weiguo   III-587
Wu, Xiang   III-397
Wu, Xiaohe   II-439
Wu, Xiaorui   I-147
Wu, Xintao   III-527

Xi, Dewei   III-81
Xi, Heran   II-300, II-406
Xia, Xiufeng   III-722
Xia, Zeyu   II-213
Xiang, Jiayan   I-237
Xiang, Yingxiao   I-660
Xiao, Bo   I-65
Xiao, Jiajian   III-772
Xiao, Limin   I-257
Xiao, Nong   II-193
Xiao, Wenjie   I-790
Xiao, Wentao   III-494
Xiao, Xi   III-494
Xie, Linyan   III-52
Xie, Mande   I-676, I-710
Xie, Ruitao   II-509
Xie, Runbin   I-237
Xie, Xuefeng   III-167
Xie, Zhiqiang   I-660
Xin, Chu   III-554
Xin, Qin   I-385
Xing, Tianzhang   II-345
Xu, Chang   III-447
Xu, Dejun   I-129, I-271
Xu, Gang   I-147
Xu, Guangping   I-222
Xu, Jia   III-52
Xu, Jianbo   II-439, II-473, III-632
Xu, Lin   III-648
Xu, YiFan   II-65
Xu, Zisang   III-632
Xue, Guangtao   III-152
Xue, Yanbing   I-222
Xue, Zhengyuan   I-775

Yan, Jie   III-587
Yan, Longchuan   III-245, III-293
Yang, Canqun   II-213
Yang, Cheng   III-620
Yang, Fan   II-18
Yang, Hao   I-100, I-288, I-304

Yang, Qing   II-345
Yang, Shijun   II-555
Yang, Shipeng   II-18
Yang, Shiwen   II-300
Yang, Tao   I-162
Yang, Xi   II-53
Yang, Yingyao   I-627
Yang, Zhao   II-391
Yao, Muyan   III-331
Yao, Yan   III-278
Yao, Ye   II-586
Ye, BaoLiu   II-144
Ye, Jiaxin   I-271
Yin, Jia-Li   I-178
Yin, Jiaying   I-564
Yu, Aimin   III-196
Yu, Jiguo   III-278
Yu, Xi   II-532
Yu, Zhi   I-402
Yu, Zhipeng   I-288
Yuan, Liang   III-133
Yuan, Liujie   II-274
Yuan, Tianyi   III-245
Yuan, Zheng-Yi   II-709
Yue, Yue   III-133

Zang, Liangjun   I-790
Zeng, Deze   II-108
Zeng, Wenhua   II-18
Zeng, Yingming   I-726
Zhang, Ang   II-213
Zhang, Bin   III-494
Zhang, Boyu   I-743
Zhang, Chaokun   III-313
Zhang, Chi   III-587
Zhang, Chuan   III-447
Zhang, Dafang   I-3
Zhang, Dunbo   I-336, II-33
Zhang, Haibin   I-726
Zhang, J. I. N.   I-18
Zhang, Jianmin   III-231
Zhang, Jiayue   I-370
Zhang, Jifeng   II-257
Zhang, Kai   I-645, III-19
Zhang, Lei   III-19, III-346, III-362
Zhang, Li   II-473
Zhang, Lijun   III-116
Zhang, Meng   II-391
Zhang, Mingwu   III-411
Zhang, Peng   II-213

Zhang, Pengcheng   I-319
Zhang, Rui   I-257
Zhang, Shaobo   II-274
Zhang, Shengbing   II-391
Zhang, Shigeng   II-230
Zhang, Shiwen   II-3
Zhang, Shukui   I-597
Zhang, Shuo   I-222, II-682
Zhang, Weijie   II-108
Zhang, Wenbo   III-35
Zhang, Xiang   III-101
Zhang, Xingjun   II-178
Zhang, Xingxu   I-402
Zhang, Xuyun   I-494
Zhang, Yang   I-597
Zhang, Yi   III-81
Zhang, Yinghan   II-317
Zhang, Yongting   III-397
Zhang, Yuhao   III-691
Zhang, Yunquan   III-133
Zhang, Zejian   III-737
Zhao, Baokang   I-385
Zhao, Caidan   III-362
Zhao, Chen   II-317
Zhao, Fengjun   II-421
Zhao, Haoyan   I-370
Zhao, Jie   III-167
Zhao, Ming   II-144
Zhao, Qingchao   I-85
Zhao, Qiting   I-676
Zhao, Shuang   I-660
Zhao, Wentao   III-509
Zhao, Yanfeng   I-422
Zhao, Yawei   I-210
Zhao, Yonghao   I-304
Zhao, Yunfeng   I-549
Zheng, Jianbing   III-602
Zheng, Junyao   II-555
Zheng, Shiming   I-564
Zheng, Shiqiang   II-53
Zheng, Wenguang   I-222
Zheng, Xuda   III-587
Zheng, Yicheng   III-362
Zheng, Zhonglong   III-152
Zhong, Ping   I-578
Zhou, Aoying   III-602
Zhou, Biyu   I-790, III-293
Zhou, Houquan   I-50
Zhou, Jieying   II-555
Zhou, Jingya   I-529

Zhou, Junqiang   I-115
Zhou, Kuanjiu   III-648
Zhou, Teng   II-53
Zhou, Tongqing   I-162
Zhou, Wei   I-494
Zhou, Xiaobao   II-334
Zhou, Xiaobo   III-313
Zhou, Xiaojun   II-453
Zhou, Zhi   I-460
Zhu, Bing   II-230
Zhu, Jinbin   I-257
Zhu, Jinghua   II-300, II-406

Zhu, Licai   I-100, I-288, I-304
Zhu, Liehuang   III-447
Zhu, Linghe   I-710
Zhu, Liubin   I-422
Zhu, Minghua   I-65
Zhu, Rui   III-722
Zhu, Shunzhi   III-737
Zhu, Xiaomin   III-707
Zhu, Yani   II-586
Zhu, Yi-hua   III-554
Zhu, Ziyan   III-479
Zong, Chuanyu   III-722